Our Sexuality

Third Edition

Our Sexuality

Third Edition

Robert Crooks

Oregon Health Sciences University, School of Medicine
Portland Community College

Karla Baur

The Benjamin/Cummings Publishing Company, Inc.

Menlo Park, California • Reading, Massachusetts
Don Mills, Ontario • Wokingham, U.K. • Amsterdam • Sydney
Singapore • Tokyo • Madrid • Bogota • Santiago • San Juan

Sponsoring Editor: Diane Bowen
Production Supervisor: Betsy Dilernia
Developmental and Copy Editor: Robin Fox
Designer: Detta Penna
Photo Researcher: Lindsay Kefauver
Cover Artist: Valerie Willson
Interior Artists: Edith Allgood, Barbara Hack, Heather Preston, Connie Warton, Martha Weston
Compositor: Jonathan Peck Typographers, Ltd.

Credits for photographs and excerpts appear after the Bibliography.

Library of Congress Cataloging-in-Publication Data

Crooks, Robert, 1941–
  Our sexuality.

  Bibliography: p. 720
  Includes index.
    1. Sex.   2. Sex customs—United States.   I. Baur,
Karla.   II. Title.   [DNLM: 1. Sex—popular works.
2. Sex Behavior—popular works.   WQ 21 C773o]
HQ21.C98   1987   612.6   86-21598
ISBN 0-8053-1909-3

CDEFGHIJ-HA-89876

The Benjamin/Cummings Publishing Company, Inc.
2727 Sand Hill Road
Menlo Park, California 94025

About the Authors

The integration of psychological, social, and biological components of human sexuality in this text is facilitated by the blending of the authors' academic and professional backgrounds. Robert Crooks has a Ph.D. in psychology. His graduate training stressed clinical and physiological psychology. In addition, he has considerable background in sociology, which served as his minor throughout his graduate training. He is currently involved in a number of research and writing projects, and teaches sexuality and psychology classes at Oregon Health Sciences University, School of Medicine, and Portland Community College.

Karla Baur has a master's degree in social work; her advanced academic work stressed clinical training. She is currently in private practice as a clinical social worker and is the training director at the Elahan Center for Mental Health and Family Living. Karla is certified as a sex therapist and educator by the American Association of Sex Educators, Counselors, and Therapists. She has instructed sexuality classes at Portland Community College and has been a Clinical Associate Professor of Obstetrics and Gynecology at Oregon Health Sciences University, School of Medicine.

The authors have a combined total of 29 years of teaching, counseling, and research in the field of human sexuality. Together they team taught sexuality courses at Portland Community College for a number of years. They present workshops and guest lectures to a wide variety of professional and community groups, and they counsel individuals, couples, and families on sexual concerns. The authors are also involved in ongoing research pertaining to sexual attitudes and behaviors of college students. Their combined teaching, clinical, and research experiences, together with their graduate training, have provided them with an appreciation and sensitive understanding of the highly complex and personal nature of human sexuality.

It is the authors' belief that a truly sensitive understanding of our sexuality must be grounded in *both* the female and the male perspectives and experiences. In this sense, their courses, their students, and this text have benefited from a well-balanced perception and a deep appreciation of human sexual behavior.

Foreword

The first time I taught an undergraduate course on human sexual behavior was in 1970, at the University of Oregon. Since then I have taught the course many times, to many students, at four different universities. In the development of courses on human sexuality over the years, the search for the best textbook has been a recurring issue. In the early years of teaching this course, and to a lesser degree today, most of the books available were basically sex education texts. Rather than focusing on human sexuality—attitudes, emotions, behavior patterns, and so forth—these books dealt mainly with the "plumbing" aspects of sex—anatomy and physiology of the reproductive system. Furthermore, many of these books were really very value laden, often with basically conservative and sexist values.

After using this type of sex education-oriented text over a few semesters, I received feedback from students that confirmed my initial misgivings. They did not find the anatomy and physiology very interesting—they wanted to know about *sexuality*, not about reproduction. The conservative values struck many of the students as hopelessly out of touch with current reality, and many students were offended by the implicitly sexist views in these books.

Not being too obtuse or a terribly slow learner, I eventually stopped using this sort of text, and instead began to use collections of articles from professional journals. However, this alternative turned out to have two problems. First, the articles were often overly detailed and uninteresting to students. Second, without the use of a text that covered anatomy and physiology, many students lacked the basic knowledge required to understand the lecture material. This sort of material is a very necessary, if not sufficient, part of a course on human sexuality.

I eventually arrived at a combination of a basic sex education text, a collection of readings, and some mimeographed material gathered from a variety of sources. What this combination did not cover was the *human* or personal side of human sexuality. Obviously, a course in sexuality has enormous personal relevance to the students, and their reactions to both readings and lecture material are often more personal than intellectual. My office hours began to assume certain aspects of a sex counseling service. I reached the point where I was actually *glad* when a student would come in merely to complain about a grade. Reflecting on their reactions to the course and readings, I realized the students needed and wanted something that would help them integrate their own life experiences—exciting, confusing, gratifying, or frustrating—with the academic material.

During this period, I often found myself wishing that my life could be much less complicated. If there were a single really good sexuality text available, it would be much easier to teach human sexuality. In thinking about what would constitute an ideal text, I came up with a shopping list:

1. The basic biology of sexuality must be thoroughly covered.
2. The psychology and sociology of human sexuality must be emphasized, covering behavior patterns, emotions, sociocultural factors, and so forth.
3. There should be some integration of both sorts of academic material with personal experiences of real people.
4. Self-help problem-solving advice in the text would be useful.
5. The text should not be overly political or stridently polemical about sexual and sex-role values, in either conservative or liberal directions. Instead, the text should be value-free as much as is possible. Given that some values obviously must appear when presenting life histories and self-help material (points 3 and 4 above), my preference would be for a book committed to equality in male and female roles and relationships, and to acceptance of a wide range of sexual lifestyles as normal and healthy.

Over the next few years, I evaluated each new textbook that appeared against this five-item shopping list. Some excellent texts appeared, including ones that met almost all of my criteria. What never did appear was a solid academic text with a personal focus; that is, one that included life history and personal problem-solving material. Thus, when I first saw a new text by Robert Crooks and Karla Baur, I was immediately intrigued. Here, at last, seemed to be two people who had obviously taught human sexuality for some time and had been willing to listen to their students and respond to *their* needs in writing a text.

The first edition of this text was an excellent book, and was very well received. Indeed, this book has become one of the most widely used (if not *the* most widely used) texts in college level courses in human sexuality. This success has been well deserved. Among the book's virtues is the fact that the academic material is presented clearly, yet is not oversimplified. The personal material is fascinating, and makes the text one that students read out of interest rather than to study for the exams. The self-help material is very straightforward and is useful and relevant to students. The values of the authors are not presented in a strident way, and are indeed egalitarian and nonjudgmental.

Not content to rest on their laurels, Crooks and Baur eventually produced a second, and now a third edition. These editions have updated, revised, and added to an already outstanding book. The latest advances in sex research have been integrated into the existing chapters, and much new material has been added. While the book has always been strong in both personal relevance and scholarship, its academic value has now been increased by the addition of over 600 new reference citations to recent research. Major new sections have been added on hormone-behavior relationships, homosexuality, love, marriage, divorce, and sexual communication. Crooks and Baur have also done an excellent job of including new material on rape, incest, child sexual abuse, laws regarding pornography, and sexually transmitted diseases, including AIDS. These are all topics of great interest, and about which much current sex research and public policy debate centers.

In closing my Foreword to the first and second editions, I concluded that at last an academically sound, personally relevant teaching package was available for courses in human sexuality. This third edition only improves on an already excellent text. The current generation of students taking a course in human sexuality—and their instructors—are indeed fortunate to have this book available.

Joseph LoPiccolo
Texas A&M University

Preface

Our major goal for the third edition of *Our Sexuality* is essentially the same as for the first two editions: To provide a *comprehensive* and *academically sound* introduction to the biological, psychosocial, behavioral, and cultural aspects of sexuality, in a way that is *personally meaningful to students*. The enthusiastic response to the earlier editions of our text has been gratifying, and has encouraged us to revise the book with the dual aim of updating it and making it even more effective as a learning tool.

Like the previous two editions, the third edition covers a broad array of subjects in considerable detail. We have included some topics that are frequently either omitted or discussed superficially in other texts—for example, gender identity and gender roles, methods of sex research, love and the development of relationships, communicating about sex, improving sexual satisfaction, sexuality throughout the life cycle, and cross-cultural variations in sexual expression. While we have avoided being overly technical in our presentation of data, we have been scholarly and thorough in our review of the human sexuality research. The third edition has been updated in every area and includes over 600 new citations from the recent literature.

New in This Edition

This new volume has benefited greatly from the comments and suggestions of the many instructors and students who have used previous editions of the book. Several additions, modifications, and new features are worthy of special mention.

- Over 600 *new citations* from the recent literature.
- *Thought Provokers* at the conclusion of each chapter—questions designed to stimulate thought and discussion.
- Increased *cross-cultural and historical information* integrated into individual chapters in "Other Times, Other Places" boxes.
- Two new *full-color inserts*: one depicting reproduction; the other, manifestations of sexually transmitted diseases.
- Enhanced focus on *health concerns* related to sexuality—for example, genital self-exam, hysterectomy, mammography, PMS, ERT, STDs, and urinary tract infections.

- Expanded discussion of *sexual arousal and response*, including the role of hormones, the impact of chemicals, and female orgasm.
- New research on *love*: love and sex, and factors related to happy marriages.
- Additional material dealing with *sexual communication*: accepting criticism, and saying no.
- Greatly enlarged coverage of *fantasy*.
- Expanded discussion of *bisexuality*.
- Significantly increased discussion of issues pertaining to *homosexuality*, including religious perspectives on homosexuality, and homosexual parents.
- Updated information of *birth control methods*, with recent material on the issues concerning IUDs and their distribution.
- Increased discussion of *abortion*—now included in Chapter 12, Conceiving Children: Process and Choice.
- Discussion of *fitness and pregnancy*.
- Expanded coverage of *teenage pregnancy*: causes and prevention.
- More information about *sex education*.
- Enlarged discussion of *extramarital relationships*: their incidence, and their impact on primary relationships.
- Increased discussion of *divorce*: its causes, and trends.
- More information on *aging and androgyny*.
- Updated categorization of *sexual difficulties*.
- Extensive elaboration on approaches to *treatment of sexual problems*.
- Greatly expanded *STD chapter*: the latest information on causes, treatment, and prevention. Several new topics, including AIDS, chlamydial infection, *Gardnerella vaginalis*, and viral hepatitis.
- Coverage of six additional *atypical sexual behaviors*; new perspectives on sadomasochism.
- Greatly expanded discussion of *rape*: date rape, the psychosocial bases of rape, classification of rapes and rapists, rape of males, and new issues in the treatment of rapists.
- Expanded and upgraded discussion of *incest*.
- A new section on the prevention of *child sexual abuse*.
- Extensive focus on the *legal aspects of pornography*, including information from the July 1986 Report of the U.S. Attorney General's Commission on Pornography.
- Greatly enhanced *text supplements*: new self-surveys and supplementary readings in the Study Guide, and completely new questions in the Test File, rated by level of difficulty.

Continuing Features

A Personal Approach

Users of the text have responded very favorably to our attempts to humanize and personalize the subject matter, and in the third edition we have retained and strengthened the main elements that contribute to our approach.

- **Readable, Personal Style.**   The book is written in a clear and interesting style that facilitates understanding. We have maintained a personal focus throughout its pages. For example, when we present the anatomy and physiology of sexual functions, we frequently provide perspectives of people's feelings about their bodies.
- **Authors' Files.**   Excerpts from our files relating experiences and observations by students, clients, and colleagues are interspersed throughout the text. In some instances, they were provided to us in the form of written personal reflections. Here, only minor changes have been made to preserve anonymity (any names that appear are fictitious). In other cases, where they were related verbally, we have recorded the accounts as accurately as our memories allow. These quotations, printed in color, help dramatize important concepts and the many dimensions of human sexuality.
- **Nonjudgmental Perspective.**   Consistent with our personal focus, we have avoided a prescriptive stance on the issues introduced in the text. We have attempted to provide information in a sensitive, nonsexist, nonjudgmental manner that assumes the reader is best qualified to determine what is most valid and applicable to his or her life.
- **Psychosocial Orientation.**   We focus on the roles of psychological and social factors in human sexual expression, reflecting our belief that human sexuality is governed more by psychosocial factors than by biological factors. At the same time, we provide the reader with a solid basis in the anatomy and physiology of human sexuality.
- **Practical Information.**   Many chapters offer practical information and suggestions for readers to use, if they wish. Some examples include: how to enhance sexual communication, options for contraception and childbirth, how to improve sexual satisfaction, how to avoid contracting sexually transmitted diseases, when and where to seek professional counseling, guidelines for parents and other caregivers who wish to reduce a child's vulnerability to sexual abuse, and suggestions for how to deal with sexual harassment in the workplace.
- **Superb Illustrations.**   The biological and diagrammatic art is clear and instructive. Enhancing the text are sensitive drawings and photographs, many of them new to this edition. The illustrations are not limited to portrayals of young and attractive couples but include a wide variety of individuals.

Organization

The organization of the book has been designed to reflect a logical progression of topics. We begin, in Part One, with the social and cultural legacy of sexuality in our society. We then describe how major research studies have increased our knowledge in recent years, and discuss the difficulties of gathering information in this sensitive area of human behavior. We conclude the opening unit with a detailed exploration of a variety of gender issues. The three chapters of Part Two present the biological foundations of sexuality, with sexual arousal and sexual response patterns integrated into one chapter, Chapter 6. A variety of sexual behaviors are discussed in Part Three. In Part Four, we discuss contraception, pregnancy, and issues pertaining to sexuality throughout the life cycle. The sources and nature of sexual problems and their treatments constitute the three chapters of Part Five. The final section, Part Six, includes discussions of atypical sexuality, sexual victimization, and the legal aspects of sexuality.

Learning Aids Within the Text

Individuals learn in different ways. We therefore provide a variety of pedagogical aids to be used as the student chooses. Each chapter opens with an **outline** of topic headings. **Key words** are boldfaced within the text. Each chapter concludes with a **Summary** in outline form for student reference, followed by several **Thought Provokers**—questions designed to stimulate thought and discussion. Annotated **Suggested Readings** are included with each chapter, and a complete **Bibliography** is provided at the end of the book. A comprehensive **Glossary** facilitates quick reference to terminology.

A Complete Set of Supplements

Lecture preparation and student understanding are enhanced when the complete teaching/learning package is employed. The main text of *Our Sexuality* is accompanied by the following:

- The student **Study Guide**, by Gary R. Lesniak of Portland Community College. In addition to its key terms and practice questions, the Study Guide now includes elements that enhance the two major objectives of the text—personal meaning and academic grounding. New *self-assessment inventories*, called Personal Reflections, and reprints of *key articles* in human sexuality can be incorporated into classroom teaching or recommended to students as an optional extension of their study.

- The **Classroom Resource Manual**, featuring learning objectives, detailed lecture outlines, classroom activities, and recommended audiovisuals.

- A **Test File**, completely revised and reformatted. The Valois Testing Program for *Our Sexuality* presents multiple-choice questions organized and keyed according to a hierarchy of recall and reasoning. The format allows instructors to create a flexible file system of questions according to their course organization and level of challenge.

- The **Slide Package**, featuring both text illustrations and additional visuals.

- **Yearly Updates**, for instructors and students alike, to keep *Our Sexuality* current throughout its life cycle. These updates, featuring key articles that have appeared during the previous year, will be accompanied by thought-provoking questions.

Feedback from Students and Instructors

We would like to hear about your experience with the third edition of *Our Sexuality*. We will incorporate your contributions and suggestions into both our Yearly Updates and our next edition. Please write to us in care of the publisher, The Benjamin/Cummings Publishing Company, 2727 Sand Hill Road, Menlo Park, California 94025, Attention D. Bowen.

Acknowledgments

This book represents a combination of talents and insights that extend beyond those of the authors. We are particularly indebted to the reviewers of our manuscripts, the staff of Benjamin/Cummings, and our students, whose combined contributions have added much to the quality of the text.

As we worked on this project, we came to appreciate the indispensable value of the review process. Individuals representing a variety of disciplines and perspectives read and evaluated our first edition manuscript at various stages of completion. For help with the first edition we owe special gratitude to Carol Ellison, author, clinical psychologist, and instructor of human sexuality. Our work on the second edition was facilitated by the suggestions of Valerie Pinhas, John Petras, and Joseph LoPiccolo, who reviewed the manuscript throughout its development. Valerie Pinhas again provided invaluable guidance on the direction of the third edition as we began to revise, and Sherman Sowby provided equally valuable feedback on our revised material. We also received important comments and suggestions from many sexuality educators who reviewed either the entire manuscript or portions of it. We appreciate the efforts of all these reviewers, whose names are listed at the end of this preface. Sally Adelman's skill and resourcefulness as a research assistant on all editions are also greatly appreciated.

The staff of The Benjamin/Cummings Publishing Company has consistently performed beyond our highest expectations. Our sponsoring editor on the first edition, Larry Wilson, maintained a sense of perspective, direction, and infectious enthusiasm and humor that saw us through many difficult times. Jane Gillen, who assumed the role of sponsoring editor on the second edition, provided invaluable direction and support. Diane Bowen, sponsoring editor on the third edition, carried on the established tradition of editorial excellence and insightful guidance. Several of the new features are the direct result of her suggestions. Margaret Moore and Pat Burner, production editors on the first and second editions, respectively, deserve a special thanks for providing the kind of organization essential to the success of a project of this nature. Betsy Dilernia performed the same critical function on the third edition in a superbly efficient manner. The developmental editing on the first two editions by Jean Stein and Beverly Azarin was extremely valuable and contributed much to the book's quality. Developmental and copy editor Robin Fox worked her special kind of magic with the third edition manuscript. We are indebted to her for contributions that ranged far beyond our expectations. Special thanks go to Valerie Willson for the art on the cover of the third edition, and to Lindsay Kefauver for new photographs.

We are deeply grateful for the support and encouragement our families and friends have so generously and patiently provided throughout the writing of this book. Karla would like to give special thanks for the active and loving support of her husband, Jim Hicks.

Finally, we owe our greatest gratitude to the thousands of students who have attended our classes. In many ways, *Our Sexuality* reflects the thoughts and experiences of this diverse group. Their contributions have enriched the text. We hope that readers of our book will derive at least a portion of the benefits that we have gathered from our opportunity to share in this collective fund of human experience.

Robert Crooks and Karla Baur

Reviewers

First and Second Editions

Jane Blackwell
Washington State University

John Blakemore
Monterey Peninsula College

Marvin J. Branstrom
Cañada College

Bruce Clear
The First Unitarian Church,
Portland

David R. Cleveland
Honolulu Community College

Brenda M. DeVellis
University of North Carolina

Judy Drolet
Southern Illinois University

Carol Ellison
Clinical Psychologist

Andrea Parrot Eggleston
Cornell University

Catherine Fichten
Dawson College

Glen G. Gilbert
Portland State University

Claudette Hastie-Beahrs
Clinical Social Worker

David Johnson
Portland State University

Richard A. Kaye
Kingsborough Community College

Miriam LeGare
California State University,
Sacramento

Roger W. Little
University of Illinois,
Chicago

Joseph LoPiccolo
State University of New York,
Stony Brook

Leslie McBride
Portland State University

John Money
Johns Hopkins University

Denis Moore
Honolulu Metropolitan Community
Church

Teri Nicoll-Johnson
Modesto Junior College

Bruce Palmer
Washington State University

Monroe Pasternak
Diablo Valley College

Third Edition

Brief Contents

Detailed Contents

PART FOUR   SEXUALITY AND THE LIFE CYCLE   341

Our Sexuality

Third Edition

Part One

Introduction

1

The type of fig leaf which each culture employs to cover its social taboos offers a two-fold description of its morality. It reveals that certain unacknowledged behavior exists and it suggests the form that such behavior takes.
Freda Adler
Sisters in Crime (1975)

Perspectives on Sexuality

The Authors' Perspectives
A Cross-Cultural Perspective: Social Norms and Sexuality
The Sex-for-Reproduction Legacy
The Gender-Role Legacy
Sexuality: Personal or Public Domain?

PERHAPS ALL OF US have had the experience of walking into a class for the first time, wondering what the course and the teacher will be like. On that first day, the instructor's candor in freely expressing the philosophy and focus of the course is a great help in setting the stage for all that is to follow. Our primary purpose for including this opening chapter is the same as that of an instructor's opening remarks—to acquaint you, the reader, with the focus, philosophy, and perspectives we bring to this text.

We offer this book as a tool for the development of your own personal perspectives on human sexuality. While we will present a wide array of information about attitudes, ideas, and behaviors, we wish to emphasize that the final expert on your sexuality is *you*. Therefore, we encourage you to evaluate all the information we present within the framework of your own experiences and convictions.

The Authors' Perspectives

It is safe to assume that any controversial topic (and what sexual topic is not controversial?) will elicit a wide range of responses. In any beginning sexuality class—or in almost any other group, for that matter—attitudes toward sexuality will likely range from very liberal to extremely conservative. It is also reasonable to assume that students in sexuality classes represent a wide range of sexual experience and preferences. Some have shared sexual encounters with one or more partners; some have had long-term partnerships in marital or other ongoing frameworks; others have not been sexually intimate with another person. Many people prefer to relate sexually exclusively to members of the other sex; some prefer sexual relations with members of the same sex; still others are comfortable relating sexually to either sex. There are virtually no universals in sexual attitudes, experiences, or preferences.

With this broad spectrum in mind, we have attempted to bring a pluralistic, nonlimiting philosophy to our book. We think a human sexuality text should be written for all prospective readers, not just for one or two groups that may happen to be statistically more common than others. We hope there will be something of value in the following pages for all our readers. At the same time, we do speak from a distinct point of view. It is appropriate to tell you about our perspective—our orientation and our biases—so you can recognize and evaluate it for yourself as you read the text.

A Psychosocial Orientation

This book has a **psychosocial** orientation, reflecting our view that human sexuality is governed more by psychological factors (motivational, emotional, attitudinal) and by social conditioning (the process by which we learn our society's expectations and norms) than by the effects of biological factors such as hormones or instincts. The psychological and social factors are so intertwined that it is often difficult to distinguish clearly between the two.

We may not always be aware of it, but our sexual attitudes and behaviors are strongly shaped by our society. The subtle ways in which we learn society's expectations regarding sexuality often lead us to assume that our behaviors or feelings are biologically innate, or natural. However, an examination of sexuality in other societies

*Sexual attitudes
and experiences
vary from person to
person.*

(or even in different cultural groups within our own society) and in other historical periods reveals a broad range of acceptable behavior. For example, lovers rubbing noses, brides experiencing coitus with many men on their wedding day, and children being masturbated by parents are all legitimate forms of sexual expression in certain other cultures, though certainly not in North American society. What we regard as natural is clearly relative.

Many contemporary sex researchers think that there has been an overemphasis on the biological determination of sexual behavior. Evidence from studies of human sexual response patterns, together with investigations of sexual behavior in different societies and in different species, shows that there is much more to human sexuality than biology. It is certainly clear that the physiology of sex plays an important role, and we will be looking in some detail at the biological foundations of sexual behavior. But understanding the impact of culture and individual experience can make it easier to make decisions about our own sexuality. Therefore, our major emphasis in this book will be on the psychosocial aspects of human sexuality.

Our Cultural Legacy: Questioning Two Themes

In addition to a psychosocial orientation, we admit to some biases. These have to do with our opposition to two themes pertaining to sexuality, themes that are of long standing in our culture and in most other Western cultures.

One of these themes is sex for reproduction, the idea that reproduction is the only legitimate purpose of sexual activity. This idea is a legacy rooted deep in our heritage. In our culture one of the most prominent ways that the reproductive theme is expressed is in the notion that sex is synonymous with penile-vaginal intercourse (or coitus). Certainly coitus can be a very fulfilling part of sexual expression. However, we believe that excessive emphasis on intercourse often has negative consequences. For one, it perpetuates the notion that sexual response and orgasm are supposed to occur during penetration. Such a narrow focus places tremendous performance pressure on both women and men and creates enormous expectations of coitus itself.

The sex-for-reproduction view also may result in devaluating other forms of sexual behavior. Some activities—for instance, affectionate kisses, body caresses, and manual or oral stimulation—are often relegated to the secondary status of *foreplay* (usually considered to be any activity before intercourse), implying that they are to be followed by the "real sex" of coitus. Many people have learned to view these and other practices—such as masturbation, sexual fantasy, and anal intercourse—with suspicion. The same is true of sexual activity between members of the same sex, which certainly does not fit into the model of intercourse for reproduction. All of these noncoital sexual behaviors have been defined at some time as immoral, sinful, perverted, or illegal. We will present them in this text as viable sexual options for those who choose them.

The other theme we oppose is the rigid distinction between male and female roles. This second legacy is based on far more than the physiological differences between the sexes. Research does show certain sex differences in behavioral predispositions, but the impact of socialization shapes and exaggerates our biological proclivities. Human beings begin learning in early infancy to be "opposites." For example, one of our students describes seeing this behavior at a baby shower for fraternal twins:

> Except for the color of their clothes, the twins sure looked the same to me. But the women handled each of them differently; they gave soft, cooing sounds and delicate touches to the girl and energetic words and bouncing to the boy. (Authors' files)

It is our belief that rigid gender-role conditioning limits each person's full range of human potential, producing a negative impact on our sexuality. For example, "appropriate" personality characteristics delegated to men and women may contribute to the notion that the man must always be the initiator and the woman must be the receiver. When this arrangement is the status quo, we believe, it places tremendous responsibility on the male and severely limits the woman's likelihood of discovering and meeting her own needs. It discourages the man from expressing his receptivity and the woman from experiencing her assertiveness.

Our psychosocial orientation and our biases—our opposition to the sex-for-reproduction theme and our belief that rigid gender roles are limiting—will appear throughout this text. In this chapter we want to explore these ideas more thoroughly, first from a cross-cultural and then from a historical perspective.

It is difficult to understand how deeply culture shapes our attitudes and feelings without some grounds for comparison. In the next section we will look at four twentieth-century societies to see how their sexual norms vary from one another and from those of our own culture. After that we will take a brief, selective look at our Western cultural heritage, searching for the roots of the two legacies: sex for reproduction and rigid gender roles. An appreciation of these two themes, as reflected in their cross-cultural and historical contexts, should help us more fully understand the conflicts they may present in our own lives.

A Cross-Cultural Perspective: Social Norms and Sexuality

What constitutes normal sexual behavior? Many of us have our own ideas about what is normal and what is not, but often the meaning of a given act (sexual or otherwise) can be fully understood only by looking at the cultural context within which it occurs. For example, North Americans often see sexual overtones in the act of two men hugging each other. In contrast, men in Iran (and in many other societies) may heartily embrace each other without any suggestion of a sexual component in their behavior. In the ancient Greek city-states of Athens and Sparta it was normal for men to engage in **pederasty**, a practice in which an older man would take a young man as a lover, providing not only affection but also intellectual and moral guidance. In fact, the Spartans encouraged pederasty for military purposes, believing that a man in love with a fellow soldier would fight more fiercely in battle to protect his lover. Today, as in Western cultures for centuries, pederasty is defined more narrowly as the sexual attraction of an adult for a child, and it has been morally condemned and made a crime. This is just one example of how the meaning of *normal* varies from one era to another.

In ancient Greece sexual relationships between men and boys, as depicted on this vase, were acceptable under certain circumstances.

A woman warrior in New Guinea. In many societies bare female breasts are not generally viewed as erotic stimuli.

There is such cultural diversity among the peoples of the world that even the idea of what is sexually arousing varies greatly. For example, exposed female breasts often trigger sexual arousal in Western males, but they induce little or no erotic interest in the males of New Guinea. Furthermore, the acceptability of sexual activity varies enormously from one culture to another. In some societies, such as the Mangaian society of Polynesia, sex is highly valued and almost all manifestations of it are considered beautiful and natural. Other societies, such as the Manus society of New Guinea, view any sexual act as undesirable and shameful.

One can take almost any specific sexual behavior and find wide differences in the ways in which it is practiced or viewed in different societies. For example, masturbation by children may be overtly condemned in one society, covertly supported in another, openly encouraged in still another, and even occasionally initiated by parental example.

The diversity of sexual expression throughout the world tends to mask a fundamental generalization that can be applied without exception to all social orders: Within the cultural mores of all societies, there are rules regulating the conduct of sexual behavior. While the exact regulations vary from one society to the next, no social order has seen fit to allow sexuality to remain totally unregulated. Thus, the sexual inclinations of human males and females are never allowed free reign within the context of any formally organized social group.

Data Sources: Methods and Limitations

Most of our data about sexual expression in other societies has been derived from the fieldwork of **ethnographers**, anthropologists who specialize in studying the cultures of different societies. Fieldwork consists of careful observation (the researcher may live with the population for several months or years) and in-depth interviews and discussions. It is a method of study that can produce detailed information about the beliefs and behaviors of a small representative group. Unfortunately, fieldwork has usually focused on religion, economics, technology, and social organization and has rarely examined sexual mores and behaviors.

The scarcity of data about sexual expression probably results in part from the cultural bias of many researchers. Most ethnographers came from Western societies, where sex was considered a private matter, not a topic of investigation. They may therefore have been reluctant to pursue the subject. Furthermore, some of these investigators were probably not entirely objective; no doubt they tended to make assumptions about other societies on the basis of their own culturally determined attitudes. Our limited information also reflects the attitudes of the people being studied. Even when field investigators are comfortable inquiring about sexual activity, their respondents may not share their comfort. In addition, investigations of other societies rely on reported rather than observed sexual behavior, and some degree of error in the data is probable, as we will discuss in Chapter 2.

This brief outline of some of the limitations of cross-cultural sex data may give you some perspective on the discussion that follows. We do not mean to imply that such information is totally untrustworthy and irrelevant. On the contrary, some of the available ethnographic descriptions contain valuable data about the richness and diversity of human sexual expression.

The rest of this section is devoted to discussions of cultural diversity in sexual attitudes and behaviors. In order to provide you with an appreciation of the tremendous diversity in human sexuality, these discussions will focus on non-Western cultures. We will look briefly at four societies—the Polynesian island of Mangaia, the Irish island known as Inis Beag, the Dani society of New Guinea, and the People's Republic of China. Additional cross-cultural and historical perspectives are presented in "Other Times, Other Places" boxes throughout the text.

Mangaia

Mangaia is the southernmost of the Polynesian Cook Island chain. The island was studied in the 1950s by anthropologist Donald Marshall, whose accounts of Mangaian sexual practices have been widely quoted.*

---

*In Mangaia, as in all human societies, behavior patterns change with the passage of time. In the years since Marshall's visit, the Mangaian lifestyle has undergone many changes, as noted during a visit in 1982 by one of the authors, Bob Crooks.

When Marshall visited Mangaia, he observed a society in which sexual pleasure and activity is a principal concern, starting in childhood (Marshall, 1971). Children have extensive exposure to sexuality: they hear folktales that contain detailed descriptions of sex acts and sexual anatomy, and they observe provocative ritual dances. During puberty, members of both sexes receive active and detailed sex instruction. Males undergo an operation called *superincision* that consists of cutting the tissue on top of the penis and folding it back, exposing the glans. During this period a boy is provided with detailed information about various sexual techniques. He is taught how to stimulate a woman's genitals and breasts with his mouth, to bring a partner to orgasm, and to control his urge to ejaculate. A Mangaian girl is also instructed in sexual activity. She is taught the importance of being responsive and active during sexual encounters.

Once their instruction is completed, boys begin to seek girls. Sex occurs in "public privacy" as young males engage in a practice called *night-crawling*. At night the boy creeps quietly into the family home of a young woman with whom he wants to have sexual intercourse. If awakened, the other 5 to 15 family members in the home politely pretend to sleep. (In the 1950s, when Marshall conducted his research, most Mangaian houses had only a single sleeping area.) Parents approve of this practice and listen for sounds of laughter as a sign that their daughter is pleased with her partner; they encourage the young woman to have several encounters so that she may find a sexually compatible marriage partner. The young men gain social prestige through their ability to please their partners. These patterns persist throughout the adolescent years for unmarried males and females.

Sexual relations continue to occur frequently after marriage. Marshall estimates that an 18-year-old male experiences three orgasms per night every day of the week—and if he is skilled, his partner experiences three orgasms for each one of his. A wide range of sexual activity is socially approved, including oral-genital sex and a considerable amount of touching before and during intercourse. The Mangaians, then, not only condone but actively encourage a high rate of sexual activity as the norm. In sharp contrast is the community of the Irish island known as Inis Beag.

Inis Beag

The inhabitants of Inis Beag (a pseudonym given to protect the privacy of this Irish island) have a very different attitude from that of the Mangaians (Messenger, 1971). Sexual expression is discouraged from infancy; mothers avoid breast-feeding their children, and after infancy parents seldom kiss or fondle them. Children learn to abhor nudity. They learn that elimination is "dirty" and that bathing must be done only in absolute privacy. Any kind of childhood sexual expression is punished.

As they grow older, children usually receive no information about sex from their parents. Young girls are often shocked by their first menstruation, and they are never given an adequate explanation of what has happened. Priests and other religious authorities teach that it is sinful to discuss premarital sexual activity, masturbation, or sex play. Religious leaders on the island have denounced even *Time* and *Life* magazines as pornographic.

The average age for marriage is older than in many societies (36 for men and 26 for women), and marriages are often arranged. One of the reasons for late marriage may be the limited land resources—a man must usually wait to own land through inheritance. Marriage partners generally know little or nothing about such precoital sex play as oral or manual stimulation of breasts and genitals. Beyond intercourse, sexual activity is usually limited to mouth kissing and rough fondling of the woman's lower body by the man. Sex usually occurs while both partners are wearing night clothes. Males invariably initiate sex, using the man-on-top intercourse position, and after ejaculation, they tend to fall asleep. Female orgasm is unknown or considered a deviant response.

Sexual misconceptions continue through adulthood. For example, many women believe that menopause causes insanity, and some women confine themselves to bed from menopause to their death. During menstruation, and also during the months following childbirth, men consider intercourse to be harmful to them. Many men also believe intercourse to be debilitating, and they avoid sex the night before a strenuous job. In general, anxiety-laden attitudes and rigid social restrictions are the normal elements of sexuality in Inis Beag.

The Dani of New Guinea

In both Mangaia and Inis Beag, sexuality receives a great deal of attention, if in different ways. Is this characteristic of all societies? A look at the Dani culture of the mountains of western New Guinea shows that it is not.

The Dani people seem to be largely indifferent to sexuality (Heider, 1976). Children are raised gently, with little stress; their toilet training and education are relaxed. Sexual activity is infrequent among adults. There is almost no premarital sex, even when courtship covers an extended period. (Marriages are held only during a certain feast that occurs every four to six years.) After marriage a couple abstains from sex for at least two years and then has infrequent intercourse. Following the birth of a child the couple abstains from sex for four to six years. During this time there is no reported masturbation, and extramarital sex is rare.

According to Karl Heider, who studied this society in the 1960s, the Dani culture does not attempt to overtly enforce these behavior patterns. Heider also saw no indications of hormonal or physiological deficiencies that could result in low sexual interest. In general, the Dani are relaxed, physically healthy people, who live in a moderate climate and have an adequate food supply. They appear to be very calm, only rarely expressing anger. Heider believes that the apparent infrequency of sexual activity reflects the Dani's relaxed lifestyle and their low level of emotional intensity.

The People's Republic of China

We will present a fourth variation on the theme that sexuality reflects society. Unlike the other societies we have discussed, the People's Republic of China has government policies designed to limit reproduction; the government considers its extensive and aggressive birth control programs essential to future social and economic development. China has 22% of the world's population and only 7% of the world's arable land. This imbalance stretches resources for basic living needs and stunts economic development (Isaacs and Cooke, 1984).

*A family planning
worker in China
provides contracep-
tive information.*

As one method of controlling the growth of China's enormous population, the government is promoting the goal of the one-child family. The 1982 constitution made practicing birth control a civic duty (Beck et al., 1984), and local employment units have family planning workers who monitor birth control use and make decisions about when a couple can have a child (David, 1980). Couples who limit their families to one child receive a monthly subsidy, higher pensions, priority for housing and health care, and free education for the child (Chen and Kols, 1982). Penalties are assessed to families who have more than one child; for instance, parents have to pay for the second child's schooling. They also lose benefits for the first child and have reduced opportunities for education, housing, and employment (Chen et al., 1982).

Extensive social policies affecting such a personal area as the number of children in a family are bound to create enormous problems, especially in a society where large families traditionally provide status and security. Since Chinese peasants rely on their sons to support them in later years, parents sometimes kill female infants or children so they can try again for a son and still adhere to the one-child policy. There are also reports that the state forces women to have abortions and sterilizations (Beck et al., 1984). In the face of widespread protests and resistance from peasants, the government adopted new rules in 1985, allowing some couples who live in rural areas to have a second child (Mann, 1985).

China provides us with a thought-provoking example of the ethical dilemma that arises when the interests of a government in limiting population growth—in order to provide its people with food, housing, employment, and education—conflict with the rights of individuals to choose the size of their families.

The broad range of sexual attitudes and behaviors among the Mangaians, the people of Inis Beag, the Dani, and the mainland Chinese helps to show how society shapes sexuality. Though we may not always look at it in the same light, our own customs, practices, and attitudes reflect a parallel process of social shaping. This becomes clearer if we explore the origins of our sexual mores in Western history.

The Sex-for-Reproduction Legacy

We have noted that a strong theme in our culture is that the purpose of sexual activity should be procreation. Where did this theme come from, and how relevant is it to us today?

The idea of sex for reproduction is associated with Judeo-Christian tradition. Childbearing was tremendously important to the ancient Hebrews. Their history of slavery and persecution made them determined to preserve their people—to "be fruitful, and multiply, and replenish the earth . . ." (Genesis 1:28). Yet to "know" a partner sexually, within marriage, was also recognized as a profound physical and emotional experience (Carswell, 1969), and the Song of Solomon in the Old Testament contains some of the most sensuous love poetry in Western literature.

The bridegroom speaks:

> *How fair is thy love, . . . my spouse!*
> *how much better is thy love than wine!*
> *and the smell of thine ointments than all spices!*
> *Thy lips, oh my spouse, drop as the honeycomb:*
> *honey and milk are under thy tongue.* (Solomon 4:10–11)

And the bride:

> *I am my beloved's and his desire is toward me.*
> *Come, my husband, let us go forth into the field;*
> *Let us lodge in the villages . . .*
> *There will I give thee my loves.* (7:10–13)

This kind of appreciation of sexuality was a part of Judaic tradition, just as was the notion of sex for procreation. It would later be eclipsed, however, by the teachings of the medieval church. To understand why this happened, it is necessary to look at the social context in which Christianity arose. By the first century B.C., after the Roman Empire had reached its height, social instability and sexual decadence were pervasive. Many exotic cults were imported to Rome from Greece, Persia, Palestine, and other parts of the empire to provide sexual entertainment and amusement. The cult of Bacchus (the god of wine) became one of the most notorious. In the Bacchanalia ceremony, which ultimately became so offensive that the Roman Senate banned it, young male initiates raced to the banks of the Tiber River, where they were forced to have intercourse with members of the cult or be killed.

We know very little about Jesus' views on sexuality. But in the years after his death his followers showed their reaction against activities like the Bacchanalia by their association of sex with sin. Paul of Tarsus, whose influence upon the early church was crucial (he died in 66 A.D., and many of his writings were incorporated into the New Testament), described the importance of overcoming "desires of the flesh," including anger, selfishness, hatred, and nonmarital sex, in order to inherit the Kingdom of God. He associated spirituality with sexual abstinence and saw **celibacy**, the state of being unmarried, as superior to marriage. Other church fathers expanded on the theme of sex as sin in the following centuries. Augustine (353–430) declared that lust was the original sin of Adam and Eve, and he formalized the notion that intercourse could take place only within marriage for the purpose of procreation.

The belief that sex is sinful persisted throughout the Middle Ages (the period from the fall of the Western Roman Empire in 476 A.D. to the beginning of the Renaissance, about 1400), and Thomas Aquinas (1225–1274) further refined this idea in a small section of his *Summa Theologica*. In a detailed list of rules about sexual behavior, Aquinas maintained that human sexual organs were designed for procreation and that any other use, as in homosexual acts, oral-genital sex, anal intercourse, or sex with animals, was against God's will and therefore heretical. Aquinas' teachings were so influential that from then on homosexuals were to find neither refuge nor tolerance anywhere in the Western world (Boswell, 1980).

The ideas of Augustine and Aquinas dominated Western thought until the Protestant Reformation in the sixteenth century. One of Martin Luther's (1483–1546) disagreements with official church doctrine centered around chastity and celibacy. Sex, he believed, was as necessary to humans as eating and drinking. He believed the clergy should be permitted to marry, and after he left the priesthood he married, and fathered several children. Another reformer, John Calvin (1509–1564), recognized that sex could have other purposes than procreation. Marital sex was permissible, he claimed, if it stemmed "from a desire for children, or to avoid fornication, or to lighten and ease the cares and sadnesses of household affairs, or to endear each other" (Taylor, 1971, p. 62). The Puritans, a group often maligned for having rigid views about sex, also shared an appreciation of sexual expression within marriage as a part of their emphasis on the importance of the family unit. One man was expelled from Boston when, among other offenses, "he denied . . . conjugal . . . fellowship unto his wife for the space of 2 years . . ." (Morgan, 1978, p. 364). Thus, the Reformation groups saw intercourse as a human necessity, not just a requirement for procreation, with marriage providing the proper outlet for it.

One other influence should be mentioned in any discussion of the sex-for-procreation legacy: the availability of modern contraception, which permits intercourse without procreation more reliably than older methods. Contraceptive devices have been used for centuries (Pomeroy, 1975). Condoms made from goat bladders were used by men in ancient times. In Rome, during the first century B.C., women used amulets, magic, and the rhythm method (which was ineffective, because the Romans believed the most fertile period was at the end of menstruation). They also inserted soft wool pads to block the cervix. The modern diaphragm, which was developed in Europe in the 1870s, was not introduced to the United States until the 1920s.

With the possible exception of the diaphragm, none of these methods was as reliable as the Pill, introduced in the late fifties and early sixties, soon to be followed by the intrauterine device (IUD), "morning after pills," and spermicides. These contraceptives have given women increased control over their reproductive capacities, and their widespread acceptance has permitted sexuality to be separated from procreation in a way that it has never been before. The world has changed, too, so that today many people are concerned with the ecological and economic costs of bearing children, costs that were not as relevant in the preindustrial world. Despite these changes, however, the legacy of the Old and New Testaments, of St. Augustine and Thomas Aquinas, and the legacy of the Reformation are still very much with us. Thus, the sex-for-reproduction issue in the twentieth-century Western world represents a complex conflict among the values of personal pleasure, practicality, and tradition.

The Gender-Role Legacy

A second issue about which we admit to a bias is the legacy of gender roles. Roles of women and men are changing in modern Western society, but each change, going as it does against tradition, has been difficult to achieve.

Other Times, Other Places

When God Was a Woman

Accurate knowledge of sexuality and gender roles in early human history is virtually impossible. Available information is sparse and subject to distorted interpretation by historians influenced by their own cultural biases. The following paragraphs summarize the provocative historical thesis of art historian Merlin Stone (1976).

In prehistoric and early historic periods of human development (about 7000 B.C.–500 A.D.), religions existed in which people revered great goddesses who had life-giving and important roles. In nearly all areas of the world, female deities were extolled as healers. Some were powerful, courageous warriors and leaders in battle. The Greek Demeter and the Egyptian Isis were both invoked as lawgivers and dispensers of wisdom and justice. In the ancient Middle East where some of the earliest evidence of agricultural development has been found, the goddess Ninlil was revered for having provided her people with an understanding of planting and harvesting.

As the role of the male in reproduction came to be understood and male kinship lines became important, religions headed by female deities were persecuted and suppressed by the newer religions, which held male deities as supreme.

Through the imposition and eventual acceptance of the male-centered religions, women came to be regarded as inferior creatures, divinely intended for the production of children and the pleasure of men. In their new role as silent and obedient vessels, women were far removed from the status of the ancient goddesses.

How far back do we have to look to find the roots of this legacy? Certainly by the time Hebraic culture was established, gender roles were highly specialized. The Book of Proverbs lists the duties of a good wife: She must instruct servants, care for her family, and keep household accounts. In addition, she must look on the future with optimism, be kind, and never be idle. Charm and beauty were not required, but bearing children (especially sons) was essential; so was obedience to the husband. In return for all this the wife was granted the right to her husband's sexual favors—although she might share this right with one or more secondary wives or concubines!

If the Old Testament seems to embody a rigid hierarchy of gender, it is egalitarian compared with the gender roles that evolved in ancient Athens, where women had no more political or legal rights than slaves. In the sixth century B.C. the lawgiver Solon institutionalized these roles, regulating women's dress, food and drink, and right to appear in public. Women were subject to the absolute authority of the male next of kin. They received no formal education and spent their lives in women's quarters within their homes.

Not all ancient societies had the same inflexible gender distinctions. In fact, the cultural climate was very different in the sixth-century Greek societies of Sparta and Lesbos. The city-state of Sparta was determined to produce the most feared and dedicated army in Greece. Women were valued. Both sexes trained from birth under severe discipline, both sexes were educated, and both were encouraged in athletics, since the Spartans believed strong women produced healthy babies. Sexual relationships between women were accepted, as well as between men. Women were also valued in the island culture of Lesbos, from whose name **lesbianism** (female homosexuality) has been derived.* What explains the difference between these two societies and Athens? Sparta and Lesbos seem to have accepted erotic attachments between women because women themselves were considered important (Boswell, 1980; Dover, 1978; Pomeroy, 1975).

Christianity reaffirmed Judaism's traditional gender roles. One of the major themes of the writings of Paul of Tarsus was the status of women. Paul used man's creation before woman's and Eve's disobedience to God to explain why women should be submissive:

> I permit no woman to teach or to have authority over men. . . . For Adam was formed first, then Eve; and Adam was not deceived, but the woman was deceived and became a transgressor. . . . (1 Timothy 2:11–15)

This was the status quo throughout the Middle Ages. During this period, however, two contradictory images of women were to evolve, gaining strength so that each had its own impact on women's place in society. The first was the image of the Virgin Mary; the second, the image of Eve as an evil temptress.

The cult of the Virgin was imported to the West by crusaders returning from Constantinople. Mary had been a vague figure of secondary importance in the Western

---

*In Greek classical literature, however, Lesbos is actually linked with both heterosexual and homosexual eroticism. Even the famous poet Sappho, who lived on Lesbos at this time, seems to have been bisexual (she had a husband and a child).

church, but now she was transformed into a gracious, compassionate mother of the poor and wretched, an exalted focus of religious devotion. The practice of *courtly love*, which evolved at about the same time, reflected a compatible image of woman as pure and above reproach. Ideally, a young knight would fall in love with a married woman of higher rank. After a lengthy pursuit he would find favor, but his love would remain unconsummated because her marriage vows ultimately proved inviolable. How many affairs actually took this course is a rather fascinating question. However, the idea caught the medieval imagination, and troubadors performed ballads of courtly love throughout the courts of Europe.

The other medieval image provides a counterpoint to the unattainable, compassionate madonna: Eve as the evil temptress of the Garden of Eden. This image, promoted by the church, reflected an increasing emphasis on Eve's sin and an antagonism toward women. The antagonism reached its climax in the witch hunts that began in the late fifteenth century—after the Renaissance, which also elevated women's status, was well under way—and lasted for close to 200 years. Queen Elizabeth I (1533–1603) was a true "Renaissance woman," who brought England to new heights of power; yet during her reign thousands of women were tortured and executed as witches in both Europe and America.

Witch hunting had ended by the time of the eighteenth-century Enlightenment, which was partly a product of the new scientific rationalism, and women were to enjoy a new equality at least for a short time. Some women, like Mary Wollstonecraft of England, were famous for their intelligence, wit, and vivacity. Wollstonecraft's book, *The Vindication of the Rights of Women* (1792), attacked the practice whereby young girls were given dolls rather than schoolbooks. Wollstonecraft also asserted that sexual satisfaction was as important to women as to men and that premarital and extramarital sex were not sinful.

These views did not prevail. The Victorian era, which took its name from the woman who ascended the British throne in 1837, brought a sharp turnaround. The genders had highly defined roles. Victorian women were valued for their spirituality and delicacy—an image that was reinforced by clothing like corsets, hoops, and bustles, which prevented a woman from freely moving her body. Popular opinion of female sexuality was reflected by the widely quoted physician William Acton, who wrote, "The majority of women are not very much troubled with sexual feelings of any kind" (Degler, 1980, p. 250). Women's duties centered around fulfilling their families' spiritual needs and providing a comfortable home for their husbands to retreat to after working all day. Ladylike manners and domestic skills were considered very important, and magazines such as *Godey's Lady's Book* instructed women on the proper forms for such virtues. The world of women was clearly separated from that of men, and intensely passionate friendships developed between women, providing the support and comfort often absent in marriage.

Victorian men were expected to conform to the strict propriety of the age, but (alas!) they were often forced to lay aside morality in the pursuit of business and political interests. They sometimes laid aside morality in the pursuit of sexual companionship also, for the separation of the worlds of husbands and wives imposed an emotional distance on many Victorian marriages. Ironically, prostitution flourished at the same time as propriety and sexual repression. Victorian men could smoke, drink, and joke with the women who had turned to prostitution out of economic necessity. Furthermore, social pressure encouraged men to marry only after they had accumulated money and established a comfortable home. Confronted with many years without a wife, then marriage to a sheltered bride many years younger than himself, a man paid prostitutes for companionship as well as sexual contact.

Perhaps more than any age, the nineteenth century was full of contradictions.

In the Victorian era, the marriageable woman possessed morals that were as tightly laced as her corset. Ironically, prostitution flourished at this time. Clearly, a double standard existed.

Some women were put on a pedestal of asexuality and piety at the same time that others were exploited as sexual objects. Men were trapped between the ideal of purity and the frank pleasures of physical expression. The nineteenth-century French writer Gustave Flaubert captured this feeling:

> A man has missed something if he has never woken up in an anonymous bed beside a face he will never see again, and if he has never left a brothel at dawn feeling like jumping off a bridge out of sheer physical disgust with life. (Baldwick, 1973, p. 106)

The twentieth century changed this precarious status quo. The suffrage movement, which began in the late nineteenth century with the goal of giving women the right to vote, grew out of several related developments, such as the temperance movement, the abolition of slavery, and the demand that women be permitted to attend universities and hold property. The passage in 1920 of the Eighteenth Amendment enfranchising women did not usher in equality, but World War II created an environment for its growth, as thousands of women left the traditional homemaker role and took paying jobs. Not until the 1960s, after the flurry of postwar marriages, the baby boom, and widespread disappointment in the resulting domesticity, did a new movement for gender-role equality begin. This movement, still under way, has had its victories. Yet we still carry the legacy of Victorianism and earlier traditions in the gender roles we all learn as children, and this legacy limits both men and women. Chapter 3 will discuss the impact of gender roles on contemporary men and women in our society.

Sexuality: Personal or Public Domain?

The historical perspective we have used in this chapter may help us appreciate the unique position in which we currently find ourselves. Men and women today have new freedoms and responsibilities. To a far greater degree than was possible for the ancient Hebrews or Athenians, the early Christians, the Europeans of the Middle Ages, or the Victorians of a century ago, we may define our own sexuality on the basis of personal morality.

This responsibility has been hard won, and it is largely a result of psychological, scientific, and social advances that have taken place, primarily in the twentieth century. Psychological advances came with the work of people like Sigmund Freud (1856–1939) and Havelock Ellis (1859–1939), who recognized sexuality in both women and men as natural, and also recognized that different individuals have differing sexual needs; and Theodore Van de Velde (1873–1937), who emphasized the importance of sexual pleasure and satisfaction. As these ideas became accepted by more people, the result was a growing tolerance for a wider variety of behaviors.

Findings of sex researchers like Alfred Kinsey provided scientific data that brought further acceptance of masturbation, homosexuality, and nonmarital intercourse as normal expressions of sexuality; and research such as that of William Masters and Virginia Johnson brought a greater public understanding of the sexual response cycle. We will look at the work of these and other scientific researchers in Chapter 2. This new awareness of sexual interests and individual variations also contributed to a greater tolerance and respect for the individual's right to make sexual decisions.

In the early 1960s the invention of the Pill and the increased availability of other reliable contraceptive devices helped bring sexual decisions even more firmly into the personal domain. By the end of that decade contraception had become accepted as a matter of personal decision. Moreover, in 1973 the U.S. Supreme Court ruled in a landmark decision that abortion is a woman's choice, one that the government cannot prohibit. In the increasingly tolerant atmosphere of the sixties and seventies, attitudes began to change about another traditional taboo, homosexuality. Homosexual men and women began to openly declare that their sexual orientation was a personal matter and should not affect their rights and responsibilities as citizens. However, the popular stigma surrounding homosexuality has only recently begun to lessen.

These many changes have come rapidly, and society is still in a state of flux. One result has been a sense of displacement and uncertainty. At the same time that young men and women have had access to information, contraception, and medical care, there has been an epidemic of sexually transmitted diseases, a rise in births to unmarried women, and widespread confusion about personal values. Still another result has been the growing interest of some groups in limiting personal control and bringing many decisions about sexuality back into the public domain. For example, antiabortion, or "right-to-life," groups are attempting to make abortion illegal. Other groups oppose homosexuality, pornography, sex outside of marriage, contraceptives for adolescents, and easy divorce and are attempting to enact social policy to support their views. The conflicts between personal choice and social control in issues pertaining to sexuality is likely to be a recurring theme throughout the 1980s and into the 1990s.

Summary

The Authors' Perspectives

1. The authors' psychosocial orientation means that this book stresses the role of social conditioning in shaping human sexuality.

2. The book will critically explore the impact of two pervasive themes related to sexuality: sex for reproduction and inflexible gender roles. The authors' biases predispose them against these legacies of Western culture.

A Cross-Cultural Perspective: Social Norms and Sexuality

3. To appreciate the importance of social conditioning, we must look at sexual attitudes and behavior in other cultures.

4. A high rate of sexual activity and extensive sexual instruction of youths is the norm on the Polynesian island of Mangaia.

5. On the Irish island of Inis Beag, sexual expression is discouraged from infancy through old age. Sexual misinformation is common, and female orgasm is practically unknown.

6. The Dani people of New Guinea demonstrate little interest in sexual activity and abstain from sex for years at a time.

7. The government of the People's Republic of China, as a matter of social policy, limits reproductive choice.

The Sex-for-Reproduction Legacy

8. A prominent theme of Western culture is that sex is for reproduction only. This idea has deep historical roots.

9. The ancient Hebrews stressed the importance of childbearing and had an appreciation of sexuality within marriage.

10. Christian writers such as Paul of Tarsus, Augustine, and Thomas Aquinas contributed to the view of sex as sinful, justifiable only in marriage for procreation.

11. Leaders of the Reformation of the sixteenth century challenged the necessity of celibacy for clergy and recognized sexual expression as an important aspect of marriage.

12. Technical advances in contraception in the twentieth century have permitted people to separate sexuality from procreation to a degree not previously possible.

The Gender-Role Legacy

13. A second theme in our culture is that of rigid gender roles. This theme, too, goes far back in Western history.

14. Gender-role differences between men and women were well established in ancient Hebraic culture. Women's most important roles were to manage the household and bear children, especially sons.

15. Women in ancient Athens had no legal rights and spent their lives in women's quarters within their homes. In contrast, women in Sparta were educated and trained in athletics.

16. The New Testament writings of Paul emphasized the importance of submissiveness for women.

17. Two contradictory images of women developed in the Middle Ages: the pure and unattainable woman, manifest in the cult of the Virgin Mary and in courtly love, and the evil temptress represented by Eve and by the women persecuted as witches.

18. The view of women as asexual was emphasized in the Victorian era, and the lives of "proper" Victorian men and women were separate. Men often employed prostitutes for companionship and sexual relations.

Sexuality: Personal or Public Domain?

19. Greater knowledge, more reliable contraceptives, and legal decisions have increased the contemporary individual's ability to make personal decisions regarding sexuality. Our society is changing, and a result for some has been uncertainty about personal decisions. Social policies and laws can either restrict or expand personal choice.

Thought Provokers

1. If you could design and implement your ideal of sexual norms within a society, what would these be?

2. In what ways do restrictive sexual norms contribute beneficially to a society?

3. How do you think the two contradictory images of women—the Virgin Mary and the temptress Eve—are manifest in contemporary attitudes and media images?

Suggested Readings

Boswell, John. *Christianity, Social Tolerance, and Homosexuality*. Chicago: University of Chicago Press, 1980. This book is a comprehensive study of Western beliefs concerning homosexuality from ancient Greece to the fourteenth century.

Davenport, William. "Sex in Cross-Cultural Perspective." In F. Beach (Ed.), *Human Sexuality in Four Perspectives*. Baltimore: Johns Hopkins Press, 1977. (Also available in paperback from same publisher, 1978.) An eminent anthropologist provides a comparison of human sexuality in different societies around the world.

Degler, Carl. *At Odds: Women and the Family in America from the Revolution to the Present*. Oxford: Oxford University Press, 1980. A historical survey of American women and their families.

Marshall, Donald, and Suggs, Robert (Eds.). *Human Sexual Behavior: Variations in the Ethnographic Spectrum*. Englewood Cliffs, N.J.: Prentice-Hall, 1971. A superb collection of eight articles that detail the sexual attitudes, behaviors, and mores of societies around the world.

Pomeroy, Susan. *Goddesses, Whores, Wives, and Slaves: Women in Classical Antiquity*. New York: Schocken Books, 1975. A scholarly and readable work on women in ancient Greece and Rome.

I know of no inquiry that the impulse of man suggests,
which is forbidden to the resolution of man to pursue.
Margaret Fuller
Summer on the Lakes (1844)

2

Sex Research:
Methods and Problems

Research Methods
Some Well-Known Studies
What to Believe? A Statement of Perspective

ARTICLES AND BOOKS that claim to contain the latest research on human sexual behavior are plentiful, and they are readily available to anyone who is interested. "Scientific polls" urge readers to accept their findings as Truth—despite the fact that these may contradict another survey published just a month earlier. At present there is an extensive body of scientific sex research, and it is rapidly growing. Some of this research is excellent and rather remarkable; other findings have proven to be less than noteworthy. How can a reader learn to distinguish the wheat from the chaff?

You may find it helpful to keep in mind that sex research, despite its rapid growth, is still in its infancy. The pioneering work done by Kinsey, who was the first to conduct an extensive general survey of American sexual behaviors, took place only in the late 1940s and early 1950s. Sex is as old as humankind, but it is a newcomer as a subject for serious research.

It is also important to realize that the study of sexuality shares the same problems that handicap all research into human social behavior. Human subjects cannot be placed in the same kind of experimental situations as other animals; ethical considerations limit the researcher's range of options. Human thought and behavior are extremely complex, and this fact poses even more serious research problems. For instance, subjects second-guess the researcher, altering their responses to coincide with their expectations of what the researcher (or society) wants to hear. The very private and sensitive nature of human sexuality further complicates the process of data collecting: Many people simply do not want to be "researched."

Despite these problems, research provides a growing body of knowledge about human sexuality. In this chapter we will acquaint you with how we have come to know certain things about sexual behavior. As we discuss particular methods, problems, and examples of sex research, you may begin to appreciate what we know and do not know, and how confident we can be in the available knowledge. You may also begin to sense the directions we can take to further expand our scientific knowledge of sexual behavior. Perhaps at some future time you will contribute to our knowledge of this important area of human experience. We invite you to do so.

Research Methods

There are a number of methods for studying sexual behavior. They range from detailed case studies of specific individuals, often in a clinical setting where the subject is being treated for a specific behavioral or medical problem, to questionnaire or interview surveys that typically produce less depth of coverage about a much larger group of people. Two less frequently used research methods are direct observation and experimental laboratory research. Each of these strategies has advantages and disadvantages for researching various kinds of questions.

Surveys via Questionnaires or Interviews

Most of our information about human sexuality has been obtained by **surveys** that ask people about their sexual experiences or attitudes. This information may be obtained in two ways: either orally through a face-to-face interview or in written form on a paper-and-pencil questionnaire. There is no single way of administering questionnaires. Questions may range in number from a few to over a thousand; they may be multiple-choice, true-and-false, or discussion questions; they may be done at home alone or in the presence of a researcher.

Each of these survey methods has its advantages and shortcomings. Questionnaires are more anonymous, and for some people this may reduce pressures to distort information about their sex lives by boasting, omitting facts, and so on. (The presence of an interviewer may encourage such false responses.) Questionnaires have another advantage in that they are usually cheaper and quicker than interview surveys. However, interviews have the distinct advantage of flexibility. The interviewer may clarify confusing questions and vary their order, if necessary, to meet the needs of the participant. A competent interviewer can establish a sense of rapport that may encourage more candor than that produced by an impersonal questionnaire. On the other hand, data obtained through oral interviews may be subject to bias as a result of inaccurate interpretations by the researcher.

While their methods are somewhat different, the intent of written and oral surveys is the same. Each tries to use a relatively small, representative population, called the *survey sample,* to draw inferences or conclusions about a much larger population group—for instance, married adults or high school adolescents.

The ideal sample is called a **probability sample**. This term means that every individual in the total population of interest has an equal chance, or probability, of being included in the limited sample actually studied. We can use an example to show how the probability sample works.

Let us assume that you wished to survey the attitudes and behavior of American high school age males regarding birth control. In order to draw broad conclusions about the general population (all American male adolescents), your sample would need to be representative of it. How could you ensure this? You could begin by obtaining the rosters of all male high school students in a variety of geographic areas throughout the United States. These regions would be chosen very carefully to reflect the manner in which the American population is distributed. If 20% of American male adolescents live in the South, for instance, 20% of your lists would be drawn from the South. Likewise, if 30% of southern male high school students live in rural environments, 30% of your southern sample must be country dwellers. Once your rosters were compiled, the next step would be to select the actual participants by some method that would ensure equal probability of inclusion, such as a table of random numbers. Provided your final sample was sufficiently large, you could be relatively confident in generalizing your findings to the entire population of American high school age males.

In real sex research, obtaining a probability sample for this hypothetical survey would be a difficult, if not impossible, task. This is so because it is often quite difficult to get people to participate in studies of this nature. Assuming you had used proper sampling procedures to choose your target sample of male high school age students, how many do you think would actually be willing to answer your questions about their sexual attitudes and practices? (Even if the individuals were willing, how many school officials and parents would object to such participation?) **Nonresponse**, the refusal to participate in a research study, is a common problem, and one that consistently plagues sex survey research. This difficulty, together with issues related to data inaccuracy, will be explored in the following section.

*A variety of factors
may reduce the
accuracy of indi-
vidual reports of
sexual behavior.*

Problems of Sex Survey Research: Nonresponse and Inaccuracy.   No one has ever conducted a major sex survey where 100% of the randomly selected subjects voluntarily participated. In fact, some studies include results obtained from samples where only a small minority of those asked to respond actually did.

Nonresponse presents a major complication in human sexual research. No matter how careful the researcher has been in selecting the sample population, that sample may be distorted by the subjects' **self-selection**. Are the individuals who agree to participate in sex research surveys any different from those who choose not to respond? Perhaps they are a representative cross section of the population—but we have no theoretical or statistical basis for that conclusion. As a matter of fact, the opposite might well be true. People who volunteer to participate may be the ones who are the most eager to share their experiences, who have explored a wide range of activities, or who feel most comfortable with their sexuality. (Or it might be that the most experienced people are the ones who are least willing to respond, because they feel their behaviors represent atypical or extreme levels of activity.) A preponderance of experienced, inexperienced, liberal, or conservative individuals might bias any sample.

A limited amount of research on self-selection, or "volunteer bias," has provided contradictory results. For example, one study compared individuals who had volunteered for Alfred Kinsey's research with those who did not volunteer (Maslow and

Sakoda, 1952). These investigators found significant differences between the two groups: The volunteers demonstrated higher levels of self-esteem and more sexual activity than those who did not volunteer. In contrast, a more recent study found no important differences in sexual attitudes and experience between men and women who volunteered to fill out a sex survey questionnaire and those who had to be persuaded to participate (Bauman, 1973). Additional research is necessary to clarify whether people who willingly participate in sex research differ from those who do not.

Other kinds of problems might result from subject selection. For instance, **demographic bias** has been a problem in many studies. Most of the data available from sex research in the United States have come from samples weighted heavily with white, middle-class volunteers. This was certainly true of the monumental studies of the Kinsey group in the forties and fifties and of Masters and Johnson in the sixties. Typically, college students and educated white-collar workers are disproportionately represented in these samples.

How much effect do nonresponse and demographic bias have on sex research findings? We cannot say for sure. But as long as elements of American society, including the less educated and ethnic and racial minorities, are underrepresented, we must remain cautious in generalizing any findings to the population at large.

A second problem that hinders sex survey research has to do with the accuracy of information provided by subjects. Most of our data about human sexual behavior are obtained from respondents' self reports of their experiences. How closely does actual behavior correspond to these subjective, after-the-fact reports?

For many reasons, there may be considerable discrepancy between actual behavior and the way people report it. One potential complication involves the known limitations of human memory. For instance, how many people remember accurately when they first masturbated and with what frequency? Ask yourself (if it is applicable) at what age you first experienced an orgasm. It may be quite difficult to accurately recall some information.

Some people may consciously or unconsciously conceal certain facts about their sexual histories because they view them as abnormal, silly, or perhaps too painful to remember. In areas of sexual behavior where there are strong social taboos (such as those regarding incest, homosexuality, and masturbation), people may feel pressure to deny or minimize such experiences in their own lives. Others may purposely falsify their responses to inflate their own sexual experience, perhaps out of a desire to appear sexually liberal.

Occasionally, false reports may result simply from misunderstandings. For example, a person with little education might answer *no* to the question "Did you experience penile-vaginal intercourse prior to marriage?" simply because he or she was not familiar with the terminology. That same person might respond affirmatively to the question "Did you go all the way before you got married?" Language is a problem in many types of social research; this is especially true in sex research, since there is a virtual absence of any sexual language common to all groups in our society. That is why the wording of questions becomes such a critical issue.

Sample surveys via questionnaires and interviews are the most commonly used methods for studying sexual behavior and attitudes. They provide a relatively inexpensive way to obtain information about a broad range of topics from many individuals. But we cannot expect to learn all there is to know about sexuality from sample surveys. Other important sources of information include case studies, direct observation, and laboratory research.

Case Studies

There are numerous references in the existing literature to **case studies**. These are in-depth explorations of single cases or of small groups of people who were examined individually. Unlike surveys, case studies obtain a great deal of information from one or a very few individuals.

Often people become subjects for case histories because they have some physical or emotional disorder or because they have manifested a specific atypical behavior. Thus, much of our current information about sex offenders, transsexuals, incest victims, and the like has been obtained through this approach. Also, a large portion of our information about sexual response difficulties (for instance, erectile inhibition in men and lack of orgasmic response in women) has been obtained from studies of individuals seeking treatment for these problems.

The case-study approach allows for flexible data-gathering procedures. These range from well-structured questions that offer specific response alternatives to open-ended queries that provide considerable flexibility to respondents. Some researchers deplore the fact that this approach offers little opportunity for investigative control. However, unlike survey methods, case studies often provide opportunities to acquire insight into specific behaviors. The highly personal, subjective information about how individuals actually feel about their behavior represents an important step beyond simply recording activities. So, while this method sacrifices some control, it adds considerable dimension to our information. Case studies have another advantage. Because of their clinical nature and the fact that they may continue for long periods of time (months or even years), the researcher is able to explore cause and effect relationships in detail.

There are some important limitations to the clinical case study, however. Since proper sampling techniques are rarely observed (how could they be?) it is hard to draw generalizations to the rest of the population. This potential source of error is illustrated in many writings that have presented a pathological model of homosexuality based on case studies of homosexuals who had sought treatment. As in the self-selection that can take place in survey sampling, there may be pronounced differences between homosexuals who are not trying to change their sexual orientation and those who seek therapy. In other situations, where individuals with known mental or physical disorders have been studied in depth, applying the resultant information to healthy people is questionable. For that matter, how do we know that individuals under treatment or observation are representative of the subpopulation to which they belong? For example, incest-committing fathers who have been identified by the court may not be representative of all fathers who engage in incestuous relationships with their offspring. All of these general cautions can be applied to the cases we cite in our authors' files selections throughout this book. We think these cases represent especially relevant experiences and feelings, but our purpose is for readers to draw perspective from them, not conclusions. An example of case study research is provided in Box 2.1.

In 1958 Harold Greenwald, a psychologist, published an in-depth social-psychological study of call girls, appropriately titled *The Call Girl*. An updated edition of his study, *The Elegant Prostitute* (1970), describes how call girls are the elite of the world of prostitution: They make appointments by phone, dress elegantly, and live in expensive apartments. Before Greenwald's study, little was known about the factors that contribute to call girls' choice of occupation. Greenwald became interested in the subject as a result of conducting therapy with six call girl clients. These six shared certain experiences and attitudes, and Greenwald began to wonder if these similarities extended to other call girls. He explored this question by conducting in-depth interviews with 20 additional women who practiced the profession.

All 20 were working as call girls at the time of the interviews. They ranged in age from 19 to 43 years. Most had a high school education or better. A substantial majority had been reared in middle-income and upper-income families. Most of the information about these women was obtained by interviews that employed open-ended questions such as "Tell me about yourself" or "What has your life been like up to now?"

After sifting through large quantities of interview data, Greenwald made some observations about the family backgrounds, lifestyles, feelings, and attitudes of the women in his research population. There was a marked similarity among the family atmospheres in which they were reared. "I found not one example of a permanent, well-adjusted marital relationship between the parents" (p. 165). Affection between parents was rarely or never displayed, and 19 of the subjects reported feeling rejected by both parents. Fifteen found themselves in broken homes before they reached adolescence, and as a result, many were passed from family to family or lived in a succession of boarding schools.

Ten of the subjects reported that at an early age they had engaged in sexual activity with an adult that resulted in some kind of reward such as affection or privileges. Greenwald suggests that these early experiences may have established a pattern of giving sexual gratification as a way of temporarily overcoming feelings of loneliness and unworthiness. Furthermore, such experiences led the women to recognize early in life that sex was a commodity they could barter with.

Greenwald found that virtually all of his study population expressed anger and even rage over being deprived of affection and stability during their formative years. Their anger was often turned inward, resulting in very negative self-images and varying degrees of anxiety and depression. Most of them found it extremely difficult to maintain satisfactory relationships with other people.

In light of their family backgrounds and resulting negative self images, Greenwald theorized that "becoming a call girl appeared to offer a desperate hope of halting the deterioration of self, but . . . their choice of profession made these conflicts more intense and more self-destructive" (p. 187).

Direct Observation

A third method for studying human sexual behavior is **direct observation**. This type of research may vary greatly in form and setting, ranging from laboratory studies that observe and record sexual responses to participant observation where the researchers join their subjects in sexual activity.

Observational research is quite common in a variety of disciplines, particularly the social sciences of anthropology, sociology, and psychology. However, very little research of this nature occurs in the area of sexuality. Sexual expression, being a highly personal and private experience, does not readily lend itself to direct observation.

When it has been well conducted, thorough direct observation produces valuable information. There are some clear advantages to seeing and measuring sexual behavior first hand, instead of relying on subjective reports of past experiences. Firsthand direct observation virtually eliminates the possibility of data falsification through memory deficits, boastful inflation, or guilt-induced repression. Furthermore, records of such behaviors may be retained indefinitely on videotapes or films.

But there are also some disadvantages associated with this approach. A major problem lies in the often unanswerable question of just how much a subject's behavior is influenced by the presence of even the most discrete observer. This question has been asked often since the publication of the Masters and Johnson studies (1966), which used the direct observation method to document male and female sexual response patterns. Researchers employing direct observation often attempt to minimize this potential complication by being as unobtrusive as possible (for example, observing from a peripheral location or behind one-way glass, using videotapes to be viewed later, and so forth). But the subject still is aware that she or he is being observed. The reliability of recorded observations may also be compromised by preexisting biases in the researchers. For example, if the observer believes "swingers" experience only nonemotional sexual involvements, she or he may be less likely to interpret their interactions as manifestations of affectionate intimacy.

Experimental Research

A fourth method, **experimental research**, is being utilized with increasing frequency in the investigation of human sexual behavior. In experimental research, subjects must be confronted with certain specific stimuli under controlled conditions, so that their reactions can be reliably measured. For example, if you designed an experiment to compare the sexual responses of males and females to visual erotica, you would subject both sexes to the same stimuli under controlled conditions and then use a reliable method for measuring the results (such as physiological measures of penile erection, vaginal engorgement, and so forth). Several experiments of this nature have been conducted in the last few years with rather interesting results, which will be discussed in Chapter 6.

A laboratory experiment offers the major advantage of control over variables thought to influence the behavior being studied. Often such an approach allows for direct statements about cause and effect that would be more speculative with other methods of data collection. However, the somewhat artificial nature of the experimental laboratory setting may influence subjects' behavior. As in direct observation research, the very fact that people know they are in an experiment can alter their responses from those that might occur outside the laboratory. An example of experimental research is provided in Box 2.2. Box 2.3 describes some applications of technology to sex research.

Some Well-Known Studies

Studies conducted by sex researchers over the years have used all of the methods just described. A few of these studies are repeatedly cited by writers in the field of sex research. In the following pages we will examine 11 of these investigations, the main

Box 2.2

The Effects of Alcohol on Sexual Arousal: Two Examples of Experimental Research

People often report that alcohol increases their level of sexual arousal. In one major survey of 20,000 middle-class and upper middle-class Americans, 60% of the respondents reported that drinking increased their sexual pleasure (Athanasiou et al., 1970). However, most surveys have been limited to asking people what they *think* happens when they drink, and these subjective assessments may not match up with objective reality, as was found in two experiments on the actual effects of alcohol on human sexual arousal.

Both investigations were conducted at Rutgers University's Alcohol Behavior Research Laboratory. The first experiment involved 48 male college students between the ages of 18 and 22 (Briddell and Wilson, 1976). During an initial session the researchers obtained baseline data on flaccid penis diameter for all subjects. The participants were then shown a 10-minute erotic film of explicit sexual interaction between male and female partners. Penile tumescence (engorgement) was measured continuously during the film by penile strain gauges (see Box 2.3). In a second session, held one week later, all subjects drank measured amounts of alcohol prior to viewing a somewhat longer version of the erotic film. Subjects were assigned to four experimental groups, with 12 subjects in each group. Each subject, depending on his group assignment, consumed 0.6, 3, 6, or 9 ounces of alcohol. After a 40-minute "rest period" the subjects viewed the film, during which each person's sexual arousal was assessed by his score on three measures of penile tumescence: increase in diameter, time required to obtain an erection, and duration of the erection. The results indicated that alcohol significantly reduced sexual arousal, especially at higher intake levels. Even at low intake levels, alcohol did not enhance penile tumescence.

The second investigation was conducted with 16 college women between the ages of 18 and 22 (Wilson and Lawson, 1976). The research design was somewhat different from that employed in the Briddell and Wilson study of men. "During weekly experimental sessions, each of 16 university women received, in counterbalanced order, four doses of beverage alcohol prior to viewing a control film and an erotic film" (p. 489). Alcohol dosage levels were approximately 0.3, 1.4, 2.9, and 4.3 ounces. The control film was a boring 12-minute review of the computer facilities at Rutgers University. The erotic film portrayed explicit heterosexual interaction. Vaginal changes reflecting sexual arousal were measured continuously during film viewing by use of a vaginal photoplethysmograph (see Box 2.3). As expected, "subjects showed significantly more arousal in response to the erotic than the control film" (p. 493). More important, there was clear evidence that alcohol significantly reduced the sexual arousal of these women. The inhibitory effects were greater at higher dosages.

These two experiments suggest that "increasing intoxication in both men and women results in progressively reduced sexual arousal in response to visual erotic stimulation" (Wilson and Lawson, 1976, p. 495).

features of which are summarized in Table 2.1. As the table shows, all but one belong in the survey category of research methods. Findings from these studies will be cited throughout the book; outlining their scope, strengths, and weaknesses here can provide you with a solid frame of reference for making subsequent interpretations.

The Kinsey Group

Alfred Kinsey, with his associates Wardell Pomeroy, Clyde Martin, and Paul Gebhard, published two large volumes in the decade following World War II. One, on male sexuality, was published in 1948; the follow-up report on female sexuality was pub-

Box 2.3   *Sex Research and Technology*

Experimental research and direct observation studies of human sexual responses often employ measures of sexual arousal. Until recently, researchers had to rely largely on subjective reports of these responses. However, advances in technology have produced two devices for measuring sexual arousal: the *penile strain gauge* and the *vaginal photoplethysmograph*.

The penile strain gauge (sometimes called a penile plethysmograph) is a flexible loop that looks something like a rubber band with a wire attached. It is actually a thin rubber tube filled with a fine strand of mercury. A tiny electrical current from the attached wire flows through the mercury continuously. The gauge is placed around the base of the penis; as an erection occurs, the rubber tube stretches and the strand of mercury becomes thinner, changing the flow of the current. These changes are registered by a recording device called a *polygraph*. The penile strain gauge can measure even the slightest changes in penis size and, in fact, is so sensitive that it can record every pulse of blood into the penis. In the interests of privacy, a subject can attach the gauge to his own penis.

When a woman is sexually aroused, her vaginal walls fill with blood in a manner comparable to the engorgement of a man's penis. The vaginal photoplethysmograph is a device designed to measure this increased vaginal blood volume. It consists of an acrylic cylinder about the size and shape of a tampon, which is inserted into the vagina. The cylinder contains a light that is reflected off the vaginal walls and a photocell that is sensitive to the reflected light. When the vaginal walls fill with blood during sexual arousal, less light is reflected to the photocell. These changes in light intensity, continuously recorded by a polygraph, provide a measure of sexual arousal comparable to that provided by the penile strain gauge. Like the male device, the vaginal photoplethysmograph can be inserted in privacy by the research subject.

lished in 1953. These volumes contain the results of extensive survey interviews, the aim of which was to determine patterns of sexual behavior in American males and females. These remarkably ambitious investigations remain unique in the annals of sex research as the most comprehensive of all **taxonomic surveys**, that is, investigations aimed at classifying people into behavioral categories for statistical comparisons.

Kinsey and his associates believed that attempts to secure sex histories from individuals selected by random sampling methods would result in so many refusals to participate that randomness would be destroyed. To minimize this problem of nonresponse, they sought subjects in the memberships of various social groups or organizations, such as college classes, professional organizations, residents of rooming houses, and so forth. Initial contacts who willingly participated were urged to convince their friends to get involved. In some cases this use of peer-group assurances or pressure produced virtually 100% participation by members of the target group.

The final Kinsey subject populations consisted of 5300 white males and 5940 white females. They included people from both rural and urban areas in each state—people who represented a range of ages, marital status, occupations, educational levels, and religions.

Despite the wide subject variability in the two research samples, the failure to use random sampling procedures resulted in underrepresentation or overrepresentation of certain population subgroups. Specifically, the sample contained a dispro-

*Alfred Kinsey,
pioneer sex
researcher.*

portionately greater number of better-educated, city-dwelling Protestants, while older people, rural dwellers, and those with less education were underrepresented. Blacks were omitted from the sample. And finally, all the subjects were volunteers. As we saw earlier, self-selected subjects can never be viewed as a random sample. Thus, in no way can Kinsey's study population be viewed as a probability sample of the American population. But Kinsey and his associates were well aware of this shortcoming. As the following quotation shows, it is clear that his group made no claim to the contrary:

> This is a study of sexual behavior in (within) certain groups of the human species, *Homo sapiens*. It is obviously not a study of the sexual behavior of all cultures and all races of man. At its best, the present volume can pretend to report behavior which may be typical of no more than a portion, although probably not an inconsiderable portion, of the white females living within the boundaries of the United States. Neither the title of our first volume on the male, nor the title of this volume on the female, should be taken to imply that the authors are unaware of the diversity which exists in patterns of sexual behavior in other parts of the world. (Kinsey et al., 1953, p. 4)

Publication of the Kinsey findings generated strong reactions, both positive and negative. The most thorough review of the work was published by the American Statistical Association (Cochran et al., 1954). Despite the acknowledged problems with the sampling methods employed, this review praised Kinsey's group for their

Table 2.1 A Summary of Key Sex Research Studies

Names of Researchers and the Study	Year	Type of Study	Focus and Scope	Strengths and Weaknesses
Kinsey, *Sexual Behavior in the Human Male* Kinsey, *Sexual Behavior in the Human Female*	1948 1953	Interview survey	Patterns of sexual behavior, the American population	Most comprehensive taxonomic sex survey yet conducted; but the large sample overrepresented certain groups (educated, urban dwellers, young) and underrepresented others: (undereducated, older, non-Protestant, rural, and nonwhite).
Masters and Johnson, *Human Sexual Response*	1966	Direct observation	Female and male physiological responses to sexual stimulation	The only major piece of research to observe and record sexual response (over 10,000 completed response cycles); has been criticized because sample was drawn from narrow-based academic community.
Sorenson, *Adolescent Sexuality in Contemporary America*	1973	Questionnaire survey	Male and female adolescent sexual behavior, ages 13–19	Surveys a broad range of sexual behaviors; has been criticized because of nonresponse bias and length of questionnaire.
Hunt, *Sexual Behavior in the 1970s*	1974	Questionnaire survey	Patterns of sexual behavior, the American population	Much information about a broad range of adult sexual behaviors; has been criticized because of high nonresponse, sampling bias from telephone recruitment, and length of questionnaire.
The Redbook Report on Female Sexuality	1975	Questionnaire survey	Female sexuality (behavior and attitudes)	Very large sample size (100,000 women); but sample bias due to fact that respondents were *Redbook* readers, not a true cross section of American women.
The Hite Report on female sexuality	1976	Questionnaire survey	Female sexuality (behavior and attitudes)	Large number of respondents (3019) provided extensive narrative answers to questions; has been criticized because sample volunteers probably overrepresented young liberal women.

excellent use of well-planned interview techniques. While there is always the possibility of distortion whenever interviews or questionnaires are used, the Kinsey interviewers were particularly adept at establishing rapport with their subjects. They accomplished this by asking questions in a way that conveyed acceptance of any kind of response, by modifying language to fit the understanding of respondents, and by spontaneously altering the interview sequence so that particularly sensitive questions could be asked at the best time.

Table 2.1 *(Continued)*

Names of Researchers and the Study	Year	Type of Study	Focus and Scope	Strengths and Weaknesses
The Hite Report on Male Sexuality	1981	Questionnaire survey	Male sexuality (behavior and attitudes)	7239 respondents out of 119,000 questionnaires distributed; strong possibility of volunteer bias, educational levels of volunteers much higher than national average.
Zelnick and Kantner, "Sexual and Contraceptive Experiences of Young Unmarried Women in the United States, 1979, 1976, and 1971"	1971, 1976, and 1979	Questionnaire survey	Pregnancy, use of contraceptives, and premarital sex among unmarried teenage women, ages 15–19 (1979 survey included men, ages 17–21)	Good sampling techniques; but a narrow population of interest.
Bell and Weinberg, *Homosexualities: A Study of Diversities Among Men and Women*	1978	Interview survey	Homosexual lifestyles and sexual practices	Most comprehensive study of homosexuality to date; criticisms have centered on sampling biases from recruitment methods.
Bell, Weinberg, and Hammersmith, *Sexual Preference: Its Development in Men and Women*	1981	Interview survey	Causes of sexual orientation	Utilization of sophisticated statistical techniques to produce findings remarkable in what they disprove; sampling biases from recruitment methods.
George and Weiler, "Sexuality in Middle and Late Life"	1981	Questionnaire survey	Changes in sexuality in the older years	Noteworthy for use of longitudinal approach; sample limited by decision to include only married people.
Blumstein and Schwartz, *American Couples*	1983	Questionnaire survey plus some interviews	Current trends in relationships among heterosexual and homosexual couples	Excellent information about a variety of sexual and nonsexual components of relationships obtained from a large national sample; sample underrepresented certain population groups (low socioeconomic, racial minorities, undereducated).

Kinsey's findings covered a wide range of topics, including such things as frequency and kind of sexual outlet (that is, the sources of orgasm and how often experienced), nonmarital coitus, sexual orientation, and sexual techniques. Many of his conclusions produced a great deal of public furor. For example, his finding that approximately one-half of the women in his sample reported experiencing coitus before marriage contradicted the dominant cultural ideal of virgin brides. His observation that many people have varying degrees of homosexual and heterosexual tendencies also produced considerable controversy. In later portions of this book we will discuss several other major findings of the Kinsey research.

Kinsey's studies were published three decades ago, and today many people question whether their findings are applicable to contemporary society. In response to this it may be noted that information becomes obsolete at differing rates, and certainly many of the Kinsey data are still relevant. It is quite unlikely that the passage of time has altered the applicability of certain findings—for example, that sexual behavior is influenced by educational level, or that the heterosexuality or homosexuality of a person is often not an all-or-none proposition. However, certain other areas—such as coital rates among unmarried people—are more influenced by changing societal norms. Thus, one might expect the Kinsey data to be less predictive of contemporary practices in these areas. Nevertheless, even here his data are relevant, in that they provide one possible basis for estimating the degree of behavioral change over the years.

In summary, despite the problems inherent in the Kinsey research, it still remains one of the very best sources of information about patterns of human sexual behavior. If the data contained in these two volumes are interpreted cautiously, we are able to secure some important clues about the sexual behavior of white Americans, if not now, at least several decades ago.

Masters and Johnson

Along with the Kinsey research, Masters and Johnson's study of human sexual response is probably the most often mentioned sex research. The two studies represent distinctly different kinds of research, with quite different goals. Kinsey used survey

*William Masters
and Virginia
Johnson.*

interviews to trace broad patterns of sexual behavior; Masters and Johnson used direct observation in a laboratory setting to learn about physiological changes during sexual arousal. (Their study remains the only major piece of research that has done this.) The product was their widely acclaimed volume *Human Sexual Response* (1966), which was based on laboratory observations of 10,000 completed sexual response cycles. Results of these observations are presented in Chapter 6.

Masters and Johnson began their research by studying a group of prostitutes (118 female and 27 male). It was assumed that ". . . study subjects from more conservative segments of the general population would not be available (a presumption which later proved to be entirely false)" (1966, p. 10). Accordingly, they turned to the one obviously available group—professional prostitutes. However, they quickly decided prostitutes were not suitable subjects, for two reasons. First, the prostitutes tended to move from one city to another frequently, a fact that discouraged study over extended periods of time. Second, female prostitutes often develop a state of chronic pelvic congestion due to repeated sexual arousal without orgasm. As a result, their physiosexual responses were somewhat different from those of other women.

Masters and Johnson obtained their final research population by spreading the word in the academic community of Washington University in St. Louis that they were interested in studying normal volunteers. The response was quite enthusiastic. From 1273 who applied, they selected 382 women and 312 men. They excluded those unable to respond sexually and anyone who showed signs of emotional instability or exhibitionist tendencies. Their final sample was thus composed of sexually responsive volunteers, drawn largely from an academic community, with above average intelligence and socioeconomic background—obviously not a probability sample. However, the physical signs of sexual arousal, the subject of their study, appear to be rather stable across a wide range of people with diverse backgrounds.

Masters and Johnson used a number of techniques to record physiological sexual responses. These included the use of photographic equipment and instruments to measure and record muscular and vascular changes throughout the body. They also employed direct observation to record changes in the primary and secondary sex organs. An ingenious artificial coition machine was designed to record changes that had never before been observed in the internal female sex structures. It was equipped with an artificial penis that could be controlled voluntarily for size, as well as for depth and rapidity of thrust. It was constructed from clear plastic and contained photographic equipment for recording changes in the vagina and the lower portion of the uterus during sexual arousal. Masters and Johnson recorded responses in a variety of stimulus situations in their laboratory—masturbation, coitus with a partner, artificial coition, and stimulation of the breasts alone. As a follow-up to all recorded observations, each individual participant was extensively interviewed.

Employing this observational approach, Masters and Johnson obtained a wealth of information about the manner in which women and men respond physiologically to sexual stimulation. Some have suggested that their conclusions are limited because of the artificial nature of laboratory observations. While there may be some merit to this criticism, time has nevertheless demonstrated that their research findings can be beneficially applied to such areas as sex therapy, infertility counseling, conception control, and general sex education.

While Masters and Johnson are perhaps most acclaimed for their study of human sexual response, they have also contributed information in two additional areas of human sexual behavior: sexual problems and homosexuality. In 1970 they published *Human Sexual Inadequacy,* an outline of the rationale, methods, and successes of a variety of strategies for treating sexual difficulties. In this book Masters and Johnson reported that only 20% of their patients failed to improve after two weeks of therapy. This was generally interpreted to mean that they were curing 80% of their cases in a very short time, a truly impressive success story.

Masters and Johnson's claims went virtually unchallenged for the next decade, until two psychologists, Bernie Zilbergeld and Michael Evans (1980), published an incisive critique of their work. This critical review was stimulated, at least in part, by

Other Times, Other Places

Foreshadowing Masters and Johnson

The Centennial Issue of the *Journal of the American Medical Association,* which appeared on July 8, 1983, included an article written by Denslow Lewis, M.D., titled "The Gynecologic Consideration of the Sexual Act." What is unusual about this article is that Lewis submitted it for publication in 1899, 84 years before it appeared. Unfortunately, Lewis's pioneering treatise was out of step with his time and publication was denied. The unwillingness of his medical colleagues to provide a forum for the issues raised in his thoughtful article is representative of the trials faced by many pioneer sex researchers in their efforts to cope with limitations imposed by a society that is unreceptive to new and controversial information.

Lewis's article contained many sound observations that were corroborated by research conducted over half a century later. For example, he provided an illuminating description of female sexual response and suggested that it was absolutely normal for a woman to experience pleasure while actively participating in the "sexual act." Many of his observations about male-female relationships would no doubt have been considered progressive just a few years ago (perhaps even today, by some). For example, he suggested that a husband should

behave more as a companion than a master, respecting and acknowledging his wife's rights as well as his own. Lewis also recommended sex education at an early age, especially for girls. This bold idea was about 60 to 70 years ahead of its time, since sex education in the public school systems has come about only in the last 10 to 15 years.

In an editorial in the same issue of the *AMA Journal,* William Masters speculated that publication of the Lewis article in 1899 might have hastened by more than 50 years investigations of the biology and psychology of sexual functioning and significantly reduced "the incredible level of sexual myth and misconception that has so handicapped medical progress well beyond the first half of this century" (p. 244).

The trials Lewis faced took place at a time when society placed much more stringent limitations on the subject matter of scientific investigations and public discussions. However, the activities of certain nationally organized groups in recent years—for example, efforts to ban sex education in schools or to restrict teenagers' access to birth control information—suggests the possibility of new limits on our access to information about our sexuality.

Evans' discovery that he could not find out enough about Masters and Johnson's research methodology to replicate their study with a different population. **Replicability** is an important feature of research. That is, original research must be described in a clear fashion to allow for repeat experiments. Then other researchers can replicate the study, using the same methodology, to see if similar results can be obtained. Without any hope of conducting valid replication studies, Zilbergeld and Evans chose to make a close examination of the methodology of Masters and Johnson's second major research endeavor. It will be instructive for us to look at a brief synopsis of their criticisms.

It was impossible to determine how Masters and Johnson assessed the outcome of their therapeutic treatments. They did not try to measure success, only failure, and their definition of failure was vague and inexact: "Initial failure is defined as indication that the two-week rapid-treatment phase has failed to initiate reversal of the basic symptomatology of sexual dysfunction . . ." (p. 352). What exactly did they mean by "initiate reversal"? Apparently no one has been able to determine this. Without clearly defined criteria of success or failure, replication is impossible and the reliability of their outcome statistics must be questioned. In addition, since we do not know how Masters and Johnson screened applicants and how many were rejected, it is difficult to compare their results to those obtained by other investigators with different treatment populations.

Masters and Johnson report a very low relapse rate of 7%, based on a five-year follow-up of nonfailure patients. However, this figure is also difficult to interpret, since they do not specify what criteria constitute a relapse. Furthermore, follow-up data were obtained on only a limited number of cases (35% of the nonfailure group).

In 1979 Masters and Johnson published *Homosexuality in Perspective,* a book that reports their investigation of homosexual behavior over a 15-year period. In the first half of this volume they compare the sexual functioning of homosexual and heterosexual individuals as assessed by observational techniques comparable to those outlined in *Human Sexual Response* (1966). They reported observing no significant differences between homosexuals and heterosexuals in their capacity to respond to effective sexual stimulation. (For example, participants in each group seemed comparable in their ability to reach orgasm.) They did find that members of the homosexual study group seemed to exhibit better sexual communication than their heterosexual counterparts during shared sexual activity. Furthermore, the homosexual couples generally exhibited a greater range of sexual activities with their partners than did the heterosexual couples. These findings, while certainly interesting and provocative, should be interpreted with caution, since Masters and Johnson do not provide any relevant information about the subjects' sexual histories or the manner in which their sexual behaviors were rated.

The second half of *Homosexuality in Perspective* reports Masters and Johnson's treatment of troubled homosexuals, both those who wished to function better in homosexual relations and those who reportedly wished to change their sexual orientation. This portion of Masters and Johnson's research program with homosexuals had many of the methodological problems outlined earlier in our discussion of *Human Sexual Inadequacy,* including unclear criteria for subject selection and treatment assessment. In addition, it contained no information about treatment strategies. This aspect of Masters and Johnson's research will be discussed further in Chapter 10.

Hunt

One of the most widely quoted contemporary studies of human sexual behavior is reported in a book written by Morton Hunt, *Sexual Behavior in the 1970s* (1974). It contains the results of a survey commissioned by the Playboy Foundation and conducted by the Research Guild, an independent market survey and behavioral research organization. The goal of the Hunt study, like that of Kinsey's research two decades earlier, was to obtain contemporary information about a broad range of adult human sexual behaviors. But this study failed to match the comprehensiveness and thoroughness of the Kinsey research in several important areas.

Hunt's sample was obtained by randomly selecting names from phone directories in twenty-four cities that supposedly represented the diversity of American urban centers. Although Hunt claimed that his final study group (1044 females and 982 males) closely represented the national population, the sample has been criticized. Serious questions have been raised, for instance, about self-selection biases. Of the original group of people who were telephoned and asked to participate in anonymous small-group discussions of sexual behavior, only 20% agreed to take part.

In addition, the methodology itself created problems. Selecting names from city phone books can easily lead to the underrepresentation of certain categories of people, including isolated rural dwellers and people who have no phones (for instance, the poor and illiterate, people living in institutions, and young dependents). The Research Guild made efforts to rectify part of this omission by interviewing an additional sample of young adults. However, the final survey group can hardly be viewed as representing a true probability sample.

Beyond the sampling methods and the problem of nonresponse, Hunt's survey has been criticized on other grounds. These have to do with the questionnaire and the way it was administered. At the conclusion of the small-group discussion, each individual was given a questionnaire to fill out anonymously. Four separate questionnaire forms were used: for unmarried women, married women, unmarried men, and married men. The number of questions on a form ranged from 1000 to 1200, depending on the number of items applicable to a given individual. This is an incredible number of items for one person to answer, and it is questionable whether subjects could really have considered each point thoughtfully. Furthermore, the situation created by Hunt's research setting may itself have created some subject bias. To what degree did the preliminary group discussion affect the participants' responses? Certain group definitions of normality, acceptable sexual behavior, and so forth might have created considerable influence on the subjects' responses.

Despite its shortcomings, though, Hunt's analysis of the survey findings does contain some important information about the sexual practices of adult Americans. Furthermore, by contrasting Hunt's findings with Kinsey's, we may get some idea of the degree of change over several decades in such areas as variety of coital positions used, incidence of extramarital involvements, number of premarital sex partners, and many other areas of sexual conduct.

The *Redbook* Report

The October 1974 issue of *Redbook* included a sixty-item multiple-choice questionnaire on female sexual attitudes and behavior. Over 100,000 women returned the questionnaire, and analysis of the results provided the basis for two subsequent articles in the September and October 1975 issues of the magazine. The complete results of this survey were eventually published in a book titled *The Redbook Report on Female Sexuality* (Tavris and Sadd, 1977).

The certainty of anonymity was well established because responses were mailed, without names or addresses, back to *Redbook*. In spite of its prodigious size, however, the study group cannot be viewed as a random sample of all American women. Groups who were underrepresented included all those who were not likely to read the magazine—namely, women with low family incomes, women who had not finished high school, women over fifty years of age, nonwhite women, and unmarried women. Beyond the bias created by the magazine's limited audience, the ever-present problem of self-selection probably had some effect, too. Did the women who voluntarily filled out and returned the questionnaire differ greatly from those who chose not to do so?

Despite sample problems and possible volunteer bias, the *Redbook* survey is noteworthy because of its sample size. Some of its findings include the following. The majority of married women reported that they were active sex partners (initiating sexual encounters and being active during relations); oral-genital sex was almost universally experienced; 7 out of 10 respondents reported sex with their husbands to be "good" or "very good"; the more religious a woman was, the more satisfied she seemed to be with her marital sexual relations; 3 out of 10 had had intercourse after smoking marijuana; one-third had experienced extramarital intercourse; and finally, 4% had had a sexual experience with another woman by the age of forty.

Data about women who had not been married revealed that 90% had experienced intercourse. Strongly religious women were less likely than others to have experienced intercourse or to have cohabited with a man; and the younger a woman was when she had premarital intercourse, the more likely she was to have extramarital intercourse.

The Hite Report on Female Sexuality

Shortly after *Redbook* published the results of its survey, Shere Hite published her bestseller *The Hite Report* (1976), which records the detailed responses of 3019 women to an approximately sixty-item essay-type questionnaire. Hite's topic was the same as that of the *Redbook* survey—female sexuality.

The Hite Report on female sexuality has been described as a nationwide study. In the sense that responses to her questionnaire came from all over America, this is an accurate statement. However, it would be inappropriate to conclude that her subjects are a representative sample of American women. In fact, they represent a very limited and perhaps quite biased sample. Her sources for respondents were several magazines and organizations. Some people responded to notices in *The Village Voice*, *Mademoiselle*, *Brides*, and *Ms.* magazines and wrote for the questionnaire. *Oui* magazine published the entire questionnaire. Mailings to women's organizations and church organizations were also utilized. *The Hite Report* is similar to the *Redbook* survey in terms of possible volunteer bias and protection of anonymity, because again responses were mailed. The obvious sampling limitations and possible subject bias present in Hite's research strongly suggest that her findings should be interpreted with considerable caution. Nevertheless, her report has provided valuable information about how some women view sex and consequently offers important insights into female sexuality.

One major finding of Hite's report was that clitoral stimulation (whether direct, through self-stimulation, partner's manual stimulation, oral-genital stimulation, or more indirect, through pressure against the public bone during intercourse) is very important to sexual arousal and orgasm for the vast majority of the women in the survey. Second, many women reported having faked orgasm. A third important finding was that there is great diversity in female sexuality.

Comparing *The Hite Report* and the *Redbook* Survey.   There are several important differences between the *Redbook* report and *The Hite Report*. The objective of *Redbook* was to examine to what extent sexual practices of women have changed since Kinsey's research. *The Hite Report*'s objective was to find out about specific sexual behaviors and to explore women's in-depth feelings about sexuality. These different intentions are reflected by the format of the questionnaires: *Redbook*'s had multiple-choice questions, and Hite's had essay questions. Sample questions about orgasm reflect the differences. *Redbook* asked "Do you achieve orgasm . . . A. All the time? B. Most of the time? C. Sometimes? D. Once in a while? E. Never? F. Don't know?" (1975, p. 51). Hite asked "In most of your sexual encounters, does your orgasm(s) usually occur during cunnilingus, manual clitoral stimulation, intercourse, or other activity? Which of these activities usually lead to orgasm? How often?" (1976, p. 585). As a result of these differences, *Redbook* responses can be more definitively analyzed statistically, and the Hite results provide a rich narrative about many aspects of women's sexuality. A substantial portion of Hite's book is composed of personal accounts. Since Hite and *Redbook* asked questions in very different ways, many of the data are impossible to compare directly.

Although the format and perspective of the questions were different, many similar topic areas were covered in the two reports: attitudes and behaviors concerning masturbation, intercourse, oral sex, and sexual relations with women. Each report also emphasized certain areas not dealt with by the other. *Redbook* examined premarital and extramarital intercourse, marijuana use during sexual relations, marital happiness, and the effect of the strength of religious convictions. Hite explored attitudes towards the "sexual revolution," examined techniques of masturbation, and sought information about arousal and orgasm during intercourse and nonintercourse activities.

Given the difference in sources for volunteer subjects, it is likely that *Redbook* respondents would be more conservative and Hite respondents more liberal. A reflection of this difference is that 90% of *Redbook* respondents and about 35% of Hite respondents were married. *Redbook*'s ratio of married to unmarried women is higher than the 70% national average and Hite's is lower. Kinsey (1953) found that marital status was related to orgasmic response, and this factor may contribute to differences. Additionally, a higher percentage of Hite's respondents had had sexual experiences with other women or were currently in same-sex sexual relationships.

Both of these studies give us some valuable information. Since they surveyed somewhat different populations and used different types of questions, they may provide a more composite picture of female sexuality than either report alone. Their different results make the important commentary that research technique and subject selection influence research findings.

The Hite Report on Male Sexuality

In 1981 Shere Hite published *The Hite Report on Male Sexuality,* which records the responses of 7239 men to an essay-type questionnaire. Like the participants in Hite's study of female sexuality, the respondents in this investigation were far from representing a true probability sample of American men. The group consisted largely of men who answered versions of the questionnaire reprinted in magazines like *Penthouse* or who wrote for the questionnaire because they were aware of Hite's work through her previous publications or her frequent appearances on television and radio. Of the 119,000 questionnaires distributed only 7239 were returned, a fact that strongly suggests the possibility of volunteer bias. The educational levels of Hite's respondents were much higher than the national average. One critic of her research sample suggested that "her respondents seem to be mainly a sexual avant-garde" (Robinson, 1981, p. 81).

The text of Hite's report is so devoid of consistently reported statistical data that it is almost impossible to make meaningful quantitative differentiations among the responses. More than 90% of the book consists of quotations from her male respondents. However, in spite of the probable sample bias and statistical limitations of this report, it does provide some insights into how men experience their sexuality.

Sorenson

An important study of adolescent sexual behavior was conducted in the early seventies by Robert Sorenson, a social psychologist. The results were published in 1973 in a volume titled *Adolescent Sexuality in Contemporary America.* The scope of this study was not as ambitious as that of the Kinsey surveys, but within the narrower target population relatively good sampling procedures were employed. Initially, 2042 households were randomly selected from 200 urban, suburban, and rural areas throughout the continental United States. This sample yielded a potential group of 839 adolescents within the designated age range of 13 to 19. If all had agreed to fill out Sorenson's questionnaire, the final study group would have been a true probability sample.

However, the design of the study required obtaining written permission first from the parents and then from the respondents. Forty percent of the parents refused to provide their consent. Of the remaining adolescents, roughly one quarter decided not to participate. Thus, the final sample contained 411 of the originally selected 839 adolescents. Here again, the problem of self-selection is apparent. Did the nonparticipants—roughly 50%—differ in important ways from those who filled out the questionnaire? And what kind of relationship existed between parental restrictiveness (as might be suggested by refusals) and children's sex attitudes? As always, we can only speculate.

Another problem with Sorenson's research lies in the excessive length of the questionnaire, which was thirty-eight pages long. How many questions can a subject answer alertly? It is possible that some of the subjects may not have carefully considered all the items, particularly those on the later pages. Nevertheless, the Sorenson research has some strengths, including the application of basically sound methodology and a commitment to survey a broad range of adolescent sexual behaviors (including activities like petting, masturbation, coitus, and homosexual contact). His finding that 45% of his female participants and about 60% of the males reported having pre-marital coitus by age 19 is particularly noteworthy and will be discussed further in Chapter 13.

Zelnick and Kantner

In 1971, 1976, and 1979 the U.S. government sponsored national sex surveys aimed at evaluating pregnancy, the use of contraceptives, and premarital sexual activity among young, unmarried American females. The research was directed and reported by two Johns Hopkins researchers, Melvin Zelnick and John Kantner (1977, 1980). Probability sampling techniques were employed to select a subject population of several hundred women in the United States between the ages of 15 and 19. (The 1979 survey also included young men, ages 17 to 21.) The use of a well-constructed questionnaire to assess sexual behaviors and attitudes among a reasonably representative sample of American adolescent women makes this research particularly valuable. However, its results are limited by the narrow study population (teenage women) and the restricted range of behaviors evaluated.

Perhaps most noteworthy of Zelnick and Kantner's findings is the fact that by 1976, three years after the publication of Sorenson's findings, the number of 19-year-old females reporting premarital coitus had risen to 55%, an increase of 10% over Sorenson's reported figure. By 1979 this figure had risen to 69%. Zelnick and Kantner also reported a rise in the proportion of all teenage women who have become pregnant before marriage—9% in 1971 compared with 13% in 1976 and 16% in 1979.

Bell and Weinberg

Alan Bell and Martin Weinberg's *Homosexualities: A Study of Diversities Among Men and Women* (1978) was the product of a study originally commissioned a decade earlier by the National Institute of Mental Health. It was an ambitious project, the most comprehensive study of homosexuality to date.

The research team, headed by Bell and Weinberg, used extensive face-to-face, four-hour interviews to survey the sexual practices of homosexual men and women. The study group was recruited in the San Francisco area from a variety of sources, including public advertising, gay bars, personal contacts, gay baths, homophile organizations, and public places (theaters, restaurants, and so forth). The final sample of homosexual individuals contained a large number (979) of men and women, black and white, from a wide range of age, educational, and occupational levels. For comparative purposes, random probability sampling was employed to select a group of 477 heterosexuals who matched the homosexual respondents in terms of race, sex, age, occupation, and education. Most of the interviews for both groups were conducted by well-trained graduate students from universities in the San Francisco area.

The sample of homosexual individuals, although quite large, has been criticized as systematically biased by its manner of selection. Individuals who frequent gay bars, join homophile organizations, or openly acknowledge their homosexuality may not be entirely representative of the general homosexual population. Bell and Weinberg freely acknowledged that the study group was not a random sample:

The nonrepresentative nature of other investigators' samples as well as of our own precludes any generalization about the incidence of a particular phenomenon even to persons living in the locale where the interviews were conducted, much less to homosexuals in general. Nowhere has a random sample of American homosexual men and women ever been obtained, and given the variety of circumstances which discourage homosexuals from participating in research studies, it is unlikely that any investigator will ever be in a position to say that this or that is true of a given percentage of all homosexuals. (p. 22)

In spite of the sample's limitations, though, the Bell and Weinberg report is the most comprehensive examination of homosexual lifestyles to date. It is an important contribution to the literature, in an often sensationalized and misunderstood area of human experience.

To gain additional insight into the mechanisms by which people form their sexual orientation, Bell and Weinberg, in collaboration with researcher Sue Kiefer Hammersmith, employed sophisticated statistical techniques to analyze the data collected from their homosexual and heterosexual samples. The results of this effort, which put to the test popular theories about the development of sexual orientation, were published in 1981 in a book titled *Sexual Preference: Its Development in Men and Women*. In this excellent volume, the authors report that sexual orientation appears to be little influenced by parenting practices or other psychosocial factors. Rather, they suggest the possibility of a biological basis for sexual orientation, although they are unable to pinpoint causal factors. We will examine this important research on homosexuality and the development of sexual orientation in more detail in Chapter 10.

George and Weiler

Well-constructed studies designed to assess how sexuality changes in the older years have been conspicuously absent. One noteworthy exception is a study conducted by Duke University researchers Linda George and Stephen Weiler (1981). These two researchers correctly pointed out that simply asking older people how frequently they engage in coitus at a specific age does not provide adequate information about how people change their sexual behaviors. To correct this perceived limitation, George and Weiler elected to conduct a **longitudinal study** (study over time) of aging and sexuality. They surveyed 278 men and women, selected from the rosters of a local health insurance program, whose ages at the onset of the study ranged from 46 to 71 years. Each participant filled out a questionnaire at two-year intervals over a six year period.

The George and Weiler study is noteworthy for its use of a highly desirable longitudinal approach to studying changes in sexual behavior in the later years. However, their decision to include only married subjects in their sample group constitutes a serious limitation in their research design. Information about changing sexual patterns in the large segment of older people who no longer have a primary partner is also important.

Perhaps the most notable finding of George and Weiler's research is that most of their sample group reported only small declines in sexual activity over the six year period of the study.

Blumstein and Schwartz

1983 marked the publication of a highly acclaimed book titled *American Couples*. This text provides a wealth of information about current trends in relationships among couples, married and cohabitating, heterosexual and homosexual. The authors, University of Washington researchers Philip Blumstein and Pepper Schwartz, obtained their information by distributing detailed questionnaires to approximately 11,000 couples, recruited largely through the use of TV, radio, and newspaper announcements. Blumstein and Schwartz obtained an impressively high return rate of approximately 55%. Their final sample consisted of 4314 heterosexual couples and 1757 homosexual couples; of the latter, 969 were gay male couples and 788 lesbian couples. (The authors do not provide exact figures, but it appears that the ratio of married to cohabitating couples in their heterosexual sample is approximately six to one.) In addition to the data obtained from the written questionnaires, these researchers also conducted personal interviews with 129 heterosexual couples, 93 lesbian couples, and 98 gay male couples.

Strong points of the Blumstein and Schwartz research include a high response rate and the use of a large national sample. The well-designed questionnaire was constructed to reveal the interplay among a variety of sexual and nonsexual components of a relationship, and to make comparisons among the categories of couples— heterosexual married and cohabitating, gay male, and lesbian. A primary weakness, typical of most sex surveys, was the use of a sample population that underrepresented certain population groups, including people in lower socioeconomic levels, those with less education, and racial minorities.

Among the findings reported by Blumstein and Schwartz was the observation that cohabitating couples (heterosexual and homosexual) appear to have less difficulty in their relationships than married heterosexual couples, probably because their involvements are based more on equal participation by both partners. They also reported that it was very unusual to find serious conflicts in relationships where sexual sharing occurred on a regular, frequent basis and that "sex had to be really rotten before it began to take over and erode a relationship" (Schwartz, 1984).

What to Believe?
A Statement of Perspective

The preceding discussion of the methods and problems of sex research may have left you with some unanswered questions. To what degree can we rely upon the wide array of data introduced in the chapters that follow? We have learned that sex research is often hindered by difficulties in obtaining representative samples and accurate information. We have also seen that sex researchers have shown remarkable versatility in their efforts, using many different approaches to data collection. Thus, a major strength of sex research is its reliance on a wide assortment of methodological techniques.

We believe that any student of sex behavior would do well to differentiate between nonscientific polls and opinions and the results of scientific research conducted by serious investigators. However, even in the case of carefully planned investigations, it is good to maintain a critical eye and to avoid the tendency many of us have to believe something just because it is "scientific." You may find the following checklist of questions useful in evaluating any particular piece of research:

1. Who conducted the research? Are they considered to be reputable professionals?
2. What type of methodology was employed? Were scientific principles adhered to?
3. How large was the sample group, and is there any reason to suspect bias in the selection of subjects?
4. Can the results be applied to individuals other than those in the sample group? How broad can these generalizations be and still remain legitimate?
5. Is it possible that the method used to obtain information may have biased the findings? (Did the questionnaire promote false replies? Did the cameras place limitations on the response potentials? And so forth.)
6. Have there been any other published reports that confirm or contradict the particular study in question?

Keeping questions like these in mind is valuable in finding a middle ground between absolute trust and offhand dismissal of a given research study.

Summary

Research Methods

1. Research methods for studying sexuality include surveys, case studies, direct observation, and experimental research.

2. Most information about human sexual behavior has been obtained through questionnaire or interview surveys of relatively large populations of respondents. Questionnaires have the advantage of being anonymous, inexpensive, and quickly administered. Interviews are more flexible and allow for more rapport between the researcher and the subject.

3. Sex researchers who use surveys share certain problems. These include:

- The virtual impossibility of getting 100% participation of randomly selected subjects. (There has not yet been a true probability sample survey.) Self-selection of samples, or "volunteer bias," is a common problem.
- Biases created by nonresponse: Do volunteer participants have significantly different attitudes and behaviors from nonparticipants?

- Demographic biases: Most samples are heavily weighted toward white, middle-class, better-educated Americans.
- The problem of accuracy: Respondents' self-reports may be less than accurate, due to limitations of memory, boastfulness, guilt, or simple misunderstandings.

4. Case studies typically produce a great deal of information about one or a few individuals. They have two great advantages: flexibility, and the opportunity to explore specific behaviors and feelings in depth. Poor sampling techniques often limit the possibility of making generalizations from case studies to broad populations.

5. There is very little direct-observation sex research, due to the highly personal nature of the topic. When it can be done, observation significantly reduces the possibility of data falsification. However, subjects' behavior may be altered by the presence of an observer. Furthermore, the reliability of recorded observations may sometimes be compromised by preexisting researcher biases.

...mental research, while infrequently employed ...igations of human sexual behavior, offers two ...tages: control over the relevant variables, and ...ect analysis of possibly causal factors. However, the artificial nature of the experimental laboratory setting may alter subject responses from those that might occur in a natural setting.

Some Well-Known Studies

7. The Kinsey surveys remain the most ambitious and broad-scale taxonomic studies of human sexual behavior. They were somewhat limited by sampling techniques that resulted in overrepresentation of young, educated, city-dwelling people.

8. The laboratory observation research of Masters and Johnson provided excellent information about the physiosexual responses of women and men. In spite of the fact that their study population was biased toward high educational and socioeconomic levels, their findings have broad application to the general population. Their subsequently reported studies of sexual problems and homosexuality are difficult to interpret because of methodological errors and imprecise reporting.

9. Morton Hunt's survey of sexual behavior in the 1970s was compromised by several limitations, including poor sampling techniques, strong self-selection bias, and excessive questionnaire length. The major strength of the Hunt research lies in the comprehensiveness with which it explored a broad range of human sexual behaviors.

10. The *Redbook* survey utilized a huge sample of women who answered questions about female sexuality. But since the sample consisted of volunteers drawn mostly from the magazine's readership, it cannot be considered a probability sample.

11. Shere Hite's observations of female and male sexual behavior, while obtained from biased samples, provide several valuable insights into human sexuality.

12. Robert Sorenson provided an important study of adolescent sexual behavior, broader in scope than the Zelnick and Kantner surveys, but more limited by sampling bias and excessive questionnaire length.

13. Zelnick and Kantner provided survey data pertaining to the sexual activity of American teenage women in 1971, 1976, and 1979. Good sampling techniques and research methodology make this investigation particularly valuable.

14. The most ambitious study of homosexual people to date was conducted by a research team headed by Alan Bell and Martin Weinberg. Their research population was biased by sampling difficulties.

15. George and Weiler conducted a longitudinal study of aging and sexuality in which they administered questionnaires to several hundred people at two-year intervals. Their research was limited by a decision to include only married people in the study sample.

16. Philip Blumstein and Pepper Schwartz employed a well-designed questionnaire to obtain information about sexual and nonsexual components of relationships among heterosexual and homosexual couples. They obtained an excellent response rate from a large national sample that was biased by the underrepresentation of certain population groups.

What to Believe?
A Statement of Perspective

17. In evaluating any study of sexual behavior it is helpful to consider who conducted the research, to examine the methods and sampling techniques carefully, and to compare the results with those of other reputable studies.

Thought Provokers

1. Of the four research techniques discussed in this chapter—surveys, clinical case studies, direct observations, and experimental laboratory studies—survey research has provided the most data about human sexuality. Why do you think this is so? Which method do you think is best for learning about our sexuality? Why?

2. A radio talk show host informs his listening audience that women enjoy sex more in the morning than in the evening. When pressed by a questioner, he says he knows this to be true from experience. How would you go about determining the validity of this assertion? Which of the four methodologies discussed in this chapter could be effectively used to test this hypothesis? Why? Might you gain valuable information by applying more than one of these techniques?

3. In your opinion, which of the various well-known studies outlined in this chapter have provided the most useful information about human sexuality? Why? Which do you think provided the most reliable data, and why?

Suggested Readings

Brecher, Edward. *The Sex Researchers*. New York: Signet, 1969. An easy-to-read account of sex researchers and their findings. Provides a behind-the-scenes perspective and some interesting historical anecdotes.

Brecher, Ruth, and Brecher, Edward. *An Analysis of Human Sexual Response*. New York: New American Library, 1966. In addition to detailing the work of Masters and Johnson, this highly readable book deals with sex research in general, particularly emphasizing its practical applications and its impact on society.

Bullough, V. *The Frontiers of Sex Research*. Buffalo, N.Y.: Prometheus, 1979. An overview of research into various fields of sexuality. Contains several excellent articles dealing with the issues and implications of sex research.

Elias, Veronica. "A Cautionary Note on Sex Studies." *The Humanist,* March/April 1978, 23–25. A thoughtful discussion of the tendencies of some sex researchers to make unwarranted interpretations of their findings. The author urges readers to use caution in interpreting sex research findings.

Pomeroy, Wardell. *Dr. Kinsey and the Institute for Sex Research*. New York: Harper & Row, 1972. An informed and entertaining look at Kinsey and his research, as seen through the "insider" eyes of one of his original research colleagues.

Pomeroy, Wardell; Flax, Carol; and Wheeler, Connie. *Taking a Sex History: Interviewing and Recording*. New York: The Free Press, 1982. Provides excellent information about applying Kinsey's interviewing strategies to contemporary sex research.

The Journal of Sex Research, February, 1986, Volume 22. A special issue of this journal devoted entirely to issues related to methodology in sex research. The many excellent articles in this volume address such topics as sampling bias, the interaction of volunteer bias with different forms of sex research techniques, the relationship between objective and subjective measures of sexual responsiveness, and a critical analysis of sex research methodology.

3

One has noticed in a certain species the female more beautiful, stronger, more active, more intelligent, and one has noticed the opposite. One has seen the male larger, or smaller; one has seen and will see him a parasite, or provider, permanent master of the couple or the group, fugitive lover, a slave sacrificed by the female after the completion of her pleasure. All attitudes, and the same ones, are attributed by nature to either of the sexes; there is not, apart from the specific functions, a male or female role.

Remy de Gourmont
The Natural Philosophy of Love (1904)

Gender Issues

Male and Female, Masculine and Feminine

Gender-Identity Formation

Gender Roles

EXAMINE THE FOLLOWING sentence and fill in the blanks: In this particular society "the _____ is the dominant, impersonal, managing partner, the _____ the less responsible and the emotionally dependent person." Did you assume that *man* goes in the first blank space and *woman* in the second? In fact, the reverse is true. But how can this be? Is it not human nature for men the world over to take charge in their relationships with women? Are not women always the more dependent partners? Things may be getting a bit more equal between the sexes (at least in some societies), but a complete reversal of the traditional roles? How can that happen?

This is the first, incredulous comment people typically voice after being told about the Tchambuli society of New Guinea, where traditional masculine and feminine behavior patterns are complete opposites of those typical of American society (Mead, 1963). This cultural difference raises certain fundamental questions: What constitutes maleness and femaleness? What is the relationship between male-female and masculine-feminine? Which of the behavioral differences between women and men have a biological basis? A psychosocial basis? Both?

Male and Female, Masculine and Feminine

Through the ages people have held to the belief that we are born males or females and just naturally grow up doing what men or women do. The only explanation required has been a simple allusion to "nature taking its course." There is a simplicity about this viewpoint that helps make the world seem an orderly place. However, closer examination has revealed a much greater complexity in the process whereby our maleness and femaleness are determined and the way they influence our behavior, sexual and otherwise. This fascinating complexity will be our focus in the pages that follow. But first it will be helpful to clarify a few important terms.

Sex and Gender

Many writers use the terms gender and sex interchangeably. However, each of these words has a specific meaning. **Sex** refers to our biological maleness or femaleness. There are two aspects of biological sex: *genetic sex,* which is determined by our sex chromosomes, and *anatomical sex,* the obvious physical differences between males and females. **Gender** is a concept that encompasses the special psychosocial meanings added to biological maleness or femaleness. Thus, while our sex is linked to various physical attributes (chromosomes, penis, vulva, and so forth), our gender refers to the social concomitants of sex, or in other words, our masculinity or femininity. In this chapter we will be using the terms masculine and feminine to characterize the behaviors that are typically attributed to males and females. One undesirable aspect of these labels is that they may limit the range of behaviors that people are comfortable expressing. For example, a man might hesitate to be nurturing lest he be labeled feminine, and a woman might be reticent to act assertively for fear of being considered masculine. It is not our intention to perpetuate the stereotypes often associated with these labels. However, we do find it necessary to use these terms when discussing gender issues.

When we encounter people for the first time, most of us quickly note their sex and make assumptions based on their maleness or femaleness about how they are likely to behave; these are **gender assumptions**. For most people, gender assumptions are an important part of routine social interaction. For example, think back on the last time you were unable to determine someone's sex. Perhaps you were as flustered and perplexed as the man in the following account:

> One day I stopped in the park to watch a pick-up soccer game involving several men and women. One player, who immediately caught my attention, seemed to flow across the field with graceful, almost sensuous movements. From a distance this person's face was striking and incredibly androgynous. The bulky clothes being worn (cold day) didn't give me any clues as to the sex of the wearer. With all the noise and hollering going on, I couldn't distinguish this person's sex by voice. The hair was cut short in a masculine style, but the movements reminded me of a woman. When the game disbanded, she or he walked alone to the parking lot. I was torn by indecision. I wanted to go up and strike up a conversation. But what if she had been a he? What would I have said?—"Say, I followed you over here to the parking lot to tell you I liked the way you play soccer"? To this day I regret my inaction and still wonder who this person was—woman or man? (Authors' files)

Many of us may find it hard to interact with a person whose gender is ambiguous. People are either the same sex or the other sex. (We have avoided using the term *opposite sex* because we believe it overstates the differences between males and females.) When we are unsure of our identification of someone's gender we may become confused and uncomfortable.

Gender Identity and Gender Role

Gender identity refers to our own personal, subjective sense that "I am a male" or "I am a female." Most of us realize that we are either male or female, masculine or feminine, in the first few years of life. However, there is no guarantee that a person's gender identity will be consistent with his or her biological sex, and some people experience considerable confusion in their efforts to identify their own maleness or femaleness. We will look into this area in more detail later in this chapter.

Gender role (sometimes called sex role) refers to a collection of attitudes and behaviors that are considered normal and appropriate in a specific culture for people of a particular sex. Gender roles establish sex-related behavioral expectations that people are expected to fulfill. Behavior thought to be socially appropriate for a male is called masculine, for a female, feminine. When we use the terms masculine and feminine in subsequent discussions, we are referring to these socialized notions.

Gender-role expectations are culturally defined and vary from society to society. For example, the Tchambuli society considers emotionally expressive behavior appropriate for males. Obviously, American society takes a somewhat different view. A kiss on the cheek is considered a feminine act and therefore inappropriate between men in American society. In contrast, such behavior is consistent with masculine role expectations in many European and Middle Eastern societies.

In addition to being culturally based, our notions of masculinity and femininity are also era dependent. For example, if an American male went to a hairdresser for

"Well, for heaven's sakes, which one is the opposite sex, you or me?"

a permanent in the 1960s, he would probably have been ridiculed for his "effeminate" behavior. In the 1980s, an abundance of curly-headed men indicates that gender-role expectations for hair style have changed significantly. Such changes are becoming increasingly common; more than any other time in our history, the present era is marked by redefinition of male and female roles. Many people are no longer content to live with traditional gender roles. Many of us who have grown up subjected to strong gender-role conditioning are now exploring how these roles have shaped our lives and are seeking to break away from their limiting influences. Being part of this change can be both exciting and confusing. We will consider the impact of traditional and changing gender roles later in this chapter (and also throughout our text). But first let us turn our attention to the processes whereby we acquire our gender identity.

Gender-Identity Formation

How do we acquire the realization that we are a boy or a girl, masculine or feminine? Is this a natural process, or does our gender identity emerge from an array of social learning experiences? In this section we will attempt to unravel some of the mysteries surrounding these questions. The mechanisms through which people attain their gender identity have been the subject of much research and theoretical discussion. Some theorists have emphasized the role of biological development; others have argued that social learning is most crucial. Today, however, most theorists recognize the importance of both of these forces. We will begin by outlining the biological factors that affect our sense of maleness or femaleness.

Gender Identity as a Biological Process: Normal Prenatal Differentiation

Gender identity is unquestionably influenced by our biological sex, which is determined by a complex set of variables. The genetic material in the fertilized egg, organized in structures called **chromosomes**, gives rise to the process of **sexual differentiation**, whereby the individual develops physical characteristics distinct from those of the other sex. However, our physical maleness or femaleness is not simply a function of the makeup of our chromosomes. Rather, it is the result of processes that occur at six different levels of sexual differentiation. Thus, we may talk about chromosomal sex, gonadal sex, hormonal sex, sex of the internal reproductive structures, sex of the external genitals, and sex differentiation of the brain. As we shall see, the overall process of prenatal sexual differentiation is largely under the control of genetic and hormonal mechanisms.

Under normal conditions, the six levels of prenatal differentiation interact harmoniously to determine our biological sex and, later, our gender identity. However, errors can occur at each of these levels, and the resulting abnormalities in the development of a person's biological sex may seriously complicate acquisition of a gender identity. Before we discuss these problems, let us consider normal biological sex differentiation.

Chromosomal Sex.   At the first level of differentiation, our biological sex is determined by the chromosomes present in the reproductive cells (sperm and ova) at the moment of conception. With the exception of the reproductive cells, the body cells of humans contain a total of 46 chromosomes, arranged as 23 pairs (see Figure 3.1). Twenty-two of these pairs are matched; that is, the two chromosomes of each pair look almost identical. These matched sets, called **autosomes**, are the same in males and females and do not significantly influence sex differentiation. One chromosome pair, however—the **sex chromosomes**—differs in females and males. Females have two similar chromosomes labeled XX. In males the pair consists of dissimilar chromosomes and is called XY.

As noted above, the reproductive cells are an exception to the 23-pair rule. As a result of a biological process known as *meiosis,* mature reproductive cells contain only half the usual complement of chromosomes—one member of each pair. (This process is necessary to avoid a doubling of the chromosome total when sex cells merge at conception.) A normal female **ovum** (or egg) contains 22 autosomes plus an X chromosome. A normal male **sperm** cell contains 22 autosomes plus *either* an X or Y chromosome. Fertilization of the ovum by a Y-bearing sperm produces an XY combination, resulting in a male child. Fertilization by an X-bearing sperm results in an XX combination and a female child.

Science is far from a complete understanding of the role of sex chromosomes in the determination of biological sex. However, certain facts seem well established from studies of people with abnormal numbers of sex chromosomes. The Y chromosome must be present to ensure the complete development of internal and external male sex organs. The presence of at least one Y chromosome—regardless of the number of X's present—allows the development of these male structures. In the absence of a Y chromosome, an individual will develop female external genitals.

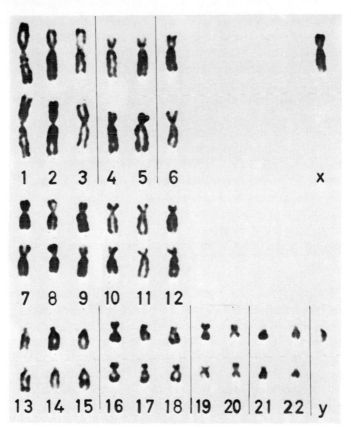

Figure 3.1

Male Human
Chromosomes

However, two X chromosomes are needed for the complete development of both internal and external female structures.

Some writers have argued that the only function of the sex chromosomes is to determine the characteristics of the sex organs. However, it now appears that this is an overly simplistic view. Both X and Y chromosomes contain **genes** (the basic units of heredity) that influence other structures and functions. Some researchers contend that the Y chromosome adds a "male" quality to development that may help account for certain physical and behavioral differences between the sexes (Hutt, 1973).

Gonadal Sex. During the first few weeks of prenatal development it is impossible to distinguish the sex of a human embryo without a chromosome analysis. The **gonads**—the structures containing the future reproductive cells—are alike in the two sexes. At this early point in development the gonads are *bipotential,* which means that they have the capacity to become either testes or ovaries, depending on events to follow.

About six weeks after conception, however, the gonads begin to differentiate. If a Y chromosome is present, the inner portion, or *medulla,* of the gonad undergoes rapid development, becoming a mature testis in several days. In the absence of a Y chromosome, the outer portion, or *cortex,* of the gonad develops into a mature ovary about 12 weeks after conception. Testes normally descend from their position inside the abdomen to the scrotum during the seventh month of prenatal development.

A great deal of research has been conducted on the process of gonadal development. It is now apparent that without specific masculinizing signals, the primitive gonads will develop as ovaries (Haseltine and Ohno, 1981). Recent evidence has implicated a substance called **H-Y antigen**, which appears to be under the control of male-determining genes on the Y chromosome. In some complex way, as yet not fully understood, this substance triggers the transformation of the embryonic gonads into testes (Bernstein, 1981; Haseltine and Ohno, 1981). In the absence of H-Y antigen, the undifferentiated gonadal tissue develops into ovaries.

As we have seen, genes on the sex chromosomes trigger differentiation of the gonads into ovaries or testes. Once this happens, the presence or absence of the fetus's own gonadal sex hormones becomes the critical factor in determining the differentiation of the internal and external sex structures and the brain.

Hormonal Sex.   As soon as the gonads differentiate into testes or ovaries, the control of biological sex determination passes to the sex hormones and genetic influence ceases. It will be easier to understand the role of hormones if we first briefly examine the endocrine system and its function in human sexual development and behavior.

The **endocrine system** consists of several ductless glands located throughout the body. The major endocrine glands include the pituitary, the gonads, the thyroid, the parathyroids, the adrenals, and the pancreas. Each of these produces hormones and secretes them directly into the bloodstream. Our interest here is in the gonads and the sex hormones they secrete that influence sexual differentiation and development. All the sex hormones belong to the general family known as *steroids.* The ovaries produce two classes of hormones: the **estrogens** and the **progestational compounds**. The estrogens, the most important of which is *estradiol,* influence development of female physical sex characteristics and help regulate the menstrual cycle. Of the progestational compounds, only *progesterone* is known to be physiologically important. Its function is to help regulate the menstrual cycle and stimulate development of the uterine lining in preparation for pregnancy. The primary hormone products of the testes are the **androgens**. The most important androgen is *testosterone,* which influences both the development of male physical sex characteristics and sexual motivation. In both sexes the adrenal glands also secrete sex hormones, including small amounts of estrogen and greater quantities of androgen.

Considerable research has shown how gonadal sex hormones contribute to differentiation of the internal and external sex structures. If fetal gonads differentiate into testes, they soon begin to secrete androgens, which in turn stimulate the development of male structures. If for some reason a male fetus does not produce enough androgen secretions, its sex organs will develop as female in form and appearance, despite the presence of the male chromosome (Money, 1968). Thus, a specific female hormone is not necessary to instigate development of female structures in a fetus; in the absence of male hormones, the developmental pattern is female. Maleness, however, depends on secretion of the right amount of male hormone at the crucial time.

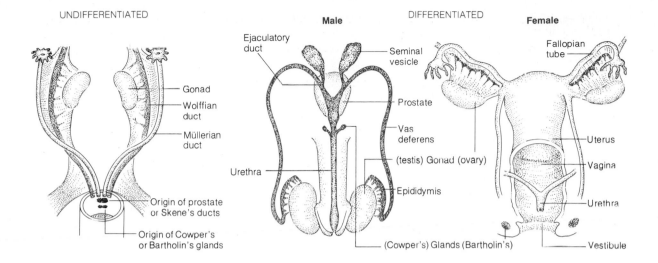

UNDIFFERENTIATED   Male   DIFFERENTIATED   Female

Ejaculatory duct
Seminal vesicle
Gonad
Wolffian duct
Müllerian duct
Prostate
Vas deferens
Urethra
(testis) Gonad (ovary)
Epididymis
Origin of prostate or Skene's ducts
Origin of Cowper's or Bartholin's glands
(Cowper's) Glands (Bartholin's)
Fallopian tube
Uterus
Vagina
Urethra
Vestibule

Sex of the Internal Reproductive Structures. At about eight weeks after conception, internal reproductive structures begin to differentiate from two paired internal duct systems, the **Müllerian ducts** and the **Wolffian ducts** (see Figure 3.2). If the embryo is chromosomally male, and if the gonads have previously differentiated into testes, the newly formed testes will begin secreting two substances. One of these chemicals, **Müllerian inhibiting substance** (MIS), causes the Müllerian ducts to shrink rather than develop into internal female structures. At the same time, the testes begin to produce androgens, primarily testosterone. These hormones stimulate the development of the Wolffian ducts into internal male reproductive structures: the vas deferens, seminal vesicles, and ejaculatory ducts.

In contrast, hormones do not guide the process of female sexual differentiation. When they are not suppressed by testis-produced MIS and testosterone, the Müllerian ducts develop into internal female structures: the fallopian tubes, uterus, and inner third of the vagina. Without testosterone to stimulate its growth, the Wolffian duct system degenerates.

Sex of the External Genitals. External genitals develop according to a similar pattern (see Figure 3.3). Prior to the completion of the sixth week of prenatal development, all human embryos possess undifferentiated rudimentary external genital tissue, located below the umbilical cord, which consists of the *genital tubercle,* the *genital folds,* and the *labioscrotal swelling.* These tissues develop into either male or female external genitals, depending on the presence or absence of testosterone. When testosterone begins circulating in the bloodstream of males, it is converted in some tissues into a hormone called *dihydrotestosterone* (DHT). DHT stimulates the labioscrotal swelling to become the scrotum and the genital tubercle and genital folds to differentiate into the glans and shaft of the penis respectively. (The genital folds fuse around the urethra to form the shaft of the penis, and the two sides of the labioscrotal

Figure 3.2

Prenatal Differentiation of Internal Sex Structures
Prenatal development of male and female internal duct systems from undifferentiated (before the sixth week) to differentiated.

Figure 3.3

Prenatal Differentiation of External Genitals

Prenatal development of external male and female genitals from undifferentiated (before six weeks) to fully differentiated stage.

UNDIFFERENTIATED BEFORE SIXTH WEEK

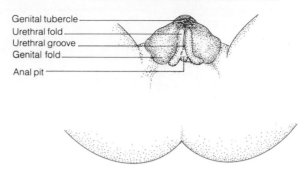

Genital tubercle
Urethral fold
Urethral groove
Genital fold
Anal pit

SEVENTH TO EIGHTH WEEK

Male   **Female**

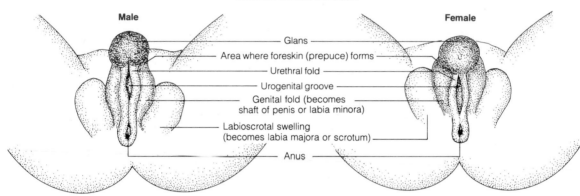

Glans
Area where foreskin (prepuce) forms
Urethral fold
Urogenital groove
Genital fold (becomes shaft of penis or labia minora)
Labioscrotal swelling (becomes labia majora or scrotum)
Anus

FULLY DEVELOPED BY TWELFTH WEEK

Male   **Female**

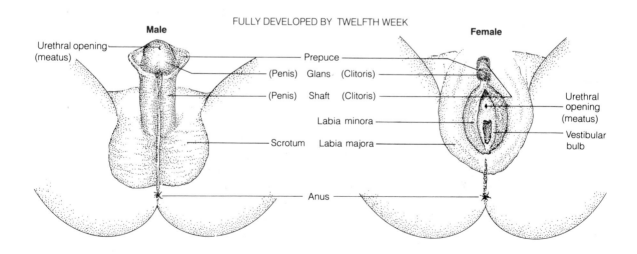

Urethral opening (meatus)

Prepuce
(Penis) Glans (Clitoris)
(Penis) Shaft (Clitoris)
Labia minora
Scrotum   Labia majora

Urethral opening (meatus)
Vestibular bulb

Anus

Table 3.1 Homologous Sex Organs

Female	Male
Clitoris	Glans of penis
Hood of clitoris	Foreskin of penis
Labia minora	Shaft of penis
Labia majora	Scrotal sac
Ovaries	Testes
Skene's ducts	Prostate gland
Bartholin's glands	Cowper's glands

swelling fuse to form the scrotum; these fusions do not occur in females.) In the absence of testosterone, female genitals evolve from the undifferentiated tissues. The genital tubercle becomes the clitoris, the genital folds become the inner vaginal lips (labia minora), and the two sides of the labioscrotal swelling differentiate into the outer vaginal lips (labia majora). By the twelfth week the differentiation process is complete: the penis and scrotum are recognizable in males; the clitoris and labia can be identified in females.

Thus, the human form is biologically sex neutral until critical physiological events in the early stages of prenatal development begin the complex process of sex differentiation. We have seen that without the additional input of certain key masculinizing influences the human embryo naturally develops in the female direction. As John Money and Anke Ehrhardt (1972) have succinctly summarized, "Nature's rule is, it would appear, that to masculinize, something must be added" (p. 7). This extra "something" is the combined input of H-Y antigen, MIS, and testosterone.

Since the external genitals, gonads, and some of the internal structures of males and females originate from the same embryonic tissues, it is not surprising that they have corresponding, or homologous, parts. Table 3.1 summarizes these male and female counterparts. We will look at the form and function of human sex organs in more detail in Chapters 4 and 5.

Sex Differentiation of the Brain. Recently, strong evidence has emerged that some important structural and functional differences exist in the brains of males and females and that the process of sex differentiation of human brains occurs largely, if not exclusively, during prenatal development. These differences appear to involve at least two major brain areas: the **hypothalamus** and the left and right **cerebral hemispheres**. Most of the evidence for sex differentiation of the brain comes from studies of nonhuman animals, particularly rats. However, "it seems likely that similar sex differences exist in the brains of all mammals" (Thompson, 1985, p. 164).

A number of studies have revealed that a marked sex differentiation occurs in the hypothalamus (see Figure 6.1 for the location of this structure) and that this process is influenced by the presence or absence of circulating testosterone, much like the differentiation of internal and external sex structures (Bloom et al., 1985; Dohanich and Ward, 1980; Gordon and Gorski, 1979; MacLusky and Naftolin, 1981). The hypothalamus is a critical brain structure; among other things, it plays a major role in controlling the production of sex hormones, and it mediates fertility and menstrual cycles through its interaction with the pituitary gland. It appears that the presence or absence of circulating testosterone during prenatal differentiation determines the estrogen sensitivity of certain cells in the hypothalamus. In the male, testosterone causes these specialized receptor cells to become insensitive to estrogen. In the female, the absence of testosterone allows these cells to develop a high level of sensitivity to estrogen in the bloodstream.

The consequences of prenatal sex differentiation of the hypothalamus become most apparent at the onset of puberty. A hypothalamus that has undergone female differentiation will direct the pituitary to release hormones in a cyclic fashion, creating the menstrual cycle. In contrast, the male-differentiated hypothalamus directs a relatively steady, or acyclic, production of sex hormones. Thus, hypothalamic sex differences are the reason why female fertility is cyclic and male fertility is not.

There is also considerable evidence for sex differences in the cerebral hemispheres of the brain (Bloom et al., 1985). If the top of a person's skull were removed and you looked straight down on the brain, you would see that it is divided into a left and a right side by a long, deep cleft running from front to back. The resulting two cerebral hemispheres are almost mirror images of each other. Though the hemispheres look alike, they are somewhat specialized in their functions. In most people the left hemisphere is more specialized for verbal functions (understanding and using language), whereas the right side of the brain is more specialized for spatial tasks (the ability to recognize objects and shapes and to perceive relationships among them).

A large body of evidence suggests that there are sex differences in verbal and spatial skills. Females frequently score higher than males on tests of verbal skills, and the reverse is often true when spatial abilities are tested (Burnstein et al., 1980; Deno, 1982; Sanders et al., 1982). Why do these differences exist? Are they primarily a function of the way males and females are socialized in this society, or are biological factors their major cause?

Several researchers have reported sex differences in the structure of the two cerebral hemispheres that suggest a possible biological basis for differences in the skills of males and females. For example, in male rats the *cerebral cortex* is thicker in the right hemisphere than in the left, with the reverse being the case for females (Diamond et al., 1979). (The cerebral cortex is the thin outer covering of the two hemispheres, the part of the brain responsible for higher mental processes like thinking, remembering, language use, and the ability to perceive spatial relationships.) Since the right hemisphere is the primary repository of spatial abilities, it is not surprising that male rats, with quantitatively superior right hemispheres, perform better than their female counterparts on maze learning tasks that require skill with spatial relationships (Beatty, 1979). Studies of human subjects who have experienced damage to one of their cerebral hemispheres have also reported evidence indicative of sex differences in the degree of hemispheric specialization (McGlone, 1978; Inglis et al., 1982).

One eminent investigator of sex differences in the brain, Norman Geschwind (1982), believes that testosterone influences the rate of hemispheric growth in the developing fetus. He suggests that the greater quantity of circulating testosterone in the brains of prenatal males slows the growth rate of the left hemisphere and results in relatively greater development of the right hemisphere; lack of testosterone in prenatal females causes the reverse development. If Geschwind's theory is ultimately supported by further research, we will have hard evidence of a biological basis for alleged sex differences in verbal and spatial skills. However, it is important to note that these reported differences are also likely to be influenced by psychosocial factors (Archer and Lloyd, 1985; Entwisle and Baker, 1983; Hyde, 1985; Paulsen and Johnson, 1983).

Some theorists have suggested that sex differences in the brain, in addition to contributing to differences in abilities, may also have a significant impact upon a variety of behaviors, most notably sexual and aggressive behaviors. However, at this time we cannot say conclusively whether sex differences in the brains of humans have any significant correlation with behavioral differences between the sexes. Certainly it is premature, and probably inaccurate, to suggest that brain differences play the most important role.

Abnormal Prenatal Differentiation

Thus far we have considered only normal prenatal differentiation. However, much of our understanding of biological sex differentiation and its impact upon the ultimate development of our gender identities comes from studies of abnormal prenatal differentiation. A detailed discussion of the vast and complex research in this field is beyond the scope of this book. However, we will examine some particularly noteworthy examples of atypical differentiation processes to broaden our understanding of gender-identity formation as a biological process.

Abnormal differentiation may be the result of an abnormal combination of sex chromosomes, but it also occurs in people with normal chromosome numbers as a result of errors at other biological levels. We will look first at several types of sex chromosome abnormalities, then follow with a more detailed examination of some biological errors that produce deviations in prenatal hormonal processes. The outstanding features of these examples are summarized in Table 3.2.

Sex Chromosome Abnormalities. Occasionally errors occur at the first level of biological sex determination, and individuals are born with one or more extra sex chromosomes or missing one sex chromosome. Over 70 abnormalities of the sex chromosomes have been identified (Levitan and Montagu, 1977). These irregularities may be associated with various physical, health, and behavioral effects. We will consider only three of the most widely researched of these abnormalities.

Turner's Syndrome. **Turner's syndrome** is a rare condition characterized by the presence of only one sex chromosome, an X. This condition results when an atypical ovum containing 22 autosomes and no sex chromosome is fertilized by an X-bearing

Table 3.2 *Summary of Some Examples of Abnormal Prenatal Sex Differentiation*

Syndrome	Chromosomal Sex	Gonadal Sex	Reproductive Internal Structures	External Genitals	Fertility	Secondary Sex Characteristics	Gender Identity
Turner's syndrome	45, XO	Fibrous streaks of ovarian tissue	Uterus and fallopian tubes	Normal female	Sterile	Underdeveloped; no breasts	Female
Klinefelter's syndrome	47, XXY	Small testes	Normal male	Undersized penis and testicles	Sterile	Some feminization of secondary characteristics; may have breast development and rounded body contours	Usually male, although higher than normal incidence of gender-identity problems
"Supermale syndrome"	47, XYY	Testes	Normal male	Normal male	Reduced fertility	Normal male	Male
Fetally androgenized females (andrenogenital syndrome and progestin induced)	46, XX	Ovaries	Normal female	Ambiguous (typically more male than female)	Fertile	Normal female (AGS females must be treated with cortisone to avoid masculinization)	Female, but significant level of dissatisfaction with female gender identity; very oriented toward traditional male activities
Androgen insensitivity syndrome	46, XY	Undescended testes	Lacks a normal set of either male or female internal structures	Normal female genitals and a shallow vagina	Sterile	At puberty breast development and other signs of normal female sexual maturation appear, but menstruation does not occur	Female
DHT deficient males	46, XY	Undescended testes at birth; testes descend at puberty	Vas deferens, seminal vesicles, and ejaculatory ducts but no prostate; partially formed vagina	Ambiguous at birth (more female than male); at puberty genitals are masculinized	Produce viable sperm but unable to inseminate	Female before puberty; become masculinized at puberty	Prepuberty gender identity difficult to ascertain (lack of data); approximately 90% have assumed traditional male gender role at puberty

sperm. (The same ovum fertilized by a Y-bearing sperm does not survive.) The resulting chromosome number in the fertilized egg is 45 rather than the normal 46; the sex chromosome combination is designated XO. People with this combination develop normal external female genitals and consequently are classified as females. However, their internal reproductive structures do not develop fully—ovaries are absent or represented only by fibrous streaks of tissue. Turner's syndrome females do not develop breasts at puberty (unless given hormone treatment), do not menstruate, and of course are sterile. As adults, women with Turner's syndrome tend to be unusually short.

Since the gonads are absent or poorly developed and hormones are consequently deficient, Turner's syndrome permits gender identity to be formed in the absence of gonadal and hormonal influences (the second and third levels of biological sex determination). Turner's syndrome individuals identify themselves as female, and as a group they are not distinguishable from biologically normal females in their interests and behavior (Money and Ehrhardt, 1972). This strongly suggests that a feminine gender identity can be established in the absence of ovaries and their hormone products.

Klinefelter's Syndrome.   A much more common sex chromosome error in humans is **Klinefelter's syndrome**. This condition results when an atypical ovum containing 22 autosomes and two X chromosomes is fertilized by a Y-bearing sperm, creating an XXY individual. In spite of the presence of both the XY combination characteristic of normal males and the XX pattern of normal females, Klinefelter's syndrome individuals are anatomically male. This supports the view that the presence of a Y chromosome triggers the formation of male structures. However, the presence of an extra female sex chromosome impedes the continued development of these structures, and Klinefelter's syndrome males typically are sterile and have undersized penises and testicles. Their interest in sexual activity is often weak or absent (Money, 1968; Rabock et al., 1979). Presumably this low sex drive is related, at least in part, to deficient production of hormones from the testes.

Klinefelter's syndrome males tend to be tall and are often somewhat feminized in their physical characteristics; they may exhibit breast development and rounded body contours. They also tend to be passive and low in ambition, and they frequently show some degree of intellectual impairment. Testosterone treatments during adolescence and adulthood can enhance the development of male secondary sexual characteristics and may increase sexual interest and assertiveness (Kolodny et al., 1979).

XYY Males.   A third type of sex chromosome error produces the **XYY male**. This chromosomal anomaly results when a normal ovum is fertilized by an atypical sperm bearing two Y chromosomes. XYY individuals develop the normal sex organs and characteristics of males and are thoroughly masculine in appearance. They are unusual in that most tend to be quite tall, over six feet on the average. These males are often somewhat below average in intelligence. They also tend to be less fertile than men with a normal XY combination, although some have fathered children. The extra Y chromosome usually is not passed on to a male offspring (Levitan and Montagu, 1977).

Some years ago the XYY condition received a great deal of publicity. Some investigators suggested a link between the so-called "supermale syndrome" and violent, aggressive, criminal behavior (Jacobs et al., 1965). This conclusion was reached largely because studies of this anomaly revealed a significantly higher proportion of XYY males in prison populations than in the general population (Gardner and Neu, 1972). However, one study of Danish prisoners found that imprisoned XYY men were no more likely to have engaged in crimes of aggression against people than were XY inmates (Witkin et al., 1976).

Some writers have proposed that the extra Y chromosome somehow adds an aggressive component to a person's character. Others have suggested that XYY males tend to be overly impulsive and that this trait, in combination with their below average intelligence, can lead to unlawful behavior. More recently a number of investigators have questioned this last interpretation, and some have noted that prison samples may be highly biased (Unger, 1979). In other words, only the most severe behavioral manifestations of the XYY condition, if there really are any, come to the attention of investigators studying prisoners. What about all the other males with the same chromosomal variation who are never identified and studied because they do not end up in prison? Perhaps further research will clarify the causal relationship, if any, between this chromosomal abnormality and behavior. Meanwhile, current thinking generally holds that the case for the alleged link between the "supermale syndrome" and violent behavior has been overstated.

Biological Errors Affecting Prenatal Hormonal Processes. As we have seen, formation of the gonads, duct development, and differentiation of the internal and external sex structures occur under the influence of timed biological cues. When these signals deviate from normal patterns, the end result can be ambiguous biological sex. People with ambiguous or contradictory sex characteristics are sometimes called **hermaphrodites**, a term derived from the mythical Greek deity Hermaphroditus, who was thought to possess attributes of both sexes. Research has demonstrated that this unusual situation can result from a variety of biological errors that produce markedly atypical patterns of hormonally induced prenatal sex differentiation.

We can distinguish between **true hermaphrodites** and **pseudohermaphrodites**. True hermaphrodites, who have both ovarian and testicular tissue in their bodies, are exceedingly rare. They may have one ovary and one testis or two ovaries and two testes. Some possess gonads called *ovotestes* that contain mixtures of ovarian and testicular tissue. Their external genitals are often a mixture of male and female structures. A vaginal opening is frequently present beneath the penis, and many true hermaphrodites menstruate. Occasionally the uterus is developed to the point of being fully functional.

Investigations of true hermaphroditism have stimulated speculation about whether such a person might both impregnate as a male and conceive as a female. Some years ago this speculation took a bizarre twist when Brazilian physicians reported the case of a pregnant true hermaphrodite who claimed to be both mother and father of the child. The uterus and ovaries of this person were fully functional and the testicles were sperm producing. While this is certainly a fascinating case, the claim of dual parenthood was not clearly substantiated and remains highly doubtful (Money, 1966).

Pseudohermaphroditism occurs much more often than true hermaphroditism. The biological sex of pseudohermaphrodites is also ambiguous. Unlike true hermaphrodites, pseudohermaphrodites are born with gonads that match their chromosomal sex. However, their internal and external reproductive anatomy may demonstrate a mixture of male and female structures, or the structures may be incompletely male or incompletely female, or inconsistent with the chromosomal sex. Such cases are particularly interesting in that they provide data that helps clarify the relative roles of biological and social-learning factors in the formation of gender identity. Let us consider some of the evidence ensuing from studies of gender-identity formation in three varieties of pseudohermaphroditism.

Fetally Androgenized Females. A number of biological accidents may result in pseudohermaphroditism. One is the situation in which a chromosomally normal female (XX) is exposed to an excessive amount of androgens or androgenlike substances during the critical period of prenatal sex differentiation. There are two possible sources of these androgens: They may be introduced as drugs the mother takes during pregnancy, or they may be produced by the fetus's own body. In the 1950s some pregnant women took a synthetic hormone drug to prevent miscarriage. The physicians who prescribed the drug (progestin) were unaware that it would have the same effect on the fetus as a dose of male hormones. Progestin and androgen have similar chemical structures, and as the drug circulated in the mother's bloodstream the developing fetus was in effect exposed to a high dose of male hormones. Sometimes a female fetus's own adrenal glands malfunction and produce abnormally high amounts of androgen. This condition, known as **adrenogenital syndrome** (**AGS**), results from an inherited genetic defect.

Regardless of the source of the prenatal androgens, the effect at birth is similar. The internal reproductive structures of these chromosomal females do not appear to be affected. However, the external genitals are masculinized and resemble those of male infants to varying degrees (see Figure 3.4). The clitoris is often enlarged and may be mistaken for a penis. The labia are frequently fused so they look like a scrotum. The masculinizing effects of AGS tend to be more pronounced than those of progestin-induced pseudohermaphroditism. Furthermore, if the problem of abnormal adrenal activity is not corrected after birth, excessive androgen secretions will continue to masculinize AGS females throughout their developmental years. In contrast, the masculinizing effects of progestin are limited to the prenatal period.

In the not-too-distant past the assignment of biological sex at birth was based solely on the appearance of a newborn's external genitals. Thus, in some cases of babies born with genital ambiguities, sex assignment was a toss-up and the assigned sex may not have been consistent with the chromosomal sex. Today, however, physicians faced with such ambiguities obtain additional information about the composition of the chromosomes and the nature of the gonads, so most masculinized female infants are correctly identified and reared as females. Corrective surgery is performed to make the appearance of their external genitals consistent with their chromosomes and internal sex structures. In addition, females with AGS are given injections of synthetic cortisone from birth on, to reduce the abnormal output of androgen from the adrenal glands. Fetally androgenized females who are provided proper medical treatment, regardless of the source of the prenatal androgens, undergo normal biological development through childhood and adolescence and become reproductively functional females.

Some years ago John Money and Anke Ehrhardt (1972) provided some fascinating data from their extensive study of 25 fetally androgenized females (10 progestin induced and 15 with AGS). These 25, all of whom had received appropriate medical treatment and had been reared as girls from infancy, were matched by age, intelligence,

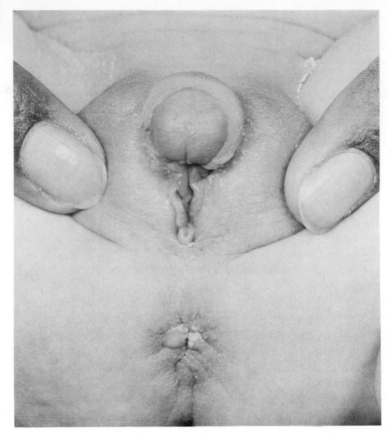

Figure 3.4

Masculinized
External Geni-
tals of a Fetally
Androgenized
Female

race, and socioeconomic status with a group of nonadrogenized girls. There were marked differences in the behaviors of these two groups. Twenty of the 25 fetally androgenized girls identified themselves as "tomboys." Their parents and friends agreed with this label. These girls tended to be active and aggressive; they preferred to engage in traditionally male activities such as rough-and-tumble athletics and pushing trucks in dirt piles. They demonstrated little interest in bride and mother roles, disliked handling infants, and were uninterested in makeup, hair-styling, and jewelry. In contrast, only a small number of the girls in the matched sample claimed to be tomboys and then only to a limited extent. The fetally masculinized girls demonstrated a significantly greater amount of dissatisfaction with their gender identity than those in the matched sample, although none expressed a desire to actually change her sex.

Androgen Insensitivity Syndrome.   The results of another study seem at odds with the observations we have just presented. Male children are occasionally afflicted with a biological anomaly known as **androgen insensitivity syndrome** (**AIS**). Individuals with this condition are chromosomally normal males (XY) whose gonads differentiate into testes that produce normal levels of prenatal androgens. However, as a result of a genetic defect their body cells are insensitive to the action of testosterone and other androgens, and consequently their prenatal development is feminized. The Wolffian duct system is unable to respond to androgens, and therefore the normal internal male structures (the epididymis, vas deferens, seminal vesicles, and ejaculatory ducts) do not develop. Furthermore, the fetal testes produce Müllerian inhibiting substance, which acts in the normal way to prevent formation of internal female structures from the Müllerian ducts. Consequently, the AIS infant is born without a normal set of either male or female internal structures.

As a result of androgen insensitivity, the external genitals of the AIS fetus fail to differentiate into a penis and a scrotum and the testes do not descend. Instead, the newborn has normal-looking female external genitals and a shallow vagina. (The inner third of the vagina is normally formed from the Müllerian system. Minor surgery can lengthen the vaginal barrel, if necessary, so that it can accommodate a penis.) Nothing unusual is suspected, and such babies are classified as girls and reared accordingly. At puberty breast development and other signs of normal sexual maturation appear, the result of estrogen production from the undescended testes. (The body tissues remain insensitive to continued production of androgens.) The error may not be discovered until adolescence or later, usually as a result of medical consultation to determine why the person has not menstruated.

Money and his colleagues reported an in-depth study of 10 individuals with androgen insensitivity syndrome (Money et al., 1968). All 10 had been reared as girls. Only one, a young girl with a very disturbed family background, showed any gender-identity confusion. The other nine were strongly identified as female by themselves and others. As a group they demonstrated strong preferences for the role of homemaker over an outside job, fantasies of becoming pregnant and raising a family, and inclinations to engage in typically female play with traditional girls' toys, such as dolls. In a word, there was nothing that could be viewed as traditionally masculine in the way the girls behaved, despite their XY chromosomes and male gonads. In this example, unlike the first, social learning factors seem to have played the decisive role.

DHT Deficient Males.   Before we discuss the apparently contradictory findings of the first two studies, let us look at our third and final example of a hormone-based differentiation error. Some of the strongest evidence for a hormone–gender-identity relationship was provided by a team of Cornell University researchers who studied 18 boys raised in two rural communities in the Dominican Republic (Imperato-McGinley et al., 1979). All of these boys were afflicted with a genetic disorder that prevents the prenatal conversion of testosterone into DHT, which as you learned earlier, is necessary for the normal development of male external genitals. Their internal sex structures developed normally, and appropriate prenatal androgen levels were present. However, at birth their testicles were undescended and their stunted penises were mistaken for clitorises. Furthermore, they had partially formed vaginas and incompletely formed scrotums that looked like labia. Consequently, these children were incorrectly identified as female, and all were apparently raised as girls. At the age of puberty, however, they showed no sign of breast development. Then, when their as-yet-undescended testes began accelerated testosterone production, the most amazing things began to happen: Their voices deepened, their clitorislike organs enlarged and became penises, and their testes finally descended.

In response to these marked biological changes in their bodies, all but two of the 18 adopted the culturally mandated male gender roles, encompassing such things as occupational inclinations and patterns of sexual activity. Of the remaining two, one acknowledged that he was male but continued to dress as a woman, while the other maintained her female gender identity and gender role, married, and sought a sex change operation to correct the inconsistencies in her body that had emerged at adolescence.

The Dominican study sparked considerable controversy in an already hotly debated area. Certain widely held assumptions of psychologists were seriously challenged by the findings of the Cornell researchers. Among them were the notions that gender identity is primarily learned and that once it is established during the critical early years of life it cannot be changed without creating severe emotional problems.

Certainly this important research suggests that gender identity may be more malleable than previously thought. However, there are important questions about the psychological environments of these Dominican youths that remain unanswered. For example, since the study was conducted after the subjects had become adults, we cannot be sure that their early gender-identity socialization was unambiguously female. It is not clear whether all the subjects, as well as others who could report on their development, were personally interviewed, and whether both parents were questioned in each case (Rubin et al., 1981). Furthermore, we must consider the possibility that these individuals converted to a male identity because of extreme social pressure (locals sometimes made the boys objects of ridicule and referred to them as *quevote,* "penis at 12" or *machihembra,* "first woman, then man") or because the environment in this Caribbean country is so openly male biased. (Some of the parents were proud to discover that their daughter was actually their son.)

These three studies of hormone-based differentiation errors in people reared as females have important implications. Chromosomal females, masculinized before birth from exposure to excessive androgens, tended to manifest typically masculine behavior in spite of having been raised as girls. In contrast, chromosomal males insensitive to androgens behaved in a typically feminine manner consistent with the way they were reared. Finally, chromosomal males whose biological maleness did not become known until puberty were able to successfully alter their gender identity to male, though they were apparently reared as girls. These findings seem to be at odds with the theory that social learning factors are the primary or sole determinants of gender-identity formation and gender-role behaviors. Proponents of this view argue that a person raised as a girl will acquire a female identity and behave in a feminine manner regardless of any biological anomalies that have arisen during prenatal development or at puberty. While this prediction holds true for those with androgen insensitivity syndrome, it is not confirmed by the Dominican research or the studies of prenatally masculinized girls.

These apparent inconsistencies may not be contradictory at all when evaluated from a biological perspective. As we discussed earlier, there is mounting evidence that prenatal androgens may masculinize the human brain as well as the sex structures. This could account for the masculine behavior of fetally androgenized females. Furthermore, the same genetic defect that prevents masculinization of the genitals of individuals with AIS may also prevent the masculinization of their brains. Finally, the Dominican boys may have been able to make the conversion from female to male identity so smoothly because their brains were already programmed along male lines by prenatal androgens. (Presumably they had normal levels of androgens during critical prenatal stages of development and were able to respond normally to these hormones; the lack of DHT affected only their external genital development.) Thus, it would appear that prenatal androgens, in addition to instigating proper differentiation of biological sex, may also masculinize the brain, thereby predisposing a person toward a male gender identity and male gender role.

The results of the investigations of these varied biological accidents raise a fundamental question. Just what makes us male or female? Our chromosomes? Our hormones? The characteristics of our sexual structures? The sex we are assigned at birth? Clearly, there is no simple answer to this question. A person's biological sex is determined by a complex process involving several interacting levels. Many steps, each susceptible to errors, are involved in sex differentiation prior to birth. We will now turn our attention to the social learning factors that influence gender-identity formation after birth. Perhaps this information will help to clarify some of the unanswered questions emerging from the biological data.

Social Learning Factors in Gender Identity

Thus far we have considered only the biological factors involved in the determination of gender identity. Our sense of maleness or femaleness is not based exclusively on biological conditions, however, and there exists an alternative explanation of the development of this sense. This social learning interpretation suggests that our identification with either masculine or feminine roles or a combination thereof (androgyny) results primarily from the social and cultural models and influences we are exposed to during our early development.

At birth parents label their children as male or female with the announcement "It's a boy!" or "It's a girl!" From this point on children are exposed to people who tend to react to them in a manner dictated by their gender-role expectations. Parents typically dress boys and girls differently, decorate their rooms differently, provide them with different toys, and even respond to them differently. Parents and others actively teach little boys and girls what gender they are by how they describe them. Expressions such as "You are a sweet little girl" or "You are a bright little boy" are common. While small children may not comprehend what makes them biologically male or female, they definitely are not confused about whether they are boys or girls—just try calling a two-year-old boy a girl, or vice versa, and observe the indignant manner in which you are set straight.

Understandably, parents and others have certain preconceived ideas about how boys and girls differ, and they communicate these views to their children from the very beginning. For example, in one study (Rubin et al., 1974) parents were asked to describe their infants within 24 hours of birth. All babies included in this sample were of approximately the same height, weight, and muscle tone. Parents of girls tended to describe their daughters as soft, sweet, fine featured, and delicate. On the other hand, parents of boys were inclined to use words like strong, well coordinated, active, and robust to describe their sons. These perceptions remain after the child is brought home from the hospital, and they may influence the nature of parent-child interaction.

A child's own actions probably strongly influence the process whereby his or her gender identity is established. Most children have developed a firm sense of being a boy or a girl by the age of 18 months. Once this takes place, they typically acquire a strong desire to adopt behaviors appropriate for their sex (Kohlberg, 1966); that is, they try to find out how boys or girls are supposed to behave and then act accordingly.

Anthropological studies of other cultures also lend support to the social learning interpretation of gender-identity formation. In several societies, the differences between males and females that we often assume to be innate are simply not evident. In fact, Margaret Mead's classic book, *Sex and Temperament in Three Primitive Societies* (1963), reveals that other societies may have very different views about what is considered feminine or masculine. In this widely quoted report of her fieldwork in New Guinea, Mead discusses two societies that minimize differences between the sexes. She noted that among the Mundugumor both sexes exhibit aggressive, non-nurturing behaviors that would be considered masculine by our society's norms. In contrast, among the Arapesh both males and females exhibit gentleness, nurturing, and nonaggressive behaviors that would be judged feminine in our society. In a third society studied, the Tchambuli, Mead observed an actual reversal of our typical masculine and feminine gender roles. You will recall from the opening page of this chapter that Tchambuli women tend to be dominant, assertive, and very much in charge, while men are quiet, undemanding, and emotionally dependent. Since there is no evidence that people in these societies are biologically different from Americans, it seems that their often diametrically different interpretations of what is masculine and what is feminine must result from different processes of social learning.

Some of the most impressive evidence in support of the social learning viewpoint has emerged from the research of John Money and his colleagues. Perhaps the most persuasive of these studies have concerned children whose external genitals represent such a mixture of male and female characteristics that biological sex identification is difficult. Money and his co-workers found that in most of the cases they evaluated, children whose assigned sex did not match their chromosomal sex developed a gender identity consistent with the manner in which they were reared (Hampson and Hampson, 1961; Money, 1965; Money et al., 1955; Money and Ehrhardt, 1972). (As we have learned, fetally androgenized females tend to manifest some dissatisfaction with their gender identity, but they do not express a desire to actually change their sex.)

One particularly unusual study of two identical twin boys (Money, 1975; Money and Ehrhardt, 1972) has frequently been cited in support of the social learning interpretation. At the age of seven months, a circumcision accident destroyed most of the penile tissue of one of the boys. Since no amount of plastic surgery could adequately reconstruct the severely damaged penis, it was recommended that the child be raised as a female and receive appropriate sex change surgery. When the child was 17 months old, the parents decided to begin raising him as a girl. Shortly thereafter initial genital surgery was performed. Follow-up studies of these unusual twins revealed that, in spite of possessing identical genetic materials, they responded to their separate social learning experiences by developing opposite gender identities. Furthermore, the child reassigned to the female gender appeared to demonstrate no confusion about her identity during her early developmental years.

If the story of these twins ended here, we would have strong evidence of the dominant role of social learning in gender-identity formation. However, in 1979, the psychiatrist following this case revealed that the assigned female member of the pair was experiencing considerable difficulty in making her adjustment as a woman (Williams and Smith, 1979). Apparently her appearance and behavior was so unfeminine during her school years that classmates heartlessly taunted her as a "cave woman" (Diamond, 1982). Thus, it appears that the efforts to alter her biological potential as a male were not completely successful. The reasons for this are not entirely clear. Maybe her parents waited too long to make their decision—the probability of successful reassignment of sex diminishes with increasing age. Perhaps prenatal masculinization of the brain by androgens is a factor in this case. If biological and social-learning factors interact in the formation of gender identity after birth, the unfolding results of this twin study may be understandable and perhaps even predictable. In the next section we will briefly explore this interactional interpretation of the formation of gender identity.

The Interactional Model

Perhaps you have already surmised, quite correctly, that an explanation of how we acquire our gender identity must involve both biology and social learning. Many social scientists have a propensity to emphasize learned over biological causes of behavior. Perhaps this may explain why some have tended to de-emphasize the biological evidence. Others may fear that acknowledging the role of biology in gender development implies that gender roles are unchangeable, or that it denies the importance of life experiences in establishing our own subjective sense of masculinity or femininity. However, few researchers today believe in an exclusively biological basis for human gender-identity formation. The evidence supporting the role of social learning is simply too pervasive. In a later section of this chapter we will consider the many forces at work in the socialization of gender roles.

Today virtually all researchers and theorists embrace the interactional model, wherein gender identity is considered to result from a complex interplay of biological and social-learning factors. The question of which plays the greater role in shaping gender identity will undoubtedly continue to be debated for years to come, as new evidence is gathered.

A Special Case of Gender Identity Difficulty: Transsexualism

The **transsexual** is a person whose gender identity is opposite to his or her biological sex. He or she feels trapped in a body of the wrong sex, a condition also known as **gender dysphoria**. Thus, a male transsexual feels that he is a woman betrayed by some quirk of fate that provided him with male genitals. He is a woman-identified man, and this is the source of his acute discomfort. He wishes to be socially identified as the woman he sincerely believes himself to be. Rather than experiencing sexual excitement when cross-dressing, as is the case with transvestism, he experiences a sense of comfort with himself. (We will discuss transvestism in Chapter 19).

In the 1960s and early 1970s, when medical procedures for altering sex were first being developed in this country, approximately three out of every four people requesting a sex change were men who wished to be women (Green, 1975). More recently, this ratio has narrowed considerably, and may now be approaching 1:1 (Dixen et al., 1984; Roberto, 1983).

A vast accumulation of clinical literature has focused on the characteristics, causes, and treatment of transsexualism. Certain things are well established: We know that most transsexuals are biologically normal individuals with healthy sex organs, intact internal reproductive structures, and the proper complement of XX or XY chromosomes. What is less understood is why the transsexual rejects his or her anatomy. Recently a leading scholar in this area, Leslie Lothstein (1984), published a critical review of 30 years of psychological evaluation of transsexuals, in which he concluded that no clear understanding of the nature and etiology of transsexualism has yet emerged. Considerable controversy also exists regarding the most appropriate clinical strategies for dealing with this condition. Keeping this continued debate in mind, we will summarize our current tenuous state of knowledge about this highly unusual gender-identity difficulty.

Many transsexuals develop a sense of being at odds with their genital anatomy in very early childhood; some recall identifying strongly with characteristics of the other sex as early as five, six, or seven years of age. In some cases these children's discomfort is partially relieved by pretending to be a member of the other sex, but many of them eventually discover that real peace with self requires advancing beyond mere pretending to actual cross-dressing. Less commonly, a strong identity with the other sex may not emerge until the adolescent or adult years.

Male-to-female transsexuals (that is, those who are anatomically male) often exhibit much more interest as children in playing dolls and dressing up in pretty dresses than in rough-and-tumble games and other typically masculine pursuits. In adolescence and adulthood many of them engage in what has been described as hyperfeminine behavior, in which their use of perfumes, cosmetics, clothing, gestures, and styles of sitting, standing, and walking represent a somewhat exaggerated expression of stereotyped femininity (Barlow et al., 1980; Pauly, 1974). They may be aware of an emotional attachment and sexual attraction to males, but typically do not view this (or even sexual activity with men) as an indication of homosexuality, since they consider themselves female. Male-to-female transsexuals who marry women before undergoing sex reassignment procedures may be able to engage in sex only by fantasizing that they are being penetrated by a penis.

Most female-to-male transsexuals recall thinking of themselves as boys long before the emergence of adolescence. Usually they dressed like boys and engaged in typically masculine activities, formed close friendships with boys rather than girls, showed no interest in babies, and expressed rejection of the wife-and-mother role. Adolescence is a particularly traumatic period for females who consider themselves male; they often feel intense revulsion at the onset of menstruation and may try to disguise their developing breasts. Female-to-male transsexuals who relate sexually to men prior to sex reassignment surgery may accept clitoral stimulation but frequently refuse to allow vaginal penetration or breast stimulation. Those who have sex with women do not typically regard such behavior as homosexual, since they consider themselves male.

What causes transsexualism? There are many theories, but at the present time there is insufficient evidence to draw any absolute conclusions about the origins of this extreme form of gender-identity difficulty. Some writers maintain that biological factors may play a decisive role. One theory suggests that prenatal exposure to inappropriate hormones of the other sex might cause improper brain differentiation (Pauly, 1974). There is no solid evidence from research with humans that supports this speculation, so it must remain merely a theory. However, research with nonhuman animals has revealed that masculine behavior can be increased in females by artificially inducing high levels of male hormones in the prenatal environment. Conversely, prenatal males who are deprived of sufficient levels of male hormones often later exhibit female behavior (Goy, 1970). Studies of prenatally masculinized human females, discussed earlier, provide additional evidence that biological errors may result in gender-identity confusion during the developmental years.

A more popular theory of the causes of transsexualism, for which there is some supporting evidence, holds that social learning experiences contribute significantly to the development of this condition. A child may be exposed to a variety of conditioning experiences that support behaving in a manner traditionally attributed to the other sex (Green, 1974; Money and Primrose, 1968). The child may develop a close, identifying relationship with the parent of the other sex that may be strongly reinforced by the adult's reaction. The little boy may play at being a girl, and the girl may be "Daddy's little man." Such cross-gender behaviors may be so exclusively rewarded that it may be difficult or impossible for the individual to develop the appropriate gender identity.

Several studies have reported unusual attachments between male-to-female transsexuals and their mothers; whereas the presence of cold, rejecting mothers and unusual identification with their fathers have been found in the early development of female-to-male transsexuals (Pauly, 1974; Stoller, 1972 and 1968). A recent study of transsexuals who were aware of their cross-gender identification during their youth revealed a high incidence of early traumatic experiences in a disturbed family environment (Meyer and Dupkin, 1985).

Difficult as it is to determine the causes of transsexualism, it is perhaps even more challenging to find ways to resolve the problem of reversed gender identity. As previously indicated, most transsexuals follow a heterosexual script and prefer to have sexual relations with a member of the other sex. However, for them the other sex happens to have the same genitals as they. Whom then do they relate to sexually? Most want to interact with heterosexuals: A male transsexual wants to be desired as a woman by a heterosexual man, and most transsexual women would not be satisfied with a lesbian relationship.

These sexual needs are often hard to meet. Heterosexuals and homosexuals can generally find willing sex partners who match their orientations, but transsexuals' most desired partners are likely to reject them offhand for making "unnatural" advances. Occasionally transsexuals try homosexual encounters, but most find them unrewarding, as revealed by the following interview:

TRANSSEXUAL: For a while I thought the homosexual life would be the answer, and it wasn't.

DOCTOR: Why wasn't it?

TRANSSEXUAL: I found it revolting. To me the idea of two men in bed with each other is sickening, while a man and a woman together is perfectly natural. I am a woman. I have a problem, a growth, but I'm a woman. I am in no way like a male.

DOCTOR: Except that you have a penis and testes, and you don't have a uterus, and you don't have ovaries.

TRANSSEXUAL: Yes.

DOCTOR: So, anatomically—

TRANSSEXUAL: Anatomically, I am female, with those things stuck on. (Green, 1974, p. 47)

Psychotherapy, without accompanying biological alterations, has generally been reported to be unsuccessful in helping transsexuals adjust to their bodies (Benjamin, 1967; Tollison and Adams, 1979). It would seem then that the best course of action might be for them to change their bodies to match their minds, through surgical and hormonal alteration of genital anatomy and body physiology. Beneficial as it may be, however, the process of medical alteration is not a simple solution, for it is both time consuming and costly.

The initial step of a sex change involves extensive screening interviews, during which the person's motivations for undergoing the change are thoroughly evaluated. Those with real conflicts about their gender identity (that is, who are not really sure which sex they are) or those seeking the operation on a whim are not considered for surgical alteration. The next step is to provide hormone therapy, a process designed to accentuate some of the person's latent other-sex traits. Transsexual males wishing to be females are given doses of estrogen that induce some breast growth, soften the skin, reduce growth of facial and body hair, and contribute to some feminization of the body contours. Muscle strength also diminishes, as does sexual interest, but there is no alteration of vocal pitch. Transsexual women who desire a male identity are treated with testosterone, which has a masculinizing effect apparent in increased growth of body and facial hair, a deepening of the voice, and a slight reduction in breast size. Testosterone also suppresses menstruation. Most professionals providing the sex change procedures require that a candidate live for a year or more as a member of the other sex, while undergoing hormone therapy, before taking the final, drastic step of surgery. At any time during this phase the process can be successfully reversed, although few transsexuals choose reversal.

The final step of a sex change is surgery (see Figure 3.5). Surgical procedures are most effective for men wishing to be women. The scrotum and penis are removed, and a vagina is created through reconstruction of pelvic tissue (Figure 3.5a). During this surgical procedure great care is taken to maintain the sensory nerves that service the skin of the penis, and this sensitive skin tissue is relocated to the inside of the newly fashioned vagina. Intercourse is possible, although use of a lubricant may be necessary, and many male-to-female transsexuals report postsurgical capacity to expe-

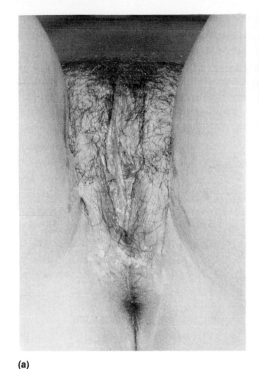

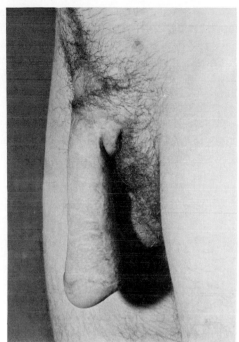

Figure 3.5

The Genitals Following Sex Change Surgery
Surgical procedures are generally more effective when applied to genitally altering a male to female (a) rather than the reverse of a female to male (b).

(a)

(b)

rience sexual arousal and orgasm (Money and Walker, 1977). Hormone treatments may produce sufficient breast development, but some individuals also receive implants. Body and facial hair, which has been reduced by hormone treatments, may be further removed by electrolysis.

Biological females who desire to be male generally have their breasts, uterus, and ovaries surgically removed and their vaginas sealed off. The process of constructing a penis is much more difficult than that of fashioning a vagina. Generally the penis is fashioned from abdominal skin or from tissue from the labia and perineum (Figure 3.5b). This constructed organ is not capable of natural erection in response to sexual arousal. However, several artificial devices are available for providing a rigid penis for purposes of intercourse. One involves fashioning a small, hollow skin tube on the underside of the penile shaft into which a rigid silicone rod may be inserted. Another alternative is to utilize an implanted inflatable device, which will be described in Chapter 17. If erotically sensitive tissue from the clitoris is left embedded at the base of the surgically constructed penis, erotic feelings and orgasm are sometimes possible.

Postoperative follow-up of transsexuals' lives reveals contradictory findings. However, several recent reports have provided some basis for optimism about the potential for success of sex reassignment surgery. One important publication summarized the conclusions that could realistically be drawn from three worldwide literature reviews on the outcome of sex change surgery (Lundstrom et al., 1984).

Among the reported findings was that approximately nine out of ten transsexuals undergoing hormonal and surgical sex reassignment procedures experience a satisfactory result. This high incidence of positive outcomes appears to be equally likely for male-to-female and female-to-male transsexuals. Another study, which utilized a large sample of males-to-females and females-to-males, reported that 94% of this study population stated that they would have the surgery again if they had it to do over (Blanchard et al., 1985).

At the time of this writing there is still considerable controversy in the scientific community over the relative benefits of sex change surgery. Clearly, we do not have the complete picture at the present time, and there is a vital need for continued research in this area. However, there does appear to be a growing trend among health professionals to accept sex reassignment surgery as an option for some individuals who experience great distress as a result of a strong identification with the other biological sex. Most professionals stress the importance of careful diagnostic screening to determine who is most likely to be aided by surgery, and the need to utilize good surgical procedures to yield an aesthetically pleasing result. Perhaps, as one writer has suggested, we may eventually come to view such procedures as "sex confirmation" rather than sex reassignment (Edgerton, 1984).

Transsexuals who have undergone surgical alteration may be confronted with a variety of legal difficulties. Questions surface over which sex they should be considered for such purposes as auto, health, and life insurance, and over their right to participate in athletic events as members of their reassigned sex. You may recall the controversy surrounding Renee Richards's attempt to compete as a woman tennis player after undergoing a male-to-female change in the 1970s. American courts have generally been unwilling to support the idea that a person's sex has been changed by surgery (Hurley, 1984). As a consequence, surgically altered transsexuals are left with serious legal difficulties as they attempt to establish their new identities. They must fight for a variety of legal rights, including being considered married should they unite with someone whose sex matches their own prior-to-surgery sex.

Many people react very strongly to the phenomenon of transsexualism, perhaps viewing it as an attack upon traditional gender assumptions. We are concerned that a backlash against sex change surgery may reduce the availability of an important option for transsexual individuals. Clearly, such an attitude is not what is needed now. Rather, we need continued careful, well-designed investigations of both the appropriateness and the effectiveness of surgical sex reassignment.

Finally, we must not overlook what transsexuals themselves have to say about this controversial process. Many finally feel "out of prison," and their accounts are often poignant. One of the most widely read personal accounts of the transsexual experience was recorded in a book titled *Conundrum,* written by Jan Morris (1974) after she had undergone the transsexual change. The photographs in Figure 3.6 show her both before and after the sex change. She summarizes her motivation for undergoing the change as ". . . mending a discrepancy. . . . I found that when people took me to be unquestionably a woman, a sense of rightness calmed and satisfied me. . . . I felt myself to be passing through an anteroom of fulfillment" (pp. 130–131).

(a)

(b)

Figure 3.6

**Sex Change:
Male to Female**
*(a) James Morris
prior to sex change
surgery. (b) Jan
Morris after sex
change surgery.*

Gender Roles

The issue of gender goes beyond the processes whereby we acquire our own subjective sense of maleness or femaleness. Society is not content merely to allow us to identify our gender. Rather, it ascribes to us a set of behaviors that are considered normal and appropriate for our particular sex. These normative standards are typically labeled gender roles (or sex roles).

The ascribing of gender roles leads naturally to certain assumptions about how people will behave. For example, men in this society are expected to act independently and aggressively, while women are supposed to be dependent and submissive. Once these expectations are widely accepted they may begin to function as **stereotypes**. A stereotype is a generalized notion of what a person is like based only on that person's sex, race, religion, ethnic background, or similar category. Stereotypes do not take individuality into account.

There are many common gender-based stereotypes that are widely accepted in our society. Some of the prevailing notions about men maintain that they are aggressive (or at least assertive), logical, unemotional, independent, dominant, competitive, objective, athletic, active, and above all, competent. Conversely, women are frequently viewed as passive, nonassertive, illogical, emotional, dependent, subordinate, warm, and nurturing. While not all people hold these gender-role stereotypes, there is strong evidence of their pervasiveness within our society (Archer and Lloyd, 1985; Doyle, 1985; Unger, 1979). A recent study that utilized several hundred respondents from vocational schools, colleges, and universities revealed that, despite claims of gender-role changes among American men and women, current conceptions of maleness and femaleness are markedly consistent with the gender-based stereotypes revealed by earlier research (Smith and Midlarsky, 1985).

Stereotyping people according to biological sex can help to make the world appear more orderly, but it may also produce a number of undesirable outcomes. Certainly it encourages us to prejudge individuals and to expect them to act in certain ways just because they happen to be female or male. Often these stereotypic assumptions limit the nature of human relationships and sexual interaction. For example, consider the following two observations expressed by former students during small-group discussions:

> If a woman makes the first move and says she would like to sleep with me, I'll probably take advantage of the opportunity. But you can bet I won't see her again. Any woman who is that easy isn't the kind of person I would really like to get to know. (Authors' files)

> Sometimes when I am making love, I would like to tell my partner how I like being touched. But I am afraid he would think I was too pushy or aggressive. Men like to run the show and they get threatened if you give them any instructions. (Authors' files)

It appears that both of these individuals are victims of societal notions about how men and women are supposed to behave. Neither seems to be looking beyond these confining assumptions, and consequently their relationship options are unnecessarily limited. The man expressing the initial observation is unwilling or unable to acknowledge that "good women" can take the lead in initiating sexual contact. Consequently, he shuts himself off from sexually assertive women who step out of the traditional gender role. The woman voicing her concerns in the second example suppresses her inclinations to be assertive during lovemaking because she assumes males see this as their role and would be threatened by any woman who crosses traditional gender-imposed boundaries.

Gender-role stereotypes also tend to restrict our opportunities. For example, a woman might not enroll in a mountaineering class because she considers mountaineering an activity within the male domain. She may be concerned that others would view her interest as a sign of masculinity. Similarly, a man might hesitate to stay at home and provide childcare and domestic services while his female partner pursued her career. Even though he might find such activities quite rewarding at some time in his life, he might still be concerned that others would think him unmasculine.

In a later section of this chapter we will consider in detail some of the possible negative effects of gender-role assumptions on sexual sharing. But first, let us examine the socialization processes that introduce these limiting roles into our lives.

The Socialization of Gender Roles

In spite of the potentially limiting impact of rigid and stereotypic gender roles on our lives, many men and women behave in a manner remarkably consistent with the norms these roles establish. Certainly many individuals are comfortable fulfilling a traditional masculine or feminine role, and we do not wish to demean or question the validity of their lifestyle. Rather, we are concerned with why these gender roles are so prevalent in our society. Are they biologically mandated or are they learned? It seems reasonable to suspect that at least some of the behavioral differences between males and females may be related to biological factors such as differences in muscle mass, hormonal variations, and brain differences (Bloom et al., 1985; Diamond, 1977 and 1979; Diamond and Karlen, 1980). Nevertheless, most theorists, including the authors, believe that gender roles result largely from the manner in which we are socialized as males and females. **Socialization** refers to the process whereby society conveys behavioral expectations to the individual. In the following sections we will examine the role of parents, peers, schools, textbooks, and television as agents in the socialization of gender roles.

Parents as Shapers of Gender Roles.   Parents play a powerful role in the socialization of gender roles in their children. The way they interact with their children, the behaviors they encourage or discourage, and the roles they model all help to shape traditional gender behaviors. Parents' influence probably begins right after birth. As we have mentioned, most parents have different perceptions and expectations of a newborn depending on his or her sex. These sex-based assumptions are likely to result in at least some differences in how parents treat boys and girls. For example, girls are often treated as if they were more fragile than boys. Instead of being subjected to the rough-and-tumble activity that often characterizes parents' play with boy children, little girls are frequently handled very delicately in the course of quiet play (Doyle, 1985; Fagot, 1978; Tauber, 1979). There is also evidence that girl babies are more likely than boy babies to be talked to and smiled at by their mothers (Thoman et al., 1972).

Research indicates that parents become increasingly likely to treat their girl and boy children differently as they grow older (Block, 1976 and 1983). "As the child moves from the infant to the toddler stage, somewhere around age two, gender typing increases. Boys are told that 'Boys don't cling to their mothers,' and 'Big boys don't cry.' Boys' independence, aggression, and suppression of emotion are rewarded, and failure to comply brings increasing disapproval. Girls are encouraged to display opposite characteristics" (Gagnon, 1977, p. 70)

Although increasing numbers of parents are becoming sensitive to the gender-role implications of a child's playthings, many others encourage their children to play with toys that help prepare them for specific adult gender roles. Girls are often given tea sets, miniature ovens, dolls, and dollhouses. Boys frequently receive things like trucks, guns, and footballs. Children who play with toys thought appropriate only for the other sex are often rebuked by their parents ("Boys who play with dolls are

sissies" or "Nice little girls don't play with guns"). Since children are sensitive to these expressions of displeasure, they usually develop toy preferences consistent with their parents' gender role expectations. There is evidence that this process takes place in children as young as 20 months (Fein et al., 1975). Certainly by the age of three children readily identify the toys appropriate for males and for females (Conner, 1980). Play activities are similarly gender stereotyped by many parents. Girls are typically encouraged to play house, change dolls' diapers, jump rope, play hopscotch, and color. Boys are more likely to receive support for building erector set bridges, exploring, playing cops and robbers, or pushing trucks around dirt piles.

These differentially rewarded toy and play preferences undoubtedly influence men and women to adopt different roles as adults. Is it surprising that boys who have been encouraged to be active and adventurous in their play activities often grow up to be comfortable with being in charge, assertive, and competitive? On the other hand, the typical play of girls certainly inclines them toward being nonassertive, compliant, and nurturing as adults.

Parents can also influence the emotional development of their children along gender lines. Boys sometimes learn that they should limit their emotional expressions ("Be strong like a man"). Girls are frequently encouraged to be nurturant ("Nice girls help others") and are allowed to express their feelings more openly. There is also evidence that from around age nine to late adolescence girls are more likely than boys to be nurtured by parental displays of affection, support, and acceptance (Armentrout and Burger, 1972; Hoffman and Saltzstein, 1967). This early socialization undoubtedly accounts, at least in part, for the fact that many adult females are more inclined toward emotional expression and nurturing behavior than their male counterparts.

The Peer Group. Parents are not the only people who are influential in the social-ization of gender roles. The peer group may exert a strong influence, particularly during the adolescent years (Adams, 1973; Doyle, 1985). Most teenagers have fairly rigid views of what constitutes gender-appropriate behavior. For girls, being popular and attractive to boys may be very important. In contrast, boys may try to prove their worth on the athletic field. Teenagers who do not conform to these traditional roles may be subjected to a great deal of peer pressure. Boys who seem sensitive or nonaggressive may be ridiculed. Girls who behave in an independent and assertive manner may be ostracized or criticized.

One particularly negative aspect of adolescent gender typing is the notion that one cannot be both feminine and an achiever. The potential impact of this limiting assumption is revealed in the following account:

> I like high school and I am a good student. In fact, I could be an outstanding student. But I am afraid of what others might think of me if I do too well. My boyfriend is into sports and not schoolwork. We take some classes together. Many times I purposely score below my ability on tests so as not to show him up. What would he think about his girlfriend being a brain? (Authors' files)

Renowned psychologist Eleanor Maccoby has noted another aspect of the peer group structure among American children that contributes to a perpetuation of tra-ditional gender roles and to misunderstandings between the sexes. In a 1985 address at Reed College she observed that there is a pronounced segregation between the sexes that begins very early in life. Research conducted by Maccoby and Carol Jacklin suggests that even preschool children select same-sex playmates about 80% of the time. By the time they enter the first grade, children voluntarily select other-sex playmates only about 5% of the time. This marked segregation of the sexes does not mean that they have no awareness of each other. Rather, Maccoby commented, "I think that children are intensely aware of each other as future sexual partners, and one force that may be pulling them apart is that awareness. It may be that our sexually explicit culture forces them to do that. It's as if they avoid each other because they aren't ready."

Schools, Textbooks, and Gender Roles. Schools may exert a particularly strong influence on a child's development. They can also be quite influential in the devel-opment and perpetuation of gender roles (Doyle, 1985; Dweck, 1975). Teachers' responses to their students are often guided by their own stereotypes about males and females. It is common for them to expect girls to excel in subjects like English and literature, while boys are often believed to be naturally more proficient in math and science. Guided by such assumptions, teachers may differentially encourage and reward boys' and girls' performances in these particular subjects. Furthermore, girls frequently learn that hanging around their teachers and acting dependent is a good way to get their attention, whereas boys learn that independent or aggressive behavior works better (Serbin, 1980).

Schoolchildren are also frequently encouraged to engage in different activities on the basis of sex. For example, boys may help move desks and tables around, while girls are encouraged to perform secretarial tasks such as making lists on blackboards. This segregation of activities on the basis of gender reinforces the notion that there are important differences in abilities between boys and girls.

Textbooks created for children have also tended to perpetuate gender-role stereotypes. In the early seventies, a task force of the National Organization for Women (NOW) conducted an extensive analysis of 134 children's readers published by 12 different companies. The results of this investigation, published in a monograph entitled *Dick and Jane as Victims* (Women on Words and Images, 1972), were quite dramatic. Extreme gender-role stereotypes were pervasive in these books, with girls portrayed as domestic, fearful, dependent, unambitious, and not very clever. In contrast, boys were brave, strong, independent, ambitious, clever, and successful. In addition to gender stereotypes, these books tended to perpetuate the notion that boys are more important than girls, as evidenced by a 5 to 2 ratio of boy-centered to girl-centered stories. The findings of the NOW task force were confirmed by another analysis of grade school textbooks (Saario et al., 1973). This study reported that boys in these books were portrayed as good at problem solving, very active (even aggressive), and in charge of their fates. Girls were depicted as followers, likely to engage in fantasy, not very successful, and less in control of their destinies.

More recently, two Oregon State University professors, Gweyneth Britton and Margaret Lumpkin (1984), completed an 11-year study of reading texts used in the United States from 1958 to 1982. In spite of massive social changes in American society, they found that these books presented the American family almost exclusively as consisting of a working father and a mother who stays home to care for two children, her husband, and the family dog. Even textbooks used from 1980 to 1982 tended to use the same traditional, gender-stereotyped stories. By far, the career role most frequently portrayed for women in these books is that of full-time, stay-at-home mother and wife. In contrast, males are typically portrayed as being soldiers, scientists, policemen, physicians, or kings. Britton and Lumpkin did find one slight improvement in recent years. In the early 1970s men were assigned the dominant roles in about four out of five stories. By the early 1980s the ratio had dropped somewhat, with approximately two out of every three stories featuring men as key characters.

These findings are somewhat tempered by recent indications that publishers of elementary and high school textbooks are reducing gender-role stereotyping somewhat in their publications. These long overdue changes are no doubt prompted, at least in part, by the fact that a number of states have recently adopted criteria for textbook adoption pertaining to the portrayal of gender roles. For example, California guidelines require that males and females be portrayed "in a wide variety of occupational, emotional, and behavioral situations, presenting both sexes in the full range of their human potential" (California State Department of Education, 1979, p. 3). Textbook publishers obviously want their books to be adopted. Therefore we can expect them to exert some effort to comply with these new guidelines.

Gender-Role Stereotypes via Television. Television is another pervasive part of our lives that may have a significant impact on the establishment of gender roles. Many children regularly spend long hours in front of a TV set, and it would hardly be surprising to discover that television portrayals of men and women influence their learning of gender-role behaviors.

Television is often quite blatant in depicting stereotyped gender roles. For example, two separate analyses of television commercials found that men were featured far more than women (particularly if any type of authoritative pronouncement was called for) and that both sexes were usually cast in roles that supported gender stereotypes (McArthur and Resko, 1975). Men are depicted as authoritative figures, while women are usually portrayed as experts only about domestic functions and feminine hygiene needs. What is the potential impact of this imbalanced treatment on the viewer? It seems probable that many watchers internalize the idea that males are more important than females.

The impact of television on gender stereotyping is not confined to commercials. The same NOW task force that examined children's readers performed a similar analysis of prime time television story lines (Women on Words and Images, 1975). They found that females were commonly portrayed as seductive sex objects, incompetent, domestically inclined, supportive, passive, and even unintelligent. Males were typically shown as being in charge, competent, brave, active, and intelligent.

There have been few notable changes in the last few years in television's gender-role stereotyping (Atkin, 1982; Kalisch and Kalisch, 1984). Men, who continue to outnumber women by a wide margin, remain typecast as strong, intelligent decisionmakers. Women, who often occupy secondary roles, continue to be depicted as passive, supportive, and dependent. However, the recent advent of several television series that portray women in active, assertive roles (programs such as "Cagney and Lacey," and "Hill Street Blues") may signal a slight shift in traditional gender-role typecasting. Nevertheless, such positive characterizations constitute only a small percentage of television's total offerings. There has also been a slight reduction in stereotyping via commercials, but men continue to sell computers and women remain entrenched in the kitchen. "One distinct sex disparity remains unchanged: more than nine of ten off-camera voices that provide the authoritative information about the product are male" (Atkin, 1982, p. 67).

We see, then, that family and friends, schools, and television frequently help develop traditional gender-role assumptions and behaviors within our lives. To some degree we are all affected by gender-role conditioning, and we might discuss at great length how this process discourages development of the full range of human potential in each of us. However, this is a text dealing with our sexuality, so it is the impact of gender-role conditioning on this aspect of our lives that we will examine in greater detail in the following section.

The Impact of Gender Roles on Our Sexuality

Gender-role expectations exert a profound impact upon our sexuality. Our beliefs about males and females, together with our assumptions about what constitutes appropriate behaviors for each, may affect many aspects of sexual sharing. Our assessment of ourselves as sexual beings, the expectations we have for intimate relationships, our perception of the quality of such experiences, and the responses of others to our sexuality, may all be significantly influenced by our identification as male or female.

In the following pages we will examine some of the potential effects of our gender-role assumptions on relations between the sexes. However, we do not mean to imply that only heterosexual couples are limited by these assumptions. Gender-role stereotypes may affect people regardless of their sexual orientation; however, homosexual couples may be affected somewhat differently by them. For example, problems of initiating may be particularly pronounced for a lesbian couple, both of whom have been socialized not to initiate, whereas a male homosexual couple may have trouble establishing an emotional bond in their relationship, since both partners have probably been socialized to hide their feelings.

Women as Undersexed, Men as Oversexed.   A long-standing, slow-to-die assumption in many societies is the mistaken belief that women are inherently less sexually inclined than men. Such gender stereotypes may result in women being subjected to years of negative socialization during which they are taught to suppress or deny their natural sexual feelings. Legions of women have been told by parents, peers, and books that sex is something a woman engages in to please a man, preferably her husband. A related gender assumption pervasive in our society is the onerous view that "normal women" do not enjoy sex as much as men.

Although these stereotypes are beginning to fade as people strive to throw off some of the behavior constraints of generations of socialization, many women are still burdened by such views. How can a woman express interest in being sexual or actively seek her own pleasure if she is laboring under the mistaken assumption that women are not supposed to have sexual needs? Some women, believing that it is not appropriate to be easily aroused sexually, may direct their energies to blocking or hiding these normal responses. Some people adhere to these stereotypes so rigidly that they believe any woman who openly expresses sexual interest or responds sexually is "easy," "sleazy," or a "slut." However, men who manifest similar behavior may be characterized as "studs," "casanovas," or "playboys," terms that are often meant to be ego enhancing rather than demeaning.

Males may be harmed by being stereotyped as supersexual. A man who is not instantly aroused by a person he perceives as attractive and/or available may feel somehow inadequate in his male role. After all, are not all men supposed to be instantly eager when confronted with a sexual opportunity? We believe that such an assumption is demeaning and reduces men to insensitive machines that respond instantly when the correct button is pushed. Male students in our classes frequently express their frustration and ambivalence over this issue. The following account is typical of these observations:

> When I take a woman out for the first time, I often am confused over how the sex issue should be handled. I feel pressured to make a move, even when I am not all that inclined to hop into the sack. Isn't this what women expect? If I don't even try, they may think there is something wrong with me. I almost feel like I would have to explain myself if I act uninterested in having sex. Usually it is just easier to make the move and let them decide what they want to do with it. (Authors' files)

Clearly this man believes he is expected to pursue sex, even when he doesn't want to, as part of his masculine role. This stereotypical view of men as the initiators of sex in developing relationships can be distressing for both sexes, as we shall see in the next section.

Men as Initiators, Women as Recipients. In our society, men traditionally initiate intimate relationships, from the opening invitation for an evening out to the first request for sexual sharing. As the following comments expressed by men during small-group discussions reveal, this can make males feel burdened and pressured:

> Women should experience how anxiety-provoking it can be to provide an invitation with the ever-present potential of being turned down. (Authors' files)

> I feel that every woman I date expects me to put the move on her. (Authors' files)

> I am never sure when I should ask a woman to sleep with me. If I am in too much of a hurry, she may say no and I'll probably feel rejected. If I wait too long, she might get the wrong idea about me. Either way, you run the risk of coming up short. What a hassle. (Authors' files)

> During lovemaking women usually expect me to make all the initial moves. Sometimes I wish I could just lie back and be taken over sexually instead of being the one who must orchestrate the whole thing. (Authors' files)

This last comment reflects a concern voiced by many of our male students and clients. Men who grow up being socialized to be active, assertive, and even aggressive are usually accustomed to being in control in most situations. It may be very difficult to relinquish this role in the bedroom. Thus, even though a man may fantasize about being taken over sexually, actually having such an experience can be stressful, as the following account reveals:

> I consider myself to be somewhat avant-garde when it comes to changing roles of men and women. I like it when a woman is assertive in her relationship with me. For quite some time I fantasized about meeting someone who would assume the role of sexual aggressor with me. Well, it finally happened with unexpected results. I was asked out by an extremely attractive, charming woman. After dinner she invited me to her place. We talked, listened to music, and drank some wine. As the evening progressed I noticed her looking kind of strangely at me. Finally, I asked her what she was thinking. Her response knocked me over. She said "I was thinking that I would like to take you into my bedroom and ball your brains out." Unreal! My fantasy translated into reality. But, alas, when we ended up in bed, my body wouldn't respond. I guess the traditional tapes are stronger than I thought. (Authors' files)

This man's candid revelation describes an event that, while unexpected by him, seems quite predictable in view of the strong impact gender roles have on our lives. We grow accustomed to behaving in certain ways that we think are consistent with our biological sex. Being asked to act in an alternative manner, while a potentially enjoyable and emancipating experience, can lead to considerable confusion and anxiety.

Even in established relationships, men are frequently expected to initiate each sexual encounter. This may result in sex becoming more of a duty than a pleasure.

> My wife never initiates sex. It is always up to me. It's almost like making decisions about sex has become my job in the relationship. I wish she would hustle my body for a change. Maybe then sex would be a little more unpredictable and exciting for me. (Authors' files)

On the other hand, it is not necessarily satisfying to be cast into the stereotypical mold of the recipient in matters of intimacy. A woman who feels compelled to accept the female role of passivity may have a very difficult time initiating sex. It could be even harder for her to assume an active role during sexual sharing. Many women are frustrated, regretful, and understandably angry that such cultural expectations are so deeply ingrained within our society. The following comments, expressed by women talking together, reflect some of these thoughts:

> I would like to ask men out, but it is real hard to take this step. Women are simply not brought up to see this as an action consistent with the female role. (Authors' files)

> It has been my experience that men may say they want women to be more assertive, but when we take the initiative they frequently act shocked, put off, or threatened. (Authors' files)

> When I feel like getting down with a man, I'd like to just let him know up front what I'm thinking. But I usually keep my mouth shut and wait for him to make the first move. What a drag, particularly if he doesn't get the message. (Authors' files)

> It is hard for me to let my man know what I like during lovemaking. After all, he is supposed to know, isn't he? If I tell him, it's like I am usurping his role as the all-knowing one. (Authors' files)

The last comment relates to another common gender myth about sexual functioning—the notion that men are more knowledgeable and better able than women to direct a sexual encounter.

Men as "Sexperts."   Considering that gender-role socialization conditions males to be competent leaders and females to be not-so-competent followers, is it any wonder that men are expected to act as experts in sexual matters? Men are not the only ones who see themselves as "sexperts"; women, in fact, may coerce them into playing the expert role by subscribing to this mistaken notion. In one study roughly one-half of the women questioned believed that a "real man" should be skilled in bed (Tavris, 1977).

Some men enjoy being cast as "teacher" or "mentor." However, others may feel quite burdened by the need to play the expert, and thus, by implication, to be responsible for the outcome of sexual sharing. As one man states:

> Sometimes sex is more like work than fun. I have to make all the decisions—when and where we are going to have sex and what we are going to do together. It's my responsibility to make sure it works out good for both of us. This can put a lot of pressure on me and it gets real tiring always having to run the show. It would be nice to have someone else call the shots for a change. Only it has been my experience that women are real reluctant to take the lead. (Authors' files)

Women may be reluctant to take the lead for good reason. They learn their roles just as well as men, and they may be just as burdened by them, perhaps more so. Some women may actually believe that men understand women's sexual needs better than women themselves. If things do not work out, they may even blame themselves for being "frigid" or unresponsive, never realizing that the real problem stems from gender-role assumptions that inhibit them from communicating their needs.

Certainly there are many women who realize that they are much more aware of their sexual needs than any partner they may encounter. Yet these women too may bolster the "men as sexperts" myth with their silence, though for a different reason. As one woman noted:

> I know what I need sexually to experience real pleasure. I have been masturbating for years and believe me, I know what feels best. The frustrating thing is that I can't bring myself to tell my boyfriend how I like to be touched. If I could just show him, our lovemaking would probably be much better. There he is, laboring away, doing all the wrong things, and me laying there with my mouth glued shut. The thing is, I'm concerned he would get real threatened or angry if I started telling and showing him what I like. It would be like I was saying he didn't know what he was doing and I'm afraid his male ego just couldn't handle it. (Authors' files)

This is not an uncommon concern of women. Many of our women students express reluctance to take responsibility for their own satisfaction during sex play because they are concerned that their partners will misinterpret active involvement as an attack on their personal prowess as lovers. Fortunately, some of these destructive patterns are showing signs of eroding. Many of our men students speak with a sense of delight and relief about their sexual encounters with women who initiate sex, play an active role during lovemaking, and assume responsibility for their own pleasure. In recent years women too have seemed more inclined to view men as sexual equals rather than all-knowing experts.

Women as Controllers, Men as Movers.   Many women grow up believing that men always have sex on their minds. For such a woman it may be a logical next step to become the controller of what takes place during sexual interaction. By this we do not mean actively initiating certain activities—she sees that as the prerogative of men, the movers. Rather, a woman may see her role as controlling her male partner's rampant lust by making certain he does not coerce her into unacceptable activities. Thus, instead of enjoying how good it feels to have her breasts caressed, she may concentrate her attention on how to keep his hand off her genitals. This concern with control may be particularly pronounced during the adolescent dating years. It is not surprising that a woman who spends a great deal of time and energy regulating sexual intimacy to preserve her "honor" (something else she learns from gender-role conditioning) may have difficulty experiencing sexual feelings when she finally allows herself to relinquish her controlling role.

Conversely, men are often conditioned to see women as sexual challenges and to go as far as they can during sexual encounters. They too may have difficulty appreciating the good feelings of being close to and touching someone when they are thinking about what they will do next. Men who routinely experience this pattern may have a hard time relinquishing the mover role and being receptive rather than active during sexual sharing. They may be confused or even threatened by a woman who switches roles from controller to active initiator.

Men as Unemotional and Strong, Women as Nurturing and Supportive.
Perhaps one of the most undesirable of all gender-role stereotypes is the notion that being emotionally expressive, tender, and nurturing is appropriate only for women. We have already seen that men are often socialized to be unemotional. This conditioning can make it exceedingly difficult for a man to develop emotionally satisfying relationships. A man who is trying to appear strong may find it difficult to express vulnerability, deep feelings, and doubts. In such a situation it can be very hard to share intimately with another person.

For example, a man who accepts the assumption of nonemotionality may approach sex as a purely physical act during which expressions of feelings have no place. This results in a limited kind of sharing that can leave both parties with feelings of dissatisfaction. Women often have a negative reaction when they encounter this characteristic in men, since they tend to place great importance on openness and willingness to express feelings in a relationship. However, we need to remember that many men must struggle against a lifetime of "Marlboro Man" conditioning when they try to express long-suppressed emotions. For some, even an expression of tenderness may be an exceedingly difficult break from the tough-guy image. Women, on the other hand, may grow tired of their role as nurturers, particularly when their efforts are greeted with little or no reciprocity. Tenderness and supportiveness can dwindle rapidly unless fueled by similar qualities in those we care for.

We have discussed how strict adherence to traditional gender roles may limit and restrict the ways we express our sexuality. While these cultural legacies may often be expressed more subtly today than in the past, rigid gender-role expectations linger on, inhibiting our growth as multidimensional people and our capacity to share intimacy with others. Also, while many people are breaking away from stereotyped gender roles and learning to accept and express themselves more fully, we cannot underestimate the extent of gender-role learning that occurs in our society. Pictures like the photographs on the next two pages underscore this point; they will probably cause most readers to do at least a slight double take.

There is growing evidence, however, that many people now are striving to integrate both masculine and feminine behaviors into their lifestyles. This new trend, often referred to as androgyny, will be the focus of the final section in this chapter.

Transcending Gender Roles: Androgyny

The word **androgyny**, meaning "having characteristics of both sexes," is derived from the Greek roots *andr* = man and *gynē* = woman. Sometimes androgyny is confused with hermaphroditism, implying a kind of mixed biological sex. More appropriately, the term is used to describe flexibility in gender role. Androgynous individuals are those who have moved beyond traditional gender roles. They are people who have integrated aspects of masculinity and femininity into their lifestyles in their pursuit of an individual sense of well-being. Androgyny offers the option of expressing whatever behavior seems appropriate in a given situation instead of limiting responses to those considered gender-appropriate. Thus, androgynous men and women might be assertive on the job and tender and nurturing with friends, family members, and lovers.

Many individuals are now expressing aspects of them-selves previously discouraged by stereotypic gender roles.

Many people hold the mistaken notion that one is either masculine or feminine and that it is not possible to be both. From this perspective, a man who chooses to do domestic chores and provide childcare is rejecting masculine traits and interests. Likewise, a woman who enrolls in auto mechanics at the local community college is seen from this viewpoint as rejecting her femininity in favor of a masculine pursuit. However, many men and women possess characteristics consistent with traditional gender assumptions but also have interests and behavioral tendencies typically ascribed to the other sex. Actually, people may range from being very masculine or feminine to being both masculine and feminine—that is, androgynous.

An eminent social psychologist, Sandra Bem (1974), has developed a paper-and-pencil inventory for measuring the degree to which individuals are identified with masculine or feminine behaviors or a combination thereof. Other devices for measuring masculine, feminine, or androgynous identifications have been developed since Bem's pioneer work (Spence and Helmreich, 1978). Research employing these devices has revealed that there are at least four primary categories of people (all categories can include people of either biological sex): those who are strongly masculine in their behaviors, those who are very feminine, those who are neither very masculine nor very feminine, and those who show a blending of both masculine and feminine behaviors (the androgynous group). Armed with these empirical devices for measuring androgyny, a number of researchers have investigated how androgynous individuals compare with strongly gender-typed people.

As we might expect, androgynous individuals of both sexes are more likely to engage in behavior typically ascribed to the other sex than are gender-typed people (Bem, 1975). A number of studies indicate that androgynous people are more flexible in their behaviors, less stifled by rigid gender-role assumptions, have higher levels of self-esteem, and exhibit more social competence and motivation to achieve than people who are strongly gender-typed or those who score low in both areas (Bem, 1979 and 1980; Bem and Lenney, 1976; Flaherty and Dusek, 1980; O'Connor et al., 1978; Spence and Helmreich, 1978). Research has also demonstrated that masculine and androgynous people of both sexes are more independent and less likely to have their opinions swayed than individuals who are strongly identified with the feminine role (Bem, 1975). In addition, feminine and androgynous people of both sexes appear to be significantly more nurturing than those who adhere to the masculine role (Bem et al., 1976).

There are indications that we need to be cautious about concluding that androgyny is an ideal state, free of potential problems. One study found that masculine-typed males demonstrated better overall emotional adjustment than androgynous males (Jones et al., 1978). A study of college professors in the early stages of their careers found that androgynous individuals exhibited greater personal satisfaction but more job-related stress than those who were strongly gender-typed (Rotheram and Weiner, 1983). In a large sample of college students, the presence of masculine personality characteristics was more closely associated with being versatile and adaptable than was the trait of androgyny (Lee and Scheurer, 1983). Clearly, more information is necessary for a complete picture of the impact of androgyny on personal adjustment and satisfaction.

What are the implications of androgyny for sexual behavior? There is evidence that androgynous individuals, both male and female, have more positive attitudes toward sexuality than those who are traditionally gender-typed (Walfish and Myerson, 1980). Androgynous people also appear to be more tolerant and less likely to judge or criticize the sexual behaviors of others (Garcia, 1982). Studies have found that androgynous women are more orgasmic and experience more sexual satisfaction than feminine-typed women (Kimlicka et al., 1983; Radlove, 1983). However, two separate investigations revealed that masculine males were significantly more comfortable with sex than were androgynous females, indicating that biological sex may still exert a stronger effect than gender typing (Allgeier, 1981; Walfish and Myerson, 1980).

Our own guess is that androgynous people tend to be flexible and comfortable in their sexuality. We would expect such people, whether men or women, to be able to fully enjoy both the emotional and the physical aspects of sexual sharing. Androgynous lovers may be comfortable both initiating and responding to invitations for sexual sharing. Perhaps such people are also less likely to be concerned about whether they happen to be on top or bottom during intercourse.

Research on androgyny is still in its infancy and we certainly have good reasons to be cautious about an unequivocally enthusiastic endorsement of this behavioral style. Nevertheless, most of the evidence thus far collected suggests that people who are able to transcend traditional gender roles may be able to function more comfortably and effectively in a wider range of situations. Androgynous individuals can select, from a broad repertoire of feminine and masculine behaviors, whatever actions seem most appropriate in a given situation. Thus, they may elect to be independent, assertive, nurturing, or tender, based not on gender-role norms but rather on what provides them and others optimum personal satisfaction and choice.

Summary

Male and Female, Masculine and Feminine

1. The process whereby our maleness and femaleness are determined and the manner in which they influence our behavior, sexual and otherwise, are highly complex.

2. Sex refers to our biological maleness or femaleness as reflected in various physical attributes (chromosomes, genitals, and so forth).

3. Gender refers to the social concomitants of sex, or, in other words, our masculinity or femininity. Our ideas of masculinity and femininity involve gender assumptions—assumptions about behavior based on a person's sex.

4. Gender identity is a term used to describe our personal, subjective sense that we are male or female, masculine or feminine.

5. Gender role refers to a collection of attitudes and behaviors considered normal and appropriate in a specific culture for people of a particular sex.

6. Gender roles establish sex-related behavioral expectations that people are expected to fulfill. These expectations are culturally defined and vary from society to society and era to era.

Gender-Identity Formation

7. Research efforts to isolate the many biological factors that influence a person's gender identity have resulted in the identification of six biological categories, or levels: chromosomal sex, gonadal sex, hormonal sex, sex of the internal reproductive structures, sex of the external genitals, and sex differentiation of the brain.

8. Under normal conditions these biological variables interact harmoniously to determine our biological sex. However, errors may occur at any of the six levels. The resulting abnormalities in the development of a person's biological sex may seriously complicate acquisition of a gender identity.

9. The social learning interpretation of gender-identity formation suggests that our identification with either masculine or feminine roles results primarily from the social and cultural models and influences we are exposed to.

10. Most contemporary theorists embrace an interactional model, in which gender identity is seen as a result of a complex interplay of biology and social learning factors.

11. Transsexualism is a special case of gender-identity difficulty in which a person's gender identity is different from his or her biological sex. The scientific community has not reached a general consensus as to the causes and best treatment of this condition. However, some transsexuals have changed their bodies to match their identities by means of surgery and hormone treatments.

Gender Roles

12. Widely accepted gender-role assumptions may begin to function as stereotypes, which are notions about what people are like based not on their individuality but on their inclusion in a general category such as age or sex.

13. There are many common gender-based stereotypes in our society that may encourage us to prejudge others and restrict our opportunities.

14. Socialization refers to the process whereby society conveys its behavioral expectations to us. Parents, peers, schools, textbooks, and television all act as agents in the socialization of gender roles.

15. Gender-role expectations exert a profound impact on our sexuality. Our assessment of ourselves as sexual beings, the expectations we have for intimate relationships, our perception of the quality of such experiences, and the responses of others to our sexuality may all be significantly influenced by our own perceptions of our gender roles.

16. Androgynous individuals are people who have moved beyond traditional gender roles by integrating aspects of masculinity and femininity into their lifestyles in their pursuit of an individual sense of well-being.

Thought Provokers

1. We have seen that gender-identity formation is influenced by both biological and social-learning factors. Do you think the evidence more strongly supports one or the other as the major contributor to gender-identity formation? Why or why not?

2. In exploring the origins of your own gender identity, do you believe that you were socialized to be strongly gender-typed, or were you raised in a manner supporting androgynous behavior? Do you believe these socialization experiences have had any impact upon how you feel about "masculinity" and "femininity" and your sexual attitudes and behaviors?

3. Which gender-role assumptions have had the least impact on your sexuality? The greatest impact? Have you ever had a relationship in which any of these assumptions became a significant issue?

Suggested Readings

Doyle, James. *The Male Experience*. Dubuque, Iowa: William C. Brown, 1983. A relatively current and comprehensive summary of what is known about men and male roles in American society.

Durden-Smith, Jo, and de Simone, Diane. *Sex and the Brain*. New York: Arbor House, 1983. A somewhat technical but concise summation of research on sex differences in the brain. Written from the perspective that some differences in mental abilities and behaviors of men and women are due to brain differences.

Gilligan, Carol. *In a Different Voice*. Cambridge, Mass.: Harvard University Press, 1982. An important, provocative work presenting the thesis that in this society men see the world in terms of their autonomy and are threatened by intimacy, whereas women view the world in terms of relationships and connectedness and are overthreatened by isolation.

Hrdy, Sarah. *The Woman That Never Evolved*. Cambridge, Mass.: Harvard University Press, 1982. A thoughtful critique of the male-oriented perspective of the world that often biases research on sex differences in the behavior of primates.

Hurley, Timothy. "Constitutional Implications of Sex-Change Operations." *The Journal of Legal Medicine*, 1984, Volume 5, 633–664. A comprehensive article that provides an illuminating discussion of the legal issues involved in sex reassignment surgery.

Hyde, Janet. *Half the Human Experience: The Psychology of Women*. Lexington, Mass.: D. C. Heath, 1985. An excellent, up-to-date summary of theories and research dealing with the psychology of women.

Mead, Margaret. *Sex and Temperament in Three Primitive Societies*. New York: Morrow, 1963. An eminent anthropologist's analysis of three societies in which male and female gender roles differ from those of North American society.

Money, John. *Love and Love Sickness: The Science of Sex, Gender Difference, and Pair-Bonding*. Baltimore: Johns Hopkins Press, 1980. A complex and scholarly text that covers a broad range of topics in human sexuality, including some provocative concepts related to gender identity and gender role.

Money, John, and Ehrhardt, Anke. *Man and Woman, Boy and Girl*. Baltimore: Johns Hopkins Press, 1972. An in-depth analysis of the psychosocial and biological factors that influence the development of gender identity. Must reading for anyone desiring a more thorough understanding of the processes of gender identity and gender role.

Morris, Jan. *Conundrum*. New York: New American Library, 1974. A widely acclaimed personal account of the transsexual experience.

Part Two

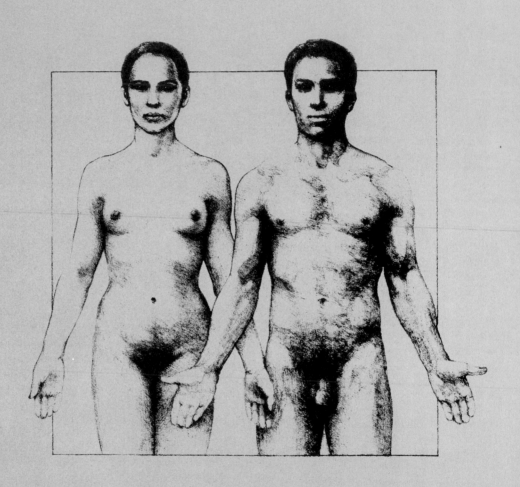

Biological Basis

4

There's the vulva, the vagina, and the jolly perineum,
There's the hymen which is sometimes found in brides,
There's the uterus, the clitoris, the ovum and the oviducts,
The ovaries and lord knows what besides—
Algernon Swinburne
"Protest by the Medical Profession" (1863)

Female Sexual Anatomy and Physiology

Genital Self-Exam
The Vulva
Underlying Structures
Internal Structures
The Breasts
Menstruation

I had three children and was 45 years old before I ever really looked at my genitals. I was amazed at the delicate shapes and subtle colors. I'm sorry it took me so long to do this because I now feel more sure of myself sexually after becoming more acquainted with *me*. (Authors' files)

Many women are as unacquainted with their genitals as this woman was. However, gaining knowledge and understanding of her body can be an important aspect of a woman's sexual well-being. This chapter presents a detailed description of all the female genital structures, external and internal. It is intended to be easy to use for reference, and we encourage women readers to do a self-exam as part of reading this chapter. We begin with a discussion of the genital self-exam and the external structures, then discuss the underlying structures and the internal organs. The chapter closes with information about the breasts and menstruation.

Genital Self-Exam

We are born with curiosity about our bodies. In fact, physical self-awareness and exploration are important steps in a child's development. Unfortunately, many of us receive negative conditioning about the sexual parts of our bodies from earliest childhood. We learn to think of our genitals as something "down there," not to be looked at, touched, or enjoyed. It is common for people to react with discomfort to the suggestion of a self-exam. A physician's experience, summarized in the following quotation, shows how much some of us learn to be alienated from our bodies:

Not infrequently when I ask a patient if she does her own breast exam, she replies, "Oh, no! I would never touch myself there!" (Authors' files)

Betty Dodson, an erotic artist and the author of *Liberating Masturbation* (1974), stresses the importance of women *un*learning negative attitudes. Although she is speaking specifically of women, this can also apply to men.

Many women feel that their genitals are ugly, funny looking, disgusting, smelly and not at all desirable—certainly not a beautiful part of their bodies. A woman who feels this way is certainly going to have reservations about sharing her genitals intimately with anyone. We therefore need to become very aware of our genitals. (p. 18)

The following paragraphs describe a self-exploration exercise designed to help you become more aware of your genitals. Some readers may choose to read about the exercises but not do them. Others may wish to try some or all of the steps. If you choose to do the exploration, you may experience a variety of feelings. Some people feel selfish for spending time on themselves. You may find it difficult to remain focused on the experience instead of thinking about daily concerns. The exercises may be enjoyable for some people and not for others. Primarily, they provide an opportunity to learn about yourself—your body and your feelings.

The exercises serve another purpose as well. Besides helping us feel more comfortable with our anatomy and sexuality, periodic self-examinations, particularly of the genitals, can augment routine medical care. (For this reason we have included other specific suggestions for self-exams throughout the text.) For self-examinations to be most effective it is best to do them regularly, at least once a month: people who know what is normal for their own bodies can often detect small changes and seek medical attention promptly. Problems usually require less extensive treatment when they are detected early. If you discover any changes, consult a health practitioner immediately. **Gynecology** is the medical specialty for female sexual and reproductive anatomy.

To begin, look at your genitals thoroughly. Use a hand mirror, perhaps in combination with a full-length mirror, to look at them from different angles and postures—standing, sitting, lying down (Figure 4.1). Notice colors, shapes, and textures. As you are looking, try to become aware of whatever feelings you have about your genital anatomy. You may find it helpful to draw a picture of your genitals and label the parts (identified in Figure 4.2, p. 98).

In addition to examining visually, use your fingers to explore the various surfaces of your genitals. Focus on the sensations produced by the different kinds of touching.

Figure 4.1

Female Genital Self-Examination
Routine self-examination is an aspect of preventive health care.

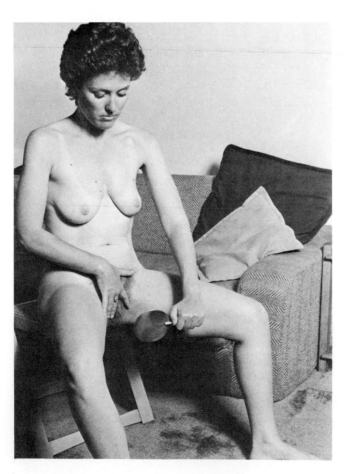

Note which areas are most sensitive and how the nature of stimulation may vary from place to place. The primary purpose of doing this exercise is to explore, not to become sexually aroused. However, if you do become sexually excited during this self-exploration, you may be able to notice changes in the sensitivity of different skin areas that occur with arousal.

After completing an initial self-exploration you may want to repeat all or parts of the exercises to become even more familiar and comfortable with your body. Women have different kinds of reactions to looking at their vulvas:

> I don't find it to be an attractive part of my body. I wouldn't go as far as to call it ugly. I think it would be easier to accept if it was something you weren't taught to hide and think was dirty, but I've never been able to understand why men find the vulva so intriguing. (Authors' files)

> I think it looks very sensuous; the tissues look soft and tender. I was told by a previous partner that my vulva was very beautiful. His comment made me feel good about my body. (Authors' files)

The Vulva

The **vulva** encompasses all of the female external genital structures—the hair, the folds of skin, and the urinary and vaginal openings. Even though vulva is a clinical term, it seems to be less impersonal than other technical words, and it lacks the derogatory connotations of street language. Vulva will be the term most frequently used in this text when we refer to the external genitals of the female. We will discuss its several parts and their functions one at a time. For reference and identification, see Figure 4.2 on the next page.

The appearance of the vulva has been likened to that of certain flowers, seashells, and other forms found in nature. Vulvalike shapes have been used in artwork, including "The Dinner Party" by Judy Chicago. This work consists of thirty-nine ceramic

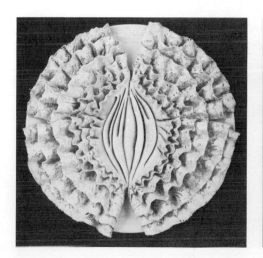 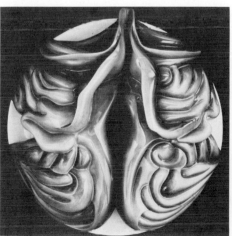

Two examples of the plates in Judy Chicago's "The Dinner Party," an exhibit symbolizing women in history. The left plate represents Emily Dickinson; the right, Georgia O'Keeffe.

plates and corresponding needlework runners representing significant women in history. Many of the plates have vulval shapes.

The Mons Veneris

Translated from Latin, **mons veneris** means "the mound of Venus." Venus was the Roman goddess of love and beauty. The mons veneris, or *mons,* is the area covering the pubic bone. It consists of pads of fatty tissue between the bone and the skin. Touch and pressure on the mons can be sexually pleasurable, due to the presence of numerous nerve endings.

Figure 4.2

**Structures and
Variations of
the Vulva**

*The vulva: (a)
external structures
and (b)–(d) differ-
ent shapes. There
are many normal
variations in shapes
of external female
genitals.*

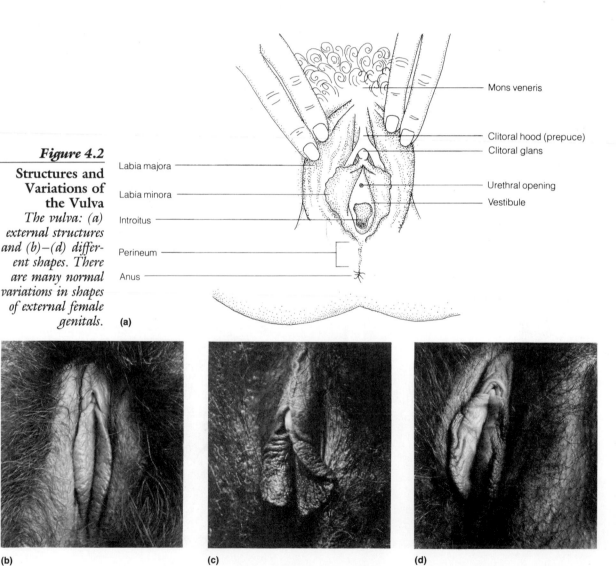

Mons veneris

Clitoral hood (prepuce)
Clitoral glans

Urethral opening
Vestibule

Labia majora
Labia minora
Introitus
Perineum
Anus

(a)

(b) (c) (d)

At puberty the mons becomes covered with hair that varies in color, texture, and thickness from woman to woman. Sometimes women are concerned about these differences:

> I always felt uncomfortable in college physical education classes because I had very thick, dark, pubic hair, more so than most other women. One day my best friend and I were talking and she mentioned that she felt self-conscious in the showers after physical education class because her pubic hair was light-colored and sparse. I told her my concerns. We laughed and both decided to stop worrying about it. (Authors' files)

During sexual arousal the scent that accompanies vaginal secretions is held by the pubic hair and can add to sensory erotic pleasure.

The Labia Majora

The **labia majora**, or outer lips, extend downward from the mons on each side of the vulva. They begin next to the thigh and extend inward, surrounding the labia minora and the urethral and vaginal openings. Next to the thigh the outer lips are covered with pubic hair; their inner parts, next to the labia minora, are hairless. The skin of the labia majora is usually darker than the skin of the thighs. The nerve endings and underlying fatty tissue are similar to those in the mons.

The Labia Minora

The **labia minora**, or inner lips, are located within the outer lips and often protrude between them. The inner lips are hairless folds of skin that join at the **prepuce** (or clitoral hood) over the clitoris and extend downward past the urinary and vaginal openings. They contain sweat and oil glands, extensive blood vessels, and nerve endings. They also vary considerably in size, shape, and color from woman to woman, as Figure 4.2 shows. In the Hottentot culture of Africa pendulous labia are considered a sign of beauty, and women start pulling on them early in childhood in an effort to increase their size.

The Clitoris

The **clitoris** is comprised of the external **shaft** and **glans** and the internal **crura**. The shaft and glans are located just below the mons area, where the inner lips converge. They are covered by the clitoral hood, or prepuce. Genital secretions, skin cells, and bacteria combine to form **smegma**, which may accumulate under the hood and occasionally form lumps and cause pain during sexual arousal or activity. Smegma can be prevented from collecting in this area by drawing back the hood when washing the vulva. If the smegma is already formed, it can be removed by a health care practitioner.

If you look at Figure 4.3, which shows the clitoris with the hood removed, you can see that the glans is supported by the shaft. The shaft can be felt and its shape seen through the hood. It contains two small spongy bodies called the **cavernous** bodies. These become the **crura** (internal leglike stalks) as they extend into the pelvic cavity. The glans is often not visible under the clitoral hood, but it can be seen if a woman gently parts the labia minora and retracts the hood as in Figure 4.2(a). The glans looks smooth, rounded, and slightly translucent. Initially it may be easier for a woman to locate her clitoris by touch rather than sight because of its sensitive nerve endings and small size. The external part of the clitoris, although tiny, has about the same number of nerve endings as the penis; the glans in particular is highly sensitive. With other factors conducive to sexual arousal present, some women find that the entire sexual response cycle can be set in motion and maintained to orgasm by light stimulation of the glans alone (Sherfey, 1972). The glans is so sensitive that women usually stimulate this area with the hood covering it to avoid direct stimulation.

Research into female masturbation patterns has produced findings in keeping with the physiological data about the location and concentrations of nerve endings. As we will see in Chapter 9, clitoral stimulation, not vaginal insertion, is the most common way women produce arousal and orgasm during self-stimulation.

While other sexual organs have additional functions of reproduction or the elimination of waste material, the only purpose of the clitoris is sexual arousal. The size, shape, and position of the clitoris varies from woman to woman. Although women are sometimes concerned that their clitorises are too small or too large, these normal differences have no known relation to sexual arousal and functioning (Money, 1970).

A good deal of controversy has surrounded the role of the clitoris in sexual arousal and orgasm. Despite long-existing scientific knowledge about the highly concentrated nerve endings in the clitoris, the erroneous belief has persisted that vaginal rather than clitoral stimulation is—or should be—exclusively responsible for female sexual arousal and orgasm. However, there are relatively few nerve endings in the vagina as compared with the clitoris. There are some nerve endings that respond to light touch in the outer third of the vagina, but almost none are present in the inner two-thirds. (This is why women do not feel tampons or diaphragms when they are correctly in place in the vagina, and some vaginal surgeries are performed painlessly without anesthesia.) Nevertheless, many women do find the internal pressure and stretching sensations during manual stimulation or intercourse highly pleasurable, and some experience more intense arousal from vaginal than from clitoral stimulation. As more and more scientific research is done, a wider range of individual variation becomes apparent (Alzate and Londono, 1984).

The Vestibule

The **vestibule** is the area of the vulva inside the labia minora. It is rich in blood vessels and nerve endings, and its tissues are sensitive to touch. In architectural terminology, the word *vestibule* refers to the entryway of a house. Both the urinary and the vaginal opening are located within the vestibule.

The Urethral Opening

Urine collected in the bladder passes out of the body through the urethral opening. The **urethra** is the short tube connecting the bladder to the urinary opening located between the clitoris and the vaginal opening.

Women sometimes develop infections of the *urinary tract,* the organ system that includes the kidneys, bladder, and urethra. About one out of every five women will have a urinary tract infection in her lifetime; some will have more than one (American College of Obstetricians and Gynecologists, 1984).

Urinary tract infections are usually caused by bacteria from the rectum or vagina, or infectious agents from a partner's sexual organs that enter the urethral opening. Coitus is the most frequent means by which pathogenic (disease-causing) bacteria enter the urinary tract (Leiter, 1984). Bacteria can be massaged into the urethra by the thrusting motions of intercourse. Bladder infections often occur during periods of frequent intercourse with a new partner and are sometimes referred to as "honeymoon cystitis." Poor hygiene or wiping the genitals from back to front after defecation can also introduce infection-causing bacteria into the urethra.

Other factors, including diabetes, pregnancy, a history of childhood urinary tract infections, and being postmenopausal increase a woman's likelihood of having a urinary tract infection. Delaying urination can also result in this problem. Repeatedly stretching the bladder muscle beyond its normal capacity (which is reached with the first urge to urinate) weakens the muscle so that it cannot expel all of the urine; some urine remains in the bladder, increasing the risk of an infection. An improperly fitting diaphragm that presses on the opening of the bladder and prevents a woman from voiding completely can also cause urinary tract infections (Gillespie, 1984).

The symptoms of urinary tract infections are usually intensely uncomfortable and include a frequent need to urinate; a severe burning sensation when urinating; blood or pus in the urine; and sometimes lower pelvic pain. A conclusive diagnosis of a urinary tract infection requires laboratory analysis of a urine sample. Such an infection generally responds to short-term antibiotic treatment. A follow-up urine test is done after treatment to assure that the infection has been cured.

Observing a few routine precautions may help women prevent urinary tract infections. Careful wiping from front to back after both urination and bowel movements helps prevent bacteria from getting close to the urethra. Washing the genital and rectal areas thoroughly each day, urinating as soon as you feel the urge, and having your health care practitioner recheck the fit of your diaphragm during your routine exam will help protect against a urinary tract infection. For those who have frequent problems with such infections, washing before and after intercourse may help. One's partner can also help by washing his or her hands and genitals before sexual contact. Using intercourse positions that cause less friction against the urethra may also help. Urinating immediately after intercourse helps wash out bacteria. Women can use sterile lubricating jelly when vaginal lubrication is not sufficient, since irritated tissue is more susceptible to infection. It can also be helpful to drink plenty of liquids, especially juices high in vitamin C, and to avoid substances like coffee, tea, and alcohol that have an irritating effect on the bladder.

The Introitus and the Hymen

The opening of the vagina is referred to as the **introitus**. It is located between the urinary opening and the anus. Partially covering the introitus is a fold of tissue called the **hymen**, which is typically present at birth and usually remains intact until initial coitus. Occasionally this tissue may be too thick to break easily during intercourse;

it may then require a minor incision by a medical practitioner. In rare cases the hymen completely covers the vaginal opening, and when the young woman begins to menstruate this *imperforate hymen* causes the menstrual flow to collect inside the vagina. When this condition is discovered, a medical practitioner can open the hymen with an incision.

Usually the vaginal opening is partially open and flexible enough to insert tampons before the hymen has been broken—contrary to the information provided by a high school physical education teacher in the 1960s:

> I'll never forget the day in class when one of the girls asked the teacher if it was OK to use tampons. She replied, "No, it's up to your husband to make you not a virgin." (Authors' files)

Contrary to the implication of the preceding quote, a person is considered a virgin until she or he has experienced coitus. And although cases have been rare, it is possible for a woman to become pregnant even if her hymen is still intact and she has not experienced penile penetration. If semen is placed on the labia minora, the sperm can swim from outside to inside the vagina and fertilize an ovum.

Although the hymen may serve to protect the vaginal tissues early in life, it has

Other Times, Other Places

Female Genital Mutilation

Some form of female genital mutilation has been practiced at some time in almost all parts of the world (including the United States, from 1890 through the late 1930s). Today it continues in many areas of Africa, the Middle East, and Asia. Women in these parts of the world undergo several types of genital mutilation. The simplest procedure, *circumcision,* consists of cutting off the clitoral hood. Another common practice is the removal of the clitoris itself, called *clitoridectomy.* In the most extreme practice, *genital infibulation,* the clitoris is entirely removed and the labia are cut off. Then both sides are scraped raw and stitched up (sometimes with thorns) so that they grow together, leaving only a small opening for urine and menstrual flow to pass through. Serious gynecological and obstetrical complications often arise from genital infibulation. Fetal death sometimes occurs because of difficult delivery due to extensive vaginal scarring. It is estimated that 30 million women and girls now living have undergone one of these "surgeries" (Brisset, 1979).

There are various rationales for performing these genital mutilations on females. Often the "surgeries" are rites of passage from childhood to adulthood. Some groups mistakenly believe that such procedures are necessary for hygiene. Others believe that contact with the clitoris is dangerous to a man, or in the case of infibulation, that the smaller vaginal opening provides greater pleasure to the male during intercourse. These "surgeries" are often thought to protect women from sexual over-excitement, ensuring their virginity before marriage and fidelity afterwards. A Somalian grandmother states that infibulation "takes away nothing that she needs. If she does not have this done, she will become a harlot" (Harden, 1985a).

A woman who has not undergone a culturally prescribed genital mutilation is often considered immature or uncouth. For example, to call a

no other known function. Nevertheless, many societies, including our own, have placed great significance on its presence or absence. (Attitudes and behavior regarding virginity will be discussed in Chapter 13.) The following quote from a woman who was an adolescent in the 1950s illustrates its importance in our own society:

> The hymen obsessed everyone, though it was never called by its proper name. It was referred to as your "innocence," your "purity," your "goodness," your "maidenhead," your "mark," as in "mark of Cain," and your "shield." . . . We were told that "men can tell" and warned not to wipe ourselves too hard, which led to untold confusion about the logistics of sexual congress. (King, 1976, p. 49)

In our society and many others, people have long believed that a woman's virginity can be proved by the pain and bleeding that may occur with initial coitus. This is not always true. Although pain or bleeding sometimes occur, the hymen can be partial, flexible, or thin enough for there to be no discomfort or bleeding; it may even remain intact after intercourse. One study found that 25% of women reported no pain with first intercourse, 40% reported moderate pain, and 33% severe pain. Women who experienced pain during first intercourse were younger than women who did not, had more conservative sexual values, more often had negative feelings

woman in Sudan *ghalfa,* meaning uncircumcised, would be a grave insult. Young girls are often considered unmarriageable if they do not have the prescribed excision. Since marriage is the most important duty of a woman in these cultures, her future and her family's pride depend upon upholding this tradition (Harden, 1985).

In addition to the numerous and severe medical problems that arise from these procedures (shock, infections, urinary retention, chronic pelvic and urinary tract infections, cyst formation, menstrual pain, childbirth complications, and infertility), African and Arab physicians and health workers report widespread sexual problems among women who have had clitoridectomies and infibulations. One physician reported that 80% of infibulated women he had examined over the years said they had never experienced any sexual pleasure. Another physician made a similar report on women who had undergone clitoridectomies. A

Middle Eastern gynecologist asked 300 men who practiced polygamy and had more than one wife whether they preferred women with or without sexual excisions. The great majority of these men (266) reported that they preferred women who had not had "surgeries" because such women enjoyed sex more (Ohm, 1980).

In recent years there has been such an outcry over female genital mutilation, particularly from women in Western nations, that the United Nations has agreed to suspend its policy of nonintervention in the cultural practices of individual nations. In 1980 the World Health Organization (WHO) and the United Nations Children's Fund (UNICEF) jointly adopted a plan to encourage leaders of nations where such practices occur to use their influence to bring them to an end. Unfortunately, the strength of cultural tradition in many societies will be difficult to overcome.

about their partner and about intercourse with him, and more often had expected no pain (Weis, 1985).

If a woman manually stretches her hymen before initial intercourse, she may be able to minimize the discomfort that sometimes occurs. To do this she first inserts a lubricated finger, using saliva or a sterile lubricant (such as K-Y jelly) into the vaginal opening and presses downward toward the anus until she feels some stretching. After a few seconds she releases the pressure and relaxes. This step is repeated several times. The next step is to insert two fingers into the vagina and stretch the sides of the vagina by opening the fingers. The downward stretching is repeated with two fingers as well.

The Perineum

The **perineum** is the area of smooth skin between the vaginal opening and the anus (the sphincter through which bowel movements pass). The perineal tissue is endowed with nerve endings and is sensitive to the touch.

During childbirth an incision called an *episiotomy* is sometimes made in the perineum to prevent the ragged tearing of tissues that may happen during delivery. Many medical practitioners believe this incision is essential, but other health care specialists disagree. We will consider this issue in more detail in Chapter 12.

Underlying Structures

If the hair, skin, and fatty pads were removed from the vulva, several underlying structures could be seen (see Figure 4.3). The shaft of the clitoris would be visible, no longer concealed by the hood. Also detectable would be the crura, or roots,

Figure 4.3

Underlying Structures of the Vulva

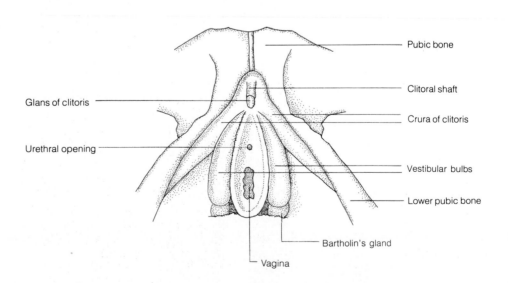

Pubic bone

Clitoral shaft

Crura of clitoris

Vestibular bulbs

Lower pubic bone

Glans of clitoris

Urethral opening

Bartholin's gland

Vagina

projecting inward from each side of the clitoral shaft. These bodies extend into the pelvic cavity to the bony pelvis, and they are part of the vast network of bulbs and vessels that engorge with blood during sexual arousal. The **vestibular bulbs** alongside the vagina also fill with blood during sexual excitement, causing the vagina to increase in length and the vulvar area to become swollen. These bulbs are similar in structure and function to the tissue in the penis that engorges during arousal and causes an erection.

The **Bartholin's glands** on each side of the vaginal opening were once believed to be the source of vaginal lubrication during sexual arousal; however, they typically produce only a drop or two of fluid just prior to orgasm. The glands are usually not noticeable, but sometimes the duct from the Bartholin's gland becomes clogged, and the fluid which is normally secreted remains inside and causes enlargement. If this occurs and the swelling does not go away within a few days, it is best to see a physician.

Besides the glands and network of vessels, a complex musculature underlies the genital area (see Figure 4.4). The *pelvic floor muscles* have a multidirectional design that allows the vaginal opening to expand greatly during childbirth and to close afterwards.

The pelvic floor muscles contract involuntarily at orgasm; they also can be trained to contract voluntarily, through a series of exercises known as **Kegel exercises**. These exercises were developed by Arnold Kegel in 1952 as a way of helping women regain control of urination after childbirth. It is common for postpartum women (women who have recently delivered babies) to lose urine when they cough or sneeze. This is due to the loss of muscle tone in the perineal area caused by the stress to the muscles during delivery. The exercises are effective in restoring muscle tone, and they have an additional bonus. Many women who practice the Kegel exercises regularly for about six weeks report an increase in sensation during intercourse, as well as a general increase in genital sensitivity. This seems to be the result of their increased awareness and sense of control of their sex organs, as well as their improved muscle tone.

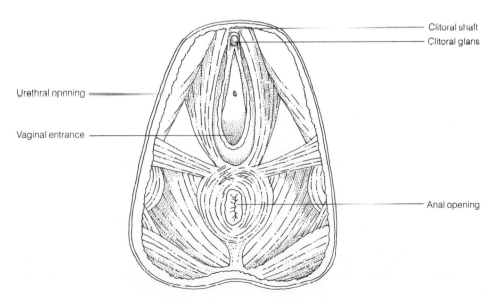

Urethral opening

Vaginal entrance

Clitoral shaft
Clitoral glans

Anal opening

Figure 4.4

Underlying Muscles of the Vulva

The steps for the Kegel exercises are:

1. Locate the muscles surrounding the vagina. This can be done by stopping the flow of urine to feel which muscles contract. The muscles that control the flow of urine are the same muscles you contract during Kegel exercises.
2. Insert a finger into the opening of the vagina and contract the muscles you located in Step 1. Feel them squeeze your finger.
3. Squeeze the same muscles for three seconds. Relax. Repeat.
4. Squeeze and release as rapidly as possible, 10 to 25 times. Repeat.
5. Imagine trying to suck something into your vagina. Hold for three seconds.
6. Push out as during a bowel movement, only with the vagina. Hold for three seconds.
7. Repeat Steps 3, 5, and 6 ten times each and Step 4 once. This exercise series should be done three times a day. (Adapted from Barbach, 1975, pp. 54–55.)

Internal Structures

Internal female sexual anatomy consists of the vagina, cervix, uterus, and ovaries. These will be discussed in the following sections. Refer to Figure 4.5 for a cross-section of the female pelvis.

The Vagina

The **vagina** opens between the labia minora and extends into the body, angling upward toward the small of the back. Women who are unfamiliar with their anatomy may have a difficult time when they first try inserting tampons:

> No matter how hard I tried, I couldn't get a tampon in until I inserted a finger and realized that my vagina slanted backwards. I had been pushing straight up onto the upper wall. (Authors' files)

The nonaroused vagina is approximately three to five inches long. The walls form a flat tube. The analogy of a glove is often used to illustrate the vagina as a potential rather than actual space, with its walls able to expand enough to serve as a birth passage. In addition, the vagina changes in size and shape during sexual arousal, as we will discuss in Chapter 6.

The vagina contains three layers of tissue: mucous, muscle, and fibrous tissue. All these layers are richly endowed with blood vessels. The **mucosa** is the layer of mucous membrane that a woman feels when she inserts a finger inside her vagina. The folded walls, or **rugae**, feel soft, moist, and warm, resembling the inside of one's mouth. The walls normally produce secretions that help to maintain the chemical balance of the vagina. During sexual arousal a lubricating substance exudes through the mucosa.

Most of the second layer, composed of muscle tissue, is concentrated around the vaginal opening. Because of the concentration of musculature in the outer one-third and the expansive ability of the inner two-thirds of the vagina, a situation often develops which can be at best funny and at worst embarrassing. During headstands and certain yoga or coital positions with the pelvis elevated, gravity causes the inner two-thirds to expand and draws air into the vagina. The outer muscles tighten and the trapped air is forced back out through the tightened muscles, creating a sound we usually associate with a different orifice. One student has suggested calling this "varting." The auditory effect is identical to that of the common fart; however, the olfactory is lacking, thereby distinguishing the two to the casual observer. Varting occurs in gym classes and bedrooms across the nation and may be cause for great consternation:

> I stopped taking gymnastics in high school because every time I did a nice tuck-roll out of a headstand, pppppppptttt! It was just too embarrassing. (Authors' files)

> When I have intercourse on my back with my legs on his shoulders, invariably my vagina fills with air. I just don't know what to do when those sounds start happening except to say, "I promise, it's not the real thing," and laugh. Only laughing just makes them louder. (Authors' files)

> When I lived in a sorority in college, one of my sisters had the amazing ability to do voluntary vaginal farts. She would sit upright, crosslegged, lift her abdominal muscles, then push them down and create that all-too-familiar sound. She could do this repeated times and provided us with great entertainment during finals week. I tried to master this skill myself but wasn't coordinated enough. (Authors' files)

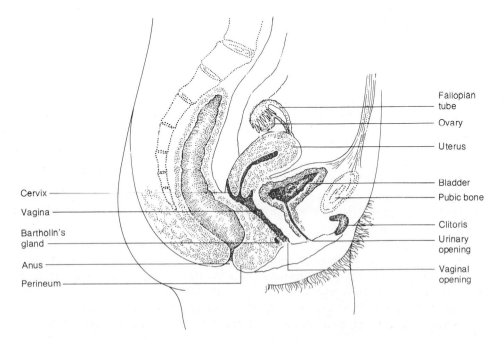

Cervix

Vagina

Bartholin's gland

Anus

Perineum

Fallopian tube

Ovary

Uterus

Bladder

Pubic bone

Clitoris

Urinary opening

Vaginal opening

Figure 4.5

Internal Female Sexual Anatomy
Cross-section side view of female internal structures.

To our knowledge, this issue has never been included in public discussions of sexuality. However, Richard Pryor, a well-known comedian, is one of the few who have been daring enough to address the subject. He discusses how women are truly amazing in their ability to recover from almost any situation. The example he relates is an experience during intercourse when suddenly, without warning, "Blaaaat." The woman calmly looked at him and said, "She's talkin' to ya, baby!" We hope that this discussion of varting will help people feel more at ease if and when it occurs.

Surrounding the muscular layer is the innermost vaginal layer, composed of fibrous tissue. This layer aids in vaginal contraction and expansion, and it acts as connective tissue to other structures in the pelvic cavity.

Arousal and Vaginal Lubrication. So far in this chapter we have described the parts of the female sexual anatomy, but we have said relatively little about how these structures function. Since lubrication is a unique feature of the vagina, it will be presented here. Other physiological aspects of female arousal will be discussed in Chapter 6.

During sexual arousal a clear, slippery fluid begins to appear on the vaginal mucosa within 10 to 30 seconds after effective physical or psychological stimulation begins. Lubrication is the first physiological sign of sexual arousal in women, and it occurs primarily in the early phase of sexual response.

Masters and Johnson's laboratory research firmly established the source of vaginal lubrication. A clear, phallus-shaped camera was inserted into the vagina and filmed the internal changes. Masters and Johnson describe the lubrication process:

> As sexual tensions rise, a "sweating" phenomenon may be observed developing on the walls of the vaginal barrel. Individual droplets of the transudation-like, mucoid material appear scattered throughout the rugae folds of the normal vaginal architecture. These individual droplets coalesce to form a smooth, glistening coating for the entire vaginal barrel. (Masters and Johnson, 1966, p. 69)

In the past, both the cervix and Bartholin's glands were believed to be the source of increased vaginal lubrication during sexual arousal. However, Masters and Johnson's research reveals that this lubrication is a result of **vasocongestion**, the pooling of blood in the pelvic area. During vasocongestion the extensive network of blood vessels in the tissues surrounding the vagina engorge with blood. Clear fluid seeps from the congested tissues to the inside of the vaginal walls to form the characteristic slippery coating of the sexually aroused vagina. (This process is discussed further in Chapter 6.)

Vaginal lubrication serves two functions. First, it enhances the possibility of conception by helping to alkalinize the normally acidic vaginal chemical balance. Sperm travel faster and survive longer in an alkaline environment than in an acidic one. (The seminal fluid of the male also helps to alkalinize the vagina.)

Second, vaginal lubrication can increase sexual enjoyment. During manual-genital stimulation, the slippery wetness can increase the sensuousness and pleasure of touching. Also, some women's partners experience the scent and taste of the lubrication during oral-genital sex as erotic. During intercourse, vaginal lubrication makes the walls of the vagina slippery, which facilitates entry of the penis into the vagina. Lubrication also helps makes intercourse pleasurable. Without adequate lubrication, entry of the penis into the vagina can be very uncomfortable for the woman and often for the man. Irritation and small tears of the vaginal tissue can result.

While lubrication helps prepare the vagina for entry of the penis, the presence of some lubrication does not automatically indicate that a woman is ready for intercourse. Some women prefer to wait until they are highly aroused before beginning intercourse. Communication, verbal and nonverbal, helps people take their partners' desires into account.

Several things can inhibit vaginal lubrication. Anxiety about oneself, one's partner, or the situation; the use of some drugs; and changes in hormone balance all can influence the vasocongestive response. Some women who take birth control pills find that vaginal lubrication is reduced; others find that for a while after childbirth lubrication is lessened. Many women experience a decrease in lubrication due to the hormonal changes after menopause. We will discuss each of these situations in more detail in later sections of the text.

There are several ways to remedy insufficient vaginal lubrication, depending on the source of the difficulty. Changing the anxiety-producing circumstances and engaging in effective stimulation are important. Saliva, K-Y jelly, or a nonirritating, water-soluble lotion can be used to provide additional lubrication. Occasionally hormone treatment is necessary.

The Grafenberg Spot.   The **Grafenberg spot** is an area located within the anterior (or front) wall of the vagina, about one centimeter from the surface and one-third to one-half way in from the vaginal opening. It is reported to consist of a system of glands (Skene's glands) and ducts that surround the urethra (Heath, 1984). This area is believed to be the female counterpart of the male prostate gland and to develop from the same embryonic tissue (Belzer, 1981; Heath, 1984).

The Grafenberg spot has generated considerable interest because of reports that some women experience sexual arousal, orgasm, or perhaps an ejaculation of fluid when stimulated there. There is wide variation in response from person to person. We will discuss the role of the Grafenberg spot in female sexual response in Chapter 6.

Vaginal Secretions and Chemical Balance of the Vagina.   Both the vaginal walls and the cervix produce secretions that are white or yellowish in color. These secretions are normal and are a sign of vaginal health. They vary in appearance according to hormone level changes during the menstrual cycle. (Keeping track of these variations is the basis for one method of birth control, discussed in Chapter 11.) The taste and scent of vaginal secretions may also vary with the time of a woman's cycle and her level of arousal. One study reports that men found vaginal secretion odors more pleasant during ovulation than during other times in the cycle (Doty et al., 1975).

The vagina's natural chemical and bacterial balance helps promote a healthy mucosa. The chemical balance is normally rather acid (pH 4.0 to 5.0).* A variety of factors can alter this balance and result in vaginal problems. Among these are too-frequent **douching** (rinsing out the inside of the vagina) and using feminine hygiene sprays. Advertising has played upon our cultural negativity about female sexual organs, turning misguided attempts to eradicate normal secretions and scents into an extremely profitable business. Women grow up hearing slogans such as "Unfortunately, the trickiest deodorant problem a girl has isn't under her pretty little arms" and "Our product eliminates the moist, uncomfortable feeling most women normally have just because they're women." However, frequent douching can alter the natural chemical balance of the vagina, thereby increasing susceptibility to infections. "Feminine hygiene" sprays can cause irritation, allergic reactions, burns, infections, dermatitis of the thighs, and numerous other problems. Deodorant tampons are another example of selling women something they do not need: menstrual fluid has virtually no odor until it is outside the body. Douching is not necessary for routine hygiene. Regular bathing with a mild soap and washing between the folds of the vulva is all that is necessary for cleanliness.

Vaginal Infections.   When the natural balance of the vagina is disturbed or a non-native organism is introduced, a vaginal infection, or **vaginitis**, can result. Usually the woman herself first notices symptoms of vaginitis: irritation or itching of the vagina and vulva, unusual discharge, and sometimes a disagreeable odor. (An unpleasant odor can also be due to a forgotten tampon or diaphragm.) Some of the different types of vaginal infections are yeast infections, bacterial infections, and trichomoniasis. These are all discussed in detail in Chapter 18.

A number of factors increase susceptibility to vaginitis: the use of antibiotics, heat and moisture retained by nylon underwear and pantyhose, emotional stress, a diet high in carbohydrates, hormonal changes caused by pregnancy or birth control pills, chemical irritants, and coitus without adequate lubrication. Menstrual flow increases the alkalinity of the vagina, which promotes yeast growth in some women. One study found that women who wear pantyhose had three times more yeast vaginitis than others (Heidrich et al., 1984).

It is important for vaginitis to be treated and cured. Chronic irritation resulting from long-term infections may play a part in predisposing a woman to cervical cell changes that can lead to cancer (Benson, 1971). Some health care practitioners provide suggestions for nondrug treatment of vaginitis. The following suggestions may help prevent vaginitis from occurring in the first place:

1. Eat a well-balanced diet low in sugar and refined carbohydrates.
2. Maintain general good health with adequate sleep, exercise, and emotional release.
3. Use good hygiene, including
   a. regular bathing with mild soap;
   b. wiping from front to back, vulva to anus;

---

*pH is a measure of acidity or alkalinity. A neutral substance (neither acid nor alkaline) has a pH of 7. A lower number means a substance is more acid; a higher number, that it is more alkaline.

    c. wearing clean cotton underpants (nylon holds in heat and moisture that encourages bacterial growth);

    d. avoiding the use of feminine hygiene sprays, colored toilet paper, bubble bath, and other people's washcloths or towels;

    e. being sure your sexual partner's hands and genitals are clean.

4. Be sure you have adequate lubrication before coitus: natural lubrication or a sterile, water-soluble lubricant such as K-Y jelly. Do not use vaseline, because it is not water-soluble and is likely to remain in the vagina and harbor bacteria.

5. Use condoms if you or your partner are nonmonogamous.

6. Women who are prone to yeast infections after menstruation may find it helpful to douch with two tablespoons of white vinegar in a quart of warm water once the flow ceases.

Self-Exams and Vaginal Health Care. A self-exam can sometimes help detect vaginal infection. The skin of the genital area may turn red instead of its usual pink, and this along with irritation is a sign that treatment may be necessary.

Many health care practitioners use a mirror to show a woman the inside of her vagina during her regular exam, and some will teach the woman how to use the **speculum**, the instrument that holds open the vaginal walls. They may also give the woman a plastic speculum that she can use during vaginal self-exams at home.

The Cervix

The **cervix**, located at the back of the vagina, is the small end of the pear-shaped uterus (Figure 4.5; see also color plates 1 and 2 in Chapter 12). It contains mucus-secreting glands. Sperm pass through the vagina into the uterus through the **os**, the opening in the center of the cervix.

A woman can see her own cervix if she learns to insert a speculum into her vagina. She can also ask for a mirror when she has her pelvic exam. A woman can feel her own cervix by inserting one or two fingers into the vagina and reaching to the end of the canal. (Sometimes squatting and bearing down brings the cervix closer to the vaginal entrance.) The cervix feels somewhat like the end of a nose, firm and round in contrast to the soft vaginal walls.

The **Pap smear**, a screening test for cervical cancer, is taken from the cervix. The vaginal walls are held open with a speculum, and a few cells are removed with a small wooden spatula; these cells are put on a slide and sent to a lab to be examined. The cells for a Pap smear are taken from the part of the cervix where long column-shaped cells called columnar cells meet flat-shaped cells called squamous cells. A Pap smear is not painful because there are so few nerve endings on the cervix.

The Pap smear is an essential part of a woman's routine preventive health care. Depending on a woman's individual situation and her health care provider's recommendation, she may have this test once every two years, every year, biannually, or even more frequently. Research indicates that women who have had genital warts (Ferenczy, 1984), smoke cigarettes, have had a large number of sexual partners (Hellberg et al., 1983), had first coitus at an early age (Clarke et al., 1985), or have husbands at increased risk of cancer from occupational contact with toxic materials (Robinson, 1983) have an increased risk of developing cervical cancer.

Pap smear results have a diagnostic range of five classes. A Class I Pap smear is considered a negative result and indicates normal tissue. A Class II is usually caused by inflammation of the cells from vaginitis. Often the specific infection is diagnosed and treated, and the Pap smear is repeated to ensure that the infection has cleared up. However, a Class II can also be caused by cells that are just beginning to change to a possibly cancerous state. Class III results usually indicate the presence of some abnormal cells on the surface of the cervix. It is important for a woman with a Class III result to be followed closely by her health care practitioner and to have more frequent Pap smears while waiting to see if the tissue returns to normal. A Class IV Pap smear indicates severe cell changes and the possibility of cancer cells on the surface of the cervix. Class V results indicate the presence of cancer cells.

When a Pap smear yields Class III, IV, or V results, further tests are necessary for a conclusive diagnosis of cancer cells. A *colposcopy* (an exam using a special microscope) and a tissue *biopsy* (surgical removal of a small piece of cervical tissue, which is examined under a microscope) are two of the kinds of further testing that can be done.

There are several simple, highly effective, life-saving treatments for cervical cancer. *Cryosurgery* (freezing of tissues) is one method of removing small numbers of cancerous cells from the surface of the cervix. Elimination of the malignant tissue by means of a biopsy is also often effective. In more severe cases a woman needs to have a complete *hysterectomy* (surgical removal of the cervix and uterus), a procedure that will be discussed further in a later section.

The Uterus

The **uterus**, or womb, is a hollow, thick, pear-shaped organ, approximately three inches long and two inches wide in a *nulliparous* woman (one who has never had a child). It is somewhat larger after pregnancy. The *fundus* is the top area of the uterus, where the uterine walls are especially thick. Longitudinal and circular muscle fibers of the uterus interweave like the fibers of a basket and enable it to stretch during pregnancy and contract during labor and orgasm.

The uterus is suspended in the pelvic cavity by six ligaments, and it is capable of some movement. It is normal for the uteri of different women to be in different positions, from tipped forward toward the abdomen (anteflexed) to tipped back toward the spine (retroflexed), as shown in Figure 4.6. At one time it was believed that a retroflexed, or tipped, uterus interfered with conception. Women with retroflexed uteri may be more likely to experience menstrual discomfort or to have difficulty with diaphragm insertion, but their fertility is not negatively affected by the position of the uterus.

Fertilization usually occurs not in the uterus but in the fallopian tubes, as the egg travels from the ovary. Once fertilization has taken place, the *zygote* (united sperm and egg) travels down the tube and becomes implanted in the uterus, where it develops into the fetus. In preparation for this event the **endometrium**, or uterine lining, becomes thickened. This thickening occurs in response to hormone changes during the monthly menstrual cycle, which will be discussed later in this chapter.

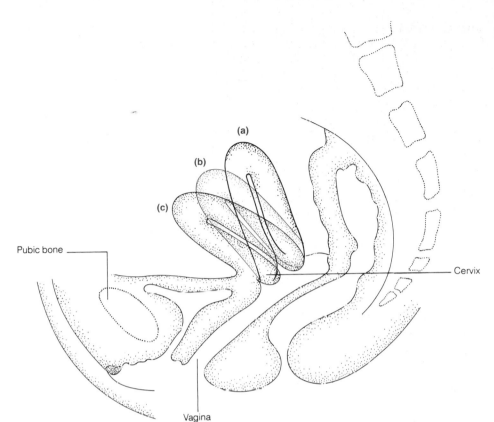

Figure 4.6

**Positions of
the Uterus**
*Various positions
of the uterus in
the pelvic cavity:
(a) retroflexed,
(b) midline, and
(c) anteflexed.*

The Fallopian Tubes

Each of the two four-inch **fallopian tubes** extends from the uterus toward the left or the right side of the pelvic cavity. The outside end of each tube is like a funnel, with fringelike projections called **fimbriae** that almost reach the ovary. When the egg leaves the ovary, it is drawn into the tube by the fimbria.

Once the egg is inside the tube, the movements of tiny, hairlike *cilia* and the contractions of the walls move it along the tube at a rate of approximately one inch per 24 hours. It remains viable for fertilization for about 24 to 48 hours. Therefore, fertilization occurs while the egg is still close to the ovary. After fertilization, the zygote begins developing as it continues traveling down the tube to the uterus.

Sometimes the zygote becomes implanted in a location outside the uterus, a condition known as an **ectopic pregnancy**. The most common site of an ectopic pregnancy is the fallopian tube, so the condition is often called a tubal pregnancy. Research indicates this occurs in one out of 100 pregnancies (Curran, 1980). A tubal pregnancy is often difficult to diagnose because some of the possible symptoms (abdominal pain, a missed menstrual period, a pelvic mass, or irregular bleeding) are similar to those found with other problems (Benson, 1974). Without surgical treatment, though, an ectopic pregnancy may ultimately rupture the tube and result in severe bleeding, shock, and even death.

The Ovaries

The two **ovaries** are structures about the size and shape of almonds. They are located at the ends of the fallopian tubes, one on each side of the uterus. They are connected to the pelvic wall and the uterus by ligaments. The ovaries are endocrine glands that produce two classes of sex hormones. The estrogens, as mentioned in Chapter 3, influence development of female physical sex characteristics and help regulate the menstrual cycle. The progestational compounds also help to regulate the menstrual cycle, and they stimulate development of the uterine lining in preparation for pregnancy. Around the onset of puberty the female sex hormones play a critical role in initiating maturation of the uterus, ovaries, and vagina and development of the **secondary sex characteristics**, such as pubic hair and breast development.

The ovaries contain 40,000 to 400,000 immature ova, which are present at birth. During the years between puberty and menopause, one ovary typically releases an egg each cycle. **Ovulation**, or egg maturation and release, occurs as the result of the complex chain of events we know as the menstrual cycle. We will look at the menstrual cycle more closely at the end of this chapter.

Surgical Removal of the Uterus and Ovaries

Sometimes a woman needs to have a **hysterectomy** (removal of the uterus), or an **oophorectomy** (removal of the ovaries), or both. Various medical problems necessitate these procedures, including cervical, uterine, or ovarian cancer; the presence of benign (noncancerous) tumors; or severe pelvic infections. The physical side effects of these operations are similar to those of any major surgery. These procedures are performed quite frequently, and it may be especially important for a woman to get a second opinion before agreeing to this type of surgery.

The effects of this type of surgery on a woman's sexuality can vary. Some women may experience alteration or decrease in their sexual response after removal of the uterus. Sensations from uterine vasocongestion and elevation during arousal, as well as contractions during orgasm, will be absent and may change the physical experience of sexual response (Zussman et al., 1981). Some changes may result from damage to the innervation of the vagina and cervix. Scar tissue or alterations to the vagina may also have an effect (Kilkku et al., 1983). Often the crucial variable in postsurgery sexual adjustment is how the woman and her partner perceive the surgery (Dennerstein et al., 1977). In a few instances continued general physical or emotional problems may interfere with sexual functioning. These problems can range from diminished vaginal lubrication (due to the absence of ovarian estrogen) to depression over the loss of reproductive ability or symbolic loss of femininity. On the other hand, some women find that the elimination of medical problems and painful intercourse, assured protection from unwanted pregnancy, and lack of menstruation may enhance their sexual functioning (Woods, 1975). Research indicates that women have intercourse as frequently after recovering from a hysterectomy as before the surgery (Kilkku, 1983). It is important for any woman facing surgical removal of her reproductive organs to obtain thorough pre- and postoperative information and counseling, along with her partner.

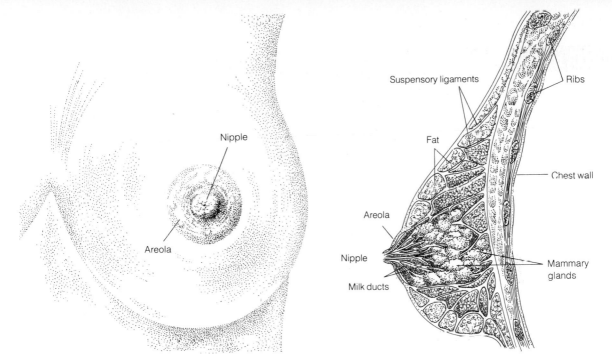

Figure 4.7

The Female Breast
External and internal structures of the female breast.

The Breasts

Breasts are not a part of the internal or external female genitalia. The **breasts** are secondary sex characteristics (physical characteristics other than genitals that distinguish male from female). In a physically mature woman they are composed internally of fatty tissue and **mammary glands**, or milk glands (see Figure 4.7). There is little variation from woman to woman in the amount of glandular tissue present in the breast, despite differences in size. This is why the amount of milk produced after childbirth does not correlate to the size of the breasts. Variation in breast size is due primarily to the amount of fatty tissue distributed around the glands. It is common for one breast to be slightly larger than the other.

Breast size is the source of considerable preoccupation for many people in our society. Large breasts are often considered to be linked with "sexiness," and cleavage is frequently depicted in advertising to help sell products. The availability of surgeries to enlarge or reduce the size of breasts reflects the dissatisfaction many women feel because their breasts do not fit the cultural ideal. (The ideal may be difficult to define because there are contradictory images of the slender, small-breasted, elegant cover girl and the buxom woman.) Many women believe that their breasts are too small, too big, or not the right shape:

> In talking with my friends about how we feel about our breasts, I discovered that not one of us feels really comfortable about how they look. I've always been envious of women with large breasts because mine are small. But my friends with large breasts talk about feeling self-conscious about their breasts too. (Authors' files)

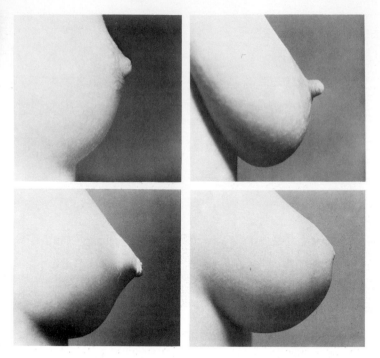

Breast size and shape vary from woman to woman.

The glandular tissue in the breast responds to sex hormones. During adolescence both the fatty and the glandular tissue develop markedly. Breasts show some size variations at different phases of the menstrual cycle and when influenced by pregnancy, nursing, or birth control pills.

The **nipple** is in the center of the **areola**, the darker area of the external breast. The areola contains sebaceous (oil-producing) glands that help lubricate the nipples during breast feeding. The openings of the mammary glands are in the nipples. Some nipples point outward from the breast, others are flush with the breast, and still others sink into the breast. When small muscles at the base of the nipple contract in response to sexual arousal, tactile stimulation, or cold, the nipples become erect.

Breast Self-Exam

A monthly breast examination is an important part of self-health care for women. This exam can help a woman know what is normal for her own breasts. She can do the breast exam herself and can also teach her partner to do it. The steps of a breast exam are illustrated in Box 4.1. Because of cyclic changes in the breast tissue, the best time to do the routine exam is following menstruation. For a woman who is not menstruating (during pregnancy, or after menopause or a hysterectomy), doing the exam at the same time each month is best. Many breasts normally feel lumpy. Once a woman becomes familiar with her own breasts, she can notice changes. If there is a change she should consult a physician, who may recommend further diagnostic testing. It is helpful to fill out a chart, like the one shown in Figure 4.8, to keep track of lumps in the breasts.

Monthly Breast Exam Record

Fill out this chart each month when you examine your breasts. Record the date you do the examination and the date your last period started. For any lump you find, mark

(a) its location
(b) its size (BB, pea, raisin, grape)
(c) its shape (rounded or elongated)

Compare each month's record with the last one, and consult your health care provider if there are any changes. A new or changing lump should be checked as soon as possible, although most such lumps will prove to be benign.

Today's date _____

Last period started _____

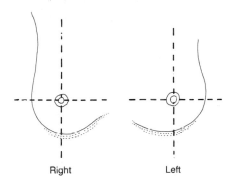

Right   Left

Today's date _____

Last period started _____

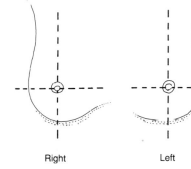

Right   Left

Today's date _____

Last period started _____

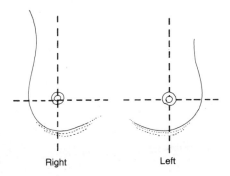

Right   Left

Today's date _____

Last period started _____

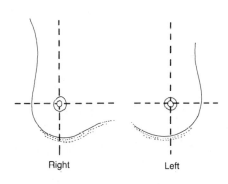

Right   Left

Concept from Kaiser Foundation Health Plan of Oregon.
Adapted with permission of Kaiser Permanente.

Figure 4.8

**Breast Exam
Chart**

1. In the shower

Examine your breasts during bath or shower; hands glide more easily over wet skin. With fingers flat, move your hands gently over every part of each breast. Use your right hand to examine your left breast, left hand for your right breast. Check for any lump, hard knot, or thickening.

2. Before a mirror

Inspect your breasts with arms at your sides. Next, raise your arms high overhead. Look for any changes in the contour of each breast: a swelling, dimpling of the skin, or changes in the nipple.

Then, rest your palms on your hips and press down firmly to flex your chest muscles. Left and right breast will not match exactly—few women's breasts do.

Mammography is a highly sensitive X-ray screening test for cancerous breast lumps. It uses low levels of radiation to create an image of the breast, called a *mammogram*, on film or paper. Mammography can often detect a breast lump before it can be felt manually. Mammography is currently the only technique that can image the breast and find a lump that is one centimeter or smaller. Some other tests can provide further diagnostic information about a lump (Kopans et al., 1984).

The American Cancer Society currently recommends a baseline mammogram between the ages of 35 and 40, a routine mammogram every one to two years during the forties, and a yearly mammogram for women over 50. Mammography is a highly effective screening test, but it is not 100% effective. The best method for early detection of breast cancer is a combination of monthly manual self-exams, routine exams by a health care practitioner, and mammography as recommended.

Breast Lumps

Three types of lumps can occur in the breasts. The two most common are *cysts* (fluid-filled sacs) and *fibroadenomas* (solid, rounded tumors). Both of these are benign (not cancerous or harmful) tumors, and together they account for approximately 80 percent of breast lumps. One study indicates that women who have benign breast lesions actually have a slightly lower incidence of breast cancer than women in the general population (Dupont and Page, 1985). Some researchers believe that caffeine in coffee, tea, cola drinks, and chocolate can contribute to the development of benign breast lumps. They report that breast lumps disappeared in many patients who eliminated

3. Lying down

To examine your right breast, put a pillow or folded towel under your right shoulder. Place your right hand behind your head—this distributes breast tissue more evenly on the chest. With your left hand, fingers flat, press gently in small circular motions around an imaginary clock face. Begin at the outermost top of your right breast for twelve o'clock, then move to one o'clock, and so on around the circle back to twelve. A ridge of firm tissue in the lower curve of each breast is normal. Then move in an inch, toward the nipple, and keep circling to examine *every part of your breast,* including the nipple. This requires at least three more circles. Now slowly repeat this procedure on your left breast.

Finally, squeeze the nipple of each breast gently between thumb and index finger. Any discharge, clear or bloody, should be reported to your doctor immediately.

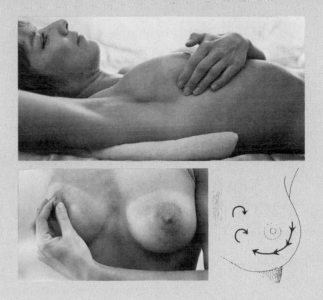

caffeine from their diet (Minton et al., 1979). The third kind of breast lump is a *malignant tumor* (a tumor made up of cancer cells). Breast cancer is the most common cancer in women, and approximately 9 percent of women will get breast cancer (American Cancer Society, 1985).

If a lump is found, further diagnostic testing is necessary. *Needle aspiration* involves inserting a fine needle into the lump to determine if there is fluid inside. If so, it is usually a cyst and can be drained. A biopsy of the tissue of any lump can be analyzed for cancer cells.

Once breast cancer has been diagnosed, several forms of treatment may be used. Radiation therapy, chemotherapy, hormone therapy, immunotherapy, surgery, or a combination of these procedures may be performed. How much of the breast and surrounding tissue is removed by surgery varies from *radical mastectomy* (entire breast, underlying muscle, and lymph nodes are removed) to a *partial mastectomy* (the lump and small amounts of surrounding tissue are removed). If the cancer has not spread too far, a partial mastectomy provides as good a chance of a cure as a radical mastectomy (Fisher et al., 1985). Research also indicates that sexual adjustment is better following partial than radical mastectomy (Steinberg et al., 1985).

Breast cancer and its treatments may affect sexual adjustment. Beyond the physical recuperation from surgery and side effects of other treatments, the loss of one or both breasts almost certainly has special meaning to a woman and her present or potential partners. In our culture the female breast is often considered a symbol of a woman's femininity and is a vital part of her body image. Breast stimulation—looking, touching, kissing—is often an important component of sexual arousal for a woman and her partner, and consequently, surgical removal of one or both breasts may create problems in sexual adjustment (Frank et al., 1978; Margolis and Goodman, 1984).

A mastectomy presents unique problems to a woman who is not in a long-term relationship. She may have difficulty deciding when to tell someone she is dating about her surgery. Her own feelings of acceptance and comfort and her judgment about timing are important. Also, she needs to understand that her partner will require some time to adjust to the information about her mastectomy. Still, it may help her to keep in mind that a loving relationship is based on more than physical characteristics.

The American Cancer Society's Reach to Recovery program provides a very important service to these women; volunteers in the program, who have all had one or both breasts removed, meet with a woman who has recently undergone a mastectomy and offer her emotional support and encouragement. They also provide positive models of women who have made a successful adjustment to their surgery.

Fortunately, reconstructive breast surgery or an external prosthesis (an artificial breast) may enhance a woman's general and sexual adjustment following a mastectomy. For example, an exterior silicone prosthesis can be matched to the other breast and worn inside a bra. In some cases a new breast can be made from a pouch containing silicone gel and placed under the woman's own skin. To improve the possibilities for breast reconstruction, it can be quite helpful to have presurgical discussions with both the surgeon removing the tissue and the plastic surgeon doing the reconstruction.

Because cancer spreads, it is especially important to remember that early detection leads to a higher survival rate, less drastic surgery, and easier and more successful breast reconstruction.

Menstruation

While **menstruation** is a sign of normal physical functioning, negative attitudes about it persist in contemporary American society. For example, in the television production, "All in the Family," Archie Bunker stated:

ARCHIE: Yes, that's right, you don't believe me. Read your Bible. Read the story about Adam and Eve there. Adam and Eve, they had it pretty soft out in Paradise. They had no problems. They didn't even know they was naked. But Eve, she wasn't satisfied with that, see. And one day, against direct orders, she made poor Adam eat that apple. God got sore. He told them to get their clothes on and get the hell outta there. And that's why Eve was cursed. And that's why they call it what he called it, the curse.

MIKE: Well, there you have it, Gloria, straight from the Reverend Archie Bunker. The true story of menstruation.

ARCHIE: SSSHHHHHHH with that kinda word!*

Archie's attitude is reflected in a survey that revealed that 66 percent of the adults sampled believe menstruation should not be discussed at work or socially, and 25 percent believed it should not be discussed within the family (Milow, 1983).

---

*Written by: Michael Ross & Bernie West © Copyright 1973. Tandem Productions, Inc. All Rights Reserved.

Common American folklore reveals many interesting ideas about menstruation. It has been thought that a woman should not bathe or wash her hair during her menstrual period because she would become ill or stop menstruation. In the 1920s women commonly believed that a permanent wave given during menstruation would not curl their hair. Other myths include the belief that it is harmful for a woman to be physically active during menstruation, that domestic animals will not obey a menstruating woman, or that a man can regain his lost ability to have erections if he performs oral sex on a menstruating woman (McCary, 1973).

In spite of these myths and negative societal attitudes toward menstruation, some women and families are redefining it more positively. For example, some may have a celebration or give a gift to a young woman when she starts her first menstrual period. One of the aspects of the menstrual cycle that people often see as positive is its cyclic pattern typical of many natural phenomena. The poet May Sarton describes the analogy of the menstrual cycle and nature in this 1937 poem:

There were seeds
within her
that burst at intervals
and for a little while
she would come back
to heaviness,
and then before a surging miracle
of blood,
relax,
and re-identify herself,
each time more closely
with the heart of life.

'I am the beginning,
the never-ending,
the perfect tree.'
And she would lean
again as once
on the great curve of the earth,
part of its turning,
as distinctly part
of the universe as a star—
as unresistant,
as completely rhythmical.

Other Times, Other Places

Menstruation

Many societies have seen menstruation as unhealthy or supernatural. Great powers and danger have both been attributed to menstruation. The Roman historian Pliny stated that bees will leave their hive, boiling linen will turn black, and razors will become blunt if touched by a menstruating woman. In some societies a menstruating woman is restricted from certain activities or from contact with men. She may also be isolated from the entire community into a menstrual hut, as with the Arapesh in New Guinea. The Bible states, "And if a woman have an issue, and her issue in her flesh be blood, she shall be put apart seven days: and whosoever toucheth her shall be unclean until the even" (Lev. 15:19). Some writers believe that menstrual myths and taboos serve to control women and maintain their inferior social status (Weidiger, 1976).

In a few cultures menstruation is described in lyrical words and positive images. The Japanese expression for a girl's first menstruation is "the year of the cleavage of the melon," and one Indian description of menstruation is the "flower growing in the house of the god of love" (Delancy et al., 1976).

Menstrual Physiology

During the menstrual cycle the uterine lining is prepared for the implantation of a fertilized ovum. If conception does not occur, the lining sloughs off and is discharged as menstrual flow. The menstrual cycle usually begins in the early teens, between the ages of 11 and 15, although some girls begin earlier or later. Menstrual cycles end at menopause, which in most women occurs between 45 and 50. The first menstrual bleeding is called the **menarche**. The timing of the menarche appears to be related to heredity, general health, altitude (the average menarche is earlier in lower altitudes), and body weight (Sullivan, 1971).

The differences in timing of menarche is often a concern for young women, especially those who begin earlier or later than the norm:

> I felt very alone when I first started my periods late in the fifth grade because none of my friends had. In our school there were no Kotex machines in the kids' bathroom stalls, so I had to carry them in my purse and was afraid someone would see them. (Authors' files)

> Almost everyone had been menstruating for years before I started. I thought something was wrong with me but Mom said she started late, too. (Authors' files)

Many young women are not adequately informed about the developments and changes that attend the onset of menstruation. One study found that 43% of women reported feeling confused, frightened, panicky, or ill when they started their first period (Research Forecasts, 1981). In another study, 20% of mothers had told their seventh-grade daughters nothing about menstruation (Block, 1978). The information girls do receive may be scanty, confusing, or frightening:

> During the time my breasts started to develop, I came home from school one day to find a pamphlet from Kotex on my bed. Mom never said anything else; I guess she was waiting for me to ask. (Authors' files)

> My mother talked to me about menstruation, but my father never did. I felt like it was something I had to hide from him. (Authors' files)

> I really avoided boys like the plague after I started because my mom said, "Now you can get pregnant." (Authors' files)

Young men are probably even less likely to receive information about menstruation. One study found that men are most likely to learn about menstruation from friends (31%), school (21%), and mothers (20%). Ninety-one percent of both men and women thought that information about menstruation should be provided in schools (Research Forecasts, 1981).

The menstrual discharge consists of blood, mucus, and endometrial membranes that sometimes form small clots. The length of the menstrual cycle is usually measured from the beginning of the first day of flow to the day before the next flow begins. It is normal for the amount of menstrual flow (usually six to eight ounces) to vary. The cycle length is often 28 days but also varies from woman to woman; it can be anywhere from 21 to 40 days. These time differences occur in the phase before ovulation. Fourteen days, plus or minus two days, is the interval between ovulation and the onset of menstruation, even when there is several weeks' difference in the total length of the cycle. If a woman experiences a dramatic change in her usual pattern, she should seek medical attention.

An interesting phenomenon known as **menstrual synchrony** sometimes occurs among women who live together and have considerable contact with each other: They develop similar menstrual cycles. The function of the uniform cycles is unknown, but the trigger is believed to be related to the sense of smell (Jarrett, 1984; McClintock, 1971). Close physical contact with men may also influence ovulation. One study showed that women who had spent two or more nights with a man over a 40-day period were almost twice as likely to ovulate as women who had spent no more than one night with a man (Veith, 1983).

The menstrual cycle is divided into three stages, or phases: the **proliferative phase**, the **secretory phase**, and the **menstrual phase**. The hypothalamus and the pituitary gland (both located within the brain), the ovaries, and the uterus are all interrelated in this cyclic pattern (see Figure 4.9). The cycle is a self-regulating and dynamic process in which the level of a particular hormone retards or increases the production of the same and other hormones. We will describe the action of the regulatory hormones briefly here and in more detail in the discussions of the three phases.

Figure 4.9

The Menstrual Cycle

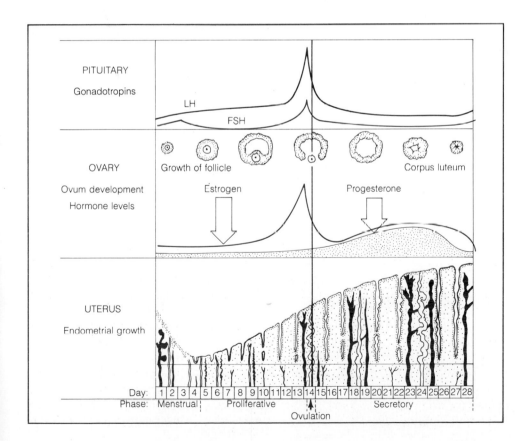

The hypothalamus monitors the levels of hormones in the bloodstream through-out the cycle, sending chemical messages to the pituitary gland, which in turn releases hormones to stimulate the ovaries. The hypothalamus produces chemicals known as *hypothalamic releasing factors*. The most important hypothalamic releasing factors related to menstruation are the *gonadotropic releasing factors*, which stimulate the pituitary to produce hormones that affect the ovaries. Once the pituitary gland receives the appropriate releasing factors from the hypothalamus, it produces **follicle-stimulating hormone (FSH)** or **luteinizing hormone (LH)**. These two hormones have the general name of *gonadotropins* because they stimulate the gonads (ovaries and testes). In the female, FSH stimulates ovarian production of estrogen and the maturation of the ova and *follicles* (small sacs, each of which contains an ovum). LH induces the mature ovum to burst from the ovary, and it stimulates the development of the **corpus luteum** (the portion of the follicle that remains after the egg has matured). The corpus luteum produces the hormone progesterone.

These glands do not produce a steady stream of hormones; there is a complex interaction among the glands that signals when to increase or decrease secretions. A

Figure 4.10

Changes During the Menstrual Cycle
The menstrual cycle during (a) the proliferative phase, including ovulation; (b) the secretory phase, and (c) the menstrual phase.

(a) PROLIFERATIVE PHASE

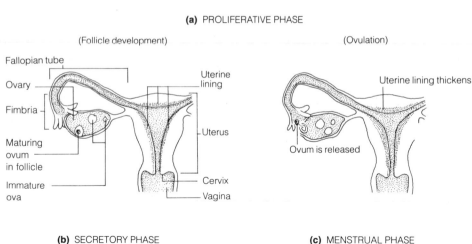

(Follicle development)

Fallopian tube
Ovary
Fimbria
Maturing ovum in follicle
Immature ova
Uterine lining
Uterus
Cervix
Vagina

(Ovulation)

Uterine lining thickens
Ovum is released

(b) SECRETORY PHASE

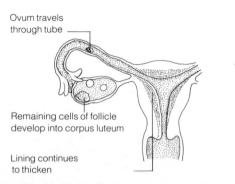

Ovum travels through tube
Remaining cells of follicle develop into corpus luteum
Lining continues to thicken

(c) MENSTRUAL PHASE

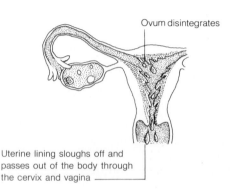

Ovum disintegrates
Uterine lining sloughs off and passes out of the body through the cervix and vagina

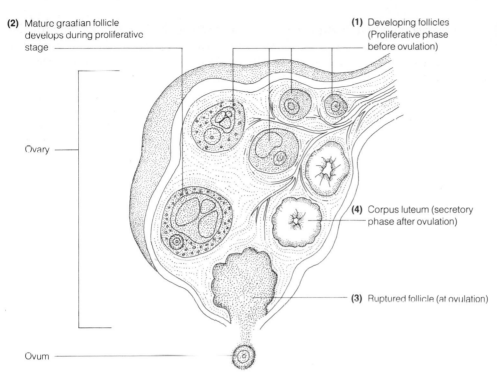

(2) Mature graafian follicle develops during proliferative stage

(1) Developing follicles (Proliferative phase before ovulation)

Ovary

(4) Corpus luteum (secretory phase after ovulation)

(3) Ruptured follicle (at ovulation)

Ovum

Figure 4.11

Ovarian Follicle Development
*Cross section of
an ovary showing
different stages
of follicle
development.*

hormone is secreted until the organ it acts upon is stimulated; at that point, the organ releases a substance that circulates back through the system to reduce hormonal activity in the initiating gland. The *negative feedback mechanism* provides an internal control that regulates fluctuations of hormonal production. In addition to the hormonal and ovarian changes already mentioned, the phases of the menstrual cycle involve changes in the uterine lining. The ovarian and uterine changes, which we will now discuss, are shown in Figure 4.10. Figure 4.11 shows ovarian follicle development in more detail.

Proliferative Phase.   During the proliferative phase of the menstrual cycle [Figure 4.10(a)], the pituitary gland increases production of FSH, which stimulates the developing follicles to mature and to produce several types of estrogen. Estrogen in turn causes the endometrium to thicken. Although several follicles begin to mature, usually only one, the **graafian follicle**, reaches maturity; the other follicles degenerate. When the level of ovarian estrogen circulating in the bloodstream reaches a peak, the pituitary gland depresses the release of FSH and stimulates LH production.

At approximately 14 days before the onset of the next menstrual period, **ovulation** occurs. In response to the spurt of LH secreted by the pituitary gland, the mature follicle ruptures and the ovum is released. Some women experience a twinge, cramp, or pressure in their lower abdomen, called *mittelschmerz* (German for "middle pain") at ovulation. Mittelschmerz is caused by the swelling and bursting of the follicle or by a little fluid or blood from the ruptured follicle that can irritate the sensitive abdominal lining. The released ovum then travels to the fimbria of the fallopian tube. Occasionally more than one ovum is released. If two ova are fertilized, fraternal twins will develop. When one egg is fertilized and then divides into two separate zygotes, identical twins result.

Around the time of ovulation there is an increase and a change in cervical mucus secretions, due to increased levels of estrogen. The mucus becomes clear, slippery, and stretchy. The pH of this mucus is more alkaline; as noted earlier, a more alkaline vaginal environment contributes to sperm mobility and longevity. This is the time in the cycle when a woman can most easily become pregnant.

Secretory Phase.   During the secretory phase [Figure 4.10(b)], continued pituitary secretions of LH cause the cells of the ruptured follicle to develop into a yellowish bump called the corpus luteum. The corpus luteum secretes progesterone, which inhibits the production of the cervical mucus produced during ovulation. Progesterone, together with estrogen produced by the ovaries, causes the endometrium to thicken and engorge with blood in preparation for implantation of a fertilized egg. If implantation does not occur, the pituitary gland, in response to high estrogen and progesterone levels in the bloodstream, shuts down production of LH and FSH. This deprives the corpus luteum of the necessary chemical stimulation to produce hormones; the corpus luteum degenerates, and estrogen and progesterone production decreases. This reduction of hormone levels triggers the sloughing off of the endometrium during the menstrual phase.

Menstrual Phase.   During the menstrual phase [Figure 4.10(c)], the uterus sheds the thickened inner layer of the endometrium, which is discharged through the cervix and vagina as menstrual flow. Menstrual flow typically consists of blood, mucus, and endometrial tissue.

As we have noted, the shedding of the endometrium is the result of reduced amounts of progesterone and estrogen. As the hormone level in the bloodstream continues to fall, the hypothalamus responds to the reduction by stimulating the pituitary to release FSH. The release of FSH initiates the maturation process of several follicles, and the cycle begins again.

Sexual Activity and the Menstrual Cycle

A common taboo in our culture has to do with intercourse during menstruation. One phone interview survey found that 51% of men and 56% of women believed that women should abstain from intercourse during menstruation (Research Forecasts, 1981). Although we know today that from a medical point of view there are no health reasons to avoid intercourse during menstruation (except in the case of excessive bleeding or other menstrual problems), many couples do so.

Reasons for avoiding sex during a woman's period vary. Some women resist sexual activity because of culturally induced shame about menstruation. Uncomfortable physical symptoms of menstruation often reduce sexual desire or pleasure, and the messiness or the spilling of blood on sheets can inhibit sexual activity. Religious beliefs can also be a factor.

If people do prefer to abstain from coitus during menstruation, the remaining repertoire of sexual activities is still available:

> When I'm on my period, I leave my tampon inside and push the string in, too. My husband and I have manual and oral stimulation, *and* a great time! (Authors' files)

Some women use a diaphragm to hold back the menstrual flow during coitus. Orgasm by any means of stimulation can be beneficial to a menstruating woman. The uterine contractions and release of vasocongestion often reduce backache and feelings of pelvic fullness and cramping.

A number of studies have attempted to determine whether a correlation exists between menstrual cycle changes and sexual behavior. There is some inconsistency in the findings of various researchers. Some studies show no significant variations in sexual arousal at different points in the menstrual cycle (Morrell et al., 1984). Others indicate a pattern of increase in sexual feelings and behavior during the ovulatory phase and the *paramenstrual* phase, which includes the menstrual period and the preceding few days (Friedman, 1980). In an attempt to control for external variables such as contraceptive use, fear of pregnancy, and male influence, one study examined the relationship between cycle phase and sexual response and activity in a sample of lesbians. In this sample, partner and self-initiated sexual activity peaked at midcycle, as did orgasm, but sexual thoughts and fantasies peaked in the first three days following onset of menstruation (Matteo and Rissman, 1984). There is great individual variation from woman to woman. We encourage women readers and their partners to notice their own patterns.

Menstruation: Mood and Performance

Because so many sociocultural, psychological, and biological factors interact, no one research study can completely analyze the complex relationship between behavior and the menstrual cycle (Friedman, 1980). It appears, though, that most women experience negative mood changes during the premenstrual week and menstrual period (Dennerstein et al., 1984). Many women report an increase in feelings of anxiety, irritability, and sadness just before and during their menstrual periods.

Not all women experience negative mood changes associated with menstruation, and among women who do individual differences are considerable. Box 4.2 offers some suggestions to men on how to help their partners cope with menstruation.

Some researchers believe that self-report studies of menstrual mood changes may be biased when the subjects know the purpose of the questionnaire is to study menstrual symptoms. Cycle phase differences found in such self-reports may reflect stereotypes or social expectations of the menstrual experience (Ruble and Brooks-Gunn, 1979). When women are unaware of the nature of the study, they often fail to show cyclic fluctuations of symptoms (Brooks et al., 1977). For example, one study asked 35 male and 35 female college students to complete a daily checklist of symptoms without knowing the research was on menstrual symptoms. Subjects of both sexes were equally likely to report feeling depressed, nervous, bloated, weak, irritable, or nauseated, regardless of the time of month. Only increases in sharp cramps, dull aching cramps, backache, and facial blemishes were tied to menstruation (Cox, 1983).

Men who make love with women have to deal in some way with menstruation. Caring about a woman's experience of her period may help to avoid misunderstandings and build intimacy.

You might ask a lover if she gets cramps, and if so how they feel. Pain is not the only consideration. The bloated feeling caused by water retention may not *hurt*, but it can be fairly uncomfortable. In some women with pronounced menstrual water retention, it can feel like the flu.

A man can do several things to help a woman deal with dysmenorrhea. He might make her a cup of soothing herbal tea—chamomile and mint herb teas may be especially effective—or massage her lower back or abdomen.

Try to discuss how a lover feels about making love premenstrually or during her period. Some women prefer not to: discomfort can interfere with the undivided attention lovemaking deserves. On the other hand, some women say lovemaking right before or during menstruation helps alleviate cramps. During orgasm the uterus contracts and the cervix opens. This helps speed menstrual flow and can reduce the duration of cramps. Men should bear in mind, however, that this is not an experience shared by all women. Also, ask about breast tenderness and keep it in mind during sensual explorations.

Different cultures and religions have different perspectives on lovemaking during a woman's period. As a result, many people—both men and women—have deep feelings about it. It is important to listen carefully to a lover's feelings about making love during menstruation and to try to respect them.

For couples who do make love during a woman's period, there are several things to keep in mind. Menstruation may change a woman's natural vaginal lubrication. Menstrual fluid irritates some penises, and a man can use a condom if this is a problem. Intercourse with a tampon in place is not recommended, but a woman can use a diaphragm or cervical cap to catch the flow. Even if a barrier method is not your primary or preferred form of contraception, you may want to use one at this time.

If a couple would rather not have genital intercourse during the woman's period, there are other satisfying ways to make love, though some men prefer not to provide oral-clitoral stimulation during menstruation.

The bottom line is: Try to talk about the issues menstruation raises in your relationship and how you both feel most comfortable dealing with them. (Adapted from Michael Castleman, 1981b)

Research has also examined the relationship between menstrual changes and women's ability to perform various tasks. A review of studies that used objective performance measures like academic examinations, factory production, and reaction time shows no demonstrable changes related to the menstrual cycle. The objective measures of task performance, however, frequently differed from the women's subjective evaluations of their performance. Some women believed that their level of performance decreased during the paramenstrual period (Sommer, 1973). This discrepancy in subjective and objective evaluation of performance may be related to attitudes and expectations. One study indicated that many people believe menstruation has a significant effect on ability. For example, 26% of the respondents thought that women could not perform their jobs as well, and 35% believed that women could not think as well during menstruation (Research Forecasts, 1981). However, further research is required before we can draw conclusions about the cause of this inconsistency in subjective and objective performance.

Menstrual Cycle Problems

Most women undergo some physical or mood changes, or both, during their menstrual cycles. In many cases the changes are minor. Sometimes, however, more serious problems with the menstrual cycle occur.

Premenstrual syndrome, or **PMS**, is the term used to identify a myriad of physical and psychological symptoms that occur before each menstrual period and are severe enough to interfere with some aspects of life. It is important to identify the cyclic manifestation of the symptoms in order to differentiate PMS from other physical or psychological problems. Approximately 30% of women experience some degree of PMS (Laube, 1985). The cause, or causes, of PMS are unknown, but fluctuations in sex steroids and their effects on various organ systems is believed to be involved.

Reported PMS symptoms include psychological discomfort such as anxiety, irritability, depression, anger, insomnia, and confusion; and physical symptoms, which may include fluid retention, breast tenderness, weight gain, fatigue, headaches, increased appetite, and craving for sweets. These symptoms may vary from mild to severe, and most women experience several of them (Abraham, 1981).

Research about the nature, cause, and treatment of PMS lacks consistency and offers contradictory results. For example, the premenstrual period is defined as beginning anywhere from four to six days before menstruation and as ending at the onset or after four days of menstruation. Symptom severity is often not measured. There is no generally accepted way of rating a syndrome that more often consists of internally experienced symptoms than objective behavioral signs. There is also a lack of consistent data in support of any single cause, in part due to the differing methods used to obtain research results. And despite anecdotal reports of the successful use of hormones, medications, or vitamins, no treatment has proven effective in placebo-controlled, double-blind studies (studies in which neither experimenter nor subject knows which treatment is being given) performed to date (Rubinow and Roy-Byrne, 1984).

Painful menstruation is called **dysmenorrhea**. *Primary dysmenorrhea* occurs during menstruation and is usually caused by the overproduction of **prostaglandins**, a class of chemicals produced by body tissue. Uterine prostaglandins cause the muscles of the uterus to contract. Most uterine contractions are not even noticed, but strong ones are painful. The uterus may begin to contract too strongly or frequently and temporarily deprive the uterus of oxygen, causing pain (American College of Obstetricians and Gynecologists, 1985). Problems with primary dysmenorrhea usually appear with the onset of menses at adolescence. The symptoms are generally most noticeable during the first few days of a woman's period and include abdominal aching and/or cramping. Some women may also experience nausea, vomiting, diarrhea, headache, dizziness, fatigue, irritability, or nervousness.

Antiprostaglandin medications, which inhibit the body's production of prostaglandins, are sometimes used to treat women who experience severe, debilitating primary dysmenorrhea (Owen, 1984). Although these medications have some side effects, they are being successfully used to treat this problem. Aspirin also prevents protaglandin production and is helpful in milder cases. Oral contraceptives relieve or reduce the pain of primary dysmenorrhea by altering the normal hormonal changes of the menstrual cycle, which results in a lower level of prostaglandins.

Secondary dysmenorrhea occurs prior to or during menstruation and is characterized by constant and often spasmodic lower abdominal pain that typically extends to the back and thighs. The symptoms are often similar to those of primary dysmenorrhea and are caused by factors other than prostaglandin production; possible causes include the presence of an intrauterine device (IUD), pelvic inflammatory disease (chronic infection of the reproductive organs), endometriosis, benign uterine tumors, and obstruction of the cervical opening. *Endometriosis*, a condition in which endometrial cells from the uterine lining implant in the abdominal cavity, affects up to 15% of premenopausal women (Malinik and Wheeler, 1985). The implanted endometrial tissue often adheres to other tissue in the pelvic cavity and reduces mobility of the internal structures. In addition, the endometrial implants engorge with blood during the proliferative phase. The engorged tissues and adhesions can cause painful menstruation, lower backache, and pain from pressure and movement during intercourse. Following a diagnosis of the cause of secondary dysmenorrhea, appropriate treatment can be implemented.

Women may be able to alleviate some of the unpleasant symptoms accompanying menstruation by their own actions (Ritz, 1981; Hopson and Rosenfeld, 1984). Moderate exercise throughout the month, as well as proper diet, can contribute to improvement of menstrual-related difficulties. For example, an increase in fluids and fiber will help with the constipation that sometimes occurs before and during menstruation. Decreasing salt intake and avoiding food high in salt (salad dressing, gravies, bacon, pickles, to name a few) can help reduce swelling and bloating caused by water retention. Food supplements such as calcium, magnesium, and B vitamins also sometimes help to relieve cramps and bloating. One writer (Burdoff, 1980) recommends small, frequent meals of low-carbohydrate, low-fat, high-protein foods for women with problems of dizziness. She also suggests cutting down on daily caffeine intake to help reduce breast tenderness during the paramenstrual state. Stress reduction strategies that include relaxation training, taking time for oneself, and supportive counseling may be helpful.

When a woman experiences menstrual-related pain, it can be useful for her to keep a diary to track symptoms, stresses, and daily habits such as exercise, diet, and sleep. She may be able to note a relationship between symptoms and habits and modify her activities accordingly. The information may also be helpful for specific diagnosis if she consults a health care practitioner.

Besides discomfort or pain, another fairly common menstrual difficulty is **amenorrhea**, the absence of menstruation. There are two types of amenorrhea, primary and secondary. Primary amenorrhea is the failure to begin to menstruate at puberty. It may be caused by problems with the reproductive organs, hormonal imbalances, poor health, or an imperforate hymen. Secondary amenorrhea involves the disruption of an established menstrual cycle, with the absence of menstruation for three months or more. This is a normal condition during pregnancy and breast feeding. It is also common in women who have just begun menstruating and women approaching menopause. Sometimes poor health and emotional distress are the causes (Maddux, 1975).

Hormonal problems can also produce amenorrhea. Women with anorexia nervosa, an eating disorder that often results in extreme weight loss, frequently stop menstruating due to hormonal changes that accompany emaciation (Clappison, 1981). Women who discontinue the birth control pill occasionally do not resume menstruation for several months, but this situation is usually temporary and resolves spontaneously. It is a good idea for a woman who does not have a period when expected to consult a health care practitioner.

Amenorrhea is more common among athletes than among the general population (Shangold, 1985). For example, approximately 30 percent of a sample of American female athletes reported missed menstrual periods during training for and participation in the Montreal Olympic games (Webb et al., 1979). It is not known whether the lack of menstruation in athletes is caused by intensive exercise, low body fat, the physical or emotional stress of training and competing, or a combination of all of these (Loucks and Horvath, 1985). The amenorrhea may also be due to medical problems unrelated to athletics. Thus, it is important for a female athlete to seek medical evaluation for menstrual irregularities (Shangold, 1980a).

Toxic Shock Syndrome

In May 1980 the Centers for Disease Control published the first report about **toxic shock syndrome (TSS)** in menstruating women. Symptoms of toxic shock syndrome, which is caused by toxins produced by the bacterium *Staphylococcus aureus,* include fever, sore throat, nausea, vomiting, diarrhea, red skin flush, dizziness, and high blood pressure.

Although TSS has received a great deal of publicity, it is important to remember that it is a rare disease and the chances of contracting it are quite low. The number of TSS cases reported has fallen sharply since the peak in 1980 (Johnson, 1985). It is most likely to occur in women during menstruation and is associated with the use of tampons. However, up to 20% of all cases are nonmenstrual. Some occur postpartum and others in connection with postoperative wounds. Though TSS is predominantly a disease of women between 15 and 24 years of age, postmenopausal women, children, and men have also contracted it (Johnson, 1985). Because toxic shock syndrome progresses rapidly and can cause death, a person with several of the symptoms of TSS should immediately consult a physician (Taylor and Lockwood, 1981; Tanner et al., 1981).

Some guidelines have been developed that may help prevent toxic shock. One suggestion has been to use sanitary napkins instead of tampons. Suggestions for women who want to continue using tampons include: use regular instead of superabsorbent tampons, change them three to four times during the day, and use napkins sometime during each 24 hours during menstrual flow. A woman should consult her health care practitioner for further up-to-date suggestions pertaining to prevention and detection of TSS.

Summary

Genital Self-Exam

1. Genital self-exploration is a good way for a woman to learn about her own body and to notice any changes that may require medical attention.

The Vulva

2. The female external genitals, also called the vulva, are composed of the mons veneris, labia majora, labia minora, clitoris, and urethral and vaginal openings. Each woman's vulva is unique in shape, color, and texture.

3. The mons veneris and labia majora have underlying pads of fatty tissue and are covered by pubic hair beginning at adolescence.

4. The labia minora are folds of sensitive skin which begin at the hood over the clitoris and extend downward to below the vaginal opening, or introitus. The area between them is called the vestibule.

5. The clitoris is composed of the external glans and shaft and the internal crura. The glans contains densely concentrated nerve endings. The only function of the clitoris is sexual pleasure.

6. The urethral opening is located between the clitoris and vaginal introitus. About one out of every five women will experience a urinary tract infection caused by bacteria that enter the urethra.

7. Many cultures have placed great importance on the hymen as proof of virginity. However, there are various sizes, shapes, and thicknesses of hymens, and many women can have initial intercourse without pain or bleeding. Also, women who have decided to have coitus can learn how to stretch their hymens to help make their first experience comfortable.

Underlying Structures

8. Below the surface of the vulva are the vestibular bulbs and the pelvic floor muscles.

Internal Structures

9. The vagina, with its three layers of tissue, extends about three to five inches into the pelvic cavity. It is a potential rather than an actual space and increases in size during sexual arousal, coitus, and childbirth. The other internal reproductive structures are the cervix, uterus, fallopian tubes, and ovaries.

10. Vaginal lubrication, the secretion of alkaline fluid through the vaginal walls during arousal, is important both in enhancing the longevity and motility of sperm cells and in increasing the pleasure and comfort of intercourse.

11. The Grafenberg spot is located about one centimeter above the surface of the top wall of the vagina. Many women report erotic sensitivity to pressure in some area of their vaginas.

12. The vaginal walls and cervix produce normal secretions. Occasionally, a vaginal infection occurs that results in irritation, unusual discharge, or a disagreeable odor.

13. A hysterectomy or oophorectomy may, in some cases, have an effect—either positive or negative—on a woman's sexuality.

The Breasts

14. The breasts are composed of fatty tissue and milk-producing glands. A monthly self-exam of the breasts is an important part of health care.

15. Three types of lumps can appear in the breasts; cysts, fibroadenomas, and malignant tumors. Careful diagnosis of a breast lump is important. Mammography, ultrasonography, and thermography can help detect and diagnose breast cancer. Less radical surgeries for breast cancer are often as effective as more severe procedures.

Menstruation

16. The menstrual cycle results from a complex interplay of hormones. The cycle is divided into the proliferative, the secretory, and the menstrual phases. While negative social attitudes have been historically attached to menstruation, some people are currently redefining it in a more positive fashion.

17. There are usually no medical reasons to abstain from intercourse during menstruation. However, many people do limit their sexual activity during this time.

18. There is conflicting evidence about the effects of the menstrual cycle on mood and performance. Many women report cyclic changes, but studies do not always confirm such reports.

19. Some women have difficulties with premenstrual syndrome or primary or secondary dysmenorrhea. Knowledge about the physiological factors that contribute to these problems is increasing, and some of the problems can be treated.

20. Amenorrhea occurs normally during pregnancy, breast feeding, and after menopause. It can also be due to medical problems or poor health.

21. Toxic shock syndrome is a rare condition that occurs most often in menstruating women. Its symptoms include fever, sore throat, nausea, red skin flush, dizziness, and high blood pressure. If untreated, it can be fatal.

Thought Provokers

1. What do you think are advantages and disadvantages to early and late physical maturation?

2. What do you observe in the media and in others' comments and reactions that indicates positive and negative attitudes about menstruation?

3. Do you think the U.S. government should take any action toward countries that practice female genital mutilation? If so, what? If not, why not?

Suggested Readings

Boston Women's Health Book Collective. *Our Bodies, Ourselves,* 3rd ed. New York: Simon & Schuster, 1984. A thorough exploration of female sexuality, anatomy, and physiology. The book has a strong emphasis on health care and covers such topics as sexual relationships, rape, VD, birth control, parenthood, and menopause.

Federation of Feminist Women's Health Centers. *A New View of a Woman's Body.* New York: Simon & Schuster, 1981. A new way of defining the clitoris. Extensive information on health care and exceptional color photographs of the vulva and cervix.

Friday, Nancy. *My Mother, Myself.* New York: Delacorte, 1977. A compelling integration of expert testimony and personal insight into many complex aspects of mother-daughter relationships, with an emphasis on the effects of this relationship on female sexuality.

Steinem, Gloria. "If Men Could Menstruate." *Ms.,* October 1978. A humorous yet provocative "political fantasy" about how menstruation would be treated in our society if men, instead of women, menstruated.

5

It is defin'd, a hollow boneless part,
Of better use, and nobler than the heart;
With mouth, but without eyes; it has a head
Soft as the lips, and as the cherry red.
Mersius
"The Cabinet of Love" (1718)

Male Sexual Anatomy and Physiology

Sexual Anatomy
Male Sexual Functions
Some Concerns About Sexual Functioning

Who needs a lecture on male anatomy? Certainly not the men in this class. It's hanging out there all our lives. We handle it and look at it each time we pee or bathe. So what's the mystery? Now the female body—that is a different story. That's why I'm in the class. Let's learn something that isn't so obvious. (Authors' files)

THE PRECEDING QUOTE, from a student in a sexuality class, illustrates two common assumptions. The first is that there is a simplicity about male sexual anatomy that requires little elaboration. A second, perhaps more subtle, implication is that female genital structures are, by comparison, considerably more complicated and mysterious. Neither of these assumptions is necessarily true. There is complexity as well as wide variation in the sexual anatomy of both men and women. Although increasing our understanding of complex biological sexual functions does not necessarily ensure sexual satisfaction, such knowledge may help us develop comfort with our bodies.

In recent years, there has been a strong movement among women to assume responsibility for understanding and influencing their own sexual health. There has not yet been an equivalent movement for men. We are hopeful that this will change; books like Zilbergeld's *Male Sexuality* (1978) may help. This text provides some excellent guidelines for a self-health program for men.

Perhaps male reluctance to move toward self-health care has been due to the fact that a male's anatomy "hangs right out there." Nevertheless, easy accessibility does not necessarily imply familiarity—and in fact, many men are quite ill at ease with the idea of a detailed self-exam. As in the preceding chapter, we encourage readers to use the pages that follow as a reference for their own self-knowledge.

Sexual Anatomy

We will begin with discussions of the various structures of the male sexual anatomy. Descriptive accounts are organized according to parts of the genital system for the reader's easy reference. Later in this chapter (and in Chapter 6), we will look more closely at the way the entire system functions during sexual arousal.

The Scrotum

The **scrotum**, or scrotal sac, is a loose pouch of skin that is an outpocket of the abdominal wall in the groin area (see Figure 5.1). Normally it hangs loosely from the body wall, although influences such as cold temperatures or sexual stimulation may cause it to move closer to the body.

The scrotal sac consists of two layers. The outermost is a covering of thin skin that is darker in color than other body skin. It typically becomes sparsely covered with hair at adolescence. The second layer, known as the *tunica dartos,* is composed of smooth muscle fibers and fibrous connective tissue.

Within the scrotal sac are two separate compartments, each of which houses a single **testis**, or testicle. (For a diagram of the testis within the scrotal sac, see Figure 5.3.) Each testis is suspended within its compartment by the **spermatic cord**. The spermatic cord contains the sperm-carrying tube, or **vas deferens**, as well as blood

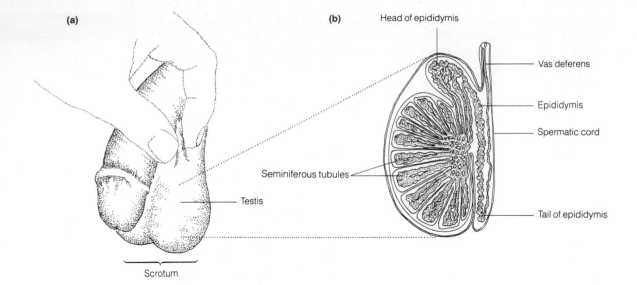

(a)

(b)

Head of epididymis

Vas deferens

Epididymis

Spermatic cord

Seminiferous tubules

Testis

Tail of epididymis

Scrotum

Figure 5.1

The Scrotum and Testes

(a) The spermatic cord can be located by palpating the scrotal sac above either testicle with thumb and forefinger. (b) Sperm is produced in the seminiferous tubules of the testes and transported to the epididymis, which serves as a storage chamber.

vessels, nerves, and **cremasteric muscle** fibers that influence the position of the testicle in the scrotal sac. These muscles can be voluntarily contracted, causing the testicles to move upward. Most males find they can produce this effect with practice; this exercise is one way for a man to become more familiar with his body. As shown in Figure 5.1, you can locate the spermatic cord by palpating the scrotal sac above either testicle with thumb and forefinger. The cord is a firm, rubbery tube that is generally quite pronounced.

The Testes

The **testes**, or testicles, have two major functions: the secretion of male sex hormones and the production of sperm. The testes form inside the abdominal cavity, and late in fetal development they migrate from the abdomen to the scrotum. The route they take is known as the **inguinal canal**.

At birth the testes are normally in the scrotum, but in some cases one or both fail to descend. This condition is known as **cryptorchidism** (meaning "hidden testis"). Estimates of the number of males born with cryptorchidism range from 1% to 7% (Campbell, 1970). Undescended testicles often move into place spontaneously sometime after birth, usually in the first year or two, and no treatment is needed. Occasionally, however, the condition is overlooked into adolescence, primarily because hormone production continues and the changes in body structures at puberty usually occur in routine fashion. The following account by a former student reflects this oversight:

> Your discussion of undescended testicles had quite an impact on me. The woman I live with has a 13-year-old son who has this condition. When I asked her about it, she just said, "That's the way it is with him." Obviously, she didn't ask the right questions or got some bad advice along the way. (Authors' files)

It is important to watch out for undescended testes, especially when both testicles are affected, because internal body temperature is too high to permit normal sperm production, and infertility may result. Surgery or hormonal treatment may be necessary to allow the testes to descend.

We are not certain of the exact relationship between heat and sperm production, but we do know that average scrotal temperature is approximately 3.1°C (5.6°F) lower than body temperature (Tessler and Krahn, 1966). In fact, both early and contemporary writers have suggested that hot baths may be an effective method of male contraception. There is some supporting evidence for this notion; for example, it has been reported that a 30-minute exposure to heat within a tolerable temperature range can arrest sperm production for as long as several weeks (Dickinson, 1949). Even so, sitting in the health spa steam room or a hot tub is not a recommended method of birth control. Considering the wide range of variables involved (for instance, temperature, frequency of exposure, or time in the bath), it would be reckless to rely on such a procedure to provide sufficient protection against conception.

In recent years there has been considerable speculation that higher-than-normal scrotal temperature may be related to male infertility. Tight clothing has been implicated by more than one writer. One study demonstrated that men who wore a specially designed jock strap had significant increases in scrotal temperature, with a corresponding lowering of their sperm count (Robinson and Rock, 1967). While it is unlikely that hot baths or tight garments have a significant effect on sperm production in most men, these conditions should not be overlooked as possible contributors in some cases of infertility.

The scrotum is very sensitive to any temperature change, and numerous sensory receptors in its skin provide information that prevents the testicles from becoming either too warm or too cold. When the scrotum is cooled, the tunica dartos contracts, wrinkling the outer skin layer and pulling the testicles up closer to the warmth of the body. This process is involuntary, and the reaction sometimes has amusing ramifications:

> When I took swimming classes in high school, the trip back to the locker room was always a bit traumatic. After peeling off my swim togs, it seemed like I had to search around for my balls. The other guys seemed to have the same problem, as evidenced by their frantic tugging and pulling as they tried to get everything back in place. (Authors' files)

Another kind of stimulation that causes the scrotum to draw closer to the body is sexual arousal. One of the clearest external indications of impending male orgasm is the drawing up of the testicles to a position of maximum elevation. The major scrotal muscle involved in this response is the cremasteric muscle, mentioned earlier. Sudden fear may also cause strong contractions of this muscle, and it is also possible to initiate contractions by stroking the inner thighs. This response is known as the **cremasteric reflex**.

The movements of the testes and scrotal sac are influenced by factors other than temperature change, sexual arousal, and strong emotion. These structures have the rather amazing property of virtually constant movement, a result of the continuous contraction-relaxation cycles of the cremasteric musculature.

Another testicle characteristic in most men is asymmetry. Note that in Figure 5.1 the left testicle hangs lower than the right. This is the case for most men, as the left spermatic cord is generally longer than the right. This difference in positioning has often been attributed to excessive masturbation, but there is no truth to this assertion. The difference is no more unusual than a woman having one breast larger than the other. Our bodies simply are not perfectly symmetrical.

We encourage you to become familiar with the geography of your testicles and to examine them on a regular basis. Recent research suggests that only a very small percentage of male college students, perhaps fewer than 10%, engage in regular self-examination of the genitals (Goldenring and Purtell, 1984). This is unfortunate, because a variety of diseases attack these organs, including cancer, venereal disease, and an assortment of infections. (Infections of the sex organs will be discussed in Chapter 18.) Most of these conditions produce observable symptoms, and early detection allows for rapid treatment and the prevention of more serious complications.

You may examine your testicles in a sitting position (see Figure 5.2), standing, or lying on your back. A good time for this exploration is after a hot shower or bath, since the heat causes the scrotal skin to relax and the testes to descend. With the scrotum in this relaxed, accessible state it may be easier to detect anything unusual. First, notice the cremasteric cycles of contraction and relaxation, and experiment with

Figure 5.2

Male Genital Self-Examination
Self examination can increase a man's familiarity with his genitals. Any irregularity, such as a lump or tender area, should be examined immediately by a physician.

initiating the cremasteric reflex. Then explore the testicles one at a time. Place the thumbs of both your hands on top of a testicle and the index and middle fingers on the underside. Then apply a small amount of pressure and roll the testicle beneath your fingertips. The surface should be fairly smooth and firm in consistency. There are individual variations in the contour and texture of male testicles, and it is important to get to know your own anatomy so that you can note changes. Having two testicles allows you the opportunity for direct comparison, and this is helpful in spotting abnormalities (although it is common for them to be slightly different in size).

Areas that appear swollen or are painful to the touch may indicate the presence of an infection. Along the back of each testicle lies a structure called the **epididymis**, from which the vas deferens carries sperm upward to the urethra. This structure occasionally becomes infected, sometimes causing an irregular area to become tender to the touch.

Testicular cancer accounts for approximately 1% of all cancers that occur in men. The probability that a man will develop this form of cancer sometime during his life is only about one in 500 (Altman, 1983). About 5000 American males are afflicted by this disease each year and most are 20 to 40 years old, although it can occur in men of any age. During the early stages of testicular cancer there usually are no symptoms beyond a mass within the testicle. The mass will feel hard or irregular to the fingertips and will be distinguishable from surrounding healthy tissue. It may be painless to touch, but some men do report tenderness in the area of the growth. Occasionally other symptoms are reported; these may include fever, tender breasts and nipples, and painful accumulation of fluid or swelling in the scrotum. Some types of testicular cancers tend to grow more rapidly than any other tumors that have been studied. Therefore, for successful treatment, it is important to detect the mass as soon as possible and to seek medical attention immediately. Improved therapeutic procedures have reduced the death rate to less than 15% among men treated for testicular cancer. Some men may be inclined to procrastinate in seeking medical treatment because they are afraid such procedures may create erectile problems or reduce their capacity to enjoy sexual pleasure. In fact, this occurs only rarely.

The Seminiferous Tubules. Within and adjacent to the testes are two separate areas involved in the production and storage of sperm. The first of these, the **seminiferous tubules** (sperm-bearing tubules), are thin, highly coiled structures located in the approximately 250 cone-shaped lobes that make up the interior of each testicle (see Figure 5.1). **Spermatogenesis**, or sperm production, takes place within these tubules. For most males this process begins sometime after the onset of puberty. Men continue to produce viable sperm cells well into their old age, often until death, although the production rate does diminish with aging. The **interstitial cells**, or **Leydig's cells**, are located between the seminiferous tubules. These cells are the major source of androgen, and their close proximity to blood vessels allows for direct secretion of their hormone products into the bloodstream. (We will discuss the role of hormones in sexual behavior in Chapter 6.)

The Epididymis. The second important area for sperm processing is the **epididymis** (literally, "over the testes"). The developed sperm move out of the seminiferous tubules through a maze of tiny ducts into this C-shaped structure that adheres to the back and upper surface of each testis (Figure 5.1). Evidence suggests that the epididymis serves primarily as a storage chamber where the sperm cells undergo additional maturing, or ripening, for a period of several weeks. During this time they are completely inactive. Researchers have theorized that a selection process also occurs in the epididymis, in which abnormal sperm cells are eliminated by the body's waste removal system.

The Vas Deferens

Eventually the sperm move through the epididymis and drain into the **vas deferens**, or ductus deferens, a long thin duct which travels up through the scrotum inside the spermatic cord. The vas deferens is close to the surface of the scrotum along this route, and this makes the common male sterilization procedure, **vasectomy**, relatively simple. (Vasectomy will be described in Chapter 11.)

The spermatic cord exits the scrotal sac through the inguinal canal, an opening that leads directly into the abdominal cavity. From this point the vas deferens continues its upward journey, looping over the ureter and behind the back of the bladder as shown in Figure 5.3. (This pathway is essentially the reverse of the route taken by the testis during its prenatal descent.) Turning downward, the vas deferens reaches the base of the bladder, where it is joined by the excretory duct of the **seminal vesicle**, forming the **ejaculatory duct**. The two ejaculatory ducts (one from each side) are very short, running their entire course within the **prostate gland**. At their termination they open into the prostatic portion of the **urethra**.

Figure 5.3

**Male Sexual
Anatomy**

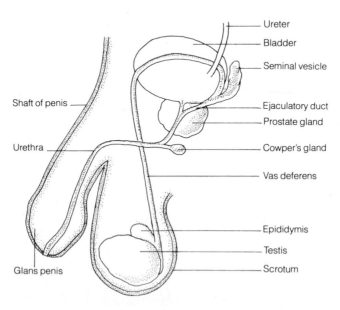

The Seminal Vesicles

The **seminal vesicles** are two small glands adjacent to the terminals of the vas deferens (Figure 5.3). Their role in sexual physiology is not completely understood at the present time. It was once assumed that they functioned primarily as storage centers for sperm. However, it is now known that they secrete an alkaline fluid that is very rich in fructose sugar. This secretion constitutes a major portion of the **seminal fluid**, perhaps as much as 70%, and its sugar component seems to contribute to sperm nutrition and motility (Spring-Mills and Hafez, 1980). Up to this point in its journey from the testicle, a sperm cell is transmitted through the elaborate system of ducts by the continuous movement of **cilia**, tiny hairlike structures that line the inner walls of these tubes. Once stimulated by the energy-giving secretions of the seminal vesicles, sperm propel themselves by the whiplike action of their tails.

The Prostate Gland

The **prostate gland** is a structure about the size and shape of a walnut, located at the base of the bladder (Figure 5.3). As described earlier, both ejaculatory ducts and the urethra pass through this organ. It is made up of smooth muscle fibers and glandular tissue, whose secretions account for about 30% of the seminal fluid released during ejaculation.

While the prostate is continually active in a mature male, it accelerates its output during sexual arousal. Its secretions flow into the urethra through a system of sievelike ducts, and here they combine with sperm and the seminal vesicle secretions to form the seminal fluid. The prostatic secretions are thin, milky, and alkaline in nature. This alkalinity helps to counteract the unfavorable acidity of the male urethra and the female vaginal tract, making a more hospitable environment for the sperm.

The prostate gland is the focal point of some of the more common physiosexual problems in the human male. Occasionally, it becomes enlarged and inflamed as a result of various infectious agents (such as the gonococcus bacterium and *Tricho-monas*). This condition, known as **prostatitis**, may occur in a man of any age. The symptoms of prostatitis may include any or all of the following: pain in the pelvic area or base of the penis, lower abdominal ache, backache, aching testicles, feelings of urgency (needing to urinate frequently), burning sensation while urinating, a cloudy discharge from the penis, and difficulties with sexual functions, such as painful erections or ejaculations and reduced sexual interest.

Some men also develop cancer of the prostate, and the potential for this becomes greater with increasing age. According to the American Cancer Society, approximately 20,000 men die each year from prostate cancer, the majority of whom would have been saved by early diagnosis and treatment. Consequently, it is very important for men to be aware of the early symptoms of this disease, which may include many of those listed for prostatitis (particularly pain in the pelvis and lower back and urinary complications). However, prostate cancer often lacks easily detectable symptoms in its early stages, and an early diagnosis may be accomplished only by a physical examination.

A physician examines the prostate by inserting a finger into the rectum. Under normal conditions this is only mildly uncomfortable. During this procedure the physician may also detect signs of cancer in the colon or rectum. The American Cancer Society recommends an annual digital rectal examination for men and women age 40 and older. Women too develop cancers of the rectum and colon—about 50,000 men and women die of these diseases each year.

Many men are reluctant to have this examination. They may be uncomfortable about homosexual associations when the examining physician is male, or they may fear what the examination might reveal. False information abounds in the area of prostate disease, and many men incorrectly believe that prostate surgery will inevitably block sexual functioning. The reality is that surgery on the prostate only occasionally results in major impairment of the biological aspects of male sexual function. We will say more about this in Chapter 15, in which we will discuss sexuality and aging.

The Cowper's Glands

The **Cowper's glands**, or **bulbourethral glands**, are two small structures, each about the size of a pea, located one on each side of the urethra just below where it emerges from the prostate gland (Figure 5.3). Tiny ducts connect both glands directly to the urethra. When a man is sexually aroused these organs often secrete a slippery, mucoid substance that appears in droplet form at the tip of the penis. Like the prostatic secretions, this fluid is alkaline in nature and helps to buffer the acidity of the urethra. Furthermore, it is thought to provide lubrication for the flow of seminal fluid through the penis. Contrary to some reports, though, it has virtually no function as a vaginal lubricant during coitus. In many men this secretion does not appear until well after the beginning of arousal, often just prior to orgasm. Other men report that it occurs immediately after they get an erection, and some individuals rarely or never produce these pre-ejaculatory droplets. All of those experiences are normal variations of male sexual functioning.

While the fluid from the Cowper's glands should not be confused with semen, it does occasionally contain active, healthy sperm. This is one reason among many why the withdrawal method of birth control is not highly effective. (Withdrawal and other methods of birth control will be discussed in Chapter 11.)

Semen

As we have seen, the **semen** ejaculated through the opening of the penis comes from a variety of sources. Fluids are supplied by the seminal vesicles, prostate, and Cowper's glands, with the seminal vesicles providing the greatest portion. The amount of seminal fluid a man ejaculates—roughly a teaspoonful on the average—is influenced by a number of factors, including the length of time since last orgasm; the duration of arousal time before ejaculation; and age (older men tend to produce less fluid). The semen of a single ejaculation typically contains between 200 and 500 million sperm, which account for only about one percent of the total volume of semen. Chemical analysis shows that semen is also made up of acids (ascorbic and citric), water, enzymes, fructose sugar, bases (phosphate and bicarbonate buffers), and a variety of other substances. None of these materials is harmful if swallowed during oral sex.

The Penis

The **penis** consists of nerves, blood vessels, fibrous tissue, and three parallel cylinders of spongy tissue. It does not contain a bone; neither does it possess an abundance of muscular tissue, contrary to some people's beliefs. However, there is an extensive network of muscles around the base of the penis, and these help to eject both semen and urine through the urethra.

A portion of the penis extends internally into the pelvic cavity. This part, including its attachment to the pubic bones, is referred to as the **root**. When a man's penis is erect he can feel this inward projection by pressing a finger up between his anus and scrotum. The external, pendulous portion of the penis, excluding the head, is known as the **shaft**. The smooth, acorn-shaped head is called the **glans**.

Running the entire length of the penis are the three chambers referred to earlier. The two larger ones, the **cavernous bodies** (corpora cavernosa), lie side by side above the smaller third cylinder called the **spongy body** (corpus spongiosum). At the root of the penis the innermost tips of the cavernous bodies, or **crura**, are connected to the pubic bones. At the head of the penis the spongy body expands to form the glans. It also enlarges at its base to form the **bulb** of the penis. These three structures are shown in Figure 5.4.

All of these chambers are similar in structure. As the terms *cavernous* and *spongy* imply, they are made of vast arrays of irregular spaces and cavities with spongelike properties. Each chamber is also richly supplied with blood vessels. When a male is sexually excited the chambers become engorged with blood, resulting in penile erection. During sexual arousal the spongy body may stand out as a distinct ridge along the underside of the penis.

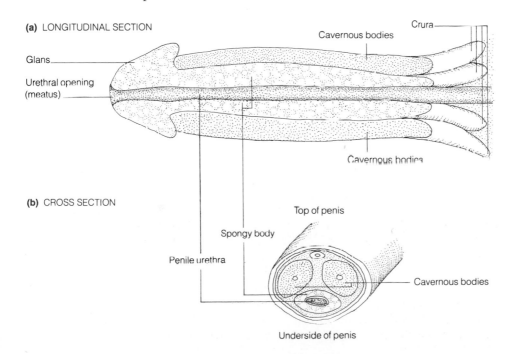

(a) LONGITUDINAL SECTION

Glans

Urethral opening
(meatus)

Crura

Cavernous bodies

Cavernous bodies

(b) CROSS SECTION

Top of penis

Spongy body

Penile urethra

Cavernous bodies

Underside of penis

Figure 5.4

Interior Structure of the Penis
Three parallel cylinders of erectile tissue (the cavernous bodies and spongy body) run the entire length of the penis.

The skin covering the penile shaft is usually hairless and quite loose, which allows for some expansion when the penis becomes erect. Though the skin is connected to the shaft at the neck (the portion just behind the glans), some of it folds over and forms a cuff, or hood, over the glans. This loose covering is called the **foreskin**, or **prepuce**. In some males it covers the entire head, while in others only a portion is covered. Typically, the foreskin can be retracted (drawn back from the glans) quite easily. **Circumcision**, discussed later in the chapter, involves the permanent removal of this sleeve of skin.

While the entire penis is sensitive to tactile (touch) stimulation, the greatest concentration of nerve endings is found in the glans. Although the entire glans area is extremely sensitive, there are two specific locations that many men find particularly responsive to stimulation. One is the rim, or crown, that marks the area where the glans rises abruptly from the shaft. This distinct ridge is called the **corona**. The other is the **frenum**, or **frenulum**, a thin strip of skin connecting the glans to the shaft on the underside of the penis. The location of these two areas is shown in Figure 5.5.

While most men enjoy stimulation of the glans, particularly the two areas mentioned above, individuals vary in their preferences. Some may occasionally or routinely prefer stimulation in genital areas other than the glans of the penis. The mode of stimulation, either manual (by self or partner) or oral, may influence the choice of preferred sites. Some of these variations and individual preferences are noted in the following accounts:

> When I masturbate I frequently avoid the head of my penis, concentrating instead on stroking the shaft. What happens is that the stimulation is not so intense, and that allows a longer time for build-up to orgasm. The end result is that the climax is generally more intense than if I focus only on the glans. (Authors' files)

Figure 5.5

Location of the Corona and Frenum
The corona and frenum are two areas on the penis that contain a great concentration of sensitive nerve endings.

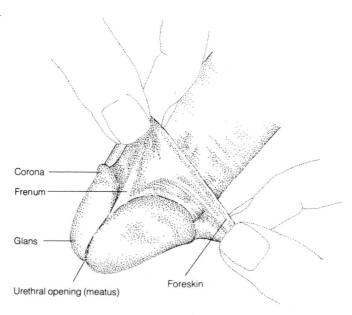

Corona

Frenum

Glans

Urethral opening (meatus)

Foreskin

Occasionally, when I make love for an extended period of time, my glans gets so sensitive that I can't stand to have it touched or sucked by my partner. In such cases I either have to stop for awhile or start having intercourse so the stimulation is not quite so intense. (Authors' files)

When I started making love with men rather than women, it was so much easier to get and give sexual pleasure. We both know where those special pleasure spots are and how a man likes to have them touched. Before, with women, it was always a hassle trying to get the message across. (Authors' files)

During oral sex with my girlfriend I sometimes have to put my hand around my penis, leaving just the head sticking out, so she will get the idea what part feels best to me. Otherwise, she spends a lot of time running her tongue up and down the shaft which just doesn't do it for me. (Authors' files)

In addition to demonstrating an array of stimulation preferences in men, these anecdotes, particularly the last two, reveal a common concern or difficulty that many of us experience in our sexual lives; namely, that it is often awkward to communicate our sexual needs and preferences. We live in a culture that provides few models of effective sexual communication. We will address this vital area in Chapter 8.

As previously mentioned, the internal extension of the penis is surrounded by an elaborate network of muscles. This musculature, the most important of which is the pubococcygeus (PC) muscle, is comparable to that in the female body, and strengthening these muscles by doing Kegel exercises may produce benefits for men similar to those experienced by women. In most men these muscles are quite weak, since they are usually only contracted during ejaculation. The following is a brief outline of how these muscles may be located and strengthened, adapted from *Male Sexuality* (Zilbergeld, 1978, p. 109):

1. Locate the muscles by stopping the flow of urine several times while urinating. The muscles you squeeze to accomplish this are the ones you will concentrate on. If you do a correct Kegel while not urinating, you will notice your penis move slightly. Kegels done when you have an erection will cause your penis to move up and down.

2. Begin the exercise program by squeezing and relaxing the muscles 15 times, twice daily. Do not hold the contraction at this stage. (These are called "short Kegels.")

3. Gradually increase the number of Kegels until you can comfortably do 60 at a time, twice daily.

4. Now practice "long Kegels" by holding each contraction for a count of three.

5. Combine the short and long Kegels in each daily exercise routine, doing a set of 60 of each, once or twice a day.

6. Continue with the Kegel exercises for at least several weeks. You may not notice results until a month or more has passed. By this time the exercises will probably have become automatic, requiring no particular effort.

Some of the positive changes men have reported after doing the male Kegels include stronger and more pleasurable orgasms, better ejaculatory control, and increased pelvic sensation during sexual arousal. In addition, some fascinating new research suggests that men can learn to experience multiple orgasms without ejaculating by tightening the PC and related muscles each time they reach the point of ejaculation (Hartman and Fithian, 1984). (Chapter 6 has a more detailed discussion of multiple orgasmic response in men and women.)

Caring for the penis is an important aspect of sexual self-health. Washing the penis regularly with soap and water, at least once a day, is an excellent self-health practice. (There is also evidence, discussed in Chapter 18, that washing the genitals before and after sex may reduce the chances of exchanging infectious organisms with your partner.) If you are uncircumcised, pay particular attention to drawing the foreskin back from the glans and washing all surfaces, especially the underside of the foreskin. Be aware of any unusual changes in your penis. A sore or unusual growth anywhere on its surface may be a symptom of a sexually transmitted disease. Sometimes the glans or shaft of the penis may develop an eczema-like reaction—"weepy" and sore. This may result from an allergic reaction to the vaginal secretions of your partner. Wearing a condom may help to alleviate this condition, but it is important that you consult a physician to clarify its origin and treatment. (**Urology** is the medical specialty that focuses on the male reproductive structures.)

It is wise to avoid abusing your penis by putting it in potentially harmful places, such as partners' mouths that have herpes blisters, or vaginas that manifest unusual sores, growths, odors, or discharges. There are some sexual gadgets that may also be quite hazardous to penile health. For example, never use a "cock ring" (a tight-fitting ring that encircles the base of the penis). Though this device may be successful in accomplishing its intended purpose of sustaining erections, it may also destroy penile tissue by cutting off the blood supply (Schellhammer and Donnelley, 1973). In recent years, sexually oriented magazines like *Penthouse* have published testimonials attesting to the pleasure of masturbating with a vacuum cleaner. This is not a good idea! A recent article by a Mayo Clinic urologist suggests that severe penile injuries (including decapitation of the glans) resulting from masturbating with vacuum cleaners and electric brooms may be much more common than reported (Benson, 1985).

On rare occasions, the penis may be fractured. This injury involves a rupture of the cavernous bodies when the penis is in an erect state. A review of the cases reported in the literature reveals that this injury most commonly occurs during coitus (Desterwitz et al., 1984). Recently a student reported his encounter with this painful injury.

> I was having intercourse with my girlfriend in a sitting position. She was straddling my legs and using the arms of the chair and her legs to move her body up and down on my penis. In the heat of passion she raised up a little too far and I slipped out. She sat back down hard, expecting me to repenetrate her. Unfortunately, I was off target and all of her weight came down on my penis. I heard a cracking sound and experienced excruciating pain. I bled quite a bit inside my penis and I was real sore for quite a long time. (Authors' files)

This account suggests that it is wise to take some precautions during coitus. This injury usually happens "in the heat of passion" and often involves putting too much weight on the penis when attempting to gain or regain vaginal penetration.

When the woman is on top, the risk increases. Communicating the need to go slow at these times can avert a painful injury. Treatment of penile fractures varies from measures like splinting and ice packs to surgery. Most men injured in this fashion regain normal sexual function, and surgical treatment generally provides the best results (Kalash and Young, 1984).

Male Sexual Functions

Up to this point in the chapter we have looked at the various parts of the male sexual system, but we have not described their functioning in much detail. In the following pages, we will examine two of these functions, erection and ejaculation.

Erection

An **erection** is essentially an involuntary process coordinated by the autonomic nervous system. When a male becomes sexually excited, the nervous system transmits messages that induce expansion of the arteries leading to the three erectile chambers in the penis. This increases the rate of blood flow into these parallel cylinders. The blood flowing out of the penis through the veins cannot keep up with the dramatically increased inflow, so blood accumulates in the spongelike tissues. The penis remains erect until the messages from the nervous system stop and the inflow of blood returns to normal.

The capacity for erection is present at birth. It is very common and quite natural for infant boys to experience erections during sleep or diapering, from stimulation by clothing, and later by touching themselves. Nighttime erections occur during the REM, or dreaming, stage of sleep (Fisher et al., 1965; Karacan, 1970). While erotic dreams may play a role, the primary mechanism seems to be physiological, and erections often occur even when the dream content is clearly not sexual. Often a man awakens in the morning just after completing a REM cycle. This explains the phenomenon of morning erections, which in the past have been erroneously attributed to a full bladder.

While an erection is basically a physiological response, it also involves psychological components. In fact, some writers distinguish between psychogenic (from the mind) and physiogenic (from the body) erections—although in most cases of sexual arousal there are simultaneous inputs from both thoughts and physical stimulation.

How great an influence does the mind have on erections? We know that it can inhibit the response: When a man becomes troubled by erection difficulties, the problem is often of psychological origin, as we will discuss in Chapter 16. It is even conceivable, given the developing science of biofeedback, that men might be trained to "think" an erection. However, this is an unlikely eventuality, at least for most men. Therefore, a man's penis, unlike other appendages of his body, will continue to act as though it has a will of its own, not always behaving in a way the mind might prefer.

Logically, one might expect erection to occur only in response to obvious sexual stimuli. That this is not always the case can be embarrassing, perplexing, amusing, or anxiety-arousing. Nearly every man can recall scenes of unwanted erections during adolescent school days—the teacher saying "Bob, come up here and do the math problem on the board," when math was the farthest thing from Bob's mind; the trips down school halls with a notebook held in a strategic location; the delayed exit from the swimming pool after playful frolicking.

Sometimes erections happen in situations that seem entirely nonsexual, such as riding a bike, lifting heavy weights, or straining during defecation (particularly in little boys). Occasionally, the occurrence of an erection produces considerable anxiety and causes a man to question his own motivations. This is evident in the following report offered by a father and former student in our sexuality class:

> Sometimes when my little girl crawls up on my lap to be cuddled, I find myself getting an erection. This bothers me greatly. Does it mean I have some kind of unconscious, incestuous craving for my daughter? (Authors' files)

This kind of experience, and the anxiety associated with it, is not unusual. It is possible to experience a reflex erection from direct physical stimulation during cuddling with a child. The response may also be psychologically induced by the association of physical closeness with sex, and thus it is probably a predictable event in our culture. Consider the following account:

> When I was a little boy my father would go away on extended business trips. I missed him terribly, and when he returned I wanted to rush across the room and catapult myself into his arms. Instead, like a man, I shook his hand and said "Hi, Dad, good to see you." (Authors' files)

Like this person, many men learn very early that it is not "masculine" to cuddle and embrace those near and dear to us. Among adult males in our society, intimate physical contact occurs primarily or exclusively within a sexual context. With this kind of conditioning, the association of warm embraces and sexual excitation will be quite strong. In this sense, it is not "unnatural" at all for a father to experience an erection when he holds his child closely.

Ejaculation

Besides erection, the second basic male sexual function is **ejaculation**—the process whereby the semen is expelled through the penis to the outside of the body. Many writers equate orgasm and ejaculation in the male. However, these two processes do not always take place simultaneously. Prior to puberty a boy may experience hundreds of orgasms without any ejaculation of fluid. Occasionally a man may have more than one orgasm in a given sexual encounter, with the second or third producing little or no expelled semen. Conversely, recent research reveals that some men may experience a series of nonejaculatory orgasms culminating in a final orgasm accompanied by expulsion of semen (Hartman and Fithian, 1984; Robbins and Jensen, 1978). Thus, it is clear that while male orgasm is generally associated with ejaculation, these two processes are not one and the same and they do not necessarily occur together.

From a neurophysiological point of view ejaculation, like erection, is basically a spinal reflex. Effective sexual stimulation of the penis (manual, oral, or coital) results in the buildup of neural excitation to a critical level. When a threshold is reached, this triggers several internal physical events.

The actual ejaculation occurs in two stages (see Figure 5.6). During the first stage, sometimes called the **emission phase**, the prostate, seminal vesicles, and **ampulla** (upper portions of the vas deferens) undergo contractions. This forces their various secretions down into the ejaculatory ducts and prostatic urethra. At the same time, both internal and external **urethral sphincters** (two muscles, one located where the urethra exits from the bladder and the other below the prostate) are closed, trapping seminal fluid in the **urethral bulb** (the prostatic portion of the urethra, between these two muscles). The urethral bulb expands like a balloon. A man typically experiences this first stage as a subjective sense that orgasm is inevitable, the so-called "point of no return."

In the second stage, sometimes called the **expulsion phase**, the collected semen is expelled out of the penis by strong, rhythmic contractions of muscles that surround the internal bulb and crura of the penis. In addition, there are contractions along the entire urethral route. The external urethral sphincter relaxes, allowing fluid to pass

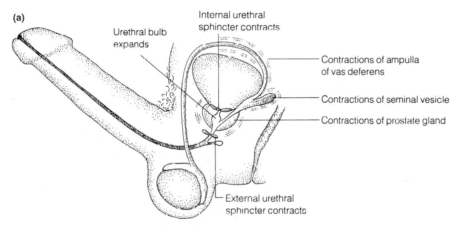

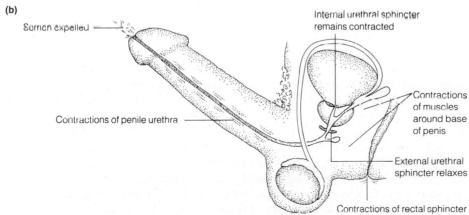

Figure 5.6

Ejaculation
*Male sexual
anatomy during
ejaculation:
(a) the emission
stage and (b)
the expulsion stage.*

through, while the internal sphincter remains contracted to prevent the escape of urine. The first two or three muscle contractions around the base of the penis are quite strong and occur at close intervals. Most of the seminal fluid is expelled in spurts corresponding to these contractions. Several more muscle responses typically occur, with a gradual diminishing of intensity and lengthening of time intervals between contractions. The entire expulsion stage usually takes place in three to ten seconds.

It is often assumed that once a man enters the emission phase, ejaculation inevitably follows. Well-known research, including the Masters and Johnson study, has supported this view:

> In contrast to the fact that orgasmic experience of the human female can be interrupted by extraneous psychosensory stimuli, the male orgasmic experience, once initiated by contractions of the accessory organs of reproduction, cannot be constrained or delayed until the seminal-fluid emission has been completed. Regardless of intensity of extraneous sensory stimuli, the male will carry the two-stage ejaculatory process to completion. (Masters and Johnson, 1966, p. 217)

This observation seems inconsistent with experiences occasionally related to us. The following describes one of these supposed biological impossibilities:

> Occasionally, when I feel like I'm going to orgasm, I stop all movement. If my partner cooperates, I have what seems like a little climax, with a contraction or two. Unlike with a normal, complete orgasm, I have no problem maintaining interest and an erection after this "false start." (Authors' files)

We have surveyed large numbers of our male students over the years and have found this experience to be somewhat uncommon but by no means rare.

Some men have an experience known as **retrograde ejaculation**, in which the semen is expelled into the bladder rather than through the penis (see Figure 5.7). This results from a reversed functioning of the two urethral sphincters. The condition sometimes occurs in men who have undergone prostate surgery. In addition, illness, congenital anomaly, and certain drugs, most notably tranquilizers, can induce this reaction. Some men have allegedly developed the voluntary ability to produce retrograde ejaculations as a method of birth control. As yet, though, training techniques for acquiring this capability have not been clearly outlined. While retrograde ejaculation is not harmful itself (the seminal fluid is later eliminated with the urine), a man who consistently experiences this response would be wise to seek medical attention to rule out the possibility of an underlying health problem.

Sometimes a man experiences orgasm without direct genital stimulation. The most familiar of these occurrences are **nocturnal emissions**, commonly known as "wet dreams." The exact mechanism that produces this response is not fully understood. Women also have the capacity for experiencing orgasm during sleep. The possibility of a man using fantasy alone to reach orgasm in a waking state is exceedingly remote, and we have never heard a firsthand account of this phenomenon. Kinsey (1948) stated that only three or four of the males in his sample of over 5000 reported this experience. In contrast, significantly greater numbers of women in his sample (roughly 2%) reported orgasms from fantasy alone (Kinsey et al., 1953). Another

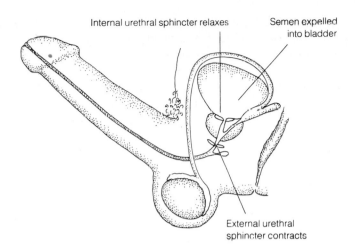

Internal urethral sphincter relaxes

Semen expelled
into bladder

External urethral
sphincter contracts

Figure 5.7

**Retrograde
Ejaculation**
*A reversed
functioning of the
urethral sphincters
(internal relaxes,
external contracts)
results in semen
being expelled into
the bladder.*

kind of nongenitally induced ejaculation that men sometimes report is reaching orgasm during sex play (activities such as mutual kissing or manual or oral stimulation of their partner) when there is no penile stimulation.

Some Concerns About Sexual Functioning

Men frequently voice a variety of concerns about sexual functioning. Several of these will be addressed throughout our text. At this point we will discuss two areas that receive considerable attention—the significance of penis size and the necessity and impact of circumcision. Claims are frequently made that one or both of these physical characteristics may influence the sexual pleasure of a man or his partner. In the following sections we will examine the available evidence.

Penis Size

> When I was a kid my peers were unmerciful in their comments about my small size. They would say things like, "I have a penis, John has a penis, but you have a pee-pee." Needless to say, I grew up with a very poor self-image in this area. Later it was translated into anxiety-ridden sexual encounters where I would insist that the room be completely dark before I would undress. Even now, when I realize that size is an irrelevant factor in giving sexual pleasure, I am still worried that a new partner will comment unfavorably about my less than impressive natural endowment. (Authors' files)

This man is not alone in his discomfort. His feelings are echoed in more accounts than we can remember. Penis size has occupied the attention of most men and many women at one time or another. Generally, it is more than mere idle curiosity that stimulates interest in this topic. For many it is a matter of real concern, perhaps even cause for apprehension or anguish.

A man's self-esteem and sense of identity often are influenced by how he views his penis (Comfort, 1972). We have all heard accounts of the little boy's reaction upon viewing the much bigger penis of his father or older brother. Allegedly, the marked contrast in size may lead to anxiety that affects future well-being. Although this early experience may be important in some cases, in general its effects seem to be a bit overstated. Consider the following account:

> One day, while taking a shower with my son, I noticed that he seemed to be overly intrigued by my penis. After his eyes had shifted back and forth between his and mine several times, he expressed the following. "Dad, how come yours is so much bigger than mine?" The unspoken part of this question seemed to be "Will mine ever be as big as yours?" I responded, "Like every other part of the body, it takes time to grow. But yours is a really nice size now, just right for you." He seemed quite content with this simple answer. At least, the big smile he flashed did not indicate the presence of any internal conflict, anxiety, envy, or regret. (Authors' files)

It does not take much imagination to understand why penis size often takes on great importance. As a society, we tend to be overly impressed with size and quantity. Bigger cars are better than compacts, the bigger the house the better it is, and by implication, big penises work better than smaller ones. Certainly the various art forms, such as literature, painting, sculpture, and movies, do much to perpetuate this obsession with big penises. Consider the following excerpt from Mario Puzo's novel *The Godfather* (1969), which describes a sexual encounter between Sonny and Lucy:

> She felt something burning pass between her thighs. She let her right hand drop from his neck and reached down to guide him. Her hand closed around an enormous, blood-gorged pole of muscle. It pulsated in her hand like an animal and almost weeping with *grateful ecstasy* she pointed it into her own wet, turgid flesh. The thrust of its entering, the *unbelievable pleasure* made her gasp, brought her legs up around his neck, and then like a quiver, her body received the savage arrows of his lightning-like thrusts; innumerable, torturing; arching her pelvis higher and higher until for the *first time in her life* she reached a shattering climax, felt his hardness break and then the crawly flood of semen over her thighs. (p. 28, italics ours)

The modern Western world is not alone in its preoccupation with penis size, as the photographs on the next page illustrate. Even the fascinating Indian sex manuals, the *Ananga Ranga* and the *Kama Sutra,* classify men according to three categories: the hare-man, whose erect penis measures six finger-widths; the bull-man (nine finger-widths long); and the horse-man (12 or more finger-widths long). In ancient Greek mythology, preoccupation with penis size found a focal point in Priapus, son of the goddess Aphrodite and the god Dionysus, who was usually portrayed as a lasciviously grinning little man with a greatly oversized penis.

The result of all this attention to penis size is that men often come to view it as an important attribute in defining their masculinity or their worth as a lover. Such a concept of virility can contribute to a poor self-image. Furthermore, if either a man or his partner views his penis as being smaller than it should be, this can decrease sexual satisfaction for one or both of them—not because of physical limitations, but rather as a self-fulfilling prophecy.

*Preoccupation with
penis size is evident
in a variety of art
forms. On the left
is a pottery lamp
in the form of
Priapus, the Greek
god of fruitfulness.*

What are the simple physiological facts of sexual interaction and penis size? We will focus on heterosexual penile-vaginal intercourse, since concerns about penis size most often relate to this kind of sexual activity.

As we learned in Chapter 4, the greatest sensitivity in the vaginal canal is concentrated in its outer portion. While some women do find pressure and stretching deep within the vagina to be pleasurable, this is not usually requisite for female sexual gratification. In fact, some women may even find deep penetration painful, particularly if it is quite vigorous:

> You asked if size was important to my pleasure. Yes, but not in the way you might imagine. If a man is quite large, I worry that he might hurt me. Actually, I prefer that he be average or even to the smaller side. (Authors' files)

There is a physiological explanation for the pain or discomfort some women feel during deep penetration. Since the female ovaries and male testicles originate from the same embryonic tissue source, they share some of the same sensitivity. If the penis bangs into the cervix and causes the uterus to be slightly displaced, this may in turn jar an ovary. The resulting sensation is somewhat like a male's experience of falling off a bike seat onto the crossbar. Fast stretching of the uterine ligaments has also been implicated in deep penetration pain. However, some women find slow stretching of these same ligaments to be pleasurable.

These observations indicate the importance of being gentle and considerate during intercourse. If one or both partners want deeper or more vigorous thrusting, they can experiment by gradually adding these components to their coital movements. It may also be helpful for the woman to be in an intercourse position other than female supine (see Figure 9.6), so she has more control over the depth and vigor of penetration.

Occasionally people are concerned about penis diameter rather than length. There is no physiological reason for diameter to appreciably affect sensations during coitus. The vagina is amazingly adjustable—it can nicely and firmly accommodate objects ranging in size from one finger to a baby's head.

Most textbooks report average dimensions of penises. We will not do this, because such information seems unimportant. Figure 5.8 shows several flaccid (nonerect) penises of different sizes, all well within the normal range. It is worth noting that penis size is not related to body shape, height, length of fingers, race, or anything else (Money et al., 1984). It should also be mentioned that small flaccid penises tend to increase more in size during erection than penises that are larger in the flaccid state (Masters and Johnson, 1966). These collective facts are reflected in the comment offered by an extremely tall, husky male:

> I think most people just naturally assumed, judging from my large stature, that I would have a big penis. Such is not the case. In fact, when I'm flaccid it looks like all I have is testicles and a glans. My shaft is practically invisible. However, when I get hard I know my penis is quite adequate in size. When I was a teenager the problem was how to let my buddies know this when it's not really cool to walk around with a hard-on. What I did was simply avoid taking showers with others if at all possible. Now I feel OK about my body but for awhile there I was really self-conscious. (Authors' files)

One of the most extreme manifestations of preoccupation with penis size is the development of an industry devoted to exploiting this anxiety through advertisements for gadgets that artificially increase a man's dimensions. For instance, a mail-order

Figure 5.8

Variations in Male Genitals
There are many normal variations in the shape and size of the male genitals. The penis in the right photo is uncircumcised.

catalog originating in Los Angeles listed among its products the "Super Cock," "Big Fat Freddy," the "Super Double Dong," and the "Extensifier." Clearly there is no lack of a market for "easy" ways to enhance one's penis size.

Circumcision

A characteristic that many people associate with differences in male sensitivity—and also differences in hygiene—is the absence or presence of the foreskin.

Circumcision is the surgical removal of the foreskin, shown in Figure 5.9. It is widely practiced throughout the world for religious, ritual, or hygienic reasons. In the United States this operation is performed on the majority of male infants (with parental consent), generally on the second day after birth. In certain other cultures the procedure is performed when a boy reaches adolescence, as part of the rituals of entering manhood. Some religions, including both the Jewish and Moslem faiths, require circumcision.

In this country routine circumcision has reflected concern by the medical profession about hygiene. There are a number of small glands located in the foreskin (*preputial glands*) and under the corona, on either side of the frenum (*Tyson's glands*). These glands secrete an oily, lubricating substance. If these secretions are allowed to accumulate under the foreskin, they combine with sloughed off dead skin cells to form a cheesy substance known as **smegma**. When it builds up over a period of time, smegma generally develops a strong, unpleasant odor, becomes grainy and irritating, and can serve as a breeding ground for infection-causing organisms.

There are unsubstantiated claims that penile cancer is more frequent among uncircumcised males (Hand, 1970). There are additional claims that smegma may harbor organisms that can cause a variety of infections in the female vaginal tract. Furthermore, some investigators have suggested that cervical cancer is more frequent in women who have sexual relations with uncircumcised partners. However, these assertions have been contradicted by research. For example, one study of Lebanese Moslems and Christians showed that the wives of the rarely circumcised Christians

Figure 5.9

Circumcision
*Circumcision,
the surgical removal
of the foreskin,
is practiced
throughout the world.*

(a)   (b)   (c)   (d)

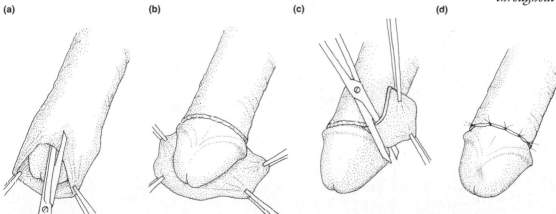

had no greater incidence of cervical cancer than their Moslem counterparts, whose husbands had been circumcised early in life (Abou-David, 1967). Perhaps the best compilation and interpretation of circumcision research is contained in a recent book by Edward Wallerstein (1980), titled *Circumcision*. After carefully analyzing the available data, Wallerstein concludes that there is absolutely no causal relationship between circumcision or lack of it and any kind of cancer.

There are several arguments against routine circumcision, many of which have been raised with greater frequency in recent years. First, it is possible that the foreskin serves some important function yet to be determined. Second, some have expressed concern that sexual function may be altered by excising the foreskin; we will consider this question later in this discussion. Finally, some think performing such an unpleasant procedure on a newborn is unnecessarily traumatic and an invitation to possible surgical complications. Some of the health risks of circumcision include hemorrhage, infections, mutilation, shock, psychological trauma, and even death in rare cases. Certainly the whole question of circumcision as a preventive medical practice is now being seriously questioned. One writer compared the practice of circumcision to pulling out children's teeth when they first appear to avoid possible tooth decay in the future (Street, 1959).

One other critical point should be mentioned. The vast majority of uncircumcised males who practice routine hygienic care are no more likely to encounter health problems than are circumcised males. If this were not so we would expect the rate of penile infections to be higher in Europe, where circumcision is an uncommon practice. This is not the case. It is interesting that even though the medical profession has tended to perpetuate the idea that circumcision equals cleanliness, there is no solid evidence to back up this claim. In 1975 the American Academy of Pediatrics asked its Committee on the Fetus and Newborn to review the evidence supporting circumcision as a routine medical practice. After thoroughly examining the available research, the committee concluded that there is no medical indication for circumcision of the newborn, and they recommended that it not be performed routinely (Kirkendall, 1981). Nevertheless, a recent nationwide survey of several hundred obstetricians and pediatricians revealed that 60% of the obstetricians surveyed and 38% of the pediatricians thought that there are good medical reasons for routine circumcision (Herrera and Macaraeg, 1984).

In recent years several American hospitals have established policies whereby circumcisions are performed only at the request of parents or as elective surgery. However, circumcision is still widely practiced. One of the reasons may be simply that established medical procedures are often slow to change. On the other hand, circumcision, a 10-minute operation, may generate fees of up to $100 for the surgeon and $300 for the hospital. As one observer wrote, "With more than 1 million babies circumcised in the United States each year, that makes circumcision at least a $55 million business" (Bolch, 1981, p. 4).

In 1984 Canadian researchers examined the circumcision literature to determine if it was appropriate for the government medical plan to continue footing the bill for this procedure. They concluded that no significant health benefits could be demonstrated and that circumcision should be classified as cosmetic surgery, to be paid for by parents wanting their sons circumcised (Cadman et al., 1984).

It seems that the widely held justification for circumcision creates unnecessary potential for anxiety. In our own classes most students assume that circumcision is important for hygiene. How do assumptions like these affect a person's self-image and sexual relations? Consider the following report provided by a surgeon:

> When I was serving a stint as ship's surgeon on a large carrier, during the Vietnam conflict, I had a very interesting experience. A young sailor came to me requesting circumcision. When I queried him as to his motivation for undergoing such an operation, he stated that his wife refused to engage in oral sex because she viewed him as unclean. After performing the simple operation, an amazing thing happened. Many more men came with the same request. Apparently the word had circulated rapidly. Their reasons were essentially the same as the first seaman. They either felt unclean themselves or were viewed in this way by partners. (Authors' files)

Accounts like this one are echoed in numerous other reports. With the increasing availability of accurate information, we hope to see a time when the absence of a flap of skin will no longer be considered a sign of personal cleanliness or sexual attractiveness.

Beyond the issue of hygiene, another question has often been raised about circumcision. Do circumcised men enjoy any erotic or functional advantages over uncircumcised men (or vice versa)? Some people assume that the circumcised male responds more quickly during penile-vaginal intercourse because of the fully exposed glans. However, except when there is a condition known as **phimosis** (an extremely tight prepuce), there is no difference in contact during intercourse. The foreskin of an uncircumcised man is retracted during coitus, so the glans is exposed. It might be assumed, in fact, that the glans of a circumcised man is less sensitive, due to the toughening effect of constant exposure to chafing surfaces. Masters and Johnson investigated both of these questions, and they found no evidence of differences in responsiveness:

> The thirty-five uncircumcised males were matched at random with circumcised study subjects of similar ages. Routine neurologic testing for both exteroceptive and light tactile discrimination were conducted on the ventral and dorsal surfaces of the penile body, with particular attention directed toward the glans. No clinically significant difference could be established between the circumcised and the uncircumcised glans during these examinations. (1966, p. 190)

Undoubtedly influenced by this report, many writers have concluded that the presence or lack of a foreskin does not influence sexual function. However, the Masters and Johnson data fail to include the all-important dimension of subjective assessment by men who have experienced both conditions after achieving sexual maturity. Occasionally we have encountered men in our classes who have been circumcised during their adult years. Some of these men have reported experiencing physiological differences in sexual arousal—such as a decrease in sensitivity of the glans—as a result of circumcision. But these reactions have not been consistent. Other men afforded this unique comparative opportunity have found no perceivable differences in sexual excitability. It would seem that there are still unanswered questions about the relationship between circumcision and sexual arousability.

Summary

Sexual Anatomy

1. The scrotum is a loose outpocket of the lower abdominal wall, consisting of an outer skin layer and an inner muscular layer. Housed within the scrotum are the two testes, or testicles, each suspended within its respective compartment by the spermatic cord.

2. Human testes have two major functions: sperm production and secretion of sex hormones.

3. Sperm development requires a scrotal temperature slightly lower than body temperature.

4. The interior of each testicle is divided into a large number of chambers that contain the thin, highly coiled seminiferous tubules, in which sperm production occurs.

5. Adhering to the back and upper surface of each testicle is a C-shaped structure, the epididymis, within which sperm maturation occurs.

6. Sperm travel from the epididymis of each testicle through a long, thin tube, the vas deferens, which eventually terminates at the base of the bladder, where it is joined by the excretory duct of the seminal vesicle.

7. The seminal vesicles are two small glands, each near the terminal of a vas deferens. They secrete an alkaline fluid that constitutes about 70% of the semen and appears to nourish and stimulate sperm cells.

8. The prostate gland, located at the base of the bladder and traversed by the urethra, provides about 30% of the seminal fluid released during ejaculation.

9. Two pea-sized structures, the Cowper's glands, are connected by tiny ducts to the urethra just below the prostate gland. During sexual arousal they often produce a few drops of slippery, alkaline fluid which appear at the tip of the penis.

10. Semen consists of sperm cells and secretions from the prostate, seminal vesicles, and Cowper's glands. The sperm component is only a tiny portion of the total fluid expelled during ejaculation.

11. The penis consists of an internal root within the body cavity; an external, pendulous portion known as its body, or shaft; and the smooth, acorn-shaped head, called the glans. Running the length of the penis are three internal chambers filled with spongelike tissue, which become engorged with blood during sexual arousal.

Male Sexual Functions

12. Penis erection is an involuntary process which results from adequate sexual stimulation—physiological, psychological, or both.

13. Ejaculation is the process by which semen is transported out through the penis. It occurs in two stages: the emission phase, when seminal fluid is collected in the urethral bulb; and the expulsive phase, when strong muscle contractions expel the semen. In retrograde ejaculation, semen is expelled into the bladder.

Some Concerns About Sexual Functioning

14. Penis size does not significantly influence ability to give or receive pleasure during penile-vaginal intercourse. Neither is it correlated with other physical variables such as body shape or height.

15. Circumcision, the surgical removal of the foreskin, is widely practiced in this country. Medical evidence supporting its hygienic benefits is scanty at best, as is data concerning its effect on erotic or functional elements of sexual expression.

Thought Provokers

1. If you had a newborn son, would you have him circumcized? When? Why or why not?

2. Do you believe that penis size is an important factor in a woman's coital satisfaction? What effect, if any, has the "bigger is better" view of penis size had upon your own sexual functioning?

3. What are some of the possible negative or positive effects of nocturnal emissions in an adolescent male? What can be done to minimize any adverse consequences of this natural occurrence?

Suggested Readings

Blank, Joani. *The Playbook: For Men/About Sex*. Burlingame, Calif.: Down There Press, 1975. This is an informally written self-awareness workbook for men. It includes topics such as body image, genital awareness, masturbation, sexual response, relationships, and fantasy.

Kinsey, Alfred C.; Pomeroy, Wardell B.; and Martin, Clyde E. *Sexual Behavior in the Human Male*. Philadelphia: W. B. Saunders, 1948. In addition to extensive data on male sexual behaviors, this volume contains an abundance of details about a male's sexual anatomy and the manner in which he responds physiologically to sexual stimulation.

Simon, William. "Male Sexuality: The Secret of Satisfaction." *Today's Health*, April 1975, 32–34, 150–152. A noted sex researcher interviews four men of diverse lifestyles who candidly discuss the meaning of sexual satisfaction in their lives with attention paid to their sexual joys, needs, uncertainties, and fears.

Zilbergeld, Bernie. *Male Sexuality: A Guide to Sexual Fulfillment*. Boston: Little, Brown, 1978. An exceptionally well written and informative treatment of male sexuality, including such topics as sexual functioning, self-awareness, and overcoming difficulties.

6

But mark you, Venus' joys must not be hurried,
But softly coaxed in dalliance unflurried.
The spot once found wherein 'tis woman's joy
To be caressed, caress it; ne'er be coy.
Ovid
"The Art of Love" (English translation, 1931)

Sexual Arousal and Response

Sexual Arousal
Sexual Response

SEXUAL AROUSAL AND RESPONSE in humans are influenced by many factors: hormones; our brain's capacity to recall experiences and engage in fantasy; our emotions; various sensory processes; the level of intimacy between two people; and a host of other influences. We will begin this chapter by discussing some of the things that influence sexual arousal. We will then turn our attention to the ways in which our bodies respond to sexual stimulation. We will concentrate primarily on biological factors and events associated with human sexual arousal and response, but this focus on physiology is not meant to minimize the importance of psychological and cultural influences. In fact, psychosocial factors probably play a greater role than biological ones in the extremely varied patterns of human sexual response, as we shall discover in later chapters.

Sexual Arousal

In this section we will single out a number of factors as we explore the complexity of human sexual arousal: the role of hormonal influences; the impact of brain functions; sensory input and the individual ways we interpret it; and finally, the reputed effects of certain foods and drugs.

The Role of Hormones

For years sex researchers have held differing opinions about the relative importance of hormones in human sexual arousal and behavior. These differences exist for several good reasons. For one, it is extremely difficult to distinguish between the effects of physiological processes, especially hormone production, and those of psychosocial processes such as early socialization, peer group learning, and emotional development. Furthermore, until recently much of the data relating sexuality and hormones was derived from poorly controlled studies of limited research populations. However, in recent years a number of well designed, carefully implemented investigations have yielded data that have given us a better understanding of the complex relationship between hormones and sexual activity. As we consider this information we shall see that the evidence linking hormones to sexuality is considerably more substantial for males than for females.

Hormones in Male Sexual Behavior.   We learned in Chapter 3 that the general term for male sex hormones is **androgens**. About 95% of the androgens produced by a male are secreted by the testes in the form of testosterone. The remaining 5% are produced by the adrenal glands. A number of experimental investigations have linked androgens with sexual activity. Some of the most illuminating of these are studies of the effects of castration, androgen-blocking drugs, reduced gonadal function, and hormone replacement therapy.

A number of studies evaluating the effects of **castration** (removal of the testes) have provided evidence of the connection between androgen and sexual function. Castration has been practiced since ancient times for a variety of reasons: to prevent sexual activity between harem guards and their charges; to render war captives docile; as part of religious ceremonies (in ancient Egypt, hundreds of young boys would be castrated in a single ceremony); and after the rise of the church, to preserve the soprano voices of European choirboys.

Castration, called **orchidectomy** in medical language, is performed today primarily as medical treatment for such diseases as genital tuberculosis and prostatic cancer. Castrations have also occasionally been performed for legal reasons, either as a method of eugenic selection (to prevent reproduction in, say, a mentally handicapped person) or as an alleged deterrent to sex offenders. The ethical status of such operations is highly controversial.

Research into the effect of castration has produced somewhat inconsistent findings. A major investigation that studied a large group of castrated Norwegian males found that a substantial majority of these men showed significantly reduced sexual interest and activity within the first year after the operation (Bremer, 1959). A more recent study of 39 West German sex offenders who voluntarily agreed to surgical castration while in prison obtained similar results (Heim, 1981). This offender population, consisting predominantly of rapists and child molesters, was evaluated over a period of several years after release from prison. Overall, sexual arousability and activity were strongly reduced by castration. However, the impact of this surgical procedure was varied. Sixteen of the subjects reported that their sexual behavior was extinguished soon after they were castrated. On the other hand, 11 individuals continued to engage in both masturbation and intercourse throughout the follow-up period, although with diminished frequency. Heim concluded that "sexual manifestations caused by castration vary considerably and that castration effects on male sexuality are not predictable with certainty" (p. 19). Other studies have revealed that the effect of castration on sexual desire and erotic functioning in men is highly variable. In one case a 43-year-old man, castrated 18 years previously, reported having intercourse one to four times weekly (Hamilton, 1943). Other writers have recorded incidences of continued sexual desire and function for as long as 30 years following castration, without hormone treatment (Ford and Beach, 1951).

In interpreting this evidence investigators need to take a number of possibilities into account. In cases where sexual activity does diminish after castration, how much of that reduction is attributable to hormone deficit and how much is psychological? It is reasonable to suspect that psychological inhibition is sometimes a side effect of castration—a result of embarrassment due to a sense of physical mutilation; the self-fulfilling belief in the myth that castration abolishes erectile response; or perhaps a combination of these and other factors.

Another finding linking androgen to sex behavior in men concerns the use of drugs to reduce sexual activity. In recent years a class of drugs known as **antiandrogens** have been used experimentally in Europe and America for the treatment of sexual offenders and individuals reporting extreme frequency of sexual activity. Antiandrogens drastically reduce the amount of testosterone circulating in the bloodstream. One of these drugs, medroxyprogesterone acetate (MPA), also known by its trade name, Depo-Provera, has received a great deal of attention from the American media in the last few years. Findings from both European and American investigations have revealed that antiandrogens such as Depo-Provera may be effective in reducing both sexual interest and activity in human males (Berlin, 1981; Lunde, 1972; Walker, 1982). However, altering the sex hormones is no guarantee of reduced activity of a sexual offender, particularly when the assaultive acts stem from nonsexual motivation. More information about the use of Depo-Provera in the treatment of sexual offenders will be included in Chapter 20.

There are several diseases of the endocrine system that impair hormone production in the testes. The result is a state of androgen deprivation called **hypogonadism**. The effects of hypogonadism show the importance of androgens. If this condition occurs before puberty, maturation of the primary and secondary sex characteristics will be retarded, and the individual may never develop an active sexual interest. If androgen deficiency occurs after a male reaches adulthood, the results are far more variable. However, extensive studies of hypogonadal men conducted by a number of researchers, including eminent Scottish endocrinologist John Bancroft (1984) and noted Stanford University physiologist Julian Davidson (1984), have provided "unequivocal evidence that androgens are necessary for normal male sexuality" (Bancroft, 1984, p. 4).

Hypogonadal men are often provided hormone replacement therapy, in which circulating androgens are artificially restored to normal levels. Such treatment often restores normal sexual interest and activity. When androgen replacement is temporarily suspended, sexual interest and associated sexual activity declines in two or three weeks. The capacity of a hypogonadal man to reach orgasm and ejaculate also usually ceases when his hormone treatments are interrupted. However, both Bancroft and Davidson have demonstrated that androgens are probably not necessary for erectile function. "Our studies of hypogonadal men have shown that in the laboratory, erections to erotic films occur to a normal extent, even though the men are androgen deficient and are experiencing a marked loss of sexual interest and activity" (Bancroft, 1984, p. 4). This finding demonstrates that androgen deficient men are capable of sexual function even though their interest in such activity is markedly diminished.

The vast majority of evidence linking androgens to male sexual functioning has been obtained from studies of adult clinical populations. However, a recent investigation provided very strong evidence of a relationship between blood androgen levels and sexual motivation and behavior in adolescent males (Udry et al., 1985). These researchers found that the higher the level of circulating androgens in the bloodstreams of their teenage subjects, the more time they spent thinking about sex and the more likely they were to have engaged in coitus, noncoital sex play, and masturbation.

Hormones in Female Sexual Behavior. When we ask our students to indicate which hormones they believe play a major role in female sexual behavior, the most common answer is **estrogens**. We do know that estrogens help maintain the elasticity of the vaginal lining, contribute to the production of vaginal lubricant, and help preserve the texture and function of the breasts. However, the role the ovarian estrogens play in female sexual motivation, arousal, and behavior is far from clear. Many writers have maintained that estrogens play an insignificant role in female sexual activity. In support of this viewpoint they have quoted data from studies of postmenopausal women (Masters and Johnson, 1966) and women who have had their ovaries removed for medical reasons (Kinsey et al., 1953). Neither change seems to have significant adverse effects on sexual arousal. However, more recent evidence calls this conclusion into question. For example, two well-designed studies revealed that not only vaginal lubrication but also sexual motivation, pleasure, and orgasmic capacity were improved with estrogen replacement therapy (Dennerstein et al., 1980; Dow et al., 1983). Findings such as these suggest that "it may well be . . . that a certain amount of estrogen is necessary for maintenance of normal sexual interest, in a way comparable to the male's need for testosterone" (Bancroft, 1984, p. 15).

For many years it has been widely assumed that androgens produced by the adrenal glands play an important role in female sexuality. Much of the evidence cited to support this viewpoint is of an anecdotal nature, derived from the reports of gynecologists and endocrinologists. For example, the clinical literature on gynecology contains many references to the fact that women undergoing androgen therapy for a variety of problems often report an increase in sexual interest and activity (Carter et al., 1947; Dorfman and Shipley, 1956; Kupperman and Studdiford, 1953). A reduction in female sexual arousal and response has also been linked to androgen deprivation. One study compared the effects of removing the ovaries with those of an adrenalectomy (removal of the adrenal glands). While sexual activity remained stable in the former case, the adrenalectomy produced profound decreases in sexual desire and behavior (Waxenberg et al., 1959). A related study reported similar adverse effects of terminated adrenal activity (Schon and Sutherland, 1960). A word of caution about interpreting these findings: It is quite possible that the reduced sexual activity may have also reflected other factors. The trauma of the surgery itself, and of the disease (often cancer) for which it was prescribed, could easily have influenced sexual behavior.

Recently, better controlled experimental evaluations of the effects of androgens on female sexuality have yielded a different picture. For example, three systematic investigations compared the effects of androgens on female sexuality with those of a *placebo* (a pharmocologically inert substance such as a sugar pill or an injection of sterile water). In all three experiments androgens proved no more effective than placebos (Mathews, 1981).

Future research may clarify the relationship, if any, between sex hormones and female sexual interest and behavior. At present the picture is much less clear for women than for men. An abundance of inconsistent and often contradictory data reveals a very unpredictable relationship between female sexuality and hormones. Even in the case of male sexuality, where the role of hormones is now becoming clearer, we must continue to be aware that human sexual behavior is so tremendously individual that it is difficult to specify the precise effects of hormones on erotic arousal and expression.

The Brain

From our experience, we know that the brain plays an important role in our sexuality. Our thoughts, emotions, and memories are all mediated through its complex mechanisms. Sexual arousal can occur without any sensory stimulation; it can be produced

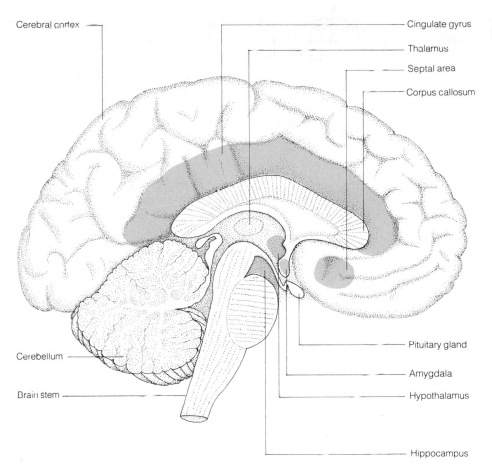

Cerebral cortex

Cingulate gyrus

Thalamus

Septal area

Corpus callosum

Cerebellum

Brain stem

Pituitary gland

Amygdala

Hypothalamus

Hippocampus

Figure 6.1

The Limbic System of the Human Brain
The limbic system, a region of the brain associated with emotion and motivation, is important in human sexual function. Key structures, shaded in color, include the cingulate gyrus, septal area, portions of the hypothalamus, amygdala, and the hippocampus.

by the process of *fantasy* (in this case, thinking of erotic images or sexual interludes), and some individuals may even reach orgasm during a fantasy experience (Kinsey et al., 1948 and 1953).

We know that specific events can cause us to become aroused. Less apparent is the role of individual experience and cultural influence, both of which are mediated by our brains. Clearly, we do not all respond similarly to the same stimuli. Some people may be highly aroused if their partner uses explicit sexual language. Others may find such words to be threatening or a sexual turn-off. Similarly, the smell of genital secretions may be more arousing to many Europeans than to members of our own deodorant-conscious society. The brain is the storehouse of our memories and cultural values, and consequently its influence over our sexual arousability is profound.

Strictly mental events like fantasies are the product of the **cerebral cortex**, the "gray matter" that controls higher functions like reasoning and language abilities. But the cortex represents only one level of functioning at which the brain influences human sexual arousal and response. At a subcortical level, the **limbic system** seems to play an important part in determining sexual behavior, both in humans and in other animals.

Figure 6.1 shows some key structures in the limbic system. These include the cingulate gyrus, the septal area, the amygdala, the hippocampus, and parts of the hypothalamus, which plays a regulating role. There is evidence linking various sites in this system with sexual behavior. For instance, several animal studies have implicated the hypothalamus in sexual functioning. Researchers have reported increased sexual activity in rats, including erections and ejaculations, triggered by stimulation in both anterior and posterior regions of the hypothalamus (Caggiula and Hoebel, 1966; Van Dis and Larsson, 1971; Vaughn and Fisher, 1962). When certain parts of the hypothalamus are surgically destroyed, there may be a dramatic reduction in the sexual behavior of both males and females of several species (Hitt et al., 1970; Sawyer, 1960).

In the 1950s, James Olds conducted a series of experimental investigations of brain stimulation in rats. He implanted electrodes in various regions of their limbic systems and wired the electrodes in a way that allowed the rats to stimulate their own brains by pressing a lever. When the electrodes were placed in the hypothalamus and the septal areas, the rats seemingly could not get enough stimulation. They would press the lever several thousand times per hour, often to the point of exhaustion. These animals were clearly experiencing something akin to intense pleasure, which led Olds to call these regions of the limbic system "pleasure centers" (Olds, 1956). Olds's rats were unable to tell him whether the pleasure they were experiencing was sexual in nature. Subsequent research with humans, outlined in the following paragraphs, is more enlightening.

For ethical reasons, few experiments have attempted to study the effects of brain stimulation on humans. In some cases, however, electrical and chemical brain stimulation of humans has been done for therapeutic purposes. Robert Heath, a Tulane University researcher, is one of the pioneers in this area. In the early 1970s he experimented with limbic system stimulation of a female epileptic and a man troubled with emotional problems. He hypothesized that the pleasure associated with stimulation of these areas would prove to be of therapeutic value to these patients. When stimulation was delivered to the septal area, both individuals reported intense sexual pleasure. The female patient experienced multiple orgasmic response as a direct result of septal area stimulation. Provided with a self-stimulating transistorized device, the male patient stimulated himself incessantly (up to 1500 times per hour). "He protested each time the unit was taken from him, pleading to self-stimulate just a few more times" (p. 6).

In a related investigation, Yale physiologist José Delgado (1969) recorded the following responses of two female patients undergoing limbic system stimulation during exploration of their epileptic conditions:

> [One patient] reported a pleasant tingling sensation in the left side of her body "from my face down to the bottom of my legs." She started giggling and making funny comments, stating that she enjoyed the sensation "very much." Repetition of these stimulations made the patient more communicative and flirtatious, and she ended by openly expressing her desire to marry the therapist.
>
> [A second female patient described] a pleasant sensation of relaxation and considerably increased her verbal output, which took on a more intimate character. This patient openly expressed her fondness for the therapist (who was new to her), kissed his hands, and talked about her immense gratitude for what was being done for her. (p. 145)

It is doubtful that researchers will ever find one specific "sex center" in the brain. However, it is clear that both the cerebral cortex and the limbic system play important roles in initiating, organizing, and controlling human sexual arousal and response. In addition, the brain interprets a variety of sensory inputs that often exert a profound influence upon sexual arousal. We will examine this topic in the next section.

The Senses

It has been said that the brain is the most important sense organ for human sexual arousal. This observation implies that any sensory event, if properly interpreted by the psyche, can serve as an effective sexual stimulus. The resulting variety in the sources of erotic stimulation helps to explain the tremendous sexual complexity of humans.

Of the major senses, touch tends to predominate during sexual sharing. However, all of the senses have the potential to become involved, and sights, smells, sounds, and tastes all may be important contributors to erotic arousal. There are no blueprints for the what and how of sensory stimulation. Each of us is unique, with our own individual triggers of arousal. There can be a special joy in discovering these "magic buttons" in ourselves or a sexual partner.

Touch. Stimulation of the various skin surfaces is probably a more frequent source of human sexual arousal than any other type of sensory stimulus. The nerve endings that respond to touch are distributed unevenly throughout the body, and this explains why certain areas are more sensitive than others. Those locations that are most responsive to tactile pleasuring are commonly referred to as the **erogenous zones**. A distinction is often made between **primary erogenous zones**—those areas that contain dense concentrations of nerve endings—and **secondary erogenous zones**, which include other areas of the body that have become endowed with erotic significance through sexual conditioning.

A list of primary erogenous zones generally includes the genitals, buttocks, anus, perineum, breasts (particularly the nipples), inner surfaces of the thighs, armpits, navel, neck, ears (especially the lobes), and the mouth (lips, tongue, and the entire oral cavity).

It is important to remember, however, that just because a given area qualifies as a primary erogenous zone, there is no guarantee that stimulating it will produce arousal in a sexual partner. What is intensely arousing for one person may produce no reaction in another; it may even be irritating to people.

The secondary erogenous zones include virtually all other regions of the body. For example, if your lover tenderly kissed and stroked your upper back during each sexual interlude, it is distinctly possible that this area would soon be transformed into a powerful erogenous zone. These secondary locations become eroticized because they are touched within the context of sexual intimacies.

While there is no limit to the amount of body surface that can become part of our own private erogenous maps, it seems that women are more likely than men in this society to realize the erotic potentials that exist throughout their bodies. This tentative conclusion is based on a few observations. First, females in our society are

*Erotic
sensual touching.*

touched more than males. This is particularly true during the early formative years. Second, females are also touched more during sexual encounters. Stereotypic gender roles dictate that men do the touching, rather than be touched, during sex play. Finally, men are typically more genitally focused than women during sexual interaction.

These are generalized observations and certainly not true for all individuals. Furthermore, we are not suggesting that women are totally free of the burden of bodies made dormant through lack of sensual attention. Many of us, men and women alike, may benefit from exploring the potentials for erotic arousal in the skin surfaces throughout our bodies. A helpful way of doing this for many is the process of **sensate focus**, which was defined by Masters and Johnson (1970). The process involves a couple sharing the experience of body exploration and pleasuring. Chapter 17 will discuss this and other methods for enhancing our erotic potentials.

Vision.   In our society we seem to be preoccupied with visual stimuli. Prime evidence is the importance we often place on physical appearance, including such activities as personal grooming, wearing the right clothes, and the extensive use of cosmetics. Therefore, it is not surprising that vision is second only to touch in the hierarchy of stimuli that most people view as sexually arousing.

The popularity of sexually explicit men's magazines in our society suggests that the human male is more aroused by visual stimuli than the female. Early research seemed to support this conclusion. Kinsey found that more men that women reported being sexually excited by visual stimuli such as pin-up erotica and stag shows (Kinsey et al., 1948 and 1953). However, this finding reflects several social influences, including the greater cultural inhibitions attached to such behavior in women at the time of his research, and the simple fact that men had been provided far more opportunities to develop an appetite for such stimuli. This interpretation is supported by later research that employed physiological recording devices (see Chapter 2) to measure sexual arousal under controlled laboratory conditions. These studies have demonstrated strong similarities in the responses of males and females to visual erotica (Abramson et al., 1981; Fisher, 1983). Recent research findings suggest that when sexual arousal is measured by self-reports rather than physiological devices, women are less inclined than men to report being sexually aroused by visual erotica (Kelley, 1985; Przybyla and Byrne, 1984). This finding may reflect the persistence of cultural influences that make women reluctant to acknowledge being aroused by filmed erotica, or it may indicate that females have greater difficulty than males identifying signs of sexual arousal in their bodies, or it may be due to a combination of these factors.

Smell. A person's sexual history and cultural conditioning often influence what smells he or she finds arousing. We typically learn through experience to view certain odors as erotic and others as offensive. From this perspective there may be nothing intrinsic to the fragrance of genital secretions that might cause them to be perceived as either arousing or distasteful. We might also argue the contrary—that the smell of genital secretions would be universally exciting to humans were it not that some people learn to view them as offensive. This latter interpretation is supported by the fact that some societies openly recognize the value of genital smells as a sexual stimulant. For example, on the European continent, where the deodorant industry is less pervasive, some women use the natural bouquet of their genital secretions, strategically placed behind an ear or in the nape of the neck, to induce arousal in their sexual partners.

Among other animals, smells are often more important than visual stimuli in eliciting sexual response. The females of many species secrete certain substances, called **pheromones**, during their fertile periods. Any of you who have had a female dog in heat and observed male dogs coming from miles around to scratch at your door will not doubt for a moment the importance of smell in sexual arousal. In early 1970s researchers isolated fatty acids called *copulins* from vaginal secretions of female rhesus monkeys; these pheromones are very strong smelling and a potent sexual attractant (Michael et al., 1971). Some years later it was discovered that sexually aroused human females secrete a vaginal substance similar to the rhesus monkey pheromone (Michael et al., 1974; Morris and Udry, 1976; Sokolov et al., 1976). Another substance that has commanded attention in the search for erotic odors in humans is a powerful pheromone called *alpha androstenal,* secreted by pigs. This substance has also been found in some human secretions, including perspiration. One investigation revealed that men and women who wore surgical masks sprayed with alpha androstenal rated women in photographs as more attractive than did subjects in a control group who wore untreated masks (Kirk-Smith et al., 1978).

In spite of these suggestive results, most researchers believe that there is no convincing evidence that any smells are natural attractants for humans (Hassett, 1978; Rogel, 1978; White, 1981). Undaunted by this general skepticism, a major perfume manufacturer began in 1983 to market a women's cologne and a men's aftershave containing alpha androstenal. If you choose to wear this perfume or cologne (assuming it is still available), do not expect miracles, since the effect of pheromones on humans, if it exists at all, is probably quite weak. Also, since alpha androstenal is a powerful pheromone for pigs, it would be a good idea to stay away from pig farms.

The near obsession of many people in our society with masking natural body odors makes it very difficult to study the effects of these smells. Any natural odors that might trigger arousal tend to be well disguised with armpit and genital sprays. Nevertheless, each person's unique experiences may allow certain smells to acquire erotic significance, as the following anecdotes reveal:

> I love the smells after making love. They trigger little flashes of erotic memories and often keep my arousal level in high gear, inducing me to go on to additional sexual activities. (Authors' files)

> During oral sex the faint odor of musk from my lover's vulva drives me wild with passion. I guess it is all the memories of special pleasures associated with these smells that produces the turn-on. (Authors' files)

In a society that is so concerned about natural odors, it is nice to see that some individuals appreciate the scents associated with sexual sharing and their lover's body.

Taste.   As with smell, taste seems to play a relatively minor role in human sexual arousal. This is no doubt influenced, at least in part, by an industry that promotes breath mints and flavored vaginal sprays. In addition to making many individuals extremely self-conscious about how they taste or smell, such commercial products may mask any natural tastes that relate to sexual activity. Nevertheless, some people are still able to detect and appreciate certain tastes they learn to associate with sexual sharing:

> When I am sucking my man I can taste the salty little drops that come out of his penis just before he comes. I get real excited about that time, because I know he is about to take that sweet ride home. (Authors' files)

> I have noticed that my wife often tastes different to me at different times in her cycle. I have asked her about it and she doesn't know why. One thing is a cinch; the taste is always arousing to me. (Authors' files)

Hearing.   Whether people make sounds during sexual sharing is highly variable; so is their partner's response. Some people find words, moans, and orgasmic cries to be highly arousing; others prefer that their lover keep silent during sex play. A range of opinions is expressed in the following quotes from a *Playboy* magazine sex poll:

> I love hearing things like, "Open wider," "You're so warm and wet," "Do you want me to come in your mouth?" The more my lover tells me, the more wanted and desirable I feel.

If I want to hear talking while I'm making love, I leave the radio on. My lover's mouth should be busy doing exciting things to my body with lips and tongue.

Silence is so boring, and talking when making love fills the gap. I like practically anything—from "I love the feel of your cock sliding in and out of my pussy" to "What did you think of Woody Allen's latest film?"

The only words I want to hear from him while fucking are, "Let's do it some more." (Smith, *Playboy* Sex Poll, February 1978, pp. 47–50)

Some people may make a conscious effort to suppress spontaneous noises during sex play. If this is a result of the silent, stoical image accepted by many males, it may be exceedingly difficult for men to talk, cry out, or groan during arousal. In one research study many women reported that their male partner's silence hindered their own sexual arousal (DeMartino, 1970). Female reluctance to emit sounds during sex play may be influenced by the belief that "nice" women are not supposed to be so passionate that they make noises.

In addition to being sexually arousing, talking to each other during a sexual interlude can be informative and helpful ("I like it when you touch me that way," "A little softer," and so on). If you happen to be a person who enjoys noise making and verbalizations during sex, your partner may respond this way if you discuss the matter beforehand. We will talk about discussing sexual preferences in Chapter 8.

Sensory stimulation will usually not be effective unless the appropriate emotional conditions are also present. Feelings of trust, of being wanted and cared for, and affection for one's partner often enhance our sexual response; in fact, they may be necessary ingredients. In contrast, feelings of being used, lack of emotional rapport, or negative emotions like guilt and anxiety often eliminate or restrain our capacity for erotic arousal.

Foods and Chemicals

Up to this point we have considered the impact of hormones, brain processes, and sensory input on human sexual arousal. There are other factors, though, that may affect a person's arousability in a particular situation. Some of these directly affect the physiology of arousal; others can have a strong impact on a person's sexuality through the power of belief. In the pages that follow, we will examine the effects of a number of products people use to attempt to heighten or reduce sexual arousal.

Aphrodisiacs: Do They Work?   An **aphrodisiac** (named after Aphrodite, the Greek goddess of love and beauty) is a substance that supposedly arouses sexual desire or increases a person's capacity for sexual activities.

Almost from the beginning of time, people have searched for magic potions and other agents able to revive flagging erotic interest or produce Olympic sexual performances. That many have reported finding such sexual stimulants bears testimony, once again, to the powerful role played by the mind in human sexual activity. We will first consider a variety of foods that have been held to possess aphrodisiac qualities, then turn our attention to other alleged sexual stimulants, including alcohol and an assortment of chemical substances.

Foods. Almost any food that resembles the male external genitals has at one time or another been viewed as an aphrodisiac. Many of us have heard the jokes about oysters, although for some a belief in the special properties of this particular shellfish is no joking matter. One wonders to what extent the oyster industry profits from this pervasive myth. Other foods sometimes considered aphrodisiacs include bananas, celery, tomatoes, and potatoes. Particularly in Asian countries, there is a widespread belief that the ground-up horns of animals such as rhinoceros and reindeer are powerful sexual stimulants. Have you ever used the term "horny" to describe a sexual state? Now you know its origin.

A number of drugs are also commonly thought to have aphrodisiac properties. Some of these are discussed in the following section and are summarized in Table 6.1.

Alcohol. More has been written about the supposed stimulant properties of alcohol than about any other presumed aphrodisiac substance. In our culture there is widespread belief in the erotic enhancement properties of alcoholic beverages:

> I am a great believer in the sexual benefits of drinking wine. After a couple glasses I become a real "hound in bed." I can always tell my wife is in the mood when she brings out a bottle of chilled rosé. (Authors' files)

In a survey of 20,000 middle-class and upper middle-class Americans, 60% of the respondents reported greater sexual pleasure after drinking (Athanasiou et al., 1970). There was a pronounced sex difference, with significantly greater numbers of women reporting this effect. This latter finding may be explained by the impact of alcohol on sexual inhibitions. Far from being a stimulant, alcohol has a depressing effect on higher brain centers, thus reducing cortical inhibitions such as fear and guilt that often block sexual expression. Alcohol may also stimulate sexual activity by providing a convenient rationalization for behavior that might normally conflict with one's values ("I just couldn't help myself with my mind fogged by booze"). If our culture produces more sexual inhibitions in females than in males—a reasonable assumption held by many—it seems logical that alcohol is more likely to facilitate sexual activity in women than in men.

A recent study has revealed that alcohol consumption may inhibit a person's ability to consciously suppress sexual arousal. In this investigation, male college students were told to try as hard as they could to suppress sexual arousal while listening to an audiotape that described an explicit sexual experience. Some of the subjects were sober and some were under the influence of alcohol when they listened to the tape. Penile tumescence, or engorgement, was measured by penile strain gauges (described in Box 2.3). Subjects who consumed alcohol developed erections significantly sooner than those who did not drink (Wilson and Niaura, 1984). This finding might account, at least in part, for an inebriated person's responding sexually in a situation where sexual arousal would normally be inhibited—for example, during contact with a sibling or child.

Consumption of significant amounts of alcohol can have serious negative effects on sexual functioning. Research has demonstrated that with increasing levels of intox-

Table 6.1 Some Alleged Aphrodisiacs and Their Effects

Name (and Street Name)	Reputed Effect	Actual Effect
1. Alcohol	Enhances arousal; stimulates sexual activity	Can reduce inhibitions to make sexual behaviors less stressful. It is actually a depressant and in quantity can impair erection ability, arousal, and orgasm.
2. Amphetamines ("uppers"; includes Benzedrine, Dexedrine)	Elevate mood; enhance sexual experience and abilities	Central nervous system stimulants; they reduce inhibitions. Long-term use impairs sexual functioning and can reduce vaginal lubrication in women.
3. Amyl nitrite ("snappers," "poppers")	Intensifies orgasms and arousal	Dilates arteries to brain and also to genital area; produces time distortion, warmth in pelvic area. It can produce dizziness, headaches, and fainting.
4. Barbiturates ("barbs," "downers")	Enhance arousal; stimulate sexual activity	Reduce inhibitions in similar fashion to alcohol. They are physically addictive, and overdose may produce severe depression and even death due to respiratory failure.
5. Cantharides ("Spanish fly")	Stimulates genital area, causing person to desire coitus	Not effective as a sexual stimulant. It acts as a powerful irritant that can cause inflammation to lining of bladder and urethra; can result in permanent tissue damage and even death.
6. Cocaine ("coke")	Increases frequency and intensity of orgasm; heightens arousal	Central nervous system stimulant; it loosens inhibitions and enhances sense of well-being. Regular use can induce depression and anxiety. Chronic sniffing ("snorting") can produce lesions and perforations of the nasal passage.
7. LSD and other psychedelic drugs (includes mescaline, psilocybin)	Enhance sexual response	No direct physiological enhancement of sexual response. They may produce altered perception of sexual activity and are frequently associated with unsatisfactory erotic experiences.
8. L-dopa	Sexually rejuvenates older males	No documented benefits to sexual ability. It occasionally produces a painful condition known as priapism.
9. Marijuana	Elevates mood and arousal; stimulates sexual activity	Enhances mood and reduces inhibitions in a way similar to alcohol. It may distort the time sense, with the resulting illusion of prolonged arousal and orgasm.
10. Yohimbine	Induces sexual arousal and enhances sexual performance	Appears to have genuine aphrodisiac effect on rats. Effect on humans undetermined at the present time (currently being evaluated).

ication, both men and women experience reduced sexual arousal (as measured physiologically), decreased pleasurability and intensity of orgasm, and increased difficulty in attaining orgasm (Briddell and Wilson, 1976; Malatesta et al., 1979 and 1982; Wilson and Lawson, 1976). Heavy alcohol use may also result in general physical deterioration, a process that commonly reduces a person's interest in and capacity for sexual activity.

Drugs and Other Chemicals. Perhaps the most famous drug considered to be an aphrodisiac is *cantharides,* also known as "Spanish fly." This substance is derived from the ground-up bodies of a species of beetle found in southern Europe (Spain and France). Taken internally, it travels to the bladder and is excreted in the urine. It acts as a powerful irritant, causing acute inflammation of the lining of the bladder and urethra as it passes out of the body. This stimulation of genital structures has resulted in the widespread reputation of cantharides as an aphrodisiac. In reality, "Spanish fly" can be extremely painful to people of both sexes, producing effects ranging from mild irritation to extensive tissue destruction and even death, depending on the dose. It is completely useless as a sexual stimulant, and its dangerous side effects make it a substance to be avoided.

Marijuana has also been widely extolled for its sexual enhancement properties. It acts similarly to alcohol to reduce inhibitions. In addition, marijuana may increase empathy with others, distort time perception (often with the resulting illusion of prolonged arousal and orgasm), and increase suggestibility—all of which may act independently or in combination to produce a sense of heightened sexual ecstasy. A number of studies have revealed that a majority of males and females who have combined marijuana use with sexual expression report that the drug enhances their sexual pleasure (Halikas et al., 1982; Weller and Halikas, 1984). However, this effect appears to be of a subjective, psychological nature, in that marijuana possesses no chemical attributes that qualify it as a true sexual stimulant (Mendelson, 1976).

Amphetamines such as Benzedrine and Dexedrine (commonly known as "uppers") are central nervous system stimulants favored by some for their presumed sexual enhancement properties. Their general effect is to elevate mood, which may in turn act to diminish inhibitions. In addition, amphetamines often energize behavior, producing an increase in confidence. This can lead to a person overestimating his or her sexual prowess.

There is no experimental evidence attributing genuine aphrodisiac properties to amphetamines. It is important to note that these drugs are psychologically addictive and that continued chronic use is known to impair sexual functioning (Kaplan, 1974). Furthermore, amphetamine use often dries the natural secretions of mucous membranes, which may lead to diminished vaginal lubrication and painful intercourse.

Cocaine, a drug extracted from the leaves of the coca shrub, is a powerful central nervous system stimulant reputed by some to be an aphrodisiac. It is usually taken either by injection or sniffing ("snorting"). Some users claim it induces an immediate "orgasmlike rush." Others report that orgasms increase in frequency and intensity while a person is under its influence. However, as with all drugs previously discussed, there is no legitimate biological evidence establishing cocaine as an aphrodisiac. Any reported improvements generally belong to the "loosening of inhibitions" or "enhancement of well-being" categories. Recent evidence suggests that frequent use of cocaine may have a number of negative effects upon sexual functioning, including reduced vaginal lubrication, inhibited erectile response, and diminished sexual interest (Siegel, 1982; Wesson, 1982).

Amyl nitrite, known on the streets as "snappers" or "poppers," is a drug often linked with intensified orgasmic experience. It is used medically by cardiac patients to prevent heart pain (angina). Inhaled from small ampules which are "popped" open for quick use, it causes a rapid dilation of the arteries that supply the heart and other organs with oxygen. Amyl nitrite also produces a sudden dilation of arteries in the brain, a response that often induces a feeling of giddiness and euphoria. In addition, there is a sense of warmth created in the pelvis and genitals due to dilation of the arteries of the genitourinary tract.

Occasionally people report that inhaling a "popper" at the moment of orgasm dramatically intensifies and prolongs the experience. However, time is distorted and perceptions altered after inhalation, and it is unlikely that this effect can be attributed to an actual prolongation of orgasm. Furthermore, amyl nitrite is a highly volatile drug that may produce a variety of negative side effects, including severe headaches, dizziness, and fainting. It is hazardous to use such a drug without the supervision of a competent physician. Recent evidence has linked amyl nitrite use with the development of Kaposi's cancer, a disease that occurs frequently among people who have AIDS (Communicable Disease Summary, 1985).

L-dopa, a drug frequently employed in the treatment of *Parkinson's disease* (a neurological disorder), received considerable publicity a few years ago when researchers reported an apparent sexual rejuvenation in older male patients taking the medication. However, research failed to confirm its suggested aphrodisiac qualities. Occasionally, it has been known to produce *priapism* (prolonged penile erection), a painful condition quite independent of genuine arousal.

Barbiturates (commonly called "barbs" or "downers"), used in the treatment of a variety of mental and physical conditions, may subjectively enhance sexual pleasure in some individuals by lessening inhibitions in a way similar to alcohol.

Since the 1920s there have been reports of the aphrodisiac properties of *yohimbine hydrochloride,* or yohimbine, a crystalline alkaloid derived from the sap of the tropical evergreen yohimbe tree that grows in West Africa. Until recently most of these claims were dismissed by serious researchers. However, in the late 1970s scientists at Stanford University received a grant from the National Institutes of Health to conduct research aimed at finding a drug that might be helpful in treating sexual difficulties. Experiments conducted by the Stanford team with male rats have found that injections of yohimbine induce intense sexual arousal and performance in these animals (Clark et al., 1984). The data suggest that this drug may be a true aphrodisiac, at least for rats. However, the Stanford researchers are cautious in assuming yohimbine will have the same effects on humans. They have begun investigations with human male subjects: Advertisements in newspapers circulated near the Stanford campus produced a flood of volunteers.

Finally, most *psychedelic drugs,* including LSD, mescaline, and psilocybin, are not generally linked with enhanced sexual response. Some people have reported very unsatisfactory erotic experiences while under the influence of these drugs.

In view of the evidence against many of the commonly held beliefs about aphrodisiacs, why do so many people around the world swear by the effects of a little powdered rhino horn, that special meal of oysters and banana salad, or the marijuana cigarette before an evening's dalliance? The answer lies in faith and suggestion—these are the ingredients frequently present when aphrodisiac claims surface. If a person believes something will improve his or her sex life, this faith is often translated into the subjective enhancement of sexual pleasure. From this perspective, literally anything has the potential of serving as a sexual stimulant.

We are not implying that all alleged aphrodisiacs owe their effects strictly to suggestion. As we have seen, several substances (including alcohol, marijuana, and barbiturates) may increase sexual motivation and arousal by reducing inhibitions. However, their effects are variable and may be greatly influenced by both the particular situation and the attitudes of the person using the drug.

Anaphrodisiacs. Several drugs are known to inhibit sexual behavior. Substances that have this effect are called **anaphrodisiacs**.

A great deal of evidence indicates that regular use of *opiates,* such as heroin, morphine, and methadone, often produces a significant—and sometimes a dramatic—decrease in sexual interest and activity in both sexes (Abel, 1984). Serious impairment of sexual functioning associated with opiate use may include erectile problems and inhibited ejaculation in males and reduced capacity to experience orgasm in females.

Tranquilizers, used widely in the treatment of a variety of emotional disorders, have been shown to reduce sexual motivation in some cases. They are occasionally prescribed by physicians for this purpose, though their effects are variable and they may also increase sexual arousal by lessening inhibitions.

Many *antihypertensives,* drugs used for treating high blood pressure, have been experimentally demonstrated to seriously inhibit erection and ejaculation and to reduce the intensity of orgasm in male subjects (Kaplan, 1979; Money and Yankowitz, 1967).

Undoubtedly, the most widely used and least recognized anaphrodisiac is *nicotine.* There is evidence that smoking can significantly retard sexual motivation and function by constricting the blood vessels (thereby retarding vasocongestive response of the body to sexual stimulation) and by reducing testosterone levels in the blood (Subak-Sharpe, 1974). In one study sexual arousal was physiologically monitored in 42 males while they viewed erotic films, before and after inhaling different amounts of nicotine. Subjects who smoked two low-nicotine cigarettes between viewings demonstrated no more variation in sexual responsiveness than control subjects who ate candy. However, men who smoked two high-nicotine cigarettes experienced both delay of and decrease in sexual arousal (Hagen and D'Agostino, 1982).

Paradoxically, the most widely known substance used as an anaphrodisiac, *potassium nitrate,* or saltpeter, is completely ineffective as a sexual deterrent. Many of us have heard the joke about the newlyweds being dosed with saltpeter on their wedding night. In reality, there is no physiological basis for this kind of tale, unless the need for frequent urination can be viewed as a sexual deterrent (potassium nitrate increases urine flow through diuretic action).

Sexual Response

Human sexual response is a highly individual physical, emotional, and mental process. Nevertheless, there are a number of common physiological changes that allow us to outline some general patterns of the sexual response cycle.

In the years before Masters and Johnson began their research, writers often

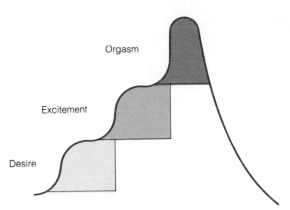

Figure 6.2

Kaplan's Three-Stage Model of the Sexual Response Cycle
This model is distinguished by its identification of desire as a prelude to sexual response. (Kaplan, 1979)

referred to the various phases of sexual response with terms like "foreplay," "the prelude," "the union" or "communion," and "afterplay." One particularly influential writer, Havelock Ellis (1906), coined the terms "tumescence" and "detumescence" to describe the process whereby blood flows into and out of the pelvic area during sexual arousal and response.

With widespread acceptance of the work of Masters and Johnson (1966), we find that their descriptive language has replaced most of the earlier terminology. However, their work does not stand alone in recent developments in the study of human sexual response. Particularly noteworthy are the views of sex therapist Helen Kaplan (1979). We will briefly outline her ideas before turning to a detailed analysis of Masters and Johnson's work.

Kaplan's Three-Stage Model

Kaplan's model of sexual response, an outgrowth of her extensive experience as a sex therapist, contains three stages: **desire**, **excitement**, and **orgasm** (see Figure 6.2). She suggests that sexual difficulties tend to fall into one of these three categories and that it is possible for a person to have difficulty in one while continuing to function normally in the other two.

One of the most distinctive features of Kaplan's model is that it includes desire as a distinct stage of the sexual response cycle. Many other writers, including Masters and Johnson, do not discuss aspects of sexual response that are separate from genital changes. Kaplan's description of desire as a prelude to physical sexual response corrects this omission and consequently stands as a welcome addition to the literature on sexual response. However, not all sexual expression is preceded by desire. For example, a couple may agree to engage in sexual sharing even though they may not be feeling sexually inclined at the time. Frequently they may find that their bodies begin to respond sexually to the ensuing activity, in spite of their lack of initial desire.

Masters and Johnson's Four-Phase Model

Masters and Johnson distinguish four phases in the sexual response patterns of both men and women: **excitement**, **plateau**, **orgasm**, and **resolution**. In addition, they

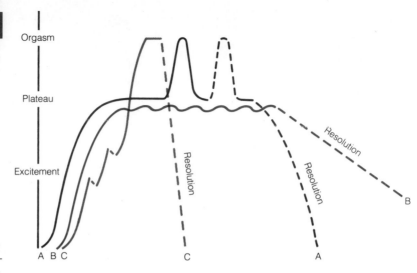

Figure 6.3

Female Sexual Response Cycle
Masters and Johnson identified three basic patterns in female sexual response. Pattern A most closely resembles the male pattern, except that a woman can have one or more orgasms without dropping below the plateau level of sexual arousal. Variations include an extended plateau with no orgasm (Pattern B), and a rapid rise to orgasm with no definitive plateau and a very quick resolution (Pattern C). (Masters and Johnson, 1966)

include a **refractory period** (a recovery stage in which there is a temporary inability to reach orgasm) in the male resolution phase. Figures 6.3 and 6.4 illustrate these four phases of sexual response in women and in men. These charts provide basic "maps" of common patterns, but a few cautions to the reader are in order.

First, the simplified nature of these diagrams can easily obscure the richness of individual variation that can and does occur. Masters and Johnson were charting only the physiological responses to sexual stimulation. While our biological reactions may follow a relatively predictable course, there is tremendous variability in our own subjective responses to sexual arousal. These personal differences are suggested in the several individual reports of arousal, orgasm, and resolution included later in this chapter.

The second caution has to do with a too-literal interpretation of the so-called plateau stage of sexual response. In the behavioral sciences the term *plateau* is typically used to describe a leveling-off period where no observable changes in behavior can be detected. For example, it might refer to a flat spot in a learning curve where no new behaviors occur for a certain period of time. It has been diagrammed in just this manner in the male chart and in pattern A of the female chart. Actually, the plateau level of sexual arousal involves a powerful surge of sexual tensions that are definitely measurable (for example, as increased heart and breathing rates), so it is far from an unchanging state.

Our third caution is a warning against a tendency to use charts like these as personal checklists. While we encourage self-references throughout this book, this is one area where a too enthusiastic self-checking can lead to potential problems in the form of "spectatoring." The following quote illustrates:

> After learning about the four stages of sexual response in class, I found myself "standing back" and watching my own reactions, wondering if I had passed from excitement into plateau. Also, I began to monitor the responses of my partner, looking for the

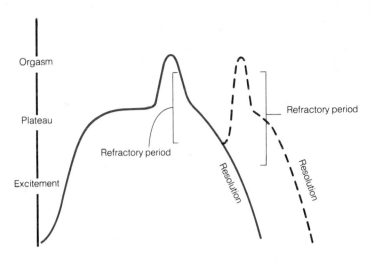

Figure 6.4

**Male Sexual
Response Cycle**
*Only one male
response pattern
was identified
by Masters and
Johnson. However,
men do report con-
siderable variation
in their response
patterns. Note the
refractory period:
Males do not have
a second orgasm
immediately after
the first. (Masters
and Johnson,
1966)*

tell-tale signs that would tell me at what point he was. Suddenly I found myself doing clinical observations rather than allowing myself to fully experience the good feelings. It was a real put-off and I had to force myself to stop being the observer and become more of a participant. (Authors' files)

The descriptions in the following pages should not be viewed as standards for analyzing or intellectualizing your feelings or for evaluating how "normal" your reactions are. We stress that there are many natural variations from these patterns. Perhaps familiarity with these generalized descriptions may help to illuminate some of the complexity of your own responses.

In much of the discussion that follows we will be looking at the physiological reactions and subjective reports of women and men. Before we become too involved in the several specific processes of sexual response, it is important to note that the basic responses of men and women are very similar—a point that was stressed by Masters and Johnson in their research:

Certainly there are reactions to sexual stimulation that are confined by normal anatomic variation to a single sex. There also are differences in established reactive patterns to sexual stimuli—for example, duration and intensity of response—that usually are sex-linked in character. However, parallels in reactive potential between the two sexes must be underlined. Similarities rather than differences of response have been emphasized by this investigation. (Masters and Johnson, 1966, p. 273)

Two fundamental physiological responses to effective sexual stimulation occur in both women and men. These are *vasocongestion* and *myotonia*. These two basic reactions are the primary underlying sources for almost all biological responses that take place during sexual arousal.

Vasocongestion is the engorgement with blood of body tissues that respond to sexual excitation. Usually the flow of blood into organs and tissues through the arteries is balanced by an equal outflow through the veins. However, during sexual arousal the dilation of arteries increases the inflow beyond the veins' draining capacity. This results in widespread vasocongestion in both superficial and deep tissues. The congested areas that are visible may feel warm and appear swollen and red, due to their increased blood content. The most obvious manifestations of this vasocongestive response are the erection of the penis in men and lubrication of the vagina in women. In addition, other body areas may become engorged—the labia, testicles, clitoris, nipples, and even the earlobes.

The second basic physiological response is **myotonia**, the increased muscle tension that occurs throughout the body during sexual arousal. Myotonia is evident in both voluntary flexing and involuntary contractions. Its most dramatic manifestations are facial grimaces, spasmodic contractions of the hands and feet, and the muscular spasms that occur during orgasm.

The phases of the response cycle follow the same general patterns regardless of the method of stimulation. Masturbation, manual stimulation by one's partner, oral pleasuring, penile-vaginal intercourse, dreaming, fantasy, and in some women breast stimulation can all result in completion of the response cycle. Often the intensity and rapidity of response vary according to the kind of stimulation.

In the next several pages we outline the major physiological reactions to sexual stimulation that occur during each of the four phases of the sexual response cycle. Subjective reports of several individuals will be included. For each stage we list reactions common to both sexes and those unique to just one. You will note the strong similarities in the sexual response patterns of men and women. We will discuss some important differences in greater detail at the conclusion of this chapter.

Excitement. The first phase of the sexual response cycle is the excitement phase. As Table 6.2 indicates, it is characterized by a number of responses common to men and women, including muscle tension and some increase in the heart rate and blood pressure. In both sexes several areas of the sexual anatomy become engorged. For example, the clitoris, labia minora, vagina, nipples, penis, and testes all increase in size, and most of them deepen in color. Some responses, such as the appearance of a **sex flush** (a pink or red rash on the chest or breasts), occur in both sexes but are more common in women. Still other responses are specific to just one sex. These are outlined in the table; they are also illustrated in Figures 6.5 through 6.8, which show changes in the sexual anatomy of women and men throughout the phases of the cycle.

The excitement phase may vary in duration from less than a minute to several hours. Both males and females may show considerable variation in the degree of their arousal during this phase. For example, a man's penis may vary from flaccid to semierect to a fully erect state. Similarly, vaginal lubrication in women may vary from minimal to copious.

While the physiological characteristics outlined in the table and figures represent general patterns, different people experience these changes in differing ways. The following two reports give some indication of the subjective variations in how women describe their own feelings during sexual arousal:

Table 6.2   The Excitement Phase: Sexual Response Cycle

Reactions Common to Both Sexes	Female Responses	Male Responses
Increased myotonia (muscle tension), particularly in striated muscles of arms and legs. Smooth muscles of abdomen may tense somewhat, late in phase.	Clitoris swells with blood engorgement; change may be very slight to quite noticeable.	Penis becomes erect. Erection may subside and recur several times.
Moderate increase in heart rate and blood pressure.	Labia majora flatten and separate away from the vaginal opening.	Scrotum elevates; skin thickens and loses its baggy appearance.
Sex flush may appear late in phase; more common in females. Often appears sporadically and seems to be related to intensity of arousal.	Labia minora increase two or three times in size, adding about 1 cm of length to the vagina. The pinkish color begins to deepen.	Testes increase in size and elevate.
Nipple erection; more common in females.	Lubrication of the vagina begins early in phase. The inner two-thirds lengthens and expands, and the vaginal walls progressively become a deeper purple color.	Cowper's glands may produce some secretions, although these are commonly delayed until plateau phase.
	Uterus elevates and becomes engorged with blood, increasing in size up to twice its unstimulated dimensions.	
	Breasts enlarge. Superficial veins become more visible.	

Sexual arousal for me is something I look forward to when I realize my husband and I will have sex. His touching, kissing, and loving me in this way brings me to a height of excitement that is incredible. At first I felt selfish about him giving me so much satisfaction through stimulation, but he enjoys it so much, it's a wonderful time. Often we don't have intercourse because we are caught up in the "foreplay" of lovemaking. (Authors' files)

When I am aroused I get warm all over and I like a lot of holding and massaging of other areas of my body besides my genitals. After time passes with that particular stimulation, I prefer more direct manual stroking if orgasm is desired. (Authors' files)

Two men provide their descriptions of sexual arousal in the following accounts:

When I am sexually aroused, my whole body feels energized. Sometimes my mouth gets dry and I may feel a little lightheaded. I want to have all of my body touched and stroked, not just my genitals. I particularly like the sensation of feeling that orgasm is just around the corner, waiting and tantalizing me to begin the final journey. Sometimes a quick rush to climax is nice, but usually I prefer making the arousal period last as long as I can stand it, until my penis feels like it is dying for the final strokes of ecstasy. (Authors' files)

When aroused, I feel very excited and I fantasize a lot. Then all of a sudden, a warm feeling comes over me and it feels like a thousand pleasure pins are being stuck into my loins all at the same time. (Authors' files)

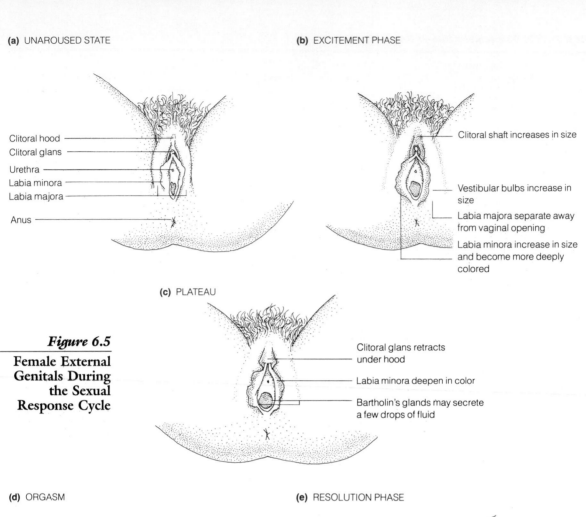

(a) UNAROUSED STATE

Clitoral hood

Clitoral glans

Urethra

Labia minora

Labia majora

Anus

(b) EXCITEMENT PHASE

Clitoral shaft increases in size

Vestibular bulbs increase in size

Labia majora separate away from vaginal opening

Labia minora increase in size and become more deeply colored

(c) PLATEAU

Figure 6.5

Female External Genitals During the Sexual Response Cycle

Clitoral glans retracts under hood

Labia minora deepen in color

Bartholin's glands may secrete a few drops of fluid

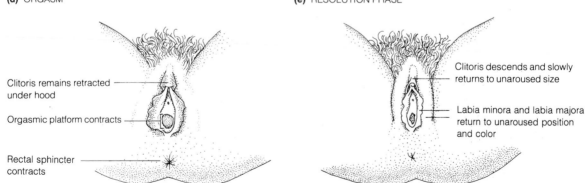

(d) ORGASM

Clitoris remains retracted under hood

Orgasmic platform contracts

Rectal sphincter contracts

(e) RESOLUTION PHASE

Clitoris descends and slowly returns to unaroused size

Labia minora and labia majora return to unaroused position and color

(a) UNAROUSED STATE

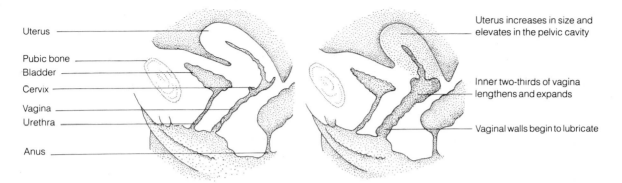

Uterus

Pubic bone
Bladder
Cervix
Vagina
Urethra

Anus

(b) EXCITEMENT PHASE

Uterus increases in size and
elevates in the pelvic cavity

Inner two-thirds of vagina
lengthens and expands

Vaginal walls begin to lubricate

(c) PLATEAU PHASE

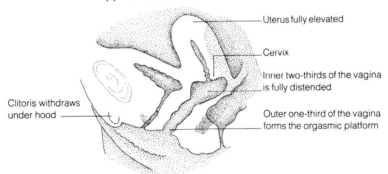

Uterus fully elevated

Cervix

Inner two-thirds of the vagina
is fully distended

Outer one-third of the vagina
forms the orgasmic platform

Clitoris withdraws
under hood

Figure 6.6

**Changes of
the Vagina and
Uterus During
the Sexual
Response Cycle**

(d) ORGASM

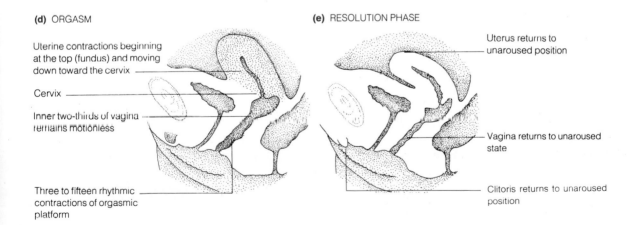

Uterine contractions beginning
at the top (fundus) and moving
down toward the cervix

Cervix

Inner two-thirds of vagina
remains motionless

Three to fifteen rhythmic
contractions of orgasmic
platform

(e) RESOLUTION PHASE

Uterus returns to
unaroused position

Vagina returns to unaroused
state

Clitoris returns to unaroused
position

(a) EXCITEMENT PHASE

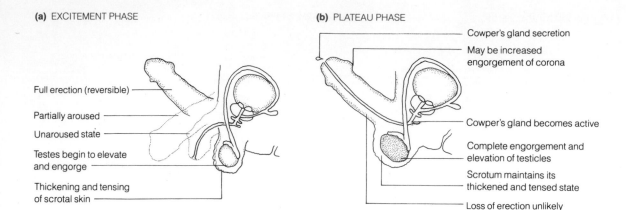

Full erection (reversible)

Partially aroused

Unaroused state

Testes begin to elevate
and engorge

Thickening and tensing
of scrotal skin

(b) PLATEAU PHASE

Cowper's gland secretion

May be increased
engorgement of corona

Cowper's gland becomes active

Complete engorgement and
elevation of testicles

Scrotum maintains its
thickened and tensed state

Loss of erection unlikely

(c) EMISSION PHASE OF ORGASM

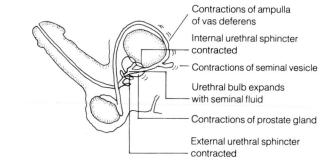

Contractions of ampulla
of vas deferens

Internal urethral sphincter
contracted

Contractions of seminal vesicle

Urethral bulb expands
with seminal fluid

Contractions of prostate gland

External urethral sphincter
contracted

Figure 6.7

**Male
Sexual Anatomy
During the Sexual
Response Cycle**

(d) EXPULSION PHASE OF ORGASM

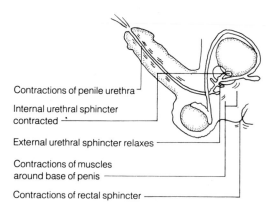

Contractions of penile urethra

Internal urethral sphincter
contracted

External urethral sphincter relaxes

Contractions of muscles
around base of penis

Contractions of rectal sphincter

(e) RESOLUTION PHASE

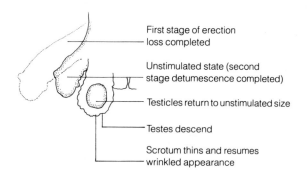

First stage of erection
loss completed

Unstimulated state (second
stage detumescence completed)

Testicles return to unstimulated size

Testes descend

Scrotum thins and resumes
wrinkled appearance

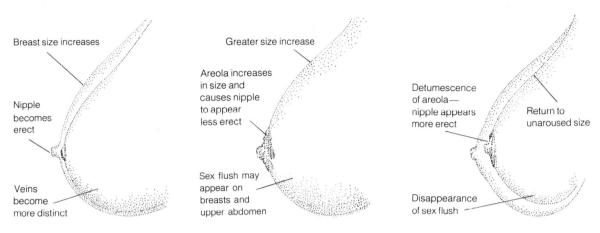

(a) EXCITEMENT PHASE

Breast size increases

Nipple becomes erect

Veins become more distinct

(b) PLATEAU AND ORGASM PHASE

Greater size increase

Areola increases in size and causes nipple to appear less erect

Sex flush may appear on breasts and upper abdomen

(c) RESOLUTION PHASE

Detumescence of areola— nipple appears more erect

Return to unaroused size

Disappearance of sex flush

Figure 6.8

Breast Changes During the Sexual Response Cycle

Plateau.   During the plateau phase, sexual tension continues to mount until it reaches the peak that leads to orgasm. It is difficult to define clearly the point at which a sexually responding individual makes the transition to this phase. Unlike the excitement phase, the plateau phase has no clear external sign such as lubrication or erection to mark its onset. Instead, a number of these signs become more pronounced as they accelerate toward the peaks reached in the next phase. Heart rate and blood pressure both continue to rise; breathing grows faster; sex flushes and coloration of the genitals become more noticeable (see Table 6.3). Muscle tension continues to build up and the face, neck, hands, and feet may undergo involuntary contractions and spasms in both the plateau phase and the orgasm phase. Among women, plateau phase is also distinguished by development of the "orgasmic platform," a term used by Masters and Johnson to describe the markedly increased engorgement of the outer third of the vagina.

The plateau phase is often very brief, typically lasting a few seconds to several minutes. However, many people find that prolonging sexual tensions at this high level produces greater arousal and ultimately more intense orgasms. This is reported in the following subjective accounts:

> When I get up there, almost on the verge of coming, I try to hang in as long as possible. If my partner cooperates, stopping or slowing when necessary, I can stay right on the edge for several minutes, sometimes even longer. I know that all it would take is one more stroke and I'm over the top. Sometimes my whole body gets to shaking and quivering and I can feel incredible sensations shooting through me like electric charges. The longer I can make this supercharged period last, the better the orgasm. (Authors' files)

When I masturbate, I like to take myself almost to the point of climaxing and then back off. I can tell when orgasm is about to happen because my vagina tightens up around the opening and sometimes I can feel the muscles contract. I love the sensations of balancing myself on the brink, part of me wanting to come and the other part holding out for more. The longer I maintain this delicate balance, the more shattering the climax. Sometimes the pleasure is almost beyond bearing. (Authors' files)

Both of the preceding accounts are by women. Men who wish to delay orgasm may need more frequent interruption of stimulation as plateau phase continues. However, men sometimes report a very different reaction, often alluding to a kind of crisis point, as suggested below:

When I first approach orgasm, it is essential to slow down or stop if I don't want to finish quickly. This is relatively easy during masturbation, but somewhat harder during intercourse. I may have to use this slow-down tactic several times in a short period. However, something then happens to me which is difficult to explain. It's almost like I pass a crisis point where, if I don't come, my staying power gets better. (Authors' files)

This is an interesting phenomenon that may be relatively common, judging from the number of our male students who have reported similar experiences. Some women also experience a more intense orgasm when they consciously move in and out of plateau phase. This is sometimes recommended for women who are first learning to experience orgasms (Barbach, 1975). We encourage you to experiment with your own (or your partner's) plateau phase to determine the potentials that exist for you.

Table 6.3   The Plateau Phase: Sexual Response Cycle

Reactions Common to Both Sexes	Female Responses	Male Responses
Myotonia becomes quite pronounced throughout the body. There may be grimaces of the face and involuntary muscular contractions in the feet and hands.	Clitoris withdraws under its hood and shortens in length.	There may be a slight increase in engorgement of corona. There may be deepening of the reddish-purple color of the glans.
Further increase in heart rate to 100–160 range just prior to orgasm. Blood pressure continues to elevate.	Labia majora undergo no further changes.	Erection is more stable in this stage.
Breathing becomes faster and deeper.	Noticeable intensification of color in the labia minora; highly colored area is called the "sex skin." Becomes bright red in nulliparous women and deep wine in parous women as orgasm approaches.	Scrotum maintains its thickened and tensed state.
Sex flush becomes more pronounced; may not appear until this phase.		Testes continue to increase to 150% of unstimulated size and continue to elevate until positioned snugly against the body wall.
Occasionally nipple erection is delayed to this stage.	Orgasmic platform develops from further vasocongestion of outer one-third of vagina. Inner two-thirds increases only slightly in width and depth. Lubrication slows considerably, particularly if plateau is extended.	Cowper's glands become active. Secretions may not be present in some men.
	The uterus is fully elevated.	
	The areola becomes more swollen; it may appear that nipple erection has subsided.	

Orgasm. As effective stimulation continues, many people move from plateau to orgasm. This is particularly true for men, who almost always experience orgasm after reaching the plateau level. In contrast, women may obtain plateau levels of arousal without the release of sexual climax. This is often the case during penile-vaginal intercourse when the man reaches orgasm first, or when effective manual or oral stimulation is replaced with penetration as the female approaches orgasm. More will be said about this later.

Orgasm is the shortest phase of the sexual response cycle, typically lasting only a few seconds. Female orgasms often last slightly longer than male orgasms. Table 6.4 summarizes the primary physiological responses during orgasm.

The experience of orgasm can be an intense mixture of highly pleasurable sensations. There has been considerable debate about whether women and men experience orgasm differently. This question was evaluated a few years ago in an experimental analysis of orgasm descriptions that were provided by college students (Wiest, 1977). Using a standard psychological rating scale, this researcher found that women's and men's subjective descriptions of orgasm were indistinguishable. Similar results were obtained in an earlier study, when a group of 70 expert judges were unable to reliably distinguish between the written orgasm reports of men and women (Proctor et al., 1974).

Beyond the question of sex differences in orgasmic experiences, it is clear that there is great individual variation in how people, both men and women, describe orgasms. In Box 6.1 some subjective accounts selected from our files illustrate the diversity of these descriptions. The first one is by a woman and the second by a man. The final three—labeled Reports A, B, and C, respectively—contain no specific ref-

Table 6.4   The Orgasm Phase: Sexual Response Cycle

Reactions Common to Both Sexes	Female Responses	Male Responses
Reduction in voluntary muscle control. Involuntary muscle spasms throughout body.	Clitoris remains retracted under the hood.	During emission phase, internal sex structures undergo contractions to cause pooling of seminal fluid in urethral bulb.
Blood pressure and heart rate reach highest levels; heart rate may increase to 180 in extreme cases.	No changes in labia majora and labia minora.	During expulsion phase, semen is expelled by strong, rhythmic contractions of penile urethra and muscles around base of penis. First 2 to 3 contractions are most intense, spaced at 0.8-second intervals; following contractions are weaker and slower.
Breathing may reach 40 breaths per minute.	Orgasmic platform contracts rhythmically 3 to 15 times. First 3 to 6 contractions are intense, spaced at 0.8-second intervals; following contractions are weaker and slower.	
Sex flush, if present during earlier stages, typically persists through orgasm.	Uterus usually contracts at orgasm.	No observable changes in scrotum, testes, or Cowper's glands.
No observable changes in the breasts or nipples.	No further changes in breasts or nipples.	
External rectal sphincter muscle contracts involuntarily at 0.8-second intervals.		

When I'm about to orgasm, my face feels very hot. I close my eyes and open my mouth. It centers in my clitoris and it feels like electric wires igniting from there and radiating up my torso and down my legs to my feet. I sometimes feel like I need to urinate. My vagina contracts anywhere from 5 to 12 times. My vulva area feels heavy and swollen. There isn't another feeling like it—it's fantastic!

Orgasm for me draws all my energy in towards a core in my body. Then, all of a sudden, there is a release of this energy out through my penis. My body becomes warm and numb before orgasm; after, it gradually relaxes and I feel extremely serene.

Report A. It's like an Almond Joy, "indescribably delicious." The feeling runs from the top of my head to the tips of my toes as I feel a powerful surge of pleasure. It raises me beyond my physical self into another level of consciousness, and yet the feeling seems purely physical. What a paradox! It strokes all over, inside and out. I love it simply because it's mine and mine alone.

Report B. An orgasm to me is like heaven. All my tensions and anxieties are released. You get to the point of no return, and it's like an uncontrollable desire that makes things start happening. I think that sex and orgasm are one of the greatest phenomenons that we have today. It's a great sharing experience for me.

Report C. Having an orgasm is like the ultimate time I have for myself. I am not excluding my partner, but it's like I can't hear anything and all I feel is a spectacular release accompanied with more pleasure than I've ever felt doing anything else. (Authors' files)

*For Reports A, B, and C from our files, decide if the subject was male or female. To find the answer, turn to the summary at the end of this chapter.

erences that identify the sex of the describer. Perhaps you would like to try to determine whether they were reported by a male or a female. The answers are given at the end of the chapter, following the summary.

Although the physiology of female orgasmic response can be clearly outlined, as it is in Table 6.4, some past and present issues about its nature need to be discussed. Misinformation about female orgasm has been prevalent in our culture. Freud, writing in the early 1900s, developed a theory of the "vaginal" versus the "clitoral" orgasm that, inaccurate though it is, has had a great impact on people's thinking about female sexual response. Freud viewed the vaginal orgasm as more mature than the clitoral orgasm, and thus preferable. The physiological basis for this theory was the assumption that the clitoris is a stunted penis. This assumption led to the conclusion that erotic sensations, arousal, and orgasm resulting from direct stimulation of the clitoris were all expressions of "masculine" rather than "feminine" sexuality—and therefore undesirable (Sherfey, 1972). At adolescence, a woman was supposed to transfer her erotic center from the clitoris to the vagina. If she was not able to do so at this time, psychotherapy was sometimes used to attempt to help her attain "vaginal" orgasms. Unfortunately, this theory led many women to believe incorrectly that they were sexually maladjusted.

Our modern knowledge of embryology has established the falseness of the theory that the clitoris is a masculine organ, as we have seen in our discussion of the genital differentiation process in Chapter 3. In one researcher's words, "to reduce clitoral eroticism to the level of psychopathology because the clitoris is an innately masculine organ . . . must now be considered a travesty of the facts" (Sherfey, 1972, p. 47). Travesty of facts or not, during Freud's time this sexual-center transfer theory was taken so seriously that surgical removal of the clitoris was recommended for little girls who masturbated, to help them later attain "vaginal" orgasms.

Surgical clitoridectomies are no longer performed in our culture. Yet social conditioning, which can be as effective as a scalpel, continues: Freud's operational definition of female sexual health is still with us in many respects. For example, a woman's reluctance to ask her partner to manually stimulate her clitoris during coitus (or to do it herself) typifies the learned belief that she "should" experience orgasm from penile stimulation alone. However, cultural conditioning can work two ways— with knowledge and support, a woman can change her attitude about her sexual feelings and behaviors.

Contrary to Freud's theory, the research of Masters and Johnson suggests that there is only one kind of orgasm in females, physiologically speaking, regardless of the method of stimulation. They state:

> From a biologic . . . [and] . . . anatomic point of view, there is absolutely no difference in the responses of the pelvic viscera to effective sexual stimulation, regardless of whether the stimulation occurs as a result of clitoral-body or mons area manipulation, natural or artificial coition, or for that matter, specific stimulation of any other erogenous area of the female body. (1966, p. 66)

While they made no anatomic distinctions between orgasms during coitus and those during noncoital activities, Masters and Johnson did note a difference between the two experiences. They found female orgasms during coitus to be measurably less intense (that is, there were slightly fewer vaginal muscular contractions), a discovery later reflected in the subjective responses of women in *The Hite Report*. In Hite's words, ". . . a clitorally stimulated orgasm without intercourse feels more locally intense, while an orgasm with intercourse feels more diffused throughout the area and/or body" (1976, p. 191).

There is considerable agreement on the existence of the difference described in the last quote, and women vary in their preferences for manual or coital orgasms.

> Clitoral orgasms (orgasms from direct clitoral stimulation) are stronger and sharper. Sometimes during intercourse I have almost a "missed" feeling. (Hite, 1976, p. 188)

> Vaginal orgasms (orgasms from coital stimulation) are deeper, more releasing, more satisfying, better both psychologically and physically. They are like an underground volcano. A manual orgasm is sharper and more piercing, more superficial. (Hite, 1976, p. 190)

As in the other phases in the human sexual response cycle, it is clear that there are wide variations in subjective feelings and preferences in female orgasms.

Masters and Johnson's view that there is no physiological basis for defining different types of female orgasms has been contested by Josephine and Irving Singer (1972). These authors contend that in addition to noting observable physiological variations, it is important to take emotional satisfaction into consideration in accounting for differences in female orgasmic response. With this in mind, the Singers have described three types of female orgasm—vulval, uterine, and blended. They suggest that a *vulval orgasm* corresponds to the type of orgasmic response described by Masters and Johnson and that it may be induced by either coital or manual stimulation. The vulval orgasm is accompanied by contractions of the orgasmic platform and typically is not followed by a refractory period. A *uterine orgasm,* in contrast, occurs only as a result of vaginal penetration and is characterized by a woman involuntarily holding her breath as orgasm approaches and explosively exhaling at climax. The Singers suggest that this type of orgasm often induces a profound sense of relaxation and sexual satiation and is typically followed by a refractory period. Finally, they describe a *blended orgasm* that is a combination of the first two types, characterized by both contractions of the orgasmic platform and breath-holding.

When the Singers' conceptualization of female orgasm was first published, many professionals in the field of sexuality assigned it little credibility. The apparent similarity of the Singers' "uterine orgasms" and Freud's "vaginal orgasms" may have caused some to fear a revival of the old theory of superior vaginal versus inferior clitoral orgasms. However, the Singers did not claim that one type of orgasm is superior to another. One of the major problems for any theory suggesting vaginal erotic response has been the widespread belief that the vagina is largely insensitive to sexual stimulation. However, this idea is being seriously called into question by the recent emergence of evidence indicating vaginal erotic sensitivity. For example, in one recent study examiners used their fingers to apply moderate to strong rhythmic pressure to all areas of the vaginal walls of 48 subjects. Over 90% of the women stimulated in this fashion reported considerable erotic sensitivity of the vagina, most commonly on the anterior (front) wall. Some reported sensitivity in more than one area. Many of the women experienced orgasm from this manual stimulation of their vaginas (Alzate and Landono, 1984).

The Grafenberg Spot.   In the last few years a number of studies have reported that some women are capable of experiencing orgasm, and perhaps ejaculation, when an area along the anterior wall of the vagina is vigorously stimulated (Addiego et al., 1981; Belzer, 1981; Perry and Whipple, 1981; Sevely and Bennet, 1978). This area of erotic sensitivity, briefly mentioned in Chapter 4, has been named the **Grafenberg spot** (or **G spot**) in honor of Ernest Grafenberg (1950), a gynecologist who first noted the erotic significance of this location within the vagina almost 40 years ago. However, the presence of glandular structures in this area was noted in the medical literature over 100 years ago (Skene, 1880). Recently it has been suggested that the Grafenberg spot is not a point that can be touched by the tip of one finger but, rather, a fairly large area composed of the lower anterior wall of the vagina and the underlying urethra and surrounding glands. Adequate stimulation of this much vaginal tissue may require use of "the full breadth of the middle two fingers and at least two thirds of their lengths" (Heath, 1984, p. 205).

Robert Mallon (1984), a pathologist and medical researcher, recently presented evidence of glandular material similar to prostate tissue in the Grafenberg area of 42 females examined by postmortem autopsies. Corroboration of this research was provided by another study in which complete urethras and surrounding tissue from 17

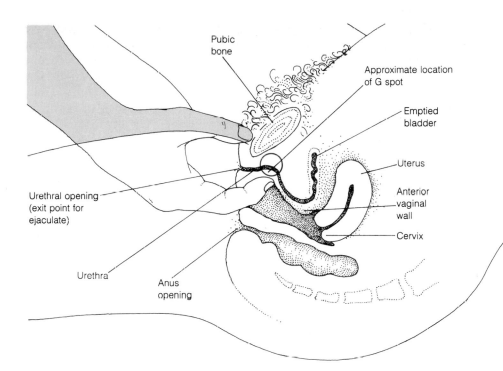

Pubic
bone

Approximate location
of G spot

Emptied
bladder

Uterus

Anterior
vaginal
wall

Cervix

Urethral opening
(exit point for
ejaculate)

Urethra

Anus
opening

Figure 6.9

Locating the Grafenberg Spot
Two fingers are usually employed, and it is often necessary to press deeply into the anterior wall of the vagina to reach the spot.

autopsied females and a portion of a urethra from one surgical specimen were examined. Over 80% of the specimens had prostatelike glandular tissue, the majority of which contained substances known to be produced by the male prostate (Heath, 1984).

The Grafenberg spot, or area, may be located by "systematic palpation of the entire anterior wall of the vagina between the posterior side of the pubic bone and the cervix. Two fingers are usually employed, and it is often necessary to press deeply into the tissue to reach the spot" (Perry and Whipple, 1981, p. 29). This exploration may be conducted by a woman's partner, as shown in Figure 6.9. Some women are able to locate their Grafenberg spot through self-exploration.

During initial searching for the sometimes elusive Grafenberg spot, a woman or her partner must rely on the sensations produced by manual stimulation. When the area is located women report a variety of initial sensations, including a slight feeling of discomfort, a brief sensation of needing to urinate, or a pleasurable feeling. After a minute or more of stroking the sensations usually become more pleasurable, and the area may begin to swell to a discernible size. Continued stimulation of the area may result in an orgasm that is often quite intense.

Perhaps the most amazing thing about Grafenberg spot orgasms is that they are sometimes accompanied by the ejaculation of fluid from the urethral opening. Four researchers describe their observation of this event:

With the aid of the subject's husband, four of us (Addiego, Belzer, Perry, and Whipple) were able to observe her response to digital massage of her Grafenberg spot, which led to expulsion of liquid, and reportedly and apparently to orgasm, on several occasions. On none of these occasions did stimulation of the clitoris, direct or otherwise, appear to occur. Orgasmic expulsions occurred after less than a minute of stimulation; they were separated in a multi-orgasmic series by similarly brief periods of time. The urethral area was clearly exposed in bright light, and there was absolutely no doubt that the liquid was expelled from the urethral meatus. Sometimes it exuded from the meatus. At other times it was expelled from one to a few centimeters. On one observed occasion, expulsion was of sufficient force to create a series of wet spots covering a distance of more than a meter. (Addiego et al., 1981, p. 17)

Research indicates that the source of this fluid is the "female prostate" discussed in Chapter 4. The ducts from this system empty directly into the urethra. In some women Grafenberg orgasms result in fluid being forced through these ducts and out the urethra. In view of the homologous nature of Grafenberg spot tissue and the male prostate, we might speculate that the female ejaculate is similar to the prostatic component of male seminal fluid. This notion has been supported by one study in which specimens of female ejaculate were chemically analyzed and found to contain high levels of an enzyme, prostatic acid phosphatase (PAP), characteristic of the prostatic component of semen (Addiego et al., 1981). Many women report that the fluid has a mild semenlike scent. A later study of six female ejaculators failed to differentiate samples of their urine and fluid they ejaculated during sexual response (Goldberg et al., 1983). However, a still more recent study of seven women who ejaculate reported that the collected urine and ejaculate samples differed substantially in the amount of prostatic acid phosphatase present (Belzer et al., 1984). The inconsistency in these findings may be due, at least in part, to a methodological problem arising from the fact that both the ejaculate and urine are delivered through the urethra. Further research may resolve this methodological problem and ultimately clarify whether or not the fluid women ejaculate is distinct from urine.

While the existence of Grafenberg spot orgasms, sometimes accompanied by ejaculation, has been reported with some degree of reliability, our understanding of this phenomenon is far from complete. For example, how common are these responses? Is there a connection between Grafenberg spot stimulation and the uterine orgasm described by the Singers? Is the female Grafenberg area a genuine homologue of the male prostate? Clearly, considerably more research is necessary before conclusive answers can be obtained for these and other questions. In the meantime, we encourage women and their partners who want to explore this intriguing new information in relation to their own sexual response and activities to do so. However, it may be self-defeating to treat Grafenberg spot orgasm as a new sexual achievement to be relentlessly pursued. It would be unfortunate if the current reexamination of some of our beliefs about female orgasm were to lead to a reemergence of attributing emotional or physiological superiority to any one orgasmic pattern.

Resolution.   During the final phase of the sexual response cycle, the sexual systems return to their nonexcited state. If no additional stimulation occurs, the resolution begins immediately after orgasm. Some of the changes back to a nonexcited state take place rapidly, while others occur more slowly. Table 6.5 summarizes the major phys-

Table 6.5   The Resolution Phase: Sexual Response Cycle

Reactions Common to Both Sexes	Female Responses	Male Responses
Usually all signs of myotonia are absent within 5 minutes after orgasm. Heart rate, blood pressure, and breathing rate begin returning to normal immediately after orgasm. Sex flush, when present, usually disappears quite rapidly. Nipple erection subsides slowly, often taking as long as one hour. Return to normal state is generally more rapid in females.	Clitoris descends to its overhanging position in 5 to 10 seconds. Engorgement of the shaft and glans takes longer to dissipate, roughly 5 to 30 minutes. Labia majora rapidly return to their unaroused size and midline position. Labia minora return to normal unstimulated size and lose their "sex skin" coloration within 10 to 15 seconds. Uterus returns to its unstimulated position in the pelvic cavity. Lack of orgasm after obtaining high levels of arousal may dramatically slow resolution. Sexual organs often remain congested, producing pressure that may result in genital and pelvic discomfort.	Erection loss occurs in two stages: During first phase, up to 50% of tumescence is lost within a minute or less after orgasm. The second stage is slower, sometimes requiring several minutes or longer for complete detumescence. The testes return to their normal size and the scrotal sac to its wrinkled appearance. This return is quite rapid in the majority of men, but is sometimes protracted.

iological changes during resolution. Skin coloration subsides quickly; and heart rate, blood pressure, and breathing all become normal almost immediately. Both the clitoris and the penis begin returning to their unstimulated position and appearance immediately, but engorgement dissipates gradually. Especially in men, two stages of erection loss can be identified, with the second much longer than the first. The duration of the resolution phase is often directly influenced by the length of the arousal period prior to orgasm.

The four self-reports that follow provide some indication of how people vary in their feelings after orgasm. The first two are by females; the second two reports are by males.

> After a satisfying experience with my husband I want to be held, as if to finalize and complete our union. Sometimes I like to talk and sometimes I just like to be able to touch him and be touched by his whole body. (Authors' files)

> After orgasm I feel very relaxed. My moods do vary—sometimes I'm ready to start all over; other times I can jump up and really get busy; and at other times I just want to sleep. (Authors' files)

> After orgasm I feel relaxed and usually very content. Sometimes I feel like sleeping and other times I feel like I want to touch my partner if she is willing. I like to hold her and just be there. (Authors' files)

> After orgasm I generally experience a brief period where my sexual interest drops dramatically. While holding and being held is nice, I prefer not to continue any sexual activity, at least not for a few minutes. Usually I feel extremely satiated, similar to the aftermath of dining on a superb meal. Talking and sharing thoughts about the experience is especially pleasant. However, sometimes I like to just roll over and quietly bask in the luxurious afterglow. (Authors' files)

These subjective reports of women and men sound very similar. But there is one significant difference in the response of men and women during this phase—their physiological readiness for further sexual stimulation. After orgasm, the male typically enters a **refractory period**—a time when no amount of additional stimulation will result in orgasm. The length of this period ranges from minutes to days, depending on a variety of factors such as the age of the man, the frequency of previous sexual activity, and the degree of his emotional closeness to and sexual desire for his partner. In contrast to men, women generally experience no comparable refractory period: They are physiologically capable of returning to another orgasmic peak from anywhere in the resolution phase. However, a woman may or may not want to do so. In the next section we will take a more detailed look at male-female differences during the resolution phase and we will consider the other differences between men's and women's patterns of sexual response.

Some Differences Between the Sexes

More and more, writers are emphasizing the basic similarities of sexual response in men and women. We see this as a positive trend away from the once-popular notion that great differences exist between the sexes—an opinion that undoubtedly helped create a big market for many "love manuals" designed to inform readers about the mysteries and complexities of the "opposite sex." Now we know that much can be learned about our partners by carefully observing our own sexual patterns. Nevertheless, there are some real and important primary differences. In the following pages we will outline and discuss some of them.

Greater Variability in Female Response.   One major difference between the sexes is the range of variations in the sexual response cycle. Although the graphs in Figures 6.3 and 6.4 do not reflect individual differences, they do demonstrate a wider range in the female response. One pattern has been outlined for the male and three for the female.

In the female chart, the sexual response pattern represented by line A is most similar to the male pattern. It differs in an important way, though, in its potential for additional orgasms without dropping below the plateau level. Line B represents quite a different female pattern: a smooth advance through excitement to the level of plateau, where the responding woman may remain for some time without experiencing orgasm. The consequent resolution phase is more drawn out. Line C portrays a rapid rise in excitement, followed by one intense orgasm and a quick resolution.

While it appears that women often have more variable sexual response patterns than men, this does not imply that all males experience the response cycle in the same way. Men report considerable variation from the Masters and Johnson standard, including several mild orgasmic peaks followed by ejaculation; prolonged pelvic contractions after the expulsion of semen; and extended periods of intense excitement prior to ejaculation that feel like one long orgasm (Zilbergeld, 1978). In other words, there is no single pattern of sexual response, nor is there one "correct way." All of the patterns and variations—including one person's different reactions to sexual stimuli at different times or in different situations—are completely normal.

The Male Refractory Period.   The presence of a refractory period in the male cycle is certainly one of the most significant differences in sexual response between the sexes. Men typically find that a certain minimum time must elapse after an orgasm before they can experience another climax. Most women have no such physiologically imposed "shutdown phase."

There is considerable speculation about why only men have a refractory period. It seems plausible that some kind of short-term neurological inhibitory mechanism is triggered by ejaculation. This notion is supported by the publication of some fascinating research conducted by three British scientists (Barfield et al., 1975). These researchers speculated that certain chemical pathways between the midbrain and the hypothalamus—pathways known to be involved in regulating sleep—might have something to do with postorgasm inhibition in males. To test their hypothesis, the researchers destroyed a specific site, the *ventral medial lemniscus,* along these pathways in rats. For comparative purposes they surgically eliminated three other areas in hypothalamic and midbrain locations in different rats. Later observations of sexual behavior revealed that the elimination of the ventral medial lemniscus had a dramatic effect on refractory periods, cutting their duration in half.

Other research with rats has provided further evidence implicating the brain in the male refractory period. In two studies, large lesions made in an area below the hypothalamus resulted in greatly increased ejaculatory behavior (Heimer and Larson, 1964; Lisk, 1966). In another investigation it was found that electrical stimulation of the posterior hypothalamus can produce dramatic declines in the intervals between a male rat's copulatory activities (Cagguila, 1970).

Some people believe that the answer to the riddle of refractory periods is somehow connected with the loss of seminal fluid during orgasm. Most researchers have been skeptical of this idea, since there is no known substance in the expelled semen to account for an energy drain, marked hormone reduction, or any of the other implied biochemical explanations. However, recent evidence that some men can avoid a refractory period by "holding back" their seminal fluid at the point of orgasm suggests a possible connection between ejaculated semen and refractory periods (Hartman and Fithian, 1984).

Another explanation suggests that there may be an evolutionary advantage in male refractory periods. According to this argument, since women have no sexual shutdown after orgasm they are able to continue copulatory activity with other males, increasing the numbers of sperm in their reproductive tracts and thus the possibility of impregnation. From this evolutionary point of view, the presence of additional sperm might also allow for increased natural selection of the fittest (the fastest swimmers, the longest living, and so forth). Admittedly, the evidence for this theory is tenuous at best, but it is nevertheless a provocative thesis. Whatever the reason for it, the refractory period is common not just to human males, but to males of virtually all other species for which data exist, including rats, dogs, and chimpanzees.

Multiple Orgasms.   There is a third area of sexual response patterns where some differences between the sexes occur: the ability to experience multiple orgasms. Technically speaking, the term **multiple orgasms** refers to having more than one orgasmic experience within a short time interval.

Although researchers differ in their views of what constitutes a multiple orgasmic experience, for our own purposes we can say that if a man or woman has two or more sexual climaxes within a short period, that person has experienced multiple orgasms. There is, however, a distinction between males and females that is often obscured by such a definition. It is not uncommon for a woman to have several sequential orgasms, separated in time by the briefest of intervals (perhaps only seconds). In contrast, the spacing of male orgasms is typically more protracted in time.

Public recognition of female capacity for multiple orgasms has only recently emerged. When the Kinsey group published their research data they were widely criticized for this "fantastic tale" of multiple response in women. There is no doubt that many individuals supported Kinsey's finding on the basis of their own experience. Nevertheless, it remained for the pioneer work of Masters and Johnson to firmly establish the legitimacy of this phenomenon.

How many women do experience multiple orgasms? Kinsey (1953) reported that about 14% of his female sample regularly had multiple orgasms. In 1970 a survey of *Psychology Today* readers revealed a 16% figure (Athanasiou et al., 1970). Surveys of our own student population over the years have produced a similar low percentage of women who regularly experience more than one orgasm during a single sexual encounter.

On the surface, it would then appear that the capacity for multiple orgasms is limited to a minority of women. However, the research of Masters and Johnson showed this assumption to be false:

> If a female who is capable of having regular orgasms is properly stimulated within a short period after her first climax, she will in most instances be capable of having a second, third, fourth, and even a fifth and a sixth orgasm before she is fully satiated. As contrasted with the male's usual inability to have more than one orgasm in a short period, many females, especially when clitorally stimulated, can regularly have five or six full orgasms within a matter of minutes. (1961, p. 792)

Thus, we find that most women have the capacity for multiple orgasms, but apparently only a small part of the female population experiences them. Why is there a large gap between capacity and experience? The answer may lie in the source of stimulation. The Kinsey report, the *Psychology Today* survey, and our own student surveys mentioned earlier, are all based on orgasm rates during penile-vaginal intercourse. For a variety of reasons—not the least of which is the male tendency to stop after his orgasm—women are not likely to continue coitus beyond their initial orgasm. In sharp contrast, several researchers have demonstrated that women who masturbate and those who relate sexually to other women are considerably more likely both to reach initial orgasm and to continue to additional orgasms (Athanasiou et al., 1970; Masters and Johnson, 1966).

We do not mean to imply by this discussion that all women should be experiencing multiple orgasms. On the contrary, many women may prefer sexual experiences during which they have a single orgasm, or perhaps no orgasm at all. The data on multiple orgasmic capacities of women are not meant to be interpreted as the way women "should" respond. This could lead to a new kind of arbitrary sexual standard. The following quotes illustrate the tendency to set such standards:

When I was growing up, people considered any young, unmarried woman who enjoyed and sought active sexual involvements to be disturbed or promiscuous. Now I am told that I must have several orgasms each time I make love in order to be considered "normal." What a switch in our definitions of normal or healthy—from the straight-laced, noninvolved person to this incredible creature who is supposed to get it off multiply at the drop of a hat. (Authors' files)

Sometimes men ask me why I don't come more than once. It is as though they want me to perform for them. The truth is, one orgasm is all I typically need to be satisfied. Sometimes it is nice not even to worry about having a climax. All this emphasis on producing multiple orgasms is a real put-off to me. (Authors' files)

As suggested earlier, multiple orgasms are considerably less common among males. They are most often reported by very young men, their frequency declining with age. Even at college age it is unusual to find men who routinely experience more than one orgasm during a single sexual encounter. However, we agree with Alex Comfort (1972), who asserts that most men are probably more capable of multiple orgasms than they realize. Many have been conditioned by years of masturbation to get it over as quickly as possible ("Hurry up and finish before I am discovered!"). Such a mental set hardly encourages an adolescent to continue experimenting after the initial orgasm. Through later experimentation, though, many men make discoveries similar to the one described in the following personal reflection of a middle-aged man:

Somehow it never occurred to me that I might continue making love after experiencing orgasm. For thirty years of my life this always signaled endpoint for me. I guess I responded this way for all the reasons you stated in class and a few more you didn't cover. My sweetheart was with me the night you discussed refractory periods. We talked about it all the way home and the next day gave it a try. Man, am I mad at myself now for missing out on something really nice all of these years. I discovered that I could have more than one orgasm in one session, and while it may take me a long time to come again, the getting there is a very nice part. My partner likes it, too! (Authors' files)

Even without a second orgasm, many men may find it pleasurable to continue sexual activity after a climax. However, some people believe it is necessary for a man to achieve orgasm whenever he interacts sexually with his partner. This idea, stemming from the pervasive myth that sex is not complete for a man unless he reaches "The Big O," may make it difficult for a man to enjoy sexual activity that does not result in a second climax. Not all males fall victim to this belief, however:

One of the best parts of sex for me is having intercourse again shortly after my first orgasm. I find it is relatively easy to get another erection, even though I seldom experience another climax during the same session. The second time round I can concentrate fully on my partner's reactions without being distracted by my own building excitement. The pace is generally mellow and relaxed, and it is a real high for me psychologically. (Authors' files)

Recent evidence suggests that some men may actually be capable of experiencing a series of orgasms in a very short time period. In one study, 13 men reported that they had the capacity to experience a series of pre-ejaculatory orgasms culminating in a final orgasm with ejaculation. Most of these men related having three to ten orgasms per sexual encounter. One man reported experiencing 30 orgasms, at intervals of one minute or less, during one intercourse session. Unfortunately, only one of these 13 individuals was studied in the laboratory, where his claim was substantiated with physiological data. Apparently the key to these multiple responses was the men's ability to withhold ejaculation, since the final orgasm in the series, accompanied by ejaculation, triggered a refractory period (Robbins and Jensen, 1978). More recently, Hartman and Fithian (1984) have reported success in teaching men to experience multiple, nonejaculatory orgasms by tightening the pubococcygeus (PC) and related muscles at the point of impending orgasm. If these findings are substantiated, and more men become aware of the possibility of experiencing multiple orgasms, future surveys may reveal that the percentage of men experiencing several orgasms during one sex session is closer to that of their female counterparts.

There is one final difference between men and women's experiences of multiple orgasms that we should mention here. It has to do with individuals' subjective assessments of sexual climaxes that occur after the first orgasm. Masters and Johnson (1966) found that women who experienced multiple responses in the laboratory reported subsequent orgasms to be more intense and pleasurable than the first. In direct contrast to this, most men who had multiple orgasms in their laboratory reported that the pleasure of the first orgasm was superior. Masters and Johnson interpreted this finding to reflect men's equating seminal fluid volume with superior orgasms, with initial ejaculation producing a larger quantity of semen.

While this finding no doubt reflects the experience of most males, it is important to note that some men report the exact opposite—namely, greater pleasure from subsequent orgasms. Some of the accounts we have heard give credit to increased sensitivity, improved staying power, more control, heightened awareness, and greater appreciation of the partner's response in later orgasms.

In all, multiple orgasms may be seen not as an ultimate goal to be sought above all else but rather as a possible area to explore. A relaxed approach to this possibility may give interested women and men an opportunity to experience more of the range of their sexual potentials.

Summary

Sexual Arousal: The Role of Hormones

1. While it is difficult to distinguish the effects of sex hormones and of learning experiences on sexual arousal, research does indicate that androgens appear to facilitate sexual interest in males. The relationship between female sexuality and hormones, if one exists, is very difficult to pinpoint.

Sexual Arousal: The Brain

2. The brain plays an important role in human sexual arousal by mediating our thoughts, emotions, memories, and fantasies.

3. There is evidence linking stimulation and surgical alteration of various brain sites with sexual arousal in humans and other animals.

4. The limbic system, particularly the hypothalamus and septal area, seems to play an important part in sexual function.

Sexual Arousal: The Senses

5. Touch tends to predominate among the senses that stimulate human sexual arousal. Locations on the body that are highly responsive to tactile pleasuring are called erogenous zones. Primary erogenous zones are areas with dense concentrations of nerve endings; secondary erogenous zones are other areas of the body that become endowed with erotic significance as the result of sexual conditioning.

6. Vision is second only to touch in providing stimuli that most people find sexually arousing. Recent evidence suggests that women respond as much as men to visual erotica.

7. It is not known whether smell and taste play a biologically determined role in human sexual arousal, but our own unique individual experiences may allow certain smells and tastes to acquire erotic significance. However, our culture's obsession with "personal hygiene" tends to mask natural smells or tastes that relate to sexual activity.

8. Some individuals find sounds during lovemaking to be highly arousing, while others prefer that their lovers be silent during love play. In addition to being sexually stimulating to some, communication during a sexual interlude can be very informative.

Sexual Arousal: Foods and Chemicals

9. At this point there is no evidence that any substance that we eat, drink, or inject has genuine aphrodisiac qualities. Faith and suggestion account for the apparent successes of a variety of alleged aphrodisiacs.

10. Certain substances are known to have an inhibitory effect upon sexual behavior. These anaphrodisiacs include some tranquilizers, a few antihypertensives, certain antiandrogenic drugs, and nicotine.

Sexual Response: Kaplan's Three-Stage Model

11. Kaplan's model of sexual response contains three stages: desire, excitement, and orgasm.

12. This model is distinguished by its inclusion of desire as a distinct stage of the sexual response cycle separate from genital changes.

Sexual Response: Masters and Johnson's Four-Phase Model

13. Masters and Johnson describe four phases in the sexual response patterns of both women and men: excitement, plateau, orgasm, and resolution.

14. During excitement, both sexes experience increased myotonia (muscle tension), heart rate, and blood pressure. Sex flush and nipple erection often occur, especially among women. Female responses include engorgement of the clitoris, the labia, and the vagina (with vaginal lubrication), elevation and enlargement of the uterus, and breast enlargement. Males experience penile erection, enlargement and elevation of the testes, and sometimes Cowper's glands secretions.

15. The plateau is marked by dramatic accelerations of myotonia, hyperventilation, heart rate, and blood pressure. In females, the clitoris withdraws under its hood, the labia minora deepen in color, the orgasmic platform forms in the vagina, the uterus is fully elevated, and the areolas become swollen. In males, the corona becomes fully engorged, the testicles continue both elevation and enlargement, and the Cowper's glands are active.

16. Orgasm is marked by involuntary muscle spasms throughout the body. Blood pressure, heart rate, and respiration rate peak. Orgasm is slightly longer in duration in females. Male orgasm typically occurs in two stages, emission and expulsion. It is difficult to distinguish subjective descriptions of female and male orgasms.

17. Masters and Johnson suggest that there is only one kind of physiological orgasm in females, regardless of the method of stimulation. Josephine and Irving Singer counter with the contention that women may experience three different kinds of orgasms.

18. Some women are capable of experiencing orgasm and perhaps ejaculation when the Grafenberg spot, an area along the anterior wall of the vagina, is vigorously stimulated.

19. During resolution, sexual systems return to their nonexcited state, a process that may take several hours, depending on a number of factors. Erection loss occurs in two stages, the first very rapid and the second more protracted.

Sexual Response: Some Differences Between the Sexes

20. Many writers now emphasize the fundamental similarities in the sexual responses of men and women. However, there are certain important primary differences between the sexes.

21. As a group, females demonstrate a wider variability in their sexual response patterns than men.

22. The presence of a refractory period in the male is one of the most significant differences in the response cycles of the two sexes. While no cause for this period has been clearly demonstrated, there is some evidence that neurological inhibitory mechanisms are activated by ejaculation.

23. Multiple orgasms occur more often in females than in males. Women are more likely to experience multiple orgasms while masturbating than during coitus. Recent evidence suggests that some men may also be capable of experiencing a series of orgasms in a very short time period. Women generally find subsequent orgasms to be more intense than the first of a series; men commonly find the opposite to be true.

Answers to Quiz:
  Report A = Male
  Report B = Female
  Report C = Female

Thought Provokers

1. Assume that research eventually reveals that yohimbine or some other substance has genuine aphrodisiac qualities. What possible benefits might be associated with its use? What possible abuses might arise? Would you consider using an aphrodisiac? If so, under what conditions?

2. It has traditionally been assumed that men have more capacity and desire for sexual expression than women. Do you believe this is a valid assumption? Why has this viewpoint been so pervasive across most Western cultures?

3. It has been said that women enjoy hugging and touching more than genital sex, whereas men have little interest in the "preliminaries," preferring to "get down to the real thing." Do you believe this statement reflects a genuine difference between the sexes? Are there sex differences in patterns of sexual turn-ons and turn-offs? If so, are they learned or biologically determined?

4. Women collectively appear to have a greater capacity for orgasm, to experience orgasm from a wider range of stimulation, and to have more problems experiencing orgasm than men. To what factors do you attribute this greater variation in female orgasmic response patterns?

Suggested Readings

Beach, Frank. "Hormonal Control of Sex-Related Behavior." In F. Beach (Ed.), *Human Sexuality in Four Perspectives*. Baltimore: Johns Hopkins Press, 1977 (also available in paperback from same publisher, 1978). A discussion of the effects of sex hormones on the behavior of humans and other animals. Although somewhat technical, this article contains a wealth of relevant facts.

Bermant, Gordon, and Davidson, Julian. *Biological Bases of Sexual Behavior*. New York: Harper & Row, 1974. Contains two excellent chapters dealing with hormonal factors in sexual expression.

Brecher, Ruth, and Brecher, Edward. *An Analysis of Human Sexual Response*. New York: New American Library, 1966. Provides a simplified and accurate reporting of the Masters and Johnson (1966) research findings.

Kaplan, Helen Singer. *Disorders of Sexual Desire*. New York: Brunner/Mazel, 1979. Deals primarily with the treatment of sexual difficulties, particularly problems of desire. It contains excellent information about the effects of a variety of drugs on sexuality.

Masters, William, and Johnson, Virginia. *Human Sexual Response*. Boston: Little, Brown, 1966. A highly technical book outlining the authors' major contributions to the understanding of the physiology of human sexual response. A good source for those readers who would like more detailed information about physiological responses to sexual stimulation.

Part Three

Sexual Behavior

7

Life has taught us that love does not consist in gazing at each other but looking outward together in the same direction.
Saint-Exupéry
Wind, Sand, and Stars (1939)

Love and the Development of Sexual Relationships

LOVE, INTIMACY, and sexual relationships are important and complex aspects of people's lives. In this chapter we will look at these interactions from various perspectives and examine some of the research dealing with them. We will consider a number of questions: What is love? How does it relate to jealousy? What does research on measuring love and on partner selection tell us? How does sex fit into relationships? Are there different kinds of love? And finally, what are some factors in developing and maintaining intimacy in a relationship?

What Is Love?

Love has intrigued people throughout history. Its joys and sorrows have inspired artists and poets, novelists, filmmakers, and other students of human interaction—indeed, love is one of the most pervasive themes in the art and literature of many cultures. Each of our own lives has likely been influenced in some significant way by love; our best and worst moments may be tied to a love relationship. Yet, although love is of great concern to humankind, little is conclusively known about it. Researchers have explored many aspects of love, however, and in the next section we will examine some of these. We will begin with a look at research related to measuring love and attraction.

Box 7.1 *Two Contrasting Definitions of Love*

1. "Love is patient and kind; love is not jealous, or conceited, or proud; love is not ill-mannered, or selfish, or irritable; love does not keep a record of wrongs: love is not happy with evil, but is happy with the truth. Love never gives up: its faith, hope and patience never fail. Love is eternal. . . . There are faith, hope and love, these three; but the greatest of these is love." (New Testament; I Corinthians 13)

2. "Love is a temporary insanity curable by marriage or by removal of the patient from the influences under which he incurred the disorder. This disease, like caries and many other ailments, is prevalent only among civilized races living under artificial conditions; barbarous nations breathing pure air and eating simple food enjoy immunity from its ravishes." (Ambrose Bierce, *The Devils' Dictionary*, 1943, p. 202)

Measuring Love

Love is a special kind of attitude with strong emotional and behavioral components. It is also a phenomenon that eludes easy definition or explanation. (Box 7.1 offers two contrasting definitions.) When asked in one study, two out of three college students were not sure they knew what love was (Kephart, 1967). Given the problematic nature of love, can it be meaningfully measured? Some social scientists have attempted to do so, with interesting results. Perhaps the most ambitious attempt to measure love was undertaken some years ago by psychologist Zick Rubin (1973). On the basis of responses to a questionnaire administered to several hundred dating couples at the University of Michigan, Rubin developed a 13-item measurement device that he called a love scale. On this scale people are asked to indicate if a particular statement accurately reflects their feelings about another person, usually someone they are interested in romantically.

Love, as measured by Rubin's scale, has three components: attachment, caring, and intimacy. *Attachment* refers to a person's desire for the physical presence and emotional support of the other person. *Caring* refers to an individual's concern for the other's well-being. *Intimacy* is the desire for close, confidential communication with the other.

Some people may argue that it is simply not possible to measure such an unfathomable emotion as love, particularly with a paper-and-pencil measurement device like the love scale. Nevertheless, Rubin did obtain some evidence supporting the validity of his scale. For example, the scale was used to investigate the popular belief that lovers spend a great deal of time looking into one another's eyes (Rubin, 1970). Couples were observed through a one-way mirror while they waited to participate in a psychological experiment. The findings revealed that "weak lovers" (couples who scored below average on the love scale) made significantly less eye contact than did "strong lovers" (those with above average scores). Another study indicated that the more two people liked each other after an initial meeting, the closer they stood together (Byrne et al., 1970).

Jealousy and Love

Many people think that jealousy is a measure of devotion and, conversely, that the absence of jealous feelings implies a lack of love. People will sometimes try to make a partner jealous to assure themselves of their partner's love or as an attempt to increase their partner's attraction to them.

> One time when I felt my girlfriend was kind of taking me for granted I felt neglected, so I flirted with another girl at a party. My girlfriend noticed that and became more attentive. Now I will occasionally deliberately flirt with someone else to get her to pay more attention to me. (Authors' files)

However, some writers believe that jealousy is related more to injured pride, or to people's fear of losing what they believe they control or possess, than to love. For example, a person who finds that a lover enjoys someone's else's company may feel inadequate and therefore jealous.

A *Psychology Today* readers' survey on jealousy defined it as the "thoughts and feelings that arise when an actual or desired relationship is threatened" (Salovey and Rodin, 1985, p. 22). The survey found that people often experience the intense emotions of jealousy because we imagine and fear the loss of the relationship. Our feelings may be further intensified by envy for the characteristics of the rival, which we may feel we lack ourselves. The survey indicated that if we want to have a particular characteristic, we are likely to be jealous of those who have this quality. In general, women were more envious of attractiveness and popularity, and men were more envious of wealth and fame. People with three specific traits were particularly prone to jealousy: having a low opinion of themselves, seeing a large discrepancy between how they are and how they would like to be, and valuing highly visible traits such as wealth, fame, popularity, and physical attractiveness.

Not everyone responds to jealousy in the same way, and according to one study (Clanton and Smith, 1977), there appear to be some differences in how women and men react. In general, women are more likely to acknowledge jealous feelings and men more likely to deny them. A jealous woman will more often focus on the emotional involvement of her partner with another person, whereas a jealous man tends to be concerned with the sexual relationship between his lover and another. Women also often blame themselves as the cause of jealousy, while men typically blame the third party or the woman. The *Psychology Today* study found few differences in men and women's jealous feelings and behaviors, except that women in the study manifested certain kinds of jealous behavior more often than men, such as secretively searching through a lover's belongings and extensively questioning a lover about a past romance (Salovey and Rodin, 1985).

Jealousy is an uncomfortable feeling that can stifle development and pleasure in a relationship. Respondents to the *Psychology Today* survey described three strategies to attempt to cope with jealousy. "Self-reliance" involved containing any expression of jealousy and becoming more committed to the loved one. "Positive comparison and self-bolstering" included thinking about one's good qualities and engaging in enjoyable activities for oneself. "Selective ignoring" involved deciding that the desired person is not particularly important. However, none of these strategies were very effective in helping the people in the study group overcome their feelings of jealousy (Salovey and Rodin, 1985). Walster and Walster (1978) offer the following suggestions to people who want to decrease feelings of jealousy. First, find out exactly what it is that makes you jealous. Examine your beliefs, thoughts, and feelings closely. Is it a matter of pride? Do you believe that the other person belongs to you like one of your possessions? Does the situation provoking jealousy lead to fears of losing this relationship? Second, it is important to put jealous feelings in perspective. One way is to ask yourself, "What is it that I want to be different? What do I really want? Why?" After understanding more fully what it is that really bothers you and leads to feelings of jealousy, the third step is for you and your partner to negotiate agreements or conditions about outside involvements. One student who did this successfully reports:

> My girlfriend and I go to a lot of parties together and have a good time—except for one thing. I find myself feeling jealous when I look across the room and see her talking and laughing with another guy. And then when I'm around her I start putting her down in subtle ways, especially to the guy she's been talking to. She pretty much ignores me when I do that, but I think it could harm our relationship. So I really gave it some thought and realized that I actually don't mind her having fun with other people, in fact it's one of the things I like about her. What I really wanted was for her to pay a little more attention to me at parties and do things like hold my arm

or give me a little kiss—little things that told others we were a couple. When I asked her to do those gestures, she was real agreeable and parties have been a lot more fun for us since. (Authors' files)

Falling in Love: Why and With Whom?

What determines why people fall in love and with whom they fall in love? These questions are exceedingly complex. Some writers believe that people fall in love to overcome a sense of aloneness and separateness. Psychoanalyst Erich Fromm (1965) suggested that union with another person is the deepest need of humans. Another psychoanalyst and writer, Rollo May, author of *Love and Will* (1969), also believes that as people experience their own solitariness, they long for the refuge of union with another through love. Others, however, see loneliness as a by-product of our individualistic and highly mobile society rather than as an inherent part of the human condition. This view emphasizes the connectedness that people have with others through all our social relationships, language, and culture, and describes love relationships as one aspect of a person's social network rather than as a cure for the "disease" of loneliness (Solomon, 1981).

For many people, falling in love may serve to justify certain behaviors—for example, being sexual with another or demanding an exclusive relationship. Sometimes when people find themselves responding sexually to someone they assume they must be in love. Frequently a person becomes convinced that he or she is in love with another after sharing a pleasant sexual encounter. Later in this chapter we will examine more fully the relationship between love and sex.

Just as we know little about why people fall in love, we have no simple explanations for why they fall in love with whom they do. There are a number of factors, however, that are often important. One of these is proximity. People often fall in love with individuals they see frequently—in school, at work, at church, or at parties. Another factor is similarity. It has been reported that people who fall in love often have very similar social backgrounds, sharing social class, religion, similar family histories, or other traits (Rubin, 1973). Commonality of interests also seems to be important to the long-term success of a relationship. People who have very similar attitudes and behavioral characteristics frequently become lovers. This does not mean that people necessarily fall in love with individuals who are like them. Frequently the needs of lovers complement each other. For example, a person who has a need to be assertive and feel in control may enter into a love relationship with someone who prefers a more passive role.

Physical attractiveness also often plays a dominant role in drawing lovers together. In spite of the saying that "beauty is only skin deep," it has been experimentally demonstrated that an individual's physical attractiveness frequently has a dramatic impact on his or her appeal to the other sex (Berscheid and Walster, 1974). One study indicated that male college students placed significantly more emphasis on physical appearance in selecting a partner for a sexual or a long-term relationship than did females. Women placed more emphasis on interpersonal warmth and personality characteristics (Nevid, 1984). Physical appearance seems to influence not only "sex appeal" but many aspects of our initial attitudes toward other people. In one study, college students were shown photographs of males and females of differing degrees of physical attractiveness and asked to provide their impression of these people. The researchers reported that the most physically appealing individuals were consistently rated as more interesting, sociable, kind, and sensitive than their less attractive counterparts (Dion et al., 1972).

Although it may be disturbing to discover that beauty is so important to others, this is most true in the early stages of a relationship. "It seems likely that the impact of physical attractiveness is greatest when we first meet someone. As a relationship progresses, physical attractiveness tends to recede in importance. And we often perceive people whom we love as being beautiful, regardless of what anyone else might think" (McNeil and Rubin, 1977, p. 581).

People's objective attractiveness appears to be only one factor in how attractive they seem to others. Subjective opinion matters too, and situational variables may significantly affect someone's opinion of how attractive or how likeable another person is. In one study, people meeting in different rooms were given the same photographs of people and asked how much they thought they would like the people in the photos. One group met in a nicely furnished, pleasant room, and the other met in a dirty, shabbily furnished, messy room. The people in the attractive room were more positive toward the photographs than the group in the unpleasant room (Maslow and Mintz, 1956). A similar study had a group of strangers meet in a cool, comfortable room and others meet in an uncomfortably hot room; the group in the comfortable room reported liking each other more than the group in the uncomfortable room (Griffitt, 1970). Research has also shown that meeting someone while experiencing physiological arousal from fear or anxiety may increase interest in and attraction to the other person (Dutton and Aron, 1974). One's pre-existing sexual arousal may also increase the subjective attractiveness of others, or one's interest in them. For example, Stephan et al. (1971) took men who were ostensibly coming to a computer dating service to see a photo of their "date" and divided them into two groups. While they were waiting, the men in one group were provided with pin-up type magazines, and the other men were given low-key, boring reading material. The men who had been reading sexually suggestive material rated their prospective date as more attractive than the others did, although they all saw the same photo. Other studies have reported similar results, and this work raises some intriguing possibilities for further research.

Love and Sex

Just what is the connection between love and sex? It is certainly true that some couples engage in sexual relations without being in love with one another. Conversely, love may exist independently of any sexual attraction or expression. Nevertheless, the feelings of being in love with and sexually attracted to another person are frequently intertwined. The complex interplay of these related mental states gives rise to many familiar questions. For example, does sexual sharing typically deepen a love relationship? Are people more likely to feel they are in love with someone after they have had sex? Is sex without love appropriate? We will attempt to shed some light on these and similar questions in this section.

One study of college students found that women were much more likely to report being in love with their partners if they had engaged in coitus than if they had not. This study found particularly high love scores (as measured by Rubin's love scale) among women whose first sexual experiences had been with their current partner. On the other hand, there seemed to be no link between a man's reported love for his partner and whether they had engaged in sexual relations (Peplau et al., 1977).

In response to questionnaires administered in our sexuality classes, women have consistently linked love with sex to a greater extent than men. In a recent survey of several hundred students, roughly 30% of the women indicated that sex was either not enjoyable or totally inappropriate without love. In contrast, only 12% of men indicated the same feelings. However, the majority of these students—70% of the women and 79% of the males—agreed that "love enriches sexual relations but is not necessary for enjoyment."

Other studies indicate a similar male-female difference. A random sample of 249 college students reported that men found it much easier than women to have sexual intercourse for pleasure and physical release without an emotional commitment (Carroll et al., 1985). When other college students were asked what the most important factors were in their decision to engage in intercourse, women reported the quality and intimacy of the relationship to more important than men did. However, men with less coital experience were more influenced by the quality and intimacy of the relationship than those with more such experience (Christopher and Cate, 1984).

Other studies suggest a shift towards a greater emphasis on love. A *Psychology Today* readers' survey indicated that love has become more important to both men and women. In 1969, 17% of men and 29% of women believed that sex without love was either unenjoyable or unacceptable. In 1983, 29% of men and 44% of women felt this way (Rubenstein, 1983). Additionally, a *Parade* magazine nationwide survey of 1100 randomly selected men and women found that 59% of men and 85% of women reported that they found it difficult to have sex without love (Ubell, 1984). (Research note: the *Parade* survey respondents were a cross-section of the U.S. population and had been contacted by the surveyers, whereas the *Psychology Today* survey respondents were mainly young, well-educated people with relatively high household incomes, who had responded to the survey on their own initiative by mailing in the

Cathy   by Cathy Guisewite

questionnaire. Therefore, the *Parade* study may be more representative of the general population.)

These findings appear to reflect a double standard that still exists in our society. Whereas men have often learned that experiencing sex in a casual relationship is acceptable, women frequently have learned that sexual sharing is appropriate only when one is in love with the other person. One might argue that men are better adjusted sexually because they express their sexuality more easily in a wider range of relationships, or that women are better adjusted because they integrate their emotional feelings and sexuality more easily. It could also be that it is not a question of adjustment but, rather, that these different tendencies of men and women stem, in part, from biological differences.

Conflict about whether or not to express oneself sexually, with or without love, can result in difficulties. It is reasonable to suspect that many women (and, to a lesser extent, men) have attempted to justify their sexual behavior by deciding they are in love. It is likely that some couples even enter into premature commitments, such as going steady, becoming engaged, or getting married, to convince themselves of the depth of their love and thus the legitimacy of their sexual involvement.

While many people enjoy sex without love, the activity frequently arouses strong feelings. We are often confronted with the question "Is it really all right for two people who are not in love to have sex?" There is no absolute answer to this question. Each of us has our own personal value system that influences the decisions we make for ourselves. Therefore, instead of attempting to answer the question about the appropriateness of sex without love, we will briefly outline a few differing views.

Albert Ellis, in his book *Sex Without Guilt* (1966), suggests that a sexual relationship between individuals who are not in love ought to be both socially and personally acceptable. After providing psychotherapy to individuals and couples for many years, Ellis concluded that sex without love can be quite satisfying, although sex with love is probably more so. In his book Ellis argues that many people, particularly young people, sometimes want sexual intimacy with someone with whom they are not in love. Many individuals, he claims, have little or no capacity for love, and these people should not be denied the satisfaction of sexual sharing. Ellis further suggests that imposing a necessary link between sex and love may result in people feeling needlessly guilty about nonloving sexual relations. If business associates, friends, and fishing partners get along excellently without loving each other, why shouldn't sex mates, who may share little else, also experience mutually gratifying encounters?

Rollo May (1969) expresses a different view about sex without love. He observes that there have been significant changes in attitudes since earlier times in our history: "The Victorian person sought to have love without falling into sex; the modern person seeks to have sex without falling into love" (p. 46). May believes that the contemporary preoccupation with technique and performance and the deemphasis of intimacy has resulted in a lack of sexual enjoyment and passion for many people. Masters and Johnson describe what they believe to be advantages of sex within a love relationship:

> Sex in a warm, emotionally committed relationship may change in character and sexual response may become diffused after a while. It may not always reach the peaks of

excitement that are sometimes experienced by a man and woman in their early, experimental encounters. But other dimensions of sexual pleasure may be discovered—the familiarity that is comforting, the safety that allows complete vulnerability, and the deepening sense of emotional intimacy, among other pleasures. (1975, pp. 99–100)

Sex and Relationships on Your Terms

The subject of sex with or without love raises the issue of decision-making regarding sexual relationships. Sexual expression can have many different meanings; for example, it can be a validation of deep intimacy within a relationship. People can choose to be sexual as a part of a friendship or as a way of getting to know someone. For some, reproduction may be the primary meaning. Reduction of sexual tension can be a motivation for sex, and sex can also be used as a way of experiencing new feelings, excitement, and risk. It can even be a kind of recreational pastime. People also use sex to try to alleviate feelings of insecurity—to prove their "manhood" or "womanhood" or to please someone or persuade them to care. Some people use sex to experience the power to attract others or to avenge earlier rejections by enticing partners and then turning them down.

Each person has the task of deciding how he or she wants to express sexuality. This important process is complicated by the fact that many of the old rules that have governed sexual relationships are changing, as reflected in these comments of a recently divorced woman:

> When I was dating 25 years ago in college, a kiss at the door on a first date was considered to mean I really liked the guy. And I was determined to be a virgin until I got married. These guidelines were held by most of my friends, and I felt a lot of security in them. Now I don't know how to behave. There really don't seem to be any standard rules. It's exciting and frightening to know I can make decisions because I want to. It is also confusing at times, and I sometimes wish the standards I used to know were still common. (Authors' files)

Some people base their decisions on sexuality on clear, pre-existing rules expressed by family, church, or peer group. Many others do not have such specific guidelines or disagree with the values they have been taught. These people need to understand their own personal values and develop their own guidelines. The following section discusses some options for establishing guidelines for decisions about sexual expression.

Know What You Want

The first step in integrating sex into your life in a meaningful way is to consider what you want in relationships before initiating sexual involvement with another. This is a variation on the theme "know thyself." Consider the following:

> Often when I meet a man for the first time I end up being swept off my feet and into bed. At the time it seems like the thing to do, but afterwards I'm often left confused and a bit empty inside. It's not that I don't like sex. I'm just not sure about what role it should play in my life. (Authors' files)

This woman might be able to reduce the confusion and discomfort she experiences by evaluating her expectations and needs in the area of sexual relationships. An important question for each of us to ask ourselves is "What role do I want relationships and sex to occupy in my life at this time?" The answer to this question will often change over time as a person faces new life situations.

As a part of this self-inventory it might be helpful to consider the following questions:

- How comfortable am I with some of the contemporary approaches to sex and relationships?
- Which of the more traditional norms do I value?
- What are my values as they pertain to sexual relationships, and where do they come from (family, church, friends, media, and so forth)?

You can further clarify your values in relation to a specific decision about sexual activity by asking another question: "Will a decision to engage in a sexual relationship—with this person and at this time—enhance my positive feelings about myself and the other person?" The answer to this question can help you act in a way that is consistent with your value system. It can also help prevent exploitative sexual encounters in which people do not consider each other's feelings.

What if the answer to the previous question is no? Then it may be appropriate to think about what kind of relationship, if any, might enhance positive feelings. Perhaps a sexual relationship is not right, but a nonsexual friendship would be. Or perhaps you do not feel ready for a sexual relationship yet, but want to leave open the possibility. At this point communication and negotiation are important.

One of the risks of understanding and acting on your own feelings, desires, and values is that someone else may not see things the same way. Unfortunately, many people take such differences to mean that either they are wrong or the other person is wrong. However, more often than not, differences simply indicate that two people do not want the same thing at the same time. Occasionally a relationship cannot be established without compromising one person's situation or values. When this occurs, one option is to end the relationship. Each person can then seek someone who has more similar perspectives. On other occasions clarification, negotiation, and compromise may establish a common bond for a relationship. However, direct communication about where one stands can be difficult. One study of college students found that only 21% of those interviewed said that they asked directly about their partners' feelings for them. Others did not let themselves be so vulnerable; they used a variety of indirect means to try to find out how their partners felt about the relationship. Thirteen percent asked a third party's opinion. Other indirect tactics students used included "endurance tests," such as asking a partner to give up a ski weekend; trying to make the partner jealous; using humor or hints about the relationship's future; or making self-deprecating comments in the hope that the person would disagree (Baxter and Wilmot, 1984). The following sections will illustrate some options for dealing with several specific relationship situations. Chapter 8 provides additional information on communication in sexual relationships.

Friendships Without Sex

Some people find it very difficult to communicate a desire for friendship without sex, especially when it appears that the other person wants a sexual relationship. Often they are concerned that the other person will feel bad or decide to end the relationship. However, most people would probably prefer to be told the truth directly rather than have to decipher the meaning of vague, confusing responses. The following comment is fairly typical of our students:

> I hate it when I find myself in a relationship and all I get is the run around. I eventually get the picture when someone else doesn't reciprocate my feelings, but what a waste of time and energy. Why can't they just come out and say what they are feeling? At least I would know where I stand and could act accordingly. (Authors' files)

This person's feeling of frustration is understandable. However, one can attempt to resolve this kind of uncertainty by asking the other person about his or her feelings. The following demonstrates how one student did this:

Nonsexual friendships can offer companionship and enjoyment.

Jake and I had gone out several times, and initially he acted like he was attracted to me. But then he began to treat me more like a sister. He continued to ask me out but made no sexual gestures. I finally told him I was confused about how he felt about me. He seemed very concerned about my feelings as he told me that he wanted a friendship with me instead of a romantic relationship. He wasn't sure why, but he had come to realize that's how he felt. I felt disappointed, and it was a little tough on my ego to not be desired sexually, but I decided that a friendship with him would be nice for me. And several years later, we are still friends. (Authors' files)

Saying "Not Yet" to a Sexual Relationship

One of the benefits of less rigid rules about "proper" sexual behavior is that they can make it easier for people to set their own pace in sexual relationships. It is common for a person to feel sexual attraction and to want a sexual relationship with someone—but not yet. The ability to delay sexual involvement until both people feel ready can do much to enhance the initial experience. Also, waiting until familiarity and trust are established, and making sure that personal values are consistent with the relationship, can enhance positive feelings about oneself.

When sexual attraction exists within a relationship, sex is not necessarily an "either-or" situation. There are progressive stages of intimacy, from holding hands to genital contact, and some people move slowly through these steps to savor and grow comfortable with the increasingly intimate contact. Gratification may be greater with a gradual progression toward intimacy than with rushed sexual contact, as the author of the following discovered:

> I felt sexually attracted to Mike the first time I met him, but somehow, almost by mutual instinct, we moved very slowly sexually. We both agreed that was how we wanted it for this relationship. We spend several extremely enjoyable months kissing, touching, holding each other, and even sleeping together before we had intercourse. The entire experience has really changed how I see "fast food sex" and has given new light to the expression "Haste makes waste." (Authors' files)

Social expectations of "instant sex" can present a challenge to those who want to move gradually into a sexual relationship. There are several things you can do to let another person know that you are not yet ready for sex or that you want the relationship to progress slowly. It is often helpful to begin by indicating that you find the person attractive. You can acknowledge your desire for greater sexual intimacy, yet be definite about not being ready. Finally, you can let a partner know what kind of physical contact you want at a given point in the relationship; this can help avoid misunderstandings and reassure the other person.

Guidelines for Casual Sex

Sometimes people are interested in a primarily sexual experience. Casual sexual encounters are characterized by a lack of deep emotional involvement, as well as by a focus on sex. The sexual relationship can be brief, or it can go on for a long time. Our students often debate whether sex can be good in this context. Some argue that without some kind of commitment the sex will be less than satisfying. Others maintain

that sexual experiences are at their best in this type of situation. Our intent is not to resolve this debate but rather to present some ideas, adapted from *Brief Encounters* (Coleman and Edwards, 1980), that can help to make casual sexual liaisons self- and other-enhancing experiences.

The basic ingredients of mutually enhancing casual sex are two people who are willing to be honest with themselves and each other. The decision to enter into such a relationship also needs to be acceptable within each person's value system. Other criteria include:

1. Both partners want to have sex.
2. Neither partner is coercing the other.
3. Both partners make it clear that their commitment is limited to mutual enjoyment.
4. Both partners are interested in their own and each other's sexual pleasure and feelings of self-worth.
5. Both partners have taken responsibility for discussing and taking any necessary precautions against sexually transmitted diseases or unwanted pregnancy.

Caring Endings

Over the years our sexuality classes have been the scene of many lively discussions of the question "How do you prefer to be informed when someone does not wish to continue a relationship with you?" While students have many different opinions and experiences, the large majority want to be told in a clear, unmistakable manner that their desire for a relationship is not reciprocated. A simple statement like "I appreciate your interest in me, but I'm not attracted to you enough to want a relationship with you" is the kind of ending that most of our students have indicated they would prefer. Most students also report that it would be more difficult to make than to hear such a direct statement; there is rarely an easy way to end a relationship when one person is interested in maintaining it. This situation requires communication that is both effective and compassionate.

Managing Rejection

Fear of rejection can often inhibit people from initiating a relationship or expressing their desires within one. The old adage "Nothing ventured, nothing gained" does not always quell the fear of venturing. One man expresses his concern as follows:

> I find it extremely stressful to ask a woman out for the first time. I just can't deal effectively with the prospect of being turned down. I know it's irrational, but when someone says, "No," I have a hard time not feeling real down. (Authors' files)

To many people, a no is tantamount to an all-out assault on their sense of self-worth. A person who is rejected may feel unattractive, boring, unsexy, unintelligent, or inherently unlovable. All of us experience rejection at some time, however, because our traits cannot match every person's preferences. The very characteristics that one person finds undesirable may well appeal to another, and the right to choose not to become involved with someone is certainly a right that most people want.

Although rejection can still be a painful experience, there are some strategies for dealing with being turned down. It is important to remember that each of us has worth, regardless of whether all people approve of us. Also, defending yourself to someone who has said no is not likely to be helpful, since being turned down is usually not a criticism but simply an expression of individual preferences. Finally, even though rejection may make us want to give up on continued attempts to form close relationships, we can avoid rejection completely only if we isolate ourselves from most kinds of social interaction. As one woman states:

> I don't like being turned down, but I like being alone even less. Life is full of risks, and the dating game has its share. It might be safer to retreat into a social vacuum and wait for something to happen. But I like making my own choices instead of hoping the right man will ask me. If I'm turned down, someone else always comes along. It's a happy hunting ground out there, filled with all kinds of prospects, some of whom will say yes. (Authors' files)

Cathy   by Cathy Guisewite

Types of Love

Love takes many forms. Two types that we will focus on in this section are *passionate love* and *companionate love*.

Passionate Love

Passionate love, also known as romantic love or infatuation, is a state of extreme absorption in another. It is characterized by intense feelings of tenderness, elation, anxiety, sexual desire, and ecstasy. Generalized physiological arousal, including increased heart beat, perspiration, blushing, and stomach churning, along with a feeling of great excitement, often accompanies this form of love. Strong sexual desire is typically a major component.

> Although I had never known him well, I had admired him from a distance for some time. When circumstances threw us together for that day, I felt strongly drawn to him and realized I was really in love with him. Being physically close to him was incredibly intense, and I felt as if I could never touch him enough or ever bring our bodies as close together as I yearned to do. (Authors' files)

A *Psychology Today* readers' survey on love and romance indicates that concepts of what is romantic are quite varied. Common romantic themes included: walking on a moonlit beach, having a quiet dinner at home, kissing in public, or making love all weekend. For many, romance was typified by heightened emotions arising from unusual sex, or by the pain of extreme suffering. About 20% described out-of-the-ordinary sex—outside during a storm, for example, or in the bathtub—as highly romantic. Many others saw the intense, painful emotions in unrequited love, being separated from a loved one, betrayal, or love doomed to failure as very romantic (Rubenstein, 1983).

Intense passionate love typically occurs early in a relationship. It sometimes seems as if the less one knows the other person, the more intense the passionate love. In passionate love, people often overlook faults and avoid conflicts. Logic and reasoned consideration are swept away by the excitement the lover evokes. One may perceive the object of one's passionate love as providing complete personal fulfillment, a situation that may have unexpected consequences:

> Romance is built on a foundation of quicksilver nonlogic. It consists of attributing to the other person—blindly, hopefully, but without much basis in fact—the qualities one wishes him to have, though they may not even be desirable, in actuality. Most people who select mates on the basis of imputed qualities later find themselves disappointed, if the qualities are not present in fact, or discover they are unable to tolerate the implication of the longed-for qualities in actual life. For example, the man who is attracted by his fiancee's cuteness and sexiness may spend tormented hours after they are married worrying about the effect of these very characteristics on other men. It is a dream relationship, an unrealistic relationship with a dream person imagined in terms of one's own needs. (Lederer and Jackson, 1968, p. 439)

Another characteristic of intense passionate love is that it often does not last very long. Love that is based on ignorance about a person's full character is bound to change with increased familiarity. Many couples choose to make some kind of commitment to each other (become engaged, move in together, get married, and so forth) while still fired by the fuel of passionate love, only to feel disillusioned later when ecstasy gives way to routine, and the everyday annoyances and conflicts typical of most ongoing relationships begin to surface. This is the time when the previously infatuated person may begin to have some doubts about his or her partner. Some couples are able to work through this period to ultimately find a solid basis upon which to build a lasting relationship of mutual love. Others discover, often to their dismay, that the only thing they ever really shared was passion.

The frequent confusion at the beginning of a relationship between passionate and companionate love is one reason a couple may find it helpful to allow their relationship to evolve over a fairly long time (months, maybe even years) before committing themselves to major lifestyle changes. They may be able to move beyond the stage of passionate love and see whether their relationship has a firm basis for a long-term commitment based on companionate love.

Unfortunately, many people who experience the lessening of passion believe that this is the end of love, rather than a possible transition into a different kind of love:

> I just don't feel the same excitement and the same passion for my lover as I used to feel. I used to feel overwhelmed waiting for her to meet me. I still look forward to seeing her, but not with breathless anticipation. I guess that I must not be in love anymore. (Authors' files)

On the other hand, some people look forward to a different kind of relationship. Erich Fromm once commented, "Romantic love is a delicious art form but not a durable one. In the end, its most persistent practitioners confess that they would like to escape from its patterned illusion into the next more realistically satisfying stage of an enduring relationship" (1965, p. 252).

Companionate Love

Companionate love is a less intense emotion than passionate love (Walster and Walster, 1978). It is characterized by friendly affection and a deep attachment that is based on extensive familiarity with the loved one. It involves a thoughtful appreciation of one's partner. Companionate love often encompasses a tolerance for another's short-comings along with a desire to overcome difficulties and conflicts in a relationship. This kind of love is committed to ongoing nurturing of a partnership. In short, companionate love is often enduring, while passionate love is almost always transitory. The qualities of companionate love were important to the respondents of the *Psychology Today* readers' survey on love and romance. Respondents said that the three most important ingredients of love were friendship, devotion, and intellectual compatibility. These rated higher than the passionate love characteristics of sexual "electricity" and longing (Rubenstein, 1983).

Sex in a companionate relationship typically reflects the feelings that familiarity provides, especially the security of knowing what pleases the other. This foundation of knowledge and sexual trust can encourage experimentation and subtle communication. Sexual pleasure in a companionate relationship strengthens the overall bond of the relationship. Although sex in companionate love is usually less exciting than in passionate love, it is often experienced as richer, more meaningful, and deeply satisfying, as the following statement reveals:

> Between my first and second marriage I really enjoyed the excitement of new sexual relationships. The passion and the challenge were all wonderful, especially after so much sexual frustration in my first marriage. Even though I sometimes miss the excitement of those times, I would never trade it for the easy comfort, pleasure, and depth of sexual intimacy I now experience in my 17-year marriage. (Authors' files)

Companionate love has also been described as a *mutative relationship* (Goethals, 1980). This notion implies that the two individuals in a love relationship, as well as the relationship itself, continually generate change. This kind of relationship has a dynamic quality that helps satisfy the often contradictory human desires for both security and excitement. The people in mutative relationships grow and change, sometimes in response to individual challenges, sometimes in response to the relationship itself. The partners share a sense of collaboration in their joint life, exhibit a great deal of empathy for each other, and demonstrate a high degree of androgyny. They are sexually exclusive by desire rather than by contractual agreement. Goethals believes that ideal mutative relationships are rare but possible.

Although most relationships begin with a period of passionate love and only later evolve into companionate love, some have the opposite history. Companionate love may develop first in, say, a situation where two people know each other for an extended period as acquaintances, friends, or coworkers. Often an initial sexual attraction is not present or is deemphasized because of circumstances. In these relationships passionate love is based on familiarity with the other person, rather than on the excitement of the unknown. One woman describes her experience:

> Jim and I had been friends for several years before I even became attracted sexually to him. We would occasionally go out to dinner together and I would always enjoy myself. We had a lot of professional interests in common, and as I came to know him more fully, I gained a deep appreciation for his personal values and integrity. But he just wasn't my "type." But one time—I'm not even sure how it happened (I guess we were both horny)—we had sex together. It was nice and comfortable, but not terrific. For some reason, we continued to be sexual and as time passed we have fallen in love, and sex between us as well as our whole relationship continues to be more and more exciting. I never expected it to happen this way. (Authors' files)

The Development of Intimacy

A question that students often ask and that interests many people is how to maintain intimacy, satisfaction, and sexual enjoyment in a relationship. There are many opinions on this subject and no conclusive answer. This may have to do with the uniqueness of each person; what is satisfying to one person may be dissatisfying to another. Each person must, in effect, reinvent the wheel and discover for him- or herself how to develop and maintain satisfactory relationships. This section will discuss some ways of thinking about developing and maintaining intimacy.

Self-Love

Satisfying intimacy within a relationship begins with self-love. How can this be? As we use the term, self-love does not mean conceit or lack of consideration of others; these qualities are usually indications of personal insecurities. By self-love we mean the kind of feeling that Leo Buscaglia (1972) describes as a genuine interest, concern, and respect for ourselves—the ability to look in the mirror and appreciate the person we see and feel excited about that person's potential.

A scholar of human development, Erik Erikson (1965), believes that positive self-feelings are a prerequisite to a satisfying relationship. Only as people begin to feel more secure in their own identity are they able to establish intimacy with others, both in friendship and eventually in a love-based, mutually satisfying sex relationship.

The Phases of Relationship

One way of understanding the development of a relationship is to examine different aspects of its growth, or phases; this may also give us some guidelines for maintaining a good relationship. As we discuss the various phases, it is important to remember that they are simply a convenient scheme; in reality, a relationship is fluid, dynamic, and frequently unpredictable. We mean to give our readers a framework for thinking about a relationship rather than a prescription for intimacy. Also, this discussion and the following section consider sex as only one part of the total context of a relationship.

Inclusion.   *Inclusion* is when one person extends some kind of invitation to relate, whether by eye contact, a smile, or a friendly "Hello." It is the first step that one person takes in meeting another. Many "how-to-pick-up-dates" books specialize in tips for initial inclusion. Often, the signs can be quite subtle:

> When I go out dancing alone and want to decide who to ask to dance, I look around the room. When I see a man who returns my glance (especially if he smiles or nods), I'll go over and ask him to dance if he isn't already on his way to ask me. (Authors' files)

Inclusion continues throughout a relationship, and the nature of inclusion behaviors provides the backbone of a positive relationship. A good morning kiss, a smile and hug after a day apart, a sincere "Tell me about your day," a compliment, or an expression of appreciation are some of the kinds of inclusions that can nourish an ongoing relationship.

Response.   How one responds to a gesture of inclusion may determine whether a relationship even begins. For example, quickly glancing away from someone's initial eye contact will likely deter any further initiation. However, if one responds in kind and goes a step further with a smile and a greeting, the other person will be more

likely to initiate further contact. Positive inclusion and responses are dependent upon each other for the interaction to progress.

As a relationship continues, certain kinds of responses will typically enhance the relationship's growth. These include listening to the other person and understanding his or her point of view, following through with agreements or plans, or being enthusiastic about seeing the other person. Positive and consistent inclusions and responses are the foundation for the next important phases—care, trust, affection, and playfulness. These phases often develop simultaneously and build on each other.

Care. Care implies a genuine concern for another's welfare. Care motivates us to consider another person's desires and interests; it creates a desire to please and contribute to another's happiness.

Trust. Trust is a feeling essential to both the ongoing development of a relationship and its satisfactory continuance. It contributes to the belief that each partner will act consistently, in ways that promote the relationship's growth and stability and that affirm each partner. It means that the partners trust each other and themselves to be positive and constructive in their inclusions and responses.

I trust my partner to:
Talk to me when she's unhappy about something I've done,
Be concerned about my satisfaction when we make love,
Feel attracted to me when I am naked,
Be honorable and fair,
Take my feelings in consideration,
Use birth control. (Authors' files)

Affection.   Affection is characterized by feelings of warmth and attachment. It evokes a desire to be physically close to another and is often expressed by touches, holding hands, sitting close, hugs, and caresses. Affection can be signalled nonverbally by smiles, winks, and tender looks, and verbally by expressions of appreciation, liking, or loving. The following comment exemplifies a high level of affection within a friendship:

> My best friend and I never get together without a hug for a greeting and a goodbye. It's also typical for us to get together at one of our houses for tea, long talks, and foot rubs. (Authors' files)

Playfulness.   This is the phase in the development of an intimate relationship in which each person exhibits delight and pleasure in the other. Exhilaration, abandon, and expansive laughter often accompany playfulness, whether it is a parent playing peek-a-boo with a small child or lovers having a pillow fight.

As you may have noted, all of the phases described to this point could characterize a variety of situations, including a good friendship, a parent-child or sibling relationship, or a close mentor-student relationship. Close nonsexual friendships with members of our own and the other sex can be a very important part of our personal lives. One study found that characteristics of close friendships include enjoying one another's company; mutual trust that each will act in the other's best interest; respecting, assisting, supporting, and understanding one another; confiding experiences and feelings to each other; and being spontaneous in the relationship. This study also found that lover and spouse relationships had these general friendship qualities as well as higher levels of passion, exclusiveness, self-sacrifice, and enjoyment of being together. They also had less acceptance than nonsexual friendships did, and more criticism, conflict, ambivalence, and discussions about the relationship and its problems (Davis, 1985).

Genitality.   The final phase extends the relationship to include genital contact. There may have been varying degrees of sexual feeling and expression in previous phases, but in the genitality phase a person has decided to express feelings through genital sex.

When people step over the genitality boundary before going through the other six phases, they may actually experience a reduction in feelings of emotional closeness. The following account illustrates this:

> I had known Chris for some time and thought I was ready to be sexual with him. So, after an evening out together, I asked him if I could stay at his place, and he said yes. I felt really aroused as we got in bed. I really enjoyed touching the shapes and tex-

tures of his previously unknown-to-me body. As we started to touch each other's genitals, I felt uncomfortable. It seemed that if we were going to proceed in the direction we were headed, we would be going beyond the level of emotional intimacy I felt—in a way, it would be a violation of my feelings. It seemed that I would have to shut out the closeness I felt in order to go further. I had to choose between intimacy and genital contact. Our closeness was more important to me, and I told him that I wanted to know each other more before going further sexually. (Authors' files)

With the foundation of the other six phases, genitality can be the culmination of deep intimacy and emotional closeness. Companionate love is an expression of all of these phases. Fromm (1965) states that the use of the body for the purpose of seeking and expressing satisfaction with one another is what sex truly is and what gives it its most deeply felt meaning. He says further that sex is important in two ways: first, through its role in initial attraction; and second, in its cementing of a relationship through the fulfillment and pleasure it offers.

An older couple's intimacy and affection develops from years of shared experiences.

Maintaining Relationship Satisfaction

Human relationships present many, many challenges. To begin, there is the challenge of building a positive relationship with oneself, as described in the section on self-love. Then, there is the additional task of establishing satisfying and enjoyable relationships with family, peers, teachers, coworkers, employers, and other people within a person's social network. We also have the challenge of developing special, intimate relationships with friends and, when we want them, sexual relationships. Finally, many people confront the challenge of maintaining satisfaction and love within an ongoing, committed relationship. Commitment in a relationship is often demonstrated by the decision to marry. However, many couples have long-term committed relationships outside of marriage. This section will present some of the factors that may contribute to ongoing satisfaction in sexual relationships. We will also discuss the value of sexual variety within the relationship.

There are many ingredients in a lasting love relationship. They include self-acceptance and appreciation of one another, commitment, good communication, realistic expectations, shared interests, and the ability to face conflict effectively (Rosenman, 1979). These characteristics are not static; they evolve and change and influence one another over time. Often they need to be deliberately cultivated. In contemporary society the efforts of the partners are probably more important to relationship stability than in the past, when marriage as an institution was sustained more strongly by culture, religion, law, and the extended family (Levinson, 1978).

A study of 300 happily married couples revealed that the most frequently named reason for an enduring and happy marriage was seeing one's partner as one's best friend. Qualities that they especially liked in one another were caring, giving, integrity, and a sense of humor. These couples were aware of flaws in their mates, but they believed that the likable qualities were more important than the deficiencies. Many said that their mates had become more interesting to them over time. They preferred shared rather than separate activities, which appeared to reflect the richness in the relationship. Another key was their belief in marriage as a long-term commitment and a sacred institution. Most of the couples were generally satisfied with their sex lives, and for some the sexual passion had become more intense over time. As one wife said, "The passion hasn't died. In fact, it has gotten more intense. The only thing that has died is the element of doubt or uncertainty that one experiences while dating or in the beginning of a marriage." However, fewer than 10% thought that good sexual relations kept their marriage together (Lauer and Lauer, 1985). Box 7.2 summarizes the major reasons these married people believed that their marriages were successful.

The Inclusion-Response Foundation

Maintaining positive inclusion and response experiences is crucial to the continued satisfaction of committed couples. The saying "It's the little things that count" is especially meaningful here. When one partner says to the other "You don't love me anymore" that often means "You are not doing as many of the behaviors you used to do that I interpret as meaning you love me." The behaviors are often so small that one may not really notice them. However, when couples do fewer things that contribute to their partner's feeling of being loved, or stop doing them, the deficit is often experienced as a lack of love. On the other hand, continuing the affectionate and considerate interactions helps maintain a feeling of love. For example:

> The kinds of things that enhance my feeling of my partner loving me may seem quite inconsequential, but to me they aren't. When he gets up to greet me when I come home, when he takes my arm crossing the street, when he asks, "Can I help you with that," when he tells me I look great, when he holds me in the middle of the night, when he thanks me for doing a routine chore—I feel loved by him. Those little things—all added up—make a tremendous difference to me. (Authors' files)

Couples may also find that talking with one another to identify especially enjoyable actions and to explore new ideas can be useful. The golden rule is not always applicable in relationships, because people's preferences are often quite different.

Enjoyment with and appreciation of one another in nonsexual areas typically enhances sexual interest and interactions. Often couples report a lack of desire for sexual intimacy when they experience a general lack of intimacy within the relationship. People may make comments like:

> I just don't feel like having sex with him when he's been at work all day, then comes home and watches TV all night. (Authors' files)

Husbands and wives listed the same reasons for the success of their marriage. These were the reasons, in descending order of the frequency with which they were mentioned:

1. My spouse is my best friend.
2. I like my spouse as a person.
3. Marriage is a long-term commitment.
4. Marriage is sacred.
5. We agree on aims and goals.
6. My spouse has grown more interesting.
7. I want the relationship to succeed.

Individual and Relationship Growth

Growth and change are important in maintaining vitality in a relationship. Each person's growth can provide an opportunity for the other partner to develop new skills within himself or herself in order to appreciate and respond positively to the changes of the beloved. Lovers can draw on emotional, artistic, intellectual, spiritual, and physical dimensions for growth, to enrich each other's mutual enjoyment. As a husband married for 30 years said, "I have watched her grow and have shared with her both the pain and the exhilaration of her journey. I find her more fascinating now than when we were first married" (Lauer and Lauer, 1985, p. 24).

At times, this dynamic of growth and change occurs without deliberate effort; at other times it requires direct attention. Couples who maintain satisfactory levels of growth will typically not let love diminish by choosing to withdraw their energy from the relationship at the first sign of strain or boredom. Rather, they will confront the difficulties and attempt to ameliorate them (Csikszentmihalyi, 1980). For example:

> My husband and I found it increasingly difficult to have time together because of our busy schedules. And then when we were together we felt a little like strangers. So we decided to structure some time together learning something new. The dancing lessons we took even rekindled some romantic feelings. (Authors' files)

Each person brings her or his strengths and weaknesses into relationships, and a relationship itself has its own combination of strengths and weaknesses. A couple is rarely fully prepared for the myriad issues that arise from this combination. It is often helpful to view problems and dissatisfactions as challenges to overcome or differences to accept, rather than as sure signs that the relationship is about to fail. Couples need to be prepared to negotiate and renegotiate what they want out of life and out of their relationship, knowing that the arrangement they work out one day may become untenable the next. At the same time, partners in a committed relationship often recognize that the love they hold for each other means accepting one another as unique human beings. These attitudes give a couple options for shaping a relationship uniquely suited to their individual and collective wants and needs (Walster and Walster, 1978).

The process of being in a committed relationship can itself be a source of growth. Such a relationship can make urgent demands on individuals so that they mature in directions and with a rapidity that would not otherwise occur. The "beneficial trauma" of confronting oneself intensely and learning to accept another deeply, as sometimes occurs within an intimate relationship, can facilitate individual growth. As Erich Fromm once wrote, "Married lovers grow within love; they develop into better human beings" (1965, p. 288).

Sexual Variety: An Important Ingredient

> There is a special little restaurant with great steaks and a cozy, intimate atmosphere that I love to visit once every few months. Good companionship, a favorite bottle of wine, a tasty cut of rare meat, and I am living. Let a friend invite me back the next day, and it is still good, but not quite so stimulating. Given an invitation for a third trip in as many days, and I might just as soon stop off for a McDonald's quarter-pounder. (Authors' files)

There is a message in this personal anecdote. Many people have a strong desire to seek variety in life's experiences. They may acquire an assortment of friends, each providing a unique enrichment to their lives. Likewise, they read different kinds of books, pursue a variety of recreational activities, eat a variety of foods, and take a mixture of classes. Yet many of these same people ignore variation in an area of life capable of providing much joy. Consider the following:

> Sex for me is a dull, boring, and uninspiring routine. My husband likes to "make love" on Saturday night (he is too tired during the week). It's always the same way— a few kisses, some mechanical manipulation of my breasts, and presto, he is in and out and finished. I rarely am satisfied, but I don't even give a damn anymore. Actually I'm glad he finishes quickly. It's never fun to prolong boring things. (Authors' files)

Unfortunately, many people enter into a committed relationship thinking that intense sexual excitement will always be a natural occurrence between two people in love. But the heart-pounding joy of initial discovery must eventually be replaced by realistic and committed efforts to maintain the vitality and rewards of a working relationship. Once a person is committed to a primary partner, and the variety offered by a succession of relationships is no longer available, it may be necessary to seek variety in other ways.

Not every couple feels the need for sexual variety. Many people may feel quite comfortable with established routines and have no desire to change them, as expressed in the following:

> We settled down into a variation of our own particular pattern, a seldom-deviated-from routine, a practice which *Cosmopolitan* warned was boring, stagnating, and ruinous to a marriage. . . . It has taken months, maybe years of persistent trial and error with shyly veiled hints and endless, polite "That was fine, really it was" from both of us before we each discovered what the other enjoyed, responded to, and wanted. Charlie, only slightly less shy than me, knew where I wanted to go and how to get me there, and in turn, over a period of time, I'd been able to reach through his natural reserve to the passionate

man underneath. Now we had an intimate knowledge of one another and our own pace, our own rhythm, our own consistent satisfaction, and to hell with the marriage manuals. In bed, at least, we trusted one another. And shared. (Rebeta-Burditt, 1978, p. 288)

However, if you prefer to develop more variety in your sexual relationship, the following paragraphs may be helpful.

Communication is critical. Talk to your partner about your needs and feelings. Share with him or her your desire to try something different. Perhaps some of the guidelines in Chapter 8 will facilitate making requests and exchanging information. You may want to try sharing fantasies and then acting them out.

Avoid the routine of time and place. Make love in unusual places (on the laundry room floor, stretched out on the kitchen counter, alongside a mountain trail) and at extraordinary times ("birdsong in the morning," a "nooner," or in the middle of the night when you wake up feeling sexual).

Some of the most exciting sexual experiences may be those that take place on the spur of the moment with little or no preplanning. It is easy to see how these encounters might occur frequently during courtship days. It is also true that they may become distant memories after couples settle into the demanding daily schedules of living together. Perhaps you may find that striving to maintain this spontaneity will stand you in good stead as your relationship is nurtured over the months or years of your time together.

Do not let questions of what is normal get in the way of an enriched and varied erotic life. Too often people refrain from experiencing something new because they feel that different activities are "abnormal" or, worse yet, "perverse." In reality, only you can judge what is normal for you. There is a consensus among contemporary writers in the field of human sexuality that any sexual activity is normal, as long as it gives pleasure and is not injurious to either partner.

Related to concerns about what is normal are concerns about frequency. Forget the magazine article that said that couples in your age category are having sex 2.7 times per week. The only right rule for you is to have sex as often as you and your partner want to.

Finally, lovers sometimes find that books dealing with sexual techniques may be beneficial to their erotic lives. We recommend that you read them together rather than separately. Discussing a particular written suggestion can often open up new vistas of sexual sharing. Such books sometimes provide the necessary approval or justification for trying something new.

We do not mean to imply that all people must have active, varied sex lives to be truly happy. This is not the case. Some, as we have already mentioned, may find comfort and contentment in repeating familiar patterns of sexual interaction. Others may consider sex relatively unimportant compared with other aspects of their lives and may choose not to exert special efforts in pursuing its pleasures. However, if your sexuality is an important source of pleasure in your life, perhaps our suggestions pertaining to variety will be valuable to you.

Summary

What Is Love?

1. Rubin's love scale is a 13-item subjective rating scale that measures what he defines as the three components of love: attachment, caring, and intimacy. Studies of eye contact and physical proximity give some support to the validity of the scale.

2. Some people consider jealousy a sign of love, but it may actually reflect fear of losing possession or control of another. Some research indicates that men and women react differently to jealousy.

Falling in Love: Why and With Whom?

3. Falling in love has been explained as resulting from the need to overcome a sense of aloneness or from the desire to justify sexual involvement, or as a consequence of sexual attraction.

4. People tend to fall in love with others with similar backgrounds.

5. Although a person's objective physical attractiveness is often important in attracting another, factors such as an anxiety-producing situation, pleasant surroundings, or preexisting sexual arousal can also affect people's interest in each other.

Love and Sex

6. There are various perspectives on the question of love and sex. Most students in our surveys report that love enriches sexual relations but is not necessary for enjoyment of sex.

7. Women consistently link love with sexual behavior more than men do.

Sex and Relationships on Your Terms

8. Deciding one's own values in relation to sexual experiences is especially important today, in a time of changing expectations. Asking yourself the question "Will a decision to engage in a sexual relationship—with this person at this time—enhance my positive feelings about myself and the other person?" can help you act in a way that is consistent with your value system.

9. There are many types of relationships, including friendships without sex; progressing slowly into a sexual relationship; and "casual sex."

10. You can develop strategies for minimizing the pain of rejection, particularly if you remember that rejection usually occurs because your traits do not match another's subjective preferences, not because you are unworthy.

Types of Love

11. Passionate love is characterized by intense, vibrant feelings.

12. Companionate love is characterized by deep affection and attachment.

The Development of Intimacy

13. Self-love, meaning positive and accepting feelings towards oneself, is an important foundation for intimacy with others.

14. The phases of a relationship are inclusion, response, care, trust, affection, playfulness, and genitality. Care, trust, affection, and playfulness usually develop at the same time and reinforce one another.

Maintaining Relationship Satisfaction

15. Maintaining positive inclusion-response experiences is crucial to continued satisfaction in an ongoing relationship.

16. Individual and relationship growth can provide challenges and stimulation to the relationship helping to maintain its vitality.

17. Sexual variety is often an important ingredient of enjoyable sex in a long-term relationship. For some, however, the security of routine is most satisfying.

Thought Provokers

1. The section on jealousy discussed research findings that women were more envious of attractiveness and popularity, while men were more likely to be envious of wealth and fame. What do you think accounts for this difference?

2. Assume you are the parent of a teenager who asks, "How do I know when I should have sex?" What would you answer?

3. What do you think are the key differences between companionate and passionate love? How do these characteristics fit into the list in Box 7.2 of things that keep a marriage going?

Suggested Readings

Coleman, Emily, and Edwards, Betty. *Brief Encounters*. New York: Anchor, 1980. An indispensable guide for dealing with relationships as a single person, with especially good chapters on the issues of money and sex.

Friday, Nancy. *Jealousy*. New York: Morrow, 1985. An exploration and analysis of jealousy.

Fromm, Erich. *The Art of Loving*. New York: Bantam, 1963. A classic on the topic of love. Fromm elucidates the power of love to develop human potential within oneself and within a relationship.

Rosenman, Martin. *Loving Styles*. Englewood Cliffs, N. J.: Prentice-Hall, 1979. This book examines what couples can do to help their relationships work better. Contains advice on working out conflict, increasing trust, and keeping a long time relationship fresh.

Singer, Laura. *Stages: The Crises That Shape Your Marriage*. New York: Grosset & Dunlap, 1980. A helpful book that discusses patterns of crisis points in marriage and ideas to deal more effectively with critical stages of marriage.

Walster, Elaine, and Walster, William. *A New Look at Love*. Reading, Mass.: Addison-Wesley, 1978. Discusses questions about love, such as sexual attraction, the dilemma of security versus excitement, and difficulties in love relationships, and reports the latest research findings through case histories and questionnaires.

Human speech is like a cracked kettle on which we tap crude rhythms for bears to dance to while we long to make music that will melt the stars.
Gustave Flaubert
Madame Bovary (1857)

Communication in Sexual Behavior

The Importance of Communication
Some Reasons Why Sex Talk Is Difficult
Talking: Getting Started
Listening and Feedback
Discovering Your Partner's Needs
Learning to Make Requests
Delivering Criticism
Receiving Criticism
Saying No
Nonverbal Sexual Communication
Impasses

THIS IS A CHAPTER about sexual communication, or *sex talk*: the ways people convey their needs and desires to sexual partners. We will consider the reasons such attempts are sometimes unsuccessful; we will also explore some ways to enhance this aspect of our sexual lives.

The Importance of Communication

Sex talk can contribute greatly to the satisfaction of an intimate relationship. We do not mean that extensive verbal dialogue is essential to all sexual sharing; there are times when spoken communication may be more disruptive than constructive. Nevertheless, partners who consistently do not talk about any sexual aspects of their relationship may be denying themselves an opportunity to learn each other's needs and desires.

Talking about sex is a unique kind of communication that presents a variety of special problems. The presence of warmth, caring, and openness in a relationship is no guarantee that the couple have good sexual communication. Furthermore, even knowledge of effective communication skills is no insurance that a couple will apply them in their relationship. Aside from the fact that it is often particularly difficult to talk about sex, some people may be unmotivated to explore this area with their partners. Sex may seem relatively unimportant to some, and therefore not worth any extra effort. Others may purposely avoid activities designed to improve sexual relations because bad sex is serving a purpose for them—perhaps to punish, put down, insult, or deprive their partners.

We have seen instances where both members of a couple have all the tools for good communication but are unable or unwilling to apply them in their relationship. The reasons for this may be far more complex than the possibilities mentioned previously suggest. Even when a climate of good will prevails, it is sometimes difficult to establish a satisfying pattern of sexual dialogue. In such circumstances, it may be undesirable for the couple to try to resolve all of their communication problems strictly on their own. Instead, they should probably seek professional counseling.*

Central to this chapter is our belief that the basis for effective sexual communication is **mutual empathy**—the underlying knowledge that each partner in a relationship cares for the other and knows that the care is reciprocated. With this perspective in mind we will discuss various approaches to sex talk that have proved helpful in the lives of many people. We do not claim to have the final word on the many subtle nuances of human communication, nor do we suggest that the ideas offered here will work for everyone. Communication strategies often need to be individually modified; and sometimes differences are so basic that even the best communication cannot ensure a mutually satisfying relationship. We hope, though, that some of these shared experiences and suggestions can be helpful in your own sex life.

---

*Chapter 17 provides some guidelines for seeking professional assistance.

Some Reasons Why Sex Talk Is Difficult

Why do so many people find it difficult to talk candidly with their companions about sexual needs? There are many reasons: Some of the most important lie in our socialization; the language available for talk about sex; and the fears many people have about losing spontancity or expressing too much of themselves.

The way we were reared as children often contributes to later difficulties in talking about sexual needs. Learning to cover our genitals, or to think that eliminative functions are "dirty," or to hide self-pleasuring for fear of adverse reactions all may contribute to a sense of shame and discomfort with the sexual areas and functions of our bodies. The development of sexual attitudes during childhood and adolescence will be discussed in Chapter 13.

There is a lack of communication about sexual matters in many American homes that is detrimental in a number of ways. Not talking about sex at home deprives a young child of one valuable source of a vocabulary for communicating about sex later in life. This lack of communication may also convey an implicit message: that sex is not an acceptable topic for conversation. Furthermore, children most effectively acquire communication skills when they are provided with models of verbal interaction followed by the opportunity to express their own thoughts in an accepting atmosphere. None of these elements is typically available in a home where people simply do not talk about sex.

The lack of positive models frequently extends beyond the home. Few individuals have access to classroom or textbook sources that portray how couples talk about sex. Neither peer groups nor the popular media fill the gap by providing realistic or positive information.

Another source of communication difficulty is related to the lack of a suitable language of sex. By the time they are grown up and eager to communicate sexual needs and feelings, many people don't know how to go about doing it. All the words may have become associated with negative rather than positive emotions. Many of us have learned to snigger over taboo sex words or to use them in an angry, aggressive, or insulting manner. Consequently, it can be very uncomfortable to use those same words to describe a sexual activity to someone we really care for.

Thus, when we want to begin engaging in sexual communication, we may find ourselves struggling to find the right language for this most intimate kind of dialogue. The range of words commonly used to describe genital anatomy gives some indication of our society's mixed messages about sexuality. Two extremes tend to predominate: street language at one end and clinical terminology at the other. Clinical and street terms are listed in Table 8.1.

One man's consternation over trying to figure out what words to use for his own genitals is revealed in the following anecdote:

> I want to talk with my girlfriend about our sex life. So many times I have made up my mind to do this, but I can't seem to come up with how I should do this. How can I tell her about my body and its needs? What words do I use? Do I say "I like it best when you caress along the entire length of my penis" or should I say "It feels good when you touch all of my cock"? The first word sounds too clinical, but I am afraid the term cock might shock her and put her off. Just what words do lovers use? (Authors' files)

As this man has discovered, our language lacks a comfortable sexual vocabulary. Many of us are not at ease with the words commonly available. We may find them to be too clinical, too harsh, or too juvenile to use in a caring way. Words like penis and vagina often seem too technical or medical; cock, prick, cunt, and snatch are expressions that are often used aggressively or insultingly. Terms describing sexual activity may create similar problems. Statements like "Let's fuck" may be lovingly delivered and excitedly received by some, but they may seem too cold, graphic, or aggressive to others. A more scientific description, such as "Let's have sexual intercourse," may seem clumsy and impersonal.

Most of us have also learned while growing up that talking about S-E-X is very different from discussing the afternoon softball game.

> When I was in early grade school, an older neighbor girl whispered to me "You have four children in the family and that means your parents fucked four times." I was quite unfamiliar with slang words; even though I didn't know what it meant, it didn't sound like a very nice thing for *my* parents to have done. I went into the house; my mother took one look at me and asked what was the matter. I said "What does fuck mean?" My memory from this point is not very clear, but when she recovered from the shock, she tried her best to explain it. The final message I received was not to ask questions about sex. (Authors' files)

Table 8.1 Sex Language, Clinical Versus Street [a]

Female		Male	
Clinical	Street	Clinical	Street
External genitals; pudendum[b]; vulva	Cunt Snatch Pussy Muff Bearded clam Beaver Hair-pie Happy Valley	External genitals; pudendum Penis	Equipment Pencil and tassles Balls and bat Cock Dick Wang Prick Reamer
Vagina	Hole Quim Cockpit	Testicles	Balls Jewels Dead meat

[a]Besides the terms listed in this table, euphemistic phrases (such as "privates," "down there," and the "wee-wee" or "pee-pee" words of childhood) can be applicable to either sex.
[b]Latin, meaning "the shamefuls." According to Webster's dictionary, the external genitals of a human being, especially of a woman.

Within the context of our culture, it is very natural—or at least common—to feel shy or embarrassed when talking about sexuality with friends and lovers. This awkwardness can often be avoided though, and people certainly find ways of learning to live with the vocabulary. For example, the context and tone in which sex terms are used may create totally different meanings and reactions, as this woman's comment shows:

> I have very different feelings about words depending on how they are used. My lover saying "I love your sweet cunt" is very different from hearing "You stupid cunt." (Authors' files)

Also, some people give their own or their partners' genitals nicknames, such as Fuzzylove, Slurpy, Artesia, Pokey, Peter, or Moby, in an attempt to avoid negative associations with much of the existing terminology.

In the absence of a better language model, each of us may benefit from seeking a vocabulary that is comfortable to use in our own intimate relationships. A helpful first step in talking about sex might be to try to determine what words are mutually agreeable. The following anecdote suggests one way of doing this:

> Whenever I am with a new person, and our relationship has progressed to the point of having sex, I suggest we play a little game where we try to come up with as many different words as we can to name a specific sexual activity or body part. As we play the game, I ask her which words she likes best, often expressing some of my own preferences. Sometimes I discover words I hadn't even heard before. It is a good way to get relaxed and begin talking about sex. Also, it helps in future discussions because we both have a sense of what words to use. (Authors' files)

Later in this book (Chapter 17) we will explore some of the benefits and joys associated with talking to our lovers while we touch their bodies. We shall see that this is a wonderful time to expand intimacy while learning about each other's needs and preferences. It is a particularly good way to discover what words are mutually acceptable.

Beyond the handicaps imposed by socialization and language limitations, difficulties in sexual communication for some people may also be rooted in fears of too much self-exposure. Any sexual communication involves a certain amount of risk: By talking, people place themselves in a position vulnerable to judgment, criticism, and even rejection. The willingness to take risks may be related to the amount of trust that exists within a relationship. Some couples lack this mutual trust, and for them the risks of openly expressing sexual needs are too great to overcome. Others have a high degree of reciprocal caring and trust, and for them the first hesitant steps into sexual dialogue may be considerably easier.

We have outlined some reasons why many people find it difficult to engage in meaningful and effective sexual communication. Despite the difficulties, communication is an important part of sexual sharing, just as it is in other aspects of a relationship. The potential rewards are enhanced sexual experiences and enriched relationships.

Talking: Getting Started

How does one begin communicating about sex? There are many ways of breaking the ice, and we will explore a few of them here. These suggestions may be useful not just at the beginning of a relationship but throughout its course.

Talking About Talking

When people feel uneasy about a topic, often the best place to start is by talking about talking. Discussing why it is hard to talk about sex can provide a good beginning. Each partner has individual reasons, and understanding those reasons can help set a relationship on a solid foundation. Perhaps you can share experiences about earlier efforts to discuss sex with parents, teachers, doctors, friends, or lovers. It may be helpful to move gradually into the arena of sex talk by directing your initial discussions to nonthreatening, less personal topics (such as new birth control methods, pornography laws, and so forth). Later, as your mutual comfort with discussing sexual matters increases, you may be able to talk about more personal feelings and concerns.

Reading and Discussing

Since many people find it easier to read than talk about sex, articles and books dealing with the subject may provide the stimulus for personal conversations. Partners can read the material separately, then discuss it together; or a couple can read it jointly and discuss their individual reactions to it. Often it is easier to make the transition from a book or article to personal feelings than to begin by talking about highly personal concerns.

*Reading together
facilitates discussion
of sensitive matters.*

Erotic Books and Movies as Stimulants

Some people find it helpful to read a sexy novel together or see an erotic film. Needless to say, this strategy is not appropriate for every couple. Some individuals may be aroused by this activity, while others may find it boring, embarrassing, offensive, or threatening. It may still be a worthwhile experience, however, in that a couple can later share their feelings about what they read or saw. It may be easy for them to discuss their overall reactions to a book or movie (bored? disgusted? excited? aroused?). Also, there may have been a particular scene that either aroused or offended one person or the other. Comparing reactions can be a helpful way of finding out about a partner's feelings about sexual matters. Books and movies can also provide ideas for exploring new behaviors: Sometimes they portray an activity that one or both partners would like to try.

Sharing Sexual Histories

Another way to start talking is to share sexual histories. There may be many questions that you would feel comfortable discussing with your partner. For instance: How was sex education handled in your home? How did your parents relate to each other—were you aware of any sexuality in their relationship? When did you first learn about sex, and what were your reactions? How did you feel about "making out" for the first time? Many other items could be added to this brief list; the questions depend on the feelings and needs of each individual.

Listening and Feedback

Communication, sexual or otherwise, is most successful when it is two-sided, involving both an active listener and an effective communicator. In this section we will focus on the listening side of this process.

From the perspective of the listener, there are a number of strategies that may facilitate communication. Have you ever wondered why certain people seem to draw others to themselves like metal to a magnet? With some thought you will probably conclude that, among other things, these individuals are often very good listeners. What special skills do they possess that make us feel they really care about what we have to say? Next time you are with such a person, observe closely. Make a study of his or her listening habits. Perhaps your list of good listening traits will include several of the following.

Be an Active Listener

Some people are passive listeners. They may stare blankly into space as their companion talks, perhaps grunting an "uh-huh" now and then. Such responses may make us think that the person is indifferent, even when this is not the case, and we may soon grow tired of trying to share important thoughts with someone who does not seem to be receptive:

> When I talk to my husband about anything really important, he just stares at me with a blank expression. It is like I am talking to a piece of stone. I think he hears the message, at least sometimes, but he rarely shows any response. Sometimes I feel like shaking him and screaming "Are you still alive!" Needless to say, I don't try communicating with him very much anymore. (Authors' files)

Being an active listener means really listening to what your partner is saying. You may communicate this by changing facial expressions, nodding your head, asking questions ("Could you give me an example?"), and making brief comments ("I see your point"). Sometimes it may be helpful to reciprocate in the conversation. For example, as your partner relates a feeling or incident you may be reminded of something in your own life that you would like to share. Making these associations and candidly expressing them to your companion can encourage her or him to continue voicing important concerns.

Maintain Eye Contact

Maintaining eye contact is one of the most vital aspects of good verbal communication. When people maintain eye contact when we are sharing with them, the message is clear: They care about what we have to say. How different we feel when the listener gazes around the room, looks out the window, or glances at a watch:

> My boyfriend averts his eyes every time I try to discuss something important about our relationship. I know he cares about me, or at least I think he does. But it sure is disconcerting when he won't look me in the eyes. I know that he is intellectually

invested in our relationship, but emotionally it seems like he leaves me when his eyes start to wander. (Authors' files)

Our eyes are wondrously expressive of feelings. When we fail to maintain eye contact we deny our partner a valuable source of information about how we are perceiving his or her message.

Provide Feedback

The purpose of communication is to provide a message that has some impact on the listener. However, a message's impact may not always be the same as its intent, for communications can be misunderstood. This is particularly true with a topic like sex, where language is often roundabout or awkward. Therefore, giving your partner some *feedback,* or reaction to her or his message, can be very helpful. In addition to clarifying how you have perceived your partner's comments, feedback shows unmistakably that you are actively listening.

We may also benefit by asking our partners to provide some response to a message we think is important. A comment like "What are your thoughts about what I have just said?" may encourage feedback that can help you determine the impact of your message on your partner.

Support Your Partner's Communication Efforts

Many of us can feel quite vulnerable when communicating important messages to our partners. Support for our efforts can help alleviate our concerns, and it can encourage us to continue building the communication skills so important for a viable relationship.

After we struggle to voice an important concern, how good it can feel to have a partner say "I really appreciate your sharing your thoughts with me" or "Thanks for caring enough to tell me what was on your mind." Such supportive comments can help foster mutual empathy, while at the same time ensuring that we will continue to communicate our thoughts and feelings candidly.

Express Unconditional Positive Regard

The concept of *unconditional positive regard* is borrowed from the immensely popular *Client-Centered Therapy,* authored by Carl Rogers (1951). In personal relationships it means conveying to our partners the sense that we will continue to value and care for them regardless of what they do or say. Unconditional positive regard may encourage a person to talk about even the most embarrassing or painful concerns. The following anecdote reveals one person's response to this valued attribute:

I know that my wife's love for me is unfaltering and that no matter what I say or reveal, she will continue to care for me. In an earlier marriage I could never express any serious concerns without my wife getting defensive or just plain mean. As a consequence, I just quit talking about things that really mattered. What a relief it is to be with someone with whom I can express what is on my mind without worrying about the consequences. (Authors' files)

Use Paraphrasing

One way to increase the probability that you and your partner will listen more effectively to each other is to use a technique called **paraphrasing**. This involves a listener summarizing, in his or her own words, the speaker's message.

BOB: Mary, I think I would enjoy our relationship more if you were more gentle. Do you understand what I mean?

MARY: I understand. You think I'm an aggressive person.

BOB: That's not quite what I mean. I mean that when you touch me when we make love, I would like you to use a lighter, softer caress.

MARY: Now I think I understand. I always thought you liked me to use firm pressure when I touched you. But now I see that light caressing is what you prefer.

BOB: That is what I meant. Thanks for understanding.

If the paraphrase is not satisfactory, the speaker can try to express the message in different words. Then the listener can try to paraphrase again. Several attempts may be necessary to clear away discrepancies between the communicator's intent and the listener's interpretation. As time goes by, a couple will typically find that the need to use this approach diminishes, as listening skills improve.

Discovering Your Partner's Needs

Discovering what is pleasurable to a sexual partner is an important part of sexual sharing. Many couples want to know each other's preferences but are uncertain how to find out. In this section we will look at some effective ways of learning about our partner's wants and needs.

Asking Questions

One of the best ways to discover your partner's needs is simply to ask. However, there are several ways of asking: Some can be helpful, while others may be ineffective or even counterproductive. We will review a few of the most common ways of asking questions and the effect each is likely to have.

Yes or No Questions.   Imagine being asked one or more of the following questions in the context of a sexual interlude with your partner:

1. Was it good for you?
2. Do you like oral sex?
3. Was I gentle enough?

4. Did you come?
5. Do you like it when I stimulate you this way?
6. Do you like being on the bottom?
7. Is it OK if we don't make love tonight?
8. Am I a good lover?

At first glance, these questions may seem reasonably worded. However, they all share one characteristic that may reduce their effectiveness: They are **yes or no questions**. Each asks for a one-word answer, even though people's thoughts and feelings are rarely so simple.

For example, consider Question 2, "Do you like oral sex?" Either answer—"Yes, I do" or "No, I don't"—gives the couple little opportunity to discuss the issue. Certainly the potential for discussion exists. Nevertheless, in a world where sexual communication is often difficult under the best of circumstances, the asker may get no more than the specific information requested. In some situations, of course, a brief yes or no is all that is necessary. But the person responding may have mixed feelings about oral sex (for example), and the phrasing of the question leads to oversimplification. Open-ended questions or questions that allow statement of a preference can make it easier for the answerer to give accurate replies.

Open-Ended Questions.   Some people find that asking **open-ended questions** is a particularly helpful way to discover their companion's desires. This approach places virtually no restrictions on possible answers; in a sense it is like responding to a general essay question on an exam. ("What are some of the important aspects of human sexuality that you have learned thus far this term?") The following list gives some examples of open-ended questions:

1. What things give you the most pleasure when we make love?
2. What aspects of our sexual sharing would you most like to have changed?
3. What parts of your body are most sensitive?
4. What variations in intercourse positions do you find pleasurable?
5. What is the easiest or most enjoyable way for you to reach orgasm?
6. What are your feelings about oral sex?

A primary advantage of open-ended questions is that they allow your partner freedom to share any feelings or information she or he thinks is relevant. With no limitations or restrictions attached, you may discover much more about your companion.

Open-ended questions can also be valuable in encouraging feedback when you are telling your partner something important. Basically, the technique of encouraging feedback involves asking for the listener's thoughts along the way, rather than waiting for a response after you have completed a lengthy monologue. Questions or statements like "What do you think about . . . ," "How do you feel about . . . ," or "I sense that you have some feelings about what I am saying" can provide opportunities for your partner to express important thoughts.

One possible drawback of the open-ended approach is that your partner may not know where to begin when asked such general questions. Consider being asked something like "What aspects of our lovemaking do you like best?" Some people might welcome the unstructured nature of this question, but others might find it difficult to respond to such a broad query, particularly if they are not accustomed to openly discussing sex. If this is the case, a more structured approach may have a better chance of encouraging talk. There are several ways of structuring your approach; one is the use of either/or questions.

Either/Or Questions. The following list gives some examples of **either/or questions**:

1. Would you like the light on when we make love, or shall we turn it off?
2. Am I being gentle enough or too gentle?
3. Is this the way you want to be touched, or should we experiment with a different kind of caress?
4. Would you like to try something different, or shall we stop and just hold each other?
5. Would you like to talk now, or would you prefer we wait for another time?

While either/or questions offer more structure than open-ended questions, they also encourage more participation than simple yes or no queries. People often appreciate the opportunity to consider a few alternatives. The either/or question also shows the questioner's concern about a partner's pleasure. Thus, this kind of question may encourage a response at a time when a more open-ended question might be overwhelming. However, either/or questions can still be somewhat restrictive. There is always the possibility that someone will not like either of the choices offered. In this case, the answerer can state another alternative that is preferable.

In addition to asking questions, there are other ways of discovering the sexual needs of a partner. We will discuss three other communication techniques here: self-disclosure, comparing notes, and giving permission.

Self-Disclosure

Often direct questions put people on the spot. Whether you have been asked "Do you enjoy oral sex?" or "How do you feel about oral sex?" it may be quite difficult to respond candidly, simply because you cannot gauge your companion's feelings on the subject. If the topic has strong emotional overtones, it may be very difficult to reply—no matter how thoughtfully the question has been phrased. It is the content, not the communication technique, that causes the problem.

With potentially loaded topics, a way to broach the subject may be to start with a self-disclosure:

> For the longest time I was reluctant to bring up the topic of oral sex with my lover. We did about everything else, but this was one area we avoided both in action and conversation. I personally was both excited and repelled by the prospect of this kind of sex. I didn't have the slightest idea what she felt about it. I was afraid to bring it up for fear she would think I was some kind of pervert. Eventually I could no longer tolerate not knowing her feelings about what might be incredibly erotic. I brought it

up by first talking about my mixed emotions, like feeling that maybe it wasn't natural but at the same time really wanting to try it out. As it turned out, she had been having similar feelings but was afraid to bring them up because of how I might react. Afterwards we laughed about how we had both been afraid to break the ice. Once we could talk freely about our feelings, it was easy to add this form of stimulation to our sex life. (Authors' files)

Personal disclosures require some give-and-take. It is much easier to share feelings about strongly emotional topics when a partner is willing to make similar disclosures. Admittedly, such an approach may have risks, and occasionally one can feel vulnerable sharing personal thoughts and feelings. Nevertheless, the increased possibility for open, honest dialogue may be worth any discomfort a person may feel about making the first disclosure.

A form of self-disclosure that some people find exciting and informative involves telling their partner about personal fantasies, as revealed in the following anecdote:

I had this sexual fantasy that kept going through my mind. I would imagine coming home after a long, hard day of classes and being met by my partner, who would proceed to take me into the bedroom and remove all my clothes. He would then pick me up and carry me into the bathroom, where a tub full of hot water and bubbles awaited. The fantasy would end with us making passionate love in the bathtub, with bubbles popping off around us. Finally, I shared my fantasy with him. Guess what happened when I came home after the next long day? It was even better than I had imagined! (Authors' files)

Understandably, many people might be concerned about the potentially adverse effects of such highly personal communication. Certain precautions may help to reduce the possibility of an unpleasant outcome.

Sharing is usually most successful when it is mutual rather than unilateral. If your partner is unwilling to engage in such talk, at least for the present, it would be wise to respect this wish. Sometimes starting out with very mild fantasies can help to desensitize fears and embarrassment and allow you to gauge the impact of such sharing on your partner and yourself. If you sense that your companion is feeling uncomfortable, it may be best not to press. It is probably advisable to avoid altogether any fantasies that you anticipate will be shocking to your companion. Fantasies that involve other lovers may be particularly threatening.

Comparing Notes

Many couples, while planning an evening out, consider it natural to discuss each other's preferences: "Do you like the symphony, the theater, movies?" "How close do you like to sit?" "Do you prefer steak or seafood?" Afterwards they may candidly evaluate the evening's events: "The orchestra was great," "I think the balcony seats would be better next time," "Boy, I wouldn't order the scampi again." Yet many of the same couples never think of sharing thoughts about mutual sexual enjoyment.

Admittedly, it may be a big step from discussing an evening out to discussing sexual preferences and evaluating sexual sharing. Nevertheless, people do engage in this type of sexual dialogue. Some people feel comfortable discussing sexual preferences with a new lover before progressing to lovemaking. They may talk about what areas of their bodies are most responsive, how they like to be touched, what intercourse positions are particularly desirable, the easiest or most satisfying way to reach orgasm, time and location preferences, special turn-ons and turn-offs, and a variety of other likes and dislikes.

The appeal of this open, frank approach is that it allows a couple to focus on particularly pleasurable activities, rather than discovering them by slow trial-and-error efforts. However, some people may feel that preparatory dialogues are far too clinical, perhaps even robbing the sexual experience of the excitement of experimentation and mutual discovery. Furthermore, what a person finds desirable may be different with different partners, so it may be difficult to assess one's own preferences in advance.

Couples may also find it helpful to share feelings after a sexual encounter. They may offer reactions about what was good and what could be better. They may use this time to reinforce the things they found particularly satisfying in their partner's lovemaking ("I loved the way you touched me with your hands"). A mutual feedback session can be extremely informative; it can also contribute to a deeper intimacy between two people.

Giving Permission

Discovering your partner's needs can be made immeasurably easier by the practice we call **giving permission**. Basically, this means providing verbal encouragement and reassurance. One partner tells the other that it is OK to talk about certain specific feelings or needs—in fact, that he or she wants very much to know how the other feels about the subject.

HE: I'm not sure how you like me to touch you when we make love.

SHE: Any way you want to is good.

HE: Well, it would be good to know what you like best, and you can help me by saying what feels good while I touch you.

Many of us have had experiences where we have felt rebuffed in our efforts to communicate our needs to others. It is no wonder people often remain silent even when they want to share personal feelings. Giving and receiving permission to express needs freely can contribute to the exchange of valuable information.

Learning to Make Requests

People are not mind readers. Nevertheless, many lovers seem to assume that their partners know (perhaps by intuition?) just what they need. People who approach sex with this attitude are not taking full responsibility for their own sexual pleasure. If sexual encounters are not satisfactory, it may be convenient to blame the other—"You don't care about my needs"—when in all probability it was one's own reluctance

to express one's needs that lay at the root of the problem. Expecting our partners to somehow know what we want without our telling them places a heavy burden on them. The alternative is to speak up and say what you want. Many people think they "shouldn't have to ask," but in fact, asking a partner to do something can be an affirmative, responsible action that is helpful to both people.

Taking Responsibility for Our Own Pleasure

> When two people are really in harmony with each other, you don't have to talk about your sexual wants. Each will sense and respond to the other's desires. Talking just tends to spoil these magical moments. (Authors' files)

The situation this person describes seems to exist more in the fantasyland of idealized sex than in the real world. As we noted earlier, people are not mind readers, and intuition leaves much to be desired as a substitute for genuine communication. A person who expects another to know his or her needs by intuition is saying "It's not my business to let you know my needs but yours to know what they are"; and by inference, "If my needs are not fulfilled it is your fault, not mine." Needless to say, this is a potentially destructive approach to sexual sharing that may lead to casting blame, misunderstandings, and unsatisfactory sex.

In a similar vein, some individuals may take too much responsibility for their partner's sexual pleasure. This behavior pattern may also be counterproductive. The person says, in effect, "It is my job to sexually satisfy you. I will make all the decisions and assume responsibility for your pleasure." Even in the best of circumstances, this can be a heavy burden. A person so intent on figuring out and fulfilling the needs of a partner may find that his or her own needs are largely overlooked. Furthermore, such a take-charge attitude encourages passivity and undermines a partner's resolve to assume responsibility for her or his own satisfaction.

In summary, the best way for us to get our needs met is to speak up with our requests. Two individuals willing to communicate their desires and take responsibility for their own pleasure create an excellent framework for effective, fulfilling sexual sharing.

Of course, even with the strongest resolve, many of us may still find it difficult to ask our partner for a particular kind of stimulation during sexual sharing. There may be several reasons for this reluctance, not the least of which is the fear that our partner may be offended or threatened by our boldness. This is shown in the following account:

> I know what I need in a sexual relationship, but how do I get this message across to my partner? I'm afraid if I were to come right out and state my requests he would feel inadequate—like why didn't he think of it without me needing to tell him? But the truth of the matter is, he usually doesn't come up with it on his own. So what do I do—keep my mouth shut and hope he will eventually figure it out? Or do I state specifically what I would like, with the possibility of turning him off by being too demanding? At this point in my life I generally opt for the former. Obviously, it is easier and less risky to say nothing. But I'm not sure I can go on much longer with my needs not being met. (Authors' files)

In thinking about this account, one fact stands out. If this woman's partner had encouraged her to share her sexual needs, much of her frustration might have been alleviated. However, the reality is that often we are not provided with a clear mandate to reveal our needs. Do we then remain silent, or should we trust our lover to be accepting of our self-revelations? One woman states her experience with assuming responsibility for her own pleasure:

> For much of my life sex has been a hit-or-miss proposition, with the miss part pre-dominating. Only recently have I discovered how to change this pattern. I know what I need sexually to be satisfied. I am very good at giving myself pleasure. Finally it occurred to me how futile it was to hope that my partners would somehow automati-cally possess this knowledge that took me years to discover for myself. I decided that the better I could express myself about my sexual needs, the greater the likelihood they would be fulfilled. Assuming this responsibility for my own pleasure was a big step that I took with a great deal of hesitancy and anxiety. But I have been pleasantly surprised by most of my subsequent lovers' reactions. They are usually quite relieved to have the guesswork taken out of our sexual experiences. One man praised me for my openness and confided that my willingness to tell him what I wanted relieved him of one of his greatest concerns, namely, not knowing what his partner desired from him during sex. (Authors' files)

Taking control of our own sexual lives and freely expressing our needs to partners can be a liberating experience, infinitely preferable to blind trust in their ability to sense these needs on their own.

Deciding to assume responsibility for one's own satisfaction is an important step. Just as important are the methods a person selects for expressing his or her needs. The way a request is made has a decided effect on the reaction it draws. Some suggestions are listed in the next two sections.

Making Requests Specific

The more specific a request, the more likely it is to be understood and heeded. This is a fact frequently noted by social psychologists and communication specialists. Nevertheless, many of us neglect to apply this sound principle to our sexual sharing. Lovers often ask for changes in the sexual aspects of their relationships in the vaguest of language. It can be quite uncomfortable, even anxiety provoking, to be on the receiving end of an ill-defined request. Just what do we do in response? Probably very little, if anything.

The key to preventing unnecessary stress for both partners lies in delivering requests in as clear and concise a manner as possible. Thus, an alternative to the vague request "I'd like you to try touching me differently" might be something like "I would like you to touch me gently around my clitoris but not directly on it." Other examples of specific requests include:

1. I would like you to spend more time touching and caressing me all over before we have intercourse.
2. I would like to be on top this time. It's real good for me and I love being able to watch you respond.
3. I like having my frenum stimulated during oral sex. If you would run your tongue back and forth over it I'll tell you if I want it harder or softer.
4. I would like you to continue with your kisses and caresses after penetration, because it makes intercourse so much better for me.
5. I would really like you to stroke my penis with your hand.

Using "I" Language

Many counselors encourage their clients to use "I" language when stating their needs to others. This forthright approach will bring the desired response more often than a general statement will. For example, saying "I would like to be on top" is considerably more likely to produce that result than "What would you think about changing positions?"

Many people find it difficult to ask for what they want in such clear, unequivocal language. Saying "I want . . ." may seem to some to be selfish. However, there is a difference between being self-centered and recognizing that "I am as important as others in my life, and my needs are worthy of being met." Individuals who experience gratification of their own needs are often able to give much of themselves to others. Conversely, the philosophy of "never put myself first" may ultimately produce so much frustration and resentment that a person is left with few positive feelings to share.

Expressing requests directly may not always be effective. Some people may want to make all the decisions during sex, and they may not take kindly to requests from their partners during lovemaking. To them a partner's assertiveness may be offensive. You may want to determine if this is your companion's attitude before an encounter, thereby avoiding an awkward situation later on. One way to do this is to ask the open-ended question "How do you feel about asking for things during lovemaking?" Or, you may choose to wait and find out during sex play. At any rate, if a person appears closed to direct requests, you may wish to reevaluate your strategy. Perhaps making your needs known at some time other than during sexual interaction may give your partner a more relaxed opportunity to consider your desires.

Delivering Criticism

Contrary to the popular romantic image, no two people can fill all of each other's needs all of the time. It seems inevitable that sometimes in an intimate relationship people will need to register some complaints and request changes. This is not an easy process for caring individuals whose involvement is characterized by mutual empathy. When the criticism pertains to the emotionally intense area of sexual sharing, it may be doubly difficult. Partners will want to think carefully about appropriate strategies and potential obstacles to accomplishing this delicate task. Perhaps the best way to begin, before verbalizing a complaint to your partner, is to examine the motivations underlying your need to criticize.

Be Aware of Your Motivation

The way criticism is offered may depend largely on the motive of the critic. Consider the following two anecdotes:

> My husband is a lousy lover. He doesn't know the first thing about how to turn me on, and when I tell him I don't get any pleasure out of our sex life he just clams up. I don't know what's the matter with him, but it sure burns me up. (Authors' files)

> A couple of years ago I found out that my wife was involved in an affair with a man she works with. She claimed he was kind and gentle and that she couldn't help being attracted to him. Faced with my ultimatum she changed jobs and stopped seeing him (I think). Since that time our sex life has been a real bust. She seems to lack enthusiasm, and we engage in sex much less frequently. Sometimes I think her having sex with the other guy has ruined our sex life. Maybe she thinks he was better than me. When I confront her with my dissatisfaction with her lack of enthusiasm she gets upset, and we usually end up having a fight. (Authors' files)

It seems clear that these people's motivations for criticizing are not based on a caring desire to make their relationships better. In the first example the aim of the woman appears to be to hurt or humiliate her husband. The man in the second anecdote seems to be motivated by a desire for revenge. If the aim is to hurt, humiliate, blame, ridicule, or get even, it is likely that criticizing a partner will prove to be far more destructive than constructive. Being aware of your motives for criticizing your partner can help you avoid this pitfall.

In this book we are concerned with constructive criticism that is prompted by a genuine desire for necessary change. It is not always easy to criticize effectively while maintaining an emphasis on sharing and building a sense of togetherness. There are, however, certain strategies that can help you to maintain empathy in a confrontational situation. One important consideration is picking the right time and place.

Choose the Right Time and Place

> Whenever my lover brings up something that is bothering her about our sex life, it inevitably is just after we have made love. Here I am, relaxed, holding her in my arms, thinking good thoughts, and she destroys the mood with some criticism. It's not that I don't want her to express her concerns. But her timing is terrible. The last thing I want to hear after lovemaking is that it could have been better. (Authors' files)

This man's dismay is obvious. His partner's decision to voice her concerns during the afterglow of lovemaking, while understandable, worked against her purpose. He may have felt vulnerable, and he clearly resented having his good mood broken by the prospect of potentially difficult conversation. Of course, other couples may find this to be a time when they are exceedingly close to each other and, thus, a good atmosphere in which to air concerns.

Many people, like the woman in the previous example, never choose the best time to confront their lover. Rather, the time chooses them: They jump right in when the problem is uppermost in their minds. There are some benefits to dealing with an issue immediately. However, a person who does this may be feeling disappointed, resentful, or angry, and these negative emotions, when running full tide, may get in the way of constructive interaction. Avoid registering complaints when anger is at its peak. Though you may have every intention of making your criticism constructive, anger has a way of disrupting a search for solutions. Sometimes, however, it may be necessary to express anger, and we will consider this process at the end of this section.

In most cases it is unwise to tackle a problem when either you or your partner has limited time or is tired, stressed, preoccupied, or under the influence of drugs or alcohol. Rather, try to select an interval when you have plenty of time and are both relaxed and feeling close to each other.

A pragmatic approach to the problem of timing is to simply ask your lover. "I really value our sexual sharing, but there are some concerns I would like to talk over with you. Is this a good time or would you rather we talk later?" Be prepared for some anxiety-induced stalling. If your partner is hesitant to talk now, support his or her right to pick another time or place. However, it is important to agree on a time, particularly if you sense your partner might prefer to let the matter go.

Choosing the right place for expressing sexual concerns can be as important as timing. Some people may find that sitting around the kitchen table while sharing a pot of coffee is a more comfortable setting than the place where they make love, while others might prefer the familiarity of their bed. A walk through a park or a

Choosing the right time and place for expressing sexual concerns can facilitate communication.

quiet drive in the country, far removed from the potential interferences of a busy lifestyle, may prove best for you. Try to sense your partner's needs. When and where is she or he most likely to be receptive to your requests for change?

Picking the right time and place to deliver criticism does not ensure a harmonious outcome, but it certainly improves the prospects of your partner responding favorably to your message. Using some other constructive strategies can also increase the likelihood of beneficial interaction. One of these is to combine criticism with praise.

Temper Criticism with Praise

The strategy of tempering criticism with praise is based largely on common sense. All of us tend to respond well to compliments, while harsh criticism untempered by praise is difficult to accept. The gentler approach of combining criticism with praise is a good way to reduce the negative impact of a complaint. It also gives the person who has been criticized a broader perspective from which to evaluate the criticism and reduces the likelihood that he or she will respond in a defensive or angry manner. Consider how you might react differently to the following criticisms depending on whether or not they are accompanied by praise:

Criticism Alone	Praise + Criticism
1. When we make love you seem so inhibited.	I appreciate the way you respond to me when we make love and I think it could be even better if you would take the initiative sometimes. Does this seem like a reasonable request?

2. I really am getting tired of your turning off the lights every time we make love.

I enjoy hearing and feeling you react when we make love. I would also like to see you respond. How would you feel about leaving the lights on sometimes?

3. I think our lovemaking is much too infrequent. It almost seems like sex is not as important to you as it is to me.

Having sex gives me a great deal of pleasure, and I value sharing it with you. My concern is that it doesn't happen as frequently as I would like. What are your thoughts about this?

Sadly, just about all of us have been on the receiving end of criticisms like those in the left column. Common reactions are anger, feeling humiliated, anxiety about our competency as lovers, and resentment. While some people may respond to such harsh complaints with a resolve to make things better, it is more likely that the opposite will occur. On the other hand, affirmative criticism, like the examples in the right column, is more likely to encourage efforts to change.

There is a good deal of wisdom in the saying "People are usually more motivated to make a good thing better than to make a bad thing good." This applies as much to sexual sharing as to any other area of human interaction. One of us was once approached by a woman who complained that her husband was often too rough with her during love play. She was reluctant to discuss her concern with her husband for fear that he would feel put down or angered. She also had mixed feelings about her husband's roughness—it was part of the unbridled enthusiasm with which he related to her sexually, a zestiness she very much enjoyed. On those rare occasions when he did take the time to be gentle with her, she was very pleased. Now, the problem: How could she tell him she didn't like his roughness, while at the same time assuring that he would maintain his enthusiasm and not feel angry or inept?

What she finally told him was essentially what she had expressed in seeking advice. Sometimes it was terrific when he was gentle. She loved being pursued with enthusiasm and vigor. It could be even better if he would include more gentleness in their lovemaking. Although he was somewhat surprised and dismayed over his inability to detect her needs, her husband's response was quite positive. What do you suppose his reaction might have been had she coldly complained "Do you have to be so rough when we make love?"

It is also a good idea to ask for feedback when delivering criticisms. Regardless of how much warmth and humanity we put into this difficult process, there is always the possibility that our partners may become silent or change the subject. Asking them to talk about their reaction to our request for change helps to reduce these prospects. (Note that in the previous list, all "Praise + Criticism" examples ended with requests for feedback.)

Nurture Small Steps Toward Change

Complete behavioral changes rarely occur immediately following criticism—no matter how positively the criticism is stated. Rather, they must be patiently nurtured, with each small step along the way properly acknowledged with words of appreciation. In the example of the woman wanting more gentleness from her husband, it would have been unreasonable for her to assume that once she expressed her criticism, her partner would completely change his ways. In fact, what occurred was a noticeable but minimal effort to be less vigorous in the next sexual encounter. Soon the old patterns ingrained over many years took over again.

Backsliding is natural and predictable and, like other unwanted behaviors, it requires tact. Have you ever heard the words "I see you didn't pay a bit of attention to what I said"? Such a negative reaction could easily cool your desire to follow through with change. It is far more encouraging and reassuring to be on the receiving end of a message like the one delivered by the wife to her "trying to be more gentle" husband: "I really appreciate the time you took to be gentle when we made love. It means a great deal that you care about my needs." With such a caring and supportive reaction, few people are likely to stick to the same old behavior.

Avoid "Why" Questions

People frequently use "why" questions as thinly veiled efforts to criticize or attack their partners while avoiding full responsibility for what is said. Have you ever been asked any of the following?

1. Why don't you make love to me more frequently?
2. Why don't you show more interest in me?
3. Why don't you get turned on by me anymore?
4. Why can't you be more loving toward me?
5. Why are you so lazy?

Such queries have no place in a loving relationship. They are hurtful and destructive. Rather than representing simple requests for information, they are typically used to convey hidden messages of anger that people are unwilling to own honestly. These are hit-and-run tactics that give pain and seldom induce positive changes. Get rid of them. They cannot help register constructive criticism.

Express Anger Appropriately

Earlier in this chapter we noted that it is wise to avoid confronting our partners when anger is riding high. However, there will probably be times when you feel compelled to express angry feelings. If so, certain guiding principles may help you defuse a potentially explosive situation.

Avoid focusing your anger on the character of your partner ("You are an insensitive person"). Instead, try directing your anger toward his or her behaviors ("When you don't listen to my concerns I think they are unimportant to you and I feel angry"). At the same time, express appreciation for your partner as a person ("You are very important to me, and I don't like feeling this way"). This acknowledges that we can he angered by our partners' behaviors and feel loving toward them as people at the same time—an often overlooked but important truth.

Anger is probably best expressed with clear, honest "I" statements rather than with accusatory and potentially inflammatory "you" statements. Consider the following:

"I" Statements	"You" Statements
1. I feel ignored.	You don't give a damn about me.
2. I don't like being blamed.	You always blame me for our problems.
3. I am upset.	You make me upset.
4. I am angry.	You make me angry.
5. I feel unloved.	You don't love me.

"I" statements are self-revelations that express how we feel without placing blame or attacking our partner's character. In contrast, "you" statements frequently are interpreted as attacks on the other person's character or attempts to fix blame.

Finally, if we become angry with our partner, it is because we choose to respond with anger. Another person cannot make us angry, although it certainly may seem that way at times. We have control over our own responses. Instead of expressing anger, we might choose from a variety of responses, including humor, silence, submission, withdrawal, or caring confrontation. The last possibility is clearly the best bet for positive change. All too often we allow ourselves to be victimized by our emotions rather than taking control of how we respond. As long as we continue to control the sentences running through our minds, we have the opportunity to harness anger and engage in constructive, caring confrontation.

Receiving Criticism

Delivering complaints to our partners is difficult for caring people; likewise, receiving criticisms from a loved one can also be an emotionally rending experience. However, as we have already said, people involved in a loving relationship will inevitably experience the need to register complaints on occasion. How we respond to such criticism may have a significant impact not only upon our partner's inclination to openly share concerns in the future but also upon the probability that the complaint will be resolved in a manner that strengthens rather than erodes our relationship.

When your partner delivers a criticism, take a few moments to gather your thoughts. A few deep breaths is probably a much better initial response than blurting out "Ya, well what about the time that you . . . !" Ask yourself "Is this person trying to give me some information that may be helpful?" In a loving relationship where mutual empathy prevails, perhaps you will be able to see some potential for positive consequences, even though you have just received a painful message. There are several ways you can respond to such a communication. We hope one or more of the following suggestions will provide you with helpful guidelines in these circumstances.

Empathize with Your Partner and Paraphrase the Criticism

Many of us have had the experience of expressing concerns to people we care about, only to have them come back with a criticism of their own. Such a response will likely result in increased defensiveness, which may precipitate withdrawal or antagonistic confrontation. Furthermore, when people match a criticism with a counter complaint, it appears that they are not trying to understand and empathize with the concern. In contrast, providing a paraphrase of your partner's criticism suggests you are making an effort to understand and appreciate what he or she is experiencing. For example, saying to your partner "It sounds like you have been frustrated with our lovemaking" will probably have a much more beneficial effect than a comment like "Well, you're not such a hot lover either!"

Paraphrasing a partner's criticism does not mean that you agree with it. Rather, you are simply saying "This is what I am hearing—do I understand correctly?" We can empathize with our lover's concerns even if we have different thoughts and feelings about them. This type of positive response increases the likelihood that your partner will voice important concerns in the future.

Acknowledge a Criticism and Find Something to Agree With

Perhaps if you open yourself to listen to a criticism, you will see that there is some basis for it. For example, suppose your partner feels victimized by your busy schedule and criticizes you for not devoting more time to the relationship. Maybe you think he or she is overreacting or forgetting all the time you have spent together. However, you also know that there is some basis for this expressed concern. It can be helpful to acknowledge this by saying something like "I can understand how you might feel neglected because I have been preoccupied lately with my new job." This constructive process can occur even if you think the criticism is largely unjustified. By reacting in a supportive manner you are conveying the message that you hear, understand, and appreciate the basis for your partner's concern.

Ask Clarifying Questions

In some cases your partner may deliver a criticism in such a vague manner that further clarification would be helpful. If this occurs, ask questions. For example, suppose your partner complains that you do not take enough time in your lovemaking. You might respond by asking "Do you mean that we should spend more time touching before intercourse, or that I should last longer before coming, or that you want to be held for a longer time after sex?"

Express Your Feelings

It can be helpful to talk about your feelings in regard to the criticism rather than letting these emotions dictate your response. For instance, your partner's criticism may cause you to feel angry, hurt, or dejected. It is probably better to verbalize these emotional reactions by expressing *feeling statements*, rather than reacting by yelling, stomping out of the room, crying, or retreating into a shell of despair. It may help to tell your partner "That was really hard to hear, and I am hurt" or "Right now I feel like flipping my lid, so I need to stop and take a few breaths and figure out what I am thinking and feeling."

Limit Criticism to One Complaint per Discussion

Many of us are inclined to avoid confrontations with our partners. This understandable reluctance to deal with negative issues may result in an accumulation of unspoken complaints. Consequently, when we finally reach the point where we need to "say something or bust," it may be difficult to avoid unleashing a barrage of criticisms that includes everything on our current list of grievances. Such a response, though understandable, may only serve to magnify rather than diffuse conflicts between lovers, as reflected in the following account:

> My wife lets things eat on her without letting me know when I do something that she disapproves of. She remembers every imagined shortcoming and blows it way out of proportion. But I never learn about it until she has accumulated a lengthy list of beefs. Then she hits me with all of them at once, dredging them up like weapons in her arsenal, all designed to make me feel like an insensitive creep. When she gets on a roll, there is no stopping her. I sometimes hear about things that happened years ago. She wonders why I don't have anything to say when she is done haranguing me. But what do you say when somebody has just given you 10 or 20 reasons why your relationship with her sucks? Which one do you respond to? And how can you avoid being pissed off when somebody rubs your face in all your shortcomings, real or imagined? (Authors' files)

We can reduce the likelihood of creating such a counterproductive situation in our own relationships by limiting our criticisms to one complaint per discussion. Even if you have a half dozen complaints you want to talk about, it will probably serve your relationship better to pick one and delegate the remaining concerns to later conversations.

Focus on Future Changes You Can Make

An excellent closure to receiving criticism is to focus on what the two of you can do to make things better. Perhaps this is the time to say that "My new job is really important to me, but our relationship is much more important. Maybe we can set aside some specific times each week where we both agree not to let outside concerns intrude upon our time together." Sometimes people agree to make things better but neglect to discuss concrete changes that will resolve the issue that triggered the complaint. Taking the time to identify and agree upon specific future changes is a process well worth the effort.

Saying No

Many of us have difficulty saying no to others. Our discomfort in communicating this direct message is perhaps most pronounced when it applies to intimate areas of relationships. This is reflected in the following anecdotes:

Sometimes my partner wants to be sexual when I only want to be close. The trouble is, I can't say no. I am afraid she would be hurt or angry. Unfortunately, I am the one who ends up angry at myself for not being able to express my true feelings. Sex sure isn't very good under such circumstances. (Authors' files)

It is so hard to say no to a man who suggests having sex at the end of a date. This is especially true if we have had a good time together. You never know if they are going to get that hang-dog hurt look or become belligerent and angry. (Authors' files)

These accounts reveal some of the common concerns that may inhibit our inclinations to say no. We may believe that saying no will hurt the other person, or perhaps cause him or her to become angry or even combative. Laboring under such fears, it may seem less stressful to simply comply with the requests of others. Unfortunately, this reluctant acquiescence can cause us to have such negative feelings that the resulting shared activity may be less than pleasurable for both ourselves and our partners.

Many of us have not learned that it is OK to say no, and perhaps more important, we have not learned strategies for doing so. In the following section we will consider some potentially useful ways to say no.

A Three-Step Approach to Saying No

Many people have found it helpful to have a definite plan or strategy in mind for saying no to invitations for intimate involvements. This can help prevent being caught off guard and not knowing how to handle a potentially unpleasant task with tact. One approach you may find helpful involves three distinct steps, or phases, outlined as follows:

> ***Step 1.*** Express appreciation for the invitation ("Thanks for thinking of me," "I appreciate your attraction to me, your interest in _____ with me," and so forth). Perhaps you may also wish to validate the value of the other person ("You are a good person").
>
> ***Step 2.*** Say no in a clear, unequivocal fashion ("I would prefer not to make love, go dancing, get involved in a dating relationship," and so forth).
>
> ***Step 3.*** Offer an alternative, if applicable ("I would like to have lunch sometime, give you a backrub," etc.).

The positive aspects of this approach are readily apparent. We first indicate our appreciation for the expressed interest in us. At the same time, we clearly state our wish not to comply with the request. Finally, we end the exchange on an upbeat note by offering an alternative. Of course, this last step will not always be an option (for example, when turning down a request from someone with whom we wish to have no further social contact). Between lovers, however, there is often a mutually acceptable alternative.

Avoid Sending Mixed Messages

Saying no in clear, unmistakable language is essential to the success of the previously outlined strategy. Nevertheless, many of us are probably guilty, at least sometimes, of sending mixed messages about our sexual and other intimate needs. Consider, for example, someone who responds positively to an expressed desire for sexual sharing but then spends an inordinate amount of time soaking in the bathtub while a patiently waiting partner falls asleep. Another version of this story involves the person who expresses a desire to have sex but instead gets engrossed in a late-night talk show. Both of these people are sending mixed messages to their partners that may reflect some of their own ambivalence about engaging in sexual relations.

The effect of such mixed messages is usually less than desirable. The recipient is often confused about the other person's intent. He or she may feel uncertain or even inadequate ("Why can't I figure out what you really want?"), and these feelings may evolve into anger ("Why do I have to guess?") or withdrawal. These reactions are understandable in such circumstances. What should a person faced with contradictory messages do—act on the first message or on the second one? Consider the following:

> It really bothers me when my partner says we will make love when I get home from night school and then she is too busy studying to take a break. Sometimes I wonder if she had any intention in the first place to follow through on her suggestion. (Authors' files)

All of us may benefit from taking stock from time to time to see if we send mixed messages. Try looking for inconsistencies between your verbal messages and your subsequent actions. Does your partner seem confused or uncertain when interacting with you? If you do spot yourself sending a double message, decide which one you really mean, then state it in unmistakable language. It may also be helpful to consider why you sent contradictory messages.

If you are the recipient of such contradictory messages, it may help to discuss your confusion over the mixed communication and ask your partner which one of the two messages she or he would like you to act upon. Perhaps your partner will recognize your dilemma and act to resolve it. If you detect an apparent unwillingness to acknowledge the inconsistency, it may help to express your feelings of discomfort and confusion as the recipient of the two messages.

Nonverbal Sexual Communication

Sexual communication is not confined exclusively to words. Sometimes a touch or smile may convey a great deal of information. Tone of voice, gestures, facial expression, and changes in breathing may also be important elements of the communication process:

> I can usually tell when my sweetheart is in the mood for some loving. There is a certain softness about her face and a huskiness which comes into her voice. She touches me more with her hands and it almost seems like she presents her body as more open and vulnerable. Believe me, there is some truth to all this stuff about body language. She rarely needs to verbalize her desire for sex because I usually get the message. (Authors' files)

Sometimes when I want my lover to touch me in a certain place, I move that portion of my body closer to his hands or just shift my position to make the area more accessible. Occasionally I will guide his hand with mine to show him just what kind of stimulation I want. (Authors' files)

These examples reveal some of the varieties of nonverbal communication that may have particular significance for our sexuality. In this section we will direct our attention to four important components of nonverbal sexual communication: facial expression, interpersonal distance, touching, and sounds.

Facial Expression

Facial expressions often communicate the feelings a person is experiencing. While there is certainly variation in people's expressions, most of us have learned to identify particular emotions from facial expression with a high degree of accuracy. The rapport and intimacy between lovers may further increase the reliability of this yardstick.

A look into the face of our lover during sexual sharing will often give us a quick reading of his or her pleasure quotient. If we see a look of complete rapture, we will likely continue providing the same type of stimulation. However, if the look conveys something less than ecstasy, we may decide to try something different or perhaps encourage our partner to provide some verbal direction.

Facial expressions can also provide helpful cues when talking over sexual concerns with a partner. If our lover's face reflects anger, anxiety, or some other disruptive emotion, it might be wise to deal with this emotion immediately ("I sense that you are angry with me. Would you like to talk about your feelings?"). Conversely, a face that mirrors interest, enthusiasm, or appreciation can encourage us to continue expressing a particular feeling or concern. It is also a good idea to be aware of the nonverbal messages you are giving your partner when she or he is sharing thoughts or feelings with you. Sometimes we may inadvertently shut down potentially helpful dialogue by setting our jaw or frowning at an inappropriate time.

Interpersonal Distance

Social psychologists and communication specialists have much to say about *personal space*. In essence, this idea suggests that each of us tends to maintain differing degrees of *interpersonal distance* between ourselves and the people we have contact with, depending on the nature of our relationship with them (actual or desired). The intimate space to which we admit close friends and lovers restricts contact much less than the distance we maintain between ourselves and the general public.

It is instructive to watch what takes place between people meeting each other at places like singles bars and parties. Consider the following:

When I meet someone I am attracted to I pay close attention to body language. If they seem uneasy or retreat when I move closer, it is a pretty good indication my interest is not reciprocated. (Authors' files)

When someone attempts to decrease interpersonal distance, it is generally interpreted as a nonverbal sign that she or he is attracted to or desirous of more intimate contact with the other person. A person's withdrawal from another's efforts to establish greater body closeness is usually interpreted as lack of interest or a gentle kind of rejection.

Lovers, whose interpersonal distance is generally at a minimum, may use these cues to signal desire for intimacy. When your lover moves in close, making his or her body available for your touches or caresses, the message of wanting physical intimacy (not necessarily sex) is quite apparent. Similarly, when he or she curls up on the other side of the bed, it may be a way of saying "Please don't come too close tonight."

Touching

Touch is a powerful vehicle for nonverbal sexual communication between lovers. Hands can convey special messages. For example, increasing or decreasing the tempo with which a lover's back is kneaded may signal a desire for more or less intense reciprocated stimulation. Reaching out and pulling someone closer can indicate desire and readiness for more intimate contact.

Touch can also defuse anger, heal rifts, and close the gap between temporarily alienated lovers. As one man states:

> I have found that a gentle touch, lovingly administered to my partner, does wonders in bringing us back together after we have exchanged angry words. Touching her is my way of reestablishing connection. (Authors' files)

Touch is a powerful vehicle for nonverbal sexual communication.

In the early stages of a developing relationship, touch can also be used to express a desire for more intimate involvement.

> When I meet a man and find myself attracted to him, I use touch to convey my feelings. Touching him on the arm to emphasize a point or letting my fingers lightly graze across his hand on the table generally lets my feelings be known. (Authors' files)

We can be thankful for the delights that touch can bring us. Sounds can also be powerful vehicles for nonverbal sexual communication.

Sounds

Many people, though by no means all, like making and hearing sounds during sexual sharing. Some individuals find increased breathing, moans, groans, and orgasmic cries to be extremely arousing. Also, such sounds can be helpful indicators of how a partner is responding to lovemaking. Some people find the absence of sounds to be quite frustrating:

> My man rarely makes any sounds when we make love. I find this to be very disturbing. In fact it is a real turn-off. Sometimes I can't even tell if he has come or not. If he wasn't moving I'd think I was making love to a corpse. (Authors' files)

Some people make a conscious effort to suppress spontaneous noises during sex play. In doing so they deprive themselves of a potentially powerful and enjoyable form of nonverbal sexual communication. Not uncommonly, their imposed silence also hinders their partner's sexual arousal, as the foregoing example illustrates.

In this section we have acknowledged that not everything has to be spoken between lovers. However, facial expression, interpersonal distance, touching, and sounds cannot convey all of our complex needs and emotions in a close relationship: Words are needed too. One writer observes, "As a supplement to verbal communication, acts and gestures are fine. As a substitute, they don't quite make it" (Zilbergeld, 1978, p.158).

Impasses

Candid communication between caring supportive partners often leads to changes that are mutually gratifying. However, even an ample supply of openness, candor, support, and understanding cannot assure a meeting of the minds on all issues: You may reach impasses. Your partner may simply not want to try a new coital position. Or your suggestion to incorporate a vibrator into shared sex play may be just a bit too threatening. Perhaps the two of you cannot agree on the question of other relationships.

What does one do when communication results in a standoff? Continued discussion may be helpful. However, it is self-deceiving to assume that talk, even the most open and compassionate, will always lead to desired changes.

Sometimes it is useful to try to put yourself in your partner's shoes. Try to see things from the other person's perspective. If you have some difficulty with this, ask your companion for help ("I am having some trouble seeing this from your perspective—can you help me out?"). If you can understand his or her point, by all means say so. Indicating that you see how reasonable the other's viewpoint must seem is a process called **validating** (Gottman et al., 1976). Validating does not mean that you will give up your own position. You are not saying "I am wrong and you are right." You are simply admitting that another point of view may make sense, given some assumptions that you may not share with your partner. Sometimes this process of trying to see the validity of another viewpoint may lead to new perspectives that can end the deadlock. However, if you continue to disagree after this effort, it may be easier to accept the idea that you can both be right.

At a time of impasse it may also be beneficial for a couple to take a break from each other for awhile. Sometimes forced continuation of a discussion, particularly when emotions are strong, is counterproductive. Scheduling another time to talk can be a good tactic. Perhaps in the future, after each has had the opportunity to privately consider the other's feelings, it may be possible to readdress the issue with more tangible results.

Sometimes people cannot or will not change, often for justifiable reasons. Certainly all of us cherish our right to refuse to do something we consider undesirable. Granting the same right to someone close to us is an important ingredient in a relationship characterized by mutual respect.

Failure to reach a solution to an impasse is not necessarily cause for despair. At least a problem has been brought out into the open and the couple has discussed a sensitive issue. Possibly they have also increased their understanding of each other and the level of intimacy between them. In the event that unresolved impasses threaten to erode a relationship, professional counseling may be desirable. (Chapter 17 includes guidelines for counselor selection.)

Summary

The Importance of Communication

1. Sexual communication often contributes positively to the contentment and enjoyment of a sexual relationship; infrequent or ineffective sex talk is a common reason for people feeling dissatisfied with their sexual lives.

2. An excellent basis for effective sexual communication is mutual empathy—the underlying knowledge that each partner in a relationship cares for the other and knows that care is reciprocated.

Why Sex Talk Is Difficult

3. Childhood training, which often creates a sense of discomfort with sexual matters, may contribute to later difficulties in engaging in sex talk.

4. Our language is characterized by a conspicuous absence of an effective, comfortable sexual vocabulary.

5. Some people object to sex talk on the grounds that it disrupts spontaneity or that it may place one in a position of increased vulnerability to judgment, criticism, or rejection.

Talking: Getting Started

6. It is often difficult to start talking about sex. Some suggestions for doing this include talking about talking; reading about sex, then discussing the material; seeing erotic movies or reading explicit novels; and sharing sexual histories.

Listening and Feedback

7. Communication is most successful with an active listener and an effective communicator.

8. The listener may facilitate communication by maintaining eye contact with the speaker; providing some feedback, or reaction to the message; expressing appreciation for communication efforts; maintaining an attitude of unconditional positive regard; and using paraphrasing effectively.

Discovering Your Partner's Needs

9. Efforts to seek information from sexual partners are often hindered by the use of yes/no questions, which encourage limited replies. Effective alternatives include open-ended queries and either/or questions.

10. Self-disclosure may make it easier for a partner to communicate his or her own needs. Sharing fantasies, beginning with mild fantasies, may be a particularly valuable kind of exchange.

11. Comparing notes about sexual needs, preferences, and reactions, either before or after a sexual encounter, may be beneficial.

12. Giving permission encourages partners to share feelings freely.

Learning to Make Requests

13. Making requests is facilitated by (a) taking responsibility for one's own pleasure; (b) making sure requests are specific; and (c) using "I" language.

Delivering Criticism

14. Be aware of your motives for criticizing. Criticism that aims to hurt or blame a partner is likely to be destructive.

15. It is important to select the right time and place for expressing sexual concerns. Avoid registering complaints when anger is at its peak.

16. Criticism is generally most effective when tempered with praise. People are usually more motivated to make a good thing better than a bad thing good.

17. It is beneficial to reward each small step in the process of changing undesirable behavior.

18. "Why" questions have no place in the process of registering constructive criticisms.

19. It is wise to direct anger toward behavior rather than toward a person's character. Anger is probably best expressed with clear, honest "I" statements, not with accusatory "you" statements.

Receiving Criticism

20. Paraphrasing a partner's criticisms and acknowledging an understanding of the basis for his or her concerns can help to establish a sense of empathy and lead to constructive dialogue.

21. It can be helpful to ask clarifying questions when criticisms are vague and to express the feelings that are aroused when one is criticised.

22. Relationships are better served when criticisms are limited to one complaint per discussion.

23. An excellent closure to receiving criticism is to focus on what can be done to make things better in a relationship.

Saying No

24. One three-step strategy for saying no to invitations for intimate involvements includes: expressing appreciation for the invitation; saying no in a clear, unequivocal fashion; and offering an alternative, if applicable.

25. To avoid sending mixed messages, occasionally check for inconsistencies between verbal messages and subsequent actions. Recipients of mixed messages might find it helpful to express their confusion and to ask which of the two messages they are expected to act on.

Nonverbal Sexual Communication

26. Sexual communication is not confined to words alone. Facial expression, interpersonal distance, touching, and sounds also convey a great deal of information.

27. The value of nonverbal communication lies primarily in its ability to supplement—not to replace—verbal exchanges.

Impasses

28. Sex talk, no matter how candid and compassionate, does not always lead to solutions. Trying to see things from a partner's perspective may be beneficial when deadlocks occur, and it may also be helpful to temporarily suspend the discussion so that each person can privately consider the other's point of view. An unresolved impasse does not necessarily threaten a relationship; if it does, counseling may be desirable.

Thought Provokers

1. Assume that you are in the early stages of a developing relationship and anticipate making love the next time you are with your new companion. In your opinion, which technique(s) described in this chapter might be most helpful in contributing to satisfying sexual relations? Which suggestion(s) would be the most difficult for you to implement? Explain.

2. Some people think that combining praise with criticism is a manipulative technique, designed to coerce behavior changes by tempering requests with insincere praise. Do you agree with this observation? Why or why not?

3. What do you think about sharing sexual fantasies as a way for intimate partners to discover each other's needs?

Suggested Readings

Alberti, Robert, and Emmors, Michael. *Your Perfect Right: A Guide to Assertive Behavior*, 3rd ed. San Luis Obispo, Calif.: Impact Publications, 1978. Contains excellent suggestions for how to be assertive without being exploitative or overpowering.

Brenton, Myron. *Sex Talk*. Greenwich, Conn.: Fawcett Publications, 1973. Provides some good ideas for improving sexual communication between partners and between parents and children.

Gottman, John; Notarius, Cliff; Gonso, Jonni; Markman, Howard. *A Couple's Guide to Communication*. Champaign, Ill.: Research Press, 1976. This book, while not focused on sex talk per se, provides some excellent suggestions for enhancing couple communication. Includes such topics as hidden agendas, negotiating agreements, listening, getting through a crisis, and so forth.

Langer, Ellen, and Dweck, Carol. *Personal Politics: The Psychology of Making It*. Englewood Cliffs, N.J.: Prentice-Hall, 1973. A well-written book containing some valuable strategies for improving interpersonal communication, several of which may be applied directly to the sexual aspects of human relationships.

McKay, Matthew; Davis, Martha; Fanning, Patrick. *Messages: The Communication Book*. Oakland, Calif.: New Harbinger Publications, 1983. A practical, skills-oriented book that addresses such topics as sexual communication, conflict resolution, and family communication.

9

. . . alone I enjoy, with another I enjoy . . . (in essence) . . . twofold.
William Carlos Williams
"The Embodiment of Knowledge" (1977)

Sexual Behavior Patterns

Celibacy
Erotic Dreams and Fantasy
Masturbation
Shared Touching
Oral-Genital Stimulation
Anal Stimulation
Coitus and Coital Positions
Sexual Adjustment and Disability

PEOPLE EXPRESS THEIR SEXUALITY in many ways. The emotions they attach to sexual behavior also vary widely. In this chapter we will define and explain some of the varieties of sexual expression, looking first at individuals and then at couples. We will also consider some of the feelings and attitudes people have about these specific behaviors. Celibacy, the first topic we will consider, may not commonly be thought of as a form of sexual expression. However, when it represents a conscious decision not to engage in sexual behavior, this decision in itself is an expression of one's sexuality.

Celibacy

A physically mature person who does not engage in sexual behavior is said to be **celibate**. There are two degrees of celibacy. In **complete celibacy** a person neither masturbates nor has interpersonal sexual contact. In **partial celibacy** he or she engages in masturbation but does not have sexual contact with another person.

Celibacy is most commonly thought of in connection with religious devotion: Joining a religious order or becoming a priest or nun often includes a vow of celibacy. But individuals may choose celibacy for other reasons as well. The following statements reflect a variety of decisions to be celibate:

> I had painfully ended a long-term marriage. Celibacy was a good option for me because I needed time of my own to resolve my feelings about my ex-wife. I wasn't ready for another relationship and I do not like casual sex. (Authors' files)

> I've been working on a very important project for several months. Sexual relationships seem to have a way of becoming complicated and time-consuming. Since deciding to be celibate, I've established some good friendships and have had more time and energy for my project. (Authors' files)

Many factors may lead a person to be celibate. Health considerations, such as concerns about recurring vaginal infections or sexually transmitted diseases, may prompt a decision to stop having sexual intercourse. Some people choose to be celibate until marriage because of religious or moral beliefs. Some people maintain celibacy until their personal criteria for a good sexual relationship have been met. Others may choose celibacy because they have experienced confusion or disappointment in past sexual relationships, and they want to spend some time establishing new relationships without the complicating factor of sexual interaction. At times a person can be so caught up in other aspects of life that sex is simply not a priority (Laws and Schwartz, 1977).

Some people find that a period of celibacy can be quite rewarding. There is often a refocusing on oneself during such a period: exploring self-pleasuring; learning to value one's aloneness, autonomy, and privacy; or giving priority to work and nonsexual relationship commitments. Friendships may gain new dimensions and fulfillment. The following comment provides an example:

> When I began to be celibate, I really missed affectionate physical contact that had been part of sex. So I began hugging, doing massage, and even sleeping—and I mean *just* sleeping—together in an affectionate way with good friends. (Authors' files)

Many people do not choose to be celibate, however, for despite its rewards for some individuals, celibacy also has a number of disadvantages. These can include lack of physical affection and loneliness for sexual intimacy. Coming out of a period of celibacy may be difficult, too, for re-establishing sexual relationships can be awkward and frightening. Being celibate is not made easier by the fact that many people today are not accepting or supportive of celibacy or virginity. The historical ideal that people should not be sexual except for procreation has been replaced by an expectation that individuals should freely and frequently express their sexuality. Rollo May observes that "our contemporary Puritan holds that it is immoral not to express your libido" (1969, p. 45). It is interesting that of the many options for self-expression, celibacy is one choice that people sometimes have considerable trouble understanding. However, both virginity and celibacy can be personally valuable choices.

Erotic Dreams and Fantasy

Some forms of sexual experience occur within a person's mind, with or without accompanying sexual behavior. These are erotic dreams and fantasies. Fantasies are mental experiences that may arise from our imagination or be stimulated by books, drawings, or photographs.

Sexual fantasies and erotic dreams take many forms. This is a detail from The Garden of Delights *by Hieronymous Bosch.*

Erotic dreams and occasionally orgasm may occur during sleep without a person's conscious direction. Almost all of the males and two-thirds of the females in Kinsey's research populations reported experiencing erotic dreams. A person may waken during such a dream and notice signs of sexual arousal: erection, vaginal lubrication, or pelvic movements. If orgasm occurs, males usually notice the ejaculate—hence the label "wet dreams." Female orgasm may be more difficult to determine, due to the absence of such a visible sign. In one study of college women, 30% reported having experienced nocturnal orgasm. Another 30% had never heard of nocturnal orgasm. Women who had a higher frequency of intercourse and of orgasm with masturbation were more likely to experience and be aware of orgasms during sleep (Wells, 1983).

As with other dreams, the content of erotic dreams may be logical or quite nonsensical. Explicit sexual expression in the dreams varies widely, from common sexual activities to behaviors considered to be taboo. Both erotic dreams and waking fantasy can be ways to express and explore dimensions of experiences, feelings, and desires.

Erotic waking fantasies commonly occur during daydreams, masturbation, or sexual encounters with a partner. In the Kinsey studies, 84% of men and 67% of women reported ever having sexual fantasies. A more recent study of college students found that 60% of both men and women reported fantasizing specifically during intercourse (Sue, 1979). Greater sexual experience may contribute to increased sexual fantasizing, since women with more sexual experience report more frequent use of sexual fantasies than women who are virgins (Brown and Hart, 1977) or who have less sexual experience (Knafo and Jaffe, 1984).

The content of sexual fantasies varies greatly and can range from vague, romantic images to graphic representations of imagined or past actual experiences. Research on fantasy content reveals this diversity, as shown in Tables 9.1 and 9.2. The tables provide an idea of the range of content and suggest some male and female differences, which we will discuss later in this chapter.

Table 9.1 Male and Female Sexual Fantasies During Masturbation

Fantasy Content	% Men	% Women
Intercourse with loved one	75	70
Intercourse with strangers	47	21
Sex with more than one person of the other sex	33	18
Sexual activities that would not be done in reality	19	28
Forcing someone to have sex	13	3
Being forced to have sex	10	19
Homosexual activity	7	11

Source: Hunt, 1974.

Table 9.2 Male and Female Sexual Fantasies During Intercourse

Fantasy Content	% Males	% Females
Sex with a former lover	43	41
Sex with an imaginary lover	44	24
Oral-genital sex	61	51
Group sex	19	14
Being forced into a sexual relationship	21	36
Being observed engaging in sexual intercourse	15	20
Being found sexually irresistible by others	55	53
Being rejected or sexually abused	11	13
Forcing others to have sexual relations with you	24	16
Having others give in to you after resisting	37	24
Observing others engaging in sex	18	13
Sex with a member of the same sex	3	9
Sex with animals	1	4

Source: Sue, 1979.

Functions of Fantasy

Erotic fantasies serve many functions, some of which are listed in Table 9.3. First of all, they can be a source of pleasure and arousal. Erotic thoughts typically serve to enhance sexual arousal during masturbation or partner sexual activities. The following two accounts, the first by a woman, and the second by a man, show how fantasy can amplify pleasurable physical and emotional feelings:

> When my partner and I make love, I let my mind leave all other thoughts behind and totally experience and feel what is happening. All aromas become much more noticeable and pleasurable. The warmth increases, and I imagine my lover and I suspended in mist upon a bed of clouds. Our bodies come close together in my mind as arousal increases, and at the moment of orgasm it is as if we were mentally and physically one. I caress my lover's body, but it is as if it were part of my own. (Authors' files)

> The fantasy that recurs most when I am making love is a visualization of being on an isolated tropical beach. The warm sun is baking our bodies golden brown. The rhythmic pounding of the waves eliminates all tension and worries. My partner and I are one. (Authors' files)

Both men and women college students reported that the most common purpose of their fantasies during intercourse was to facilitate sexual arousal (Sue, 1979).

Frequency of fantasy appears to be related to increased ability for genital arousal. One study found that women who reported more frequent use of fantasy during masturbation outside the laboratory also demonstrated greater genital arousal in the laboratory from both self-generated fantasy and erotic tapes than did women who used masturbatory fantasy less frequently (Stock and Geer, 1982).

Sexual fantasies may also help overcome anxiety and facilitate sexual functioning (Coen, 1978) or compensate for a somewhat negative sexual situation (Knafo and Jaffe, 1984). For example, a woman who is bored with her marital relationship states:

> When having intercourse with my husband of 17 years, I often fantasize that I am taking a young virgin male to bed for his first time. I show him what I want done to me just the way I like it, while at the same time giving this poor young boy an experience he will long remember. (Authors' files)

The ability to fantasize appears to be an important component of sexual interest and arousal; a deficit of erotic fantasy is often present with problems of low sexual desire and arousal (Nutter and Condron, 1983).

Fantasies can also be a way to mentally rehearse and anticipate new sexual experiences. Imagining seductive glances, that first kiss, or a novel intercourse position may help a person more comfortably implement these activities. As one student wrote:

> I'd gone through a period of several months of celibacy and found myself feeling more reserved sexually with my new boyfriend than I liked. So I started fantasizing intimate, passionate sex with him and found it easier to be more open and affectionate. Things moved forward easily from that point. (Authors' files)

Sexual fantasies can serve to bolster a person's self-image and one's sense of femininity or masculinity. In our fantasies we can be incredibly attractive, desired, loved, or powerful. For example:

> I'm at a fancy party and am a bit underdressed. As I walk around I notice that the most beautiful woman in the room is staring at me. I look back at her; she walks away from the people she's talking with, comes up to me and says, "I want *you*." She leads me into a back room and devours me like a tigress. (Authors' files)

Table 9.3   Stated Purpose of Fantasies During Intercourse

Purpose	% Males	% Females
To facilitate sexual arousal	38	46
To imagine activities my partner and I do not engage in	18	13
To increase my partner's attractiveness	30	22
To relieve boredom	3	5
Uncertain	10	15

Source: Sue, 1979.

Some sexual fantasies allow for tolerable expression of "forbidden wishes." The fact that a sexual activity in a fantasy is "forbidden" may make it more exciting. People in sexually exclusive relationships can fantasize about past lovers or others to whom they feel attracted, even though they are committed to a single sexual partner. In a fantasy a person can experience lustful group sex, cross-orientation sexual liaisons, brief sexual encounters with strangers, erotic relations with friends and acquaintances, incestuous experiences, sex with animals, or any other sexual activities they can imagine, without actually engaging in them. The following are examples of the variety of "forbidden wishes" fantasies. A woman's masturbation fantasy:

> I fantasize about being seduced by another woman. Although I've never had an affair with another woman, it really makes me sexually excited to think of oral sex being performed on me or vice versa. (Authors' files)

A man's masturbation fantasy:

> I usually think of some woman (no one that I know), blond, beautiful, lowering herself onto me, letting me eat her out in a 69. Often times a strong and bearded man is involved and gives me oral stimulation at the same time the woman is kissing me or letting me eat her. (Authors' files)

Another man's masturbation fantasy:

> My favorite fantasy is to imagine myself with two women friends, who begin the sexual interlude by making love to each other as I observe. As their excitement heightens I join in, and we do every imaginable act together. (Authors' files)

Another function of erotic fantasy can be to provide relief from gender-role expectations (Pinhas, 1985). In fact, a degree of gender-role deviation in women may contribute to increased fantasizing. One study found that college women with more traditional feminine attitudes report fewer sexual fantasies than women who are more independent and hold more liberal views of women's roles (Brown and Hart, 1977). Women's fantasies of being the sexual aggressor and men's fantasies of being forced to have sex can offer alternatives to stereotypical roles. Three percent of women in Hunt's (1974) study and 16% in Sue's (1979) study reported fantasizing forcing others to have sex. For example, a woman college student fantasizes an aggressive and powerful role:

I walk into a male locker room and tell them to drop their shorts. I proceed to suck them off one by one. All the others are watching and panting in anticipation. When I am done with all of them, I take off my clothes, and they all begin to kiss me and touch me very slowly. I get hotter and hotter and we all end up in a sweaty orgy. (Authors' files)

Ten percent of men in Hunt's study and 21% in Sue's study reported fantasizing about being forced to have sex. In her book about male sexual fantasy, Nancy Friday reports that one of the major themes is men's abdication of activity in favor of passivity:

It may seem lusty and dashing always to be the one who chooses the women, who decides when, where, and how the bedroom scene will be played. But isn't her role safer? The man is like someone who has suggested a new restaurant to friends. What if it doesn't live up to expectations he has aroused? The macho stance makes the male the star performer. The hidden cost is that it puts the woman in the role of critic. (1980, p. 274)

The following fantasy represents an escape from the male role of initiator and director of sexual activity:

She pulls my [bathing] suit down with one hand, twisting my arm as I try to resist. I try to push her off, but she is stronger, and it is no use. She mounts me as she holds both my hands down, and I can see her large oily breasts flopping as she moves up and down on me. She looks down at me in triumph and excitement, and breathes deeply with each stroke. I am willing now, and I feel the tightness of her cunt around my shaft as she works me up to a beautiful climax. (Friday, 1980, p. 284)

While fantasies of being forced to have sex provide an alternative to gender-role expectations for men, the same type of fantasy typically means something different to women. For women, who often learn to have mixed feelings about being sexual, this type of fantasy offers sexual adventures free from the responsibility and guilt of personal choice. One study found that submission fantasies among women were more common during intercourse than during masturbation or daydreaming (Knafo and Jaffe, 1984). Enjoyment of forced sex fantasies does *not* mean women really want to be raped. A woman is in charge of her fantasies, but as a victim of sexual aggression she is not in control.

Male-Female Similarities and Differences

Research indicates several basic similarities between men's and women's fantasy lives. First, the frequency of fantasy is similar for both sexes during daydreams, masturbation, and sexual activity with a partner (Knafo and Jaffe, 1984). Second, both men and women indicate a wide range of fantasy content, as seen in Tables 9.1 and 9.2. Third, similar percentages of research subjects fantasize while masturbating about having intercourse with a loved one.

The frequency of fantasies of being forced or forcing someone to have sex differs significantly between males and females. Research indicates that almost twice as many women as men fantasize about being forced to have sex. Conversely, more men than women fantasize about forcing someone to have sex (Hunt, 1974; Sue, 1979). These types of fantasies probably reflect an exaggeration of stereotypical gender roles of the male as active and the female as receptive.

One study of college undergraduates found that men fantasize more about past experiences and current behavior, while women fantasize more about imaginary experiences. These researchers hypothesize that due to the female script of passivity and acquiescence, women are less able than men to initiate and act out their impulses except in their fantasy lives (McCauley and Swann, 1978). Other male-female differences are shown in Tables 9.1 and 9.2.

Fantasies: Help or Hindrance?

Erotic fantasies are generally considered a healthy and helpful aspect of sexuality. Many sex therapists encourage their clients to use sexual fantasy as a source of stimulation to help them increase interest and arousal (Barback, 1976; Heiman et al., 1976; Lentz and Zeiss, 1984).

Although most of the available research supports erotic imagining as helpful, sexual fantasy has also been considered symptomatic of poor heterosexual relations or other problems (Hollender, 1970; Horney, 1967; Shainess and Greenwald, 1971). Private fantasies during sex with a partner may lessen the trust and intimacy in a relationship (Apfelbaum, 1980). On the other hand, fantasies about a partner other than the one present may provide needed distance from uncomfortably intense intimacy (Coen, 1978). As with most other aspects of sexuality, what determines whether fantasizing is helpful or disturbing to a relationship is its meaning and purpose for the individuals concerned.

Some people may decide to incorporate a particular fantasy into their actual sexual behavior. Acting out a fantasy can be pleasurable; on the other hand, if a fantasy is counter to one's value system or has possible negative consequences, one should consider the advantages and disadvantages of doing so. For some people fantasies are more exciting when they remain imaginary and are a disappointment in actual practice.

Most people draw a distinct boundary between their fantasy world and the real world. For example, a woman who enjoys fantasizing about having intercourse with her partner's best friend might never really consider doing so. However, some people feel guilty about fantasizing; almost 20% of college men and women felt uneasy or ashamed about their fantasies during intercourse (Sue, 1979). For people who experience guilt over their fantasies, it is important to remember that thinking is not the same as doing. As long as people feel in control of their actions —that is, able not to act on a fantasy that would hurt themselves or others—they probably do not need to be concerned.

In some cases, fantasy may contribute to a person acting in a way harmful to others. This is of particular concern with people who may sexually molest children or sexually assault adults. A person who thinks that he or she is in danger of committing such an act should seek professional psychological assistance. Chapter 20 provides further information about fantasy and sexual offenders.

Masturbation

In this text, the term **masturbation** is used to describe self-stimulation of one's genitals for sexual pleasure. We will discuss some perspectives on and purposes of masturbation, patterns of self-stimulation through the life cycle, and specific techniques used in masturbation.

Perspectives on Masturbation

Masturbation has been a source of social concern and censure throughout Judeo-Christian history. This state of affairs has resulted in both misinformation and considerable personal shame and fear. Many of the negative attitudes toward masturbation are rooted in the early Judeo-Christian view that procreation was the only legitimate purpose of sexual behavior. Since masturbation obviously could not result in conception, it was condemned. The "evils" of masturbation received a great deal of publicity in the name of science during the mid-eighteenth century, due largely to the writings of a European physician named Tissot. He wrote vividly about the mind- and body-damaging effects of "self-abuse." This view of masturbation became part of social and medical attitudes.

In the 1800s sexual abstinence, simple foods and fitness were lauded as crucial to health. The Reverend Sylvester Graham, who promoted the use of whole grain flours and whose name is still attached to Graham crackers, wrote *A Lecture to Young Men*. He proclaimed that ejaculation reduced precious, health-preserving "vital fluids" and beseeched men to abstain from masturbation and even marital intercourse to avoid moral as well as physical degeneracy. John Harvey Kellogg, M.D., carried Graham's work further and developed the corn flake as an antimasturbation food and extinguisher of sexual desire (Money, 1983). False beliefs about masturbation, fostered by medical authorities and popular writings well into this century, may be one reason earlier generations of men in Kinsey's study reported less masturbation and more concern about it than did later generations (Downey, 1980).

Freud and most other early psychoanalysts recognized that masturbation does not harm physical health, and they saw it as normal during childhood. However, they believed that masturbation in adulthood could result in "immature" sexual development and in the inability to form good sexual relationships. Current research indicates that masturbation does not prevent people from developing positive social and sexual relationships. In a national sample of male and female college students, a greater frequency of dating, kissing, breast and genital touching, and intercourse was found to correlate with a higher likelihood and increased frequency of masturbation (Atwood, 1981).

Contemporary views reflect conflicting beliefs about masturbation, and much of the traditional condemnation still exists. In 1976 the Vatican issued a "Declaration on Certain Questions Concerning Sexual Ethics," which described masturbation as an "intrinsically and seriously disordered act."

On the other hand, many writers today view masturbation as a positive aspect of sexuality. For example, Betty Dodson, author of *Liberating Masturbation,* states:

> Masturbation, of course, is our first natural sexual activity. It's the way we discover our eroticism, the way we learn to respond sexually, the way we learn to love ourselves and build self-esteem. Sexual skill and the ability to respond are not "natural" in our society. Doing what "comes naturally" for us is to be sexually inhibited. Sex is like any other skill—it has to be learned and practiced. (1974, p. 13)

Other Times, Other Places

Masturbation: A Historical Opinion

There are various names given to the unnatural and degrading vice of producing venereal excitement by the hand, or other means, generally resulting in a discharge of semen in the male and a corresponding emission in the female. Unfortunately, it is a vice by no means uncommon among the youth of both sexes, and is frequently continued into riper years.

Symptoms—The following are some of the symptoms of those who are addicted to the habit: . . . becoming timid and bashful, and shunning the society of the opposite sex; the face is apt to be pale and often a bluish or purplish streak under the eyes, while the eyes themselves look dull and languid and the edges of the eyelids often become red and sore: the person can not look anyone steadily in the face, but will drop the eyes or turn away from your gaze as if guilty of something mean.

The health soon becomes noticeably impaired; there will be general debility, a slowness of growth, weakness in the lower limbs, nervousness and unsteadiness of the hands, loss of memory, and inability to study or learn, restless disposition, weak eyes and loss of sight, headache and inability to sleep or wakefulness. Next come sore eyes, blindness, stupidity, consumption, spinal affection, emaciation, involuntary seminal emissions, loss of all energy or spirit, insanity and idiocy—the hopeless ruin of both body and mind . . .

The subject is an important one. Few, perhaps, ever think, or ever know, how many of the unfortunate inmates of our lunatic asylums have been sent there by this dreadful vice. Were the whole truth upon this subject known, it would alarm parents, as well as the guilty victims of the vice, more even than the dread of the cholera or smallpox . . .

Source: Vitalogy, described as an "encyclopedia of health and home" (Wood and Ruddock, 1918, p. 812).

"Now they tell us masturbation is harmless!"

Purposes of Masturbation

People masturbate for a variety of reasons. Not the least of these is the pleasure of arousal and orgasm. In one study (Clifford, 1978), college women reported that experiencing pleasurable sensations and physical release of sexual tension were their primary motives for masturbation. At certain times the satisfaction from an autoerotic session may be more rewarding than an interpersonal sexual encounter, as the following quote illustrates:

> I had always assumed that masturbation was a second-best sexual expression. One time, after reflecting back on the previous day's activities of a really enjoyable morning masturbatory experience and an unsatisfying experience that evening with a partner, I realized that first- and second-rate was very relative. (Authors' files)

Furthermore, some people find that the independent sexual release available through masturbation can help them make better decisions about relating sexually with other people. Within a relationship, too, masturbation can help to even out the effects of dissimilar sexual interest. Masturbation can be a shared experience:

> When I am feeling sexual and my partner is not, he holds me and kisses me while I masturbate. Also, sometimes after making love I like to touch myself while he embraces me. It is so much better than sneaking off to the bathroom alone. (Authors' files)

Beyond these reasons, some people find masturbation to be valuable as a means of self-exploration. Sex educator Eleanor Hamilton recommends masturbation to adolescents as a way to release tension and to become "pleasantly at home with your own sexual organs" (1978, p. 33). Indeed, people can learn a great deal about their sexual responses from masturbation. Self-stimulation is often helpful for women learning to experience orgasms and for men experimenting with their response patterns to increase ejaculatory control. (Masturbation as a tool for increasing sexual satisfaction is discussed in Chapter 17.) Finally, some people find that masturbation helps to induce sleep at night, for the same generalized feelings of relaxation that often follow a sexual encounter can also accompany self-pleasuring.

While masturbation is a widely existing practice that is being recognized more and more as a normal activity, guilt about it is still common:

> Every time before I would masturbate I would pray and say "I promise, God, this will be the last time." (Authors' files)

Most people have "done it," but many people feel uncomfortable about it. However, it is possible to feel uneasy about *not* doing it, too!

> I was with a group of friends who started talking and joking about masturbation. I knew what they were talking about, but I had never done it. I didn't want to say so, though. (Authors' files)

Most people who masturbate probably view the behavior with a mix of pleasure and a socialized sense of uneasiness or guilt.

A common concern about masturbation is "doing it too much." Even in writings where masturbation is said to be "normal," masturbating "to excess" is often presented as a problem. A definition of excess rarely follows. If a person were masturbating so much that it significantly interfered with daily life, there might be cause for concern. However, in that case masturbation would be a manifestation of the problem rather than the problem itself. For example, someone who is experiencing intense emotional anxiety may use masturbation as an attempt to release the anxiety or as a form of self-comforting. The problem is the source of the anxiety rather than the masturbation.

Masturbation Through the Life Cycle

Masturbation often continues as part of a person's sexual expression throughout his or her life. It is normal for infants to touch their genitals and respond pleasurably to self-stimulation. Most children soon learn, though, to be secretive about masturbation.

Few receive permission for or information about self-stimulation from their parents. On the contrary, parents may not address the topic at all or may express direct disapproval by a look, a slap, or moving the child's hands away from his or her genitals. In some cases parents punish or chastise the child severely. One woman reports:

> When I was about eight years old my mother caught me masturbating in bed. She told me that I was a very bad girl and made me sleep in the hallway that night. The next weekend we had our aunt and uncle over for supper, and she told everyone at the dinner table what I had done. (Authors' files)

Even children who experience no direct disapproval from their parents or others will usually learn quickly that masturbation must be done in secret and kept private, as reflected by the following comment:

> I didn't even know there was a word to describe what I was doing when I touched myself. I don't even remember being told not to, but somehow I knew I had to be very careful not to be caught. (Authors' files)

The perception that masturbation must be kept secret can produce feelings of guilt and shame and make it difficult for a child to ask clarifying and potentially useful questions about masturbation.

During adolescence the number of boys who masturbate increases dramatically. Kinsey's figures estimated that only 21% of 12-year-old boys masturbated, compared with 82% of 15-year-old boys (1948). Corresponding statistics for girls were much lower: an initial 12% at 12 years of age, increasing to only 20% by the age of 15 (1953). More recent statistics have higher percentages for both boys and girls, but there is still a wide discrepancy between the sexes (Hunt, 1974). The reasons masturbation is more common among males are unknown. One factor may be that young boys are taught to hold their penises during toilet training, thus receiving some degree of encouragement to touch themselves. Girls, however, learn to use toilet tissue to wipe their genitals, and this may make it less likely for girls to discover the pleasurable sensations in their genitals.

During adolescence the social expectations for gender-role stereotyped behavior often become stronger and more rigid, and these stereotypes may also contribute to lower masturbation rates among females. Masturbation is a direct statement of desire for one's own sexual pleasure and orgasm. It does not conform to gender-role stereotypes in which males obtain sexual satisfaction and females provide it. The lower percentage of adolescent girls who masturbate may also reflect the idea that "good girls" are not sexual. In other words, masturbation does not fit into the expectations that females often learn to have about sex. In contrast, the value of sex for pleasure and release of sexual tension meshes more closely with stereotypical male attitudes about sexuality. Adolescent males are probably more likely to experience peer support for masturbation, and it is not uncommon for boys to show each other how to masturbate. For females, however, the situation is often quite different; some women in Kinsey's study masturbated for the first time only after their partners manually stimulated them. A more recent study also found that approximately 20% of women learned to masturbate by copying their partner's petting technique (Clifford, 1978). These sex differences in masturbation behavior extend into young adulthood: college age men are more likely to masturbate and do so more often than college age women (Atwood, 1981).

In adulthood the majority of men and women, both married and unmarried, masturbate on occasion. Women tend to masturbate more after they reach their twenties. Kinsey hypothesized that this phenomenon was due to increased erotic responsiveness, opportunities for learning about the possibility of self-stimulation through sex play with a partner, and a reduction in learned sexual inhibitions.

It is common for people to continue masturbation even when involved in a committed relationship. Hunt's 1974 survey reported that 72% of young husbands and 68% of young wives (in their twenties and early thirties) masturbate, on the average, twice and once a month respectively. However, masturbation is often not considered appropriate if a person has a sexual partner. Some people believe that they should not engage in a sexual activity that excludes their partner or that experiencing sexual pleasure by masturbation deprives their partner of pleasure. Others mistakenly interpret their desire to masturbate as a sign that there is something wrong with their relationship. But unless it interferes with enjoyable sexual sharing in a relationship, masturbation can be considered a normal part of each partner's sexual repertoire.

During the adult years people who are not in a sexual relationship may use masturbation as a primary sexual outlet. Masturbation may be particularly valuable to older people as a way of continuing sexual expression when illness, absence, death, or divorce deprive them of a partner.

Self-Pleasuring Techniques

This section offers descriptions of self-pleasuring techniques. Self-exploration exercises can help a person become more aware of genital and whole-body sensations, and readers who would like to experiment with some or all of the steps are invited to do so. It is not unusual for someone first trying self-pleasuring to feel anxious. If this happens to you, two suggestions may be helpful. First, focus for a minute on physical relaxation: take a few slow breaths, extending your belly outward as you inhale. Another way to relax yourself is to tense a body part, like an arm and hand, for a few seconds and then release it. Second, try to clear your mind of thoughts related to the "rightness" or "wrongness" of self-pleasuring, and allow yourself to concentrate instead on the positive physical sensations that can come from self-stimulation.

Since the genitals are only one part of the body, we suggest involving the entire anatomy in the self-exam, to explore your sensuality as well as specific structures. Both men and women often report that their sexual feelings are enhanced by learning to be less genitally focused and more in touch with the sensual potentials that exist throughout their bodies.

Set aside a block of time (at least one hour for the entire exercise) when you will have privacy. Allow several minutes for your mind to quiet down from the noisy clatter of the day. A good way to begin is with a relaxing bath or shower. You can start the self-exploration while bathing, washing with soap-covered, slippery hands in an unhurried manner. Towel off leisurely and then explore all areas of your body

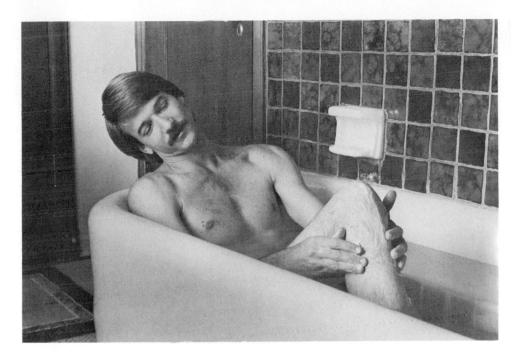

*A relaxed bath
can be a way to
get in touch with
one's sensuality.*

with your fingertips, gently touching and stroking the skin of your face, arms, legs, stomach, and feet.

As you are touching, focus on the various textures and shapes. Compare the sensations when you have your eyes open and closed. You may wish to experiment with using a body lotion, oil, or powder. After the gentle stroking try firmer, massaging pressures, paying extra attention to areas that are tense. You might like to allow yourself some pleasurable fantasies during this time. Notice whether your breathing is relaxed; let it be deep and slow. When you have completed this part, notice how you feel.

For the next step we recommend that you return to the genital self examination exercises in Chapters 4 and 5. Once you have completed the exploration, continue experimenting with various kinds of pressure and stroking. Pay attention to what feels good. The following paragraphs are descriptions of ways of touching that some people use during masturbation.

Specific techniques for masturbation vary. Males commonly grasp the penile shaft with one hand, as shown in Figure 9.1. Up-and-down motions of differing pressures and tempos provide stimulation. A man may also stroke the glans and frenum or caress or tug the scrotum. Or, rather than using his hands, he may rub his penis against a mattress or a pillow.

Women enjoy a variety of stimulation techniques. Typically, the hand provides circular, back-and-forth, or up-and-down movements of the mons and clitoral area (see Figure 9.2). The glans is rarely stimulated directly, although it may be touched rhythmically when covered by the hood. Some women thrust their clitoral area against

Figure 9.1

**Male
Masturbation**

an object such as bedding or a pillow. Others masturbate by pressing the thighs together and tensing the pelvic floor muscles that underlie the vulva. Contrary to what is often portrayed in pornography, few women use vaginal insertion to produce orgasm during masturbation. Only 1.5% of women in Hite's survey (1976) used vaginal insertion of a finger or penis-shaped object; over half of this small group had also used clitoral stimulation prior to insertion.

Individuals and couples also use vibrators for added enjoyment or variation. Although some men enjoy using a vibrator on their genitals, women tend to be greater enthusiasts of this technical advancement. If you want to use a vibrator for sexual pleasure, experimentation is in order. By placing it on different areas of the body or genitals you can find what is particularly arousing. Moving the pelvis or the vibrator may or may not enhance enjoyment.

There are several different types of vibrators available (see Figure 9.3), and people's preferences vary. The penis-shaped, battery-operated ones usually have less intense vibrations than the others. These vibrators do not require an electrical outlet, and they are also the least expensive type.

Electric vibrators are either held in the hand or strapped to the back of the hand. Two basic kinds of hand-held vibrators are the wand-shaped and the multiple-attachment type, both of which usually have two speeds. A variety of shapes of attachments come with the vibrator unit. One brand has a special clitoral attachment. Electric vibrators should never be used in or around water, as lethal electric shock may result.

Hand-strapped vibrators attach to the back of the hand and cause the fingers to vibrate. The vibrations transmitted this way are generally less intense than with hand-held vibrators, and some people prefer this. In addition, some prefer receiving indirect stimulation, through their own or their partner's fingers, to direct application

Figure 9.2

**Female
Masturbation**

of the vibrator to their genitals. However, the hand attached to the vibrator can become numb or uncomfortable. The recent development of detachable, hand-held pulsating shower heads has added another alternative. Some women have long known that a stream of water over their genitals is very arousing.

Vibrators are available in department and hardware stores, by mail order, and in adult bookstores. If possible, compare different models for strength of vibrations and ease in handling. Vibrators with more than one speed are most likely to meet individual needs. You may find that you sometimes prefer different intensities of vibration.*

Although masturbating is valuable for many people in varied situations, not everyone wants to do it. Sometimes, in our attempts to help people who would like to eradicate their negative feelings about self-stimulation, it may sound as if the message is that people *should* masturbate. This is not the case. Masturbation is an option for sexual expression—not a mandate.

---

*An excellent book on vibrators is *Good Vibrations* by Joani Blank (Burlingame, Calif.; Down There Press, 1976).

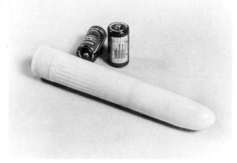

(a)

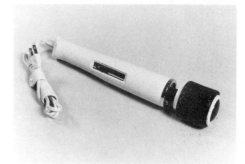

(b)

Figure 9.3

Vibrators
Four types of vibrators: (a) phallic-shaped with batteries; (b) wand-shaped; (c) hand strap; (d) hand-held with attachments.

(c)

(d)

Up to this point in the chapter, we have been looking at ways that people express themselves individually or find solitary sexual outlets. However, many of the sexual behaviors with which we are concerned in this book take place as interactions between people.

In the sections that follow, we will discuss some of the commoner forms of shared sexual behavior. The sequence in which they are presented does not mean that such a progression is "best" in a particular sexual encounter; for example, a heterosexual couple may desire oral-genital stimulation after coitus rather than before. Nor is any one of these activities necessary in a given encounter: complete sexual experience may consist of any or all of them. The discussions of shared sexual activities, with the exception of coitus, are directed toward all individuals, regardless of their sexual orientation.

Although the following sections include discussions of sexual technique, a technique is not able to stand on its own; it is part of the framework of the relationship in which it occurs. Feelings, desires, and attitudes strongly influence choices about sexual activity. Sensitivity to a person's sexual needs will help develop shared pleasure and arousal more effectively than any specific technique. Mutual consent is an important aspect of a sexual relationship, and sexual activities that both partners are willing to engage in are likely to provide a couple with enjoyable sexual experiences.

There may be some male-female differences to consider in regard to feelings about various sexual activities. A research study asked college students about their preferences regarding "foreplay," coitus, and "afterplay" and found that males were more likely to say they preferred coitus, and females that they preferred foreplay and afterplay (none of the males said afterplay). Furthermore, females wanted to spend more time in foreplay and afterplay than males (Denny et al., 1984). There is, of course, great individual variation. Open communication can greatly help couples establish their unique and changing preferences.

Shared Touching

> i like my body when it is with your
> body. It is so quite new a thing.
> Muscles better and nerves more.
> i like your body. i like what it does,
> i like its hows. i like to feel the spine
> of your body and its bones, and the trembling
> -firm-smooth ness and which i will
> again and again and again
> kiss, i like kissing this and that of you,
> i like, slowly stroking the, shocking fuzz
> of your electric fur, and what-is-it comes
> over parting flesh. . . . And eyes big love-crumbs,
>
> and possibly i like the thrill
>
> of under me you so quite new*

Touch is one of the first and most important senses that we experience when we emerge into this world. Infants who have been fed but deprived of this basic stimulation have died for lack of it. Touch also forms the cornerstone of sexuality shared with another. In Masters and Johnson's evaluation:

> Touch is an end in itself. It is a primary form of communication, a silent voice that avoids the pitfall of words while expressing the feelings of the moment. It bridges the physical separateness from which no human being is spared, literally establishing a sense of solidarity between two individuals. Touching is sensual pleasure, exploring the textures of skin, the suppleness of muscle, the contours of the body, with no further goal than enjoyment of tactile perceptions. (1976, p. 253)

Touch does not need to be directed at an erogenous area of the body to be sexual. The entire body surface is a sensory organ and touching—almost anywhere—can enhance intimacy and sexual arousal. It is important to remember that partners

---

*Reprinted from *Tulips & Chimneys* by e. e. cummings, by permission of Liveright Publishing Corporation. Copyright 1923, 1925 and renewed 1951, 1953 by e. e. cummings. Copyright © 1973, 1976 by the Trustees for the e. e. cummings Trust. Copyright © 1973, 1976 by George James Firmage.

*Sensual touching
can be pleasurable
to both the giver
and the receiver.*

may like different kinds of touching. It is helpful for couples to openly discuss their preferences, to avoid the frustration that can result when one partner touches the other the way that the toucher would like instead of the way the touched one enjoys.

While the entire body responds to touching, some specific areas are, of course, more receptive to sexual feelings than others. Preferences vary from one person to another. Many men and women report breast stimulation (especially of the nipple) to be arousing; others find it unenjoyable or unpleasant. A few women reach orgasm from breast stimulation alone (Masters and Johnson, 1966). The size of the breasts is not related to how erotically sensitive they are. Some women's breasts become more sensitive, even tender, during certain times of their menstrual cycles. A woman may find that a firm touch that is highly arousing one week feels uncomfortable and harsh the next. Once again, ongoing communication is important. Masters and Johnson's sensate focus exercises, described in Chapter 17, give an opportunity to explore and experience the pleasurable sensations from giving and receiving touching.

Genital stimulation is often highly pleasurable to women and men. Many people's first experience with manual genital stimulation comes from masturbation, and this self-knowledge can form the basis of further learning with a partner. People who have not previously masturbated can explore and learn what is enjoyable with each other. One partner can touch the other, or they can explore each others' sensations simultaneously. Manual stimulation can provide pleasure or orgasm by itself, or it can be a step towards other activities.

Manual Stimulation of the Female Genitals

The vulva tissues are delicate and sensitive. If there is not enough lubrication to make the vulva slippery, it can become easily irritated. A lubricant such as K-Y Jelly, a lotion without alcohol, or saliva can be used to moisten the fingers and vulva.

There is great variation from one woman to another in the kind of touches that create arousal. Even the same woman may vary in her preference from one moment to another. Women may prefer gentle or firm movements on different areas of the vulva. Direct stimulation of the clitoris is uncomfortable for some women; touches above or along the sides may be preferable. Insertion of a finger into the vagina may enhance arousal. Anal stimulation is erotic to some women but not to others. It is important not to touch the vulva or vagina with the same finger used for anal stimulation, because bacteria that are normal in the rectum can cause infections if introduced into the vagina.

Manual Stimulation of the Male Genitals

Men also have individual preferences for manual stimulation, and as with women, the pace of the movements may vary as arousal increases. Gentle or firm stroking of the penile shaft and glans and light touches or tugging on the scrotum may be desired. Some men experience uncomfortable sensitivity of the penile glans when it is touched immediately following orgasm. Some men find that lubrication with a lotion or saliva increases pleasure. With heterosexual couples, if intercourse might follow, the lotion should be nonirritating to the woman's genital tissues. Some men also enjoy manual stimulation or penetration of the anus.

Oral-Genital Stimulation

Both the mouth and genitals are primary biological erogenous zones, areas of the body generously endowed with sensory nerve endings. Therefore, couples who are psychologically comfortable with oral-genital stimulation often find both giving and receiving to be highly pleasurable. Oral-genital contact is used to produce pleasure, arousal, or orgasm. As one woman states:

> At first, I was very uncomfortable with the idea of oral sex. After some explanations and some showing by my partner, I realized that maybe this wasn't so bad after all. In fact, for the first time in my life, I reached orgasm. (Authors' files)

Oral-genital stimulation can be done individually (by one partner to the other) or simultaneously. Some people prefer oral sex individually because they can focus on either giving or receiving. Others especially enjoy the mutuality of simultaneous oral-genital sex. Simultaneous stimulation is sometimes referred to as "69" because of the body position suggested by the numbers (see Figure 9.4). A variety of positions can be used; lying side by side and using a thigh for a pillow is another option. As arousal becomes intense during mutual oral-genital stimulation, partners need to be careful not to suck or bite too hard.

Different terminology is used to describe oral-genital stimulation of women and oral-genital stimulation of men. **Cunnilingus** (Latin *cunnus,* "vulva," and *lingere,* "to lick") is oral stimulation of the vulva—the clitoris, labia minora, vestibule, and vaginal opening. Many women find the warmth, softness, and moistness of the partner's lips and tongue to be highly pleasurable and effective in producing sexual arousal or orgasm. Variations of stimulation include rapid or slow circular or back-and-forth tongue movement on the clitoral area, sucking the clitoris or labia minora, and thrusting the tongue into the vaginal opening. Some women are especially aroused by simultaneous manual stimulation of the vagina and oral stimulation of the clitoral area.

Fellatio (Latin *fillare,* "to suck") is oral stimulation of the penis and scrotum. Both of Kinsey's studies found that, in heterosexual couples, women were less likely to stimulate their partners orally than the reverse. Options for stimulation include gently or vigorously licking and sucking the glans, the frenum, and the penile shaft, and licking or enclosing a testicle in the mouth. Some men enjoy combined oral stimulation of the glans and manual stroking of the penile shaft, testicles, or anus.

Couples differ in their preference for including ejaculation into the mouth as a part of male oral stimulation. Many find it acceptable and some find it exciting; others do not. An occasional couple avoids fellatio entirely because they want to avoid ejaculation into the partner's mouth. However, a couple can agree beforehand that the one who is being stimulated will indicate when he is close to orgasm and withdraw from his partner's mouth. For couples who are comfortable with ejaculation into the mouth, the ejaculate can be swallowed or not according to one's preference. In either

Other Times, Other Places

Noncoital Sex Play

In some societies, noncoital sexual interaction is virtually nonexistent; in others, a broad repertoire of sexual techniques may be used. Touching, oral stimulation, manual stimulation, and mutual masturbation are not commonly employed as substitutes for coitus among heterosexual lovers in most societies. While these activities may be common, they are usually part of sexual encounters that also include coitus. Orgasm resulting from noncoital sex play is probably much more frequent in the United States than in most less industrialized societies (Gebhard, 1971).

Kissing on the mouth, universal in Western societies, is rare or absent in many other parts of the world. Male fondling of the female body, particularly of the breasts, is apparently common to all cultures. Male oral stimulation of the female breast is somewhat less universal. Manual stimulation of a partner's genitals is commonly practiced by both males and females in the majority of researched societies (Gebhard, 1971).

Oral sex, both cunnilingus (oral stimulation of the vulva) and fellatio (oral stimulation of the penis), is quite common among island societies of the South Pacific, in the industrialized nations of Asia, and in much of the Western world. In Africa the practice is most prevalent in northern regions. In societies that accept the practice of cunnilingus, fellatio is also almost always practiced. However, the reverse is not necessarily the case.

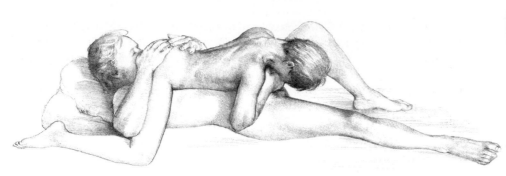

Figure 9.4

Simultaneous Oral-Genital Stimulation in the "69" Position

case, it is usually best for the partner who is doing the oral stimulation to control the movements. During oral sex this partner can grasp the penis manually below his or her lips to prevent it from going further into the mouth than is comfortable. This will help avoid difficulty with a gagging reflex. Also, vigorous thrusting may result in lacerations of the partner's lips as he or she attempts to protect the penis from the teeth.

Some people have reservations concerning oral-genital stimulation. These views or preferences come from a number of sources. As we have seen, sexual behaviors that do not have the potential of resulting in a pregnancy within marriage have historically been labeled immoral, and many people believe that oral sex is wrong. This notion of immorality has been institutionalized into law, and sexual behaviors other than coitus are still illegal in many states.

Other reservations have to do with the belief that oral-genital stimulation is unsanitary or that genitals are unattractive. It may be difficult for someone who has a negative image of his penis or her vulva to feel comfortable with receiving oral sex. Many people have also acquired the attitude that the genitals are "dirty," since they are close to the urinary opening and the anus. However, routine thorough washing of the genitals with soap and water is adequate for cleanliness.

Other reasons some people object to oral sex stem from the belief that it is a homosexual act—even when experienced by heterosexual couples. Although many homosexual people do engage in oral sex, the activity is not homosexual by nature. Rather, its homosexuality or heterosexuality depends on the sexes of the partners involved.

Despite these negative attitudes, oral-genital contact is quite common and has become even more so in recent years. In this period, too, it seems to have gained acceptance through a larger cross-section of educational levels. Kinsey's research in the late forties and early fifties revealed that 60% of college-educated couples, 20% of high-school-educated couples, and 10% of grade-school-educated couples had experienced oral-genital stimulation as part of their marital sex. Hunt's 1974 investigations indicated that by the 1970s, 90% of married couples under 25 years of age—regardless of educational level—had experienced oral-genital sex. While it is likely that these different figures reflect a degree of sample bias (see Chapter 2), it also seems probable that oral-genital contact is gaining more widespread acceptance and practice. A study of 203 Canadian college women found that 61% had experienced fellatio and 68% had experienced cunnilingus. Of those who had experienced fellatio, 97% had also experienced cunnilingus (Herold and Way, 1983). Surveys administered to several thousand students enrolled in our sexuality classes over the last 15 years reveal that approximately 89% of women and 82% of men have experienced both fellatio and cunnilingus (Crooks, 1986a).

Anal Stimulation

Like oral-genital stimulation, anal stimulation may be thought by some to be a homosexual act. However, penile penetration of the anus is practiced by both heterosexual and male homosexual couples; so is the use of small penis-shaped vibrators for anal insertion. The anus has dense supplies of nerve endings that can respond erotically. Some women report orgasmic response from anal intercourse (Masters and Johnson, 1970), and heterosexual and homosexual men often experience orgasm from stimulation during penetration.

Individuals or couples may also use anal stimulation for arousal and variety during other sexual activities. Manually stroking the outside of the anal opening or inserting one or more fingers into the anus can be very pleasurable for some people during masturbation or partner sex. Others may engage in oral-anal stimulation, called *analingus* or "rimming." Hunt's (1974) survey reported that various forms of anal stimulation had been used, at least experimentally, by many of his respondents. Over half of the men and women under 35 in his sample had experienced oral-anal contact. Approximately 25% of married couples under 35 reported that they used anal intercourse occasionally.

Besides the sphincter muscle, the anus is composed of delicate tissues, and some special care needs to be taken in anal stimulation. A nonirritating lubricant and gentle penetration are necessary to avoid discomfort or injury to these tissues. It is helpful to use lubrication on both the anus and the penis or object being inserted. The partner receiving anal insertion can bear down (as with a bowel movement) to relax the sphincter. The partner inserting needs to go slowly and gently, keeping the penis or object tilted to follow the direction of the colon (Morin, 1981).

There are some important health risks to consider in connection with anal sex. Various intestinal infections, hepatitis, and sexually transmitted diseases can be contracted or spread through oral-anal contact. Anal intercourse is one of the riskiest of all sexual behaviors associated with transmission of the AIDS virus. Consequently, both heterosexual and homosexual people who wish to reduce their risk of transmitting or contracting this deadly virus should refrain from anal intercourse or use a condom and practice withdrawal prior to ejaculation. (Precautions against transmission of AIDS will be discussed more fully in Chapter 18.) Heterosexual couples should never have vaginal intercourse directly following anal intercourse, since bacteria that are normal in the anus often cause vaginal infections. To prevent vaginal infections from this source, a couple may choose to use a condom during anal intercourse. Alternatively, the penis should be washed thoroughly after anal intercourse. Bacteria may, however, remain harbored in the penile urethra. Another alternative is for vaginal intercourse to precede anal intercourse.

Coitus and Coital Positions

There is a wide range of positions a couple may choose for penile-vaginal intercourse, or coitus. Many people may have a favored position, yet enjoy others. A 30-year-old man states:

> Different intercourse positions usually express and evoke particular emotions for me. Being on top I enjoy feeling aggressive; when on the bottom I experience a special kind of receptive sensuality. In the side-by-side position I easily feel gentle and intimate. I like sharing all these dimensions of myself with my lover. (Authors' files)

In the pages that follow we will describe some of the basic coital positions and their potential advantages and disadvantages. These are meant only as general descriptions, not inflexible guidelines. As in all areas of sexuality, individual preferences vary. Furthermore, the desirability of a particular position may change with health, age, weight, pregnancy, or different partners. Therefore, the points in our discussion of potential advantages and disadvantages will not be true for everyone.

We can make one other general statement about coitus. Beyond technique, cooperation and consideration are important, particularly at certain times. Some couples may find that mutual cooperation during **intromission** (entry of the penis into the vagina) is helpful. Often the woman can best guide her partner's penis into her vagina by moving her body or using her hand. If his penis slips out of the vagina, which can occur fairly easily in some positions, a helping hand will most likely be welcome. Furthermore, both nonverbal and verbal communication about preferences of position, tempo, and movement can enhance the pleasure and arousal of both partners. Coitus can occur with or without orgasm for one or both partners.

Man Above, Face-to-Face

The most familiar coital position in our society, sometimes known as the "missionary position," is with the man above and the couple facing each other (see Figure 9.5). There are several potential advantages of this position. First of all, the man is typically the more active partner in our society, and many couples are most comfortable with

Figure 9.5

Man-Above, Face-to-Face, Intercourse Position

the man having the initiative. In this position, he has maximum freedom and control over coital movements. Kinsey's research in the late 1940s indicated that a large majority of males predominantly or exclusively experienced coitus in this position.

Closeness of upper bodies and opportunity for kissing and eye contact are also benefits of this position. The woman's hands are free to manually caress and hold her partner. If the man is raised on his hands, she can stimulate her clitoris. This is also a good position for maintaining penetration after ejaculation. This position increases the possibility of conception, an advantage if pregnancy is desired. (Improving the chances of conception will be discussed in more detail in Chapter 12.)

The position also has disadvantages. The man usually supports his weight on his knees and hands or elbows, limiting his ability to caress his partner. Also, the strain of both supporting himself and actively moving increases muscle tension, and this may hasten ejaculation. He may find it more difficult to control his orgasm and prolong intercourse. For this reason, most sex therapists working with men who want to establish ejaculatory control suggest positions other than man-above.

This position is also limiting for the woman, whose control over her own pelvic movements is often restricted. It may be more difficult for her to experience the pressures and movements that are most arousing to her. If her partner is much heavier than she, his weight may be uncomfortable. Also, she has little control over penetration, and deep penetration is uncomfortable for some women. Finally, this position is a poor one during pregnancy, once the woman's abdomen has enlarged, as pressure on the abdomen is uncomfortable then.

Woman Above, Face-to-Face

An alternative to the man-above position is for the woman to be on top. As Figure 9.6 shows, she may either be prone or sitting upright. Some of the advantages of either of these positions are the converse of when the man is on top. The woman can control the tempo, direction, and depth of movement. Many women find pressure against their partner's pubic bone stimulating, and this position allows for the woman to adjust her body to provide the kind of pubic bone contact that is especially arousing to her. Her partner can assume a more receptive role. These combined factors are the reasons that most sex therapists ask heterosexual clients to use this position as an aid to modifying a variety of difficulties.

Apparently "primitive" humans were aware of what modern sex therapists know. The woman-above position is common in prehistoric drawings that show intercourse scenes. In Kinsey's survey (1948), this position was reported to be used occasionally, with frequency varying somewhat according to education level. Thirty-five percent of college-educated men, 28% of high-school-educated men, and 17% of grade-school-educated men reported having used this position. The use of the woman-above position has been increasing, as indicated by Kinsey's 1953 findings that 35% of women born before 1900 and 52% born after 1900 had used it frequently. In 1974 Morton Hunt found that nearly three-quarters of married couples reported using this position occasionally.

Particularly when the woman is sitting upright, the position has another advantage in that the woman or her partner can stimulate her clitoris. A vibrator can also be used. When she is sitting upright, the woman is free to touch her partner; and whether she is prone or sitting, the man's hands are free to caress much of her body. When she is prone, full-body contact can be enjoyable. It is a good position for looking at and talking to each other.

One of the disadvantages of the woman-above position is that one or both partners may be uncomfortable with the woman assuming a more active role. The woman may also find this position tiring. If the male attempts to maintain a very active role, he may find the muscle tension created by moving both his body and hers results in his orgasm occurring sooner than desired. Finally, even if both partners are comfortable with this position, the woman may need some time at first to experiment and learn how to move her pelvis.

Figure 9.6

**Two Variations
of the Woman-
Above Position**

Figure 9.7

**Face-to-Face
Side Intercourse
Position**

Side Position, Face-to-Face

In this position the partners face each other, but they lie on their sides (see Figure 9.7). One of the primary advantages of this position is that neither partner must support the other's weight. Each has one hand available to caress and fondle the partner, and manual clitoral stimulation can be included. This is typically a relaxed, unhurried position; talking, looking at each other, even sipping something to drink are all options. Intercourse can often be prolonged, due to the relaxed nature and mutual control over pelvic movements. A couple can remain intertwined after completing intercourse, if they wish, and fall asleep in each other's arms. This can be a good position in late pregnancy, because depth of penetration can be easily regulated and there is no extra pressure on the woman's abdomen.

A possible disadvantage of the face-to-face side position is difficulty with intromission. For this reason some couples prefer to begin in either the woman- or man-above position, then roll over to the side position. Another disadvantage is that it is not a good position for vigorous pelvic thrusting, due to the limited mobility of both partners. Also, it may be difficult to make the kind of pubic bone contact that is often arousing for the woman.

Rear-Entry Position

One of the potential advantages of a rear-entry intercourse position is the number of possible variations. Depending on the option selected, intercourse can be vigorous or relaxed. The woman or her partner can easily stimulate her clitoris, and she can also stroke his scrotum. The side-by-side, back-to-belly variation shown in Figure 9.8 can be a good position during pregnancy. In the kneeling position, where the woman is on her knees and the man enters from behind, the man has considerable ease of penetration.

Figure 9.8

**Rear-Entry
Intercourse
Position,
with Pregnant
Woman Using
Simultaneous
Manual
Stimulation**

One common objection to rear-entry coitus is the feeling of lack of intimacy without face-to-face contact. Others believe it is "animalistic," because animals copulate in a similar position. Furthermore, it is sometimes associated with anal intercourse, which as we have discussed, has negative overtones for some people.

Sexual Adjustment and Disability

People with disabilities often have special needs in relation to their sexual behavior. This section will discuss some of the special needs of people with spinal injuries, cerebral palsy, blindness, deafness, and developmental disabilities. (The sexual impact of illnesses like diabetes, arthritis, heart attack, and multiple sclerosis will be discussed in Chapter 16.) Before we consider specific disabilities, we will examine some of the sexual concerns that people with disabilities have in common.

Stereotypes About Sexuality and Disability

Most disabled people must confront prevalent myths about their sexual nature and abilities. These myths often have their basis in the notion, common in our society, that the only people who have the right to be sexual are those who are young and beautiful. "Barbie and Ken" images of sexually active people are constantly reinforced by the popular media; people who are obese, old, or do not conform to current standards of sexual attractiveness are usually presented as asexual or ludicrous. This narrow stereotype has been particularly damaging to physically or mentally disabled people. In one writer's words: "Society has placed an added handicap on the already handicapped person by helping to deny two basic needs—a realistic and positive identity as a sexual being, and the opportunity for sexual expression and fulfilling sexual relationships" (Bidgood, 1974, p. 1). The belief that those with certain disabilities are not sexual beings is an important myth for both able-bodied and disabled people to examine and reject.

The stereotype of the asexual disabled may also be based on incorrect assumptions about the sexual limitations that certain disabilities present. These assumptions commonly focus on lack of genital sensation; inability to have an erection, orgasm, or ejaculation; inability to have penile-vaginal intercourse or to use the male-on-top position; or the presence of bowel or bladder apparatus, braces, or prostheses. Infertility as a result of disability may also be interpreted as a loss of sexuality. However, as we stress throughout this text, sexuality is integral to all of us—regardless of whether erection, intercourse, orgasm, or pregnancy can occur and in spite of crutches, braces, or wheelchairs. People are sexual beings no matter what their physical appearance or level of functioning.

Certainly the limitations and special circumstances that disabilities present are often a challenge for sexual adjustment. Special information and teaching tools may be needed for appropriate sex education. Good communication within relationships is especially important, because a nondisabled partner is unlikely to know what the disabled partner can or cannot do. Disabled people can greatly benefit from flexibility in sexual roles and innovation in sexual technique. As a woman with cerebral palsy explains:

> My disability kind of makes things more interesting. We have to try harder and I think we get more out of it because we do. We both have to be very conscious of each other— we have to take time. That makes us less selfish and more considerate of each other which helps the relationship in other areas beside sexuality. (Shaul et al., 1978, p. 5)

A disability does not eliminate the human need and capacity for shared intimacy.

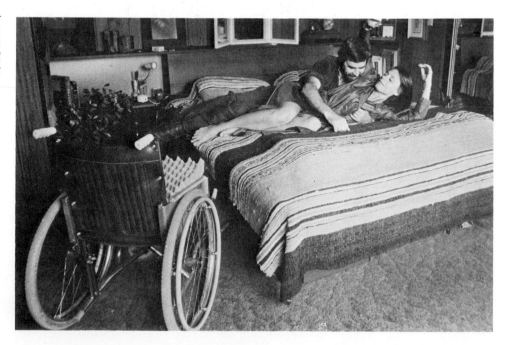

This kind of exploration, experimentation, communication, and learning together are ways of relating that can contribute to pleasure and intimacy in the relationships of nondisabled couples too.

Body Image

Physical disabilities often affect a person's body image. Accepting and positive feelings about one's physical self are an important part of sexuality; a good body image contributes to a person's perception of him- or herself as a sexual, and sexually attractive, individual. People who believe that they are unattractive may avoid social situations or feel inadequate in a sexual relationship. Body image also influences how much attention a person pays to grooming and other aspects of personal physical care. A positive body image can contribute to how lovable and worthwhile one feels and what kinds of relationships a person chooses.

For individuals with physical disabilities and limitations, developing a positive body image may be difficult. It can be emotionally painful to compare oneself to nondisabled people, or to oneself prior to becoming ill or injured. Impaired mobility and limitations in recreation, self-care, and work performance can generate resentment and anger towards one's body. These feelings can be exacerbated by juxtaposing media images of attractiveness and one's own attributes: scars from injuries or surgery, lack of muscle tone from paralysis, or involuntary muscle spasms from neurological damage. Yet these characteristics are very much a part of a person and need to be accepted along with his or her other attributes. As one person who had polio noted:

> Before my disability I was very active. I figure skated, danced, played the piano. After I was disabled, it changed my body so much. Well, it happened at 17 and was quite a shock . . . at the present time I'm working on trying to accept my body and to be more aware of it. It is really part of my self-image. Sometimes I'd like to put it [my body] out there somewhere and act as if it's not part of me, but I'm working to admit that it's there and trying to include it as part of me. (Shaul et al., 1978, pp. 6–7)

Body image often can be improved for both disabled and nondisabled people. Many people have negative feelings about their bodies, and all of us will eventually confront body image changes caused by wrinkles, gray hair, and reduced speed and agility. The following suggestions for helping disabled individuals improve their body image (adapted from Shaul et al., 1978) can be helpful for others as well:

1. Using a mirror, note your positive features and think about how they can be enhanced.
2. Explore and become acquainted with the features or body parts you consider least attractive.
3. Put up photographs of yourself that you like.
4. Say out loud to the mirror, the next time you go to extra effort to look good, "I look great today."
5. Pamper your body with relaxing baths, fragrances, backrubs, a new haircut, and new clothes.
6. Ask people what they find physically attractive about you.

7. Develop your physical potential with exercise and diet.
8. Talk with other people with disabilities to help overcome a sense of isolation.
9. Shop for prostheses or braces where the sales people are concerned with appearance as well as function.
10. Pay attention to the ways you've grown and improved.

Sometimes a person will face body image changes due to a disability with previously unknown reserves of emotional strength. Meeting such a challenge can promote a re-evaluation of personal values and priorities. A young woman who broke her neck in a car accident reports:

> I went through enormous personal changes after my accident. I had been working as a model prior to my accident and was very sought after socially, mainly because of my physical attractiveness. I didn't really reach out to others to get to know them; I always got enough attention by being pretty. But after my accident, with my hair shaved for the halo-type metal band that screwed into my skull and attached to a shoulder-neck brace, I wasn't very pretty. I had to learn to reach out to others to help them feel comfortable with me, so that I wouldn't be so alone and lonely. It has been the most valuable, and most difficult, experience in my life. (Authors' files)

Sexuality and Medical and Institutional Care

Most individuals with a disability will have contact with medical or institutional care. Health care professionals may pay attention to reproductive concerns of disabled people but ignore the emotional and social effects of a disability on sexuality. They sometimes mistakenly assume that they should not talk about sexuality with disabled patients to avoid adding to their problems and anxieties. Although those responsible for health care of the disabled have become more sensitive to their patients' needs in this area, there is still a great need for sexuality education for the staff and clients of hospitals and institutions. Perhaps most important for disabled people are opportunities to explore options for sexual expression—solitary and interpersonal—within their capabilities. One writer clearly outlines some of the current issues and decisions about sexuality and the disabled:

> Slowly, as society is coming to grips with its own sexuality . . . we are beginning to realize fully that all human beings are sexual by nature from the moment of birth to the moment of death, including those who by birth, accident or disease live in deformed or crippled bodies or possess incomplete faculties. "Privacy rooms" are beginning to appear in institutional settings. In the Netherlands, in England, and in Cincinnati, Ohio, apartment units designed for handicapped couples have been built and are staffed by professionals. Various non-marital heterosexual and homosexual relationships are being tolerated, and eventually accepted among handicapped couples. In a few institutions, those individuals too handicapped even to masturbate are having masturbation prescribed and provided. Interest in sex education programs for the handicapped is increasing greatly as this acceptance of them grows, and as the options for them broaden. (Bidgood, 1974, p. 14)

The next sections briefly describe several disabilities and their possible impact on sexuality. We will also discuss some of the sexual adjustments that people with these disabilities can make.

Spinal Cord Injury

People with spinal cord injuries (SCI) have reduced motor control and sensation because the damage to the spinal cord obstructs the pathway between body and brain. The parts of the body that are paralyzed vary according to the location of the injury. A person can be *paraplegic* (loss of feeling and voluntary muscle function of the trunk and legs) or *quadraplegic* (loss of feeling and voluntary muscle function of the arms or hands, as well as of the trunk and legs). Injuries lower on the spine result in paraplegia, and higher injuries cause quadraplegia.

An SCI person may have impaired ability for arousal and orgasm; this varies according to the specific injury. Some men and women are able to experience arousal or orgasm from psychological or physical stimulation and others are not. Furthermore, an SCI person may or may not be able to feel the arousal that he or she experiences. Some SCI people report that the sensations they experience change or increase slightly over time. Typically, men with injuries to the spinal cord in the neck and upper back are not able to experience erections from psychological stimulation (*psychogenic erections*), but often can become erect from physical stimulation (*reflex-stimulated erections*). Conversely, individuals with lesions in the lower spinal cord sometimes experience psychogenic erections, but rarely have reflex-stimulated erections (Boller and Frank, 1982). There is great individual variation in sexuality among those with spinal cord injuries. Therefore, an individual's sexual capacity cannot be predicted solely on the basis of the nature of the injury (Narum and Rodolfa, 1984).

Lack of erection in the SCI male usually requires some sexual adjustments, and it is important to experiment with positions that work for a given couple. A couple can use the "stuffing technique" when erection does not occur (Mooney et al., 1975). In this method the woman uses her fingers to stuff the flaccid penis into her vagina, in order to experience intravaginal sensations. Surgically inserted implants are sometimes used to make the penis erect. However, SCI males and their partners often re-evaluate the importance of penile-vaginal intercourse and develop other viable options for pleasure, such as manual and oral stimulation or the use of vibrators.

Much of the professional and personal sexual education for SCI individuals and couples consists of redefining and expanding sexual expression. For example, genital sensations may be very slight or nonexistent, but other areas of the body may increase in sexual responsiveness and may cause intense pleasure. The book *Sexual Options for Paraplegics and Quadraplegics* describes techniques to increase feelings of pleasure:

> Sensory amplification, the method used by some disabled men and women to achieve the most pleasure and satisfaction from a sensory input, is the act of thinking about a physical stimulus, concentrating on it, and amplifying the sensation in your mind to an intense degree. Thus, it is possible to achieve a higher level of satisfaction and possibly a mental orgasm. Some who have lost physical sensation in the genital area substitute

or transfer a sensation to an area of the body that has retained some feeling, such as the inside of an arm, the neck, breasts, buttocks, or around the anal area. By transposing these sensations mentally, or by using your imagination to create a fantasy, you may find intense satisfaction. (Mooney et al., 1975, p. 5)

Observing their partner's responses to sexual pleasure can heighten the satisfaction and enjoyment of people with spinal cord injuries. Some disabled people have developed the ability to "feel" what their partners are feeling and share intensely in their excitement (Mooney et al., 1975). Most spinal cord injured people have able-bodied partners who can enhance the sexual relationship by taking an active role in sex play.

Cerebral Palsy

Cerebral palsy (CP) is caused by damage to the brain before or during birth or during early childhood; it is characterized by mild to severe lack of muscular control. Involuntary muscle movements may disrupt speech, facial expressions, balance, and body movement. Involuntary, severe muscle contractions may cause limbs to jerk or assume awkward positions. A person's intelligence may or may not be affected. Unfortunately, it is often mistakenly assumed that people with CP are mentally handicapped because of their physical difficulty in communicating.

Genital sensation is unaffected by CP. Spasticity and deformity of arms and hands may make masturbation difficult or impossible without assistance, and the same problems in the hips and knees may make certain intercourse positions painful or difficult. Anxiety or sexual arousal may stimulate an increase in involuntary muscle movements (Shaul et al., 1978).

The sexual adjustment of a person with cerebral palsy is contingent upon what is physically possible and the extent of environmental support for social contacts and privacy. People with CP and spinal cord injuries may require the help of someone who can assist in preparation and positioning for sexual relations.

Blindness and Deafness

The sensory losses of blindness and deafness can affect a person's sexuality in several ways. A woman with visual impairment comments:

> When I am trying to meet a person for the first time, I do not have access to eye contact. For example, I can't flirt with my eyes . . . A new experience I had last year was being in a hot tub for the first time with three friends. I was really looking forward to this experience. I would have liked being able to see the other bodies, but I could not. I mentioned this to my boyfriend afterward. So the next time we did this, he described these people to me in graphic detail: "Her nipples point up; he's got a roll around his middle; he's got a large penis . . . it makes mine look like . . ." His descriptions really made the experience fun for me. (Straw, 1981, pp. 37–38)

A great deal of information and many attitudes and social interaction skills are acquired by seeing or hearing others, and visual or hearing deficits can impair this learning process. Deafness or blindness that occurs in adolescence or adulthood may cause depression, lowered self-esteem, and social withdrawal during the adjustment period. If the sensory losses are a result of disease, the disease itself may have deleterious effects on sexual functioning. In themselves, blindness and deafness do not appear to physically impair sexual interest or response.

Developmental Disabilities

Developmentally disabled people have below average intellectual functioning. A person with an IQ of below 70 is usually classified as developmentally disabled. However, the learning capabilities of such people vary greatly from one person to the next. The ability to meet age-appropriate standards of independence and responsibilities depends somewhat on intelligence, but with repetition and guidance many people with intellectual deficits can learn adaptive behaviors related to daily living and to sexuality.

Unfortunately, there are strong stereotypes that imply that developmentally disabled people are unable to learn and are either asexual or unable to control their sexual impulses. More often than not, developmentally disabled people have not had adequate learning opportunities, because parents or health-care providers have attempted to deny or repress any sexual expression and have not provided adequate teaching of appropriate sexual behavior. The result is a lack of effective social-sexual skills.

Sex education is particularly important for both developmentally disabled people and their families. Sexual development of the developmentally disabled follows the typical patterns (initial involvement with masturbation followed by heterosexual and/ or homosexual exploration), but with a lag in time compared with nondisabled children. A crucial point in sex education is that developmentally disabled people have a basic right to sexual expression. Thorough teaching of important areas of responsibility, including self-care, menstrual hygiene, use of contraceptives, and appropriateness of time and place, is essential. Developmentally disabled people, their parents, and health-care professionals need to be taught that masturbation is normal (Kolodny et al., 1979). Judgment in social situations is also a part of sex education.

In institutional settings where privacy is at a minimum, "appropriateness" in terms of privacy for sexual activities should be liberally defined. The bathroom, bedroom, or secluded outdoor places can be considered appropriate for masturbation or intimacy with others. The developmentally disabled share the usual human interest in and desire for closeness, affection, and physical contact, and institutions need to be sensitive to this aspect of their residents' lives (Johnson, 1971).

Summary

Celibacy

1. Celibacy means not engaging in sexual activities. Celibacy can be complete (no masturbation or interpersonal sexual contact) or partial (the person masturbates).

Erotic Dreams and Fantasy

2. Erotic dreams often accompany sexual arousal and orgasm during sleep. Erotic fantasies serve many functions. They can enhance sexual arousal, help overcome anxiety or compensate for a negative situation, allow rehearsal of new sexual experiences, permit tolerable expression of "forbidden wishes," and provide relief from gender-role expectations.

Masturbation

3. Masturbation is self-stimulation of the genitals, intended to produce sexual pleasure.

4. Past attitudes toward masturbation have been highly condemnatory. However, the meaning and purposes of masturbation are currently being more positively re-evaluated.

5. Masturbation is an activity that is continuous throughout the life cycle, although its frequency varies with age and sex.

Shared Touching

6. The entire body's surface is a sensory organ, and touch is a basic form of communication and shared intimacy.

7. Breast stimulation is arousing to most men and women, but some people find it unenjoyable.

8. Preferences as to the tempo, pressure, and location of manual genital stimulation vary from person to person. A lubricant, a nonirritating lotion, or saliva on the genitals may enhance pleasure.

Oral-Genital Stimulation

9. Oral-genital contact has become more common in recent years. Concerns about oral-genital stimulation usually stem from ideas that it is immoral, unsanitary, or a homosexual act.

10. Cunnilingus is oral stimulation of the vulva and fellatio is oral stimulation of the male genitals.

Anal Stimulation

11. Couples may engage in anal stimulation for arousal, orgasm, and variety. Careful hygiene is necessary to avoid introducing anal bacteria into the vagina. To reduce the chances of transmitting the AIDS virus, couples should avoid anal intercourse or use a condom and practice withdrawal before ejaculation.

Coitus and Coital Positions

12. The diversity of coital positions offers potential variety during intercourse. The man-above, woman-above, side-by-side, and rear-entry positions are common.

Sexual Adjustment and Disability

13. A disability may influence the ways in which a person expresses his or her sexuality, but does not alter the inherent sexual nature of the person.

14. Development of a positive body image can be an important component of sexuality for a physically disabled person.

15. Institutional care does not generally allow for the sexual needs of disabled residents, although the situation is slowly improving.

Thought Provokers

1. If your 10-year-old son asked you what you thought about masturbation, what would you say? And if your 10-year-old daughter asked?

2. What helpful functions, if any, do you think sexual fantasies have? When do you think a person's fantasies indicate a problem?

3. Research indicates that men prefer coitus and women prefer "foreplay" and "afterplay." Why do you think this is so?

Suggested Readings

Comfort, Alex. *The Joy of Sex: A Gourmet Guide to Love Making*. New York: Simon & Schuster, 1974. A well-illustrated adult "sex education" guide to erotic techniques, described in intimate detail with an emphasis on enhancing pleasure.

Friday, Nancy. *My Secret Garden.* New York: Simon & Schuster, 1973. A collection of women's sexual fantasies that reflects the diversity among women.

Friday, Nancy. *Men In Love*. New York: Delacorte, 1980. A collection of men's sexual fantasies and interpretations of their meaning.

Mooney, Thomas. *Sexual Options for Paraplegics and Quadraplegics*. Boston: Little, Brown, 1975. A non-technical and explicit book written for spine-injured persons to help them deal with the impact of the injury on their sexuality.

10

The lover takes courage in her certainty of caressing a body whose secrets she knows, whose preferences her own body has taught her.
Colette
Ces Plaisirs (1932)

Homosexuality

A Continuum of Sexual Orientations
Defining Bisexuality
Societal Attitudes
Development of Homosexuality
Lifestyles
Gay Rights and the Antigay Movement

MOST PEOPLE THINK of homosexuality as sexual contact between individuals of the same sex. However, this definition is not quite complete. It does not take into account two important dimensions—the context within which the sexual activity is experienced and the feelings and perceptions of the people involved. Nor does it encompass all of the meanings of the term **homosexual**, which can refer to (a) sexual behavior, (b) emotional affiliation, and (c) a definition of self. The following definition incorporates a broader spectrum of elements: A homosexual person is an individual "whose primary erotic, psychological, emotional, and social interest is in a member of the same sex, even though that interest may not be overtly expressed" (Martin and Lyon, 1972, p. 1).

A homosexual person's gender identity agrees with his or her biological sex. That is, a homosexual person perceives him- or herself as male or female, respectively, and feels attraction toward a same-sex person.

A word commonly used for homosexual is *gay*. Gay was initially used as a code word between homosexuals, and it has moved into popular usage to describe homosexual men and women, as well as social concerns related to homosexual orientation. Gay women are often referred to as *lesbians*. Pejorative words like faggot, fairy, homo, queer, lezzie, or dyke have traditionally been used to demean homosexuality. However, within certain gay subcultures, gay people use these terms with each other in a positive or humorous way.

A Continuum of Sexual Orientations

Homosexuality, bisexuality, and heterosexuality are words that identify one's **sexual orientation**—that is, to which of the sexes one is attracted. Attraction to same-sex partners is a homosexual orientation, and attraction to other-sex partners is a heterosexual orientation. **Bisexuality** refers to attraction to both same- and other-sex partners. Since sexual orientation is only one aspect of a person's life, this text will use these three terms as descriptive adjectives rather than as nouns that label one's total identity.

In our society we tend to make clear-cut distinctions between homosexuality and heterosexuality. Actually, the delineation is not so precise. A relatively small percentage of people consider themselves to be exclusively homosexual; a greater number think of themselves as exclusively heterosexual. These groups represent the opposite ends of a broad spectrum. Individuals between the ends of the spectrum exhibit varying mixtures of preference and experience, which may also change over time.

Figure 10.1 shows a seven-point continuum Kinsey devised in his analysis of sexual orientations in American society (1948). The scale ranges from 0 (exclusive contact with and erotic attraction to the other sex) to 6 (exclusive contact with and attraction to the same sex). In between are varying degrees of homosexual and heterosexual orientation; category 3 represents equal homosexual and heterosexual attraction and experience.

How many people in our society fall into the exclusively homosexual category on the continuum? According to the Kinsey data, this category comprised 2% of women and 4% of men. Although this percentage of people who identified themselves as having had exclusively homosexual experiences appears small, slightly less than 3% of the 226 million people in the United States is over six million people. The number of predominantly homosexual people may be 10% of the population. Accurate statistics are hard to obtain, since social pressures cause many homosexual people to conceal their orientation (a behavior known as being "in the closet"). This can be done in a number of ways, including having heterosexual experiences. Social pressure for heterosexual conformity often results in homosexual people dating, having sexual experiences with, and marrying partners of the other sex.

Between the extreme points on the continuum are many individuals who have experienced sexual contact with or been attracted to people of the same sex. Kinsey's estimate of this group's number was quite high: 37% of males and 13% of females in his research population reported having had overt homosexual experiences at some time in their lives, and even more had experienced erotic psychological responses to the same sex.

Kinsey's estimates were made some time ago, and they have come in for some criticism since then. It has been suggested that the study's sample techniques (for example, making interview contacts in gay bars) produced an inflated estimate of the number of homosexual people in our society. Hunt's more recent report (1974) revealed a somewhat lower incidence of homosexuality among his respondents, who were contacted by telephone. However, Hunt has criticized his own study for being somewhat underweighted with homosexual people. He has suggested adjusting his data upward and Kinsey's data downward to arrive at what may be more accurate figures. The revised estimates after this adjustment are that approximately 2% of men and 1% of women are exclusively homosexual; about 75% of men and 85% of women are exclusively heterosexual; and roughly 23% of men and 14% of women have had both types of experience.

Figure 10.1

**Continuum
of Sexual
Orientation**
*Adapted from
Kinsey et al.,
1948, p. 638.*

Defining Bisexuality

In interpreting the continuum shown in Figure 10.1, we want to caution against too broad a use of the term *bisexual*. There is a tendency to use behavior as the only

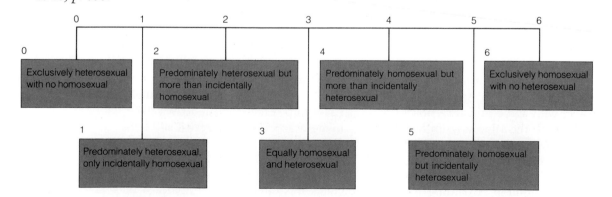

criterion for sexual orientation and to use *bisexual* as a catch-all to describe the considerable number of people who fall between exclusive heterosexuality and exclusive homosexuality. This grouping fails to take into account the context within which the sexual experiences occur and the feelings and thoughts of the individuals involved. It is the context, not the contact, that may be most significant. Bisexuality can be considered as a behavior or as an identity, and the two are not always the same. As one bisexual woman states:

> My dreams and fantasies could remain bisexual; I could continue to be sometimes equally attracted to the male and female star at the movies; still, the world would define me, not by my own sexuality, but by my lover's gender. (Orlando, 1978, p. 60)

Kinsey's model of sexual orientation has been questioned, especially in regards to bisexuality (Storms, 1978). On Kinsey's scale individuals lose degrees of one orientation as they move toward the opposite end of the scale; thus, bisexual individuals are seen as a compromise between the two extremes. In another model a bisexual orientation is viewed as showing high, rather than moderate, degrees of both homosexuality and heterosexuality. This view is supported by the type and frequency of sexual fantasies reported by study subjects in the various groups. As might be expected, homosexual subjects reported more fantasy about the same sex than about the other sex, while heterosexual subjects reported the reverse. But contrary to what one might predict from the Kinsey model, bisexual subjects reported as much same-sex fantasy as homosexual individuals and as much opposite-sex fantasy as heterosexual individuals. In other words, bisexual people seem to have a high degree of general erotic interest (Storms, 1980).

According to one definition, a bisexual person is one who can "enjoy and engage in sexual activity with members of both sexes, or recognizes a desire to do so" (MacDonald, 1981). There has been little research on bisexuality, and much remains to be learned about people who fit this definition. Researchers have had a tendency to categorize people who engage in sexual activity with both sexes as homosexual, when they would be more accurately understood as bisexual (Dixon, 1985).

There are several different types of bisexuality: bisexuality as a real orientation, as a transitory orientation, as a transitional orientation, or as homosexual denial (MacDonald, 1981). Bisexuality as a real orientation means that some people are born with a natural attraction to both sexes, and this attraction continues into adulthood. An individual with this orientation might or might not be sexually active with more than one partner at a time but would continue to have feelings of attraction to both sexes.

Bisexual behavior can also be transitory—a temporary involvement by people who are actually heterosexual or homosexual. These individuals will return fully to their original orientation after a period of bisexual experimentation or experiences. Transitory homosexual behavior may occur in single-sex boarding schools and in prisons, yet the people involved resume heterosexual relationships when the opportunity is once again available. Some prostitutes or male hustlers may do business with either sex and yet be involved in only heterosexual or homosexual relationships in their personal lives.

Bisexuality can also be a transitional state in which a person is changing from one exclusive orientation to another. This person will remain in the new orientation, as illustrated in the following account:

> I had led a traditional life with a husband, two kids, and community activities. My best friend and I were very active in the PTA together. Much to our surprise, we fell in love. We were initially secretive about our sexual relationship and continued our marital lives, but then we both divorced our husbands and moved away to start a life together. The best way I can describe being with her is that life is now like a color TV, instead of a black and white. (Authors' files)

Finally bisexuality may sometimes be an attempt to deny exclusive homosexual interests and to avoid the full stigma of homosexual identity (MacDonald, 1981). Gay men and lesbians sometimes view the bisexual person as someone who really is homosexual but lacks the courage to identify him- or herself as such. For example, there are a number of people who marry to maintain a facade of heterosexuality but continue to have strong homosexual desires or secretive homosexual contacts.

Sexual orientation is often viewed as an either-or situation—one is either heterosexual or homosexual. Consequently, self-identified bisexual individuals may be met with ambivalence and suspicion and are often pressured by heterosexual or homosexual people to adhere to one orientation. Even without pressure they may experience self-doubt and distress due to the cultural message that one must choose between orientations (Klein, 1978). Bisexual individuals "who associate with the gay/lesbian community as well as with the heterosexual mainstream may find themselves shifting social identities: the attempt to bridge both worlds with a single identity can be a source of stress and discomfort in both social arenas" (Paul, 1984, p. 54).

Societal Attitudes

In our own Judeo-Christian tradition, homosexuality has been viewed negatively. Many religious scholars believe that the condemnation of homosexuality stems from a reformation movement beginning in the seventh century B.C., through which Jewish religious leaders wanted to develop a distinct, closed community that was different from others of the time. Homosexual activities were a part of the religious services of many groups of people, including the Jewish people, in that era. Rejecting religious rituals involving homosexual activities that had previously been considered sacred was one way of establishing the uniqueness of a religion. Homosexual behaviors were then condemned as a form of pagan worship (Kosnik et al., 1977). Strong prohibitive biblical scriptures were written: "You shall not lie with a man as one lies with a female, it is an abomination" (Leviticus 18:22).

In the Judeo-Christian tradition, the purpose of sexual interaction is procreation, not pleasure. Nonprocreative sexual behavior, whether practiced by homosexual or heterosexual individuals, was viewed as immoral within this philosophical framework:

> St. Thomas [Aquinas] treats of homosexual acts in connection with the sins against temperance, specifically lust . . . His judgment is predicated on the Stoic assumption that

any pursuit of sexual pleasure outside of the purpose of all sexual acts, namely procreation, offends against nature and reason. (Kosnik et al., 1977, p. 198)

A prominent modern historian (Boswell, 1980) states that there has been more widespread and vehement intolerance toward gay people during the first half of the twentieth century than at any other time in Western history. He also maintains that religious belief was not the cause of intolerance, but that biblical strictures have been employed selectively in Christian countries to justify personal and popular prejudice.

Current theological positions towards homosexuality demonstrate a great range of convictions. Theologian James B. Nelson (1980) describes four stances represented in contemporary Christianity. The first is a *rejecting-punitive* orientation, which unconditionally rejects homosexuality and bears a punitive attitude toward gay people. This position is the predominate one in Christian history. For many centuries the church ostracized homosexual people from church and community life and gave its blessings to civil persecutions, including killing discovered homosexuals. The theology of this position rests on selective biblical literalism. Most churches' formal statements have moved away from the rejecting-punitive position. However, in practice and attitude it may still be by far the most common stance of churches in our society. The Greek Orthodox church's statement from the Biennial Clergy-Laity Congress of 1976 exemplifies this theological position:

> Thus the function of the sexual organs of a man and a woman . . . are ordained by nature to serve one particular purpose, the procreation of human kind. Therefore, any and all uses of the human sex organs for purposes other than those ordained by creation, runs contrary to the nature of things as decreed by God. . . . The Orthodox Church believes that homosexuality should be treated by society as an immoral and dangerous perversion and by religion as a sinful failure. In both cases correction is called for. Homosexuals should be accorded the confidential medical and psychiatric facilities by which they can be helped to restore themselves to a self-respecting sexual identity that belongs to them by God's ordinance. (Batchelor, 1980, p. 237)

The *rejecting-nonpunitive* position maintains that homosexuality is inherently unnatural and must be condemned, but because of Christ's grace, the homosexual person must not be condemned. This position supports the civil liberties of gay people, recognizing the injustice and hypocrisy in their persecution.

The third position is *qualified acceptance*. It maintains that homosexuality is a sin, but acknowledges that homosexuality is largely unsusceptible to change by contemporary medical and psychological science. Therefore, homosexual people who cannot refrain from sexual interaction should maintain fully committed relationships.

The fourth major theological position is *full acceptance*. This perspective views sexuality as intrinsically important to the capacity for human love. It maintains that ethical sexual relationships include commitment, trust, tenderness, and respect for the other regardless of the sex of the partners. Full acceptance includes providing a church blessing of the union of those who vow a lifelong commitment. As another aspect of complete acceptance, gay Christians are welcomed into every aspect of the life of the congregation, including ordination as ministers. (The first major American denomination to ordain an openly gay candidate was the United Church of Christ in 1972; it was followed four years later by an Episcopalian church.) Full acceptance also includes support for the civil rights of gays and lesbians. The advocates of full acceptance are still a minority but increasing in number. The widely read *Towards a Quaker View of Sex* stated:

> One should no more deplore homosexuality than left-handedness. . . . Homosexual affection can be as selfless as heterosexual affection, and therefore we cannot see that it is in some way morally worse. (Friends Home Service Committee, 1963, p. 45)

Other Times, Other Places

Homosexuality in Cross-Cultural Perspective

Attitudes towards homosexuality have varied considerably. A number of research studies of other cultures have revealed widespread acceptance of homosexual activities. One survey of 190 societies found that two-thirds of them considered homosexuality socially acceptable for certain individuals or on specific occasions (Ford and Beach, 1951). Homosexuality has been widely accepted in many earlier cultures. For example, over half of 225 Native American tribes accepted male homosexuality, and 17 percent accepted female homosexuality (Pomeroy, 1965). With the exception of ceremonial heterosexual contacts, homosexuality was the primary form of sexual expression among a group of eastern Peruvian native males (Schneebaum, 1975). In ancient Greece homosexual relationships between men were considered a superior intellectual and spiritual expression of love, whereas heterosexuality provided the more pragmatic benefits of children and a family unit.

Certain general findings emerge from cross-cultural comparisons of homosexual behavior. First, male homosexuality is more common than lesbianism in most societies. Second, the percentage of males in a given society who participate in homosexual activity sometime during their lives varies from nearly 100%, as in the Melanesian island society of East Bay (Davenport, 1965), to virtually none, as in Mangaia. Third, it appears that the societies with the lowest proportions of people who are exclusively or nearly exclusively

homosexual are nonindustrialized societies like those of Africa and the South Pacific. Finally, homosexual activity has never been the predominant form of adult sexual behavior in any society for which we have data.

Some societies require their members to engage in homosexual activities. For example, all male members of the Sambia society of about 2300 people in the mountains of New Guinea engage in exclusively homosexual activities from approximately seven years of age until they get married, in their late teens or early twenties. The Sambia men believe that a prepubertal boy becomes a strong warrior and hunter by drinking as much semen as possible from postpubertal boys' penises. Once a boy reaches puberty, he must no longer fellate other boys but experiences erotic pleasure from fellatio by boys who can not yet ejaculate. From the start of their erotic lives and during the years of peak orgasmic capacity, young men engage in frequent, obligatory, and gratifying homoeroticism. During the same period, looking at or touching females is taboo. Yet as they approach marriage, these youths create powerful erotic daydreams about women. During the first weeks of marriage they experience only fellatio with their wives, but they then change to include intercourse as a part of their heterosexual activity. Following marriage they stop homosexual activity, experience great sexual desire for women, and engage exclusively in heterosexual activity for the rest of their lives. (Stoller and Herdt, 1985).

The religious mandates of morality often become translated into law. In the United States today it is not illegal to be a homosexual person, but sexual acts other than heterosexual coitus are still illegal in many states. The illegal status of homosexual acts and the social stigma attached to homosexuality often make the homosexual individual wary of law enforcement personnel or agencies. If a homosexual person is a victim of an assault, homicide, robbery, or other crime related to his or her sexual orientation, he or she may conceal the incident out of fear of legal reprisal or indifferent prosecution. In the past few years, about half of the states have replaced these antiquated laws with statutes that legalize all private sexual behaviors between consenting adults. However, in July 1986 the Supreme Court upheld states' rights to prosecute consenting adults who engage in oral and anal sex.

In recent times there has been a shift in attitudes toward homosexuality. The belief that homosexual people are sinners has been replaced to some degree by a belief that they are mentally ill. This notion that homosexuality is a sickness is quite common. In a survey conducted in the 1970s, the majority of respondents believed that homosexual people were sexually abnormal, perverted, or mentally ill (Weinberg and Williams, 1976).

The medical and psychological professions have used drastic treatments in attempting to cure the "illness" of homosexuality. Surgical procedures such as castration were performed in the 1800s. Lobotomy (brain surgery that severs nerve fibers in the frontal lobe of the brain) was performed as a "cure" for homosexuality as late as 1951. Psychotherapy, drugs, hormones, hypnosis, shock treatments, and aversion therapy (pairing nausea-inducing drugs or electric shock with homosexual stimuli) have all been used to the same end (Katz, 1976).

Actually, much of current research contradicts the notion that homosexual people are mentally ill. The first major research to compare the adjustment of nonpatient heterosexual and homosexual individuals found no significant differences between the two groups (Hooker, 1967). Further research has supported these findings (Wilson, 1984). Bell and Weinberg summarize that ". . . homosexual adults who have come to terms with their homosexuality, who do not regret their sexual orientation and who can function effectively sexually and socially, are no more distressed psychologically than are heterosexual men and women" (1978, p. 216).

Attitudes toward homosexuality continue to change. For example, about 50% of Hunt's respondents thought that homosexual acts between consenting adults should be legal (1974). Many churches have endorsed gay rights legislation. Also, in 1973 the American Psychiatric Association, after great internal conflict, removed homosexuality per se from the category of a mental disorder. In 1975 the American Psychological Association urged ". . . all mental health professionals to take the lead in removing the stigma of mental illness that has long been associated with a homosexual orientation" (American Psychological Association press release, January 24, 1975).

Homophobia

Some of society's antihomosexual attitudes stem from what Weinberg (1973) labels **homophobia**. Homophobia is defined as irrational fears of homosexuality in others, the fear of homosexual feelings within oneself, or self-loathing because of one's ho-

A researcher has developed the following scale to identify homophobia. Respondents answer yes or no to the following statements:

1. Homosexuals should be locked up to protect society.
2. It would be upsetting for me to find out I was alone with a homosexual.
3. Homosexuals should be allowed to hold government positions.
4. I would not want to be a member of an organization which had any homosexuals in its membership.
5. I find the thought of homosexual acts disgusting.
6. If laws against homosexuality were eliminated, the proportion of homosexuals in the population would probably remain the same.
7. A homosexual could be a good President of the United States.
8. I would be afraid for a child of mine to have a teacher who was homosexual.
9. If a homosexual sat next to me on a bus, I would get nervous.

The key for interpreting responses appears at the end of the Summary at the end of this chapter.

Source: Smith, 1973, pp. 129–130.

mosexuality. It stems from ignorance and popular myths that give rise to homosexual prejudice. Box 10.1 presents one scale that has been used to measure homophobic tendencies. Perhaps you may want to use it to examine your own attitudes.

The recent recognition and discussion of homophobia represents a significant shift in the view of homosexuality: It implies that homophobic attitudes are the problem, rather than the sexual orientation itself. However, fear of homosexuality is still the most prevalent attitude, and it is not typically classified as a problem (Weinberg, 1973). Some reactions to AIDS have reflected strong antihomosexual bias. Jerry Falwell, founder of the fundamentalist political group called the "Moral Majority," called the outbreak of AIDS a "form of judgment of God upon a society." An executive in this same group criticized federal spending for medical research on AIDS: "What I see is a commitment to spend our tax dollars on research to allow these diseased homosexuals to go back to their perverted practices without any standards of accountability" (*U.S. News and World Report*, Sept. 2, 1985). This view assumes that homosexuality, rather than a virus, is the cause of AIDS (Brandt, 1985).

Homophobia can be exhibited in many ways, both subtle (even unconscious) and blatant. Telling "queer" jokes and belittling homosexuality expresses an element of hostility that is part of the homophobic attitude. This hostility can be overt, and people who are suspected of being homosexual are sometimes subjected to verbal or physical assault:

> The group I ran around with in high school used to drive downtown to where the gay bars were, pick up a swishy-looking one, beat him up, and dump him back on the street. (Authors' files)

Many psychologists believe that such aggression toward homosexuality is an attempt to deny or suppress homosexual feelings in oneself.

Another expression of homophobia may be the careful avoidance of any behavior that might be interpreted as homosexual. In this sense homophobia can restrict the lives of heterosexual people. For example, one may avoid manual-genital or oral-genital contact with an other-sex partner if one believes that these activities are inherently homosexual. During lovemaking, sexual receptivity in men and assertiveness in women may be viewed as threatening if these behaviors are believed to demonstrate homosexual tendencies. Same-sex friends or family members may refrain from spontaneous embraces, people may shun "unfeminine" or "unmasculine" clothing, or a woman may decide not to march in a women's movement demonstration because she fears being called a lesbian. Homophobia may have an especially significant impact on the depth of intimacy in male friendships. Men's fear of same-sex attraction often prevents them from allowing the emotional vulnerability required for deep friendship and limits their relationships largely to competition and "buddyship" (Nelson, 1985).

Any gender role reversal can be perceived as threatening. According to some research, homophobia may be related to rigid gender-role stereotypes (MacDonald and Games, 1974). This study found a correlation between attitudes about gender roles and attitudes toward homosexuality, with respondents who supported rigid gender-role stereotypes having more negative feelings about homosexuality than other respondents. Bell, Weinberg, and Hammersmith (1981) discuss the idea that homosexuality confronts people with their ability to tolerate diversity in gender roles:

> In a society such as ours a special loathing is reserved for any male who appears to have forfeited the privileges and responsibilities associated with upholding the conventional imagery of males. The spectre of a group of males living outside the strict confines of "masculinity" can appear as a threat to men who are not entirely certain about their own maleness and thus heighten whatever antagonisms are expressed toward those who do not follow male "rules." Similarly, to the degree that lesbianism is associated with the rejection of traditionally "feminine" roles and responsibilities, heterosexual women may feel threatened by those who do not join their ranks. (p. 221)

Homophobic attitudes can change over time, with experience or deliberate thought. One of our students describes this process:

> My own reaction to learning that one of my fraternity brothers was gay was discomfort. I increasingly avoided him. I am sorry now that I didn't confront myself as to why I felt that way at that time. I had an opportunity to explore a part of myself with another person whom I cared about. I was homophobic. And because I didn't deal with that then, the process of resolving it psychologically took a long time for me. It also kept me from developing a closeness with my other men friends, which I regret since many of them are now gone. I lost something in those relationships simply because I was afraid that being physically and emotionally close to another man meant that I, too, was homosexual.
>
> As with everybody, ideas and concepts change. I gradually became aware of myself and comfortable with my own heterosexuality. I finally began to explore why I felt so uncomfortable touching or being touched by another man. Not consciously, perhaps, I began exploring the idea of touching with others who I was comfortable with. And it worked.
>
> Today I think nothing of hugging or otherwise showing a person, male or female, that I care about them. I can do it without threatening their sexuality or worrying about my own. I am no longer threatened or frightened by physical closeness from another man, even if I know his preference is other men. I am secure enough to deal with that honestly. (Authors' files)

Development of Homosexuality

What determines sexual orientation? A variety of theories have attempted to explain the origins of sexual orientation, particularly homosexuality. Considerable research has been done over the years, but there are still no definitive scientific answers. In the next few pages we will consider some common notions about the causes of homosexuality and evaluate some of the research that has attempted to substantiate these ideas.

Bell, Weinberg, and Hammersmith (1981) have done the most comprehensive study to date about the development of sexual orientation. They used a sample of 979 homosexual people matched to a control group of 477 heterosexual people. All research subjects were asked questions about their childhood, adolescence, and sexual practices during four-hour, face-to-face interviews. The researchers then used sophisticated statistical techniques to analyze possible causal factors in the development of homosexuality or heterosexuality. This research will be cited frequently throughout this section because of its excellent methodology.

Psychosocial Theories

Some of the theories about the development of a homosexual orientation relate to life incidences, parenting patterns, or psychological attributes of the individual. Unhappy heterosexual experiences or the inability to attract partners of the other sex are sometimes believed to cause a person to become homosexual. Stereotypes that homosexuals are less attractive than others are common. For example, in one study college students of both sexes were shown photographs of 22 women and asked to identify the half who were reputed to be homosexuals. The students tended to identify people they perceived as less attractive as the homosexuals (Dew, 1985). Statements like "All a lesbian needs is a good lay" or "He just needs to meet the right woman" reflect the notion that homosexuality is a poor second choice for people who lack satisfactory heterosexual experiences. Such beliefs may attach particularly to lesbian behavior because of the societal tendency to define female sexuality in relation to the male. It is often assumed that lesbianism is due to resentment, dislike, fear, or distrust of men rather than attraction toward women. The illogic of this argument is clear if we turn it around and say that female heterosexuality is caused by a dislike and fear of women. Actually, research indicates that up to 70% of lesbians have had sexual experiences with men, and many report having enjoyed them. However, they prefer to be sexual with women (Klaich, 1974; Martin and Lyon, 1972). Bell and his colleagues' analysis of their data indicates that "homosexual orientation among females reflects neither a lack of heterosexual experience nor a history of particularly unpleasant heterosexual experiences" (1981, p. 176).

Bell and his colleagues also found that the homosexual and heterosexual groups did not differ in the frequency of dating during high school. This refutes the belief that lack of heterosexual opportunity causes homosexuality. The male and female homosexual subjects did tend, however, to feel differently about dating than their heterosexual counterparts; fewer homosexual subjects reported that they enjoyed dating. Their feelings likely indicated less interest in heterosexual activity. For example, although the homosexual males dated as much as the heterosexual males in the study, they tended to have fewer sexual encounters with females and to have engaged in fewer types of heterosexual activities such as manual stimulation of genitals, oral-genital sex, or intercourse. The Bell et al. data suggest "that unless heterosexual encounters appeal to one's deepest sexual feeling, there is likely to be little about them that one would experience as positive reinforcement for sexual relationships with members of the opposite sex" (p. 108). On the other hand, some researchers conclude that learning from intense and pleasurable sexual experiences is the strongest antecedent to later sexual orientation. Their research found that those who learned to masturbate by being manually stimulated by a person of the same sex and those whose first orgasm is in homosexual contact are more likely to have a homosexual orientation as adults (VanWyk, 1984). This is a classic "Which came first, the chicken or the egg?" question. Do the feelings guide the behavior (and what causes the feelings?), or does the behavior shape the feelings? How do the feelings and the behavior interact and how significant is each in developing sexual orientation? These are questions for continued research.

Another myth that the Bell et al. study shows to be false is that young men and women become homosexual because they have been seduced by older homosexuals. Their data indicate that most homosexual males and females had their first homosexual encounter with someone, usually a friend or acquaintance, about the same age as themselves. In fact, homosexual people were less likely than heterosexual people to have had initial sexual encounters with a stranger or an older person.

Some people may believe that homosexuality can be "caught" from someone else. People seem especially concerned about the influence of homosexual teachers;

they are afraid that exposure to a homosexual teacher, especially a well-liked and respected teacher, will cause students to model after him or her and become homosexual. However, a homosexual orientation appears to be established even before school age, and modeling is not a relevant factor (Marmor, 1980).

Another prevalent theory concerning the development of homosexuality has to do with certain patterns in a person's family background. Speculation about environmental causes of homosexuality can be found in the literature of psychoanalysis. Psychoanalytic theory implicated both childhood experiences and relationships with parents. Freud (1905) maintained that the relationship with one's father and mother was a crucial factor in the development of homosexuality. He believed that men and women were innately bisexual but, with "normal" developmental experiences, passed through a "homoerotic" phase in the process of establishing a heterosexual orientation. However, he thought that people could become "fixated" at the homosexual phase if certain kinds of life experiences occurred, especially if a male had a poor relationship with his father and an overly close relationship with his mother. Later clinical research attempted to confirm these hypotheses. A study by Irving Bieber (1962), for instance, compared homosexual and heterosexual men who were undergoing psychoanalysis. Bieber's data indicated that certain patterns were frequently found in the family backgrounds of homosexual clients—most typically, a dominant and overprotective mother and a passive and detached father. Another study gave some support to Bieber's finding. It compared homosexual and heterosexual men who had lost one or both parents before the age of 15. More of the homosexual group reported that their mothers had been overcontrolling or that their fathers had been emotionally distant toward them (Saghir and Robins, 1973).

It has not been clearly established, however, that certain childhood factors are the critical determinants in the development of a homosexual orientation. Many homosexual people do not have a family background of a dominant mother and emotionally detached father, just as many heterosexual people have been reared in families where this pattern prevailed. Bell and his colleagues (1981) reported some interesting findings on the role of family patterns in the development of sexual orientation. Although there was some evidence that male homosexuality was related to poor father-son relationships, they state that the traditional psychoanalytic model of the impact of parents is exaggerated. On the basis of their findings, no particular phenomenon of family life can be singled out as "especially consequential for either homosexual or heterosexual development" (p.190). These researchers also stress the variations in patterns of homosexual development.

Implicit in many psychosocial explanations of homosexuality is the assumption that homosexuality is a less permanent condition than heterosexuality. Some therapists provide therapeutic intervention for homosexual and bisexual people who are highly distressed by their orientation and want to develop a heterosexual preference. Masters and Johnson have done some preliminary work in this area, described in their publication, *Homosexuality in Perspective* (1979). However, Masters and Johnson have come under heavy criticism for their claim of converting "homosexuals" to heterosexual functioning and for their research reporting and methodology (Barlow et al., 1980; Zilbergeld and Evans, 1980; Bell et al., 1981). For example, many of the subjects may have been incorrectly labeled as homosexual individuals, when they were in fact bisexual or heterosexual people who had turned to homosexual behavior because of sexual problems in heterosexual relationships. Most therapists agree that exclusive homosexuality is extremely difficult, if not impossible, to change to functional and satisfactory heterosexuality.

Due partly to recent research—and due also to the removal of homosexuality from the category of mental illness by the American Psychiatric and Psychological Associations—many therapists and counselors have changed the focus of therapy. Rather than making the assumption that their homosexual clients must be "cured," therapists have made it an objective to assist them to love, live, and work in a society that harbors considerable hostility toward them (Milligan, 1975). This change in therapeutic practice is significant, in that it defines the problem as society's negativity toward homosexuality, rather than homosexuality itself.

Biological Theories

Researchers have looked into a number of areas in an effort to establish physiological causes for sexual orientation. One biological theory centers on the possibility of a genetic factor. Is there something in a person's genetic inheritance that influences or determines homosexuality? A 1952 study tried to answer this question by comparing sexual orientations in groups of fraternal and identical twins. Each pair of twins had been reared together, so they had minimal differences in prenatal and postnatal environments. The primary difference between the two groups lay in the genetic inheritance of each twin pair, which was identical in one group but not in the other. The study reported a 95% *concordance* (the frequency of both twins showing the trait) for homosexuality in the identical twins group. In marked contrast, the fraternal twins had a concordance rate of only 12% (Kallman, 1952a and 1952b). These findings are intriguing, but they have been criticized because of the sources of the twin pairs: Many subjects came from correctional, psychiatric, and charitable organizations. A more recent investigation reported concordance rates for homosexuality of approximately 75% and 19% respectively among populations of identical and fraternal twins (Whitman and Diamond, 1986). However, other research has failed to find evidence that hereditary factors directly determine sexual orientation (Money, 1981).

Other researchers have studied hormonal imbalances, both before birth and during adulthood, to see if they might be a cause of homosexuality. Some writers speculate that prenatal hormone imbalances can alter the masculine and feminine development of the fetal brain and that this may contribute to a homosexual orientation (Murphy and Fain, 1978). They base their speculations primarily on other people's research into the effects of prenatal androgen deficiency in animals (Dörner, 1976; Money and Ehrhardt, 1972). This research demonstrates that female mating behavior can be produced in male animals as a consequence of experimentally induced androgen deficiency during prenatal development. The writers speculate that there is a critical period in which the fetus is particularly sensitive to levels of sex hormones and hypothesize that a prenatal androgen deficiency in human males could contribute to homosexuality. However, it is highly questionable to draw conclusions about humans from animal studies. Dörner and his associates (1975) also did some research with humans that uncovered differences in the ways homosexual and heterosexual males' hormones respond to injections of estrogen. They believe that this work supports the theory of prenatal hormonal influences on male-female brain differentiation.

A more recent study comparing men with lifelong homosexual orientations to men and women with lifelong heterosexual orientations points in the same direction. This investigation measured the effect of administered estrogen on LH (luteinizing hormone) and testosterone secretions. Normally females secrete LH in a cyclic pattern (see Chapter 4) and males secrete LH in a relatively steady pattern; however, these patterns can be altered by estrogen. The patterns of LH secretion in homosexual men who were given estrogen were between those of heterosexual men and heterosexual women who also received estrogen. In addition, testosterone levels remained lowered for longer periods in homosexual than in heterosexual men. There was greater variability in response among the homosexual men than among the heterosexual men. These findings may not apply to all male homosexuals. Whether a different hormonal response is present in men of less exclusive homosexual orientation remains to be determined (Gladue et al., 1983).

Other researchers have speculated that hormone levels in adults may contribute to homosexuality. Some have compared hormone levels in adult homosexual men and women with those in heterosexual adults. Here, too, the data have been contradictory (Meyer-Bahlburg, 1977; Tourney, 1980). Some studies report that homosexual males have less androgen than heterosexual males; others indicate just the opposite; and still others reveal no difference. There have been only a few studies exploring hormone levels in lesbians, and just as in male homosexual studies, the results have been inconsistent (Gaitwell et al., 1977; Griffiths et al., 1974; Loraine et al., 1971). One researcher suggests that future research needs to control for the many variables operating in this experimental area (Tourney, 1980). Proposed controls include establishing adequate criteria for selection of subjects; use of control subjects matched for age, sex, education, and other factors; and compiling thorough sexual histories of those being studied. More comprehensive studies may clarify some of the conflicting reports of the relationship of homosexuality to hormone levels in adults.

Even if consistent differences were found in the hormonal patterns of homosexual and heterosexual adults, it would remain unknown whether the differences were a cause or a result of sexual orientation. Testosterone levels are sensitive to a number of variables, including general health, diet, drug use, marijuana use, cigarette smoking, sexual activity, and physical and emotional stress (Marmor, 1980). Many of these variables can be controlled for in careful research. However, it is important to note that the stress and anxiety many homosexual people experience as a result of societal oppression may itself have an impact on hormone levels.

Although Bell and his co-workers did not do any hormonal studies, they believe that their research also suggests biological causes, especially for Kinsey's category of exclusive homosexuality. They write that, in general, homosexuality "is a pattern of feelings and reactions within the child that cannot be traced back to a single social or psychological root" (1981, p. 192) and that "a boy or girl is predisposed to be homosexual or heterosexual, and during childhood and adolescence this basic sexual orientation begins to become evident" (p. 187).

These researchers believe that evidence for a biological predisposition for homosexuality is the strong link between adult homosexuality and **gender nonconformity** as a child. Gender nonconformity is a variable the researchers used that measured the extent to which the research subjects conformed to stereotypic notions

of masculinity or femininity during childhood. Respondents were asked their own
perceptions of how masculine or feminine they were as children and how much they
enjoyed conventional boys' or girls' activities (see Box 10.2 for examples of responses).
Both male and female homosexuals were more likely to have experienced far-ranging
and deep-seated gender nonconformity than were heterosexuals. One-half of homosexual males and one-fourth of heterosexual males did not conform to a typical
"masculine" identity pattern, while about four-fifths of homosexual females and two-
thirds of heterosexual females were not highly "feminine" during childhood. Childhood gender nonconformity in homosexual people also occurs in societies other than
the United States. A comparative study of males in the United States, Guatemala,
and Brazil indicated that gender nonconformity related to childhood toy and activity
interests, as well as sexual interest in other boys, were behavioral indicators of adult
homosexual orientation (Whitam, 1980). Bell and his colleagues speculate that "if
there is a biological basis for homosexuality, it probably accounts for gender nonconformity as well as for sexual orientation" (p. 217).

The question of biological causation of homosexuality raises some important
issues. On one hand, if homosexuality were found to be biologically based, the
assumption that homosexuality is "unnatural" would be challenged, because something biologically innate is natural for that person. Parents who have blamed them-

selves or have been blamed by others for causing what they view as an aberration could be relieved of their guilt. Society's expectations for gender-role behaviors might become more flexible given the acceptance of biologically based gender nonconformity. On the other hand, if homosexuality were shown to be biologically caused and homosexuals were labeled as biologically "defective," attempts to use biology to prevent homosexuality might be implemented through such procedures as fetal monitoring and medical intervention related to prenatal hormone levels (Bell et al., 1981). During the 1930s and 1940s hormone therapy (consisting of androgen supplements) was used to try to "cure" male homosexuality, although the data were inconsistent regarding homosexuality and hormone imbalance. Such medical intervention, while it sometimes increased sexual interest, did not result in significant changes in sexual orientation (Money and Ehrhardt, 1972).

In conclusion, research is beginning to suggest that there is a biological predisposition to exclusive homosexuality. However, the causes of sexual orientation in general, and homosexuality specifically, remain speculative at this point. It seems more appropriate to think of the continuum of sexual orientation as influenced by a variety of psychosocial and biological factors, which may be unique for each person, than to think in terms of a single cause for sexual orientation.

Lifestyles

As we have discussed in the preceding section, people whose sexual orientation is homosexual cannot be clearly distinguished from heterosexual people on the basis of hormonal balance or mental health. This leads to another observation: that homosexual lifestyles are as varied as heterosexual lifestyles. All social classes, occupations, races, religions, and political persuasions are represented among homosexual people. The only elements they necessarily have in common are their desire for emotional and sexual fulfillment with someone of the same sex and their shared experience of oppression from a hostile social environment.

Despite their many similarities to heterosexual people and the wide variety of their lifestyles, stereotypes about homosexual people exist. Many of these concern their physical appearance. It is true that there are some homosexual individuals who dress and act according to commonly held stereotypes. Characteristics often associated with an identifiable homosexual man include exaggerated "feminine" gestures, tight and flashy clothing, and earrings; in contrast, the image of a stereotypically recognizable lesbian includes such attributes as short hair and highly "masculine" clothing and gestures. Although the incidence of people who fit the stereotypes is small, the stereotypes persist. This is in part because people who believe that homosexual individuals look a certain way notice and categorize (sometimes erroneously) those who seem to fit the image. The fact that many homosexual people may not fit the stereotype at all often goes unnoticed. One study measured general sex-role attributes and found no significant differences in characteristics of masculinity and femininity between homosexual, bisexual, and heterosexual male and female college students (Storms, 1980).

There are far more basic elements of a homosexual lifestyle than how a person dresses. We will look briefly at some of these in the next few pages.

Homosexual Relationships

Some people mistakenly think that homosexual partners always enact the stereotypical active "male" or passive "female" roles. This notion stems in part from the pervasive heterosexual model of relationships. Because this model of male-female role playing has historically been the predominant one in our culture, both heterosexual and homosexual intimate relationships have typically been patterned after it. However, options for more egalitarian relationships have increased in recent years, and these are being followed by both heterosexual and homosexual couples. In this regard, a homosexual relationship may well be the more flexible in our society. Some adults state that they have made a conscious decision to follow their homosexual rather than heterosexual feelings, partly because of their belief that more equal relationships are possible between same-sex than other-sex partners.

One research study that compared characteristics of homosexual and heterosexual relationships found major differences in gender roles. The study reported that heterosexual couples were likely to adhere more closely to traditional gender-role expectations than were homosexual couples. Most of the homosexual relationships studied resembled "best friendships" combined with romantic and erotic attraction. The researcher suggests that studies of homosexual couples can provide insights and models for heterosexual couples who are trying to establish more egalitarian relationships (Peplau, 1981).

There are some differences between homosexual men and women in the number of their sexual partners. Lesbian women are likely to have had fewer than 10 sexual partners, and lesbian couples are more likely than male couples to contract for monogamy (Thoresen, 1984). Homosexual men are more often involved in casual sexual encounters, sometimes with hundreds of partners (Bell and Weinberg, 1978; Kinsey, 1948). These encounters are sometimes exceedingly brief, occurring in public restrooms or in film booths in pornography shops. This difference may reflect traditional gender-role definitions. Males learn initially to be interested in sex; females learn initially to be interested in love.

One study found that homosexual women differed from homosexual men in the extent to which they associated love with sex. Most of the lesbians waited to have sex with a partner until they had developed emotional intimacy. Although 46% of gay men had become friends with their partner before having sex, as a group they were more likely than lesbians to have had sexual experiences with casual acquaintances or people they had just met. In addition, gay men with primary partners were much more likely to have sexual experiences with others than were lesbians or heterosexual women and men. What explains the tendency to less sexual exclusiveness among gay men? The researcher suggests that the gender-role socialization of males places more emphasis on and gives more permission for casual sex for males than for females. Heterosexual relationships are to some extent a compromise between male and female gender-role expectations, and thus may include exclusiveness for both partners. However, with gay relationships this particular compromise is not typically as necessary, and casual sex outside of an intimate relationship can occur more easily (Peplau, 1981).

However, sexual involvement with many partners is not universal among homosexual men. Many men feel no urge for such multiple relationships, and others have decided that they do not adequately meet their needs. Some men want to have a strong emotional relationship before becoming sexually involved. And for some men, being involved in an ongoing relationship eliminates sexual interest in other men (Tripp, 1975). In some cases the growing desire of homosexual men to modify the definition of masculinity has encouraged them to develop committed, multi-dimensional relationships rather than pursuing casual sexual encounters. Also, many gay men are reducing the numbers of their sexual partners or establishing monogamous relationships because of concerns about contracting AIDS (Schecter et al., 1984).

Although marriage between two people of the same sex is not legally recognized by any state, many homosexual couples share significant one-to-one relationships. Half of the lesbians and one-quarter of the homosexual men in Bell and Weinberg's study were in primary relationships. Lesbian pairs are more likely than male homosexual couples to share a household, perhaps partly because less suspicion is aroused by women living together (Bell and Weinberg, 1978). The Metropolitan Community Church, which primarily serves gay people, performs holy unions (this term is used because marriage is a legal contract) that provide the spiritual significance of marriage for homosexual couples.

Bell and Weinberg's 1978 research concluded that homosexual relationships and lifestyles could be classified into five basic categories that reflect the many variations in homosexuality. Seventy-one percent of the people in their study fit into these five groups; the remaining 29% were too diverse to be easily grouped.

1. *Close-coupled:* People in this group had a close bond within a relationship. They were less likely to seek partners outside the relationship and tended to look to

A holy union performed by the Metropolitan Community Church in Honolulu, Hawaii.

each other for sexual and interpersonal satisfaction. They reported having gratifying sex lives and had the fewest sexual problems of the people studied. They were unlikely to regret being homosexual and had rarely experienced difficulties in their jobs or outside lives because of their orientation. The close-coupled men and women were the happiest and least lonely of any in the study. Using a heterosexual framework, one might call them "happily married." About 28% of lesbians and 10% of gay males were close-coupled.

2. *Open-coupled:* Open-coupled individuals were living with a primary partner and also sought and engaged in numerous sexual experiences outside of the primary relationship. Open-coupled individuals reported broad sexual repertoires, but the men had concerns about getting their primary partners to meet their sexual requests, and the women worried about their primary partners wanting them to engage in unwelcome sexual activities. This lifestyle also appeared to be more difficult and less satisfying for females than for males who engaged in it. About 17% of lesbians and 18% of gay men were open-coupled.

3. *Functionals:* People in this group were "single" and reported more sexual activity with a greater number of partners than did those in any other group. They reported the most interest in sex and had few, if any, sexual problems. They also appeared uninterested in establishing a committed relationship. These individuals were highly involved in the gay world and were the least likely to regret being homosexual. They were also likely to have had contact with the legal system for a "homosexual" offense. Approximately 10% of lesbians and 15% of gay men fit into this category.

4. *Dysfunctionals:* Individuals in this group were regretful about their homosexuality and reported more sexual problems than people in any other group. Their overall psychological adjustment was poor, and they encountered many difficulties and dissatisfactions in daily living. About 5% of lesbians and 12% of male homosexuals fit into this group.

5. *Asexuals:* People in this group tended not to be involved with others. They reported less interest in sex, fewer sex partners, and more narrow sexual repertoires than those in other groups. They typically spent leisure time alone and described themselves as lonely but were not interested in becoming involved with others. About 11% of lesbians and 16% of male homosexuals were in this category.

Another study has examined characteristics of homosexual love relationships. This study found many similarities between homosexual and heterosexual relationships, and it reported that most differences in relationships have more to do with whether the partners are men or women than with whether they are homosexual or heterosexual. Matched samples (overrepresented by young, well-educated, middle-class whites) of homosexual females and males and heterosexual females and males all indicated that "being able to talk about my most intimate feelings" with a partner was most important in a love relationship. Using Rubin's love scale (discussed in Chapter 7), the researcher found no differences in the depth of love and liking experienced by homosexual or heterosexual individuals in the study. The research also found that partners in a love relationship, regardless of sexual orientation, must deal with and attempt to reconcile desires for togetherness and independence. For many individuals, these desires were not mutually exclusive; some people wanted both a secure love relationship and meaningful activities and friendships separate from the relationship. Responses from homosexual and heterosexual women were different in some ways than those from homosexual and heterosexual men. Women placed greater importance on emotional expressiveness within a relationship than did men. Women also gave higher ratings to the importance of having an egalitarian relationship and having similar attitudes and political beliefs (Peplau, 1981).

Homosexual Parents

Traditionally a family has been considered to consist of a heterosexual couple and their offspring, but this is not the only form of family life available. Single-parent families have become more predominant as the divorce rate has increased and as more women have decided to have children outside of marriage. Homosexual individuals also form family units, either as single parents or as couples, with children brought into the family or born through a variety of circumstances.

Some homosexual individuals or couples become parents with adopted or foster children, and many homosexual people have children who were born in previous heterosexual marriages. The custody of children in divorce proceedings is commonly biased toward the mother. However, if the mother is an acknowledged lesbian, this may jeopardize her claim to custody. A homosexual father attempting to gain custody has the double disadvantage in court of being a man and a homosexual. There has been considerable controversy over the ability of homosexual parents to provide a positive family environment for children. Some research has been done with lesbian mothers, and studies show that children of lesbian mothers are essentially no different

Families headed by homosexual parents are one of several forms of nontraditional families.

from other children in terms of gender-related problems and sex-role and general development (Kirkpatrick et al., 1981; Hoeffer, 1981; Green, et al., 1986). Lesbian mothers have been found to be similar to heterosexual mothers in lifestyle, maternal interests, and parenting behavior (Kirkpatrick, 1982; Lewin, 1981).

Children may also be conceived by lesbians through artificial insemination, either by standard procedures with semen obtained from a sperm bank or by individual arrangements with a selected donor. One woman who became pregnant through this second process shares her experience:

> My partner and I wanted to have a child, and we decided to ask a close male friend to be the donor. We charted my ovulation cycle for several months and then got together with him monthly for the artificial insemination. He ejaculated in privacy and brought his semen to our bedroom. We put the sperm in a cervical cap and inserted it to insure contact between the semen and the cervix. It took me about five months to become pregnant, and now we have a beautiful baby boy. (Authors' files)

A homosexual man who wants to be a father may make a personal agreement with a woman that he will act as a sperm donor and have an ongoing relationship with the child. If a woman wants a known donor, it is important for the future parents to discuss their rights and responsibilities, and a legal document supporting the agreement is advisable. Many new concepts of family are emerging in our society as people expand their definition of parenting.

Sexual Expression

Homosexual individuals who are in sexual relationships engage in sexual behaviors similar to those of heterosexual persons, with the exception of penile-vaginal intercourse. Touching, kissing, body contact, manual-genital stimulation, oral-genital contact, and anal stimulation are techniques that are used during sexual interactions. Younger homosexual people are typically more likely to have experienced a greater variety of sexual behaviors than older people (Bell and Weinberg, 1978), as is the case with the heterosexual population.

Sexual Behaviors Among Women.   Several misconceptions exist regarding lesbian sexual expression. One is the notion that sex between women is unsatisfactory. For example, one sex book states, "One vagina plus one vagina equals zero" (Reuben, 1969, p. 269). This implies that sexual relating between women is unsatisfactory because a penis is lacking. Kinsey's 1953 study indicated that lesbian women had orgasms in a greater percentage of sexual encounters than did heterosexual married women. After five years of marriage, 55% of heterosexual women had orgasms in 60%–100% of sexual contacts. After five years of homosexual experience, 78% of homosexual women had orgasms in 60%–100% of their sexual encounters. Kinsey has suggested that these results may be due to better understanding of sexual and psychological response between members of the same sex than between those of different sexes. Hite (1976) states that greater sexual satisfaction between women may occur because "lesbian sexual relations tend to be longer and involve more all-over body sensuality" (p. 413).

Another mistaken belief is that dildoes (penis-shaped devices) are used exten-sively among lesbians. In fact, only 2% of the homosexual women in Hunt's 1974 survey had ever used a dildo. Manual stimulation, oral contact, and rubbing genitals together or against the partner's body are included in lesbian sexual behaviors (Hite, 1976; Hunt, 1974; Kinsey, 1953). Rubbing genitals against someone's body or their genital area is called *tribadism*. Many lesbians like this form of sexual play because it involves all-over body contact and a generalized sensuality. Some women find the thrusting very exciting; others straddle their partner's leg and rub gently. Some rub the clitoris on their partner's pubic bone (Loulan, 1984).

It may be more difficult for lesbians to initiate a sexual relationship than for either heterosexual or male homosexual persons. One explanation for this is that society conditions women to respond to sexual initiation rather than to take the lead. Without the familiar cues of "being pursued," women may not even be aware of a mutual attraction; each is waiting for the other person to take a first step to demonstrate interest. Consequently, the sexual relationship may not even begin (Schwartz and Blumstein, 1973). A woman explains:

> Initiating dates is difficult for lesbians because most of us never learned how to ask someone out. We were supposed to wait for the boys to ask us! This skill that most men began to develop gradually at about age thirteen is expected to bloom suddenly in a lesbian who comes out at eighteen or twenty-nine or forty-two. Two women attempting to get together face this process with little experience and a lot of awkwardness. (Loulan, 1984, p. 20)

A survey comparing heterosexual and homosexual patterns concluded that lesbian couples have sex less frequently than heterosexual couples. The gap between the lovemaking frequency of lesbian and heterosexual couples widens dramatically as the relationships continue over time. In the first two years of the relationship, 76% of lesbians and 83% of heterosexual couples reported making love one or more times per week. After two years 37% of lesbians and 73% of heterosexual couples reported that same frequency (Blumstein and Schwartz, 1983).

Sexual Behaviors Among Men.   Contrary to the stereotype that sexual experiences between men are completely genitally focused, extragenital eroticism and affection are important aspects of sexual contact for many homosexual men:

No doubt most people will always conceive of male sexuality in general, and male homosexuality in particular, in terms of phallic actions. Certainly this focus invites the kinds of misconceptions which, in turn, tend to obscure the meaning homosexuality has for those who practice it . . . These and similar ideas have led to a widely held impression that homosexual practices lack precisely those kinds of affection which, in fact, are usually the main motives behind them. (Tripp, 1975, p. 102)

Hugging, kissing, and total-body caressing are important, as one homosexual man clearly states:

> One of the best parts of making love is the time we spend holding each other, touching each other's faces and looking into the other's eyes. (Authors' files)

Anal intercourse is often thought to be the most prevalent sexual behavior between homosexual men. However, the Bell and Weinberg study (1978) found that fellatio is the most common mode of expression. Partner manual stimulation is the next most common, and anal intercourse is least common. Almost all of the homosexual men in the study had used a considerable variety of sexual techniques. Since AIDS is contracted through body fluids, some gay men are changing their patterns of sexual activity by using condoms and avoiding any exchange of semen during sexual activity (Schecter et al., 1984). (Chapter 18 has a detailed discussion of AIDS prevention strategies.)

Coming Out

The extent to which a homosexual person decides to be secretive or open about his or her sexual orientation has a significant effect on the person's lifestyle. There are various degrees of being "in the closet," and there are several steps in the process of *coming out*—acknowledging, accepting, and openly expressing one's homosexuality. Although these decisions are unique to each individual and situation, there are often some common components.

Self-Acknowledgment. Very "closeted" homosexual men and women may attempt to suppress their sexual orientation even from their own awareness. These people may actively seek sexual encounters with members of the other sex, and it is not uncommon for them to marry in an attempt to convince themselves of their "normalcy." Some of the homosexual people who have previously been married (one-third of the women and one-fifth of the men in the Bell and Weinberg study) may have done so to avoid openly confronting their sexual orientation. As one man, now openly homosexual, states:

> As I look back now, I can see that my playboy lifestyle was really an attempt to convince myself that the nagging attraction I felt for John was just a good friendship. It was as if I thought I could change my feelings by having sex with enough women. (Authors' files)

The initial step in coming out is usually a person's realization that she or he feels different from the heterosexual model. Some people report knowing they were

homosexual when they were small children. Others realize during adolescence that something is missing in their heterosexual involvements.

Not just when, but how a person becomes aware of being homosexual varies from one person to another. It is not unusual for people to engage in explicit sexual behavior with same-sex partners without thinking of themselves as homosexual. For others, the initial homosexual experience represents the acknowledgment of this orientation.

Self-Acceptance. Accepting one's homosexuality is the next important step after realizing it. Self-acceptance is often difficult, for it involves overcoming the internalized negative societal view of homosexuality:

> Initially a homosexual person often has difficulty from the pervasive condemnatory attitudes toward homosexuality. Like the prejudiced heterosexual, his early impressions about homosexuality came from the culture around him. As a child he heard the same nasty references to homosexuals. He has heard them called "queers," seen them portrayed as dissolute and sad, on stage and screen, in novels, in newspaper articles. His own attitude toward homosexuality has evolved out of a context almost wholly derogatory. His prejudice against himself is an almost exact parallel to the prejudice against homosexuals held in the larger culture. (Weinberg, 1973, p. 74)

The term *gay* is commonly used to describe homosexual people who see their homosexuality as a positive part of their identity.

Disclosure.   Related to acknowledgment and self-acceptance is the decision to be secretive or open. Deciding to remain in the closet may erode a person's pride and self-respect, yet concerns about consequences from disclosure often encourage secrecy. As a result, interpersonal relationships may remain distant:

> To avoid awkwardness or dishonesty, many of us just refrain from talking openly about our personal lives. Our co-workers and co-students see us as shy, withdrawn, reserved, snobbish—when actually we are trying to protect ourselves from *their homophobia!* (Loulan, 1985, p. 17)

Concealment can intensify social isolation and personal loneliness; it also inhibits participation in any gay rights activities. Whatever security is gained by concealment can also be jeopardized by discovery at any time (Milligan, 1975). **Passing** is a term sometimes used for maintaining the false image of heterosexuality. Passing as heterosexual is usually quite easy, since most people have learned to assume everyone is heterosexual.

Being homosexual usually requires a lifelong process of decision-making about whether to be in or out of the closet, as new relationships and situations unfold. Heterosexuals sometimes do not understand this, as exemplified by the following comment:

> I don't see any reason why they have to tell anyone. They can just lead their lives without making such a big deal out of it. (Authors' files)

In most daily interactions, sexual orientation is irrelevant. However, imagine being a closeted homosexual person listening to a friend tell a "queer" joke, being asked "When are you going to settle down and get married?" or being invited to an office party for couples. In one writer's words, "Because of its devalued status, affirmation of homosexuality (or disclaiming it) becomes a more significant act than the same would be for a heterosexual, with significant consequences for a lifestyle" (Gagnon, 1977, p. 248). A lesbian author writes about how concealing one's homosexuality can affect the intimate relationship:

> The daily act of having to live a double life—one that you show in public, one that you act in private—negatively influences our sexual expression. It is difficult to be sexual with someone you have denied all week at work. Switching gears from being "friends" outside your home to passionate lovers inside has a devastating effect on our ability to be sexually free. (Loulan, 1984, p. 23)

With some exceptions, the more within "the system" a person is or desires to be, the more risk there is in not concealing one's sexual orientation. Jobs, social position, and friends may all be placed in jeopardy. Bell and Weinberg (1978) confirm this notion with their findings that relatively overt homosexual men and women are more likely to have lower social status (less education and income) than those who remain covert. The conservativeness of the surrounding community may further affect one's decisions.

Coming out may be a particularly difficult issue for homosexual adults who are parents. Approximately 60% of homosexual men and women who have been married have at least one child (Bell and Weinberg, 1978). The difficulties a gay parent meets in attempting to attain custody or visitation rights may be severe. It is not unusual for gay parents to lose these rights strictly on the basis of their sexual orientation, regardless of their fitness as parents. Yet some courts hold that homosexuality itself is not proof of unfitness. The pattern of decisions at this time is arbitrary and uncertain (Stevens, 1978).

Telling the Family.   Coming out to one's family and friends is a particularly significant step, as the following account by a 35-year-old man illustrates:

> Most of my vacation at home went well, but the ending was indeed difficult. Gay people kept cropping up in conversation. My mother was very down on them (us), and I of course was disagreeing with her. Finally she asked me if I was "one of them." I responded that I was. It was very difficult for her to deal with. She asked a lot of questions which I answered as calmly, honestly, and rationally as I could. We spent a rather strained day together. It was so painful for me to see her suffering so much heartache over this, and not even having a clue that the issue is the oppression of gay people. I just wish my mother didn't have to suffer so much from all this. I feel very down on our society. (Authors' files)

Parents often do experience difficult feelings from the revelation that a child is homosexual. They may react with anger, or with guilt about what they "did wrong" (see Box 10.3). Because telling the family is so difficult, many homosexual people do not do so. Approximately half of the respondents in the Bell and Weinberg survey believed that their parents did not know about their homosexuality. Fathers were somewhat less likely to know than mothers.

Each person decides if, when, and how to come out (except when homosexuality is discovered by accident). For those who decide to disclose their sexual orientation to their parents, Weinberg (1973) offers some suggestions, qualified with the statement that none are universally applicable. In the following list, the term *parents* can be translated to brothers, sisters, or friends:

1. Initiating discussions about homosexuality in general may help a gay person to test parents' openness. It may also provide the opportunity to give information to them about homosexuality.
2. Literature about homosexuality may also be helpful in facilitating their comfort and knowledge.
3. In telling parents about being homosexual, avoiding both blame and apologies can help maintain the dignity of both parties.
4. The person should make explicit the goodwill and desire for increased closeness that has motivated the disclosure.
5. Some parents may initially react explosively. It may be best to end the discussion at this point to give parents a chance to think it over. If parents

Dear Abby: Some time ago you made the statement in your column that lesbians are born, not made.

Abby, I have a beautiful, talented 30-year-old daughter who is a lesbian, and I have always blamed myself for that. When she was little, she hated dresses, so I let her wear blue jeans and T-shirts just like her brothers wore. I didn't think a thing of it at the time, but now I realize I helped to make a tomboy out of her. I blame myself for not insisting that she dress and act like a girl instead of putting her in boys' clothes and encouraging her to play boys' games with her brothers and their friends.

So, my question is, if I didn't contribute to the way she turned out, how in the world did it happen?—Puzzled in Hope, Ark.

Dear Puzzled: Don't blame yourself. Millions of little girls are tomboys and prefer jeans to dresses, yet the vast majority of them do not become lesbians. The causes of lesbianism, like those of male homosexuality, are complex and not fully understood, but there is growing evidence that many lesbians are born with a predisposition in that direction.

The important thing to remember is that sexual preference is not a matter of choice; it is determined at a very early age. Children who grow up to be homosexuals need their parents' love and understanding no less than other children do. In fact, they need it more.

become vindictive, the person may decide to remove himself or herself from the relationship until the parents indicate a willingness to resume communication.

Weinberg also offers some suggestions for parents whose child has told them about being homosexual. Given the negative cultural stereotypes about homosexuality, it is understandable that a parent, sibling, or friend may have difficulty accepting the news calmly. Weinberg suggests that the parents keep in mind that the son or daughter is exactly the same person they have known and loved. The only difference is that she or he is being more honest than before. Parents who have severed their relationship with a homosexual son or daughter can attempt to reestablish the relationship. Box 10.4 is a letter from a gay son that addresses many of these issues.

Involvement in the Gay Community. Involvement with homosexual people as a group may be another step in coming out. Weinberg describes issues such as "[w]hether to ridicule homosexuals. Whether to disparage other people called deviates by society. Whether to avoid homosexuals who are outspoken, who are gay and proud, or to join them. Whether to join the gay liberation movement" (1973, p. 87).

Some aspects of homosexual lifestyles center around various gay subcultures. In larger cities, gay bars and cafes cater to different groups or clientele. As with heterosexual bars, these gathering places range from low-key socializing spots to establishments with reputations for casual pickups. Lesbian women are far less likely to "cruise" in search of casual encounters than are homosexual males. However, many homosexual men do not cruise either. Particularly in past years, homosexual bars, as

Box 10.4

A Letter from a Gay Man to His Parents

Dear Mom and Dad,

Hi! I hope that all is well with you.

Well, I was waiting to tell you about my sexuality—waiting for a time when it would be best for you to deal with it. But now that it is out in the open I'm happy that I can share that part of my life with you. My relationship with Bob is a big part of what is positive in my life, so not being able to share that has really been difficult for me.

I would hope that my sharing this with you will bring us closer together. I would like to do anything I can to help you understand me and to understand what it's like to be gay. Please realize that you are in no way responsible for my sexual preference. What you did or didn't do as parents is not what determined my sexuality. I want to be absolutely clear—you are not to "blame," it is not your "fault"—it's just part of who I am and it is a beautiful part of me. So do not feel guilty. Besides, accepting my feelings has made me truly happy for the first time in my life. My being gay is not a tragedy—it's just part of who I am.

I know that my preference to be in a relationship with a man is going to be difficult for you to understand and difficult to accept. There is a lot of social pressure and programming against it. For that reason I had a hard time accepting it myself. I tried to deny it, in fact, for 29 years. I didn't want to disappoint you as parents and I wanted to be "normal" and accepted by those around me. As I said, it was not easy to accept the social context, but I firmly believe, deep in my heart and soul, that being with another man is going to make me happy and fulfilled (it has already).

My feelings for a man are deeper, more beautiful and more intense than anything I have felt with a woman. How can it be wrong if it fills me full of joy and happiness? How can it be wrong when being with a man is just so comfortable and easy?

How can it be wrong? Because Anita Bryant says so? Because the Catholic Church says so? Because ignorant people who know nothing about it and are afraid of looking at their own sexuality say so? *Who has the right to tell me that my feelings are wrong?*

I hope you can accept my relationship because it is the most important aspect of my life—that love and caring form a base for everything else that I do. I would very much like you to share my life and I hope that you can see that I'm still the same person that you have always loved and cared about. I definitely do not want to be in the position of having to choose between your approval and my happiness—because from my perspective, the choice would be an obvious but unfortunate one.

Also, please try to react out of love, not fear, guilt or sadness. I tried to write this letter from my heart and I hope that you will receive it in the same spirit in which it was written.

I love you very much,

Don   (Authors' files)

---

well as certain recreational areas, restaurants, or steam baths, served an important function—often they were the only place where the patrons could drop the facade of heterosexuality. In recent years this need has diminished to some extent. Gay people have helped to found service organizations, educational centers, and professional organizations. Religious organizations for gay people have been established, including the Metropolitan Community Church and denominational groups such as Dignity for Roman Catholics and Integrity for Episcopalians. Political interest groups concerned with gay rights have also been formed. Since its beginning in the 1960s, the growing gay rights movement has provided support for many homosexual men and women to be more open about their sexual orientation. The following section describes some of the movement's activities.

This gay men's chorus is one of many community activities available to homosexual people.

Gay Rights and the Antigay Movement

In the 1950s some organizations for gay people were established, in spite of the very conservative atmosphere of the times. The Mattachine Society had chapters in many cities, providing a national network for support and communication among homosexuals. The Daughters of Bilitis, an organization of lesbians, also published a journal called *The Ladder,* which contained fiction, poetry, and political articles. The goals of both organizations were to educate homosexual and heterosexual people about homosexuality, increase understanding of homosexuality, and eliminate discriminatory laws toward homosexual individuals (Katz, 1976).

During the 1960s many people began to question traditional aspects of American life in all areas, including the sexual. In this atmosphere more gay people began to respond to social and political changes and to question and challenge the social problems they faced. The symbolic birth of gay activism occurred in 1969 in New York City, when police raided a gay bar, the Stonewall. Police raids on gay bars were common occurrences, but this time people in the bar resisted and fought back. A riot followed and did not end until the next day. The Stonewall incident acted as a catalyst for the formation of gay rights groups, and activities such as Gay Pride Week are held in yearly commemoration of the Stonewall riot (Hankel and Cunningham, 1979).

Since the early 1970s, groups have worked to end various kinds of discrimination against homosexual people. Some organizations have lobbied for more accurate coverage of homosexual lifestyles in the media, and gay people have organized to confront prejudice within their own professions. The National Gay Task Force was founded in 1973 to work with homosexual men and women around the country to help achieve legal rights.

The gay rights movement has been primarily concerned with legislation related

to consensual sex and civil rights. Both of these legal areas are seen as essential to providing homosexual people the same legal protection that heterosexual people enjoy. The desired legislation aims to prevent harassment and discrimination based on sexual orientation. The movement's central philosophy is that private consensual sexual expression is not a matter of legal concern, nor is it adequate reason to deny or rescind housing or employment.

Many states have passed legislation legalizing private sexual behavior between consenting adults. In many other states, however, sexual behaviors such as oral-genital contact, manual-genital stimulation, and anal intercourse are still illegal, whether performed by same- or other-sex partners. These laws are most commonly enforced against homosexual men. Some states have meted out life imprisonment to convicted homosexual "offenders." *Entrapment*, the practice of undercover police enticing propositions from homosexual men, is a major source of arrests.

A major legislative goal of gay rights advocates is an amendment to the 1964 Civil Rights Act that would broaden it to include "affectional or sexual preference" along with race, creed, color, and sex. This would make it illegal to discriminate in housing, employment, and public accommodations on the grounds of sexual orientation. Such a bill was introduced into Congress in 1975, but the legislation has not yet been passed, nor has such civil rights legislation passed in any state legislatures. However, some local governments have adopted laws prohibiting discrimination on the basis of sexual orientation. Additionally, several large private corporations and the Federal Civil Service Commission have established equal opportunity employment in regard to homosexuality. This means that it is illegal for an employer to discriminate against anyone in hiring or firing on the basis of sexual orientation.

These gains have been countered by the antigay movement. Opponents of gay rights typically believe that homosexuality is a sin. Does the belief that homosexual behaviors are sinful provide grounds for discriminatory laws against homosexuals? This question represents another basic issue. As discussed at the beginning of this chapter, the biblical condemnation of homosexuality stems from a unique historical context. The implications of these prohibitions for today's world are questioned by religious scholars:

> There is no doubt that the Old Testament condemns homosexual practice with the utmost severity. The reason for the condemnation, however, and the severity of the punishment cannot be appreciated apart from the historical background that gave rise to them. Simply citing verses from the Bible outside of their historical context and then blithely applying them to homosexuals today does grave injustice both to scripture and to people who have already suffered a great deal from the travesty of biblical interpretation. (Kosnik et al., 1977, p. 188)

Whatever the correct interpretation may be, the question remains whether anyone's interpretation should influence the legal system. If the religious beliefs of some were codified into law for all, then eating pork, drinking coffee, and driving a car would be illegal. "Those who argue that our law is based on the Judeo-Christian ethic sometimes are highly selective in their application of biblical sanctions" (The Portland Town Council, 1976, p. 13).

The gay rights position maintains that the United States Constitution upholds the separation of church and state. A crucial point is that civil rights legislation provides legal protection in housing, employment, and public accommodations—not necessarily moral sanction for homosexuality. The American Civil Liberties Union stated in 1975: "Homosexuals are entitled to the same rights, liberties, lack of harassment, and protections as are other citizens" (The Portland Town Council, 1976).

Another basic issue has concerned the reputed dangers of permitting homosexual people to work as teachers or childcare providers, or in other positions where they would have contact with children. Some groups' support for continued discrimination in employment is based on the belief that many homosexual adults sexually molest children. Antigay groups are afraid that contact between homosexual people and children might result in "recruitment" of children into homosexuality.

These fears are groundless, for several reasons. First, as we will discuss in Chapter 20, child molestation is committed primarily by heterosexual male adults who are family members or friends of the children. Protecting children from sexual abuse is a concern shared by homosexual and heterosexual adults. Civil rights employment protection for homosexual teachers absolutely does not give them any more rights than heterosexual teachers to make sexual advances to students. Second, it is untrue that homosexual people attempt to increase their numbers by "recruitment." Even if they did, sexual orientation is much too complex a phenomenon to be readily changed by seduction or example. In fact, recent preliminary research indicates that even children who live with a homosexual parent are not likely to adopt a homosexual orientation (Green, 1978).

Antigay sentiment can escalate to drastic proportions. Many cities are reporting an increase in physical assaults on gays and others suspected of being gay. These events indicate a pathological fear and hatred of homosexuality, and they deepen the commitment of gays and others sympathetic to their concerns to eradicating the attitudes that contribute to such violence. The National Gay Task Force has started a major project to monitor and document violence against homosexuals. The data will be used as a tool for civil rights advocacy and to help reduce gay victimization (Gurel, 1982). Many gay men have become involved in gay rights advocacy for the first time as a result of their concerns about AIDS (Clarke, 1985). Much recent gay activism has focused on funding for AIDS research; providing support organizations for victims and their friends and families; and public education about AIDS.

The struggle for gay rights is far from ending. Gay rights supporters and antigay groups are attempting to pass or restrict antidiscriminatory legislation in various places throughout the country. It is our hope that gay civil rights will prevail, and that homosexual Americans will be freer to live, work, and contribute to society.

Summary

1. The term *homosexual* can be an objective or subjective appraisal of sexual behavior, emotional affiliation, and/or self-definition.

A Continuum of Sexual Orientations

2. Kinsey's seven-point continuum ranges from exclusive heterosexuality to exclusive homosexuality. Kinsey based his ratings on a combination of overt sexual behaviors and erotic attractions

3. According to estimates based on methodological adjustments between Kinsey and Hunt, approximately 2% of men and 1% of women are exclusively homosexual; about 23% of men and 14% of women have both homosexual and heterosexual experiences; and roughly 75% of men and 85% of women are exclusively heterosexual.

4. Bisexuality can be characterized by overt behaviors and/or erotic responses to both males and females. As with heterosexuality and homosexuality, a clear-cut definition is difficult to establish.

5. Four types of bisexuality include bisexuality as a real orientation, as a transitory orientation, as a transitional orientation, or as homosexual denial.

Societal Attitudes

6. Cross-cultural attitudes toward homosexuality vary from condemnation to acceptance. Negative attitudes toward homosexuality still predominate in our society.

7. Homophobia is the irrational fear of homosexuality, the fear of homosexual feelings within oneself, or self-loathing because of one's own homosexuality.

8. Current theological positions towards homosexuality include the rejecting-punitive, rejecting-nonpunitive, qualified acceptance, and full acceptance stances.

Development of Homosexuality

9. There are a number of psychosocial and biological theories that attempt to explain the development of homosexuality. Some of the psychosocial theories relate to parenting patterns, life experiences, or the psychological attributes of the person. Theories of biological causation look to genetic causation or prenatal or adult hormone differences.

10. Various "treatments" have been used to attempt to change homosexual orientation to heterosexual. Such attempts in the past have not been particularly successful, and much controversy surrounds current therapy designed to develop heterosexual functioning in homosexually oriented individuals.

11. Sexual orientation, regardless of where it falls on the continuum of heterosexuality and homosexuality, seems to be formed from a composite of inconsistent and undetermined elements.

Lifestyles

12. Contrary to popular stereotypes, homosexual individuals exhibit a wide variety of lifestyles.

13. As gender-role stereotyping has decreased, many homosexual and heterosexual couples have developed more egalitarian relationships. Some of the differences reported between homosexual men and homosexual women may be attributed to general gender-role differences between men and women.

14. Bell and Weinberg classified homosexual relationships and lifestyles into five basic categories: close-coupled, open-coupled, functionals, dysfunctionals, and asexuals.

15. The choice of coming out or being "in the closet" often has a significant impact on a homosexual person's lifestyle. The steps of coming out involve recognizing one's homosexual orientation, deciding how to view oneself, and being open about one's homosexuality.

Gay Rights and the Antigay Movement

16. Gay rights activists have been promoting consenting adult and civil rights legislation. These activities have met with opposition from various individuals and groups.

Key to Box 10.1, "The Homophobic Scale": According to Smith, yes responses to questions 1, 2, 4, 5, 8 and 9 and no responses to questions 3, 6 and 7 indicate homophobic attitudes.

Thought Provokers

1. What do you think are the advantages and disadvantages of being bisexual, homosexual, heterosexual, or asexual?

2. How have you observed homophobia being expressed?

3. How do you think the emergence of AIDS has affected attitudes towards homosexuality? What do you think the longer term changes will be?

Suggested Readings

Clark, D. *Loving Someone Gay*. Millbrae, Calif.: Celestial Arts, 1979. A book designed to increase understanding and communication between homosexual people and their friends and families.

Hall, Marny. *The Lavender Couch*. Boston: Alyson, 1985. A book to help guide gay people in choosing a therapist and evaluating their therapy experience.

Hanckel, Frances, and Cunningham, John. *A Way of Love, A Way of Life*. New York: Lothrop, Lee & Shepard, 1979. This book is written to inform people, especially young people, about what it means to be gay. It discusses how young people who are gay can know that they are, how to develop positive attitudes about themselves, how to tell family and friends, where to go for help, the history of gay rights, and variations in lifestyles.

Loulan, JoAnn. *Lesbian Sex*. San Francisco: Spinsters Ink, 1984. An excellent book about lesbian sexual activities, relationships, and lifestyles, with exercises designed to enhance self-awareness and sexual expression.

McWhirter, David, and Mattison, Andrew. *The Male Couple*. Englewood Cliffs, N.J.: Prentice-Hall, 1984. This book about the developmental stages of gay relationships examines the intimate and daily lives of male couples who have been together for one to thirty-seven years.

Schulenberg, Joy. *Gay Parenting*. New York: Anchor Books, 1985. This book is a practical and comprehensive guide to dealing with becoming a parent, coming out to children, and custody issues.

Zinik, Gary. "Identity Conflict or Adaptive Flexibility? Bisexuality Reconsidered." *Journal of Homosexuality*, 1985, 11, 7–19. An article about two opposing models of bisexual functioning, the "conflict model" and the "flexibility" model.

Resources

The National Gay Task Force, 80 Fifth Avenue, New York, N.Y. 10011. (212)741-5800. This group will provide information about social, political, and educational organizations in a particular locale.

Parents and Friends of Lesbians and Gays (Parents FLAG), P.O. Box 24565, Los Angeles, CA 90024. This group provides support and counseling for parents, and public education on gay rights.

Part Four

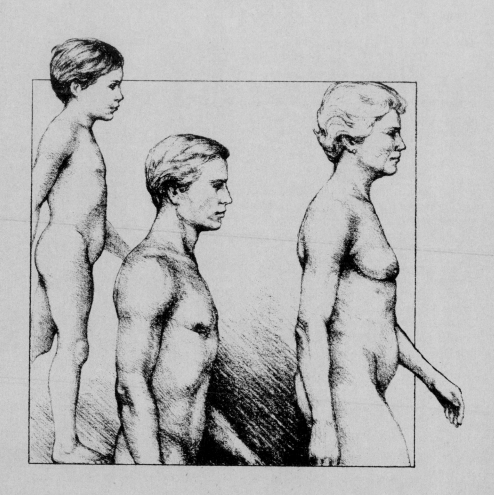

Sexuality and the Life Cycle

11

No woman can call herself free who does not own and control her body. No woman can call herself free until she can choose consciously whether she will not be a mother.
Margaret Sanger
Parade (Dec. 1, 1963)

Contraception

Historical and Social Perspectives
Shared Responsibility
Currently Available Methods
Sterilization
New Directions in Contraception

Historical and Social Perspectives

HUMANKIND'S CONCERN with controlling conception goes back at least to the beginning of recorded history. In ancient Egypt women placed dried crocodile dung next to the cervix to prevent conception (Zatuchni, 1984). In sixth-century Greece, eating the uterus, testicle, or hoof paring of a mule was recommended. In more recent historical times, the eighteenth-century Italian adventurer Giovanni Casanova was noted for his animal membrane condoms tied with a ribbon at the base of the penis. In seventeenth-century Western Europe, condoms, withdrawal of the penis from the vagina before ejaculation, and vaginal sponges soaked in a variety of solutions were used for contraception.

Contraception in the United States

Although we may take for granted the variety of contraceptive, or birth control, methods available in the United States today, this phenomenon is quite recent in our history. Through the years, both the methods available and the laws concerning their use have been restrictive. In the 1870s Anthony Comstock, then secretary of the New York Society for the Suppression of Vice, succeeded in having national laws enacted which prohibited disseminating contraceptive information through the United States mail on the grounds that such information was obscene. (The laws became known as the Comstock Laws.) At that time the only "official," legitimate form of birth control was abstinence, and reproduction was the only acceptable reason for sexual intercourse.

Margaret Sanger was the person most instrumental in promoting the changes in birth control legislation and availability in the United States. She opened an illegal clinic in 1915 where women could obtain and learn to use the diaphragms she had shipped from Europe. She also published birth control information in her newspaper, *The Woman Rebel*. As a result, Sanger was arraigned for violating the Comstock Laws. She fled to Europe to avoid certain prosecution but later returned to promote birth control hormone research, a project financed by her wealthy friend Katherine Dexter McCormack. These women wanted to develop a reliable method by which women could control their own fertility. However, it was not until 1960 that the first birth control pills came on the U.S. market, after limited testing and research in Puerto Rico.

In 1966 the last major law regulating the sale of contraceptives was revoked. Laws governing contraceptive availability continue to change. Recently many states have liberalized their laws to allow the dispensing of contraceptives to adolescents without parental consent and the displaying of condoms and foam on open pharmacy shelves rather than behind the counter. On the other hand, controversy continues on the national level about whether to require parental notification when minors receive contraceptive services from government-funded organizations. Even today, the availability and acceptability of contraception is still a contested issue.

Contraception as a Contemporary Issue

In recent years the availability and use of reliable birth control has been seen as increasingly desirable for a variety of reasons. There has been a growing emphasis on having planned and wanted children. Many couples who want children wait for some years to establish their relationship and their financial stability. Birth control also enables couples and individuals to limit the size of their families. Women who want to combine a career and parenthood depend for this on birth control. Finally, men and women who choose not to be parents at all have been able to accomplish this more easily since the development of more effective birth control methods.

The use of birth control can also contribute to the physical health of the mother. Pregnancy itself has health risks, and spacing pregnancies usually means better health for the mother and children. In some cases birth control is used to avoid the possibility of bearing children with hereditary diseases or birth defects.

Population growth is another concern that plays a part in some people's decision to limit their family size. The world's natural resources are not unlimited, and a continually increasing population may precipitate a crisis. For this reason, some people see population control through the use of birth control as a social necessity.

Objections to contraception often stem from religious mandate. The official doctrine of the Roman Catholic church, as well as some other religions, holds that the use of means other than abstinence and methods based on the menstrual cycle is immoral. However, many contemporary religions favor the use of birth control. Furthermore, there is great diversity of views among leaders of the Catholic church. For example, a study commissioned by the Catholic Theological Society of America states: "The mere fact that a couple is using artificial means of birth control cannot provide a sufficient basis to make a judgment about the morality or immorality of their married life and sexual expression" (Kosnik et al., 1977, p. 127). Also, the discrepancy between doctrine and practice is wide. The majority of church members in the United States use some kind of artificial contraception. In fact, the difference

Other Times, Other Places

The Burden of Fertility

Millions of women around the world lack the cultural support and money necessary to limit the number and timing of their children. The story of Dora Ayonga, a 23-year-old woman who lives in a village in Kenya, typifies the lives of women in many countries of the world. Her ability to have babies is her key to acceptance in the community. Dora has been pregnant five times in the last five years. One child has died, and the living children have the bloated bellies and skinny legs of malnourishment. Dora earns about 48 cents a day hoeing cornfields. A trip to the nearest family planning clinic would cost her five days' salary, equal to a week's supply of food for her family. In addition, her husband, who is out of work, wants her to have another baby. The more children he has the higher his status in the village, where the average family has 12 children (Harden, 1985b).

*Margaret Sanger
helped make birth
control available
for American
women.*

between Catholic and non-Catholic use of contraceptive devices is minimal. A recent investigation of birth control practices among a large sample of women of childbearing age found that 88.7% of Protestant women and 88.3% of Catholic women used some contraceptive method (Bachrach, 1984).

Shared Responsibility

In promoting the pill, it was Margaret Sanger's idea to give women control over their own fertility. However, control does not necessarily mean total responsibility by the woman. It may not be wise for a man to assume that a woman has "taken care of herself." Many women do not regularly practice birth control, especially if they are not engaged in a long-term relationship, and some use various methods incorrectly.

Would you be more careful if it were you that got pregnant?

If there is any uncertainty about using birth control, the relationship may suffer. Decisions about an unwanted pregnancy are not easy, and fear of pregnancy can negatively affect both partners' sexual experience.

Sharing the responsibility of contraception can enhance a relationship. Talking about birth control can be a good way to practice discussing personal and sexual topics. A man who takes an active interest in contraception is not likely to be affected by the resentment women often feel for men who put the entire responsibility on them. As one writer states, "Taking care of business before you get down to pleasure often enhances lovemaking by reducing stress and building trust" (Castleman, 1980a). For these reasons, we recommend that responsibility for birth control be shared.

The first step in sharing contraceptive responsibility may simply be for either partner to ask the other about birth control before the first time they have intercourse. In our experience talking with students and clients, this initial question is rarely asked. (Chapter 13 has a discussion of nonuse of contraception.) Openness on the part of the male partner to using condoms or noncoital sexual activities, whether as the method of choice or as a backup or temporary method, is one way to share responsibility for birth control. Reading about and discussing the various alternatives and choosing the one that seems best is an important way for both partners to be involved. Most birth control clinics offer classes that are open to partners. The man can also participate by accompanying his partner when a medical exam is needed. Some physicians or nurse practitioners are comfortable with the woman's partner being present during the exam. Expenses for both the exam and the birth control method can also be shared. Further suggestions for sharing responsibility will be included in the discussion of specific methods. We believe that sharing the responsibility for birth control can help provide both better sexual relationships and improved contraceptive effectiveness.

Currently Available Methods

There are many forms of birth control. However, a perfect method—one that permits any sexual activity, yet is 100% effective, reversible, without side effects, convenient, and usable by either sex—is not available now or in the foreseeable future. Each of the methods currently available has advantages and disadvantages with regard to effectiveness, safety, and convenience. It is a good idea to be familiar with the various methods available, because most people will use several of them during their active sex lives.

Considerations in Choosing a Method

How do people go about choosing a method of birth control? A number of criteria are important, including convenience, safety, expense, and effectiveness. Details relating to specific birth control methods will be discussed later in this section. Here we will present only a brief comparison.

Convenience.   What is convenient or easy for one person to use may be inconvenient or difficult for another. Because this factor is so subjective, we will discuss ways of using each contraceptive in the following pages to permit readers to judge for themselves.

Safety.   Every method of contraception except abstinence has health risks. Some of the dangers are directly due to the method; others are due to failure of the method and resulting birth complications. One study compared the annual risk of death of women from birth control methods and from births following contraceptive failure in the United States and Britain (Tietze et al., 1977). The major findings were that barrier methods (condom and diaphragm), with abortion backup, are the safest methods of reversible fertility control. Deaths associated with both the method and its failure increase for barrier methods, the IUD, and the pill as a woman becomes older. The most important point is that the overall risk to life from any birth control method is very small. There is one exception: Women over 40 years of age who smoke cigarettes and use the pill have a substantially increased risk of death.

Expense. There are several factors involved in comparing the costs of different contraceptives, and these make direct comparisons difficult. Pills, IUDs, and diaphragms require examinations by a health-care specialist, whereas foam and condoms do not. Yet a woman needs to have yearly or biannual Pap smears even when she is not using a prescription method of birth control. When a method causes side effects or is personally unsatisfactory, visits to the doctor to deal with the problems will add expense. Frequency of intercourse will affect how expensive some methods are. For example, foam and condoms would cost less per month with infrequent intercourse. Finally, one should keep the emotional and financial cost of an unplanned pregnancy in mind when considering the various contraceptive methods.

Effectiveness. Several variables influence the effectiveness of birth control. The theoretical effectiveness of a method does not take into account human error. Physician mistakes (such as improper IUD insertion or poor fitting of a diaphragm, discussed later in this chapter), lack of knowledge of correct method use, negative attitudes about using the method, an uninvolved partner, forgetfulness, or deciding "this time it won't matter" greatly increase the chances of pregnancy. Contraceptive effectiveness is best compared by seeing how many women out of 100 get pregnant by the end of the first year of using a particular method. Table 11.1 shows the failure rates (pregnancies per 100 women per year) for a large number of women using several of the most commonly used methods. As Box 11.1 suggests, many couples may want to use backup methods to provide greater protection under certain circumstances. Many additional factors influence people in their decisions about whether to use a birth control method and which methods to use. As we discuss a number of commonly used methods in the paragraphs that follow, we will present more specific information on how to use each method, how it works, how a couple may share responsibility, and the potential advantages and disadvantages of each option.

Table 11.1 *Birth Control Method Effectiveness*
Number of pregnancies during the first year of use per 100 nonsterile women initiating the method.

Method	Theoretical Number If Method Is Used Correctly and Consistently	Actual Number in Sample of U.S. Women Who Wanted No More Children
"Outercourse"	0	0
Tubal sterilization	0.4	0.4
Vasectomy	0.4	0.4
Estrogen/progesterone pills	0.5	2
Progestin-only pills	1	2.5
IUD	1.5	5
Foam and condom	less than 1	5
Condom	2	10
Diaphragm and spermicide	2	19
Cervical cap	2	13
Foam, creams, jellies, and vaginal suppositories	3–5	18
Sponge with spermicide	9–11	10–20
Withdrawal	16	23
Fertility awareness: "rhythm," calendar, basal body temperature, cervical mucus	2–20	24
Douching	?	40
No method	90	90

Source: Adapted from Hatcher et al., 1986, p. 102. Foam and condom data from Hatcher et al., 1980.

"Outercourse"

Noncoital forms of sexual intimacy, called "outercourse," can be a viable form of birth control (Hatcher et al., 1986). **Outercourse** includes all avenues of sexual intimacy other than penile-vaginal intercourse, such as kissing, touching, petting, holding, massage, and oral sex. Many couples have very pleasurable memories of highly erotic sexual interaction in their initial courtship phase before they began having intercourse. Returning to outercourse activities can often enhance sexual enjoyment (Greenwood and Margolis, 1981). As a man in his mid-twenties states:

> Right now in this relationship I'm very sexual; I'm just not "intercoursal."
> (Authors' files)

The voluntary avoidance of coitus offers effective protection from pregnancy, is free from side effects, and reduces the chances of sexually transmitted diseases. Outercourse can be used as a primary or temporary means of preventing pregnancy, and it can also be used when it is inadvisable to have intercourse for other reasons—for example, following childbirth or abortion, or during a herpes outbreak.

Oral Contraceptives

There are three basic types of oral contraceptives currently on the market: the combination pill, the progestin-only pill (currently called the mini-pill), and the multiphasic pill. The **combination pill** contains two hormones, synthetic estrogen and progestin. It is the most commonly used oral contraceptive in the United States and has been on the market since the early 1960s. There are more than twenty different varieties, containing varying amounts and ratios of the two hormones. The **progestin-only pill** contains only 0.35 mg of progestin (a progesteronelike substance)—about one-third of the amount in an average-strength combination pill. There is no estrogen in the progestin-only pill. This pill has been on the market since 1973. Both the combination pill and the progestin-only pill are constant-dose formulations. The most recent addition to oral contraceptive formulations is the **multiphasic pill**. Unlike constant-dose formulations, this type of pill provides fluctuations of estrogen and progesterone levels that simulate those of the natural menstrual cycle. It is also designed to reduce the total steroid dose and side effects while maintaining contraceptive effectiveness (Pasquale, 1984).

How Pills Work.　The combination and multiphasic pills (estrogen-progesterone pills) prevent conception primarily by inhibiting ovulation. The estrogen in the pill affects the hypothalamus, inhibiting the release of the pituitary hormones LH and FSH that would otherwise begin the chain of events culminating in ovulation (see Chapter 4). After a woman stops taking estrogen-progesterone pills it may take time for her ovaries to resume normal functioning. The progesterone in the pill provides secondary contraceptive protection by thickening and chemically altering the cervical mucus so that it hampers the passage of sperm into the uterus. Progesterone also causes changes in the lining of the uterus, making it less receptive to implantation. In addition, progesterone may inhibit ovulation by mildly disturbing hypothalamic-pituitary-ovarian function (Hatcher et al., 1980).

The progestin-only pill works somewhat differently. Most women who take the progestin-only pill probably continue to ovulate at least occasionally. The primary effect of this pill is to alter the cervical mucus to a thick and tacky consistency that effectively blocks sperm. As with the combination pill, secondary contraceptive effects may be provided by alterations in the uterine lining that make it unreceptive to implantation.

How to Use the Pill.　There are several acceptable ways to start taking pills, and a woman who uses the pill should carefully follow suggestions of her health care practitioner. A woman takes estrogen-progesterone pills for only 21 days of the 28-day pill cycle (although most packets contain seven inert "reminder" pills for the remaining days). She will usually experience a menstruationlike flow that results from the hormone withdrawal each month. Progestin-only pills are taken every day, even during menstruation.

Forgetting pills reduces the effectiveness of this method; taking the pill at approximately the same time each day maximizes it. Since the pills maintain a particular hormone level in the body, missing one or more pills can alter the hormone level and allow ovulation to occur. A woman must take a missed pill as soon as she remembers it; she then takes the next pill at the regular time. If she forgets more than one pill, it is best for her to consult her health care practitioner. She should use a backup method such as foam or condoms for the remainder of her cycle.

Shared Responsibility.   The woman's partner can share in the responsibility of oral contraceptive use by understanding the manifestations and consequences of potential side effects and by sharing the expense of the exam and pills. He can also use condoms as a backup method for the rest of the cycle if the woman forgets one or more pills and during the initial month of pill use, when the risk of pregnancy is higher. Sharing responsibility may be more important with the progestin-only pill than with the combination pill, as the progestin-only pill is slightly less effective (see Table 11.1). Condoms and noncoital sexual sharing, as well as the use of diaphragm and foam, can help ensure contraception during the midcycle ovulation phase.

Potential Advantages of Oral Contraceptives.   Birth control pills have several advantages. They can be taken at a time separate from sexual activity, which many people believe helps maintain sexual spontaneity. If the combination pill is used correctly, it is a highly effective method, as Table 11.1 shows. Some women who experience breast enlargement from the pill consider this a positive side effect. Acne is often improved by taking oral contraceptives. The pill also often eliminates *mittelschmerz* (pain at ovulation) and reduces menstrual cramps and the amount and duration of the flow. Some women notice that taking oral contraceptives diminishes premenstrual tension symptoms. Iron deficiency anemia is decreased in pill users. Oral contraceptives can be effective in treating endometriosis or cysts of the ovary and may decrease the incidence of benign breast disease (Franceschi et al., 1984). The incidence of rheumatoid arthritis and of ovarian, endometrial, and breast cancers is also lower in users than in nonusers of the pill (Hatcher et al., 1986; Kols et al., 1982). A woman who is pleased with this method states:

> I really like the pill I'm taking. My periods are light and the bad cramps I used to have are gone. I hadn't been using anything before taking the pill. It's a tremendous relief to make love and not be afraid of getting pregnant. (Authors' files)

These advantages explain, in part, why the pill is more commonly used than any other temporary method of birth control. One study reported that over 12% of women who use the pill do so exclusively for the various noncontraceptive benefits (The Walnut Creek Contraceptive Drug Study, 1981).

The progestin-only pill has the advantage that it eliminates estrogen-related side effects and reduces the likelihood of progestin-related problems because of the low progestin dosage. Adverse reactions to the combination pill, including carbohydrate metabolism alterations, yeast infections, nausea, weight gain, acne, and depression, may be reduced by switching to the progestin-only pill, and it is often recommended for women over 35 or for women who have a history of headaches, hypertension, or bad varicose veins (Hatcher et al., 1986).

Cautions in Using Oral Contraceptives.   A woman should have a complete medical and family history taken before using oral contraceptives. She should also have a physical exam (including a Pap smear, blood pressure, urinalysis, a gonorrhea culture, and breast and pelvic exams) before starting pills and at least once a year while taking them. In fact, all women should have yearly breast, Pap, and pelvic exams, regardless of whether they use pills.

Women vary in their responses to the hormone combinations of the different pills. Some of the side effects such as nausea, fluid retention, increased appetite, acne, depression, spotting, or lack of "menstruation" (withdrawal bleeding), can be eliminated by changing the type of pill. Generally, a woman will be given a type of pill that works well for her and that has the lowest practical hormonal potency to reduce the possibility of side effects.

Some women are much less prone than others to experience problems with the pill. Women who are least likely to have serious problems are under 30, are non-smokers, are of normal weight, have regular menstrual cycles, and have a medical history with no contraindications for the pill. For most healthy young women, the benefits of oral contraceptives outweigh the risks (Ory et al., 1980).

Potential Disadvantages of Oral Contraceptives.   Because the hormones in birth control pills circulate in the bloodstream through the entire body, there are a variety of potential side effects. Much is yet unknown, and the risks and rewards of oral contraception remain controversial. It is not wise to consider the pill to be completely harmless, as some do. A nurse practitioner reports:

> It's frightening to me to realize than many women on the pill don't consider it to be medication. When I take their medical histories and ask if they are taking any medications, they say no or ask "Does aspirin count?" When I later ask if they have ever taken birth control pills, they answer "Yes, I'm taking them now." (Authors' files)

Serious problems associated with the pill can be summarized by the acronym ACHES (Table 11.2). We will look first at some of the problems that have been associated with the estrogen-progestin pills, then examine possible side effects of the progestin-only pill.

The combination pill has been associated with an increased risk of blood clots in users. If a clot forms and travels to the lung or the brain, it can cause crippling or death. The symptoms of a blood clot may include severe leg or chest pains, coughing up blood, breathing difficulty, severe headache or vomiting, dizziness, fainting, disturbances of vision or speech, and weakness or numbness of an arm or leg. If a woman using an oral contraceptive experiences one or more of these symptoms, she should obtain immediate medical attention. Women who are immobilized or confined to a wheelchair are often advised against using the pill because poor circulation (sometimes related to lack of physical activity) can increase the potential for developing blood clots. Research indicates that the risk of a fatal blood clot is 15 times greater during pregnancy than with the pill. However, it is also important to compare side effects of the pill to risks from other methods of birth control. Pregnancy is not the only other option.

Another risk associated with the combination pill is increased likelihood of heart attacks, particularly for women over 40. For this reason, the U.S. Food and Drug

Table 11.2 Remember "ACHES" for the Pill
Symptoms of possible serious problems with the birth control pill,
represented by their initials.

Initial	Symptom	Possible Problem
A	Abdominal pain (severe)	Gallbladder disease, liver tumor, or blood clot
C	Chest pain (severe) or shortness of breath	Blood clot in lungs or heart attack
H	Headaches (severe)	Stroke, high blood pressure, or migraine headache
E	Eye problems: blurred vision, flashing lights, or blindness	Stroke, high blood pressure, or temporary vascular problems of many possible sites
S	Severe leg pain (calf or thigh)	Blood clot in legs

Source: Adapted from Hatcher et al, 1986.

Administration (FDA) has urged physicians not to prescribe the pill to women past 40 years of age. The risks are especially high for women over 40 who smoke cigarettes. Some research indicates that women who have used oral contraceptives for more than 10 years continue to be more susceptible to heart attack even after discontinuing the pill (Slone et al., 1981). Oral contraceptives containing low doses of estrogen (less than 50 micrograms) and of progestin may provide more safety from cardiovascular (heart and blood vessel) complications than higher dose pills (The Medical Letter, 1983).

High blood pressure (hypertension) is another potential risk of taking the pill. One in 20 pill users develops this complication. Pill-related high blood pressure can be reversed by discontinuing use. Periodic blood pressure measurements are important in pill users, and women who already have high blood pressure are usually advised to use another form of contraception.

The FDA has also listed an increased risk of noncancerous liver tumors as a potential side effect of oral contraceptives. These tumors are very rare but can be fatal. Women 27 years old and older who have used high dose oral contraceptives for seven years or more run the greatest risk of developing liver tumors (Centers for Disease Control Morbidity and Mortality Report, September 1977). Other researchers have found some liver tumors associated with oral contraceptives to be cancerous (Neuberger, 1980).

In some women the pill affects carbohydrate metabolism. These changes may lead to a prediabetic or diabetic condition or may aggravate already-existing diabetes. A careful medical history taken when birth control pills are first prescribed may reveal the need for glucose tolerance testing. Some women experience an increase in vaginal discharge as a side effect of the pill. The pill does alter the chemical balance of the vagina, and this causes women to develop yeast infections more easily.

The pill may also be related to emotional changes, although it is difficult to establish a definitive cause for any emotional state. Many women, however, see a correlation between their moods and use of oral contraceptives. Some studies have shown an increase in depression in women on the pill (Hatcher et al, 1986); since depression can affect all aspects of a woman's life, it is not to be taken lightly. A woman who suspects her depression may be pill-related can use another method for a time and observe any changes in her mood.

Many women take the pill to increase their enjoyment and the spontaneity of their sexual expression. Some women on the pill experience an increase in sexual desire (Hatcher et al., 1986). However, a decrease in sexual motivation may also occur. A decline in sexual interest may be influenced by a variety of side effects, including frequent yeast infections, a reduction of vaginal lubrication, and depression. Hormonal and other psychological factors may also contribute.

There are still other potential adverse effects. First, use of oral contraceptives for two or more years doubles the risk of developing gall bladder disease (Boston Collaborative Drug Surveillance Program, 1973) and also increases the incidence of bladder and kidney infections. Some conditions—including migraine headaches, asthma, epilepsy, and cardiac or kidney dysfunction—may be aggravated by the fluid retention that accompanies the pill. (When these conditions are related to hormone imbalance, however, the pill is sometimes used to alleviate the difficulty.) The hormones in the pill can also alter the way in which the body assimilates vitamins and minerals that are essential for optimal health.

A summary study of oral contraceptive research turned up some contradictory information (Ory et al., 1980). The authors cite a lack of confirmation for several side effects, including impaired fertility and an increase in diabetes, gall bladder disease, and urinary tract infections. They also suggest that past research findings may overstate the risks for today's young women for two reasons. First, the pills used in the 1960s and early 1970s usually had higher doses of estrogen than do pills today. Higher levels of estrogen are linked with increased risk of most side effects. Second, most of the studies have been done with women older than 25, and the results may reflect that influence to some extent.

While the reduced amounts of hormones in the progestin-only pill causes it to have fewer potential side effects, this pill too has some disadvantages associated with it. Irregular and "breakthrough" bleeding (a light flow between menstrual periods) happens more frequently with the progestin-only pill than with the combination pill. However, the bleeding irregularities usually diminish in two or three months, as they do with the combination pill.

A Comment on Oral Contraceptives.   The long list of potential side effects of oral contraceptives makes it difficult to not sound alarmist. However, informed choice depends on thorough information and weighing of the alternatives. Much remains to be learned about the effects of oral contraceptives, and studies are still contradictory.

Many informed women continue to choose the pill as their best contraceptive alternative. The physical risks associated with the pill are still lower than those of pregnancy, although a Gallup poll found that 84% of women incorrectly believe that the risks of the pill are greater than the risks of pregnancy and delivery (American College of Obstetricians and Gynecologists, 1985). However, since the pill can aggravate some medical problems, a woman with a history of certain conditions should use a different method of contraception. These conditions include blood clots, strokes, circulation problems, heart problems, jaundice, cancer of the breast or uterus, and undiagnosed genital bleeding. In addition, a woman who currently has a liver disease, who suspects or knows she is pregnant, who is nursing her child, or who is 40 years of age or older should not take the pill.

Finally, women who should weigh the potential risks most carefully and use the pill only under close medical supervision are those who have problems with migraine headaches, depression, high blood pressure, epilepsy, diabetes or prediabetes symptoms, asthma, and varicose veins.

Diaphragms

The **diaphragm**, shown in Figure 11.1(a), is a round, soft latex dome with a thin, flexible spring around the rim. It is inserted into the vagina along with a spermicidal contraceptive cream or jelly that comes in a tube. The diaphragm rim fits around the back of the cervix, and underneath and behind the pubic bone, as shown in Figure 11.1(b). Some women's cervixes are located farther back in the vagina, and others are closer to the opening. Therefore, diaphragms vary in size from 2 to 4 inches in diameter to fit each individual correctly. Diaphragms are also made with different kinds of springs: the coil spring, the flat spring, or the arcing spring. Some women find one style easier to insert and better fitting than another. For example, the arcing spring may stay in place better than a coil spring for a woman with reduced vaginal muscle tone.

How the Diaphragm Works.   The cervix lies within the dome of the diaphragm, which covers it. When the diaphragm is used with the cream or jelly, it provides a chemical as well as a mechanical barrier to prevent sperm from entering the cervix and uterus.

How to Use the Diaphragm.   The diaphragm must be fitted by a skilled practitioner. A size estimate is made during the pelvic exam; then different sizes and types are inserted until the best fit is found. It is very important for the examiner to thoroughly instruct the woman on how to insert and care for her diaphragm. Then the woman practices inserting it herself in the examination room until she is able to do so. The examiner makes a final check to see if she has correctly learned the insertion technique.

Figure 11.1(b) shows how the diaphragm is used. First, a tablespoon of the spermicidal cream or jelly (available at pharmacies without a prescription) is put into the cup of the diaphragm. Some of the spermicide should also be spread around the inside of the rim. The sides of the rim are then squeezed together with one hand, while the other hand opens the inner lips of the vulva. Some women prefer to use a plastic diaphragm introducer while others find this more difficult than manual insertion. The diaphragm is then pushed into the vagina, with the cream side facing upwards. The woman may be standing, lying, or squatting while she or her partner inserts the diaphragm.

After the diaphragm is inserted, it is important for the woman or her partner to feel it with the fingers to determine whether the dome covers the cervix. Occasionally the back rim lodges in front of the cervix, so that the diaphragm offers no

Figure 11.1

**Diaphragm and
Contraceptive
Cream or Jelly**
*(a) The dia-
phragm is made of
a soft latex dome
on a coil and is
used with contra-
ceptive cream or
jelly. (b) Insertion
and checking of
diaphragm.*

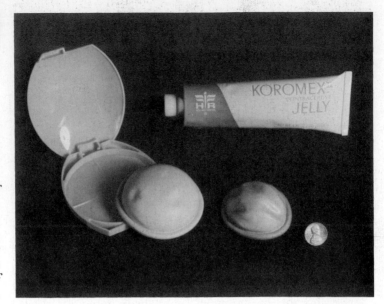

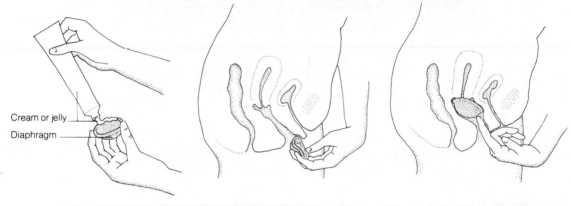

Cream or jelly
Diaphragm

Squeeze spermicide into
dome of diaphragm and
around the rim

Squeeze rim together;
insert jelly-side up

Check placement to make
certain cervix is covered

contraceptive protection. When the diaphragm is placed correctly, it rarely can be felt by the woman or her partner during intercourse.

Some sources state that the diaphragm can be inserted up to six hours prior to intercourse; others recommend no more than two hours prior without an additional application of spermicide. The shorter time span may afford better protection. The diaphragm can also be inserted just before intercourse. Some women prefer to insert the diaphragm ahead of time in privacy, while others share this experience with their partner. As one man explains:

I have had a traditional repulsion of "just-before" birth control devices such as con-doms and diaphragms. However, with my present partner the use of the diaphragm is part of sexual excitement for us. We usually become quite stimulated before reaching for the good old jelly and diaphragm, and then I continue with manual clitoral stimulation while she inserts the device. I have also learned to put it in while she continues to stimulate herself and me at the same time. Also, any leftover jelly works nicely as a lubricant. The pause between being ready for intercourse and actually doing it seems to heighten the whole thing. (Authors' files)

The diaphragm should remain in the vagina for at least six hours following intercourse to assure that the spermicide has killed all the sperm in the vaginal folds. It is important not to douche during this time. If intercourse occurs again before six hours elapse, the diaphragm can be left in place, but additional cream or jelly needs to be inserted with an applicator tube. Reusable plastic applicators can be purchased with the creams and jellies.

Several cases of toxic shock syndrome have been reported in association with diaphragm use. Therefore, a diaphragm should not be left in the vagina for more than 24 hours (Hatcher et al., 1986). To remove it, a finger is inserted into the vagina under the front rim of the diaphragm. Squatting or bearing down may make it easier to find the rim. After a gentle pull with one finger to break the air seal, it is easier to grasp the rim with two fingers and pull the diaphragm out. After removal the diaphragm should be washed with a mild soap and warm water. Then it should be carefully and thoroughly dried, dusted with cornstarch, and returned to its plastic case.

A well cared-for diaphragm can last for several years. It should remain soft, flexible, and free of defects. To make certain of this, the woman should check it periodically. She can detect tiny leaks by placing water in the dome or by holding it up to the light, stretching it slightly and checking for any defects. She should bring along her diaphragm when she has her yearly Pap smear so that its fit and condition can be evaluated. A woman may need a different diaphragm after a pregnancy (including an aborted pregnancy) or a weight loss or gain of 10 pounds or more.

A most important point in using the diaphragm is to have it available. It simply will not do a woman any good at home in a drawer when she is at the beach for the weekend. Depending on a woman's lifestyle, the best place for it may be in her purse, bedroom, bathroom—wherever is most convenient for her situation. Some women prefer to own two diaphragms to assure availability.

Shared Responsibility. As the earlier anecdote indicates, inserting the diaphragm can be a shared experience. A woman's partner can learn to insert the diaphragm in the examination room if the health care practitioner agrees, or later, from the woman herself. Checking to see if it is in correctly and helping remove it can also be a mutual responsibility. Both remembering to use the diaphragm and a commitment to do so are very important.

Potential Advantages of the Diaphragm. The recent resurgence of the diaphragm is most likely due to concern about pill and IUD side effects, coupled with reports of high rates of contraceptive effectiveness with diaphragm use. In studies where women were thoroughly instructed in the use and care of the diaphragm, its effectiveness was roughly comparable to that of the pill and the IUD. Another study of diaphragm effectiveness reported that 80% of the women who began using the diaphragm were still doing so at the end of one year (Lane et al., 1976). Most important, there are no potentially dangerous side effects comparable to those encountered when using pills and IUDs.

Through learning to use the diaphragm a woman may become more knowledgeable and comfortable with her body. She may also find it helpful in making decisions about relating sexually with others. For example:

> Since I've been using the diaphragm, I've moved more slowly into sexual relations. I want to discuss my method with a new partner before we have intercourse. When I'm feeling like I'm not comfortable enough to talk about birth control, I'm not ready to have intercourse. (Authors' files)

Some people think that there may be some additional positive side effects to proper use of the diaphragm. They speculate that some spermicidal jellies and creams may promote vaginal health and decrease the incidence of vaginal infections. There is also some evidence that certain contraceptive creams, jellies, and foams may help prevent gonorrhea and pelvic inflammatory disease (Hatcher et al., 1986).

Potential Disadvantages of the Diaphragm.   The diaphragm is not without disadvantages, however. Some people may find that it is inconvenient, that using it interrupts spontaneity, or that the cream or jelly is messy. The cream or jelly can also interfere with oral-genital sex. However, a couple can engage in oral-genital contact before inserting the diaphragm, or the woman's partner can focus stimulation on the clitoral rather than vaginal area. Occasionally women or their partners experience irritation from a particular cream or jelly. Usually switching to a different brand will take care of any difficulty. In rare instances a woman is allergic to the latex of the diaphragm. Using a plastic diaphragm can eliminate this problem.

Poor diaphragm fit may occasionally cause problems. Since diaphragms are fitted when a woman is not sexually aroused, they may not fit as well during arousal due to the vaginal expansion that occurs. The penis may then be placed between the diaphragm and cervix. This is most likely to happen during position changes, with reinsertion of the penis, and in the woman-above position. The cream or jelly will still provide some contraceptive protection if this occurs. If either partner feels the diaphragm during intercourse, she or he should check to see if it is correctly in place. Some women report bladder discomfort, urethral irritation, or recurrent cystitis from rim pressure. Using another diaphragm size or rim type may eliminate these difficulties (Gillespie, 1984; Hatcher et al., 1986). A few women with certain pelvic-structure problems, like marked loss of vaginal muscle tone and support, cannot use the diaphragm effectively.

Cervical Caps

The **cervical cap** is a thimble-shaped cup made of rubber or plastic (see Figure 11.2). The cap is like a miniature diaphragm, but it fits only over the cervix and can be left in place longer. Like the diaphragm, the cap comes in different sizes. Although it can

Figure 11.2
Cervical Caps

be used alone, it is usually recommended that a spermicide be used with the cap (Cappiello and Grainger-Harrison, 1981).

Different versions of the cervical cap have been used for centuries. In ancient Sumatra women molded opium to fit over their cervixes. In the Orient an oiled, silky paper called *musgami* was made into cup shapes to be used in the same manner. European women melted beeswax into cervical discs. In eighteenth-century Europe, Casanova promoted the idea of using a squeezed-out lemon half to cover the cervix. The modern cervical cap was developed in 1838 by a German gynecologist, who took a wax impression of each patient's cervix and made custom cervical caps out of rubber (Seaman and Seaman, 1978).

The cervical cap is widely used in Europe today, but is relatively unknown in the United States. The cap is not recognized by the FDA as a birth control method, and perhaps as a result, there has been little research done on it. Some writers believe that research and development of the cervical cap has lagged because it is not as profitable for drug companies as other contraceptive methods (Seaman and Seaman, 1978). However, some health clinics and physicians are distributing cervical caps, and in early 1981 the FDA began to study this method's contraceptive effectiveness (Cappiello and Grainger-Harrison, 1981).

How to Use the Cervical Cap.   The cervical cap comes in different sizes and must be individually fitted by a skilled practitioner. When a woman uses the cap, she or her partner fills it one- to two-thirds full of spermicide. The cap is inserted by folding its edges together and sliding it into the vagina along the vaginal floor. The cup is then pressed onto the cervix. The woman or her partner then sweeps a finger around the cap to see if the cervix is covered and depresses the dome of the cap to feel the cervix through the rubber. A woman can usually reach her cervix most easily if she is in a squatting or upright sitting position. The cap can be inserted up to six hours before intercourse. It should not be removed for at least six hours following intercourse, and douching should be avoided during this period. Pulling on one side of the rim will break the suction to permit easy removal of the cap from the vagina. After removal, the cap should be washed with warm water and soap and dried.

Shared Responsibility.   A woman's partner can learn to insert, remove, and care for the cervical cap. He can also help her to remember to use it.

Potential Advantages of the Cervical Cap.   A major advantage of the cervical cap is the lack of side effects. Another is its low cost. Women who cannot use the diaphragm because of pelvic structure problems or loss of vaginal muscle tone or support can often use this method. The cap is less expensive because it requires less spermicide.

Potential Disadvantages of the Cervical Cap.   A woman who has distortions of her cervix from cysts or lacerations is usually an unsuitable candidate for cervical cap use. Currently available caps will fit only 60%–75% of women (Cappiello and Grainger-Harrison, 1981). The cap is usually more difficult to learn to use than the diaphragm, and for some people it is uncomfortable to wear. There is some concern that wearing the cap for prolonged periods may cause problems by damaging the cervix or interrupting the normal discharge of secretions from the cervix, although there are no clear data on this matter. The cap may also become dislodged during intercourse, greatly reducing its contraceptive effectiveness (Johnson, 1984; Lehfeldt and Sivin, 1984). Currently, two major disadvantages of the cervical cap are the difficulty in obtaining one and the lack of extensive scientific research on the effectiveness of this method.

Vaginal Spermicides

There are several types of **vaginal spermicides**: foam, suppositories, the contraceptive sponge, and creams and jellies (see Figure 11.3). *Foam*, the most widely used, is a white substance resembling shaving cream. It comes in pressurized cans and has a plastic applicator. Foam is available in pharmacies without a prescription. (Feminine hygiene products, although often displayed along with various brands of foam, are *not* contraceptives.) *Vaginal suppositories* have an oval shape and contain the same spermicidal chemical found in foam. The *contraceptive sponge* is made of polyurethane and is impregnated with spermicide. It is shaped like a mushroom cap and fits in the upper vagina. Some *contraceptive creams and jellies* are made to be used without a diaphragm. However, they are not as effective as foam, and many health care practitioners recommend that they not be used without a diaphragm. Therefore, we will not discuss them in detail.

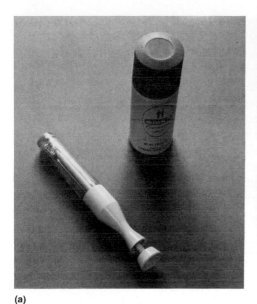

(a)

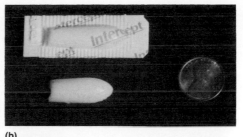

(b)

(c)

Figure 11.3
Vaginal
Spermicides
*Vaginal spermi-
cides are available
in pharmacies
without a prescrip-
tion. (a) Foam
and applicator.
(b) Suppositories.
(c) Sponge.*

How Spermicides Work.   Foam, suppositories, creams and jellies, and the sponge contain a *spermicide*, a chemical that kills sperm. When foam is inserted with the applicator, it rapidly covers the vaginal walls and the cervical os. By contrast, contraceptive vaginal suppositories take about 20 minutes to dissolve and cover the walls. One brand of suppositories, Encare, effervesces and creates a foam inside the vagina. Other brands melt. The sponge works by releasing spermicide, absorbing semen, and blocking the cervical opening.

How to Use Vaginal Spermicides.   Some brands of foam come with an applicator that can be filled ahead of time; other applicators are prefilled. For maximum effectiveness foam should be inserted into the vagina no more than a half hour before intercourse, and preferably as close to intercourse as possible. First, the can should be shaken well to mix the spermicide. Depending on the brand, the nozzle on the top of the can is either pressed or tilted against the applicator. The foam then enters the applicator, pushing the plunger upwards. (It is a good idea to have an extra can on hand in case one becomes empty.) To insert the foam, the woman first lies down. The vaginal lips can be opened with one hand and the applicator inserted with the other, in the same way that tampons are inserted (aiming towards the small of the back). Once the tip of the applicator is well inside the vagina, the plunger is pushed to deposit the foam next to the cervix, as shown in Figure 11.4(a). The foam quickly disperses to cover the vaginal walls. If intercourse is delayed beyond a half hour, another application should be inserted prior to coitus.

     Proper use of the spermicidal vaginal suppository is somewhat different from that of foam. The suppository must be inserted at least 20 minutes before intercourse to allow it to dissolve in the warmth and moisture of the vagina. It should be placed at the back of the vagina by the cervix rather than at the vaginal opening. The couple must either have intercourse within an hour of inserting the suppository or insert another 20 minutes before intercourse.

As with spermicides used with the diaphragm, another application of foam or another suppository is necessary before each further act of intercourse. If a woman douches, she needs to wait eight hours after intercourse to assure that the spermicide has killed the sperm. It is probably better to shower than to take a bath, to prevent the spermicide from being rinsed out of the vagina.

The sponge is moistened with a few drops of water, which activates the spermicide. It is then inserted high in the vagina, as shown in Figure 11.4(b). It can be kept in place for 24 hours for continuous protection (Sherris et al., 1984). The FDA recommends not leaving the sponge inserted for more than 30 hours (Centers for Disease Control, 1984a).

Figure 11.4

Insertion of Vaginal Spermicides
(a) Insertion of foam: The filled applicator is inserted into the vagina, and the foam is deposited at the back of the vaginal canal. (b) Insertion of sponge: The sponge is moistened with tap water and then inserted deep into the vagina.

Shared Responsibility. A partner can share in purchasing the spermicide or sponge, remembering to use it, and inserting it. Using condoms along with foam, suppositories, or the sponge, particularly during ovulation, will increase the overall contraceptive effectiveness.

Potential Advantages of Vaginal Spermicides. Since spermicides and contraceptive sponges are available in pharmacies, this method does not require a visit to a physician's office. They have no known dangerous side effects to the woman, and some couples welcome the additional lubrication spermicides provide. As with the diaphragm cream or jelly, spermicidal foam, suppositories and sponges may give some protection against vaginal infections, sexually transmitted diseases, and pelvic inflammatory disease (Austin et al., 1984). The suppository has the advantage of being small and convenient to use.

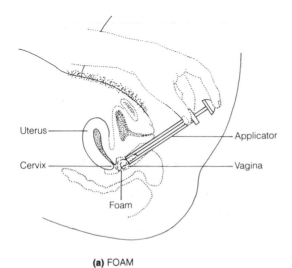

(a) FOAM

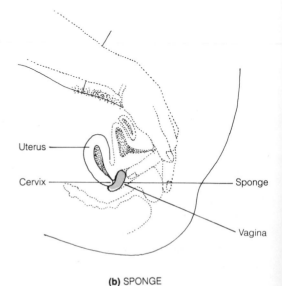

(b) SPONGE

Potential Disadvantages of Vaginal Spermicides. Occasionally a woman or her partner may report irritation of genital tissues from the foam, suppositories, or sponge. Changing brands will often alleviate this difficulty, but in some cases any brand causes discomfort. Some of the suppositories may not dissolve completely and therefore feel gritty. Some women or couples dislike the additional lubrication during intercourse or the postcoital discharge following intercourse. Because of the unpleasant taste, using vaginal spermicides may limit couples who engage in cunnilingus after intercourse. (A couple can still have oral sex before inserting the foam or suppositories.) These products may also have a soaplike scent that is disagreeable to some users. Also, some people feel that insertion of spermicides, even though the procedure takes only about 30 seconds, interrupts spontaneity. Some women and their partners report difficulty in removing the sponge.

Spermicides should not be used if a pregnancy is suspected, until research clears up the question of the effects of spermicides on the developing fetus (Hatcher et al., 1986).

Condoms

Condoms, also called "safes," prophylactics, and rubbers, are currently the only temporary method of birth control available for men. A condom is a sheath that fits over the erect penis and is made of thin surgical latex or sheep membrane. This approach to contraception has a long history. A penile sheath was used in Japan during the early 1500s, and in 1564 an Italian anatomist, Fallopius, described a penile sheath made of linen. Mass production of inexpensive modern condoms began after the development of vulcanized rubber in the 1840s (Zatuchni, 1984).

Condoms are available without prescription at pharmacies, from family planning clinics, by mail order, and in some areas in vending machines. Recent changes in the laws of some states have made condoms more accessible by placing them on drugstore shelves rather than behind the counter, much to the relief of some customers:

> The rubber-buying scene of the movie *Summer of '42* was hilariously similar to the first time I bought rubbers in our local small pharmacy: waiting until no one else was in the store, trying to look casual, and really not knowing how to ask for them. (Authors' files)

Most condoms are packaged—rolled up and wrapped in foil or plastic—and come lubricated or nonlubricated. There is less chance of the condom breaking if it is lubricated, and some men report less reduction of penile sensation during intercourse with lubricated condoms. The sheep membrane, natural skin condoms are more expensive but often interfere less with sensation than do the latex ones. Some condoms have a small nipple on the end, called a reservoir tip, and others have a contoured shape or textured surface (see Figure 11.5). Some are also made with spermicide on their inner and outer surfaces. Condoms have an average shelf life of about five years, although not all packages are dated. They should not be stored in hot places like the glove compartment of a car or a back pocket, because the heat can deteriorate the latex.

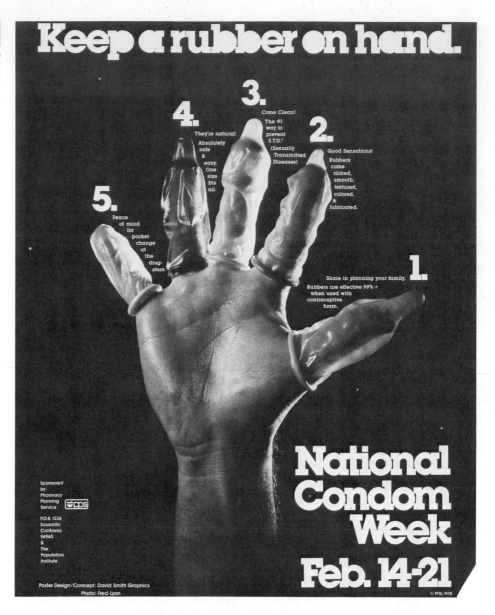

Keep a rubber on hand.

4. They're natural! Absolutely safe & easy. One size fits all.

3. Come Clean! The #1 way to prevent S.T.D.* (Sexually Transmitted Diseases)

2. Good Sensations! Rubbers come ribbed, smooth, textured, colored, & lubricated.

5. Peace of mind for pocket change at the drug-store.

1. Share in planning your family. Rubbers are effective 99%+ when used with contraceptive foam.

National Condom Week Feb. 14-21

Sponsored by Pharmacy Planning Service ⊟pps

P.O.B. 1336 Sausalito California 94965 & The Population Institute

Poster Design/Concept: David Smith Graphics
Photo: Fred Lyon

© PPSI, 1978

How the Condom Works. When a condom is used properly, both the ejaculate and the fluid from Cowper's glands secretions are contained within the tip. Therefore, the sperm are inside the condom rather than the vagina.

How to Use the Condom. Most condoms are packaged rolled up. Correct use includes unrolling the condom over the erect penis before any contact between the penis and the vulva occurs. Sperm in the Cowper's gland secretions or in the ejaculate can travel from outside the labia to inside of the vagina. For maximum comfort and

(a)

(b)

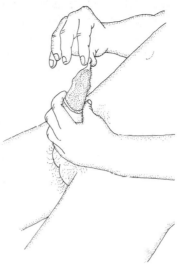

The end of a plain-end condom needs to be twisted as it is rolled onto the penis in order to leave space at the tip.

(c)

Figure 11.5

Condoms
(a) Unrolled condom with plain end. (b) Unrolled condom with reservoir tip. (c) Correct use of a plain-end condom.

sensation an uncircumcized man can retract the foreskin before rolling the condom over the penis. With plain-ended condoms (without the reservoir tip) the end needs to be twisted before rolling the condom down over the penis as shown in Figure 11.6(c). This leaves some room at the end for the ejaculate and reduces the chances of the condom breaking. If a condom breaks or slips off, contraceptive foam, cream, or jelly should be inserted into the vagina immediately.

If the condom is nonlubricated, some vaginal secretion, saliva, or K-Y jelly needs to be put on the outside of the condom before insertion of the penis into the vagina. After ejaculation, due to detumescence of the penis, it is important to hold the condom at the base of the penis before withdrawing it from the vagina. Otherwise it may slip off and spill semen inside the vagina:

> The first time I used a rubber, I relaxed inside her after I came, holding her for a while. Then I withdrew, leaving the rubber behind. My first thought was "Oh, no, it's dissolved." I reached inside her vagina and found the rubber. We used some foam right away but were nervous until her next period started. (Authors' files)

Condoms are best disposed of in the garbage rather than in the toilet, because they have been known to clog plumbing.

Shared Responsibility. The woman can share the responsibility for this method of birth control by helping pay for the condoms, remembering to use them, putting them on, or holding on to the base after ejaculation before her partner withdraws. Women who want their prospective partners to use condoms may wish to carry them, since there is no guarantee that the man will be prepared.

Potential Advantages of Condoms. Condoms are available without prescription. There are no harmful side effects associated with their use. If condoms are not the primary method of birth control, they are useful as a backup. Some men prefer the slightly lessened sensation they experience with condoms, because they find that the duration of intercourse before ejaculation is prolonged. Since the semen is contained inside the condom, some women appreciate the tidiness:

> I really like the juiciness of sex when I can bathe afterwards, but when we go camping and don't have a stream or shower handy, my husband uses condoms so it's not as messy. (Authors' files)

Condoms provide protection from contracting and spreading sexually transmitted diseases and vaginal infections. For this reason, venereal disease experts advocate their use by anyone who has coitus or anal intercourse with more than one partner, including heterosexual men and women and homosexual men.

Potential Disadvantages of Condoms. Unless putting on the condom is incorporated as part of sexual interaction, it can interrupt spontaneity. Some men see reduced penile sensitivity as a disadvantage. Condoms can break or slip off, but this is not common. Also, a few people are allergic to rubber condoms.

Intrauterine Devices

Intrauterine devices, commonly referred to as **IUDs**, are small plastic objects that are inserted into the uterus through the vaginal canal and cervical os. Although IUDs did not become widely available until the 1960s, people have used the technique of inserting an object into the uterus to prevent pregnancy for a long time. For example, Middle Eastern camel drivers would insert a smooth stone into their female camels' uteri so the camels would not become pregnant during desert crossings. Several types of IUDs were available in this country during the 1960s and 1970s, but as of spring 1986 the only IUD distributed on the U.S. market was the Progestasert T (see Figure 11.6). All other companies had removed their IUDs from the market because of numerous lawsuits charging that the devices caused infections, infertility, or death from infection when pregnancy occurred with an IUD in place. The Progestasert T has slow-releasing progesterone embedded in the plastic. It has fine plastic threads attached to it, cut to hang slightly out of the cervix into the vagina.

How the IUD Works. Exactly how an IUD works has not been scientifically established. The most widely held theory suggests that the uterine lining is slightly irritated and inflamed due to the presence of this foreign object, and that as a result the fertilized ovum does not implant. The IUD also alters the delicate timing of ovum transport through the tubes. In addition, the progesterone in Progestasert T may have some of the contraceptive effects of the progestin-only birth control pill.

How to Use the IUD. The IUD is inserted by a trained health care professional using sterile instruments. Most IUDs come with an inserter. The inserter and IUD are introduced through the os and into the uterus; the inserter is then withdrawn,

Figure 11.6

**The Progestasert
T Intrauterine
Device**

leaving the IUD in place. A woman should be screened for gonorrhea before she has an IUD inserted, since the procedure may cause the bacteria to be pushed farther into the uterus. The Progestasert T needs to be replaced yearly, because the progesterone gradually loses its effectiveness. IUDs should be removed when a woman reaches menopause and stops menstruating (Hatcher et al., 1986).

Shared Responsibility.   A backup method such as foam, condoms, or the diaphragm is recommended for the first one to three months after an IUD has been inserted. Some women and their partners choose to continue using a backup method each month during the fertile midcycle.

While a woman is using an IUD, she or her partner needs to check each month after her menstrual period to see that the string is the same length as when the device was inserted. To do this, one of them reaches into the vagina with a finger and finds the cervix. If the cervix is far back in the vagina and difficult to reach, the woman can squat or bear down to make it more accessible. The string should be felt in the middle of the cervix, protruding out of the small indentation in the center. Occasionally it curls up in the os and cannot be felt, but any time a woman or her partner cannot find it, she needs to check with her health care specialist. She should also seek attention if the string seems longer or the plastic protrudes out of the os. This probably means that the IUD is not correctly placed.

Potential Advantages of the IUD.   The primary advantage of the IUD is that it provides a woman with contraceptive protection with little inconvenience beyond the monthly checking of the string. In one woman's words:

> The IUD insertion was uncomfortable to me and my periods are now longer, but all I have to do is to check the IUD string once a month instead of taking a pill every day or using the diaphragm each time. (Authors' files)

The IUD allows uninterrupted sexual interaction. Beyond the initial cost for the exam and insertion, there are no further supplies to be purchased. Although an IUD is usually not inserted until two to three months after childbirth, it does not interfere with nursing once it is in place. Some women who experience initial discomfort after the insertion find that this decreases in a month or two. The ideal candidate for an IUD is a woman who has given birth; has no history of pelvic inflammatory disease, has normal menstrual cycles, with mild or moderate menstrual flow and no dysmenorrhea; is willing to check the string; has easy access to medical care; and is in a monogamous relationship, reducing her chance of exposure to sexually transmitted diseases (Tyrer, 1983).

Potential Disadvantages of the IUD. Discomfort, cramping, bleeding, or pain may occur during insertion. The discomfort or bleeding sometimes continues for a few days and occasionally much longer. The IUDs that have been withdrawn from the market typically caused increased menstrual bleeding, but the Progestasert T usually diminishes bleeding by half of the regular menstrual flow (Hatcher et al., 1986).

From 5% to 20% of users will expel their IUD within the first year following insertion (Hatcher et al., 1986). The uterus reacts to the IUD as a foreign body, contracting and sometimes pushing it out. This is most likely to occur during menstruation, so a woman needs to check her tampons or sanitary napkins before disposing of them. Also, her partner might feel the IUD protruding out of the cervix during intercourse. It is wise to check the string several times a month at first, because if the IUD is incorrectly positioned in the uterus or is expelled, the woman will not be protected against an undesired pregnancy.

As discussed in Chapter 4, the multidirectional muscles of the uterus are interwoven. In rare cases, the IUD breaks through the uterine wall. This perforation can partially extend through the wall, or the IUD can slip completely through the uterus into the abdominal cavity. When this occurs, surgery may be necessary to remove it. Occasionally (although rarely) a woman may require a hysterectomy as a result of this type of complication. In a small number of cases the IUD perforates both the uterus and the bladder (Zakin, 1984). If an IUD string seems to become shorter, this may be an indication that the IUD is perforating, and the woman should seek immediate medical attention.

Another significant disadvantage associated with the IUD is that it increases a woman's chances of pelvic inflammatory disease, or PID (McCarthy et al., 1984). PID can occur if bacteria are introduced into the sterile environment of the uterus during insertion. The string of the IUD has also been suspected of providing an entryway for bacteria. An IUD is likely to aggravate a gonorrhea infection and make treatment more difficult. Most physicians recommend removal of an IUD when a woman is being treated for a uterine infection.

One of the complications associated with PID is partial or complete blockage of the fallopian tubes and a resultant increased chance of ectopic pregnancy. It is believed that the overall rate of ectopic pregnancies is higher for women who use the IUD than for those who do not (Hatcher et al., 1986). Fallopian tube problems resulting from IUD use can also be a contributing factor in infertility (Daling et al., 1984).

Other problems may occur if a woman becomes pregnant with an IUD in place. Her chances of a miscarriage in the first six months of pregnancy are twice as high as those of a woman who is using other methods or no contraception when she conceives (Hatcher et al., 1986). Because of some reports of deaths of pregnant IUD users in 1974, removal of the IUD when a woman becomes pregnant is now recommended. It is thought that as the uterus enlarges during pregnancy, the string in

Table 11.3 Remember "PAINS" for the IUD
Symptoms of possible serious problems with the IUD, represented by their initials.

Initial	Symptom
P	Period late, no period
A	Abdominal pain
I	Increased temperature, fever, chills
N	Nasty discharge, foul discharge
S	Spotting, bleeding, heavy periods, clots

Source: Adapted from Hatcher et al., 1986.

the vagina is drawn into the uterus and carries bacteria with it. The string may also act as a wick for bacteria, facilitating the spread of any infectious organisms. Due to the increased blood flow in the tissues of the uterus during pregnancy, such an infection travels rapidly through the woman's bloodstream and may cause death within 24 to 48 hours. If an IUD is removed during the first three months of pregnancy, the risk of a subsequent miscarriage is only slightly higher than for nonusers of IUDs (Foreman et al., 1981).

Finally, a number of previous or current conditions seem to be related to heightened risks in using an IUD. A woman should consult a health-care practitioner if any of these conditions apply to her: a history of ectopic pregnancy, active PID or gonorrhea; current or suspected pregnancy; or current conditions such as endometriosis, anemia, heavy menstrual flow or cramping, a very small or malformed uterus, heart disease, or the use of anticoagulants.

Serious problems associated with the IUD can be summarized by the acronym PAINS (Table 11.3). Besides the IUD and the pill, a number of other methods are available that may have fewer potential complications for some women. We will look at these in the paragraphs that follow.

Methods Based on the Menstrual Cycle

The birth control methods we have already discussed require use of pills or devices. Some of these methods have side effects in some users, and there may be health risks in the use of the pill and the IUD. Other methods that we have looked at—condoms, foam, the diaphragm—have fewer side effects, but they require that the couple use them each time they have intercourse.

Many couples are interested in a birth control method that has no side effects, is inexpensive, and does not interrupt spontaneity during sexual interaction. In the next paragraphs we will look at some methods of birth control based on the menstrual cycle, which may answer some of these couples' needs. These methods are sometimes referred to as *natural family planning*, or *fertility awareness* methods. A fertile woman's body reveals subtle and overt signs of cyclic fertility that can be used both to help prevent and to plan conception. The three methods—mucus, calendar, and basal body temperature—are most effective when used together.

Mucus Method.   The **mucus method**, also called the *ovulation method*, is based on the cyclic changes of the cervical mucus. (See color plates 1 and 2 in Chapter 12.) These natural changes, if carefully observed, will reveal periods of fertility in a woman's cycle. To use this method a woman learns to "read" the amounts and textures of vaginal secretions and to maintain a daily chart of the changes. A woman reads her mucus by wiping herself every time she goes to the toilet and observing the secretions on the tissue. After menstruation there are usually some "dry days" when there is no vaginal discharge on the vulva. When a yellow or white sticky discharge begins, the fertile time is considered to have started, and unprotected coitus should be avoided. (Some ovulation method teachers say that abstinence from intercourse is preferable.) Several days later the ovulatory mucus appears. It is clear, stringy, and stretchy in consistency, similar to egg white. A drop of this mucus will stretch between an open thumb and forefinger. A vaginal feeling of wetness and lubrication accompanies this discharge, which has a chemical balance and texture that facilitate the entry of sperm into the uterus. Four days after the ovulatory mucus begins and a cloudy discharge resumes, it is considered safe to resume unprotected intercourse. The fertile period usually totals 9 to 15 days out of each cycle. The temperature method, discussed later in this section, is often combined with the mucus method to better estimate the time of ovulation.

In many cities, classes in this method are offered at a hospital or clinic. Each woman's mucus patterns may vary, and a class is the best way to learn to interpret the changes.

The Calendar Method.   With the **calendar method**, also called the *rhythm method*, a woman estimates the calendar time during her cycle when she is ovulating and fertile. To do this she keeps a chart, preferably for one year, of the length of her cycles. (She cannot be using oral contraceptives during this time, for they impose a cycle that may not be the same as her own.) The first day of menstruation is counted as day number one. The woman counts the number of days of her cycle, the last day being the one before the onset of menstruation. To determine the high-risk days, on which she should avoid unprotected coitus, she subtracts 18 from the number of days of her shortest cycle. For example, if her shortest cycle was 26 days, day number 8 would be the first high-risk day. To estimate when nonprotected coitus could resume, she subtracts 10 from the number of days in her longest cycle. For example, if her longest cycle is 32 days, she would be able to resume intercourse on day 22. In this fashion, she avoids coitus without birth control protection during the midcycle ovulation. The pattern for this woman would be either to abstain from coitus or to use another method from days 8 through 22. Forms of lovemaking other than intercourse can continue during the high-risk days.

The Basal Body Temperature Method.   Another way of estimating high-fertility days is through temperature. Immediately prior to ovulation, the **basal body temperature** (BBT, the body temperature in the resting state upon waking in the morning) drops slightly. After ovulation, the corpus luteum releases more progesterone, which causes the body temperature to rise slightly ($0.2°$–$0.6°F$). Since these temperature changes (shown in Figure 11.7) are slight, a thermometer with easy-to-read gradations must be used. An electronic device (Rite Time) has been developed for measuring BBT and appears to be effective in indicating infertile and fertile times in the cycle (Royston et al., 1984).

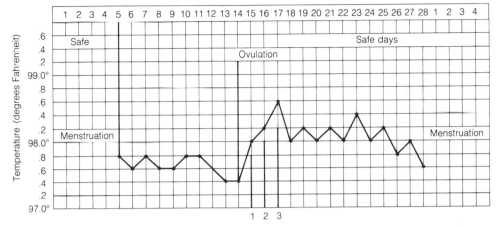

Figure 11.7

Basal Body Temperature During a Model Menstrual Cycle

Shared Responsibility. The man can share in these methods by learning to recognize the mucus changes, helping to chart menstrual cycles, and reminding his partner to take morning temperatures. If the couple does not abstain from coitus during the fertile days, he can participate in the use of a barrier method. (However, it is usually recommended that the couple not use foam or diaphragms with the mucus method, because they interfere with interpreting the mucus.) For those who abstain from coitus, mutual cooperation and sexual experimentation can greatly enhance the use of these methods.

Potential Advantages of Menstrual Cycle Based Methods. Major advantages of methods based on the menstrual cycle are that there are no side effects and that they are free or very inexpensive. Some women and their partners report increased comfort and appreciation of their bodies' cycles and processes when they use these methods. If they choose abstinence from penile-vaginal intercourse during the fertile days, this interval can provide time and motivation for noncoital sexual relating. Knowledge of cyclic changes can also help a couple to plan a pregnancy. Also, these methods are acceptable to some religious groups that oppose other contraceptive methods.

Potential Disadvantages of Menstrual Cycle Based Methods. Methods based on the menstrual cycle may restrict spontaneity of intercourse and ejaculation during fertile times. Furthermore, learning to accurately detect the mucus and temperature changes involves practice, and with all of these methods a couple must keep accurate records for several cycles before beginning to rely on them for contraception. Considerable commitment is essential to maintain daily observation and charting. These methods are more difficult for women who have irregular cycles, and some women are unable to see mucus and temperature patterns clearly. Also, vaginal infections, semen, and contraceptive foams, jellies, and creams make it more difficult to accurately interpret mucus.

    While temperature changes are often good indicators of ovulation, this method is fallible. Slight temperature variations can result from many conditions— a low-grade infection or cold, unrestful sleep, and so forth. Also, because sperm can remain alive in the fallopian tubes for up to 72 hours, the preovulation temperature drop does not occur far enough ahead of time to safely avoid coitus. Although the temperature method is more effective in preventing an undesired pregnancy than no method, it is quite unreliable.

Even after careful arithmetic, the calendar method is very unreliable. Ovulation usually occurs about 14 days before the onset of menstruation; however, even with a woman who ordinarily has regular cycles, the timing of ovulation and menstruation may vary due to factors such as illness, fatigue, or excitement. For a woman who routinely or periodically has irregular cycles, the calendar method is even less safe and requires longer abstention from coitus.

Present research indicates that methods based on the menstrual cycle are considerably less effective than most others (Hatcher et al., 1986). A 1978 World Health Organization survey concluded that "failure to implement the abstinence required . . . renders the method relatively ineffective in general use for preventing pregnancy" (World Health Organization, 1978).

Other Methods

There are other contraceptive methods that are less commonly used than the ones we have been discussing. We will mention some of them here, partly because they are used both as primary birth control methods and as backups for other methods, and partly because people may have misconceptions about their effectiveness. We will discuss nursing, withdrawal, and douching as methods of birth control.

Nursing.   Nursing a baby delays the return to fertility after childbirth; however, it is not a reliable method of birth control, because there is no way of knowing when ovulation will resume. Amenorrhea (lack of menstruation) usually occurs during nursing, but it is not a reliable indication of inability to conceive. Nearly 80% of breast-feeding women ovulate before their first menstrual period. The longer a woman breast-feeds, the more likely it is that ovulation will occur (Hatcher et al., 1986).

Other Times, Other Places

Worldwide Contraceptive Use in 1980

Method	Millions of Couples	Method	Millions of Couples
Sterilization	80	Condoms	40
Female	45	IUD	35
Male	35	Vaginal barrier/spermicides	25
Abortion	55		
Birth control pills	44	Withdrawal/rhythm	Unknown but extensive

Source: Zatuchni, 1983.

Withdrawal.   The practice of the man removing his penis from the vagina just before he ejaculates is known as *withdrawal*. The oft-unfulfilled hope is that there will be no sperm present to fertilize an ovum. However, withdrawal is not very effective. It may be difficult for the man to judge exactly when he must withdraw. His tendency is likely to be to remain inside the vagina as long as possible, and this may be too long. Both partners may experience pleasure-destroying anxiety about whether he will withdraw in time. Furthermore, even withdrawal before ejaculation is not insurance against pregnancy. The pre-ejaculatory Cowper's gland secretions may contain sperm that can fertilize the egg; and if sperm are deposited on the labia after withdrawal, they can swim into the vagina.

Douching.   *Douching* after intercourse is very ineffective as a method of birth control. After ejaculation, some of the sperm are inside the uterus in a matter of minutes. The movement of the water from douching may actually help sperm reach the opening of the cervix. Furthermore, frequent douching can irritate vaginal tissues.

Postcoital Contraception

Women or couples may seek some kind of postcoital contraception following unprotected midcycle intercourse. The risk of pregnancy from unprotected midcycle intercourse is up to 17% (Hatcher et al., 1986). For contraception after intercourse, administration of high levels of hormones and insertion of an IUD are the methods most commonly used.

Morning-After Pills.   Recent studies show that taking Ovral, a brand of birth control pills, within 72 hours following unprotected midcycle intercourse has been effective in preventing pregnancy. High doses of estrogens or progestins are also given as "morning-after" contraceptives. These hormone treatments are presumed to work by affecting the uterine lining so that the developing embryo cannot implant in it. Nausea or vomiting are potential side effects of morning-after pills. Long-term health effects on the woman or the fetus are unknown, and cancer in sons and daughters of women who take morning-after pills but continue the pregnancy has not been ruled out. If a woman uses any kind of morning-after pill, she should be aware of and watch for pill-related side effects (Hatcher et al., 1986).

Morning-After IUD Insertion.   Inserting an IUD within 24 hours following unprotected midcycle intercourse can prevent pregnancy. IUDs are believed to work by preventing implantation of the fertilized ovum, and they can be kept as an ongoing method. An IUD should not be used as morning-after protection if there has been a high risk of exposure to a sexually transmitted disease.

Shared Responsibility.   The partner can help with postcoital contraception in several ways. He can be aware of the options and risks of the various methods or be willing to help find the necessary information. He can be supportive and encourage the woman to obtain immediate medical advice. He can also help in planning future before-the-fact contraceptive protection for his partner and himself.

Sterilization

One other method of contraception has become common in recent years, due to improved surgical techniques and increasing societal acceptance. *Sterilization* is the most effective method of birth control except abstinence from coitus, and its safety and permanence appeal to many who want no more children or prefer to remain childless. Sterilization is the leading method of birth control in the United States. Although some research is being conducted on ways of reversing sterilization, at present the procedures involve complicated surgery and their effectiveness is not guaranteed. Therefore, sterilization is recommended only to those who desire a permanent method of birth control. Since sterilization is best considered permanent, a person should carefully explore his or her situation and feelings before deciding on the procedure. Questions to consider include: Are there any circumstances under which I would want (more) children (for example, if my child dies, or if I begin a new relationship)? Is my sense of masculinity or femininity tied to my fertility? What are my alternatives to sterilization? In the following paragraphs we will look at the procedures for sterilization of females and males.

Female Sterilization

In recent years female sterilization has become a relatively safe, simple, and inexpensive procedure. Sterilization can be accomplished by a variety of techniques that use small incisions and either local or general anesthesia.

Tubal sterilization can be done in several ways. A *minilaparotomy* involves a small abdominal incision. Each fallopian tube is gently pulled to this incision; then it is cut and tied, or clips or rings are applied. The tubes are then allowed to slip back into place within the abdomen (Liskin et al., 1985). Another procedure, *laparoscopy*, is shown in Figure 11.8. One or two small incisions are made in the abdomen, usually at the navel and slightly below the pubic hair line. A narrow, lighted viewing instrument called a laparoscope is inserted into the abdomen to locate the fallopian tubes. The tubes are then tied off, cut, or cauterized to block passage of sperm. Other methods have also been developed to block the tubes. A band or a clip is sometimes applied to a tube instead of removing a segment (Brenner, 1981; Penfield, 1981). The ligated (cut) or blocked tubes prevent the sperm and egg from meeting in the tube, thus preventing pregnancy. The incisions are generally so small that bandaids rather than stitches are used after surgery. Sometimes the incision is made through the back of the vaginal wall, and the procedure is called a *culpotomy*.

Sterilization acts only as a roadblock in the tubes. It does not further affect a woman's reproductive and sexual system. Until menopause, her ovaries continue to release their eggs. The released egg simply degenerates, as do millions of other cells daily, and it is carried away by the circulatory system. The woman's hormone levels remain the same, and the timing of menopause will not be altered. Her sexuality will not be physiologically changed, but she may find that her interest and arousal increase because she no longer is concerned with pregnancy or birth control methods. Most of the 208 Scandinavian women in one study reported an improvement in their sex lives and in their marriages after tubal sterilization (Børdahl, 1984).

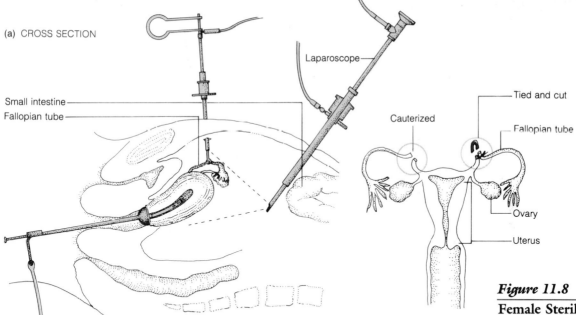

(a) CROSS SECTION

Laparoscope

Small intestine

Fallopian tube

Cauterized

Tied and cut

Fallopian tube

Ovary

Uterus

(b) FRONT VIEW

Figure 11.8

**Female Steriliza-
tion by Laparo-
scopic Ligation**
*(a) Cross section:
The tubes are
located by the lapa-
roscope and cut,
tied, or cauterized
through a second
incision. (b) Front
view: The tubes
after ligation.*

Following a tubal ligation, a woman should usually wait to resume normal activities for two to three days, or until she feels comfortable doing so. She should avoid strenuous lifting for about a week. She can resume sexual intercourse when it is comfortable.

Some discomfort or complications can occur from female sterilization. A woman may experience some pain at the site of the incision, and if the tubes are sealed by burning, other tissue in the pelvic cavity may be accidently burned. Postsurgical bleeding is also a possible complication. To minimize the possibility of complications, it is important for a woman to choose a doctor who is experienced in sterilization procedures.

Surgical reversal of female sterilization is sometimes successful. Rates of post-surgery pregnancy vary from about 50% to 70% (Liskin et al., 1985). One researcher found that women were most likely to have successful reversal if the previous sterilization procedure had removed or blocked only a small portion of the tube on the end close to the uterus (Silber and Cohen, 1984).

Male Sterilization

In general, data indicates that male sterilization is safer, considerably less expensive, and as effective as female sterilization (Smith et al., 1985). **Vasectomy** is a minor surgical procedure that involves cutting and tying the vas deferens, the two sperm-

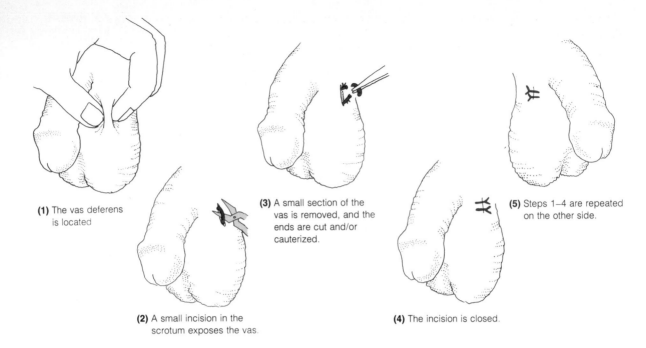

(1) The vas deferens is located

(2) A small incision in the scrotum exposes the vas.

(3) A small section of the vas is removed, and the ends are cut and/or cauterized.

(4) The incision is closed.

(5) Steps 1–4 are repeated on the other side.

Figure 11.9
Male Sterilization by Vasectomy

carrying ducts (see Figure 11.9). The operation is typically performed in a physician's office. Under a local anesthetic, a small incision is made in the scrotal sac, well above the testicle. The vas is lifted out and a small segment is removed. The free ends are tied off, clipped, or cauterized to prevent rejoining. After the procedure is repeated on the opposite side, the incisions are closed and the operation is completed, usually in less than 20 minutes.

Vasectomy prevents sperm produced in the testes from entering the semen produced by the internal reproductive organs (see Chapter 5). However, since a significant number of sperm are stored beyond the site of the incision, a man remains fertile for some time after the operation. Studies have shown that sperm may be present in the first 10 to 20 postoperative ejaculations, or for up to several months (Sivanesaratham, 1985). Therefore, effective alternative methods of birth control should be employed until semen analysis reveals no sperm present in the seminal fluid. Many physicians recommend that a vasectomized man have two consecutive negative evaluations before engaging in unprotected intercourse. Generally these checks occur six to eight weeks after the operation. In rare cases the two free ends of the severed vas grow back together (this is called **recanalization**), and once in a very great while a man will be found who has more than one vas on one or both sides.

Unlike castration, vasectomy does not alter testicular production of male sex hormones or absorption of the hormones into the bloodstream. A vasectomized man will also continue to produce sperm that are absorbed and eliminated by his body. His ejaculations will contain almost as much semen after the operation as before, since sperm constitute less than 5% of the total ejaculate. The characteristic odor and consistency of the semen will also remain the same.

Most men report that vasectomy does not affect their sexual functioning. Some report improvements, often due to greater spontaneity of sexual expression and less fear of impregnating their partners. A few report a reduction in sexual desire, which may be related to concerns about their continued masculinity.

At present there are no known physical side effects of vasectomy that compromise its value as a permanent method of contraception. There may be some short-term postoperative problems, such as swelling, inflammation, or bruising in the region of the surgery (Massey et al., 1984; Philip et al., 1984).

Some men request a **vasovasectomy**, a reversal of a vasectomy. Approximately 80% of vasovasectomies are done for men in a second marriage following divorce (Fallon et al., 1981). With selected patients and experienced microsurgeons, the chances of reconnecting the vas have increased (Hatcher et al., 1984). The shorter the interval between vasectomy and vasovasectomy, the better the outcome (Cos et al., 1983). However, the major problem complicating vasovasectomy is reduced fertility following reconnection. After vasovasectomy many men have low sperm counts, reduced sperm motility, or both. Another factor in reduced postvasovasectomy fertility may be the antisperm antibodies that develop in some vasectomized men (Smith and Paulson, 1980). The best measure of vasovasectomy success is subsequent pregnancy; various studies report a pregnancy rate of 35% to 82% using current vasovasectomy techniques (Martin, 1981; Owen and Kapila, 1984).

New Directions in Contraception

The spectrum of choices available for contraception has widened markedly in the past few decades. Several overall trends emerge. First, options continue to increase, as older methods change and new methods are developed. Second, there is increased concern regarding the effects of prolonged use of contraception on health and fertility as women delay childbearing. The trend in hormonal contraceptives is toward "less is better"; we now have lower dose oral contraceptives, injectible preparations, and subcutaneous capsules. Finally, user information and education is increasingly emphasized by professionals in the contraceptive field (Hatcher et al., 1986). As we have seen in this chapter, however, there are still potential health hazards and inconveniences associated with available methods. A great deal of research is being done to improve the safety, reliability, and convenience of birth control. We will look at some projected improvements for both men and women.

New Directions for Men

Presently, male contraception is limited to condoms, vasectomy, and the highly unreliable withdrawal method. However, there are some research efforts currently underway that suggest other methods may be available in the future. These efforts have concentrated on the development of a male pill that would work by inhibiting sperm production, motility, or maturation (Linde et al., 1981).

Some years ago it was shown that the conventional estrogen-progesterone female birth control pill will induce temporary sterility in men by curtailing sperm production. This effect was presumed to result from suppression of pituitary gonadotropins, the same mechanism by which the pill induces temporary sterility in women. Unfortunately, men often reported markedly reduced sex interest while taking the pill, a fact that seriously limited its practicality. The idea of giving men a contraceptive pill that will cause modified hormone levels still holds some promise, and research with various substances is under way (Nieschlag et al., 1981).

A gonadotropin-releasing hormone inhibitor (LHRH agonist) is currently under study as a male contraceptive. LHRH agonist has been shown to reduce the number and motility of sperm in men who received daily injections of the substance. Testosterone levels also dropped, and inability to achieve an erection occurred in more than half of the men in the study. This side effect disappeared after treatment stopped. Further research is being done to see whether testosterone combined with LHRH agonist could be effective in maintaining sexual functioning while producing temporary infertility (Linde et al., 1981).

Another substance under research as a male contraceptive is *gossypol*, a compound derived from the seeds, stems, or roots of cotton plants. Gossypol was first identified as an antifertility agent in China. Investigators found that there was an extremely low birthrate in an area where the local people used cottonseed oil for cooking. Clinical trials in China began in 1972, and more than 10,000 men have been studied. Among the first 400 men who received the drug for six months to four years, gossypol was reported to be 99.89% effective. Gossypol apparently inhibits enzyme activity necessary for sperm production and reduces sperm count dramatically, without affecting sex hormone levels. Some of the side effects reported included transient weakness, an increase or decrease in appetite, gastrointestinal disturbances, and a small incidence of decreased sexual interest and functioning (Nieschlag et al., 1981). Although there have been several births of healthy babies from wives of men who stopped taking gossypol (Maugh, 1981), recovery of complete sperm counts did not occur in 25% of the 2000 men who were followed up after stopping (Nieschlag et al., 1981). A great deal of further research is needed to determine the safety of gossypol as a contraceptive agent (Liskin et al., 1983).

Many scientists are concerned about the potential long-range effects of hormone-based contraceptives for males. One concern is the possibility that complications associated with the female pill may also occur in men. Furthermore, it is feared that the hormones might produce genetic damage, and that fertilization by any sperm that might still be produced could result in fetal abnormalities.

Several researchers are considering the possibility of developing a vaccine to immunize a man against his own sperm. The idea is to introduce a substance into the male system that would induce him to develop antibodies against his sperm cells. There has even been some effort to develop an antisperm vaccine for women. However, there are still some unresolved problems with this approach, including possible genetic damage and unhealthy reactions of body tissue to the vaccine.

New Directions for Women

An array of contraceptive methods for women is currently under experimentation. All of the hormonal methods have potential side effects similar to those of the pill, but these vary with the manner of administration. Injections of progesterone, given every one to three months, are used in many countries (Garza-Florez et al., 1984; Saxena, 1984). Also, a time release capsule containing progesterone embedded in a woman's arm or leg can remain effective for months or years (Diaz et al., 1984). The capsule can be removed if a woman desires a pregnancy before the capsule loses its effectiveness. There is still the possibility of infertility after using either of these methods. Another recently developed female contraceptive device is the "vaginal ring," which is something like a diaphragm. Each month a new ring is inserted, and it slowly releases low doses of estrogen and progesterone, or progesterone alone (Liskin and Quillin, 1983). The hormone is absorbed into the bloodstream through the vaginal mucosa.

As mentioned earlier, another possibility is a vaccination to develop a woman's immunity to her partner's sperm. This method is still in the experimental stages, and effective reversal of the immunity has not yet been firmly established. The use of a luteinizing hormone–releasing factor inhibitor (LRF agonist) as a method of contraception is also under study. Injections of LRF agonist for three successive days, beginning with the first day of menstruation, has been shown to induce a chain of hormonal events that results in inadequate maturation of the ovarian follicle and also of the uterine lining. Either of these effects would act to prevent conception. It may also be possible to use LRF agonist in a birth control pill taken monthly at the beginning of menstruation (Sheehan et al., 1982).

Female sterilization by injection of liquid silicone into the fallopian tubes, where it hardens and blocks passage of the sperm and egg, is also under study (Loffer, 1984). Another futuristic technique is a test for hormones in saliva that can indicate ovulation (Zorn et al., 1984).

Summary

Historical and Social Perspectives

1. From the beginning of recorded history, human-kind has been concerned with birth control.

2. Margaret Sanger opened the first birth control clinics in the United States at a time when it was illegal to provide birth control information and devices.

Shared Responsibility

3. The male partner can share contraceptive responsibility by being informed, asking a new partner about birth control, accompanying his partner to her exam, using condoms and/or coital abstinence if the couple chooses, and sharing the expense of the exam and method.

Currently Available Methods

4. Comparison of relative convenience, safety, cost, and effectiveness may influence the choice of contraception.

5. Three types of oral contraceptives are currently available. The combination pill contains both estrogen and progestin. The progestin-only pill consists of a low dosage of progestin. The multiphasic pill varies the amounts of estrogen and progesterone during the cycle.

6. Potential advantages of oral contraceptives are high effectiveness and lack of interference with sexual activity. An additional potential advantage of the combination pill and multiphasic pill is reduction of menstrual flow and cramps. The potential advantage of the progestin-only pill is the reduced chance of harmful side effects.

7. Some of the potential disadvantages of the combination and multiphasic pill include possible side effects such as blood clots, increased probability of heart attack, high blood pressure, liver disease, diabetes, more rapid growth of cancer of the breast and uterus, fetal abnormalities if pregnancy occurs, infertility, depression, and reduced sexual interest. Potential disadvantages of the progestin-only pill include irregular bleeding and the possibility of additional side effects.

8. Diaphragm use is currently increasing. Potential advantages include lack of side effects, high effectiveness with knowledgeable and consistent use, and possible promotion of vaginal health. Some potential disadvantages are interruption of sexual activity, irritation from the cream or jelly, and misplacement during insertion or intercourse.

9. The cervical cap is not widely available in the United States. Some women who have problems fitting the diaphragm can use the cervical cap, but cervical caps will not fit all women.

10. Vaginal spermicides, including foam, vaginal suppositories, and the sponge, are available without a prescription. Potential advantages are lack of serious side effects, added lubrication, and promotion of vaginal health. Potential disadvantages include possible irritation of genital tissues and interruption of sexual activity.

11. Condoms are available in a variety of styles. Potential advantages include protection from venereal diseases, improved ejaculatory control, and ready availability as a backup method. Potential disadvantages include interruption of sexual activity and reduced penile sensation.

12. The Progestasert T is currently the only intrauterine device (IUD) on the U.S. market. Potential advantages of the IUD include uninterrupted sexualinteraction and simplicity of use. Potential disadvantages include the possibility of increased cramping, spontaneous expulsion, uterine perforation, tissue changes and infection, and pregnancy complications.

13. Methods based on the menstrual cycle, including the mucus, calendar, and basal body-temperature methods, help in planning coital activity to avoid a woman's fertile period.

14. Nursing, douching, and the withdrawal method are not reliable for contraception.

15. Postcoital ("morning-after") contraception may be used following unprotected midcycle intercourse. Various types of hormone administration and IUD insertion are the available methods.

Sterilization

16. At this time, sterilization should be considered permanent. A decision to be sterilized should be carefully evaluated.

17. Tubal ligation is the sterilization procedure most commonly done for women. It does not alter a woman's hormone levels, menstrual cycle, or menopause.

18. Vasectomy, the sterilization procedure for men, is not effective for birth control immediately after surgery, because sperm remain in the vas deferens above the incision. Most men report that vasectomy does not affect their sexual functioning.

New Directions in Contraception

19. Possible contraceptive methods for men in the future include a male pill or a sperm-immunization vaccine.

20. Possible contraceptive methods for women in the future include several hormonal alternatives and a vaginal ring.

Thought Provokers

1. What do you think are the positive and negative effects of modern contraception on relationships and sexuality?

2. If you could design an ideal contraceptive, what would it be like?

3. What criteria should a married couple who do not want more children use to decide which one of them should be sterilized?

Suggested Readings

"Condoms." *Consumer Reports*, October 1979. This article describes and compares different brands of condoms and thoroughly discusses various advantages and disadvantages reported by the magazine's survey.

Hatcher, Robert et al. *Contraceptive Technology: 1986–1987.* New York: Irvington, 1986. A comprehensive, up-to-date book about birth control, which includes a section about birth control and nutrition. A must for anyone who wants the latest information about the technology and effects of contraception.

12

A baby is an inestimable blessing and bother.
Mark Twain
Letters (1876)

Conceiving Children: Process and Choice

Parenthood as an Option
Becoming Pregnant
Spontaneous and Induced Abortion
A Healthy Pregnancy
The Experience of Pregnancy
Childbirth
Postpartum

ONE OF THE MOST important decisions you will probably make in your lifetime is whether or not to become a parent. In this chapter we address the pros and cons of parenthood. We also discuss the processes of conception, pregnancy, and birth and some of the emotions that accompany them, from the points of view of the mother and the involved father. The discussions that follow are not intended to be complete, but are meant to give an overview of a number of processes and options. We encourage people who desire further information on one or more topics to seek more extensive references or to consult a health care practitioner. As a starting point we will look at the option of parenthood and some of the alternatives that are available for people who want to become mothers and fathers.

Parenthood as an Option

Parenthood is changing in contemporary American society, both in the degree of choice we have about becoming parents and with regard to the definition of parenthood itself. Until recently, highly effective birth control methods were not available, and parenthood was an expected consequence of marriage. Today, however, adults have more choice about becoming parents. Couples may make conscious decisions about when or whether they would like to have children. One result of this freedom of choice is that an increasing number of married people are deciding not to have children at all.

However, people who choose childless marriage often experience external pressure about their decision. **Pronatalism** is a word used to describe policies and attitudes that encourage parenthood for all couples. Childless married couples are routinely asked questions like "When are you going to start your family?" or "You're *not* going to have children? Why aren't you?" (Rarely when someone says they *are* planning to have children does someone ask "Why?") Other manifestations of pronatalism are commonly held stereotypes about people, especially women, who choose not to be parents. Many women have learned to believe that motherhood is essential to their personal fulfillment and that they are selfish or "unnatural" if they choose not to be mothers. One study of college students and their parents indicates that these stereotypes may be becoming less prevalent. Only 22% of people surveyed agreed that having babies was totally fulfilling for women, and 88% disagreed that women who do not want children are selfish or unnatural. However, males were more likely than females to endorse stereotypical attitudes about women and motherhood and these differences in attitude may be a source of relationship conflict when choices about parenting are made (Hare-Mustin and Broderick, 1979). The unfortunate consequence of pronatalism may be that individuals or couples who really do not want children have them anyway and then find that this negatively affects the quality of their own and their children's lives. On the other hand, some couples who have children without fully desiring them discover enjoyment and fulfillment in their parenting roles.

Couples who decide not to have children may do so before or after marriage. One study found that one-third of 52 voluntarily childless couples had made premarital agreements not to have children (Veevers, 1973). The other two-thirds had remained childless after a series of postponements and a later decision. Initially, the women in the second group did not have strong feelings about parenthood and assumed that they eventually would have one or two children. However, unlike many other couples, they and their husbands used contraception conscientiously and continuously during the early years of marriage. At some point, the couples openly acknowledged the possibility that they might choose to remain childless and began to examine the pros and cons of bringing children into their lives and relationships. The couples in this study appeared content with the implications of their choice.

A recent study reported that voluntarily childless women tended to be both very involved in their marriages and to feel a great deal of ambivalence about the conflict between work and motherhood. These women believed that their own parents had made financial sacrifices and had limited their travels, careers, and mobility for the sake of their children. Many of their mothers had longed for careers that they had never had or had cut short when they became parents. Most said that they themselves had not had babies because of their careers. Voluntarily childless women viewed careers and childrearing as full-time commitments, and many feared that choosing one would close off the other. As one subject stated:

> I wish I could decide once and for all to have a baby, or even figure out whether I want one. Then I could plan the rest of my life. . . . One day I'm so absorbed by my career that I think I can't possibly have a child. Then the next day, I'm staring somewhat jealously at pregnant women. I see mothers and babies everywhere. It looks good to me. But I always scare myself away before I actually do anything about it. (Faux, 1984, p. 167)

Since parenthood is much more a choice today than in the past, many people are taking the time to carefully consider the question of child-free living versus parenthood. Many individuals and couples are ambivalent about these alternatives. There are gains and losses with each choice, and regardless of the one selected there is a large element of chance in what the actual, rather than the predicted or assumed, consequences of the decision will be.

There are many potential advantages to not having children. Childless individuals and couples have much more time for themselves and do not have worries about providing for the physical and psychological needs of children. Nonparents can continue more spontaneous recreational, social, and work patterns. They can more fully pursue careers and may experience a great deal of challenge and fulfillment in their professional lives. There is usually more time and energy for companionship and intimacy in an adult relationship when there are no children. There is often less stress on marriages, and some studies show that marriages without children are happier and more satisfying than marriages with children (Campbell, 1975). Nonparents also have more financial resources available to them.

There are, however, many potential advantages to having children. Children themselves give and receive love, and their presence may enhance the love between couples as they share in the experiences of raising their offspring. Managing the challenge of parenthood can also be a source of self-esteem and give a sense of accomplishment. Parenthood is often an opportunity for discovering new and untapped dimensions of oneself that can give one's life greater meaning and satisfaction. Many parents say that they have become better people through parenthood.

Are We Parent Material?
(Or, Am I? in the Case of Single Parenthood)

1. Are my partner and I willing to devote at least 18 years of our lives to being responsible for a child?
2. How would a child affect our growth and development as individuals and as a couple? How would a child affect our careers, education, social life, recreational interests, and privacy?
3. Do my partner and I understand each other's feelings about religion, careers, family, child-raising, future goals? Will children fit into these feelings, hopes, and plans?
4. Could we give a child a good home? Is our relationship basically happy and strong?
5. Do we like children? Do we enjoy activities that children can do?
6. How would we feel if our child's ideas and values turn out to be different from our own?
7. Do I expect a child to make up for happiness I feel is missing from my life?

Source: Adapted from a pamphlet by the National Alliance for Optional Parenthood.

Children offer ongoing stimulation and change as they develop through childhood and may also provide financial or emotional support in the parents' old age (Mayleas, 1980).

The potential rewards of a particular decision may be romanticized or unrealistic for a given person or couple. There are no guarantees that the benefits of either children or childless living will meet one's expectations. For example, children may not provide companionship in a parent's old age, or a career may be much less personally rewarding than anticipated. Still, it is important to assess the choice of parenthood, because it is a permanent and major life decision. Box 12.1 presents some important considerations for people making decisions about having children. There are no "right" or "wrong" answers; these questions are merely a tool to help you explore your feelings about parenthood. And since we all change, your feelings about parenthood may very well change during your life.

Although more people today are deciding not to have children, there has also been an increase in the number of couples and single women who are having children outside of legal marriage. Unmarried women, including lesbians, sometimes choose to become pregnant by means of natural or artificial insemination. Most unmarried mothers now keep their babies, whether the pregnancy was planned or not. Other couples or single men and women are bringing already-born children into their homes to form or enlarge their families. This may be done in a variety of ways. In adoption, a child becomes the legal daughter or son of one or two adults. An available option is subsidized adoption, legal adoption with continued partial government financial aid to the child. This takes place when legislated funds are made available to help families who want to adopt "hard-to-place" (older or handicapped) children but who have limited financial resources to meet these children's special needs. Another option besides adoption is to provide homes for foster children. Foster children usually have legal parents who are also their biological parents, but for various reasons their parents' home environment is temporarily unavailable or unacceptable.

There are many reasons why adults may want to raise children who are not biologically their own. They may be partly motivated by a concern with overpopulation and a desire to give homeless children love and security. Another common reason is that a couple is unable to have children due to infertility or medical problems. Currently, potential adoptive parents outnumber the healthy newborn infants available for adoption. However, children or adolescents who are older, handicapped, or previous foster children are being placed more and more frequently in adoptive homes.

Becoming Pregnant

We have seen that there are a number of options for becoming parents without experiencing the process of pregnancy and childbirth. Most people who have children, however, are biological parents. In the remainder of this chapter, we will look at some of the developments, experiences, and feelings that are involved in the physiological process of becoming parents, starting with becoming pregnant. This first step may be difficult for some couples.

Infertility

It has been estimated that as many as 10%–15% of the couples who want to be parents are unable to conceive. If their attempts at impregnation are unsuccessful after a reasonable period of time (usually a year), a couple should consult a physician. Since approximately 40% of infertility cases result from male factors, it is important that both partners be evaluated (Speroff et al., 1978). The causes of infertility are sometimes difficult to determine and rectify (10%–20% of infertile couples have no diagnosable cause for their infertility), and in many cases both partners have problems that impede conception. Couples who seek help are often under tremendous psychological stress and their sexual relationships may be disrupted. In this section we will look briefly at some common causes of female and male infertility.

Female Infertility. A woman may have difficulty conceiving or be unable to conceive for a number of reasons. Failure to ovulate at regular intervals is quite common. Basal body-temperature charts, hormonal tests, and endometrial biopsies are used to document ovulation. A lack of ovulation may be caused by a variety of factors, including hormone imbalances, severe vitamin deficiencies, metabolic disturbances, poor nutrition, genetic factors, emotional stress, or medical conditions. Women who smoke cigarettes are less fertile and take longer to become pregnant than nonsmokers (Baird and Wilcox, 1985). A variety of so-called "fertility drugs" are sometimes used to stimulate ovulation. These drugs are often successful in accomplishing their purpose. However, they may produce certain undesirable side effects, including multiple births.

If tests indicate that the woman is ovulating and the man is producing adequate numbers of viable sperm, the next step is a postcoital test to see whether the sperm remain viable and motile in the cervical mucus. A woman's cervical mucus may contain antibodies against her partner's sperm, and it may form a plug that blocks their passage.

In such cases, several months of using condoms or abstaining from intercourse may reduce the level of sperm antibodies in the mucus sufficiently to allow fertilization (Fraser et al., 1980; Speroff et al., 1978).

Infections of the vagina, uterus, fallopian tubes, or ovaries can destroy sperm or prevent them from reaching the egg. Scar tissue from old infections—in the fallopian tubes or in or around the ovaries—can block the passage of sperm and eggs. Reproductive tract infections from sexually transmitted diseases (STDs) are a major cause of infertility (Curran, 1980). IUD use increases the risk of tubal infection and fertility problems (Cramer et al., 1985; Daling et al., 1985). Growths in the tubes can also block the passage of sperm and eggs, while growths in the uterus can prevent implantation of the fertilized egg. Endometriosis can also result in infertility (Malinak and Wheeler, 1985).

Male Infertility. On rare occasion a man with normal sperm production may have a fertility problem due to ejaculatory inhibition, a condition we will discuss in Chapter 16. However, most causes of male infertility are related to low sperm count or, less frequently, to abnormal sperm (sperm cells that do not propel themselves with sufficient vigor). Infectious diseases of the male reproductive tract can alter sperm production, viability, and transport. For example, infectious diseases of the testes, particularly mumps, can reduce sperm output; an infection of the vas deferens can block the passage of sperm. Fertility may be decreased when a genital tract infection produces an immune response that affects sperm (Witkin and Toth, 1983). STD-caused infections are a major cause of male infertility. Environmental toxins such as toxic chemicals, pollutants, radiation, and drugs, may also produce reduced sperm counts and abnormal sperm cells (Castleman, 1980b).

A major cause of infertility in men is a damaged or enlarged blood vein in the testes or vas deferens, called a varicocele. The varicocele causes blood to pool in the scrotum, which elevates heat in the area, impairing the shape and reducing the number of sperm produced. Varicoceles can usually be corrected surgically, and the postsurgery pregnancy rate is about 50% (Crocket, 1984). Another cause of male sterility may be undescended testes. If this condition is not corrected before puberty, sperm will be less likely to mature because of the higher temperatures within the abdomen. Hormone deficiencies may also result in an inadequate number of sperm cells in the semen. This situation can sometimes be remedied by hormone therapy.

Discovery or treatment of male infertility is sometimes hampered by psychological factors. Some men are quite reluctant to subject themselves to fertility evaluation. The following account reveals one possible motivation for this reluctance:

> My wife and I have been trying to have a baby for over a year without success. Both physicians she has seen have assured her that nothing is wrong with her reproductive system. The doctors want me to come in for a checkup. What if they find out I'm not making enough sperm? There is nothing wrong with my drive or capabilities. Somehow, the idea of a low sperm count suggests I am sexually inadequate. How can a man with a high sex drive be shooting blanks? (Authors' files)

It is not uncommon for a man to relate his masculinity or virility to his ability to produce babies. However, it is uncommon to find a relationship between capacity for sexual response and production of sperm. Male sterility can occur among men who are highly sexually active as well as among individuals with infrequent outlets. Occasionally, however, low sperm count and reduced sexual interest may both stem from the same cause, insufficient hormone output.

Infertility and Sexuality. Couples may experience various reactions to their difficulty or inability to become pregnant, and problems with infertility can have profoundly negative effects on a couple's sexual functioning (Menning, 1979). When a couple is first informed of their infertility, they may deny it or downplay their desire to have children. As knowledge of their infertility becomes more evident, they may feel a great sense of isolation from others during social discussions of pregnancy, childbirth, and childrearing. As one woman who has been unable to conceive states:

> Coffee breaks at work are the worst times; everyone brings out their pictures of their kids and discusses their latest trials and tribulations. I can't help feeling like there's something wrong with me for not being able to get pregnant. When one of the women complains about having problems with something like childcare, I just want to shout at her and tell her how lucky she is to be able to have such a "problem." (Authors' files)

Couples may also become isolated from each other and believe that the partner does not really understand. Each may feel inadequate about his or her masculinity or femininity due to problems with conceiving. Each may feel anger and guilt and wonder "Why me?" Finally, the couple may feel grief over their losses: biological children, the pregnancy experience, and the option to conceive. Intercourse itself may evoke these uncomfortable feelings and become an emotionally painful rather than pleasurable experience.

Also, the medical procedures used in fertility diagnosis and treatment are often disruptive to the couple's sexual spontaneity. Sex can become very stressful and mechanical. Taking basal body-temperature daily and timing intercourse according to ovulation can create tremendous sexual performance anxiety that can interfere with arousal and response.

Because of these psychological and sexual stresses, health care practitioners who work with infertility problems need to be sensitive to and skilled in helping affected couples. The nationwide organization *Resolve* (P.O. Box 474, Belmont, MA 02178) offers support groups, counseling, and referrals for people with infertility problems.

Enhancing the Possibility of Conception

If a couple is having difficulty conceiving a child, both partners should be medically evaluated. Before extensive medical evaluation and treatment is begun, they may be told to follow certain steps to maximize the possibility of conception. Modifying both coital position and the timing of coitus can sometimes increase the chances of fertilization. The recommendations that follow may be helpful for couples who are trying to become pregnant.

A woman's position during intercourse can affect the likelihood of conception. For most women, the best position is to lie on the back, with knees drawn up. This

REPRODUCTION: THE INSIDE STORY

These images depict reproductive processes occurring inside the mother's body. Refer to the chapter narrative for a complete description of these and other reproductive events.

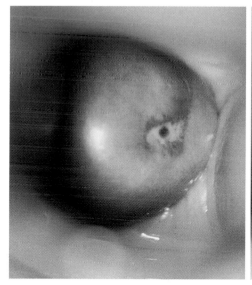 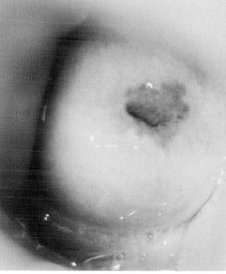

Plate 1 (left) Cervix at day 6 of the menstrual cycle. Secretions are minimal.

Plate 2 (right) Cervix at ovulation on day 14. Fertile mucus is secreted from the os. The squamocolumnar junction is visible.

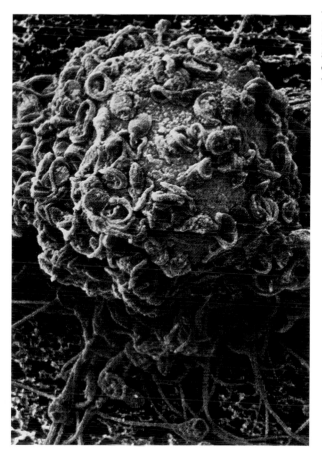

Plate 3 Human sperm surrounding an ovum. Only one will fertilize it.

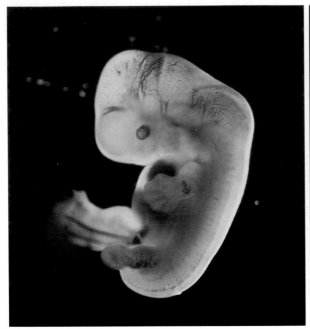

Plate 4
Fetal development
at 5 weeks.

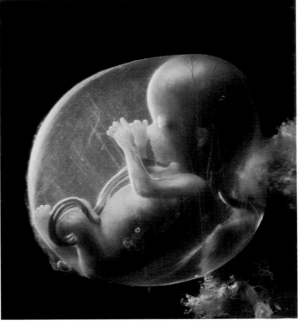

Plate 5
Fetal development
at 14 weeks.

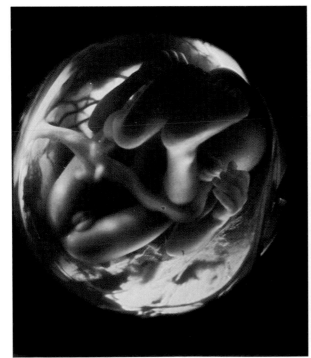

Plate 6
Fetal development
at 20 weeks.

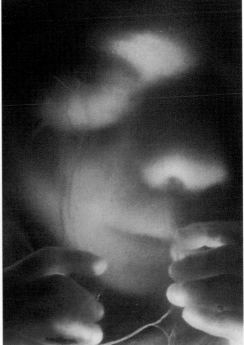

Plate 7
Closeup of fetal development
at 22 weeks.

allows the cervix to dip down into the pool of semen. Some fertility counselors recommend placing a pillow under the woman's buttocks. The added elevation helps prevent semen from escaping out of the vagina. For a woman with a severely retro-flexed (backward-tipped) uterus, where the cervix is on a straight line with the vagina rather than at right angles to it, it may be best to use the knee-chest position for coitus. The woman kneels face down, supporting her weight on her elbows and knees, as the man enters from behind. This position allows gravity to help keep the semen in the vagina. In both cases, when the man's orgasm is imminent he should penetrate as deeply as is comfortable to his partner and stop moving once he has begun expelling seminal fluid. After ejaculation, he should make no further movements other than a careful withdrawal of his penis (additional movements may disperse the seminal pool). The woman should remain in her position for 30 minutes (Culverwell, 1983).

Picking the right time to have coitus is also important in increasing the prob-ability of conception. While it is difficult to predict the exact time of ovulation, several methods permit a reasonable approximation. Perhaps the best is the mucus method discussed in the previous chapter, where the couple times coital activity according to the fertile period in the woman's menstrual cycle. (See color plates 1 and 2.) Body temperature and the principles of the calendar method may also be used in estimating ovulation time. Ovulation predictor tests that measure the rise in luteinizing hormone in urine prior to ovulation can also help identify the best time for conception.

In cases where low sperm count is suspected, the optimal frequency of ejaculation during intercourse is usually every other day during the week of ovulation (Speroff et al., 1978). In such circumstances it is especially important for a couple to chart the woman's cycle so that they can reasonably predict her most fertile time. A man with a borderline sperm count might also want to avoid taking hot baths and wearing tight clothing and undershorts, since these and similar environments expose the tes-ticles to higher than normal temperatures.

Alternatives to Couple Intercourse for Conception

In recent years various alternatives have been developed to help couples overcome the problem of infertility. Artificial insemination is one option to be considered in cases of an abnormality related to sperm motility. In this procedure, semen from a woman's partner is mechanically introduced into her vagina or cervix by a health care practitioner. If the man is not producing adequate viable sperm, or if a woman does not have a partner, artificial insemination with a donor's semen is another option.

Various procedures are being developed to allow a woman who cannot conceive through intercourse or artificial insemination to have a child. The world's first "test-tube baby," born in England in 1978, provided impetus to research in this area. In this method, called *in vitro fertilization* (IVF), mature eggs are removed from the woman's ovary and are fertilized in a laboratory dish by her partner's sperm. Several fertilized eggs are then introduced into the woman's uterus and, if the procedure is successful, at least one will implant and develop. This method can be used for a woman whose infertility is due to blocked fallopian tubes. In a variation called donor IVF, an ovum from a woman other than the one who will carry the pregnancy is used. Another method under study for women with blocked tubes is called *low tubal ovum transfer*. It involves using a laparoscope to remove a mature egg from the ovary.

The egg is then inserted by a syringe into a fallopian tube on the uterus side of the blocked area. Another method, *embryo transfer*, also called *artificial embryonation*, may be a possibility for women who are unable to produce an egg due to diseased or absent ovaries. In embryo transfer a volunteer female donor is artificially inseminated by the sperm of the infertile woman's partner. Approximately five days following fertilization the tiny embryo is removed from the donor and transferred into the uterus of the mother-to-be, who then carries the pregnancy. At present, these techniques are still experimental and quite costly, and success rates are low. However, they do provide hope for infertile individuals and couples in the future.

Surrogate mothers are women who are willing to be artificially inseminated by the male partner of a childless couple, carry the pregnancy to term, deliver the child, and give it to the couple for adoption. This is sometimes done anonymously through a health care practitioner or privately by arrangement between the woman and the couple. There are many unresolved legal ramifications to surrogate motherhood, especially when the surrogate mother is paid for her services.

In general, the area of nontraditional conception and birth raises complex ethical and legal issues. For example, if a surrogate mother has a baby with birth defects, and neither party wants the child, who is ultimately responsible for the child? If a deformed child is born following donor artificial insemination, is the sperm bank liable? With in vitro fertilization procedures more ova are fertilized in the laboratory medium than are implanted, and the extra ones are discarded—is this immoral destruction of human life? What will be the long-term emotional effects on children, parents, and donors involved in surrogate motherhood, artificial insemination, in vitro fertilization, and embryo transfer? These and many other considerations will become more salient as reproductive technology continues to expand (Elias and Annas, 1986).

Preconception Sex Selection

The desire to select the sex of a child has existed since ancient times. Superstitions about this are part of our folk tradition; for example, the belief that if a man wears a hat during intercourse he will father a male child, or that hanging his trousers on the left bedpost will produce a girl. In contemporary times, an obstetrician-gynecologist, Dr. Landrum Shettles (1972), basing his techniques on the premise that female-producing sperm travel slower, live longer, and survive better in the acid environment of the vagina than do male-producing sperm, reported that a precoital baking soda and water douche and intercourse with deep vaginal penetration near ovulation would increase chances of conceiving a boy. Conversely, douching with vinegar and water prior to intercourse, shallow penetration, and intercourse two to three days prior to ovulation would increase the chances of a girl. However, other researchers have not found these approaches to be reliable (Karp, 1980; Simcock, 1985).

Some researchers are experimenting with techniques to separate Y- from X-bearing sperm in ejaculates. The male- or female-producing sperm would then be introduced into the vagina by artificial insemination. The most promising method for obtaining viable, undamaged, and well-separated sperm samples is to induce sperm migration through progressively denser solutions of albumen (egg white). This procedure yields primarily Y-bearing sperm (Glass and Ericsson, 1982).

Other researchers contend that a woman can preselect the sex of her child by taking mineral supplements and regulating her diet, beginning one and one-half menstrual cycles before conception. According to this method, a woman who wants to conceive a girl should eat foods rich in calcium and magnesium, such as milk, cheese, nuts, beans, and cereals; a woman who wants a boy should eat foods rich in potassium and sodium, such as meat, fish, vegetables, chocolate, and salt. The researchers claim an 80% success rate but are not certain by what mechanism the selection occurs (Stolkowski and Choukroun, 1981).

If preconception sex selection became effective and easy, what would the impact be on society? An imbalance in sex ratios, probably in favor of males, might result. The overall birth rate could also be reduced, because once they got what they wanted parents would no longer continue having more children in hope of conceiving a child of the desired sex. The potential societal impact of scientific developments in human reproduction is well illustrated by preconception sex determination.

Pregnancy Detection

The initial signs of pregnancy may provoke feelings ranging from joy to dread, depending on the woman's desire to be pregnant and a variety of surrounding circumstances. Although some women may have either a light blood flow or "spotting" (irregular bleeding) after conception, usually the first indication of pregnancy is the absence of the menstrual period at the expected time. Breast tenderness, nausea, vomiting, or other nonspecific symptoms (such as tiredness or change in appetite) may also accompany pregnancy in the first weeks or months.

Any or all of these clues may cause a woman to suspect she is pregnant. Urine tests and pelvic exams are medical techniques used to make the determination with a greater degree of certainty. The urine of a pregnant woman contains a hormone, **human chorionic gonadotropin (HCG)**, secreted by the **trophoblast cells** of the placenta. HCG is detectable in a testing solution about a month after conception or two weeks after the expected date of menstrual onset. Recently, sensitive blood assays for HCG have become available that can detect pregnancy by about 10 days after conception. Also, around the sixth week after conception an experienced practitioner can feel a softening of the uterus during a pelvic exam (see Figure 12.1).

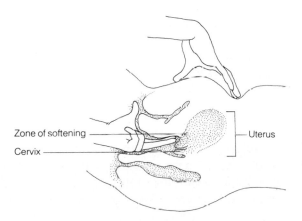

Zone of softening

Cervix

Uterus

Figure 12.1

Pelvic Exam Pregnancy Detection
One sign of pregnancy is a softening of the uterus.

Spontaneous and Induced Abortion

Even when pregnancy has been confirmed, complications may prevent full-term development of the fetus. Sometimes genetic or physical defects in a fetus will cause **spontaneous abortion**, or **miscarriage**, to occur, terminating the pregnancy. Although the exact frequency of spontaneous abortion is unknown, it is estimated that 10%–40% of pregnancies end in miscarriage. The majority of these occur within the first trimester.

Early miscarriages may appear as a heavier than usual menstrual flow; later ones may involve uncomfortable cramping and profuse bleeding. Fortunately for women who desire a child, one miscarriage rarely means that a later pregnancy will be unsuccessful.

In contrast to a spontaneous abortion, an **induced abortion** involves a decision to terminate a pregnancy by medical procedures. A recent investigation indicates that approximately 26% of pregnancies occurring among American women were terminated by abortion. About 3 percent of all women aged 15–44 obtained abortions, and most abortions were obtained by young, unmarried, white women (Henshaw et al., 1985).

Induced abortion continues to be a controversial issue in the United States and other countries. Beliefs regarding the beginning of life, the reproductive choice of women, and the quality of life influence the stand one takes regarding elective termination of pregnancy.

Laws regulating abortion continue to change. Abortion early in pregnancy was legal in ancient China and Europe. In the thirteenth century, St. Thomas Aquinas delineated the Catholic church's view that the fetus developed a soul 40 days after conception for males and 90 days for females. Abortion after ensoulment (development of the soul) became a serious crime. Early American common law allowed abortion until the pregnant woman felt fetal movement, or quickening. Quickening usually occurs during the fourth or fifth month after conception.

In the late 1860s, Pope Pius IX decreed abortion a sin. During the 1860s abortion became illegal in the United States, except when it was necessary to save the woman's life. Some of the reasons given for making abortion illegal included the high mortality rate from abortion due to scarcity of antiseptics and to crude abortion procedures. Also, population growth was seen by some decision-makers as important to the country's developing economy (Lader, 1966).

In contemporary times, before abortion became legal again, women desperate to terminate their unwanted pregnancies sought illegal abortions or attempted to abort themselves. Women with money could fly to Europe or Japan or persuade an American physician to perform an abortion. Low-income women often resorted to unskilled, unsanitary, medically unsafe procedures. By 1967, due to the advocacy of women and men who organized to lobby for change, a few states began altering their abortion laws. In 1973 the Supreme Court legalized a woman's right to decide to terminate her pregnancy before the fetus has reached the age of viability. *Viability* is defined as the fetus's ability to survive independently of the woman's body. This usually occurs by the sixth or seventh month of pregnancy, but most abortions are done before the third month.

The legalization of abortion in 1973 has not been the end of the story. Legislation in the late 1970s greatly curtailed the availability of medically safe abortions to low-income women. In July 1977 the Hyde Amendment was passed, and the Supreme Court ruled to prohibit federal Medicaid funds for abortions. (Medicaid is a state and federal joint program to provide payment of medical services for low-income citizens.) The Court also established that states are not required to provide Medicaid funds for the purpose of elective pregnancy termination. Before this legislation, one-third of the approximately one million annual abortions had been paid for by Medicaid. Many of the low-income women who carry their unwanted pregnancies to term and do not give the child out for adoption will have larger families, making it more difficult for them to break out of the cycle of poverty. While low-income women may not have the financial resources to choose a medical abortion, middle and upper income women are able to continue to obtain medically safe abortions.

Antiabortion Versus Prochoice

Currently, induced abortion is a major social and political issue in the United States, characterized by highly polarized opinions for and against. The antiabortion, or "right to life," advocates argue that life begins at conception and abortion is immoral. One of their pamphlets states:

> At the moment of conception, all the elements that create a new human life are present. When the life-giving forces of the father and the mother unite, they form a unique human person. Life begins and from that moment, your formation has been purely a matter of development, growth and maturation. [Source not available]

Antiabortion groups want to re-establish national legislation, by constitutional amendment, if necessary, to make abortion illegal and to establish the constitutional rights of the unborn fetus. Although surveys show clearly that the overwhelming majority of Americans believe abortion should be legal, and a majority also oppose cutting off of public funding of abortion for poor women (Family Planning Perspectives, 1983), members of the antiabortion minority are waging an active battle against legal and available abortion. One of their primary tactics has been to target prochoice incumbents in Congress to attempt to prevent their reelection. Some extreme antiabortion activists have burned or bombed abortion clinics and harassed clinic patients and staff. This activity has increased, and there were 24 incidents of arson or bombing of abortion facilities in 1984 (Donovan, 1985).

Prochoice advocates see abortions as a social necessity, due to imperfect and sometimes unavailable birth control methods and lack of education. They want abortion to be an option for women who are faced with the dilemma of an unwanted pregnancy and who decide that terminating it is their best alternative. Prochoice forces support a woman's choice *not* to have an abortion, but they are strongly opposed to antiabortion legislation restricting others' choices. Many prestigious organizations have made public statements opposing antiabortion bills, including the National Academy of Sciences, the American Public Health Association, the American Medical

Antiabortion activists are bombing or burning clinics where abortions are performed.

Association, the American College of Obstetricians and Gynecologists, and many religious organizations. For example, a rabbi states:

> My religious tradition is one which has revered and sanctified human life for nearly four thousand years. . . . It is that regard for the sanctity of human life which prompts us to support legislation enabling women to be free from the whims of biological roulette and free mostly from the oppressive, crushing weight of ideologies and theologies which . . . continue to insist that in a world already groaning to death with overpopulation, with hate and with poverty, there is still some noble merit or purpose to indiscriminate reproduction. (Hamilton, 1983, pp. 30–31)

One study of recent trends in abortion attitudes found that people who approve of legally available abortions are more likely to support civil liberties and women's rights than those who disapprove. People who disapprove of legal abortion are more likely than others to have strongly committed Catholic or fundamentalist Protestant affiliations (Granberg and Granberg, 1980); to have disapproving attitudes towards premarital sex, homosexuality, and government spending; to be politically conservative; and to have traditional attitudes about the female role (Deitch, 1983). Another study found that women who were prochoice activists tended to be college educated, to have well-paid careers and few children, to have few ties to formal religion, and to have a strong vested interest in their work roles. The antiabortion activist women were more likely to be practicing Roman Catholics with large families, have low-paying or no employment outside the home, and to base their self-esteem on their maternal roles. In addition, prochoice activists believe that intimacy is the most important purpose of sexuality, while antiabortion activists believe that the primary purpose of sexuality is procreation. It is likely that the abortion debate will remain passionate and bitter because of fundamental differences in life circumstances and values (Luker, 1984).

Medical Procedures for Abortion

There are several different abortion procedures used at different stages of pregnancy. The most common are *suction curettage, D and E, prostaglandin induction*, and *saline injection*. Suction curettage is usually done from 7 to 13 weeks after the last menstrual period. About 90% of abortions are done at or before 12 weeks (Henshaw et al., 1985). With suction curettage the cervical os is usually dilated by graduated metal dilators or by a *laminaria*, a small cylinder of seaweed stem (*Laminaria digitata*), inserted hours earlier. The laminaria slowly expands as it absorbs cervical moisture, and it gently opens the os. This gradual expansion reduces the chance of cervical trauma. During the abortion, a small plastic tube is inserted into the uterus. The tube is attached to a vacuum aspirator, which draws the fetal tissue, placenta, and built-up uterine lining out of the uterus. The suction curettage is done by physicians at clinics or hospitals, and the procedure takes about 10 minutes. However, admission, preparation, counseling, and recovery take longer. A local anesthetic may be used. There are minor risks of uterine infection or perforation, hemorrhage, or incomplete removal of the uterine contents. If a pregnancy progresses past approximately 12 weeks, the suction curettage procedure can no longer be performed as safely. The uterine walls have become thinner, and perforation and bleeding are more likely.

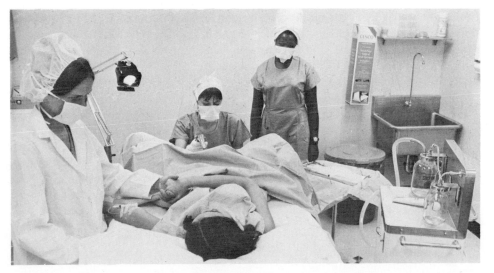

A first-trimester abortion procedure.

D and E, or dilation and evacuation, is used commonly between 13 and 16 weeks of pregnancy. A combination of suction equipment, special forceps, and a curette (a metal instrument used to scrape the walls of the uterus) is used. General anesthesia is usually required, and the cervix is dilated wider than with suction curettage (Hatcher et al., 1984). Since all of the abortion procedures performed after 13 weeks are riskier and more complicated, they are usually done in hospitals.

Prostaglandins (a type of human hormone) are currently among the most commonly used compounds to induce termination of second trimester pregnancies. (They are also sometimes used to induce full-term labor.) The appropriate type of prostaglandin can be introduced into the vagina as a suppository or into the amniotic sac by inserting a needle through the abdominal wall. These hormones cause uterine contractions, and the fetus and placenta are usually expelled from the vagina within 24 hours (Embrey, 1977).

Two other methods for pregnancy termination after 13 weeks are the saline and urea injection procedures. These are similar to intra-amniotic prostaglandin injection, but either a saline or a urea solution is injected into the amniotic cavity. These procedures kill the fetus and cause contractions to begin, expelling the fetus. An increasing number of abortions after 13 weeks are being performed by combined use of two or three of these substances (Hatcher et al., 1984). Complications from abortion procedures that induce labor contractions can include nausea, vomiting, and diarrhea; tearing of the cervix; excessive bleeding; and the possibility of shock and death.

Shared Responsibility. The decision-making process begins when a woman discovers that she is pregnant. After she has confirmed her suspicions with a pregnancy test, the woman will have to decide whether to carry the pregnancy and keep the child, to give it up for adoption, or to have an abortion. There are several ways in which a couple can share responsibility for abortion. First, the man can help his partner clarify her feelings and can express his own in the decisions to be made about an unwanted pregnancy. One study of 1000 men interviewed in abortion clinics stressed the importance of men talking about their own feelings (Shostak et al., 1984). Important topics for a couple to discuss include each person's life situation at the time; their feelings about the pregnancy, possible choices, and each other; and their future plans as individuals and as a couple. If the couple disagrees on what to do, the final decision rests with the woman. Male partners do not have a legal right to demand or deny abortion for the woman.

Once the woman has made a decision for abortion, the man can help pay medical expenses and accompany her to the clinic or hospital. According to several studies, about three-fourths of male partners of pregnant women agreed to the abortion decision and helped pay for the procedure (Pfuhl, 1978; Shostak, 1979). The man can also be understanding about not having intercourse for at least a week following the abortion and can help in planning effective postabortion contraception. Since the abortion process is likely to evoke some difficult emotions, the couple may find it useful to continue to talk with each other about their reactions.

Potential Advantages of Abortion. The most important advantage of abortion is that it is the only procedure that can terminate an unwanted pregnancy. It allows a woman the choice of having a child only if she truly wants one. For many women, abortion eliminates the severe stress of an unwanted pregnancy, and most women report a sense of relief following abortion (Freeman et al., 1980). Another advantage is that the medical risks involved in abortion, especially early abortion, are minimal. Abortion does not reduce fertility (Stubblefield et al., 1984; WHO Task Force on Sequelae of Abortion, 1984).

Potential Disadvantages of Abortion. A woman will usually experience bleeding and cramps for the first two weeks following an abortion. During this time she should use sanitary pads instead of tampons, to help protect against infection. She should not douche for at least a week for the same reason.

Some medical complications can result from abortion. Infection, intrauterine blood clots, cervical or uterine trauma, excessive bleeding, incomplete abortion, or continued pregnancy are some of the short-term problems that can occur. Research data about long-term medical complications following abortion is inconclusive and contradictory (Hatcher et al., 1986), but research does indicate that having two or more abortions may lead to a higher incidence of miscarriages in subsequent pregnancies (Levin et al., 1980; Madore et al., 1981).

Abortion is usually a difficult decision for a woman and her partner to make. It means weighing and examining highly personal values and priorities. When made, the decision is usually the "best of the bad alternatives." Even if the pregnancy was unwanted, both the woman and the man may feel loss and sadness. They may also feel regret, depression, anxiety, guilt, or anger about the abortion or what led to needing to have the abortion. Research indicates that women who have abortions usually experience emotional distress before and after the procedure, but that the distress tends to disappear within several months. Women who have repeat abortions experience higher emotional distress in interpersonal relationships than do women having a first abortion (Freeman et al., 1980). Men often find themselves experiencing feelings of hurt, guilt, and anger following their partners' abortions (Shostak et al., 1984).

A great many factors can affect the woman and the man's emotional response to the abortion. The reactions of close friends and family, the attitude of the medical staff and physician performing the abortion, the individuals' values about abortion, the voluntariness or pressure from others about the decision, the nature and strength of the relationship of the woman and her partner all can contribute to positive or negative reactions. One study has found that support from partners, friends, and families was the most important variable in the degree of anxiety and depression women felt before and after abortion (Moseley et al., 1981). One study found that women who become pregnant while using contraception tended to be more depressed after an abortion than women who did not use contraception. The women who had used contraception believed that they would be unable to avoid future pregnancies, whereas those who blamed themselves for not using contraception said they planned to avoid future pregnancies by using birth control (Janoff-Bulman and Golden, 1984).

The timing of the abortion may also be important: Early abortions are medically, and usually emotionally, much easier than later abortions. A woman who has had a legal abortion is also less likely to be as upset as with an illegal, clandestine abortion.

Pregnancy Risk Taking and Abortion

In many cases an unwanted pregnancy is clearly a matter of contraceptive failure. A woman and her partner can face a situation in which they have used an effective method of birth control correctly and consistently and the woman still became pregnant. For other women or couples seeking abortions, contraceptive risk taking can be common.

To better understand the issues in unwanted pregnancies not related to method failure, one researcher studied 500 women who had abortions. This research showed that there can be various kinds of "costs" to contraceptive use. Some women stop using a method because they fear side effects. Obtaining birth control from a pharmacy or health care practitioner can mean acknowledging one's intent to engage in or continue nonmarital intercourse, which may conflict with one's value system, cause guilt, and result in risk taking (Luker, 1975). Another study found that college women with low degrees of guilt about sex were more likely to use effective contraception than were women with high degrees of guilt (Mosher and Vonderheide, 1985). Actively seeking and using contraception is also contrary to the traditional role of female passivity. Pregnancy prevention may interfere with romantic passion, and in some cases a woman may fear alienating her partner by asking for cooperation in contraceptive planning and implementation. Using drugs and alcohol also increases the chances of risk taking unless a woman uses the pill or IUD.

"Getting away with" contraceptive risk taking often increases carelessness. For example, a couple who does not use the diaphragm on a few occasions during one month without a pregnancy resulting is likely to increase nonuse the following month. In some cases lack of information about contraceptive methods results in risk taking. Although the majority of women in the sample of 500 had previously demonstrated contraceptive skills, they began to take contraceptive risks, either believing that they were unlikely to become pregnant or because they placed a high social value on pregnancy. Two-thirds of the women interviewed reported that a gynecologist had told them that they would have difficulty becoming pregnant, and many were consequently not careful about birth control (Luker, 1975).

Some women may take contraceptive risks because of the high social value placed on pregnancy. Pregnancy connotes fertility, womanhood, and adulthood in our society and is accordingly often considered a measure of a woman's worth. Pregnancy can also be a bargaining chip for marriage, or be used to test or coerce a man's commitment to a relationship or parenthood, or to prevent an impending breakup. Pregnancy can be a plea for help or an attempt to punish someone—usually the woman's parents. Life transitions may also affect risk taking—the mother who has just sent her last child off to school or the woman past 30 who has never been pregnant may become more careless in contraceptive use (Luker, 1975).

Repeat Abortions.   Approximately one-third of abortions are performed for women who have had at least one previous abortion (Henshaw et al., 1985). Although there is limited data about women who have had more than one abortion, the available research findings are interesting. First, the data indicate that contraceptive method failure is a major contributor to repeat abortions. Another study found that repeat abortions are not the consequence of women's psychological maladjustment or negative attitudes toward using contraceptives; rather, they occur due to frequency of sexual activity during relationships of long duration and imperfect birth control methods (Berger et al., 1984).

A Healthy Pregnancy

Once a woman becomes pregnant, her own health care plays an important part in the development of a healthy fetus. Countless books have been written about pregnancy and prenatal care (a few are listed in the Suggested Readings); we will mention only a few important points here.

Fetal Development

The nine-month span of pregnancy is customarily divided into three three-month segments called *trimesters*. Characteristic changes occur in each trimester.

As with all mammals, humans begin as a **zygote** (a united sperm cell and ovum), which develops into the multicelled **blastocyst** that implants on the wall of the uterus about a week after fertilization (see Figure 12.2). Growth progresses steadily. (See color plates 4–7.) By 9 to 10 weeks after the last menstrual period, the fetal heartbeat can be heard with a special stethoscope known as the *Doppler*. By the beginning of the second month from the time of conception, the fetus is 1½ inches long, grayish, and crescent-shaped. During this same month the spinal canal and rudimentary arms and legs form, as do the beginnings of recognizable eyes, fingers, and toes. During the third month internal organs such as the liver, kidneys, intestines, and lungs begin limited functioning in the 3-inch fetus.

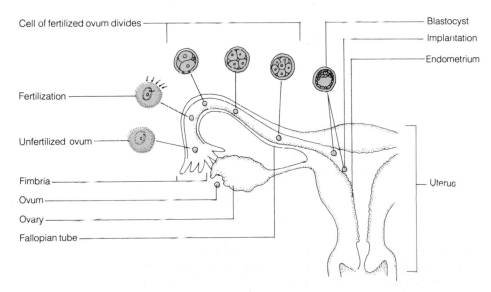

Cell of fertilized ovum divides
Blastocyst
Implantation
Endometrium
Fertilization
Unfertilized ovum
Uterus
Fimbria
Ovum
Ovary
Fallopian tube

Figure 12.2

From Ovulation to Implantation
The egg travels into the tube where fertilization occurs. The fertilized ovum divides as it travels toward the uterus where it implants on the wall.

The second trimester begins with the fourth month of pregnancy. By now the sex of the fetus can often be distinguished. External body parts, including fingernails, eyebrows, and eyelashes, are clearly formed. The fetus's skin is covered by fine, downlike hair. Future development will primarily consist of growth in size and refinement of the features that already exist. Fetal movements can be felt by the end of the fourth month, and the fetal heartbeat can be heard slightly later with a regular stethoscope. The fetus's weight has increased to one pound by the end of the fifth month. Head hair may appear at this time, and subcutaneous fat develops. By the end of the second trimester, the fetus has opened its eyes. (See color insert for stages of fetal development.)

In the third trimester the fetus continues to grow and to develop the size and strength it will need to live on its own, apart from the mother's warmth and sustenance. It increases in weight from four pounds in the seventh month to an average of seven pounds at birth. The downlike hair covering its body disappears, and head hair continues growing. The skin becomes smooth rather than wrinkled. It is covered with a protective waxy substance, the **vernix caseosa**.

Prenatal Care

The developments just described take place in most pregnancies. Occasionally, however, something may go wrong. The fetus may not develop normally, or the pregnancy may terminate early, as we discussed previously. The causes of these problems may be genetic and unpreventable; but the mother's own health and nutrition are also crucial in providing the best environment for fetal development. This is one reason why it is important for a woman to have a complete physical examination before becoming pregnant. She also needs to have a test to determine her immunity to rubella (German measles), a disease which may cause severe fetal defects if the mother contracts it while she is pregnant.

Thorough prenatal care is essential for promoting the health of both the mother and the fetus. Components of optimal prenatal care include good nutrition, general good health, adequate rest, routine health care, exercise, and childbirth education. Early in the pregnancy the woman, her partner, and her health care practitioner should discuss the health needs of both the mother and the developing fetus; they can also begin to make plans for the birth.

As women have increasingly taken up athletic activities, many have had questions about the effects of exercise on pregnancy. Moderate exercise is commonly recommended as important to a healthy pregnancy. See Box 12.2 for current guidelines.

Risks to Fetal Development.   The fetus is dependent upon the mother for nutrients, oxygen, and waste elimination as substances pass through the cell walls of the **placenta** (a disc-shaped organ attached to the wall of the uterus, shown in Figure 12.3). The fetus is joined to the placenta by the umbilical cord. The fetal blood circulates independently within the closed system of the fetus and the inner part of the placenta. Maternal blood flows in the uterine walls and outer part of the placenta. Fetal and maternal blood do not intermingle. All exchanges between the fetal and maternal blood systems occur by passage of substances through the walls of the blood vessels.

Pregnancy: Latest Fitness Thinking

The American College of Obstetricians and Gynecologists has issued safety guidelines for women who wish to continue exercising during pregnancy.

- Consult your doctor first. (Certain factors may be reasons to avoid exercise during pregnancy.)
- Limit aerobic exercise to 15-minute sessions and monitor your heart rate regularly. Keep it below 140 beats per minute. (Animal studies indicate that increased body temperatures induced by too-vigorous exercise can have adverse effects on the fetus.)
- Avoid jerky stretches and exercises. (The hormonal changes caused by pregnancy loosen the soft tissue that links bones within the joints, making a woman more susceptible to joint injury.)
- Drink fluids before and after exercise; stop immediately to drink if you become thirsty. (Dehydration occurs much more rapidly than usual during pregnancy.)
- After the fourth month of pregnancy, don't do any exercises that are performed lying down on your back. (The increased size of the uterus can interfere with the flow of blood to a woman's heart and to the fetus.)
- Have reasonable expectations from exercise. (Exercise can boost a pregnant woman's energy level; help her maintain muscle tone, strength, and endurance; and lessen chances of back pain.)

Nutrients and oxygen from the maternal blood pass into the fetal circulatory system; carbon dioxide and waste products from the fetus pass into the maternal blood vessels, to be removed by the maternal circulation.

Although the placenta prevents some kinds of bacteria from passing into the fetal blood system, many bacteria do cross through the placenta. Furthermore, many substances ingested by the mother easily cross through the placenta and can be damaging to the developing fetus. Certain medications, as well as drugs, alcohol, and tobacco are all potentially dangerous, and there have been a number of tragic situations where children have been damaged by medications taken by their mothers during pregnancy. For example, the drug *thalidomide*, prescribed as a sedative to pregnant women during the early 1960s, was absorbed into the circulatory systems of fetuses, causing severe deformities to the extremities. A drug used to treat severe acne, Accutane, creates a risk of having a baby with a major malformation almost as high as did thalidomide (Lammer et al., 1985). In the last few years some daughters and sons of women who took diethylstilbestrol (DES) while pregnant have developed cancer of the vagina or testicle. Tetracycline, a frequently used antibiotic, can damage an infant's teeth and cause stunted bone growth if it is taken during pregnancy. In animal studies, even nonprescription drugs such as aspirin have been implicated in fetal abnormalities.

Some substances known to cause harm to the mother also pose serious hazards to a developing fetus. The babies of mothers who regularly use an addictive drug such as heroin, cocaine, codeine, morphine, or opium during pregnancy are often born addicted. Withdrawal from the drug can be fatal to a newborn, so the drug must often be continued until the infant is strong enough to be taken off it. Another health hazard for the fetus is cigarette smoking. Maternal smoking increases the chances of spontaneous abortion and of pregnancy complications that can result in fetal or infant death. Smoking reduces the amount of oxygen in the bloodstream, and this may adversely affect the fetus by slowing its growth. Infants of mothers who smoked during pregnancy often weigh less and are in poorer general condition than infants of nonsmoking mothers.

Fetal alcohol syndrome (FAS) is the leading cause of developmental disabilities and birth defects in the U.S. (Centers for Disease Control, 1984b). Heavy alcohol use can cause intrauterine death and spontaneous abortion, premature birth, con-

Figure 12.3

The Placenta Attached to the Uterine Wall
The placenta exchanges nutrients, oxygen, and waste products between the maternal and fetal circulatory systems.

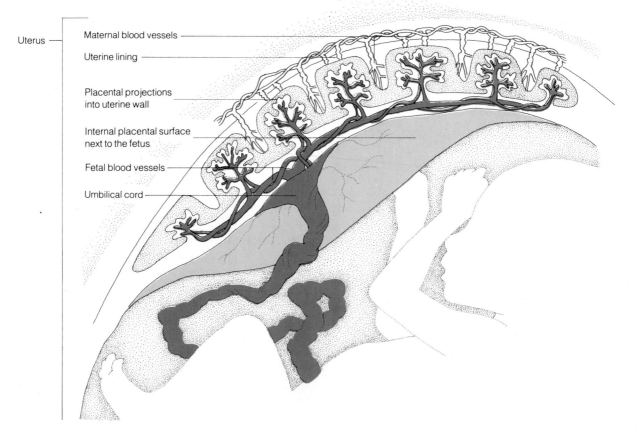

Uterus

Maternal blood vessels

Uterine lining

Placental projections into uterine wall

Internal placental surface next to the fetus

Fetal blood vessels

Umbilical cord

genital heart defects, damage to the brain and nervous system, and numerous physical malformations of the fetus. Most babies with FAS have below normal IQs. Infants may be born addicted to alcohol and, consequently, experience alcohol withdrawal for several days following birth (Clarren and Smith, 1978). The fetus is at risk of developing FAS if the mother drinks six or more drinks per day during her pregnancy. However, lesser amounts of alcohol can also impair the fetus (Abel, 1980). In 1981 the Food and Drug Administration advised women to abstain completely from alcohol use during pregnancy to avoid the risk of damage to their babies. Research also indicates that heavy marijuana use may cause problems similar to fetal alcohol syndrome (Hingson et al., 1982).

The extent of our knowledge about the effect of most of the drugs and other substances consumed by pregnant women is very limited; little is known of the exact risk of a given drug taken during pregnancy. What we do know at this point is that we are learning of more and more potential hazards. For this reason, *no* drugs should be used during pregnancy unless they are absolutely necessary and are taken under close medical supervision.

Detection of Birth Defects

If a woman and her physician have some reason to suspect that there may be fetal abnormalities, a reliable and accurate test known as **amniocentesis** can help establish whether a problem exists. The test is done during the fourteenth to sixteenth week of pregnancy. The procedure consists of inserting a needle through the woman's abdominal wall and into the uterine cavity to draw out a sample of the **amniotic fluid** (fluid surrounding the fetus). Fetal cells from the fluid are cultured for chromosome analysis and the fluid is tested in procedures that take two to three weeks to produce results. A variety of birth defects can be detected by this means. Although amniocentesis cannot detect all fetal abnormalities, the number is increasing as techniques become more sophisticated.

Another technique for detection of birth defects is called **chorionic villi sampling** (CVS). The chorionic villi are threadlike protrusions on a membrane surrounding the fetus. This test involves inserting a thin catheter through the vagina and cervix into the uterus, where a small sample of the chorionic villi is removed for analysis. This procedure has several advantages over amniocentesis: it can be done as early as the eighth week instead of the fourteenth, and the results are available in 6 to 24 hours rather than two to three weeks (Cadkin et al., 1984).

Circumstances in which amniocentesis or CVS may be of benefit include: maternal age over 35 years, a parent with a chromosome defect, a previous child with Down's syndrome, a previous child with certain defects of the spine or spinal cord, or a familial background that suggests a significant risk of other disorders related to chromosome abnormalities. If the test results reveal a serious untreatable birth defect, the mother can have the pregnancy terminated. Amniocentesis and CVS involve some risks, including damage to the fetus, induced miscarriage, and infection; for this reason the procedures are not used unless there is a likelihood of a problem.

Pregnancy After 35

Increasing numbers of women are deciding to have children after 35 years of age. Projections for the 1980s indicate that the percentage of births to women 35 years and older will increase by 37% (Adams et al., 1982). Some couples are delaying childbearing for career, financial, or other reasons (Howley, 1981).

There are some greater risks to the fetus and mother with pregnancy in increased age. The rate of fetal defects due to chromosomal abnormalities rises with maternal age: The estimated rate of such fetal defects per 1000 women is 2.6 up to age 30, 5.6 at age 35, 15.8 at age 40, and 53.7 at age 45 (Hook, 1981). *Down's syndrome*, the most common condition caused by a chromosome abnormality, results in impaired intellectual functioning and various physical defects. Women 35 and older may also be more likely to experience pregnancy and delivery complications. However, medical advances have greatly reduced the risks of childbearing after 35. For women between 35 and 44 years, amniocentesis and elective abortion reduce the risk of bearing an infant with a severe birth defect to a level comparable with that for younger women (Goldberg et al., 1979). Furthermore, with careful monitoring and management, risks to the newborn and mother from complications of labor and delivery can also be reduced almost to the level for the younger population (Kujansuu et al., 1981).

Another concern that women and their partners have when they consider postponing having a child until the woman is past her twenties is that her ability to become pregnant may be lessened. Current research indicates that as women become older they have a slightly increased chance of infertility. However, "for the majority of women who want to postpone childbearing until they have completed their education and established themselves in a career, the risks they are running may be quite small compared with the benefits" (Bongaarts, 1982, p. 78).

The Experience of Pregnancy

Pregnancy is a unique and significant experience for both the woman and her partner, especially if he is involved throughout the pregnancy. In the following pages we will look at the experience and at the impact it may have on the woman and the man.

The Woman's Experience

Each woman has different emotional and physical reactions to pregnancy, and the same woman may react differently to different pregnancies. Factors influencing a woman's emotional reactions can include how the decision for pregnancy was made, current and impending lifestyle changes, her relationship with others, her financial resources, her self-image and hormonal changes. The woman's acquired attitudes and knowledge about childbearing and her hopes and fears about parenthood will also contribute to her experience.

Women sometimes feel they should experience only positive emotions when they are pregnant. However, the physical, emotional, and situational aspects of a pregnancy often elicit an array of contradictory emotions, including joy, depression, excitement, impatience, and fear. As one writer states:

That calm, sure, unambivalent woman who moved through the pages of the manuals I read seemed as unlike me as an astronaut. Nothing, to be sure, had prepared me for the intensity of relationship already existing between me and a creature I had carried in my body and now held in my arms and fed from my breasts. Throughout pregnancy and nursing, women are urged to relax, to mime the serenity of madonnas. No one mentions the psychic crisis of bearing a first child, the excitation of long-buried feelings about one's own mother, the sense of confused power and powerlessness, of being taken over on the one hand and of touching new physical and psychic potentialities on the other, a heightened sensibility which can be exhilarating, bewildering, and exhausting. No one mentions the strangeness of attraction—which can be as single-minded and overwhelming as the early days of a love affair—to a being so tiny, so dependent, so folded-in to itself—who is, and yet is not, part of oneself. (Rich, 1976, p. 36)

The marked changes that occur also have a significant effect on the experience of pregnancy. Several changes take place during the early stages of the first trimester. Menstruation ceases. As the milk glands in the breasts develop, the breasts increase in size. The nipples and areola usually become darker in color. Nausea, sometimes called "morning sickness," may occur. Many women experience a marked increase in tiredness:

> I'm ordinarily a very energetic woman, but during the first two months of my pregnancy I couldn't get enough sleep. This meant a drastic change in my daily routine. (Authors' files)

Vaginal secretions may change or increase. Urination may be more frequent and bowel movements more irregular. These physical changes may pass unnoticed, however, for there will be little increase in the size of the woman's abdomen during these first three months.

In the second trimester there are more outward signs of pregnancy. The waistline thickens and the belly begins to protrude. For some women, looking pregnant provides a sense of confirmation:

> Even though I knew I was pregnant, I somehow really didn't believe it until my stomach started to grow. (Authors' files)

Fetal movements may be felt in the fourth or fifth month. First trimester nausea and tiredness usually disappear by now, and a woman may experience heightened feelings of well-being. The breasts may begin to secrete a thin yellowish fluid called **colostrum**.

During the last trimester the uterus and abdomen increase in size (see Figure 12.4). The muscles of the uterus occasionally contract painlessly. The enlarged uterus produces pressure on the woman's stomach, intestines, and bladder. This may cause discomfort, indigestion, and frequent urination. Fetal movements can be seen and felt from the outside of the abdomen.

Fatherhood does not involve the same physical experiences (although occasionally a "pregnant father" may report psychosympathetic symptoms such as the nausea or tiredness his partner is experiencing). However, the experiences of pregnancy and birth are often profound for the father.

The Man's Experience

Significant changes have occurred in the last several decades in the role of the woman's partner during pregnancy, childbirth, and childrearing. Pregnancy, once seen as predominantly the woman's domain, is now commonly viewed as a shared experience:

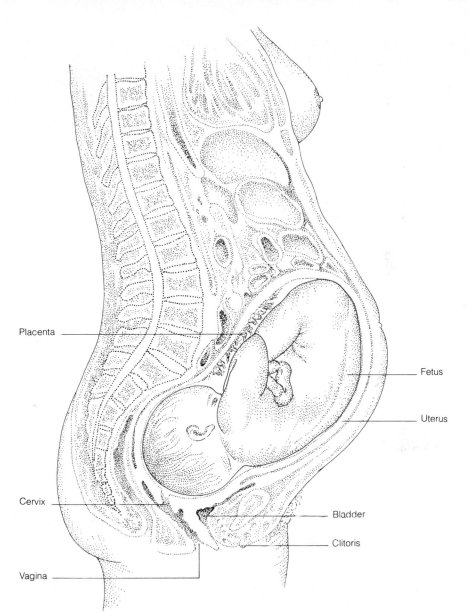

Figure 12.4

**Pregnancy at
the Ninth Month**

Placenta

Fetus

Uterus

Cervix

Bladder

Clitoris

Vagina

For many couples the proposition is now *our* pregnancy and birth. With the advent of the Lamaze method and the prepared natural-childbirth movement, the man became more intimately involved in the pregnancy and childbirth experience. He attended pregnancy and childbirth classes, and even watched childbirth films. He became an aide in the process, helping with breathing exercises, listening to little heartbeats, learning to comfort and cope with the experience of the woman. There is no question that this movement brought the male closer to the pregnancy and birth experience in some cases. For that special group there is a very real sense of "our pregnancy and birth" which represents a substantial departure from the traditional involvement of the male. (Dailey, 1978, p. 43)

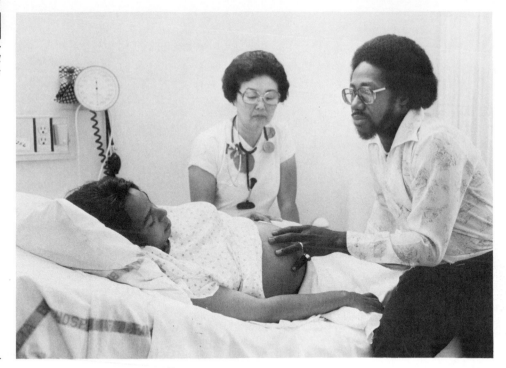

The author of the preceding quote is describing some of the unique emotional experiences of the male in what he terms the "male pregnancy." Like the woman, her partner often reacts with a great deal of ambivalence. He may feel ecstatic, but he may also be fearful about the pregnancy or the woman's safety. He may feel especially tender toward his partner, and he may become more solicitous. At the same time he may feel a sense of separateness from the woman because of the physical changes only she is experiencing. He may be proud at the prospect of becoming a father, but he may question his parenting ability and feel concern over the impending increase in responsibility. In all, the "pregnant male" has special needs, as does his partner, and in Dailey's view it is important that the woman be aware of these needs and be willing to respond to them. This "two-way" support and comfort can enhance "the level of sharing, support, and mutuality. . . and for many parents, the notion of 'our' child seems much more real" (Dailey, 1978, p. 44).

Sexual Interaction During Pregnancy

During pregnancy it may be necessary for a couple to modify intercourse positions. The side-by-side, woman-above, and rear-entry positions are generally more comfortable than the man-above position as pregnancy progresses. Oral and manual genital stimulation as well as total body touching and holding can continue as usual. In fact, pregnancy is a time when a couple may explore and develop these dimensions more fully; even if coitus is not advised, intimacy, eroticism, and sexual satisfaction can continue.

A woman's sexual interest and responsiveness may change through the course of her pregnancy. In limited studies, Masters and Johnson report no increase in sexual desire and activity during the first trimester (Masters and Johnson, 1966). Nausea, breast tenderness, and fatigue may inhibit sexual interest during this time. However, they report that increased sexual tension and response is common for some women during the second trimester. Some women may experience orgasm for the first time and others develop a multiorgasmic response. This change in sexual response may be due to the increases in pelvic vascularity during pregnancy and the resulting intensification of sexual vasocongestion. During this time the duration and intensity of orgasmic contractions are increased and resolution is slowed. During the third trimester, a decrease in sexual interest may occur.

Most other studies confirm the third trimester decline in sexual interest and activity reported by Masters and Johnson. However, other research that examined the influence of pregnancy on sexuality did not show a second trimester increase for most women; on the contrary, the study reported that the level of sexual interest and activity declined progressively over the pregnancy (Calhoun et al., 1981). Some of the most common reasons women gave for decreasing sexual activity during pregnancy included physical discomfort, feelings of physical unattractiveness, and fear of injuring the unborn child. Research indicates that a planned pregnancy results in fewer sexual problems than an unplanned pregnancy, and women who experience more sexual arousal prior to pregnancy do not lose interest in sex as much as those who experience less sexual arousal. Many women also have increased desire for nonsexual affection as pregnancy progresses (Walbroehl, 1984).

There is currently disagreement in the medical community about the safety of intercourse or orgasm late in pregnancy. Some evidence suggests that sexual intercourse during the last weeks of pregnancy may be related to greater fetal distress and to greater frequency of infections of amniotic fluid (Naeye, 1979). More recent research finds no correlation between sexual activity and orgasm, and problems with fetal heart rate or premature labor (Georgakipoulos et al., 1984; Reamy and White, 1985). Masters and Johnson state that "frequently, blanket medical interdiction of coital activity for arbitrarily established periods of time both before and after delivery has done far more harm than good" (1966, p. 168). They believe that sexual intercourse may be continued as desired until the onset of labor, with some exceptions. No coital contact should take place if spotting or vaginal or abdominal pain occur, or if the amniotic sac ("water bag") breaks. As with many other areas of sexual health care, a woman, her partner, and her health care practitioner can make an informed decision.

Childbirth

The full term of pregnancy usually lasts about nine months, although there is some variation in length. Some women may have longer pregnancies; others may give birth to fully developed infants up to a few weeks before the nine-month term is over. There is a good deal of variation in the experience of childbirth also, depending on many factors: the woman's physiology, her emotional state, the baby's size and posi-

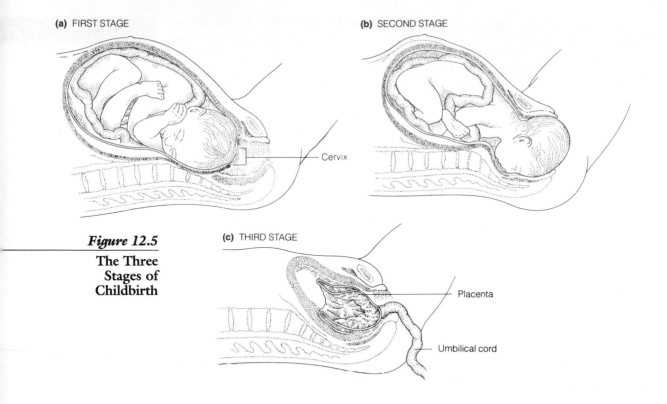

(a) FIRST STAGE

(b) SECOND STAGE

Cervix

Figure 12.5

**The Three
Stages of
Childbirth**

(c) THIRD STAGE

Placenta

Umbilical cord

tion, and the kind of childbirth practices she employs. Despite the variations, there are three generally recognizable stages in the process of childbirth (see Figure 12.5).

Stages of Childbirth

A woman can often tell that labor has begun when regular contractions of the uterus begin. Another indication of beginning **first-stage labor** may be the "bloody show" (discharge of the mucus plug from the cervix). The amniotic sac may rupture in the first stage of labor, an occurrence sometimes called "breaking the bag of waters." The first stage is shown in Figure 12.5(a).

Before the first stage begins, the cervix usually has already **effaced** (flattened and thinned) and dilated slightly. It continues to dilate throughout the first stage, and it is the extent of dilation that defines the early, late, and "transition" phases of first-stage labor. The cervix is dilated up to 5 centimeters during the early phase, 5 to 8 centimeters in the late phase, and 8 to 10 during the final, or transition, phase of the first stage. Each phase becomes shorter and the contractions become stronger; transition is usually the most intense. The first stage is the longest of the three stages, usually lasting 10–16 hours for the first childbirth, and 4–8 hours in subsequent deliveries.

The **second stage** begins when the cervix is fully dilated and the infant descends further into the vaginal birth canal. Usually the descent is head first, as shown in Figure 12.5(b). The second stage often lasts from a half hour to two hours—although it may be much shorter or longer. During this time the woman can actively push to help the baby out, and many women report their active pushing to be the best part of labor:

> I knew what "labor" meant when I was finally ready to push. I have never worked so hard, so willingly. (Authors' files)

The second stage ends when the infant is born.

The **third stage** of labor consists of the delivery of the placenta, shown in Figure 12.5(c). With one or two more uterine contractions, the placenta usually separates from the uterine wall and comes out of the vagina, generally within a half hour after the baby is born. The placenta is also called the **afterbirth**.

Childbirth Practices: Past and Present

In Europe before the 1600s women usually gave birth in their own homes, assisted by a birth attendant, a woman called a **midwife**. Childbirth generally took place with the woman in a sitting or squatting position that permitted gravity to help the child exit from the birth canal.

This practice began to change during the 1600s, however, when male "physicians" (often students, barbers, butchers, and hog gelders) began replacing midwives. Many women then went to hospitals in large cities. These hospitals were primarily charity institutions where souls could be saved as people died. There was no knowledge of the principles by which infectious diseases spread, and laboring women were examined by the unwashed hands of a "physician"—who may have just examined someone with syphilis, cholera, smallpox, or typhoid, or perhaps had recently completed dissecting a diseased cadaver. Sometimes entire wards of new mothers died from infections spread in this way. In the mid-1800s, a physician in Vienna discovered the link between childbirth fever and the infected hands of examiners. Even with minimal changes in hygienic procedures, childbirth fever deaths were eliminated in his hospital within a year (Arms, 1975).

However, other developments began that reinforced the notion that birth is painful and dangerous, necessitating extensive medical intervention. The supine position, anesthesia, and forceps all came into common use in the mid-1800s. Louis XIV initiated the use of the supine position. He found it sexually arousing to hide behind a screen and watch his various mistresses give birth. Louis had the court physician convince women to lie on their backs on a table, in full view of the hidden king, rather than sitting as they had previously done (a position which obstructed his view). The supine position then became fashionable and was widely adopted. Similarly, when Queen Victoria was convinced to use chloroform during birth, anesthesia became popular. Most of the opposition to its use came from religious leaders who said it was God's will for women to suffer in childbirth (Arms, 1975).

By the mid-1800s, forceps and the supine position had come to have a counteracting relationship. Forceps (tongs applied to the sides of the baby's head) speeded delivery, while the supine position slowed it down. The woman lying on her back works against gravity rather than with it, losing its natural assistance during delivery. The supine position also puts pressure on the blood vessels, which may slow the return of blood to the heart and thereby decrease blood availability to other organs, including the uterus. The reduction of blood flow can cause fetal distress.

By the 1900s even uncomplicated childbirth was treated as risky, requiring hospitalization, anesthetics, instruments, and machines. Technically trained medical practitioners offered a new sanitized, mechanized, controlled, physically and emotionally detached birth. Although many of the technical advancements can be helpful and frequently are life saving in problem situations, their routine use in problem-free births has become increasingly unpopular. Today, obstetric technology is still an available option in cases where complications arise, but there are also many alternatives that can make problem-free childbirth simpler, less expensive, and for some people, more pleasant.

The best-known advocates of contemporary childbirth alternatives are Grantly Dick-Read and Bernard Lamaze, who began presenting their ideas about childbirth in the late 1930s and early 1940s. Basically, they thought that certain attitudes and practices could help make childbirth a better experience. Dick-Read believed that most of the pain during childbirth stemmed from the muscle tension caused by fear. In an effort to reduce anxiety, he advocated education about the birth process and relaxation with calm, consistent support during a woman's labor. The Lamaze philosophy is similar. The method consists of learning to voluntarily relax abdominal and perineal muscles and to use breathing exercises to dissociate the involuntary labor contractions from pain sensations. Both of these methods are incorporated into childbirth education classes throughout the United States.

Although they are sometimes referred to as "natural" childbirth, **prepared childbirth** is a more appropriate label for the Dick-Read and Lamaze methods. A woman and her partner are indeed preparing themselves when they rehearse these techniques. An additional benefit of prepared childbirth is the company and support of the labor coach, often the woman's partner. Only in the past 10 years or so have hospitals routinely permitted labor coaches in the delivery room for uncomplicated vaginal, and in some cases cesarean, deliveries.

Another birth technique has been developed by a French physician, Frederick LeBoyer (1975). Instead of focusing on the parents' preparation, it is concerned primarily with the birth experience of the infant. The LeBoyer techniques can be suitable for hospital, home, or clinic delivery. (In anticipation of possible policy conflicts, permission and arrangements should be made beforehand with a hospital.) LeBoyer's basic philosophy is that the newborn's transition from the inner world of the uterus to the outer world should be made as nontraumatic as possible. Techniques such as lowered lights and hushed voices, immediate skin contact on the mother's belly, not cutting the umbilical cord until after it has stopped pulsing, and a body temperature water bath are used to soothe the senses of the newborn and reduce the shock of birth. How effective these techniques are is undetermined.

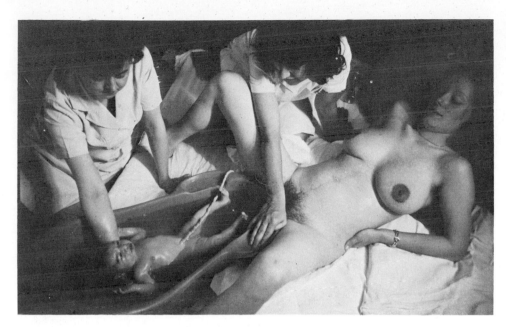

Birthplace Alternatives

Along with more options for childbirth practices have been new options for places where childbirth occurs. Not many years ago, having a baby invariably meant a stay in the hospital. But in the last few years the alternatives for location of labor and delivery facilities have increased greatly and include birthing clinics and private homes as well as hospitals. Each birthplace is unique in terms of what it offers the parents and the infant.

Hospital Births.   Hospitals have grown more receptive to individualized birth in recent years, and many hospitals now have birthing rooms with a homelike atmosphere. Participation of partner, labor coach, and others; nondrug deliveries; delivery techniques such as LeBoyer; and immediate postdelivery maternal-infant physical contact are increasingly available. The following account describes a hospital birth experience:

> My husband and I had a great deal of privacy during labor. We had consulted with our doctor prior to delivery. She agreed to use no medications unless I agreed, and to let me use the sitting-up and holding-my-knees position during second-stage pushing. We also used LeBoyer's water bath. It really felt like *our* delivery rather than "being delivered." (Authors' files)

Regulations vary among physicians and hospitals, so that experiences like this one are not always permitted. Therefore, it is important to discuss and agree upon childbirth plans with the practitioner before the time of delivery.

The hospital setting provides emergency medical care should birth complications arise. The hospital is the appropriate place for delivery in any high-risk pregnancy. Conditions that raise the risk of complication include premature labor; the infant in other than the head-first presentation; blood incompatibility between mother and fetus; **toxemia** (water retention and high blood pressure are early symptoms—the condition may result in convulsions if untreated); **placenta previa** (the placenta positioned over the cervical opening); multiple births; five or more previous deliveries; too small a pelvis; illness; or advanced age (Boston Women's Health Book Collective, 1976). Competent and thorough prenatal screening can detect most of these complications.

Most pregnancies can be delivered normally with no medical interventions. However, some women welcome extensive medical intervention in a hospital delivery:

> I want to have my second child the way I had my first. General anesthesia when things get rough—then I wake up as if nothing happened and see my beautiful baby, all clean and dressed in, hopefully, her new clothes. I don't understand women who want to go through all that work, panting, and pain when the doctor can simply take care of it all. (Authors' files)

Birthing Clinics. Birthing clinics or centers are beginning to appear in the United States. Some are adjoined to hospitals and others are separate organizations. The birthing clinic rooms are furnished more like a home than a hospital, and the pregnant

*The birth of
a child in a
birthing room
within a hospital.*

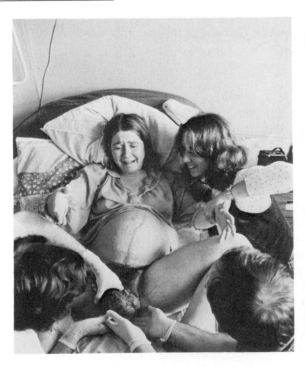
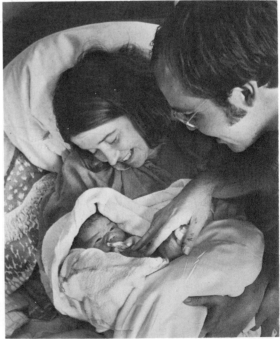

woman can arrange to have family members and friends with her. Women and their chosen attendants have the use of a room throughout labor and delivery, and some emergency medical equipment is available. A woman who delivered her second child in such a setting reports her experience:

> I was delighted to learn about the family-oriented maternity center. When labor began, my husband and three-year-old girl drove there and moved into our room. At first, between contractions, I would go to the communal kitchen to make some tea or to the playroom to chat with my daughter. When Jason was born my family, a long-time woman friend, and the doctor were all there. The doctor was supportive, yet he never interfered with my previously clarified wishes. Knowing that emergency equipment was readily available helped me to be even more relaxed. (Authors' files)

Home Birth.   Home birth has become more common over the last few years. With precautions—careful prenatal screening for complications, thorough preparations, a skilled attendant, and available emergency transportation—home birth can be safe. However, it may still be difficult to find doctors or midwives who will deliver at home. Midwives are illegal in some states, and in some cases doctors who do home deliveries may have their hospital privileges revoked. The primary advantages of home birth are the familiar surroundings, the ability to make decisions about delivery, the initial contact with the newborn independent of institutional policies, the involvement of other children or friends, the limited exposure of the newborn to strangers, and the reduced cost. To many people, the relaxed home setting is particularly valuable:

> When my contractions began, I called the midwife, my mother, and my husband to come over to the house. Supplies were already on hand. When my contractions stopped for a while, my husband and I curled up and took a nap while the others visited in the living room. The delivery went fine. I was glad I had taken the prepared childbirth classes and learned the breathing to help me over the rough spots. Afterwards, as I was lying in my husband's arms holding our new baby I felt—at home. (Authors' files)

The greatest risks with a home birth are that life-saving emergency equipment is not readily available and that emergencies are not always predictable.

Medical Interventions: Pros and Cons

Women and their partners should be aware of possible benefits and side effects of medical procedures used during childbirth. Often an initial minor intervention will result in other procedures becoming necessary. Furthermore, there is some evidence that the receptivity and contact between parent and child immediately after delivery may have an effect on the formation of their relationship. The conditions in which a woman gives birth greatly affect the course of her labor, the normalcy of her delivery, the health of her baby, and the relationship of parents and child (Klaus and Kenell, 1982). Drugs, fetal heart monitors, forceps, cesarean delivery, and episiotomies are common medical interventions whose advantages and disadvantages need to be evaluated carefully.

Most drugs given to the woman during childbirth cross the placental barrier. As a result, they can affect not only the mother but also the fetus during labor, and often after delivery. Research indicates that drugs can slow, lengthen, or stop labor; cause maternal convulsions and lowered blood pressure; eliminate the urge to push during second stage labor, and affect fetal heart rate and oxygen supply (Willson et al., 1983). Newborn sucking behavior, responsiveness to cuddling, and muscular, visual, and neural development have been shown to be retarded by the use of certain obstetrical medications (Kron et al., 1966; Scanlon, 1974). Drugs may inhibit the newborn's responsiveness to its parents, which may negatively affect the parent-child attachment.

In addition to the administration of drugs, other procedures are frequently used during deliveries. An **episiotomy**, an incision in the perineum from the vagina toward the anus, is often made in hospital deliveries. The rationale for episiotomies is that they reduce the pressure on the infant's head and also help prevent vaginal tearing, which is more difficult to suture than a straight incision and often heals less well. Episiotomies also are thought to help preserve pelvic muscle tone and support. While the procedure is common in the United States, it is not considered necessary in most other societies. Only 8% of birthing women in Holland have episiotomies. Relaxation, proper breathing and pushing, physician patience, manual stretching of the perineum, and freedom of leg movement can eliminate the need for many routine incisions.

Forceps, shaped like salad tongs, fit alongside the baby's head and are used to assist the infant out of the birth canal. Forceps are often used after analgesics and anesthetics have reduced the strength of uterine contractions. Careful use of forceps is justified with certain complications but not with routine, normal deliveries, for they pose some risks of injury to the woman and baby.

A **cesarean delivery**, in which the baby is removed through an incision made in the abdominal wall and uterus, can be life-saving surgery for the mother and child. Cesarean birth may be recommended in a variety of situations, including a fetal head that is too large for the mother's pelvic structure, maternal illness (including herpes in the vaginal tract), birth complications such as breech-fetal position (feet or bottom coming out of the uterus first), and many others. Mothers who do have a cesarean delivery often have a spinal anesthetic and are awake to greet their infant when she or he is delivered. A woman may have more than one baby by cesarean delivery. Also, many women can have subsequent vaginal deliveries, depending on the circumstances of the earlier cesarean delivery(s) and of the subsequent delivery (Lavin et al., 1982; Porreco and Meier, 1983).

The percentage of cesarean deliveries performed in the United States has increased dramatically over the last 15 to 20 years. In 1970 approximately 5.5% of deliveries were cesarean; in 1978 this figure had more than doubled to 15.2% (NIH Cesarean Birth Task Force, 1980). In 1984 approximately 15%–20% of deliveries were cesarean (Pritchard et al., 1985). The increase in the incidence of cesarean deliveries has evoked controversy. While some maintain that the increase reflects better use of medical technology in the management of childbirth, others believe that cesarean deliveries are aggressive medical interventions that are being too readily used.

Postpartum

The first several weeks following birth are referred to as the **postpartum period**. It is a time of both physical and psychological adjustment for each family member and is likely to be a time of intensified emotional highs and lows. Understanding that these feelings are a common response to adjustments to the new family member may help new parents cope with the stresses involved. Combined with the excitement and pleasures of the arrival of the long-awaited infant are often other feelings. The mother may experience what is described as "postpartum blues," during which she may cry easily and feel fearful or sad. Such reactions may be partly due to the sudden physical and hormonal changes following delivery.

The new baby also affects the roles and interactions of all the members of the family. The mother and father may experience an increased closeness to each other as well as some troublesome feelings. New fathers sometimes feel jealous of the relationship between the mother and child. Both the man and the woman may want extra emotional support from the other, but each may have less than usual to give. The time and energy demands of caring for an infant can contribute to weariness and stress—feelings that may be compounded by the impact of the responsibility of caring for this new addition for the next 20 years. Brothers and sisters may also be affected, as they often have some negative feelings about the attention given the new family member.

Each of these feelings and concerns gradually tends to lessen as the family makes adjustments to new roles and expectations. Often, too, the adjustment is easier when family members have accurate expectations (or previous experience) to prepare them for the demands as well as the pleasure of the new arrival.

Parent-Child Contact

Not just the first weeks after birth but also the first few minutes after birth may be a very important period. There has been a growing interest and concern about the parent-child contact that takes place following birth and the impact that this contact has on parent-child attachment. The reciprocal attachment may influence the developing child's behavior and may help the parent make the adjustment to the nurturing role, providing motivation to meet the insistent demands of a helpless infant.

Some hospitals are changing the traditional postpartum separation of infant and mother. In others, however, standard procedure is similar to that in the following description:

> In many hospitals, the newborn, after the cord is tied, is given to a nurse. She takes him to a table where a radiant heat panel avoids chilling his wet skin. A footprint is taken so no confusion is possible later on. Soon the baby, wrapped in a blanket, is brought to the mother. In some places, a 5–10 minute visit is allowed, but in others the nurse merely shows the baby to her. Then the child is taken to the nursery, washed, weighed and placed in a crib—alone again. (Spezzano and Waterman, 1977, p. 110)

*Many men share
in caring for their
children.*

One study compared groups of infant-mother pairs where different amounts of contact were experienced (Klaus and Kenell, 1982). Some mothers were given more contact with their newborns both immediately after birth and during their hospital stay than is the usual hospital procedure. These extended-contact mothers consequently engaged in more holding, fondling, kissing, eye contact, talking to the infant, and successful and lengthy breast feeding than other mothers. These infants were found to cry less and to smile and laugh more. At five years of age, the children of extended-contact mothers had significantly higher IQs and more advanced scores on language tests than children who were treated according to standard hospital procedures. In this same study, fathers who were asked to establish eye contact for one hour during the first day of life and to dress their children twice a day during the hospital stay also demonstrated an increase in their caretaker role at home.

Attachment depends, in part, on complex interactions between parent and child that begin immediately after birth. The mother, when she is alert during delivery, often wants to have the closest possible contact with her newborn. The immediate interaction can be a profound experience that initiates a "series of reciprocal interactions" (Klaus and Kenell, 1976, p. 11). The timing of the initial close physical contact appears to be important to the infant too:

Right after a drug-free, uncomplicated delivery, the baby is quite alert—even more so than he will be later on. Evidence shows that he responds to a moving face and to sounds near his ear. If the corner of his mouth is touched, he reflexively turns his head to that side and starts to suck. Rub his palm, especially between thumb and forefinger, and he will hold on to whatever is tickling him. His senses and reflexes mark him as a responsive human being in need of human contact, and the contact he needs is right there—mother. She has the rhythmic heartbeat he is accustomed to, eyes to look at, a warm body to touch, breasts to suck. (Spezzano and Waterman, 1977, p. 110)

The father can also provide this kind of contact. Therefore, the maximum potential for parent-child attachment depends partly on an environment that encourages physical closeness of the parents and child.

Once again, prospective parents who are informed about the choices can discuss their needs with the physician before the delivery. Even in cases of cesarean delivery or of premature babies who must be in incubators, adjustment of hospital routines can sometimes be made to maximize parent-child contact if the parents wish.

Breast Feeding

Production of breast milk does not take place as soon as the infant is born. Right after delivery the breasts produce a yellowish liquid called **colostrum**, which contains antibodies and protein. Lactation, or milk production, begins about one to three days after delivery. Pituitary hormones stimulate milk production in the breasts in response to the stimulation of the infant suckling the nipple. If a new mother does not begin or continue to nurse, milk production subsides within a matter of days.

Nursing may temporarily inhibit ovulation. However, it is highly unreliable as a method of birth control (see Chapter 11). Birth control pills should not be used during nursing, because the hormones (as well as other drugs) are transmitted to the infant in the mother's milk.

Closely related to the concern with postpartum contact is the renewed interest in breast feeding over the last several years. For women who decide to nurse, breast feeding is another opportunity for close physical contact. It also has other advantages. It provides the infant with a digestible food filled with antibodies and other immunity-producing substances. Nursing also induces uterine contractions that help speed the return of the uterus to its pre-pregnancy size. Breast feeding can be an emotional and sensual experience for the mother. Masters and Johnson (1966) found that sexual interest often returns more rapidly in women who breast-feed than in those who bottle-feed. However, most women in another study reported that breast feeding had no effect on their sexual relationship. When a negative effect was reported it was usually due to decreased sexual enjoyment due to breast tenderness, decreased vaginal lubrication, or milk leakage (Ellis and Hewat, 1985).

Nursing has some disadvantages. The nursing mother's genitals may be oversensitive and become sore from intercourse because of the reduction of estrogen that nursing creates (estrogen conditions and maintains vulvar tissue) (Walbroehl, 1984). Her breasts may also be tender and sore. Milk may be ejected involuntarily from her nipples during sexual excitement and be a source of embarrassment. Also, the tasks of caring for a baby and the physical demands of producing milk may leave the woman with little energy for sexual activities.

Some women may have negative feelings about breast feeding. Many women feel ambivalent about this activity, perhaps partly because of our society's emphasis on breasts as sex symbols. Furthermore, some mothers' lives may be too disrupted

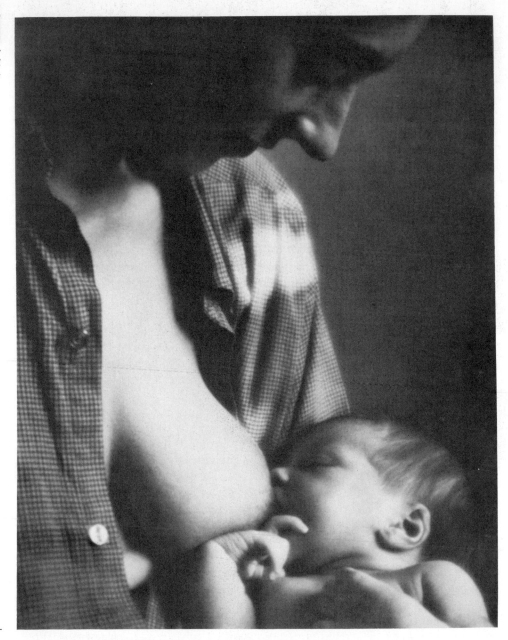

by the sole feeding responsibility of nursing, particularly if they have to return to work shortly after childbearing. It is often easier to share childcare responsibilities by bottle feeding rather than nursing, and a father can play a greater role by holding and feeding the infant. However, a nursing mother can use a breast pump to extract her milk, so that it is available to her partner or another caretaker for bottle feeding the baby. Like other aspects of childcare, breast feeding is a matter of exploration and personal preference.

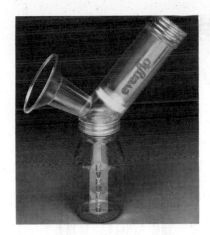

*A breast pump
extracts breast milk
to be fed to the
baby by bottle.*

Sexual Interaction After Childbirth

In the past, many physicians prohibited intercourse until six weeks after delivery. Currently, couples are commonly advised that intercourse can resume after the flow of the reddish uterine discharge, called **lochia**, has stopped and after episiotomy incisions or vaginal tears have healed (Masters and Johnson, 1966). An important factor to consider is when intercourse is physically comfortable for the woman. This will depend on the type of delivery, the size and presentation of the baby, the extent of episiotomy or lacerations, and the individual woman's rate of healing. There is also a postpartum decrease in estrogen, especially pronounced with breast feeding, that can lead to thinning of the vaginal mucosa and reduction in vaginal lubrication, which in turn can cause discomfort in intercourse (Walbroehl, 1984). After a cesarean delivery the couple needs to wait until the incision has healed enough for intercourse to occur without discomfort. Other sexual and affectionate relations can be shared while waiting.

Psychological readiness for sexual activity is another important factor. The significant changes in daily life that a new baby brings can effect sexual intimacy. There is some evidence that desire for and frequency and satisfaction of sexual activity decline during the first year following birth (Fischman and Rankin, 1983). An obstetrician comments:

> Planned spontaneity is now the order. Between the baby's schedule, her husband's working hours, and all her chores, there is precious little time left for love. It usually comes last, when everyone is fatigued. In general, the breastfeeding woman is far more tired. There is an actual drain on her body to produce the milk, and unless the baby will take a supplementary bottle or stored breast milk, no one else can feed the baby at odd hours. . . .

Couples whose sexual activity has been disrupted by pregnancy and birth may feel "out of practice" with their sexual relationship. It is often helpful for couples to slowly resume sexual activity in an explorative manner, as if they were first initiating a sexual relationship (Murray, 1976). Once intercourse is resumed, contraception is necessary for as long as the couple wants to avoid another pregnancy.

Summary

Parenthood as an Option

1. Increasing numbers of couples are choosing not to be parents and others are adopting children or providing homes for foster children.

Becoming Pregnant

2. Failure to ovulate and blockage of the fallopian tubes are typical causes of female infertility. Low sperm count is the most common cause of male infertility.

3. The emotional stress and the disruption of a couple's sexual relationship caused by infertility can result in sexual difficulties.

4. The man-above intercourse position, deep penetration at ejaculation, and staying still after ejaculation may enhance chances of conception.

5. Techniques for selecting the sex of a child are not highly effective.

6. The first sign of a pregnancy is usually a missed menstrual period. Urine tests and pelvic exams are used to determine pregnancy.

Spontaneous and Induced Abortion

7. Spontaneous abortion, or miscarriage, sometimes occurs during pregnancy. Often the aborted tissues are abnormal.

8. Induced abortion is a controversial issue in the United States today. Suction curettage, D and E, intra-amniotic injections, and intravaginal suppositories of prostaglandins are the medical techniques used for pregnancy termination.

9. Contraceptive risk-taking sometimes precedes an unplanned pregnancy and consequent abortion. There are different kinds of "costs" and "benefits" to contraceptive use for each woman and in each relationship.

A Healthy Pregnancy

10. Pregnancy is divided into three trimesters, each of which is marked by fetal changes.

11. Nutrients, oxygen, and waste exchange between the woman and fetus occurs through the placental cell walls. Substances harmful to the fetus can pass through the placenta from the mother's blood.

12. In amniocentesis, cells and the amniotic fluid are examined to detect birth defects. The number of problems that can be detected by this means is constantly increasing.

13. More women are deciding to have children after age 35. These women have slightly decreased fertility and a somewhat higher risk of conceiving a fetus with abnormalities and of having pregnancy and delivery complications. However, with careful monitoring of pregnancy and childbirth, their risks can be reduced almost to the level of risks for younger women.

The Experience of Pregnancy

14. Some first trimester physical changes include cessation of menstruation, tiredness, and breast size increase. In the second trimester the woman's belly begins to protrude and she can feel fetal movements. By the third trimester the abdomen is enlarged and fetal movements are pronounced.

15. Men have become increasingly involved in the prenatal, childbirth, and childrearing processes.

16. Although changes of position may be necessary, sensual and sexual interaction may continue as desired during pregnancy, except in occasional cases of medical complications.

Childbirth

17. Indications of first-stage labor are regular contractions of the uterus, discharge of the mucus plug, rupture of the amniotic sac, and cervical effacement and dilation of up to five centimeters.

18. Second-stage labor is the descent of the infant into the birth canal, ending with birth. The placenta is delivered in the third stage.

19. Prepared childbirth, popularized by Bernard Lamaze and Grantly Dick-Read, has changed childbirth practices, as have LeBoyer birth techniques.

20. The birthing clinic combines a home setting and limited emergency backup equipment.

21. Home births are becoming more common. A woman or couple have maximum control of the birth experience in the home; however, medical emergency backup equipment is not available.

22. Hospital delivery procedures have become more flexible for noncomplicated deliveries and provide the safest place for problem deliveries.

23. Medical interventions during birth (drugs, forceps, cesarean delivery, and episiotomies) can be helpful in the delivery process, but many people believe that they are overused.

Postpartum

24. Extended postdelivery parent-child contact may positively influence the quality of the relationship.

25. Breast feeding is regaining popularity in the United States. There are advantages and disadvantages to breast or bottle feeding.

26. Intercourse after childbirth can usually resume once the flow of lochia has stopped and any vaginal tears or the episiotomy incision have healed.

Thought Provokers

1. If you were in a position of deciding whether a large research grant would go towards developing a perfect contraceptive or a cure for infertility, what would you decide? Why?

2. If preconception sex selection became accurate, easy, and inexpensive, what do you think the consequences would be?

3. What laws, if any, should be established regarding surrogate motherhood, in vitro fertilization, artificial insemination, and embryo transfer?

Suggested Readings

Dornbaser, Carole, and Landy, Ute. *The Abortion Guide: A Handbook for Women and Men*. Rockville Center, N.Y.: Playboy Paperbacks, 1982. The medical and emotional aspects of abortion, including a focus on decision making.

Gerson, Kathleen. *Hard Choices*. Berkeley, Calif.: University of California Press, 1985. An in-depth analysis of the individual and social forces which influence how women decide about work, career, and motherhood.

Herzfeld, Judith. *Sense and Sensibility in Childbirth*. New York: Norton, 1985. A book that offers insights and advice on childbirth concerns.

Luker, Kristin. "The War Between Women." *Family Planning Perspectives*, 1984, 16, 105–110. An illuminating article about the basic lifestyle and value differences between prochoice and antiabortion activists.

Parke, Ross. *Fathers*. Cambridge, Mass.: Harvard University Press, 1981. A discussion of how an involved and caring father can make a difference in his family in a variety of fathering roles: divorced, stepparenting, house husband, or traditional.

Rubin, Sylvia. *It's Not Too Late for a Baby*. Englewood Cliffs, N.J.: Prentice-Hall, 1980. A practical guide to childbirth for the expectant parent over the age of 35. Includes a section on fathers over 35; has illustrative case examples.

Resources

International Childbirth Education Association, P.O. Box 20048, Minneapolis, MN 55420. Provides information and resources for childbirth education.

La Leche League, P.O. Box 1209, Franklin Park, IL 60131-8209. Provides education and encouragement for breastfeeding.

National Association of Parents and Professionals for Safe Alternatives in Childbirth, P.O. Box 429, Marble Hill, MO 63764. Provides information about alternatives to traditional hospital delivery.

13

If men and women are to understand each other, to enter into each other's nature with mutual sympathy, and to become capable of genuine comradeship, the foundation must be laid in youth.
Havelock Ellis
The Task of Social Hygiene (1912)

Sexuality During Childhood and Adolescence

Sexual Behavior in Childhood
The Physical Changes of Adolescence
Sexual Behavior During Adolescence
Adolescent Pregnancy
Some Key Influences on Psychosexual Development
Sex Education
Androgynous Child-Rearing and Sexuality

IN MANY WESTERN SOCIETIES, including the United States, it has been traditional to view childhood as a time when sexuality remains unexpressed and adolescence as a time when sexuality needs to be restrained. These viewpoints no doubt reflect, at least in part, the sex-for-procreation philosophy that has long influenced American sexual attitudes and behaviors. The opinion that adolescent sexual behavior should be curtailed continues to receive considerable support. However, with the widespread circulation of the findings of Alfred Kinsey and other distinguished investigators, the false assumption that childhood is a period of sexual dormancy is gradually eroding. In fact, it is now widely recognized that infants of both sexes are born with the capacity for sexual pleasure and response.

Signs of sexual arousal in infants and children, such as penile erection, vaginal lubrication, and pelvic thrusting, are often misinterpreted or unacknowledged. However, careful observers may note these indications of sexuality in the very young. In some cases infants, both male and female, have been observed experiencing what appears to be an orgasm. The infant, of course, cannot offer spoken confirmation of the sexual nature of such reactions. However, the behavior is so remarkably similar to that exhibited by sexually responding adults that little doubt exists about its nature. The following two quotations offer evidence for this conclusion:

Orgasm has been observed in boys of every age from 5 months to adolescence. Orgasm is in our records for a female babe of 4 months. The orgasm in an infant or other young male is, except for the lack of ejaculation, a striking duplicate of orgasm in an older adult. The behavior involves a series of gradual physiologic changes, the development of rhythmic body movements with distinct penis throbs and pelvic thrusts, an obvious change in sensory capacities, a final tension of muscles, especially of the abdomen, hips, and back, a sudden release with convulsions, including rhythmic anal contractions—followed by the disappearance of all symptoms. A fretful babe quiets down under the initial sexual stimulation, is distracted from other activities, begins rhythmic pelvic thrusts, becomes tense as climax approaches, is thrown into convulsive action, often with violent arm and leg movements, sometimes with weeping at the moment of climax. After climax the child loses erection quickly and subsides into the calm and peace that typically follows adult orgasm. It may be some time before erection can be induced again after such an experience. There are observations of 16 males up to 11 months of age, with such typical orgasm reached in 7 cases. In 5 cases of young pre-adolescents, observations were continued over months or years, until the individuals were old enough to make it certain that true orgasm was involved and in all of these cases the later reactions were so similar to the earlier behavior that there could be no doubt of the orgastic nature of the first experience. (Kinsey et al., 1948, p. 177)

The typical reactions of a small girl in orgasm, seen by an intelligent mother who had frequently observed her three-year-old in masturbation, were described as follows; "Lying face down on the bed, with her knees drawn up, she started rhythmic pelvic thrusts, about one second or less apart. The thrusts were primarily pelvic, with the legs tensed in a fixed position. The forward components of the thrusts were in a smooth and perfect rhythm which was unbroken except for momentary pauses during which the genitalia were readjusted against the doll on which they were pressed; the return from each thrust was convulsive, jerky. There were 44 thrusts in unbroken rhythm, a slight momentary pause, 87 thrusts followed by a slight momentary pause, concentration and intense breathing with abrupt jerks as orgasm approached. She was completely oblivious to everything during these later stages of the activity. Her eyes were glassy and fixed in a vacant stare. There was noticeable relief and relaxation after orgasm. A second series of reactions began two minutes later with series of 48, 18, and 57 thrusts, with slight momentary pauses between each series. With the mounting tensions, there were audible gasps, but immediately following the cessation of pelvic thrusts there was complete relaxation and only desultory movements thereafter."

We have similar records of observations made by some of our other subjects on a total of 7 pre-adolescent girls and 27 pre-adolescent boys under four years of age. These data indicate that the capacity to respond to the point of orgasm is certainly present in at least some young children, both female and male. (Kinsey et al., 1953, pp. 104–105)

It is impossible to determine what such early sexual experiences mean to infants, but it is reasonably certain that these activities are gratifying. Many infants of both sexes engage quite naturally in self-pleasuring unless such behavior produces strong negative responses from parents or other caretakers.

As this information demonstrates, we cannot accurately view sexuality as something that remains dormant during the early years of life. A variety of behaviors and body functions, including sexual eroticism, develop during infancy and childhood. In some ways sexuality may be especially important during this period, as many experiences during these formative years may have great impact on the later expression of adult sexuality. In the opening section of this chapter we will briefly outline some typical sexual behaviors during childhood.

Sexual Behavior in Childhood

People show considerable variation in their sexual development during childhood, and many diverse influences are involved. Despite these differences, however, certain common features in the developmental sequence tend to emerge. In the next few pages we will briefly outline some of these typical behaviors, keeping in mind that each person's unique sexual history may differ from one or more of the following points. As you consider this information, it is also important to realize that most of the data about childhood sexual behavior is based on the recollections of adults who are asked to recall their childhood experiences. As we noted in Chapter 2, it may be quite difficult to remember accurately experiences that occurred many years earlier.

In the first few years of life many girls and boys discover the pleasures of genital stimulation. This activity often involves rubbing the genital area against an object such as a doll or pillow. With the development of coordinated hand movements, manual stimulation may become a preferred method for producing sexual pleasure. In all probability, such activity is more likely to be observed in children raised in home environments where adults hold permissive attitudes toward genital touching.

A child may also learn to express his or her affectionate and erotic feelings through activities like kissing and hugging. The responses the child receives to these expressions of intimacy may have a strong influence on the manner in which he or she expresses sexuality in later years. The inclinations we have as adults toward giving and receiving affection seem to be related to our early opportunities for warm, pleasurable contact with significant others, particularly parents. A number of researchers believe that children who are deprived of "contact comfort" (being touched and held) during the first months and years of life may have difficulty establishing intimate relationships later in their lives (Harlow and Harlow, 1962; Money, 1980; Montagu and Matson, 1979; Trause et al., 1977).

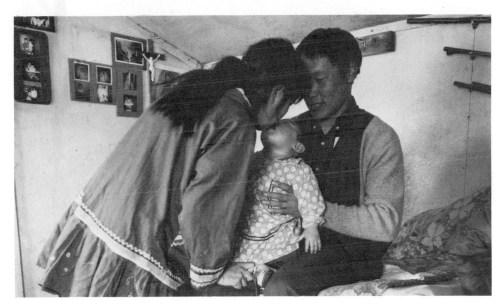

Sharing sexual intimacies as adults may be related to childhood experiences of warm, pleasurable contact, particularly with parents.

In addition to self-stimulation, prepubertal children often engage in play that may be viewed as sexual in nature. Such play takes place with friends or siblings of the same or the other sex. It may occur as early as the age of two or three, but it is more likely to take place between the ages of four and seven. Kinsey (1948 and 1953) noted that 45% of the females and 57% of the males in his sample reported having these experiences by age 12. In a more recent survey, parents of six- and seven-year-old children reported that 76% of their daughters and 83% of their sons had participated in some sex play with friends or siblings (Kolodny, 1980). The activities may range from exhibition and inspection of the genitals, often under the guise of "playing doctor," to simulating intercourse by rubbing genital regions together. While most adults, particularly parents, tend to react to the apparent sexual nature of this play, for many children the play aspects of the interaction may be far more significant than any sexual overtones:

> The sexual nature of these games is not always understood by the child and even when the small boy lies on the top of the small girl and makes what may resemble copulatory movement, there is often no realization that genital contact might be made, or that there might be an erotic reward in such activity. (Kinsey et al., 1953, p. 108)

> When we think of preadolescent activities that look sexual—we, as adults, looking back on it, or as parents looking at it in our children—we respond to the sexual aspect; the sex is very important; the play is unimportant. To the child, however, the balance is exactly the opposite. The play is the major part; whatever sex might be in it, is mainly interesting because it is forbidden, like mommy's jewel box or daddy's tool chest. (Gagnon, 1977, p. 85)

As this last quote suggests, curiosity about what is forbidden probably plays an important role in encouraging early sexual exploration. Curiosity about the sexual

*Many children
find the play
aspects of interac-
tions like this one
more important
than any sexual
overtones.*

equipment of others, particularly the other sex, is quite normal. Many daycare centers and nursery schools now have bathrooms open to both sexes so that children can learn about sexual differences in a natural, everyday way.

Besides showing interest in sexual behaviors, many children in the five-to-seven age range begin to act in ways that mirror the predominant heterosexual marriage script in our society. This is apparent in the practice of "playing house," which is typical of children of this age (Broderick, 1966). Some of the sex play described earlier occurs within the context of this activity.

By the time children reach the age of eight or nine, there is a pronounced tendency for boys and girls to begin to play separately, although romantic interest in the other sex may exist at the same time. Furthermore, in spite of an apparent decline

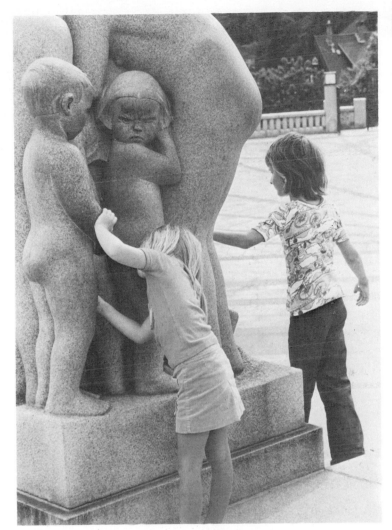

in sex play with others, curiosity about sexual matters remains high. This is an age when many questions about reproduction and sexuality may be asked.

Most 10- and 11-year-olds are keenly interested in body changes, particularly those involving the genitals and secondary sex characteristics. They often wait in eager anticipation for these signs of approaching adolescence. Many prepubescent children may become extremely self-conscious about their bodies and may be quite reticent about exposing them to the view of others. Segregation from the other sex is still the general rule, and children of this age often strongly protest any suggestions of romantic interest in the other sex. Nonetheless, most girls and boys of this age have already decided they want to get married (Broderick, 1971).

Sex play with friends of the same sex is common during the late childhood years. In fact, during this time when the segregation of the sexes is particularly strong, homosexual activity is probably more common than heterosexual encounters (Comfort, 1963). In one survey of 432 white children, conducted by Kinsey and his associates, 52% of males and 35% of females reported homosexual experiences prior to puberty (Elias and Gebhard, 1969). In most instances these childhood homosexual encounters are transitory and are soon replaced by the heterosexual courting of adolescence. We encourage parents who become aware of these behaviors to avoid responding in an overly negative fashion or labeling such activity as homosexual in the adult sense (Carrera, 1981; Gadpaille, 1975).

Masturbation is one of the most common sexual expressions during the childhood years. In Kinsey's study of children 30% of the females and 56% of the males reported masturbating prior to adolescence (Elias and Gebhard, 1969). In a more recent survey, one-third of the female respondents and two-thirds of the males reported having masturbated by the age of 13 (Hunt, 1974). For both sexes masturbation is the most frequent source of preadolescent orgasm (Kinsey et al., 1948 and 1953). Most boys learn about it from friends, and some may even receive instruction in the particulars of self-stimulation, as the following account indicates:

Children are naturally curious about the naked human body.

My introduction to the fine art of masturbation was provided by an older buddy. One day in his basement, while changing from wet swim suits, he asked me if I had ever "jerked off." Well, I hadn't and he proceeded to soap up his penis and demonstrate his technique. When I tried it, the sensations were very good but, unlike my friend, nothing came out of my penis. He told me to keep practicing and I did. Several months later I had my first ejaculation. (Authors' files)

In contrast to males, most young girls do not discuss masturbation with friends. For them, discovery of this activity is usually a solitary and often an accidental event:

I discovered the delights of masturbation when I was about eight years old. My mother always encouraged me to thoroughly wash my "privates." One day in the tub I decided to make them "squeaky clean." I slid my bottom under the faucet and directed a stream of warm water over my vulva. Wow! That was one kind of washing I really liked. In short order I experienced my first orgasm. I didn't even know what you called it, but the sensations were great. I soon improvised all kinds of ways to squirt water over my clitoris. I never told anyone about my "discovery," but continued masturbating regularly with this water-spray technique. Today I have no problem understanding the popularity of hand-held water massagers. (Authors' files)

As these accounts and the preceding discussion have indicated, self-discovery and peer interactions are very important during childhood development of sexuality. These factors continue to be influential during the adolescent years, as we shall discover in later portions of this chapter. But first we will turn our attention to the physical changes that accompany the onset of adolescence.

The Physical Changes of Adolescence

Adolescence is a time of dramatic physiological changes and social-role development. In Western societies it is the transition between childhood and adulthood that typically spans the period from 12 to 20 years of age. Most of the major physical changes of adolescence take place during the first few years of this period. However, important and often profound changes in behavior and role expectations occur throughout this phase of life. By cross-cultural standards, adolescence in our society is rather extended. In many cultures (and in Western society in preindustrial times) adult roles are assumed at a much earlier age. Rather than undergoing a protracted period of child-adult status, the child is often initiated into adulthood upon reaching puberty.

Puberty (Latin *pubescere*, to be covered with hair) is a term frequently used to describe the period of rapid physical changes in early adolescence. The onset of puberty is approximately two years earlier for girls than for boys. Before puberty, both boys and girls have been growing taller and stronger. It is not known what mechanism triggers the chain of developments that follow, but we do know that the hypothalamus plays a part (Katchadourian, 1977). In general, when a child is between 8 and 14 years old, the hypothalamus increases secretions that cause the pituitary to release larger amounts of **gonadotropins** into the bloodstream. The gonadotropins, hormones that stimulate activity in the gonads, are chemically identical in men and women. However, in males they cause the testes to increase testosterone production, while in females they act on the ovaries to produce elevated estrogen levels.

At this point, external signs of characteristic male and female sexual maturation begin to be manifest in response to higher levels of the male and female hormones. The resulting developments—breasts, deepened voice, and facial, body, and pubic hair—are called **secondary sex characteristics**. Growth of pubic hair in both sexes and breast budding (slight protuberance under the nipple) in girls are usually the earliest signs of puberty. A growth spurt also follows. This spurt eventually terminates, again under the influence of the sex hormones, which send signals to close the ends of the long bones. The growth spurt usually occurs earlier in females than in males (on the average, age 12 versus 14) and often results in girls being taller than boys during early adolescence (Marshall, 1977). External genitals also undergo enlargement; the penis and testes increase in size in the male, and the labia become enlarged in the female.

Under the influence of hormone stimulation, the internal organs of the male and female undergo further development during puberty. In girls, the vaginal walls become thicker and the uterus becomes larger and more muscular. The vaginal pH changes from alkaline to acidic as vaginal and cervical secretions increase in response to the changing hormone status. Eventually menstruation begins; the first menstrual period is called **menarche**. Initial menstrual periods may be irregular and occur without ovulation. Some adolescent females may experience irregular menstrual cycles for several years before their periods become regular and predictable. Consequently, so-called "natural" methods of birth control based on the menstrual cycle can be particularly unreliable for females in this age group. Most girls begin menstruating around the age of 12 or 13, but there is widespread variation in the age of menarche. Research suggests that menarche may be triggered when a certain minimum percentage of body fat is present (Frisch and McArthur, 1974). At the onset of puberty the average ratio of lean to fatty tissue in females is 5 to 1 (that is, approximately one-sixth of the total body weight is fat). At menarche it is about 3 to 1 (about one-fourth of body weight is fat). In support of the suggested connection between body fat and menarche, research has revealed that female athletes and ballet dancers who engage in prolonged and strenuous training frequently experience delayed menarche or interrupted menstruation (Frisch et al., 1980; Warren, 1982). Presumably this results from having a low proportion of body fat.

In boys, the prostate gland and seminal vesicles increase noticeably in size during this time. Although boys may experience orgasms throughout childhood, ejaculation is not possible until the prostate and seminal vesicles begin functioning under the influence of increasing testosterone levels. Typically, the first ejaculation occurs a year after the growth spurt has begun, usually around age 13 or 14, but as with menstruation, the timing is highly variable. Kinsey (1948) reported that in two out of three boys initial ejaculation occurred during masturbation. There appears to be a period of early adolescent infertility in many girls and boys following initial menstruation or ejaculation. However, this should not be depended upon for birth control. In some males sperm production occurs in the early stages of puberty, and even the first ejaculation may contain viable sperm (Abrahams, 1982).

Voice changes caused by growth of the voice box (larynx) occur in both sexes, but they are more dramatic in boys, who often experience an awkward time when their speech alternates between low and high pitch. Facial hair in boys and axillary (underarm) hair in both sexes usually appears approximately two years after the pubic hair. Increased activity of oil-secreting glands in the skin can cause facial blemishes, or acne.

Many of these physical developments may be sources of concern or of pride to the adolescent and his or her family and friends. Feeling self-conscious is a common reaction, and individuals who mature early or late often feel particularly self-conscious:

> I was the first one to get hair on my chest. At first I would cut it off so I wasn't different from everyone else in the shower room. (Authors' files)

> All my friends had started menstruating a long time before and I still had not. I started wearing pads and a belt once a month so I wouldn't feel so out of it. (Authors' files)

The physical changes we have been describing are quite dramatic and rapid. Suddenly the body one has been living in for years undergoes mysterious changes that are often disconcerting:

> If given the chance, I would never repeat my early teen years. My body was so unpredictable. At the most inopportune moments my voice was cracking, my penis was erect, or a pimple was popping out on my face. Sometimes, all these things would happen at the same time! (Authors' files)

These physical changes do not go unnoticed by adolescent peers. Boy-girl friendships often change, and adolescents are likely to become—at least temporarily—more **homosocial**, relating socially primarily with members of the same sex. A young woman clarifies:

> When I was growing up a neighbor boy and I were best buddies. We spent our summers exploring nearby fields, wrestling, and building a great tree house. When I started developing breasts it all changed, and we didn't seem to know how to talk to each other any more. (Authors' files)

Adolescent relationships often do not remain homosocial for very long. The period of adolescence is marked not only by physical changes, but also by important behavioral changes. In the following pages we will look at some important areas of adolescent sexual behavior.

Sexual Behavior During Adolescence

Adolescence is a period of exploration, when sexual behavior—both self-stimulation and partner-shared—generally increases. While much of teenage sexuality represents a progression from childhood behaviors, a new significance is attached to sexual expression. We will look at some areas in which important developments take place during adolescence, including masturbation, petting, development of on-going relationships, intercourse, pregnancy and the use of birth control, and homosexuality. In most areas of adolescent sexuality the male-female double standard is a pervasive influence. Another powerful influence is peer pressure. We will consider these two influences before turning to specific behaviors.

The Double Standard

Although children have been learning gender-role stereotypes since infancy, the stress on gender-role differentiation often increases during adolescence. One way that the gender-role expectations for males and females are revealed is through the double standard. As we will see in Chapter 16, the double standard has profound effects on both male and female sexuality throughout our lives. The sexually emerging adolescent receives the full brunt of this polarizing societal belief.

For males, the focus of sexuality may be sexual conquest. Young men who are nonexploitative or inexperienced are often labeled with highly negative terms like "sissy." On the other hand, peers often provide social reinforcement for stereotypical "masculine" attitudes and behaviors; for example, approval is given to aggressive and independent behavior. For some young men, telling their peers about their sexual encounters is more important than the sexual act itself. As one young man states:

> My own self-image was at stake. There I was—good looking, humorous, athletic, liked to party—but still a virgin. Everybody just assumed that I was an expert at making love. I played this role and, without a doubt, always implied "Yes, we did and boy was it fun." (Authors' files)

For females, the message and the expectations are often very different. The following account illustrates one woman's view of both sides of the double standard:

> It always seemed so strange, how society encouraged virginity in girls but it was OK for boys to lose theirs. I came from a large family, my brother being the oldest, and we girls followed him. I can remember when word got around how much of a playboy my brother was (he was about 18). My parents were not upset, but rather seemed kind of tickled. When we girls were ready to go out, our parents became suspicious. I can always remember how I felt and how if I ever became a parent I wouldn't allow such an inequality and emphasis on female virginity to take place. (Authors' files)

Many girls face a dilemma. They may learn to appear "sexy" to attract males, yet they often experience ambivalence about overt sexual behavior. A young woman expresses this feeling:

> Going out with boys is hard for me when it comes to making a decision about sex. I'm afraid if I don't hold out long enough they'll think I'm easy and if I wait too long they'll lose interest. (Authors' files)

The double-standard dilemma often encompasses far more than sexual behavior. Girls may begin to define their worth by their boyfriends' accomplishments rather than their own. Wearing the quarterback's letter jacket may bring a girl infinitely more status than earning one herself. Her abilities may even be seen as liabilities rather than assets. She may be concerned, for example, about getting better grades than her boyfriend.

Virginity or "Sexual Liberation"?

While the double standard is still influential, both males and females today are also affected by another societal influence—the increase in permissive attitudes toward sex. This greater tolerance for and increased expectation of sexual behavior sometimes goes by the label *sexual liberation*. A dimension of this so-called liberation is the considerable pressure many adolescents feel to be sexually active. While peers are most often the source of this pressure, even parents may attempt to push their adolescent children into sexual activity (Anthony et al., 1982). Teenagers who resist being pressured into becoming sexually experienced run the risk of being labeled "up-tight," moralistic, or old-fashioned. On the other hand, teenagers who respond to these pressures by becoming sexually active may feel anxious, confused, guilty, or inadequate as lovers.

As a result of the new expectations, boys and girls in some schools or peer groups see virginity as something to be eliminated as soon as possible. This pressure, however, varies according to place and time:

> My older sister says she used to lie to her friends and say she was a virgin to protect her reputation. It is just the opposite for me. I lie to my friends claiming I'm not a virgin. (Authors' files)

In view of these kinds of pressures, how appropriate is the term *sexual liberation*? It is our belief that true liberation means promotion of choice rather than coercion to say yes instead of no to sexual intercourse or other activities. Given the current pressure in some peer groups to have intercourse, saying no is often difficult.

However, many adolescents have not experienced intercourse. In Sorenson's 1973 study, 55% of females and 41% of males between 13 and 19 had not had intercourse. Other studies have produced varying findings, as Table 13.1 shows later in this chapter. These statistics indicate that many adolescents are remaining virgins. Major reasons given by adolescents who have not experienced sexual intercourse include (a) not being ready for it, (b) not having met a girl or boy they would like to have sex with, and (c) not having met a girl or boy who wants to have sex with them (Sorenson, 1973).

Other factors undoubtedly influence an adolescent's inclination to experience sexual relations. For example, a recent survey of several hundred middle-class high school students in suburban Chicago suggested that a teenager's decision to engage in sexual intercourse is strongly related to his or her home life and scholastic status (Ostrov et al., 1985). Adolescents participating in the survey who lived with both biological parents were decidedly less likely to have experienced intercourse than those who did not live with both biological parents. The authors of this study speculate that adolescents in intact homes tend to internalize their parents' values more and to have less need for emotional gratification and support from relationships outside the family. The data from this survey also revealed that the teenagers who performed at an average or lower academic level were about twice as likely to have experienced intercourse than those whose performance was above average. The latter finding may indicate that adolescents with higher than usual scholastic aptitude may be more aware of the potential negative consequences of sexual activity (for example, unwanted pregnancies or contracting diseases). Of course, it may also reflect the fact that high-achieving students have less time to devote to the development of social-sexual relationships.

Masturbation

Although a significant number of adolescents do not experience sexual intercourse by the age of 19, many masturbate. As we saw earlier in this chapter, masturbation is a common sexual expression during childhood. During adolescence the behavior tends to increase in frequency. A recent survey of teenage males revealed an average masturbation frequency of five times per week (Lopresto et al., 1985). Masturbation frequency rates among females are notably lower among all age groups, including adolescents. Studies indicate that by the time they have reached the end of adolescence, almost all males and two-thirds of females have masturbated to orgasm (Hunt, 1974; Sorenson, 1973). A more recent survey of 580 women revealed that approximately three out of four had masturbated sometime during their adolescence, a result that suggests an upward trend in the incidence of masturbation among teenage females (Kolodny, 1980). Although masturbation is the primary sexual expression for many adolescents, approximately half of those who masturbate experience anxiety about doing so (Hass, 1979; Sorenson, 1973). Chapter 9 discussed this behavior and the mixed feelings many people have about it.

Masturbation can serve as an important avenue for sexual expression during the adolescent years. In addition to providing an always available outlet for sexual tension, self-stimulation is an excellent way to learn about one's body and its sexual potential. Teenagers can experiment with different ways of pleasuring themselves, thereby increasing their self-knowledge. This information may later prove helpful during sexual sharing with another. In fact, many sex therapists believe that people who do not masturbate during adolescence may be omitting an important element in their sexual development.

Petting

Another form of noncoital sexual expression provides an important way for many couples to relate to one another, often as an alternative to intercourse. A man describes this alternative:

> My fiancee and I agreed that it was important for both of us to remain virgin before marriage. Neither of us felt it was a particular hardship to wait until we were married to experience coitus. Instead, we engaged in lots of necking and heavy petting, often to orgasm. (Authors' files)

Petting refers to erotic physical contact that may include kissing, holding, touching, manual stimulation, or oral-genital stimulation—but not coitus. "Necking," "making out," and "messing around" are other expressions for petting. Even very "heavy" petting is a common activity among teenagers. According to the 1974 Hunt survey, during adolescence approximately one-half of girls and two-thirds of boys have experienced some type of petting to the point of orgasm.

Perhaps one of the most noteworthy recent changes in the pattern of adolescent petting behaviors involves oral sex. A number of surveys show that the incidence of oral-genital stimulation among teenagers has risen dramatically, to a level two or three times higher than the rates reported in the Kinsey studies (Delamater and MacCorquodale, 1979; Hass, 1979; Newcomer and Udry, 1985). Cunnilingus is more frequently reported than fellatio by adolescents of both sexes.

"How far to go" in petting is often an issue. It can become a contest between the young man and woman, he trying to proceed as far as possible and she attempting to go only as far as is "respectable." Since "love" often motivates or justifies sexual behavior for girls, he may say "I love you" as a ploy to engage in further sexual behaviors.

However, petting is often not so narrowly goal oriented, and it may provide a form of sexual expression that offers both members of a couple the highly valued combination of safety and enjoyment. Petting can be an opportunity for young people to experience sexual sharing while technically remaining virgins. The steps from holding hands to genital stimulation can progress with increasing emotional intimacy. Through petting adolescents begin to learn, within the context of an interpersonal relationship, about their own and their partner's sexual responses. They can develop a repertoire of pleasurable sexual behaviors without the risk of pregnancy, as the following account shows:

> One boy I went out with in high school and I had a great understanding. We both knew we were not ready for intercourse. Because of this mutual decision—and our mutual affection—we felt very free to experiment together and spent most of our dates making out for hours. (Authors' files)

This account illustrates not just the function petting serves as a sexual outlet but also the importance of a partner relationship in adolescent sexual behavior.

Ongoing Sexual Relationships

Despite the lingering double standard, data indicate that early petting and intercourse experiences are now more likely to be shared within the context of an ongoing relationship than they were in Kinsey's time. It appears that contemporary adolescents are most likely to be sexually intimate with someone they love or feel emotionally attached to. Furthermore, there are noteworthy changes in both sexes that are narrowing the gender gap. There are indications that adolescent females are becoming more comfortable with having sex with someone they feel affection for rather than feeling they need to "save themselves" for a love relationship. At the same time, adolescent males are becoming increasingly inclined to have sex with someone they feel emotional connections with (affection or love) rather than engaging in sex with a casual acquaintance or stranger, which was once a typical pattern for adolescent males (Delamater and MacCorquodale, 1979; Sorenson, 1973; Zabin et al., 1984a).

One major study (Sorenson, 1973) revealed that many adolescents (40% of

*Many adolescents
form caring
relationships with
each other.*

nonvirgin adolescents) are involved in one-to-one, sexually exclusive relationships. Slightly over half of these relationships continue for a year or more. There is also some indication of differences between monogamous and nonmonogamous relationships. Adolescents in monogamous pairs are more likely to use contraceptives consistently than are nonmonogamous young people. Also, approximately half of the monogamous females report that they usually or always have an orgasm, as compared to 29% of nonmonogamous females. These data suggest that many adolescents are expressing their sexuality within a framework of developing intimacy.

Sexual Intercourse

Before beginning to discuss adolescent coital behavior, it is worthwhile to note a basic point of semantics that places some limitations on our interpretations of data.

A frequently quoted statistic in sex research is the number of people in a given category who have engaged in "premarital sex." As a statistic in sex surveys, *premarital sex* is defined as penile-vaginal intercourse that takes place between a couple before they are married. For two reasons, however, the term is somewhat misleading. First, as a measure that is frequently used to indicate the changing sexual or moral values of American youth, it excludes a broad array of noncoital heterosexual and homosexual activities. We saw in the previous discussion that petting can include extensive noncoital types of sexual contact, and that it often produces orgasm. For some people maintaining virginity prior to marriage may not reflect a lack of sexual activity.

Second, the term *premarital* has connotations that may seem highly inappropriate to some people:

> I really hate those survey questions that ask, "Have you engaged in premarital coitus?" What about those of us who plan to remain single? Does this mean we will be engaging in premarital sex all of our lives? I object to the connotation that marriage is the ultimate state that all are supposed to evolve into. (Authors' files)

In spite of these limitations of the term premarital sex, most of the statistics we have are based on this measure. We will now turn to some of the available data on sexual intercourse during adolescence; then we will look at two related areas, adolescent pregnancy and the use of contraceptives.

Incidence of "Premarital Sex."   Kinsey's 1953 data revealed that half of the women in his sample had experienced coitus before marriage. (This statistic includes women whose initial coital experience occurred after adolescence but before marriage.) Social class, as determined by educational level, did not significantly influence this figure. Slightly over half of these women had had premarital coitus with only one partner, typically the man they later married. Kinsey's findings revealed that a major change in the sexual activity of young women had occurred in the 1920s. Less than one-quarter of the women in his sample who had married prior to 1920 had had intercourse before marriage. In sharp contrast, about half of those married after 1920 had experienced premarital coitus. These figures remained fairly constant until the middle 1960s, when another significant increase occurred (Cannon and Long, 1971).

As one might anticipate, there were higher premarital coital rates among men than among women in Kinsey's surveys. Approximately three out of four males in his total sample stated that they had participated in sex before marriage. The frequency of this behavior was significantly related to education, with 67% of college educated, 84% of high school educated, and 98% of elementary school educated men reporting premarital coitus. Besides being more likely to have premarital intercourse than the women in the sample, Kinsey's male respondents also reported having more partners. However, in contrast to the women in his sample, men showed significant correlation between premarital coital rates and the decade in which they were born.

In spite of the fact that no contemporary studies match the scope and comprehensiveness of Kinsey's efforts, there is evidence of significant increases in the sexual activity of unmarried adolescent females in recent years. All of the data presented here are drawn from studies discussed in some detail in Chapter 2. A revealing comparison can be made between the Kinsey findings and the results of three more contemporary studies, Sorenson's 1973 work and the 1976 and 1979 surveys of Zelnick and Kantner, reported in 1977 and 1980, respectively. All three of these investigations employed good methodology, and the Zelnick and Kantner surveys came reasonably close to utilizing probability samples. However, the extent of nonrespondent bias is unknown in all of these studies. Their findings about coitus among unmarried adolescents are summarized in Table 13.1.

Sorenson's study was a national survey of adolescent sexual behavior in the early 1970s, and as the table shows, it found that 45% of the females reported having premarital coitus by age 19. The later national surveys conducted by Zelnick and

**Table 13.1   Percentage of Adolescents Who Reported
Having Premarital Intercourse by Age 19**

	Females	Males
Kinsey (1948, 1953)	20%	45%
Sorenson (1973)	45%	59%
Zelnick and Kantner (1977)	55%	No males in survey
Zelnick and Kantner (1980)	69%	77%

Kantner reported that 55% of unmarried women in their national sample had experienced intercourse by age 19, a figure that increased to 69% in their 1979 sample. By sharp contrast, Kinsey's earlier sample revealed that slightly fewer than 20% of women reported premarital coitus by age 19. Thus, the surveys by Sorenson and Zelnick and Kantner demonstrate pronounced increases in premarital coital rates of American adolescent women through the 1970s. Unfortunately there have been no recent large-scale national surveys that would allow us to determine if the upward trend in premarital coitus rates among teenage women has continued in the 1980s. However, some relatively small-scale studies have indicated a possible leveling off of this trend, with only small increases occurring in the early 1980s (Ostrov et al., 1985).

Throughout the 1960s, when the percentage of adolescent women who had experienced premarital coital activity was increasing, the male rates showed little change from the earlier Kinsey figures (Davis, 1971). However, in the 1970s there was some evidence of a significant increase in the incidence of coitus among young unmarried males. In Sorenson's national sample 59% of adolescent males reported experiencing premarital intercourse by age 19, as compared with 45% from the Kinsey survey. The 1979 survey by Zelnick and Kantner reported that 77% of adolescent males in their sample had experienced intercourse by age 19. Overall, these data on males do not show increases as dramatic as the comparable figures for adolescent females. However, these statistics do reveal a marked upward trend in the incidence of premarital intercourse among adolescent males. It is particularly interesting to note the apparent convergence in the rates for adolescent men and women over the last 30 to 40 years: Male rates were more than double female rates in Kinsey's studies, while a mere eight percentage points separated males and females in Zelnick and Kantner's 1979 survey population.

In broad terms, we can briefly summarize the major changes in adolescent coital activities in the last four decades as follows. First, there has been an increase in the percentages of both young men and young women who have experienced coitus. Second, these increases have been considerably larger for females than for males. Finally, there are still fewer women than men who have "premarital sex." However, this difference between the sexes has been diminishing at a very rapid rate.

Homosexuality

The 1973 Sorenson research indicated that about 6% of adolescent females and 11% of adolescent males in the study group had experienced same-sex contact during their adolescent years. The great majority of these contacts took place between peers. These data, or the behaviors they describe, do not entirely reflect later orientation. Same-sex contact with the intent of sexual arousal can be either experimental and transitory or an expression of a lifelong sexual orientation. As we saw in Chapter 10, many homosexual individuals do not act on their sexual feelings until adulthood, and many people with heterosexual orientations have one or more early homosexual experiences.

Some people, however, do define themselves as homosexual during adolescence. This realization may create severe problems for the young person. It may begin with an awareness of having different feelings about sexual attractions than those commonly verbalized by peers; often a person will have a homosexual experience before she or he either applies a label of homosexuality to the behavior or understands its significance. Not being "part of the crowd" can be emotionally painful. It may be very difficult for young people to find confidants with whom they can share their concern or find guidance. Parents, ministers, doctors, and teachers often are unable to offer constructive help or personal support:

> Since most school counselors are heterosexual and relatively few have been formally sensitized to homosexuality, they can relate to the problems of acne-prone, obese, or other physically problem-stricken youths who feel socially ostracized, but when confronted by a young person acknowledging her/his homosexuality, few counselors know what to say. Most gay high schoolers at present would hesitate even to confide, knowing that homophobic school officials might contact homophobic parents and start a personally disastrous chain of events. (Portland Town Council, 1976, p. 57)

The adolescent's problem is further complicated by the fact that homosexual organizations, although designed to provide assistance and support, are often reluctant to offer help to underage people because of possible legal action for "contributing to the delinquency of a minor" (Martin and Lyon, 1972). Still, as with many of the other areas of sexuality discussed in this chapter, homosexual expression is gaining more widespread acceptance in many areas of society. We hope that growing acceptance will help make this time of life easier for adolescents with homosexual orientations.

Adolescent Pregnancy

As premarital intercourse has become more common among adolescents in the United States, the rate of teenage pregnancy has increased sharply and has become a matter of urgent social concern. There are approximately one and a quarter million adolescent pregnancies each year, and it has been conservatively estimated that a pregnancy occurs in at least one out of every ten unmarried American teenage women each year (Kisker, 1985). Recent statistics provided by the Alan Guttmacher Institute indicate that of the teenagers who become pregnant each year, almost half give birth and approximately 40% obtain abortions. About 10% of pregnancies end in spontaneous abortions or stillbirths.

These statistics represent a great deal of human suffering. A pregnant adolescent is four to five times more likely to have pregnancy complications than a woman in her twenties. These include toxemia, hemorrhage, miscarriages, and even maternal

*At least one out of
every ten unmar-
ried American
teenage women
become pregnant
each year, many of
whom experience
considerable hard-
ship as a result of
their pregnancies.*

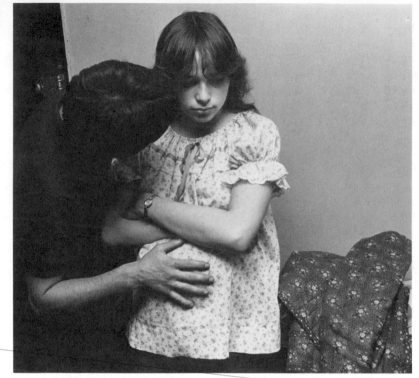

death (Fielding, 1978). Furthermore, the younger the adolescent, the higher the risk (La Barre, 1969). Biological immaturity and lack of prenatal health care contribute to these problems.

Unintended pregnancy and the decision to keep her child often have a serious negative impact upon the adolescent mother's educational progress and financial resources. Almost 90% of unmarried adolescent mothers who give birth choose to keep their babies. It is now illegal to bar teenagers who are pregnant or already mothers from public school. Nevertheless, a large number of these young women, perhaps as many as 80%, drop out of school and do not return (McGee, 1982; Furstenberg et al., 1981). Faced with the burden of childcare duties and an inadequate education, teenage mothers are highly likely to be underemployed or unemployed and dependent upon welfare services (Delatiner, 1978; McGee, 1982). Furthermore, low education levels and limited employment skills severely limit the efforts of these young mothers to obtain economic independence as they move beyond their teenage years.

Use of Contraceptives

Despite the economic, lifestyle, and emotional stress pregnancy and parenthood often bring, and the availability of birth control today, contraceptive use is not widespread among nonvirgin American adolescents. A number of studies have revealed that most teenagers do not use any contraception at all the first few times they have sexual intercourse. Only a minority of teenagers consistently use a reliable method of birth control even after they have been sexually active for some time (Byrne, 1977; Furstenberg, 1984; Kisker, 1985; Zabin et al., 1984b). Even adolescent couples involved in monogamous relationships in which contraception is discussed often use ineffective methods or are inconsistent in their use of more reliable techniques. The authors of a recent in-depth study of teenage couples, in which each member of the pair was interviewed separately, estimated that 22% of the adolescent women were likely to become pregnant within one year, given the assumption that current contraceptive behavior would continue (Polit-O'Hara and Kahn, 1985).

Many professionals knowledgeable about teenage pregnancy believe that American culture contributes greatly to the high rate of adolescent pregnancies. The following quote provides a summary of this point of view:

> American teenagers seem to have inherited the worst of all possible worlds regarding their exposure to messages about sex: Movies, music, radio and TV tell them that sex is romantic, exciting, titillating; premarital sex and cohabitation are visible ways of life among the adults they see and hear about; their own parents or their parents' friends are likely to be divorced or separated but involved in sexual relationships. Yet, at the same time, young people get the message good girls should say no. Almost nothing that they see or hear about sex informs them about contraception or the importance of avoiding pregnancy. For example, they are more likely to hear about abortions than about contraception on the daily TV soap opera. Such messages lead to an ambivalence about sex that stifles communication and exposes young people to increased risk of pregnancy, out-of-wedlock births and abortions. (Jones et al., 1985, p. 61)

The preceding quote is from an article describing the results of an extensive, comparative study of adolescent pregnancy in a number of developed countries (Jones et al., 1985). In addition to the United States, five nations were studied in depth: Canada, England, France, Sweden, and the Netherlands. All five of these countries were found to have lower adolescent pregnancy rates than the United States. The incidence of teenage pregnancy in England, the nation with the second highest rate among the six, is less than half that of the United States. The two countries with the lowest incidence, Sweden and the Netherlands, have adolescent pregnancy rates less than one fifth of the American rate. Yet the available evidence indicates that the level of sexual activity among young people in these six nations is comparable. What then accounts for the pronounced differences in pregnancy rates? The authors of this landmark study suggested several possible contributing factors, three of which we will discuss here.

First, "teenagers are much less likely to get free or very low-cost contraception services in the United States than in the other five countries studied in detail" (p. 54). One of the major problems with the American family planning clinic system is that it was originally developed primarily as a service to the poor. Consequently, teenagers often avoid birth control clinics, regarding them as places that serve only people on welfare. In contrast, adolescents in countries like Sweden and the Netherlands have access to a dense network of clinics, many of which are directed largely toward meeting the special needs of youth. Sweden is exemplary in having established a link between schools and contraceptive clinic services for adolescents. This link was initiated in 1975, just after Sweden liberalized its abortion laws. Many were concerned that increasing the availability of abortion might result in a marked rise in the number of abortions performed on teenagers. In fact, the adolescent abortion rate in Sweden has declined dramatically since school-clinic networking was established in 1975.

Second, the research team determined that use of birth control pills is much less common among American teenagers than among the youth of the other five countries. This difference suggests that American adolescents use less effective birth control methods when they use anything at all.

Third, with the exception of Canada, school and community sex education programs in the other five nations are much more extensive than in the United States. Sweden has established a compulsory sex education curriculum in every school that extends to all grade levels. Sex education is enthusiastically supported by the vast majority of Swedish parents, most of whom had sex education while they were in school. The Netherlands government encourages teaching of contraception by subsidizing mobile educational teams. The Dutch media also presents extensive information about contraception and other aspects of sexuality. Surveys of Dutch adolescents reveal that knowledge of how to avoid pregnancy is virtually universal among them. In England and France there is a national policy supporting the inclusion of sex education in the school curriculum. There is no such national policy in our country or Canada.

This comparative study of adolescent pregnancy demonstrates that we need more readily available contraception and improved sex education if we are to reduce the increasing numbers of unwanted pregnancies. A number of surveys have revealed that many American adolescents, perhaps the majority, have little accurate knowledge about effective birth control. In addition, certain myths abound, such as the belief that a woman cannot get pregnant the first time she has intercourse, or that infrequent coitus will not result in a pregnancy (Kisker, 1985; Ostrov et al., 1985).

Lack of knowledge is by no means the only reason for not using contraception. Another reason teenagers avoid birth control is that its use is an acknowledgement that one is planning to have intercourse. Some young people's attitudes reflect the value that the teenage woman who "does it" without contraceptive evidence of premeditation is more moral than the young woman who assumes responsibility for her sexual activity and uses birth control. This theme emerges in the responses we received from high school students when we asked them "Why would a high school age woman who didn't want to become pregnant not use birth control?"

> She may feel guilty about planning ahead about sex.
>
> She feels guilty. If she uses birth control, then she is admitting she is having sex.
>
> Maybe people would think of her as a big sleaze if the word got out that she was on the pill or something.
>
> Because she wants to consider it making love. (Authors' files)

Strategies for Reducing the Teenage Pregnancy Rate

What can be done to reverse the trend of escalating teenage pregnancies in America? Many authorities on adolescent sexuality agree that educational programs designed to increase adolescents' awareness of contraception and other aspects of sexuality will

A COMMON METHOD OF BIRTH CONTROL,

THAT DOESN'T WORK.

be much more effective if they treat sexuality as a positive aspect of our humanity rather than something that is wrong or shameful. An adolescent who has a positive and accepting attitude toward her or his sexuality is more likely to use contraceptives in an effective manner (Oettinger, 1979). In the European countries included in the previously discussed research, sex is viewed as natural and healthy, and there is wide-spread acceptance of teenage sexual activity. This stands in sharp contrast to America, where sex is romanticized and flaunted but also portrayed as something sinful or dirty that should be hidden (Jones et al., 1985).

We offer a list of suggestions for reducing teenage pregnancy, gleaned from the writings and research of several eminent investigators of adolescent sexuality.

1. The American family planning clinic system needs to be upgraded to provide free or low-cost contraceptive services to *all* adolescents who want them. The school and other media should become more involved in publicizing the fact that these services are not limited to the poor. Of equal importance is the need to publicize the fact that clinics maintain the confidentiality of their clients. Many adolescents are reticent about visiting a family planning clinic because they think the clinic staff might contact their parents. A survey of 1200 teenage women, conducted during their first visit to a family planning clinic, revealed that 84% were already sexually active prior to seeking professional birth control help. Fear that parents would find out about their sexual activity was a major reason these women reported for delaying their visit to a clinic (Zabin and Clark, 1981).

2. America should follow the lead of several European nations, most notably Sweden, in establishing a compulsory national sex education curriculum that is extended to all grade levels. Research data clearly reveal that teenagers who have been exposed to sex education are considerably less likely to become pregnant than those who have had no such education (Jones et al., 1985; Zelnick and Kim, 1982). These sex education programs will be more effective if they stress the healthy, natural, and enriching aspects of sexuality. As we pointed out earlier, teenagers who accept their sexual behaviors as positive are more likely to use contraceptives than those who believe that adolescent sexual expression is inappropriate and shameful.

3. Ideally, sex education programs provided by local school districts would be linked to family planning clinic services in a manner similar to the Swedish approach. A pilot program incorporating in-school sex education and counseling with adjacent clinic services was recently designed and implemented in Baltimore by Johns Hopkins University School of Medicine researchers (Zabin et al., 1984b). We hope the data obtained from the first American effort of its kind will encourage other communities within our nation to adopt a similar approach.

4. Efforts to educate adolescents in ways to prevent unwanted pregnancies must recognize that male attitudes are important for the practice and effectiveness of birth control. Adolescent boys often consider birth control to be their partner's responsibility (Cohen and Rose, 1984). When we asked teenage men "Why would a high school age man who did not want to be a father have sexual intercourse and not use a condom?" their responses included:

He may have thought that it was the girl's problem, not his.

He probably didn't want it to seem planned.

Because he didn't like the feeling of the rubber.

Embarrassed about putting them on. (Authors' files)

School sex education programs should stress that responsibility for contraception is best shared by both parties. A recent survey of several thousand American teenagers revealed that respondents who believed responsibility for pregnancy prevention should be shared were more likely to have used effective contraception than those who felt the responsibility belonged to one or the other partner (Zabin et al., 1984a).

5. Government agencies should relax the restrictions on distribution and advertising of nonprescription contraceptives, particularly the condom. Recent television ads for vaginal spermicides suggest that the United States is moving in this direction. However, we have a long way to go before matching the widespread availability of condoms and other devices—in clinics, pharmacies, supermarkets, and vending machines—in many European countries. Many health practitioners also believe that a widespread campaign should be launched to inform teenagers and physicians that the pill is generally the most effective contraception method for adolescents (Jones et al., 1985; Kisker, 1985). This educational effort should also provide information about potential health risks of the pill and what factors might rule out its use by some teenage women. The campaign should try to counteract a common adolescent assumption that the pill is only for people who are having regular sex with a steady boyfriend. This attitude is reflected in the following comment by an 18-year-old woman:

I wouldn't go on the pill only if I was going to meet somebody, maybe to have sex casually, you know, like once a month or once every two months. I feel it's more for somebody who has a steady boyfriend. (Kisker, 1985, p.84)

In summary, we hope that in the years to come we will see widespread efforts to increase the legitimacy and availability of contraception, as well as broadly focused sex education programs that will help reverse the upward trends in teenage pregnancy rates in America.

Some Key Influences on Psychosexual Development

We began this chapter with a look at sexual behavior in childhood and adolescence, and at the physical changes that take place as a person begins to mature sexually. In this section we will retrace our steps, considering some of the important psychological and social influences on a person's sexual development, beginning with early childhood.

Of the variety of factors and conditions that are influential in shaping early psychosexual development, parenting and family practices appear to be of great importance. In the pages that follow, a considerable portion of our discussion will be directed toward the potential impact of these influences upon the sexual development of children. Some of our discussion is based on established facts. Other observations are anecdotal or speculative in nature, drawn primarily from interactions with our own children and from the experiences of friends, colleagues, and students who share the common bond of concerned parents. We will look at a few important areas: toilet practices, adult reactions to children's masturbation, the modeling parents provide through their own behaviors, the treatment of nudity, independency issues, and privacy concerns.

Dirty Diapers, Going Potty, and Related Issues

An influential area in which adults may mold children's attitudes about sexuality is treatment of eliminative functions. Have you ever watched a parent changing a diaper with a disgusted expression on his or her face, or perhaps gagging? Were you ever scolded for relieving yourself behind a bush because you played one minute too long? Or were words like "stinky," "messy," or "ugh" ever used when there was a setback in your toilet training program?

We can only guess the impact of such reactions on an infant or toddler. Certainly, however, it does not promote the development of positive feelings about the natural eliminative functions of the genitals. It might possibly even be one factor in the development of an association between discomfort with elimination and with later sexual functioning. (Other factors are also involved, however, and undoubtedly many people who have had these experiences in their infancy do nevertheless function in a sexually healthy manner as adults.)

Home environments that treat eliminative functions as secretive or dirty may foster feelings of discomfort with the body and its natural processes. Furthermore, there is the possibility that children raised in such surroundings may learn to associate the guilt, shame, or embarrassment connected with genital elimination to genital sex.

These are some of the reasons why it may be helpful for parents to create a relaxed and open atmosphere in the area of toilet practices.

Reactions to Masturbation

A second, often important, influence on developing sexuality is parental reaction to self-pleasuring. In our society, comments about masturbation that pass from parent

Other Times, Other Places

Cultural Variations in Childhood and Adolescent Sexuality

Humans are capable of experiencing sexual arousal and pleasure in the very earliest stages of their lives. However, adult acceptance of youthful sexuality, as well as the actual expression of such activity, shows enormous variation from one society to another. A few examples provide some indication of cultural diversity in this area of sexual behavior.

Many of the island societies of the South Pacific are very permissive about youthful sexual activity. Children of both sexes may engage in solo masturbation, group masturbation, and sex play with others, including manual manipulation, oral-genital contacts, and coitus. Children may receive extensive verbal instructions about sexual matters. In some areas, they may be allowed to observe adult sexual activity.

Among the Mangaians of the South Pacific, children acquire a great deal of information about sexuality during their early years, as evidenced by their use of detailed vocabulary for describing sexual anatomy and function. (For example, they learn several different terms for the clitoris.) In the 1950s Donald Marshall (1971) noted that it was quite common for an entire Mangaian family of 5 to 15 members to sleep in one room. Since a good deal of sexual activity occurred at night in this room, Mangaian children had innumerable opportunities to see and hear sexual sharing. One of us, Bob Crooks, visited Mangaia in 1982 and noted that in recent years many of the island inhabitants have moved into larger homes with multiple sleeping areas, a change that may reduce

the exposure of young people to sexual activity.

Like the Mangaians, the children of the Marquesas Islands in French Polynesia develop remarkable sophistication about sex early in life. They also sleep with their parents and siblings in one room, with ample opportunity to observe sexual activity. Marquesan boys begin masturbating around the age of two or three and may engage in same-sex group activities involving genital fondling by the age of five or six. Boys may also engage in casual homosexual contacts during their youth. Marquesan girls also experience self-stimulation and homosexual contacts from an early age (Suggs, 1962).

Early childhood masturbation is common in other areas besides the South Pacific. Among the African Bala, children of both sexes are given free reign to engage in self-stimulation from an early age. As in the Marquesas, Bala boys commonly engage in group masturbation.

Some of these permissive societies provide a rationale for prepubertal sexual activity. For example, the Chewa of Central Africa believe that sexual activity in children is essential to ensure adult fertility. The Lepcha of the southeastern Himalayas maintain that girls must be sexually active if they are to undergo normal growth as they develop into adulthood.

A few non-Western societies have strong prohibitions against self-stimulation similar to those of North American societies. For example, the African Ashanti forbid their children to masturbate.

to child are typically either nonexistent or negative. Think back to your youth. Did your parents ever express to you that they accepted this activity? Or, did you have an intuitive sense that your parents were comfortable with self-pleasuring in their children? Probably not. Most often, a verbal message to "stop doing that," a disapproving look, or a slap on the hand are the responses children receive to masturbation. These gestures may be noted even by a young child who does not yet have language capabilities.

Little boys growing up in the Kwoma society of New Guinea live in fear of being caught with an erection. If they are, they may have their penises struck with a stick! Some Kwoma boys become so concerned about this possibility that they learn to urinate without touching their penises.

As with childhood sexual activity, an enormous cultural diversity exists in both attitudes toward and expression of adolescent premarital coital activity. Some societies, more restrictive than our own, apply strong punishments to individuals caught indulging in such behavior. At the other extreme, some societies encourage coital expression in unmarried young people.

The inhabitants of Romonum Island in the Truk group of the South Pacific are representative of some of the more permissive societies in this regard. The Romonum consider premarital coital activity to be both natural and desirable for both sexes starting in early adolescence. Teenage males are often introduced to coitus by older women. Initiation into coitus by older adults is also common among the Lepcha of the Himalayas. However, in the Lepcha society it is typically the young female who, by age 11 or 12, may be engaging in intercourse with adult males.

First coital experiences occur at an even younger age in the Trobriand Islanders society, located in a group of islands off the coast of New Guinea. Here, girls as young as 6 and boys of 10 or 11 years have their first coital experiences with other children under adult tutelage.

The Marquesans also openly encourage coitus before marriage. Throughout adolescence, it is considered normal for girls and boys to have frequent sexual relations. This is generally accomplished through the practice known as night-crawling, where boys enter their chosen lover's house at night and have sexual relations while other family members are sleeping nearby. The practice of night-crawling also occurs on the island of Mangaia. However, it appears that night-crawling has lost some of its appeal in the years since Marshall studied Mangaian society. Several of Crooks's adult informants in 1982 stated that it is now an uncommon practice. Some flatly denied it occurs. However, numerous youthful informants confirmed its continued existence, although in significantly altered form. It seems that parents have become less accepting of such behavior. An adolescent male caught in his lover's bedroom stands a good chance of being punished. Apparently some Mangaian adolescents also disapprove of night-crawling. One 17-year-old woman adamantly stated to Crooks: "I'm a good girl—I'm not one of those."

What happens in permissive societies like those of Mangaia and the Marquesas when an "illegitimate" birth occurs? William Davenport provides a general answer. "Societies that permit or encourage premarital sex freedom are organized so that all children born outside marriage are fully provided for and in no way suffer social disabilities or stigma" (1978, p. 146).

In writing about the issue of early alienation from such an important part of our bodies as our genitals, the words of Mary Calderone, executive director of the Sex Information and Education Council of the United States, come to our minds. "We should see this [genital fondling] as normal and human. The body of a child belongs to him or her and each should have the right to experience pleasure with it" (1978). In many children's and parents' lives, though, there is probably much confusion and anxiety surrounding this very natural form of sexual expression.

How can adults convey their acceptance of masturbation? One way to begin is by not reacting negatively to the genital fondling that is typical of infants and young children. Later, as we respond to children's questions about their bodies, it may be desirable to mention the potential for pleasure that exists in their genital anatomy ("It feels good when you touch it"). Respecting privacy—for example, knocking before entering a child's room—is another way to foster comfort with this very personal activity. Perhaps you may feel comfortable with making specific accepting responses to self-pleasuring activity in your children, as did the parents in the following accounts:

> One day my seven-year-old son joined me on the couch to watch a football game. He was still in the process of toweling off from a shower. While appearing to be engrossed in the activity on the screen, I noticed one hand was busy stroking his penis. Suddenly his eyes caught mine observing him. An uneasy grin crossed his face. I wasn't sure how to respond so I simply stated, "It feels good, doesn't it?" He didn't say anything, nor did he continue touching himself but his smile grew a little wider. I must admit I had some initial hesitancy in openly indicating my approval for such behavior. I was afraid he might begin openly masturbating in the presence of others. However, my fears were demonstrated to be groundless in that he continues to be quite private about such activity. It is gratifying to know that he can experience the pleasures of his body without the unpleasant guilt feelings that his father grew up with. (Authors' files)

> The first time my 10-year-old daughter and I took a shower together, after purchasing a hand-held water massager, I told her it felt good when directed toward her vulva. While I only spoke about this potential, feeling uncomfortable about conducting an actual demonstration, the message seemed to sink in, judging from the long showers she often took from that date forward. (Authors' files)

Many parents are reluctant to openly express their acceptance of masturbation, afraid that their children, armed with this parental stamp of approval, will go off to some cloistered area and masturbate away the hours. While this is an understandable concern, available evidence does not suggest that this response is likely. Children have many other activities to occupy their time.

Another concern, voiced in the first anecdote, is that children will begin masturbating openly in front of others if they are aware that their parents accept such behavior. This also is a reasonable concern. Very few of us would be enthusiastic about needing to deal with Johnny or Suzie masturbating in front of Grandma. However, children are generally aware enough of social expectations to maintain a high degree of privacy in something as emotionally laden and personal as self-pleasuring. Most of them are much more capable of making important discriminations than parents sometimes acknowledge. In the event that children do masturbate in the

*Parents may pro-
vide their children
with positive models
of shared sensual
intimacies.*

presence of others, it would seem reasonable for parents to voice their concerns, taking care to label the choice of location and not the activity as inappropriate.

Most children masturbate. Telling them to stop this behavior will rarely eliminate it, even if such requests are backed with threats of punishment or claims that masturbation causes mental or physical deterioration. Rather, these negative responses will most likely succeed only in greatly magnifying the guilt and anxiety associated with this behavior.

Positive Models

Most adult behavior is strongly influenced by models identified with or emulated during the growing-up process. We need only observe the little girl combing her hair like mother or the young boy imitating his father's walk to sense how powerful this modeling process is. The question for us is, where does a child find positive models for caring, nonexploitive, joyful sexual interaction? Not typically in the popular media. (When is the last time you saw a movie or read a novel that made you feel good about the potential for joy in intimate relationships?) The peer group often leaves something to be desired, with its rudimentary or inaccurate knowledge, its tendency toward sexism and narrow views of morality, and its often competitive view of sexual interaction ("How many times have you 'scored'?" "How many invitations did you get to the dance?") What then is left as a potential source for positive models? One answer is the relationships between adults who are significant in a child's life.

Among American parents there seems to be a marked reluctance to reveal to children the sensual or intimate aspects of the parents' relationship. Parents may show this reluctance in several ways: by hiding spontaneous displays of affection for each other, refraining from talking about loving each other in front of the children, or avoiding acting "turned on" in their presence. This reluctance to display such natural feelings and behaviors may stem from attitudes such as discomfort with sexuality in general, concern that such displays will lead to embarrassing questions, and worry that children may learn about sexual experimentation too early in life. Thus, these potentially positive models may be unavailable to children, as perhaps they were to their parents and their parents' parents.

How many of us grew up with a realization that our parents were sexual and that they were still "doing it"? Student surveys in our classroom suggest that very few can respond affirmatively to this question. Consider the following account:

> One day when I was 15, my Mom phoned me at home and asked if I would gather some information contained in papers located in her bedroom chest of drawers. This was her private space that I had never before invaded. But with permission, I proceeded to look for the papers. During the course of my explorations I was amazed and horrified to discover a box of condoms. I couldn't believe she and Dad were still doing it. However, I opened it up and found some were missing. Then I knew for sure! (Authors' files)

We wonder what the world would be like if such a discovery failed to produce surprise in the majority of developing children. Why not allow them to witness desire, caring, and sharing between adults? To the extent that parents' relationships are characterized by mutual caring and warmth, what better model can be made available to them?

For parents who feel comfortable about expressing affection in front of their children, what limits are there to such expression? The major concern here is the potential damaging impact of observing parents engaged in sexual contact, especially coitus. Some writers, particularly those of a psychoanalytic orientation, have expressed concern about such a practice, stating that severe psychological trauma may result in children who see their parents having sex. The following experience exemplifies a negative reaction to witnessing parental coitus:

> When I was still a little girl, I guess about 10 or 11, I walked in on my Mom and Dad while they were having intercourse. They failed to hear me enter and I didn't announce my presence. Something was going on that I didn't understand, but I knew it made me feel real uncomfortable. It seemed like Dad was hurting Mom, banging up and down on top of her, and from the look on her face, it certainly didn't seem like she was enjoying it. And yet, something about the scene kept me from asking what was going on. Instead, I quietly slipped out being careful not to let them know they had been observed. I was bothered by my memory of this experience for a long time after. I guess the hardest part was not having anyone to talk to about what I had seen and wondering if Dad always hurt my mother when they went into their bedroom to be alone. (Authors' files)

Here the child had misinterpreted the sexual activity as aggressive and abusive behavior on the part of her father. The misunderstanding was complicated by the fact that there was enough ambiguity in the situation that the girl was unwilling to ask her parents about what she had seen. This is the potential problem in a child surreptitiously observing parents involved in sex play. We wonder how much of this child's bewilderment stemmed from a general lack of knowledge about sexuality. It seems less likely that such confusion and discomfort would exist in a young person whose parents regularly maintained open communication about sexual or intimate matters. In fact, in families where good communication exists, so that a child could ask about what she or he has seen, it seems probable that little or no harm would result from accidental witnessing of parental coitus (Hoyt, 1982). Such an event may provide parents an opportunity to tell the child that shared sexuality is pleasurable and an expression of mutual caring. Conversely, parents who become angry or upset over the accidental intrusion may foster guilt and anxiety in their child.

We are not advocating exposing children to the sexual play of their parents. Such a decision is a highly individual matter, with many ramifications. But neither do we think that such an experience is inevitably damaging. The following report of a woman in one of our sexuality classes is relevant to this issue:

> I live in a tiny apartment with my six-year-old son and my lover. It offers virtually no privacy, consisting of one large room with pull-down beds and a small bathroom. We can't afford anything bigger, since we are both going to school. It really presented problems when it came to lovemaking. It was always at night after my son was asleep, and then we had to be careful about the sounds we made. Finally we got tired of the lack of spontaneity and limited nature of our responses. One morning, while my boy was watching TV, we decided to have sex. Halfway through he came over and stood by the bed and watched us moving under the covers for a few moments. Finally he said, "What are you doing?" I answered, "Making love." His response to this was "Oh," followed by watching for a couple more minutes and then back to the TV set. It just wasn't any big deal for him. However, later he did ask me some questions, which I thought was real good in that it started us talking about sex. (Authors' files)

Many people would not be comfortable with the explicitness of this scene. However, direct observation is not the only vehicle through which parents can model positive aspects of sexuality to their children. Consider the following scenario. It is a lazy Saturday afternoon, and parents and children have spent time together having lunch and working in the yard. Mom and Dad are unashamedly expressing mutual affection, periodically kissing and hugging, clearly taking pleasure in each other's company. Eventually they slip off to their bedroom, making no effort to conceal their excitement and anticipation from the children. Later they return, arm in arm, contentment mirrored in their faces. With repeated exposure to such scenes the children are likely to realize that their parents are sexual, and furthermore, that sexual activity brings them great pleasure and happiness. The children will also have the somewhat unusual opportunity to observe such behavior in a caring, nonexploitive, and joyful relationship. The many benefits that may result from such early modeling are well worth considering before parents elect to bar their children from all awareness of intimate or sexual aspects of their relationship.

Single parents often ask us if it is healthy to reveal to their children that they are sharing an intimate relationship with someone they see regularly. There are factors here that are not present in the intact nuclear family situation. It is possible that children may feel quite uncomfortable with their parents' relationship with someone other than the original spouse. This may involve feelings of loyalty to the absent parent, a sense of betrayal, or even the feeling of futility that results when hope for a reconciliation is shattered. Nevertheless, it is possible that surreptitious behavior, in some circumstances at least, may create more problems than open and honest acknowledgement of feelings. Consider the following experience:

> After I was divorced from my husband I felt very uncomfortable displaying any affection for my men friends in the presence of my children. It was very awkward to have them over to the house. The kids never said anything, but I always felt they were disapproving of me becoming involved with men other than their father. When I met the man I am with now it became a real problem. While he and I prefer not to marry, at least in the immediate future, we have made a personal commitment to each other. I love him very much and the kids seem to enjoy his company. It was very hard having him over for dinner and treating him like a casual friend rather than the man I dearly love. On those rare occasions when we spent an entire night together, it was always at his place after making up some trumped-up excuse. Finally, it all came to a head one evening when my 16-year-old got up in the middle of the night and discovered us making love in front of the fireplace. It was terrible. I was so shook up I didn't know what to say. He just went back to bed without saying anything. The next day I mustered up my courage to ask him what he thought about last night. He simply said, "Mom, I think it's great that you two get it on together. Me and the rest of the kids have always thought it was kind of silly you pretended you didn't have something going." I didn't say much of anything, but believe me it was a relief to know that I didn't have to go on acting out some charade. (Authors' files)

Clearly, a great deal of individual discretion is necessary in deciding whether (and how much) children should know about a sexual relationship; specific family circumstances and the nature of the outside relationship are important considerations. Children do not always react as reasonably as did the son in the preceding account. Occasionally a child will emotionally pressure his or her single parent into curtailing, if not totally eliminating, involvement with potential lovers. This highly undesirable behavior is revealed in the following anecdote:

> Whenever I have a male friend over, my little boy undergoes a personality change. He becomes sullen, belligerent, and verbally abusive. I am at my wits' end trying to deal with such behavior. Under any other circumstance he is a beautiful person, sweet, attentive, and very helpful. It's getting so that I just avoid dating so that I don't have to deal with his strange and unpleasant behavior. (Authors' files)

We suggest that this child's behavior is not so strange—particularly in view of the fact that it proved successful in curtailing his mother's relationships with other men. Not uncommonly, scenarios like these are enacted in the lives of divorced, widowed, or separated parents. Many factors may be operating. The child or children may have a strong desire to occupy a position of sole preeminence in the life of the parent with whom they are living. Resistance to the "intrusion" of another important person may also involve elements of jealousy, loyalty to the absent parent, or fear that the new relationship will only be transitory and the loss will be repeated. When a child has concerns like these, it may be helpful to acknowledge them and attempt to open lines of communication. However, it seems unnecessary for single parents to restrict their pursuit of new relationships even if their children resist such activities. As long as the children receive a fair share of loving attention, the parent need not feel uncomfortable about satisfying his or her own relationship needs.

The Question of Nudity

Related to modeling is the manner in which nudity is treated in the household. Over the years we have asked thousands of human sexuality students the question "Did you feel comfortable with nudity around the home while you were growing up?" In a class of 75, the number of hands raised often can be counted on the fingers of one hand. Consider the following accounts:

> I can remember accidentally walking in on my father when he was shaving, naked as a jaybird. His response was off the wall. I got the message loud and clear that there was something wrong about a little girl seeing her father naked. My mother was quite prudish too, as I think back on it. I didn't see another adult male naked, I mean close up so I could really look him over, until I was involved in my first heavy sex experience. (Authors' files)

> As early as I can remember, we kids were told to always lock the bathroom door when showering or taking care of nature's calling. We were in real trouble if we forgot to knock when someone else was using the john. They didn't even like the sounds. We flushed the toilet so someone else would not hear the pee hit the pot. It's crazy, but I'm still compulsive about flushing at the strategic moment. (Authors' files)

These accounts are typical of many stories related to us. To the extent that the home environments of our students are reasonably representative of cultural values about nudity, it would seem that the majority of us either were or are exposed to at least some family taboos in this area. Do you remember being told to cover up? What was it that you were supposed to cover? Your neck, face, feet, or arms? More likely, it was the "down-theres." Somehow it was okay to expose the rest of the body, but for many of us the genitals (and breasts for girls) needed to be covered up at all times, even in the privacy of our own homes.

What kind of message does this convey? For many of us, the taboo against self-exposure became translated into a sense of shame or discomfort about these areas of our bodies. Certainly we do not compulsively cover up that which is healthy and acceptable. Therefore, by implication, there must be something basically unpleasant or dirty about our genital anatomy. Later in life, when we become aware that sexual expression is often related to these hidden unmentionables, it is easy to see how sexuality becomes by association "dirty," or something to be ashamed of.

*Growing up in a
family that is at
ease with nudity
may contribute to
a positive sexual
awareness.*

It is not uncommon for people to feel anxious during the early stages of sexual intimacies with others. These feelings may stem from many factors—performance anxiety, guilt, conflict, and for some, basic discomfort with their own bodies. It is difficult to feel good about exposing parts of our anatomy that we have been told to cover up since we could barely walk. A person can feel incredibly vulnerable in such a circumstance, with the old associations ("it's dirty," "cover up," "lock the door," "flush the toilet") clanging away in his or her head like alarm bells.

Acquiring good feelings about nudity, and particularly one's own sexual anatomy, can contribute to an overall positive sexual awareness. Parents who feel at ease with nudity within the home can help foster these same feelings in their children by exhibiting an open comfort with their own bodies and those of their children. A variety of activities shared by a family—bathing together, dressing together, skinny-dipping in a mountain lake—may encourage the process whereby young family members acquire more positive body images. Consider the following:

> Some of our most joyous family times were those spent crowded together, all four of us, in one large shower or bathtub. We talked, and joked, and just felt good together. Our nakedness was a natural thing, so common as to be undeserving of mention. (Authors' files)

Understandably, many parents may find it difficult to implement these suggestions about nudity, particularly if their own experiences make such activities seem inappropriate or uncomfortable. We are not suggesting that lack of open nudity around the house will inevitably be detrimental to the sexual development of a child. In fact, parents who try to be open about nudity when they are not personally convinced of its appropriateness may inadvertently communicate this discomfort to their children. There are alternatives. Parents who wish to maintain privacy about their own bodies can still avoid directing negative comments toward their children when, for example, they forget to dress completely before entering the family room. Acceptance of nudity does not necessarily imply open display. This is a matter of individual choice.

It can be detrimental to force nudity upon a child who feels uncomfortable without clothing. Sometimes children who have been previously comfortable with nudity will begin to show some reluctance about being naked around family members. This change in attitude is most likely to occur during the period of rapid body changes characteristic of early adolescence. We caution parents to respect these emerging needs for privacy and to not chide their children about becoming self-conscious.

Independency Issues

Late childhood and most of adolescence is a time of life characterized by a great deal of ambivalence or confusion about appropriate behavior. One important consequence of this is that the child-parent relationship is often stressful during adolescence. Adolescents are neither entirely dependent nor entirely independent, yet often they want to be both:

> I used to harass my mother to let me do things I was really a little afraid of doing. Although I would feel inner relief when she said no, I would belligerently tell her how mean she was. (Authors' files)

When dependency versus independency conflicts increase, tension within the family often rises. Culturally defined "adult" behaviors, such as driving, drinking, smoking, and sexual intercourse are sometimes used by adolescents as symbols of maturity or as a form of rebellion against parental authority.

Parents (or other caretakers of adolescents) may greet their children's sexual maturation with a mixture of emotions, including avoidance, ambivalence, concern, and pride. At the same time, they may have dilemmas about their own role, for as their children change and become more independent, the nature of the parent-child relationship and of their adolescents' needs also changes.

One of the most difficult problems for parents is how to help adolescents make decisions about sexual matters. Parents are often caught in conflicts between their own attitudes toward sexuality and social pressures they and the adolescents experience. There is a sharp discrepancy between the societal ideal of sex within marriage and the societal reality of adolescent sexual behavior. These two factors are typically not easy to reconcile, even by the most concerned and caring adults. Furthermore, many adults understandably experience an uncomfortable gap between their intellectual ideas and their emotional reactions to their children's sexuality. For example:

I told my daughter that when she decided she was ready to have intercourse to let me know and we would make arrangements for birth control. Well, several years later she said it was time. I couldn't help it—I became upset with her. (Authors' files)

Many adults express the desire to help their children be positive and comfortable with their sexuality. However, as the foregoing account illustrates, parents are often in a confusing double bind. The traditional role of the parent in our society has been to suppress and control children's sexuality rather than to encourage overt sexual expression. Some people believe that even talking about sex may precipitate adolescent sexual activity. And so, although parents may want to encourage open communication and positive feelings, they may feel inhibited by dominant societal attitudes and their own family backgrounds.

Privacy Concerns

Another issue that is often troublesome to parents concerns privacy, which may take on a new meaning with the onset of adolescence. During childhood, one's bedroom is often a special place to take friends. At the onset of sexual maturity, however, many parents become uncomfortable with allowing this same privacy to the adolescent. They may make the bedroom off limits to other-sex friends, out of fear that their children will now interpret such privacy as a license to engage in intercourse. The adolescent, however, may perceive an entirely different message, welcoming the security offered by the home setting:

> While I was growing up, my Mom and Dad always allowed me to entertain friends of both sexes in my room. The neat thing was that they didn't eliminate this opportunity when I started dating. It was OK to have my boyfriends in the bedroom with me, and with the door closed. Most of the time we just watched TV, talked, or listened to my stereo. Sometimes we did a little heavy necking and petting. As crazy as it may sound, it was great knowing my Mom was just a few steps away if things got a little out of hand. Also, I think it encouraged my boyfriends to be a little more responsible. None of that back seat scene and being pressured into something I didn't want. I love my Mom and Dad for treating me like an adult, someone capable of making responsible choices. (Authors' files)

A variety of decisions relate to the issue of privacy in the home; for example, whether children can have guests when adults are not home (if so, it may be wise to ask that the friend's parents be informed), the hours of visiting, or use of various rooms. Particular rules may seem appropriate in a particular family.

Sex Education

Today many parents want to provide some input into the sexual education of their children. Societal values about sex are rapidly changing, and we are all exposed to an abundance of contrasting opinions. How much should children see, or how much should they be told? Many parents—even some of those who are comfortable with their own sexuality—have difficulty judging the "best" way to act and react toward their children's sexuality.

Perhaps the information that we offer in the following paragraphs will help to modify some of this uncertainty. We do not profess to have the last word on raising sexually healthy children, so we advise you to read this material with a critical eye. Along the way, however, you may acquire some new insights that will aid in your efforts to provide meaningful sex education for your children, either now or in the future.

We are often asked the question "When should we start telling our kids about sex?" One answer to this inquiry is "When the child begins to ask the questions." It seems typical for children to inquire about sex along with the myriad of other questions they ask about the world around them. Research indicates that by about age four, most children begin asking questions about how babies are made (Martinson, 1980). What is more natural than a query about where you came from? Yet this curiosity is often stopped short by parental response. A flushed face and a few stammering words, a cursory "Wait till your mother (or father) comes home to ask that question," or "You're not old enough to learn about such things" are a few of the common ways communication in this vital area is blocked before it has a chance to begin. Putting questions off at this early age means that you may be confronted with the potentially awkward task of starting a dialogue on sexual matters at a later point in your children's development.

Earlier, we discussed the value of parental modeling. One important application of this principle is for parents to include information about sex (when appropriate) in everyday conversations that their children either observe or participate in. Accomplishing this with a sense of ease and naturalness may increase the comfort with which the children introduce their own questions or observations about sex.

If a child's questions either do not arise spontaneously or get sidetracked at an early age, there may be a point when you as a parent will feel it is important to begin to talk about sexuality. Perhaps a good starting point is to share your true feelings with your child—that possibly you are a bit uneasy about discussing sex with them, or that maybe you are confused about some of your own beliefs or feelings. There is something very human about a parent who can express his or her own indecision or vulnerability to a child. This may be all you will say during this initial effort, simply indicating your feelings and leaving the door open to future discussions. An incubation period is often valuable, allowing a child to reassess her or his interpretation of your willingness to talk about sexuality. If no questions follow this first effort, it might be wise to select a specific area for discussion. Some suggested open-ended questions for a not too stressful beginning might be (a) How do you feel about the changes in your body? (b) What are some of the things that the kids at school say about sex? and (c) What are your feelings about birth control? Is it "proper"? Who should be responsible, male or female or both?

Understandably, parents sometimes have a tendency to overload a child who asks a question expecting a relatively brief, straightforward answer. For example, when a five-year-old inquires "Where did I come from?" he or she is probably not asking for a detailed treatise on the physiology of sexual intercourse and conception. In such cases it may be more helpful to just briefly discuss the basics of sexual intercourse, perhaps including the idea of potential pleasure in such sharing. It is also a good idea to check to see if your child has understood your answer to his or her question. In addition, you might wish to inquire if you have provided the information that was desired and also to indicate that you are open to any other questions. When young children want more information they will probably ask for it, provided an adult has been responsive to their initial questions.

Some parents may feel that it is inappropriate to tell their children that sexual interaction is pleasurable. Others may conclude that there is value in discussing the joy of sex with their offspring, as revealed in the following account:

> One evening, while sitting on my daughter's bed and discussing the day's events, she expressed some concern over her next-door playmate's announcement that her father was going to purchase a stud horse. Apparently, she had been told to have me build a higher fence to protect her mare. She asked why this was necessary. Actually, she knew all about horses mating, as evidenced by her quick acknowledgment of my brief explanation. However, such commentary on my part did produce the following inquiry, "Do you and Mom do that?" to which I replied, "Yes." "Do my uncle and aunt do that?" Again the affirmative response which produced the final pronouncement, "I don't think I'll get married." Clearly, she was experiencing some strong ambivalence about what this sexual behavior meant to her. It seemed of critical importance to make one more statement, namely that not only did we do this, but that it is a beautiful and pleasurable kind of sharing and lots of fun! (Authors' files)

Reluctance to express the message that sex can be enjoyable may stem from parents' concern that their children will rush right out to find out what kind of good times they have been missing. However, there is little evidence to support such apprehension. On the other hand, there are many unhappy lovers striving to overcome early messages about the dirtiness and immorality of sex.

There are some topics that may never get discussed, at least not at the proper time, unless parents are willing to take the initiative. We are referring to certain aspects of sexual maturing that the child may not consider until he or she experiences them. These include menstruation, first ejaculation, and nocturnal orgasms. The desirability of preparing girls for their first period well in advance of the event has been well documented. Nevertheless, a majority of women students in our classes have said that they knew little or nothing about menstruation until they were given sketchy accounts by peers or actually had their first period. It is also typical for males to be unaware of their potential for ejaculating when masturbating. Experience with first menstruation or ejaculation can come as quite a shock to the unprepared, as revealed in the following two anecdotes:

> I hadn't even heard of menstruation when I first started bleeding. No one was home. I was so frightened I called an ambulance. (Authors' files)

> I remember well the first time I ejaculated during masturbation. At first I couldn't believe it when something shot out of my penis. The only thing I could figure is that I had whipped up my urine. However, considering earlier lectures from my mother about the evils of "playing with yourself," I was afraid that God was punishing me for my sinful behavior. (Authors' files)

It is important that youngsters be aware of these impending changes before they actually happen. A child's natural curiosity about the other sex may cause him or her to discuss these topics with friends, who are usually not the most reliable sources of information. It is certainly better for parents to provide a more accurate description of natural events like menstruation and ejaculation.

Some parents may find it relatively easy to discuss menstruation, but quite difficult to discuss nighttime orgasms or first ejaculations because of their associations with sexual activity. However, discussion of these events may also provide an opportunity to talk about self-pleasuring. Females also may experience nighttime orgasms. The fact that girls have no seminal traces to deal with in the morning does not eliminate possible confusion or guilt over the meaning of these occurrences.

> When I was a little girl I began to have these incredibly erotic dreams that sometimes produced indescribably good sensations. Looking back on it now, I realize these were my first experiences with nighttime orgasms. At the time I thought it was awful to have such good feelings connected with such wicked thoughts. I wish someone had told me then that my experiences were normal. It certainly would have eliminated a lot of unnecessary anxiety. (Authors' files)

Most young people prefer that their parents be the primary source of sex information, and that their mothers and fathers share equally in this responsibility (Bennett, 1984). To the extent that parents do take an active role in the sex education of their children, mothers are far more likely than fathers to fulfill this function (Coreil and Parcel, 1983; Thornburg, 1981). Unfortunately, most American parents do not provide sex education to their children. Several studies have revealed that friends are the principal source of information about sex for young people in this country (Gebhard, 1977; Sorenson, 1973; Thornburg, 1981). Thus, the gap created by lack of information in the home is likely to be filled with incorrect information from peers and other sources. Such information can have serious consequences; for example, an adolescent may hear from friends that a girl will not get pregnant if she only has intercourse "now and then." Peers may also encourage traditional gender-role behavior, and they often put pressure on each other to become sexually active. The issue facing parents is whether they want to become actively involved in their children's sex education, thereby minimizing some of the pitfalls faced by children and adolescents who turn to their peers for sex information.

Parents may hesitate to discuss sex with their children because they are concerned that such communication may encourage early sexual experimentation. However, there is no evidence that sex education leads to sexual activity. This inaccurate assumption may stem, at least in part, from the tendency of adults to overestimate teenagers' interest in sex. The truth is that there are many things that adolescents typically consider to be more important issues in their lives. In a nationwide survey of teens, 13- to 18-year-olds ranked sex seventh in a list of major concerns—behind school, parents, money, friends, siblings, and drinking or drugs (Norman and Harris, 1981). In another survey, girls ranked sex last and boys placed it fourth in order of importance on a list of six activities which included sex, doing well in school, athletics, friendships with their own sex, friendships with the other sex, and romantic involvement with someone (Hass, 1979).

In response to the frequent lack of information from the home and the inaccuracy of much of the information from peers, other social institutions are attempting to provide sex education. Some schools have included sex education as part of the curriculum, although the quality and extent of these programs varies considerably from place to place.

Various surveys have revealed that a majority of parents support the idea of having sex education in schools but that only a minority of American schools offer sex education courses, many of which are woefully incomplete (Alexander, 1984; Orr, 1982). Public school sex education programs are often hampered by pressures from well-organized and highly vocal minorities. In response to these pressures, many school systems completely omit sex education from their curricula, and others attempt to avert controversy by allowing only discussions of "safe" topics such as reproduction and anatomy. As a consequence, some important areas for discussion, such as interpersonal aspects of sexuality and preventing pregnancy are entirely overlooked. In a recent survey of several hundred adolescents, only about one out of ten indicated that their school was teaching them what they wanted to know about sex. The top five topics they wanted to learn about, in order of importance, included feelings about the other sex, birth control, pregnancy and parenthood, abortion, and how to decide about sex (Ostrov et al., 1985). School sex education is further limited by the fact that it is typically provided during the late stages of high school, a time when most adolescents have already begun sexual experimentation.

Individuals who are pondering whether it would be beneficial to discuss sexuality with their children might wish to consider the following information. The World Health Organization has stated that sexual ignorance is a major cause of "sexual misadventures" (Calderone, 1965). These "misadventures" may include such things as unwanted pregnancies, exploitive relationships, contracting sexually transmitted diseases, and nonfulfilling sexual experiences. Numerous studies have revealed a connection between lack of education and these undesirable occurrences, particularly unwanted pregnancy and sexual disease. Our experiences, and those of other therapists and educators, have demonstrated the strong relationship that often exists between lack of knowledge of sexual matters and sexual maladjustment.

On the brighter side, researchers have shown that providing people with factual sex information contributes positively to their psychological and sexual adjustment (McCary and Flake, 1971; Wright and McCary, 1969). Furthermore, studies indicate that young people whose parents play a major role in their sex education are not as likely to engage in early sexual activity as are their less-informed counterparts (Lewis, 1973). They are also more likely to use effective birth control when they do begin sexual sharing than are adolescents reared in families that do not discuss sex (Fox, 1980). One survey of 600 teenagers indicated that if a young person obtained "sex knowledge from parents or adults with whom a positive identification exists, there appeared to be less tendency toward involvement in promiscuity" (Deschin, 1963). Thus, in sharp contrast to what many believe, it seems that talking with our children about sex is more likely to discourage rather than encourage premature or irresponsible sexual involvement with others.

People who do not
conform to tradi-
tional role stereo-
types have more
alternatives avail-
able to them.

Androgynous Child-Rearing and Sexuality

The idea of raising children in an androgynous fashion has much to offer to parents anxious to minimize the limiting influence of gender-role expectations in the lives of their children. As discussed in Chapter 3, the term androgyny is used to describe flexibility in gender roles. In this sense, androgynous child-rearing means raising a child in a way that encourages selection of whatever feminine or masculine behaviors feel good to him or her.

On numerous occasions in this text we have expressed our belief that strict adherence to stereotypic gender roles may have a detrimental effect upon sexual functioning. The examples are many, ranging from the man who is unable to express emotion and tenderness because it is not "masculine" to the woman who has great difficulty communicating her sexual needs because she has been conditioned to be passive. Many parents may wish to counteract these limiting influences by the manner in which they rear their children. Perhaps such things as reassuring little boys that it is okay to cry and reinforcing girls for expressions of appropriate assertiveness will help to offset the impact of rigid gender roles.

Encouraging a child to develop as a human being first and a male or female second is a developmental goal that is receiving increasing support in our society. Those inclined to agree with the philosophy and intent of this evolving concept of androgyny may find the most fertile ground for its implementation in the home environment.

One of the truly striking aspects of a gender role dominated society is that boys and girls grow up playing primarily with same-sex peers. Little girls get together to

*Parents can
provide models of
nonstereotyped
behavior for
their developing
children.*

see who has the latest Barbie doll fashions and boys shoot each other with mock guns. Other than dating in adolescence, this same-sex pairing generally holds up throughout the developmental years. There may be many effects of this sex segregation, not the least of which is the awkwardness and lack of spontaneity that characterizes many man-woman relationships. The segregation may often seem to be self-imposed—girls frequently do not *want* to play with boys and vice versa. However, a contributing factor may sometimes be adult approval of sex-specific play activities. Many now believe that it is acceptable for boys to play with dolls and girls to push trucks through dirt piles. Would children play so consistently in same-sex groups if gender-neutral activities were encouraged more?

In addition to encouraging or discouraging types of play, parental modeling is also an important influence in raising children in an androgynous fashion. Parents who feel comfortable sharing childcare and housework can provide models of androgynous behavior for their developing children. It may be particularly valuable to engage in behaviors that are markedly different from traditional gender-role stereotypes. For example, Dad may cook dinner or change diapers, while Mom works late at the office, changes the oil in the car, and so on.

We believe that people raised in an androgynous fashion may enjoy freedom to behave sensitively and sensibly, and that by lifting restrictive notions about "acting like a lady" or "being a man," adults can encourage their children to have a broader outlook. This potential is one of the possible benefits of this alternative approach to parenting.

Summary

1. The traditional view of infancy and childhood as a time when sexuality remains unexpressed is not supported by research findings.

2. Infants of both sexes are born with the capacity for sexual pleasure and response, and some experience observable orgasm.

Sexual Behavior in Childhood

3. Self-administered genital stimulation is common among boys and girls during the first two years of life.

4. Sex play with other children, which may occur as early as the age of two or three, increases in frequency during the five-to-seven age range.

5. Segregation of the sexes becomes pronounced by the age of eight or nine. However, romantic interest in the other sex and curiosity about sexual matters are typically quite high during this stage of development.

6. The ages of 10 and 11 are marked by keen interest in body changes, continued segregation of the sexes, and a substantial incidence of homosexual encounters.

7. Masturbation is one of the most common sexual expressions during the childhood years. It is the most frequent source of preadolescent orgasm for both sexes.

The Physical Changes of Adolescence

8. Puberty refers to the physical changes that occur in response to increased hormone levels. These physical developments include maturation of the reproductive organs and consequent menstruation in girls and ejaculation in boys.

Sexual Behavior During Adolescence

9. The double standard often pressures males to view sex as a conquest and places females in a double bind about saying yes or no.

10. Peer pressure among adolescents may cause both males and females to engage in sexual activities in the name of "sexual liberation."

11. The number of adolescents who masturbate increases between the ages of 13 and 19.

12. Petting is a common sexual behavior among adolescents. One-half of adolescent girls and two-thirds of adolescent boys have engaged in petting to the point of orgasm.

13. Adolescent sexual expression is now more likely to take place within the context of an ongoing monogamous relationship than it was during Kinsey's time.

14. A significant increase in the number of both young men and young women who experience intercourse by age 19 has occurred since Kinsey's research was conducted. These increases have been considerably more pronounced among females.

15. Homosexual experiences during adolescence can be experimental or an expression of permanent sexual orientation.

Adolescent Pregnancy

16. One in 10 adolescent females becomes pregnant each year. Pregnancy usually compounds social, medical, educational, and financial difficulties.

17. The majority of adolescents who have intercourse do not regularly use contraceptives.

18. The low rate of contraceptive use among American adolescents seems to be related to a number of factors, including inadequate availability of free or low-cost contraceptive services, minimal use of the most effective birth control methods, inadequate school sex education programs, and an attitude among teenagers that assuming responsibility for birth control implies an immoral character.

19. Strategies for reducing the teenage pregnancy rate in America include upgrading the family planning clinic system, establishing a compulsory national sex education curriculum, linking school programs to clinics, educating males about their contraceptive responsibility, and relaxing government restrictions on the distribution and advertising of nonprescription contraceptives.

Some Key Influences on Psychosexual Development

20. Negative feelings about one's own sexual anatomy may stem from adverse parental reactions to eliminative functions and punitive or disapproving responses to early genital fondling.

21. Much of the anxiety children experience over their masturbation practices is related to real or imagined parental disapproval. Expressing acceptance of masturbation, while unlikely to appreciably increase its incidence, may allow a child to feel less guilty and more comfortable with this form of self-discovery.

22. Many parents are reticent about revealing to their children the sensual and intimate aspects of their relationship. This is an area that merits careful consideration, in that parents can often provide a far more positive model of caring, nonexploitive sharing than is typically offered by a young person's peer group or the popular media.

23. Many individuals acquire a sense of shame or uneasiness about the genital areas of their bodies, feelings that may be fostered by a lack of comfort with nudity around the home.

24. Dependency versus independency conflicts between parents and children often become pronounced during adolescence. Parents may find it particularly difficult to encourage adolescents to make independent decisions pertaining to sexual expression.

25. Another issue that is often troublesome to parents concerns privacy, which may take on a new meaning with the onset of adolescence. Many parents may be uncomfortable about granting privacy to teenage children who bring their other-sex friends home.

Sex Education

26. One answer to the question of when to start discussing sex with our children is "When they start asking questions." If communication does not spontaneously occur, it may be helpful for parents to initiate dialogue, perhaps by simply sharing their feelings or asking non-stressful, open-ended questions.

27. Some important topics—particularly menstruation, first ejaculation, and nocturnal orgasms—are rarely discussed unless parents take the initiative.

28. Although the majority of adolescents prefer their parents to be the primary source of sex information, evidence indicates that peers are considerably more likely than parents to provide this information, often in a biased and inaccurate manner.

29. Several studies have revealed a connection between sexual "misadventures" and an inadequate sex education. Furthermore, research indicates that individuals who receive factual sex education, in contrast to their uninformed counterparts, demonstrate better psychological and sexual adjustment and a reduced tendency to engage in premature or irresponsible sexual activity with others.

Androgynous Child-Rearing and Sexuality

30. In addition to encouraging a child to develop his or her potential, androgynous child-rearing practices help to break down the stereotypic gender roles that often have a negative effect upon sexual functioning.

Thought Provokers

1. Assume you are a parent of a seven-year-old and that one day you find your child "playing doctor" with a playmate of the same age of the other sex. Both have lowered their pants and they seem to be involved in visually exploring each others' bodies. How would you respond to this situation? Would you react differently according to the sex of your child?

2. Should parents provide birth control devices to their teenage children who are actively dating or going steady?

3. It has been suggested that raising children in an androgynous fashion may foster uncertainty and lead to confusion over their proper roles in society. Do you agree with this assertion? Why or why not?

4. There is evidence that women who have had a history of masturbating to orgasm during their childhood or adolescence have an increased probability of experiencing satisfactory sexual relations as adults. In view of this finding, do you think it is appropriate for parents to encourage their female children to engage in self-pleasuring?

Suggested Readings

Anthony, James; Green, Richard; and Kolodny, Robert. *Childhood Sexuality*. Boston: Little, Brown, 1982. Provides comprehensive information about childhood and adolescent sexuality.

Bryne, Dann, and Fisher, William (Eds). *Adolescents, Sex, and Contraception*. Hillsdale, N.J.: Erlbaum, 1983. A thoughtful, accurate discussion of many aspects of adolescent sexuality.

Calderone, Mary, and Johnson, Eric. *The Family Book About Sexuality*. New York: Harper & Row, 1981. This excellent book, helpful for both parents and children, offers practical advice and valuable insights into childhood sexuality.

Calderone, Mary, and Ramey, James. *Talking With Your Child About Sex*. New York: Random House, 1982. This excellent book provides practical and wise advice for parents who wish to raise sexually healthy children.

Hanckel, Frances, and Cunningham, John. *A Way of Love, A Way of Life*. New York: Lothrop, Lee and Shepard, 1979. A sensitive, thoughtful book that gives young people information about what it means to be homosexual.

Pogrebin, Letty. *Growing Up Free: Raising Your Child in the '80s*. New York: McGraw-Hill, 1980. An important source of information for parents who wish to raise their children in an androgynous fashion.

14

Love seems the swiftest, but it is the slowest of all growths.
No man or woman knows what perfect love is
until they have been married a quarter of a century.
Mark Twain
Notebook (1935)

Sexuality and the Adult Years

Single Living
Cohabitation
Marriage
Relationship Contracts
Extramarital Relationships
Divorce
Widowhood

INTIMATE RELATIONSHIPS occupy a position of considerable significance in many adults' lives. An adult's relationship status—as single, married, or living with someone—becomes an important social concern, as well as an important element in that person's self-identity. A person's relationship status may also have considerable influence on the kinds of sexual interactions he or she experiences during the adult years. This chapter will examine several alternatives for lifestyles and intimate relationships, which have been undergoing transition in recent years.

Single Living

Increasing numbers of people in our society live alone. This increase is most pronounced among people in their twenties and early thirties. For example, a comparison of 1970 and 1980 census figures reveals that the percentage of men in the 20 to 24 age range who were single increased from 55% in 1970 to 69% in 1980. Comparable figures for women demonstrated an increase from 36% to 50%. In 1970, 17.1% of all American households were comprised of only one person. This figure increased by almost 40% over the ensuing 14 years, so that by the end of 1984 single adults constituted 23.4% of the households in the United States (Bureau of the Census, 1985). The proportion of individuals who have never married has approximately doubled since 1970 for men and women in their late twenties and early thirties (Current Population Reports, 1985).

These figures seem to represent a shift in adult living patterns. In the past, a far smaller percentage of adults either divorced or remained unmarried. Various factors contribute to the increasing numbers of single adults; these include people marrying at a later age, a slight increase in the numbers of those who never marry, more women placing career objectives ahead of marriage, rising divorce rates, a greater emphasis on advanced education, and an increase in the number of women who no longer must depend on marriage to ensure their economic stability (Current Population Reports, 1985; Glick and Norton, 1979). The figures also reflect what may be a change in societal attitudes. Until recently in the United States a stigma was often attached to remaining single. This stigma attached itself particularly to women, as terms such as "old maid" and "spinster" indicate. (Single men would most likely be referred to by the less negative term "bachelor.") Today these terms are heard less frequently, and it is quite possible that remaining single, either as an option to first marriage or following termination of a marriage, will play an increasingly prominent role in American culture. If this happens, we may also witness a reduction in the number of people who marry primarily for convention's sake or to avoid the negative perception of the single state. Nevertheless, single life is still often seen as the period before, in between, or after marriage.

A recent survey of 482 single Canadian adults in several major population centers provided both indications of what motivates people to remain single and a sense of how satisfied they are with single life (Austrom and Hanel, 1985). Almost half of the respondents considered themselves single by deliberate choice and not as a result of chance or circumstances beyond their control. The vast majority of the 482 did not believe they were single because they were reluctant to be committed to an exclusive relationship, because they lacked desire for sexual relations with the other sex, or because high divorce rates made them apprehensive about marriage. Rather, most indicated that they were unmarried "simply because they had not met the right person and also because their expectations of a marriage partner were very high" (p. 17). There were some sex differences in the reasons expressed for being single. Women had a greater tendency to attribute their singleness to caution due to bad experiences with previous relationships. On the other hand, men were more inclined to say that there were too many interesting people to choose among. There were no sex differences in reported satisfaction with single life. Forty-seven percent indicated dissatisfaction with their present status and the rest were either neutral (28%) or satisfied (25%). Levels of satisfaction did not seem to be a function of whether the respondents were never-married, divorced, or widowed. Being satisfied with the number and types of friends they had was positively correlated with feeling good about being single. "These results suggest that satisfaction with single life is, to some degree, a function of expressive social support, especially in the interpersonal areas of friendship and community life . . ." (p. 19).

Single living encompasses a range of sexual lifestyles and differing levels of personal satisfaction. Levels of sexual activity among single people vary widely, just as they do among marrieds. However, evidence suggests that singles are likely to be as sexually active as married people (Petersen et al., 1983). Some people who live alone remain celibate by choice or because of lack of available partners. Others may be involved in a long-term, sexually exclusive relationship with one partner. Some practice serial monogamy, moving through a succession of sexually exclusive relationships. Still others prefer concurrent sexual and emotional involvements with a number of different partners. Some single people develop a primary relationship with one partner and have occasional sex with others.

Single adults often initially react like "children in a candy factory" to society's loosened restraints on sexual behavior. However, with time, many of these same people become disillusioned with their frequent involvement in casual sex (Simenauer and Carroll, 1982). Others find that a climate of increased sexual freedom and choices may be just as likely to lead to pressure, conflict, and disappointment as it is to promote satisfaction and a sense of personal fulfillment (Marin, 1983).

Meeting people for prospective social contacts, sexual partners, or marriage is often important to single people. Singles bars and singles apartment complexes often serve this purpose, especially among middle- and upper-income, urban, unmarried individuals. Singles bars may also offer people an opportunity to enjoy socializing and to overcome boredom and loneliness. However, the singles bar atmosphere may provoke anxieties, prompt people to assume roles they are not comfortable with, and generally increase feelings of alienation and isolation (Allon and Fishel, 1979). People who dislike the "heavy hustle" scene and superficiality that sometimes characterize such places may prefer to develop contacts through common activities or through work, friends, or family.

The survey of Canadian singles found that the most frequently used means for meeting people were introductions by mutual friends (experienced by 92% of the respondents), parties (90%), the workplace (82%), and activities such as hobbies or sports (80%). The least employed methods for meeting available singles were dating services (10%), classified companion or love ads (20%), church groups (26%), and singles clubs (27%). Dating services and love ads were rated by the respondents as

Many cities have
singles bars.

the least effective means of meeting a desirable person, whereas sports and hobby activities and meeting people at work were considered the most promising options for establishing a romantic relationship. However, even the best methods for meeting people were rated little better than neutral on an 11-point scale ranging from complete dissatisfaction to complete satisfaction (Austrom and Hanel, 1985).

Single living is becoming more acceptable in our society. However, the majority of people still choose to enter into a long-term relationship with a partner, even though it may not be a lifelong bond. There are several kinds of long-term sexual relationships, and we will examine these various options in most of the remainder of this chapter.

Cohabitation

When I was a college student in the early 1960s, the possibility of living with someone dear to me, without the sanctity of marriage, simply never entered my mind. When I met a very special person and found myself wishing for the intimacy of sharing a home together, marriage was my only option. Although we were sexual prior to marriage, there were no occasions when we even took a weekend trip together. The topic of unmarrieds living together was never discussed, although I did occasionally hear a hushed reference to someone "living in sin." (Authors' files)

This account reflects a prevalent societal attitude toward **cohabitation** (living together in a sexual relationship without being married), and this attitude has only recently begun to undergo change. In the past few decades there has been a significant increase in both the number of people choosing this living arrangement and societal acceptance of what was once an unconventional practice. Census Bureau figures reveal that by 1984 the number of unmarried couples living together in the United States numbered 1,988,000—nearly triple the number in 1970 (Current Population Reports, 1985). It appears that cohabitation is now well established as a social phenomenon. In 1980 the U.S. Census Bureau formally acknowledged it by announcing a new category: POSSLQ ("person of opposite sex sharing living quarters").

This dramatic increase in cohabitation has been attributed to American youth's growing inclination to question traditional mores, particularly those pertaining to the value of marriage. These questioning attitudes are supported by an expanding societal awareness that sexuality is an important part of a person's life and that marriage is not the only lifestyle that legitimizes sexual relations. In addition, some social theorists have pointed to the increased availability and variety of birth control methods as influencing people's decision to live together outside of matrimony. Beyond these factors, there are a number of personal reasons why people choose to live together as a temporary or permanent alternative to marriage. We will look at some of these reasons before examining the impact of this trend on the more traditional lifestyle of marriage.

Personal Reasons for Living Together

There are several reasons why a couple may choose to live together without marriage. Many people are waiting longer to get married and delaying having their first child, factors that increase the attractiveness of cohabitation as a lifestyle option. Older people may elect to cohabit because they simply cannot afford marriage. (If a widow remarries she may lose half or all of her Social Security pension, but if she cohabits with her male partner the two can pool their incomes without suffering a financial loss.)

An important factor influencing the decision to live together is the desire for sexual fulfillment. In a survey of 100,000 readers of *Playboy* magazine, the cohabitators in the study population reported more satisfaction with their sex lives than either the single or the married respondents (Petersen et al., 1983). In a study of college students who were living together (Macklin, 1976), 96% of respondents reported having sexually satisfying relationships. Some sexual difficulties were acknowledged, however. The most common of these were differing degrees of sexual interest, fear of pregnancy, and occasional failure to reach orgasm. It appears that most cohabiting couples, particularly young adults, prefer to have a sexually exclusive relationship (Macklin, 1978).

The sexual involvement of couples living together is only one element of the desire to share a home with a partner. Other reasons for choosing this lifestyle may include a desire for a meaningful relationship, a need for companionship, an attempt to secure more intimacy and emotional security, and dissatisfaction with the "dating game." For many cohabitants living together provides an opportunity to determine their suitability for a long-term commitment before entering into the more binding partnership of marriage (Clarke, 1978). However, marriage is usually not the initial goal at the time a couple enters into a cohabitation relationship, and most individuals do not believe that a long-term commitment is necessary to begin a living-together relationship (Hobart, 1979; Macklin, 1976 and 1978).

Many couples prefer the relative informality of cohabitation arrangements to the more official aspects of a marriage. They appreciate the sense of living together because they want to, not as a result of the binding power of a legal contract, as the following account demonstrates:

> I object to people constantly asking us when we are going to get married. We live together because it feels good and because it seems like a reasonable thing to do. Neither one of us have any intention of ever getting married, to each other or to anyone else. We have been together for over two years and plan to continue for a long time. One thing is certain. We are together because we want to be, not because we are in some kind of "training for marriage." (Authors' files)

The informality of living together may have other advantages. A couple may not feel as pressured to take on the new and demanding roles of wife and husband. As a result, the relationship is less likely to produce the sort of "identity crisis" that may follow when people try to live up to the social expectations attached to these roles. Another perceived advantage may be that if the relationship is not satisfactory, the stigma of failure is less than with a divorce. This does not necessarily mean that it is easy to break up after living together. Terminating such a relationship can be very traumatic.

While living together offers some advantages to many couples, it also poses certain unique problems. Many of these problems stem from lack of social acceptance for this arrangement. Disapproval on the part of parents and other family members

Many college students who cohabit value sharing the day-to-day activities of living together.

can sometimes be severe—a situation that can place considerable emotional strain on one or both partners. Some couples may also have difficulty in renting or buying property, although this problem is becoming less common. Owning property does present other potential difficulties, however. Who owns the property and financial assets a former couple have shared? Without a clear written contract, legal rights upon dissolution of the partnership are less clear than with a divorce. Death of one or both partners can result in legal confusion in addition to the emotional trauma. Again, unless the couple has had the foresight to write a contract, there is no clearly established legal definition of partnership rights.

In addition to social disapproval and possible legal difficulties, there may also be financial disadvantages to living together. For instance, unmarried couples often receive discriminatory treatment under the tax laws. Despite the potential disadvantages, however, the practice of living together is a growing trend. In the next few paragraphs, we will look at this trend's impact.

The Social Impact of Living Together

It is still too early to assess what impact the experience of living together may have on relationship satisfaction, the stability of partnerships, and the marriage institution itself. There are those who view cohabitation as a clear sign of moral decay. Others applaud the advent of a new alternative to the narrow restrictions of a traditional life script.

A question arising from the increase in cohabitation is whether this experience has a measurable effect upon the longevity and happiness of any subsequent marriage. At present, with very little available evidence, there are two opposing hypotheses. One holds that positive outcomes will prevail, with happier and more stable marriages emerging as a result of living together. Trial experiences of the struggles and joys of an everyday relationship can allow a person to better identify his or her own needs and expectations. In this view, living-together arrangements provide the couple an opportunity to explore their compatibility before making a long-term commitment.

The opposing hypothesis suggests that living together will have an overall negative impact upon the institution of marriage, particularly its long-term stability. When people who are living together are faced with conflict, they may find it easier to end the relationship than to exert an effort to resolve the problems. A marriage relationship often carries with it a greater commitment to solving problems, in part because termination of marriage carries with it legal complications and social stigma. Those who hold this view are concerned that once the pattern of breaking up has been established, people will be more likely to respond to marital conflict in the same way. The following account expresses the basic rationale behind this view:

> Many times during our marriage I have thought seriously about leaving. I am quite certain, had it not been for the moral commitment of the marriage contract and the legal and family hassles I could expect from divorce, our marriage would have ended long ago. It may sound strange, based on what I just said, but I am thankful that being married helped to keep us together. It takes one heck of a lot of work to make a marriage work. My guess is that people who just live together have much less incentive to struggle to keep things good. I'm glad I am still married. We have something really worth holding onto. (Authors' files)

It is possible that neither of these opposing hypotheses is correct. Cohabitation may have no demonstrable effect upon the longevity or satisfaction of any subsequent marriage. There is some limited evidence that supports this contention. In one study, couples who had cohabited before marriage were just as likely to divorce as those who did not (Newcomb and Bentler, 1980). Another study, conducted among university students, examined whether cohabitation (with the future spouse or someone else) had any influence on subsequent marital happiness. This investigation revealed no differences after marriage on several measures of marital success, which included indicators of relationship stability, sexual satisfaction, physical intimacy, and openness of communication (Jacques and Chason, 1979). However, in contrast to these two studies, a more recent survey of over 300 couples found that cohabitation with one's future spouse was associated with significantly lower perceived quality of communication for wives and significantly lower marital satisfaction for both partners (DeMaris and Leslie, 1984).

Clearly, further research is necessary to clarify the impact, if any, of cohabitation on marriage. One thing we can say with some confidence: People do not appear to be permanently substituting living-together arrangements for marriage (Macklin, 1980). In spite of the rapidly changing societal mores pertaining to human relationships and sexual expression, Census Bureau statistics reveal that about nine out of every ten adults in the United States marry, some more than once. Statistics released in 1985 show that the number of new marriages each year per 1000 resident U.S. population has remained relatively constant in the period from 1970 to 1984 (see Table 14.2 later in the chapter). A closer look at the institution of marriage may provide some insight into its continuing appeal.

Marriage

Marriage is an institution that is found in virtually every society. It has traditionally served several functions, both personal and social. It provides societies with stable family units that help to perpetuate social norms, as children are typically taught society's rules and expectations by parents or kinship groups. In many cultures, marriage defines inheritance rights to family property. Marriage performs an important function by structuring an economic partnership that ties child support and subsistence tasks into one family unit. Marriage regulates sexual behavior to maintain the family line. It also provides a framework for fulfilling people's needs for social and emotional support.

Although marriage is integral to most cultures, it assumes many different forms. Our society has defined its own marriage ideal. Within this ideal we can isolate a number of elements that many people take for granted—for instance, legality, permanence, heterosexuality, sexual exclusivity, emotional exclusivity, and monogamy (one man and one woman). But the elements that are traditional to marriage in our society are not necessarily the same in other societies. For example, some societies have marriages between one man and several women (polygamy); others (far less common) have recognized unions between one woman and several men (polyandry).

In our own society, there are several modifications of the marriage ideal, although changing one element is still often seen as a radical departure from the

Marriage is a traditional and deeply ingrained institution in American society.

norm. Yet even when one element is changed, other elements of a partner relationship are often expected to remain the same. For example, the extramarital sexual behavior known as "swinging" (discussed later in this chapter) theoretically alters only the sexual exclusivity of the marriage ideal. Other elements, including emotional exclusivity, are expected to remain constant in the relationship. Likewise, a couple living together often adheres to virtually all aspects of the marriage ideal except for its legal sanction. (In this case, even legality is granted in many states, where the relationship becomes a common-law marriage after a certain number of years.) The same assumptions sometimes hold true when the element of gender is changed. Some homosexual couples want their unions to be legally recognized marriages. In spite of the fact that homosexual marriages are not accepted as legal by the judicial system, some same-sex couples nevertheless have wedding ceremonies and adopt the marriage ideal for their relationships.

Changing Expectations and Marital Patterns

The institution of marriage has been both condemned and venerated in contemporary America. Currently, a large discrepancy exists between the American marriage ideal and actual marriage practices. Cohabitation, high divorce rates, widespread extramarital sexual involvements, and the increasing popularity of personalized relationship contracts are all developments that are antithetical to the traditional ideal of marriage.

Some of the reasons for contradictions between the ideal and actual marriage practices have to do with changes that have been taking place, both in expectations for marriage and in the social framework of marriage. Historically, the function of marriage has been to provide a stable economic unit in which to raise children. People who did not want to have children were often admonished not to marry (Ritter, 1919). In many societies, and in some groups within our own society in the past, marriages were arranged through contracts between parents; "romance" was not expected to play a part. Today, however, most people expect more from marriage, as they seek fulfillment for their social, emotional, financial, and sexual needs—all within the marriage relationship. Happiness itself is sometimes thought to be an automatic outcome of marriage. These are high expectations, and they are difficult to meet. As one observer states, "Marriage was not designed as a mechanism for providing friendship, erotic experience, romantic love, personal fulfillment, continuous lay psychotherapy or recreation" (Cadwallader, 1975, p. 134). However, many modern couples expect a satisfactory degree of all these benefits from the marital relationship.

At the same time that people's expectations for marriage have increased, our society's supportive network for marriage has decreased. Extended families and small communities have become less prevalent, and many married couples are isolated from their families and neighbors. In effect, this places further demands on the marriage to meet a variety of human needs, for there is often no place else to turn for such things as childcare assistance, emotional support, and financial or housework help. Another development that is influencing marital patterns is increased longevity. "Till death do us part" now means many more years than it did in the past. This raises the question of how long even the best marriage can be expected to fulfill all of these functions.

At a personal level, courtship experiences before marriage also contribute to the discrepancy between expectations and reality. Dating rarely offers a couple the kinds of experiences that would enable them to draw a realistic picture of the marriage relationship or learn the skills that may help resolve later difficulties. Both partners frequently present their more likeable, sociable side. The focus of their time together is usually on pleasurable activities, with day-to-day problems kept separate from their interactions. The fairy-tale ending to their courtship—"they married and lived happily ever after"—is often difficult to achieve. While the challenges of sharing everyday life can provide enrichment and meaning to some couples, the lack of preparedness may be cause for disillusionment for others.

There are many things a couple can do that may help prepare them for the experience of marriage. Some not yet married couples make an effort to talk about such things as finances, children, and daily tasks that frequently are basic to disagreements. They may plan the handling of finances for shared activities or a vacation. They may also decide to divide living expenses equally, or on a percentage basis relative to their respective incomes.

A couple contemplating marriage needs to discuss their desires and decisions about children—whether each person wants them, how many, and when. If neither partner has children at the time, they may want to make arrangements to share volunteer childcare work or babysitting for friends, to help assess and discuss their childrearing attitudes. They may also need to plan the logistics of caring for their own children. The importance of becoming clear about aspirations and expectations concerning children is made evident by the fact that married couples tend to disagree frequently about childrearing practices (Klagsbrun, 1985).

Some couples may work on a cooperative project or share homemaking activities. Building something together, organizing a party, trading work days at each other's houses, or cooking meals for each other are samples of activities that may help couples learn more about how well they can work together.

Situations in which the pair discovers problems can make the couple aware of what differences they bring into the marriage. A "good marriage" is not necessarily a problem-free marriage but rather a relationship in which two people are committed to working with the problems that invariably arise.

Francine Klagsbrun (1985) recently conducted in-depth interviews with 90 couples, married 15 years or more, who rated their marriages as happy and successful. Some of the traits she found to be associated with good marriages included spending focused time together, such as might occur during the courtship days, sharing values (more important than sharing interests), and flexibility—the ability to accept change both in one's partner and in the nature of the relationship. Other research studies have provided strong evidence that positive communication, high levels of physical intimacy, and perceptions of emotional closeness and mutual empathy are highly correlated with marital happiness (Tolstedt and Stokes, 1983; Zimmer, 1983).

Why Do People Marry?

While both individual and societal expectations have undergone important changes, marriage remains a dominant lifestyle in our culture. Certainly the majority of Americans marry, some several times. The fact that marriage is such a traditional and deeply ingrained institution in American society at least partly answers the question "Why do people marry?" The following list includes some additional reasons people often give for entering wedlock:

1. Marriage can provide a feeling of permanence in one's life and a very reassuring sense of belonging and being needed.
2. The closeness and trust engendered by marriage may lead to richer relationships and deeper caring.
3. Sexual interaction is legally and socially sanctioned in marriage.
4. With the greater familiarity provided by marriage, people may develop better understanding of each other's needs and thus a more harmonious relationship.
5. There are some monetary and legal advantages granted married people under present legal codes.

Marriage itself has changed in the face of changing expectations and needs, and there is a growing interest in making the most of the institution in a changing society. The popularity of "marital enrichment" programs is one indication of the desire of many couples to improve their relationships. The aim of these programs is usually to teach the couple to be more responsive and accepting of each other's needs, to improve communication, and to deepen intimacy. Other couples seek professional counseling to improve the way they relate to each other. The large number of "make your marriage better" books and magazine articles also reflects the importance placed on "good" marriages. Sexual behavior has also changed within the marriage structure, and this is another area that has come under professional scrutiny.

Sexual Behavior Within Marriage

Contemporary developments and changes in sexual mores and behavior are often discussed in the context of nonmarital or extramarital activities. However, the greatest impact of increased sexual liberalization may be on the marital relationship itself. As compared with the people in Kinsey's research groups, contemporary American married men and women appear to be engaging in sexual intercourse more often, experiencing a wider repertoire of sexual behaviors, and enjoying sexual interaction more. Several surveys have revealed significant changes in sexual activity among married couples in the years since Kinsey collected his data. The frequency and duration of precoital activity has increased, with more people focusing on enjoyment of the activities themselves rather than viewing them as preparation for coitus. Oral stimulation of the breasts and manual stimulation of the genitals has increased; so has oral-genital contact, both fellatio and cunnilingus (Blumstein and Schwartz, 1983; Frank and Enos, 1983; Hunt, 1974; Rubin, 1976; Petersen et al., 1983).

Married couples' experiences with coitus also seems to have changed over the years. Today's couples report using a wider variety of intercourse positions and prolonging coitus to several times longer than the two-minute average reported in Kinsey's 1948 study (Hunt, 1974; Petersen et al., 1983). The average frequency of marital coitus also appears to have increased to approximately two or three times per week for couples in their twenties and thirties, a frequency that gradually declines with increasing age (Frank and Enos, 1983; Petersen et al., 1983; Pietropinto and Simenauer, 1979; Trussel and Westoff, 1980).

Philip Blumstein and Pepper Schwartz (1983), in their landmark study of American couples, found that the frequency of marital sexual interactions was strongly associated with how the over 7000 married respondents in their sample group rated their sexual satisfaction. Nine out of ten of the marrieds who were having sex three or more times a week reported satisfaction with the quality of their sex lives. In contrast, only half of those individuals who were having sex one to four times a month were satisfied. Furthermore, only a third of those with frequency rates of once a month or less reported satisfaction. As we might expect, Blumstein and Schwartz also found that sex is more exciting at the outset of marriage, and that in long-term relationships sex tends to be more "bread and butter" rather than "champagne and caviar."

A number of factors other than frequency of sexual interaction have also been linked to satisfaction with marital sex. Mutuality in initiating sex may be an important contributor to sexual satisfaction of both wives and husbands (Blumstein and Schwartz, 1983; Tavris and Sadd, 1977). It also appears that women who take an active role during sexual sharing are more likely to be pleased with their sex lives than those who assume a more passive role (Tavris and Sadd, 1977). Research also suggests a positive correlation between marital happiness and female orgasm. In one survey of over 1000 women, orgasm frequency was considerably higher among those women reporting marital happiness than in those who indicated they were unhappily married (Gebhard, 1966). There is evidence that orgasm frequency is increasing among married women (Hunt, 1974; Petersen et al., 1983; Pietropinto and Simenauer, 1979; Tavris and Sadd, 1977).

It appears that good communication contributes greatly to sexual satisfaction within marriage. In the *Redbook* survey, 88% of the women who reported always discussing their sexual feelings with their partners described their sex lives as good or very good. In contrast, only 30% of women who reported never discussing sex with their partners described their sex lives as good or very good (Tavris and Sadd, 1977). A recent study of married couples found that those participants who enjoyed a high-quality marital relationship also reported good sexual communication (Banmen and Vogel, 1985).

Morton Hunt's (1974) research indicates that a positive relationship exists between subjective ratings of sexual pleasure and emotional closeness within marriage. Couples who rated their marriage as very close emotionally almost always rated marital coitus in the year preceding the study as highly pleasurable, while three-fifths of women and two-fifths of men who rated their marriages "not close" considered marital coitus to be unpleasant or not pleasant enough. (This still indicates that for two-fifths of women and three-fifths of men in this study, sexual pleasure was present despite a lack of emotional closeness.) The *Redbook* survey also suggests an apparent relationship between women's subjective assessments of the quality of their marriages and the degree of satisfaction in their sex lives. Eighty percent of women who reported happy marriages also said their sex life was good. On the other hand, 70% of women reporting poor marriages indicated that sex was poor (Tavris and Sadd, 1977).

After reviewing the information just presented, one might be tempted to conclude that all is well with marital sex. However, we caution against such a generalization. One of the shortcomings of much of the available data is that it is generally collected from people involved in intact marriages, as opposed to those whose marriages have ended. This is an important biasing influence that quite possibly leads to a more positive image of marital sexual satisfaction than is justified. Furthermore, most studies focus on the frequencies of certain behaviors and attitudes rather than on people's feelings about various aspects of their marriages, including sex. One notable exception is the work of sociologist Lillian Rubin (1976). She interviewed 50 working-class and 25 professional middle-class couples living in the San Francisco Bay area. Her interviews explored not only how her respondents behaved sexually but, perhaps more important, how they felt about sex in their marriages. Each of the 75 couples in her study population reported some problems in sexual adjustment. Masters and Johnson (1970) also state that marital sexual problems are quite common, and they estimate that approximately half of all American married couples experience difficulties with sexual adjustment.

A number of factors may interfere with marital sexual enjoyment. When people marry, their relationship often changes. They suddenly find themselves confronted with a new set of role expectations. They are no longer just friends and lovers but also husband and wife, and the romance of the former condition may be replaced by the stress of role adjustments to the latter. They no longer have the independence of living separately, and day-to-day togetherness may erode their sense of individuality and autonomy. Unfortunately, many people are less motivated to maintain personal attractiveness once they have secured a marriage partner; being overweight, out of shape, and poorly groomed may reduce one's sexual attractiveness and pleasure during sexual activity. People often get caught up in a "rat race" life style that can seriously erode the quality of marital sex. Holding down a job, doing laundry, fixing the lawn mower, socializing with two sets of relatives and friends, and countless other tasks can reduce the time a couple has for intimate sharing. Couples who become parents may discover that children can place unexpected strains on their relationship, in addition to interfering with their privacy and spontaneity. Finally, boredom can be a devitalizing factor. Sex may become routine and predictable. The discussion in Chapter 7 on maintaining relationship satisfaction may be helpful in enhancing sexual enjoyment in marriages and other long-term relationships.

Relationship Contracts

Another contemporary development is the use of relationship contracts to define particular aspects of both marital and nonmarital relationships. A **relationship contract** is a mutually agreed-upon set of rules, plans, or philosophies related to the relationship, and it can be either written or verbal. Some contracts may include legal documentation that spells out particular points.

The notoriety of certain court cases dealing with the dissolution of long-term cohabiting relationships, such as the break-up of Michele Triola and actor Lee Marvin, have inspired some couples to sign legal contracts before entering into a cohabiting relationship. This may be particularly advisable for couples who anticipate acquiring a considerable amount of property or financial assets during the course of their relationship. Couples planning to get married may also wish to follow this advice, since decisions about division of property and acquired income will be made in accordance with the laws of their state of residence unless they have entered into their own premarital contractual agreement.

Developing an individualized contract can be potentially useful to the couple. Such a contract might include the woman's right to use her own last name if they marry; an agreement about the children's names; decisions concerning reproduction, such as method of birth control and number and timing of natural, adoptive, or foster children; childrearing practices; divisions of labor for housework or other work; financial arrangements; living location and decision-making process for moving; agreements and commitments regarding sexual, social, and emotional exclusivity or nonexclusivity; and any other issues of importance to an individual couple (Edmiston, 1972). One person expressed the following feelings about writing a contract: "What we are really doing in thrashing out a contract is finding out where we stand on issues, clearing up all the murky, unexamined areas of conflict, and unflinchingly facing up to our differences" (Edmiston, 1972, p. 67). Many couples who implement individualized contracts renew, revise, or amend them on an ongoing basis to fit the changing needs of the relationship.

Extramarital Relationships

The term **extramarital relationship** is a label for sexual interaction experienced by a married person with someone other than his or her spouse. The term is a general one that makes no distinction among the many ways in which extramarital sexuality occurs. Such activity can be clandestine; it can also be based on an open agreement between the married partners. The extramarital relationship may be a casual encounter, or it may involve deep emotional commitment; it may last for a brief or extended time period. Sometimes this form of sexual sharing occurs within the context of an alternative lifestyle, as in the case of group marriages. The following discussions will examine extramarital relationships, both nonconsensual and consensual.

Nonconsensual Extramarital Relationships

In **nonconsensual extramarital sex**, the married person engages in an outside sexual relationship without the consent (or presumably the knowledge) of his or her spouse. This form of behavior has been given many labels, including "cheating," adultery, infidelity, having an affair, and "fooling around."

Why do people enter into nonconsensual extramarital relationships? The reasons are varied and complex. Sometimes such relationships are motivated by a desire for excitement and variety. The person may have no particular complaints about the marital relationship but may want to enrich or broaden his or her emotional or sexual life with extramarital encounters. Some may be motivated to engage in extramarital relationships to secure evidence that they are still desirable to members of the other sex. In other cases, people may be highly dissatisfied with their marriage. If emotional needs are not being met within the marriage, having an "illicit lover" may seem particularly inviting. Occasionally the reason for outside involvements may be the unavailability of sex within the primary bond. A lengthy separation, a debilitating illness, or an inability or unwillingness of the partner to relate sexually may all contribute to a person deciding to look elsewhere for sexual fulfillment. An affair may also be motivated by a desire for revenge. In such instances, the offending party may be quite indiscreet, to ensure that the "wronged" spouse will discover the infidelity.

It is difficult to estimate the incidence of extramarital sexual involvements. Kinsey's surveys reported that approximately half of the men and a quarter of the women in his samples admitted to experiencing extramarital sexual intercourse at least once by age 40. The term *admitted* is a significant qualifier. Many writers and researchers believe that a considerable number of people are reluctant to acknowledge this kind of behavior, which may contribute to low estimates of its prevalence. This speculation receives some support from a survey of 750 individuals undergoing psychotherapy (Greene et al., 1974). Thirty percent of the sample initially admitted to having experienced extramarital involvements. After a period of extensive psychotherapy, however, an additional 30% revealed previous affairs. Furthermore, many sex surveys fail to distinguish between consensual and nonconsensual relationships—although it is reasonable to assume that the substantial majority of extramarital sexual contacts are nonconsensual. In Hunt's 1974 study, only one in five spouses whose partners had had such contacts had been told of the occurrence by their partner.

A number of surveys conducted in more recent times have yielded varying estimates of the frequency of extramarital involvements among American couples. None of these investigations were conducted with true probability samples of the U.S. population. Furthermore, each is biased by certain characteristics of its sample. However, in spite of drawing upon widely divergent sample populations, all of these surveys yield consistent evidence of an increasing incidence of extramarital sexual involvements, particularly among women. The following list gives the pertinent statistics from several of these investigations:

1. Of 106,000 female respondents to a *Cosmopolitan* sex survey, 50% under age 35 indicated they had experienced one or more extramarital affairs. The figure for women over age 35 jumped to 69% (Wolfe, 1981).

2. Of 100,000 respondents to a *Playboy* sex survey, all age groups combined, 45% of the men and 34% of the women reported one or more extramarital involvements. When only the older respondents were evaluated, the number of those experiencing extramarital sex by age 50 rose to 70% of the men and 65% of the women (Petersen et al., 1983).

3. The *Redbook* survey of 100,000 women reported that approximately 30% of the overall study population had engaged in one or more extramarital involvements. However, approximately half of those respondents who worked outside the home had experienced affairs. Furthermore, women in their late teens and twenties were almost three times as likely to have experienced extramarital sex as women of the same age in Kinsey's study population (Tavris and Sadd, 1977). This latter finding of a dramatic escalation of extramarital activity among young women was duplicated by Morton Hunt's 1974 research and a *Psychology Today* survey (Athanasiou et al., 1970).

When all of these statistics are considered collectively, it seems reasonable to conclude that a substantial majority of married American men and women will experience one or more extramarital involvements during their lifetime. Furthermore, there is clear evidence that the double standard for male and female marital infidelity that was clearly evident in Kinsey's time has been quite notably eroded over the last few decades. Recent evidence suggests that middle-aged women are almost as likely as their husbands to have extramarital sexual relationships.

It is quite possible that future sex surveys will reveal pronounced increases in extramarital sexual activity. This prediction is based on the many social changes evident in contemporary American life. For instance, greater mobility has increased people's opportunities to establish relationships away from home. Another factor is the increased number of women in the work force—a trend that has increased the potential for close daily relationships and sexual contacts between men and women. As more women enter into work situations that provide personal autonomy, we can expect that many will avail themselves of "legitimized" opportunities for exercising their extramarital sexuality. Furthermore, recent research has indicated that "if women perceive that interaction with other attractive men is available to them, they are likely to be more permissive in their attitudes towards extramarital coitus" (Saunders and Edwards, 1984, p. 831).

The effects of extramarital sex on a marriage vary. When secret involvements are discovered, the "betrayed" spouse may feel devastated. He or she may experience a variety of emotions, including feelings of inadequacy and rejection, extreme anger, resentment, shame, and jealousy. This last emotion can be very difficult to deal with, particularly when one partner has remained faithful while the other has "cheated." Jealousy may emerge from a sense of betrayal—the belief that the spouse is giving away something that belongs exclusively to the other partner. The fear that another person will usurp one's position of preeminence in the life of one's spouse may also be involved. Particularly for men, part of sexual jealousy may stem from a sense of ownership. However, the discovery of infidelity does not necessarily erode the quality of a marriage. In some cases it motivates a couple to search for sources of discord in their relationship, a process that may ultimately lead to an improved marriage.

Only minimal research efforts have been directed toward assessing the impact of extramarital sex on the individual participant. Perhaps the most noteworthy study to date is the work of Lynn Atwater (1982), who interviewed a sample of 50 women in depth about their extramarital experiences. These women, who lived primarily in urban and suburban areas in 17 states, represented a wide range of personal and socioeconomic characteristics. A majority of the respondents indicated that curiosity and a desire for personal growth, rather than marital unhappiness, motivated their decisions to become involved in extramarital relationships. Furthermore, most reported positive consequences for their sexual and self-identity, rather than the traditionally expected negative consequences. Ninety-three percent of Atwater's sample reported increased feelings of self-esteem, self-confidence, autonomy, power, and resourcefulness.

Consensual Extramarital Relationships

Consensual extramarital relationships occur in marriages where both partners are informed about and supportive of sexual involvements outside their primary marriage bond. These mutually agreed-upon experiences may be primarily emotional, primarily sexual, or they may involve the couple's whole lifestyle. There are indications of increasing societal tolerance of this type of extramarital sexual activity. A number of organizations have emerged that facilitate the movement of people into such experiences or lifestyles. This is a significant departure from the traditional covertness of extramarital sexual experiences, and in effect it gives some societal legitimacy to nonmonogamy. A variety of arrangements fall under the category of consensual extramarital involvements. We will examine three: open marriage, swinging, and group marriage.

Open Marriage. The concept of **open marriage** received widespread public attention with the 1972 publication of George and Nena O'Neill's book *Open Marriage*. For many people who are not aware of the broad scope of this concept, open marriage has become synonymous with consensual sexual involvements. However, this is an incomplete view of the open marriage idea. The essence of the O'Neills' thesis is that one relationship is unlikely to fulfill a person's total intimacy needs throughout the adult years. The concept of open marriage is people allowing each other the freedom to have intimate emotional relationships with members of either sex without compromising their primary relationship. These intimacies do not necessarily include sexual sharing. This is a matter for an individual couple to determine.

Those who support open marriage believe that it is confining to limit emotional or sexual sharing to only one person. Some have even argued that it is "essentially absurd to expect that all physical sexual expression for a fifty-year period will be confined to the marriage partner" (Roy and Roy, 1973, p. 144). Other advocates of open marriage are committed to sexual exclusivity, but they find it stressful to avoid nonsexual intimacies with individuals other than their spouse. As the following anecdotes reveal, a marriage relationship that is too "closed" can have a confining and potentially negative effect:

> When I married my husband it was with the intention of being totally faithful to him. I couldn't imagine myself wanting sex with another man. However, I was unprepared for the jealous way he reacts to anybody I show an interest in. If I talk too long to another man at a party, he comes unglued. He doesn't even like me to spend time with my girlfriends, and I lie to him on those rare occasions I go out to lunch or shopping with a friend. I long for the companionship of others. I still love my husband, but sometimes I just need to be close to someone else. Sometimes I think his extreme possessiveness will be the end of us. (Authors' files)

> In my job I form close working relationships with both men and women. A couple of the women have become very dear friends. I wish I could feel comfortable taking them out to lunch on occasion or having them call me at home like good friends do. But my wife raises hell even when their names come up in conversation. I guess she thinks being friends and crawling into bed go hand-in-hand. (Authors' files)

Open Marriage maintains that people who are allowed the freedom to form close, meaningful relationships with others are often able to bring more contentment and satisfaction to the primary relationship with their spouse. As an alternative to the resentment and frustration evident in the preceding accounts, open marriages attempt to foster mutual trust, support, and appreciation. *Eternity*, a poem by William Blake, perhaps captures the essence of loving with open arms:

> *He who binds to himself a joy,*
> *Does that winged life destroy,*
> *But he who kisses the joy as it flies*
> *Lives in eternity's sunrise.*

We have very limited information on the incidence of sexually open relationships in American society. Blumstein and Schwartz (1983) found that in 15% of 3,574 heterosexual married couples, both partners indicated having "an understanding that allows nonmonogamy under some circumstances." Nearly twice as many cohabitors (28%) had a similar understanding, while 29% of lesbian couples and 65% of male homosexual couples reported sexually open relationships.

A few studies have attempted to assess the impact of nonmonogamy agreements on the primary relationship. In one investigation, individuals who were involved in sexually open marriages reported several benefits from this arrangement, including greater personal fulfillment, the excitement of new experiences, and improved sex with the marital partner. Problems were also reported, such as jealousy, time-sharing difficulties, and resentments growing out of differing expectations (Knapp and Whitehurst, 1977). Another researcher conducted a three-year evaluation of the progress of 19 couples involved in sexually open marriages. At the end of this investigative period all the marriages were still intact, but only one couple was still actively involved in extrarelationship sexual sharing. None of these individuals regretted their experiences and the majority were still committed to the importance of sharing sexual intimacy with others. The concept of open marriage was still favored by all, and most felt that at some time in the future they would again avail themselves of opportunities for consensual extramarital sexual sharing (Watson, 1981).

A few researchers have attempted to determine if the outcomes of sexually open marriages and sexually exclusive marriages are different. Arline Rubin (1982) found no appreciable differences in the levels of marital adjustment of 130 couples with sexually open marriages and 130 couples who were sexually exclusive. A follow-up study of 34 sexually open couples and 39 sexually exclusive couples, from Rubin's original sample population, revealed no generalized differences between the open and the exclusive couples in the area of marital adjustment. Eighty percent of the sexually open couples and 86% of the sexually exclusive couples rated their marriages as happy. However, there was a noteworthy, although not statistically significant, difference between the two groups in the category of marital stability. At the end of a five-year follow-up, 32 (82%) of the 39 sexually exclusive couples were still together in contrast to 23 (68%) of the 34 sexually open couples (Adams and Rubin, 1984).

Swinging.   **Swinging** refers to a form of consensual extramarital sex that a married couple shares. Husband and wife participate simultaneously and in the same location, and this distinguishes swinging from the extramarital sexual contact that might occur in an open marriage, where mutual participation is not usual. This activity has been labeled "wife-swapping" in the past, but this term came into disrepute among swingers because of its implications of male property rights. Most participants also object to labeling this activity as "extramarital" sex. Since they do it together, they do not consider it extraneous to, but rather part of, their marriage. Furthermore, many believe it to be far more acceptable morally than a secretive affair. In the words of one male swinger, "The hypocrisy that you find in the country club set—where everybody knows that everyone is balling everyone else, but it's clandestine—simply doesn't exist here" (Lewis, 1971, p. 33).

Only a few large-scale sex surveys have included questions about swinging. Data gleaned from these surveys suggest that between 2% and 5% of American men and women have experienced swinging (Athanasiou et al., 1970; Hunt, 1974; Tavris and Sadd, 1977). Much of the data about the motivations and traits of swingers comes from four major studies. These are the research by Bartell (1970), by Smith and Smith (1970), by Palson and Palson (1972), and by Gilmartin (1977). A review of these investigations and several lesser studies in the literature on swinging provides a composite picture of typical swingers, who tend to be predominantly middle-class and upper middle-class whites with above average educations and incomes and minimal religious and political affiliations (Jenks, 1985). The reasons respondents most commonly gave for becoming involved in swinging were boredom with their partner and a desire to introduce excitement into their sex life.

There are a number of ways a couple may "swing." They may get together for weekends with a few like-minded couples, or they may visit local nightclubs known to cater to such activities. Swinging may also involve more formal prearrangements, including highly organized club activities. Most participants carefully avoid emotional involvements with their sexual partners. For them, swinging is "designed to make extramarital sex safe for marriage by defusing emotional involvement and exclusivity" (Gagnon, 1977, p. 230).

The general prohibition against emotional involvement ultimately leads to boredom for some individuals:

> At first swinging was a real high. The sex was much better than I expected. Some of the men I encountered were really expert lovers, at least from a technique point of view. But as the initial excitement wore off, the whole scene became jaded. Finally I realized that instead of standing around making meaningless small talk, as is typical of cocktail parties, we were lying around and engaging in meaningless screwing. I got out, and I can't say that I miss it. (Authors' files)

Swinging seems to affect individuals and couples in a variety of ways, however. Some suggest that it improves the sexual aspects of the marriage, increases togetherness, and broadens social horizons. Gilmartin (1977) reported that the swingers in his research population, compared with a matched control group of nonswingers, had sex more often with their spouse, were slightly more happily married, and generally seemed to be less bored. However, swinging is not without potential hazards. Some of its participants report extreme sexual performance pressures (this is particularly true of men), guilt, jealousy, and feeling threatened. It appears that swinging does not maintain its appeal for very long; most couples terminate their participation after a brief period of experimentation (Murstein, 1978).

Group Marriage. **Group marriage** refers to a living and sharing arrangement where several people live together with commitment to each other. Each member of the group maintains what the group considers marriage relationships with more than one other person. Usually three or four people enter into such a group relationship, but sometimes there is a larger membership. Some of the people may be legally married to each other. (This activity may not be accurately classified as extramarital sex if none of the participants is legally married.)

There is very little available information about this rare social phenomenon. The most frequently quoted source is one in-depth study of slightly more than 100 group marriages (Constantine and Constantine, 1973). These writers outline a number of factors that lead individuals to enter such expanded family groups. For some, the primary advantage lies in having more people to relate to intellectually, socially, emotionally, and sexually. Many participants in group marriages want the unique opportunities for personal growth offered by close, intimate contact with a group of like-minded companions. Others believe that children profit from having more siblings and parent models with whom to interact. (Most of the children included in group marriages were born into nuclear families before their parents entered a group marriage.) Other benefits to group marriage may come from pooling economic resources.

Not uncommonly, couples who enter into group marriages have had a prior pattern of consensual extramarital sex. Each partner may have experienced periodic outside involvements with the consent of his or her spouse, or perhaps the couple shared these experiences by participating in swinging. However, the couple may have been dissatisfied with the emotional and relational limitations of such arrangements.

The realities of group marriage are not always consistent with the expectations of participating members (Constantine and Constantine, 1973; Constantine, 1978;

Other Times, Other Places

Adult Sexuality in Other Cultures

Marital coitus is the most common form of adult sexual activity in virtually all societies for which we have information. However, there is widespread variation in both the types of coital positions used and the frequency of sexual contact. While data are limited, there is evidence that each society tends to favor a particular coital position. Whether it is man-above, woman-above, or some other variation is greatly influenced by the relative social status of the sexes in the society. In places like the Trobriand Islands off the coast of New Guinea, where women are valued, the female-above position is quite common. In societies where women are assigned low social status (for example, Inis Beag, off the coast of Ireland), the male-above position seems to be preferred. It is interesting to note that improved social status of American women has been paralleled by an increase in the use of coital positions other than the man-above (Hunt, 1974).

It has been estimated that most married couples around the world engage in coitus between two and five times per week (Gebhard, 1971). However, in some societies the frequency may range as high as ten times a night or as low as once or twice a month. Married couples on the Polynesian island of Mangaia, while somewhat less active than during their premarital days, maintain a coital frequency far greater than that of most Western couples. With marriage, coital emphasis tends to shift from the number of times a man can bring his partner to orgasm during a single session to whether he can copulate with her every night in the week (Marshall, 1971). Somewhat higher frequencies are reported among the Australian Aranda, who report as many as three to five coital contacts per night. Even higher rates (up to ten times per night) are reported by the Chagga farmers of Tanzania. The Lepcha of the southeastern Himalayas report having intercourse five to nine times a night during the early years of marriage. At the other extreme, there are societies that report an exceedingly low rate of marital coitus. Couples in the Dani culture of New Guinea seem rarely to have sexual interactions. Newlyweds wait for an average of two years for their first coital experiences, and both men and women abstain from intercourse for a period of four to six years after the birth of a child. Married couples in another New Guinean society, the Kerakis, report relatively low coital frequencies of once a week.

Most societies have more restrictive norms pertaining to extramarital than to premarital sex. Nevertheless, many societies impose fewer restrictions on extramarital activity than does our own. Some societies even have formal rules allowing such behavior under special circumstances—during celebrations, as part of the marriage ceremony, or as a form of sexual hospitality. With very few exceptions, men around the world are allowed greater access to extramarital coitus than are women. However, it appears that as many as 60% of non-Western societies studied allow some form of extramarital coitus for wives (Gebhard, 1971).

Salsberg, 1973). Conflicts may emerge in a number of areas: differing life styles, privacy, division of labor, childrearing practices, financial arrangements, and other issues. The difficulties encountered when living with one other person are compounded in group marriages. Not infrequently, jealousy becomes a disruptive influence. Not all members may be in equal demand for emotional or sexual sharing. Some groups seek to avoid this potential difficulty by setting up sleeping together on a rotational basis. However, the resulting lack of spontaneity may also be a problem.

A few examples will illustrate the diversity of this activity in other societies.

The aborigines of western Australia's Arnhem Land openly accept extramarital sexual relationships for both wives and husbands. They welcome the variety in experience and the break in monotony offered by extramarital involvements. Many also report increased appreciation of and attachment to the spouse as a result of such experiences (Berndt and Berndt, 1951). The Polynesian Marquesans, while not open advocates of extramarital affairs, nevertheless exhibit covert acceptance of such activity. A Marquesan wife often takes young boys or her husband's friends or relatives as lovers. Conversely, her husband may have relations with young unmarried girls or with his sisters-in-law. Marquesan culture openly endorses the practices of partner swapping and *sexual hospitality,* where unaccompanied visitors are offered sexual access to the host of the other sex. Sexual hospitality is also practiced by some Eskimo groups, where a married female host has intercourse with a male visitor. The Turu of central Tanzania regard marriage primarily as a cooperative, economic, and social bond. Affection between husband and wife is generally thought to be out of place; most people believe that the marital relationship is endangered by the instability of love and affection. The Turu have evolved a system of romantic love, called *Mbuya,* that allows them to seek affection outside the home without threatening the stability of the primary marriage relationship. Both husband and wife actively pursue these outside relationships.

Culture also seems to exert an impact on the orgasmic response of sexually active adult women. With no recorded exceptions, males from virtually every society typically experience orgasm as part of sexual expression. In contrast, the frequency of female orgasm is quite variable, and some writers have suggested that orgasmic response among women is largely culturally determined. According to Margaret Mead, "there seems . . . to be a reasonable basis for assuming that the human female's capacity for orgasm is to be viewed much more as a potentiality that may or may not be developed by a given culture" (1949, p. 217).

There has been a general tendency in Western societies to consider female sexual gratification unimportant. While this is changing, particularly in the United States, there are still significant numbers of Western women who seldom experience orgasm, particularly in repressive cultures. In Inis Beag, where women are ascribed the status of second-class citizens, female orgasm is virtually unknown. In marked contrast, most island societies of the South Pacific value female sexual pleasure, and here female orgasm during sexual activity is routine. An example is provided by Mangaian culture, where "the Mangaian male lover aims to have his partner achieve orgasm two or three times to his once" (Marshall, 1971, p. 122).

Most participants in group marriages see their involvement as a positive experience. However, many of these evaluations are obtained in retrospect. Most group marriages have a short life span, generally lasting a few months to a few years (Macklin, 1980; See, 1975).

Divorce

We have seen that people today may interpret marriage in a variety of ways, according to particular needs. Despite this increased flexibility, however, a significant number of marriages are ending in divorce. Rising divorce rates are a common topic in the popular media, and they are often presented as a sign of societal rejection of the institution of marriage. This interpretation is not necessarily accurate. Available divorce statistics are not an entirely reliable indicator of the current state of American marriage.

Interpreting Divorce Statistics

There are several factors that have some bearing on how we interpret divorce statistics. The rise in divorce rates may reflect the increased ease of obtaining a legal marital dissolution more than a rise in dissatisfaction with marriage. Obtaining a legal divorce has become a simpler, less expensive process in recent years. Furthermore, a significant percentage of divorces involve people who have had more than one marriage and divorce. Therefore, a higher percentage of first marriages remain intact than a quick glance at the statistics indicates.

Research does confirm that the proportion of marriages ending in divorce has increased dramatically since the 1950s, as shown in Table 14.1. The ratio of divorce

Table 14.1   Number and Ratio of Divorces to Marriages, 1950, 1977, and 1984

	1950	Ratio	1977	Ratio	1984	Ratio
Number of divorces	385,000	1	1,097,000	1	1,160,000	1
Number of marriages	1,667,000	4	2,176,000	2	2,440,000	2

Sources: U.S. Bureau of the Census, 1978, and National Center for Health Statistics, 1982 and 1985.

Table 14.2   Number of Marriages and Divorces Per 1000 Resident Population, 1970–1984

	1970	1971	1972	1973	1974	1975	1976	1977	1978	1979	1980	1981	1982	1983	1984
Marriages	10.6	10.6	10.9	10.8	10.5	10.0	9.9	9.9	10.3	10.4	10.6	10.6	10.6	10.5	10.5
Divorces	3.5	3.7	4.0	4.3	4.6	4.8	5.0	5.0	5.1	5.3	5.2	5.3	5.0	5.0	4.9

Source: U.S. Bureau of the Census, 1985.

© Engleman/Rothco.

ROTHCO
ORIGINAL

ENGLEMAN

"Playing house is old-fashioned . . .
let's play divorce!"

to marriage was 1:4 in 1950; by 1977 the ratio was one divorce to every two marriages. More recent statistics reveal that there were approximately 1.2 million divorces and 2.4 million marriages in 1984, still a ratio of 1:2. In the last few years the divorce rate has begun to level off and even decline somewhat. As you can see in Table 14.2, there were 3.5 divorces per 1000 resident population in 1970, and this figure increased steadily until 1981, at which time it was 5.3 per 1000 (an increase of 51%). However, in the next three years the rate dropped 7.5%.

Suggested Causes for High Divorce Rates

Several large scale investigations have reported the demographic characteristics of divorced people, such as age, length of marriage, number of children, education level, profession, income, and so on. These demographic studies do provide worthwhile data that can be used to predict probabilities of divorce for groups of individuals sharing particular characteristics. However, they generally rely on data provided by county, state, and federal bureaus, which almost never include reasons for divorce except for occasional reporting of legal grounds. In the absence of hard data, a number of writers have speculated on the factors responsible for the high divorce rates in America. Some of the causes frequently mentioned include the comparative ease of obtaining divorces since the liberalization of divorce laws during the 1970s; a reduction in the social stigma attached to divorce; increasing expectations for marital and sexual fulfillment, which have caused people to become more disillusioned with and less willing to persist in unsatisfying marriages; the increased economic independence of women; a greater abundance of wealth, which makes it easier for some people to maintain multiple families; and an attitude of "me first," which places personal fulfillment ahead of the compromises and hard work that relationships often require.

A recent study conducted by Margaret Cleek and Allan Pearson (1985) provided some much-needed empirical evidence of what divorced people perceive to be the cause of their break-up. These researchers administered a survey containing 18 "cause-of-divorce" items to a sample of over 600 divorced men and women. The men indicated an average of 3.2 causes, and the women 4.2. Communication difficulties was the most frequently checked item for both sexes, followed by basic unhappiness and incompatibility.

There were some sex differences in the constellation of factors indicated by the men and women in this research population. Males indicated their own alcohol abuse and "women's lib" (the feminist movement) more often than females. In contrast, women indicated basic unhappiness, incompatibility, emotional and physical abuse, and spouse's infidelity as causes of their divorce more often than did men.

Adjusting to Divorce

Although the chain of events leading to marriage is unique for each individual, most people marry with the hope that the relationship will last. Divorce often represents loss of this hope and other losses as well: one's spouse, lifestyle, the security of familiarity, sometimes one's children, and often part of one's identity. Many people who terminate nonmarital intimate relationships also share this experience.

The loss a person feels in divorce is often comparable to the sense of loss when a loved one dies. In both cases, the person undergoes a grieving process. There are important differences, however. When the grief is caused by death, there are rituals and social support available which may be helpful to the survivor. In contrast, there are no recognized grief rituals to help the divorced person. Initially, a person may experience shock: "This cannot be happening to me." Disorganization may follow, a sense that one's entire world has turned upside down. Volatile emotions may unexpectedly surface. Feelings of guilt may become strong. Loneliness is common. Finally (usually not for several months or a year), a sense of relief and acceptance may come (Krantzler, 1974). If after several months of separation a person is not developing a sense of acceptance, she or he may need professional help. Although many of the feelings triggered by divorce are uncomfortable, even painful, they can be steps toward resolving the loss so that a person can reestablish intimate relationships. Grieving can lead to healing.

Separation and divorce represent a major life transition. Even in a mutually agreed-upon, friendly termination of a legal marriage, many significant lifestyle changes usually occur. The newly single person often faces adjustments in social and sexual relationships, financial and living arrangements, and if applicable, parenting roles. Extensive changes such as these, even if accompanied by the relief of ending an undesirable situation, typically cause stress. Of course, many divorces are not peaceful agreements but conflicts full of bitter contention. A person's self-confidence may also be negatively affected if the divorced individual believes he or she has "failed" in the marriage.

Other difficulties may arise with the change of status from being married to being single. Many married people have established friendships and social relationships as couples rather than as individuals, and the divorced person may feel awkward being alone with others who are in pairs. At the same time, other couples may not be comfortable including a single person in their activities. The sense of security or belonging that often accompanies being in an established pair is replaced by sudden autonomy. People who become divorced often need to find new groups of other single people to establish social contacts. Many cities have organizations where single people can meet and form new friendships.

There is a potential for personal growth in the adjustment process that accompanies divorce. Many people experience a sense of autonomy for the first time in their lives. Others find that being single presents opportunities to experience more fully dimensions of themselves that had been submerged in their identity within a couple. Learning to reach out to others for emotional support can help diminish feelings of aloneness. Divorce can offer an opportunity to reassess oneself and one's past, a process that may lead to the evolution of a new life. One person describes the experience as very positive:

> Today I look back on the last three years as the most personally enriching period in my life. Through a painful emotional crisis, I have become a happier and stronger person than I was before. I learned that what I went through was what all divorced people, men and women, go through to a greater or lesser degree—first a recognition that a relationship has died, then a period of mourning, and finally a slow, painful emotional readjustment to the facts of single life. I experienced the pitfalls along the way—the wallowing in self-pity, the refusal to let go of the old relationship, the repetition of old ways of relating to new people, the confusion of past emotions with present reality— and I emerged the better for it. (Krantzler, 1975, p. 30)

Making the transition from marital to postmarital sexual relationships often presents a challenge to divorced individuals. The newly divorced person may experience considerable ambivalence about intimacy. Feelings of anger, rejection, or fear remaining from the trauma of the divorce may inhibit openness to intimate relationships. To protect themselves from emotional vulnerability, some people may withdraw from potential sexual relationships. Others may react by seeking many superficial sexual encounters.

Despite the problems newly single people often encounter in establishing nonmarital sexual expression, Morton Hunt's research revealed considerable sexual satisfaction and activity among the divorced people in his volunteer subject group (1974). Specific data on the sexual activity of divorced men indicated a slightly higher frequency of coitus than for married men of the same age, while the rate for divorced women was approximately the same as for married women of the same age. In this same study, divorced respondents reported greater participation in noncoital sexual activities and more variety in intercourse positions than did married respondents. There is also evidence that divorced women may be more orgasmic in their postmarital relationships than in their previous marriages (Gebhard, 1970). In one national survey it was reported that a majority of divorced individuals become sexually active within the first year following break-up of their marriages (Hunt and Hunt, 1977).

The majority of both men and women remarry after a divorce (Cherlin, 1981). Many remarried people report that their second marriage is better than the first, but hard evidence indicates that second marriages are more likely to end in divorce than first marriages (Blumstein and Schwartz, 1983; Brooks, 1985; Cox, 1983; Spanier and Furstenberg, 1982). Remarried people may be inclined to rate second marriages

higher because they strive harder to achieve good communication, have fewer romantic illusions, and are more committed to effectively resolving conflicts. However, such people are also inclined to monitor second marriages more closely than initial marriages, and are less willing to stick around when things turn sour (Cox, 1983; Spanier and Furstenberg, 1982). Some researchers also believe that second marriages are more prone to fail because the trauma of divorce has been lessened somewhat by having gone through it once already (Blumstein and Schwartz, 1983).

Widowhood

Although a spouse can die during early or middle adult years, widowhood usually occurs later in life. In most cases it is the man who dies first, a tendency that has become more pronounced during this century. The ratio of widows to widowers has increased from less than 2 : 1 in the early 1900s to almost 6 : 1 by the 1980s (Statistical Abstract of the U.S., 1985).

The postmarital adjustment of widowhood is different in some ways from that of divorce. Widowed people typically do not have the sense of having failed at marriage. However, the anger and resentment that often help to ease the emotional separation after a divorce is frequently lacking when a partner dies. The grief may be more intense, and the quality of the emotional bond to the deceased mate is often quite high. For some people this emotional tie remains so strong that other potential relationships appear dim by comparison.

Many widowers and widows experience the same lifestyle adjustments and grieving processes described in our discussion of divorce, often to a greater degree. Further information on widowhood is included in the next chapter's discussion of aging and sexuality.

Summary

Single Living

1. Although single living is often seen as a transition period before, in between, or after marriage, some people choose it as a permanent lifestyle.

2. The proportion of individuals who have never married has approximately doubled since 1970 for men and women in their late twenties and early thirties.

Cohabitation

3. The number of couples who cohabit (live together without marriage) almost tripled in the period from 1970 to 1984.

4. Research indicates that most college students who cohabit do not have plans to marry when they first enter into this arrangement.

5. The possible effect of cohabitation on subsequent marriage stability is unknown at present.

Marriage

6. The primary elements in the marriage ideal of our society are a permanent and exclusive legal relationship between two heterosexual adults.

7. The reasons people give for entering marriage vary widely and may include one or more of the following: a desire to achieve a sense of permanence and belonging; a response to social pressures to conform and be traditional; a need to obtain legally and socially sanctioned sexual interaction; a desire for a closer and deeper relationship; and wanting the monetary and legal advantages granted to married people.

8. Recent changes in sexual behaviors can be observed within the marital relationship. Married couples are engaging in a wider variety of sexual behaviors and experiencing coitus more often and with greater duration than in the past.

Relationship Contracts

9. Individualized contracts attempt to outline mutually agreed-upon rules, plans, or philosophies related to the relationship.

Extramarital Relationships

10. Nonconsensual extramarital relationships occur without the partner's consent.

11. Kinsey found that approximately 50% of married males and 25% of married females had experienced sexual intercourse outside of marriage by age 40.

12. The results of several contemporary surveys suggest that a substantial majority of married American men and women will experience one or more extramarital involvements during their lifetime.

13. The most notable increase in extramarital sexual intercourse in current studies is among young women.

14. Consensual extramarital relationships occur with the spouse's knowledge and agreement. Examples of these involvements include open marriage, swinging, and group marriage.

15. The open marriage concept can include emotional, social, and sexual components in the extramarital relationship.

16. Swinging is structured to facilitate sexual expression and inhibit emotional involvement between the participants.

17. Group marriage is seen by participants as a commitment to live as if the several people involved were married to each other.

Divorce

18. The ratio of divorces to marriages has increased from 1:4 (1950) to 1:2 (1984).

19. In the last few years the divorce rate has begun to level off and even decline somewhat.

20. Some of the causes of high divorce rates may include the liberalization of divorce laws, reduction in the social stigma attached to divorce, unrealistic expectations for marital and sexual fulfillment, increased economic independence of women, and a "me first" attitude.

21. One important study found that the most common reasons given by men and women for their divorces was communication difficulty, followed by basic unhappiness and incompatibility.

22. Divorce typically involves many emotional, sexual, interpersonal, and lifestyle changes and adjustments.

Widowhood

23. The ratio of widows to widowers is now close to 6:1.

Thought Provokers

1. Which of the following lifestyles do you consider to be viable options for your adult years: single living, cohabitation, "traditional" monogamous marriage, open marriage limited to emotional intimacy with others, open marriage that allows both emotional and sexual intimacy with someone other than your spouse, swinging, and group marriage? What are some of the benefits and potential problems associated with each lifestyle?

2. You and an intimate companion have decided to live together. What aspects of your cohabitation relationship would you want to discuss and reach agreement on first? What problems would you expect to face as a result of your changed relationship? Do you think that cohabitation might affect any future marriage you enter into?

3. Among the aborigines of western Australia's Arnhem Land, extramarital relationships contribute to increased appreciation of and attachment to one's spouse. Do you think that if such involvements received more support within American society, married couples in this country would experience similar benefits?

4. Consider your married friends and relatives. Of those that have happy marriages, what seem to be the major factors that contribute to their satisfaction? What about those that are experiencing poor adjustment within their marriages? What appear to be the primary causes for their lack of happiness?

Suggested Readings

Atwater, Lynn. *The Extramarital Connection: Sex, Intimacy, and Identity*. New York: Irvington, 1982. This book provides enlightening insights into the motivations underlying women's decisions to become involved in extramarital relationships and the effect of such involvements on their marriages and their self-concepts.

Blumstein, Philip, and Schwartz, Pepper. *American Couples*. New York: Morrow, 1983. This highly acclaimed book provides a wealth of information about current trends in relationships among couples—married and cohabitating, heterosexual and homosexual.

Colgrove, Melba; Bloomfield, Harold; and McWilliams, Peter. *How To Survive the Loss of A Love*. New York: Bantam, 1977. A sensitive, warm, and practical book that can assist people in the process of emotional healing after experiencing loss.

Krantzler, Mel. *Creative Divorce*. New York: Signet, 1975. This book views divorce as an opportunity for personal growth and learning. It also gives readers support during the difficulties usually accompanying divorce.

Masters, William, and Johnson, Virginia. *The Pleasure Bond*. New York: Bantam, 1976. An exploration of the meaning of sexual exclusivity in a marital relationship and of the ways in which it serves to solidify the couple's bond.

Sarrel, Lorna, and Sarrel, Philip. *Sexual Turning Points: The Seven Stages of Adult Sexuality*. New York: Macmillan, 1984. An enlightening, sensitive book by respected sex therapists that provides thought-provoking discussions of many important aspects of adult sexuality, including initial pairing with an intimate companion, the experience of being a parent, divorce, and sex in the middle years and beyond.

Shahan, Lynn. *Living Alone and Liking It*. New York: Stratford Press, 1981. This book examines some of the potential advantages of living alone and provides excellent advice on how to combat loneliness.

Singer, Laura. *Stages: The Crises That Shape Your Marriage*. New York: Grosset & Dunlap, 1980. This book discusses the evolving pattern of predictable crisis points in marriage and provides positive suggestions to help resolve problems.

Old age has its pleasures, which, though different, are not less than the pleasures of youth.
W. Somerset Maugham
The Summing Up (1938)

15

Sexuality and Aging

Sexuality in the Later Years: Examining the Myths
Physiosexual Changes and Sexual Response: The Older Female
Physiosexual Changes and Sexual Response: The Older Male
Sexual Development in the Later Years
Maximizing Sexual Functioning in the Later Years

DURING THE YOUNG ADULT YEARS, the prospect of altered sexual expression with aging may seem remote and unimportant. However, in the later years of life most people begin to note that certain changes are taking place in their sexual response patterns. Some women and men who understand the nature of these variations may accept them with equanimity. Others will observe them with alarm and perhaps even respond with deep concern. People of both sexes may begin to worry about the possibilities of being rejected or of developing problems with sexual functioning.

An important source of the confusion, frustration, and perhaps outrage many aging people feel is the prevailing notion that old age is a sexless time. However, as one author states:

> The needs for an intimate relationship, for touch, caress, companionship, caring, love, dignity, identity, self-esteem, intellectual growth, and overall human interaction begin very early in human development and continue until death in old age. These needs and their realization may be even more critical in the later years, as other roles and relationships slip away. (Weg, 1983, p. 46)

In this chapter we will examine some facts about aging and sexuality.

Other Times, Other Places

Sexuality and Aging in Other Cultures

We have only limited cross-cultural data about sexual expression among older men and women. However, there is some evidence to suggest that frequency of activity is related to the status assigned older members of the community. It seems that cultures that value older people tend to be characterized by more frequent sexual expression among aging individuals.

For example, the mountain people of Abkhasia, in the Caucasus region of the Soviet Union, enjoy tremendous longevity as well as prolonged sexual activity. Sex among married couples is considered a primary pleasure in life, to be pursued for as long as possible. Most Abkhasian couples remain quite active sexually beyond the age of 70, and some even after the age of 100. Aging individuals are ascribed valued social status. They are expected to continue making productive contributions to the family and community—there is no retirement in this society. Moderation is the key cultural ethic: Older folks "continue to do what they have always done, but in gradually diminishing amounts" (Beach, 1978, p. 118).

The African Bala also seem to maintain a high degree of sexual vigor in the older years. Ethnographer Alan Merriam (1971) reported asking a small sample of men how many times they had experienced intercourse in the preceding 24 hours. The data, collected each morning for a period of 10 days, revealed that the average frequency for several men over the age of 45 (the oldest was 66) was about 1.5 times each 24-hour period. Some caution in interpreting this finding seems necessary. It is possible that being asked daily to report the frequency of coital encounters may have induced Merriam's respondents to temporarily increase or to misreport their activity levels.

Sexuality in the Later Years: Examining the Myths

Some people begin to deny their sexuality as they grow older. This change in sexual identity often starts at about age 50, or sometime thereafter, and it may occur as part of an overall shift that takes place to a greater or lesser degree when a person realizes he or she is growing old.

Why is aging in our society often associated with sexlessness? There are a number of reasons. Part of the answer is that American culture is still influenced by the philosophy that equates sexuality exclusively with procreation. For older people, whose prospects for having babies are either nonexistent or unrealistic, this viewpoint offers little beyond self-denial.

Society also suppresses sexuality in its older members by disproportionately focusing on youth. The media usually link love, sex, and romance together with the implicit assumption that all three belong exclusively to the young. There is also a pervasive, often unspoken, assumption in American society that it is not quite acceptable for older people to have sexual needs. In all probability, attitudes like these at least partly account for the infrequency with which older couples publicly display expressions of affection such as hugging, kissing, or holding hands.

With such widespread denial of the validity of sexual expression in the "golden years," it is not surprising that many individuals are confused about aging and sexuality. Unfortunately, some older people may accept the cultural mandate for a sexless old age and as a result may actively suppress their natural urges. Others may not deny their continued sexuality as they grow older, but they may feel conflict or be concerned that they are either morally decadent or physically abnormal (Rubin, 1965).

In examining the myth of sexless old age, two notable societal phenomena merit some special attention. These are, first, the double standard as it relates to the aging process and, second, the way nursing homes deal with the sexual needs of their residents.

The Double Standard of Aging

We have discussed the double standard as it relates to male and female sexual expression during adolescence and adulthood. The assumptions and prejudices implicit in the double standard continue into old age, imposing a particular burden on women.

Although a woman's erotic and orgasmic capabilities continue after menopause, it is not uncommon for her to be considered past her "sexual prime" relatively early in the aging process. Women are often considered to be less sexually attractive as they grow older. The cultural image of an erotically appealing woman is commonly one of youth, as exemplified by the statement of a 30-year-old man who told one of the authors with delight about the woman he had started seeing. "She's 22," he said, "but she has the body of a 16-year-old." As a woman grows further away from this nubile image, she is usually considered less and less attractive. In our society even young girls are sometimes told not to frown ("You'll get wrinkles"); cosmetics, specially designed clothing, and even surgery are often used to maintain a youthful appearance for as long as possible.

In contrast, the physical and sexual attractiveness of men is often considered to be enhanced by the aging process. Gray hair and facial wrinkles may be thought to look "distinguished" on men—signs of accumulated life experience and wisdom.

Likewise, while the professional achievements of women may be perceived as threatening to a potential male partner, it is relatively common for a man's sexual attractiveness to be closely associated with his achievements and social status, both of which may increase with age.

The pairings of powerful, older men and young, beautiful women reflect this double standard of aging. The marriage of a 60-year-old man and a 20-year-old woman would probably generate a much smaller reaction than if the sexes were reversed—a situation that was portrayed in the 1972 film *Harold and Maude*. In reality, pairing of older women and younger men occurs much less commonly than the reverse.

One research study (Stimson et al., 1981) suggests that the aspects of sexuality that contribute to a general feeling of well-being among the aged are different for men and women. For the older man, pride in his sexual performance and attractiveness to the other sex appeared to be crucial to his general feeling of well-being. In contrast, sexual performance did not seem related to general feelings of well-being for the older woman. However, feeling sexually attractive to the other sex was important; when the older woman no longer felt attractive, her general feelings of well-being decreased.

The need for affection and sexual intimacy extends to the older years, which can be a time of sharing and closeness.

Given that attractiveness in women is often equated with youthfulness, aging may affect a woman's sense of well-being more than a man's.

It is our opinion that exaggerated attempts at remaining perpetually youthful are both a losing battle and a denial of a woman's full humanity. Susan Sontag presents an alternative:

> Women have another option. They can aspire to be wise, not merely nice; to be competent, not merely helpful; to be strong; not merely graceful; to be ambitious for themselves; not merely themselves in relation to men and children. They can let themselves age naturally and without embarrassment, actively protesting and disobeying the conventions that stem from this society's double standard about aging. Instead of being girls, girls as long as possible, who then age humiliatingly into middle-aged women and then obscenely into old women, they can become women much earlier—and remain active adults, enjoying the long, erotic career of which women are capable, for longer. Women should allow their faces to show the lives they have lived. (Sontag, 1972, p. 38)

Sexuality and Aging in Nursing Homes

The double standard, especially as it relates to aging, has been so ingrained in our social traditions that until recently it has rarely been questioned. In the past decade, however, the treatment that older people receive in some nursing homes has come under increasing public scrutiny. Nursing homes have been criticized for their insensitivity to the human rights of aged individuals. Our concern here is specifically with antisexual prejudice and practices, which are clearly demonstrated in many nursing home facilities. For example, researchers often find that administrators and personnel in senior facilities resist programs having to do with sexuality (Starr and Weiner, 1981). Sometimes staff in nursing homes separate married couples who engage in sexual activities (Falk and Falk, 1980). Of the 5% of the population over 65 who live in nursing homes at a given time, many are denied the adult rights of sexual opportunity and privacy. One writer describes the situation:

> Their environment is almost totally desexualized. It is considered progress when dining room or recreation halls and residential wings are not sex-segregated. Privacy is virtually nonexistent . . . [O]nly a minority of institutions make an effort to provide areas where a couple can be alone to talk, much less to court. Even married couples may be separated; some state institutions segregate them or permit the sexes to mix only under "supervision." If only one spouse is in a home, the other seldom has the right to privacy during a visit. (Lobsenz, 1974, p.30)

These problems can be especially acute for older homosexual partners. Antihomosexual prejudice may make it extremely difficult for a gay person to express affection and to be involved with his or her lover or friend in hospital or nursing room settings (Kassel, 1983). Even nursing homes that allow conjugal visits for their heterosexual residents are unlikely to do this for a homosexual couple (Kimmel, 1978).

Because older people are often assumed not to be sexual, medications are sometimes prescribed without consideration of their effects on sexuality. Some tranquilizers, antidepressants, and high blood pressure and arthritis medications can have an inhibiting effect on sexual interest and arousal. In cases where drug therapy is indicated, these factors should be discussed with each person and adjustments made. It is also desirable for older people to be thoroughly educated about the potential effects on sexuality of suggested surgeries, particularly those that involve the reproductive organs (Page, 1977).

Some relatives of nursing home residents and the staffs of such facilities help to perpetuate difficulties like those just outlined, perhaps in part because of their own lack of knowledge or discomfort about sexuality and aging. Concerned individuals, progressive nursing-home personnel, and organizations such as the Gray Panthers and Services to Ongoing Mature Aging are beginning to have some effect on restrictive practices in nursing homes. Staff education, programs on sexuality for the residents, private lounges, and acceptance of affectional and sexual rights of residents are important elements of care in these facilities. Perhaps as these alternatives are made increasingly available, they will help maintain the important option of sexual expression for the aged who are in institutions. As one writer states:

> The aged in nursing homes have minimal opportunity for many satisfying experiences and enjoyable pursuits. Within all of the limitations, sex is an opportunity for good, clean entertainment that provides laughter and joy in the heart and the intimate giving of one person to the other. (Kassel, 1983, p. 182)

We have been looking at some of the myths about sexuality and aging that have had a particularly oppressive impact on some older people. One of the foundations of these myths is a widespread ignorance of the facts about sexual functioning in aged people. The rest of this chapter will examine some of the physiosexual changes and altered sexual responses that take place as part of the aging process.

Physiosexual Changes and Sexual Response: The Older Female

The term **climacteric** refers to the physiological changes that occur during the transition period from fertility to infertility. **Menopause**, one of the events of the female climacteric, refers to the cessation of menstruation. Menopause occurs as a result of certain physiological changes that take place at around 45–50 years of age. Although the pituitary continues to secrete follicle-stimulating hormone (FSH), the ovaries cease production of mature ova. Ovarian estrogen output also slows down, although the adrenals, liver, and adipose (fat) tissue produce some estrogen after menopause (Mosher and Whelan, 1981).

The cessation of menstruation and fertility do not eradicate sexual desire and response. In fact, the altered ratio of hormones and the elimination of fear of pregnancy may sometimes increase sexual interest. As discussed in Chapter 6, the role of estrogen in sexual interest and response is not clearly understood. Research does indicate that for some women supplemental estrogen following menopause improves sexual functioning (Dennerstein et al., 1980).

During menopause women may experience some physical symptoms other than cessation of menstruation. However, only 25% of all women seek medical consultation due to difficulties related to menopause (Perlmutter, 1978). For many, the "event" is surprisingly uneventful:

> After hearing comments for years about how menopause was so traumatic, I was ready for the worst. I was sure surprised when I realized I had hardly noticed it happening. (Authors' files)

Women who do experience problems report symptoms such as changes in vaginal tissues, menstrual irregularities, headaches, insomnia, and "hot flashes." Hot flashes may occur sporadically, and there is a physiological explanation for them. Hormones influence the nerves that control the blood vessels, so that as hormone levels fluctuate during menopause, the diameter of the blood vessels may change. Rapid dilation of the vessels may cause a woman to experience a momentary rush of heat, typically in the face. The sensation can be quite disconcerting. Hot flashes occur several times a day and during sleep; they usually cease within two years. About 10% to 20% of women report extreme discomfort from hot flashes (Seaman and Seaman, 1978). Some women report a decrease in frequency of intercourse during the time they are experiencing hot flashes (McCoy et al., 1985).

Changes in the vaginal tissues are also hormonally caused. They result from a decrease in circulating hormones. The vaginal mucosa becomes thinner and changes to a lighter pinkish color. Both the length and the width of the vagina decrease, and these changes contribute to the diminished expansive ability of the inner vagina during sexual arousal. There may also be diminished lubrication during sexual response. Both of these changes can result in uncomfortable or painful intercourse.

The Sexual Response Cycle of the Older Female

Prior to Masters and Johnson's (1966) research, the sexual response cycle of menopausal and postmenopausal women had not been studied. Sixty-one women between the ages of 41 and 78 were in Masters and Johnson's research population. In the following paragraphs we will contrast the sexual response cycles of these postmenopausal women with patterns that typically occur in premenopausal women, as described in Chapter 6. For the most part, the changes that accompany aging have to do with somewhat decreased intensity rather than with significant alterations of response.

Excitement Phase.   The first physiological response to sexual arousal, vaginal lubrication, typically begins more slowly in an older woman. Instead of 10–30 seconds, it may take several minutes or longer before vaginal lubrication is observed. In most cases, the amount of lubrication is reduced. Studies using the vaginal photoplethysmograph found that postmenopausal women's vaginal blood volume increase during sexual arousal is smaller than in premenopausal women. However, women of both age groups reported similar levels of sexual activity and enjoyment, indicating that the somewhat lowered vasocongestion response is within the range necessary for normal function (Morrell et al., 1984; Purifoy et al., 1983). In addition, some older women do not experience lessening of physiological arousal. The Masters and Johnson group included three subjects who had maintained active sexual involvement through-out their adult years and had rapid, full lubrication.

Other characteristic changes of excitement phase, such as the sex flush and expansion of vagina, are often less pronounced than in earlier years. Clitoral sensitivity and nipple erection remain the same.

Plateau Phase.   During the plateau phase, the vaginal orgasmic platform develops and the uterus elevates. In a postmenopausal woman, these changes occur to a some-what lesser degree than before menopause. However, the vaginal opening is con-stricted to the same degree as with a younger woman, and the clitoris withdraws under the hood as before.

Orgasm Phase.   Contractions of the orgasmic platform and the uterus continue to occur at orgasm, although the number of these contractions is typically reduced in an older woman. In some menopausal women the uterine contractions that take place at orgasm can be painful. This typically results from a hormone deficit or imbalance, a condition that can usually be corrected by providing a proper balance of both estrogen and progesterone. The capacity for multiple orgasms continues, and several of the older women in the Masters and Johnson study experienced multiple orgasmic response.

Orgasm appears to be an important aspect of sexual activity to older women. One survey (Starr and Weiner, 1981) found that 69% of women aged 60 to 91 listed "orgasm" first in response to the question "What do you consider a good sexual experience?" Only 17% of the women answered "intercourse" to this same question. Additionally, "orgasm" was the most frequent response to the question "What in the sex act is most important to you?" Compared with when they were younger, 65% of the women reported that the frequency of orgasm was the same, and 20% said it was increased. About 14% reported that they now experienced orgasms less often, but only 1.5% of the sample said they never experienced orgasm.

Resolution Phase.   Resolution phase typically occurs more rapidly in postmeno-pausal women. Labia color change, vaginal expansion, orgasmic platform formation, and clitoral retraction all disappear soon after orgasm. This is most likely due to the overall reduced amount of pelvic vasocongestion during arousal.

In summary, complete sexual response can continue throughout a woman's lifetime. As Masters and Johnson state, "The aging human female is fully capable of sexual performance at orgasmic response levels, particularly if she is exposed to reg-ularity of effective sexual stimulation" (1970, p. 238).

Estrogen Replacement Therapy

Estrogen replacement therapy (**ERT**) may alleviate some of the problems resulting from the significant reduction in estrogen after menopause. These difficulties can include hot flashes, inelastic and thin vaginal tissues, reduction in vaginal lubrication, and *osteoporosis* (abnormal bone loss). The benefits of ERT can contribute to general health and sexual functioning. However, there are also risks involved. The risks and benefits of ERT vary from person to person.

A significant increase in the incidence of endometrial cancer was associated with ERT consisting of exclusive and continuous use of estrogen. Now it is common practice to combine progestin with estrogen for about 10 days out of a 30-day cycle. The addition of progestin has almost eliminated the risk of endometrial cancer with ERT (Cali, 1984). The progestin causes the uterine lining to shed each month, and a monthly flow results. When this occurs, it is highly unlikely that the lining will develop cancer from estrogen stimulation.

The potential effects of ERT on the development of breast cancer are a controversial issue. Some studies have shown a small increased risk after long-term use (Judd et al., 1983), whereas others have shown no link between ERT and breast cancer (Kelsey et al., 1981; Stadel et al., 1985), and others show a decreased risk of breast cancer when a combination of estrogen and progestin are used (Gambrell, 1984). Women who need to be most cautious about ERT are those who have benign breast lumps, have not borne children, or have mothers or sisters with breast cancer (Greenwood, 1984).

Liver tumors are a rare complication of ERT (Judd et al., 1983). Estrogen administered orally appears to have a greater effect on the liver than estrogen introduced directly into the bloodstream, so methods involving skin patches, subcutaneous capsules, or vaginal tablets are under study (Cardozo et al., 1984; Judd et al., 1983; Laufer et al., 1983). An increased incidence of gallbladder disease may also occur with ERT. Some studies show that ERT reduces the risk of developing high blood pressure and heart disease, whereas other investigations have shown the opposite (Judd et al., 1983). Part of the confusion stems from the fact that studies have involved different types and amounts of estrogen or combinations of estrogen and progestin. Estrogen alone, in small doses, may provide some protection against heart disease. However, the progestin added during each cycle to prevent endometrial cancer may increase the risk of stroke and heart attack by unfavorably altering the type of fats in the bloodstream. These risks are significantly increased in smokers, diabetics, the very obese, women who do not exercise, and women with high blood pressure and high cholestrol levels (Greenwood, 1984).

The current research suggests that a menopausal woman should carefully weigh the potential benefits and risks of ERT against the symptoms of hormone deficiency. We recommend thorough discussions of the matter with one's health care practitioner. When ERT is determined to be appropriate, low-dose, short-term treatment is generally advisable.

There are some alternatives to ERT. Continued frequent sexual activity helps maintain vaginal lubrication during sexual arousal. Research has found that changes due to aging are less pronounced in women who are sexually active through intercourse or masturbation than in sexually inactive women (Lieblum et al., 1983). Creams containing estrogen can be inserted directly into the vagina, and these topical medications can sometimes effectively counteract the drying of vaginal tissues. Although some of the locally applied estrogen will be absorbed into the bloodstream, the amount is less than with oral estrogen. Physical exercise, good nutrition, and food supplements can also sometimes alleviate some menopausal symptoms (Ritz, 1981).

Physiosexual Changes and Sexual Response: The Older Male

As a man grows older, certain physiosexual changes occur that are in large part related to decreased production of testosterone. In most men the male hormones reach their peak level sometime between the ages of 17 and 20. Hormone output then steadily but slowly declines until around age 60, after which it remains fairly constant.

With aging, a man may note several changes in his sexual anatomy or functioning. The size and firmness of his testicles diminishes somewhat. This is a normal change in body anatomy that is unlikely to impair his ability to function sexually. There is also a thickening and gradual degeneration of the seminiferous tubules, and this generally results in reduced sperm production. However, many men retain their fertility well into the older years. There are numerous recorded cases of men older than 80 who have fathered children. Besides the reduction in sperm production, changes in orgasmic and erectile function also accompany the male aging process, and specific alterations occur in the prostate gland. We will look at some of these changes in the following two sections.

The Sexual Response Cycle of the Older Male

Masters and Johnson studied 39 men between the ages of 51 and 89 and found that, as with the female, most changes in the sexual response cycle involve alterations in the intensity and duration of response.

Excitement Phase.   During youth, many males are capable of achieving an erection in a few seconds. This ability is typically altered with the aging process. Instead of 8 or 10 seconds, a man may now require several minutes of effective stimulation to develop an erect penis. More direct stimulation may also be desirable or necessary. This slowed rate of erectile response may cause alarm, stimulating the fear of impotence that some men experience:

> I guess it was the little things adding up that finally made me realize it was taking me longer to get a hard-on—the fact that I could go to bed with an extremely desirable woman and still be flaccid; that kissing and hugging often wasn't enough to get me started. At first I was real shook up at this discovery, thinking that maybe I would lose my potency. However, I received some good advice from my physician, who assured me that while things may slow down a bit, they continue to remain functional. (Authors' files)

Fortunately, this man received good advice. Others, fearful that they will ultimately lose their erectile function, may develop such anxiety that their fears become reality. However, most men retain their erectile capacities throughout their lifetime. The slowed rate of obtaining an erection is a natural occurrence within the aging process. When a man understands this, the altered pattern has little or no effect on his enjoyment of sexual expression.

Plateau Phase.   Older men do not typically experience as much myotonia (muscle tension) during plateau phase as when they were younger. The testes may not elevate as close to the perineum. Complete penile erection is frequently not obtained until late in the plateau phase, just prior to orgasm.

One result of these changes is that the older man is often able to prolong the plateau phase much longer than he did when he was younger, which may significantly enhance his pleasure. Many men appreciate this prolonged opportunity to enjoy other sensations of sexual response besides ejaculation. When a man engages in intercourse, his partner also may appreciate his greater ejaculatory control.

Orgasm Phase.   Most aging males continue to experience considerable pleasure from their orgasmic responses. In fact, about 73% of older men in one study reported that orgasm was "very important" in their sexual experiences (Starr and Weiner, 1981). However, they may note a decline in intensity. Frequently absent are the sensations of ejaculatory inevitability that correspond with the emission phase of ejaculation. The number of muscular contractions occurring during the expulsion stage are typically reduced, and so is the force of ejaculation. The seminal fluid is usually less copious and somewhat thinner in consistency.

Resolution Phase.   Resolution typically occurs more rapidly in older men. Loss of erection is usually quite rapid, perhaps bypassing altogether the two stages of penile detumescence characteristic of younger men. The testicles generally descend immediately after ejaculation.

While resolution becomes faster with aging, the refractory period between orgasm and the next excitement phase gradually lengthens. Men may begin to notice this as early as their thirties or forties. Often by age 60 the refractory period may last for several hours, even days in some cases. Some men may be quite philosophical about this increased time span between ejaculations. As one 70-year-old man stated:

> I can still shoot just as good—it just takes me longer to reload. (Authors' files)

The Prostate Gland

One of the most common physiosexual changes encountered by men during the aging process involves the prostate gland. This structure produces a large portion of the fluids contained in the ejaculate. Inflammation of the prostate, a condition known as **prostatitis**, is a difficulty that may occur in young and old alike, but it is considerably more common in aging men. In most cases it results from a bacterial or viral infection, although occasionally it may be attributed to a disruption in the usual pattern of sexual behavior (either an increase or decrease in frequency). Some common symptoms of prostatitis include pain in the pelvic area, backache, urinary complications, and occasionally a cloudy discharge from the penis. In the case of a bacterial infection, medical treatment generally involves the administration of antibiotics. Nonbacterial prostatitis often responds to prostatic massage (the physician inserts a finger into the rectum and presses rhythmically against the prostate).

As men grow older the prostate gland tends to increase in size, a condition called benign prostatic hypertrophy. The enlarged prostate tends to put pressure on the urethra and decreases urine flow (Ritz, 1981). Also, it is not uncommon for aging men to develop benign or malignant tumors of the prostate. Early detection of prostatic cancer is important to its successful treatment. Therefore, it is good preventive practice for all men past the age of 40 to have yearly prostate evaluations.

The usual treatment for prostate cancer is surgical removal of the entire gland (*prostatectomy*) or treatment with female sex hormones (Kolodny et al., 1979; Ritz, 1981). These treatments may contribute to a variety of problems in sexual functioning. Hormone treatments sometimes result in difficulty in achieving an erection. Surgically removing portions of the prostate via the urethral tract damages the urethral sphincter valves, and this can result in retrograde ejaculation. This produces sterility, although in some cases artificial insemination can be successfully performed with sperm removed from the man's urine. Although some prostate surgery may cause erection problems, new surgical techniques that avoid cutting a small group of nerves involved in erection can maintain erectile functioning for many men following prostate surgery (Goldsmith, 1983).

Sexual Development in the Later Years

As the preceding discussion of sexual responses indicates, most people retain the capacity for sexual expression throughout their lives. As we grow older, all of us will experience some physical changes that will affect our sexual functioning. However, it is unlikely that these natural alterations will eliminate our capacity to maintain a rewarding and satisfying sex life. In the following sections we will examine some of the many factors that impact on sexual development during the later years.

Sexual Expression in the Later Years

The options for sexual expression may change in the later years. Men die an average of eight years earlier than women, and women accustomed to expressing their sexuality exclusively within a marriage may find themselves suddenly alone. Furthermore, older males without partners often seek younger female companions, whereas women are less likely to be involved with younger men.

For some older women and men, widowed or divorced, masturbation can become or continue to be a form of sexual release and expression. A study of 800 people between 60 and 91 years of age reports that women are becoming more accepting of masturbation as a means of sexual expression (Starr and Weiner, 1981). As a woman of 60 states:

> I thought my life was over when my husband of 35 years died two years ago. I have learned so much in that time. I learned to masturbate. I had my first orgasm. I had an "affair." I have established intimate relationships with women for the first time in my life. And most of all, I have survived. (Authors' files)

One survey found that more older people approved of masturbation (62%) than engaged in it (Brecher, 1984). This study also found that the incidence of masturbation among both male and female respondents declined with age and that a greater proportion of men than of women, at all ages, reported masturbating (see Table 15.1).

Table 15.1   Percentage of Older People Who Report That They Masturbate

	Men	Women
Age 50–59	66	47
Age 60–69	50	37
Age 70 and above	43	33
Married	52	36
Unmarried	63	54

Source: Brecher, 1984.

Being married is no guarantee of the availability of a satisfying sexual relationship. One partner's sexual interest may lag behind the other's. A woman who finds that her sexual needs are more demanding than those of her male partner may find it quite difficult to seek more frequent sexual activity with her partner, particularly if a pattern of male initiation has long been established. Misunderstandings about altered patterns of sexual response may give rise to difficulties. A woman may misinterpret the slower erectile and ejaculation response of her male partner as signs of waning interest or rejection. Similarly, a man may believe that reduced vaginal lubrication is an indication that his female lover is less aroused by him than formerly. However, many couples find ways to successfully cope with lubrication and erection problems, as discussed later in this section (Brecher, 1984).

On the other hand, both well-established and new relationships may blossom during the later years. The opportunities for sexual expression in a relationship are often increased, as pressures from work, children, and fulfilling life's goals may be reduced, and more time is available for sharing with a partner. Although it was not a representative study, one survey found that 66% of women and 80% of men age 70 and older experience intercourse, and 50% do so at least once a week (Brecher, 1984). Couples may increasingly emphasize quality rather than quantity of sexual experience. For example, one study of heterosexual men found that for younger men the amount of sexual activity they engaged in was an important aspect of their social confidence. However, for older men the quality of their sexual activity was the most crucial factor (Stimpson et al., 1981). A small study of older gay men found this same trend. Most of the homosexual respondents indicated that sex was less frequent than when they were younger, but half felt that it was more satisfying than before. As one 63-year-old man said, "Less accent on the genitals, more on the total person now" (Kimmel, 1978, p.199).

The stereotypic view that homosexual people as a group face a lonely and unhappy old age is not suggested by the limited research available. Gay men and lesbians may be better prepared for coping with the adjustments of aging than are heterosexual men and women. Many homosexual individuals have planned for their own financial support and have consciously created a network of friends. Having successfully faced the adversities of belonging to a socially stigmatized group may also help them deal with the losses that come with aging (Dawson, 1982). One study found that older homosexual males match or exceed comparable groups in the general population on a measure of life satisfaction (Berger, 1982). The majority of these men reported that they socialized primarily with age peers. There was a change over time toward fewer sexual partners, but frequency of sexual activity remained quite stable, and 75% were satisfied with their current sex life (Berger, 1982). Another study of over 4000 gay men found no age-related differences in amount of sexual activity or of social interaction with other gay men. Research has also revealed that most older lesbians prefer women of similar ages as partners (Raphael and Robinson, 1980). Furthermore, lesbians do not have the same limitations as heterosexual women on the number of same-age eligible partners, since their potential partners do not die younger than they do (Laner, 1979).

Intimacy, a lifelong need, may find new and deeper dimensions in later years. Some people find their sex lives markedly improved by the greater opportunities to explore relaxed and prolonged lovemaking. A few may even have more frequent sexual encounters, as revealed in one survey of people more than 65 years old (Pfeiffer, 1975). For others, genital sexual activity may become less frequent, but interest, pleasure, and frequency of nonintercourse activity, like caressing, embracing, and kissing, may remain stable or increase (Foster, 1979). As a 73-year-old man expressed it:

> I don't know if I'm oversexed, but I'm a lover. I like to pet, kiss, hug. I have more fun out of loving somebody I love than the ultimate end. You know, some people want sex and forget the rest of it—the hugging and the petting—and I think that's wrong. People say, "What will happen to me when I get older?" Well, I'm still alive! (Vinick, 1978, p. 362)

Nonsexual friendships often provide affection and closeness.

One survey found that, while sexual frequency declines, enjoyment of sex sometimes increases with age. Many of the respondents found techniques for maintaining or enhancing their enjoyment of sex despite the progressive physiological changes. For example, 43% of women and 56% of men provided oral sex to their partners. Some used fantasy or sexually explicit materials; others engaged in manual and oral stimulation of the breasts and genitals, anal stimulation, use of a vibrator, various coital positions, sex in the morning, or exclusive fondling and cuddling (Brecher, 1984).

Older people may redefine their sexual and affectional relationships. Nonsexual friendships with either sex can offer affectionate physical contact, emotional closeness, intellectual stimulation, and opportunities for socializing. One survey found that a supportive network of close friends helped to minimize loneliness and maintain life enjoyment, especially for the unmarried (Brecher, 1984).

Most people who regularly hike, fish, play golf, or till a garden during their youth will continue to do so in their later years, although often with somewhat reduced vigor. Far from developing a total incapacity for these activities, older people may simply pursue them at a more leisurely pace. The same can be true of one's sexuality, particularly if misconceptions and anxieties are avoided or resolved. As one woman explains:

> Sex isn't as powerful a need as when you're young, but the whole feeling is there; it's as nice as it ever was. He puts his arms around you, kisses you, and it comes to you—satisfaction and orgasm—just like it always did . . . don't let anybody tell you different. Maybe it only happens once every 2 weeks, but as you get older, it's such a release from tensions. I'm an old dog who's even tried a few new tricks. Like oral sex, for instance. . . . We weren't too crazy about it though. . . . We take baths together, and he washes my body, and I wash his. I know I'm getting old and my skin could use an ironing, but we love each other—so sex is beautiful. (Wax, 1975, p. 43)

A review of the literature on sexuality and aging notes the following trends:

1. In the presence of reasonably good health and available partners, sexual activity among older people continues into the seventies, eighties, and nineties. Among those who are no longer sexually active, it is not uncommon to find a continuation of sexual interest.
2. Within the older age group, the range of sexual drive varies from very great to very little. Sexual capacity varies from individual to individual, and from time to time in a particular individual.
3. There is an overall pattern of decline in sexual interest and activity with advancing age. However, sexuality continues to hold a place of importance in the lives of most older people.
4. Among older men and women, sexual interest and activity are directly related to individual sexual histories. Those who describe their sexual urges as strongest in youth tend to describe them as moderate in old age. Those who describe their sexual feelings in youth as weak to moderate describe themselves as being without sexual feelings in old age.
5. Maintenance of sexual capacity depends upon regular sexual expression. (Dressel and Avant, 1983, pp. 199–200)

Toward Androgyny in Later Life

Development toward androgyny in personal, interpersonal, and sexual styles occurs for many people in later life. On a biological level, there is a lessening of the hormonal differences between women and men. Estrogen levels in women diminish rapidly following menopause, and androgen levels decline gradually in men from about age 30 on. The extent to which these hormonal changes contribute to the movement towards androgyny is unknown.

The older years usually bring with them a lessening of the demand for the traditional roles of early adulthood: career building, marriage, and parenting. For people who have followed stereotypic role patterns, the nurturing role for women and the achieving role for men often lessen after their children leave home and they retire. There is also often a shift in power within the marital relationship, with women being more likely to have increased power in later than in earlier life stages (Chiriboga and Thrunher, 1980). One study found that older men and women develop other-sex characteristics by age 50 without relinquishing same-sex characteristics:

> Individuals who were psychologically healthiest at age 50 showed increased androgyny over time. Women became more assertive and analytic while remaining nurturant and open to feelings. Men became more giving and expressive while they continued to be assertive and ambitious. (Livson, 1983, p. 112)

These developments can help set the stage for a merging of sexual styles that may occur in later years. Older males often become more like women in their sexual behavior, in that fantasy and ambience become more important in their lovemaking, and they become less preoccupied with orgasm. Older adults may move away from the stereotypical focus of women on the relationship and men on genital sex. Over the lives of many of the subjects, women developed a greater interest in genital sex and men in nongenital sexuality (Bangs, 1985).

Maximizing Sexual Functioning in the Later Years

We have seen that most people retain the capacity for sexual expression throughout their lives. However, it is important to distinguish between capacity and desire. Some individuals or couples may not wish to maintain or renew sexual activity in their later years. The following information is directed toward those who are interested in continued or renewed sexual expression.

There are certain conditions, other than those discussed earlier, that may reduce the pleasures of sex in later years. A brief discussion of these potential deterrents, and some ways of minimizing them, may help older people to enjoy their sexuality more. Research has shown that both men and women continue to engage in and enjoy sex in the older years by finding ways to circumvent or adapt to limitations and illnesses that may occur (Bangs, 1983; Brecher, 1984).

Older people may experience the same sexual problems as younger ones. One study found that in individuals over 50 years of age seeking treatment for sexual difficulties, the most common were erectile problems in men and lack of orgasm and sexual desire in women (Wise et al., 1984). Sex therapy can help people resolve or adjust to these problems.

Like all physical expressions, sexual activity may become increasingly fatiguing to the person who allows his or her physical condition to deteriorate markedly through lack of exercise. Consequently, maintaining a regular program of physical activity (walking, jogging, swimming, and so forth) may enhance erotic abilities, in addition to contributing to one's general health.

Related to the value of maintaining physical exercise are the known benefits of sexual regularity. Masters and Johnson (1966) maintain that regularity of sexual expression throughout the adult years (whether by masturbation or activity with a partner) is a crucial factor in maintaining satisfactory sexual functioning beyond one's youth and middle age. This conclusion is supported by data from Kinsey's studies

As one grows older, an active physical life can contribute to self-satisfaction.

(1948 and 1953) that reveal a close correlation between sexual activity levels in the earlier years and those in the later years. Another researcher's work corroborated Kinsey's findings and found that the differences among men in levels of sexual activity before middle age tended to be maintained as the men grew older (Martin, 1981). These findings do not necessarily demonstrate a direct cause-and-effect relationship; it may simply be that those people with the strongest sex interest in their youth maintain that interest into old age. However, some theorists believe that regular functioning of the sex organs is a key factor that directly affects sexual ability in the later years. According to their argument, regularity helps maintain sexual vigor by preventing the deterioration of the sex organs with aging (Rubin, 1965).

Overindulgence in food or drink has frequently been linked with declining sexuality. Overeating may become a major problem in older people, who often slip into a sedentary lifestyle. In Chapter 6 we pointed out the potentially adverse effects of excessive alcohol consumption. Moderation in both eating and drinking can indirectly contribute to healthier sexual funtioning.

The monotony of a repetitious sexual relationship, often exaggerated after long years of living with the same person, may also significantly reduce an older couple's sexual ardor. The need for experimentation and variety, discussed in Chapter 7, may be particularly important at this time. Certainly, not all long-term couples report problems with boredom. For some, who may have grown to understand and adjust to each other's needs over the years, familiarity may breed contentment.

Summary

Sexuality in the Later Years: Examining the Myths

1. American culture continues to be influenced by the philosophy that equates sexual expression with procreation and youth.

2. The double standard continues into old age. It often affects both sexes adversely, but may impose a particular burden on women.

3. Antisexual prejudice against older people is particularly pronounced in some nursing home facilities.

Physiosexual Changes and Sexual Response: The Older Female

4. Menopause is the cessation of menstruation and signals the end of female fertility. The level of estrogen output is reduced by the end of menopause.

5. Some women experience menopause-related symptoms such as hot flashes, menstrual irregularity, headaches, insomnia, and changes in the vaginal tissues.

6. With aging a woman typically requires more time to achieve vaginal lubrication.

7. The sexual response cycle of the older woman is also characterized by less vaginal expansion, reduced sex flush, diminished orgasmic intensity, and a more rapid resolution. The capacity for multiple orgasmic response is typically maintained.

8. Estrogen replacement therapy (ERT) is a medical treatment for menopausal symptoms. Potential side effects necessitate careful use of this medication.

Physiosexual Changes and Sexual Response: The Older Male

9. After early adulthood, testosterone production declines steadily, until approximately age 60. Many physiosexual changes in the aging male result from this decreased hormone output.

10. Common physiosexual changes in the older male include reduction in the size and firmness of the testicles, lowered sperm production, and difficulties with the prostate gland.

11. The older male typically requires longer periods of time to achieve erection and reach orgasm. Greater ejaculatory control may be beneficial to both his partner and himself.

12. The sexual response cycle of the aging male is also characterized by less myotonia, reduced orgasm intensity, more rapid resolution, and longer refractory periods.

Sexual Development in the Later Years

13. The options for sexual expression may change in the older years, as many individuals find themselves without a sexual partner. Masturbation may serve as one alternative.

14. Sexual relationships may improve during later years when individuals focus on intimacy and redefine their sexual and affectional relationships.

15. A lessening of stereotypical sex roles and an increase in androgyny often occurs in later life.

16. It is unlikely that the physiosexual changes of aging alone will eliminate one's capacity to maintain a satisfying sex life.

Maximizing Sexual Functioning in the Later Years

17. Continued physical exercise may help to maintain sexual functioning, and evidence suggests that regularity of sexual expression throughout the adult years may be another crucial factor.

18. Overindulgence in food or drink has frequently been linked with declining sexuality in the later years.

19. Boredom with a repetitious sexual relationship may inhibit sexual ardor in older couples. However, routine and familiarity may also bring contentment.

Thought Provokers

1. Television programs featuring older adults, such as "Murder, She Wrote," with Angela Lansbury, and "The Golden Girls" (about four female housemates over 50), have become more common. Why do you think these changes have occurred, and what impact might they have on attitudes toward sexuality and older adults?

2. What policies and practices do you think nursing homes should follow regarding their residents' sexual behavior?

3. Are there any advantages that you are looking forward to in being older? Can you imagine yourself as a "sexy senior citizen"? What do you think the potential advantages and disadvantages of the development toward androgyny might be?

Suggested Readings

Berger, Raymond. *Gay and Gray*. Urbana, Ill.: University of Illinois Press, 1982. An informative book based on research that examines lifestyles, sexuality, relationships, and life satisfaction of older homosexual men.

Butler, Robert, and Lewis, Myrna. *Sex After Sixty: A Guide for Men and Women for Their Later Years*. New York: Harper & Row, 1976. Extensive, down-to-earth health and living-adjustment information related to sexuality. Many useful suggestions within a context of individual differences, with encouragement for personal and relationship growth.

Greenwood, Sadja. *Menopause, Naturally*. San Francisco: Volcano Press, 1984. An informative, enlightening book about psychological, sexual, and biological aspects of menopause.

Starr, Bernard, and Weiner, Marcella. *The Starr-Weiner Report on Sex and Sexuality in the Mature Years*. New York: Stein & Day, 1981. An informative report on the personal responses to questions about sexuality of more than 800 people between the ages of 60 and 91.

Weg, Ruth (Ed.). *Sexuality in the Later Years: Roles and Behavior*. New York: Academic Press, 1983. A multifaceted approach to the understanding of sexual roles and behavior in the later years, including perspectives from anthropology, psychology, sociology, and physiology.

Part Five

Sexual Problems

16

For some years she had been thinking she was not much inclined toward sex. . . . It is not merely a lack of pleasure in sex, it is dislike of the excitement. And it is not merely dislike, it is worse, it is boredom.

Muriel Spark
Collected Stories: I (1968)

The Nature and Origins of Sexual Difficulties

Origins of Sexual Difficulties
Desire Phase Difficulties
Excitement Phase Difficulties
Orgasm Phase Difficulties
Coital Pain

THE NEXT THREE CHAPTERS are concerned with some of the difficulties that can hinder sexual functioning and some ways of preventing or resolving these difficulties. This chapter looks at a number of relatively common sexual problems and the factors that frequently contribute to them. First we discuss some common origins of such problems—cultural, personal, interpersonal, and organic. Then we look at a number of specific problems related to sexual desire, arousal, orgasm, and at problems that cause painful intercourse. Chapter 17 outlines several ways for enhancing sexuality and overcoming specific difficulties. In Chapter 18 we will turn our attention to understanding and preventing sexually transmitted diseases.

Origins of Sexual Difficulties

What are the causes of sexual difficulties? This may sound like a simple question, but finding origins to sexual problems is often complex. There are several reasons for this. First of all, even when a sexual difficulty has been clearly identified, it is often hard to isolate the specific causes, because many varied influences and experiences contribute to sexual feelings and behavior. Second, it is difficult to identify a clear and consistent cause-and-effect relationship, because the experiences that contribute to a specific sexual difficulty in one person may produce no such effects in another individual (LoPiccolo, 1985). Finally, people who do not demonstrate any specific, objectively measurable sexual difficulty may still experience dissatisfaction with their sexuality.

The following paragraphs will examine several factors, each of which can either interfere with sexuality or enhance it. We hope that a clearer understanding of the events that shape sexuality will lead to increased satisfaction, communication, and pleasure. Cultural, personal, interpersonal, and organic factors can each contribute to sexual difficulties. Significant interaction among these areas also occurs. Therefore, the separate categories that we describe in the following pages are somewhat arbitrary.

In reading this chapter, it is important to remember that sexual satisfaction is a subjective perception. A person or couple could experience some of the problems described in this chapter, and yet be satisfied with their sex lives. In fact, some research has indicated that many of the happily married couples studied experienced problems with arousal and orgasm but felt very positive about their sexual relations and marriages (Frank et al., 1978). Research does indicate that sexual problems are quite common. A random, nationwide survey done by *Parade Magazine* found that one in seven people reported problems in their sex lives. The rate was the same for men and women. Table 16.1 shows percentages of people with specific sexual problems.

Cultural Influences

Culture strongly influences both the way we feel about our sexuality and the way we express it. At times, because cultural influences are so pervasive, it is easy to think of them as innate, or natural, rather than learned. Yet, in another time or culture, a quite different sexual behavior or attitude may be viewed as the norm. These cross-cultural inconsistencies clearly reveal the powerful shaping impact that society has upon sexuality. This section will examine some influences in Western society—and particularly in the United States—that affect our sexuality and may contribute to sexual problems in some people.

Table 16.1   Prevalence of Sexual Problems in Nonclinical Sample
Percentage of patients who reported specific sexual problems
during a routine sexual history by physicians.

	Men	Women
Lack of sexual desire	13	27
Erection difficulties	12	—
Inorgasmia	0	25
Premature ejaculation	14	—
Pain during intercourse	0	20
Concern with frequency of intercourse	18	23

Source: Ende et al., 1984.

Negative Childhood Learning.   We learn many of our basic, important attitudes about sexuality during childhood. Some people's views are strongly influenced by our cultural legacy that sex is sinful. It has been widely reported by a variety of therapist researchers that severe religious orthodoxy equating sex with sin is common to the backgrounds of many sexually troubled people. One researcher found that the more rigidly orthodox married members of Jewish, Protestant, and Catholic churches were, the less sexual interest, response, frequency and pleasure they reported in marital sex and the more sexual inhibitions, anxiety, guilt, shame, and disgust they experienced (Purcell, 1985).

A child may or may not be directly told that sex is shameful or sinful, but the groundwork of such a belief can be laid in other ways. Helen Singer Kaplan describes some aspects of childhood sexuality and the response it often evokes in our society:

> Infants seem to crave erotic pleasure. Babies of both genders tend to touch their genitals and express joy when their genitals are stimulated in the course of diapering and bathing, and both little boys and girls stimulate their penis or clitoris as soon as they acquire the necessary motor coordination. At the same time, sexual expression is, in our society, systematically followed by disapproval and punishment and denial. (1974, p. 147)

The results are often guilt feelings about sexual pleasure from touching one's genitals. Conflict about erotic pleasure may thus be initiated early in a person's life. Kaplan summarizes: "The interaction between the child's developing sexual urges and the experiences of growing up in our sexually alienating society probably produces some measure of sexual conflict in all of us" (p. 145).

Negative attitudes about childhood masturbation appear to be still quite common among American parents. One study found that almost 35% of parents of preteens said their children's masturbation was wrong. Fewer than half of the parents wanted their adolescent children to have positive attitudes about masturbation. When parents were confronted with their children's masturbation, common responses were "don't touch," and "that's not nice" (Gagnon, 1985).

Not only do children often learn that it is wrong to touch their genitals; they may also learn that their genitals are "down there" and somehow dirty. Rather than

The way others react to childhood genital exploration may affect how children learn to feel about their sexual anatomy.

understanding that their sexual anatomy is one more part of their body to learn about and explore, they may begin to have strong negative feelings about their genitals. These can carry over to adult life and influence feelings towards self-exploration and sharing their body with another person.

The availability of accurate and appropriate information about sexuality can influence sexual attitudes and behaviors. Boys generally acquire more knowledge (but not necessarily good feelings) about their sex organs than girls do. It is quite typical, for example, for a girl not to learn she has a clitoris, as the following report illustrates:

> It wasn't until the first time that a man touched my clitoris with his hand that I knew I had anything down there so special. This new knowledge really paid off when I realized I could do for myself what he had done to me. (Authors' files)

Children begin early on to develop a sense of whether it is acceptable to ask questions about sex. Schools and parents typically contribute only in a limited way to a child's understanding of sex, and by and large peers are the most frequent providers of sexual information (Hunt, 1974). Unfortunately, much of the information a child receives from his or her friends is incorrect. Also, since sexuality is an emotionally laden topic, many young people learn *not* to talk about sex. It is no wonder that by the time people reach adulthood, sharing needs and discussing information about sex is often difficult.

While growing up we learn important lessons about human relationships. We observe and integrate the models we see around us. During this time we are also forming our sense of self. Both of these elements, the sense of self and relationships with others, contribute to the meaning and expression of sexuality. As children we often had limited choices about what we learned. However, this learning and development continues throughout our lives, and as adults we are more able to choose what information and experiences are valuable to us.

The Double Standard. Although the rigidity of the double standard appears to be lessening somewhat, opposite sexual expectations for women and men are still quite prevalent in our society. Despite recent changes in societal views, the notion that women should be sexually passive still lingers. Masters and Johnson noted that "sociocultural influence more often than not places a woman in a position in which she must adapt, sublimate, inhibit or even distort her natural capacity to function sexually. . . . Herein lies a major source of woman's sexual dysfunction" (1970, p. 218).

The "good girl" facade and pervasive cultural repression of female sexuality affects most girls and women to some degree—both those with and those without definable sexual problems. Women often are held responsible for controlling the sexual advances of men, who, they are told, "are only after one thing." As the Boston Women's Health Book Collective describes it, women "are always so busy setting limits and holding off this powerful sexuality coming from [men] that [they] never get a chance to explore [their own sexuality]" (1973, p. 26).

In our recent history, marriage has given permission for female sexual expressiveness. The contradictory message is "Sex is dirty, save it for someone you love." However, as many women find, such a rapid transition from sexual repression to responsiveness is not easy to make:

> I dutifully followed the expectation to be chaste until marriage. However, a 15-minute ceremony did not make me instantly sexually responsive. My inhibition was a great disappointment to my husband and myself. (Authors' files)

Research does indicate that women with nontraditional gender-role orientation are more likely to have positive attitudes about sexual activities, including oral sex, petting, intercourse using different positions, initiating sexual encounters, and being the more assertive partner (Koblinsky and Palmeter, 1984).

The male side of the double standard is also a function of cultural expectations. Men frequently learn that sexual conquest is a measure of "manliness"; as a result, they should be interested in enticing as many women as they can into sexual relationships. According to this image, a man is supposed to be always ready for sex:

> Erotic materials portray men as always wanting and always ready to have sex, the only problem being how to get enough of it. We have accepted this rule for ourselves and most of us believe that we should always be capable of responding sexually, regardless of the time and place, our feelings about ourselves and our partners, or any other factors. We have thus accepted the status of machines, performing whenever the right button is pushed. (Zilbergeld, 1978, p. 41)

Differing expectations can lead to difficulties in intimate relationships.

As a result of these expectations, men have often assumed that intercourse was primarily for their own pleasure and sexual release. This was true especially in the past. However, today men frequently feel responsible for the woman's sexual pleasure as well.

These cultural expectations can produce discomfort, frustration, and resentment for men as well as for women. Often a man may feel overburdened by his responsibility for sexual activity. At times, his feeling that he must perform and the resulting lack of spontaneity may obliterate his sexual arousal and pleasure. His sense of responsibility for the success of the sexual relationship may also result in psychological distress if his partner has a sexual problem. One research study (Derogatis et al., 1977) that examined psychological distress in couples in which one of the partners had a diagnosed sexual problem found some gender differences in the reactions of the other partner. Men partners without sexual problems indicated more feelings of depression, anxiety, and self-deprecation than did women partners without sexual problems. In fact, the former demonstrated as much psychological distress as did male subjects with diagnosed sexual problems. In contrast, women partners without sexual problems had significantly lower levels of psychological problems than did women with sexual problems.

A Narrow Definition of Sexuality.   Besides early socialization experiences and continuing exposure to the double standard, popular opinions about the appropriateness of sexual behaviors also influence our expressions of sexuality. Although attitudes about what is "normal" appear to have changed in recent years, certain assumptions still strongly affect sexual expression.

The notion that "real sex" equals penile-vaginal intercourse is pervasive in our society, and this assumption can significantly affect erotic behavior. Fewer than 5% of respondents to Hite's survey (1976) described their patterns of sexual encounters as something other than the standard one of (a) foreplay, (b) penetration, (c) thrusting, and (d) orgasm, especially male orgasm (lesbian responses excepted).

Certainly coitus is a viable option. However, it is one alternative—rather than the only, most important, or best avenue for experiencing sexual pleasure. A strong inclination to view coitus as synonymous with sex can place burdensome and anxiety-provoking expectations on intercourse. It can also lead people to overlook other sensual enjoyments in relating sexually. In Zilbergeld's words, "Many men, when asked how it felt to touch their partners or be touched by them, have said that they didn't know because they were so busy thinking about getting to intercourse. In this way we [men] rob ourselves of pleasure and of fully experiencing the stimulation necessary for an enjoyable sexual response" (1978, p. 45).

The sex-equals-coitus model in heterosexual relating may greatly reduce the eroticism of the experience for both people. Nevertheless, the stimulation of the penis provided by the vaginal walls is likely to be adequate for inducing male orgasm. The problem may be greater for women, who are less likely to experience orgasm from intercourse alone. Therefore, this model is one in which many women are left with the specific sexual dissatisfaction of not experiencing orgasm with a partner. This important topic will be discussed in a later section dealing with female orgasm difficulties.

Goal Orientation.   There has been a wide variety of goals prescribed for sexuality throughout history. Certainly a common one has been reproduction. Another is the man's biological release, with the woman providing it as her duty. Once the woman's pleasure began to be considered a legitimate aspect of sexual contact, the simultaneous orgasm became the pinnacle of achievement. As women are increasingly viewed as sexual beings, "vaginal" orgasms and, currently, multiple orgasms may be seen as essential to sexual experience. Contemporary magazines and sex manuals provide the latest in acrobatic positions, techniques, and gadgets. The "modern" message about sexuality often appears to be "Sex is OK for both males and females, and you better be good at it" (LoPiccolo and Heiman, 1978, p. 56). It sometimes seems as if the pursuit of bigger, better, and more orgasms has become a consuming American pastime—and shame on the couple who used only one intercourse position last time! As Philip Slater (1973) in his article "Sexual Adequacy in America" aptly states:

> Discussions of sexuality in America have always centered on the orgasm rather than pleasure in general. This seems to be another example of our tendency to focus on the *product* of any activity at the expense of the *process*. It may seem odd to refer to orgasms as a product, but this is the tone taken in such discussions. Most sex manuals give the impression that the partners in lovemaking are performing some sort of task; by dint of great cooperative effort and technical skill (primarily the man's), an orgasm (primarily the woman's, which masculine mystification has made problematic) is ultimately produced. The bigger the orgasm, the more "successful" the task performance. (p. 19)

We do not intend to demean sexual exploration and variety. Nor, by any means, do we mean to criticize the orgasm. We do believe, however, that arbitrary definitions of sexuality that impose external standards for measuring "success" or "failure" reduce the opportunity for individuals and couples to determine what is satisfactory based on their own feelings.

Personal Factors

Beyond the cultural setting and the influence it has on sexual feelings and expression, sexual difficulties may also stem from other factors. Each of us is a unique, complex blend of biological, cultural, and emotional elements. Our sexuality is an expression of all these aspects of ourselves that begin forming in childhood and continue to develop throughout our lives.

Personal factors are important, for human reactions to life experiences are highly variable. Two individuals may respond in totally different ways to the same situation. It is in this light that we present a discussion of some of the personal influences that help mold an individual's sexual expression and satisfaction.

Sexual Knowledge and Attitudes.   The knowledge and attitudes we acquire about sex have a direct influence on our sexual options. For example, if a woman knows about the function of her clitoris in sexual arousal and believes her own sexual gratification is important, she will most likely have experiences different from a woman who has neither this knowledge nor this belief. Even education and social class have an impact on sexual attitudes and behaviors. For example, Kinsey's study found that the higher the educational and occupational level of a couple the greater their tendency to use a variety of noncoital stimulation and intercourse positions (Kinsey et al., 1948 and 1953). In certain cases where difficulties are based on ignorance or misunderstanding, accurate information can sometimes alleviate sexual dissatisfaction.

Self-Concept.   Self-concept is a term that refers to the feelings and attitudes we have about ourselves. These feelings influence the kinds of decisions we make about expressing our sexuality. For example, one man may decline a sexual proposition because he lacks confidence. Another man's reasons for saying no in the same situation may be based on an entirely different attitude; for example, he may have found casual sexual encounters to be unrewarding.

Sexual difficulties may often be tied to problems of self-concept. Some studies have found that men and women with sexual problems are likely to have more feelings of depression and anxiety and to have less self-confidence than men and women without sexual problems (Clement and Pfafflin, 1980; Derogatis et al., 1977). In addition, women who report disliking themselves indicate that they experience less sexual satisfaction than do women who have more positive feelings about themselves (Frank et al., 1979).

Self-concept combined with social skills also affects the ease or difficulty with which people begin, maintain, and end relationships. People often feel more at ease relating to others (sexually and socially) after having had some experience and having gained a sense of confidence in their own feelings and abilities.

Emotional Difficulties.   Often related to poor self-concept are personal emotional difficulties, such as anxiety or depression. These difficulties can be a response to a current situation or they may stem from unresolved past events. Whatever the source, emotional states have a strong impact on sexuality. However, once again this impact depends on the individual. One person who is feeling a generalized kind of anxiety may respond by becoming exceptionally sexually active. Another may withdraw from sexual encounters in an attempt to reduce anxiety or as a reaction to his or her emotional state.

Discomfort with certain emotions can also affect sexuality. Particularly important are one's feelings about intimacy and about lessening of control. The desire for intimacy, and apprehension about it, can significantly influence sexual encounters. An individual who experiences intimacy in a sexual relationship as threatening may have considerable sexual difficulty (Kaplan, 1979). On the other hand, being sexual with someone does not result in automatic intimacy. In fact, sexual encounters can be used to increase or decrease interpersonal closeness. For example, people can use their sexuality to increase warmth and involvement with another person or to express hostility and rejection. The issue of control also frequently contributes to the quality of a sexual experience. Arousal is usually accompanied by a reduction in control, and fear of sexual arousal underlies many sexual problems (Appfelbaum, 1985). For some people, arousal may provoke some anxiety, and they may inhibit their sexual response by maintaining control over their arousal.

Sexual Victimization.   A traumatic sexual experience, such as rape or incest, may contribute to sexual difficulties. One study of 83 female sexual assault victims found that 56% experienced sexual problems as a result of the assault; fear of sex and lack of desire or arousal were the most frequently mentioned problems. Incest victims commonly reported never having experienced orgasm (Becker et al., 1982). Another study found that 71% of rape victims had decreased sexual activity four to six years after the assault (Burgess and Holmstrom, 1979).

Interpersonal Factors

In addition to personal feelings and attitudes, a variety of interpersonal factors can strongly influence the satisfaction or dissatisfaction couples experience from a sexual relationship. These factors often vary according to the couple and their particular circumstances. For example, one couple may find that an argument typically ends with passionate lovemaking, whereas another couple moves to separate bedrooms for a week after a disagreement.

Judging from the popular media, it would almost seem that our sexuality is separate from the context in which we express it. Movies, magazines, and novels perpetuate the belief that if we are "sexually liberated" we can turn ourselves on and off regardless of our feelings of the moment. It is sometimes jarring to realize that as real people we cannot always relate this way. A lack of trust, dislike of a partner, boredom, fear, or rejection can easily lead to sexual dissatisfaction or disinterest. The dynamics of a whole relationship are highly significant in determining sexual satisfaction or dissatisfaction, and this fact is reflected in the strong emphasis in sex therapy on working with the couple rather than the individual. In many cases a sexual difficulty is a symptom of a more general relationship problem.

How a person reacts to a partner's sexual problem can be extremely important. For example, demanding and critical responses to a lover's sexual difficulty may magnify the problem by increasing anxiety. Likewise, a partner's sexual problem may become worse when we interpret it to mean that he or she "doesn't love me" or "doesn't find me attractive." As we will see in Chapter 17, an informed and caring response to a partner's difficulties may produce quite different results.

Gender-role orientation and expectations may affect how a person reacts to a partner's sexual difficulty. One study found that feminist women were more supportive of men with sexual problems than nonfeminist women. These researchers hypothesized that feminists are less likely to pressure men to perform according to a traditional gender role (Daniel et al., 1984).

Many interpersonal issues can affect sexual satisfaction. Among the more important are ineffective communication, fear of pregnancy, and sexual orientation.

Ineffective Communication.   Ineffective communication can contribute to and perpetuate sexual dissatisfaction. As we discussed in Chapter 8, verbal communication between partners is a basic tool for learning about needs and sharing desires. Without effective verbal communication, couples must base their sexual encounters on assumptions, past experiences, and wishful thinking—all of which may be inappropriate in the immediate situation. Nonverbal communication is also important. One study found that sexually distressed couples exhibited more negative nonverbal expression than a group of happily married couples (Zimmer, 1983).

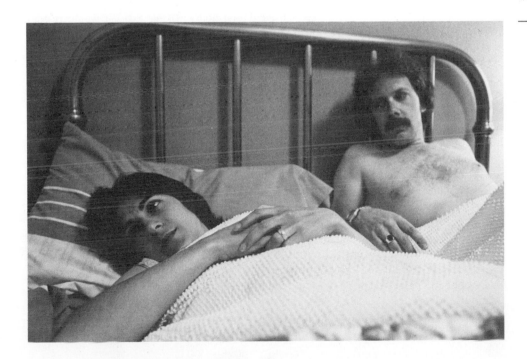

A frequent source of communication problems is stereotyped gender roles—in particular, the myth that ". . . sex is exclusively the man's responsibility and that sexual assertiveness in a woman is 'unfeminine' " (Kaplan, 1974, p. 350). A woman who believes that it is not her "place" to tell her partner that she is or is not in the mood to make love, or that she would like another kind of stimulation (or any other sex-related desire), may find that their relationship becomes increasingly frustrating, simply because her partner does not know what she wants. How could he?

For many reasons—limited communication skills, stereotyped gender roles, stereotyped images of romance, misplaced assumptions about the other person—couples sometimes operate under the belief that communication is unnecessary in a good sexual relationship. However, communicating sexual needs is often the first step in having them met. Communication is also the basis for the negotiation often necessary to reach compromises over individual differences.

Fears About Pregnancy.   The fear of an unwanted pregnancy may interfere with coital enjoyment in a heterosexual relationship. If a couple uses no birth control, this may result in a pairing of intercourse with thoughts such as "I sure hope I don't get pregnant." It is not easy to enjoy sex with that concern in the back of one's mind. Furthermore, a 100% effective temporary method of birth control is simply not available at this time. The reality is that unless one of the partners is surgically sterilized, there is a risk of impregnation, however small, in heterosexual intercourse.

An unwanted pregnancy has historically been the "punishment" for nonmarital sexual intercourse. If a woman experiences guilt about being sexual, it follows that she might expect consequences for her "transgression." Sometimes women may fear that simply being aroused or pleasured sexually can result in pregnancy:

> When I was in high school, I would spend long hours making out. We wouldn't even touch each other's genitals. Although I *knew* how women got pregnant, and that I hadn't done what was necessary for a pregnancy to occur, I still worried that I might get pregnant, simply because I had been turned on. (Authors' files)

The relationship between pregnancy anxiety and arousal can sometimes be seen in women who are completely freed from the possibility of pregnancy through sterilization or menopause. It is not at all uncommon for sexual activity and desire to increase at this point.

On the other hand, fears about not being able to become pregnant can create sexual difficulties. Many couples who want to conceive and have difficulties with infertility often find that their sexual relationship becomes anxiety-ridden, especially if they have to modify and regulate the timing and pattern of sexual interaction to enhance the possibility of conception.

Sexual Orientation.   Another reason a woman or man may not experience sexual satisfaction in a heterosexual relationship can be a preference to be involved with individuals of the same sex. It is understandable that a person with a homosexual orientation experiences sexual difficulty or a lack of satisfaction in heterosexual relations (Ross, 1983). Sexual difficulties with heterosexual partners are most likely to be considered problems by homosexual people who are attempting to conceal their orientation by relating sexually to partners of the other sex, or by people who want to change their orientation to heterosexual. Although some progress has been made by gay rights groups, a homosexual lifestyle is not generally accepted in our society. Following one's homosexual inclinations still involves severe societal pressures and repercussions, and many homosexual people attempt to relate heterosexually in spite of their lack of desire for such a relationship. Others have a commitment and a desire for the heterosexual relationship (often marriage) to continue and to be sexually fulfilling. Sex therapists are increasingly attempting to provide services for individuals and couples to resolve these complex difficulties (Gochros, 1978; Masters and Johnson, 1979).

Organic Factors

Organic, or physiological, conditions are estimated to be the primary cause of a sexual problem in 10%–20% of cases (Kolodny et al., 1979; Munjack and Oziel, 1980). In other situations, physiological factors contribute to a problem. Various illnesses, drugs, and physical problems—many of them seemingly unrelated to sexuality—can result in pain or discomfort during intercourse and can influence sexual interest, arousal, or orgasmic response. A person's psychological reaction to an organic disorder can often magnify or lessen its effect upon his or her sexual functioning. Consulting a physician may provide useful information about necessary sexual adjustments and options for people with temporary or permanent organic problems.

Illness. Diseases of the neurological, endocrine, and vascular systems can interfere with sexual functioning. An illness that is painful or debilitating may inhibit sexual interest, or the illness may directly affect physiological sexual response. For cancer patients the physiological effects of the disease and treatments, the threat of surgery, depression, and related stresses may negatively affect sexuality (Walbroehl, 1985). Surgical or medical treatments can also physically or emotionally impair sexual functioning. For example, people with kidney failure who undergo renal dialysis may have significant difficulty with sexual response. Prostate surgery can impair sexual functioning, but recent surgical techniques that do not injure the pelvic nerves involved in erection help to preserve erectile functioning (Goldsmith, 1983).

Multiple sclerosis (MS) is a neurological disease of the brain and spinal cord in which damage occurs to the myelin sheath that covers nerve fibers; vision, sensation, and voluntary movement are affected. The person with MS may experience either reduction or loss of sexual interest, genital sensation, arousal, or orgasm, as well as uncomfortable hypersensitivity to genital stimulation. Sexual arousal may not be possible by genital stimulation because of sensory losses (Hill and Kassam, 1984). One study of MS patients found that 62% experienced some sexual problem (Valleroy and Kraft, 1984).

Nerve damage or circulatory problems from diabetes can also cause sexual problems (Lin and Bradley, 1985; McCulloch et al., 1984). Many diabetic men experience reduction or loss of their capacity for erection, and a few diabetic men ejaculate into the bladder. Heavy alcohol use and poor blood sugar control increase the chances of erectile problems in men with diabetes (McCulloch et al., 1984). Much less research has been done with women than with men on the role of diabetes in sexual problems. Many studies report no reduction in vaginal lubrication in diabetic women (Schreiner-Engel, 1984). However, one study found that diabetic women do experience vaginal dryness during sexual activity and pain during intercourse. These problems were more likely to occur the longer a woman had diabetes (Whitley and Berke, 1983). Women with diabetes may also experience an absence of or decrease in the frequency of orgasm.

Cerebrovascular accidents (CVA), commonly called strokes, often result in residual impairments of motor, sensory, emotional, and cognitive functioning that can have a negative effect on sexuality. Stroke survivors frequently report a decline in the frequency of interest, arousal, and sexual activity. Some of the factors that commonly influence the sexual behavior of people who have experienced a stroke include limited mobility, altered or lost sensation, impairment in verbal communication, and depression. Role changes that occur when one of the partners assumes the role of caretaker and nurse can interfere with the adult-to-adult relationship (Emick-Herring, 1985).

Rheumatoid arthritis is a progressive, systemic disease that results in inflammation of the joints. Chronic inflammation can cause pain, destruction of the joint, or reduced joint mobility. Nerves and muscle tissue surrounding the affected joints are also often damaged. Rheumatoid arthritis does not directly impair sexual response, but chronic pain and fatigue may lessen a person's sexual interest. Pain or deformities in the hands may also make masturbation difficult or impossible without assistance. Arthritic impairment of hips, knees, arms, and hands may interfere with certain intercourse positions.

Sexual problems following a heart attack are usually due to anxiety and misinformation rather than to organic causes. A person may be worried that sexual excitement will bring on another heart attack and consequently be fearful of and avoid sexual activity. Research measuring cardiac effects in men during masturbation, noncoital stimulation, and intercourse in both the male- and the female-above intercourse positions found that cardiac expenditure was equivalent to light to moderate exercise (Bohlen et al., 1984). It is essential for someone who has had a heart attack to consult a physician about sexual activity, to secure individualized, accurate information.

Medication and Drugs. In some cases medication causes sexual problems. For example, certain drugs used to treat gastrointestinal problems, some drugs prescribed for high blood pressure, and some medications used for psychiatric disorders may impair vasocongestion and orgasmic response (Brass, 1984; Stevenson and Umstead, 1984; Shen et al., 1984). A new antidepressant medication, buproprion, that appears not to impair sexual functioning has been developed recently (Gardner and Johnston, 1985).

Barbiturates and narcotics (heroin, morphine, codeine, and methadone) depress the central nervous system and can seriously inhibit sexual interest and response (Abel, 1984). Chronic alcohol abuse results in physiological disturbances that can cause a variety of sexual difficulties. Alcoholism often presents personal and interpersonal disruptions in addition to physical problems (Bertello et al., 1983). For example, it can diminish female sexual satisfaction when either the woman or her partner is alcoholic (Peterson et al., 1984). Estrogen, sometimes used to treat prostate cancer or as replacement therapy after menopause, often decreases sexual interest. Birth control pills may also decrease sexual interest and arousal in some women.

It is important to remember that physiological factors can cause or contribute to sexual problems. We advise people who are concerned about a sexual problem to consult their physicians, especially if they have unsuccessfully attempted to resolve their difficulties by some of the methods described in these chapters. A sex therapist may also help direct a person to health care facilities where he or she may obtain the appropriate exam and screening tests.

It may be desirable to have a general physical and a gynecological or urological exam to help rule out organic factors in sexual difficulties. Tests for diabetes, endocrine and neurological problems, or other illnesses may be indicated. Special procedures have been developed to evaluate physical factors in erection problems (Zorgniotti, 1984). Instruments designed to measure penile blood pressure and flow can help evaluate possible vascular problems (Langone, 1981; Tordjman et al., 1980). A *nocturnal penile tumescence* (NPT) test can also be performed to help assess physiological erectile capability, although results of this procedure are not always reliable (Dhabuwala et al., 1983).

We have looked at some general factors that may influence sexual functioning and cause difficulties. The remainder of this chapter deals with some of the specific problems people encounter. We will treat these problems according to whether they have to do with the desire, excitement, or orgasm phases of sexual response. In reality, there is considerable overlapping of the problems. Problems with desire and arousal also affect orgasm, and orgasm difficulties can easily have an impact on a person's interest and ability to become aroused.

The sexual problems we shall discuss can vary in duration and focus from person to person. A specific difficulty can be of lifelong duration (primary) or appear after a certain time (secondary). A person may experience the problem in all situations with all partners (global) or only in specific situations or with specific partners (situational) (Kaplan, 1977; LoPiccolo, 1980a). A given individual may also have more than one identifiable problem. For example, a woman who does not experience orgasm may also have painful intercourse.

The categories and labels for the following problems are an integration of those in the American Psychiatric Association's Diagnostic and Statistical Manual (DSM III) and of a sex therapy research group from the Stony Brook Sex Therapy Center in New York State (Schover et al., 1982), with a few additions of our own.

Desire Phase Difficulties

Problems with sexual desire have received increased attention in recent years. This section will discuss inhibited sexual desire, difficulties with differences in sexual desire in a couple, and sexual aversion.

Inhibited Sexual Desire

Inhibited sexual desire (**ISD**) is a common sexual difficulty experienced by both men and women. Kaplan (1979) describes it as a lack of "sexual appetite." ISD is characterized by a lack of interest in initiation and participation in sexual fantasy and activity. Inhibited sexual desire can be distinct from excitement and orgasm difficulties. In fact, some people who are uninterested in sex become aroused and experience orgasm when they engage in a sexual encounter. Others may experience pleasure from touching and physical closeness but have no desire for erotic excitement. Still others with inhibited sexual desire feel tension and anxiety with physical and sexual contact and do not experience arousal and orgasm.

Primary ISD is rare. People with this condition did not masturbate or exhibit sexual curiosity in childhood, and as adults they do not develop interest in sexual fantasy, sexual activity, or the sexual aspects of a relationship. More commonly, however, people develop secondary inhibited sexual desire at a specific point in their lives. Some people may experience ISD in a particular situation, such as with a spouse but not with masturbation or with a lover.

A precise definition of inhibited sexual desire is difficult to establish. First of all, there is great variation in the level of sexual desire from person to person. Second, lack of desire is a realistic response to many situations; when a sexual situation or partner is negative or disadvantageous, sexual interest normally diminishes. For example, it would be adaptive to lose sexual interest in a person one does not like, a partner with poor hygiene, or someone who is verbally or physically abusive (Kaplan, 1979). The Stony Brook group considers less than one orgasm every two weeks from masturbation or partner sexual activity as one marker of low desire (Schover et al., 1982). This definition is not applicable to people who are quite interested in sexual activity but do not experience orgasm. In general, inhibited sexual desire is most commonly presented as a problem when it causes distress in a relationship.

Common psychological and physiological factors associated with ISD are depression, severe stress, low testosterone levels, and certain drugs and illnesses. A marked decrease in or absence of sexual interest often accompanies depression. Severe life problems such as death in the family, divorce, or extreme family or work difficulties can create stress that results in lack of sexual interest, as can illness (Kaplan, 1979). Insufficient testosterone levels resulting from surgical removal of testosterone-producing glands or from medications that counter the action of testosterone can also reduce sexual desire. Other factors that negatively affect desire include narcotics, high doses of sedatives or alchohol, and certain high blood pressure medications.

Inhibited sexual desire frequently reflects relationship problems. Often a person who experiences a lack of power and control in a relationship unintentionally loses sexual desire and then has some control in the sexual aspect of the relationship. Partners need a balance of togetherness and separateness, and ISD may occur when there is insufficient independence and an overabundance of dependency and closeness within the relationship (Fish et al., 1984). For some couples, hostility or lack of trust or respect in a relationship may inhibit sexual desire. It is usually difficult to feel desire for someone who arouses strong negative feelings. The following anecdote describes this common situation:

> Over the years of our marriage my sexual desire for my wife has diminished gradually to the point that it is presently almost nonexistent. There have been too many disputes over how we raise the children, too many insensitive comments, too many demands, not enough freedom to be my own person. When I look at her I have to

acknowledge that she is a remarkably beautiful woman, just as lovely as the day I was first attracted to her. I certainly feel no physical repulsion to her body. I guess it would be more accurate to say that I simply no longer have sexual feelings for her. One feeling I do have plenty of is hostility. I suspect it is this largely suppressed anger that has been the killer of my sexual interest. (Authors' files)

One partner may even use his or her lack of sexual interest, consciously or unconsciously, to punish or "get back at" the other. A person who is frequently pressured to engage in sex or who feels guilty about saying no may become less and less interested and feel increasingly diminished desire (Kolodny et al., 1979).

Some of the anxieties and conflicts that form the basis for ISD may be more complex. Some people may unconsciously be so fearful of sexual pleasure or intimacy that they prevent themselves from feeling sexual desire. One study of individuals whose inhibited sexual desire did not improve with therapy found that they had negative feelings about closeness and intimacy in general (Chapman, 1984). These individuals may have developed a "turn off" mechanism, described by Kaplan:

> Most of the patients I have studied tend to suppress their desire by evoking negative thoughts or by allowing spontaneously emerging negative thoughts to intrude when they have a sexual opportunity. They have learned to put themselves into negative emotional states. . . . In this manner they make themselves angry, fearful, or distracted, and so tap into the natural physiologic inhibitory mechanisms which suppress sexual desire. (1979, p. 83)

Kaplan further explains that people are usually not aware of the active role they play in creating their inhibitions. Their lack of desire appears to emerge automatically and involuntarily, and they do not realize that they have control over the focus of their thoughts.

Some people with ISD either do not perceive or misperceive internal and external cues associated with sexual arousal. They may not have learned to notice their own genital sensations of arousal or to generate interest and arousal within themselves. They also tend not to notice the potential sexual nature of situations or to consider themselves as sexual people (LoPiccolo, 1980a).

Inhibited sexual desire sometimes occurs following prolonged frustration from lack of arousal and orgasm. By not being interested and avoiding sexual activity, the person protects him- or herself from experiencing embarrassment or a sense of failure from unsatisfying sexual experiences.

Dissatisfaction with Frequency of Sexual Activity

Sexual partners may have discrepancies in their preferences for amount, type, and timing of sexual activities. In fact, some therapists believe that most desire problems are due to these differences within a relationship. "It is not that one person has too much desire and another too little on some absolute scale; it is rather a discrepancy in two people's styles or interests" (Zilbergeld and Ellison, 1980, p. 69). It is probably rare to find a couple with identical sexual preferences. One partner may prefer oral sex to intercourse and enjoy sexual activity only once a week in the morning, while the other delights in prolonged intercourse that occurs several times a week at night.

Sometimes the relationship can accommodate these individual differences. However, when sexual differences are a source of conflict or significant dissatisfaction, a couple can experience considerable discomfort.

Instead of moving toward some compromise, the couple may polarize in opposite directions. Feelings of resentment and power struggles may then develop. As two men state:

> I've never been wild about oral sex, but since my wife won't do it for me, I've stopped doing it to her.
>
> I'd like to have sex about two times a week, but my wife wants it every night. It seems like I can never satisfy her, so now I'm not interested even once a week. (Authors' files)

A common pattern that often emerges in these situations is that one partner feels constantly deprived and the other constantly pressured. Usually both feel unloved and guilty—one for asking too much and the other for not giving enough (Zilbergeld and Kilmann, 1984).

Sexual Aversion

When low desire for sexual activity includes a negative reaction to sex, it is considered **sexual aversion** (Schover et al., 1982). Sexual aversion can range from feelings of disgust to extreme, irrational fear of sexual activity. Even the thought of sexual contact can result in intense anxiety. A person who experiences sexual aversion may exhibit physiological symptoms such as sweating, increased heartbeat, nausea, or diarrhea as a consequence of fear. Both men and women experience sexual aversion, but it is more common among women (Kolodny et al., 1979).

Several factors appear frequently in the histories of people with sexual aversion. Severely negative parental sexual attitudes are common. Sexual trauma, such as incest or rape, often precedes sexual aversion (LoPiccolo, 1985). A pattern of constant pressuring, coercion, or bargaining for sex in a relationship can also precede the development of this problem. Repeated unsuccessful attempts to please a sexual partner or "working at sex" to overcome a sexual difficulty may generate intense anxiety about sexual relations. Anxiety about unresolved conflicts in sexual identity or orientation may surface in anticipation of a sexual experience and also create intense fear (Kolodny et al., 1979).

Excitement Phase Difficulties

Both men and women can experience difficulties in sexual arousal. Of course, most of us are not responsive sexually all of the time. Sometimes we may be too preoccupied with another aspect of our lives, too fatigued, or feeling somewhat distant from our partner. However, when physiological arousal, erotic sensations, or the subjective feeling of being "turned on" are chronically diminished or absent, inhibited sexual excitement exists (Schover et al., 1982). We will focus here on lack of vaginal lubrication in women and inability to secure or maintain an erection in men. These respective difficulties are particular to just one sex, but in many cases the reader may note similarities between the sexes in the origins of these conditions.

Inhibited Sexual Excitement in Women (Lubrication Inhibition)

As we saw in Chapters 4 and 6, vaginal lubrication is a woman's first physiological response to sexual arousal. For some women, inhibited lubrication is only an occasional problem. They become sufficiently aroused to experience lubrication in certain situations but not in others. Other women have never experienced vaginal lubrication during a sexual encounter. Biological factors, including low estrogen levels, can be a factor in lack of lubrication. As discussed in the origins section, nonphysiological factors such as years of learning not to experience sexual arousal frequently contribute to this difficulty. Feelings of apathy, anger, or fear may also inhibit arousal and lubrication.

Lack of lubrication in a particular situation does not necessarily mean something is wrong. Vaginal lubrication frequently decreases during prolonged coitus. This may be due to a long plateau phase (during the plateau phase, lubrication typically decreases). Or it may be the result of exclusive coital stimulation that may not be stimulating enough to induce continued lubrication. In the latter case, if continued sexual contact is desired, simultaneous manual stimulation of the clitoris or other parts of the body or changing to noncoital activities may increase lubrication.

Inhibited Sexual Excitement in Men (Erectile Inhibition)

Engorgement and erection of the penis are the physiological correlates of vaginal lubrication and an early indication of sexual arousal in men. The term most commonly applied to male erection difficulty is *impotence*. The origin of this word suggests the primary reason for our opposition to its use: It comes from Latin and literally means "without power." The implication is that a man without an erection is without power or potency as a lover. It is likely that a man who experiences lack of erection as a problem is often deeply anguished; the implication that he is without value as a lover contributes to this distress. As the following account indicates, however, this interpretation can be far from reality:

> I met a man once whose erectile capacity was completely destroyed by a cord injury in the precise region of the lower spine where erectile function is controlled. While he couldn't get it up, he certainly had no trouble getting it on! I've often wondered if his acquired status of highly desired lover had something to do with his discovery that erections are not essential to meaningful sexual interaction. (Authors' files)

Instead of the term impotence, we will use the more descriptive phrase **erectile inhibition**, which adequately describes a major male difficulty without the implications just mentioned.

Erectile inhibition problems may be broadly classified into two types. Men with *primary erectile inhibition* have attempted but never experienced maintained penetration (either vaginally or anally) with a sexual partner their entire lives, although they may routinely experience nighttime erections and have erections during masturbation.

Box 16.1   *A Case Study in Psychologically Based Erectile Inhibition*

The following case is a composite of several actual situations described to the authors by students and clients. At the end are some questions that may prove helpful as you analyze both the source(s) and potential remedies for the difficulties encountered by this hypothetical couple.

Bill and Karen attended a party, during the course of which she became quite angry over his lack of attention. As the evening wore on her anger mounted, ultimately resulting in an argument with Bill. On the drive home neither talked. Both felt somewhat responsible, but neither was willing to apologize. Bill was actually feeling some guilt over his actions and was determined to make up in bed. At the same time, he was still angry at Karen. He brought these conflicting feelings to bed with him and was unable to get an erection. Now Karen became openly angry and suggested that Bill's present ineptness, together with his earlier indifference at the party, clearly indicated a lack of caring on his part. He feebly assured her that this was not the case, that he was just tired, and that everything would be back to normal next time. But would it really be fine the next time? This question bothered him as he lay awake, long after Karen had fallen asleep by his side.

The next day he could think of little else. "I have got to make it right tonight—must show her that I still care." However, as the evening approached, his anxiety

mounted. By the time he was driving home, the pressure was really intense. He stopped at Joe's Bar for a drink or two to soothe his growing fears. Finally, after an evening spent trying to appear casual and collected, it was time for bed—time for him to function as a lover.

Instead of being spontaneously swept away by the passions of lovemaking, he remained focused on his penis, willing it to respond and to become erect. He had now become a spectator to his own performance, cursing his flaccid penis, sick with frustration and concern over Karen's response to his repeated failure. Unexpectedly, but perhaps more damaging, her reaction was not overtly accusatory. Rather she simply withdrew in brooding silence, leaving him alone with his acute misery. At this point, he was on the merry-go-round of the failure-fear-failure syndrome.

Some questions for analysis:

1. What does this case illustrate about the relationship between emotional conflicts and sexual sharing?
2. In what ways do you think Bill and Karen's expectations of love and intimacy may have contributed to the development of their shared problem?
3. How might this situation have been averted?
4. What do you think Bill and Karen could do to resolve their sexual problem?

The label *secondary erectile inhibition* is applied to the man who has previously had erections with his partner(s), but finds himself presently unable to consistently experience a functional erection. This condition is far more prevalent than primary erectile difficulty (Kaplan, 1974). It is common for men to occasionally be unable to achieve or maintain an erection due to minor factors like fatigue or stress. Masters and Johnson state that if a man is unable to have an erection in 25% or more of his sexual experiences, this label is appropriate for him. We believe that the percentage is not as important as whether the individual or couple sees this occurrence as a problem.

The underlying factors in erectile inhibition are many. Frequently, erectile problems are due to a combination of organic and psychogenic factors. From 50% to 60% of erection difficulties are estimated to be partially or totally caused by physiological factors (Crenshaw, 1984). Biological factors that may contribute to erectile difficulty include the effects of certain drugs (for example, alcohol, narcotics, amphetamines, and some prescription medications), severe diabetes (Maatman and Montague, 1985), and a wide variety of anatomic, endocrine, vascular, neurological, cardiorespiratory, and infectious conditions (Goldstein et al., 1985; Kaplan, 1974; Masters and Johnson, 1970). Approximately 25% of erection problems are caused by medications and illicit drug use (Crenshaw, 1985).

Erection difficulties can also occur as a result of problems that affect blood flow into and out of the penis (Tordjam et al., 1980; Wagner et al., 1982; Wespes and Shulman, 1985). Chronic kidney failure can create erectile problems by causing blood vessel or nerve damage and hormonal abnormalities. Surgeries performed in the pelvic area can damage nerves and blood vessels and result in erectile failure. Injury to the spinal cord can affect the ability to have an erection, depending on the location of the injury and the nerve damage involved. Increasingly refined and sophisticated methods for diagnosing organic causes of erection problems have been, and continue to be, developed (Zorgniotti, 1984).

Fatigue, worry, and relationship conflict typically produce only transitory episodes of erectile inhibition. However, occasionally these experiences may produce such concern and anxiety that they develop into a pattern. His own anxiety, his partner's response, or the combination of the two can turn a man's transitory difficulty into a serious problem. The composite case presented in Box 16.1, drawn from several such cases we have dealt with over the years, illustrates some of the ways psychological factors can escalate a situational difficulty. A history of premature ejaculation (described later in this chapter) is common among men with secondary erectile inhibition. If a man has developed a lot of anxiety about ejaculating too soon, he may become very susceptible to erection difficulties.

Occasionally, a traumatic first sexual experience can cause erectile inhibition. A response from a man's partner that he interprets as an attack on his self-worth may be particularly damaging. The following account illustrates this situation:

> I was with this woman for the first time. Other than being a little nervous, I was really looking forward to a good time. When I took my clothes off my penis was still soft (the room was cold!). She said, "Where is it!" Well, let me tell you, she didn't see much that night. Neither did anyone else for quite awhile. It even took a long time for me to feel comfortable again about undressing in full view of my partner. (Authors' files)

Women are sometimes concerned that assertiveness on their part during sexual activity with a male partner will inhibit his sexual arousal. However, one study in which male college students listened to audio tapes depicting various female sexual behaviors, found that men experienced the highest levels of enjoyment and sexual arousal with depictions of female sexual assertiveness. This finding contradicts the notion that gender roles of the assertive male and nonassertive female are necessary for male sexual security (Sirkin and Mosher, 1985).

Orgasm Phase Difficulties

The problems we have been discussing have primarily been ones of desire and excitement. Some other sexual difficulties specifically affect orgasmic response, and a variety of different problems are reported by both men and women. Some of these are infrequency of orgasms and their total absence. Others involve reaching orgasm too rapidly or delayed climaxes. Sometimes a partner may fake orgasm to conceal its absence.

Inhibited Female Orgasm

The term *frigidity* has been used as a general, descriptive label for female sexual problems, including lack of interest, arousal, or orgasm. It is both imprecise and pejorative, mistakenly implying that women with these difficulties are totally sexually unresponsive and emotionally cold or unloving. Many sexuality educators and therapists now use the word **inorgasmia**, meaning the absence of orgasm.

Women who do not achieve orgasm may experience arousal, lubrication, and enjoyment from sexual contact. However, their sexual response does not increase to the point of experiencing orgasm. Some women who do not have orgasms enjoy sexual encounters. Many others are highly disappointed and distressed. They view their lack of orgasm as failure, and the lack of physical release from orgasm results in experiences that are less and less enjoyable.

Inorgasmia can be primary, secondary, situational, or coital. A woman who has *primary inorgasmia* has never experienced orgasm by masturbation or with a partner. *Secondary inorgasmia* refers to a woman who has previously experienced orgasm but no longer does so. A woman who has *situational inorgasmia* experiences orgasm rarely, or in some situations but not in others; for example, she may be orgasmic with masturbation but not with a partner. *Coital inorgasmia* refers to women who are orgasmic with manual or oral partner stimulation but not during intercourse.

It is rare for inorgasmia to be due to physiological causes. However, conditions that impair the vascular system or nerve supply of the genital area can inhibit orgasmic response. Disorders of the endocrine system or chronic illnesses can also interfere with arousal and orgasm.

Primary inorgasmia is quite common; surveys indicate that approximately 10% of adult women in the United States have never experienced orgasm by any means of self- or partner stimulation (Hite, 1976; Kaplan, 1974; Kinsey, 1953). This 1-out-of-10 figure is especially noteworthy when compared with the number of men who have never experienced orgasm in their lifetime. We don't know exactly how many this is: Because it is assumed that males have orgasms, the question is rarely even asked. Nevertheless, some men are totally inorgasmic, although the incidence is extremely low.

There are some indications that the number of primary inorgasmic women is decreasing, and some sex therapy clinics are seeing a smaller percentage of women with primary inorgasmia (LoPiccolo, 1980b). This apparent decrease may be due to the accessibility of excellent self-help books for women who want to learn to experience orgasm.

Women with primary inorgasmia often lack knowledge of their sexual response patterns that others have learned through self-stimulation. Few of these women masturbate. Lacking masturbation experiences, a woman misses a potentially important opportunity to learn about and become comfortable with her orgasmic response. Most men have had these intitial learning experiences provided by self-stimulation.

The absence of routine orgasm during coitus without additional manual-clitoral stimulation is not an unusual pattern for women. The Hite Report (1976) asked women if they routinely experienced orgasm during coitus without simultaneous manual stimulation of the clitoral area; only 30% responded that they did. Another study found that fewer than half (44%) of 141 women attending human sexuality workshops usually or always experienced orgasm during intercourse without simultaneous manual clitoral stimulation (Ellison, 1980). Kaplan states, "There are millions of women who are sexually responsive, and often multiply orgasmic, but who cannot have an orgasm during intercourse unless they receive simultaneous clitoral stimulation" (1974, p. 397). For many women the indirect clitoral stimulation that occurs during coitus is less effective than direct manual or oral stimulation of the clitoral area.

During coitus, the clitoris may be stimulated indirectly in two ways. First, coital thrusting can create tension of the labia minora which extends to the clitoral hood. Clitoral stimulation thereby occurs from pressure and movement of the hood (Masters and Johnson, 1966). Second, pressure on the mons and clitoral area from the partner's pubic bone may provide stimulation (Hite, 1976; Masters and Johnson, 1966). Although this indirect clitoral stimulation is often not sufficiently intense to result in orgasm, most women, as indicated in *The Hite Report*, report intercourse to be highly enjoyable and desirable. Most sex therapists do not believe that a woman has a sexual problem if she enjoys intercourse and experiences orgasm in some other way than during coitus (LoPiccolo, 1985).

Copyright 1986, John Caldwell.

The Hite Report raises an important question about a definition of sexuality that says women must have orgasms during intercourse. In Hite's view, we should not be asking why women aren't having orgasms from intercourse ". . . but rather: Why have we insisted women should orgasm from intercourse? And why have women found it necessary to try everything in the book, from exercises to extensive analysis to sex thereapy to make it happen?" (Hite, 1976, p. 236). Once again, this issue reflects the sex-equals-coitus model of sexuality, which is inadequate in indicating how to provide effective stimulation for female orgasmic release.

Unfortunately, many women believe there is something wrong with them for not conforming to this model—even though it does not fully take into account their physiological needs. The painfully asked question "I come when he touches me but not when he's inside me. What's wrong with me?" is very common. Women who require clitoral stimulation to reach orgasm may feel pressured to fake climax at the "appropriate" moment. In addition, they may be reluctant to ask for or engage in manual stimulation or to request noncoital stimulation after their partner ejaculates.

Besides lack of clitoral stimulation, insufficient duration of coitus is another factor that may contribute to lack of orgasm during intercourse (Jayne, 1985). This is especially true if a woman's partner has difficulty controlling his ejaculation. Worry about whether coitus will last long enough can also inhibit arousal. Given the direct stimulation of the penis by the vaginal walls versus the indirect clitoral stimulation from the hood and pubic bone pressure, it is predictable that unless modifications are incorporated the male will often reach orgasm more rapidly than his partner.

A less frequently expressed difficulty is the lack of orgasm from manual or oral stimulation by the partner. Some women prefer and respond more readily to stimulation from intercourse, and the internal stretching and pressure sensations from intercourse can trigger orgasm (Ellison, 1980). On the other hand, lack of orgasm from partner manual or oral stimulation can be rooted in negative attitudes about self-stimulation that affect feelings about noncoital stimulation from sexual partners.

Another frequent factor in nonorgasmic response with a partner may be ineffective sexual techniques; many women have not requested or received effective stimulation by a partner (Newcomb, 1984). Lack of self- or partner stimulation is not always the cause, however, and supplying stimulation does not always solve what may be a more complex problem. Experiencing orgasm usually involves a lessening of conscious control. Feelings of anxiety, fear, or anger, or guilt about her sexual expression, situation, or relationship, can interfere with a woman's ability to "let go," and this can inhibit orgasmic response. One study found that women who were more willing to relinquish control, as demonstrated by hypnotic susceptibility and liking the feeling of getting "carried away" while drinking alcohol, reported experiencing orgasm more consistently than women who were less willing to "let go." A woman may be ambivalent about the relationship or have negative feelings about her partner. A woman who does not want to lose control of her feelings or behavior in front of her partner may consent to sexual interaction while simultaneously saying no to orgasm. Performance pressure to have an orgasm can also interfere with her arousal; anxiety about having an orgasm may diminish the pleasurable sensations that create it.

Inhibited Male Orgasm

Ejaculatory inhibition, sometimes called retarded ejaculation, generally refers to the inability of a man to ejaculate during coitus. Unlike premature ejaculation, it is generally considered an uncommon condition. However, some clinicians think that mild forms of this difficulty may actually be quite prevalent (Kaplan, 1974).

Most men who are troubled by retarded ejaculation are able to reach orgasm by masturbation or by manual or oral stimulation by their partner. In some cases, however, a man may not ejaculate at all during a sexual encounter, as revealed in the following account.

> I began a sexual relationship several months ago with a man who has a problem I've never before encountered. He has no difficulty getting an erection. In fact, he usually seems real excited when we make love. But he never comes. The first time I thought it was great—he seemed to be able to go on forever. But, after awhile it started getting to me. I've tried everything—going down on him, using my hand, stroking his scrotum when he is inside me—nothing works. He doesn't want to talk about it, but I sense he is as frustrated as I am, maybe more. Once I got him to admit he climaxes when he masturbates. Why can't he come with me? (Authors' files)

Many researchers and therapists distinguish between primary and secondary ejaculatory inhibition. *Primary ejaculatory inhibition* refers to men who have never been able to experience intravaginal ejaculation. Most of these men are capable of ejaculation outside the vagina, through stimulation by a partner or through masturbation. However, there are extremely rare cases of men who have never experienced ejaculation in their entire lives (Kaplan, 1974).

When retarded ejaculation develops in a man who has a past history of normal ejaculatory functioning, it is classified as *secondary ejaculatory inhibition*. A variation of this is *partial ejaculation*. Here, the man experiences the sensations of ejaculatory inevitability but fails to have the strong muscle contractions and intense pleasure associated with the expulsion stage of orgasm. Instead of spurting out, the semen seeps from the penis during such a "half" orgasm. Chronic partial ejaculation is very rare. However, many men report having this experience occasionally, particularly when they are tired or under stress. Sometimes when a man is trying to delay ejaculation he will go "one stroke too far" and experience a seeping emission rather than a full orgasm.

Ejaculatory inhibition may be related to a variety of factors. In isolated cases the problem is associated with a physical condition. Disease may cause damage to the neurological structures that coordinate ejaculation, and certain prescription drugs used in the treatment of emotional problems or hypertension have occasionally been known to induce retarded ejaculation.

Far more frequently, ejaculatory inhibition has a psychological cause. Some of the more common psychological factors are guilt over sexual activities (often stemming from strict religious training), conflict with a partner, fear of the partner getting pregnant, and lack of interest in or dislike for a partner. Another cause may be unconscious feelings of anxiety, fear or resentment associated with ejaculation

(Libman et al., 1984). Masters and Johnson (1970) report instances in which men dislike their partners so much that they attempt to frustrate them by withholding their ejaculate. If the couple is involved in a high-conflict relationship (particularly one in which the man feels overpowered or dominated), his retarded ejaculation may represent an act of defiance or rebellion in the power struggle.

Occasionally, inhibited orgasm may be traced to a particularly traumatic event early in a man's sexual development. For example, he may have suffered severe punishment at the hands of a parent after being discovered masturbating, or perhaps he was acutely embarrassed when intercourse in a car was interrupted by a law officer's spotlight. The ejaculatory response may also be inhibited later on by association with a psychologically painful experience. Masters and Johnson (1970) report one case in which a man discovered his wife having intercourse with her clandestine lover. His first view of the scene was seminal fluid dripping out of her vagina. While the marriage was maintained, the man was not longer able to ejaculate intravaginally. Apparently he felt that his wife's vagina had been made unclean by the other man's semen, and he could not tolerate the thought of allowing his seminal fluid to mix, even symbolically, with her lover's ejaculate.

Premature Ejaculation

An orgasm difficulty found commonly in men is **premature ejaculation**. We define premature ejaculation as consistently reaching orgasm so quickly that the rapidity significantly lowers a man's own enjoyment of the experience, impairs a partner's gratification, or both. This definition eliminates arbitrary time goals, takes into account the partner's pleasure, and views the person's own subjective needs as an important determinant of what constitutes reaching orgasm too fast.

The Stony Brook group divides premature ejaculation into a continuum of severity, from ejaculation before intromission to ejaculation within seven minutes of commencing intercourse. However, the premature ejaculation label is not applied if neither the man nor his partner considers the rapidity of ejaculation a problem (Schover et al., 1982). While most people who encounter this problem do so during heterosexual coitus, too-rapid climax is sometimes a difficulty in homosexual relationships or noncoital heterosexual activity. Thus, speed of response may be considered an issue whenever people, including women, reach orgasm sooner than they want to during sexual activity.

While there are no statistics establishing exactly how many people experience premature orgasm, it is an extremely common problem among men in our society. Masters and Johnson state that it is the most prevalent sexual problem of men, estimating that millions are troubled by it. In anonymous surveys of students enrolled in our human sexuality classes over the last several years, we have consistently found that fewer than 25% of men report that premature ejaculation is never a problem. One-quarter of our male students report it to be an ongoing difficulty, and the other 50% is distributed between these two extremes.

Biological factors, such as an overly sensitive penile glans, are rarely the primary cause of this difficulty. However, a low amount of vaginal lubrication can increase friction of the penis during intercourse and cause rapid ejaculation (Steege, 1981).

Men with premature ejaculation often have fewer orgasms in a given time period and may ejaculate at a lower level of arousal than men who do not experience rapid ejaculation (Geer and O'Donohue, 1984; LoPiccolo, 1980b). Usually past experiences are more likely to contribute to the pattern of rapid ejaculation—for instance, striving to reach orgasm quickly to alleviate anxiety or to demonstrate sexual prowess.

In our society, early sexual experiences—both coital and noncoital—are frequently anxiety producing and thus completed as quickly as possible. For many men, self-stimulation is not a relaxed, leisurely episode of discovery and delight but is often a brief and furtive experience designed solely to release sexual tension:

> Masturbation for me consisted of jerking off in the shower as fast as possible (no lock on bathroom door) or under the covers at night, holding my breath and making certain no weird groans signaled my solitary vice. (Authors' files)

Perhaps less significant, but by no means uncommon, is the adolescent male practice of group masturbation, often referred to graphically as a "circle jerk." Typically, several friends get together to see who can ejaculate first. After "Ready, set, go" the quickest finisher wins. Such experiences may provide peer-group esteem for a person who is able to ejaculate rapidly.

Young people often have their first sexual encounters in an atmosphere that is not at all conducive to relaxed exploration. It has been reported that an individual's first heterosexual coital experience takes place most commonly in either the home or the back seat of an automobile. Both settings can establish patterns of anxious and pressured sexual expression. A typical scene in the home might involve a young couple ostensibly watching Johnny Carson, while furtively having intercourse on the living room sofa, one ear listening for the sounds of distant stirring (what a time for Dad to decide to have a late night ham sandwich!). The back seat of a car is often no better. Consider the following account:

> When I was young, the logical choice of locations for sexual intimacy was the local lovers' lane, a tall butte in the middle of suburbia we called "the rock." The county sheriff's department took their role as protectors of the public morality quite seriously, patrolling this area with precision regularity, every 7 to 10 minutes as I recall. The criterion for not being hassled was two or more heads visible. Quite obviously, one's capacity for relaxed sharing was seriously damaged by such close scrutiny unless he or she was content to restrict the evening's activities to stargazing! (Authors' files)

Situations like these may have powerful conditioning effects: The sooner ejaculation occurs and intercourse is over, the quicker will be the relief from the unpleasant state of anxiety. Such early experiences may establish a strong tendency toward rapid ejaculation, which can be quite difficult to overcome later in life.

Any one or a combination of the situations just outlined may lead to prematurity difficulties, and anxiety may further strengthen the pattern. This is particularly true in situations where the individual or couple attempt changes that result only in additional, frequently magnified, failures. The consequent anxiety often promotes muscle tension (myotonia), which tends to hasten orgasm.

Premature Orgasm in Women

The problem of female prematurity has not received a great deal of attention, but conversations with colleagues, students, and friends have convinced us that some women do have concerns about too-rapid orgasms. Surveys of our women students indicate that 32% occasionally reach orgasm sooner than desired, and 8% report this to occur frequently. Prematurity may be a problem when the woman reaches orgasm before her partner and does not want to continue (women sometimes find that their clitoris or vulva becomes extremely sensitive after orgasms). More commonly, however, it is a problem for a different reason—it happens to some women when they feel the pressure to have an orgasm sooner than they want to:

> Sometimes when we make love, with him using his mouth to pleasure me, and I'm really getting into it, bang, he wants me to come just like that! I mean, sometimes I just want to lay back, fantasizing and enjoying, making it last and last. When he says "What's the matter, what am I doing wrong?" it really ruins it for me. He's not doing anything wrong with his mouth. It's the head trip he is laying on me—like I've got to produce the big O instantly or his ego or masculinity will be threatened. All I want to do is enjoy for awhile. Is that asking too much? Why does lovemaking have to be so product-oriented? (Authors' files)

Often only the woman is aware of and concerned about her prematurity. Considering the emphasis on sexual performance in our society, it is unlikely that most male partners would view female orgasm, regardless of the speed with which it occurs, with concern. Quite the contrary, as the preceding account illustrates, a man might even view his partner's rapid orgasm as a sign of his skill.

Faking Orgasms

A final orgasmic difficulty we will discuss is **faking orgasms**—pretending to experience orgasm without actually doing so. This kind of sexual deception is typically discussed in reference to women, and it happens quite often. According to a recent survey of female students in our sexuality classes, 62% have faked an orgasm at some time. This statistic is comparable to Hite's 1976 findings.

Unlike some of the other difficulties discussed in this chapter, faking orgasm reflects a conscious decision. A person is often motivated to engage in such deception by real or imagined performance pressures. Some additional factors related to faking orgasms may include a lack of communication or knowledge about sexual techniques, a need for partner approval, little hope about changing the partner's behavior, or an attempt to hide a deteriorating relationship or to protect a partner's ego (Lauersen and Graves, 1984). The following comments, all by women, reveal some of these motivations:

> He feels badly if I don't have an orgasm during intercourse, so I fake it, even though I have real ones from oral sex. (Authors' files)

> I get tired of intercourse after a certain period, and there he is, still pumping away, determined not to stop until I come, so I pretend to climax. (Authors' files)

I don't know my partner well enough to tell her what I like, but I don't want her to think it's her fault that I don't come. (Authors' files)

I figure if I don't have orgasms with him, he'll go find someone who does. (Authors' files)

I started our sexual relationship faking, and I don't know how to stop. (Authors' files)

Although some women may find faking orgasm to be an acceptable solution in their individual situation, others find that faking itself becomes troublesome, as revealed in the last of the preceding comments. The effects of faking orgasm can include increased resentment, guilt, anger, and fear of being discovered (Lauersen and Graves, 1984). At the least, faking orgasms creates emotional distance at a time of potential closeness and satisfaction (Masters and Johnson, 1976).

In recent years we have heard an increasing number of reports of men faking orgasms. One survey found that 30% of males reported having faked orgasm (Peterson et al., 1983). Some of this behavior may be related to feeling pressured to reveal virility through multiple orgasmic responses, as revealed in the following account:

Sometimes when I am having sex I feel like my partner wants me to perform like an orgasm machine, pumping them out in rapid succession, both hers and mine. Recently I was with a woman who kept asking "Has it happened for you yet?"—and this after I had already come once and was doing good just to get it up again. Occasionally in these situations I just fake it. I figure since I've come already, she won't know the difference. Also, it is hard for me to admit that one or maybe two orgasms is all that I can produce in a given session. (Authors' files)

Occasionally men who have difficulty with ejaculatory inhibition may fake orgasms in an attempt to hide the problem. This creates another problem in itself, however, for "if their deception is to be successful, they must either forego orgasm altogether or masturbate in solitude later, after their wives are asleep" (Kaplan, 1974, p. 320).

There is often a vicious circle involved in faking orgasms. The person's partner is likely not to know that his or her partner has pretended to climax. Consequently, the deceived partner continues to do what he or she has been led to believe is effective, and the other partner continues to fake to prevent discovery of the deception. This makes it more difficult for the couple to talk about and discover what is gratifying to both of them. Once established, a pattern of deception may be quite difficult to break.

How to best change this pattern of interaction is a matter of personal decision. Some people may not want to change, because faking orgasms serves a purpose in a relationship. A person who does want to change might decide to discontinue faking orgasms without discussing the decision with his or her partner. Under such circumstances, some of the procedures for enhancing sexual pleasure outlined in the next chapter might prove helpful. Another alternative would be to inform one's partner of one's past deception and to discuss the reasons why pretending to climax seemed necessary. Some of the communication strategies outlined in Chapter 8 may help this process along. Maybe some specific difficulties will surface as the motivation for deception, such as female orgasm problems, or retarded ejaculation. It may be helpful, or perhaps necessary, to engage a counselor to help communicate with a partner. Doing this may also facilitate efforts to establish more rewarding sexual behaviors.

Coital Pain

Both men and women can experience coital pain, although it is more common for women to have this problem. The medical term for painful intercourse is **dyspareunia**.

Painful Intercourse in Women

Experiencing pain with intercourse is very likely to affect a woman's sexual arousal. Coital discomfort stems from a variety of causes, and for this reason it is important for the woman to determine specifically where the pain is.

Discomfort at the vaginal entrance or inside the vaginal walls is commonly due to a lack of adequate lubrication. Typically this occurs because a woman has been insufficiently aroused. There are many reasons why a woman may not become aroused—a lack of effective stimulation, the myriad of cultural inhibitions that affect sexual responsiveness, or possibly relationship difficulties with her partner. Physiological conditions, such as insufficient hormones, may also reduce lubrication. The use of a lubricating jelly can provide a temporary solution so that intercourse can take place comfortably, but this may bring only short term relief. It would no doubt be better if the woman could discover the cause of her discomfort, and then take steps to remedy the situation. A woman can consult a physician for help with physiological causes of this difficulty.

There are also a variety of other causes for vaginal discomfort during intercourse. Yeast, bacterial, and trichomoniasis infections cause inflammations of the vaginal walls and may result in painful intercourse. This problem is often related to the one just described: Intercourse with insufficient lubrication irritates the walls and increases the possibility of vaginal infections. Foam, contraceptive cream or jelly, condoms, and diaphragms may irritate the vaginas of some women. Pain at the opening of the vagina may also be attributed to an intact hymen, a Bartholin's gland infection, or scar tissue at the opening.

Another area where there may be discomfort is the clitoral glans. Occasionally smegma collects under the clitoral hood and may cause distress when the hood is moved during sexual stimulation. Gentle washing of the clitoris and hood may help prevent this.

Pain deep in the pelvis during coital thrusting may be due to jarring of the ovaries or stretching of the uterine ligaments. A woman may experience this type of discomfort only in certain positions or at certain times. Some women report that it only occurs around the time they are ovulating. Avoiding positions or movements that aggravate the pain is the first solution, and if a woman has more control of the pelvic movements during coitus, she may feel more secure about being able to avoid pain. If the discomfort is difficult to remedy, she should probably consult a physician, for pain during intercourse can also be caused by medical problems.

Another source of deep pelvic pain is *endometriosis*, a condition in which tissue that normally grows on the walls of the uterus implants on various parts of the abdominal cavity. The endometrial tissue can prevent the internal organs from moving freely, resulting in pain during coitus. Birth control pills are sometimes prescribed to control the buildup of tissue during the monthly cycle.

Infections in the uterus, such as gonorrhea, may also result in painful intercourse. In fact, pelvic pain may often be the first physical symptom noticed by a woman who has gonorrhea. If the infection has caused considerable scar tissue to develop, surgical treatment may be necessary. Childbirth and rape may tear the ligaments that hold the uterus in the pelvic cavity, which can result in pain during coitus. Surgery can relieve this difficulty partially or completely.

Vaginismus

Vaginismus is characterized by strong involuntary contractions of the muscles in the outer third of the vagina (see Figure 16.1). The contraction can be so strong that attempts at inserting a penis into the vagina are very painful to the woman. A woman with vaginismus will usually experience this same contracting spasm during a pelvic exam. Even the insertion of a finger into her vagina can cause great discomfort.

Milder forms of vaginismus can produce minor unpleasant sensations that are chronically irritating—enough to have an inhibiting effect on a woman's sexual interest and arousal. It is important for women and their partners to know that intercourse, tampon use, and pelvic exams should not be uncomfortable. If they are, investigating the cause of the discomfort is essential (Kessler, 1985).

Masters and Johnson (1970) state that vaginismus is often linked with chronic painful intercourse, repeated erectile difficulties of a woman's partner, strong orthodox religious taboos about sex, a homosexual orientation, past physical or sexual assault,

Figure 16.1

Constriction of Vaginal Muscles During Vaginismus
Vaginismus, characterized by strong involuntary contractions of the muscles in the outer third of the vagina, is a relatively uncommon sexual difficulty.

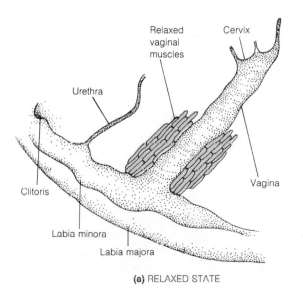

(a) RELAXED STATE

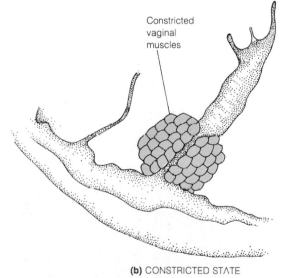

(b) CONSTRICTED STATE

or feelings of hostility or fear toward a partner. It is important to note that although a woman who experiences vaginismus can learn to prevent the contractions, she does not consciously will them to occur. Rather, they are a conditioned, involuntary response to fearful, painful, or conflicted situations or feelings. When a woman experiences physical pain from vaginismus, she will probably be anxious about pain occurring the next time she attempts intercourse. Her apprehensions will increase the likelihood of involuntary muscle contractions, and when her expectations are once again met, she will be even more anxious on subsequent occasions.

The incidence of vaginismus is believed to be very low. Some women who experience vaginismus are sexually responsive and orgasmic with manual and oral stimulation. However, since most couples regard coitus as a highly important aspect of their sexual relationship, this difficulty typically causes great concern.

Painful Intercourse in Men

Dyspareunia in men is unusual, but it does occur. If the foreskin of an uncircumcised male is too tight, he may experience pain during sexual arousal and difficulty reaching orgasm. In such circumstances minor surgery may be called for. Inadequate hygiene of an uncircumcised penis can result in the accumulation of smegma or infections beneath the foreskin, causing irritation of the glans during sexual stimulation. This problem can be prevented by routinely pulling back the foreskin and washing the glans area. Another possible source of pain or discomfort is **Peyronie's disease**, where fibrous tissue and calcium deposits may develop in the space above and between the cavernous bodies of the penis. Medical treatments can sometimes be effective in treating this condition. Finally, infections of the urethra, bladder, prostate gland, or seminal vesicles may induce burning, itching, or pain during or after ejaculation (Masters and Johnson, 1970). Proper medical attention can generally alleviate this source of discomfort during coitus.

This chapter has outlined some of the reasons people encounter dissatisfactions, problems, or discomfort in what can be an experience of great pleasure and joy. It remains for us to explore ways of preventing or overcoming these difficulties. This will be our focus in the next chapter.

Summary

Origins of Sexual Difficulties

1. Sexual problems in the general population appear to be common. For example, a nationwide random survey found that one in seven people reported problems in their sex lives.

2. Cross-cultural variations in sexual attitudes and behaviors reflect the powerful impact of culture and society on sexuality.

3. The acquired attitude that sex is sinful and negative feelings about one's genitals can be detrimental to acceptance of one's body and sexual feelings.

4. The double standard prescribes opposite expectations of sexual behavior for males and females. Both sets of expectations can have negative effects on sexuality.

5. The cultural notion that "real sex" equals coitus often limits the erotic potential of sexual interaction.

6. Goal orientation in sexual expression is a culturally acquired attitude that can increase performance pressure.

7. Sexual difficulties can be related to personal factors such as lack of sexual knowledge, problems of self-concept, or emotional difficulties. Experiencing sexual assault often leads to sexual problems.

8. Ineffective communication can often inhibit sexual satisfaction.

9. Fear of pregnancy or a homosexual orientation can negatively affect heterosexual experiences.

10. Illnesses, drugs, and painful intercourse are organic difficulties that can interfere with sexual response.

Desire Phase Difficulties

11. Inhibited sexual desire (ISD) is characterized by a lack of interest in sexual fantasy and activity. ISD sometimes stems from fear of sexual intimacy.

12. Dissatisfaction with frequency of sexual activity occurs when a couple is not able to compromise about their individual preferences.

13. Sexual aversion is an extreme, irrational fear or dislike of sexual activity.

Excitement Phase Difficulties

14. A lack of vaginal lubrication indicates an inhibition of the vasocongestive response. This inhibition may be caused by physiological or psychological factors.

15. Erectile inhibition can be primary (never having completed vaginal or anal penetration) or secondary (having previously been able to maintain erections during intercourse). Perhaps 50%–60% of erection difficulties are partially or totally caused by physiological problems.

Orgasm Phase Difficulties

16. Inhibited orgasm, or inorgasmia, occurs mostly in women. Inorgasmia can be primary, secondary, situational, or coital.

17. Primary inorgasmia means that a woman has never experienced orgasm by any means of self or partner stimulation.

18. Secondary inorgasmia means a woman has experienced orgasm but no longer does so.

19. Situational inorgasmia describes a woman who can experience orgasm in one situation but not another; for example, during masturbation but not with a partner.

20. Coital inorgasmia refers to a woman having orgasm with a partner, but not during intercourse. Coitus provides mostly indirect clitoral stimulation, and for many women is not sufficient to result in orgasm.

21. Ejaculatory inhibition is the inability of a man to ejaculate (usually during coitus).

22. This text defines premature ejaculation as reaching orgasm so quickly as to significantly reduce enjoyment of the experience or to interfere with the partner's gratification. This problem is a common one.

23. Many men establish patterns of ejaculating rapidly from hurried masturbation, "circle jerks," and furtive sexual experiences.

24. Both men and women fake orgasm. Pretending may perpetuate ineffective patterns of relating.

Coital Pain

25. Pain during coitus, or dyspareunia, is very disruptive to sexual interest and arousal in both men and women. Numerous physical problems can cause painful intercourse.

26. Vaginismus is an involuntary contraction of the outer vaginal muscles that makes penetration of the vagina difficult and painful.

Thought Provokers

1. What positive and negative effects do you think traditional gender roles can have on sexual functioning?

2. Describe a hypothetical example of an individual with a sexual problem stemming from a combination of cultural, personal, interpersonal, and organic factors.

3. Do you think men or women are more prone to sexual problems? Why?

Suggested Readings

Albee, George; Gordon, Sol; and Leitenberg, Harold (Eds.). *Promoting Sexual Responsibility and Preventing Sexual Problems*. Hanover, Mass.: University Press of New England, 1983. This book offers an excellent overview of philosophical, social, and theological issues related to sexual responsibility and difficulties.

Belliveau, Fred, and Richter, Lin. *Understanding Human Sexual Inadequacy*. New York: Bantam, 1970. A conversationally written analysis of Masters and Johnson's work with sexual problems.

Kaplan, Helen. *The Evaluation of Sexual Disorders*. New York: Brunner/Mazel, 1983. A thorough and scholarly presentation of information about psychosexual and medical evaluation of sexual problems.

Zilbergeld, Bernie. *Male Sexuality: A Guide to Sexual Fulfillment*. Boston: Little, Brown, 1978. An exceptionally well-written and informative treatment of male sexuality, including such topics as sexual functioning, self-awareness, and overcoming difficulties.

We have been led astray by our economic and biological models to think that the aim of the love act is the orgasm. The French have a saying which, referring to eros, carries more truth: "The aim of desire is not its satisfaction but its prolongation."

Rollo May
Love and Will (1969)

Increasing
Sexual Satisfaction

The PLISSIT Model of Sex Therapy
Basics of Sex Therapy
Specific Suggestions for Women
Specific Suggestions for Men
Treatment for Inhibited Sexual Desire
Guidelines for Seeking Professional Assistance

THIS CHAPTER FOCUSES on approaches in sex therapy and methods for increasing sexual satisfaction. The activities we discuss may be pursued individually or by a couple; they range from expanding self-knowledge to sharing more effectively with a partner. Much of what follows embraces our belief that all of us have the potential for self-help. The various suggestions offered here have proved helpful in the lives of many people. However, the same techniques do not work for everyone, and exercises often need to be individually modified. Furthermore, professional help may be called for in those cases where individual efforts, couple efforts, or both do not produce the desired results. Recognizing that therapy is sometimes necessary to promote change, we have included guidelines for seeking sex therapy in the last section of this chapter.

The PLISSIT Model of Sex Therapy

There are many approaches to sex therapy. However, most sex therapies have several elements in common. The PLISSIT model of sex therapy (Annon, 1974) specifies four levels of treatment; each successive level provides increasingly in-depth therapy. PLISSIT is an acronym for permission, limited information, specific suggestions, and intensive therapy.

Although PLISSIT describes formal levels of sex therapy, many people find similar kinds of help in informal ways. A trusted friend saying "I feel the same way too," a lover enjoying our body in spite of our insecurities about size or shape, a television interview with someone in a situation similar to ours, or books we read at the right time can give us needed permission and useful information and suggestions.

Permission

A therapist can play an important role in reassuring clients that thoughts, feelings, fantasies, desires, and behaviors that enhance their satisfaction and do not have potentially negative consequences are normal. Helping individuals and couples to appreciate their unique patterns and desires instead of comparing themselves with friends or national averages of frequency is sometimes all the help they need. Another aspect of this level of therapy is giving people permission *not* to engage in certain behaviors unless they choose to do so. For example, a therapist can support a person's desire to set limits about sexual relationships, not have orgasms with every sexual encounter, or not engage in an undesired sexual activity.

Limited Information

In the limited information level of treatment a therapist provides the client with information that is specific to his or her sexual concern. A person can use information, as well as permission, to change thoughts and feelings that impede his or her sexual satisfaction. Information that helps a person to view sexuality as positive and to think, talk, and fantasize about sex is a major component in treatment of many sexual problems. Factual information about concerns with penis size, clitoral sensitivity, or effects of medications on sexual response can alleviate anxiety and problems related to lack of knowledge.

Specific Suggestions

Specific suggestions are the activities and "homework" exercises that therapists recommend to clients to help them reach a goal. These behavioral approaches form the foundation of contemporary sex therapy and were initially popularized by Masters and Johnson (1970). Other therapists have modified and developed further techniques discussed in this chapter. Most are designed to reduce anxiety, enhance communication, and to teach new, arousal-enhancing and -enabling behaviors. Masturbation techniques, sensate focus, and the squeeze technique described later in this chapter are examples of specific suggestions common in sex therapy.

A therapist may also suggest that a client read books that give permission, information, and specific suggestions. In fact, some therapists ask potential clients to read certain books before their first therapy appointment. In some cases, an appropriate book can help resolve problems so that therapy is no longer needed. In others, it can enhance the therapy process (McGovern, 1982).

Intensive Therapy

If a client's problem has not been resolved by the first three therapy levels, intensive therapy may be required. According to Annon (1974), intensive therapy is needed in about 1 out of 10 sexual problem cases. These are likely to be situations in which

Professional assistance can be helpful in resolving sexual difficulties.

personal emotional difficulties or significant relationship problems interfere with sexual expression. In these instances, behavioral techniques alone are not adequate to help the person resolve her or his difficulties.

Treatment that combines behavioral techniques with the development of insight into unconscious conflicts is a recent development in the sex therapy field. In insight-oriented therapy, the therapist provides interpretations and reflection to help clients gain awareness and understanding of the unconscious feelings and thoughts that have been contributing to their sexual difficulties. Helen Singer Kaplan (1974) calls this **psychosexual therapy**. Kaplan believes that many people's sexual behavior is governed by unconscious guilt and anxiety. These people often unconsciously avoid sexually exciting positive relationships or effective forms of stimulation. For example, a woman who becomes aroused from light touching, but unconsciously is anxious about feeling "turned on," may interfere with her partner touching her in such a manner. When he begins to stroke her lightly, she may immediately think "Oh, he's bored" and request intercourse, denying herself an opportunity to respond to his touches. The integration of sex therapy exercises with insight can be especially useful: Discussions about clients' reactions to the behavioral touching experiences often help them realize the extent to which they avoid receiving and giving pleasure.

Insights gained in this type of intensive therapy often pertain to patterns developed in childhood that are the root of current problems. In psychosexual therapy, the therapist helps the client examine how present feelings relate to childhood influences. Since intimate adult relationships can be greatly affected by the first significant relationships with parents, awareness and insight into these are sometimes necessary for resolution of a sexual difficulty.

Another addition to the sex therapy methods is **systems theory** (LoPiccolo, 1985). In contrast to Kaplan's psychosexual therapy, which emphasizes insight into the historical causes of a sexual problem, systems theory is based on the concept that the identified problems serve important current functions in the relationship. For example, in one case a woman's inhibited sexual desire helped to maintain some separateness in an otherwise overly-close relationship:

> Brad and Lisa had an almost nonexistent boundary between them as individuals. When not working, they were always together, and when at home, they would stay in the same room. There was rarely a division of labor; instead, they did everything together. They shared the same soda in the therapist's office, smoked the same cigarette, talked for each other, and knew everything about their mate. They had stopped seeing old friends and had only a few acquaintances. They both . . . admitted to an almost phobic response to strangers. . . . Thus Lisa's inhibited sexual desire was an attempt to correct too much intimacy in the relationship. (Fish et al., 1984, pp. 9–10)

An important part of systems therapy is to gain understanding about the function(s) that the sexual problems serve. This can enable the couple to make changes so that they no longer need the sexual difficulty. For example, in the case of Brad and Lisa, the therapist would help them to be more separate in their daily lives so they could be intimate and close sexually.

Psychosexual therapy and systems theory are two methods of helping individuals and couples who need more intensive approaches to resolving their sexual difficulties.

Let us now return to examine some of the specific behavioral methods used in sex therapy. These techniques need not be limited to the setting of formal sex therapy; they can also be used on one's own to enhance sexual awareness and satisfaction and to add variety to a sexual relationship. Many of these suggestions are equally applicable to heterosexual and homosexual couples. Some specific approaches for homosexual people, similar to those developed for heterosexual couples, are outlined in Masters and Johnson's publication, *Homosexuality in Perspective* (1979).

Basics of Sex Therapy

Many people's childhood sexual development is influenced by negative conditioning, limiting attitudes, and a lack of self-exploration. All of these factors can hinder later sexual enjoyment or functioning; however, increased self-knowledge may help to modify negative preconceptions and feelings. With this in mind, we briefly outline procedures for improving awareness of your body and of activities that provide the most pleasurable stimulation.

Self-Awareness

People who know themselves—their sexual feelings, their needs, and how their bodies respond—are often better able to share this valuable information with a partner than people who are unaware of their sexual needs and potentials. A good way to increase self-awareness, as well as comfort with our sexuality, is to become well-acquainted with our sexual anatomy. It is not unusual for women to report never having looked at their own vulvas. While men may not feel quite so alienated from their bodies, many are not comfortable with their genital structure. The following anecdote reveals the extent of the negative feelings that some people experience:

> I find it difficult to undress in the presence of my lover. I guess this has a lot to do with how I feel about my body. Every time I look at my genitals in the mirror I think "My God, how ridiculous they look. Here is this funny little shriveled-up thing hanging between my legs." It doesn't look much better when erect. I can't remember when I first got the idea my genitals were dirty. I even perfected a technique where I could unzip and whip it out without touching the nasty little thing. (Authors' files)

We strongly recommend becoming familiar with your genitals by looking and touching, as a process for increasing comfort with your body. It can be helpful to include all areas of your anatomy, not just the genital region. Examine yourself visually and experiment with different touches, perhaps using a massage lotion to make the movements more pleasant.

Some people find that knowledge obtained during self-exploration exercises may later be shared with a partner. Explorations of one's own body may provide the motivation to apply the same process to exploring and examining the body of a partner. Exchanging information can be immensely valuable in increasing both comfort with and knowledge about each other. A later section, "Sensate Focus," elaborates on mutual exploration.

Masturbation Exercises

Masturbation exercises are an effective way for a person, male or female, to learn about and experience sexual response. They can be enjoyed for themselves and the knowledge they provide can be shared with a partner. Many people have some negative feelings about masturbation that intrude on sensations of pleasure. Changing these negative attitudes and increasing self-knowledge may take some time, but the rewards can be worth the effort.

There are many variations of masturbation, and you can experiment to find what is most enjoyable. Some people think of masturbation as making love to themselves. They treat themselves as they would a special lover, with soft lights, music, clean sheets, fragrant oils, and lots of time to develop arousal slowly and tenderly. It may be helpful to include several erogenous zones. Concentrate your stroking on areas that feel particularly pleasurable. While lubricating materials like body lotion, oil, or saliva will often improve sensations, women should be careful to avoid using any lubrications that are not water soluble (such as vaseline) in the vagina, because they may cause irritation or infection.

If you choose to experiment with masturbation exercises, it is important to remember that the major purpose of the experience is to become more aware of your body's sensations. You may find it helpful to experiment with several positions. Some people find that lying on their back is best; others prefer to stand or sit. Many people use sexual fantasy to enhance the sensual experience. Further information on masturbation has been provided in Chapter 9, and there is more discussion later in this chapter in the section "Specific Suggestions for Women, Becoming Orgasmic."

Communication

Before discussing specific ways of dealing with sexual difficulties, we want to stress again the importance of communication. Many people find it difficult to talk about the sexual area of their relationships, but failure to communicate needs and expectations can hinder the resolution of sexual problems and may even contribute to some difficulties.

One of the primary benefits of sex therapy, whether it is learning to have orgasms with partners, how to overcome premature ejaculation, or almost any other shared problem, is that couples participating together in the treatment process often develop more effective communication skills. The following account, from one of our students, reflects this potential benefit:

> When you first discussed the "squeeze technique" [discussed later in this chapter] in class, I was excited to try it out with my partner. However, I didn't know how to talk about it. It wasn't like he had never mentioned his problem before. He would say he was sorry he was so fast, and that maybe it would get better with time. Finally, I asked him to come to class with me the day you showed the film demonstrating the technique. Man, did we do a lot of talking after it was over. He was anxious to give it a try, and we felt that with your lectures and the movie, we could do it on our own. At first we made some mistakes, like not doing enough sensate focus and him waiting too long to tell me to put the squeeze on. In fact, it was only when we were really talking openly that things began to work well. He showed me how he liked to be

stimulated, things he had never told me before. During sensate focus we shared a lot of feelings. He became much more aware of my needs and what I needed to be satisfied. We really started getting into a lot of variety in our lovemaking, whereas before it had usually consisted of just kissing and intercourse. By the way, the squeeze technique did work in slowing him down, but I think the biggest benefit has been breaking down the communication barriers. Now the talking is almost as fun as the doing and it sure makes sex a whole lot better! (Authors' files)

Communication itself may not solve a sexual difficulty. It is, however, a very important element, for it is helpful not only in working out a specific problem but also in establishing and maintaining mutual understanding that can make a relationship stronger. In a study of college students, general assertiveness was a significant predictor of sexual satisfaction (Laflin, 1985).

Sensate Focus

One of the most useful couple-oriented activities for mutually enhancing sexual enjoyment is a series of touching experiences called **sensate focus** (see Figure 17.1). Masters and Johnson labeled this technique and use it as a basic step in the treatment of many sexual problems. It can be extremely helpful in reducing anxiety caused by goal orientation and in increasing communication, pleasure, and closeness. It is by no means a technique only appropriate for sex therapy but is rather an activity all couples can use to enhance sexual relationships. In the sensate focus touching experiences, partners take turns touching each other while following some essential guidelines. We shall assume in the following descriptions that the one doing the touching is a

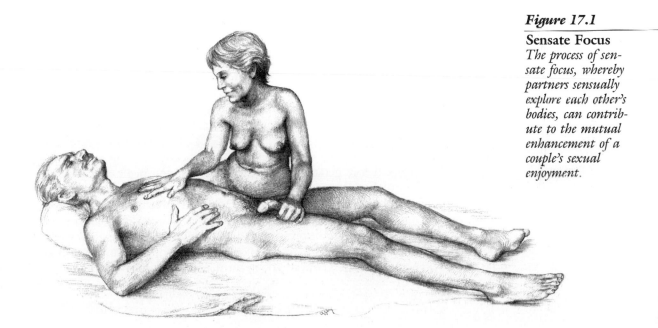

Figure 17.1

Sensate Focus
The process of sensate focus, whereby partners sensually explore each other's bodies, can contribute to the mutual enhancement of a couple's sexual enjoyment.

woman and the one being touched is a man. Of course, homosexual as well as heterosexual couples can do these exercises, and in either case the partners periodically change roles.

To begin with, the person who will be doing the touching takes some time to "set the scene" in a way that is comfortable and pleasant for herself; for example, by unplugging the phone and arranging a warm, cozy place with relaxing music and lighting. The couple then undresses and the toucher begins to explore her partner's body, following this important guideline: She is *not* to touch to please or arouse her partner, but for her *own* interest and pleasure. The goal is for the toucher to focus on her perception of textures, shapes, and temperatures. The nondemand quality of this kind of touching is what helps both partners to remove performance pressure obstacles to arousal. The person being touched remains quiet except when any touch is uncomfortable. In that case he describes the uncomfortable feeling and what the toucher could do to make it more comfortable; for example, "That feels ticklish—please touch the other side of my arm." This guideline helps the toucher attend fully to her own sensations from touching rather than worry about whether or not something is unpleasant to the other person.

In the next sensate focus experience the couple changes roles of touching and being touched, following the same guidelines as before. In these first sensate focus experiences, intercourse and touching breasts and genitals are "off limits." After the couple has been able to focus on touch and to communicate uncomfortable feelings, they include breasts and genitals. Again, the toucher explores for her own interest and pleasure. Once the couple is comfortable including breasts and genitals, they learn a "hand riding" technique in order to learn more about what is pleasurable to one another. The person being touched places his hand over his partner's hand and gently guides the location, movement, and strength of the caresses. Following this step, the partners progress to a simultaneous sensate focus experience. Now they touch one another at the same time and experience feelings from both touching and being touched.

Sensate focus is an excellent way to learn to respond erotically with all areas of the body. It is also a good vehicle for learning the exquisitely sensitive areas on one's partner's body. We strongly recommend it as an ongoing practice to enhance sexual sharing and maintain total body sensuality. In therapy sensate focus experiences usually precede and form the foundation for specific techniques for resolving arousal and orgasm difficulties. These techniques are discussed later in the text.

A modified sensate focus approach can be an excellent way to begin a sexual relationship with a new partner. We suggest that at an early point in a developing intimate relationship, before genital contact has occurred, you begin sexual sharing with a period of mutual exploration, a time when each may acquire knowledge about the other's body, feelings, sensitivities, and needs. Make an agreement to avoid genital sex during the initial stages. This can reduce anxiety and give you a chance to experience mutual discovery without the pressure of goal orientation. For a man or woman who has had difficulties in previous sexual encounters, the opportunity to feel and respond spontaneously, with no need to perform, can be a particularly valuable experience.

Masturbation with a Partner Present

It can be particularly valuable for couples to let each other know what kind of touching they find arousing. Masturbating in the presence of a partner may be a way to share this kind of information (see Figure 17.2). A woman describes how she accomplished this:

> When I wanted to share with my partner what I had learned about myself through masturbation, I felt super uptight about how to do it. Finally, we decided that to begin with, I would be in the bedroom and he would be in the living room, knowing I was masturbating. Then he would sit on the bed, not looking at me. The next step was for him to hold and kiss me while I was touching myself. Then I could be comfortable showing him how I touch myself. (Authors' files)

Couples who feel comfortable incorporating self-stimulation into their sexual relationship open many options for themselves. When only one of them feels sexual, that person can masturbate with the other present, perhaps touching, perhaps kissing. This may sometimes lead to shared sexual activity:

> Occasionally, when I don't feel like having sex, my wife will coax me into taking a shower with her while she masturbates with the shower head massager. Sometimes it's just nice to hold her and feel her respond. Other times, watching her getting turned on gets me going and we end up making love in the shower. (Authors' files)

Figure 17.2

Masturbation with Partner Present
Masturbating in the presence of a partner can be an effective way for an individual to indicate what kind of touching she or he finds arousing.

The experiences suggested in the preceding pages may all be helpful in increasing sexual satisfaction, whether an individual or couple have a specific difficulty or their goal is simply to find out more about themselves. Beyond these general exercises, though, specific exercises or techniques can sometimes aid in reducing or overcoming particular sexual difficulties that can be highly troublesome. We described some of these difficulties in Chapter 16, and in the remainder of this chapter we will look at some strategies that have been used to deal with them. For purposes of clarity and easy reference, these strategies are organized according to whether they deal with primarily female or primarily male sexual problems, except treatment of ISD. As in the previous chapter, however, we should stress that these discussions are not only applicable to one gender. Men can gain some understanding of both themselves and female partners from reading the section on specific female strategies; women can gain similarly from reading the discussions of techniques for men.

Specific Suggestions for Women

The following paragraphs suggest procedures that may be helpful to women in learning to increase sexual arousal and to reach orgasm by themselves or with a partner. They also include suggestions for dealing with vaginismus.

Becoming Orgasmic

Learning effective self-stimulation is often recommended for women who have never experienced orgasm. One advantage to self-stimulation is that a woman without a partner can learn to become orgasmic. For a woman with a sexual partner, becoming orgasmic first by masturbation may help to develop a sense of sexual autonomy that can increase the likelihood of satisfaction with a partner.

Therapy programs for inorgasmia are based on progressive self-awareness activities that a woman does at home between therapy sessions. The step-by-step activities are often presented by a therapist in a small group of women who want to learn to experience orgasm. Women in the group also provide each other with support and encouragement. These same steps are also used in individual sex counseling. Both individual and group counseling for inorgasmic women can provide information, permission-giving, and individualized problem-solving.

Another source of guidance for learning to experience orgasms comes from books such as *For Yourself; The Fulfillment of Female Sexuality* by Lonnie Barbach (1975) or *Becoming Orgasmic: A Sexual Growth Program* by Julia Heiman and Leslie and Joseph LoPiccolo (1976). The following is a brief outline of the therapy program presented in Barbach's book:

1. *Time commitment.* Set aside one hour every day to do the following "home-play" exercises.
2. *Mirror exercise.* Using a full-length mirror, look at your nude body from all angles. Examine uncritically the shapes, colorations, and textures of the different areas.

3. *Body exploration.* Using your hands, and body lotion or powder if desired, explore your entire body, from your face to your toes. Take lots of time and focus on the feelings in your fingertips and in your body. Notice differences in sensation. Compare doing this with your eyes open and closed.

4. *Vulva self-exam.* Locate and explore the different structures of the vulva. Learn and practice Kegel exercises (outlined in Chapter 4).

5. *Self-stimulation.* Find and use a lotion or oil which contains no alcohol and is water soluble. Use this on your vulva to enhance the touch sensations. For the first several sessions, experiment and discover genital touches that are pleasurable, but do not attempt to reach orgasm. It's very important to remove the goal orientation of orgasm at this point. If you feel yourself becoming aroused, reduce the stimulation. Then begin again, allowing yourself to become slightly more aroused than previously. Focus on the pleasurable sensations. Allow yourself to have erotic fantasies if you so desire. Experiment with Kegel squeezes during stimulation.

6. *Orgasm.* Once you are becoming aroused from self-stimulation and believe you want to proceed to orgasm, continue the touching that is most arousing. If interfering thoughts or feelings arise, allow yourself to be aware of them and then refocus on the sensations. If you experience difficulty "letting go," it may be helpful to try acting out an orgasm—exaggerate the movements and sounds you associate with orgasm.

7. *Use of a vibrator.* Vibrators are a potentially pleasurable option for self-stimulation. They are sometimes used to help an inorgasmic woman experience sexual climax for the first time so she knows that she can experience this response. A vibrator is often less tiring to use and supplies more intense stimulation than the fingers, and it is sometimes recommended for a woman who has not experienced orgasm after a couple of weeks of daily self-stimulation exercises. After she has a couple of orgasms with the vibrator, it is helpful for her to stop using it and return to manual stimulation, so she can learn to respond in this manner too. This is important, because it is easier for a partner to replicate a woman's own touch than the stimulation of a vibrator.

If following these exercises does not result in orgasm and this concerns you, that does not necessarily mean that something is "wrong." It may be that you could benefit by reading more. The books listed earlier should be helpful, and your sexuality course teacher may have other suggestions. Counselors are also available, as mentioned earlier, to answer questions and provide more personal assistance. Sharing discoveries with a partner may be another area to explore.

Experiencing Orgasm with a Partner

As we saw in Chapter 16, the origins of difficulties in reaching orgasm may be highly complex, involving conditioning and experiences of which a person may not even be consciously aware. This is one reason why any step-by-step guidelines for learning to reach orgasm should be thought of as aids, not solutions. The steps that follow are intended to help a woman experience orgasm with a partner. They are based on techniques developed in a therapy context.

After the couple is comfortable with the sensate focus exercises described earlier, they proceed to genital exploration. The exercise is called a *sexological exam*. Each partner takes turns visually exploring the other's genitals, locating all the parts discussed in Chapters 4 and 5. After looking thoroughly they experiment with touch, noticing and sharing what different areas feel like (Barbach, 1975).

The next step is for the woman to stimulate herself in her partner's presence. The woman can use self-stimulation methods that she has learned are effective and share her arousal with her partner. Her partner can be holding and kissing her or lying beside her, as was shown in Figure 17.2. This step is often a difficult one, and some women begin by asking their partners to be in another room while they are masturbating. Slowly, as the woman determines she is ready for the next step, her partner can be progressively closer and more involved (Barbach, 1975).

Next the partner begins nondemanding manual-genital pleasuring. The couple can do this in any position that suits them. Masters and Johnson (1970) recommend the position illustrated in Figure 17.3. (We are supposing in this discussion that the partner is a man.) The partner leans slightly back, propped with pillows; the woman

Figure 17.3

Back-to-Chest Position for Genital Sensate Focus

sits between his legs with her back supported by his chest. The woman places her hand over the partner's hand on her genitals to guide the stimulation. They can use lotion or oil to increase sensation. The partner is to make no assumptions about how to touch, but rather to be guided by the woman's words and hand. The purpose of initial sessions is for the partner to discover what is arousing to the woman, rather than to produce orgasm. If the woman thinks she is ready to experience orgasm, she indicates to her partner to continue the stimulation until climax is achieved. Orgasm will probably not occur until after several sessions.

There are several specific techniques that couples can use to increase a woman's arousal and the possibility of orgasm during intercourse. The first has to do with initiating intercourse. Rather than beginning intercourse after a certain number of minutes of "foreplay" or when there is sufficient lubrication, a woman can be guided by her feeling of what might be called "readiness." Not all women experience this feeling of readiness, but for those who do, beginning intercourse at this time may enhance the resultant erotic sensations.

A woman who wants increased stimulation during coitus may benefit from direct manual stimulation of her clitoris (see Chapter 9, Figures 9.6 and 9.8). This often results in greater arousal and sometimes in orgasm. The woman-above intercourse position is commonly used in this situation. After both partners are aroused— the man with an erection and the woman with adequate lubrication—and feel ready for intercourse, she sits astride and guides his penis into her vagina. She remains motionless for several moments, allowing both of them to be aware of sensations. Then she begins slow, exploring pelvic movements with the intention of discovering what is pleasurable to her. Her partner is to be receptive to her movements rather than actively initiating his own (Masters and Johnson, 1970). *The Hite Report* emphasizes the imporance of female-initiated movements:

> Orgasms during intercourse in this study usually seemed to result from a conscious attempt by the woman to center some kind of clitoral area contact for herself during intercourse, usually involving contact with the man's pubic area. This clitoral stimulation during intercourse can be thought of then as basically stimulating yourself while intercourse is in progress. Of course, the other person must cooperate. This is essentially the way men get stimulation during intercourse. They rub their penises against our vaginal walls so that the same area they stimulate during masturbation is being stimulated during intercourse. In other words, you have to get the stimulation centered where it feels good. (Hite, 1976, p. 276)

Additionally, a woman can experiment with positions and pelvic thrusts that create more intense internal sensations. Research indicates that conscious actions on the woman's part to facilitate orgasm are important. A sample of college women reported that in order to experience orgasm, they initiated the intercourse position that was most stimulating, concentrated on sensations, stimulated themselves manually, and fantasized (Sholty et al., 1984).

The next step is for the woman to stimulate her clitoris manually during intercourse. She can also use a vibrator, as shown in Figure 17.4. Some men report the vibrations transmitted to their penis as pleasurable. Then she teaches her partner to touch her clitoris (Barbach, 1975). One way for him to be able to touch her clitoris is to turn his hand slightly and use his thumb. The side-to-side coital position also

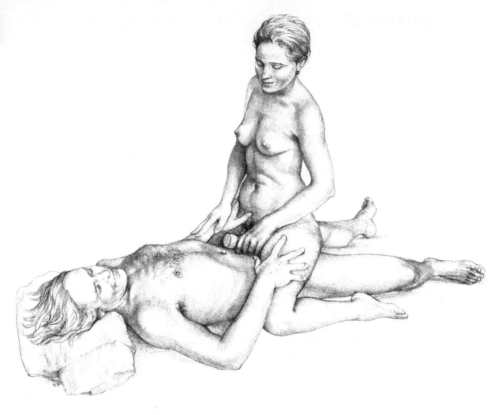

Figure 17.4

The Use of an
Electric Vibrator
for Clitoral
Stimulation
During Coitus

works well for either of them to touch her clitoris. The woman may also find it helpful to experiment with Kegel exercises during penetration.

After several sessions of the woman's controlling pelvic movements and incorporating manual stimulation, the man initiates nondemanding thrusting. The couple can also experiment with other coital positions. For women who wish to try experiencing orgasm without direct clitoral stimulation, Kaplan (1974) suggests the use of the *bridge maneuver*. In this, manual stimulation during intercourse is employed until the woman is very close to climaxing. Then manual stimulation is stopped, and she actively moves her pelvis to provide sufficient stimulation to induce orgasm. In suggesting this maneuver we do not mean to imply that this is "better" than continuing manual stimulation to orgasm. As Kaplan comments:

> We reassure her and her husband that their reliance on clitoral stimulation to achieve orgasm is a normal and authentic response. . . . We emphasize that it is possible for partners . . . [who use these techniques] . . . to have a gloriously rich and fulfilling sex life, providing neither feels that this is an inferior mode of sexual expression. We try in this way to undo the myths surrounding "vaginal" orgasm and the unrealistic ideal of invariable simultaneous orgasms and universal female orgasm on intercourse. (pp. 398–99)

The techniques just described are useful in exploring ways of relating sexually, and they may allow a woman to experience orgasm in some cases. A number of books are available for couples who want more information than we have had space to present here; some of these are listed in the Suggested Readings at the end of this chapter.

Dealing with Vaginismus

Treatment for vaginismus usually begins during a pelvic exam, with the therapist or a consulting physician demonstrating the vaginal spasm reaction to the couple. The woman is then sometimes given relaxation and self-awareness exercises to do in the privacy of her own home. These include a soothing bath, general body exploration, and manual external genital pleasuring. The next steps pertain specifically to resolving the vaginismus. She puts some lubricant, such as K-Y Jelly, at the vaginal opening and practices inserting a fingertip gently into her vagina. This may take several sessions. Once she can do this comfortably, she inserts her entire finger into the vaginal canal. After relaxing with her finger inside, she is to consciously contract and relax the vaginal muscles as with Kegel exercises. The next step is for her to insert two, then three, fingers and continue to practice vaginal muscle contractions and relaxation. Dilators, cylindrical rods of graduated sizes that the woman inserts into her vagina, are also sometimes used to accustom the vaginal muscles to stretching. Once she can comfortably insert one size, she allows it to remain in her vagina for several hours. Concurrently with these "homeplay" exercises she will meet with her therapist to discuss her reactions.

When the woman has completed the preceding steps, her partner joins her in "homeplay" assignments. He visually examines her vulva and proceeds to insert his fingers or dilators, following the same steps she did. Open communication between the partners is essential during these steps. After the man can insert three fingers without inducing a vaginal muscle spasm, the couple continues to the next step, vaginal-penile penetration. The penis and the vaginal opening are well lubricated and the woman slowly guides the penis into her vagina. Once it is inside, the couple remain motionless while she experiences vaginal containment of the penis. After a few moments, he withdraws his penis. The couple will repeat this procedure, and as they continue to be comfortable with penetration they will add pelvic movements and pleasure focusing. Masters and Johnson (1970) report 100% success in alleviating vaginismus using this method. However, more current research indicates that vaginismus can be difficult to treat successfully, especially in relationships in which couples have never had penile-vaginal intercourse (LoPiccolo, 1982).

Specific Suggestions for Men

In the following paragraphs we outline methods for dealing with the common difficulties of premature ejaculation and erectile inhibition. We also discuss a way of treating the less common condition of ejaculatory inhibition. As in the preceding discussion of women's sexual difficulties, we caution that the origins of such problems are complex and that solutions are frequently not simple. Again, we refer readers who are interested in pursuing this topic to Suggested Readings and also to the discussion about therapy assistance.

Lasting Longer

Although premature ejaculation is a common dissatisfaction, the prospects for positive change are good. Most professional sex therapists use a multiphased program that focuses on the stop-start or squeeze techniques. These successful approaches to learning ejaculatory control are quite easy to implement, even, in some cases, without professional guidance. There are also simpler strategies for helping to delay ejaculation, and we will discuss these first. Women readers and men for whom premature ejaculation is not a problem may find the following discussion valuable simply because they would sometimes like sexual interactions to last longer.

Ejaculate More Frequently.   Men with premature ejaculation problems sometimes find that they can delay ejaculation when they are having more frequent orgasms (Geer and O'Donohue, 1984). If partner sex is not a viable option, frequent masturbation to orgasm can be helpful.

Change Positions.   Excessive muscle tension is detrimental to a man who ejaculates rapidly. All things being equal, increased muscle tension is typically associated with a rapid sexual response cycle. Aside from certain exotic acrobatic positions, the man-above position is about the worst way to have intercourse for a man who wants to delay ejaculation. The muscle tension from supporting his own weight as he thrusts results in a more rapid ejaculation.

Many men gain a desirable amount of control by lying on their backs (see Figure 9.6 for variations of the woman-above position). An important point to note is that this position by itself is not sufficient; another essential aspect is relaxation. One couple who reported a lack of success with the position told us that the male partner's orgasm was occurring more rapidly than before. Closer questioning revealed that he was maintaining his old custom of energetic pelvic movements. Thus, he was moving not only his own weight but that of his partner as well, increasing muscle tension to even higher levels than before. Encouraged to relax during coitus, he found that he was able to prolong intercourse. Both partners were then able to fully enjoy what had once been a fleeting and anxiety-ridden experience.

Immediate results do not always follow this position modification. Sometimes a man will experience increased arousal, stemming from the novelty of the position, that will temporarily counteract its tendency to delay ejaculation. Also, his partner may be more responsive, and he may be further excited by the increased opportunity to observe her reactions. However, after some experience with this change in position, he often experiences the advantages of increased relaxation.

"Come Again!"   In view of our earlier discussion of the male refractory period, it is clear that sexual activity that follows initial male orgasm will not typically be characterized by rapid ejaculation. However, few men or their partners consider or explore the potential for slowed responsiveness after first climax. This is largely due to the belief that male orgasm is the end point of sexual interaction. Many men might be pleased with the results of exploring the potential for continued interaction.

Talk with Each Other.   Communicating during coitus may help the couple prolong the experience. It is often essential to slow down or completely cease movements if climax is to be delayed. A partner may find it difficult to anticipate the precise moment to reduce or stop stimulation unless she or he is clearly informed by the other.

Some men find that intercourse can be maintained for very long periods of time if they allow sexual tension to rise and fall between plateau and excitement phase levels of arousal. Not uncommonly, men report an added sense of control that comes with repeated episodes of going to the brink of orgasmic release, reducing stimulation to allow tensions to subside somewhat, and then moving once again to the edge. Often, time and practice facilitate this modulated form of activity, particularly if the partners continue to communicate.

Consider Alternatives.   In minimizing performance anxiety about rapid ejaculation (and most of the other problems discussed here), it is often useful to think of intercourse as just one of the several options for sexual sharing. Many people have discovered that reaching orgasm during intercourse is not necessary to pleasure, particularly if other successful methods of orgasm-producing stimulation are used. Occasionally, a man will find that manual stimulation, oral-genital contact, using a vibrator, and so forth will reduce his performance anxiety enough to considerably improve his staying power. It can be comforting to know that there are many options for obtaining and giving sexual pleasure. It is also important to realize that an activity may be very enjoyable even when it does not produce orgasm.

Have a "Small Orgasm."   According to Masters and Johnson and many other researchers, when a man reaches the point of "ejaculatory inevitability" (synonymous with the emission stage of orgasm, described in Chapter 6), nothing can be done to avert a complete ejaculation. However, there is more recent evidence that some men have the ability to shut down the second stage of ejaculation, right at its beginning, and experience what amounts to a "small orgasm." This typically takes the form of one or two muscle contractions and a small amount of seminal fluid emission. Such an experience is often followed by the continued ability to keep a complete erection and increased ejaculatory control. A full ejaculation almost always occurs following the initial small orgasm(s), but often after a long period of continued coital activity.

We have surveyed several hundred of our male students about the occurrence of small orgasms. Ten to fifteen percent have consistently reported this phenomenon in their sex lives; some practice it with a high degree of regularity. Of this group, many have remarked on the "staying power" advantages of having small orgasms. Some students have experimented with this response after first learning about it in class. In the following account one male student relates his experience:

> I first experimented in this area with masturbation. At the point of climax, I would relax the muscles in my penis and slightly apply pressure as if trying to urinate. The feeling was good, and some semen was released. I was able to do this a total of three times before reaching a complete orgasm. The amount of semen released each time was less than my usual ejaculation; however, the total amount expelled was greater than ever before. (Authors' files)

The reports we have received are only tentative evidence, and experimental investigation is needed to find out more about small male orgasms and their incidence. However, enough men have spoken convincingly of the benefits of small orgasm to convince us that it does deserve further evaluation. At present, our best suggestion is for personal exploration and experimentation, either with a partner or during masturbation.

The Stop-Start and Squeeze Techniques.   The method most commonly associated with treatment for premature ejaculation is the **squeeze technique** popularized by Masters and Johnson (1970). Their approach is a modification of a technique developed earlier by James Semans (1956). Semans, a urologist, hypothesized that premature ejaculation stems from a man's lack of awareness of the neuromuscular sensations that precede orgasm and ejaculation. The man who ejaculates rapidly, for whatever reasons, has not noticed this sensory feedback, yet such awareness is essential to bringing any reflex function under control.

Working from this assumption, Semans developed a stop-start technique. This technique is learned in several training sessions and is designed to prolong the sensations prior to orgasm, thereby affording the man a chance to become acquainted with, and ultimately to control, his ejaculatory reflex. The partner is instructed to stimulate the man's penis, either manually or orally, to the point of impending orgasm. At this time, stroking is stopped until the preejaculatory sensations subside.

The strategy advocated by Masters and Johnson follows essentially the pattern developed by Semans, with the added component of squeezing the penis. When the man is on the brink of orgasm, he signals his partner to cease stimulation and to squeeze. Figure 17.5 illustrates the proper application of this technique. As indicated, the thumb is placed on the frenum and two fingers are positioned on the other side of the penis, one above and one below the corona. Strong pressure must then be applied for a few seconds until the man loses the urge to ejaculate. (At the same time, a portion of his erection is typically lost.) Sometimes, two hands are required to apply sufficient pressure. This squeezing will not cause pain or injury, and occasionally the partner who is squeezing needs to be assured of this. A man with rapid ejaculation can place his fingers directly over his partner's fingers, demonstrating how hard to squeeze to produce the desired results. After applying the squeeze, his partner should refrain from further stimulation for a period of 15–30 seconds. While a variety of postions can be used during these training sessions, most commonly couples will use an approach approximating that shown in the figure.

Masters and Johnson have introduced another type of squeeze technique, called the *basilar squeeze*. After the man has practiced with the regular squeeze technique and has developed some ejaculatory control, either he or his partner can apply firm pressure on the top and bottom of the base of the penis. This technique has the advantage of not requiring the man to remove his penis from the vagina during intercourse to apply the squeeze.

It is generally suggested that training sessions such as those just described last around 15–30 minutes and occur as often as once a day for several days or weeks. During each session the couple repeats the stimulation and squeeze or stop-start procedure several times and then allows ejaculation to occur on the last cycle. The couple should reach an agreement about sexual stimulation and orgasm for the man's partner. If this is desired, they can engage in noncoital activity.

A man undergoing this procedure will usually experience immediately observable benefits. As his ejaculatory control improves appreciably, the couple progresses to coital interaction, employing the woman-above position shown in Figure 17.6, with the woman sitting astride. This position is especially well suited for this stage because

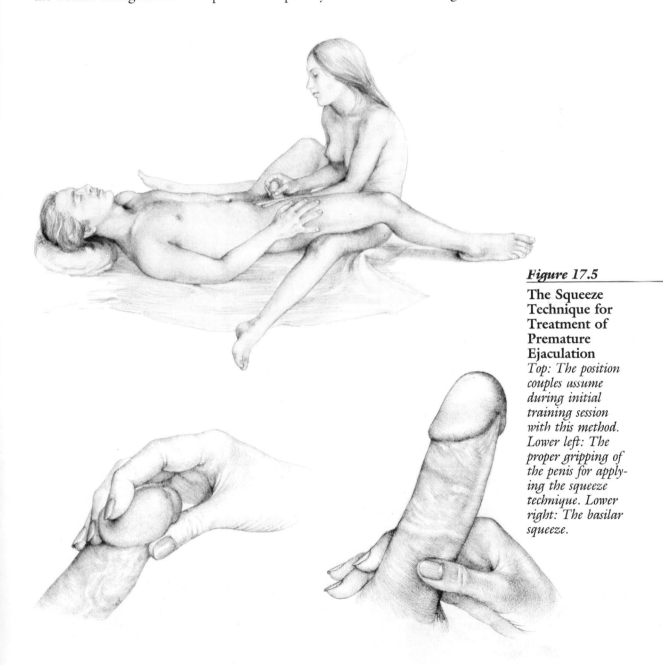

Figure 17.5

The Squeeze Technique for Treatment of Premature Ejaculation
Top: The position couples assume during initial training session with this method. Lower left: The proper gripping of the penis for applying the squeeze technique. Lower right: The basilar squeeze.

Figure 17.6

Woman-Above Intercourse Position

a slight shift of the woman's pelvis permits the man's penis to be withdrawn so the squeeze can be applied. The couple can also stop moving if they are using the stop-start technique. This technique is continued as the man experiences progressive improvement. In most cases the man is able to prevent a too-hasty orgasm (Masters and Johnson report a 98% success rate).

A major advantage of Seman's stop-start technique and the "squeeze" variations is the almost inevitable improvement of communication that results when two people treat premature orgasm. As Masters and Johnson note, "Aside from the obvious control improvement, the greatest return from use of the squeeze technique is improved communication both at verbal and non-verbal levels for the marital unit" (1970, p. 105).

Recently it has been demonstrated that a man can benefit from using the squeeze technique on himself during solo sessions of masturbation. However, to gain the full returns of improved communication, we encourage couples to share in this experience whenever it is practical.

We have considered several approaches to overcoming the problem of premature ejaculation. Although couple-oriented approaches such as the stop-start and the squeeze technique have the advantages of leading to better communication and cooperation, any of the other suggested avenues of change may be enough to reduce or resolve this difficulty, and combinations of techniques are often even more effective.

[However, do not combine the squeeze technique and having a "small orgasm" because there is some chance of rupturing the seminal vesicle (LoPiccolo, 1982).] For example, it is unlikely that a man will experience a hasty climax during intercourse when he is relaxing in the male supine position and recovering from the refractory effects of an earlier orgasm. There is a wide array of possible combinations. Experiment a little to find what works best for you. Most important, trust that change can occur. Once you begin to experience some improvements, one powerful benefit will most likely become apparent, namely a marked lowering of performance anxiety. The reduction of this pressure undoubtedly accounts, at least in part, for continued long-term gains you can expect to maintain.

Dealing with Erectile Difficulties

With the exception of organically caused erection difficulties, anxiety is the major stumbling block to erectile response. Therefore, all behaviorally focused approaches to this problem concentrate on reducing or eliminating anxiety. A major goal is to create an atmosphere in which the man is able to achieve some success with obtaining an erection, thus restoring his confidence and diminishing performance fear.

Initially, a couple should spend their intimate moments engaged in nondemanding caresses. The sensate focus experiences discussed earlier are ideally suited to this purpose. Often it is helpful not to touch the genitals during these first encounters. The emphasis is placed on sensual pleasure as each person lightly touches, strokes, and explores his or her partner's body. It is also important that both members of the pair understand that these exercises are not designed to produce an erect penis. Neither person should enter into the experience expecting this. If an erection should occur, fine; if it goes away, do not worry. The main point is that the time spent touching is not goal oriented. For this reason, therapists restrict coitus and ejaculation during these exercises. The following account shows how one man reacted to the regimen imposed by his therapist:

> When I was told that intercourse was off-limits, at least for the time being, I couldn't believe how relieved I felt. After years of trying to make my body get up for a performance, suddenly the doctor's advice eliminated this pressure. It was like being given permission to feel again. If I couldn't get hard, so what? After all, I was told not to use it even if it happened. Looking back, I think those first few times touching and getting touched by my wife were the first really worry-free pleasurable times I had experienced in years. Soon I was getting erections all over the place, and the problem was resisting the urge to jump the gun on the therapy timetable. (Authors' files)

An urge to take shortcuts on the therapy timetable can be a potential problem. Such impulsiveness may be counterproductive. However, avoiding intercourse and ejaculation does not necessarily mean that a man's partner may not have an orgasm. If a couple wants to, they can agree in advance for the partner to have an orgasm at the close of a session by whatever mode of stimulation seems comfortable to both (self-stimulation, being touched by the partner, oral stimulation, and so on). One key restriction is that such activity is noncoital and does not result in ejaculation by the man who has the erectile difficulty.

When anxiety is reduced and the couple has progressed to a point where both feel comfortable with the newly discovered pleasures of body exploration, it is time to move to the next phase. Note that while the man who has experienced arousal difficulties will probably have begun to have spontaneous erections by this time, their occurrence is not essential to deciding to move forward. The critical condition is that both partners feel relaxed and positive about their mutually experienced sensuality. In the next phase, the couple directs their attention toward whatever kinds of genital stimulation are particularly arousing to the man. This may consist of manual or oral pleasuring, or both. The intercourse ban is still in effect. If the man achieves a complete erection, his partner should stop whatever actions have aroused him.

Sometimes people are perplexed at this suggestion, thinking that the logical next step would be to progress to penetration. However, in view of the past history of the vast majority of men troubled by erectile inhibition, it is critical that the erection be allowed to subside at this point. The purpose of this is to alter the man's belief that once an erection is lost it will not return. When his partner stops providing optimal stimulation, the man allows his erection to subside. This may take several minutes of nonstimulation if the level of arousal is very high. This time can be spent holding each other close or exchanging nongenital caresses. When his erection has completely gone down, the man's partner again resumes the genital pleasuring that produced the original reaction. Once he experiences that erections can be lost and regained, the fear that he has "had it" if he loses the first one is diminished.

Occasionally, a man will experience a recurrence of erection-inhibiting fears during these exercises. In such cases, it is helpful to remind him to relax and focus his attention on touching his partner, following the sensate focus guidelines. It may sometimes be necessary to move back a step to emphasize nondemand pleasuring if he continues to have difficulty responding to the stimulate-stop-restimulate phase of treatment.

The final phase of treatment, for heterosexual couples who desire intercourse, involves penetration and coitus. A good procedure for this is to begin with sensate focus, with the man on his back and his partner astride. The couple can then move to genital stimulation; then, when he has an erection, she lowers herself onto his penis, maintaining stimulation by gentle movements of her pelvis. If his penis remains erect, vaginal stimulation should be continued until he reaches orgasm. Permission to be "selfish" is quite helpful at this point (Kaplan, 1974). By this, we mean that the man should be instructed to concentrate exclusively on his own erotic pleasures. If worries such as "Is she going to come?" or "Am I doing well?" intrude on his own sensual feelings, he should shift his attention back to his own sensations. Sometimes this concern for self is easier to put into practice if the partners have agreed to consider her orgasm after he has experienced his.

Occasionally a man will lose his erection after penetration. If this happens, it is good procedure for his partner to again provide the kind of oral or manual stimulation that originally produced his erection. If his response continues to be blocked, it is wise to stop genital contact, returning once again to the original nondemand pleasuring of sensate focus rather than forcing efforts to "make it happen." Erection loss after penetration is not uncommon, and couples should not be overly anxious if it happens. A few successful coital encounters will generally alleviate erectile inhibition.

Should the problem recur, the couple is now experienced in techniques they can use to avoid establishing a pattern of difficulty.

Some men who have impaired erectile functioning as the result of a medical problem make a very satisfactory sexual adjustment to the absence of erection by emphasizing and enjoying other ways of sexual sharing. In cases where illness or injury have left a man permanently unable to have erections, the option of a surgically implanted penile prosthesis is also available. Since the surgery is expensive and involves some risks, it is wise to carefully evaluate this option. There are two basic types of penile implants. One consists of a pair of semirigid rods placed inside the cavernous bodies of the penis. A potential disadvantage to this method is that the penis is always semierect. The second type of penile prosthesis is an inflatable device that enables the penis to be either flaccid or erect (see Figure 17.7). Two inflatable cylinders are implanted into the cavernous bodies of the penile shaft. They are connected to a fluid-filled reservoir located near the bladder and to a pump in the scrotal sac. When a man wants an erection, he squeezes the pump several times, and the fluid fills the collapsed cylinders and produces an erection. When an erection is no longer desired, a release valve causes the fluid to go back into the reservoir. Neither of these devices can restore sensation or the ability to ejaculate if these have been lost due to medical problems. They do, however, provide an alternative for men who want to mechanically restore their ability to have erections.

A review of research on postsurgical adjustment and satisfaction following implantation of penile prosthesis found that 64% to 100% of implant patients and their partners were satisfied with the results (Collins and Kinder, 1984). A majority of the respondents also reported positive changes in the nonsexual aspects of their relationships. Some implant recipients were more likely to experience adjustment problems and dissatisfaction than others, including maladjusted couples and men who had a low level of sexual interest prior to their erectile difficulties. Dissatisfaction with

Figure 17.7

A Penile Prosthesis
This inflatable device enables the penis to be either flaccid or erect.

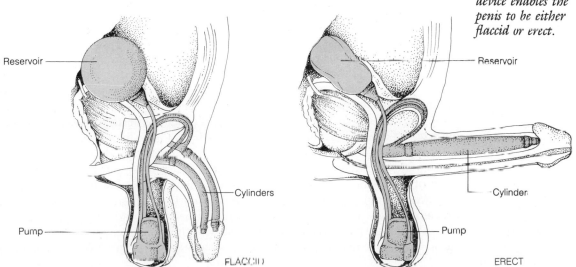

Reservoir — Cylinders — Pump — FLACCID — Reservoir — Cylinder — Pump — ERECT

the surgery can be due to mechanical problems with the implant, loss of sensation in the glans of the penis, and physical discomfort when using the device. It is important for men who are considering implants to be aware that any ability they have to experience natural erection prior to surgery will be impaired postoperatively. Also, implant erections will not be as long, wide, or firm as natural erections (Kraus, 1985).

Medical treatments for organically based erection problems have increased in recent years. A variety of innovative microsurgical procedures to repair vascular problems in the penis can be helpful (Kudish, 1983). In addition, increased knowledge about the pelvic nerves that affect erection have resulted in nerve-sparing techniques during pelvic, rectal, prostatic, and urethral operations (Lue, 1985). Drug treatments are also being developed. Papaverine, a smooth muscle relaxant that produces vasodilation, causes erection when injected into the corpora cavernosa of the penis. Papaverine injections result in erection in some men with diabetes and vascular and neurological impairments. The physician injects the drug or, in some cases, men inject it themselves. Erection typically occurs within 4 to 10 minutes and lasts approximately two hours. Some complications reported from papaverine injections include transitory numbness of the penile glans, difficulty reaching orgasm and ejaculation, infection, and prolonged erection. Only small numbers of men have used papaverine injections, and at this time the long-term effects are unknown (Zorgniotti and Lefleur, 1985). Yohimbine, a drug occasionally prescribed for hypertension, helps induce erection in some cases. This drug is believed to work by stimulating the nerves that affect the penile blood vessels, increasing blood flow into and decreasing blood flow out of the penis (Kudish, 1983). A further development is an electronic device known as the male electronic genital stimulator. Electrodes are implanted around the cavernous nerves of the penis, and the electronic impulses stimulate the nerves, muscles, and vessels to cause increased net blood flow into the penis, resulting in erection (Lue, 1985). If these innovative medical treatments are developed further, they may provide more options for treatment of erection problems caused by physiological factors.

Reducing Ejaculatory Inhibition

As with erectile difficulties, a behavioral approach is generally used in the treatment of ejaculatory inhibition. In addition, psychotherapy aimed at reducing resentment in the relationship may be helpful when dislike or anger toward a partner contributes to a man's difficulty with ejaculatory inhibition. The program outlined in the following paragraphs is suitable for either a heterosexual or a homosexual couple; however, for purposes of descriptive simplicity, we will assume a male-female pair.

Therapy usually begins with few days of sensate focus, during which time the man should not attempt to have an ejaculation, either intravaginally or by some other form of stimulation. If his partner desires orgasm, this may be accomplished in whatever fashion is comfortable to both, excluding coitus. It is desirable for a man to maintain this consideration for his partner's needs throughout the program.

When they have become comfortable with the nondemand pleasuring of sensate focus, the couple may move on to the next phase of treatment. Now the man should experience ejaculation by whatever method is most likely to be successful. Ideally, this will involve his partner, so that he may begin to associate his orgasmic pleasure with her. Frequently the man begins by masturbating himself after first being stimulated to a highly aroused state by his partner. If he is uncomfortable masturbating in her presence, he can leave the room after being aroused by her touch and immediately stimulate himself to orgasm. Perhaps after some experience with this activity, he will feel comfortable remaining in her presence while he masturbates, preferably with her participation through kissing, fondling, or holding him. The essential idea is for him to begin connecting his partner's presence and activity with his own pleasure. Many couples may find that they can move successfully from sensate focus to partner stimulation without the intervening step of solo masturbation.

Once both partners feel comfortable with the man's self-stimulation in the woman's presence, the couple may move on to the next phase, where she attempts to bring him to orgasm with manual or oral stimulation. Communication is especially important at this time. The man can greatly heighten his pleasure and arousal by demonstrating or verbalizing what feels best to him. It may take several days or longer before his partner's stimulation produces an ejaculation—there is no need to rush or feel panicked if it does not happen immediately. Most therapists agreed that once he can reach orgasm by her touch, an important step has been accomplished.

When the man is ejaculating consistently in response to partner stimulation, the couple may move on to the final phase of treatment, in which ejaculation takes place during penetration. The female partner assumes the woman-above position, sitting astride the man, who is lying on his back. She then stimulates him to the point where he signals that he is about to reach orgasm, at which time she inserts his penis and begins active pelvic thrusting. If he starts to ejaculate before insertion is completed, this should not be viewed as a cause for concern. If he does not ejaculate shortly after penetration, she should withdraw his penis and resume manual stimulation. When he is again about to ejaculate, she reinserts his penis and they continue stimulation by pelvic thrusting.

Once the man experiences a few intravaginal ejaculations, the mental block that is usually associated with ejaculatory inhibition often disappears. After a few experiences with penetration followed immediately by ejaculation, he may acquire confidence in his capacity to ejaculate intravaginally. At this point the couple may wish to concentrate on prolonging coital contact. Typically the man will begin to enter his partner at lower levels of excitement rather than at the moment of impending orgasm. It may be useful to apply some of the techniques for lasting longer that we discussed earlier. It frequently happens that a couple reaches a stage during which no noticeable improvement occurs, and this can take place at any point in the program. In this case, they may need to let some time pass before trying to move on to the next stage.

Ejaculatory inhibition may involve complex factors. Nevertheless, based on limited clinical data, it appears that the probability of overcoming the problem in a therapy program is high. Masters and Johnson (1970) report success with 10 of the 17 men they treated for this difficulty. Generally the prognosis is better when the condition occurs independently of severe relationship problems.

A sexual surrogate is a person who is paid to teach sex therapy clients social and sexual skills. Surrogates work with people who do not have a sexual partner willing to participate in sex therapy. The goal of therapy with a surrogate is to resolve sexual problems and to help clients function in relationships with others outside of therapy. Surrogates work under the direction of a therapist. They have private sessions with clients using treatment techniques such as communication skills training and sensate focus, depending on the client's problem and the treatment goals. Intercourse may or may not be a part of therapy with the surrogate.

The use of sexual surrogates is not widespread at this time, primarily due to legal and therapeutic issues. The legal question of whether the therapist, surrogate, and client could be prosecuted for prostitution-related offenses remains unanswered. There is controversy in the sex therapy field about the benefits and risks to clients engaging in physical intimacy in the context of a professional relationship. In what ways could working with a surrogate, who is not emotionally involved with the client, be helpful or harmful to a client with a sexual problem? What influence does the separation of sexual contact from an ongoing, "real" relationship have? Research results regarding the effectiveness of sex therapy with surrogates and its positive or negative impact on clients' post-therapy functioning will help influence how significant a role surrogates will have in sex therapy.

Treatment for Inhibited Sexual Desire

Many aspects of treatment for inhibited sexual desire are similar to specific suggestions for resolving other sexual problems. These include encouraging erotic responses through self-stimulation and arousing fantasies; reducing anxiety with appropriate information and sensate focus exercises; and enhancing sexual experiences by improving communication, increasing skill in initiation and refusal of sexual activity, and expanding one's repertoire of affectionate and sexual activities (LoPiccolo, 1980a).

Inhibited sexual desire appears to be more difficult to treat than other sexual problems, and it is more likely to require intensive therapy than problems like rapid ejaculation, primary inorgasmia, or vaginismus (Kaplan, 1979). The goal for treatment of ISD is to modify the person's pattern of inhibiting his or her erotic impulses. To achieve this, the therapist helps the client to understand the underlying motivation to suppress sexual feelings and the reasons he or she refuses sexual intimacy. Kaplan combines suggestions for specific activities with insight therapy that may help the person understand and resolve unconscious conflicts about sexual pleasure and intimacy. In cases where the inhibited sexual desire is a symptom of a relationship problem, focusing on the relationship is an essential part of treatment (Fish et al., 1984).

Guidelines for Seeking Professional Assistance

After exploring the information and suggestions in this text and other readings, you may continue to experience considerable sexual dissatisfaction. Perhaps you may find it difficult to progress beyond a particular stage in an exercise program. Although some people with sexual problems improve over time without therapy (De Amicis et al., 1984), you may decide to seek professional help. A skilled therapist can offer useful information, emotional support, a perspective other than your own, and specific problem-solving techniques, all of which may help you make the desired changes in your sex life.

Many people are apprehensive about going to see a sex therapist, and it can be helpful to have some idea about what to expect. Each therapist works differently, but most follow certain steps. At the first interview the therapist will help the person or couple to clarify the problem and their feelings about it, and to understand what their goals are for therapy. The therapist will usually ask questions about when the difficulty first began, how it has developed over time, what the person thinks has caused it, and what he or she has already tried to resolve the problem. The therapist will likely gather some information about medical history and current physical functioning and then make referrals, if necessary, for further physical screenings. Increasingly sophisticated and refined techniques for diagnosing vascular, neurological,and endocrine causes of sexual problems have been and continue to be developed (LoPiccolo, 1985).

Over the next few sessions the therapist may gather more extensive sexual, personal, and relationship histories. During the history the therapist will screen for severe depression and other major psychological problems that would interfere with therapy, explore whether the clients have a lifestyle conducive to a good emotional and sexual relationship, and determine whether they are involved in substance abuse or domestic violence (LoPiccolo, 1985). Some therapists use written questionnaires to help gather information and clarify problems.

Once the therapist and the individual or couple more fully realize the nature of the difficulty and have defined the therapy goals, the therapist helps the client understand and overcome obstacles to meeting the goals as the sessions continue. Most therapy occurs in one-hour weekly sessions, although the Masters and Johnson Institute has daily appointments for a two-week period. The therapist will often give "homework" assignments such as masturbation or sensate focus exercises for the client(s) to do between therapy sessions. Successes and difficulties with the assignments are discussed at subsequent meetings. Therapy is terminated when the clients reach their goals. It is often helpful for clients to leave with a plan for continuing and maintaining progress. The therapist and clients may also plan one or more follow-up sessions.

Selecting a Therapist

Depending on your situation, you may wish to see a therapist alone or with your partner. Many women who want to learn to experience orgasm may not have an available partner or may decide they prefer to attain orgasm initially by self-stimulation; the same may be true for men with ejaculation or erection problems. Masters and Johnson believe that a couple's sexual functioning, including difficulties one or the other may experience, is based on the interaction between the two people. Therefore, their counseling is done with both partners. Masters and Johnson have also promoted the use of male and female cotherapists to work with heterosexual couples, but research does not indicate that cotherapy is more effective than an individual therapist (Arentewicz and Schmidt, 1983; Marks, 1981).

Another option in some areas is small-group therapy. Small groups in sex therapy were first extensively used with women who had not yet experienced orgasm. These women's groups combine in-group sharing and support with self-discovery exercises (Barbach, 1975). This model is also being used for groups of men (Zilbergeld, 1975) and couples (Baker and Nagata, 1978; McGovern et al., 1976). One advantage of group therapy is that it is usually less expensive than individual therapy. Also, group members often gain knowledge and support from sharing with each other.

Once a person has determined she or he wants help from a sex therapist, how is a therapist selected? To locate a therapist, you might ask your sexuality course instructor or health care practitioner for referrals. Also, the American Association of Sex Educators, Counselors and Therapists (AASECT) can send you the names of therapists in your area who have applied and qualified for AASECT certification.* If you are concerned about having a nonsexist focus to your therapy, you can call your local National Organization for Women (NOW) chapter, which may have a list of therapists from whom to choose. Homosexual individuals or couples may find it helpful to contact a gay rights organization for names of therapists who are supportive of their clients' sexual orientations. Your doctor or friends may know therapists whom they might recommend, and your county or state psychological association can also provide names of licensed clinical psychologists in your area. County medical societies have lists of names of psychiatrists.

After consulting some of these sources you will have several choices. There are many factors to consider in making your selection. A basic criterion is training. Professionals from a variety of backgrounds do sex therapy. The title *sex therapist* does not assure competence: There are few regulations on use of that title. At this time, there are few advanced degree programs in sex therapy. Rather, a professional who has specialized in this area is likely to have credentials as a psychiatrist, psychologist, social worker, or educational or pastoral counselor. To do sex therapy, he or she should also have participated in sex therapy training, supervision, and workshops. It is highly appropriate for you to inquire about the specific training and certification of a prospective therapist.

To help determine if a specific therapist will meet your needs, you may wish to establish the following points at your first meeting:

1. What do you want from therapy? You and your therapist should reach an agreement on your and his or her goals. This agreement is sometimes referred to as the therapy contract.
2. What is the therapist's approach? You can ask about the general process (what the therapist will do) in the therapy sessions and what kind of participation is expected of you.
3. How do you feel about talking with the therapist? Therapy is not intended to be a light social interaction. It can be difficult. At times it may be quite

---

*The address is AASECT, 11 Dupont Circle N.W., Suite 200, Washington, D.C., 20036.

uncomfortable for a client to discuss personal sexual concerns. However, for therapy to be useful, you will want to have the sense that the therapist is open and willing to understand you.

After the initial interview you can decide to continue with this therapist or ask for a referral more appropriate to your needs. If you become dissatisfied once you begin therapy, discuss your concerns with your therapist. Decide jointly, if possible, whether to continue or to seek another therapist. It is usually best to continue for several sessions before making a decision to change. Occasionally clients expect magic cures rather than the hard and rewarding work therapy often demands.

Another consideration may be the cost of therapy. Fees vary considerably. Psychiatrists are usually on the upper end of the fee scale, psychologists are in the middle, and social workers and counselors are usually on the lower end. A higher fee does not necessarily indicate better sex therapy skills. Some mental health agencies and private practitioners offer sliding fee schedules based on the client's income.

Professional Ethics

It is considered highly unethical for professional therapists to engage in sexual relationships with clients. If a sexual relationship develops in the context of therapy, attention would likely be diverted from the client's original concerns, and the preexisting problems would not be resolved. In addition, the sexual involvement can have negative effects. Research indicates that women who experienced sexual contact with their therapists (including psychotherapists in general, not only sex therapists) felt greater mistrust of and anger toward men and therapists than a control group of women. They also experienced a greater number of psychological and psychosomatic symptoms, including anger, shame, anxiety, and depression (Feldman-Summers and Jones, 1984). If at any time your therapist makes verbal or physical sexual advances toward you, you have every right to leave immediately and terminate therapy. It would be helpful to others who may be victims of this misuse of professional power if you report this incident to local professional organizations.

In conclusion, sex therapy can be a useful tool for individuals and couples who want to resolve their sexual difficulties. The process of sex therapy may also have additional benefits. Clients often experience reduced anxiety, as well as improved communication, marital adjustment, and satisfaction following sex therapy (Zilbergeld and Kilmann, 1984). Couples may be more assertive and emotionally expressive with each other (Tullman et al., 1981). One study reported that women who completed a treatment group for primary inorgasmia exceeded a control group in many areas, including feeling desirable, feeling positive about how they looked nude in the mirror, telling their preferences during sexual activity, and initiating sexual activity (Cotten-Houston and Wheeler, 1983). Individuals and couples who have met their goals may experience increased self-confidence and emotional satisfaction (Clement and Pfäfflin, 1980). The combined efforts of the therapist and client can replace doubt and anxiety with the joy of satisfying sexual intimacy.

Summary

The PLISSIT Model of Sex Therapy

1. The PLISSIT model outlines four progressive levels of sex therapy: permission, limited information, specific suggestions, and intensive therapy.

2. Intensive therapy often combines sex therapy behavioral techniques with insight-oriented psychosocial therapy or with a systems theory approach that focuses on the function of the problem within the relationship.

Basics of Sex Therapy

3. Self-awareness is a good beginning for therapy. Exploring one's own body increases one's knowledge and comfort and may prepare one for exploring a partner's body.

4. Masturbation exercises are an effective way for an individual to learn about and experience sexual response. They can be enjoyed for themselves and the acquired knowledge can be shared with a partner.

5. Communication between partners is an important element of therapy. It can help work out specific problems and foster stronger relationships.

6. The experience of sensate focus, nondemand pleasuring shared by sexual partners, is an excellent vehicle for mutually enhancing sexual potentials.

7. Masturbating in each other's presence may be an excellent way for a couple to indicate to each other what kind of touching they find arousing.

Specific Suggestions for Women

8. Therapy programs for inorgasmic women are based on progressive self-awareness activities.

9. Women who wish to become orgasmic while sharing with a partner may benefit from programs that commence with sensate focus, mutual genital exploration, masturbation, and nondemand genital pleasuring by the partner.

10. A couple may increase the probability of female orgasm during penetration by incorporating knowledge acquired during sensate focus and nondemand pleasuring, and by combining manual stimulation with penetration.

11. Treatment for vaginismus generally involves promoting increased self-awareness and relaxation. Insertion of a lubricated finger (first one's own and later the partner's) into the vagina is an important next step in overcoming this condition. Penile insertion is the final phase of treatment for vaginismus.

Specific Suggestions for Men

12. A variety of approaches may help a man learn to delay his ejaculation. Potentially helpful suggestions include ejaculating more frequently, using a more relaxed intercourse position, having a second orgasm, openly communicating a need to modulate movements, including noncoital activity in sexual sharing, and experimenting with "small orgasms."

13. If a couple has the time and inclination to work together in resolving premature ejaculation difficulties, application of the stop-start or squeeze methods is usually effective.

14. A behavioral approach designed to reduce anxiety has proven quite successful in treating psychologically based erectile inhibition. This treatment method has several phases: sensate focus, followed by genital stimulation, then penetration.

15. Surgically implanted penile prostheses are options for men who have a permanent, physiologically caused inability to experience erections.

16. A behavioral approach for the treatment of ejaculatory inhibition combines sensate focus with self- and partner manual stimulation to ultimately lead to intravaginal ejaculation.

Treatment for Inhibited Sexual Desire

17. Problems with inhibited sexual desire often require more intensive therapy to help people understand and change their suppression and avoidance of sexual feelings.

Guidelines for Seeking Professional Assistance

18. Professional counseling is often helpful and sometimes necessary in overcoming sexual difficulties.

19. A skilled therapist can offer useful information, emotional support, a perspective other than your own, problem-solving strategies, and specific sex therapy techniques.

20. A lack of regulations governing sex therapy suggests that we should be careful in selecting a therapist or cotherapists. Referrals may be given by sex educators, physicians, or a variety of organizations, including AASECT or women's groups.

21. It is highly unethical for therapists to have sexual relationships with clients. A sexual advance is grounds for immediate termination of the therapy.

Thought Provokers

1. Why might someone be reluctant to seek professional assistance for a sexual difficulty?

2. How do you think the sensate focus experience challenges sex-role stereotyped behavior of men and women?

3. What do you think would be the risks and benefits of a sex therapy client working with a sex surrogate?

Suggested Readings

Castleman, Michael. *Sexual Solutions*. New York: Simon & Schuster, 1980. An excellent book that encourages readers to clarify their personal conditions for positive sexual experiences.

Kaplan, Helen. *The Illustrated Manual of Sex Therapy*. New York: Quadrangle/New York Times, 1975. A readable and beautifully illustrated book with clearly explained steps in the behavioral treatment of sexual difficulties.

Kilmann, Peter, and Mills, Katherine. *All About Sex Therapy*. New York: Plenum, 1983. This book is especially helpful to anyone considering sex therapy.

LoPiccolo, Joseph, and LoPiccolo, Leslie (Eds.). *Handbook of Sex Therapy*. New York: Plenum, 1978. An edited text that synthesizes research and writing in the field of sex therapy. It is somewhat technical but highly appropriate reading for the student who is seriously interested in the field of sex therapy.

McCarthy, Barry; Ryan, Mary; and Johnson, Fred. *Sexual Awareness: A Practical Approach*. San Francisco: Boyd & Fraser, 1975. A straightforward and sensitive guide to improving self-awareness and pleasure in sexuality. The book offers suggestions for enhancement programs for men, women, and couples.

Westheimer, Ruth. *Dr. Ruth's Guide to Good Sex*. New York: Warner Books, 1983. This book offers straightforward information and advice on a myriad of sexual topics.

18

Say, Goddess, to what cause shall we at last
Assign this Plague, unknown to Ages past;
If from the Western climes was wafted o'er,
When daring Spaniards left their native shore;
Resolv'd beyond th' Atlantick to descry,
Conjectur'd Worlds, or in the search to dye.
For Fame reports this Grief perpetual there,
From Skies infected and polluted air:
For whence 'tis grown so Epidemical,
Whole Cities Victims to its Fury fall.

Fracastorius
Syphilis (1686)

Sexually Transmitted Diseases

Common Vaginal Infections

Chlamydial Infection

Gonorrhea

Syphilis

Nongonococcal Urethritis

Herpes

Viral Hepatitis

Pubic Lice

Genital Warts

Acquired Immune Deficiency Syndrome (AIDS)

Other Sexually Transmitted Diseases

Prevention of Sexually Transmitted Diseases

IN THIS CHAPTER we will discuss a variety of diseases that can be transmitted through sexual interaction. These are commonly called **STDs**, or **sexually transmitted diseases**. Some of these conditions can be spread nonsexually as well as through sexual contact (for example, pubic lice, herpes, and genital warts). The term *venereal disease* (VD) is sometimes used interchangeably with STD. However, the VD label is traditionally applied only to those conditions whose mode of transmission is almost always sexual contact (for example, gonorrhea and syphilis). Thus, the title of this chapter, "Sexually Transmitted Diseases," is a much broader topic that includes the more limited category of VD.

Chlamydia, gonorrhea, and herpes affect large numbers of people and are major health problems in the United States. Other STDs, such as *Gardnerella vaginalis*, candidosis, and trichomoniasis are also quite prevalent. It is quite possible that you will experience at least one of the STDs described in this chapter. The probability of this occurring is greatest if you are (or have sexual contact with) a sexually active, nonmonogamous individual.

Our purpose in including a chapter on STDs is not to scare readers into celibacy or monogamy. Rather, we would like to present a realistic picture of what a sexually transmitted disease is, how it can be recognized, what should be done to treat it, and what preventive measures can be taken. Furthermore, we trust that increased knowledge about STDs will lead to thoughtful consideration of other people who might be involved. There are good reasons for letting them know if they might be affected and for taking proper preventive action and treatment. These are our motives for including a chapter on this topic in this book—particularly considering that many STDs are on the increase, that relatively little prevention is currently practiced, and that most of these diseases can be successfully treated.

It is not entirely clear why the incidence of STDs is so high. Undoubtedly, a number of factors are operating in what many writers and health authorities have labeled an epidemic. Increasing sexual activity among young people has commonly been advanced as a prime reason for the accelerating rate of STDs. A related contributory effect of "sexual liberation" has been an increasing tendency to have multiple sexual partners, particularly during one's youth, when the incidence of STDs is the highest. It is also believed that increased use of birth control pills has contributed to the rising rates by reducing the use of vaginal spermicides and the condom, contraceptive methods known to offer some protection against sexually transmitted diseases.

The spread of STDs is facilitated by the unfortunate fact that many of these diseases do not produce obvious symptoms. In some cases, particularly among women, there may be no outward signs at all. Under these circumstances people may unknowingly infect others. In addition, feelings of guilt and embarrassment that often accompany having an STD may prevent people from seeking adequate treatment or informing their sexual partners.

It is possible that the effect of these factors could be counterbalanced through general public understanding of STDs and their prevention. Unfortunately, this has not happened. We hope the present widespread ignorance will eventually be overcome by the development of more meaningful sex education at all levels of society.

The following sections focus on the most common sexually transmitted diseases. There is also a section on AIDS, a relatively uncommon disease that has received more attention than any other STD in the last few years. Table 18.1 summarizes the sexually transmitted diseases discussed in this chapter. If you want more information, we recommend contacting your county health service or VD clinic or calling the VD National Hotline.* These services will answer questions, send free literature, and most important, give you the name and telephone number of a local physician or public clinic that will treat STDs free or at minimal cost.

Common Vaginal Infections

There are several kinds of vaginal infections that may be transmitted through sexual interaction. Because they are also frequently contracted through nonsexual means, they are not generally referred to as venereal diseases. Vaginitis and leukorrhea are general terms applied to a variety of vaginal infections characterized by a whitish discharge. The secretion may also be yellow or green in color because of the presence of pus cells, and it often has a disagreeable odor. Additional symptoms of vaginitis may include irritation and itching of the genital tissue, buring during urination, and pain around the vaginal opening during intercourse.

Vaginal infections are far more common than some of the more serious STDs like gonorrhea and syphilis. Practically every woman experiences one or more of these infections during her life. In fact, vaginitis is one of the most common reasons women consult physicians. Under typical circumstances, many of the organisms that cause vaginal infections are relatively harmless. In fact, some routinely live in the vagina, and they cause no trouble unless something alters the normal vaginal environment and allows them to overgrow. The vagina normally houses bacteria (lactobacilli) that help to maintain a healthy vaginal environment. The pH of the vagina is usually sufficiently acidic to ward off most infections. However, certain conditions may alter the pH toward the alkaline side, and this may leave a woman vulnerable. Some factors that increase the likelihood of vaginal infection include antibiotic therapy, use of contraceptive pills, menstruation, pregnancy, wearing panty hose and nylon underwear, douching, and lowered resistance from stress or lack of sleep. A few women appear to have such a delicately balanced vaginal ecosystem that even a brief change in vaginal pH is sufficient to allow pathogenic (infection-causing) organisms to overwhelm the protective lactobacilli. These women may develop symptoms of vaginitis after each coital encounter, because the alkalinity of semen may reduce vaginal acidity enough to allow the pathogenic organisms to gain control. The use of condoms or a postcoital vinegar douche will usually overcome this problem (Friedrich, 1985).

Approximately 90% of women with vaginitis have an infection caused by *Gardnerella*, *Candida*, or *Trichomonas*, either alone or in combination (Friedrich, 1985). Of the infections caused by these organisms, *Gardnerella vaginalis* is the most common, followed in order of frequency by candidosis and trichomoniasis (Brown et al., 1984).

---

*The VD National Hotline can be dialed toll free from 8:00 A.M. to 8:00 P.M. weekdays and from 10:00 A.M. to 6:00 P.M. weekends. The number is 1–800–227–8922 (in California, 1–800–982–5883).

Gardnerella vaginalis

Gardnerella vaginalis (formerly known as *Hemophilus vaginalis*) is a vaginal infection caused by a bacterium of the same name.

Incidence and Transmission. Not long ago the *Gardnerella vaginalis* bacterium was dismissed as a harmless organism in the normal vaginal flora. However, physicians are now well aware that this organism acts as a pathogen (infection-causing agent) in women and men alike, producing an array of effects ranging from aesthetically displeasing symptoms to serious clinical complications. There is evidence that *Gardnerella* infection is the most common cause of vaginitis in American women and that it is present in as many as 50% of sexually active unmarried women who consult a physician about gynecological problems (Brown et al., 1984). A large majority of male partners of women with diagnosed *Gardnerella* also harbor the organism usually without any clinical symptoms. In fact, evidence suggests that asymptomatic males in the general population are serving as a primary reservoir for this infectious organism (Watson, 1985). Coitus is the primary mode of transmitting the infection in the vast majority of women and men.

Symptoms and Complications. The most predominant symptom of *Gardnerella* in women is a foul smelling, thin discharge that resembles flour paste in consistency. The discharge is usually gray, but it may also be white, yellow, or green. The disagreeable odor, often noticed first by an infected woman's sexual partner, is typically described as fishy or musty. This smell may be particularly noticeable after coitus, because the alkaline seminal fluid reacts with the bacteria, causing the release of the chemicals that produce the smell (Friedrich, 1985). A small number of infected women experience irritation of the genital tissues and mild burning during urination. As mentioned earlier, most men are asymptomatic. However, some males infected with *Gardnerella* develop inflammation of the foreskin and glans of their penis, **urethritis** (inflammation of the urethral tube), and **cystitis** (bladder infection) (Watson, 1985).

Treatment. The treatment of choice for *Gardnerella vaginalis* is metronidazole (Flagyl) by mouth for seven days (Friedrich, 1985; Centers for Disease Control, 1985a). When this drug is contraindicated (inadvisable) because of pregnancy or other factors, ampicillin or amoxicillin may be used. To avoid "ping-ponging" the disease back and forth, the male sexual partner(s) of an infected woman should be treated at the same time.

Moniliasis

Moniliasis, also commonly referred to as *candidosis* or a *yeast infection*, is caused by a yeastlike fungus called *Candida albicans*.

Incidence and Transmission. The microscopic *Candida* organism is normally present in the vagina of many women; it also inhabits the mouth and large intestine of large numbers of men and women. A disease state results only when certain conditions

(Text continues on p. 588)

Table 18.1   Common Sexually Transmitted Diseases (STDs):
Mode of Transmission, Symptoms, and Treatment

STD	Transmission	Symptoms	Treatment
Gardnerella vaginalis	The *Gardnerella vaginalis* bacterium is transmitted primarily by coitus.	In women, a fishy or musty smelling, thin discharge, like flour paste in consistency and usually gray. Most men are asymptomatic.	Metronidazole (Flagyl), ampicillin, or amoxicillin
Moniliasis (yeast infection)	The *Candida albicans* fungus may accelerate growth when the chemical balance of the vagina is disturbed; it may also be transmitted through sexual interaction.	White, "cheesy" discharge; irritation of vaginal and vulvar tissue.	Vaginal suppositories or cream, such as nystatin and miconazole, or oral ketoconazole
Trichomoniasis	The protozoan parasite *Trichomonas vaginalis* is passed through genital sexual contact, or less frequently by towels, toilet seats, or bathtubs used by an infected person.	White or yellow vaginal discharge with an unpleasant odor; vulva is sore and irritated.	Metronidazole (Flagyl), effective for both sexes
Chlamydial infection	The *Chlamydia trachomatis* bacterium is transmitted primarily through sexual contact. It may also be spread by fingers from one body site to another.	In men, chlamydial infection of the urethra may cause a discharge and burning during urination. *Chlamydia*-caused epididymitis may produce a sense of heaviness in the affected testicle(s), inflammation of the scrotal skin, and painful swelling at the bottom of the testicle. In women, PID caused by *Chlamydia* may include disrupted menstrual periods, abdominal pain, elevated temperature, nausea, vomiting, and headache.	Tetracycline, doxycycline, erythromycin, or trimethoprim-sulfamethoxazole
Gonorrhea ("clap")	The *Neisseria gonorrhoeae* bacterium ("gonococcus") is spread through genital, oral-genital, or genital-anal contact.	Most common symptoms in men are a cloudy discharge from the penis and burning sensations during urination. If disease is untreated, complications may include inflammation of scrotal skin and swelling at base of the testicle. In women, some green or yellowish discharge is produced but commonly remains undetected. At a later stage, PID may develop.	A single-dose regimen for eradicating gonorrhea (oral amoxicillin or ampicillin or injected procaine penicillin G) followed by seven days of medication effective against *Chlamydia* (tetracycline, doxycycline, or erythromycin)
Syphilis	The *Treponema pallidum* bacterium ("spirochete") is transmitted from open lesions during genital, oral-genital, or genital-anal contact.	*Primary stage:* A painless chancre appears at the site where the spirochetes entered the body. *Secondary stage:* The chancre disappears and a generalized skin rash develops. *Latent stage:* There may be no observable symptoms. *Tertiary stage:* Heart failure, blindness, mental disturbance, and many other symptoms may occur. Death may result.	Benzathine penicillin, tetracycline, or erythromycin

Table 18.1 (*Continued*)

STD	Transmission	Symptoms	Treatment
Nongonococcal urethritis (NGU)	Primary causes are believed to be the bacteria *Chlamydia trachomatis* and *Ureaplasma urealyticum*, most commonly transmitted in coitus. Some NGU may result from allergic reactions or from *Trichomonas* infection.	Inflammation of the urethral tube. A man has a discharge from the penis and irritation during urination. A woman may have a mild discharge of pus from the vagina, but often shows no symptoms.	Tetracycline or erythromycin
Herpes	The genital herpes virus (*Herpes simplex* type 2, or HSV-2) appears to be transmitted primarily by vaginal, oral-genital, or anal sexual intercourse. The oral herpes virus (HSV-1) is transmitted primarily by kissing.	One or more small red, painful bumps (papules) appear in the region of the genitals (genital herpes) or mouth (oral herpes). The papules develop into painful blisters that eventually rupture to form wet, open sores.	No known cure; a variety of treatments may reduce symptoms; oral acyclovir (Zovirax) may promote healing and suppress recurrent outbreaks
Viral hepatitis	The hepatitis B virus may be transmitted by blood, semen, vaginal secretions, and saliva. Manual, oral, or penile stimulation of the anus are practices strongly associated with the spread of this viral agent. Hepatitis A seems to be primarily spread via the fecal-oral route. Oral-anal sexual contact is a common mode for sexual transmission of hepatitis A.	Vary from nonexistent to mild, flulike symptoms to an incapacitating illness characterized by high fever, vomiting, and severe abdominal pain.	No specific therapy; treatment generally consists of bedrest and adequate fluid intake
Pubic lice ("crabs")	*Phthirus pubis*, the pubic louse, is spread easily through body contact or through shared clothing or bedding.	Persistent itching. Lice are visible and may often be located in pubic hair or other body hair.	Preparations such as A-200 pyrinate or Kwell (gamma benzene hexachloride)
Genital warts (venereal warts)	The virus is spread primarily through genital, anal, or oral-genital interaction.	Warts are hard and yellow-gray on dry skin areas; soft pinkish-red, and cauliflower-like on moist areas.	Topical agents like podophyllin; cauterization; freezing; surgical removal; or vaporization by carbon dioxide laser
Acquired immune deficiency syndrome (AIDS)	Blood and semen are the major vehicles for transmitting the AIDS virus, which attacks the immune system. It appears to be passed primarily through sexual contact, needle sharing among IV drug abusers, or less commonly through administration of blood products.	Vary with the type of cancer or opportunistic infections that inflict an AIDS virus victim. Common symptoms include fevers, night sweats, weight loss, loss of appetite, fatigue, swollen lymph nodes, diarrhea and/or bloody stools, atypical bruising or bleeding, skin rashes, headache, chronic cough, a whitish coating on the tongue or in the throat.	At present, therapy limited to specific treatment(s) of opportunistic infections and tumors; no drugs shown to have antiviral impact on the AIDS virus

allow the yeast to overgrow other microorganisms in the vagina. This accelerated growth may result from pregnancy, use of birth control pills, or diabetes—conditions that increase the amount of sugar stored in vaginal cells (*Candida albicans* thrives in the presence of sugar). If a nonpregnant woman has repeated yeast infections, it may be advisable for her to be tested for diabetes or other blood sugar disorders. Another factor is the use of oral antibiotics that reduce the number of lactobacilli, mentioned earlier as important for a healthy vaginal environment. This permits *Candida* to multiply rapidly. In one study, women who wore panty hose were found to be three times more likely to have yeast vaginitis than women who did not wear panty hose (Heidrich et al., 1984).

Recently it has become clear that diet can play an important role in this disease. The ingestion of large amounts of dairy products, sugar, and artificial sweeteners leads to the excessive excretion of urine sugars that may promote *Candida* overgrowth. Reducing the intake of these substances can lead to a dramatic reduction in the frequency of recurrences of yeast infections (Friedrich, 1985).

If the yeast organism is not already present in the woman's vagina, it may be transmitted to this area in a variety of ways. It may be conveyed from the anus by wiping back to front or on the surface of a menstrual pad, or it can be transmitted through sexual interaction, since the organism may be harbored under the foreskin of an uncircumcised man. It may also be passed from a partner's mouth to a woman's vagina during oral sex (Blum, 1984; Friedrich, 1985).

Symptoms.   A woman with a yeast infection may notice that she has a white, clumpy discharge that looks something like cottage cheese. In addition, moniliasis is often associated with intense itching and soreness of the vaginal and vulval tissues, which typically become red and dry. A woman who has a yeast infection may find coitus quite painful, and irritation from intercourse may worsen the infection.

Treatment.   A variety of different treatments may prove effective in combating yeast infections. Traditional treatment strategies consist of vaginal suppositories or cream, such as clotrimazole, miconazole, or nystatin. In recent studies it has been found that orally administered ketoconazole tablets are as effective as intravaginal treatments (better than 90% cure rate) and that patient compliance with the treatment is much higher for the oral drug (Bingham, 1984; Puolakka and Tuimala, 1983). Since *Candida* is a hardy organism, treatment should be continued for the prescribed length of time (usually two to four weeks) even though the symptoms may disappear in two days.

Trichomoniasis

Trichomoniasis is caused by a one-celled protozoan parasite called *Trichomonas vaginalis*.

Incidence and Transmission.   In females, trichomoniasis accounts for about one fourth of all cases of vaginitis. Not all infected women have noticeable symptoms. Men may carry the infection, too, but it is quite difficult to spot this condition in men, because they generally have no observable symptoms. Nevertheless, some authorities believe that most male sex partners of infected women carry the trichomonas organism in their urethra, and under the foreskin if they are uncircumcised.

The trichomonas organism is hardy and can survive outside the body for several hours on a moist object or in tap water, soapy water, chlorinated water, or hot water (Friedrich, 1985). Thus, it is possible for a woman to become infected if her genitals come in close contact with a towel, washcloth, toilet seat, or other object used by an infected person. It is also believed that the organism may enter a woman's vagina if she uses a swimming pool or bathtub that has been used by an infected individual. However, the main mode of transmission appears to be through genital sexual contact.

Symptoms and Complications. The most common symptom of trichomoniasis infection in women is an abundant, frothy, white or yellow vaginal discharge with an unpleasant odor. The discharge frequently irritates the tissues of the vagina and vulva, causing them to become inflamed, itchy, and sore. The infection is usually limited to the vagina and sometimes the cervix, but occasionally the organism may invade the urethra, bladder, or Bartholin's glands. Some health specialists believe that long-term trichomonal infection may damage the cells of the cervix and increase susceptibility to cervical cancer. However, prompt, effective treatment prevents permanent cervical damage.

Infected males generally have no observable symptoms. Occasionally, there may be a slight, whitish discharge from the penis, accompanied by some sensations of tickling, itching, or burning in the urethral tract.

Treatment. To avoid passing the disease back and forth, it is important that the male partner(s) of the infected woman be treated even if asymptomatic. If a male partner is not treated, the couple should use condoms to prevent reinfection. The recommended drug regimen for both sexes is a single 2 gram dose of metronidazole (Flagyl) taken by mouth (Centers for Disease Control, 1985a). Metronidazole is strongly contraindicated in the first trimester of pregnancy and should be avoided throughout pregnancy. Topical creams, such as clotrimazole, may provide symptomatic improvement and some cures in women unable to take metronidazole.

Chlamydial Infection

Chlamydial infection is caused by *Chlamydia trachomatis*, a bacterial microorganism. Although classified as a bacterium, *C. trachomatis* is like viruses in that it only grows intracellularly. This organism is now recognized as the cause of a diverse group of genital infections. *Chlamydia* is also involved in a number of infections of newborns and is "the greatest single worldwide cause of preventable blindness" (Crum and Ellner, 1985).

Incidence and Transmission. It is now widely recognized that *C. trachomatis* infections are the most prevalent and among the most damaging of all sexually transmitted diseases (Centers for Disease Control, 1985b; Judson, 1985). An estimated three to four million American men, women, and infants are infected with *Chlamydia* each year. Data obtained from STD clinics throughout the United States indicate marked increases in the incidence of chlamydial infections in the period from the mid-1970s to the mid-1980s (Centers for Disease Control, 1985b). Studies of different research populations have provided a range of chlamydial infection rates. For example, chlamydial infection was isolated in approximately 7% of women attending a health clinic at UCLA (Wiesmeier et al., 1984), but it was found in 40% of the males and 26% of the females among a group of inner-city adolescents attending a clinic for genitourinary complaints (Jaffe et al., 1985). Chlamydial infections are diagnosed one to three times more frequently than gonorrhea in public STD clincs, and up to 10 times more frequently in university student health clinics and in private practice (Bowie, 1984).

In men, the *Chlamydia* organism is estimated to be the cause of approximately half of the cases of **epididymitis** (infection of the epididymis) and **nongonococcal urethritis** (infection of the urethral tube not caused by gonorrhea) (Crum and Ellner, 1985; Centers for Disease Control, 1985b). Chlamydial infections among women are of even greater clinical importance because of the increased risk of adverse reproductive consequences. There are two general types of genital chlamydial infections in females—infections of the mucosa of the lower reproductive tract, commonly manifested as urethritis or **cervicitis** (infection of the cervix), and invasive infections of the upper reproductive tract, which are expressed as **pelvic inflammatory disease** (PID). PID typically occurs when chlamydial or other infectious organisms spread from the cervix upward, infecting the lining of the uterus (*endometritis*), the fallopian tubes (*salpingitis*), and possibly the ovaries and other adjacent abdominal structures. *Chlamydia* may account for as many as one-half of the one million recognized cases of PID that occur annually in the United States (Centers for Disease Control, 1985b). At least one-quarter of the one million American women who develop this disease each year suffer long-term consequences (Washington et al., 1986). "Pelvic inflammatory disease is one of the most widespread and debilitating diseases affecting women today" (Washington et al., 1986, p. 1735).

C. trachomatis is also the most common cause of eye infections in newborns, who can become infected as they pass through the birth canal. Various studies estimate that sometime in the first three weeks of life, one-fifth to one-half of infants born to infected mothers will develop **conjunctivitis** (inflammation of the mucous membrane that lines the inner surface of the eyelid and the exposed surface of the eyeball) (Centers for Disease Control, 1985b). In addition, 3% to 18% of the babies of infected mothers will develop chlamydial pneumonia during the first few months of their lives (Centers for Disease Control, 1985b). This disease is generally mild, but in some instances it can be severe and require hospitalization.

Chlamydial disease is transmitted primarily through sexual contact. It may also be spread by fingers from one body site to another, such as the genitals to the eyes. In areas of the world where people live in conditions of poor santitation and overcrowding (such as the Middle East, Africa, and India) the disease is commonly spread through sexual activity and by nonsexual modes of transmission such as by hands, flies, and contact with human waste (Bowie, 1984). In the United States, the major mode of transmission is sexual relations. Approximately 70% of female sex partners of men with confirmed chlamydial urethritis have *C. trachomatis* in their reproductive tract; and as many as 50% of male partners of women with confirmed chlamydial infection have *Chlamydia* in their urethras (Centers for Disease Control, 1985b). Genital chlamydial infection rates appear to be most prevalent among young people with multiple sexual partners. The risk of acquiring this infection rises in proportion to the number of sex partners one has (Bowie, 1984; Centers for Disease Control, 1985b).

One of the most disheartening aspects of this disease is that the majority of females with lower reproductive tract chlamydial infection have few or no symptoms. This is also true of most men and women with rectal chlamydial infection and as many as 30% of men with chlamydial urethritis (Centers for Disease Control, 1985b). Laboratory diagnostic tests are necessary to confirm the presence of *C. trachomatis*. At the present time, a cell culture is the best of several labor intensive and hence expensive diagnostic procedures.

The risk of acquiring chlamydial infection can be reduced by using a barrier method of contraception (condoms, condoms plus foam, diaphragm, or diaphragm plus foam) (Bowie, 1984; McCormack et al., 1985; Centers for Disease Control, 1985b). Women who use oral contraceptives have an increased risk of becoming infected with *Chlamydia* (Jaffe et al., 1985; Centers for Disease Control, 1985b; Washington et al., 1985).

Chlamydial and gonorrheal infections are known to play a major role in the causation of PID. For many years medical experts speculated about how these bacteria ascend through the cervical mucus to the upper reproductive tract. A popular hypothesis about how this process occurs suggests that these microorganisms adhere to sperm cells, thereby hitching a ride to the uterus and fallopian tubes (Droegemueller, 1984; Keith et al., 1984). Two in vitro ("test tube") experiments demonstrated that *C. trachomatis* bacteria do in fact adhere to sperm cells (Wolner-Hanssen and Mardh, 1984). The observation that female partners of men who do not produce sperm rarely develop salpingitis provides further evidence that sperm are a factor in the transmission of bacteria from the lower to upper female reproductive tract (Toth et al., 1984). There is also good evidence that the highly motile *Trichomonas* organisms may carry attached bacteria to the upper reproductive tract (Keith et al., 1984).

There is a marked tendency for a chlamydial infection to coexist with other STDs. It is estimated that 15%–30% of men with gonococcal urethritis have simultaneous chlamydial urethral infections and that 25%–50% of women with gonorrhea also have chlamydial infections (Centers for Disease Control, 1985b). Women who have other STDs, such as trichomoniasis and several bacterial types of vaginitis, are also at increased risk of developing chlamydial infection.

Symptoms and Complications. *Nongonococcal urethritis* (NGU) in males is commonly caused by chlamydial infections. Symptoms of NGU include a discharge from the penis and burning during urination (more details about symptoms are provided in a later section on NGU). An appreciable minority of men with NGU caused by *Chlamydia* are asymptomatic. The other major syndrome associated with *C. trachomatis* infection in men is epididymitis, the symptoms of which may include a sensation of heaviness in the affected testicle(s), inflammation of the scrotal skin, and the formation of a small area of hard, painful swelling at the bottom of the testicle.

Most women with lower reproductive tract chlamydial infections have few or no symptoms. Symptoms, when they do occur, may include mild irritation or itching of the genital tissues, burning during urination, and a slight discharge. PID resulting from invasion of the upper reproductive tract by *C. trachomatis* often produces a variety of symptoms, which may include disrupted menstrual periods, pain in the lower abdomen, elevated temperature, nausea, vomiting, and headache. Chlamydial salpingitis is a major cause of infertility and ectopic pregnancy (Crum and Ellner, 1985; Kane et al., 1984; Centers for Disease Control, 1985b). Even after PID has been effectively treated, residual scar tissue in the fallopian tubes leaves some women sterile. "The risk of infertility is significantly higher with chlamydial PID than with gonococcal PID, perhaps because the symptoms of chlamydial PID tend to be milder and are often ignored" (Crum and Ellner, 1985, p. 158). A woman who has had PID should be cautioned about the use of the IUD as a method of birth control. An IUD does not prevent fertilization (see Chapter 11 for an explanation of how the IUD prevents pregnancy); thus, a tiny sperm cell may negotiate a partially blocked area and fertilize an ovum that, because of its larger size, subsequently becomes lodged in the scarred tube. The result is an ectopic pregnancy, a serious hazard to the woman.

Chlamydial infections also contribute to a variety of pregnancy complications, which may include postpartum *endometritis* (inflammation of the lining of the uterine walls), spontaneous abortion, premature labor, and possible death of the newborn (Faro, 1985; Centers for Disease Control, 1985b). One study found that stillbirth or infant death occurred ten times more frequently than the norm in women with chlamydial infections (Martin et al., 1982).

Treatment. Drugs effective against *C. trachomatis* include tetracycline, doxycycline, erythromycin, and trimethoprimsulfamethoxazole. Penicillin is not effective. Since chlamydial infection often coexists with gonorrhea, it is advisable to employ a drug regimen that is effective against both infectious organisms. Tetracycline is the treatment of choice for men, and for nonpregnant women with uncomplicated infections of the lower reproductive tract. For pregnant women and others for whom tetracycline is contraindicated, an effective alternative drug is erythromycin (Centers for Disease Control, 1985a and 1985b). All sex partners exposed to *C. trachomatis* should be examined for STDs and treated if necessary.

To reduce the risk of an infant developing chlamydial conjunctivitis after passing through the birth canal of an infected woman, either erythromycin or tetracycline ointment is put into the eyes of exposed newborns as soon as possible after delivery.

Gonorrhea

Gonorrhea, known in street language as "clap," is an STD caused by the bacterium *Neisseria gonorrhoeae* (also called "gonococcus").

Incidence and Transmission. Gonorrhea is a very common communicable disease. During the period 1980 to 1984 approximately one million cases of gonorrhea were reported annually in the United States, a figure which is no doubt much smaller than

Table 18.2   *Incidence of Reported Gonorrhea and Syphilis in the 1980s*

Year	Gonorrhea[a]	Syphilis[a]
1985	861,000	25,000
1984	878,000	28,000
1983	898,000	32,000
Median 1980–1984	989,000	32,000

[a]Annual incidence of reported cases rounded to the nearest thousand. The actual incidence of gonorrhea may be 4 to 10 times the reported incidence.

Source: Centers for Disease Control, 1985c, p. 756; Fitzgerald, 1984, p. 91.

the number of actual cases. (The Centers for Disease Control estimates the true incidence of gonorrhea to be three to five million cases annually.) Recently there has been an encouraging, albeit slight, decline in the number of reported gonorrhea infections (see Table 18.2). The 861,000 cases reported in 1985 represents a 13% decline from 989,000 cases, the median number of annually reported cases for the years 1980–1984.

Evidence suggests that women have a slightly greater than 50% chance of developing gonorrhea after a single exposure to an infected partner. In contrast, a man who has intercourse once with an infected woman has a lower risk, probably around 20% to 25%, of contracting the disease (Platt et al., 1983; Rein, 1977). The risks for both sexes increase with repeated exposures.

Survival of the gonococcus bacterium is facilitated by the warm mucous membranes found in the tissues of the genitals, anus, and throat. Its mode of transmission is by sexual contact—penile-vaginal, oral-genital, or genital-anal. Until recently health professionals believed that gonococci do not survive when removed from the body's mucous membranes and, thus, that one cannot contract this disease from toilet seats, towels, and other objects used by an infected person. However, research has shown that gonococci may survive for up to 24 hours on towels, 3 hours on toilet paper, and 2 to 24 hours on toilet seats (Neinstein et al., 1984). In one study, researchers found that gonococci contained in the urethral discharge from male patients with diagnosed gonorrhea remained viable on a toilet seat and toilet paper for several hours. However, these researchers caution that though "the ability of the gonococcus to survive for several hours in dried purulent discharge on toilet seats or toilet paper suggests a possible source for nonsexual acquisition of gonorrhea," their data "in no way prove that such transmission can occur . . ." (Gilbaugh and Fuchs, 1979, p. 93). It is noteworthy that these investigators were unable to find any gonococci in random samplings from toilet seats in 72 public restrooms.

Symptoms and Complications.   Early symptoms of gonorrheal infection are more likely to be evident in men than women. The majority of men who experience gonococcal urethritis will have some symptoms, ranging from mild to quite pronounced. However, it is not uncommon for men with this type of infection to be asymptomatic.

Most of us would find it difficult to discuss with our lover(s) the possibility that we have transmitted a disease to him or her during sexual sharing. Due to the stigma often associated with STDs, it can be bad enough admitting to having one of these diseases. The need to tell others that they may have "caught" something from you may seem to be a formidable task. You might fear that such a revelation will jeopardize a valued relationship, or worry that you will be considered "dirty." In relationships presumed to be monogamous, a person might fear that telling his or her partner about an STD will threaten mutual trust. "However, lovers who attempt to conceal a sex-related illness risk a good deal more in the long run than those who have the courage to discuss the situation right away" (Castleman, 1980, p. 230).

Not disclosing the existence of an STD risks the health of one's partner(s). Many people may not have symptoms and thus may not become aware that they have contracted a disease until they discover it for themselves,

perhaps only after they have developed serious complications. Furthermore, if a lover remains untreated, she or he may reinfect you even after you have been cured. Unlike some diseases (like measles and chicken pox), STDs do not provide immunity against future infections. You can get one, give it to your lover, be cured, and then get it back again if he or she remains untreated (a process some health authorities call "ping-pong VD").

The following suggestions may provide some guidelines for telling a partner about your STD. Remember, these are only suggestions that have worked for some people; they may need to be modified to fit your particular circumstances. This is a sensitive issue that requires thoughtful consideration and planning.

1. Be honest. There is nothing to be gained by downplaying the potential risks associated with STDs. If you tell a partner, "I have this little drip, but it probably means nothing," you may

---

In one study approximately 40% of the sexual partners of women with diagnosed gonorrhea were found to have asymptomatic gonorrhea (Starcher et al., 1983). The incidence of asymptomatic gonorrhea is considerably greater in women; as many as 80% will not detect the disease until it has progressed considerably.

The high frequency of infections without symptoms makes it imperative for infected individuals to tell their sexual partners once they are diagnosed as having gonorrhea. The same thing can be said for all of the other STDs discussed in this chapter. One cannot assume that a partner who has been infected with a disease during sexual sharing will have symptoms, or that he or she will understand the meaning of any symptoms that might occur and seek proper medical treatment. Box 18.1 offers some suggestions that may be helpful when telling a partner about an STD infection.

Early Symptoms in the Male.   In men, early symptoms typically appear within three to five days after sexual contact with an infected person. However, symptoms may show up as early as one day or as late as two weeks after contact. The two most common signs of infection are a bad-smelling, cloudy discharge from the penis (see color plate 8) and burning sensations during urination. About 30%–40% of infected men also have swollen and tender lymph glands in the groin. These early symptoms

regret it. Stick with the facts and be sure your partner understands the importance of obtaining a medical evaluation.

2. Even if you suspect that your partner may have been the source of your infection, there is little to be gained by blaming him or her. Instead, you may wish to simply acknowledge that you have the disease and are concerned that your partner gets proper medical attention.

3. Your attitude may have considerable impact upon how your partner receives the news. If you display high levels of anxiety, guilt, fear, or disgust, your partner may reflect these feelings in her or his response. Try to simply present the facts in as clear and calm a fashion as you can manage.

4. Be sensitive to your partner's feelings. Be prepared for reactions of anger or resentment. These are understandable initial responses. Being supportive and demonstrating a willingness to listen without becoming defensive may be the best tactics for diffusing negative responses.

5. Engaging in sexual intimacies after you become aware of your condition and before you obtain medical assurances that you are no longer contagious is clearly inappropriate.

6. Medical examinations and treatments for STDs, when necessary, can be a financial burden. Offering to pay for some or all of these expenses may help to maintain (or re-establish) good will in your relationship.

7. In the case of herpes, where recurrences are unpredictable and the possibility of infecting a new partner is an ongoing concern, it is probably a good idea to tell him or her about your herpes before sexual intimacies take place. You may wish to preface your first sexual interaction by saying "There is something we should talk over first." Be sure to emphasize that herpes is usually preventable when proper precautions are taken.

often clear up on their own without treatment. However, this is no guarantee that the disease has been eradicated by the body's immune system. The bacteria may still be present, and a man may still be able to infect a partner.

Complications in the Male.   If the infection goes without treatment for two to three weeks, it may spread up the genitourinary tract. Here, it may involve the prostate, bladder, kidneys, and testicles. Most men who continue to harbor the gonococcus have only periodic flareups of the minor symptoms of discharge and burning during urination. In a small number of men, however, the bacteria cause abscesses to form in the prostate. These may result in fever, painful bowel movement, difficulty in urinating, and general discomfort. In approximately one out of five men who remain untreated for longer than a month, the bacteria move down the vas deferens to infect one or both of the epididymal structures that lie along the back of each testicle. Generally only one side is infected initially, usually the left. The symptoms of *epididymitis* were described in the discussion of chlamydial infection. Even after successful treatment, gonococcal epididymitis leaves scar tissue, which can block the flow of sperm from the affected testicle. Sterility does not usually result, since this complication is usually restricted to only one testicle. However, if treatment is still not carried out after epididymitis has occurred on one side, the infection may spread to the other testicle, rendering the man permanently sterile.

Early Symptoms in the Female.   As mentioned earlier, women are often unaware of the early signs of gonorrheal infection. The primary site of infection, the cervix, may become inflamed without producing any observable symptoms. A green or yellowish discharge usually results, but since this is rarely heavy, it commonly remains undetected. A woman who is very aware of her vaginal secretions (perhaps from using the mucus method of birth control), is more likely to note the infection during these early stages. Sometimes the discharge may be irritating to the vulva tissues. However, when a woman seeks medical attention for an irritating discharge, her physician may fail to consider gonorrhea, since many other infectious organisms produce this symptom. Also, many women who have gonorrhea also have trichomoniasis, and this condition may mask the presence of gonorrhea. Consequently, it is essential for any woman who thinks she may have gonorrhea to make certain that she is tested for gonorrhea when she is examined. (A Pap smear is not a test for gonorrhea.)

Complications in the Female.   It is not uncommon for the Bartholin's glands to be invaded by the gonococcus organism. When this happens there are usually no symptoms. Far more serious complications result from spread of the disease to the upper reproductive tract, where it often causes pelvic inflammatory disease. The symptoms of PID, discussed in the previous section on chlamydial infection, are often more severe when the infecting organism is gonococcus rather than *C. trachomatis*. Sterility and ectopic pregnancy are very serious consequences occasionally associated with gonococcal PID. Another serious complication that may result from PID is the development of tough bands of scar tissue adhesions that may link several pelvic cavity structures (tubes, ovaries, uterus, and so forth) to each other, to the abdominal walls, or to both. These adhesions can cause severe pain during coitus or when a woman is standing or walking.

Other Complications in Both Sexes.   In about 1% of adult men and women with gonorrhea, the gonococci enter the bloodstream and spread throughout the body to produce a variety of symptoms, including chills, fever, loss of appetite, skin lesions, and arthritic pain in the joints (Fitzgerald, 1984). If arthritic symptoms develop, quick treatment is essential to avoid permanent joint damage. In very rare cases, the gonococcus organism may invade the heart, liver, spinal cord, and brain.

An infant may develop a gonococcal eye infection after passing through the birth canal of an infected woman. The use of silver nitrate or penicillin eye drops immediately after birth averts this potential complication. There are a few rare cases recorded where adults have transmitted the bacteria to their eyes by touching this region immediately after handling their genitals. That is one reason it is important to wash with soap and water immediately after self-examination.

Oral contact with infected genitals may result in transmission of the gonococcal bacteria to the throat, causing pharyngeal gonorrhea. Most people who have pharyngeal gonorrhea are asymptomatic, but a few may have a sore throat. Rectal gonorrhea may be caused by anal intercourse or, in a woman, by transmission of the bacteria from the vagina to the anal opening in menstrual bleeding or vaginal discharge. This form of gonorrhea is often asymptomatic, particularly in females, but it may be accompanied by itching, rectal discharge, and bowel disorders.

Because infections of the throat or anus often do not produce observable symptoms, it is very important to examine laboratory cultures taken from the throats or anuses of people who have engaged in oral-genital or anal intercourse with those suspected of having gonorrhea. Health practitioners often overlook these important tests unless a person requests them.

Treatment. Since gonorrhea is often confused with other ailments, it is important to make the correct diagnosis. This can be accomplished by culturing material taken from the male urethra or female cervix. One disadvantage of the culture method is that it takes 24 to 72 hours to isolate the gonococcus organism. Consequently, a much quicker laboratory procedure called a Gram stain is often employed, in which genital discharge is examined microscopically. This procedure works well in males but it is not sensitive in females. Recently a new approach involving an enzyme immunoassay procedure has been shown to be highly sensitive for both sexes (Demetriou et al., 1984). This test is inexpensive and the results are available in three hours.

An important consideration in gonorrhea treatment is the fact that a coexisting chlamydial infection has been shown to be present in up to 45% of gonorrhea cases when adequate *Chlamydia* cultures are performed (Centers for Disease Control, 1985a). Consequently, many health practitioners utilize a treatment strategy that is effective against both gonorrheal and chlamydial infections. Treatment guidelines recently published by the Centers for Disease Control suggest a single-dose regimen for eradicating gonorrhea followed by seven days of medication effective against *Chlamydia*. The single-dose regimen involves taking either amoxicillin or ampicillin by mouth or an injection of procaine penicillin G. (Spectinomycin, injected intramuscularly, may be substituted in cases of penicillin allergy.) In addition to taking one of these single-dose medications, the patient is also provided probenecid by mouth. The suggested medication during the follow-up period is tetracycline or doxycycline. In cases where tetracyclines are contraindicated or not tolerated, the single-dose regimen may be followed by erythromycin (Centers for Disease Control, 1985a).

In recent years we have seen the emergence of two new strains of penicillin-resistant gonococci: penicillinase-producing *N. gonorrhoeae* (PPNG) and chromosomally mediated resistant *N. gonorrhoeae* (CMRNG). People infected with PPNG or CMRNG may be treated effectively with single-dose injections of spectinomycin or ceftriaxone, followed up with seven days of tetracycline, doxycycline, or erythromycin.

A reduction in the symptoms of a gonorrheal infection does not necessarily imply total cure, and it is essential that a follow-up negative culture be obtained three to seven days after completion of treatment before a person may conclude that he or she is free of the infection. All sex partners exposed to a person with diagnosed gonorrhea should be examined, cultured, and treated prophylactically with one of the previously outlined drug regimens that covers both gonococcal and chlamydial infections.

Syphilis

Syphilis is an STD caused by a thin, corkscrewlike bacterium called *Treponema pallidum* (also commonly called a "spirochete").

Incidence and Transmission. As you can see in Table 18.2, the incidence of reported syphilis cases in the United States has dropped off rather notably in the last few years. The approximately 25,000 cases reported in 1985 represent a 22% decline from 32,000 cases, the median number of annually reported cases from 1980 to 1984. Many health officials believe that the recent decline in the rate of syphilis (and gonorrhea) may reflect a trend that began in the early 1980s, when widespread fear about the sexual transmission of viruses causing herpes and AIDS began to significantly alter sexual practices. These changes to safer sexual practices are perhaps most pronounced among gay males, who account for more than half of the syphilis cases reported in the United States (Specter, 1985). The actual incidence of syphilis is undoubtedly much higher and some STD specialists speculate that as many as nine cases go unreported for each case that is recorded (Fitzgerald, 1984). Regardless of its frequency, it should not be taken lightly: Unlike most STDs, syphilis can result in death.

Treponema pallidum requires a warm and moist environment for survival. It is transmitted almost exclusively from open lesions of infected individuals to the mucous membranes or skin abrasions of sexual partners through penile-vaginal, oral-genital, or genital-anal contacts. Syphilitic organisms may also be transmitted from an infected pregnant woman to her unborn child through the placental blood system. The resulting congenital syphilis can cause death or extreme damage to infected newborns. If the disease is successfully treated before the fourth month of pregnancy, the fetus will not be affected. Therefore, pregnant women should be tested for syphilis sometime during their first three months of pregnancy.

Symptoms and Complications. If untreated, syphilis may progress through four phases of development. These are known as the primary, secondary, latent, and tertiary stages. A brief description of each follows.

Primary Syphilis. In its initial, or primary, phase syphilis is generally manifested in the form of a painless sore called a **chancre** (pronounced "shanker"), which appears at the site where the spirochete organism enters the body (see color plates 9 and 10). In women who have coitus with infected men, this sore most commonly appears on the inner vaginal walls or cervix. It may also appear on the external genitals, particularly the labia. In men, the chancre most often occurs on the glans of the penis, but it may also show up on the penile shaft or on the scrotum. Although 95% of chancres are genital, they may occur in the mouth or rectum or on the anus or breast (Fitzgerald, 1984). People who have had oral sex with an infected individual may develop a sore on their lips or tongue. Anal intercourse may result in chancres appearing in the rectum or around the anus. The following is an excellent description of the chancre sore:

When the chancre first develops, it is a dull red bump about the size of a pea. The surface of the bump soon breaks down and the chancre becomes a rounded, dull red, open sore which may be covered by a yellow or grey crusty scab. The chancre is painless and does not bleed easily. In about 50% of cases, the chancre is surrounded by a thin pink border. The edges of the chancre are often raised and hard, like the edges of a button. The hardness may spread to the base of the chancre and eventually to the surrounding tissue, making the whole area feel hard and rubbery. (Cherniak and Feingold, 1973, p. 30)

In view of the typically painless nature of the chancre, it often goes undiscovered when it occurs on internal structures like the rectum, vagina, or cervix. (Occasionally chancres may be painful and they may occur in multiple sites.) Even when it is noticed, some people do not seek treatment. Unfortunately (from the long term perspective), the chancre generally heals without treatment in one to five weeks after its initial appearance. For the next few weeks the person usually has no symptoms but may infect an unsuspecting partner. After about six weeks (sometimes as little as two weeks or as long as six months), the disease progresses to the secondary stage.

Secondary Syphilis.   This phase is characterized by the appearance of a skin rash on the body that may range from barely noticeable to severe, with raised bumps that have a rubbery, hard consistency. While the rash may look terrible, it typically does not hurt or itch. If it is at all noticeable, it generally prompts a visit to a physician, if the earlier appearance of a chancre did not. In addition to a generalized rash, a person may have flulike symptoms such as fever, swollen lymph glands, tiredness, and weight loss. Even if treatment is not provided, these symptoms eventually subside, usually within a few weeks. Rather than being eliminated, however, the disease may enter the potentially more dangerous latent phase.

Latent Syphilis.   This stage can last for several years, and during this time there may be no observable symptoms of the disease. Nevertheless, the infecting organisms may continue to multiply, preparing for the final, most horrendous stage of syphilitic infection. After one year of the latent stage has elapsed, the infected individual is no longer contagious to sexual partners (Cherniak and Feingold, 1973). However, a pregnant woman with syphilis in any stage can pass the infection to the fetus.

Tertiary Syphilis.   A small percentage of those individuals who do not obtain effective treatment during the first three stages of syphilis are affected by the tertiary stage later in life. The final manifestations of syphilis can be severe, often resulting in death. They occur anywhere from 3 to 40 years after initial infection and may include such conditions as heart failure, blindness, ruptured blood vessels, paralysis, skin ulcers, liver damage, and severe mental disturbance. Depending on the extent of the damage, treatment even at this late stage may be beneficial.

Treatment.   Primary, secondary, or latent syphilis of less than one year's duration may be effectively treated with a single intramuscular injection of benzathine penicillin. People allergic to penicillin may be treated with tetracycline or erythromycin. Syphilis of more than one year's duration is treated with intramuscular injections of benzathine penicillin once a week for three successive weeks. People with long-duration syphilis who are allergic to penicillin may be treated with tetracycline or erythromycin (Centers for Disease Control, 1985a).

All sex partners exposed to a person with infectious syphilis within the preceding three months should be treated, using the drug regimen for syphilis of less than one year's duration. All individuals who have been treated for this disease should have several diagnostic blood tests after the completion of treatment to make certain that they are completely free of the *Treponema pallidum* organism.

Nongonococcal Urethritis

Any inflammation of the urethra tube that is not caused by gonorrhea is called **nongonococcal urethritis** or *NGU*. Until 1974 it was not known what organisms were the cause of this very common condition. Prior to this time it was also common to call it nonspecific urethritis, or NSU. Now it is believed that two separate microscopic organisms, *Chlamydia trachomatis* and *Ureaplasma urealyticum* (a member of a group of bacteria called mycoplasmas) are the primary causes of NGU. Occasionally NGU may result from invasion by other infectious agents, such as trichomonas, fungi, or bacteria; allergic reactions to vaginal secretions; or irritation by soaps, vaginal contraceptives, or deodorant sprays.

Incidence and Transmission. NGU is quite common among men: It has an estimated incidence 2.5 times that of gonococcal urethritis (Centers for Disease Control, 1985b). While it generally produces urinary tract symptoms only in men, there is evidence suggesting that women harbor the chlamydia or mycoplasma organisms. The most common forms of NGU, caused by these two organisms, are no doubt transmitted by coitus. The fact that NGU rarely occurs in men who are not involved in sexual interaction supports this contention.

Symptoms and Complications. Men who contract NGU often manifest symptoms similar to those of gonorrheal infection, including discharge from the penis and mild burning during urination. Often the discharge is less pronounced than that which occurs with gonorrhea; it may be evident only in the morning before urinating.

Women infected with *Chlamydia* or *Ureaplasma* are generally unaware of the disease until they are informed that NGU has been diagnosed in a male partner. They frequently show no symptoms, although there may be some itching, burning on urination, and a mild discharge of pus from the vagina. (Cultures may reveal the presence of the causative organism.) An infected woman may have the infection for a long period of time, during which she may pass it to sexual partners. *Chlamydia* present in the cervix of a pregnant woman may contaminate the eyes of her infant at birth and produce a chronic infection that can result in mild scarring of the cornea of the eyes.

The symptoms of NGU generally disappear after two to three months without treatment. However, the disease may still be present. If left untreated in women it may result in cervical inflammation or pelvic inflammatory disease; in men it may spread to the prostate, epididymis, or both (Holmes and Stamm, 1981). In rare cases NGU produces a form of arthritis.

Treatment.   Many physicians assume that any penile discharge is caused by gonorrhea, and thus they may fail to diagnose NGU. Some even begin treatment for gonorrhea before confirming its existence with laboratory tests. Because penicillin, the common treatment for gonorrhea, is not effective against NGU, it is important that an infected person make certain there has been a laboratory diagnosis before receiving treatment. Tetracycline or doxycycline usually clears up the condition. Erythromycin is used for people who are allergic to tetracyclines. All sex partners of individuals diagnosed as having NGU should be examined for the presence of an STD and treated if necessary.

Herpes

Herpes is caused by a virus called *Herpes simplex* (HSV). A virus is a parasite that invades, reproduces, and lives within a cell, thereby disrupting normal cellular activities. There are five different herpes viruses that infect humans, the most common being type 1 (HSV-1) and type 2 (HSV-2). Type 1 is generally confined to nongenital areas and is typically manifested as lesions of the type called "cold sores," or "fever blisters" in the mouth or on the lips (oral herpes). Type 2 generally causes lesions (sores) on and around the genital areas (genital herpes). Occasionally, type 1 affects the genital area, and conversely, type 2 may produce a sore in the mouth area.

Incidence and Transmission.   In the spring of 1986 the Centers for Disease Control estimated that 98 million Americans are afflicted with oral herpes and that 9 million people in the U.S. have genital herpes. During the period from the mid-1960s to the early 1980s, there was a tenfold increase in the number of cases of genital herpes seen by private physicians in this country. Current estimates suggest that there are between 300,000 and 600,000 new cases of genital herpes annually in the United States (Becker et al., 1985).

Genital herpes appears to be transmitted primarily by penile-vaginal, oral-genital, or genital-anal sexual contact. Oral herpes may be transmitted by kissing, sharing towels, drinking out of the same cup, and so on. A person who has oral sex performed on her or him by a partner who has a cold sore or fever blister in the mouth region may develop genital herpes of either the type 1 or type 2 variety.

Herpes simplex viruses have been shown to survive for up to 72 hours on dry gauze and two to four hours on toilet seats, gloves, and a speculum (Neinstein et al., 1984). Those of you who enjoy using hot tubs at home or at health spas will be encouraged to hear that one well-controlled study found that no HSV could be isolated from hot-tub water with high levels of chlorine and bromine (commonly employed purifying agents). In contrast, HSV was found to survive for four hours in tap water and 24 hours in distilled water. These same researchers found that herpes viruses were able to survive for over four hours on plastic surfaces in a humid atmosphere typical of a spa facility (Nerurkar et al., 1983). This latter finding suggests a possible nonsexual mode of HSV transmission. Consequently, avoiding direct contact between skin and plastic-coated benches and seats in a spa facility seems to be a prudent precaution.

When any herpes sores are present, the infected person is highly contagious, and it is extremely important that he or she avoid bringing the lesions into contact with someone else's body through touching, sexual interaction, or kissing. It was once believed that a person could transmit herpes only when symptoms are present. However, it has recently been demonstrated that "transmission of *Herpes simplex* virus occurs during asymptomatic periods, but the relative risk is undefined" (Centers for Disease Control, 1985a, p. 88). A recent study of the sexual partners of persons with first-episode genital herpes revealed that the frequency of HSV transmission from asymptomatic individuals may be quite high (Mertz et al., 1985).

Research has shown that HSV-2 will not pass through either latex or natural membrane condoms (Conant et al., 1984). The use of condoms may be highly effective in preventing transmission from a male whose only lesions occur on the shaft or glans of the penis. Condoms are helpful but less effective in preventing transmission from a female to a male, due to the fact that vaginal secretions containing the virus may wash over the male's scrotal area.

People may also spread the virus from one part of their body to another by touching a sore and then scratching or rubbing somewhere else, a process referred to as *autoinoculation*. It is very important for people with herpes to wash their hands thoroughly with soap and water after touching a sore. It is better to avoid touching the sores if possible.

Symptoms and Complications.   The symptoms associated with HSV-1 and HSV-2 infections are quite similar.

Genital Herpes Symptoms.   Genital herpes symptoms consist of one or more small, red, painful bumps, called *papules*, that usually appear in the genital region. In women, the areas most commonly infected are the labia. The inner vaginal walls and cervix may also be affected. In men, the infected site is typically the glans or shaft of the penis. Homosexual men and heterosexual women who have engaged in anal intercourse may develop eruptions in and around the anus.

Soon after their initial appearance, the papules rapidly develop into tiny painful blisters filled with a clear fluid containing highly infectious virus particles (see color plates 11 and 12). The body then attacks the virus with white blood cells, causing the blisters to become filled with pus. Soon the blisters rupture to form wet, painful, open sores surrounded by a red ring (health practitioners refer to this as the period of "viral shedding"). A person is highly contagious during this time. About 10 days after the first appearance of the papule, the open sore forms a crust and begins to heal, a process that may take as long as 10 more days. There may be other symptoms accompanying genital herpes, including swollen lymph nodes in the groin, fever, muscle aches, and headaches. In addition, urination may be accompanied by a burning sensation, and women may experience increased vaginal discharge.

Oral Herpes Symptoms.   Oral herpes is characterized by the formation of papules on the lips, and sometimes on the inside of the mouth and on the tongue and throat.

(HSV-1 only infrequently occurs within the mouth, and it should not be confused with canker sores.) These blisters tend to crust over and heal within 10 to 16 days. Other symptoms of oral herpes include fever, general muscle aches, swollen lymph nodes in the neck, flulike symptoms, increased salivation, and possible bleeding in the mouth.

Recurrence. After complete healing, one cannot assume that one will not experience a recurrence of the infection. Unfortunately, the herpes virus does not typically go away; instead, it retreats up the nerve fibers leading from the infected site. Ultimately the genital herpes virus finds a resting place in nerve cells adjacent to the lower spinal column, while the oral herpes virus becomes lodged in nerve cells in the cheek. The virus may remain dormant in these cells, without causing any apparent damage, perhaps for the person's entire lifetime. However, in many cases there will be periodic flareups as the virus retraces its path back down the nerve fibers leading to the genitals or lips.

Many people never experience a recurrence of herpes following the initial or primary infection. Research suggests that 10% to 40% of people who have undergone a primary episode of oral herpes experience at least one recurrence. The comparable figures for genital herpes are 30% to 70% (Gunn and Stenzel-Poore, 1981; Straus et al., 1984a). Individuals who experience recurrences may do so frequently or only occasionally. Studies have shown that the more extensive the primary attack, the greater the chance of recurrence (Holmes, 1982). The symptoms associated with recurrent attacks tend to be milder than primary episodes, and the disease tends to run its course more quickly, averaging 7 to 10 days (Gunn and Stenzel-Poore, 1981; Holmes, 1982; Straus et al., 1984a).

A variety of factors may trigger reactivation of the herpes virus, including emotional stress, acid food, sunburn, cold, poor nutrition, being overtired or "run down," and trauma to the skin region affected. One person noted:

> For several years I have been having a herpes outbreak on my lips. It usually happens just once a year and coincides with the start of fishing season when I sit in a boat too long without protection from the sun. Now that I am aware of the pattern, I plan to take proper precautions in the future. (Authors' files)

Recurrences may also be more frequent in cases where the genitals are kept tightly enclosed and warm, as by wearing panty hose, nylon underwear, or tight jeans (Gunn and Stenzel-Poore, 1981). There is a wide individual variation in triggering factors, and it is often difficult to associate a specific event with the onset of a recurrent herpes infection.

The majority of people prone to recurrent herpes outbreaks, perhaps as many as 75%, experience some type of **prodromal symptoms** that give advance warning of an impending eruption (Grossman, 1981). These indications include itching, burning, throbbing, or "pins and needles" tingling at the sites commonly infected by herpes blisters, and sometimes pain in the legs, thighs, groin, or buttocks. Many health authorities believe that a person's degree of infectiousness increases during this stage and that it further escalates when the lesions appear. Consequently, a person should be particularly careful to avoid direct contact from the time he or she first experiences prodromal symptoms until the sores have completely healed. Even during an outbreak it is possible to continue intimacies with a partner, as long as infected skin does not come in contact with healthy skin. During this time partners may wish to experiment with other kinds of sensual pleasuring, such as sensate focus (see Chapter 17), hugging, and oral or manual stimulation.

Some people may not experience a relapse of genital herpes until several years after the initial infection. Therefore, if you have been in what you believe is a sexually exclusive relationship and your partner shows symptoms or transmits the virus to you, it does not necessarily mean that he or she contracted the disease from someone else during the course of your relationship. Furthermore, one study revealed that a majority of subjects experiencing their first symptomatic outbreak of genital herpes already had HSV-2 antibodies present in their blood, indicating that they had previously experienced an asymptomatic herpes infection. Clearly then, a first episode of symptomatic genital herpes may not be due to recent sexual contact with an infected person (Bernstein et al., 1984).

During their initial episode of genital herpes infection, most women have blisters on the cervix as well as the labia (see color plate 13). The cervical sores may continue to produce infectious viral material for as long as 10 days after the labial sores have completely healed. Consequently, it is wise during an initial episode to avoid coitus for a 10-day period after any external sores heal. Recurrent episodes of genital herpes in women do not typically involve the cervix.

Other Complications. While the sores are painful and bothersome, it is very unlikely that men will experience any major physical complications of herpes. Women, however, may be faced with two very serious, although quite uncommon, complications: cancer of the cervix and infection of the newborn. There is strong evidence that the risk of developing cervical cancer is higher among women who have had genital herpes (Rapp, 1982; Wear and Holmes, 1976). Fortunately, the great majority of women infected with herpes will never develop cancer of the cervix. Nonetheless, it is advisable for all women, particularly those who have had genital herpes, to obtain an annual cervical Pap smear for the rest of their lives. Some authorities recommend that women with genital herpes should have this test every six months (Gunn and Stenzel-Poore, 1981).

A newborn may be infected with genital herpes while passing through the birth canal. Many newborns infected with herpes will be severely damaged or die (Sweet, 1985). Studies of infant HSV infections reveal that a majority of infected newborns are born to mothers without symptoms of the disease (Vontver, 1982). It is believed that asymptomatic viral shedding from the cervix, vagina, or vulva play the primary role in transmission of the disease from mother to infant. Therefore, it is very important that the cervix, vagina, and vulva of a pregnant woman with a history of herpes infections be cultured frequently during the last four to six weeks of pregnancy. These cultures, together with an assessment of the woman's clinical condition at the onset of labor, provide a reasonable basis for choosing an appropriate delivery route. When sufficient risk exists for transmission of HSV from a delivering mother to her baby, a cesarean delivery is often performed to avert this possibility.

There is one additional serious physical complication of herpes that both women and men should be aware of. Occasionally a person will transfer the virus to an eye after touching a virus-shedding sore. This may lead to a severe eye infection known as ocular herpes or *herpes keratitis* (usually caused by HSV-1). Ocular herpes is the most common cause of cornea transplants in the United States (Fraunfelder, 1982). This complication may be best prevented by not touching the herpes sores. If you cannot avoid contact, thoroughly wash your hands with hot water and soap immediately after touching the lesions. There are effective treatments for this condition, but they must be started quickly to avoid eye damage.

Many people who have recurrent herpes outbreaks are troubled with mild to severe psychological distress. Some health authorities believe that emotional pain is the biggest problem associated with herpes. One survey of 3148 individuals with recurrent herpes revealed that 84% attributed periodic episodes of depression to herpes, 70% experienced a definite sense of isolation, 53% said they avoided potentially intimate situations, and 25% indicated that at one time or another they had experienced self-destructive feelings (American Social Health Association, 1981). In view of the physical discomfort associated with the disease, the unpredictability of recurrent outbreaks, and the lack of an effective cure (see next section), it is no small wonder that people who have herpes undergo considerable stress. We believe that becoming better informed about herpes may help to alleviate some of these emotional difficulties. Certainly, herpes is not the dread disease that some people believe it to be. In fact, countless numbers of individuals have learned to cope quite effectively with it, as did the person in the following account:

> When I first discovered I had herpes several years ago my first reaction was "Oh no, my sex life is destroyed!" I was really depressed and angry with the person who gave me the disease. However, with time I learned I could live with it, and I even began to gain some control over it. Now, on those infrequent occasions when I have an outbreak, I know what to do to hurry up the healing process. Most of the time things are just the same as before I got it, and my sex life is only occasionally disrupted. (Authors' files)

Treatment. The most common method of diagnosing herpes is direct observation by a physician. In most cases the clinical symptoms accompanying a herpes outbreak, together with a thorough patient history, will yield an accurate diagnosis. There are also a number of laboratory tests designed to detect herpes virus infections, and one or more of these may be used in cases where the diagnosis is in question. The most accurate of these tests involves culturing a small sample taken from the base of an active lesion (Loveless, 1982). If the virus grows in the culture medium, a definitive diagnosis of HSV can be made.

At the time of this writing there is no medical treatment proven to be effective in curing either oral or genital herpes. However, there is mounting optimism among medical researchers who are pursuing an effective treatment on many fronts. Current treatment strategies are designed to reduce discomfort and to speed healing during an outbreak.

There are a number of ways to obtain relief from the discomfort associated with herpes. The following list of suggestions may be helpful. The effectiveness of these measures varies from person to person, and we encourage people to experiment with the various options available to find an approach to symptom relief that best meets their needs.

1. Keeping herpes blisters clean and dry will lessen the possibility of secondary infections, significantly shorten the period of viral shedding, and reduce total time of lesion healing (Grossman, 1981; Straus et al., 1984a). Washing the area with warm water and soap two to three times daily is adequate for cleaning. After bathing, dry the area thoroughly by patting it gently with a soft cotton towel or by blowing it with a hair dryer set on cool. Since the moisture that occurs naturally in the genital area may slow the healing process, it can be helpful to sprinkle the dried area liberally with cornstarch or baby powder. It is desirable to wear loose clothing that does not trap the moisture (cotton underwear absorbs moisture, but nylon traps it).

2. A number of health practitioners recommend a soothing soak in a warm bath to which a drying agent such as Epsom salts or Burow's solution has been added. This can help to relieve local pain and discomfort while increasing circulation in the infected area. However, there is some evidence that after prolonged soaking the normal skin adjacent to infected areas may become more susceptible to invasion by the herpes virus (Straus, et al., 1984a). Consequently, it is probably wise to limit the frequency and duration of these soaks.

3. Two aspirin every three to four hours may help to reduce the pain and itching. Ice packs applied directly to the lesions (avoid wetting with melt water) may also provide temporary relief. Keeping the area liberally powdered may also alleviate itching.

4. Some people have an intense burning sensation when they urinate if the urine comes into contact with herpes lesions. This discomfort may be reduced by pouring water over the genitals while you void or by urinating in a bathtub filled with water. It may help to dilute the acid in the urine by drinking lots of fluids (avoid liquids that make the urine more acidic, like cranberry juice).

5. Since stress has been implicated as a triggering event in recurrent herpes, it is a good idea to try to reduce this negative influence. There are a variety of approaches to stress reduction, including learning relaxation techniques, practicing yoga or meditation, and obtaining counseling about ways to cope with daily pressures.

6. If you are prone to repeated relapses of herpes, you may obtain some benefit from recording events that occur immediately before an eruption (either after the fact or as part of an ongoing journal). You may be able to recognize common precipitating events like fatigue, acid food, or sunlight that you can avoid in the future.

Until the early 1980s, no drug was shown to have any consistent beneficial effect upon the duration or severity of HSV infections. However, a recently developed antiviral drug, acyclovir, sold under the trade name Zovirax, is often highly effective in the management of herpes. There are two forms of the drug, topical (ointment) and oral. The ointment, while beneficial in the treatment of initial outbreaks of HSV infections, has not proven to be particularly helpful in the management of recurrent herpes outbreaks (Straus et al., 1984a). A number of clinical trials with humans have found that oral acyclovir dramatically reduces the length and severity of initial outbreaks of herpes infections (Mertz, 1984; Centers for Disease Control, 1985a). The evidence is less clear how effective it is in treating recurrent episodes. Some research has reported that oral acyclovir, like its topically applied counterpart, is ineffective in treating recurrent episodes (Mertz, 1984). Other research has indicated that people who take this drug by mouth at the onset of a recurrent attack experience briefer viral shedding and faster crusting and healing than subjects who take a placebo drug (Reichman et al., 1984).

One of the most promising recent research findings is that continuous treatment with oral acyclovir reduces the frequency of genital herpes outbreaks by at least 75% among people prone to frequent (at least six per year) recurrences (Douglas et al., 1984; Centers for Disease Control, 1985a; Straus et al., 1984b). However, it is appropriate to offer a word of caution about the continuous use of oral acyclovir to suppress recurrent herpes outbreaks. Although use of the drug for a period as long as six months has not been shown to produce harmful side effects, the long-term impact of continuous use is not yet known (Centers for Disease Control, 1985a). Some researchers in the STD field have raised concerns that using oral acyclovir as a palliative suppressant may have adverse effects on a person taking the drug, or that widespread use will lead to the emergence of HSV strains resistant to acyclovir (Guinan, 1985). Guidelines issued by the Centers for Disease Control (1985a) state that this suppressive regimen is definitely contraindicated in women who may become pregnant during treatment.

Perhaps by the time you read this an even more effective drug for treating herpes will be widely used. Recent clinical research has revealed that when intervir-A ointment was applied to herpes sores, the amount of time to complete healing was dramatically decreased, and the number of recurrent outbreaks was greatly reduced (Goldberg, 1986). Researchers are very hopeful about this new drug, and some consider it to be "the most effective treatment to date" (Goldberg in Ricks, 1986). At the time of this writing, clinical tests continue with intervir-A, and it has not been approved by the Food and Drug Administration for sale to the general public. If approval is eventually granted, the drug is expected to be sold over the counter rather than by prescription.

Viral Hepatitis

Viral hepatitis is a disease in which liver function is impaired by a viral infection. There are three major types of viral hepatitis: hepatitis A (formerly called infectious hepatitis), hepatitis B (formerly called serum hepatitis), and non-A/non-B hepatitis. Each of these forms of viral hepatitis is caused by a different virus.

Incidence and Transmission. Hepatitis B is the most common form of viral hepatitis in the United States, followed in order of frequency by hepatitis A and non-A/

non-B hepatitis. In 1985 approximately 26,000 cases of hepatitis B, 23,000 cases of hepatitis A, and 4000 cases of non-A/non-B hepatitis were reported in the United States (Centers for Disease Control, 1985c). Both A and B types can be sexually transmitted, but the non-A/non-B type is not thought to be sexually transmitted. It is believed that hepatitis B is more often transmitted by sexual activity than hepatitis A. The A and B forms of viral hepatitis appear to be proportionately more common among homosexual males than among heterosexuals of either sex (Francis et al., 1984).

Hepatitis B may be transmitted by blood or blood products, semen, vaginal secretions, and saliva. Manual, oral, or penile stimulation of the anus are practices strongly associated with the spread of this viral agent. Hepatitis A seems to be primarily spread via the fecal-oral route. Consequently, epidemics often occur when infected food handlers do not wash their hands properly after using the bathroom. Oral-anal sexual contact seems to be the primary mode for sexual transmission of hepatitis A.

Symptoms and Complications. The symptoms of viral hepatitis may vary from nonexistent to mild flulike symptoms (poor appetite, upset stomach, diarrhea, sore muscles, fatigue, headache) to an incapacitating illness characterized by high fever, vomiting, and severe abdominal pain. One of the most notable signs of viral hepatitis is a yellowing of the whites of the eyes; the skin too may take on a yellow, or jaundiced, look. Hospitalization is required only in severe cases. There is some evidence that people who have had hepatitis B are at increased risk for developing cancer of the liver. On rare occasions severe medical complications associated with viral hepatitis infections result in death.

Treatment. At the present time there is no specific therapy available for the various types of viral hepatitis (Centers for Disease Control, 1985a). Consequently, treatment generally consists of bed rest and adequate fluid intake to prevent dehydration. The disease generally runs its course in a matter of a few weeks, although complete recovery may take several months in cases of severe infections. Recently an effective and safe vaccine has been developed to prevent hepatitis B infections. Many health experts believe that if this vaccine (called Heptavac B) were widely employed in high risk populations—such as homosexual men, intravenous drug users, and health care professionals—the incidence of hepatitis B infections could be reduced dramatically (Littenberg and Ransohoff, 1984; Sacks et al., 1984).

Pubic Lice

Pubic lice, more commonly called "crabs," belong to a group of parasitic insects called biting lice. They are known technically as *Phthirus pubis*. Although very tiny, adult lice are visible to the eye. They are yellowish-gray in appearance, and under magnification they resemble a crab, as Figure 18.1 shows. A pubic louse generally grips a pubic hair with its claws and sticks its head into the skin, where it feeds on blood from tiny blood vessels.

Incidence and Transmission. Pubic lice are quite common and are seen frequently in public health clinics and by private physicians. They are frequently transmitted

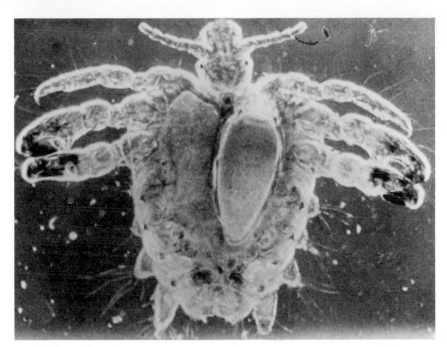

during sexual contact when two people bring their pubic areas together. Crabs may live away from the body for as long as one day, particularly if their stomachs are full of blood. They may drop off onto underclothes, bedsheets, sleeping bags, and so forth. Eggs deposited by the female louse on clothing or bedsheets may survive for several days. Thus, it is possible to get pubic lice by sleeping in someone else's bed or by wearing his or her clothes. Furthermore, a successfully treated person may be reinfected by being exposed to her or his own unwashed sheets or underclothes. Pubic lice do not necessarily limit themselves to the genital areas. They may be transmitted, usually by fingers, to the armpits or scalp.

Symptoms.   Most people begin to suspect something is amiss when they start itching. Suspicions become stronger when scratching brings no relief. However, a few people seem to have great tolerance for the bite of a louse, experiencing very little if any discomfort. Self-diagnosis is possible simply by locating a louse on a pubic hair.

Treatment.   Self-treatment for pubic lice can be done with an over-the-counter preparation known as A-200 pyrinate. Another commonly employed treatment is Kwell (gamma benzene hexachloride), available by prescription (often a phone call to your physician will be sufficient). Be sure to follow the accompanying instructions carefully. It is advisable to apply the solution to all areas where there are concentrations of body hair—the genitals, armpits, scalp, and even eyebrows. This should be followed by a reapplication seven days later (eggs take seven days to hatch). Be sure to wash all clothes and sheets that were used prior to treatment.

Genital Warts

Warts that appear on the genitals, sometimes called venereal warts or condylomata acuminata, are caused by a virus similar to that which produces warts on other parts of the body (see color plate 14).

Incidence and Transmission. The incidence of genital warts has been increasing so rapidly in both sexes that they have reached "epidemic proportions in recent years" (Ferenczy, 1984). It is believed that they are primarily transmitted by vaginal, anal, or oral-genital sexual interaction. However, warts have been known to appear on people who are not sexually active or whose only sexual partner shows no sign of the condition.

Symptoms and Complications. The average incubation period for genital warts, after contact with an infected person, is about three months. In women they most commonly appear on the bottom part of the vaginal opening. They may also occur on the perineum, the vaginal lips, the inner walls of the vagina, and the cervix. In men they commonly occur on the glans, foreskin, or shaft of the penis. In moist areas (such as the vaginal opening and under the foreskin) they are pink or red and soft, with a cauliflower-like appearance. On dry skin areas, they are generally hard and yellow-gray.

Genital warts are occasionally associated with serious complications. Sometimes they invade the urethra, where they may cause urinary obstruction and bleeding. There is also good evidence that some warts progress to cancerous states in both women and men (Ferenczy, 1984).

Treatment. Genital warts may spontaneously disappear, but this is a relatively rare event. Therefore, it is good idea to obtain treatment so they will not enlarge and spread to healthy tissue. Many methods have been used for removing genital warts, including topical applications of podophyllin (widely used), trichloroacetic acid, and 5-fluorouracil cream (Efudex). Sometimes a second or extended period of treatment with these topical medications is necessary. Podophyllin should not be used during pregnancy, and it is not recommended for treatment of cervical warts (Centers for Disease Control, 1985a). Cauterization by electric needle, freezing with liquid nitrogen, or surgical removal is sometimes necessary with very large or persistent warts. Recently a highly effective technique has been employed, involving vaporization of the warts with a carbon dioxide laser (Ferenczy, 1984; Grundsell et al., 1984; Kryger-Baggesen et al., 1984). This treatment is essentially bloodless, healing is rapid, scarring does not occur, and recurrence of warts is very minimal.

Acquired Immune Deficiency Syndrome (AIDS)

No disease in modern times has received more attention or produced such hysteria as **acquired immune deficiency syndrome** (**AIDS**). An unprecedented, all-out research assault on this deadly disease is being conducted throughout the world, and new findings are surfacing with startling rapidity. Consequently, it is very likely that some of the information that follows, a summation of the state of knowledge in the late spring of 1986, will be obsolete by the time you read it.

It is widely believed that AIDS results from infection with a virus that has been variously labeled human T-lymphotropic virus III (HTLV-III), lymphadenopathy-associated virus (LAV), and AIDS-related virus (ARV). Recently an international committee recommended a new name, human immunodeficiency virus (HIV), intended to replace the three other labels (Marx, 1986). To simplify our discussion of AIDS, we will refer to the infectious agent simply as the AIDS virus.

In some people this virus invades and destroys the body's T-4 helper lymphocytes ("T-helper cells"), which in healthy people stimulate the immune system to fight disease. The resulting impairment of the immune system leaves the body vulnerable to a variety of cancers and opportunistic infections. Some scientists believe that the AIDS virus may ultimately prove to be just one, albeit probably the most important, of several causative agents in the AIDS epidemic and that other viruses or infections may be prerequisites for developing the deadly syndrome.

A person is considered to have AIDS when the T-4 helper lymphocyte population is so seriously depleted that he or she has developed one or more characteristic diseases. These include Kaposi's sarcoma (a form of cancer that accounts for many AIDS deaths), pneumocystic carinii pneumonia (a lung disease that is also a major cause of AIDS deaths), and a variety of other generalized opportunistic infections such as shingles (herpes zoster), encephalitis, cryptococcus fungal infections that cause a type of meningitis, and cytomegalovirus infections of the lungs, intestines, and central nervous system. Some people infected with the AIDS virus do not develop a full blown case of AIDS but manifest a less severe immune system disease called *AIDS-related complex* (ARC), which unfortunately often culminates in the development of AIDS itself.

Incidence and Transmission. By June 1986 more than 21,000 cases of AIDS had been reported in this country since the disease was first diagnosed in 1981. This number is expected to exceed 30,000 by the end of 1986, according to estimates made by the Centers for Disease Control (CDC). Approximately half of all AIDS victims in this country have already died. The average survival time after the disease is diagnosed is estimated to be 56 weeks (Hardy, 1986). The CDC has projected that 270,000 cumulative cases of AIDS will have occurred in the U.S. by the end of 1991, including 74,000 that year alone. By comparison, about 16,000 new cases are expected in 1986.

Evidence presented at an international scientific conference on AIDS in January of 1986 provided further reason to anticipate a more ominous future for this disease than previously predicted by health officials. One important paper presented at this conference reported on a study of New York homosexuals that revealed that approximately one-third of those exposed to the AIDS virus have developed AIDS (Blattner, 1986). This finding stands in marked contrast to the previous estimates by the CDC that 5% to 10% of those who test positive for exposure to the AIDS virus eventually will contract AIDS. At the time of this writing, the CDC has announced that it is about to revise its estimates upward. In addition, the CDC previously estimated that about 25% of those exposed to the AIDS virus develop ARC; it has indicated that this figure is also about to be increased.

These trends are of particular concern in view of the fact that about 2 million Americans were estimated to be infected with the AIDS virus by mid-1986 and that this number is growing by more than 1000 per day. Health officials fervidly hope that most people who are infected with the AIDS virus will never develop AIDS or ARC. However, because this virus may take years to take its toll on the immune system, it is too early to determine what percentage of people who test positive for antibodies to the AIDS virus (evidence of infection) will develop serious disease processes. A recently published long-term study of a population of Danish homosexuals suggests that a very large percentage of people infected with the AIDS virus will eventually experience serious health consequences. At the onset of the study in 1981, all of the subjects who tested positive for AIDS virus antibodies were healthy. Data collected over the ensuing three and a half years revealed that 92% of these subjects experienced marked decreases in the number of T-helper cells in their immune systems. Furthermore, half of them developed at least one of five clinical symptoms: diarrhea, oral thrush (yeast infection), herpes, fever, or weight loss. These conditions are commonly associated with a general decline in health prior to the onset of diagnosed AIDS (Melbye et al., 1986).

James Curran (1985), director of the CDC AIDS Task Force, has stated that the presence of AIDS virus antibodies should be taken as "presumptive" evidence that a person can transmit AIDS and that he or she will be infected for life. We can only hope that a successful method for eradicating this deadly virus from a person's system will be developed in the not too distant future, thereby negating this grim prediction.

The AIDS virus has been isolated from the semen, blood, vaginal secretions, saliva, tears, urine, and breast milk of infected individuals (Communicable Disease Summary, 1985; Lourea et al., 1986; Vogt et al., 1986; Wofsy et al., 1986). Blood and semen are the major vehicles for transmitting the virus, which appears to be passed primarily through sexual contact, needle sharing among intravenous drug abusers, or less commonly, through administration of blood products. It is believed that the risk, if any, of transmitting the AIDS virus via saliva, tears, or urine is extremely low (Communicable Disease Summary, 1985).

Transmission of AIDS by sexual contact is by no means limited to homosexual men. It is true that the greatest percentage of AIDS victims in the United States to date are gay men. This may be a function, at least in part, of the fact that AIDS was first transmitted to this country by gay men who had vacationed in Haiti (see Box 18.2). Furthermore, as we shall see, anal intercourse, a common practice among some male homosexuals, is one of the highest risk sexual behaviors for contracting AIDS. However, a recently reported study in Haiti found that although AIDS was once primarily a disease of Haitian men, it is now spreading rapidly to women via heterosexual transmission. At the beginning of 1980 only 12% of Haitian AIDS victims were women; this figure rose to 30% by the end of 1985 (Pape, 1986).

Evidence from studies in central Africa indicates that AIDS afflicts African men and women in roughly equal numbers and that heterosexual contact is the primary mode of transmission of the AIDS virus in Africa (Altman, 1985; Norman, 1986). This has led some researchers to suggest that a different transmission mechanism may be operating among Africans. However, it was recently pointed out that "the spread

SEXUALLY TRANSMITTED DISEASES

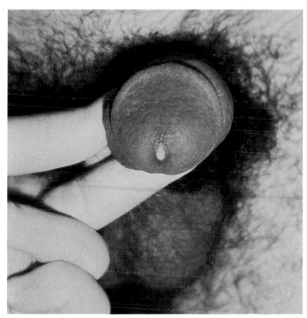

While unpleasant, these pictures impart important information on the external manifestations of some sexually transmitted diseases. Refer to the chapter narrative for a complete description of these symptoms.

Plate 8
A cloudy discharge symptomatic of gonorrheal infection.

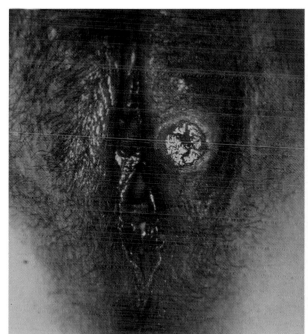

Plate 9
Syphilitic chancre as it appears on the labia.

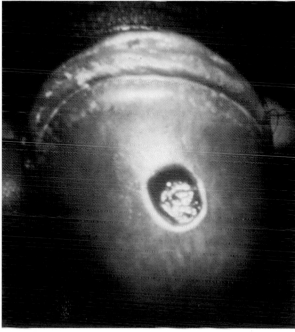

Plate 10
Syphilitic chancre as it appears on the penis.

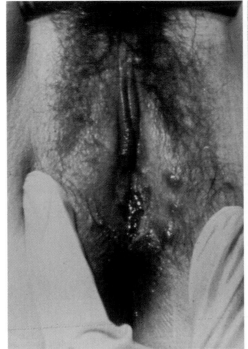

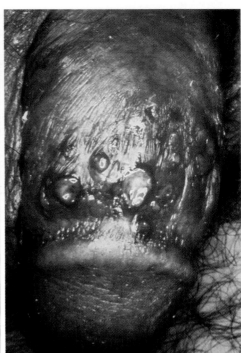

Plate 11 (left)
Genital herpes
blisters as they
appear on the labia.

Plate 12 (right)
Genital herpes
blisters as they
appear on the penis.

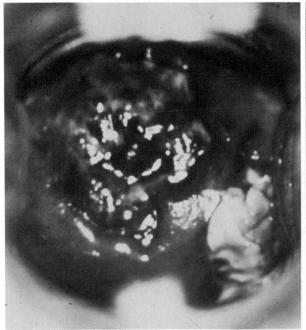

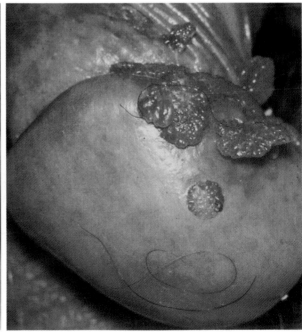

Plate 13
Cervical involvement is
common in genital herpes.

Plate 14
Genital warts.

Various theories have been proposed as to the origin of AIDS. Some researchers believe that it originated in Africa (Norman, 1986). Others point out that it was first recognized in the United States, not Africa, and that "no scientific evidence has proved any theories about where it originated" (Altman, 1985, p. 2).

One of the most widely held theories is that the AIDS virus was first transmitted to humans from the central African green monkey. A virus essentially identical to human AIDS virus is quite common among the green monkeys of central Africa. About 70% of the green monkeys studied have tested positive for the virus antibodies, and yet they are healthy, suggesting that they have evolved some kind of mechanism that controls the virus (Essex, 1985). It is also possible that the "monkey virus itself may not be pathogenic but it may have mutated in man and acquired some destructive properties" (Norman, 1986, p. 1141). Recently a team of scientists reported discovering a new strain of AIDS virus that may constitute the long-sought "missing link" between the viral strain that infects healthy green monkeys and the more virulent form that causes AIDS in humans. They theorize that the virus "jumped" from monkeys to people, becoming more virulent along the way (Kanki et al., 1986).

It is further theorized that AIDS was carried to the Caribbean country of Haiti by Haitians who once lived in central Africa. From Haiti it is presumed to have moved to the United States via Haitian immigrants, and perhaps more importantly, via homosexual males—until recently Haiti was a popular vacation spot for American gay men.

of the disease among heterosexuals in Africa and homosexuals in the West may point to a common factor in their sexual practices" (Linke, 1986, p. 203). Contact with blood during anal intercourse is thought to be a major mode of transmission of the AIDS virus among gay men in the United States (anal penetration causes small tears in rectal tissues that may result in bleeding). The same principle may apply to heterosexuals in central Africa, where female genital mutilations are still widely practiced (see Chapter 4). These procedures often result in severe gynecological complications (constricted vaginal opening, extensive scarring, etc.) that can either make penile-vaginal intercourse impossible or cause it to be chronically associated with tissue damage and bleeding. Because of these complications, a common recourse for heterosexual partners in central Africa is anal intercourse, which while it may not be painful, is often associated with bleeding (Linke, 1986).

Recent studies in the United States are reporting a significant increase in the number of cases of AIDS attributed to heterosexual contact (Centers for Disease Control, 1985d). For example, in one study of 41 AIDS patients admitted to Walter Reed Hospital, it was found that 15 cases (37%) resulted from exposure to heterosexual contact. Nine of these 15 victims reported sexual contact with prostitutes (Redfield et al., 1985). There has been increasing concern that female prostitutes may provide a primary reservoir of the AIDS virus. Two studies in Africa that found high levels of AIDS virus infection among prostitutes lend credence to this concern. Eighty percent of a group of 84 prostitutes examined in Rwanda tested positive for viral antibodies and 54% of 90 Kenyan prostitutes were infected with the AIDS virus (Altman, 1985).

The continued spread of AIDS among sexually active women in central and eastern Africa has caused many babies to be born with the disease (Altman, 1985; Norman, 1986). The AIDS virus can pass from mother to fetus during pregnancy, and through breast milk to a nursing infant. Maternal transmission to a fetus has been reported very infrequently in the United States. However, such accounts are occurring in the scientific literature with increasing frequency. One recent article reported that three half sisters were all born with AIDS; their mother was an AIDS virus–infected intravenous·drug using prostitute (Cowan et al., 1984).

No cases of AIDS have been attributed to transmission by casual contact (Communicable Disease Summary, 1985; Friedland et al., 1986). A recent report by the CDC summarized nine studies of family members of AIDS patients that failed to find any evidence of transmission to other members of the household who were not sexually involved with the infected person (Centers for Disease Control, 1985e). "Based on current evidence, non-sexual person-to-person contact such as occurs in offices, restaurants, schools, and even homes appears to pose no risk of infection" (*Communicable Disease Summary*, 1985, p. 3).

There also appears to be no danger of being infected with the AIDS virus as a result of donating blood (Communicable Disease Summary, 1985). Blood banks, the Red Cross, and other blood collection centers use sterile equipment and disposable needles. Recently the American Association of Blood Banks announced the development of a serious national shortage of donated blood for transfusions (Furlow, 1986). This shortage was attributed to the unfounded belief that people can contract AIDS by giving blood. Blood bank officials hope to dispel this myth with a national media campaign. There is a small risk associated with receiving blood or blood products. However, this risk has been greatly reduced with the development of procedures for screening for the AIDS virus. It has been estimated that no more than 2% of the approximately 20,000 U.S. cases of AIDS to date have resulted from people receiving transfusions of blood or blood products tainted with the virus (Furlow, 1986).

Symptoms and Complications.   The symptoms of AIDS or ARC are many and varied, depending on the degree to which the immune system is compromised and on the particular type of cancer or opportunistic infection(s) that afflict a victim. The following symptoms are commonly associated with AIDS or ARC. However, it must be emphasized that many of these physical manifestations may only indicate common, everyday ailments that are by no means life threatening. Observing that you have one or more of these symptoms can alert you to seek out a medical diagnosis of your ailment. However, do not be needlessly alarmed, because the risk of contracting AIDS at the present time is extremely low. Some common symptoms include: (1) persistent or periodically repeating fevers or night sweats, (2) unexplained weight loss, (3) loss of appetite, (4) chronic fatigue or a tendency to tire quickly when performing routine tasks, (5) swollen lymph nodes in the neck, armpits, or groin, (6) persistent and unexplained diarrhea or bloody stools, (7) easy bruising or atypical bleeding from any body opening, (8) skin rashes or discoloration of the skin, (9) persistent severe headaches, (10) a chronic dry cough unrelated to smoking or a cold, and (11) a persistent whitish coating on the tongue or throat.

AIDS patients experience a multitude of serious, life-threatening complications. As mentioned earlier, approximately half of the AIDS victims in the United States have already died, which means the mortality rate is at least 50%. Many AIDS researchers believe that the true mortality rate is closer to 100%. Thus far, no victims have experienced the reestablishment of effectively functioning immune systems.

Treatment and Prevention.   At the present time, therapy for AIDS is limited to specific treatment(s) of opportunistic infections and tumors that occur in AIDS patients. No drugs have been demonstrated to have significant anti-viral impact on the AIDS virus. Research has made it abundantly clear that any successful treatment that may ultimately be developed will involve both rebuilding disabled immune systems (for example, by bone marrow transplants) and the use of effective antiviral drugs to eradicate the deadly AIDS virus.

Many AIDS researchers are reasonably optimistic that an effective vaccine against the AIDS virus will be developed within the next few years. Scientists at the New England Regional Primate Center in Southboro, Massachusetts recently identified a virus in macaque monkeys that is essentially identical to the virus that causes AIDS. Researchers are hopeful that these animals will provide a beneficial study population for developing and testing an AIDS vaccine. Another promising line of research was recently reported by a team of scientists who demonstrated that vaccinating mice with a smallpox vaccine modified to include part of the AIDS virus produced some immunity to AIDS (Chakrabarti et al., 1986). Researchers are hopeful that this technique, or a similar one, might also protect against the deadly disease in humans.

At the present time the best hope for curtailing the epidemic spread of AIDS is through education and behavior changes. AIDS can definitely be prevented. The following list provides suggestions that will dramatically reduce your chance of being exposed to the AIDS virus if you follow them. Most of these recommendations offer ways to avoid exchanging semen and blood, the two body secretions associated with the vast majority of AIDS virus transmissions. The first two recommendations apply to all people, regardless of the nature of their sex lives. The remaining 12 suggestions are particularly directed at people who are sexually active and not involved in a monogamous relationship with a noninfected partner.

1. If you use IV drugs, do not share needles or syringes (boiling does not guarantee sterility).
2. Do not share razor blades, toothbrushes, or other implements that could become contaminated with blood.
3. Do not have sexual contact with persons known or suspected of having AIDS.
4. Do not have sex with people who use IV drugs.
5. Do not have sex with prostitutes.
6. You may wish to reevaluate the importance of sex with multiple partners at this point in your life, in view of the clear evidence that one of the

strongest predictors of being infected with the AIDS virus is a large number of sexual partners (*Communicable Disease Summary*, 1985; Goedert et al., 1984). You may also elect to not have sex with individuals you know or suspect have had multiple partners.

7. Avoid oral, vaginal, or anal contact with semen.

8. Use condoms. Recent research has demonstrated that the AIDS virus cannot pass through the fine membranes of condoms made of latex, synthetic skin, or natural skin (Conant et al., 1986).

9. Avoid anal intercourse, since this is one of the riskiest of all sexual behaviors associated with transmission of the AIDS virus (Goedert et al., 1985; Goedert et al., 1984). The high risk associated with this activity is thought to be related to the fact that anal penetration causes small abrasions in the rectal tissues, through which the AIDS virus in an infected partner's semen may be injected directly into the recipient's blood.

10. In view of the remote possibility that the AIDS virus may be transmitted via saliva, it might be wise to avoid prolonged open mouth kissing.

11. Do not allow a partner's urine to enter your mouth, anus, eyes, or open cuts or sores.

12. Do not engage in the insertion of fingers or fists ("fisting") into the anus as active or receptive partner. Fingernails can cause tears in the rectal tissues, allowing direct access to the blood system.

13. Avoid oral contact with the anus (a practice commonly referred to as "rimming").

14. Do not use amyl nitrite (poppers), unless you need it to control a heart condition. There is evidence that this drug may be associated with the development of Kaposi's cancer (*Communicable Disease Summary*, 1985).

A number of studies of high risk populations of gay males have shown that fear of contracting AIDS has resulted in significant changes in sexual behavior. Many of these men have reduced the number of their sexual partners or entered into monogamous relationships. There also seems to be a marked reduction in the frequency of certain high risk activities, such as anal intercourse, fellatio, and "fisting" (Lourea et al., 1986; Centers for Disease Control, 1985f; Schechter et al., 1984). Masturbation with partner(s) present, or manual stimulation by a partner, has become a very common activity in the San Francisco gay male community (Lourea et al., 1986).

Virginia Prince (1986) advocates a form of sexual sharing without fear of AIDS, herpes, or pregnancy. She calls this form of sharing SMILES, which stands for simultaneous, mutual, intimate, loving, erotic self-stimulation. "Each person is responsible for their own genital stimulation but does so in a physically close and caring relationship with another." Partners touch, caress, communicate with their eyes, talk, and otherwise share in each other's pleasure in a way that transforms the solitary act of masturbation into a joyous expression of shared sexual intimacy. We certainly believe that this is a viable alternative to more conventional sexual interaction that you may wish to consider, particularly if you choose to be sexual with someone in a high risk category.

Other Sexually Transmitted Diseases

In this section we will briefly comment on several STDs that receive less attention in the popular and professional literature than the ones we have already discussed.

Molluscum contagiosum is a disease caused by a pox virus. It produces small, painless lesions that are firm, elevated, rounded, smooth, shiny, and waxy on top. These lesions usually appear on the genitals, thighs, buttocks, or lower abdomen three to six weeks after exposure to an infected person. Serious complications are rarely associated with this disease, which often disappears spontaneously in a few months. Treatment typically consists of nicking the top of each lesion with a needle and squeezing out the white center or core, much as you might pop a blackhead. Some health professionals freeze the lesions with topical applications of liquid nitrogen.

Scabies is a highly contagious infestation by tiny, parasitic mites known technically as *Sarcoptes scabiei*. These pesky little creatures may be transmitted sexually or nonsexually, in much the same manner as pubic lice. Since they are too tiny to be seen with the naked eye, diagnosis is generally made by microscopic examination of scrapings from skin surfaces irritated by the mites. Treatment and tactics for preventing recurrences of the infestations are similar to those suggested for pubic lice.

Shigellosis is caused by the bacterium *Shigella* and is characterized by diarrhea, fever, and inflammation of the large intestine. It may be transmitted by contact with infected feces or by oral stimulation of the anal area. It is treated with tetracycline or ampicillin.

Chancroid is an infection caused by the bacterium *Hemophilus ducreyi*. It is characterized by the formation of small bumps, usually in the region of the genitals, perineum, or anus, that occur a few days after contact with an infected person. These lesions eventually rupture and form painful, soft, craterlike ulcers that emit a foul discharge. The softness and painfulness of the chancroid ulcers distinguish them from the hard, painless chancres of syphilis. Frequently chancroid infection is accompanied by swollen lymph nodes. This disease is usually transmitted by sexual interaction, although nonsexual physical contact can also spread the infecting organism. Chancroid infection can be effectively treated with erythromycin or sulfa drugs.

Lymphogranuloma venereum (LGV) is a very rare STD caused by several strains of *Chlamydia trachomatis*. It is characterized by the appearance of small, painless papules or ulcers on the genitals within three days to three weeks after exposure. These sores usually heal quickly. However, a few weeks later the disease may remanifest itself in the form of systematic symptoms, such as swollen lymph nodes, fever, chills, or loss of appetite. Later, more serious ulcerations or swelling may recur in the genital region. LGV may be treated with doxycycline, erythromycin, or sulfamethoxazole.

Granuloma inguinale is an even rarer infection caused by the bacterium *Calymmatobacterium granulomatis*. This disease, which may be spread either sexually or nonsexually, is first evident in the appearance of one or more small, painless, pimplelike bumps on the genitals or thighs. Eventually the lesions ulcerate, emit a sour, pungent odor, and spread to adjacent healthy tissue. Treatment should be implemented at the earliest possible stage to prevent extensive tissue destruction and permanent scarring of the genitals. Tetracycline, gentamicin, streptomycin, or erythromycin may be effective in stopping further spread of the infection, but these medications will not eradicate the permanent damage already inflicted.

*Health depart-
ments often provide
screening and
treatment for
sexually transmitted
diseases.*

Prevention of Sexually Transmitted Diseases

Many approaches to curtailing the spread of sexually transmitted diseases have been advocated. These range from attempting to prohibit sexual activity among young people to providing easy public access to information about the symptoms of STDs, along with free medical treatment. Consistent with the latter approach is an effort by most public health agencies to trace and treat any sexual partners with whom an infected person has had contact. While public health codes require physicians to report all cases of venereal disease, in practice it seems that the majority of cases go unreported. With nonsexually transmitted diseases like influenzas, chicken pox, or measles, this method of reporting and tracing potentially infected individuals has proved extremely successful in curtailing widespread epidemics. However, STDs present unique problems. Beyond embarrassment, there may be fear of the reactions of infected partners. In many states nonmarital sex is against the law, creating the added problem of implicating a partner in crime. Fortunately these laws are rarely enforced, and most public clinics are willing to treat patients even if they refuse to reveal the names of sexual partners.

Unfortunately, the efforts of public health agencies have not been successful in curbing the rapid spread of sexually transmitted diseases. For this reason it is doubly important to stress a variety of specific preventive measures that may be taken by an individual or couple. Clearly, abstinence is one virtually sure-fire method to avoid an

STD infection. However, this alternative is not especially popular. Being monogamous yourself and having a disease free partner who is also monogamous is another way to prevent contracting a sexually transmitted disease. Yet sometimes it is difficult to be certain your partner is monogamous, even if you are. In addition, many people do not find either abstinence or monogamy an acceptable alternative. The following suggestions are primarily directed toward those of you who have more than one sexual partner, or whose partner is nonmonogamous.

Prostitutes and certain medical practitioners have known for a long time that a collection of specific procedures, some of which are quite simple to put into effect, can help to reduce a person's chances of getting an STD. Unfortunately, preventive measures (other than abstinence) have not been stressed publicly with the same enthusiasm that has been directed toward dispensing information on the symptoms and treatment of STDs. The lack of emphasis on practical preventive techniques often reflects an underlying societal attitude that STDs are "little helpers" in scaring off young people who might otherwise experiment with sex. For example, in California before 1971 it was a criminal offense for an individual to provide another with a VD preventive. Furthermore, some people feel quite uncomfortable with promoting prevention, because of the supposed implication that they condone nonmarital intercourse. However, the reality of contemporary sexual behavior indicates a need for some practical preventive procedures.

Some Steps for Prevention

We will discuss several methods of prevention—steps that can be taken before, during, or shortly after sexual contact to reduce the likelihood of contracting an STD. Many of these methods are effective against the transmission of a variety of diseases. Several are applicable to oral-genital and anal-genital contacts in addition to genital-genital interaction. None is 100% effective, but each acts to significantly reduce the chances of infection. Furthermore—and this cannot be overemphasized—the use of preventive measures may help to curtail the booming spread of STDs. Since most infected people have sexual contact with one or more partners before they realize they have a disease and seek treatment, improved prevention rather than better treatment seems to hold the key to reducing these unpleasant accompaniments to sexual expression.

Inspection of Your Partner's Genitals.   Examining your partner's genitals prior to coital or oral contact may reveal the symptoms of an STD. Herpes blisters, vaginal and urethral discharges, chancres and rashes associated with syphilis, genital warts, and pubic lice may be easily seen. In most cases, symptoms will be more evident in a man. If he is uncircumcised, be sure to retract the foreskin. The presence of a discharge, unpleasant odor, sores, blisters, rash, warts, or anything else out of the ordinary should be viewed with some concern. "Milking" the penis is a particularly effective way to detect a suspicious discharge. This technique, sometimes called the "short arm inspection," involves grasping the penis firmly and pulling the loose skin up and down the shaft several times, applying pressure on the base-to-head stroke. Next, part the urinary opening to see if any cloudy discharge is present.

People may frequently find it difficult to conduct such an inspection before sexual sharing. Occasionally just the request "let me undress you" will provide some opportunity to examine your partner's genitals. Perhaps some sensate focus pleasuring, discussed in Chapter 17, will provide the opportunity for more detailed visual exploration. Some people suggest a shower before sex, with an eye toward examining their partner. While this may be quite helpful for noting visible sores, blisters, and so forth, the soap and water may also remove the visual and olfactory cues associated with a discharge.

If you note signs of infection, you may justifiably and wisely elect not to have sexual relations. Your intended partner may or may not be aware of his or her symptoms. Therefore, it is important that you explain your concerns. Some people may decide to continue their sexual interaction, using some of the methods of protection described in the following sections. Others might choose a form of sexual sharing that avoids either coitus or oral-genital contact, like the SMILES technique discussed previously.

Washing the Genitals Before or After Sexual Contact. There is some difference in opinion about the effectiveness of soap and water washing of the genitals before sexual interaction. One problem is that the organisms infecting a man are often harbored within the urethra even when removed from the external penis, and they may be forced to the outside during sexual arousal or ejaculation. However, there can be little doubt that washing has some benefits (Buchan, 1973). This technique is generally more effective when applied to the man, although washing the vulva can also be helpful.

Some people may find it difficult to suggest that their partner allow them to wash their genitals before having sex. However, this may be accomplished unobtrusively by including the washing of the penis and vulva in the sex play that occurs in the shower or bathtub. Others may quite frankly announce that they are cleansing their partner's genitals for their mutual protection. Some individuals suggest that a woman douche before coitus as a preventive measure. However, frequent douching may be harmful to a woman, and its effectiveness in preventing transmission of an STD is likely to be quite limited.

After sexual contact, thorough washing of the genitals and surrounding area with soap and water is highly recommended as a preventive procedure when transmission of an infection is a possibility. We are not suggesting that this procedure should always follow sexual sharing. In fact, many lovers with long-term relationships would find it unnecessary and possibly even offensive, implying that a person is somehow unclean after sex.

Promptness is very important in postsex washing, probably as important as thoroughness. However, some people might object to jumping out of bed to wash, as it may break the relaxed mood. For those uncomfortable with letting their partner know they are taking this precaution, perhaps simply announcing you need to go to the bathroom (a not uncommon need after sex) will be enough. Sometimes a partner will be pleased with the suggestion of a postsex shower. Women and men can also wash their genitals while sitting over the washbowl. First fill it with warm soapy water, then turn your back to it and boost yourself up to straddle it. In this position it is relatively easy to thoroughly wash your exposed genitals with a soapy washcloth.

It has been suggested that women douche after intercourse with a partner who may have an STD. This procedure may be somewhat effective in preventing disease, particularly when a medicated douche preparation is used (Singh et al., 1972). However, as with douching before coitus, the preventive value of this procedure should be carefully weighed against its potentially damaging effects.

Urination after coitus may have some limited benefits, particularly to men. Many infectious organisms do not survive in the acid environment created by urine. Urinating may also flush out disease-causing organisms.

Vaginal Prophylaxis During Coitus.   Most women and men, when they consider the range of available birth control options, are not aware that the foams, creams, and jellies currently on the market offer some protection against a variety of sexually transmitted diseases, including gonorrhea, syphilis, trichomoniasis, and possibly the AIDS virus (Bolch and Warren, 1973; Lourea et al., 1986; Centers for Disease Control, 1985a; Singh et al., 1972). This is an important additional benefit of vaginal contraceptive products.

The Condom as a Prophylactic Device.   It has been known for decades that condoms effectively prevent transmission of some STDs. Unfortunately, this benefit has not been as actively promoted in the United States as it has been in other countries, most notably Sweden. The condom seems to be one of the great underrated aids to sexual interaction. Used in combination with vaginal spermicides, it is effective in preventing both undesired conception and transmission of many diseases. It is most valuable in the prevention of gonorrhea, trichomoniasis, moniliasis, syphilis, NGU, and AIDS. It is less effective against warts and herpes and has no value in combating pubic lice. Condoms are particularly practical in sexual encounters where the couple has not thoroughly evaluated a method of birth control appropriate for their respective lifestyles and where the lack of a monogamous affiliation increases the possibility of contracting a sexually transmitted disease.

Postcontact Medication.   Occasionally a person may engage in sexual relations where the possiblity of contracting an STD seems quite high. Perhaps certain symptoms were detected during or after the sexual sharing. What can be done? Observing a period of abstinence while waiting for symptoms to appear seems a good practice to follow. In addition, it has long been known that taking tetracycline after high risk exposure dramatically reduces the possibility of developing a variety of STDs (Wear and Holmes, 1976). A word of caution is in order here, however. Routine prophylactic treatment with any antibiotic you might have around the house is not advisable. It is much better to consult with your private physician or local VD clinic.

Routine Medical Evaluations.   Many authorities recommend that sexually active people with multiple partners routinely visit their physician or local VD clinic for periodic checkups, even when no symptoms of disease are evident. In view of the number of people, both women and men, who are symptomless carriers of STDs, this seems like very good advice. How often these examinations should be conducted is a matter of opinion. Our advice to people in this category is that they should have checkups preferably every three months and certainly no less often than twice a year.

Summary

1. In the United States there is an increasing incidence of sexually transmitted diseases (STDs). However, public understanding of STDs, particularly of preventive measures, has not shown a comparable increase.

Gardnerella vaginalis

2. *Gardnerella vaginalis*, a bacterium, is the most common cause of vaginitis (vaginal infection) in American women. A large majority of male partners of infected women also harbor the organism, usually without clinical symptoms. Coitus is the primary mode of transmission of this infection.

3. The most prominant symptom of *Gardnerella* in women is a fishy or musty smelling, thin discharge that is like flour paste in consistency. Women may also experience irritation of the genital tissues. A small number of men may develop inflammation of the foreskin and glans, urethritis, or cystitis.

4. The treatment for *Gardnerella* is Flagyl. To avoid "ping-ponging" the disease back and forth, partners of infected individuals should be treated.

Moniliasis

5. Moniliasis is a yeast infection that affects many women. The *Candida* organism is commonly present in the vagina, but causes problems only when overgrowth occurs. Pregnancy, diabetes, using birth control pills, treatment with oral antibiotics, and the ingestion of large amounts of dairy products, sugar, and artificial sweeteners are conditions often associated with yeast infections. The organism can be transmitted by sexual or nonsexual means.

6. Symptoms of yeast infections include a white, clumpy discharge and intense itching of the vaginal and vulvar tissues.

7. Traditional treatment for moniliasis infection consists of vaginal suppositories or cream such as clotrimazole, miconazole, or nystatin.

Trichomoniasis

8. Trichomoniasis accounts for about one-fourth of all cases of vaginitis. Male partners of infected women are thought to carry the *Trichomonas* organism in the urethra, and under the foreskin if they are uncircumcized. The primary mode of transmission of this infection is through sexual contact.

9. The primary symptom of trichomoniasis in women is an abundant, unpleasant-smelling vaginal discharge, often accompanied by inflamed, itchy, and painful genital tissues. Men are rarely symptomatic.

10. Infected women and their male sexual partners may be successfully treated with the drug Flagyl.

Chlamydial Infection

11. Chlamydial infections are the most prevalent and among the most damaging of all sexually transmitted diseases. In men, the *Chlamydia* bacterium is a common cause of epididymitis and NGU. In women, this organism is a frequent cause of cervicitis and pelvic inflammatory disease. Babies born to women with chlamydial infections may develop eye infections or pneumonia.

12. Chlamydial disease is transmitted primarily through sexual contact. It may also be spread by fingers from one body site to another, as from the genitals to the eyes.

13. The symptoms of chlamydial infections in men may involve a discharge from the penis and burning during urination. Most women with lower reproductive tract chlamydial infections have few or no symptoms. Symptoms of *Chlamydia*-caused PID include disrupted menstrual periods, abdominal pain, elevated temperature, nausea, vomiting, and headache.

14. Chlamydial salpingitis (infection of the fallopian tubes) is a major cause of infertility and ectopic pregnancy.

15. The treatment of choice for men and nonpregnant women with uncomplicated chlamydial infections is tetracycline. Penicillin is not effective.

Gonorrhea

16. Gonorrhea, a very common communicable disease in the United States, is a bacterial infection transmitted by sexual contact. The infecting organism is commonly called a gonococcus bacterium.

17. Early symptoms of gonorrheal infection are more likely to be manifested by men, who will probably have a discharge from the penis and burning during urination. The early sign in women, often not detectable, is a mild vaginal discharge that may be irritating to vulvar tissues.

18. Complications of gonorrheal infection in men include prostate, bladder, and kidney involvement, and infrequently, gonococcal epididymitis that may lead to sterility. In women, gonorrhea may lead to pelvic inflammatory disease, sterility, and abdominal adhesions.

19. Most cases of gonorrhea respond well to penicillin treatment. Because chlamydial infection often coexists with gonorrhea, many health practitioners utilize a treatment strategy that is effective against both infectious organisms.

Syphilis

20. Syphilis is far less common, but potentially more damaging, than gonorrhea. It is almost always transmitted by sexual contact.

21. If untreated, syphilis may progress through four phases: primary, characterized by the appearance of chancre sores; secondary, distinguished by the occurrence of a generalized skin rash; latent, a several-year period of no overt symptoms; and tertiary, during which the disease may produce cardiovascular disease, blindness, paralysis, skin ulcers, liver damage, and severe mental pathology.

22. Syphilis may be treated with penicillin at any stage of its development. People allergic to penicillin may be treated with tetracycline or erythromycin.

Nongonococcal Urethritis

23. Nongonococcal urethritis (NGU) is a very common infection of the urethral passage typically seen in men. It is primarily caused by two infectious organisms transmitted during coitus.

24. Symptoms, most apparent in men, include penile discharge and slight burning during urination. Women may have a minor vaginal discharge and are thought to harbor the infecting organisms.

25. Penicillin is not effective against NGU, making definitive diagnosis essential. Tetracycline therapy usually clears up the condition.

Herpes

26. There are five different herpes viruses, the most common being type 1, which generally produces cold sores, and type 2, which generally infects the genital area. Occasionally, type 1 is found in the genital area and type 2 in the mouth area. Type 2 is transmitted primarily by sexual contact; type 1 may be passed by kissing, or by using toilet articles or utensils of an infected person.

27. It has been estimated that 98 million Americans are afflicted with oral herpes and that 9 million people in the U.S. have genital herpes.

28. The presence of painful sores is the primary symptom of herpes. A person is highly contagious during a herpes eruption.

29. There is evidence that herpes may also be transmitted during asymptomatic periods, but the relative risk is undefined.

30. Genital herpes may predispose a woman to cervical cancer. It may also infect her newborn child, producing severe damage or death of the infant.

31. There is no known cure for herpes. Treatment is symptomatic, aimed at reducing pain and speeding the healing process. Oral acyclovir is effective in promoting healing during first episodes and, if taken continuously, in suppressing recurrent herpes outbreaks.

Viral Hepatitis

32. Hepatitis A, hepatitis B, and non-A/non-B hepatitis are three major types of viral infections of the liver. Both the A and the B types can be sexually transmitted.

33. Hepatitis B may be transmitted by blood or blood products, semen, vaginal secretions, and saliva. Manual, oral, or penile stimulation of the anus are practices strongly associated with the spread of this viral agent.

34. Oral-anal contact seems to be the primary mode of sexual transmission of hepatitis A.

35. The symptoms of viral hepatitis may vary from mild to incapacitating illness. There is no specific therapy available to treat this disease. Most infected people recover in a few weeks with adequate bedrest.

Pubic Lice

36. Pubic lice ("crabs") are tiny biting insects that feed on blood from small vessels in the pubic region. They may be transmitted through sexual contact or by using sheets or clothing contaminated by an infested individual.

37. The primary symptom is severe itching that is not relieved by scratching. Sometimes pubic lice can be seen.

38. A variety of prescription and nonprescription medications effecively kill pubic lice.

Genital Warts

39. Genital warts are primarily, but not exclusively, transmitted by sexual contact. They are successfully treated by applications of topical agents, cauterization, freezing, surgical removal, or vaporization by a carbon dioxide laser.

Acquired Immune Deficiency Syndrome (AIDS)

40. AIDS appears to be caused primarily or exclusively by infection with a virus, which destroys the immune system, leaving the body vulnerable to a variety of cancers and opportunistic infections.

41. Some individuals infected with the AIDS virus manifest a less severe immune system disease called AIDS-related complex (ARC).

42. Researchers cannot determine what percentage of the almost two million Americans infected with the AIDS virus will develop serious disease processes.

43. The average survival time after AIDS is diagnosed is 56 weeks.

44. The AIDS virus has been isolated from the semen, blood, vaginal secretions, saliva, tears, urine, and breast milk of infected people. Blood and semen are the major vehicles for transmitting the virus, which appears to be passed primarily through sexual contact and through needle sharing among IV drug abusers.

45. Transmission of AIDS by sexual contact occurs in both homosexuals and heterosexuals. The virus can also pass from mother to fetus during pregnancy and through breast milk to a nursing infant.

46. No cases of AIDS have been attributed to transmission by casual contact, and there is no danger of being infected with the AIDS virus as a result of donating blood.

47. The symptoms of AIDS and ARC are many and varied, depending on the degree to which the immune system is compromised and the particular type of cancer or opportunistic infection(s) that inflict an AIDS virus victim.

48. No drugs have been demonstrated to have significant antiviral impact on the AIDS virus. At the present time, therapy for AIDS is limited to specific treatment(s) of opportunistic infections and tumors that occur in AIDS patients.

49. AIDS can definitely be prevented through widespread educational efforts and changed behaviors, primarily in the realm of sexual activity.

Other Sexually Transmitted Diseases

50. Other, less frequently discussed, STDs include molluscum contagiosum, caused by a pox virus; scabies, an infection by parasitic mites; shigellosis, a bacterial disease of the large intestine; and chancroid, lymphogranuloma venereum, and granuloma inguinale, all bacterial diseases that affect the external genital areas.

Prevention of STDs

51. Combined efforts to curtail the spread of STDs, including increasing the public's knowledge about them, offering free medical care, and requiring physicians to report all cases of VD, have not been successful.

52. To curb the rising tide, more emphasis needs to be placed on prophylactic (preventive) measures.

53. Besides abstinence and monogamy, both unacceptable to many sexually active people, there are a variety of potentially valuable preventive measures that concerned individuals or couples can take. These include inspection of a partner's genitals, disinfection of the genitals prior to or after sexual contact, vaginal prophylaxis during coitus, use of a condom, routine medical evaluations, and in certain cases of high-risk exposure, the use of postcoital medication.

Thought Provokers

1. Do you think that the threat of contracting STDs like AIDS, herpes, or *chlamydia* will alter or has already altered patterns of sexual interaction among college students and other young adults? Explain.

2. Many individuals with herpes have very rare outbreaks of the disease. It is also true that some people afflicted with this disease have experienced rejection by prospective sexual partners when they explain their condition. In view of these facts, do you believe that people who carefully monitor their health and take proper precautions can justifiably enter into sexual relationships without revealing that they have herpes?

3. It has been suggested that all adolescents and adults should be required to undergo screening for the presence of the AIDS virus. Do you agree with this recommendation? How might this information be effectively employed to reduce the transmission of AIDS? What problems might occur as a result of this compulsory screening? Do you believe that such mandatory testing would be an unjustifiable violation of human rights?

4. Assume that you are in the preliminary stages of an episode of sexual sharing and you notice one or more symptoms of an STD in your partner. What course of action would you pursue at this point? Would you make up an excuse for not continuing with sexual sharing, or would you tell your companion the true basis for your concerns? Would your response be different with a first-time versus a repeat lover?

Suggested Readings

Centers for Disease Control. *1985 STD Treatment Guidelines. MMWR Supplement*, September 1985. An excellent document that contains up-to-date information on the treatment of a broad spectrum of STDs. The *MMWR* (*Morbidity and Mortality Weekly Report*) of the national Centers for Disease Control is available in most major library systems (particularly medical libraries) and frequently contains valuable information about the nature, transmission, prevention, and treatment of STDs.

Langston, D. *Living with Herpes*. Garden City, N.Y.: Doubleday, 1983. A comprehensive discussion of herpes, of value to those who have the disease as well as those to whom they relate.

Lumiere, Richard, and Cook, Stephani. *Healthy Sex and Keeping It That Way*. New York: Simon and Schuster, 1983. A valuable resource guide to genital health and disease for the layperson. Contains an excellent chapter on informing sexual partners about an STD.

Warren, Terri Gunn, and Warren, Ricks. *The Updated Herpes Handbook*. Portland, Oregon: Portland Press, 1985. A superb comprehensive guide to the physical and emotional aspects of genital and oral herpes. An entire chapter is devoted to how to tell a partner one has herpes. Price of $2.00 per copy includes mailing in an unmarked envelope. Make checks payable to Portland Press, 6728 S.W. Miles, Portland, OR 97223.

Resources

AIDS national hotline, 800-342-AIDS. An informative recording with current information. Those who have specific questions not answered by the recording may call 800-447-AIDS. Many cities have a local AIDS information hotline.

The Herpes Resource Center (formerly HELP), 260 Sheridan Avenue, Palo Alto, California 94306; (415) 328-7710. For an annual membership fee, this excellent service provides a quarterly journal complete with up-to-date information about herpes, access to local chapters (support groups), and a private telephone information, counseling, and referral service.

Part Six

Social Issues

19

There's nothing the world loves more than a ready-made description which they can hang on to a man, and so save themselves all trouble in the future.
W. Somerset Maugham
Mrs. Dot (1912)

Atypical Sexual Behavior

Exhibitionism

Obscene Phone Calls

Voyeurism

Sadomasochism

Fetishism

Transvestism

Other Atypical Behaviors

IN THIS CHAPTER we will focus on a number of sexual behaviors that have been variously labeled as deviant, perverted, aberrant, or abnormal. More recently, the terms *variant* and *paraphilia* (meaning "beyond usual or typical love") have been used to describe these somewhat uncommon types of sexual expression. These labels are less emotionally laden and judgmental, and therefore preferable to the others. However, in our experience of dealing with and discussing variant sexual behaviors, only one common characteristic seems to stand out. Simply stated, each behavior in its fully developed form is not typically expressed by most people in our society. Therefore, we have elected to use the label **atypical** to describe these behaviors.

There are several points we should raise about atypical sexual expression in general, before we discuss specific behaviors. First, like many other sexual expressions discussed in this book, the behaviors singled out in this chapter represent extreme points on a continuum. In reality, atypical sexual behaviors exist in many gradations, ranging from mild, infrequently expressed tendencies to full-blown, regularly manifested behaviors. Despite the term atypical, many of us may recognize some degree of such behaviors or feelings within ourselves—perhaps manifest at some point in our lives, or mostly repressed, or emerging only in very private fantasies.

A second point has to do with the state of our knowledge about these behaviors. In most of the discussions that follow the person who shows the atypical behavior is assumed to be male. For some of the activities discussed in this chapter, this is an accurate portrayal. In other instances, however, the tendency to assume that males are predominantly involved may be influenced by the somewhat biased nature of differential reporting and prosecution. Female exhibitionism, for example, is far less likely to be reported than is a similar kind of behavior in a male. John Money (1981) suggests that atypical sexual behavior may be decidedly more prevalent among males than females because "male erotosexual differentiation is more complex than that of the female, and subject to more errors" (p. 79). In support of this contention Money notes that nature seems to have more difficulty producing males than females. For example, males have higher prenatal and postnatal mortality rates; and masculine development will not even occur unless triggered by sufficient levels of male hormones, since the basic developmental pattern is female (see Chapter 3). Money theorizes that these facts may demonstrate that males are more susceptible to a variety of errors affecting survival, sexual differentiation, and erotosexual differentiation (development of sexual arousal in response to various kinds of images or stimuli).

A third consideration is the impact of atypical behaviors both upon the person who exhibits them and upon others to whom they may be directed. People who manifest unusual sexual behaviors often depend upon these acts for sexual satisfaction. The behavior is an end in itself. It is also likely that their unconventional behavior will alienate others. Consequently, these people often find it very difficult to establish satisfying relationships with partners. Instead, their sexual expression may assume a solitary, driven, even compulsive quality. Research also suggests that such acts may have harmful effects upon others (Altrocchi, 1980). People who are unwilling recipients of variant sexual expressions, such as peeping or exposing, may be psychologically traumatized. They may feel that they have been violated or that they are vulnerable to physical abuse, and they may develop fears that such unpleasant episodes will recur. This is one reason many of these behaviors are illegal. On the other hand, many people who encounter such acts are not adversely affected. Because of this, and the fact that many of these behaviors do not generally involve physical or sexual contact with another, many authorities view them as minor sex offenses (sometimes called "nuisance" offenses). However, recent evidence suggests that some people progress from nuisance offenses to more serious forms of sexual abuse, a finding that may lead to a reconsideration of their classification as minor. We will examine this issue in more detail later in this chapter and in the next.

Finally, please note that the terms we use in this chapter refer to behaviors, not to people. While it may be convenient to label people as transvestites, voyeurs, fetishists, and the like, such labeling is inappropriate and potentially oppressive. For example, even when a person's primary mode of sexual expression is genital exposure, it would be misleading to label him or her an exhibitionist. This would be comparable to labeling someone who has a tendency to squint an eye squinter. "Hi, Jack, I would like you to meet Tom—he is an eye squinter." Sounds ludicrous, doesn't it? Is it any more sensible to label people by how they express their sexuality? Many of the individuals you will read about in the following pages live productive lives, exhibiting no overtly detectable behaviors that result in their being labeled abnormal or undesirable by the general public. It is much more appropriate to speak of voyeuristic or masochistic behavior than to call people voyeurs or masochists.

In the following pages we will discuss in some detail six of the most frequently expressed atypical behaviors in our society. We will examine how each of these behaviors is expressed, some of the common characteristics of those exhibiting it, and the various factors thought to contribute to its development. More severe forms of sexual victimization, such as rape, incest, and child abuse, will be discussed in the next chapter.

Exhibitionism

Exhibitionism, often called "indecent exposure," refers to behavior where an individual (usually a male) exposes his genitals to an involuntary observer (usually an adult woman or female child). Typically, a man who has exposed himself obtains sexual gratification by masturbating shortly thereafter, using mental images of the observer's reaction to increase his arousal. Some men may fantasize about exposing themselves or replay mental images from previous episodes while having intercourse with a willing partner (Money, 1981). Still others may have orgasm triggered by the very act of exposure, and a few may masturbate while exhibiting themselves. The reinforcement of associating sexual arousal and orgasm with the actual act of exhibitionism, or with mental fantasies of exposing oneself, contribute significantly to the maintenance of exhibitionistic behavior (Blair and Lanyon, 1981). Exposure may occur in a variety of locations, most of which allow for easy escape. Subways, relatively deserted streets, parks, and cars with a door left open are common places for exhibitionism to occur. However, sometimes a private dwelling may be the scene of an exposure, as revealed in the following account:

> One evening I was shocked to open the door of my apartment to a naked man.
> I looked long enough to see that he was underdressed for the occasion and then

slammed the door in his face. He didn't come back. I'm sure my look of total horror was what he was after. But it is difficult to keep your composure when you open your door to a naked man. (Authors' files)

Certainly many of us have exhibitionistic tendencies—we may go to nude beaches, parade before admiring lovers, or wear provocative clothes or scanty swim wear. However, such behavior is considered appropriate by a society that in many ways exploits and celebrates the erotically protrayed human body. The fact that legally defined exhibitionistic behavior involves generally unwilling observers sets it apart from the more acceptable variations of exhibitionism just described.

Exhibitionism accounts for more arrests for sexual offenses than any other single form of behavior (American Psychiatric Association, 1980; McWorter, 1977). Our knowledge of who displays this behavior is based almost exclusively on studies of the arrested offender, a fact that may make the sample unrepresentative. This sampling problem is common to many forms of atypical behavior that are defined as criminal.

From the available data, however limited, it would appear that most people who exhibit themselves are adult males in their twenties or thirties and over one-half are or have been married. They are often very shy, nonassertive people who feel

A calm response to an act of exhibitionism is not likely to reinforce such behavior.

Spencer— © Punch/Rothco.

"You don't often see a real silk lining, these days . . ."

inadequate and insecure (Maletzky and Price, 1984). They may function quite efficiently in their daily lives and be commonly characterized by others as "nice, but kind of shy." Their sexual relationships with others are likely to have been quite unsatisfactory. Many were reared in atmospheres characterized by puritanical and oppressive attitudes toward sexuality.

There are a number of hypotheses about the factors that influence the development of exhibitionistic behavior. Many of the individuals manifesting such behavior may have such powerful feelings of personal inadequacy that they are afraid to reach out to another person out of fear of rejection. Their exhibitionism may thus be a limited attempt to somehow involve others, however fleetingly, in their sexual expression. Limiting contact to briefly opening a raincoat before dashing off minimizes the possibility of overt rejection. Some men who expose themselves may be looking for affirmation of their masculinity. Others, feeling isolated and unappreciated, may simply be seeking attention they desperately crave. A few may feel anger and hostility toward people, particularly women, who have failed to notice them or who they believe have caused them emotional pain. In these circumstances exposure may be a form of reprisal, designed to shock or frighten the people they see as the source of their discomfort. It is not uncommon to observe exhibitionism in emotionally disturbed, intellectually handicapped, or mentally disoriented individuals. In these cases the behavior may reflect a limited awareness of what society defines as appropriate actions, a breakdown in personal ethical controls, or both.

In contrast to the public image of an exhibitionist as one who lurks about in the shadows, ready to grab hapless victims and drag them off to ravish them, the majority of men who engage in exhibitionism limit their illegal behaviors to exposing themselves (Langevin et al., 1979; Radar, 1977). Yet the word "victim" is not entirely inappropriate, in that observers of such exhibitionistic episodes may be emotionally traumatized by the experience. Some may feel that they are in danger of being raped or otherwise harmed. A few, particularly young children, may develop negative feelings about genital anatomy from such an experience.

Investigators have noted that some people who expose themselves, probably a small minority, may actually physically assault their victims. Furthermore, it also seems probable that a minority of men who engage in exhibitionism progress from exposing themselves to more serious offenses such as rape and child molesting. In a one-of-a-kind study, Gene Abel (1981), a Columbia University researcher, conducted an in-depth investigation of the motives and behavior of 207 men who were admitted perpetrators of a variety of sexual offenses, including child molesting and rape. This research is unique in that all participants were men outside of the legal system who voluntarily sought treatment after being guaranteed confidentiality. Abel found that 49% of the rapists in his sample had histories of other types of variant sexual behavior, generally preceding the onset of rape behavior. The most common of these were child molestation, exhibitionism, voyeurism, incest, and sadism. These findings do not imply that people who engage in activities like exhibitionism and voyeurism will inevitably develop into rapists. However, it seems clear that some people may progress beyond these relatively minor acts to far more severe patterns of sexual aggression.

While perhaps all of us would like protection against being sexually used without our consent, it seems unnecessarily harsh and punitive to imprison people manifesting exhibitionistic behavior, particularly first-time offenders. In recent years, at least in some locales, there has been some movement toward therapy as an alternative to incarceration. Often therapy is directed toward fostering feelings of personal worth and adequacy, together with supporting the development of more acceptable modes of sexual expression. In addition, various behavioral therapy methods are sometimes used to help the offender gain control over his urge to expose (Rooth and Marks, 1974). A recent extensive review of the literature revealed that men undergoing treatment for exhibitionism are often able to successfully modify their behavior and overcome their inclinations to exhibit their genitals to involuntary observers (Kilman et al., 1982).

A final note about exhibitionism has to do with ways of responding to it. Most people who express this behavior want to elicit reactions of shock, disgust, fear, or terror. Although it may be difficult not to react in any of these ways, a better response to exhibitionism is to calmly ignore it and casually go about your business. In this way you avoid reinforcing the behavior. Of course, it is also important to report such acts to the proper authorities as soon as possible.

Obscene Phone Calls

The characteristics of people who make obscene phone calls seem to be similar to those of people who engage in exhibitionism. They typically experience sexual arousal when their victim reacts in a horrified or shocked manner, and many masturbate during or immediately after a "successful" phone exchange. As one extensive study has indicated, people who manifest this behavior are typically male, and they often suffer from pervasive feelings of inadequacy and insecurity (Nadler, 1968). Obscene phone calls are frequently the only way they can find to have sexual exchanges. However, when relating to the other sex they frequently show greater anxiety and hostility than do people inclined toward exhibitionism. This is revealed in the following account:

> One night I received a phone call from a man who sounded quite normal until
> he started his barrage of filth. Just as I was about to slam the phone down, he
> announced, "Don't hang up. I know where you live (address followed) and that
> you have two little girls. If you don't want to find them all mangled up, you will hear
> what I have to say. Furthermore, I expect you to be available for calls every night at
> this time." It was a nightmare. He called night after night. Sometimes he made me
> listen while he masturbated. Finally, I couldn't take it any longer and I contacted the
> police. They were unable to catch him, but they sure scared him off in short order,
> thank heaven. I was about to go crazy. (Authors' files)

Fortunately, a caller rarely follows up his verbal assault with a physical attack on his victim.

Information about how to deal with obscene phone calls is available from most local phone company offices. Because they are commonly besieged by such queries, you may need to be persistent in your request. A few tips are worth knowing; they may even make it unnecessary to seek outside help.

First, quite often the caller has picked your name at random from a phone book, or perhaps knows you from some other source and is just trying you out to see what kind of reaction he can get. Your initial response is critical in determining his subsequent actions. He wants you to be horrified, shocked, or disgusted, so the best response is usually not to react overtly. Slamming the phone down may reveal your emotional state and provide reinforcement to the caller. Simply set it down gently and go about your business. If the phone rings again immediately, ignore it. Chances are he will seek out other, more responsive victims.

Other tactics may also be helpful. One, used successfully by a former student, is to feign deafness. "What is that you said? You must speak up. I'm hard of hearing, you know!" Setting down the phone with the explanation that you are going to another extension (that you never arrive at) may be another practical solution.

If you are persistently bothered by repeated calls, you may need to take additional steps. There are several possible ways of dealing with the situation. Your telephone company may cooperate in changing your number to an unlisted one at no charge. Another option is to have the police try to trace the call (phone-call tracing has become exceedingly efficient in recent years). Some people report success with tapping a ring or some other metallic object against the mouthpiece to simulate connecting a recording device. Others cover the mouthpiece partially, announcing "He is on the line again, officer." It is probably not a good idea to heed the commonly given advice to blow in the mouthpiece with a police whistle (which may be quite painful and even harmful to the ear), since you may end up receiving the same treatment from your caller.

Voyeurism

Voyeurism refers to deriving sexual pleasure from looking at the naked bodies or sexual activities of others, usually strangers, without their consent. A degree of voyeurism is socially acceptable (witness the popularity of R- and X-rated movies and magazines like *Playboy* and *Playgirl*), and it is sometimes difficult to determine when voyeuristic behavior becomes a problem. To qualify as atypical sexual behavior, voyeurism must be preferred to sexual relations with another or indulged in with some risk (or both). People who engage in this behavior are often most sexually aroused when the risk of discovery is high, and this may explain why most are not attracted to places like nudist camps and nude beaches, where looking is acceptable (Tollison and Adams, 1979).

The common term "Peeping Tom" correctly implies that this behavior is typically, although not exclusively, expressed by males. Voyeurism includes peering in bedroom windows, stationing oneself by the entrance to women's bathrooms and boring holes in walls of public dressing rooms. Some men have elaborate routes that they travel several nights a week, being occasionally rewarded by a glimpse of bare anatomy or, rarely, by a scene of sexual interaction. The following account reveals one such pattern of repetitive, ritualized voyeuristic behavior:

> During my teenage years I never expressed any sexual needs to another person—not that I had any real opportunities. You could count the dates I had all through high

school on one hand. But I did have my secret nightlife. Almost every evening, after Mom and Dad were asleep, I would slip out my bedroom window and make the rounds. Sometimes I would only do a "short-circuit," covering just the local neighborhood. Other times I would branch out, traveling for miles over a familiar route. Sometimes days would go by and I wouldn't see anything. Other nights I would get real lucky. There was a high school girl who lived down the street who persisted in undressing in front of her bedroom window. I guess she thought her backyard was secluded enough for such activities. I wonder what she would have thought if she had seen me masturbating in the darkness below? I would fantasize that she would invite me in to share her bed. Actually, if she had made such an offer, I would probably have run the other way. Finally, I tired of such activity. But for a while, it was the major part of my sex life. (Authors' files)

Most people inclined toward voyeurism tend to have some of the same characteristics as people who expose themselves (Gebhard et al., 1965). They often have poorly developed sociosexual skills, with strong feelings of inferiority and inadequacy, particularly as directed toward potential sexual partners. They tend to be very young men, usually in their early twenties. They rarely "peep" at someone they know, preferring strangers instead. Voyeurism is not typically associated with other antisocial behavior. Most individuals who engage in such activity are content merely to look, preferring to keep their distance. However, in some instances people who engage in voyeurism go on to more serious offenses such as burglary, arson, assault, and even rape (Abel, 1981; Gebhard et al., 1965; MacNamara and Sagarin, 1977).

It is difficult to isolate specific influences that trigger voyeuristic behavior, particularly since so many of us demonstrate these tendencies in somewhat more controlled fashion. The adolescent or young adult male who displays this behavior is often an individual who feels great curiosity about sexual activity (as many of us do) but at the same time feels very inadequate or insecure. Peeping becomes a vicarious fulfillment because he may be unable to consummate sexual relationships with others without experiencing a great deal of anxiety. Some people may also have their voyeuristic behavior reinforced by feelings of power and superiority over those they secretly observe.

Sadomasochism

We have chosen to discuss sadism and masochism under the common category **sadomasochistic** behavior (also known as SM) because they are mirror images of the same phenomenon, the association of sexual expression with pain. Furthermore, the dynamics of the two behaviors are similar and overlapping. Technically, sadomasochism may be defined as obtaining sexual arousal through giving or receiving physical or mental pain (Gebhard et al., 1965).

Labeling behavior as sadistic or masochistic is complicated by the fact that many people enjoy some form of aggressive interaction during sexual sharing (such as "love bites") for which the label SM seems inappropriate. Kinsey (1953) found that 22% of the males and 12% of the females in his sample responded erotically to stories with SM themes. Furthermore, over 25% of both sexes reported erotic response to receiving love bites during sexual interaction. More recently, Hunt's survey (1974) found that 10% of males and 8% of females in his sample (under age 35) reported obtaining sexual pleasure from SM activities during interaction with a partner. Although sadomasochistic practices have the potential for being physically dangerous, most people who indulge in these behaviors generally stay within mutually agreed-upon limits, often confining their activities to mild or even symbolic SM acts with a trusted partner. In mild forms of sadism the pain inflicted may often be more symbolic than real. For example, a willing partner may be "beaten" with a feather or a soft object designed to resemble a club. Under these conditions, the receiving partner's mere feigning of suffering is sufficient to induce sexual arousal in the individual inflicting the symbolic pain.

People with masochistic inclinations may be aroused by such things as being whipped, cut, pierced with needles, bound, or spanked. The degree of pain one must experience to achieve sexual arousal varies from symbolic or very mild to, on rare occasions, severe beatings or mutilations. Masochism is also reflected in individuals who achieve sexual arousal as a result of "being held in contempt, humiliated, and forced to do menial, filthy, or degrading service" (Money, 1981, p. 83). There is a common misconception that any kind of pain, physical or mental, will sexually arouse a person with masochistic inclinations. This is not true. The pain must be associated with a staged encounter whose express purpose is sexual gratification.

Many individuals who engage in SM activities do not confine their participation to exclusive sadistic or masochistic behaviors. Some are able to alternate between the two roles, often out of necessity, since it may be difficult to find a partner who prefers only to inflict or to receive pain. A majority of these people seem to prefer one or the other role, but some may be equally comfortable in either role (Spengler, 1977; Weinberg et al., 1984).

There are some indications that individuals with sadistic tendencies are less common than their masochistic counterparts (Gebhard et al., 1965). This imbalance may reflect a general social script—certainly it is more virtuous to be punished than to be the perpetrator of either physical or mental aggression toward another. A person who needs severe pain as a prerequisite to sexual response may have difficulty finding a cooperative partner. Consquently, such individuals may resort to causing their own pain by burning, mutilating, or hanging themselves (which sometimes causes death). A person who needs to inflict intense pain in order to achieve sexual arousal may find it very difficult to find a willing partner, even for a price. We occasionally read of sadistic assaults against unwilling victims: The classic sex murder is often of this nature. In these instances, orgasmic release may be produced by the homicidal violence itself.

Many people in contemporary Western societies view SM in a very negative light. This is certainly understandable, particularly when those who see it this way regard sexual sharing as a loving, tender interaction between partners who wish to exchange pleasure, not pain. However, much of this negativity stems from a generalized societal perception of sadomasochistic activities as perverse forms of sexual expression involving severe pain, suffering, and degradation. There is a further assumption that many individuals caught up in such activities are victims rather than willing participants.

Martin Weinberg, Colin Williams, and Charles Moser (1984) maintain that these conceptions of sadomasochism are misleading "because they are not based on close examination of what the majority of SM participants actually do and how they interpret their own behavior" (p. 379). These researchers suggest that the traditional medical model of SM as a pathological condition is based on a limited sample of individuals who practice SM activities and who also have personality disorders or severe emotional problems that cause them to come to the attention of clinicians. In contrast to this clinically biased sample, Weinberg, Williams, and Moser conducted extensive fieldwork in nonclinical environments, in which they interviewed a variety of SM participants and observed their behaviors in many different settings. They did find that some of these individuals engaged in "heavy SM" that was consistent with traditional conceptions. However, for the majority of these participants, "SM was simply a form of sexual enhancement which they voluntarily and mutually choose to explore" (p. 388).

Weinberg, Williams, and Moser found that this majority form of SM activity was characterized by five social features: dominance and submission, role playing, consensuality, a sexual context, and mutual definition. The feature of dominance and submission was present in all the SM activities they observed. Typically this was manifested in the form of a dominant partner inflicting moderate pain or humiliating the submissive partner. Bondage—the restraint of one partner by another through the use of ropes, chains, suspension, and so forth—was also widely employed as a means of making a person feel physically and sexually at the mercy of another. These dominance and submission sexual fantasy themes were acted out through elaborate role playing; participants called the activity a "scene" and their involvement in it "play." SM was definitely a consensual activity among the vast majority of individuals interviewed, who collectively maintained that a nonconsenting person would not be considered "into SM" or sexually desirable. Most of the SM participants defined their activities as sexual in some way and engaged in such behavior in a setting or context that supported this assigned meaning. Finally, for such activities to be defined as SM, both partners had to mutually agree that what they were engaging in was SM.

Studies of sexual behavior in other species reveal that many nonhuman animals engage in what might be labeled combative or pain-inflicting behavior before coitus. Many observers theorize that such activity has definite neurophysiological value in that it heightens many of the biological accompaniments of sexual arousal, including blood pressure, muscle tension, and hyperventilation (Gebhard et al., 1965). It may be that a number of people engage in this behavior because, for a variety of reasons (such as guilt, anxiety, or apathy), they need additional nonsexual stimuli to achieve sufficient arousal. It has also been suggested that resistance or tension between partners enhances sex and that SM is just a more extreme version of this ordinary principle (Tripp, 1975).

Many people, perhaps the majority, who participate in SM are not dependent upon these activities to achieve sexual arousal and orgasm. Those for whom it is only an occasional pursuit may find that at least some of its excitement and erotic allure stems from the fact that it represents a marked departure from more conventional sexual practices. Other people who indulge in SM acts may have acquired strong negative feelings toward sex, often believing it is sinful and immoral. For such people masochistic behavior provides a guilt-relieving mechanism: Either they get their pleasure simultaneously with punishment, or they first endure the punishment to entitle them to the pleasure. Similarly, people who indulge in sadism may be punishing partners for engaging in anything so evil. Furthermore, people who have strong feelings of personal or sexual inadequacy may resort to sadistic acts of domination over their partners to temporarily alleviate these feelings of inferiority.

It has also been suggested that sadomasochism may provide participants with an escape valve and an opportunity to temporarily assume a role that may be the exact opposite of the rigidly controlled, restrictive one they manifest in their everyday, public life. Thus, there are "men who may be brokers of immense political, business or industrial power by day, and submissive masochists begging for erotic punishment and humiliation by night" (Money, 1984, p. 169). Conversely, individuals who are normally meek may welcome the temporary opportunity to assume a powerful, dominant role within the carefully structured role playing of SM.

Clinical case studies of individuals who engage in SM sometimes reveal early experiences that may have established a connection between sex and pain. For example, being punished for engaging in sexual activities, such as masturbation, might result in a child or adolescent associating sex with pain. A child might even experience sexual arousal while being punished—for example, getting an erection or lubricating when one's pants are pulled down and a spanking is administered (spanking is a common SM activity). Paul Gebhard (1965) reported one unusual case in which a man developed a desire to engage in SM activities following an episode during his adolescence in which he experienced a great deal of pain while a fractured arm was set without the benefit of anesthesia. During the ordeal he was comforted by an attractive nurse, who caressed him and held his head against her breast in a way that created a strong conditioned association between sexual arousal and pain.

Fetishism

Fetishism refers to sexual behavior in which an individual becomes sexually aroused by focusing on an inanimate object or a part of the human body. As has been the case with the behaviors we have considered so far, it is often difficult to draw the line between normal activities that may have fetishistic overtones and those that are genuinely atypical. Many people are erotically aroused by the sight of undergarments and certain specific body parts like legs, buttocks, thighs, and breasts. Many men and some women may use articles of clothing and other paraphernalia as an accompaniment to masturbation or sexual activity with a partner. It is only when a person becomes focused on these objects or body parts to the exclusion of everything else that the term fetishism is truly applicable. In some instances a person may be unable to experience sexual arousal and orgasm in the absence of the fetish object. In other situations, where the attachment is not so strong, sexual response may occur in the absence of the object, but often with diminished intensity. For some people fetish objects serve as substitutes for human contact and are dispensed with if a partner becomes available. Some common fetish objects include women's lingerie, shoes (particularly high-heeled), boots (often affiliated with SM themes of domination), hair, stockings (especially black mesh hose), and a variety of leather, silk, and rubber goods.

How does fetishism develop? Perhaps the most common way is through incorporating the object or body part, often through fantasy, in a masturbation sequence where the reinforcement of orgasm strengthens the fetishistic association. This is a kind of classical conditioning in which some object or body part becomes associated with sexual arousal. This pattern of conditioning was demonstrated some years ago by Rachman (1966), who created a mild fetish among male subjects under laboratory conditions by repeatedly pairing a photograph of women's boots with erotic slides of nude females. The subjects soon began to show sexual response to the boots alone. This reaction also generalized to other types of women's shoes.

Only rarely does fetishism develop into an offense that might harm someone. Occasionally, an individual may commit burglary to supply an object fetish, as in the following account:

> Some years ago we had a bra stealer loose in the neighborhood. You couldn't hang your brassiere outside on the clothesline without fear of losing it. He also took panties, but bras seemed to be his major thing. I talked to other women in the neighborhood who were having the same problem. This guy must have had a roomful. I never heard anything about him being caught. He must have decided to move on, because the thefts stopped all of a sudden. (Authors' files)

Burglary is the most frequent serious offense to be associated with a fetishist inclination. Uncommonly, a person may do something bizarre, such as cut hair from an unwilling person. In extremely rare cases, a man may murder and mutilate his victim, preserving certain body parts for fantasy-masturbation activities.

Transvestism

The term **transvestism** is applied to behaviors whereby an individual obtains sexual excitement from putting on the clothes of the other sex. In defining transvestism, it is important to emphasize the differences among people who cross-dress to experience sexual arousal, female impersonators (who cross-dress to entertain), male homosexuals who occasionally "go in drag" (cross-dress), and transsexuals who, as we discussed in Chapter 3, cross-dress to obtain a partial sense of physical and emotional completeness rather than for sexual titillation.

A range of behaviors fall under the category of transvestism. Some people prefer to don the entire garb of the other sex. This is often a solitary activity, occurring privately in their homes. Occasionally a person may go out on the town while so attired, but this is unusual. Generally the cross-dressing is a momentary activity, producing sexual excitement that often culminates in gratification through masturbation or sex with a partner. In many cases of transvestism a person becomes aroused by wearing only one garment, perhaps a pair of panties or a brassiere. There is a strong element of fetishism in this behavior that has led many writers to link the two conditions. A distinguishing feature of transvestism is that the article is actually worn instead of just being viewed or fondled.

It would appear that in the majority of instances it is men who are attracted to transvestism. This seems to be true of all contemporary societies for which we have

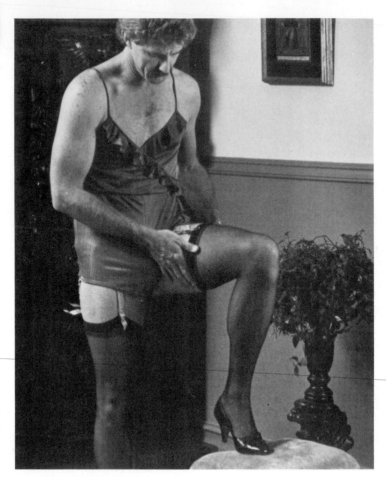

Transvestism is usually a solitary activity expressed by a heterosexual male in the privacy of his own home.

data. However, there have been a few isolated cases of female transvestism in the clinical literature (Stoller, 1982). Some writers contend that transvestism is more common among females than we are aware of, since the opportunities for cross-dressing without detection are obviously much greater for women. While this may be true, we know that males who cross-dress are not aroused by wearing ambiguous or unisex attire. Rather, they prefer feminine apparel that only women wear, such as panties, bras, or nylons. Consequently, we might expect women engaging in transvestism to become sexually aroused while wearing something strictly identified with males, such as a pair of jocky undershorts or a jock strap, rather than jeans or a flannel work shirt. These behaviors among women are extremely rare in the clinical literature.

Several studies of both clinical and nonclinical populations indicate that cross-dressing occurs primarily among married men with predominantly heterosexual orientations (Buhrich, 1976; Prince and Bentler, 1972; Stoller, 1971; Wise and Meyer, 1980). A survey of 504 subscribers to the magazine *Transvesti* provided some of the best evidence we have about the characteristics of individuals who practice transvestism. Nine out of ten respondents described themselves as heterosexual and 64% were married at the time of the survey. Only 22% had never been married. Roughly one out of four had experienced sexual contact with the same sex at some time in their lives, a percentage comparable to that reported for the general male population. Over 80% said they were treated as boys, not girls, during their childhood, and approximately three out of four said their father modeled a typically masculine role. Three-quarters of these men had not sought treatment for their atypical pattern of sexual arousal (Prince and Bentler, 1972). Another survey of over 200 members of an Australian male transvestite club also revealed that the majority of the respondents were married and heterosexual in orientation (Buhrich, 1976). The majority of these individuals had begun cross-dressing before they were nine years old. As adults, most practiced their atypical behavior once or twice a month.

The majority of men in both studies just described had not told their wives about their interest in cross-dressing prior to marriage, primarily because they thought their urge to engage in such behavior would disappear once they settled into married life. This did not happen, and most of the wives eventually found out. Of the 80% of wives of the *Transvesti* respondents who made this unsettling discovery about their husbands, 23% were accepting, 20% antagonistic, and the rest somewhere between these two extremes. Even when the initial reaction of the partner is not particularly negative, resentment and disgust may sometimes develop, as revealed in the following account:

> The first time my husband asked if he could wear my panties I thought he was joking. When he put them on I could see that he wasn't kidding around. Actually, we had a real good session that night and I guess this kind of blunted my concern. After a while it just started really bugging me. It seems like we can never just make love without his first putting on my underthings. Now I'm sick and tired of it. The whole thing seems real weird. (Authors' files)

As with fetishism and some other atypical behaviors, the development of transvestism often reveals a pattern of conditioning. Reinforcement, in the form of arousal and orgasm, may accompany cross-dressing activities at an early point in the development of sexual interest. This is portrayed in the following anecdote:

> When I was a kid, about 11 or 12, I was fascinated and excited by magazine pictures of women modeling undergarments. Masturbating while looking at these pictures was great. Later, I began to incorporate my mother's underthings in my little masturbation rituals, at first just touching them with my free hand, and later putting them on and parading before the mirror while I did my hand-job. Now, as an adult, I have numerous sexual encounters with women that are quite satisfying without the dress-up part. But, I still occasionally do the dress-up when I'm alone, and I still find it quite exciting. (Authors' files)

Many males who engage in transvestism report having dressed up as girls during their childhood for a variety of reasons (Bullough et al., 1983). Occasionally parents initiate this behavior by cross-dressing their boy child in dainty girl's clothes because they think it is "cute" or because they wanted a little girl rather than a boy. Often the case histories of men who engage in transvestism reveal that as boys they were punished by being forced to dress in girl's clothes (Stoller, 1977). This attempt to punish by humiliation is sometimes the first step toward transvestism as revealed in the following case history:

> When he was four years old (his stepmother) dressed him in girl's clothes to punish him for getting dirty. . . . She did this several times subsequently, and within two years he had arranged with a neighbor girl to dress him up regularly during their after school play. The dressing-up died away for several years, but at age 12, he did it once again, almost casually. On starting to put his stepmother's panties on, he suddenly became intensely sexually excited and masturbated for the first time. For several years thereafter, he would only put on his stepmother's underwear and either masturbate or spontaneously ejaculate. Then, in mid-teens, he began taking underwear from the homes of friends' sisters, and in a year or so increased this activity to stealing women's underwear wherever he could find it. . . . He was attracted to girls and went out on dates, but being shy, he had less sexual experience than some of his friends.
>
> He proposed to the first girl with whom he had a serious affair, confessed his fetishistic cross-dressing to her, and was surprised and relieved when she not only was not upset but assisted him by offering her underwear and by purchasing new pairs for him as he wished. Starting within a year after marriage, he found it more exciting to put on more of his wife's clothes than just her underwear, and now he prefers dressing completely in her clothes and having her assist him in putting on makeup and fixing his wig.
>
> He feels completely male and is accepted by all who know him as a masculine man. He does not desire sex transformation. He has never had homosexual relations and is sexually attracted only by women's bodies. (Stoller, 1977, p. 210)

Occasionally transvestism is a behavior of the heterosexual male who is striving to explore the feminine side of his personality, an often difficult effort in a society that extols the "Marlboro Man" image. In essence, such men create two separate worlds—the one dominated by the masculine image they exhibit on the job and in most relationships, and the private world of dress-up at home, where they can express their gentle, sensuous "feminine" self.

Anthropologist Robert Munroe (1980) has noted that transvestism tends to appear most frequently in cultures where males shoulder a greater portion of the economic burden than their female counterparts. Munroe speculates that in some instances transvestism may allow men in these cultures to temporarily unburden themselves from perceived pressures of responsibility by escaping into the female role, complete with feminine attire and behaviors.

Most people who engage in transvestism are not inclined to seek professional help. Even when therapy is undertaken, it is unlikely that the behavior will be appreciably altered (Wise and Meyer, 1980).

Other Atypical Behaviors

The six paraphilias discussed in the preceding pages, while among the most common of the atypical sexual behaviors, by no means exhaust the list of variant ways in which humans express their sexuality. John Money (1984), who has written extensively about the nature and origins of the paraphilias, has categorized over 30 of these conditions. In this final section we will briefly describe six paraphilias not previously

Table 19.1   Miscellaneous Paraphilias

Apotemnophilia: Being sexually excited by the fantasy or reality of being an amputee. This behavior is often accompanied by obsessional scheming to convince a surgeon to perform a medically unnecessary amputation.

Acrotomophilia: Being sexually aroused by a partner who is an amputee.

Asphyxiophilia: A condition in which a person, most commonly an adolescent male, employs partial asphyxiation, as by hanging, in order to achieve and maintain sexual arousal or as a way to facilitate or enhance orgasm.

Gerontophilia: The condition in which a young adult may become sexually aroused primarily or exclusively via sexual conduct with a much older person.

Mysophilia: Being sexually turned on by something soiled or filthy, such as smelly underwear or used menstrual pads.

Narratophilia: The need to listen to erotic narratives (stories) in order to achieve sexual arousal.

Pictophilia: Being dependent upon sexy pictures for sexual response.

Somnophilia: Being dependent upon the fantasy or actuality of intruding upon and fondling a sleeping stranger in order to achieve sexual arousal.

discussed. In addition, Table 19.1 lists several less common forms of variant sexual expression not discussed below.

Zoophilia

Zoophilia, sometimes called *bestiality*, involves sexual contact between humans and animals. Eight percent of the males and almost 4% of the females in Kinsey's sample populations reported having had sexual experience with animals at some point in their lives. The frequency of such behavior among males was highest for those raised on farms (17% of these men reported experiencing orgasm as a result of animal contact). The animals most frequently involved in sex with humans are calves, sheep, donkeys, large fowl (ducks and geese), dogs and cats. Males are most likely to have contact with farm animals and to engage in penile-vaginal intercourse, or to have their genitals orally stimulated by the animals (Hunt, 1974; Kinsey et al., 1948). Women are more likely to have contact with household pets involving the animals licking their genitals or masturbation of a male dog. Less commonly, some adult women have trained a dog to mount them and engage in coitus (Kinsey et al., 1953).

Sexual contact with animals is commonly only a transitory experience of young people to whom a sexual partner is inaccessible or forbidden (Money, 1981). Most adolescent males and females who experiment with zoophilia make a transition to normal adult sexual relations with human partners. Occasionally an adult may engage in such behavior as a "sexual adventure," or because a human partner is unavailable (Tollison and Adams, 1979). True zoophilia exists only when sexual contact with animals is preferred regardless of what other forms of sexual outlet are available (American Psychiatric Association, 1980). Such behavior, which is quite rare, is generally only expressed by people with deep-rooted psychological problems or distorted images of the other sex. For example, a man who has a pathological hatred of women may be attempting to express his contempt for them by choosing animals in preference to women.

Necrophilia

Necrophilia is a rather bizarre and extremely rare sexual variation in which a person obtains sexual gratification by viewing or having intercourse with a corpse. This paraphilia appears to occur exclusively among males, who may be driven to remove freshly buried bodies from cemeteries or to seek employment in morgues or funeral homes (Tollison and Adams, 1979). However, the vast majority of people who work in these settings do not have tendencies toward necrophilia.

Due to the obvious difficulties associated with gaining access to dead bodies, some men with necrophilic preferences limit their atypical behavior to contact with simulated corpses. Some prostitutes cater to this desire by powdering themselves to produce the pallor of death, dressing in a shroud, and lying very still during intercourse. Any movement on their part may inhibit their customer's sexual arousal.

People who engage in necrophilia almost always manifest severe emotional disorders. Such men many see themselves as sexually and socially inept and may both hate and fear women. Consequently, the only "safe" woman may be one whose lifelessness represents the epitome of a nonthreatening, totally subjugated sexual partner (Mathis, 1972; Stoller, 1977).

Klismaphilia

Klismaphilia is a very unusual variant in sexual expression in which an individual obtains sexual pleasure from receiving enemas. Less commonly, the erotic arousal may be associated with giving enemas. The case histories of many individuals who express klismaphilia reveal that as infants or young children they were frequently administered enemas by concerned and affectionate mothers. This association of loving attention with the erotic pleasure of anal stimulation may eroticize the experience for some people, so that as adults they may manifest a need to receive an enema as a substitute for or necessary prerequisite to genital intercourse.

Coprophilia and Urophilia

Coprophilia and **urophilia** refer to activities in which people obtain sexual arousal from contact with feces and urine, respectively. Individuals who exhibit coprophilia achieve high levels of sexual excitement from watching someone defecate or by defecating upon someone. In rare instances they may achieve arousal when they are defecated upon. Urophilia is expressed by urinating upon someone or being urinated upon. This activity has been referred to as "water sports" and "golden showers." There is no consensus opinion as to the origins of these highly unusual paraphilias.

Frotteurism

Frotteurism may be a fairly common paraphilia that goes largely unnoticed. It involves an individual, usually a male, who obtains sexual pleasure by pressing or rubbing against a full clothed female in a crowded public place like an elevator, bus, or subway. The most common form of contact is between the man's clothed penis and a woman's buttocks or legs. Often the contact seems to be inadvertent and the woman who is touched may not notice or pay little heed to the seemingly casual contact. On the other hand, she may feel victimized and angry. In rare cases, she may reciprocate (Money, 1984).

The man who engages in frotteurism may achieve arousal and orgasm during the act. More commonly, he incorporates the mental images of his actions into masturbation fantasies at a later time. Men who engage in this activity have many of the characteristics manifested by those who practice exhibitionism. They are frequently plagued with feelings of social and sexual inadequacy. Their brief, furtive contacts with strangers in crowded places allows them to include others in their sexual expression in a safe, nonthreatening manner.

Summary

1. Atypical sexual behavior refers to a variety of sexual activities that in their fully developed form are statistically uncommon in the general population.

2. Such behaviors exist in many gradations, ranging from mild, infrequently expressed tendencies to full-blown, regularly manifested behaviors.

Exhibitionism

3. Exhibitionism refers to behavior where an individual, almost always a male, exposes his genitals to an involuntary observer.

4. People who exhibit themselves are usually young, adult males who have strong feelings of inadequacy and insecurity. Sexual relationships with others, either past or present, are likely to be unsatisfactory.

5. Gratification is usually obtained when the reaction to exhibitionism is shock, disgust, or fear. Physical assault is generally associated with such behavior.

Obscene Phone Calls

6. The characteristics of individuals who make obscene phone calls are similar to those who engage in exhibitionism.

7. While there may be an element of vicious verbal hostility in obscene phone calls, the caller rarely follows up his verbal assault with a physical attack on his victim.

Voyeurism

8. Voyeurism refers to obtaining sexual pleasure from looking at the exposed bodies or sexual activities of others, usually strangers.

9. People inclined toward voyeurism, typically males, are often sociosexually underdeveloped, with strong feelings of inferiority and inadequacy.

Sadomasochism

10. Sadomasochism (SM) may be defined as obtaining sexual arousal through receiving or giving physical and/or mental pain.

11. The majority of participants in SM view it as a form of sexual enhancement that they voluntarily and mutually choose to explore. This majority form of SM is characterized by five social features: dominance and submission, role playing, consensuality, a sexual context, and mutual definition.

12. Individuals who engage in SM behavior may be seeking additional nonsexual stimuli to achieve sufficient arousal. They may also be acting out of deeply rooted beliefs that sexual activity is sinful and immoral.

13. For some participants, SM may act as an escape valve whereby they are able to temporarily step out of the rigid, restrictive role they play in their everyday life.

14. Individuals who engage in SM sometimes describe early experiences that may have established a connection between sex and pain.

Fetishism

15. Fetishism is a form of atypical sexual behavior wherein an individual obtains arousal by focusing on an inanimate object or a part of the human body.

16. Fetishism often is a product of conditioning, where the fetish object becomes associated with sexual arousal through the reinforcement of masturbation-produced orgasm.

Transvestism

17. Transvestism involves obtaining sexual excitement by cross-dressing. It is usually a solitary activity, expressed by a heterosexual male in the privacy of his own home.

18. As with fetishism, transvestism often evolves through an early pattern of conditioning. In this case, reinforcement in the form of arousal and orgasm accompanies cross-dressing activities.

19. Many males who engage in transvestism were dressed up as girls by parents who thought it was cute or who wanted a girl, or perhaps as a form of punishment.

20. Transvestism may allow some men to unburden themselves from the pressures of responsibility by temporarily escaping into the female role.

Other Atypical Behaviors

21. Zoophilia involves sexual contact between humans and animals; it occurs most commonly as a transitory experience of young people to whom a sexual partner is inaccessible or forbidden. Necrophilia involves obtaining sexual gratification by viewing or having intercourse with a corpse. Klismaphilia involves achieving sexual pleasure from receiving enemas. Coprophilia and urophilia refer, respectively, to obtaining sexual arousal from contact with feces or urine. Frotteurism involves obtaining sexual pleasure by pressing or rubbing against a person in a crowded public place.

Thought Provokers

1. Which of the atypical sexual behaviors discussed in this chapter do you find to be the most unacceptable? Why?

2. Do you think that social and cultural conditioning contributes to the much higher incidence of atypical sexual behavior among men than among women? Explain.

3. People typically are much less concerned about female exhibitionism than they are about male exhibitionism. For example, if a woman were seen observing a man undressing in front of a window, the man might be accused of being an exhibitionist. However, if the roles were reversed and the woman was undressing, the man would probably be labeled a voyeur. What do you think of this sex-based inconsistency in labeling these behaviors?

Suggested Readings

Gebhard, Paul H.; Pomeroy, Wardell B.; Gagnon, John H.; and Christenson, Cornelia V. *Sex Offenders: An Analysis of Types*. New York: Harper & Row, 1965 (also available in paperback from Bantam Books, 1967). A thorough analysis of many types of atypical sexual behaviors which come under the criminal code. Contains excellent information about a variety of psychosocial factors implicated in the development of these behaviors.

Stoller, Robert. "Sexual Deviations." In F. Beach (Ed.), *Human Sexuality in Four Perspectives*. Baltimore: Johns Hopkins Press, 1977 (also available in paperback from same publisher, 1978). Provides a review of several common atypical sexual behaviors with accompanying case examples.

Weinberg, Thomas, and Kamel, G.W. Levi (Eds.). *Studies in Sadomasochism*. Buffalo, New York: Prometheus Books, 1983. A collection of 18 articles that provide a considerable amount of thought-provoking information about sadomasochism.

The maiden I wronged in Peninsular days . . .
You may prate of your prowess in lusty times,
But as years gnaw onward you blink your bays
And see too well your crimes! . . .

Afeared she fled, and with heated head
I pursued to the chamber she called her own;
When might is right no qualms deter,
And having her helpless and alone
I wreaked my will on her. . . .

So, to-day I stand with a God-set brand
Like Cain's, when he wandered from kindred's ken. . . .
I served through the war that made Europe free,
I wived me in peace-year. But, hid from men,
I bear that mark on me. . . .

Thomas Hardy
San Sebastian (1813)

20

Sexual
Victimization

Rape
Pedophilia
Incest
Prevention of Child Sexual Abuse
Sexual Harassment in the Workplace

A PERSON BECOMES a sexual victim when he or she is deprived of free choice and coerced or forced to comply with sexual acts under duress. Sexual victimization takes many forms; for example, a teenager may threaten to break up with his girlfriend if she doesn't "put out," or an adult may feel compelled to perform a personally repugnant sexual act because his or her partner has threatened to "find it somewhere else." In this chapter we will focus on four particularly abusive and exploitive forms of sexual victimization: rape, pedophilia (child molestation), incest, and sexual harassment. All of these behaviors involve strong elements of coercion, sometimes even violence.

Rape

Rape, commonly thought of as sexual relations forced by a man upon an unconsenting woman, has occurred throughout history. It is exceedingly difficult to obtain accurate statistics on the number of rapes and rape survivors in America due to the reticence of many people to report being assaulted. It has been conservatively estimated that a woman is raped every seven minutes in this country and that at least three and a half million rapes of females occur each year in the United States (Mahoney, 1984; Seligmann, 1984). A number of contemporary surveys of various populations of women have provided indications of the numbers of American women who have experienced attempted or completed rape. The population size and victim percentages from three of these studies are as follows: 24% of 500 women (DeVisto et al., 1984); 25% of 404 women (Mims and Chang, 1984); 19% of 2000 women (Crooks, 1986).

Obtaining an estimate of the prevalence of rape in our society is further complicated by the fact that a majority of rapes are committed by someone who is known to the raped woman, not (as in the popular stereotype) by a stranger lurking in the bushes. These "acquaintance rapes," or "date rapes," as they are commonly labeled, are much less likely to be reported than stranger rapes (Burkhart, 1983; Lizotte, 1985; Williams, 1984). A recent survey of several hundred Cornell University students revealed that 16% of the women in the sample reported that they had been forced to have intercourse against their will in dating or acquaintance situations. However, only 2% said they had been raped (Parrot and Allen, 1984). Follow-up interviews with the women suggested several reasons why they did not classify these assaults as rape. The misconception that one can only be raped by a stranger under conditions of extreme violence is common in our society, and unfortunately this viewpoint appeared to be prevalent among the Cornell women who experienced acquaintance rape. Another major reason these women did not define being sexually coerced as rape was to protect themselves from the mental anguish associated with being classified as a rape victim. Apparently many of these women felt that if they could assume some of the responsibility for the event (I invited him back to my room; I let him touch me in a sexual way, and so forth), they would not need to define the forced sex as rape, thereby avoiding the severe emotional aftermath of rape—feelings of loss of control, powerlessness, and so forth.

The legal definition of rape varies from state to state. Varying degrees of rape are also defined, depending on the particular sexual act or the age of the person who is raped. Most laws define rape as sexual intercourse that occurs under actual or threatened forceable compulsion that overcomes earnest resistance of the victim.

Statutory rape is intercourse with a person who is legally defined as under the age of consent. The age of consent varies in different states but is generally 18. Statutory rape is considered to have occurred regardless of the apparent willingness of the underage partner. Even if the young person lies about his or her age, the older person can be prosecuted for this activity.

Many contemporary attitudes, issues, and laws regarding rape stem from the historical status of women. Until very recently, rape has been institutionalized by law as a violation of male property rights. For example, in ancient Babylonian law women were considered to be their father's possessions until sold to their husband for a bride price. The amount of payment for the bride was contingent upon her virginity. Therefore, rape of an unmarried woman was considered as theft of the father's market price for his daughter. In England at the close of the thirteenth century, punishment that had previously been reserved only for forcible rape of virgins was extended to include the rape of married women by men other than their husband. The law still maintained that a husband could not legally rape his own wife, since she was his possession and sexual relations were his right (Brownmiller, 1975).

The viewpoint that a husband should be allowed unrestricted sexual access to his wife has come under sharp attack in recent years in this country. By 1985, 23 states and the District of Columbia had established statutes permitting the prosecution of husbands who rape their wives, and 15 more states were considering similar laws to provide a woman legal recourse against her spouse if he forces her to engage in sex without her consent. A major study by Diana Russell (1982), published in her book *Rape in Marriage*, provided strong evidence that one out of every seven American women who have ever been married has been raped by a husband or ex-husband. Lenore Walker (1979), author of *The Battered Woman*, found that 60% of 430 battered women she interviewed had been raped by their husbands. These grim statistics reveal the need for legislation to make spousal rape a crime in all states of the union.

Both rape and the threat of rape have served to control female sexuality and behavior for centuries. Throughout history, if a woman was to expect even a modicum of protection or recourse against rape, her sexual behavior had to remain within narrowly defined limits; that is, she must have been a virgin or a monogamous wife. The "protection" of women from rape has often been a way of preserving exclusive male sexual rights to chaste women. In the following discussions, we will examine the effects of these historical attitudes on contemporary rape issues.

Contemporary Issues

Significant changes in rape laws and services to those who are raped have occurred in the past several years. Legal reform is taking place in the areas of redefinition of the crime and revision of the rules of evidence during rape trials. A few important changes have been made in some states. One is the provision that the *threat* of force is sufficient coercion—that is, that personal injury does not have to occur for an act to be considered rape. Second, the accusor's prior sexual conduct is not admitted as

*Boston women
protest night
assaults
with a mass
march.*

evidence in the trial. Third, the accused man's past sexual offenses may be discussed in court. A fourth reform recognizes the woman's right not to have her name printed in the newspaper.

An important impetus for legal reforms has come from the women's movement, which has also challenged societal assumptions about rape. When women organized in the early 1970s to deal with rape issues, they asserted first that the problem of rape stems from the way society deals with it. The women's movement involvement began with consciousness-raising groups and conferences. Grass-roots community outreach programs, rape crisis centers, and hotlines were established to provide education, counseling, and procedural information to women who are raped and to the community. Groups of women began to patrol high-rape areas of cities. Legislative task forces were implemented to change laws. Programs were established in conjunction with police forces, hospitals, and legal systems to provide advocate and support services to women who reported being raped. In some cities men have formed groups to support the women's movement efforts and to examine male attitudes that perpetuate rape.

Recently women who have been raped have begun to fight back in civil court. Several have successfully sued their assailants. Property owners and institutions may also be found liable in such procedures. In one landmark case in California, a woman who had been raped in her own apartment won the right in appeals court to bring charges against her landlord for negligence in failing to provide adequate safety measures. Colleges and universities have also had legal judgments rendered against them for failure to provide adequate protection for women students who were raped on campus. These developments in rape litigation may prompt insurance companies to demand stricter enforcement of security measures before providing coverage for property owners and institutions.

False Beliefs About Rape

As attitudes have begun to change and research has correspondingly improved, many past beliefs about the crime of rape, the person who rapes, and the person who is raped have been shown to be inaccurate. However, many false beliefs about rape still persist. In the following paragraphs we will consider some of the more common of these misconceptions.

False Belief: "You Can't Thread a Moving Needle."   The belief that women can always successfully ("if they *really* want to") resist a rape attempt is false, for several important reasons. First, men are usually physically larger than women. They have been encouraged to develop their physical strength and agility throughout their lives. Boys' rough-and-tumble play and athletics encourage them to be physically forceful and confident. On the other hand, stereotypical female gender-role conditioning trains a woman to be passive—the recipient rather than the initiator of action. Smaller stature is a physical reality, but the way women feel about and use their bodies is learned. Muscles may be admired on men, but they are typically considered unattractive on women. Soft skin and physical weakness are "feminine." Furthermore, a woman's clothing and shoes typically inhibit her efforts to fight or to run. Yet these are only exterior symbols of passivity, compliance, and submission that "good girls" are encouraged to incorporate in their behavior. (Paradoxically, "good girls" are also supposed to actively defend their "honor"!) These elements of gender-role conditioning limit the options a woman believes she has in resisting a rape attack. It simply may not be in her repertoire of behavior to be offensive or aggressive, or to resort to socially unacceptable behaviors to defend herself against the person attacking her.

Second, the man who rapes chooses the time and place. He has the element of surprise on his side. The fear and intimidation a woman usually experiences when attacked works to the assailant's advantage. His use of weapons, threats, or physical force further encourages her compliance. One study revealed that some type of weapon is used in 50% of rapes reported to the police. Furthermore, strong-arm force was present in 75% of reported rapes (National Institute of Law Enforcement and Criminal Justice, 1978). Many rapes are perpetrated by two or more attackers (Steen and Price, 1977). Increased physical violence is more likely to occur in situations with multiple rapists (Rada, 1977); the intimidation the woman feels is likely to be greater as well.

To state that a woman who wishes to avoid rape can do so is to misunderstand the realities of this crime:

> Rape can be the most terrifying event in a woman's life. The sexual act or acts performed are often intended to humiliate or degrade her: bottles, gun barrels and sticks may be thrust into her vagina or anus. She may be compelled to swallow urine or perform fellatio with such force that she thinks she might strangle or suffocate; her breasts may be bitten or burned with cigarettes. In many instances, her hope is to save her life—not her

chastity. Her terror may be so overwhelming that she urinates, defecates or vomits. If she escapes without serious outward signs of injury, she may suffer vaginal tears or infections, contact venereal disease, or become impregnated. For months or years afterward, she may distrust others, change residences frequently and sleep poorly. Her friends and family may blame or reject her. (National Institute of Law Enforcement and Criminal Justice, 1978, p. 15)

As the preceding report illustrates, women who are attacked often believe their only choices are to be killed, seriously injured, or raped.

Courses on rape prevention sometimes advise women to be passive when attacked, on the assumption that resistance or fighting might increase the potential for violence. Yet such compliance often results in difficulties for a rape survivor if she prosecutes. Without clear signs of resistance on her part, chances of a conviction are often reduced. Statistically, rape murders are rare. Serious physical injury occurs in a small minority of cases. Two recent studies demonstrated no relationship between a rape survivor's resistance tactics and subsequent injury (Cohen, 1984; Quinsey and Upfold, 1985). There was no evidence that physical resistance increases or decreases the likelihood of injury. However, women who physically resist their attacker may experience less postassault depression than those women who do not use physical force in an effort to escape their attacker (Bart and O'Brien, 1984).

False Belief: Many Women "Cry Rape." Historically, women may have chosen to "cry rape" because they were severely condemned when they overstepped the boundaries of virgin or wife. Today false accusations rarely occur, and they are even less frequently carried as far as prosecution. Given the difficulties that exist in reporting and prosecuting a rape, few women or men could successfully proceed with an unfounded rape case.

False Belief: "All Women Want to Be Raped." Novels and films perpetuate the notion that women want to be raped. Typically, fictionalized rape scenes begin with a woman resisting her attacker, only to melt into passionate acceptance. In the rare cases where male-to-male rape is shown, as in the film *Deliverance*, the violation and humiliation of rape is more likely to be truthfully portrayed.

The fact that some women do occasionally have rape fantasies is sometimes used to support the idea that women want to be sexually assaulted. However, there are several factors that clearly discredit this belief. First of all, in a fantasy a person still retains ultimate control. It is important to understand the distinction between an erotic fantasy and a conscious desire to lose one's free will to someone whose intent is to inflict harm. A basic element in an actual rape is the terrifying powerlessness of the woman. A fantasy carries no threat of physical harm or death; a rape does. Furthermore, many women have internalized ambivalent "good girl versus bad girl" messages about expressing their sexuality. Fantasizing about intense seduction can be a way for a woman to feel accepting of her sexual feelings without having to assume active responsibility for them.

An extremely negative consequence of the belief that women want to be raped is that many rape survivors may believe that the rape was basically their fault. Even when they may have simply been in the wrong place at the wrong time, a pervasive sense of personal guilt may remain. Unfortunately, when a woman continues to feel self-blame following a rape, the man who raped her is still indirectly maintaining some control over her life. Rape self-help groups or personal counseling may help a woman resolve these feelings.

False Belief: "It Could Never Happen to Me."   Many women may think that because they are too young, too old, too fat, married, "not that kind of girl," exceedingly cautious, or possess any of a variety of unique characteristics, they will not be raped. This belief may promote a false sense of security. It also tends, once again, to place blame for the rape on some characteristic or behavior of the woman herself. The truth is that any female is a potential victim.

Rapists show a high degree of arbitrariness in selecting their targets. Victim precipitation (behaviors which contribute to the occurrence of a crime) has been analyzed for a variety of crimes, and a Federal Commission on Crimes of Violence study indicates that only 4% of rapes involve precipitant behavior by the woman. In fact, rape victims engaged in less precipitant behavior than victims of homicide, assault, or robbery (Brownmiller, 1975).

Even women who are never raped live daily with the threat of a sexual attack. The possibility of rape makes it more difficult for women to lead independent lives. Although rape can happen to virtually any woman, there are some things that can be done to reduce (but not eliminate) the chance of its occurrence. Some suggestions for prevention, and for coping with the situation if it cannot be prevented, appear in Box 20.1.

Female Rape Survivors

The vast majority of rapes that occur outside prisons and jails are perpetrated by males upon female victims. However, as we shall see in a later section of this chapter, the research and treatment community is becoming increasingly aware that nonimprisoned men also can be raped by either males or females. Since the majority of people who are raped are females, it follows that most of our knowledge about the short- and long-term effects of rape have been gleaned from studies of female survivors of rape.

Given the characteristics of rape—the physical violation and psychological trauma it inflicts, and our societal attitudes about it—it is understandable that many rape survivors suffer long-lasting emotional effects. The emotional repercussions women experience following rape or attempted rape have been labeled *rape trauma syndrome* (Burgess and Holmstrom, 1974a and 1974b).

There are usually two phases of rape trauma. The first, known as the *acute phase*, begins immediately following the rape and may continue for hours, days, or often several weeks. During the first few hours after the attack a woman will tend to react in either an expressive or controlled manner. In the expressive reaction she will likely be crying and obviously upset. In the controlled reaction a woman will appear subdued and matter-of-fact. She may, however, experience the expressive reaction at a later time. The feelings many victims report during the acute phase cover a wide range, often including shame, anger, fear, nervousness, guilt, self-blame, and a sense of

Box 20.1   *Dealing with Rape*

While rape is a society-wide problem, it is the rape victim who experiences the direct, personal violation. The suggestions offered below may reduce a woman's chances of being raped. *However, these suggestions are no guarantee of avoiding rape.* Even a woman who leads an extremely cautious and restricted life may be raped.

Reducing the risk of rape

Rape prevention consists primarily of making it as difficult as possible for a rapist to make you his victim. Many of the following suggestions are common-sense measures against other crimes as well as rape.

1. Do not advertise living alone. Use initials on your mailbox and in the phone book. You may also wish to add a fictitious name.
2. Install and use secure locks on doors and windows, changing door locks after losing keys or moving into a new residence. A peephole viewer in your front door can be particularly helpful.
3. Do not open your door to strangers. If a repairman or public official is at your door, ask him to slide his ID card under the door and call his office to verify he is a reputable person on legitimate business.

Many women take self-defense training to protect themselves.

654

4. Lock your car when it is parked, and drive with locked car doors.

5. Avoid dark and deserted areas, and be aware of the surroundings where you are walking. This may help if you need an opportunity to escape. Should a driver ask for directions when you are a pedestrian, avoid approaching his car. Instead, call out your reply from a safe distance.

6. Have house or car keys in hand before coming to the door, and check the back seat before getting into your car.

7. Should your car break down, attach a white cloth to the antenna and lock yourself in. If someone other than a uniformed officer in an official car stops to render assistance, ask this person to call the police or a garage, but do not open your locked car door.

8. Wherever you go, it can be very helpful to carry a device for making a loud noise, like a whistle, or even better, a small purse-sized compressed air horn available in many sporting goods and boat supplies stores. Sound the noise alarm at the first sign of danger.

Many cities have crime-prevention bureaus that will provide further suggestions and home safety inspections.

What to do in a threatening situation

When a woman is approached by a man or men who may intend to rape her, she will have to decide what to do. *Each situation, assailant, and woman is unique: There are no absolute rules.*

1. Run away if you can.

2. Resist if you cannot run. Make it difficult for the rapist. Many men, upon locating a potential victim, test her to see if she is easily intimidated. Resistance by the woman is responsible for many of the thwarted attempts (Brownmiller, 1975; Bart and O'Brien, 1984; Cohen, 1984). Active and vociferous resistance—shouting, being "rude," causing a scene, running away, fighting back—may deter the attack.

3. Ordinary rules of behavior do not apply. Vomiting, screaming, acting "crazy," or being passive—whatever you are willing to try—can be appropriate responses to a rape situation.

4. Talking can be a way to stall and give you a chance to think about what your next move might be.

5. Self-defense classes are a resource for learning techniques of physical resistance that can injure the attacker(s) or distract them long enough for you to escape.

6. Remain alert for an opportunity to escape. In some situations it may be initially impossible to fight or elude an attacker. However, you may later have a chance to deter the attack and escape—for example, if the rapist becomes distracted or a passerby comes on the scene.

What to do if you have been raped

If a woman has been raped, she will have to decide whether to report the attack to the police.

1. It is advisable to report a rape, even an unsuccessful rape attempt. The information a woman provides may prevent another woman from being raped. Ninety-eight percent of women who reported being raped recommended that other victims report to protect other women (Forcible Rape: Final Project Report, 1978).

2. When she reports a rape, any information the woman can remember about the attack will be helpful—the assaulter's physical characteristics, voice, clothes, car, even an unusual smell.

3. A woman who has been raped should call the police as soon as possible; she should not bathe or change her clothes. Semen, hair, and material under her fingernails or on her apparel—all may be useful in identifying the man who raped her.

4. Finally, it is important to remember that many women will mistakenly blame themselves for the rape. However, the victim has not committed a crime—the man who raped her has.

powerlessness (Roehl and Gray, 1984). Physical symptoms, such as nausea, headaches, and sleeplessness, are also commonly associated with the emotional trauma. Some physical symptoms may be due to the assault itself and not to the emotional trauma. Injuries such as bruises, abrasions, and vaginal or rectal tears may require a period of healing.

Fear and nervousness often continue during the second phase, called the *long-term reorganization phase*, which may last for several years (Sales et al., 1984). The woman may fear retaliation by the rapist, and she may change her place of residence frequently during this time. She may have fearful or negative feelings about sexual relations, particularly intercourse. One long-term study of rape survivors revealed that 40% refrained from sexual contact for six months to a year after the assault. Almost three out of four of these women reported that the frequency of their sexual activity remained below pre-assault levels for as long as four to six years after the attack. Their major sexual problems occurred in the area of sexual desire and arousal. Orgasmic difficulties, painful intercourse, and vaginismus were less common (Burgess and Holmstrom, 1979). A more recent study provided similar evidence. Out of a sample of 222 rape survivors, 60% reported one or more sexual problems that surfaced after the attack. The most common difficulties were fear of sex and lack of arousal and desire (88% reporting). Only a quarter of the women in this sample indicated having orgasm problems (Becker et al., 1984). These findings suggest that a rape interferes less with the survivor's physiosexual response than with the psychological aspects of her sexual activity. Rape survivors may associate sexual touches or sex talk with the trauma of their assault. As a result, these sexual stimuli may be more likely to induce anxiety than sexual desire or arousal in the post-assault period.

Estimates of how many rapes of women are reported to the police or other public agencies range from 10% of all such attacks (Seligmann, 1984) to as high as 50% (Feldman-Summers and Norris, 1984). A recent survey of several hundred victims of rape revealed that individual characteristics of the rapists and the victims had no appreciable impact on the probability that a rape would be reported to the police. Rather, how a woman perceived the legal strength of her case appeared to exert the greatest influence on her decision whether to report the assault. Women in this sample were inclined to report the rape when one or more of the following conditions were met: when the rapist was a stranger, when he stole a significant amount of personal property, when there was serious injury, and when the woman was married (Lizotte, 1985). Another study found that rapes perpetrated by strangers in which the victim's home was broken into, a weapon employed, or significant personal injury incurred, were much more likely to be reported than rapes that occurred in a dating or social situation (Williams, 1984).

Women who report a rape to the police and prosecute the offender will be involved in legal proceedings that will include a recounting of the assault. In the past the judicial system has been insensitive and sometimes psychologically brutal to rape survivors. In recent years there has been considerable improvement as the police and court system have attempted to be more sensitive and supportive. A few cities have instituted *rape victim advocate programs*. These provide a counselor to work with the woman, beginning with the initial report and continuing throughout the prosecution process.

Supportive counseling can help ease the trauma suffered by a rape victim.

Women who choose not to report a rape to the police or to tell anyone else are likely to have the same traumatic psychological reactions to their experience as women who report rape. Furthermore, they may have even more problems coping, since they do not have the opportunity to express and resolve their feelings. Sometimes the trauma of the rape surfaces later, when a woman seeks help for a problem apparently unrelated to the attack.

In summary, rape is usually a very traumatic experience. The passage of time combined with support from others can help alleviate its effects, and counseling can be useful. We hope that the many women who are survivors of this crime will seek help in resolving a trauma that can interfere with their lives.

A Partner's Response to Rape

The rape of his partner may be a difficult experience for a man. In a sense he also is victimized by the assault. He may feel a range of emotions including rage, disgust, and helplessness. He may be confused and unsure about how he should react to his lover's victimization. This lack of direction may prove costly, because his reactions can have a profound impact upon both his lover's recovery and the future of their relationship. A recent survey of several hundred female survivors of sexual assault revealed that female friends were the most frequent source of post-assault help, followed by mothers and male friends, but that the most helpful people were male friends, followed by psychologists and female friends (Mims and Chang, 1984). In the following paragraphs we will offer some suggestions for how a man may participate meaningfully in his partner's recovery. These recommendations are adapted from *Sexual Solutions*, an excellent book by Michael Castleman (1980). Though they are directed to the male partners of female victims, they are also applicable to people whose same-sex partners have been violated and to female partners of male assault victims.

The last thing a rape survivor needs is to have her judgment questioned ("Why did you park on a dark side street?"). Equally counterproductive is the response of the partner who gets sidetracked by focusing his attention on his own imagined shortcomings ("I should have been along to protect you"). The woman has just finished dealing with a violent man (or men), and being confronted with a similar emotional state in her partner (motivated by his desire for revenge against the assailant) is probably not in her best interests.

What she does need is to be listened to. A person comforting a rape survivor might understandably try to divert her attention from the terrible event. However, professionals who work with survivors of sexual assault have found that many of these people need to talk repeatedly about the assault to come to terms with it. A partner can help by encouraging his lover to discuss the rape in any way that she is able.

A rape survivor may recover more quickly when she is able to decide for herself how to deal with the assault. A man may be inclined to ease his partner's burden by taking charge and deciding what should be done in the aftermath of a rape. However, "she should make every decision in reponse to the assault. She was the person attacked. The important thing is for her to regain a sense of control over her life after being stripped of that control by her attacker(s)" (Castleman, 1980, p.177). Her partner may suggest alternatives and act as a sounding board while she weighs her options. Nevertheless, the woman should ultimately make all the decisions, unless she is unable to do so.

In the days, weeks, and even months following the rape, a partner can continue to provide empathy, support, and reassurance to a rape victim. He can encourage her to resume a normal life and support her at those moments that she feels particularly vulnerable, fearful, or angry. He can be there to listen, even if it means hearing the same things over and over again. In the event that her assailant is prosecuted, she may be in particular need of support and understanding throughout the often arduous legal proceedings.

Rape victims may need more than their lovers or families can provide. Some may require short- or long-term therapy to help ease the trauma of rape and reconstruct their lives. Partners may recognize these needs and encourage their lovers to seek professional help. Similarly, partners of sexually assaulted women may also experience severe conflicts and deep feelings of rage and guilt that they need help coping with. These men may find that a close friend, family member, or professional therapist will listen as they voice their pain and anger. "Men who take care of their own emotional needs tend to provide better support to their lovers" (Castleman, 1980, p. 181).

Resuming sexual activity after a rape may present problems for both the victim and her partner. Rape may precipitate sexual difficulties for the woman; she may not want to be sexually intimate for quite a while. However, some women may desire relations very soon after the attack, perhaps for assurance that their lovers still care for them and do not consider them "tainted." Some women may prefer not to have intercourse for awhile, but instead just want to be close and affectionate. Deciding when and how to engage in intimate sharing is best left up to the woman. Her partner's support in this matter is very important. Even when sexual sharing resumes, it may be some time before she is able to relax and again respond the way she did before the attack. A patient, understanding, sensitive partner can help her reach the point where she is again able to experience satisfying sexual sharing.

The Psychosocial Bases of Rape

Why do men rape women? This is a question that researchers have attempted to find an answer to for many years. Until very recently, many of these investigative efforts were hindered by both a narrow conceptualization of rape and inadequate research methods. Our awareness of the characteristics and motivations of men who rape has been based, until recently, largely on studies of men convicted of the crime, a sample group that probably represents fewer than one percent of all males who rape. We cannot say with certainty that men who rape without being prosecuted and convicted demonstrate traits similar to those of convicted rapists. In fact, there is good reason to believe that convicted rapists are less educated, are more inclined to commit other antisocial or criminal acts, and tend to be more alienated from society than rapists who do not pass through the criminal justice system (Smithyman, 1979).

Many of the men incarcerated for rape offenses appear to have a strong proclivity toward violence that is often reflected in their act of rape. This fact, along with certain assumptions about male-female relationships, resulted in a number of feminist writers taking the position that rape is not sexually motivated, but rather an act of power and domination (Brownmiller, 1975). This viewpoint prevailed for a number of years, during which time the sexual component of rape and other assaultive offenses was deemphasized. However, recent research has made it clear that while power and domination is often involved in sexual coercion, such acts are also frequently motivated by a desire for sexual gratification. Our awareness of this fact has been enhanced by several excellent recent studies of the incidence and nature of sexual coercion among populations of nonincarcerated males.

It is becoming increasingly apparent that rape is more often a product of socialization processes that occur within the fabric of "normal" society than of severe pathology of the individual rapist. Strong support for the view that rape is in many ways a cultural phenomenon was provided by the research of Peggy Reeves Sanday, an anthropologist who compared the incidence of rape in 95 societies. A recently published summary of Sanday's important research reported that women in America are several hundred times as likely to be raped as are women in certain other societies (Benderly, 1984). Her research indicates that the incidence of rape in a given society is influenced by several important cultural factors: the nature of relations between the sexes, the status of women, and the attitudes boys acquire during their developmental years. Sanday found that societies with a high incidence of rape, which she labeled "rape-prone," tolerate and even glorify masculine violence. These societies encourage men and boys to be aggressive and competitive and to view physical force as a natural and exemplary expression of their nature. Men in such societies generally have special gathering spots, like a men's club or corner tavern, and women generally have less power in the economic and political aspects of life. Men in these societies also frequently demean the judgments of women as well as remaining aloof from childrearing and household duties, which they may consider to be "women's work."

In contrast, Sanday reported on 44 "rape-free" societies where there is virtually no rape. Her observations contradicted the hypothesis of a number of feminist writers that rape is inherent in the nature of the relations between men and women. Apparently this is not true in a significant number of societies within the world community. What is the nature of a society in which men do not rape women? Women and men in rape-free societies share power and authority and both contribute equally to the community welfare. In addition, children of both sexes in these societies are raised to value nurturance and to avoid aggression and violence. With this cultural framework in mind, let us take a closer look at some of the aspects of male socialization within our own culture that contribute to the occurrence of rape and other forms of sexual coercion.

Attitudes Toward Rape in American Society.   Males in our society often learn that power, aggressiveness, and getting what one wants are all part of the proper male role. Furthermore, they frequently learn that they should seek sex and expect to be successful in this endeavor. It is widely recognized that many males receive a great deal of pressure from their peers to acquire sexual experiences. When this pressure is combined with callous attitudes toward women and a belief that "might makes right," we have a cultural foundation for rape and other acts of sexual coercion.

Research has revealed that some rapists have distorted perceptions of their interactions with the women they rape, both before and during the assault. They may believe that women want to be coerced into sexual activity, even to the extent of being physically abused (Abel, 1981). These distorted beliefs may help the rapist justify his reprehensible behavior; his acts are not rape but rather "normal" courtship behavior. Such a man might meet a woman in a bar, take her for a drive, park, and attempt intercourse, which he would force if she resisted. Even if he has to "slap her around" to convince her to have sex, he believes he is only acting in accordance with her wishes and expectations. Afterwards, he may have little or no guilt about his behavior, since in his own mind it was not rape. Of 114 imprisoned rapists who were interviewed recently, over 80% did not see themselves as rapists. Those who did not deny having sexual contact with their accuser used a variety of explanations to make her appear guilty, including such distorted perceptions as women say no when they mean yes, women are seducers who "lead you on," and most women eventually relax and enjoy it (Scully and Morolla, 1984). Unfortunately, there seems to be considerable support for such attitudes in the general population. Many people believe that roughing up women is acceptable, that many women get "turned on" by such activity, and that it is impossible to rape a healthy woman against her will (Burt, 1980; Malamuth et al., 1980). Thus, a rapist may find both the impetus for and support of his behavior within the fabric of society.

A number of investigations have revealed that an alarming number of American men sexually victimize women. A recent survey of 190 male college students found that a significant number had engaged in a variety of sexually coercive behaviors ranging from grabs and feels (61%) to forced intercourse (15%). Men who were inclined to engage in these coercive acts tended to view relations between the sexes as adversarial, considered the use of force to be legitimate in certain sexual situations, and viewed women as manipulative and untrustworthy (Rapaport and Burkhart, 1984). Another survey of several hundred male college students revealed that 25% of the respondents reported attempting or completing forced intercourse (Kanin, 1967).

A survey of over 400 women, drawn primarily from college and military settings, revealed that 59% had experienced some type of forced, unwanted sexual encounter including unwanted vaginal intercourse (25%), attempted or completed rape (25%), genital fondling (21%), and a variety of other coercive sexual acts. The majority of offenders in these acts were relatives, friends, dating partners, and lovers (Mims and Chang, 1984). If we consider rape to be any act of forced intercourse upon an unconsenting woman, then the actual incidence of attempted or completed rape in this sample group was 50%. However, as we have seen, many women who are forced to submit to intercourse by their dates, fiances, or spouses do not define the act as one of rape. Another recent survey of 500 women revealed that 59.6% had been victims of some form of sexual coercion. Twenty-four percent of the respondents in this sample group reported attempted or completed rape (Devisto et al., 1984). These depressing statistics reveal that rape is an act that involves an abundance of victims and perpetrators from the mainstream of American life.

To obtain a better sense of why men rape, let us examine some recent comparative analyses of populations of rapists and nonrapists. Eugene Kanin (1985) recently reported the results of an in-depth comparison study of 71 self-disclosed date rapists (male college students who forced their female dates to engage in coitus) with a control sample of 227 nonrapists (also male college students). This important study provided several noteworthy findings.

1. The rapists were not sexually deprived—in fact, their average levels of current sexual activity and previous experiences were much greater than those of the control subjects. However, the rapists were over twice as likely to report dissatisfaction with their sex lives than the nonrapist controls (79% vs. 32%).

2. The rapists were much more exploitive of women in their attempts to achieve sexual contact. For example, almost 80% reported attempting to get a female drunk to gain sexual access, whereas only 23% of the nonrapist controls reported similar behavior. In addition, 86% of the rapists had falsely expressed love for this purpose, compared to 25% of the controls.

3. There was strong evidence that the rapists were much more likely to have a peer group that legitimized "rough sex" and labeled certain types of females as legitimate targets for rape. Over half of the rapists (54%) indicated they believed their peer group reputation would be enhanced if they tried to rape a "bar pick-up," whereas 16% of the controls embraced this repugnant attitude. Eighty-one percent of the rapists thought they would enhance their reputation by raping a known "teaser," whereas 40% of the controls expressed this belief; and 73% versus 39% thought their reputation would be enhanced by raping a woman who economically exploited men.

4. The rapists also reported considerable more peer group pressure than the controls to acquire sexual experience. Almost half of the rapists had been involved with their peers in a sequential sex episode with one female (frequently called a "gang bang"). In addition, significantly more rapists than controls had experienced sex with a woman recommended for such purposes by a friend.

5. Finally, 86% of the rapists indicated believing that rape is justified under some circumstances, whereas 19% of the controls embraced this reprehensible viewpoint.

Another recent study found similar correlates of male sexual aggression in a sample of 237 subjects. In this investigation, sexual aggression was defined as physically forced sexual activity carried to the point where the woman was crying, fighting, or screaming. Three variables were shown to distinguish men who reported sexually aggressive behavior from those who did not. Having male friends who were sexually aggressive was the most predictive factor, followed by having served in Vietnam and by seeing women as legitimate targets for sexual assault. Seventy-five percent of the men in the sample who were characterized by all three of these factors had engaged in sexually aggressive behavior (Alder, 1985). These recent studies of samples of nonincarcerated males support the earlier findings of UCLA researcher Neil Malamuth (1981 and 1982), who found that a man's perception of peer group acceptance of rape is the best predictor of his inclination to engage in rape, followed by the presence of callous attitudes toward women.

As the evidence about cultural influences accumulates, we are beginning to understand why the United States is among the societies identified by Sanday as rape-prone. Sadly, many American men seem to be socialized to view aggression as a legitimate means to achieve sexual access to women and to treat with callous disregard women's right to maintain the integrity and privacy of their bodies. Men who are products of a peer subculture that openly legitimizes and supports these attitudes and behaviors are particularly prone to sexually victimize women.

Specific Influences on Men Who Rape. In addition to the different socialization processes that often distinguish rapists from nonrapists, a number of other characteristics have been linked to men who rape. Several studies have noted that rapists are frequently socially inept, have difficulty establishing meaningful interpersonal relationships, have low self-esteem, and feel inadequate (Baxter et al., 1984; Groth and Burgess, 1977; Marshall and Barbaree, 1984; Pepitone-Rockwell, 1980). To the extent that rapists lack social competence they may be unable to establish satisfying heterosexual relationships, which may increase their negative attitudes toward women and their inclination to perpetrate acts of sexual violence (Marshall and Barbaree, 1984). Rapists may also be characterized by a tendency to hold rather conservative attitudes toward a variety of sexual topics such as masturbation and the appropriateness of family nudity (Allford and Brown, 1985). Many rapists were subjected to sexual abuse during childhood (Delin, 1978; Groth, 1979; Petrovich and Templer, 1984). In one study of 83 imprisoned male rapists, 59% reported having been heterosexually abused during childhood. In most of these cases, the female perpetrator was a family member, friend, or neighbor (Petrovich and Templer, 1984). Alcohol use may also contribute to rapist behavior; rapists have often been drinking just prior to assaulting their victims (Ladouceur and Temple, 1985; Rada, 1975).

A number of researchers have provided compelling indications that sexually violent pornography may contribute to more accepting attitudes toward rape. In 1979 Neil Malamuth and James Check recruited 271 college men and divided them into two groups. Subjects in one group were shown movies with nonviolent erotic themes. Participants in the other group were shown movies in which men commit sexual violence against women who eventually experience a transformation from victim to willing erotic partner—a theme reinforcing the culturally perpetuated myth that women welcome violence. Several days after the film-viewing sessions all subjects completed a questionnaire, the results of which demonstrated that the men who viewed the violent erotica were much more inclined to have an accepting attitude toward sexual violence than those subjects exposed to consensual, nonviolent erotic themes. The results of this study, considered collectively with a number of other investigations, led Malamuth to conclude that "certain types of violent porn do encourage attitudes of violence against women" (in Japenga, 1981, p. 1).

Research has demonstrated that exposure to even a few minutes of violent pornography can decrease one's sensitivity to the tragedy of rape and the damaging impact on the victim, increase the viewer's acceptance of a variety of rape myths (for instance, that women want to be coerced into sexual activity), and perhaps most alarming, increase the willingness of a man to admit that he would commit a rape if he thought he could get away with it (Donnerstein and Linz, 1984). Furthermore, a number of investigators have demonstrated that repeated exposure to violent pornography and other films where violence and sex are associated may result in males becoming desensitized to violence (particularly against women), more callous in their attitudes toward women, and less inclined to see rape as a crime (Gray, 1984; Donnerstein and Linz, 1984).

Several researchers have provided evidence that men who rape have sexualized violence. Two separate studies compared the erectile responses of matched groups of rapists and nonrapists to taped descriptions of rape and of mutually consenting sexual activity (Abel et al., 1977; Barbaree et al., 1979). Both experiments found that rapists obtained erections while listening to violent scenes of rape while their nonrapist counterparts did not. Descriptions of consenting sexual activity produced similar levels of arousal in both groups of men. A more recent study compared the responses of convicted rapists and non–sex offenders to audio descriptions of a variety of sexual activities that ranged from consenting heterosexual contact to rape. As in the two previously mentioned experiments, the description of rape produced greater arousal in the rapists than in the controls. However, unlike those in the earlier studies, the rapists in this experiment manifested significantly less arousal than the nonrapists to descriptions of consenting sex (Quinsey et al., 1984).

Some particularly illuminating evidence pertaining to the psychosocial bases of rape was provided by Gene Abel (1981), a Columbia University researcher who developed an elaborate system of confidentiality that allowed over 200 New York men who engaged in a variety of sexual victimization behaviors to participate in his research without being identified by the criminal justice system. Abel found that some of the rapists in his sample had extensive histories of fantasizing about rape and violence long before becoming rapists. Such a man might have begun masturbating frequently to the accompaniment of rape fantasies as early as his mid-teens. As he continues this pattern, his deviant urges to rape become progressively stronger. Ultimately his attempts to resist acting on his impulses fail, and he becomes a rapist in fact. Earlier we suggested that some men sexualize the violence of rape. These observations by Abel suggest at least one mechanism whereby this effect may occur. Approximately half of the rapists in Abel's sample had histories of other types of sexual offenses, most notably child molestation, exhibitionism, voyeurism, incest, and sadism. This suggests that the behavior of at least some rapists may escalate through a series of progressively more violent sexual offenses.

Abel also found that rapists are frequently motivated by displaced anger toward women. For example, a man who is unable to express his anger directly to his wife or girlfriend may inappropriately and violently direct that anger at another woman by raping her. The relationship between anger and rape was demonstrated in an experimental laboratory study. Marshall (1981) measured sexual arousal to rape stimuli before and after his subjects were confronted by a hostile, angry woman (actually a research colleague who pretended anger toward the subjects). The results indicated that many of his male subjects, following their confrontation with an angry woman, experienced significant increases in their sexual arousal to descriptions of rape. Similar results were obtained in a more recent investigation, in which male college students were exposed to brief audio descriptions of both mutually consenting sex and rape while their sexual arousal was monitored via a penile strain gauge. Some of the subjects had been insulted by a female prior to their exposure to the audio tapes. Descriptions of rape produced significantly less sexual arousal than accounts of consensual sex in subjects who had not been insulted, whereas the insulted subjects responded in a similar manner to both rape and mutually consenting sex descriptions (Yates et al., 1984). These investigations strongly suggest that anger reduces the tendency for sexual arousal to be inhibited when men are confronted with rape cues. It might follow that men who experience generalized anger toward women would be less likely than others to experience inhibition of their sexual responses in situations that suggest the possibility of sexually victimizing a woman.

Classification of Rapes and Rapists

One fact that has become clear in our evolving understanding of the psychosocial bases of rape is that there is no singular pattern that characterizes the violent act of rape or the men who perpetrate this crime. Rather, there is a wide range of individual differences among rapists based on the motivation underlying the sexual assault and the kinds of behavior that occur in the rape situation. From this perspective we may differentiate among four types of rape: sexual gratification rape, anger rape, power rape, and sadistic rape. The typology for the last three types of rape in this categorization was developed by Nicholas Groth and William Hobson (1983), based on over 16 years of extensive clinical experience with more than 1,000 rapists in a variety of institutional and community-based settings.

Sexual Gratification Rape.   The motivation propelling this type of rape is primarily sexual in nature. A man who perpetrates this act of sexual coercion is interested in obtaining sexual gratification and willing to use varying degrees of force to obtain it. Since sexual gratification is the primary goal, this type of rapist is likely to use no more force than necessary to accomplish this end. If it becomes clear that an excessive amount of force or violence is necessary to overcome the woman's resistance, the sex gratification rapist may terminate his assaultive act.

It is likely that a majority of the so-called date rapes fit into this category. Many men who force an acquaintance or date companion to submit to unwanted sexual intercourse may be acting out some of the male themes common in our culture that were discussed earlier. These include glorifying the virtues of being a strong, virile, aggressive male who gets what he wants by taking it. The caveman mentality of dragging a woman off by her hair for sexual conquest is, unfortunately, all too prevalent in our rape-prone society.

The sexual gratification rape is likely to be impulsive rather than planned. For example, a man may take a woman to dinner, spend some money, perceive her interactions with him as seductive, assume that he will "score" when he takes her home, and end up deciding impulsively when aroused that his desire for sexual gratification will not be thwarted by his date saying no. He perceives that "she really means yes," or that she deserves what she gets because "she led me on all evening." Less commonly, sexual gratification rape may occur when a man happens on an unexpected opportunity for sexual activity and uses force to obtain it. For example, a woman in a rural community in the state of Washington was recently raped by three men who met her in a bar when she was in an intoxicated state. Testimony of the assailants indicated that they believed she was a "loose woman" who was asking for it by being in a bar alone and behaving in a flirtatious manner. It is also likely that these assailants presumed that the intoxicated state of their victim would reduce her resistance and preclude her identifying and pressing charges against her attackers.

In light of the previously mentioned statistics suggesting a high incidence of date rape and rape by family members and friends, it is possible, even probable, that sexual gratification rapes represent the most common kind of rape in American society.

Anger Rape.   According to Groth and Hobson, "The anger rape is an unpremeditated, savage, physical attack prompted by feelings of hatred and resentment" (p. 163). The assailant is motivated to vent his rage and contempt, and sexual gratification has little or nothing to do with his assaultive behavior. Anger rape is often characterized by the use of physical violence far in excess of the amount necessary to force sexual submission. Many anger rapists exhibit a pattern of long-term hostility toward women. They perceive the rape as an act of revenge in which they attempt to get even for the "putdowns," humiliation, and rejection they believe they have suffered at the hands of women.

The victim of anger rape is usually a total stranger to the perpetrator. She is often subjected to physical injury and extreme degradation. She may be forced to engage in acts such as fellatio and anal intercourse, and sometimes foreign objects are used to penetrate her vagina or anus. The anger rapist often has difficulty obtaining sufficient sexual arousal to achieve and sustain an erection, and he usually does not find the rape to be sexually gratifying.

As mentioned previously, an anger rape is not premeditated, but rather occurs impulsively when some triggering event, like a conflict with a lover or spouse, causes a man to reach a breaking point under an accumulated load of anger and resentment. An anger rapist's assaults tend to be episodic in nature, which is to say they occur on an irregular schedule, often separated by months and even years.

Power Rape.   A power rape is an act motivated primarily by a desire to exert control over another human being. Sexual gratification may be an aspect of this type of rape, but it is secondary to the power rapist's desire to demonstrate that he has more power than his victim and that he is able to dominate and control her. Such an offender may rape women in an ". . . effort to resolve disturbing doubts about his masculine identity and worth," or in an attempt "to combat deep-seated feelings of insecurity and vulnerability" (p. 165). A power rapist often presents a picture of a man overwhelmed by an increasing sense of failure. His psychological makeup, socioeconomic background, or both ill equip him to cope with economic and social stresses in his life. He may feel powerless, hopeless, and unable to effectively deal with escalating stress. Rape may represent his attempt to regain some of the power absent from his life.

The power rapist usually employs only enough force to cause the woman to cooperate in a submissive fashion. His intention is not to physically injure her, but rather to achieve control over her. Power rapes are typically premeditated and often highly repetitive, and they may exhibit a pattern of increasing frequency over time.

Sadistic Rape.   "The sadistic rape is a preplanned, ritualistic assault, frequently involving bondage, torture, and sexual abuse, in which aggression and sexuality become inseparable" (Groth and Hobson, 1983, pp. 167–168). In this type of rape, aggression is an erotic experience. Power and anger or both may be eroticized. If power is the primary source of sexual arousal, the victim may be subjected to certain ritualistic acts such as bondage, being shaved, or being assaulted with an instrument. If the anger components of rape are sexualized, the victim is likely to be subjected to torture, such as having her breasts or genitals bitten, burned, or otherwise mutilated.

The motivational forces underlying sadistic rape are complex and more difficult to delineate than in the three previously discussed types of rape. Groth and Hobson suggest that for this type of assailant, rape may represent a perverse attempt to regain some sense of control and psychological equilibrium, while at the same time discharging pent-up frustration over unresolved conflicts. This type of rapist is likely to exhibit a particularly strong preoccupation with violent pornography. Explicit erotica without a component of violence is unlikely to hold the interest of a sadistic rapist.

It is important to note that these four types of rape are not necessarily mutually exclusive. Any act of rape may involve components from one or more of these forms of sexual assault. However, the characteristics and motivational dynamics of one type are frequently predominant in a given assault. Thus, we are often able to describe various types of rapes and rapists in accordance with the dominant aspects of the assault.

Treatment of Rapists

Statistics show that most rapists are repeat offenders, and imprisonment does not typically stop them from raping again. These grim facts have prompted the development of specialized treatment programs for convicted rapists in a handful of states, most notably Connecticut, Florida, Minnesota, Oregon, and Washington. One approach in these programs is the use of conditioning procedures designed to create aversion to deviant arousal. For example, a man who is sexually aroused when exposed to slides and narrative tapes of violent sexual interaction might be subjected to a putrid odor through a tube in his nose at the precise moment a penile strain gauge registers erectile response. Repeated sessions of this aversion conditioning frequently reduce inappropriate arousal patterns. At the same time the offender's deviant sexual arousal is being reduced, therapists strive to establish or increase his arousal to slides and tapes depicting caring, mutually consensual sexual sharing.

Treatment programs also attempt to teach offenders more appropriate ways to deal with their anger. In the cases of men whose rape behavior is motivated by deeply rooted hatred for people, particularly women, long-term psychotherapy may be required. Sometimes combining reconditioning trials with in-depth psychotherapy is the best approach.

As stated earlier, rapists are sometimes socially inept individuals who have difficulty establishing and maintaining relationships. When these traits are present, treatment may involve teaching the rapist useful social skills and how to develop warm and loving relationships with people. This can be an extremely difficult task in view of the marked amount of emotional deprivation and abuse that distinguishes the backgrounds of many rapists.

The distorted beliefs that often support rape behavior must also be eliminated in effective treatment programs. The rapist needs to learn that actual rape is not like his distorted perception of a woman becoming sexually aroused after being roughed up a bit. He must be taught to view rape as it actually is—a dehumanizing, terrifying experience for a woman, who after being forced against her will may suffer long-lasting psychological damage.

In recent years a controversial new approach to treating rapists and other sex offenders has received considerable media attention. In Chapter 6 we mentioned the use of antiandrogen drugs to lower male hormone levels in repeat sex offenders. The drug used most extensively in America for this purpose is medroxyprogesterone acetate (MPA), commonly known by its trade name, *Depo-Provera*. This drug, a synthetic version of the hormone progesterone, was originally developed in 1957 by UpJohn as a female contraceptive. Its effect upon men is to dramatically lower the production of testosterone. As we learned previously, when testosterone levels are drastically reduced in men, sexual motivation is also diminished, but the capacity for sexual response remains intact. The theory behind the use of Depo-Provera with male sex offenders is that reducing sexual motivation may serve to break the grip of the deviant sexual fantasies with which these men are so frequently obsessed.

Thus far the evidence is incomplete, and the value of incorporating Depo-Provera in sex offender treatment programs has received mixed reviews. Johns Hopkins University researchers John Money and Richard Bennet (1981) described a long-term study of 20 male sex offenders treated with Depo-Provera in combination with psychotherapy. These researchers reported that while the drug had modest overall success, "for some patients it proved to be the only form of treatment that induced a long-term remission of symptoms and kept them off a treadmill of imprisonment" (p. 132). Our home state, Oregon, recently began to incorporate the use of Depo-Provera in a treatment program for incarcerated sex offenders. The director of this program has expressed considerable optimism, commenting that "we have a very valuable new tool which, when used with other methods, has great promise in reducing sexual problems" (Smith in Manzano, 1984, p. 1).

There have been some legal issues raised by the use of Depo-Provera. There are some indications that the drug may be a cancer-inducing agent, and for this reason the U.S. Food and Drug Administration has not allowed UpJohn to market the drug for contraceptive use. In addition, other negative side effects, such as headaches and cramps, are sometimes associated with Depo-Provera treatment. Civil rights advocates have expressed concern about a prison inmate's opportunity to exert free choice by refusing to take the drug. Offenders theoretically must give informed and voluntary consent to drug treatment, but one might question how voluntary this decision actually is when the alternative may be incarceration or increased prison time (Demsky, 1984).

Rape of Males

Health professionals who work with rape survivors know that men are raped. However, statistics on the frequency of rapes of males are extremely difficult to obtain. Men are probably less likely than women to report that they have been raped. However, there is evidence "that men may be at the same point women were ten years ago on the subject of rape—more assertive, willing to talk and beginning to realize that the victim is not the criminal" (*Sexuality Today*, 1982, p. 1).

A large percentage of the rapes of males are perpetrated by heterosexual men, who often commit their crime with one or more cohorts. As in rape of women, violence and power is often associated with the sexual assault of men. The possibility of being raped is a very serious issue among male homosexuals, since they are often the victims of such attacks.

Rape of inmates in penal institutions is a serious problem. Men who do the raping typically consider themselves to be heterosexual. When released, they usually resume sexual relations with women. The men who are raped often experience brutal gang assaults. Such a man may become the sexual partner of one particular dominant inmate for protection from others (Braen, 1980).

The idea that mature males can be raped by women has been largely rejected, because it has been assumed that a man cannot function sexually in a state of extreme anxiety or terror. However, this common impression is not accurate, as indicated by the account of a 27-year-old, 178-pound male truck driver:

> One night he had been drinking and left a bar with a woman companion he had not known previously. They went to a motel where he was given another drink and shortly thereafter fell asleep. He awoke to find himself naked, tied hand and foot to a bedstead, gagged, and blindfolded. As he listened to voices in the room, it was evident that several women were present.

When the women realized that he was awake, he was told that he had to have sex with all of them. He thinks that during his period of captivity four different women used him sexually, some of them a number of times. Initially he was manipulated to erection and mounted. After a very brief period of coitus, he ejaculated. He was immediately restimulated to erection and the performance was repeated. Following the first two coital episodes, he did not ejaculate again until he was seen in therapy. After several more coital experiences, it became increasingly difficult for him to maintain an erection. When he couldn't function well, he was threatened with castration and felt a knife held to his scrotum. He was terrified that he would be cut and did have some brief improvement in erective quality. (Sarrel and Masters, 1982, pp. 121–122)

Only rarely do men report being sexually coerced by women, and this type of assault is undoubtedly an extremely uncommon phenomenon. However, it is very difficult to assess just how rare this offense is, since most men would probably be intensely embarrassed or humiliated to acknowledge that their presumed male prerogative to initiate and control sexual encounters had been usurped by one or more female assailants. Philip Sarrel and William Masters (1982) reported on eleven men who had been raped by women. None of the victims reported the assault and none were able to talk about it until they became involved in therapy several years after the offense was committed. A common feeling among the male victims was that there was something drastically wrong with them, since they had responded sexually in circumstances they thought would render any normal man incapable of erection. Labeling themselves as abnormal kindled sexual performance anxieties and feelings of inadequacy as men. All of these victims suffered from a "post-assault syndrome," characterized by impaired sexual functioning and emotional distress, which was comparable to the rape trauma syndrome previously described for women.

Alfred Kinsey and his associates were perhaps the earliest sex researchers to acknowledge the ability of the human male to function sexually in a variety of severe emotional states, when they noted that "the record suggests that the physiologic mechanism of any emotional response (anger, fright, pain, etc.) may be the mechanism of sexual response" (Kinsey et al., 1948, p. 165). More recently the eminent Scottish endocrinologist John Bancroft (1980) cited evidence from human and other animal research indicating that sexual responses can occur in situations that induce extreme anxiety. This finding that males may respond sexually in situations involving intense fear and degradation is paralleled by the observation that "most women lubricate and some women respond at orgasmic levels while they are being sexually molested" (Sarrel and Masters, 1982, p. 118). Sexual response during an assault, particularly if it is at an orgasmic level, may be a source of great confusion and anxiety to both female and male rape survivors. In some instances they may find their sexual response to be more upsetting than the physical trauma and social humiliation produced by the assault.

Pedophilia

Child molestation, or **pedophilia** (derived from the Greek "lover of children"), refers to sexual contact between an adult and a child. The definition of pedophilia depends to some extent on how one defines a child and an adult. For example, if an adult male has sexual intercourse with a 15-year-old female, is he guilty of pedophilia, statutory rape, or simply bad judgment? The issue may be further complicated when his partner willingly participates and may, in fact, have been the initiator. Each state has its own legal codes that specify at what age interaction between an adult and a younger person is considered **child molestation** (usually if the younger person is under age 12), **statutory rape** (generally 12 to 17), and a consenting sexual act (often 18 or older, but in some states the age of consent may even be 21). The legal code may appear quite ludicrous at times, particularly in cases involving teenage sex where one partner is technically an adult and the other a minor, even though only one or two years separate their ages.

It is difficult to obtain accurate estimates on the frequency of pedophilia in our society. Relatively few people are actually imprisoned for this offense (and these few are likely to be ostracized and abused by an inmate population that takes a dim view of child molesters). Acts of child molestation are unlikely to be reported, for several reasons. First, a child may not recognize that what has transpired is improper behavior. He or she may be unable to distinguish between expressions of affection and illicit sexual contact. The fact that the offender is often a friend may further confuse the child. A second reason for low reporting stems from the fact that even when a child does inform his or her parents of improper sexual advances, the parents may not believe the child or may be reluctant to expose the child to the stress of legal proceedings. This reluctance to prosecute may be strengthened when the offender is a "friend" or acquaintance of the family.

Most researchers in the field of child sexual abuse distinguish between pedophilia and incest (sex between relatives). However, many of the published statistics on the overall incidence of child sex abuse do not differentiate between these two offenses. Consequently, when you read a statement like "One out of four American females is sexually abused during her youth," keep in mind that this estimate represents the combined statistics of sex abuse by relatives and nonrelatives. The greatest portion of the overall abuse rate is accounted for by incestuous abuse by relatives, which we will discuss in the next section. To get a sense of the magnitude of child sex abuse, consider the following statistics, obtained from two recent surveys:

1. A report issued in the spring of 1985 by Margaret Heckler, the Secretary of Health and Human Services, estimated that one in every four or five girls and one in every nine or ten boys is sexually abused before the age of 18. In over 90% of the cases of sex abuse uncovered by this investigation, the child was abused in the home by close relatives, family friends, or neighbors.

2. A recent comprehensive telephone survey of almost 3,000 adults, commissioned by the Los Angeles Times in July of 1985, revealed that 22% of the respondents indicated being sexually abused as children (27% of women and 16% of men). Almost 70% of the abuse was perpetrated by friends and relatives. Ninety-three percent of the victims said the abusers were men.

Child molestation is considered by many to be one of the most heinous of crimes. Many states have meted out life sentences for this crime, and in a few the death penalty may be applied. Who is the "horrible person" who commits sexual offenses against children? A range of studies have revealed that the offender is most commonly a male, perhaps a teenager but often middle-aged or older, who is shy, lonely, conservative (particularly in the area of sexual attitudes), possesses limited sexual knowledge, and is often very moralistic or religious (Bauman et al., 1984). Typically people who engage in child molestation are family friends, neighbors, or acquaintances of the victim. They are likely to have poor interpersonal and sexual relations with other adults, and they may feel socially inadequate and inferior (Alford et al., 1984; Bauman et al., 1984). Alcoholism, severe marital problems, sexual difficulties, and poor emotional adjustment are additional problems frequently exhibited by people who molest children (Kolodny et al., 1979; Rada, 1976). Not uncommonly, these offenders have been sexually victimized themselves during their childhood (Gafney et al., 1984; Groth, 1979). Occasionally pedophilia involves adult-child homosexual contacts, but the vast majority of such acts are heterosexual in nature, between an adult male and a female child or, less commonly, between an adult female and a male child (Alford et al., 1984; Rush, 1980).

In an effort to explain this behavior, many writers have suggested that relating to children represents a way of coping with powerful feelings of inadequacy that are likely to emerge in social-sexual relationships with adults. Many people who seek sexual contacts with children do not relate well to other adults, particularly sexually. A child, as a nonadult, is less threatening. Thus, sexual behavior directed at a child may be an attempt to establish a relationship seemingly unavailable in the adult world, and an individual who lacks the appropriate interpersonal skills to relate effectively with adults may be drawn to a child because he feels more comfortable.

Most adults who relate sexually to a child do not inflict physical harm (McCaghy, 1971). The sexual interaction usually consists of touching and fondling of the child's genital organs (often without removing undergarments). Sometimes the child touches the offender's genitals. Vaginal intercourse and anal penetration are not very common. However, the potential for violent abuse is present, and evidence suggests that some child molesters may progress to more violent sexual offenses, such as rape (Abel, 1981).

The emotional trauma a child experiences as a result of a sexual encounter with an adult may be magnified by excessive parental reactions to revelations or discovery of such an activity. The child, when reporting to the parent, may merely be relaying a sense of discomfort over something he or she does not fully understand. When the parents understandably react with extreme agitation, the child is likely to react with increased emotional negativity. He or she may now have a sense of being implicated in something terrible and may come to feel extremely guilty over having participated in such an event. Children may feel guilty about such experiences even without parental displays of distress, because they sense the guilt of the person who molests them.

It is important that parents respond appropriately to instances of pedophilia involving their children. Such acts should not be ignored! While parents can try to remain calm in the face of their child's revelation, they should take great precautions to see that the child is not alone with the offending party again. In many instances children are repeatedly molested by the same person, and they may come to feel a sense of obligation and guilt. It is essential to see that the child is protected from further experiences of this kind. Specific suggestions for prevention of child abuse are presented later in this chapter.

Incest

Incestuous behavior is sexual interaction between relatives. Specifically, this includes contact between siblings, or between children and their parents, grandparents, uncles, or aunts. All of these behaviors are illegal in every state. (Sexual contact between first cousins is a gray area, and not all state legal codes contain laws against these unions.) Although its definitions may vary slightly from place to place, incest is one of the few sexual behaviors that is prohibited in every known society.

Despite universal prohibitions against incest, the behavior occurs—although it is difficult to estimate how frequently. Concealment by families and the powerful social taboos against such activity dramatically reduce the chances that incestuous behavior will come to public attention. However, recent attention to the problem of sexual abuse in the home has led some writers to conclude that incest occurs with a much higher frequency than was previously imagined (Stark, 1984). Morton Hunt's 1974 study revealed that 15% of the 2026 subjects in his sample group reported sexual contacts with relatives. Some researchers estimate that incest in its various forms may occur in 10% of American families (Justice and Justice, 1979). In a survey of 952 college students, 7.7% of the women in the sample and 4.8% of the men reported being sexually molested as children, usually by relatives such as parents, grandparents, aunts, and uncles (*Sexuality Today*, 1981). This study suggests that the incidence of male victimization may be much greater than previously believed. Most of the male victims in the study had been molested by females.

Incest occurs at all socioeconomic levels (Meiselman, 1978). However, it appears to occur with greater frequency in families disrupted by a variety of problems, including severe marital conflict, spouse abuse, alcoholism, unemployment, and emotional illness.

While it is commonly assumed that father-daughter incest is the most prevalent, studies have shown that brother-sister and first-cousin contacts are far more common (Finkelhor, 1979; Hunt, 1974; Stark, 1984). However, father-daughter sex is far more likely to be reported to authorities, a fact that has no doubt led to the confusion over which type of incestuous pattern occurs most frequently.

Sexual relations between brothers and sisters are seldom discovered, and when they are, they do not typically elicit the extreme adverse reactions that father-daughter sexual contact often does. Furthermore, it is not uncommon for participating siblings to look favorably upon their shared experiences, particularly if no coercion is involved (Justice and Justice, 1979). In one survey of 796 college students, 15% of the women and 10% of the men reported some type of sexual experience involving a sibling. Reactions to the experiences were equally divided among those who considered them positive and those who considered them negative (Finkelhor, 1980). A survey of a randomly selected sample of 927 university students revealed that 21.9% of the males and 20.9% of the females had experienced one or more incestuous involvements

(Story and Story, 1983). (These researchers included first cousins, step-parents, step-siblings, and half-siblings in their definition of incest.) Sibling sex was by far the most common form of incest experienced by both the female and male respondents (45% and 68% respectively). Father and step-father accounted for 38% of the women's contacts and 10% of the men's. Mothers accounted for an additional 6% of the male contacts. Overall, 52% of the respondents rated the incest experience as slightly to extremely negative, 18% rated it as neutral, and 30% rated it as slightly to extremely positive. Sibling incest accounted for almost all of the positively rated incestuous involvements.

Sex between a parent and child is often a different matter. At the time of this writing little is known about mother-son sex. Perhaps the recent evidence that victimization of boys by adult female relatives is more common than previously thought will stimulate more investigations of this pattern of incest. Much more is currently known about father-daughter sex, since this is the type of incest that most frequently leads to intervention by child-protection agencies and the legal system (Stark, 1984).

The incestuous involvement of a father and his daughter often begins before the female child understands its significance. Frequently it starts as a kind of playful activity involving wrestling, tickling, kissing, and touching. Over time the father may gradually include touching of the genitals and breasts, perhaps followed by oral or manual stimulation of the genitals and intercourse. In most cases the father does not need to use physical force, but relies on his position of authority or the pair's emotional closeness. He may pressure his daughter into sexual activity by reassuring her that he is "teaching" her something important, by offering rewards, or by exploiting her need for love. Later, when she discovers that the behavior is not appropriate, or finds her father's demands to be unpleasant or excessive, it may be difficult for her to escape from a well-established pattern of sexual activity. Occasionally a daughter may value the relationship for the special recognition or privileges it brings her. The incestuous involvement may come to public attention when she gets angry with her father, often for nonsexual reasons, and "tells on him." Sometimes a mother may discover, much to her horror, what has been transpiring between her husband and daughter. However, just as often she may be aware of such behavior but remain quiet for various reasons. These may include shame, fear of reprisals, concern about having her family disrupted if her husband is jailed, or the fact that the incestuous activity allows her to avoid her husband's sexual demands.

The man who is prosecuted for having an incestuous relationship with his child is often economically disadvantaged, a heavy drinker, unemployed, devoutly religious, emotionally immature, and very conservative (Gebhard et al., 1965; Furniss, 1985; Meiselman, 1978; Stark, 1984). His behavior may result from general tendencies toward pedophilia, severe feelings of inadequacy in adult sexual relations, or rejection by a hostile spouse; or it may be an accompaniment to alchoholism or other psychological disturbances. Not uncommonly, he is a product of a family where patterns of incest were modeled for him by parents, other siblings, or both (Nelson and Clark, 1981). He also frequently has certain distorted ideas about child-adult sex; for example, that a child who does not resist desires the sexual contact, that child-adult sex is an effective way for children to learn about sex, that a father's relationship with his daughter is enhanced by having sexual contact with her, and that a child does not report contact because she enjoys it (Abel, 1984).

Once detected, a father who engages in sexual relations with his child may be prosecuted under state criminal codes. Sometimes an entire family may be disrupted, with the father imprisoned, the mother faced with economic difficulties, and perhaps the victim and other siblings being placed in foster homes. Separation or divorce may result. These potential consequences of revealing an incestuous relationship place tremendous pressure on the child. For these and other reasons she may be extremely reluctant to tell anyone else in her family, let alone public authorities. Many professionals are hard-pressed to decide which is more traumatic to the victim: the incestuous experience itself or the consequences of its revelation.

There is increasing evidence that father-daughter incest can be a severely traumatizing and emotionally damaging experience with long-term consequences for the child. Many of these victims have difficulty forming intimate adult relationships, particularly with men (Janeway, 1981; Summit and Kryso, 1978). When relationships with men are established, they are frequently devoid of emotional and sexual fulfillment (Meiselman, 1978). Sexual molestation by fathers (or other adults) is not uncommon in the histories of women who seek treatment for sexual difficulties (McQuire and Wagner, 1978). Other difficulties commonly found in these victims include low self-esteem, guilt, shame, a sense of alienation from others, revulsion at being touched, drug and alcohol abuse, elevated suicide rates, and a predisposition to becoming repeatedly victimized in a variety of ways (Gomes-Schwartz et al., 1985; Stark, 1984).

We conclude our discussion of incest with one woman's account of her incestuous victimization:

> I was subjected to sexual pressures and advances by my father throughout adolescence, although it seems to have started much earlier with a disarming and subtle conditioning and progression. My feeling of having been betrayed and made unclean and unworthy by these experiences was almost overwhelming. I was so shocked by what was happening that I could find no words to express it. I wanted desperately to be rescued and protected. But I was sure that no one would believe me. I was right. In a desperate moment I confided in one of my brothers. He rejected with disbelief and anger what I said, and told me never to mention it again . . .
>
> It was not easy, at the age of 11, to try alone to cope with my father's sexual advances. He was a very authoritarian father, but he had always been abundantly affectionate and protective. I hardly knew how to resist. He always made sure that no one was at home when he approached me. I had absolutely no frame of reference by which to judge this experience. I clung desperately to an instinctive conviction that this was not normal, although my father tried to convince me that it was. It was a long, exhausting struggle—mine was an adolescence without joy. I grew sullen and solitary and felt I bore a peculiar mark of shame. I feared that people would shrink away from me if they knew what I had experienced, but at the same time and for years afterward I wanted someone to talk to.
>
> I am almost 40 now, and I'm happily married. But sometimes when I look at little girls, I wonder how many of them are trapped in incestuous situations and don't know how to ask for help. (Name withheld, *Ms.*, September 1977, p. 89)

Prevention of Child Sexual Abuse

Specialists in the field of child sexual abuse are becoming increasingly focused on developing more effective strategies for preventing the sexual victimization of children.

This is essential, since the available evidence indicates that most children do not reveal that they have been victimized, and when they do, families are often reticent to seek outside help (Finkelhor, 1984a). The experiences of health professionals who work with victims suggests that many children could have avoided being victimized if they had been provided with some important messages, such as their right to say no, the difference between "OK" and "not OK" touches, and how to cope with an adult's attempt to coerce them into inappropriate intimate contact.

Perhaps the best prospects for reducing the high levels of child sexual abuse in our society lie in developing effective programs to be implemented in the early stages of a child's public education. As indicated in Chapter 13, American parents are very reticent to talk about sex with their children. Therefore, it is probably unrealistic to expect better parent-child communication to resolve the issue. Furthermore, parents are often the perpetrators of the sexual abuse of children. The following list of suggestions, drawn from the writings of a number of child abuse specialists, offer some suggestions for preventing child sexual abuse that may be helpful to parents, educators, and other adult caretakers of children:

1. It is important to present prevention-oriented material to children when they are still very young, since as many as 25% of child sex abuse victims are younger than seven (Finkelhor, 1984a). Be sure to include boys, since they too may be abused.

2. Educators and parents will be more effective if they avoid complicated discussions of ethics, social responsibility, and complex notions of appropriate sexual activity. A more realistic approach is to keep things simple and "to translate the notions of sexual abuse into concepts that make sense within the world of the child" (Finkelhor, 1984b, p. 3).

3. It is wise to avoid making a discussion of child sex abuse unduly frightening. A child may develop so much fear that she or he will feel powerless and incapable of acting effectively in an abuse situation. It is important that children be sufficiently concerned so that they will be on the lookout for potentially abusive adult behavior. However, we also want them to have a sense of optimism about their ability to avoid such a suituation should it occur.

4. Take time to carefully explain the differences between "OK touches" (pats, snuggles, and hugs) and "not OK touches" that make a child feel uncomfortable or confused. Not OK touches can be explained as touching under the panties or underpants or touching areas that bathing suits cover. In discussing touches that are not OK, be sure to indicate that a child does not have to touch an adult in these same areas even if the adult says it is all right. It is also a good idea to talk about not OK kisses (prolonged lip contact or tongue in mouth).

5. Encourage children to believe that they have rights—the right to control their bodies and the right to say no when they are being touched in a way that makes them uncomfortable.

6. Encourage children to tell someone right away if an adult has touched them in a way that is inappropriate or has made them do something they are

Specialists in the field of child sexual abuse sometimes use anatomically correct dolls to educate children about "OK touches." These dolls may also be used in discussions with very young victims to help them understand the nature of abuse that has occurred.

uncomfortable about. Emphasize that you will not be angry with them and that they will be okay when they tell, even if someone has told them they will get in trouble. Stress that no matter what happened, it was not their fault and they will not be blamed. Also, alert them to the fact that not all adults will believe them. Tell them to keep telling people until they find someone like you who will believe them.

7. Discuss with children some of the strategies that adults may use to gain compliance with their deviant sexual demands. For example, tell them to trust their own feelings when they think something is wrong, even if an adult who is a friend or relative says that it is okay and that they are "teaching" them something they need to learn about. In view of the fact that many adults use the "this is our secret" strategy, it can be particularly helpful to explain the difference between a secret (something they are never to tell—a bad idea) and a surprise (a good idea, because it is something they tell later to make someone happy).

8. Discuss strategies for getting away from uncomfortable or dangerous situations. Let them know that it is okay to scream, yell, run away, or get assistance from a friend or trusted adult.

9. Perhaps one of the hardest things to incorporate in this prevention discussion, particularly for parents, is the message that private touching can be a very joyous and pleasurable experience, as they shall discover when they grow older and meet someone they care for or love. Without some discussion of the positive aspects of sexuality, there is a risk that a child will develop a very negative view of any kind of sexual act between people, regardless of the nature of their relationship.

Sexual Harassment in the Workplace

Working Women United Institute, a New York based research and resource center founded in 1975 to deal exclusively with sexual harassment on the job, offers a brief and succinct definition of this behavior: "Sexual harassment is any unwanted attention of a sexual nature from someone from the workplace that creates discomfort and/or interferes with the job" (Bartlett, 1982, p. 22).

Many working people are subjected to sexual coercion on the job. This form of sexual victimization, while perhaps not as shocking as child molestation, incest, or rape, is nevertheless a major concern that is receiving increasing attention. Some people may consider sexual harassment to be an unimportant or trivial issue. However, victims present a different picture, as the following account reveals:

> A woman in her late forties was hired as an executive secretary to the head of a small business in California. Her duties included a heavy correspondence load, keeping the social schedule of her boss and his wife, paying all his personal and household bills, and also arranging dates with, buying gifts for, and making motel reservations for the many young women whom he recruited for one-night stands. She was then summoned in the morning to hear about his sexual exploits, and to rehearse with him the details of an overnight business trip he had concocted as an excuse for his wife.
>
> When she objected to such nonbusiness duties, she was told that she was lucky, at her age, to hear about sex at all. When he began to accompany his morning rehearsals with pats on her buttocks and requests for blow jobs, she objected more strongly, but still she felt guilty about having gone along with his lies up to then. He told her she was a "dirty old woman," and she felt ashamed, as if she might somehow have invited his advances. After a number of incidents in which he unzipped his pants in front of her, she finally quit the job she badly needed. Though she had done the secretarial work with great efficiency (and he had hired two women to replace her), he gave her poor work references, and wouldn't support her claim for unemployment insurance. (Lindsey, 1977, p. 47)

How common are such experiences? A number of studies have shown that sexual harassment is extremely widespread. A recent survey of more that 17,000 federal employees found that 42% of the women and 15% of the men surveyed had been sexually harassed (Bartlett, 1982). (Working men are not as likely as women to be victims of sexual coercion. However, men are occasionally sexually harassed by their female or male bosses.) In 1976, *Redbook* magazine printed a questionnaire on sexual harassment that was returned by 9000 women. Approximately 88% of these women said they had personally been subjected to sexual harassment at work (Safran, 1976). The *Redbook* respondents were certainly not a probability sample of the general population. However, the high incidence revealed by the survey suggests that sexual harassment is a very common problem for working women. More recently, interviews with several hundred randomly selected Connecticut women revealed that 50% of the interviewees who had ever been employed had experienced sexual harassment in the workplace (Loy and Stewart, 1984).

How do people at the top of the corporate ladder view this problem? A 1981 survey of almost 2000 business executives revealed an apparent difference in how women and men in high level positions assess sexual harassment on the job. Two-thirds of the men indicated they felt that the extent of the problem "is greatly exaggerated" while only one-third of the women respondents agreed with this statement (Safran, 1981).

In the last few years there have been a number of court decisions that have interpreted Title VII of the 1964 Civil Rights Act, which prohibits discrimination in employment on the basis of sex, as also prohibiting unwelcome sexual advances or requests for sexual favors. In 1980 the Equal Employment Opportunity Commission issued guidelines derived from the Civil Rights Act that impose liability on companies for sexual harassment by supervisors unless the company takes immediate and appropriate action. These guidelines emphasize that both verbal and physical harassment are illegal. Furthermore, they also provide legal recourse for other employees if a coworker uses sex to obtain job advancement. Thus, if employee A has sex with a boss and gets promoted, employee B, who is equally qualified for the higher level position, may file suit against the employer for sexual discrimination.

There is evidence that employers are becoming increasingly sensitive to the issue of sexual harassment, perhaps motivated in part by a number of court decisions that have awarded large payments to victims. More and more large companies (including CBS, General Electric, General Motors, IBM, and General Telephone) are establishing programs for supervisors that clarify what harassment is and when a company can be liable for such coercive actions by its supervisors, coworkers, and even customers.

Sexual harassment creates anxiety and tension in the workplace.

Varieties of Sexual Harassment

Sexual harassment on the job can appear in many forms. A common situation involves a boss or supervisor who requires sexual services from an employee as a condition for keeping a job or promotion. This is a particularly insidious form of harassment, because when an employee is fired for noncompliance, the supervisor may invent a reason for the termination that can be damaging to the victim's future employment prospects. Employees are well aware of this possibility and thus may feel great pressure to go along with their employers' demands. Retaliation may also occur in other, less dramatic ways that are nevertheless quite damaging. A person may be denied promotion, be demoted to a lesser job, receive a reduction in pay, have vacation requests denied, and so forth. Sometimes job seekers find that sexual availability is a condition for being hired. A prospective employer may even require a "sample" before putting a new person on the payroll.

What if a worker is subjected to obscenities or made the constant target of sexual jokes? Is this sexual harassment? We certainly believe so, and apparently the courts share this view. In one case a woman engineer—whose coworkers made her job intolerable by such abusive behaviors as loudly speculating about whether she was a virgin and passing around an obscene cartoon about her—complained to her supervisor and was then promptly fired. After several years of trying to obtain legal redress, she was compensated on all counts. The coworkers were found guilty of sexual harassment, and each had to pay her $1,500. The company was required to reinstate her in a higher position and pay all back wages.

Sometimes workers are coerced into providing sexual services to customers or clients of the firm they work for. This is also clearly a form of sexual harassment, for which a company can be liable.

Effects of Sexual Harassment on Victims

The financial ramifications of not complying with sexual coercion on the job may be devastating, especially for people in lower level positions such as clerical and blue-collar workers. Many victims, particularly if they are supporting families, cannot afford to be unemployed. Many find it exceedingly difficult to look for other jobs while maintaining their present employment. If they are fired for refusing to be victimized, they may be unable to obtain employment compensation (unfortunately, harassment is sometimes seen as insufficient reason for quitting a job), and when they do, compensation will probably provide only half of their former income. Thus, a person who quits or is fired as a result of sexual harassment faces the prospect of severe financial difficulties.

The victim of sexual harassment may also suffer a variety of adverse emotional and physical effects. In two separate surveys of sexually harassed women, 75% and 78% respectively reported experiencing some negative effects, including feeling angry, humiliated, ashamed, embarrassed, cheap, nervous, irritable, and unmotivated (Loy and Stewart, 1984; McKinnon, 1979). Many of these women also felt guilty, as though they had done something to encourage the harassment; some felt that they alone had been singled out for such abuse, an often mistaken notion that can result in a sense of alienation from coworkers. The sense of degradation and helplessness reported by many victims of sexual harassment is similar to that experienced by many rape victims (Safran, 1976). These feelings of isolation, helplessness, and guilt, together with the very real threat of financial disaster, may cause a victim to acquiesce to the exploitive sexual demands encountered on the job. Very few comply because they feel "flattered" by the sexual attention they receive (McKinnon, 1979; Safran, 1976).

Finally, many victims of sexual harassment report a variety of psychosomatic symptoms that stem directly from the pressures associated with their victimization. These include headaches, stomach ailments, back and neck pain, and a variety of other stress-related ailments.

How to Deal with Sexual Harassment

If you face sexual harassment at work, a number of options are available to you. The suggestions listed below, some of which are adapted from an excellent article by Karen Lindsey (1977), provide guidelines for dealing with this exploitive abuse:

1. If the harassment includes actual or attempted rape or assault, you can file criminal charges against the perpetrator.

2. If the coercion has stopped short of attempted rape or assault, you may wish to confront the person who is harassing you. State in clear terms that what he or she is doing is clearly sexual harassment, that you will not tolerate it, and that if it continues you will file charges through appropriate channels. You may prefer to document what has occurred and your response to it in a letter directed to the harasser (keep a copy). In such a letter you should include specific details of previous incidents of harassment, your unequivocal rejection of such inappropriate overtures, and your intent to take more serious action if they do not stop immediately.

3. If the offender does not stop the harassment after direct confrontation, it may be helpful to discuss your situation with your supervisor and/or the supervisor of the offender.

4. If neither the harasser nor the appropriate supervisors respond appropriately to your concern, you may want to gather support from your coworkers (you may not be the only victim in your company). Discussing the offense with other sympathetic men and women in your place of work may produce sufficient pressure to terminate the harassment. Be sure of your facts, since such actions could result in a slander lawsuit.

5. Sometimes you can get results by using unorthodox tactics, such as an anonymous posting of the offender's name or picture along with the message, "Warning: This person is a sexual harasser."

6. If your attempt to deal with this problem within your company does not work, or if you are fired, demoted, or refused promotion because of your efforts to end harassment, you may file an official complaint with your city or state Human Rights Commission or Fair Employment Practices Agency (the names may vary locally). You may also ask that the local office of the federally funded Equal Employment Opportunity Commission investigate the situation.

7. Finally, you may wish to pursue legal action to resolve your problem with sexual harassment. Lawsuits may be filed in federal courts under the Civil Rights Act. They may also be filed under city or state laws prohibiting employment discrimination. One lawsuit can be filed in a number of jurisdictions. A person who has been a victim of such harassment is most likely to receive a favorable court judgment if she or he has first tried to resolve the problem within the company before taking the issue to court.

Summary

Rape

1. Rape is a crime of violence. It is highly underreported. It has been conservatively estimated that 3.5 million rapes of females occur each year in the United States.

2. Significant changes are occurring in rape laws regarding legal definition and prosecution proceedings.

3. The many false beliefs about rape tend to hold the victim responsible for the crime and excuse the attacker.

4. There are some rape prevention tactics that may help reduce the chances of a woman being raped.

5. Rape survivors often suffer severe emotional difficulties that are manifested in the two phases of the rape trauma syndrome, the acute phase and the long-term reorganization phase.

6. A rape survivor's recovery from her ordeal may be facilitated by a partner who listens and provides support and encouragement.

7. Rape is often a product of socialization processes that occur within certain rape-prone societies—societies that glorify masculine violence, teach boys to be aggressive, and demean the role of women in economic and political aspects of life.

8. Many rapes occur in dating situations in which men socialized by a peer subculture that legitimizes rough sex exercise their perceived masculine prerogative to "take what they want."

9. Men who are convicted of rape are frequently poor, young, socially inept individuals who feel inadequate. Many have a prior history of sexual offenses.

10. Rapists frequently reveal extensive histories of rape and violence fantasies. They also may exhibit displaced anger toward women and distorted perceptions of their rape behavior.

11. There is no singular pattern that characterizes the violent act of rape and there is a wide range of individual differences among rapists. From the perspective of motivational intent, rapes can be categorized as sexual gratification rapes, anger rapes, power rapes, or sadistic rapes.

12. There are a few specialized treatment programs for convicted rapists that attempt to reduce deviant arousal patterns, modify distorted belief systems, and teach rapists more appropriate ways of relating to people.

13. Rape of men is a serious problem, particularly in penal institutions. Most of the perpetrators of male rape are heterosexual men.

14. On rare occasions women rape men, and survivors of such assaults suffer from sexual and emotional trauma comparable to that experienced by female rape survivors.

Pedophilia

15. Pedophilia, or child molestation, refers to sexual contact between an adult and a child. The exact definition varies, since state legal codes vary as to the age they consider a young person to be a child.

16. It is estimated that one in every four or five girls and one in every nine or ten boys is sexually abused before the age of 18. The majority of child abusers are male relatives, friends, or neighbors of the victims.

17. Most individuals who engage in pedophilia are middle-aged or older males who are shy, lonely, conservative, and often very moralistic or religious. They frequently have poor social and sexual relations with other adults and may feel inadequate and inferior.

18. Most adults who relate sexually to children do not inflict physical damage. The emotional trauma a child experiences as a result of a sexual encounter with an adult may be magnified by excessive parental reactions.

Incest

19. Incestuous behavior is sexual interaction between relatives. Brother-sister and first-cousin contacts are the most prevalent forms of this activity.

20. Most incestuous activity that is legally prosecuted is father-daughter sexual contact. The fathers in such cases are often economically disadvantaged, heavy drinkers, unemployed, religious, and very conservative.

21. Father-daughter incest can be an emotionally damaging experience for the child victim, with long-term negative consequences such as low self-esteem and difficulty establishing satisfying sexual and emotional relationships as an adult.

Prevention of Child Sexual Abuse

22. It is important to talk to children about protecting themselves from sexual abuse. Things children need to know include: the difference between "OK touches" and "not OK touches"; the fact that they have rights; that they can report abuse without fear of blame; and strategies for getting away from uncomfortable situations.

Sexual Harassment in the Workplace

23. Sexual harassment is any unwanted attention of a sexual nature from someone on the job that creates discomfort and/or interferes with the job.

24. Title VII of the 1964 Civil Rights Act prohibits sexual harassment in all its forms. A company can be liable for such coercive actions by its supervisors, coworkers, and customers.

25. Victims of sexual harassment may experience a variety of negative financial, emotional, and physical effects.

Thought Provokers

1. How do false beliefs about rape perpetuate the idea that the victim is responsible, rather than the attacker? In your opinion, what effect does this attitude have on the prosecution of rape? On the incidence? On the survivor?

2. If your child was a victim of sexual abuse, what would you do to reduce the potentially adverse effects of such an experience? What steps would you take to prevent the recurrent victimization of your child?

3. Do you believe that sexual harassment by professors is a significant problem on your campus? What experience, if any, have you or your friends had with this form of sexual victimization? How might a student effectively deal with instances of sexual harassment by a professor?

Suggested Readings

Beneke, Timothy. *Men on Rape*. New York: St. Martin's Press, 1982. A provocative book that deals with men's responsibility in stopping rape. Beneke provides numerous insights into what men think about women and rape.

Brady, Katherine. *Father's Days*. New York: Dell, 1979. A courageous and powerful true story of a woman's sexual victimization by her father.

Brownmiller, Susan. *Against Our Will: Men, Women, and Rape*. New York: Simon & Schuster, 1975. A powerful, illuminating examination of rape from the feminist perspective that rape is an act of power and domination.

Colao, Flora, and Hosansky, Tamar. *Your Children Should Know*. New York: Bobbs-Merrill, 1983. A very fine book written in an engaging style that provides a wealth of information about preventing child sexual abuse and strategies for coping with such occurrences. Children, parents, educators, and health professionals all might profit from reading this excellent text.

Demsky, Linda. "The Use of Depo-Provera in the Treatment of Sex Offenders." *The Journal of Legal Medicine*, 1984, 5, 295–322. This article provides an excellent discussion of the complex legal issues involved in the use of Depo-Provera in the treatment of sex offenders.

Groth, A. Nicholas. *Men Who Rape*. New York: Plenum, 1979. Written by the director of a sex offender program in Conecticut, this book provides important insights into the character and motivation patterns of rapists.

MacKinnon, Catherine. *Sexual Harassment of Working Women*. New Haven, Conn.: Yale University Press, 1979. An excellent, comprehensive discussion of the nature, extent, and impact of sexual harassment.

McGovern, Kevin. *Alice Doesn't Baby-Sit Anymore*. Portland, Oreg.: McGovern and Mulbacker Books, 1985. A children's storybook designed to teach children, parents, and educators how to avoid child sexual abuse. The author of this superb book is a clinical psychologist with extensive experience in the treatment of sex offenders and survivors of sexual victimization. $8.95, which includes handling and shipping. Make checks payable to Alternatives to Sexual Abuse, P.O. Box 25537, Portland, OR 97225.

Rush, Florence. *The Best Kept Secret: Sexual Abuse of Children*. New York: Atlantic, 1981. A superb, painfully illuminating discussion of the sexual abuse of children. The author details the historical, political, social, and even religious factors that have sanctioned and perpetuated child-adult sex through the ages.

Russell, Diana. *Rape in Marriage*. New York: Macmillan, 1982. This book summarizes the results of a comprehensive study of marriage rape. Russell provides an excellent analysis of the prevalence of wife rape, its connection to wife battery and alcoholism, and the underlying cultural attitudes that contribute to what she calls "the crime in the closet."

Thorman, George. *Incestuous Families*. Springfield, Ill.: Charles C. Thomas, 1983. This text provides detailed information about the family dynamics of incest and suggests strategies for dealing with the disturbed family system.

Resources

Rape crisis centers are listed in the white pages of the phone books of many cities.

21

Senator Smoot (Republican, Ut.)
Is planning a ban on smut.
Oh rooti-ti-toot for Smoot of Ut.
And his reverent ossiput.
Smite, Smoot, smite for Ut.,
Grit your molars and do your dut.,
Gird up your l**ns,
Smite h*p and th*gh,
We'll all be in Kansas
By and by.
Ogden Nash
"Invocation" (1979)

Sex and the Law

Adult Consensual Sexual Behaviors

Pornography

Prostitution

Sex Law Reform

EVERY SOCIETY has certain norms for sexual behavior. Some of these sexual norms are codified in law. This chapter presents a discussion of some of the laws that relate to sexuality in the United States and some of the social issues that pertain to these laws.

Laws generally attempt to regulate the behavior of members of society in order to protect individuals and property and to ensure continuation of the society itself. Sex laws endeavor to serve these and other purposes, as indicated by the many areas of sexuality that are under legal jurisdiction. Some laws pertaining to sexuality attempt to protect the public from acts that have been identified as offensive; for instance, exhibitionism, solicitation, sexual harassment, and voyeurism. Child molestation legislation tries to control exploitation of children. Rape laws are concerned with forcible and coercive sexual relations. Other laws pertaining to consensual acts between adults aspire to define and prevent "immorality." Laws about procreation determine which contraception, abortion, and conception practices are legal. For example, anti-abortion legislation would give the fetus constitutional rights and might make IUD use as well as abortion illegal. Laws regarding commercialized sex regulate prostitution and pornography. Considering the broad gamut of laws pertaining to sexuality, it may not be too surprising that Kinsey (1948) estimated that 95% of the males in his sample had experienced sex acts defined as illegal.

Many of the legal issues of sexuality do not apply equally in all parts of the country. Some sex laws are federal, covering all the states, while others are determined by the individual states and vary from one state to another. Penalties for breaking sex laws also differ greatly. Additionally, many of the laws are in a state of flux. For example, the legal status and funding of abortion, the availability of contraceptives to adolescents without parental consent, and federal funding for birth control clinics that provide abortion information and referrals are currently being challenged.

Adult Consensual Sexual Behaviors

Consensual sexual behavior between adults consists of activities in which the individuals agree to participate. Such acts may be designated as illegal on the grounds of "immorality." We will discuss three categories of consensual behavior—nonmarital intercourse, specific sexual behaviors, and homosexual behaviors—in the following sections.

Nonmarital Intercourse

Contemporary laws in our society reflect the Judeo-Christian ethic that sexual intercourse is only permissible within the institution of marriage. These laws reflect long-standing societal concerns for the stability of the family and for property rights. Laws against nonmarital intercourse attempt to ensure that those to whom property is passed are the legitimate heirs. Consequently, married women often have been more harshly prosecuted than married men for engaging in extramarital intercourse.

There are two legal categories for nonmarital sexual intercourse. **Fornication** is intercourse between unmarried adults, and **adultery** is intercourse by a married person with someone other than his or her spouse. In states where fornication and adultery are both crimes, fornication is usually the lesser crime. Laws against **co-habitation** (unmarried people living together) also exist in some states. Laws about nonmarital sex as well as other sexual activities have tended to become less severe through the years. For example, in early American times, adultery was punishable by death (Taylor, 1970).

People are rarely prosecuted for nonmarital intercourse. However, the illegality of sex between unmarried people can have adverse effects. It sometimes provides justification in court for discriminating in employment or is used to demonstrate the "bad character" of a rape victim or a parent seeking custody. Adultery is also often not prosecuted, although adultery was used as grounds for thousands of divorces before divorce by mutual consent became widely available. Although criminal prosecution for cohabitation is unlikely, other difficult legal matters may arise. Property and inheritance rights and responsibility for debts may be difficult to establish after the death of or separation from an unmarried partner (MacNamara and Sagarin, 1977).

Specific Sexual Behaviors

Many of the laws concerning specific sexual behaviors of consenting adults in private are derived from the Judeo-Christian ethic that viewed procreation as the only justification for sex. In this view, any sexual act that did not provide the possibility of conception was "sinful." In Europe during medieval times the Catholic church placed very severe restrictions on marital sexual behaviors. Intercourse was legal only in one position, and it was illegal on Sundays, Wednesdays, and Fridays and during the days before Easter and Christmas. Church confessors were required to inquire specifically about these and other behaviors of their parishioners (Taylor, 1970).

"Immorality" has been codified into laws that define many nonprocreative behaviors as criminal, and many of these laws are still in effect. Although definitions are often vague and vary from state to state, oral-genital intercourse and anal intercourse are categorized as **sodomy**. In the 24 states where such laws exist, it is important to note that they usually pertain to all adults—married, nonmarried, heterosexual, and homosexual. Often the penalties for these "crimes" (described in many statutes as "crimes against nature") are very severe. The maximum jail sentence for sodomy is 20 years in Georgia and Rhode Island, and 10 years in several other states (Press et al., 1986). See Table 21.1 for further specifics.

In June 1986 a heavily disputed U.S. Supreme Court decision upheld states' rights to have sodomy laws and to impose penalties, stating in its decision that "the proposition that any kind of private sexual conduct between consenting adults is constitutionally insulated from state proscription is unsupportable" (Hardwick v. Georgia, 85–140). In his dissenting opinion, Justice Harry Blackmun emphasized the right to privacy and stated, "What the court really has refused to recognize is the fundamental interest all individuals have in controlling the nature of their intimate associations" (Hardwick v. Georgia, 85–140). Blackmun's views appear to be supported by the majority of the population. A Gallup Poll found that 57% of those surveyed thought that states should not prohibit private sexual practices between consenting adult homosexual individuals, and 74% took the same position regarding

Table 21.1   States' Penalties for Sodomy in 1986

States with Sodomy Laws	Maximum Jail Sentences for Sodomy	States with Sodomy Laws	Maximum Jail Sentences for Sodomy
Alabama	1 year	Mississippi	10 years
Arizona	30 days	Missouri	1 year
Arkansas	1 year[a]	Montana	10 years[a]
Florida	60 days	Nevada	6 years[a]
Georgia	20 years	North Carolina	10 years
Idaho	5-year minimum	Oklahoma	10 years
Kansas	6 months[a]	Rhode Island	20 years
Kentucky	12 months	South Carolina	5 years
Louisiana	5 years	Tennessee	15 years
Maryland	10 years	Texas	$200 fine[a]
Michigan	15 years (anal sex), 5 years (oral sex)	Utah	6 months
		Virginia	5 years
Minnesota	1 year	D.C.	10 years

[a]For homosexual sodomy only.
Source: Press et al., 1986.

Table 21.2   States with Consenting Adult Laws as of 1986

Alaska	Maine	Oregon
California	Massachusetts	Pennsylvania
Colorado	Nebraska	South Dakota
Connecticut	New Hampshire	Texas
Delaware	New Jersey	Vermont
Hawaii	New Mexico	Washington
Illinois	New York	West Virginia
Indiana	North Dakota	Wyoming
Iowa	Ohio	

Source: National Gay Task Force.

heterosexual activity (Alpern, 1986). By 1986, 26 states have repealed their sodomy laws (Press et al., 1986), as shown in Table 21.2.

Miscegenation refers to a sexual relationship, marital or nonmarital, between people of different races. Prior to the mid-1960s when antimiscegenation laws were declared unconstitutional in the United States, laws in most southern and several other states forbade sexual relations between whites and nonwhites, especially whites and blacks. These laws were enforced selectively; white males were rarely prosecuted for having interracial relationships. Although miscegenation is no longer illegal in the United States, interracial couples often face considerable social pressure.

Homosexual Behaviors

The laws against homosexual behaviors stem from biblical injunctions against same-sex contact. Laws against homosexual behaviors have been exceedingly punitive. People with a homosexual orientation have been tortured and put to death throughout Western history. In the American colonies homosexual people were condemned to death by drowning and burning. In the late 1770s Thomas Jefferson was among the political leaders who suggested lessening the punishment from death to castration for men who committed homosexual acts (Katz, 1976).

Today official views and actions on homosexuality reflect changed attitudes. The British Wolfenden Report of 1957 was based on a 10-year study by the Committee on Homosexual Offenses and Prostitution. The report maintains that there is no evidence that homosexual behavior contributes to "societal decay"; that personal revulsion by those who believe homosexual behavior to be unnatural or sinful is not a valid reason to override personal privacy or to make an act criminal; that the removal of criminal sanctions against homosexual behaviors in private between consenting adults will not result in an increase in homosexuality; and that private morality is not the law's business. The report recommended that sexual behavior in private between consenting adults should not be a criminal offense, and the British Parliament eventually supported this position.

As we have seen, sodomy laws are still in the legal codes in many states in our own country. Although they apply to heterosexual as well as homosexual behavior, these statutes are invoked more against homosexual people. For example, the 1986 U.S. Supreme Court hearing was precipitated by a police officer entering a bedroom and seeing two men engaged in oral sex. Most arrests for sodomy between same-sex (usually male) partners take place when the act occurs in a public place such as a restroom, theater, or park. In these cases, sexual conduct in public may be the issue rather than (or as well as) homosexuality.

The majority of homosexual arrests are made not for sodomy but for solicitation or for loitering in public places. Most homosexual solicitation is based on subtle gestures and comments that are not highly offensive to public decency—certainly no more so than catcalls, whistles, and comments directed at women by heterosexual men. However, the judicial system in some cities has occasionally used controversial practices to make arrests for homosexual solicitation. Policemen dress in plain clothes and attempt to entice homosexual men to make sexual propositions. If the proposition or "solicitation" occurs, another policeman standing nearby arrests the homosexual man. The police regard this practice as enticement. Others call it entrapment—in other words, inducing people to commit illegal acts. Entrapment is illegal and enticement is legal. The controversy over the definition of this procedure continues in the legal system. (The same practices and issues pertain to prosecution of prostitutes.)

The great majority of homosexual people are never arrested for either solicitation or sodomy, because the behaviors occur in private. However, living under the threat of prosecution for being sexual with another consenting adult is an uncomfortable position, especially given the negative attitudes toward homosexuality in our society. As we saw in Chapter 10, one of the goals of the gay rights movement is to repeal sodomy laws and establish **consensual adult statutes** that decriminalize sexual activity between consenting adults in private.

*Erotic scenes on
a Greek vase.*

Pornography

Pictorial and written representations of sexuality are not a modern invention. Cave drawings depicted sexual activity. Ancient Greek and Roman societies used sexual themes to decorate housewares and public architecture. The ancient Indian love manual *Kama Sutra*, dating from about 400 A.D., summarized philosophies of sexuality and spirituality in its description of specific sexual techniques. Graphic representations of coitus in Japanese *schunga* paintings and woodcuts from the 1600s and 1700s were regarded as art masterpieces.

A clearcut contemporary definition of **pornography** is difficult to establish. The United States judicial system has not been able to establish a consistent definition, and individual opinions vary greatly on what is considered to be pornography. Generally speaking, pornography is written, visual, or spoken material, depicting or describing sexual conduct or genital exposure, that is arousing to the viewer. This definition is broad, however; within it, the continuum could range from suggestive advertisements commonly seen in the media to the explicit portrayal of sexual interaction and sexually oriented violence, including torture and murder. The legal controversies about pornography center on what is to be legally defined as "obscene," a term that implies a personal or societal judgment that something is offensive. For

A Japanese
schunga *painting.*

purposes of this section on legal issues, *pornography* will be used as a collective term for visual and written materials sold for the purpose of sexual arousal. We will further refine this definition in a later section on effects of sexually explicit materials.

Four Legal Issues

The legal controversies relating to pornography have centered on four issues: the evaluation of what is obscene, regulations concerning dissemination of sexually explicit materials, the constitutional right of free speech, and sexual discrimination ordinances.

Attempts at a Legal Definition.   Pornography itself is not illegal, but materials considered to be obscene are. This leads us to the dilemma faced by the courts in determining what constitutes obscenity. Early American courts considered material to be obscene if it depraved and corrupted the user. The courts then faced the problem of establishing that a person had been depraved by the materials. The first major challenge to this legal definition of obscenity occurred in the Roth v. United States case (354 US 476), decided by the Supreme Court in 1957. This and subsequent decisions have established three criteria for evaluating obscenity. First, the dominant theme of the work as a whole must appeal to prurient interest in sex. Second, the work must be patently offensive to contemporary community standards. Third, it must be without serious literary, artistic, political, or scientific value (Miller v. California 413 US 15, 1973).

The subjectivity of these criteria is reflected in Supreme Court Justice Potter Stewart's comment that obscenity is difficult to define intelligently, "but I know it when I see it" (Jacobelis v. Ohio, 379 US 197, 1965), as well as in local differences in interpretation. Community standards of obscenity can vary dramatically. In some areas, particularly in large cities, all manner of explicit sexual films are openly advertised

"Obviously been too long in the making. What was obscene enough
when you started isn't obscene enough now."

and shown. In other areas, particularly in small communities, magazines like *Playboy* have been banned. Some school boards eliminate books they find objectionable from classrooms and libraries (see Box 21.1). Courts, communities, and pornographic entrepreneurs still struggle with the legal definition of obscenity. The Report of the 1986 Attorney General's Commission on Pornography did not expand or clarify the legal definition of obscenity.

Regulating Pornography Dissemination. There have been several legal approaches to the regulation of obscene materials. In 1969, the United States Supreme Court ruled that private possession in the home is not a crime, nor is it subject to government regulation (Stanley v. Georgia, 394 US 557). However, dissemination of pornography is closely regulated. Federal laws prohibit broadcasting, mailing, importation, and interstate transport of obscene materials.

Most of these pornography dissemination statutes stem from the Comstock Act of 1873 (mentioned in Chapter 11), which made it a felony to deposit any materials

Box 21.1   *Books Banned in Schools*

School boards and their appointed book review committees can legally ban books from classroom use or from the library. Many books have been banned from various schools. John Steinbeck's *Grapes of Wrath* was banned from classroom use in Kanawha, Iowa because a parent complained that the work was "profane, vulgar, and obscene"; his book *Of Mice and Men* was removed from a high school library in Oil City, Pennsylvania on the basis that it refers to prostitution and contains "vulgarity and profanity." A high school library in Milton, New Hampshire removed Alexander Solzhenitsyn's work *One Day in the Life of Ivan Denisovitch* because it contained "language you wouldn't allow to be used in the home." The school board of Issaquah, Washington removed *The Catcher in the Rye* by J. D. Salinger from classroom use, claiming that it represents an "overall Communist plot" and contains numerous profanities. The Middleville, Michigan school board banned the same book after several parents complained that it "violates the word of God." Pressure from parents caused a school board to ban *Flowers for Algernon* (on which the movie *Charly* was based) because parents believed that a scene in the book would stir students' "natural impulses." The school board of Miller, Missouri banned Huxley's *Brave New World* because many parts of the book "make that kind of sex look like fun." Finally, *The American Heritage Dictionary* was removed from a high school because, among other things, a "bed" was defined as a "place for lovemaking." The school board in Anchorage, Alaska also removed this dictionary because it contained too many "dirty words" (Doyle, 1982).

of "indecent character" in the U.S. mail. During the first eight years of his involvement in the New York Society for the Suppression of Vice, some of self-appointed censor Anthony Comstock's activities included destroying 27,584 pounds of books; confiscating 1,376,939 "obscene" songs, poems, pamphlets, and catalogs; and recording 976,125 names and addresses of people on mailing lists for pornography (Kilpatrick, 1960). Federal mailing laws have also been invoked in contemporary times in the prosecution of purveyors of obscene materials, and the 1986 Commission on Pornography recommends increasing funds for enforcement of these laws.

There are other ways of regulating dissemination of pornography. Many cities limit the areas where adult bookstores and movie houses can be located. Containment of bookstores and movie houses by zoning and land-use regulations attempts to protect nonusers of pornography from being visually assaulted by offensive material on the basis of the right to freedom from involuntary exposure to pornography. Because of zoning ordinances, high concentrations of pornographic establishments have arisen in some cities. The "Combat Zone" in Boston and North Beach in San Francisco are examples of such areas.

Freedom of Speech.   In its 1957 decision the Supreme Court declared that the U.S. Constitution's First Amendment guarantee of freedom of speech and of the press did not apply categorically to obscene materials. Vigorous argument against this position has been presented by civil libertarians as well as by some of the justices of the Supreme Court. They maintain that any censorship is unconstitutional and support the unre-

Areas such as North Beach in San Francisco have high concentrations of "adult" entertainment establishments.

stricted availability of pornography to adults. The American Civil Liberties Union opposes many of the recommendations of the 1986 Commission on Pornography as "unconstitutional proposals which strike not only the First Amendment directly, but intrude upon civil liberties values like due process, privacy, and choice" (American Civil Liberties Union, 1986, p. 4).

Sexual Discrimination.   A number of communities across the U.S. have considered laws establishing pornography as a form of sexual discrimination. These laws would be similar to those that allow people to file complaints against discrimination in employment: Individuals could press civil suits against the makers, distributors, or exhibitors of sexually explicit depictions of the subordination of women. Proponents of such laws and ordinances maintain that pornography harms a woman's opportunities for equal rights because it fosters exploitation and subordination based on sex.

Opponents of this type of legislation believe that such laws would infringe on freedom of personal choice by giving the courts power to interpret and rule on a wide variety of sexual images. They are also concerned about the antisexual bias in the proposed laws: Sexual explicitness is singled out as the target of these proposed laws and defined as degrading to women, rather than sexist images in general (Vance, 1985). They also maintain that eliminating pornography would not alleviate discrimination towards women. Historically, women have been oppressed when pornography was not evident as a significant part of the culture. For example, pornography did not lead to the burning of witches in early American times (Duggan et al., 1985).

Effects of Sexually Explicit Materials

Questions about the effects of pornography have been debated extensively in recent years from different philosophical perspectives, and a considerable body of research is emerging. Some of the key questions being raised have to do with whether sexually explicit materials have significant effects on behavior, what those effects are, and what messages pornography may transmit about human relationships.

In the late 1960s President Johnson appointed a Commission on Obscenity and Pornography to study the effects of sexually explicit materials. The commission studied events following the legalization of pornography in Denmark, analyzed findings of various self-report and survey research studies in the United States, and offered recommendations. The commission found that after pornography was legalized in Denmark in the late 1960s there was an initial increase in the number of Danish people who purchased pornographic materials. After a few years, however, sales to Danes decreased, and foreign tourists purchased most of the pornography. The commission noted that legalization and increased availability of pornography did not result in an increase in reported sex offenses, although a cause-and-effect relationship is difficult to establish. (For example, there may have been increased tolerance and reduced prosecution of lesser offenses such as exhibitionism.) Also, the commission's analysis of current research found that imprisoned sex offenders had not had more exposure to pornography than had other prison inmates or nonprison populations. In its summary of research on the effects of sexually explicit materials, the commission concluded that no significant, long-lasting changes in behavior were evident in college student volunteer research subjects after being exposed to pornography. On the basis of this information the commission's 1970 report recommended repealing all laws prohibiting access to pornography for adults. However, the U.S. Senate and President Nixon rejected the commmission's recommendations.

Controversy and concern about the effects of pornography have continued, and research in this area has expanded. [However, research results are limited by several factors. Most subjects are undergraduate male college students rather than a sample of the general population. In addition, the experimental setting is artificial, and it is difficult to know how reported attitudes will affect actual behavior in daily life (Green, 1985).] As research has increased, the categorization of sexually explicit materials has become more distinct. Much of the current research separates sexually explicit materials into three groups: violent and aggressive pornography, degrading and dehumanizing pornography, and mutually consenting and pleasurable erotica. Central to both violent and degrading pornography is the depiction of an unequal balance of power for the purpose of sexual stimulation and entertainment (Dworkin, 1979). Violent pornography involves aggression or brutality; the violence takes the form of rape, beatings, dismemberment, and even murder. Degrading pornography portrays objectification and denigration of a person (Dworkin, 1979). In contrast, "erotica can be defined as depictions of sexuality which display mutuality, respect, affection, and a balance of power" (Stock, 1985, p. 13). Erotica offers "a spontaneous sense of people who are there because they want to be, out of shared pleasure" (Steinem, 1980, p. 37).

The prevalence of violence towards women in pornography and mass media depictions in magazines, record covers, film and video has increased significantly in recent years (Check, 1984; Malamuth and Spinner, 1980; Penrod and Linz, 1984). For example, one study found that one-third of sex episodes in pornographic books involved some type of emotional or physical force, and the number of sex acts depicting rape doubled from 1968 to 1974 (Smith, 1976). Another study found that in 1977 about 15% of the pictures in *Playboy* and *Penthouse* magazines contained sexual violence; this represents a significant increase over the percentage five years earlier (Malamuth and Spinner, 1980). These magazines are read by more men than *Newsweek* and *Time* combined (Target Group Index of 1978). A great deal of violent pornography depicts the myth that women enjoy rape and are willing participants in their own abuse (Stock, 1985). In Chapter 20 we presented research indications that exposure to depictions of violent sex may, in some cases, encourage men to commit rape.

A newer focus of research has been to examine the effects of degrading pornography. Sexual depictions that degrade, debase, and dehumanize women are a common pornographic theme. Women are presented as sexual playthings, eager to accommodate every sexual urge of any man (Zillman and Bryant, 1982). This type of material may be most prevalent in mainstream X-rated videos. One study found that subjects who viewed pornography videos or films on their own initiative at least once a month were more accepting of rape myths, more accepting of violence against women, and more likely to report that they would rape women and force them to engage in unwanted sex acts (Check, 1985a).

Many of the studies examining the effects of nonviolent but degrading pornography show results similar to the effects of exposure to violent pornography. One study found that after about five hours of exposure to nonviolent stag films, subjects considered rape to be a lesser offense than prior to viewing the films. Men's sex callousness toward women also increased, as indicated by their increased support of such statements as "A woman doesn't mean no until she slaps you." In addition, subjects were less compassionate toward rape victims and less supportive of the women's movement after seeing the films (Zillman and Bryant, 1982). Another study demonstrated that increased acceptance of the rape myth remained two months after exposure to degrading pornography (Linz, 1985).

An important question about changes in attitudes that occur in research experiments is whether or not these attitudes influence "real life" behavior. A leading researcher hypothesizes:

> The data suggest that the type of media effects found in the research . . . may indirectly affect actual aggression against women. This may occur in two ways. First, it appears that in combination with other factors, attitudes that are relatively accepting of violence against women may contribute to the likelihood that a person will commit aggressive acts. Of course, media messages are only one of the many sources that can influence attitudes and in many cases changed attitudes will not necessarily alter behavior. A second way in which the media may indirectly affect behavior is by contributing to the social climate. For example, if a person's attitudes become more tolerant of violence against women this may not necessarily affect his own aggressive behavior but may influence how he reacts to a friend's boasting about sexual aggression, his reactions to a rape victim or even his vote as a member of a jury in a rape trial. Such responses may influence the aggressive behavior of others. Clearly, there is a need for additional research concerning these propositions. (Malamuth, 1985, p. 110)

In addition to the questions already raised about the effects of violent or degrading pornography are concerns about its impact on intimate relationships between men and women. One criticism of pornography is that it contributes to unrealistic expectations about sexuality. Pornography often stresses performance and conquest rather than pleasure. It perpetuates the myth that a "real man" is always ready for sex and that sex can be obtained without regard for the other person or the complex nature of the man himself (Zilbergeld, 1978). Women are often portrayed as intensely responsive to just about any stimulation from men. When women do not react in such a manner, men may feel cheated, and both may doubt their own perfectly normal sexuality (Zillman and Bryant, 1982). Sexual expectations derived from pornography may cause conflict in relationships. For example, 10% of a randomly selected group of women said that they had been upset by being asked to do something their male partner had seen in pornographic pictures, movies, or books (Russell, 1980).

In contrast to research on violent and degrading pornography, studies of exposure to erotica have shown no negative effects. In addition, men in one study reported that they found erotica just as sexually arousing, exciting, and stimulating as violent and degrading pornography (Check, 1985b). A partial solution to the potential problems with pornography would be for erotica to be as available as sexually violent and degrading materials (Check, 1984). Research also suggests that education dispelling rape myths changes attitudes in a more positive direction (Donnerstein and Linz, 1985). Sex education programs for children and adolescents that deal with the myths and stereotypes about women and rape may reduce the negative impact of violent and dehumanizing media images of sexuality (Donnerstein and Linz, 1985).

In 1986 the Report of the U.S. Attorney General's Commission on Pornography addressed numerous issues, and it reached drastically different conclusions and made radically different recommendations than the 1970 Commission. The report concluded that violent pornography causes sexually aggressive behavior toward women, and that degrading pornography fosters accepting attitudes toward rape and has some causal relationship to sexual violence. The Commission members disagreed substantially about the effects of mutually consensual sexually explicit erotica; some viewed erotica as harmless and potentially beneficial, and others believed it to be destructive to the moral environment of society by promoting "promiscuity" and sex outside of marriage. Among the 92 recommendations in the report were many advocating more vigorous law enforcement and prosecution related to obscene materials. It recommended citizen activity to file complaints, to pressure the legal system, and to monitor and boycott newsstands, videocassette stores, and bookstores selling objectionable sexually explicit materials. Additional recommendations included prohibiting obscene cable television programming and "Dial-a-Porn" telephone services, and prosecuting consensual sexual activity occurring in "adults only" bookstores. The report placed special emphasis on child pornography and encouraged increased enforcement efforts of the criminal laws now in place related to the production, sale, and distribution of child pornography. In addition, contrary to earlier Supreme Court rulings that private possession of pornography in the home is not a crime, the report recommended that possession of child pornography become a felony (U.S. Attorney General's Commission on Pornography, 1986).

Many of the report's conclusions and recommendations have generated considerable dissent and disagreement. To begin with, the composition of the Commission

Pornography: The Feminist Dilemma

Box 21.2

Feminists have developed diverse perspectives on the issues surrounding sexually explicit materials. The release of the Report of the U.S. Attorney General's Commission on Pornography has sharpened the focus of some of these points of view.

"According to various feminists, the Meese commission report was good for the women's movement (Law Professor Catharine MacKinnon), bad for the movement (A.C.L.U. Attorney Nan Hunter) or basically irrelevant to feminist interests (Movement Pioneer Betty Friedan). 'Today could be a turning point in women's rights,' MacKinnon told a news conference in a cramped storefront near the Times Square porno district that

serves as the offices of Women Against Pornography. 'Women actually succeeded in convincing a national governmental body of a truth that women have long known: pornography harms women and children.' Hunter tapped a different strand of feminist thinking: women should seek liberation, not special protection from the state. 'Protectionist attitudes,' she said, 'ultimately hurt women.' Friedan once again declared that the war against porn is a woeful waste of energies needed on the economic and legal fronts. Said she, 'As repulsive as pornography can be, the obsession with it is a dangerous diversion for the women's movement'" (Leo, 1986, p. 18).

---

was biased; six of the eleven members had been involved in some type of opposition to sexually explicit materials prior to their appointments, and none of the members had a history of opposition to restriction of sexually explicit materials (Kurtz, 1985; American Civil Liberties Union, 1986). In addition, many critics maintain that the Commission's goal was to establish the dangers of sexually explicit materials and to justify greater governmental control, rather than to engage in an objective, balanced inquiry (American Civil Liberties Union, 1986; Wooster, 1986).

Two Commission members, behavioral scientist Judith Becker and journalist and editor Ellen Levine, wrote a dissenting opinion to the report in which they expressed concern that the materials presented in the hearings were not representative of materials available, nor did they accurately represent the positive and negative effects of sexually explicit materials. The American Civil Liberties' critique stated, "Materials which presented alternative viewpoints [or] reached conclusions not consistent with the presuppositions of the Commission . . . were suppressed or ignored" (1986, p. 1). Becker and Levine further protested that the Commission lacked sufficient time and money to adequately address the complicated issues involved in such a controversial and complex issue as pornography. They also disagreed with a major conclusion of the report—that sexually violent and degrading pornography causes sexually aggressive behaviors toward women. They declared this conclusion to be simplistic and not supported by social science, stating, "We still have more questions than answers" (Becker and Levine, 1986, p. 20).

The American Civil Liberties Union summary and critique of the Commission's report echoes the previous concerns and raises many more. Their primary objection is to the potential infringements of First Amendment rights to free speech. Their critique also emphasized constitutional rights to privacy, and the fact that this report and many of the measures it recommends threaten these rights. The A.C.L.U. also raised the possibility of misallocation of public monies, if the Commission's recom-

Experts estimate that there may be as many as 2.4 million teenage prostitutes in the United States (United States General Accounting Office, 1982). Teenagers often become prostitutes as a means of survival after they have run away from home. There are extreme instances, such as a seven-year-old boy selling his sexual services for 25¢ to buy food. Many of these young prostitutes have been abused or neglected at home, did not perform well in school, and have poor self-images. They are often seeking adult attention and affection, and they believe at first that prostitution is a life of glamour and adventure. One study of adolescent male prostitutes found two dominant themes in their earlier lives. They were likely to have an unstructured and unsupervised home life, and they also felt rejected by peers at school and had few friends (Price et al., 1984).

Pornographers are able to find children—usually between the ages of eight and 16—who will participate in making pornographic photographs, video tapes, or movies in exchange for friendship, interest, or money, or as a result of threats. One study found that many of the children were related by blood to the pornographers

(Burgess et al., 1984). Some children, particularly the very young, may not know their photographs are used as pornography. Commercially produced child pornography has declined due to the Protection of Children Against Sexual Exploitation Act of 1977, stricter enforcement, and media attention; but homemade, underground child pornography is still produced (Baker, 1980). Many children who have been involved in pornography suffer from depression, anxiety, guilt, and self-destructive and antisocial behavior (Burgess et al., 1984). The 1986 U.S. Attorney General's Commission on Pornography Report focused a great deal of attention on prevention of and intervention in this problem.

Children involved in prostitution and pornography often suffer emotional distress and have a poor life adjustment. Many develop a concept of themselves as objects to be sold. They frequently have problems with employment because of the stigma of their past and their dissatisfaction with the lower pay of a regular job. They may have difficulty establishing meaningful relationships and are likely to become involved in crime.

mendations were followed: "Every dollar spent on the legal 'fight' against pornography is a dollar taken from the struggle against murder, rape, robbery, extortion, and the corruption of public institutions. A decision to expend scarce enforcement resources on 'crimes' of consensual individual behavior in preference to other priorities ought to be rejected" (1986, p. 155).

The 1986 Commission on Pornography Report and its advocates and critics have intensified the issue of government regulation and enforcement of "morality." The social significance of the report goes beyond its specific findings, and is much more a documentation of evolving attitudes toward sexual morality and the role of government that have gained acceptance during the Reagan era than of current scientific knowledge. A journalist explains, "The findings of presidential commissions are often a kind of mirror of the public sensibility of the time—one reason, perhaps, that the latest porn report is so different from the 1970 one" (Stengle, 1986, p. 17).

Definitions of and perspectives on pornography, as well as pornography itself, have changed with time. However, the issues involved, such as freedom of speech, the role of law, effects on human relationships, and considerations of personal and public morality, remain controversial.

Prostitution

Prostitution refers to the exchange of sexual services for money. It is typically thought of in terms of a woman selling sexual services to a man, although transactions between two males are also common. Payment for a man's services to a woman are less usual. Involvement of children in prostitution also occurs (see Box 21.3). Prostitution is generally characterized by sexual contacts with multiple partners, with whom the contract for the exchange of sexual services for money is explicit. Prostitution is illegal in every state of the United States except Nevada.

Prostitution has existed throughout history. However, the significance and meaning of prostitution have varied in different times and societies. In ancient Greece the practice was tolerated. During some periods of Greek history prostitutes were valued for their intellectual, social, and sexual companionship. Prostitution was part of revered religious rituals in other ancient societies. Sexual relations between prostitutes and men often took place within temples and were seen as sacred acts; in some cultures the man in this transaction was considered to be a representative of the deity. In medieval Europe prostitution was tolerated, and the public baths provided a flourishing opportunity for contacts between customers and prostitutes. And in England during the Victorian era, prostitution was viewed as a scandalous but necessary sexual and social outlet for men: It was a lesser evil for a man to have sexual relations with a prostitute than with another man's wife or daughter (Taylor, 1970).

Prostitutes exist because there is a demand for their services (Cohen, 1980). Customers of prostitutes are usually white, middle-aged, middle class, and married (James et al., 1975), and they patronize prostitutes for various reasons. Sex with a prostitute can provide sexual contact or release without any expectation of intimacy or future commitment, or it may offer an opportunity to engage in sexual techniques that a partner will not permit.

Prostitutes may be delinquent school dropouts and runaways or well-educated adults. No single theory can explain the motivation for being a prostitute. A combination of psychological, social, environmental, and economic factors is involved. However, studies report a high incidence of childhood sexual abuse in the history of female prostitutes (James and Meyerding, 1977; Satterfield and Listiak, 1982). Many are prostitutes on a part-time basis and otherwise pursue conventional school, work or social lifestyles. People who work as prostitutes on a temporary, part-time basis and have other occupational skills can more easily leave prostitution. Many of these men and women have not identified themselves as prostitutes, or "professionals" (Davis, 1978). The full-time prostitute, who is alienated from traditional values, has identified him- or herself as part of the subculture (being arrested facilitates this identification); this person may have little education and no other marketable skills, and usually finds it very difficult to become successfully independent of prostitution.

Female Prostitutes

There are various types of female prostitutes who service male customers. The variations relate to a number of characteristics, including public visibility of the woman, the amount of money she charges, and her social class. We will look at a few different categories, defined roughly in terms of the method a woman uses to contact customers.

Other Times, Other Places

Prostitution in the American West in the Late 1800s

Prostitution permeated both the rural and the urban American West in the 1800s. Prostitutes gravitated toward mining towns, construction sites, military outposts, cattle terminals, supply stations, and larger urban centers of the frontier. They sold companionship and sex in dance halls and gambling joints, in brothels, in shacks and tents off the streets, or in travelling "cat" wagons. Prostitutes were among the poorest women on the frontier, and they usually remained destitute throughout their lives. They were often European immigrants or from ethnic groups such as Oriental, Mexican, or Native American, and their cultural backgrounds made prostitution a likely outgrowth of their life experiences. For example:

Black women entered the ranks of prostitution after the close of the Civil War. Their previous experiences in American society exposed them to unskilled or agricultural labors. Some few escaped this destiny during slavery, but most black women remained uneducated and untrained. Thrust into a society that did not want them, left with no means of support, some black women turned to prostitution in the West. The appearance of the black brothel represented an extension of the cultural interaction that generations of black women had been taught in slavery. Sexual availability without matrimonial protection permeated the experiences of female slaves. Long eliminated from the inner circles of profit, advancement, and status, black women did nonetheless understand the art of survival. For some the transformation from slave to prostitute flowed from the debilitating social and economic effects of bondage (Butler, 1985, p. 13).

These include *streetwalkers*, women who work in brothels or massage parlors, and *call girls*.

Streetwalkers can be seen on the streets of most large cities. They solicit customers on the street or in bars. They are often from lower socioeconomic backgrounds, and they charge less than other types of prostitutes for their services. Because of their visibility, streetwalkers are easily subject to arrest. Most streetwalkers repeat the cycle of arrest, short jail sentences, and release many times throughout their careers. Even in the few cities where laws inflict penalties on the customer as well as the prostitute, the male customers of streetwalkers and other prostitutes are rarely arrested.

A **brothel** is a house in which a group of prostitutes work. Brothels were common in earlier American history and remain so in some other countries. They are legal in some areas of Nevada today. Brothels range from expensive establishments to run-down, seedy places. They are usually managed by a "madam" who acts as a hostess and business manager of the house. Prostitutes who work in brothels are somewhat more protected from arrest than streetwalkers because they are less visible to the police.

Massage parlors are often seen as a modern "quick service" version of brothels. Some massage parlors offer legitimate massages, nothing more. However, many also provide some sexual services. Intercourse is illegal and may or may not occur as part of the "massage." Manual stimulation (a "local" or "hand finishing") or oral stimulation to orgasm is often arranged for a fee once the customer is in the massage room. The customer also can often dictate in what state of dress or undress he would like his masseuse to be. Most of the massage parlor customers in one study were white-

Prostitutes' "cribs" like these were common throughout the West in the 1890s. This photo was taken in the Yukon Territory.

collar businessmen over the age of 35 (Velarde and Warlick, 1973). Zoning and business license laws are sometimes used to attempt to control the location or existence of massage parlors.

Call girls generally earn more than prostitutes. They often come from middle-class backgrounds. Call girls frequently offer social companionship as well as sexual services for their customers. Their customer contacts are usually made by personal referral, and they often have several regular customers. Their public visibility is minimal, and their risk of arrest is much less than that of the streetwalker. Call girls charge more for their services and provide themselves with attractive wardrobes and apartments—all part of their business expenses. They are also more likely than other types of prostitutes to be given goods such as clothing or living accommodations by regular customers. A case study of call girls is described in Box 2.1.

Male Prostitutes

Men who provide sexual services for women in exchange for money and gifts are called **gigolos**. The role of a gigolo is most similar to that of a call girl, because he usually acts as a social companion as well as sexual partner to his customers. Customers are usually wealthy middle-aged women seeking the attentions of attractive young men. There is often a pretense on the gigolo's part of romantic interest in the woman. The exchange of money for services is less explicit than in most interactions between female prostitutes and male customers. It is unknown how common this type of male prostitution is, but it is probably far less common than female prostitution.

Male prostitutes who exchange their sexual services for money with homosexual customers are probably as numerous as female prostitutes, but they have not been studied as extensively. As with female prostitutes, male prostitutes who cater to homosexual men can be classified into different groups. *Hustlers* make contact with customers on the streets, in gay bars or steam baths, or in public parks or toilets. *Call boys* work similarly to call girls. They have regular customers and are often social companions as well as sexual partners. Call boys find their customers by newspaper advertising or through someone who refers the customer to them. *Kept boys* are partially or fully supported by an older male. *Peer-delinquent prostitutes* often work in small groups and use homosexual prostitution as a vehicle for assault and robbery. Most peer-delinquent prostitutes are between 14 and 17 years old. Their usual modus operandi is for one or more of them to solicit a customer who is willing to pay to perform fellatio on them; they then rob and physically assault the customer. Peer-delinquent prostitutes often define their contacts with customers as a demonstration of their masculinity and heterosexuality to their peers. However, beneath this facade many have strong homosexual feelings (Allen, 1980).

Some male prostitutes consider themselves to be heterosexual. They have concurrent female sexual partners and usually return to a heterosexual lifestyle after a brief career in prostitution. Like the peer-delinquent prostitutes, they often restrict the nature of the sexual activities so that they assume the more "masculine" role; for example, allowing customers to perform fellatio on them, but not reciprocating (Reiss, 1964).

Economics and Profit from Prostitution

For many men and women who sell sexual services, prostitution is a way of earning a living; most view their work as an economic opportunity. Recognizing the connection between prostitution and economic disadvantage, the 1959 United Nations Commission study of prostitution concluded that creating other economic opportunities for women is important for its prevention.

While women and men usually become prostitutes to earn money for themselves, the practice provides business for many other parties. In fact, it may not be as lucrative for the prostitute as it is for the other people involved, either directly or indirectly. Pimps, the criminal justice system, referral agents, and hotel operators all benefit financially from prostitution (Sheehy, 1973). Pimps are men who "protect" the prostitutes (usually streetwalkers) and live off their earnings. (Women are more likely than men to have pimps.) The illegality of prostitution contributes to the prostitutes' need for a pimp. Pimps bail the women in their "stables" out of jail when they are arrested. They may offer companionship, a place to live, clothing, food, and in some cases, drugs. They often assume a highly controlling, authoritarian relationship with their prostitutes while being supported by the women's earnings. Pimps may keep as much as 95% of the streetwalkers' earnings, which they often invest in ostentatious clothing and cars that represent the pimp's status and the prostitute's earning power (Young, 1970).

Because prostitution is illegal, police officers, attorneys, judges, bail bondsmen, and jailers spend part of their work time attempting to control, litigate, or process prostitutes through the judicial bureaucracy. In this way, prostitution provides some of the business for the criminal justice system. (Some people argue that the time and money spent in actions against prostitution impedes the judicial system's effectiveness in working with more serious crimes.) On the other side, organized crime is also often involved in prostitution and profits from it (Sheehy, 1973).

Referral agents also make money from prostitution. Cabdrivers, hotel desk clerks, and bartenders get cash tips from customers as well as from prostitutes for helping establish the contact. Prostitutes who work out of their apartments may have to give doormen, hotel proprietors, and elevator operators an ongoing supply of tips, high rental fees, or sexual services (or any combination thereof) so that they will not report them to the authorities.

Issues of Legal Status

Questions on the legal status of prostitution have been debated for some time in the United States. There are several arguments for maintaining its status as a criminal offense. One view is that if prostitution were not a punishable offense many women would take it up, and it would be more difficult to enforce any restrictions on prostitution activities. (This same argument is sometimes offered regarding legal sanctions against homosexual behavior.) Another argument is that it is the responsibility of government to regulate public morals and the absence of laws against prostitution signifies governmental tolerance of commercialized vice (United Nations Study on Traffic in Persons and Prostitution, 1959).

There are also arguments against the criminal status of prostitution. Some of these center on the difficulty of effective prosecution. Prostitution flourishes despite criminal sanctions against it, as it has throughout history in most societies where it has been prohibited. Other arguments are concerned with the possible negative results of outlawing prostitution. For instance, its criminal status may encourage connections with organized crime, contribute to the use of police entrapment, and hamper the rehabilitation of prostitutes (who may find it difficult to find other kinds of work once they have a criminal record). There are also arguments that center on discrimination in applying penalties. Customers and prostitutes are equally responsible in the vast majority of cases, but it is the prostitute, not the customer, who is arrested and prosecuted. Many people who argue for the legalization of prostitution have a different view of the role of government from that held by people who favor its proscription. They maintain that the appropriate role of penal codes is to protect minors and to maintain public order, not to penalize prostitution because it is seen as immoral (United Nations Study on Traffic in Persons and Prostitution, 1959).

There are at least two alternatives to the criminal status of prostitution. One is its **legalization**; the other is **decriminalization**. If legalized, prostitution could be regulated, licensed, and taxed by the government. In some European cities prostitutes are registered and required to follow certain procedures, such as periodic STD checks, to maintain their licenses. If prostitution were decriminalized, criminal penalties for engaging in prostitution would be removed; however, prostitutes would be neither licensed nor regulated. Laws concerning solicitation and laws against involvement of minors would remain, even if prostitution were legalized or decriminalized.

Some writers favor decriminalization and oppose legalization. The primary objection to legalization is that prostitutes would still be "owned" and controlled, but now by the government and its regulations instead of pimps and their rules. Some people see decriminalization as a better way to allow women control over the use of their own bodies (Millett, 1976).

The rationale for legalization or decriminalization is based on several factors. Prostitution is usually considered a "victimless crime," an act that does not harm the people engaged in it. (However, prostitution may not be victimless in all senses, since as we have seen, the prostitute is often the victim of abuse from customers and pimps and of discriminatory laws and social stigma.) There is a legislative trend toward giving victimless crimes (including such acts as gambling, alcohol use, and drug use) regulatory rather than criminal status. In changing these laws, it is hoped that the criminal justice system can expend more efforts on protection from crimes that harm people or property (Morris, 1973). Also, if prostitution were legal, its association with organized crime might be weakened. Victimization of prostitutes by pimps, customers, the judicial system, and others who profit at their expense would perhaps be reduced.

Some prostitutes have begun to organize for political change and mutual support. The prostitutes' union, COYOTE (Cast Out Your Old Tired Ethics), acts as a collective voice for the prostitutes' concerns. We still do not know what impact this organization will have on laws pertaining to prostitution.

Sex Law Reform

There are several important questions to be considered in the discussion of sex law reform. These include the right to sexual privacy, attitudes toward victimless crimes, and equality before the law. None of these questions has a simple answer, due partly to the conflicting values within our pluralistic society.

The right of personal sexual privacy is violated by many of the existing sex laws. Statutes regulating private, consensual sexual behavior between adults are an example. Some legislative action has been taken along these lines. In Griswold v. Connecticut in 1965, the United States Supreme Court ruled that the state of Connecticut could not prohibit the use of contraceptives by married people, basing the decision on the right to privacy of married couples (381 US 479). This decision set a precedent and led to the challenging of remaining laws that regulate marital sexual relations. In 1972 the Supreme Court ruled against a statute that prohibited distribution of contraceptives to unmarried people (Eisenstadt v. Baird, 405 US 438).

The right to privacy in consensual adult sexual behavior increased as more states repealed their sodomy laws. In 1962, Illinois became the first state to remove criminal offense status from adult consensual behavior. The American Law Institute's Model Penal Code recommends removing criminal sanctions from all private adult consensual sexual behavior except prostitution (1962). However, trends in the mid-1980s indicate increased government involvement in private behavior. For example, the June 1986 Supreme Court decision supported states' rights to impose sodomy laws, and many of the recommendations of the U.S. Attorney General's Commission on Pornography Report raised concerns about the rights to privacy and free speech (American Civil Liberties Union, 1986; Stengel, 1986). In addition, numerous activities on local levels, such as citizen action to restrict the sale of sexually explicit materials in stores, have increased (Stengle, 1986).

Victimless crimes are another focus for law reform. Prostitution is most commonly thought of in this connection, but consensual adult sexual behaviors, also victimless, are still legally defined as criminal in many states. Pornography might also be considered in this category. The argument for decriminalization of victimless crimes is twofold. The first point is based on the principle that if an act does not harm anyone, it should not be considered as a crime. The second is based on the expense to the already overextended judicial system of prosecuting acts that are not harming anyone. There is also the argument that time and money spent on victimless crimes would be much better used to attack crimes that do endanger others.

The arbitrariness and inequality of many sex laws are of further concern. For example, although prostitutes and their customers commit the act together, usually only the woman is arrested. Homosexual people are more likely to be brought to trial for sodomy than heterosexual people. These inequalities violate our constitutional right to equal protection under the laws. The dramatic variations in laws and penalties from state to state are another form of inequality. Changes in sex laws are, in part, an attempt to achieve increased legal equality.

Summary

1. The laws about sexuality cover many areas, including reproduction, exhibitionism, child molestation, rape, voyeurism, pornography, prostitution, and consensual adult behaviors.

2. Kinsey (1948) estimated that 95% of the males in his sample had broken some sex law.

Adult Consensual Sexual Behaviors

3. Fornication laws cover intercourse between unmarried adults, and adultery laws pertain to intercourse by a married person with someone other than the spouse. Miscegenation refers to a sexual relationship between people of different races.

4. Sodomy laws prohibit oral-genital intercourse and anal intercourse. In some states penalties for these activities are severe.

5. Sodomy laws and solicitation statutes are used in arrests of homosexual people.

6. The Wolfenden Report from Great Britain recommended the removal of private homosexual behavior between consenting adults as a criminal offense.

Pornography

7. A clear definition of pornography and obscenity has yet to be established by the judicial system. The criteria established by the Supreme Court in attempting to decide what is obscene decree that the dominant theme of the work as a whole must appeal to prurient interest, be offensive to contemporary community standards, and be without serious literary, artistic, political, or scientific value.

8. Legal regulation of pornography occurs through mailing laws and zoning of pornography outlets.

9. The increased availability and legalization of pornography in Denmark was not followed by an increase in reported sex offenses.

10. There is conflicting data on the effects of pornography. The 1970 Commission on Obscenity and Pornography reported that it does not have significant, long-lasting effects. However, more recent research suggests that sexually violent and degrading materials have a significant impact on attitudes toward women and promote rape myths. The controversial 1986 Attorney General's Commission on Pornography Report maintains that sexually violent and degrading pornography causes sexual aggression toward women.

11. Characteristics of erotica include affection, respect, and pleasure. Unlike violent and degrading pornography, erotica has no known long-term effects.

Prostitution

12. Streetwalkers, women in brothels or massage parlors, and call girls are general categories of female prostitutes.

13. Male prostitutes who service women are called gigolos. Male prostitutes who service men may be categorized as hustlers, call boys, kept boys, or peer-delinquent prostitutes.

14. Women or men who turn to prostitution do so, in part, for economic opportunity. However, pimps, the criminal justice system, organized crime, referral agents, and hotel operators also profit from prostitution.

15. Alternatives to the criminal status of prostitution include legalization and decriminalization.

Sex Law Reform

16. Questions concerning personal privacy, victimless crimes, and equal application of the law are important in considering sex law reform.

Thought Provokers

1. If you were on a city council that was voting on a sexual discrimination antipornography ordinance, how would you vote? Why?

2. What effects, if any, do you think violent and degrading pornography and erotica have on intimate relationships between men and women?

3. What kinds of laws about prostitution make sense to you? How do you justify this point of view?

Suggested Readings

American Civil Liberties Union. *Polluting the Censorship Debate*. Washington D.C.: American Civil Liberties Union, 1986. A summary and critique of the Final Report of the Attorney General's Commission on Pornography.

Butler, Anne. *Daughters of Joy, Sisters of Mercy*. Urbana, Ill.: University of Chicago Press, 1985. A detailed book about the lives and the socioeconomic impact of prostitutes in the American West in the late 1800s.

Great Britain Committee on Homosexual Offenses and Prostitution. *The Wolfenden Report*. New York: Stein and Day, 1963. A thorough and thoughtful investigation into sex laws pertaining to homosexuality and prostitution, with concluding recommendations for sex law reform.

Malamuth, Neil, and Donnerstein, Edward (Eds.). *Pornography and Sexual Aggression*. Orlando, Fla.: Academic Press, 1984. The research presented in this book analyzes various facets of pornography and sexual aggression.

Millett, Kate. *The Prostitution Papers*. New York: Ballantine, 1976. A critical exploration into the social role of prostitutes in our society which presents an argument against legalization and for decriminalization.

Schultz, Leroy (Ed.). *The Sexual Victimology of Youth*. Springfield, Ill.: Charles C. Thomas, 1980. A variety of papers on various aspects of sexual victimization and young people, including incest, sexual abuse, and pornography.

U.S. Attorney General's Commission on Pornography. *Final Report of the Attorney General's Commission on Pornography*. Washington D.C.: U.S. Justice Department, 1986. A two-volume, 1960-page report of the testimony, analysis, and recommendations of the Commission. Includes dissenting opinions of Commission members.

Glossary

Abortion The spontaneous or medically induced removal of the contents of the uterus during pregnancy.

Abstinence Not engaging in sexual interaction or intercourse.

Acquired immune deficiency syndrome (AIDS) A catastrophic illness in which a virus invades and destroys the ability of the immune system to fight disease. The AIDS virus appears to be passed primarily through sexual contact, needle sharing among intravenous drug abusers, or less commonly, through administration of contaminated blood products.

Adolescence The period of life between the onset of puberty and the cessation of major body growth changes.

Adrenogenital syndrome A condition that results when a female fetus's adrenal glands malfunction and produce abnormally high amounts of androgen, inducing masculinization of the external genitals.

Adultery Coitus experienced by a married person with someone other than his or her spouse.

Afterbirth The placenta and amniotic sac following their expulsion through the vagina after childbirth.

AIDS. *See* Acquired immune deficiency syndrome.

Amenorrhea The absence of menstruation.

Amniocentesis A procedure in which amniotic fluid is removed from the uterus and tested to determine if certain fetal birth defects exist.

Amniotic fluid The fluid inside the amniotic sac surrounding the fetus during pregnancy.

Amniotic sac A sac of tissue inside the uterus that encloses the fetus and the amniotic fluid.

Ampulla Upper portions of the vas deferens that undergo muscle contractions during the emission phase of ejaculation.

Anaphrodisiac A substance that allegedly inhibits sexual desire and behavior.

Androgen insensitivity syndrome A condition resulting from a genetic defect that causes chromosomally normal males to be insensitive to the action of testosterone and other androgens. These individuals develop female external genitals of normal appearance.

Androgens A class of hormones that promotes the development of male genitals and secondary sex characteristics and influences sexual motivation in both sexes. These hormones are produced by the adrenal glands in males and females and by the testes in males.

Androgyny A blending of typical male and female behaviors in one individual.

Antiandrogens A group of drugs that blocks the action of testicular and adrenal androgens.

Aphrodisiac   A substance that allegedly arouses sexual desire and increases the capacity for sexual activity.

Areola   The darkened circular area surrounding the nipple of the breast.

Artificial insemination   Introducing semen into the vagina or uterus by means other than coitus to induce conception.

Autoinoculation   A process whereby an individual may spread the herpes virus from one part of the body to another by touching a sore and then scratching or rubbing somewhere else.

Autosomes   The twenty-two pairs of human chromosomes that do not significantly influence sex differentiation.

Bartholin's glands   Two small glands slightly inside the vaginal opening that secrete a few drops of fluid during sexual arousal.

Basal body temperature birth control   A method of birth control based on temperature changes before and after ovulation.

Bisexual   A person who feels sexual attraction to or has sexual contact with members of both sexes.

Blastocyst   Multicellular descendant of the united sperm and ovum that implants on the wall of the uterus.

Brothel   A house in which a group of prostitutes works.

Calendar method   A method of birth control based on abstinence from intercourse during calendar-estimated fertile days.

Candida albicans   A yeastlike fungus ordinarily found in the vagina. When excessive amounts of it develop, a vaginal inflammation called moniliasis results.

Castration   Surgical removal of the testes or ovaries.

Cavernous bodies   The structures in the shaft of the penis and clitoris that engorge with blood during sexual arousal.

Celibacy   Historically defined as the state of being unmarried, currently defined as not engaging in sexual behavior.

Cervical cap   A plastic or rubber cover for the cervix that provides a contraceptive barrier to sperm.

Cervicitis   Infection of the cervix.

Cervix   The small end of the uterus, located at the back of the vagina.

Cesarean delivery   A childbirth procedure in which the infant is removed through an incision in the abdomen and uterus.

Chancre   A raised, red, painless sore that is symptomatic of the primary phase of syphilis.

Chancroid   A bacterial STD characterized by small bumps in the region of the genitals, perineum, or anus that eventually rupture and form painful ulcers with a foul discharge.

Chastity   Abstention from sexual interaction.

Chlamydial infection   Urogenital infection caused by the bacterium *Chlamydia trachomatis*. Chlamydia infections are the most prevalent and among the most damaging of all STDs.

Chorionic villi sampling   A prenatal test that detects some birth defects.

Circumcision   Surgical removal of the foreskin of the penis.

Climacteric   Physiological changes that occur during the transition period from fertility to infertility in both sexes.

Clitoral hood   The skin that covers the clitoris.

Clitoris   A highly sensitive structure of the female external genitals, the only purpose of which is sexual pleasure.

Cohabitation   Living together and having a sexual relationship without being married.

Coitus   A technical term for penile-vaginal intercourse.

Colostrom   A thin fluid secreted by the breasts during late pregnancy and the first few days following delivery.

Combination pills   Contraceptive pills containing both estrogen and progestin.

Complete celibacy Engaging neither in masturbation nor in interpersonal sexual contact.

Condom *See* Prophylactic.

Conjunctivitis Inflammation of the mucous membrane that lines the inner surface of the eyelid and the exposed surface of the eyeball.

Consensual adult statutes Laws that maintain that private, consensual sexual behavior between adults is not illegal.

Consensual extramarital relationship A sexual and/or emotional relationship that occurs outside the marriage bond with the consent of one's spouse.

Contraception Techniques, drugs, or devices to prevent conception.

Coprophilia A sexual paraphilia in which a person obtains sexual arousal from contact with feces.

Corona The rim of the penile glans.

Corpora cavernosa *See* Cavernous bodies.

Corpus luteum A yellowish body that forms on the ovary at the site of the ruptured graafian follicle and secretes progesterone.

Corpus spongiosum *See* Spongy body.

Cowper's glands Two pea-sized glands located alongside the base of the urethra in the male that secrete an alkaline fluid during sexual arousal.

Cremasteric muscle A muscle located in the spermatic cord that elevates the testicles when voluntarily or involuntarily contracted.

Cremasteric reflex Involuntary contractions of the cremasteric muscle induced by stroking the inner thigh.

Crura The innermost tips of the cavernous bodies that connect to the pubic bones.

Cryptorchidism A condition in which the testicles fail to descend from the abdominal cavity to the scrotal sac.

Culture A society's shared patterns of belief, thought, speech, and behavior.

Cunnilingus Oral stimulation of the vulva.

Cystitis An inflammation of the urethra or bladder, characterized by discomfort during urination.

Decriminalization Removing criminal penalties for activities previously defined as criminal.

Diaphragm A birth control device consisting of a latex dome on a flexible spring rim. The diaphragm is inserted into the vagina with contraceptive cream or jelly and covers the cervix.

Dildo A penis-shaped device used for vaginal or anal insertion.

Douching Rinsing out the vagina with plain water or a variety of solutions. It is usually unnecessary for hygiene, and too-frequent douching can result in vaginal irritation.

Ductus deferens *See* Vas deferens.

Dysmenorrhea Pain or discomfort before or during menstruation.

Dyspareunia Pain or discomfort during intercourse.

Ectopic pregnancy Implantation of a fertilized ovum in a location other than the uterus, usually in the fallopian tubes.

Effacement of the cervix Flattening and thinning of the cervix that occurs before and during childbirth.

Ejaculation The process whereby semen is expelled from the body through the penis.

Ejaculatory ducts Two short ducts located within the prostate gland.

Ejaculatory inhibition A sexual difficulty whereby the male does not ejaculate inside the vagina.

Emission phase The first stage of male orgasm, in which the seminal fluid is gathered in the urethral bulb.

Endocrine system A system of ductless glands that produces hormones and secretes them directly into the bloodstream.

Endometriosis A condition in which uterine tissue grows on various parts of the abdominal cavity.

Endometrium The tissue that lines the inside of the uterine walls.

Epididymis The structure along the back of each testicle in which sperm maturation occurs.

Episiotomy An incision in the perineum that is sometimes made during childbirth.

Erectile inhibition A sexual difficulty whereby a man's penis does not become erect in response to sexual stimulation.

Erection The process of the penis or clitoris engorging with blood and increasing in size.

Erogenous zones Areas of the body that are particularly responsive to sexual stimulation.

Estrogen replacement therapy (ERT) The use of supplemental estrogen during and after menopause.

Estrogens A class of hormones that produces female secondary sex characteristics and affects the menstrual cycle. Also found in lesser amounts in males.

Ethnographers Anthropologists who specialize in studying the cultures of different societies.

Excitement phase Masters and Johnson's term for the first phase of the sexual response cycle, in which engorgement of sexual organs and an increase in muscle tension, heart rate, and blood pressure occur.

Exhibitionism The act of exposing one's genitals to an unwilling observer.

Expulsion phase The second stage of male orgasm, during which the semen is expelled from the penis by muscular contractions.

Faking orgasms A sexual difficulty whereby a person pretends to experience orgasm during sexual interaction.

Fallopian tubes Two tubes in which the egg and sperm travel, extending from the sides of the uterus.

Fellatio Oral stimulation of the penis.

Fetishism Obtaining sexual excitement primarily or exclusively from an inanimate object or a particular part of the body.

Fimbriae Fringelike ends of the fallopian tubes into which the released ovum enters.

First-stage labor The initial stage of childbirth, in which regular contractions begin and the cervix dilates.

Follicle-stimulating hormone (FSH) A pituitary hormone. Secreted by a female during the secretory phase of the menstrual cycle, it stimulates the development of ovarian follicles. In males, it stimulates sperm production.

Foreplay Usually defined as the kissing, touching, or oral-genital contact preceding coitus.

Foreskin A covering of skin over the penile or clitoral glans.

Fornication A pejorative (also legal) term sometimes used to label coitus between two unmarried persons.

Frenulum *See* Frenum.

Frenum A highly sensitive, thin fold of skin that connects the foreskin with the underside of the penile glans.

Frotteurism A fairly common paraphilia in which a person obtains sexual pleasure by pressing or rubbing against another in a crowded public place.

Fundus The upper, rounded portion of the uterus.

Gardnerella vaginalis A vaginal infection, caused by a bacterium of the same name, that may be the most common form of vaginitis among American women.

Gender assumption Assumptions about how people are likely to behave based on their maleness or femaleness.

Gender identity How one psychologically perceives oneself as either male or female.

Gender nonconformity A lack of conformity to stereotypic masculine and feminine behaviors.

Gender role A collection of attitudes and behaviors that are considered normal and appropriate in a specific culture for people of a particular sex.

Genes The basic units of heredity, carried on the chromosomes.

Genitals The sexual organs of males and females.

Genital tubercle The area on a fetus that develops into the male or female external genitals. It is undifferentiated prior to six weeks of fetal age.

Gigolos Men who provide social companionship and sexual services to women for financial gain.

Glans The head of the penis or clitoris; richly endowed with nerve endings.

Gonadotropins Pituitary hormones that stimulate activity in the gonads (testes and ovaries).

Gonads The male and female sex glands—ovaries and testes.

Gonorrhea A sexually transmitted disease that initially causes inflammation of mucous membranes.

Graafian follicle A small swelling on the ovary from which a mature ovum is discharged.

Grafenberg spot Glands and ducts located in the anterior wall of the vagina below the urethra. Some women may experience sexual pleasure, arousal, orgasm, and an ejaculation of fluids from stimulation of the Grafenberg spot.

Granuloma inguinale A very rare disease that may be spread either sexually or nonsexually. Initial symptoms are small, painless, pimplelike bumps on the genitals or thighs that eventually ulcerate and emit a sour odor. The disease may result in extensive tissue destruction and permanent scarring of the genitals.

Group marriage Several adults living together, each maintaining what are considered marital relationships with more than one other group member.

Gynecology The medical practice specializing in women's health and in diseases of the female reproductive and sexual organs.

Hermaphroditism A condition in which biological characteristics of both sexes are present.

Herpes A disease, characterized by blisters on the skin in the regions of the genitals or mouth, that is caused by a virus and is easily transmitted by sexual contact.

Heterosexual person A person whose primary social, emotional, and sexual orientation is toward members of the other sex.

Homophobia Irrational fears of homosexuality, the fear of the possibility of homosexuality in one-self, or self-loathing toward one's own homosexuality.

Homosexual person A person whose primary erotic, psychological, emotional, and social orientation is toward members of the same sex.

Homosocial Relating socially primarily with members of the same sex.

Hormones Chemical substances produced by endocrine glands that affect the functioning of other organs.

Human chorionic gonadotropin (HCG) A hormone that is detectable in the urine of a pregnant woman about a month after conception.

H-Y antigen A substance present in males that triggers the transformation of the embryonic gonads into testes.

Hymen Tissue that partially covers the vaginal opening.

Hypogonadism Impaired hormone production in the testes that results in androgen deprivation.

Hypothalamus A critical brain structure that plays a major role in controlling the production of sex hormones and the regulation of fertility and menstrual cycles through its interaction with the pituitary gland.

Hysterectomy The surgical removal of the uterus.

Imperforate hymen A hymen that completely seals the vaginal opening.

Incest Sexual interaction between close relatives other than husband and wife.

Induced abortion Medically induced removal of the contents of the uterus during pregnancy.

Inferior vena cava A large blood vessel that is a major source of blood supply to and from the uterus.

Inguinal canal The canal through which the testes travel during fetal development from inside the abdomen to the scrotum.

Inhibited sexual desire (ISD) A sexual difficulty involving lack of interest in sexual fantasy and activity.

Inorgasmia A sexual difficulty involving the absence of orgasm in women.

Interstitial cells Cells located between the seminiferous tubules that are the major source of androgen in males.

Intrauterine device (IUD) A small plastic device that is inserted into the uterus for contraception.

Introitus The opening to the vagina.

Intromission Insertion of the penis into the vagina.

IUD. *See* Intrauterine device.

Kegel exercises A series of exercises that strengthen the muscles underlying the external female or male genitals.

Klinefelter's syndrome A rare condition characterized by the presence of two X chromosomes and one Y (XXY).

Klismaphilia A very unusual variant in sexual expression in which an individual obtains sexual pleasure from receiving enemas.

Labia majora The outer lips of the vulva.

Labia minora The inner lips of the vulva, one on each side of the vaginal opening.

Lactobacilli Bacteria that help maintain a healthy vagina.

Legalization Making legal previously defined illegal activities and regulating, licensing, or taxing the activities.

Leukorrhea A general term applied to a variety of vaginal infections characterized by an excessive discharge.

Leydig's cells *See* Interstitial cells.

Libido A term commonly used to denote sexual motivation.

Limbic system A subcortical brain system composed of several interrelated structures that influences the sexual behavior of humans and other animals.

Lochia A reddish uterine discharge that occurs following childbirth.

Lubrication inhibition A sexual difficulty that involves a lack of lubrication during sexual interaction.

Luteinizing hormone (LH) The hormone secreted by the pituitary gland that stimulates ovulation in the female. In males it is called interstitial cell hormone (ISCH) and stimulates production of androgens by the testes.

Lymphogranuloma venereum A rare STD that first appears as small painless papules on the genitals.

Mammary glands Milk glands in the female breast.

Mammography A highly sensitive X-ray test for the detection of breast cancer.

Masturbation Stimulation of one's own genitals to create sexual pleasure.

Menarche The initial onset of menstrual periods in a young woman.

Menopause Cessation of menstruation due to the aging process or surgical removal of the ovaries.

Menstrual synchrony The development of congruent menstrual cycle timing that sometimes occurs among women who live in close proximity.

Menstruation The sloughing off of the built-up uterine lining that takes place if conception has not occurred.

Midwife A woman who has had training as a birth attendant.

Miscarriage The spontaneous expulsion of the fetus from the uterus early in pregnancy, before it can survive on its own.

Miscegenation Sexual relationships between persons of different races.

Molluscum contagiosum A sexually transmitted disease, caused by a pox virus, that is characterized by small, painless lesions.

Moniliasis An inflammatory infection of the vaginal tissues caused by the yeastlike fungus *Candida albicans*.

Mons veneris A triangular mound over the pubic bone above the vulva.

Mores Established customs and beliefs in a given culture.

Mucosa Collective term for the mucous membranes, moist tissue that lines certain body areas such as the penile urethra, vagina, and mouth.

Mucus method A birth control method based on determining the time of ovulation by means of the cyclical changes of the cervical mucus.

Müllerian ducts A pair of ducts in the embryo that develop into female reproductive organs.

Müllerian inhibitory substance A substance secreted by the fetal testes that causes the Müllerian ducts to shrink rather than develop into internal female structures.

Multiparous Refers to a woman who has given birth more than once.

Multiphasic pills Birth control pills that vary the dosages of estrogen and progestin during the cycle.

Multiple orgasms More than one orgasm experienced within a short time period.

Mutual empathy The underlying knowledge that each partner in a relationship cares for the other and knows that the care is reciprocated.

Myotonia Muscle tension.

Necrophilia A rare sexual paraphilia in which a person obtains sexual gratification by viewing or having intercourse with a corpse.

Neisseria gonorrhoeae The name of the bacterium that causes a gonorrhea infection.

Nocturnal emission Involuntary ejaculation during sleep, also known as a "wet dream."

Nocturnal penile tumescence (NPT) test An erection-monitoring procedure done during sleep in a specially equipped lab.

Nonconsensual extramarital sex Engaging in an outside sexual relationship without the consent (or presumably the knowledge) of one's spouse.

Nongonococcal urethritis (NGU) An inflammation of the male urethral tube caused by other than gonorrhea organisms.

Nulliparous Refers to a woman who has never given birth.

Oophorectomy Surgical removal of the ovaries.

Open marriage A marriage in which spouses, with each other's permission, have intimate relationships with other people as well as the marital partner.

Oral-genital stimulation Mouth to genital contact to create sexual pleasure.

Orchidectomy The surgical procedure for removing the testes.

Orgasm A series of muscular contractions of the pelvic floor muscles occurring at the peak of sexual arousal.

Orgasm phase A term coined by Masters and Johnson to describe the third phase of the sexual response cycle in which rhythmic muscular contractions of the pelvic floor occur.

Os The opening in the cervix that leads to the interior of the uterus.

Outercourse Noncoital forms of sexual intimacy.

Ovary Female gonad that produces ova and sex hormones.

Ovulation The release of a mature ovum from the graafian follicle of the ovary.

Ovum The female reproductive cell.

Pap smear A screening test for cervical cancer.

Paraphrasing A listener summarizing the speaker's message in his or her own words.

Partial celibacy Not engaging in interpersonal sexual contact but continuing to engage in masturbation.

Passing Appearing to be heterosexual and avoiding presenting oneself as homosexual.

Pederasty A practice in ancient Greece in which an older man would take a young man as a lover and student.

Pedophilia Sexual contact between an adult and a child.

Pelvic inflammatory disease (PID)   An infection in the uterus and pelvic cavity.

Penis   A male sexual organ consisting of the internal root and external shaft and glans.

Perineum   The area between the vagina and anus of the female and the scrotum and anus of the male.

Petting   Physical contact including kissing, touching, and manual or oral genital stimulation but excluding coitus.

Peyronie's disease   Abnormal fibrous tissue and calcius deposits in the penis.

Pheromones   Certain odors produced by the body that relate to reproductive functions.

Phimosis   A condition characterized by an extremely tight penile foreskin.

Pituitary gland   A gland located in the brain that secretes hormones that influence the activity of other endocrine glands.

Placenta   A disc-shaped organ attached to the uterine wall and connected to the fetus by the umbilical cord. Nutrients, oxygen, and waste products pass between mother and fetus through its cell walls.

Placenta previa   A birth complication in which the placenta is between the cervical opening and the infant.

Plateau phase   Masters and Johnson's term for the second phase of the sexual response cycle, in which muscle tension, heart rate, blood pressure, and vasocongestion increase.

Pornography   Visual and written materials of a sexual nature that are used for purposes of sexual arousal.

Postpartum period   The first several weeks following childbirth.

Premarital sex   A term commonly used to categorize coitus that occurs before marriage.

Premature ejaculation   A sexual difficulty whereby a man ejaculates so rapidly as to impair his own or his partner's pleasure.

Premenstrual syndrome (PMS)   Symptoms of physical discomfort and emotional irritability, also called premenstrual tension, that occur 2 to 12 days prior to menstruation.

Prepared childbirth   Birth following an education process that can involve information, exercises, breathing, and working with a labor coach.

Prepuce   *See* Foreskin.

Preputial glands   Small lubricating glands located in the foreskin of the penis.

Priapism   Prolonged and uncomfortable penile erection.

Primary erogenous zones   Areas of the body that contain dense concentrations of nerve endings.

Probability sample   A type of limited research sample in which every individual in the total population about which one wishes to draw inferences has an equal chance (probability) of being included.

Prodromal symptoms   Symptoms that give advance warning of an impending herpes eruption.

Progesterone   The hormone produced by the corpus luteum of the ovary that causes the uterine lining to thicken.

Progestin-only pills   Contraceptive pills that contain a small dose of progestin and no estrogen.

Proliferative phase   The phase of the menstrual cycle in which the ovarian follicles mature.

Pronatalism   Attitudes and policies that encourage parenthood for all couples.

Prophylactic   A latex or membrane sheath that fits over the penis and is used for protection against unwanted pregnancy and sexually transmitted diseases. The term is also used in a general sense to mean anything that aids in disease prevention.

Prostaglandins   Hormones that are used to induce uterine contractions and fetal expulsion for second trimester abortions.

Prostate gland   A gland located at the base of the bladder that produces the greatest portion of the volume of seminal fluid released during ejaculation.

Prostatitis   Inflammation of the prostate.

Prostitution   The exchange of sexual services for money.

Pseudohermaphrodites   Individuals whose gonads match their chromosomal sex, but whose internal and external reproductive anatomy has a mixture of male and female structures or structures that are incompletely male or female.

Psychosexual therapy Treatment designed to help clients gain awareness of their unconscious thoughts and feelings that contribute to their sexual problems.

Psychosocial Refers to a combination of psychological and social factors.

Puberty The stage of life between childhood and adulthood during which the reproductive organs mature.

Pubic lice Lice that primarily infest the pubic hair and are transmitted by sexual contact.

Pubococcygeal (PC) muscle A muscle surrounding the vaginal opening.

Rape Sexual intercourse that occurs without consent as a result of actual or threatened force.

Rape trauma syndrome The emotional difficulties women experience after they have been raped.

Recanalization The spontaneous rejoining of the vas deferens following sterilization.

Refractory period The period of time following orgasm in the male during which he cannot experience another orgasm.

Relationship contract A mutually agreed upon set of rules, plans, and philosophies related to an interpersonal relationship.

Resolution phase The fourth phase of the sexual response cycle as outlined by Masters and Johnson, in which the sexual systems return to their nonexcited state.

Retrograde ejaculation Process by which semen is expelled into the bladder instead of out of the penis.

Rugae The folds of tissue in the vagina.

Sadomasochism (SM) The act of obtaining sexual arousal through receiving (masochism) or giving (sadism) physical or psychological pain.

Scabies A highly contagious infestation by tiny, parasitic mites that may be transmitted by sexual contact.

Scrotum The pouch of skin of the external male genitals that encloses the testicles.

Secondary erogenous zones Areas of the body that have become erotically sensitive through learning and experience.

Secondary sex characteristics The physical characteristics other than genitals that indicate sexual maturity, such as body hair, breasts, and deepened voice.

Second-stage labor The middle stage of labor, in which the infant descends through the vaginal canal.

Secretory phase The phase of the menstrual cycle in which the corpus luteum develops and secretes progesterone.

Semen A viscous fluid ejaculated through the penis that contains sperm and fluids from the prostate, seminal vesicles, and Cowper's glands.

Seminal fluid *See* Semen.

Seminal vesicle A small gland adjacent to the terminal of the vas deferens that secretes an alkaline fluid conducive to sperm motility.

Seminiferous tubules Thin, coiled structures in the testicles in which sperm are produced.

Sensate focus A process of touching and communication used to enhance sexual pleasure and to reduce performance pressure.

Sex chromosomes A single set of chromosomes that influences biological sex determination.

Sex flush A pink or red rash that appears on the chest or breasts during sexual arousal.

Sexual aversion Extreme and irrational fear of sexual activity.

Sexual differentiation The process whereby the individual develops physical characteristics distinct from those of the other sex.

Sexual harassment Unwanted attention of a sexual nature from someone at the workplace.

Sexually transmitted diseases (STDs) Diseases that are transmitted by sexual contact. Term includes, but is not limited to, diseases traditionally called VD.

Sexual orientation Sexual attraction to one's own sex (homosexual) or the other sex (herero-sexual).

Shaft The length of the clitoris and penis between the glans and the body.

Shingellosis A sexually transmitted bacterial infection characterized by diarrhea, fever, and inflammation of the large intestine.

Smegma A cheesy substance of glandular secretions and skin cells that sometimes accumulates under the foreskin of the penis or hood of the clitoris.

Socialization The process whereby our society conveys behavioral expectations to the individual.

Society An enduring, cooperative group of people with organized patterns of interrelationships.

Sodomy An ill-defined legal category for noncoital genital contacts such as oral-genital and anal intercourse.

Speculum An instrument with two blades used to open the vaginal walls during a gynecological exam.

Sperm The male reproductive cell.

Spermatic cord A cord attached to the testicle that contains the vas deferens, blood vessels, nerves, and cremasteric muscle fibers.

Spermatogenesis Sperm production.

Spermicides Chemical substances used in contraceptives that kill sperm.

Spongy body A chamber that forms a bulb at the base of the penis, extends up into the penile shaft and forms the penile glans.

Squeeze technique A treatment technique for rapid ejaculation, consisting of squeezing the penis at the base of the glans or at the base of the shaft.

Statutory rape Intercourse with a person under the legal age of consent.

Stereotype A generalized notion of what a person is like that is based only on that person's sex, race, religion, ethnic background, or similar criterion.

STD. *See* Sexually transmitted diseases.

Swinging The exchange of marital partners for sexual interaction.

Syphilis A sexually transmitted disease caused by an organism called *Treponema pallidum* or spirochete.

Systems theory Treatment that focuses on interactions within a couple relationship and on the functions of the sexual problems in the relationship.

Target organs Organs and cells that are influenced by certain specific hormones.

Testicle Male gonad inside the scrotum that produces sperm and sex hormones.

Testosterone A major male hormone produced by the testes.

Third-stage labor The last stage of childbirth, in which the placenta separates from the uterine wall and comes out of the vagina.

Toxemia A dangerous condition during pregnancy in which high blood pressure occurs.

Toxic shock syndrome (TSS) A disease that may cause a person to go into shock, occurring most commonly in menstruating women.

Transsexual A person whose psychological gender identity is opposite to his or her biological sex.

Transvestism Deriving sexual arousal from wearing clothing of the other sex.

Trichomoniasis A form of vaginitis caused by a one-celled protozoan called *Trichomonas vaginalis*.

Trimesters Three-month segments dividing the nine months of pregnancy.

Trophoblast cells Cells of the placenta that secrete human chorionic gonadotropin (HCG).

True hermaphrodites Exceedingly rare individuals who have both ovarian and testicular tissue in their bodies. Their external genitals are often a mixture of male and female structures.

Tubal sterilization Female sterilization accomplished by cutting the fallopian tubes.

Turner's syndrome A rare condition characterized by the presence of one unmatched X chromosome (XO). Turner's syndrome individuals have normal female external genitals, but their internal reproductive structures do not develop fully.

Tyson's glands   Small glands under the corona of the penis on either side of the frenum.

Urethra   The tube through which urine passes from the bladder to outside the body.

Urethral bulb   The portion of the urethra between the urethral sphincters in the male.

Urethral sphincters   Two muscles, one located at the base of the bladder in both sexes and another located below the prostate in the male.

Urethritis   An inflammation of the urethral tube.

Urology   The medical specialty dealing with reproductive health and genital diseases of the male and urinary tract diseases in both sexes.

Urophilia   A sexual paraphilia in which a person obtains sexual arousal from contact with urine.

Uterus   A pear-shaped organ inside the female pelvis, within which the fetus develops.

Vagina   A stretchable canal in the female that opens at the vulva and extends about four inches into the pelvis.

Vaginismus   A sexual difficulty in which a woman experiences involuntary spasmodic contractions of the muscles of the outer third of the vagina.

Vaginitis   Inflammation of the vaginal walls caused by a variety of vaginal infections.

Validating   The process of indicating that a partner's point of view is reasonable, given some assumptions that one may not share with one's partner.

Vas deferens   A sperm-carrying tube that begins at the testicle and ends at the urethra.

Vasectomy   Male sterilization procedure that involves removing a section from each vas deferens.

Vasocongestion   The engorgement of blood vessels in particular body parts in response to sexual arousal.

Vasovasectomy   Surgical reconstruction of the vas deferens after vasectomy.

Venereal disease (VD)   Contagious diseases whose mode of transmission is almost always sexual contact. The term has traditionally been limited to gonorrhea and syphilis.

Vernix caseosa   A waxy, protective substance on the fetus's skin.

Vestibular bulbs   Two bulbs, one on each side of the vaginal opening, that engorge with blood during sexual arousal.

Vestibule   The area of the vulva inside of the labia minora.

Viral hepatitis   A disease in which liver function is impaired by a viral infection.

Virgin   A person who has not experienced coitus.

Voyeurism   The act of obtaining sexual gratification by observing undressed or sexually interacting people without their consent.

Vulva   The external genitals of the female, including the mons veneris, labia majora, labia minora, clitoris, and urinary and vaginal openings.

Wolffian ducts   The internal duct system of the embryo that develops into male reproductive structures.

XYY males   A chromosomal anomaly that results when a normal ovum is fertilized by an atypical sperm bearing two Y chromosomes. XYY males develop normal sex organs and characteristics of males and are masculine in appearance.

Zoophilia   A paraphilia in which a person has sexual contact with animals.

Zygote   The single cell resulting from the union of sperm and egg cells.

Bibliography

Abel, E. Fetal alcohol syndrome. *Psychological Bulletin*, 1980, 87, 29–50.

Abel, E. Opiates and sex. *Journal of Psychoactive Drugs*, 1984, 16, 205–216.

Abel, G. The evaluation and treatment of sexual offenders and their victims. Paper presented at St. Vincent Hospital and Medical Center, Portland, Ore., Oct. 15, 1981.

———, Barlow, D., Blanchard, E., and Guild, D. The components of rapists' sexual arousal. *Archives of General Psychiatry*, 1977, 34, 895–903.

Abel, G., Becker, J., and Cunningham-Rather, J. Complications, consent, and cognitions in sex between children and adults. *International Journal of Law and Psychiatry*, 1984, 7, 89–103.

Abou-David, K. Epidemiology of carcinoma of the cervix uteri in Lebanese Christians and Moslems. *Cancer*, 1967, 20, 1706–1714.

Abraham, G. Premenstrual tension. *Current Problems in Obstetrics and Gynecology*, 1981, 1–39.

Abrahams, J. Azoospermia before puberty. *Medical Aspects of Human Sexuality* 1982, 1, 13.

Abramson, P., Perry, L., Rotblatt, A., Seeley, T., and Seeley, D. Negative attitudes toward masturbation and pelvic vascongestion: A thermographic analysis. *Journal of Research in Personality*, 1981, 15, 497–509.

ACLU of Oregon Newsletter, March/April 1982, 20.

Adams, J. *Understanding Adolescence*. Boston: Allyn and Bacon, 1973.

Adams, J., and Rubin, A. Outcomes of sexually open marriages: A five year follow up. Paper presented at the Eastern Region Annual Conference of the Society for the Scientific Study of Sex, Philadelphia, Apr. 1984.

Adams, M., Oakley, G., and Marks, J. Maternal age and births in the 1980s. *Journal of the American Medical Association*, 1980, 247, 493–494.

Addiego, F., Belzer, E., Comolli, J., Moger, W., Perry, J., and Whipple, B. Female ejaculation: A case study. *Journal of Sex Research*, 1981, 17, 13–21.

Advertising Research Foundation. *Target Group Index*, 1978.

Alder, C. An exploration of self-reported sexually aggressive behavior. *Crime and Delinquency*, 1985, 31, 306–331.

Alexander, S. Improving sex education programs for young adolescents: Parent's views. *Family Relations*, 1984, 33, 251–257.

Alford, J., and Brown, G. Virgins, whores, and bitches: Attitudes of rapists toward women and sex. *Corrective and Social Psychiatry*, 1985, 31, 58–61.

Alford, J., Kasper, C., and Baumann, P. Diagnostic classification of child sexual offenders. *Corrective and Social Psychiatry*, 1984, 30, 40–46.

Allen, D. Young male prostitutes: A psychosocial study. *Archives of Sexual Behavior*, 1980, 9, 399–426.

Allgeier, E. The influence of androgynous identification on heterosexual relations. *Sex Roles*, 1981, 7, 321–330.

Allon, N., and Fishel, D. Singles bars. In N. Allon (Ed.), *Urban Life Styles*. Dubuque, Iowa: Brown, 1979.

Alpern, D. A Newsweek poll: Sex laws. *Newsweek*, July 14, 1986, 38.

Altman, L. Increase in testicular cancer prompts call for self-examination. New York Times News Service, May 3, 1983.

———. AIDS leaves different track through Africa. *The Oregonian*, Nov. 13 and 14, 1985, A2.

Altrocchi, J. *Abnormal Behavior*. New York: Harcourt Brace Jovanovich, 1980.

Alzate, H., and Londono, M. Vaginal erotic sensitivity. *Journal of Sex and Marital Therapy*, 1984, 10, 49–56.

American Cancer Society. *1985 Cancer Facts and Figures*.

American Civil Liberties Union. *Polluting the Censorship Debate*. Washington, D.C.: American Civil Liberties Union, 1986.

American College of Obstetricians and Gynecologists. *Urinary Tract Infections*, Oct. 1984.

———. *Preventing Osteoporosis*, 1984.

———. *Dysmenorrhea*, Jan. 1985.

American Law Institute. *Model Penal Code: Proposed Official Draft*. Philadelphia: American Law Institute, 1962.

American Medical Association Council on Pharmacy and Chemistry. "Germicidal" soaps. *Journal of the American Medical Association*, 1944, 124, 1195–1201.

American Psychiatric Association. *Diagnostic and Statistical Manual of Mental Disorders*, 3rd ed. (DSM–III). Washington, D. C.: American Psychiatric Association, 1980.

American Social Health Association. Help membership HSV survey. *The Helper*, 1981, 3, 1–5.

Annon, J. *The Behavioral Treatment of Sexual Problems*, Vol. 1. Honolulu, Hawaii: Enabling Systems, 1974.

Anthony, E., Green, R., and Kolodny, R. *Childhood Sexuality*. Boston: Little, Brown, 1982.

Antunes, C., Stolley, P., Rosenshein, N., Davies, J., Tonascia, J., Brown, C., Burnett, L., Rutledge, A., Pokempner, M., and Garcia, R. Endometrial cancer and estrogen use. *New England Journal of Medicine*, 1979, 300, 9–13.

Apfelbaum, B. Why we should not accept sexual fantasies. In B. Apfelbaum (Ed.), *Expanding the Boundaries of Sex Therapy*. Berkeley, Calif.: Berkeley Sex Therapy Group, 1980.

Aquinas, T. *Summa Theologica* II, III, ed. T. Gilbey. New York: Doubleday, 1975.

Archer, J., and Lloyd, B. *Sex and Gender*. New York: Cambridge University Press, 1985.

Arentewicz, B., and Schmidt, G., (Eds.). *The Treatment of Sexual Disorders*. New York: Basic Books, 1983.

Armentrout, J., and Burger, G. Children's reports of parental child-rearing behavior at five grade levels. *Developmental Psychology*, 1972, 7, 44–48.

Arms, S. *Immaculate Deception*. Boston: Houghton Mifflin, 1975.

Arthur, C. Customized cervical cap: Evolution of an ancient idea. *Journal of Nurse-Midwifery*, 1980, 34, 25–33.

Athanasiou, R., Shaver, P., and Tavris, C. Sex. *Psychology Today*, July 1970, 39–52.

Atkin, C. Changing male and female roles. In M. Schwarz (Ed.), *TV and Teens: Experts Look at the Issues*. Reading, Mass.: Addison-Wesley, 1982.

Atwater, L. *The Extramarital Connection: Sex, Intimacy, and Identity*. New York: Irvington, 1982.

Atwood, J. The role of masturbation in sociosexual development. Ph.D. dissertation, University of New York at Stony Brook, 1981.

Austin, H., Louv, W., and Alexander, W. A case-control study of spermicides and gonorrhea. *Journal of the American Medical Association*, 1984, 251, 2822–2824.

Austrom, D., and Hanel, K. Psychological issues of single life in Canada: An exploratory study. *International Journal of Women's Studies*, 1985, 8, 12–23.

Bachrach, C. Contraceptive practice among American women, 1973–1982. *Family Planning Perspectives*, 1984, 16, 253–259.

Baird, D., and Wilcox, A. Cigarette smoking associated with delayed conception. *Journal of the American Medical Association*, 1985, 253, 2979–2983.

Baker, C. Preying on playgrounds. The sexploitation of children in pornography and prostitution. In L. Schultz (Ed.), *The Sexual Victimology of Youth*. Springfield, Ill.: Charles C. Thomas, 1980.

Baker, L., and Nagata, F. A group approach to the treatment of heterosexual couples with sexual dissatisfactions. *Journal of Sex Education and Therapy*, 1978, 4, 15–18.

Baldwick, R. *Dinner at Magny's*. London: Harmondsworth Press, 1973.

Bancroft, J. Psychophysiology of sexual dysfunction. In M. Dekker (Ed.), *Handbook of Biological Psychiatry*. New York: Dekker, 1980.

———. Hormones and human sexual behavior. *Journal of Sex and Marital Therapy*, 1984, 10, 3–21.

Bangs, L. Aging and positive sexuality: A descriptive approach. Ph.D. dissertation, U.S. International University, 1983.

Banmen, J., and Vogel, N. The relationship between marital quality and interpersonal sexual communication. *Family Therapy*, 1985, 12, 45–58.

Barbach, L. *For Yourself: The Fulfillment of Female Sexuality*. Garden City, N. Y.: Doubleday, 1975.

Barbaree, H., Marshall, W., and Lanthier, R. Deviant sexual arousal in rapists. *Behavior Research and Therapy*, 1979, 17, 215–222.

Barfield, R., Wilson, C., and McDonald, P. Sexual behavior: Extreme reduction of postejaculatory refractory period by midbrain lesions in male rats. *Science*, 1975, 189, 147–149.

Barlow, D., Mills, J., Agras, W., and Steinman, D. Comparison of sex-typed motor behavior in male-to-female transsexuals and women. *Archives of Sexual Behavior*, 1980, 9, 245–253.

———, Silverstein, C., and Bieber, I. New frontiers in human sexuality. *Contemporary Psychology*, 1980, 25, 355–359.

Bart, P., and O'Brien, P. Stopping rape: Effective avoidance strategies. *Signs*, 1984, 10, 83–101.

Bartell, G. Group sex among the mid-Americans. *Journal of Sex Research*, 1970, 6, 113–130.

Bartlett, K. Sexual harassment may be issue of '80s. *The Oregonian*, Feb. 28, 1982, A22.

Batchelor, E. (Ed.). *Homosexuality and Ethics*. New York: Pilgrim Press, 1980.

Bauman, K. Volunteer bias in a study of sexual knowledge, attitudes, and behavior. *Journal of Marriage and the Family*, 1973, 35, 27–31.

Bauman, R., Kasper, C., and Alford, J. The child sex abusers. *Corrective and Social Psychiatry*, 1984, 30, 76–81.

Baxter, D., Marshall, W., Barbaree, H., Davidson, P., and Malcolm, P. Deviant sexual behavior: Differentiating sex offenders by criminal and personal history, psychometric measures, and sexual response. *Criminal Justice and Behavior*, 1984, 11, 477–501.

Baxter, L., and Wilmot, W. "Secret tests": Social strategies for acquiring information about the state of the relationship. *Human Communication Research*, 1984, 11, 171–202.

Beach, F. (Ed.). *Human Sexuality in Four Perspectives*. Baltimore, Md.: Johns Hopkins Press, 1978.

Beatty, W. Gonadal hormones and sex differences in nonreproductive behaviors in rodents: Organizational and activational influences. *Hormones and Behavior*, 1979, 12, 112–163.

Beck, M., Rohter, L., and Friday, C. An unwanted baby boom. *Newsweek*, Apr. 30, 1984.

Becker, J., and Levine, E. A statement by Dr. Judith Becker and Ellen Levine. Personal communication, July, 1986.

Becker, J., Skinner, L., Abel, G., Axelrod, R., and Cichon, J. Sexual problems of sexual assault survivors. *Women and Health*, 1984, 9, 5–20.

———, ———, ———, and Treacy, E. Incidence and types of sexual dysfunctions in rape and incest victims. *Journal of Sex and Marital Therapy*, 1982, 8, 65–74.

Becker, T., Blount, J., and Guinan, M. Genital herpes infections in private practice in the United States, 1966 to 1981. *The Journal of the American Medical Association*, 1985, 253, 1601–1603.

Behavior Today. Leboyer babies—a first follow-up from France. Nov. 29, 1976, 3.

Beigel, H. The meaning of coital postures. *International Journal of Sexology*, 1953, 4, 136–143.

Bell, A., and Weinberg, M. *Homosexualities: A Study of Diversity Among Men and Women*. New York: Simon and Schuster, 1978.

———, ———, and Hammersmith, S. *Sexual Preference: Its Development in Men and Women*. Bloomington, Ind.: Indiana University Press, 1981.

Belzer, E. Orgasmic expulsions of women: A review and heuristic inquiry. *Journal of Sex Research*, 1981, 17, 1–12.

———, Whipple, B., and Moger, W. On female ejaculation. *The Journal of Sex Research*, 1984, 20, 403–406.

Bem, S. The measurement of psychological androgyny. *Journal of Consulting and Clinical Psychology*, 1974, 42, 155–162.

———. Sex role adaptability: One consequence of psychological androgyny. *Journal of Personality and Social Psychology*, 1975, 31, 634–643.

———. Theory and measurement of androgyny: A reply to the Pedhazer-Tetenbaum and Locksley-Colton critiques. *Journal of Personality and Social Psychology*, 1979, 37, 1047–1054.

———. Beyond androgyny: Some presumptuous prescriptions for a liberated sexual identity. In J. Sherman and F. Denmark (Eds.), *The Future of Women: Issues in Psychology*. New York: Psychological Dimension, 1980.

———, and Lenney, E. Sex typing and the avoidance of cross-sex behavior. *Journal of Personality and Social Psychology*, 1976, 33, 48–54.

———, Martyna, W., and Watson, C. Sex-typing and androgyny: Further explorations of the expressive domain. *Journal of Personality and Social Psychology*, 1976, 34, 1016–1023.

Benderly, B. Rape free or rape prone. *Science Magazine*, Oct. 1984, 40–43.

Bennett, S. Family environment for sexual learning as a function of father's involvement in family work and discipline. *Adolescence*, 1984, 19, 609–627.

Benson, R. *Handbook of Obstetrics and Gynecology*, 4th rev. ed. Los Altos, Calif.: Lange Medical Publications, 1971.

———. *Handbook of Obstetrics and Gynecology*, 5th rev. ed. Los Altos, Calif.: Lange Medical Publications, 1974.

———. Vacuum cleaner injury to penis: A common urologic problem? *Urology*, 1985, 25, 41–44.

Berg, S., and Harrison, W. Spectinomycin as primary treatment of gonorrhea in areas of high prevalence of penicillinase-producing *N. gonorrhoeae*. *Sexually Transmitted Diseases*, 1981, 8, 38–39.

Berger, C., Gold, D., Andres, D., Gillett, P., and Kinch, R. Repeat abortion: Is it a problem? *Family Planning Perspectives*, 1984, 16, 70–75.

Berlin, F., and Meinecke, C. Treatment of sex offenders with antiandrogenic medication. *American Journal of Psychiatry*, 1981, 138, 601–607.

Bermant, G., and Davidson, J. *Biological Bases of Sexual Behavior*. New York: Harper & Row, 1974.

Berndt, R., and Berndt, C. *Sexual Behavior in Western Arnhem Land*. New York: Viking Fund Publications in Anthropology, 1951.

Bernstein, D., Lovett, M., and Bryson, Y. Serologic analysis of first episode nonprimary genital simplex virus infection. *The American Journal of Medicine*, 1984, 77, 1055–1060.

Bernstein, R. The Y chromosome and primary sexual differentiation. *Journal of the American Medical Association*, 1981, 245, 1953–1956.

Berscheid, E., and Walster, E. Physical attractiveness. In L. Berkowitz (Ed.), *Advances in Experimental Social Psychology*, Vol. 7. New York: Academic Press, 1974.

Bertello, P., Gurioli, L., Faggiuolo, R., Veglio, F., Tamagnone, C., and Angeli, A. Effect of ethanol infusion on the pituitary-testicular responsiveness to gonadotropin releasing hormone and thyrotropin releasing hormone in normal males and in chronic alcoholics presenting with hypogonadism. *Journal of Endocrinological Investigation*, 1983, 6, 413–420.

Bevson, J. Lovemaking with myself. *Changing Men*, Jan. 1975, 1.

Bidgood, F. Sexuality and the handicapped. *SIECUS Report*, 1974, 2, 2.

Bieber, I., Dain, H., Dince, P., Drellich, M., Grand, H., Gundlach, R., Kremer, M., Rifkin, A., Wilbur, C., and Bieber, T. *Homosexuality*. New York: Vintage Books, 1962.

Bierce, A. *The Devil's Dictionary*. New York: World, 1943.

Billings, E., Billings, J., and Catarinch, M. *Atlas of the Ovulation Method*. Collegeville, Minn.: Liturgical Press, 1974.

Bingham, J. Single blind comparison of ketoconazole 200 mg oral tablets and clotrimazole 100 mg vaginal tablets and 1% cream in treating acute vaginal candidosis. *British Journal of Venereal Diseases*, 1984, 60, 175–177.

Blair, C., and Lanyon, R. Exhibitionism: Etiology and treatment. *Psychological Bulletin*, 1981, 89, 439–463.

Blanchard, R., Steiner, B., and Clemmensen, L. Gender dysphoria, gender reorientation, and the clinical management of transsexualism. *Journal of Consulting and Clinical Psychology*, 1985, 53, 295–304.

Blattner, W. Paper presented at an international scientific conference on AIDS, Les Trois Ilets, Martinique, Jan. 1986.

Bloch, D. Sex education practices of mothers. *Journal of Sex Education and Therapy*, 1978, 4, 7–12.

Block, J. Issues, problems, and pitfalls in assessing sex differences. *Merrill-Palmer Quarterly*, 1976, 22, 283–308.

———. Differential premises arising from differential socialization of the sexes: Some conjectures. *Child Development*, 1983, 54, 1335–1354.

Bloom, F., Lazerson, A., and Hofstadter, L. *Brain, Mind, and Behavior*. New York: W. H. Freeman, 1985.

Blum, M. Vaginal candidosis transmitted by non-coital sex. *British Journal of Sexual Medicine*, 1984, 11, 144.

Blumstein, P., and Schwartz, P. *American Couples*. New York: William Morrow, 1983.

Bohlen, J., Held, J., Sanderson, M., and Patterson, R. Heart rate, rate-pressure product, and oxygen uptake during four sexual activities. *Archives of Internal Medicine*, 1984, 144, 1745–1748.

Bolch, J. Academy questions and routine circumcision. *The Oregonian*, Oct. 20, 1981, C4.

Bolch, O., and Warren, J. In vitro effects of Emko on *Neisseria gonorrhoeae* and *Trichomonas vaginalis*. *American Journal of Obstetrics and Gynecology*, 1973, 115, 1145–1148.

Boller, F., and Frank, E. *Sexual Dysfunction in Neurological Disorders*. New York: Raven Press, 1982.

Bongaarts, J. Infertility after age 30: A false alarm. *Family Planning Perspectives*, 1982, 14, 75–78.

Bonica, J. *Principles and Practice of Obstetric Analgesia and Anesthesia*, Vols. 1 and 2. Philadelphia: F. A. Davis, 1972.

Børdahl, P. The social and gyneacological long-term consequences of tubal sterilization. *Acta Obstetrica et Gynecologica Scandinavica*, 1984, 63, 487–495.

Boston Collaborative Drug Surveillance Program. Oral contraceptives and venous thromboembolic disease, surgically confirmed gallbladder disease and breast tumors. *The Lancet*, 1973, 1, 1399–1404.

———. Surgically confirmed gallbladder disease, venous thromboembolism and breast tumors in relation to postmenopausal estrogen therapy. *New England Journal of Medicine*, 1974, 290, 15.

Boston Women's Health Book Collective. *The New Our Bodies, Ourselves*, New York: Simon and Schuster, 1984.

Boswell, J. *Christianity, Social Tolerance, and Homosexuality*. Chicago and London: University of Chicago Press, 1980.

Bowie, W. Epidemiology and therapy of *Chlamydia trachomatis* infections. *Drugs*, 1984, 27, 459–468.

Braen, G. Examination of the accused: The heterosexual and homosexual rapist. In C. Warner (Ed.), *Rape and Sexual Assault*. Germantown, Md.: Aspens Systems Corp., 1980.

Brandt, A. *No Magic Bullet*. New York: Oxford University Press, 1985.

Brass, E. Effects of antihypertensive drugs on endocrine function. *Drugs*, 1984, 27, 447–458.

Brazelton, T. Effects of prenatal drugs on the behavior of the neonate. *American Journal of Psychiatry*, 1973, 126, 1261– 1266.

Brecher, E. *The Sex Researchers*. New York: New American Library, 1971.

———. *Love, Sex and Aging*. Boston: Little, Brown, 1984.

Bremer, J. *Asexualization*. New York: Macmillan, 1959.

Brenner, W. Evaluation of contemporary female sterilization methods. *Journal of Reproductive Medicine*, 1981, 26, 439– 453.

Briddell, D., and Wilson, G. Effects of alcohol and expectancy set on male sexual arousal. *Journal of Abnormal Psychology*, 1976, 85, 225–234.

Bridges, C., Critelli, J., and Loos, V. Hypnotic susceptibility, inhibition control, and orgasmic consistency. *Archives of Sexual Behavior*, 1985, 14, 367–376.

Brisset, C. Female mutilation: Cautious forum on damaging practices. *The Guardian*, Mar. 18, 1979, 12–15.

Britton, G., and Lumpkin, M. Battle to imprint for the 21st century. *Reading Teacher*, 1984, 37, 724–733.

Broderick, C. Sexual behavior among preadolescents. *Journal of Social Issues*, 1966, 22, 6–21.

———. Heterosexual interests of suburban youth. *Medical Aspects of Human Sexuality*, 1971, 5, 83–100.

Bromberg, W. and Coyle, E. Rape: A compulsion to destroy. *Medical Insight*, 1974, 22, 21–25.

Brooks, A. Serial marriages keep divorce courts busy. *The Oregonian*, Feb. 13, 1985, B1.

Brooks, J., Ruble, D., and Clark, A. College women's attitudes and expectations concerning menstrual-related changes. *Psychosomatic Medicine*, 1977, 39, 289–298.

Brown, D., Kaufman, R., and Gardner, H. *Gardnerella vaginalis* vaginitis: The current opinion. *The Journal of Reproductive Medicine*, 1984, 29, 5, 300–306.

Brown, J., and Hart, D. Correlates of females' sexual fantasies. *Perceptual and Motor Skills*, 1977, 45, 819–825.

Brownmiller, S. *Against Our Will: Men, Women, and Rape*. New York: Simon and Schuster, 1975.

Buchan, W. *Domestic Medicine: A Treatise on the Prevention and Cure of Diseases*. Boston: Printed by Joseph Bumstead for James White and Ebenezer Larkin, 1973.

Buhrich, N. A heterosexual transvestite club: Psychiatric aspects. *Australian and New Zealand Journal of Psychiatry*, 1976, 10, 331–335.

Bullough, V., Bullough, B., and Smith, R. Comparative study of male transvestites, male to female transsexuals, and male homosexuals. *Journal of Sex Research*, 1983, 19, 238–257.

Burdoff, P. *No More Menstrual Cramps and Other Good News*. New York: Putnam, 1980.

Bureau of the Census. *U.S. Statistics at a Glance: Annual Summary of Demographic and Economic Indicators*. June 1985.

Burgess, A., Hartman, C., McCausland, M., and Powers, P. Response patterns in children and adolescents exploited through sex rings and pornography. *American Journal of Psychiatry*, 1984, 141, 656–662.

———, and Holmstrom, L. Rape trauma syndrome. *American Journal of Psychiatry*, 1974a, 131, 981–986.

———, and ———. *Rape: Victims of Crisis*. Bowie, Md.: Robert J. Brady, 1974b.

———, and ———. Rape: Sexual disruption and recovery. *American Journal of Orthopsychiatry*, 1979, 49, 648–657.

Burkhart, B. Acquaintance rape statistics and prevention. Paper presented at the Acquaintance Rape and Rape Prevention on Campus Conference, Louisville, Ky., Dec. 1983.

Burstein, B., Bank, L., and Jarvik, L. Sex differences in cognitive functioning: Evidence, determinants, implications. *Human Development*, 1980, 23, 289–313.

Burt, M. Cultural myths and supports for rape. *Journal of Personality and Social Psychology*, 1980, 38, 217–230.

Buscaglia, L. *Love*. Greenwich, Conn.: Fawcett Books, 1972.

Butler, A. *Daughters of Joy, Sisters of Mercy*. Urbana, Ill.: University of Chicago Press, 1985.

Byrne, D. A. pregnant pause in the sexual revolution. *Psychology Today*, July 1977, 67–68.

———, Ervin, C., and Lamberth, J. Continuity between the experimental study of attraction and "real life" computer dating. *Journal of Personality and Social Psychology*, 1970, 16, 157–165.

Cadkin, A., Ginsberg, N., Pergament, E., and Verlinski, Y. Chorionic villi sampling: A new technique for detection of genetic abnormalities in the first trimester. *Radiology*, 1984, 151, 159–162.

Cadman, D., Gafni, A., and McNamee, J. Newborn circumcision: An economic perspective. *Canadian Medical Association Journal*, 1984, 131, 1353–1355.

Cadwallader, M. Marriage as a wretched institution. In Jack and Joann DeLora (Eds.), *Intimate Lifestyles: Marriage and Its Alternatives*. Pacific Palisades, Calif.: Goodyear, 1975.

Caggiula, A. Analysis of the copulation-reward properties of posterior hypothalamic stimulation in male rats. *Journal of Comparative and Physiological Psychology*, 1970, 70, 399–412.

———, and Hoebel, B. Copulation-reward site in the posterior hypothalamus. *Science*, 1966, 153, 1284–1285.

Calderone, M. The sex information and education council of the U.S. *Journal of Marriage and Family*, 1965, 27, 533–534.

Calhoun, L., Selby, J., and King, E. The influence of pregnancy on sexuality: a review of current evidence. *Journal of Sex Research*, 1981, 17, 139–151.

Cali, R. Estrogen replacement therapy—boon or bane? *Postgraduate Medicine*, 1984, 75, 279–286.

California State Department of Education. Guidelines for evaluation of instructional materials with respect to social content. *Curriculum Frameworks and Instructional Materials Unit*, Mar. 1979.

Campbell, A. The American way of mating, marriage Si, children only maybe. *Psychology Today*, May 1975, 37–43.

Campbell, M. Anomalies of the genital tract. In M. Campbell and J. Harrison (Eds.), *Urology*, Vol. 2. Philadelphia: W. B. Saunders, 1970.

Cannon, K., and Long, R. Premarital sexual behavior in the sixties. *Journal of Marriage and Family*, 1971, 33, 36–39.

Caplan, B. In the foreword of Brodyaga, L., Gates, M., Singer, S., Tucker, M., and White, R. *Rape and Its Victims: A Report for Citizens Health Facilities and Criminal Justice Agents*. Washington, D.C.: U.S. Department of Justice, Nov. 1975.

Cappiello, J., and Grainger-Harrison, M. The rebirth of the cervical cap. *Journal of Nurse-Midwifery*, 1981, 26, 13–18.

Carodozo, L., Gibb, D., Studd, J., Tuck, S., Thom, M., and Cooper, D. The use of hormone implants for climacteric symptoms. *American Journal of Obstetrics and Gynecology*, 1984, 148, 336–337.

Carrera, M. *Sex: The Facts, The Acts, and Your Feelings*. New York: Crown, 1981.

Carroll, J., Volk, K., and Hyde, J. Differences between males and females in motives for engaging in sexual intercourse. *Archives of Sexual Behavior*, 1985, 14, 131–139.

Carswell, R. Historical Analysis of Religion and Sex. *Journal of School Health*, 1969, 39, 673–683.

Carter, A., Cohen, E., and Shorr, E. The use of androgens in women. *Vitamins and Hormones*, 1947, 5, 317–391.

Castleman, M. *Sexual Solutions*. New York: Simon and Schuster, 1980a.

———. Sperm crisis. *Medical Self-Care*, Spring 1980b, 26–27.

———. Men, lovemaking and cramps. *Medical Self-Care*, Spring 1981, 21.

Cautley, R., Beebe, G., and Dickinson, R. Rubber sheaths as venereal disease prophylactics. *American Journal of the Medical Sciences*, 1938, 195, 155–163.

Centers for Disease Control. Increased risk of hepatocellular adenoma in women with long-term use of oral contraception. *Morbidity and Mortality Weekly Report*, 1977, 26, 293.

———. Annual summary 1980: Reported morbidity and mortality in the United States. *Morbidity and Mortality Weekly Report*, 1981, 29, 54.

———. *Morbidity and Mortality Weekly Report*, 1984a, 33, 43–44; 49.

———. Fetal alcohol syndrome: Public awareness week. *Morbidity and Mortality Weekly Report*, 1984b, 33, 1–2.

———. 1985 STD treatment guidelines. *Morbidity and Mortality Weekly Report Supplement*, September 1985a.

———. *Chlamydia trachomatis* infections. *Morbidity and Mortality Weekly Report Supplement*, August 23, 1985b.

———. Summary—cases of specified notifiable diseases, United States. *Morbidity and Mortality Weekly Report*, 1985c, 34, 756.

———. Heterosexual transmission of human T-lymphotropic virus type III/lymphadenopathy-associated virus. *Morbidity and Mortality Weekly Report*, 1985d, 34, 561–563.

———. Education and foster care of children infected with human T-lymphotropic virus type III/lymphadenopathy-associated virus. *Morbidity and Mortality Weekly Report*, 1985e, 34, 517–521.

———. Self-reported behavioral change among gay and bisexual men—San Francisco. *Morbidity and Mortality Weekly Report*, 1985f, 34, 613–615.

Chakrabarti, S., Robert-Guroff, M., Wong-Staal, F., Gallo, R., and Moss, B. Expression of the HTLV-III envelope gene by a recombinant vaccinia virus. *Nature*, 1986, 320, 535–537.

Chapman, J. Sexual anhedonia: Disorders of sexual desire. *Journal of the American Osteopathic Association*, 1984, 82, 709–714.

Chase, H., and Ducat, C. *Constitutional Interpretation*. St. Paul, Minn.: West, 1979.

Check, J. Mass media sexual violence: Content analysis and counteractive measures. Paper presented at the meeting of the American Psychological Association, Toronto, Aug. 1984.

———. Psychoticism and habitual pornography consumption as mediators of the effects of exposure to violent and nonviolent pornography. Paper presented at the meeting of the International Society for the Study of Individual Differences, San Feliú de Guixols, Spain, June 1985a.

———. Questions of definition, harm, and community standards in obscenity cases. Symposium presented at the annual convention of the American Psychological Association, Los Angeles, August 23–27, 1985b.

Chen, P., and Kols, A. Population and birth planning in the People's Republic of China. *Population Reports*, 1982, Series J, No. 25.

———, Tian, X., and Tuan, C. 11 million Chinese opt for 'only child glory certificate.' *People*, 1982, 9, 12–15.

Cherlin, A. *Marriage, Divorce, Remarriage*. Cambridge, Mass.: Harvard University Press, 1981.

Cherniak, D., and Feingold, A. *VD Handbook*. Montreal: Montreal Press, 1973.

Chiriboga, D., and Thurnher, M. *Journal of Divorce*, 1980, 3, 379–390.

Christopher, F., and Cate, R. Factors involved in premarital decisionmaking. *Journal of Sex Research*, 1984, 20, 363–376.

Chvapil, M, and Droegemueller, V. Collagen sponge in gynecologic use. *Obstetrics and Gynecology Annual*, 1981, 10, 363–73.

Clanton, G. and Smith, L. *Jealousy*. Englewood Cliffs, N.J.: Prentice-Hall, 1977.

Clappison, V. Anorexia nervosa and related eating disorders. Unpublished manuscript, Jan. 30, 1981.

Clark, D. *Loving Someone Gay*. Millbrae, Calif.: Celestial Arts, 1977.

———. *Living Gay*. Millbrae, Calif.: Celestial Arts, 1979.

Clark, J., Smith, E., and Davidson, J. Enhancement of sexual motivation in male rats by yohimbine. *Science*, 1984, 225, 847–849.

Clarke, G. In the middle of a war. *Time*, Aug. 12, 1985, 46.

Clarke, J. The unmarried marrieds: The meaning of the relationship. In J. Eshleman and J. Clarke (Eds). *Intimacy, Commitment, and Marriage*. Boston: Allyn and Bacon, 1978.

Clarren, S., and Smith, D. The fetal alcohol syndrome. *New England Journal of Medicine*, 1978, 298, 1063–1067.

Cleek, M., and Pearson, T. Perceived causes of divorce: An analysis of interrelationships. *Journal of Marriage and the Family*, 1985, 47, 179–183.

Clement, U., and Pfäfflin, F. Changes in personality scores among couples subsequent to sex therapy. *Archives of Sexual Behavior*, 1980, 9, 235–244.

Clifford, R. Development of masturbation in college women. *Archives of Sexual Behavior*, 1978, 7, 559–573.

Cochran, W., Mosteller, F., and Tukey, J. *Statistical Problems of the Kinsey Report on Sexual Behavior in the Human Male*. Washington, D.C.: The American Statistical Association, 1954.

Coen, S. Sexual interviewing, evaluation, and therapy: Psychoanalytic emphasis on the use of sexual fantasy. *Archives of Sexual Behavior*, 1978, 7, 229–241.

Cohen, B. *Deviant Street Networks*. Lexington, Mass.: Lexington Books, 1980.

Cohen, D., and Rose, R. Male adolescent birth control behavior: The importance of developmental factors and sex differences. *Journal of Youth and Adolescence*, 1984, 13, 239–252.

Cohen, P. Resistance during sexual assaults: Avoiding rape and injury. *Victimology*, 1984, 9, 120–129.

Coleman, E., and Edwards, B. *Brief Encounters*. New York: Anchor Books, 1980.

Collins, G., and Kinder, B. Adjustment following surgical implantation of a penile prosthesis: A critical overview. *Journal of Sex and Marital Therapy*, 1984, 10, 255–271.

Comfort, A. *Sex in Society*. London: Duckworth, 1963.

———. *The Joy of Sex*. New York: Crown, 1972.

Commission on Obscenity and Pornography. *The Report of the Commission on Obscenity and Pornography*. New York: Bantam, 1970.

Commission on Population Growth and the American Future. *Population and the American Future*. Washington, D.C.: U.S. Government Printing Office, 1972.

Communicable Disease Summary. AIDS update. Oregon Health Division, Nov. 1985, 34, 1–3.

Conant, M., Hardy, D., Sernatinger, J., Spicer, D., Levy, J. Condoms prevent transmission of the AIDS-associated retrovirus. *Journal of the American Medical Association* (1986, in press).

Conant, M., Spicer, D., and Smith, C. Herpes simplex virus transmission: Condom studies. *Sexually Transmitted Diseases*, 1984, 11, 94–95.

Connor, J. In *Nova*, The Pinks and the Blues. Boston: WGBH Transcripts, 1980.

Constantine, L. Multilateral relations revisited: Group marriage in extended perspective. In B. Murstein (Ed.), *Exploring Intimate Lifestyles*. New York: Springer, 1978.

———, and Constantine, J. *Group Marriage*. New York: Collier Books, 1973.

Consumer Reports. Condoms. 1979, 44, 583–589.

Cooke, C., and Dworkin, S. *The Ms. Guide to a Woman's Health*. New York: Anchor Books, 1979.

Coreil, J., and Parcel, G. Sociocultural determinants of parental involvement in sex education. *Journal of Sex Education and Therapy*, 1983, 9, 22–25.

Cos, L., Valvo, J., Davis, R., and Cockett, A. Vasovasostomy: Current state of the art. *Urology*, 1983, 22, 567–575.

Cotten-Houston, A., and Wheeler, K. Preorgasmic group treatment: Assertiveness, marital adjustment and sexual function in women. *Journal of Sex and Marital Therapy*, 1983, 9, 296–302.

Cowan, M., Hellman, D., Chudwin, D., Wara, D., Chang, R., and Ammann, A. Maternal transmission of acquired immune deficiency syndrome. *Pediatrics*, 1984, 73, 382–386.

Cox, C. Second marriages: Better while they last. *Psychology Today*, Feb. 1983, 72.

Cox, D. Menstrual symptoms in college students: A controlled study. *Journal of Behavioral Medicine*, 1983, 6, 335–338.

Cramer, D., Schiff, I., Schoenbaum, S., Gibson, M., Belisle, S., Albrecht, B., Stillman, R., Berger, M., Wilson, E., Stadel, B., and Seibel, M. Tubal infertility and the intrauterine device. *New England Journal of Medicine*, 1985, 312, 941–947.

Crenshaw, T. Medical causes of sexual dysfunction. Paper presented at the American AASECT 1984 Regional Conference, Las Vegas, Nev., Oct. 25–28, 1984.

———. Effects of psychotropic drugs in sexual functioning. Paper presented at the 28th Annual Meeting of the Society for the Scientific Study of Sex, San Diego, Calif., Sept. 19–22, 1985.

Crocket, Takihara H., and Cosentino, M. The varicocele. *Fertility and Sterility*, 1984, 41, 5–11.

Crooks, R. Sexual attitudes and behaviors among a population of college students. Unpublished research, 1986a.

———. Incidence of rape victimization among female college students enrolled in human sexuality courses. Unpublished research, 1986b.

Crum, C., and Ellner, P. Chlamydia infections: Making the diagnosis. *Contemporary Obstetrics and Gynecology*, 1985, 25, 153–159; 163; 165; 168.

Csikzentmihalyi, M. Love and the dynamics of personal growth. In K. Pope (Ed.), *On Love and Loving*. San Francisco: Jossey-Bass, 1980.

Cummings, E. *e. e. cummings: a selection of poems*. New York: Harcourt, Brace, and World, 1961.

Curran, J. Economic consequences of pelvic inflammatory disease. *American Journal of Obstetrics and Gynecology*, 1980, 138, 848–851.

———. Paper presented at an international conference on AIDS, Atlanta, Ga., Apr. 1985.

Current Population Reports. Marital status and living arrangements: March 1984. U.S. Department of Commerce, Bureau of the Census, July 1985.

Cvetkovich, G., Grote, B., Lieberman, J., and Miller, W. Sex role development and teenage fertility-related behavior. *Adolescence*, 1978, 13, 231–236.

Dailey, D. The pregnant male. *Journal of Sex Education and Therapy*, 1978, 4, 43–44.

Dailey, J. Women and orgasm: Breakthrough discovery. *Sexology Today*, Apr. 1981, 17–20.

Daling, J., Weiss, N., Metch, B., Chow, W., Soderstrom, R., Moore, D., Spadoni, L., and Stadel, B. Primary tubal infertility in relation to the use of an intrauterine device. *New England Journal of Medicine*, 1984, 312, 937–941.

Daniel, D., Abernethy, V., and Oliver, W. Correlations between female sex roles and attitudes toward male sexual dysfunction in thirty women. *Journal of Sex and Marital Therapy*, 1984, 10, 160–169.

Davenport, W. Sexual patterns and their regulation in a society of the Southwest Pacific. In F. Beach (Ed.), *Sex and Behavior*. New York: John Wiley, 1965.

———. Sex in cross-cultural perspective. In F. Beach (Ed.), *Human Sexuality in Four Perspectives*. Baltimore, Md.: Johns Hopkins Press, 1978.

David, H. Psychological studies in abortion. In J. Fawcett (Ed.), *Psychological Perspectives on Population*. New York: Basic Books, 1973.

———. Incentives, fertility behavior, and integrated community development: An overview. Bethesda, Md.: Transnational Family Research Institute, Jan. 1980.

Davidson, J. Response to "Hormones and human sexual behavior" by John Bancroft, M.D. *Journal of Sex and Marital Therapy*, 1984, 10, 23–27.

Davis, K. Sex on campus: Is there a revolution? *Medical Aspects of Human Sexuality*, 1971, 5, 128–142.

———. Near and dear: Friendship and love compared. *Psychology Today*, Feb. 1985, 22–30.

Davis, N. Prostitution: Identity, career, and legal-economic enterprise. In J. Henslin and E. Sagarin (Eds.), *Studies in the Sociology of Sex*. New York: Schocken Books, 1978.

Dawson, K. Serving the older gay community. *SIECUS Report*, 1982, 11, 5–6.

De Amicis, L., Goldberg, D., LoPiccolo, J., Friedman, J., and Davies, L. Three-year follow-up of couples evaluated for sexual dysfunction. *Journal of Sex and Marital Therapy*, 1984, 10, 215–228.

Debrovner, C., and Shubin-Stein, R. Sexual problems associated with infertility. *Medical Aspects of Human Sexuality*, Mar. 1976, 161–162.

Degler, C. *At Odds: Women and the Family in America from the Revolution to the Present*. Oxford: Oxford University Press, 1980.

Deitch, C. Ideology and opposition to abortion: Trends in public opinion, 1972–1980. *Alternative Lifestyles*, 1983, 6, 6–26.

Delameter, J., and MacCorquodale, P. *Premarital Sexuality: Attitudes, Relationships, Behavior*. Madison, Wis.: University of Wisconsin Press, 1979.

Delaney, J., Lupton, M., and Toth, E. *The Curse, A Cultural History of Menstruation*. New York: E.P. Dutton, 1976.

DeLatiner, B. The teenage pregnancy epidemic. *McCall's*, July 1978, 45.

Delgado, J. *Physical Control of the Mind*. New York: Harper & Row, 1969.

Delin, Bart. *The Sex Offender*. Boston: Beacon Press, 1978.

Delson, N., and Clark, M. Group therapy with sexually molested children. *Child Welfare*, 1981, 50, 161–174.

DeMaris, A., and Leslie, G. Cohabitation with the future spouse: Its influence upon marital satisfaction and communication. *Journal of Marriage and the Family*, 1984, 46, 77–84.

DeMartino, M. How women want men to make love. *Sexology*, October 1970, 4–7.

Demetriou, E., Sackett, R., Welch, D., and Kaplan, D. Evaluation of an enzyme immunoassay for detection of *Neisseria gonorrhoeae* in an adolescent population. *The Journal of the American Medical Association*, 1984, 252, 247–250.

Demsky, L. The use of Depo-Provera in the treatment of sex offenders. *The Journal of Legal Medicine*, 1984, 5, 295–322.

Dennerstein, L., Burrows, G., Wood, C., and Hyman, G. Hormones and sexuality: The effects of estrogen and progestagen. *Obstetrics and Gynecology*, 1980, 56, 316–322.

———, Spencer-Gardner, C., and Burrows, G. Mood and the menstrual cycle. *Journal of Psychiatric Research*, 1984, 18, 1–12.

———, Wood, C., and Burrows, G. Sexual response following hysterectomy and oophorectomy. *Obstetrics and Gynecology*, 1977, 49, 92–96.

Denny, N., Field, J., and Quadagno, D. Sex differences in sexual needs and desires. *Archives of Sexual Behavior*, 1984, 13, 233–245.

Deno, D. Sex differences in cognition: A review and critique of the longitudinal evidence. *Adolescence*, 1982, 17, 779–788.

Derogatis, L., Meyer, J., and Gallant, B. Distinctions between male and female invested partners in sexual disorders. *American Journal of Psychiatry*, 1977, 134, 385–390.

Deschin, C. Teenagers and venereal disease: A sociological study of 600 teenagers in NYC social hygiene clinics. *American Journal of Nursing*, 1963, 63, 63–67.

Dew, M. The effect of attitudes on inferences of homosexuality and perceived physical attractiveness in women. *Sex Roles*, 1985, 12, 143–155.

Dhabuwala, C., Ghayad, P., Smith, J., and Pierce, J. Penile calibration for nocturnal penile tumescence studies. *Urology*, 1983, 22, 614–616.

Diamond, M. Human sexual development: Biological foundations for social development. In F. Beach (Ed.), *Human Sexuality in Four Perspectives*. Baltimore, Md.: Johns Hopkins Press, 1977.

———. Sexual identity and sex roles. In V. Bullough (Ed.), *The Frontiers of Sex Research*. Buffalo, N.Y.: Prometheus Press, 1979.

———. Sexual identity, monozygotic twins reared in discordant sex roles and a BBC follow-up. *Archives of Sexual Behavior*, 1982, 11, 181–186.

———, Johnson, R., and Ehlert, J. Comparison of cortical thickness in male and female rats: Normal and gonadectomized young and adult. *Behavioral and Neural Biology*, 1979, 26, 485–491.

——— and Karlen, A. *Sexual Decisions*. Boston: Little, Brown, 1980.

Díaz, S., Peralta, O., Juez, G., Herreros, C., Casado, M., Salvatierra, A., Miranda, P., and Croxatto, H. Fertility regulation in nursing women: VI. Contraceptive effectiveness of a subdermal progesterone input. *Contraception*, 1984, 30, 311–325.

Dickinson, R. *Atlas of Human Sex Anatomy*. Baltimore, Md. Anatomy: Williams and Wilkins, 1949.

Dick-Read, G. *Childbirth Without Fear*, 2d rev. ed. New York: Harper & Row, 1959.

Dion, K., Bersheid, E., and Walster, E. What is beautiful is good. *Journal of Personality and Social Psychology*, 1972, 24, 285–290.

DiVasto, P., Kaufman, A., Rosner, L., Jackson, R., Christy, J., Pearson, S., and Burgett, T. The prevalence of sexually stressful events among females in the general population. *Archives of Sexual Behavior*, 1984, 13, 59–67.

Dixen, J., Maddever, H., Van Maasdam, J., and Edwards, P. Psychosocial characteristics of applicants evaluated for surgical gender reassignment. *Archives of Sexual Behavior*, 1984, 13, 269–276.

———. Bisexual panel presentation at the Society for the Scientific Study of Sex Western Regional Conference, Palm Springs, Calif., Jan. 12, 1985.

Dodson, B. *Liberating Masturbation*. New York: Betty Dodson, 1974.

Dohanich, G., and Ward, I. Sexual behavior in male rats following intracerebral estrogen application. *Journal of Comparative and Physiological Psychology*, 1980, 94, 634–640.

Donnerstein, E., and Berkowitz, L. Victim reactions in aggressive erotic films as a factor in violence against women. *Journal of Personality and Social Psychology*, 1981, 41, 710–724.

————, and Linz, D. Sexual violence in the media: A warning. *Psychology Today*, Jan. 1984, 14–15.

————, and ————. Paper presented at a hearing of the Attorney General's Commission on Pornography, Houston, Tex., Sept. 12, 1985.

Donovan, P. The holy war. *Family Planning Perspectives*, 1985, 17, 5–9.

Dorfman, R., and Shipley, T. *Androgens: Biochemistry, Physiology and Clinical Significance*. New York: John Wiley, 1956.

Dörner, G. *Hormones and Brain Differentiation*. Amsterdam: Elsevier Publishing Co., 1976.

————. Sex-hormone-dependent brain differentiation and reproduction. In J. Money and H. Musaph (Eds.), *Handbook of Sexology*. New York: Elsevier/North-Holland Biomedical Press, 1977.

————, Rohde, W., Stahl, F., Krell, L., and Masius, W. A neuroendocrine predisposition for homosexuality in men. *Archives of Sexual Behavior*, 1975, 4, 1–8.

Doty, R., Ford, M., Preti, G., and Huggins, G. Changes in the intensity and pleasantness of human vaginal odors during the menstrual cycle. *Science*, 1975, 190, 1316–1318.

Douglas, J., Critchlow, M., Benedetti, J., Mertz, G., Connor, J., Hintz, M., Fahnlander, A., Reminton, M., Winter, C., and Corey, L. A double-blind study of oral acyclovir for suppression of recurrences of genital herpes simplex infection. *The New England Journal of Medicine*, 1984, 310, 1551–1556.

Dover, K. *Greek Homosexuality*. Cambridge, Mass.: Harvard University Press, 1978.

Dow, M., Hart, D., Forrest, C. Hormonal treatments of unresponsiveness in post-menopausal women: A comparative study. *British Journal of Obstetrics and Gynecology*, 1983, 90, 361–366.

Downey, L. Intergenerational change in sex behavior. A belated look at Kinsey's males. *Archives of Sexual Behavior*, 1980, 9, 267–317.

Doyle, J. *Sex and Gender*. Dubuque, Iowa: William C. Brown, 1985.

Doyle, R. American Library Association Office of Intellectual Freedom. Personal correspondence, 1982.

Dressel, P., and Avant, W. Range of alternatives. In R. Weg (Ed.), *Sexuality in the Later Years: Roles and Behavior*. New York: Academic Press, 1983.

Droegemueller, W. Pelvic inflammatory disease: Changing management concepts. *Drug Therapy*, June 1984, 131–147.

Duggan, L., Hunter, N., and Vance, C. False promises: New antipornography legislation in the U.S. *SIECUS Report*, 1985, 13, 1–5.

Dupont, V. and Page, D. Risk factors for breast cancer in women with proliferative breast disease. *The New England Journal of Medicine*, 1985, 312, 146–151.

Dutton, D., and Aron, A. Some evidence for heightened sexual attraction under conditions of high anxiety. *Journal of Personality and Social Psychology*, 1974, 30, 510–517.

Dweck, C. Sex differences in the meaning of negative evaluation in achievement situations: Determinants and consequences. Paper presented at a meeting of the Society for Research in Child Development, Denver, Colo., Apr. 1975.

Dworkin, A. *Pornography: On Men Possessing Women*. New York: Perigee Books, 1979.

Eastman, N., and Hellman, L. *Williams' Obstetrics*, 12th ed. New York: Appleton-Century-Crofts, 1961.

Edgerton, M. The role of surgery in the treatment of transsexualism. *Annals of Plastic Surgery*, 1984, 13, 473–476.

Edmiston, S. How to write your own marriage contract. *Ms.*, Spring 1972, 66.

Ehrhardt, A. Prenatal androgenization and human psychosexual behavior. In J. Money and H. Musaph (Eds.), *Handbook of Sexology*. New York: Elsevier/North-Holland Biomedical Press, 1977.

Elias, J., and Gebhard, P. Sexuality and sexual learning in childhood. *Phi Delta Kappan*, 1969, 50, 401–405.

Elias, S. and Annas, G. Social policy considerations in noncoital reproduction. *Journal of the American Medical Society*, 1986, 255, 62–68.

Ellis, A. *Sex Without Guilt*. Secaucus, N.J.: Lyle Stuart, 1966.

Ellis, H. *Studies in the Psychology of Sex*. New York: Random House, 1906.

Ellison, C. A critique of the clitoral model of female sexuality. Paper presented to the American Psychological Association, Montreal, Sept. 4, 1980.

Embrey, M. Oxytocins and the uterus. In E. Phillip, J. Barnes, and M. Newton (Eds.), *Scientific Foundations of Obstetrics and Gynecology*. Chicago: William Heinemann, 1977.

Emick-Herring, B. Sexual changes in patients and partners following stroke. *Rehabilitation Nursing*, 1985, 10, 28–30.

Ende, J., Rockwell, S., and Glasgow, M. The sexual history in general medical practice. *Archives of Internal Medicine*, 1984, 144, 558–561.

Erikson, E. Youth and the life cycle. In D. Hamachek (Ed.), *The Self in Growth, Teaching and Learning*. Englewood Cliffs, N.J.: Prentice-Hall, 1965.

Essex, M. Paper presented at an international conference on AIDS, Atlanta, Ga., April 1985.

Fagot, B. The influence of sex of child on parental reactions to toddler children. *Child Development*, 1978, 49, 459–465.

Falk, G., and Falk, U. Sexuality and the aged. *Nursing Outlook*, 1980, 28, 51–55.

Fallon, B., Miller, R., and Gerber, W. Non-microscopic vasovasostomy. *Journal of Urology*, 1981, 126, 361.

Faro, S. *Chlamydia trachomatis* infection in women. *The Journal of Reproductive Medicine*, 1985, 30 supplement, 273–278.

Faux, M. *Childless by Choice*. New York: Anchor Press, 1984.

Fein, G., Johnson, D., Kesson, N., Stork, L., and Wasserman, L. Sex stereotypes and preferences in the toy choices of 20 month old boys and girls. *Developmental Psychology*, 1975, 11, 527–528.

Feldman-Summers, S., and Jones, G. Psychological impacts of sexual contact between therapists and other health care practitioners and their clients. *Journal of Consulting and Clinical Psychology*, 1984, 52, 1054–1061.

———, and Norris, J. Differences between rape victims who report and those who do not report to a public agency. *Journal of Applied Psychology*, 1984, 14, 562–573.

Ferenczy, A. Laser therapy of genital condylomata acuminata. *Obstetrics and Gynecology*, 1984, 63, 703–705.

Fielding, J. Adolescent pregnancy revisited. *New England Journal of Medicine*, 1978, 299, 893–896.

Fink, P. Sexually unresponsive husbands. *Medical Aspects of Human Sexuality*, 1984, 18, 157.

Finkelhor, D. *Sexually Victimized Children*. New York: The Free Press, 1979.

———. Sex among siblings: A survey on prevalence, variety, and effects. *Archives of Sexual Behavior*, 1980, 9, 171–194.

———. *Child Sexual Abuse: Theory and Research*. New York: The Free Press, 1984a.

———. The prevention of child sexual abuse: An overview of needs and problems. *SIECUS Report*, 1984b, 13, 1–5.

Fish, L., Fish, R., and Sprenkle, D. Treating inhibited sexual desire: A marital therapy approach. *American Journal of Family Therapy*, 1984, 12, 3–12.

Fisher, B., Bauer, M., Margolese, R., Poisson, R., Pilch, Y., Redmond, C., Fisher, E., Wolmark, N., Deutsch, M., Montague, E., Saffer, E., Wickerham, L., Lerner, H., Glass, A., Shibata, H., Deckers, P., Ketcham, A., Oishi, R., and Russell, I. Five-year results of a randomized clinical trial comparing total mastectomy and segmental mastectomy with or without radiation in the treatment of breast cancer. *The New England Journal of Medicine*, 1985, 312, 665–673.

Fisher, C., Gross, J., and Zuch, J. Cycle of penile erection synchronous with dreaming (REM) sleep. *Archives of General Psychology*, 1965, 12, 29–45.

Fisher, W. Gender, gender role identification, and response to erotica. In E. Allgeier and N. McCormick (Eds.), *Changing Boundaries: Gender Roles and Sexual Behavior*. Palo Alto, Calif: Mayfield, 1983.

Fitzgerald, F. The classic venereal diseases: Syphilis and gonorrhea in the 80s. *Postgraduate Medicine*, 1984, 75, 91–98; 100–101.

Flaherty, J., and Dusek, J. An investigation of the relationship between psychological androgyny and components of self-concept. *Journal of Personality and Social Psychology*, 1980, 38, 984–992.

Fleming, M., Cohen, D., Salt, P., Jones, D., and Jenkins, S. A study of pre- and postsurgical transsexuals: MMPI characteristics. *Archives of Sexual Behavior*, 1981, 10, 161–170.

Ford, C., and Beach, F. *Patterns of Sexual Behavior*. New York: Harper & Row, 1951.

Foreman, H., Stade, B., and Schlesselman, S. Intrauterine device usage and fetal loss. *Obstetrics and Gynecology*, 1981, 58, 669–677.

Forgac, G., Cassel, C., and Michaels, E. Chronicity of criminal behaviors and psychopathology in male exhibitionists. *Journal of Clinical Psychology*, 1984, 40, 827–832.

——— and Michaels, E. Personality characteristics of two types of male exhibitionists. *Journal of Abnormal Psychology*, 1982, 91, 287–293.

Foster, A. Relationships between age and sexual activity in married men. *Journal of Sex Education and Therapy*, 1979, 5, 21–26.

Fox, G. The mother-adolescent daughter relationship as a sexual socialization structure: a research review. *Family Relations*, 1980, 29, 21–28.

Franceschi, S., LaVecchia, C., Parazzini, F., Fasoli, M., Regallo, M., Decarli, A., Gallus, G., and Tognoni, G. Oral contraceptives and benign breast disease: a care-control study. *American Journal of Obstetrics and Gynecologists*, 1984, 149, 602–606.

Francis, D., Hadler, S., Prendergast, T., Peterson, E., Ginsberg, M., Lookabaugh, C., Holmes, J., and Maynard, J. Occurences of hepatitis A, B, and non-A non-B in the United States: CDC sentinel county hepatitis study I. *The American Journal of Medicine*, 1984, 76, 69–74.

Frank, D., Dornbush, R., Webster, S., amd Kolodny, R. Mastectomy and sexual behavior: A pilot study. *Sexuality and Disability*, 1978, 1, 16–26.

Frank, E., Anderson, C., and Rubinstein, D. Frequency of sexual dysfunction in "normal" couples. *New England Journal of Medicine*, 1978, 299, 111–115.

———, ———, and ———. Marital role strain and sexual satisfaction, *Journal of Consulting and Clinical Psychology*, 1979, 47, 1096–1103.

———, and Enos, S. The love life of the American wife. *Ladies Home Journal*, Feb. 1983, 71–73, 116–119.

Fraser, I., Radonic, I., and Clancy, R. Successful pregnancy after occlusion therapy for high-titre sperm antibodies. *Medical Journal of Australia*, 1980, 1, 324–325.

Fraunfelder, F. Ocular herpes. Paper presented at the Herpes Symposium, Oregon Health Sciences University, Portland, Oreg., April 2, 1982.

Freeman, E., Rickels, K., Huggins, G., Celso-Ramon, G., and Polin, G. Emotional distress patterns among women having first or repeat abortions. *Obstetrics and Gynecology*, 1980, 55, 630–636.

Freud, S. Three essays on the theory of sexuality. In *Standard Edition*, Vol. VII. London: Hogarth Press, 1953. Originally published in 1905.

Friday, N. *My Secret Garden*. New York: Simon & Schuster, 1973.

———. *Men in Love*. New York: Delacorte, 1980.

Friedland, G., Saltzman, B., Rogers, M., Kahl, P., Lesser, M., Mayers, M., and Klein, R. Lack of transmission of HTLV-III/LAV infection to household contacts of patients with AIDS or AIDS-related complex with oral candidiasis. *The New England Journal of Medicine*, 1986, 344–349.

Friedman, R., Hurt, S., Arnoff, M., and Clarkin, J. Behavior and the menstrual cycle. *Signs*, 1980, 5, 719–738.

Friedrich, E. Vaginitis. *American Journal of Obstetrics and Gynecology*, 1985, 152, 247–251.

Friends Home Service Committee. *Towards a Quaker View of Sex*. London: Friends House, 1963.

Frisch, R., and McArthur, J. Menstrual cycles: Fatness as a determinant of minimum weight for height necessary for their maintenance or onset. *Science*, 1974, 185, 949–951.

———, Wyshak, G., and Vincent, L. Delayed menarche and amenorrhea in ballet dancers. *New England Journal of Medicine*, 1980, 303, 17–19.

Fromm, E. *The Ability to Love*. New York: Farrar, Straus and Giroux, 1965.

Furlow, R. Blood banks cite AIDS fear for drop-off. *The Oregonian*, Jan. 10, 1986, A8.

Furniss, T. Conflict-avoiding and conflict-regulating patterns in incest and child sexual abuse. *Acta Paedopsychiatrica*, 1985, 50, 299–313.

Furstenberg, F. Family communication and teenagers' contraceptive use. *Family Planning Perspectives*, 1984, 16, 163–170.

Furstenberg, F., Menchen, J., and Lincoln, R. *Teenage Sexuality, Pregnancy, and Childbearing*. Philadelphia: University of Pennsylvania Press, 1981.

Gadpaille, W. *The Cycles of Sex*. New York: Scribner, 1975.

Gaffney, G., Luries, S., and Berlin, F. Is there familial transmission of pedophilia? *The Journal of Nervous and Mental Disease*, 1984, 172, 546–548.

Gagnon, J. *Human Sexualities*. Glenview, Ill.: Scott, Foresman, 1977.

———. Attitudes and responses of parents to preadolescent masturbation. *Archives of Sexual Behavior*, 1985, 14, 451–466.

Gaitwell, N., Loriaux, D., and Chase, T. Plasma testosterone in homosexual and heterosexual women. *American Journal of Psychiatry*, 1977, 134, 117–119.

Gambrell, D. Proposal to decrease the risk and improve the prognosis of breast cancer. *American Journal of Obstetrics and Gynecology*, 1984, 150, 119–132.

Garcia, L. Sex-role orientation and stereotypes about male-female sexuality. *Sex Roles*, 1982, 8, 863–876.

Gardner, E., and Johnston, J. Bupropion: An antidepressent without sexual pathophysiological action. *Journal of Clinical Psychopharmacology*, 1985, 5, 24–29.

Gardner, L., and Neu, R. Evidence linking an extra Y chromosome to sociopathic behavior. *Archives of General Psychiatry*, 1972, 26, 220–222.

Gartrell, N., and Mosbacher, D. Sex differences in the naming of children's genitalia. *Sex Roles*, 1984, 10, 869–876.

Garza-Flores, J., Diaz-Sanchez, V., Jimenez-Thomas, S., and Rudel, H. Development of a low-dose monthly injectable contraceptive system: I. Choice of compounds, dose and administration route. *Contraception*, 1984, 30, 371–379.

Gebhard, P. Situational factors affecting human sexual behavior. In F. Beach (Ed.), *Sex and Behavior*. New York: Wiley, 1965.

———. Factors in marital orgasm. *Journal of Social Issues*, 1966, 22, 88–95.

———. Postmarital coitus among widows and divorcees. In P. Bohannan (Ed.), *Divorce and After*. New York: Doubleday, 1970.

———. Human sexual behavior: A summary statement. In D. Marshall and R. Suggs (Eds.), *Human Sexual Behavior: Variations in the Ethnographic Spectrum*. Englewood Cliffs, N.J.: Prentice-Hall, 1971.

———. The acquisition of basic sex information. *Journal of Sex Research*, 1977, 13, 148–169.

———, Gagnon, J., Pomeroy, W., and Christenson, C. *Sex Offenders: An Analysis of Types*. New York: Harper & Row, 1965.

Geer, J., and O'Donohue, W. Premature ejaculation: Investigation of factors in ejaculatory latency. *Journal of Abnormal Psychology*, 1984, 93, 242–245.

Georgakopoulos, P., Dodos, D., and Mechleris, D. Sexuality in pregnancy and premature labor. *British Journal of Obstetrics and Gyneacology*, 1984, 91, 891–893.

George, L., and Weiler, S. Sexuality in middle and late life. *Archives of General Psychiatry*, 1981, 38, 919–923.

Geschwind, N., and Behan, P. Left-handedness: Association with immune disease, migraine, and developmental learning disorder. *Proceedings of the National Academy of Science, USA*, 1982, 79, 5097–5100.

Gibb, G., and Millard, R. Research on repeated abortion: State of the field. *Psychological Reports*, 1981, 48, 415–424.

Gilbaugh, J., and Fuchs, P. The gonococcus and the toilet seat. *New England Journal of Medicine*, 1979, 301, 91–93.

Gillespie, L. The diaphragm: An accomplice in recurrent urinary tract infections. *Urology*, 1984, 24, 25–30.

Gilmartin, B. Swinging: Who gets involved and how? In R. Libby and R. Whitehurst (Eds.), *Marriage and Alternatives: Exploring Intimate Relationships*. Glenview, Ill.: Scott, Foresman, 1977.

Ginsberg, G., Frosch, W., and Shapiro, T. The new impotence. *Archives of General Psychiatry*, 1972, 26, 218–220.

Gladue, B., Green, R., and Hellman, R. Neuroendocrine response to estrogen and sexual orientation. *Science*, 1983, 225, 1496–1499.

Glass, R., and Ericsson, R. *Getting Pregnant in the 1980s*. Berkeley, Calif.: University of California Press, 1982.

Glick, P., and Norton, A. *1979 Update: Marrying, Divorcing, and Living Together in the U.S. Today*. Washington, D.C.: Population Reference Bureau, 1979.

Gochros, H. Counseling gay husbands. *Journal of Sex Education and Therapy*, 1978, 4, 6–10.

Goedert, J., Biggar, R., Winn, D., Greene, M., Weiss, S., Grossman, R., Strong, D., and Blattner, W. Determinants of retrovirus (HTLV-III) antibody and immunodeficiency conditions in homosexual men. *The Lancet*, Sept. 29, 1984, 711–715.

———, Biggar, R., Winn, D., Mann, D., Byar, D., Strong, D., DiGioia, R., Grossman, R., Sanchez, W., Kase, R., Greene, M., Hoover, R., and Blattner, W. Decreased helper T lymphocytes in homosexual men: Sexual practices. *American Journal of Epidemiology*, 1985, 121, 637–644.

Goepp, R. Personal communication, Apr. 1982.

Goethals, G. Love, marriage, and mutual growth. In K. Pope (Ed.), *On Love and Loving*. San Francisco: Jossey-Bass, 1980.

Golbus, M., Loughman, W., Epstein, C., Halbasch, G., Stephens, J., and Hall, B. Prenatal genetic diagnosis in 3000 amniocenteses. *New England Journal of Medicine*, 1979, 300, 157–163.

Goldberg, C. Controlled trial of 'intervir-A' in herpes simplex virus infection. *The Lancet*, 1986, 1, 703–706.

Goldberg, D., Whipple, B., Fishkin, R., Waxman, H., Fink, P., and Weisberg, M. The Grafenberg spot and female ejaculation: a review of initial hypotheses. *Journal of Sex and Marital Therapy*, 1983, 9, 27–37.

Goldberg, M., Edmonds, L., and Oakley, G. Reducing birth defect risk in advanced maternal age. *Journal of the American Medical Association*, 1979, 242, 2292–2294.

Goldberg, P. Are women prejudiced against women? *Transaction*, Apr. 1968, 28–30.

Goldenring, J., and Purtell, E. Knowledge of testicular cancer risk and need for self-examination in college students: A call for equal time for men in teaching of early cancer detection techniques. *Pediatrics*, 1984, 1093–1096.

Goldsmith, M. Modifications in prostate cancer operation preserve potency. *Journal of the American Medical Association*, 1983, 250, 2897–2899.

Goldstein, I., Davidson, M., de Tejada, I., Heeren, T., Siroky, M., Sax, D., and Krane, R. Dorsal nerve impotence: A clinical study using neurological somatosensory evoked potential testing. *Journal of Urology*, 1985, 133, 187A.

Goldstein, M., and Kant, H. *Pornography and Sexual Deviance*. Berkeley, Calif.: University of California Press, 1973.

Gomes-Schwartz, B., Horowitz, J., and Sauzier, M. Severity of emotional distress among sexually abused preschool, school-age, and adolescent children. *Hospital and Community Psychiatry*, 1985, 36, 503–508.

Gordon, J., and Gorski, R. Sexual differentiation of the brain—implications for neuroscience. In D. Schneider (Ed.), *Reviews of Neuroscience*, Vol. 4. New York: Raven Press, 1979.

Gordon, S. *The Sexual Adolescent*. North Scituate, Mass.: Duxbury Press, 1973.

Gorer, G. *Himalayan Village*. London: Michael Joseph Ltd., 1938.

Gottman, J., Notarius, C., Gonso, J., and Markman, H. *A Couple's Guide to Communication*. Champaign, Ill.: Research Press, 1976.

Goy, R. Experimental control of psychosexuality. *Philosophical Transactions of the Royal Society of London Biological*, 1970, 259, 149–162.

Grafenberg, E. The role of urethra in female orgasm. *International Journal of Sexology*, 1950, 3, 145–148.

Granberg, D., and Granberg, B. Abortion attitudes, 1965–1980: Trends and determinants. *Family Planning Perspectives*, 1980, 12, 250–261.

Gray, C. Pornography and violent entertainment: Exposing the symptoms. *Canadian Medical Association Journal*, 1984, 130, 769–772.

Great Britain Committee on Homosexual Offenses and Prostitution. *The Wolfenden Report* (American edition). New York: Stein and Day, 1963.

Green, R. *Sexual Identity Conflict in Children and Adults.* New York: Basic Books, 1974.

———. Sexual identity of 37 children raised by homosexual or transsexual parents. *American Journal of Psychiatry*, 1978, 135, 692–697.

———. Adults who want to change sex; adolescents who cross-dress; and children called "sissy" and "tomboy." In R. Green (Ed.), *Human Sexuality: A Health Practitioner's Text*, 2nd ed. Baltimore, Md.: Williams and Wilkins, 1979.

———. Exposure to explicit sexual materials and sexual assault: A review of behavioral and social science research. Paper presented at a hearing of the Attorney General's Commission on Pornography, Houston, Tex., Sept. 12, 1985.

———, Mandel, J., Hotvedt, M., Gray, J., and Smith, L. Lesbian mothers and their children: A comparison with solo parent heterosexual mothers and their children. *Archives of Sexual Behavior*, 1986, 15, 167–184.

Greenbank, R. Are medical students learning psychiatry? *Pennsylvania Medical Journal*, 1961, 64, 989–992.

Greene, B., Lee, R., and Lustig, N. Conscious and unconscious factors in marital infidelity. *Medical Aspects of Human Sexuality*, 1974, 8, 87–105.

Greenwald, H. *The Call Girl.* New York: Ballantine Books, 1958.

———. *The Elegant Prostitute: A Social and Psychoanalytic Study.* New York: Walken, 1970.

Greenwood, S., and Margolis, A. Outercourse. *Advances in Planned Parenthood*, 1981, 15, 4.

Griffiths, P., Merry, J., Browning, M., Eisinger, A., Huntsman, R., Lord, E., Polani, P., Tanner, J., and Whitehouse, R. Homosexual women: An endocrine and psychological study. *Journal of Endocrinology*, 1974, 63, 549–556.

Griffitt, W. Environmental effects on interpersonal behavior: Ambient effective temperature and attraction. *Journal of Personality and Social Psychology*, 1970, 15, 240–244.

Grossman, J. Herpes: Dry lesions may shorten periods of viral shedding. *Sexually Transmitted Diseases Bulletin*, 1981, 1, 4.

Groth, A. *Men Who Rape.* New York: Plenum Press, 1979.

Groth, N. Sexual trauma in the life histories of rapists and child molesters. *Victimology*, 1979, 4, 10–16.

———, and Hobson, W. The dynamics of sexual assault. In L. Schlesinger and E. Revitch (Eds.), *Sexual Dynamics of Anti-Social Behavior*. Springfield, Ill.: Thomas, 1983.

Grundsell, H., Larson, G., and Bekassy, Z. Treatment of condylomata acuminata with the carbon dioxide laser. *British Journal of Obstetrics and Gynecology*, 1984, 91, 193–196.

Guinan, M. Oral acyclovir, palliative therapy for genital herpes: Will it change the epidemiology? *Sexually Transmitted Diseases*, 1985, 12, 55–56.

Gunn, T., and Stenzel-Poore, M. *The Herpes Handbook.* Portland, Ore.: Venereal Disease Action Council, 1981.

Gurel, L. National Gay Task Force. Personal communication, March 1982.

Hagen, R., and D'Agostino, J. Smoking may be hazard to male sexual response. *Brain-Mind Bulletin*, 1982, 7, 3.

Halikas, J., Weller, R., and Morse, C. Effects of regular marihuana use on sexual performance. *Journal of Psychoactive Drugs*, 1982, 14, 59–70.

Hamburg, M. Observations concerning family planning education in China. *SIECUS Report*, 1981, 10, 23–25.

Hamilton, E. *Sex, with Love.* Boston: Beacon Press, 1978.

Hamilton, G. *The Religious Case for Abortion.* Asheville, N.C.: Madison and Polk, 1983.

Hamilton, J. Demonstrable ability of penile erection in castrate men with markedly low titers of urinary androgen. *Proceedings of the Society of Experimental Biology and Medicine*, 1943, 54, 309.

Hampson, J. L., and Hampson, J. G. The ontogenesis of sexual behavior in man. In W. Young (Ed.), *Sex and Internal Secretions*. Baltimore, Md.: Williams and Wilkins, 1961.

Hanckel, F., and Cunningham, J. *A Way of Love, A Way of Life.* New York: Lothrop, Lee & Shepard, 1979.

Hand, J. Surgery of the penis and urethra. In M. Campbell and J. Harrison (Eds.), *Urology*, Vol. 3. Philadelphia: W. B. Saunders, 1970.

Harden, B. Female circumcision: Painful, risky, and little girls beg for it. *Washington Post National Weekly Edition*, July 29, 1985a, 15–16.

———. Tradition stalls progress of Africa's women: Pregnancy, farm work fill their lives. *Oregonian*, July 9, 1985b, A2.

Hardy, A., Rauch, K., Echenberg, D., Morgan, W., and Curran, J. The economic impact of the first 10,000 cases of acquired immunodeficiency syndrome in the United States. *The Journal of the American Medical Association*, 1986, 255, 209–211.

Hare-Mustin, R., and Broderick, P. The myth of motherhood: A study of attitudes toward motherhood. *Psychology of Women Quarterly*, 1979, 4, 114–28.

Harlap, S., Shiono, P., and Ramcharan, S. Spontaneous foetal losses in women using different contraceptives around the time of conception. *International Journal of Epidemiology*, 1980, 9, 49–56.

Harlow, H., and Harlow, M. The effects of rearing conditions on behavior. *Bulletin of the Menninger Clinic*, 1962, 26, 13–24.

Hartman, W., and Fithian, M. *Treatment of Sexual Dysfunction*. New York: Jason Aronson, 1974.

———, and ———. Any man can: Multiple orgasmic response in males. Paper presented at the Regional Conference of the American Association of Sex Educators, Counselors, and Therapists, Las Vegas, Nev., Oct. 1984.

Haseltine, F., and Ohno, S. Mechanisms of gonadal differentiation. *Science*, 1981, 21, 1272–1278.

Hass, A. *Teenage Sexuality*. New York: Macmillan, 1979.

Hasset, J. Sex and smell. *Psychology Today*, Mar. 1978, 40– 45.

Hatch, J. Psychophysiological aspects of sexual dysfunction. *Archives of Sexual Behavior*, 1981, 10, 49–63.

Hatcher, R., Guest, F., Stewart, F., Stewart, G., Trussell, G., Trussell, J., and Frank, E. *Contraceptive Technology 1984–1985*, 12th rev. ed. New York: Irvington, 1984.

———, ———, ———, ———, Trussell, J., Cerel, S., and Cates, W. *Contraceptive Technology 1986–1987*, 13th rev. ed. New York: Irvington, 1986.

———, Stewart, G., Stewart, F., Guest, F., Schwartz, D., and Jones, S. *Contraceptive Technology 1980–1981*, 10th rev. ed. New York: Irvington, 1980.

———, ———, ———, ———, Stratton, P., and Wright, A. *Contraceptive Technology 1978–1979*, 9th rev. ed. New York: Irvington, 1978.

Health, R. Pleasure and brain activity in man. *Journal of Nervous and Mental Disease*, 1972, 154, 3–18.

Heath, D. An investigation into the origins of a copious vaginal discharge during intercourse—"enough to wet the bed"—that "is not urine." *Journal of Sex Research*, 1984, 20, 194–215.

Heider, K. Dani sexuality: A low energy system. *Man*, 1976, 11, 188–201.

Heidrich, F., Berg, A., and Bergman, J. Clothing factors and vaginitis. *Journal of Family Practice*, 1984, 19, 491–494.

Heim, N. Sexual behavior of castrated sex offenders. *Archives of Sexual Behavior*, 1981, 10, 11–19.

Heiman, J. The physiology of erotica: Women's sexual arousal. *Psychology Today*, Apr. 1975, 90–94.

———. Female sexual response patterns. *Archives of General Psychiatry*, 1980, 37, 1311–1316.

———, LoPiccolo, L., and LoPiccolo, J. *Becoming Orgasmic: A Sexual Growth Program for Women*. Englewood Cliffs, N.J.: Prentice-Hall, 1976.

Heimer, L., and Larsson, K. Drastic changes in the mating behavior of male rats following lesions in the junction of diencephalon and mesencephalon. *Experientia*, 1964, 20, 460–461.

Heinrichs, W., and Adamson, G. A practical approach to the patient with dysmenorrhea. *Journal of Reproductive Medicine*, 1980, 25, 236–242.

Hellberg, D., Valentin, J., and Nilsson, S. Smoking as a risk factor in cervical neoplasia. *The Lancet*, December 24–31, 1983, 1497.

Helsinga, K., Schellen, A., and Verkuyl, A. *Not Made of Stone: The Sexual Problems of Handicapped People*. Springfield, Ill.: Charles C. Thomas, 1974.

Henderson, S. Reversal of female sterilization: Comparison of microsurgical and gross surgical techniques for tubal anastomosis. *American Journal of Obstetrics and Gynecology*. 1981, 139, 73–79.

Henshaw, S., Binkin, N., Blaine, E., and Smith, J. A portrait of American women who obtain abortions. *Family Planning Perspectives*, 1985, 17, 90–96.

Herold, E., and Way, L. Oral-genital sexual behavior in a sample of unversity females. *Journal of Sex Research*, 1983, 19, 327–339.

Herrera, A., and Macaraeg, A. Physicians' attitudes toward circumcision. *American Journal of Obstetrics and Gynecology*, 1984, 148, 825.

Heston, L., and Shields, J. Homosexuality in twins. *Archives of General Psychiatry*, 1968, 18, 149–160.

Hill, J., and Kassam, S. Sexual competence in multiple sclerosis. *Female Patient*, 1984, 9, 81–84.

Hingson, R., Alpert, J., Day, N., Dooling, E., Kayne, H., Morelock, S., Oppenheimer, E., and Zuckerman, B. Effects of maternal drinking and marijuana use on fetal growth and development. *Pediatrics*, 1982, 70, 539–546.

Hite, S. *The Hite Report: A Nationwide Study of Female Sexuality*. New York: Dell Books, 1976.

———, *The Hite Report on Male Sexuality*. New York: Knopf, 1981.

Hitt, J., Hendericks, S., Ginsberg, S., and Lewis, J. Disruption of male but not female sexual behavior in rats by medial forebrain bundle lesions. *Journal of Comparative and Physiological Psychology*, 1970, 73, 377–384.

Hobart, C. Changes in courtship and cohabitation in Canada, 1968–1977. In M. Cook and G. Wilson (Eds.), *Love and Attraction*. New York: Pergamon Press, 1979.

Hoeffer, B. Children's acquisition of sex-role behavior in lesbian-mother families. *American Journal of Orthopsychiatry*, 1981, 51, 536–544.

Hoffman, M., and Saltzstein, H. Parent discipline and the child's moral development. *Journal of Personality and Social Psychology*, 1967, 5, 45–57.

Hollender, M. Women's coital fantasies. *Medical Aspects of Human Sexuality*, 1970, 4, 63–70.

Holmes, K. Natural history of herpes: Current trends in treatment. Paper presented at the Herpes Symposium, Oregon Health Sciences University, Portland, Oreg., Apr. 2, 1982.

———, and Stamm, W. Chlamydial genital infections: A growing problem. *Hospital Practice*, Oct. 1979, 105–117.

Hook, E. Rates of chromosome abnormalities at different maternal ages. *Obstetrics and Gynecology*, 1981, 282–284.

Hooker, E. The adjustment of the male overt homosexual. *Journal of Projective Techniques*, 1957, 21, 18–31.

Hoover, R., Gray, L., and Cole, P. Menopausal estrogens and breast cancer. *New England Journal of Medicine*, 1976, 295, 401–405.

Horney, K. *Feminine Psychology*. New York: Norton, 1967.

Hoult, T., Henze, L., and Hudson, J. *Courtship and Marriage in America*. Boston: Little, Brown, 1978.

Howe, B., Kaplan, R., and English, C. Repeat abortions: Blaming the victims. *American Journal of Public Health*, 1979, 69, 1242–46.

Howley, C. The older primipara: Implications for nurses. *Journal of Gynecological Nursing*, 1981, 10, 182–185.

Hoyt, M. Children's accidental exposure to parental coitus. *Medical Aspects of Human Sexuality*, 1982, 1, 64–65.

Hubbard, C. *Family Planning Education*. St. Louis, Mo.: Mosby, 1977.

Hulka, B., Chambless, L., Kaufman, D., Fowler, W., and Greenberg, B. Protection against endometrial carcinoma by combination-product oral contraceptives. *Journal of the American Medical Association*, 1982, 247, 475–477.

Hunt, M. *Sexual Behavior in the 1970s*. Chicago: Playboy Press, 1974.

———, and Hunt, B. *The Divorce Experience*. New York: Signet, 1977.

Hurley, T. Constitutional implications of sex-change operations. *The Journal of Legal Medicine*, 1984, 5, 633–664.

Hutt, C. *Male and Female*. New York: Penguin, 1973.

Hyde, J. *Half the Human Experience: The Psychology of Women*. Lexington, Mass.: Heath, 1985.

Imperato-McGinley, J., Peterson, R., Gautier, T., and Sturla, E. Androgens and the evolution of male-gender identity among male pseudohermaphrodites with 5-α-reductase deficiency. *New England Journal of Medicine*, 1979, 300, 1233–1237.

Inglis, J., Ruckman, M., Lawson, J., MacLean, A., and Monga, T. Sex differences in the cognitive effects of unilateral brain damage. *Cortex*, 1982, 18, 257–276.

Isaacs, S., and Cook, R. Laws and policies affecting fertility: A decade of change. *Population Reports*, 1984, 12, 106–151.

Jacobs, P., Brenton, M., Melville, M., Brittain, R., and McClemont, W. Aggressive behavior, mental subnormality, and the XYY male. *Nature*, 1965, 208, 1351–1353.

Jacoby, S. 49 million singles can't all be right. *New York Times Magazine*, February 17, 1974, 37–43.

Jacques, J., and Chason, K. Cohabitation: Its impact on marital success. *Family Coordinator*, 1979, 28, 35–39.

Jaffe, L., Sigueria, L., Diamond, S., Diaz, A., and Spielsinger, N. Genital chlamydia detection in inner-city adolescents. Paper delivered at the Annual Meeting of the American Pediatric Society and the Society for Pediatric Research, Washington, D. C., May 1985.

James, J., and Meyerding, J. Early sexual experience as a factor in prostitution. *Archives of Sexual Behavior*, 1978, 7, 31–42.

———, Withers, J., Haft, M., Theiss, S., and Own, M. *The Politics of Prostitution*. Seattle, Wash.: Social Research Associates, 1975.

Janeway, J. Incest: A rational look at the oldest taboo, *Ms.*, November 1981, 61 ff.

Janoff-Bulman, R., and Golden, D. Attributions and adjustment to abortion. Paper presented at a meeting of the American Psychological Association, Toronto, Aug. 24, 1984.

Japenga, A. Pornography: Fuel for rapists? *The Oregonian*, Jan. 31, 1984, C1.

Jarett, L. Psychosocial and biological influences on menstruation: Synchrony, cycle length, and regularity. *Psychoneuroendocrinology*, 1984, 9, 21–28.

Jay, K. Coming out as process. In G. Vida (Ed.), *Our Right to Love*. Englewood Cliffs, N.J.: Prentice-Hall, 1978.

Jayne, C. Time factors and female sexual response: Therapeutic, conceptual and statistical implications. Paper presented at the Society for the Scientific Study of Sex Western Region Conference, Palm Springs, Calif., Jan. 1985.

Jenks, R. Swinging: A replication and test of a theory. *The Journal of Sex Research*, 1985, 21, 199–210.

Jick, H., Alexander, W., Rothman, K., Hunter, J., Holmes, L., Watkins, R., D'Ewart, D., Danford, A., and Madsen, S. Vaginal spermicides and congenital disorders. *Journal of the American Medical Association*, 1981, 245, 1329–1332.

———, Walker, A., and Rothman, K. The epidemic of endometrial cancer: A commentary. *American Journal of Public Health*, 1980, 70, 264–267.

Johnson, J. The cervical cap: A retrospective study of an alternative contraceptive technique. *American Journal of Obstetrics and Gynecology*, 1984, 148, 604–608.

Johnson, S. TSS–Don't overlook less obvious cases. *Contemporary Obstetrics/Gynecology*, 1985, 25, 131–138.

Johnson, W. Key factors in the sex education of the mentally retarded. Keynote address of Planned Parenthood Conference, Seattle, Wash., Dec. 2, 1971.

Jones, E., Forrest, J., Goldman, N., Henshaw, S., Lincoln, R., Rosoff, J., Westoff, C., and Wulf, D. Teenage pregnancy in developed countries: Determinants and policy implications. *Family Planning Perspectives*, 1985, 17, 53–63.

Jones, W., Chernovetz, M., and Hansson, R. The enigma of androgyny: Differential implications for males and females. *Journal of Consulting and Clinical Psychology*, 1978, 46, 298–313.

Judd, H., Meldrum, D., Deftos, L., and Henderson, B. Estrogen replacement therapy: Indications and complications. *Annals of Internal Medicine*, 1983, 98, 195–205.

Judson, F. Assessing the number of genital chlamydial infections in the United States. *The Journal of Reproductive Medicine*, 1985, 30 supplement, 269–272.

Justice, B., and Justice, R. *The Broken Taboo: Sex in the Family*. New York: Human Sciences Press, 1979.

Kalash, S., and Young, J. Fracture of the penis: Controversy of surgical versus conservative treatment. *Urology*, 1984, 24, 21–24.

Kalisch, P., and Kalisch, B. Sex-role stereotyping of nurses and physicians on prime-time television. *Sex Roles*, 1984, 10, 533–554.

Kallman, F. Comparative twin study on the genetic aspects of male homosexuality. *Journal of Nervous and Mental Disease*, 1952a, 115, 283–298.

———. Twin and sibship study of overt male homosexuality. *American Journal of Human Genetics*, 1952b, 4, 136–146.

Kane, J., Woodland, R., and Forsey, T. *Chlamydia trachomatis*, and infertility. *The Lancet*, March 31, 1984, 736–737.

———, ———, ———, Darougar, S., and Elder, M. Evidence of chlamydial infection in infertile women with and without fallopian tube obstruction. *Fertility and Sterility*, 1984, 42, 843–848.

Kanin, E. Reference groups and sex conduct norm violations. *Sociological Quarterly*, 1967, 8, 495–504.

———. Date rapists: Differential sexual socialization and relative deprivation. *Archives of Sexual Behavior*, 1985, 14, 219–231.

Kanki, P., Barin, F., M'Boup, S., Allan, J., Romet-Lemonne, J., Marlink, R., McLane, M., Lee, T., Artbille, B., Denis, F., Essex, M. New human T-lymphotropic retrovirus related to simian T-lymphotropic virus type III (STLV-III). *Science*, 1986, 232, 238–243.

Kaplan, H. *The New Sex Therapy: Active Treatment of Sexual Dysfunction*. New York: Brunner/Mazel, 1974.

———. Hypoactive sexual desire. *Journal of Sex and Marital Therapy*, 1977, 3, 3–9.

———. *Disorders of Sexual Desire*. New York: Brunner/Mazel, 1979.

Karacan, I. Clinical value of nocturnal erection in the prognosis and diagnosis of impotence. *Medical Aspects of Human Sexuality*, 1970, 4, 27–34.

Karp, L. The arguable propriety of preconceptual sex determination. *American Journal of Medical Genetics*, 1980, 6, 185–187.

Kassel, V. Long-term care institutions. In R. Weg (Ed.), *Sexuality in the Later Years: Roles and Behavior*. New York: Academic Press, 1983.

Katchadourian, H. *The Biology of Adolescence*. San Francisco: W. H. Freeman, 1977.

Katz, J. *Gay American History*. New York: Avon, 1976.

Kaufman, A., Divasto, P., Jackson, R., Voorhees, D., and Christy, J. Male rape victims: Noninstitutionalized assault. *American Journal of Psychiatry*, 1980, 137, 221–223.

Kegel, A. Sexual function of the pubococcygeus muscle. *Western Journal of Surgery*, 1952, 60, 521–524.

Keith, L., Berger, G., Edelman, D., Newton, W., Fullan, N., Bailey, R., and Friberg, J. On the causation of pelvic inflammatory disease. *American Journal of Obstetrics and Gynecology*, 1984, 149, 215–224.

Kellet, J. Testosterone: Treatment for low libido in woman? *British Journal of Sexual Medicine*, 1984, 11, 106, Apr.–May, 82–84, 87.

Kelley, K. Sex, sex guilt, and authoritarianism: Differences in responses to explicit heterosexual and masturbatory slides. *The Journal of Sex Research*, 1985, 21, 68–85.

Kelsey, J., Fischer, D., Holford, T., LiVolsi, V., Mostow, E., Goldenberg, I., and White, C. Exogenous estrogens and other factors in the epidemiology of breast cancer. *Journal of the National Cancer Institute*, 1981, 67, 327–333.

Kephart, W. Some correlates of romantic love. *Journal of Marriage and the Family*, 1967, 29, 470–474.

Kessler, J. Understanding the treatment of vaginismus: Learning from clinical experience. Paper presented at the Twenty-Eighth Annual Meeting of the Society for the Scientific Study of Sex, San Diego, Calif., Sept. 19–22, 1985.

Kilkku, P. Supravaginal uterine amputation vs. hysterectomy: Effects on coital frequency and dyspareunia. *Acta Obstetricia et Gynecologica Scandinavica*, 1983, 62, 141–145.

———, Gronroos, M., Hirvonen, T., and Rauramo, L. Supravaginal uterine amputation vs. hysterectomy: Effects on libido and orgasm. *Acta Obstetricia et Gynecologica Scandinavica*, 1983, 62, 147–152.

Kilmann, P., Sabalis, R., Gearing, M., Bukstel, L., and Scovein, A. The treatment of sexual paraphilias: A review of the outcome research. *Journal of Sex Research*, 1982, 18, 193–252.

Kilpatrick, J. *The Smut Peddlers*. Garden City, N.Y.: Doubleday, 1960.

Kimmel, D. Adult development and aging: A gay perspective. *Journal of Social Issues*, 1978, 34, 113–130.

King, F. Roll me over, lay me down. In D. Stillman and A. Beatts (Eds.), *Titters*. New York: Collier Books, 1976.

Kinsey, A., Pomeroy, W., and Martin, C. *Sexual Behavior in the Human Male*. Philadelphia: W. B. Saunders, 1948.

———, ———, ———, and Gebhard, P. *Sexual Behavior in the Human Female*. Philadelphia: W. B. Saunders, 1953.

Kirkendall, L. The case against circumcision. *Sexology Today*, May 1981, 56–59.

Kirkpatrick, M. Lesbian mother families. *Psychiatric Annals*, 1982, 12, 842–845; 848.

———, Roy, R., and Smith, K. Lesbian mothers and their children: A comparative study. *American Journal of Orthopsychiatry*, 1981, 51, 545.

Kirk-Smith, M., Booth, D., Carroll, D., and Davies, P. Human social attitudes affected by androstenol. *Research Communications in Psychology, Psychiatry, and Behavior*, 1978, 3, 379–384.

Kisker, E. Teenagers talk about sex, pregnancy and contraception. *Family Planning Perspectives*, 1985, 17, 83–90.

Klagsbrun, G. *Married People: Staying Together in the Age of Divorce*. New York: Bantam Books, 1985.

Klaich, D. *Woman Plus Woman: Attitudes Towards Lesbianism*. New York: Simon and Schuster, 1974.

Klaus, M., and Kennel, J. *Journal of Maternal Infant Bonding*. St. Louis: Mosby, 1976.

———, and ———. *Parent-Infant Bonding*, 2nd ed. St. Louis, Mo.: Mosby, 1982.

Klein, F. *The Bisexual Option*. New York: Arbor House, Berkeley Books, 1978.

Knafo, D., and Jaffe, Y. Sexual fantasizing in males and females. *Journal of Research in Personality*, 1984, 19, 451–462.

Knapp, J., and Whitehurst, R. Sexually open marriage and relationships: Issues and prospects. In R. Libby and R. Whitehurst (Eds.), *Marriage and Alternatives: Exploring Intimate Relationships*. Glenview, Ill.: Scott, Foresman, 1977.

Koblinsky, S., and Palmeter, J. Sex-role orientation, mother's expression of affection toward spouse, and college women's attitudes toward sexual behaviors. *Journal of Sex Research*, 1984, 20, 32–43.

Kohlberg, L. A cognitive-developmental analysis of children's sex-role concepts and attitudes. In E. Maccoby (Ed.), *The Development of Sex Differences*. Stanford, Calif.: Stanford University Press, 1966.

Kolodny, R. Adolescent sexuality. Paper presented at the Michigan Personnel and Guidance Association Annual Convention, Detroit, Mich., Nov. 1980.

———, Masters, W., and Johnson, V. *Textbook of Sexual Medicine*. Boston: Little, Brown, 1979.

Kols, A., Rinehart, W., Piatrow, P., Doucette, L., and Quillan, W. Oral contraceptives in the 1980s. *Population Reports*, Series A(6), May-June 1982.

Kopans, D., Meyer, J., and Sadowsky, N. Breast imaging. *New England Journal of Medicine*, 1984, 310, 960–967.

Kosnik, A., Carroll, W., Cunningham, A., Modras, R., and Schulte, J. *Human Sexuality: New Directions in American Catholic Thought*. New York: Paulist Press, 1977.

Krantzler, M. *Creative Divorce*. New York: New American Library, 1975.

Krauss, D. Personal communication, December 1985.

Kreuz, L., Rose, R., and Jennings, J. Suppression of plasma testosterone levels and psychological stress. *Archives of General Psychiatry*, 1972, 26, 479–482.

Kron, R., Stein, M., and Goddard, K. Newborn sucking behavior affected by obstetrical sedation. *Pediatrics*, 1966, 37, 1012–1016.

Kryger-Baggesen, N., Larsen, J., and Pedersen, P. CO_2 laser treatment of condylomata acuminata. *Acta Obstetrica et Gynecologica Scandinavica*, 1980, 63, 341–343.

Kudish, H. Treatment of impotence: Proven and promising methods. *Postgraduate Medicine*, 1983, 74, 233–240.

Kujansuu, E., Kivinen, S., and Tuimala, R. Pregnancy and delivery at the age of forty and over. *International Journal of Gynecological Obstetrics*, 1981, 19, 341–345.

Kupperman, H., and Studdiford, W. Endocrine therapy in gynecologic disorders. *Postgraduate Medicine*, 1953, 14, 410–425.

Kurtz, H. Behind the green door: Does pornography lead to violence? *The Washington Post National Weekly Edition*, October 28, 1985, 33.

Kutchinsky, B. The effect of easy availability of pornography on the incidence of sex crimes: The Danish experience. *Journal of Social Issues*, 1973, 29, 163–182.

La Barre, M. *The Double Jeopardy: The Triple Crisis, Illegitimacy Today*. New York: National Council on Illegitimacy, 1969.

Lader, L. *Abortion*. Indianapolis, Ind.: Bobbs-Merrill, 1966.

Ladouceur, P., and Temple, M. Substance use among rapists: A comparison with other serious felons. *Crime and Delinquency*, 1985, 31, 269–294.

Laflin, M. Assertiveness as a predictor of sexual satisfaction. Paper presented at the Twenty-Eighth Annual Meeting of the Society for the Scientific Study of Sex, San Diego, Calif., Sept. 19–22, 1985.

Lamaze, F. *Painless Childbirth*. Chicago: Henry Regnery, 1956.

Lammer, E., Chen, D., Hoar, R., Agnish, N., Benke, P., Braun, J., Curry, C., Fernhoff, P., Grix, A., Lott, I., Richard, J., and Sun, S. Retinoic acid embryopathy. *New England Journal of Medicine*, 1985, 313, 837–841.

Lane, M., Arley, R., and Sobrero, A. Successful use of the diaphragm and jelly in a young population: Report of a clinical study. *Family Planning Perspectives*, 1976, 8, 81–86.

Laner, M. Growing older female: Heterosexual and homosexual. *Journal of Homosexuality*, 1979, 4, 267–275.

Langevin, R., Patich, D., Ramsay, G., Anderson, C., Kamrad, J., Pape, S., Geller, G., Pearl, L., and Newman, S. Experimental studies of the etiology of genital exhibitionism. *Archives of Sexual Behavior*, 1979, 8, 307–331.

Langone, J. A new view of impotence. *Discover*, May 1981, 74–76.

Lapides, J. The key to urinary infections. *The Female Patient*, 1980, 5, 11–14.

Larned, D. Caesarean births: Why they are up 100 percent. *Ms.*, October 1978, 24–30.

Lasswell, M., and Lasswell, T. In T. Hoult, L. Henze, and J. Hudson (Eds.), *Courtship and Marriage in America*. Boston: Little, Brown, 1978.

Laube, D. Premenstrual syndrome. *The Female Patient*, 1985, 6, 50–61.

Lauer, J., and Lauer, R. Marriages made to last. *Psychology Today*, June 1985, 22–26.

Lauersen, N., and Graves, Z. Pretended orgasm. *Medical Aspects of Human Sexuality*, 1984, 18, 74–81.

Laufer, L., DeFazio, J., Lu, J., Meldrum, D., Eggena, P., Sambhi, M., Hershman, J., and Judd, H. Estrogen replacement therapy by transdermal estradiol administration. *American Journal of Obstetrics and Gynecology*, 1983, 146, 533–540.

Lavin, J., Stephens, R., Miodovnik, M., and Barden, T. Vaginal delivery in patients with a prior cesarean section. *Obstetrics and Gynecology*, 1982, 59, 135–148.

Laws, J., and Schwartz, P. *Sexual Scripts: The Social Construction of Female Sexuality*. Hinsdale, Ill.: Dryden Press, 1977.

Leboyer, F. *Birth Without Violence*. New York: Knopf, 1975.

Lederer, W., and Jackson, D. False assumption 3: That love is necessary for a satisfactory marriage. In F. Morrison and V. Borosage (Eds.), *Human Sexuality: Contemporary Perspectives*, 2d rev. ed. Palo Alto, Calif.: Mayfield, 1977.

Lee, A., and Scheurer, V. Psychological androgyny and aspects of self-image in women and men. *Sex Roles*, 1983, 9, 289–306.

Lehfeldt, H., and Sivin, I. Use effectiveness of the Prentif cervical cap in private practice: A prospective study. *Contraception*, 1984, 30, 331–338.

Leiblum, S., Bachmann, G., Kemmann, E., Colburn, D., and Swartzman, L. Vaginal atrophy in the postmenopausal woman: The importance of sexual activity and hormones. *Journal of the American Medical Association*, 1983, 249, 16, 2195–2198.

Leiter, E. Urethritis: Clinical manifestations and interrelationship with intercourse and therapy. *Sexuality and Disability*, 1984, 6, 72–77.

Lentz, S., and Zeiss, A. Fantasy and sexual arousal in college women: An empirical investigation. *Imagination, Cognition, and Personality*, 1984, 3, 185–202.

Leo, J. Pornography: The feminist dilemma. *Time*, July 21, 1986, 18.

Levin, A., Schoenbaum, S., Monson, R., Stubblefield, P., and Ryan, K. Association of induced abortion with subsequent pregnancy loss. *Journal of the American Medical Association*, 1980, 243, 2495–2499.

Levin, R., and Levin, A. Sexual pleasure: The suprising preferences of 100,000 women. *Redbook*, Sept. 1975, 38.

———, and ———. The *Redbook* report on premarital and extramarital sex. *Redbook*, Oct. 1975, 51.

Levinson, D. *The Seasons of a Man's Life*. New York: Knopf, 1978.

Levitan, M., and Montagu, A. *A Textbook of Human Genetics*, 2nd ed. New York: Oxford University Press, 1977.

Lewin, E. Lesbianism and motherhood: Implications for child custody. *Human Organization*, 1981, 40, 6–14.

Lewis, A., and Hoghughi, M. An evaluation of depression as a side effect of oral contraceptives. *British Journal of Psychiatry*, 1969, 115, 697–701.

Lewis, M. State as an infant-environment interaction: An analysis of mother-infant interaction as a function of sex. *Merrill-Palmer Quarterly*, 1972b, 18, 95–121.

Lewis, R. The swinger. In F. Robinson and N. Lehrman (Eds.), *Sex American Style*. Chicago: Playboy Press, 1971.

———. Parents and peers: Socialization agents in the coital behavior of young adults. *Journal of Sex Research*, 1973, 9, 156–162.

Libman, E., Brender, W., Burstein, R., and Hodgins, S. Ejaculatory incompetence: A theoretical formulation and case illustration. *Journal of Behavior Therapy and Experimental Psychiatry*, 1984, 15, 127–131.

Lin, J., and Bradley, W. Penile neuropathy in insulin-dependent diabetes mellitus. *Journal of Urology*, 1985, 133, 213–215.

Linde, R., Doelle, G., Alexander, N., Kirchner, F., Vale, W., Rivier, J., and Rabin, D. Reversible inhibition of testicular steroidogenesis and spermatogenesis by a potent gonadotropin-releasing hormone agonist in men. *New England Journal of Medicine*, 1981, 305, 663–667.

Lindsey, K. Sexual harassment on the job. *Ms.*, Nov. 1977, 47 ff.

Linke, V. AIDS in Africa. *Science*, 1986, 231, 203.

Linz, D. Sexual violence in the media: Effects on male viewers and implications for society. Doctoral thesis, University of Wisconsin, Madison, Department of Psychology, 1985.

Lisk, R. Increased sexual behavior in the male rat following lesions in the mammillary region. *Journal of Experimental Zoology*, 1966, 161, 129–136.

Liskin, L., Pile, J., and Quillin, W. Vasectomy—safe and simple. *Population Reports*, 1983, 11, 5.

———, and Quillin, W. Long-acting progestins—Promise and prospects. *Population Reports*, 1983, 11, 2.

———, Rinehart, W., Blackburn, R., and Rutledge, A. Minilaparotomy and laparoscopy: Safe, effective, and widely used. *Population Reports*, 1985, 13, 2.

Littenburg, B., and Ransohoff, D. Hepatis B vaccination. *The American Journal of Medicine*, 1984, 77, 1023–1026.

Livson, F. Gender identity: A life-span view of sex-role development. In R. Weg (Ed.), *Sexuality in the Later Years: Roles and Behavior*. New York: Academic Press, 1983.

Lizotte, A. The uniqueness of rape: Reporting assaultive violence to the police. *Crime and Delinquency*, 1985, 31, 169–190.

Lloyd, C. The influence of hormones on human sexual behavior. In E. Astwood and C. Cassidy (Eds.), *Clinical Endocrinology*, Vol. 2. New York: Grune and Stratton, 1968.

Lobsenz, N. Sex and the senior citizen. *The New York Times Magazine*, Jan. 20, 1974, 87–91.

Loffer, F. Hysteroscopic sterilization with the use of formed-in-place silicone plugs. *American Journal of Obstetrics and Gynecology*, 1984, 149, 261–269.

LoPiccolo, J. Low sexual desire. In S. Leiblum and L. Pervin (Eds.), *Principles and Practice of Sex Therapy*. New York: Guilford Press, 1980a.

———. The human sexual dilemma: New clinical approaches and perspectives. Paper presented in seminar in Portland, Ore., Oct. 22, 1980b.

———. Personal communication, July 1982.

———. Advances in diagnosis and treatment of sexual dysfunction. Paper presented at the 28th Annual Meeting of the Society for the Scientific Study of Sex, San Diego, Calif., Sept. 19–22, 1985.

———, and Heiman, J. The role of cultural values in the prevention and treatment of sexual problems. In C. Qualls, J. Wincze, and D. Barlow (Eds.), *The Prevention of Sexual Disorders*. New York: Plenum, 1978.

LoPresto, C., Sherman, M., and Sherman, N. The effects of a masturbation seminar on high school males' attitudes, false beliefs, guilt, and behavior. *The Journal of Sex Research*, 1985, 21, 142–156.

Loraine, J., Adamopoulos, D., Kirkham, K., Ismail, A., and Dove, G. Patterns of hormone excretion in male and female homosexuals. *Nature*, 1971, 234, 552–554.

Lothstein, L. The postsurgical transsexual: Empirical and theoretical considerations. *Archives of Sexual Behavior*, 1980, 9, 547–563.

———. Psychological testing with transsexuals: A 30-year review. *Journal of Personality Assessment*, 1984, 48, 500–507.

Loucks, A., and Horvath, S. Athletic amenorrhea: A review. *Medicine and Science in Sports and Exercise*, 1985, 17, 56–72.

Loulan, J. *Lesbian Sex*. San Francisco: Spinsters Ink, 1984.

Lourea, D., Rila, M., and Taylor, C. Sex in the age of AIDS. Paper presented at the Western Region Annual Conference of the Society for the Scientific Study of Sex, Scottsdale, Ariz., Jan. 1986.

Loveless, M. Clinical and laboratory diagnosis of herpes. Paper presented at the Herpes Symposium, Oregon Health Sciences University, Portland, Oreg., Apr. 2, 1982.

Loy, P., and Stewart, L. The extent and effects of the sexual harassment of working women. *Sociological Focus*, 1984, 17, 31–43.

Lue, T. Evaluation and treatment of impotence—where are we going? (editorial). *Western Journal of Medicine*, 1985, 142, 546.

Luker, K. *Taking Chances: Abortion and the Decision Not to Contracept*. Berkeley, Calif.: University of California Press, 1975.

———. The war between women. *Family Planning Perspectives*, 1984, 16, 105–110.

Lumby, M. Homophobia: The quest for a valid scale. *Journal of Homosexuality*, 1976, 2, 39–47.

Lunde, D., and Hamburg, D. Techniques for assessing the effects of sex hormones on affect, arousal and aggression in humans. *Recent Progress in Hormone Research*, 1972, 28, 627–663.

Lundstrom, B., Pauly, I., and Walinder, J. Outcome of sex reassignment surgery. *Acta Psychiatrica Scandinavica*, 1984, 70, 289–294.

Maatman, T., and Montague, D. Diabetes mellitus and erectile dysfunction in men. *Journal of Urology*, 1985, 133, 191A.

Maccoby, E. Address presented at a Symposium on Issues in Contemporary Psychology, Reed College, Portland, Oregon, May 1985.

MacDonald, A., and Games, R. Some characteristics of those who hold positive and negative attitudes towards homosexuals. *Journal of Homosexuality*, 1974, 1, 9–27.

MacDonald, A., Jr. Bisexuality: Some comments on research and theory. *Journal of Homosexuality*, 1981, 6, 21–35.

MacDonald, J. *Rape: Offenders and Their Victims*. Springfield, Ill.: Thomas, 1971.

Macklin, E. Unmarried heterosexual cohabitation on the university campus. In J. Wiseman (Ed.), *The Social Psychology of Sex*. New York: Harper & Row, 1976.

———. Review of research on nonmarital cohabitation in the United States. In B. Murstein (Ed.), *Exploring Intimate Life Styles*. New York: Springer, 1978.

———. Nontraditional family forms: A decade of research. *Journal of Marriage and the Family*, 1980, 4, 11–24.

MacLean, P. New findings relevant to the evolution of psychosexual functions of the brain. In J. Money (Ed.), *Sex Research: New Developments*. New York: Holt, Rinehart, and Winston, 1965.

MacLusky, N., and Naftolin, F. Sexual differentiation of the central nervous system. *Science*, 1981, 211, 1294–1303.

MacNamara, D., and Sagarin, E. *Sex, Crime, and the Law*. New York: Free Press, 1977.

Maddux, H. *Menstruation*. New Canaan, Conn.: Tobey, 1975.

Madore, C., Hawes, W., Many, F., and Hexter, A. A study on the effects of induced abortion on subsequent pregnancy outcome. *American Journal of Obstetrics and Gynecology*, 1981, 139, 516–521.

Mahoney, E. Editor's note. *Current Research Updates*, 1984, 2, 8–12.

Malamuth, N. Rape proclivity among males. *Journal of Social Issues*, 1981, 37, 138–157.

———. Aggression against women: Cultural and individual causes. In N. Malamuth and E. Donnerstein (Eds.), *Pornography and Sexual Aggression*. New York: Academic Press, 1982.

———. The mass media as an indirect cause of sexual aggression. Paper presented at a hearing of the Attorney General's Commission on Pornography, Houston, Tex., Sept. 12, 1985.

———, and Check, J. The effects of mass media exposure on acceptance of violence against women: A field experiment. *Journal of Research in Personality*, 1981, 15, 436–446.

———, Haber, S., and Feshback, S. Testing hypotheses regarding rape: Exposure to sexual violence, sex differences, and the "normality" of rapists. *Journal of Research in Personality*, 1980, 14, 121–137.

———, and Spinner, B. A longitudinal content analysis of sexual violence in the best-selling erotica magazines. *Journal of Sex Research*, 1980, 16, 226–237.

Malatesta, V., Pollack, R., Crotty, T., and Peacock, L. Acute alcohol intoxication and female orgasmic response. *Journal of Sex Research*, 1982, 18, 1–17.

———, ———, Wilbanks, W., and Adams, H. Alcohol effects on the orgasmic-ejaculatory response in human males. *Journal of Sex Research*, 1979, 15, 101–107.

Maletzky, B., and Price, R. Public masturbation in men: Precursor to exhibitionism? *Journal of Sex Education and Therapy*, 1984, 10, 31–36.

Malinak, R., and Wheeler, J. Endometriosis. *The Female Patient*, 1985, 6, 35–36.

Mallon, R. Demonstration of vestigial prostatic tissue in the human female. Paper presented at the Annual Regional Conference of American Association of Sex Educators, Counselors, and Therapists, Las Vegas, Nev., Oct. 1984.

Mann, J. China slowly backs off from rigid population control policy. *Oregonian*, 1985, May 12, A9.

Manzano, P. Drug helps therapy in sex offender unit. *The Oregonian*, Jan. 22, 1984, B1 and B6.

Margolis, C., and Goodman, R. Psychological factors in women choosing radiation therapy for breast cancer. *Psychosomatics*, 1984, 25, 464–466; 469.

Marin, P. A revolution's broken promises. *Psychology Today*, July 1983, 50–57.

Marks, E. Review of behavioral psychotherapy (II): Sexual disorders. *American Journal of Psychiatry*, 1981, 138, 750–756.

Marmor, J. (Ed.). *Homosexual Behavior*. New York: Basic Books, 1980.

Marshall, D. Sexual behavior on Mangaia. In D. Marshall and R. Suggs (Eds.), *Human Sexual Behavior: Variations in the Ethnographic Spectrum*. Englewood Cliffs, N.J.: Prentice-Hall, 1971.

Marshall, W. *Human Growth and Its Disorders*. New York: Academic Press, 1977.

———. The evaluation of sexual aggressives. Paper presented at the Third Annual Conference on the Evaluation and Treatment of Sexual Aggressives, San Luis Obispo, Calif., 1981.

———, and Barbaree, H. A behavioral view of rape. *International Journal of Law and Psychiatry*, 1984, 7, 51–77.

Martin, C. Factors affecting sexual functioning in 60-79-year-old married males. *Archives of Sexual Behavior*, 1981, 10, 399–420.

Martin, D. Microsurgical reversal of vasectomy. *American Journal of Surgery*, 1981, 142, 48–50.

———, Kotitsky, L., Eschenbach, D., Daling, J., Alexander, E., Benedetti, J., and Holmes, K. Prematurity and perinatal mortality in pregnancies complicated by maternal *Chlamydia trachomatis* infections. *The Journal of the American Medical Association*, 1982, 247, 1585–1615.

———, and Lyon, P. *Lesbian-Woman*. New York: Bantam, 1972.

Martinson, F. Childhood sexuality. In B. Wolman and J. Money (Eds.), *Handbook of Human Sexuality*. Englewood Cliffs, N.J.: Prentice-Hall, 1980.

Marx, J. AIDS virus has new name—perhaps. *Science*, 1986, 232, 699–700.

Maslow, A., and Mintz, N. Effects of esthetic surroundings: I. Initial effects of three esthetic conditions upon perceiving "energy" and "well-being" in faces. *Journal of Psychology*, 1956, 41, 247–254.

———, and Sakoda, J. Volunteer-error in the Kinsey study. *Journal of Abnormal and Social Psychology*, 1952, 47, 259–267.

Massey, F., Bernstein, G., O'Fallon, W., Schuman, L., Coulson, A., Crozier, R., Mandel, J., Benjamin, R., Berendes, H., Chang, P., Detels, R., Emslander, R., Korelitz, J., Kurland, L., Lepow, I., McGregor, D., Nakamura, R., Quiroga, J., Schmidt, S., Spivey, G., and Sullivan, T. Vasectomy and Health. *Journal of the American Medical Association*, 1984, 252, 1023–1029.

Masters, W. Update on sexual physiology. Paper presented at the Masters and Johnson Institute's Postgraduate Workshop on Human Sexual Function and Dysfunction, St. Louis, Oct. 20, 1980.

———. Half a century of unnecessary sexual myths. *Journal of the American Medical Association*, 1983, 250, 244.

———, and Johnson, V. Orgasm, anatomy of the female. In A. Ellis, and A. Abarbonel (Eds.), *Encyclopedia of Sexual Behavior*, Vol. 2. New York: Hawthorn Books, 1961.

———, and ———. *Human Sexual Response*. Boston: Little, Brown, 1966.

———, and ———. *Human Sexual Inadequacy*. Boston: Little, Brown, 1970.

———, and ———. *The Pleasure Bond*. New York: Bantam, 1976.

———, and ———. *Homosexuality in Perspective*. Boston: Little, Brown, 1979.

Mathews, A. Treatment of sexual dysfunction: Psychological and hormonal factors. In J. Boulougouris (Ed.), *Learning Theory Applications in Psychiatry*. New York: Wiley, 1981.

Mathis, J. *Clear Thinking About Sexual Deviations*. Chicago: Nelson-Hall, 1972.

Mattco, S., and Rissman, E. Increased sexual activity during the midcycle portion of the human menstrual cycle. *Hormones and Behavior*, 1984, 18, 249–255.

Maugh, T. Male "pill" blocks sperm enzyme. *Science*, 1981, 212, 314.

May, R. *Love and Will*. New York: Norton, 1969.

Mayleas, D. The impact of tiny feet on love. *Self*, Aug. 1980, 105–110.

Mbiti, J. *African Religions and Philosophy*. New York: Praeger, 1969.

McArthur, L., and Resko, B. The portrayal of men and women in American television commercials. *Journal of Social Psychology*, 1975, 97, 209–220.

McCaghy, C. Child molesting. *Sexual Behavior*, Aug. 1971, 16–24.

McCarthy, T., Roy, A., and Ratnam, S. Intrauterine devices and pelvic inflammatory disease. *Australian and New Zealand Journal of Obstetrics and Gynaecology*, 1984, 24, 106–110.

McCary, J. *Sexual Myths and Fallacies*. New York: Schocken, 1973.

McCauley, C., and Swann, C. Male-female differences in sexual fantasy. *Journal of Research in Personality*, 1978, 12, 76–86.

McClintock, M. Menstrual synchrony and suppression. *Nature*, 1971, 229, 244–245.

McConnel, J. *Understanding Human Behavior*. New York: Holt, Rinehart, and Winston, 1977.

McCormack, W., Rosner, B., McComb, D., Evrard, J., and Zinner, S. Infection with *Chlamydia trachomatis* in female college students. *American Journal of Epidemiology*, 1985, 121, 107–115.

McCoy, N., Cutler, W., and Davidson, J. Relationships among sexual behavior, hot flashes, and hormone levels in perimenopausal women. *Archives of Sexual Behavior*, 1985, 14, 385–394.

McCulloch, D., Young, R., Prescott, R., Campbell, I., and Clarke, B. The natural history of impotence in diabetic men. *Diabetologia*, 1984, 26, 437–440.

McEwen, B. Binding and metabolism of sex steroids by the hyopothalamic-pituitary unit: Physiological implications. *Annual Review of Physiology*, 1980, 42, 97–110.

McGee, E. *Too Little, Too Late: Services for Teenage Parents*. New York: Ford Foundation, 1982.

McGinnis, T. *More Than Just a Friend*. Englewood Cliffs, N.J.: Prentice-Hall, 1982.

McGlone, J. Sex differences in functional brain asymmetry. *Cortex*, 1978, 14, 122–128.

McGovern, K. Personal communication, June 28, 1982.

———, Kirkpatric, D., and LoPiccolo, J. A behavioral group treatment program for sexually dysfunctional couples. *Journal of Marriage and Family Counseling*, Oct. 1976, 2, 397–404.

McGuire, L., and Wagner, N. Sexual dysfunction in women who were molested as children: One response pattern and suggestions for treatment. *Journal of Sex and Marital Therapy*, 1978, 4, 11–15.

McKinnon, K. *The Sexual Harassment of Working Women*. New Haven, Conn.: Yale University Press, 1979.

McNeil, E., and Rubin, Z. *The Psychology of Being Human*. San Francisco: Canfield Press, 1977.

McWorter, W. Flashing and dashing: Notes and comments on the etiology of exhibitionism. In C. Bryant (Ed.), *Sexual Deviancy in Social Context*. New York: New Viewpoints, 1977.

Mead, M. *Male and Female: A Study of Sexes in the Changing World*. New York: Morrow, 1949.

———. *Sex and Temperament in Three Primitive Societies*. New York: Morrow, 1963.

Medical Letter, The. Oral contraceptives and the risk of cardiovascular disease. 1983, 25, issue 640.

Meiselman, K. *Incest*. San Francisco, Jossey-Bass, 1978.

Melbye, M., Biggar, R., Ebbesen, P., Neuland, C., Goedert, J., Faber, V., Lorenzen, I., Skinhoj, P., Gallo, R., and Blattner, W. Long-term seropositivity for human T-lymphotropic virus type III in homosexual men without the acquired immunodeficiency syndrome: Development of immunologic and clinical abnormalities. *Annals of Internal Medicine*, 1986, 104, 496–500.

Mendelson, J. Marijuana and sex. *Medical Aspects of Human Sexuality*, 1976, 10, 23–24.

Menning, B. Counseling infertile couples. *Contemporary OB/GYN*, 1979, 13, 101–108.

Merriam, A. Aspects of sexual behavior among the Bala. In D. Marshall and R. Suggs (Eds.), *Human Sexual Behavior: Variations in the Ethnographic Spectrum*. Englewood Cliffs, N.J.: Prentice-Hall, 1971.

Mertz, G. Double-blind placebo-controlled trial of oral acyclovir in first-episode genital herpes simplex virus infection. *The Journal of the American Medical Association*, 1984, 252, 1147–1151.

———, Schmidt, O., Jourden, J., Guinan, M., Remington, M., Fahnlander, A., Winter, C., Holmes, K., and Corey, L. Frequency of acquisition of first-episode genital infection with herpes simplex virus from symptomatic and asymptomatic source contacts. *Sexually Transmitted Diseases*, 1985, 12, 33–39.

Messenger, J. Sex and repression in an Irish folk community. In D. Marshall and R. Suggs (Eds.), *Human Sexual Behavior: Variations in the Ethnographic Spectrum*. Englewood Cliffs, N.J.: Prentice-Hall, 1971.

Meyer, J., and Dupkin, C. Gender disturbance in children. *Bulletin of the Menninger Clinic*, 1985, 49, 236–269.

Meyer-Bahlburg, H. Sex hormones and male homosexuality in comparative perspective. *Archives of Sexual Behavior*, 1977, 6, 297–325.

Michael, R., Bonsall, R., and Warner, P. Human vaginal secretions; volatile fatty acid content. *Science*, 1974, 186, 1217–1219.

———, Keverne, E., and Bonsall, R. Pheromones: Isolation of male sex attractants from a female primate. *Science*, 1971, 172, 964–966.

Millett, K. *The Prostitution Papers*. New York: Ballantine Books, 1976.

Milligan, D. Homosexuality: Sexual needs and social problems. In R. Bailey and M. Brake (Eds.), *Radical Social Work*. New York: Pantheon Books, 1975.

Milow, V. Menstrual education: Past, present and future. In S. Golub (Ed.), *Menarche*. Lexington, Mass.: Lexington Books, 1983.

Minton, J., Foecking, D., Webster, D., and Matthews, R. Caffeine, cyclic nucleotides, and breast disease. *Surgery*, 1979, 86, 105–109.

Mims, F., and Chang, A. Unwanted sexual experiences of young women. *Psychosocial Nursing*, 1984, 22, 7–14.

Mittwoch, U. *Genetics of Sex Differentiation*. New York: Academic Press, 1973.

Moncrieff, M., and Pearson, D. Comparison of MMPI profiles of assaultive and non-assaultive exhibitionists and voyeurs. *Corrective and Social Psychiatry and Journal of Behavior Technology*, 1979, 25, 91–93.

Money, J. Components of eroticism in man: The hormones in relation to sexual morphology and sexual desire. *Journal of Nervous and Mental Disease*, 1961, 132, 239–248.

———. Psychosexual differentiation. In J. Money (Ed.), *Sex Research, New Developments*. New York: Holt, Rinehart, and Winston, 1965.

———. The strange case of the pregnant hermaphrodite. *Sexology*, August 1966, 7–9.

———. Cytogenetic and other aspects of transvestism and transsexualism. *Journal of Sex Research*, 1967, 3, 141–143.

———. *Sex Errors of the Body: Dilemmas, Education, Counselling*. Baltimore, Md.: Johns Hopkins Press, 1968.

———. Clitoral size and erotic sensation. *Medical Aspects of Human Sexuality*, 1970, 4, 95.

———. *Man Woman/Boy Girl*. Baltimore, Md.: Johns Hopkins Press, 1972.

———. Ablatio penis: Normal male infant sex-reassigned as a girl. *Archives of Sexual Behavior*, 1975, 4, 65–72.

———. Paraphilias: Phyletic origins of erotosexual dysfunction. *International Journal of Mental Health*, 1981, 10, 75–109.

———. Food, fitness, and vital fluids: Sexual pleasure from Graham Crackers to Kellogg's Cornflakes. Paper presented at the Sixth World Congress of Sexology, May 27, 1983.

———. Paraphilias: Phenomenology and classification. *American Journal of Psychotherapy*, 1984, 38, 164–179.

———, and Bennett, R. Postadolescent paraphilic sex offenders: Antiandrogenic and counseling therapy follow-up. *International Journal of Mental Health*, 1981, 10, 122–133.

———, and Ehrhardt, A. Prenatal hormonal exposure: Possible effects on behavior in man. In R. Michael (Ed.), *Endocrinology and Human Behavior*. London: Oxford University Press, 1968.

———, ———, and Masica, D. Fetal feminization induced by androgen insensitivity in the testicular feminizing syndrome: Effect on marriage and maternalism. *Johns Hopkins Medical Journal*, 1968, 123, 105–114.

———, Hampson, J., and Hampson, J. An examination of some basic sexual concepts: The evidence of human hermaphrodism. *Bulletin of Johns Hopkins Hospital*, 1955, 97, 301–319.

———, Lehne, G., and Pierre-Jerome, F. Micropenis: Adult follow-up and comparison of size against new norms. *Journal of Sex and Marital Therapy*, 1984, 10, 105–116.

———, and Primrose, C. Sexual dimorphism and dissociation in the psychology of male transsexuals. *Journal of Nervous and Mental Disorders*, 1968, 147, 472–486.

———, and Walker, P. Counseling the transsexual. In J. Money and H. Musaph (Eds.), *Handbook of Sexology*. Amsterdam: Elsevier/North-Holland Biomedical Press, 1977.

———, and Yankowitz, R. The sympathetic-inhibiting effects of the drug Ismelin on human male eroticism, with a note on Mellaril. *Journal of Sex Research*, 1967, 3, 69–82.

Montagu, A., and Matson, F. *The Human Connection*. New York: McGraw-Hill, 1979.

Mooney, T., Cole, T., and Chilgren, R. *Sexual Options for Paraplegics and Quadraplegics*. Boston: Little, Brown, 1975.

Morgan, E. The Puritans and sex. In M. Gordon (Ed.), *The American Family in Social-Historical Perspective*. New York: St. Martin's Press, 1978.

Morin, J. *Anal Pleasure and Health*. Burlingame, Calif.: Down There Press, 1981.

Morrell, M., Dixen, J., Carter, C., and Davidson, J. The influence of age and cycling status on sexual arousability in women. *American Journal of Obstetrics and Gynecology*, 1984, 148, 66–71.

Morris, J. *Conundrum*. New York: Harcourt Brace Jovanovich, 1974.

Morris, N. The law is a busybody. *The New York Times Magazine*, Apr. 18, 1973, 58–64.

———, and Udry, J. Pheromonal influences on human sexual behavior: An experiential search. *Journal of Biosocial Science*, 1978, 10, 147–159.

Moseley, D., Fellingstad, D., Harley, H., and Heckel, R. Psychological factors that predict reaction to abortion. *Journal of Clinical Psychology*, 1981, 37, 276–279.

Mosher, B., and Whelan, E. Postmenopausal estrogen therapy: A review. *Obstetrical and Gynecological Survey*, 1981, 36, 467–475.

Mosher, D., and Vonderheide, S. Contributions of sex guilt and masturbation guilt to women's contraceptive attitude and use. *Journal of Sex Research*, 1985, 21, 24–39.

Munjack, D., and Oziel, L. *Sexual Medicine and Counseling in Office Practice*. Boston: Little, Brown, 1980.

Munroe, R. Male transvestism and the couvade: A psychocultural analysis. *Ethos*, 1980, 8, 49–59.

Murdock, G. *Social Structure*. New York: Macmillan, 1949.

Murphy, N., and Fain, T. Psychobiological factors in sex and gender identity. Paper presented to the AASECT Conference in Portland, Oreg., Oct. 19, 1978.

Murray, M. Sexual problems in nursing mothers. *Medical Aspects of Human Sexuality*, Oct. 1976, 75–76.

Murstein, B. Swinging or comarital sex. In B. Murstein (Ed.), *Exploring Intimate Life Styles*. New York: Springer, 1978.

Nadler, R. Approach to psychodynamics of obscene telephone calls. *New York Journal of Medicine*, 1968, 68, 521–526.

Naeye, R. Coitus and associated amniotic-fluid infections. *New England Journal of Medicine*, 1979, 301, 1198–1200.

Nahmias, A. Herpes, pregnancy and the neonate. Paper presented at the Herpes Symposium, Oregon Health Sciences University, Portland, Oreg., Apr. 2, 1982.

Narum, G., and Rodolfa, E. Sex therapy for the spinal cord injured client: Suggestions for professionals. *Professional Psychology: Research and Practice*, 1984, 15, 775–784.

Neinstein, L., Goldenring, J., and Carpenter, S. Nonsexual transmission of sexually transmitted diseases: An infrequent occurrence. *Pediatrics*, 1984, 74, 67–76.

Nelson, J. Selecting the optimum oral contraceptive. *Journal of Reproductive Medicine*, 1973, 11, 135–141.

———. Gayness and homosexuality: Issues for the church. In E. Batchelor, Jr. (Ed.), *Homosexuality and Ethics*. New York: Pilgrim Press, 1980.

———. Male sexuality and masculine spirituality. *SIECUS Report*, 1985, 13, 1–4.

Nerurkar, L., West, F., May, M., Madden, D., and Sever, J. Survival of herpes simplex virus in water specimens collected from hot tubs in spa facilities and on plastic surfaces. *The Journal of the American Medical Association*, 1983, 250, 3081–3083.

Neuberger, J., Nunnerely, H., Davis, M., Portman, B., Laws, J., and Williams, R. Oral-contraceptive-associated liver tumors: Occurrence of malignancy and difficulties in diagnosis. *The Lancet*, 1980, 1, 273–276.

Nevid, J. Sex differences in factors of romantic attraction. *Sex Roles*, 1984, 11, 401–411.

Newcomb, M., and Bentler, P. Assessment of personality and demographic aspects of cohabitation and marital success. *Journal of Personality Development*, 1980, 4, 11–24.

Newcomer, S., and Udry, J. Oral sex in an adolescent population. *Archives of Sexual Behavior*, 1985, 14, 41–46.

Nieshclag, E., Wickings, E., and Breuer, H. Chemical methods for male fertility control. *Contraception*, 1981, 23, 1–10.

NIH Cesarean Birth Task Force. National Institute of Child Development statement on cesarean childbirth. U.S. Department of Health and Human Services, 1980.

Norman, C. Politics and science clash on African AIDS. *Science*, 1986, 230, 1140–1141.

Norman, J., and Harris, M. *The Private Life of the American Teenager*. New York: Rawson Wade, 1981.

Novak, E., Jones, G., and Jones, H. *Novak's Textbook of Gynecology*, 8th ed. Baltimore, Md.: Williams and Wilkins, 1970.

Nowak, J., Rodunda, R., and Young, N. *Handbook on Constitutional Law 1978*. St. Paul, Minn.: West, 1978.

Nutter, D., and Condron, M. Sexual fantasy and activity patterns of females with inhibited sexual desire versus normal controls. *Journal of Sex and Marital Therapy*, 1983, 9, 276–282.

O'Connor, K., Mann, D., and Bardwick, J. Androgyny and self-esteem in the upper middle class: A replication of Spence. *Journal of Consulting and Clinical Psychology*, 1978, 46, 1168–1169.

Oesterwitz, H., Bick, C., and Braun, E. Fracture of the penis: Report of 6 cases and review of the literature. *International Urology and Nephrology*, 1984, 16, 123–127.

Oettinger, K. *Not My Daughter*. Englewood Cliffs, N.J.: Prentice-Hall, 1979.

Ohm, W. Female circumcision, *Sexology Today*, June 1980, 21–25.

Olds, J. Pleasure centers in the brain. *Scientific American*, 1956, 193, 105–116.

O'Neill, N., and O'Neill, G. *Open Marriage*. New York: Evans, 1972.

Onlofsky, J. Sex-role orientation, identity formation, and self-esteem in college men and women. *Sex Roles*, 1977, 3, 561–576.

Orlando [pseud.] Bisexuality: A choice not an echo. *Ms.*, Oct. 1978, 60.

Orr, M. Sex education and contraceptive education in U.S. public high schools. *Family Planning Perspectives*, 1982, 14, 304–313.

Ory, H., Rosenfield, A., and Landman, L. The pill at 20: An assessment. *Family Planning Perspectives*, 1980, 12, 278–283.

Ostrov, E., Offer, D., Howard, K., Kaufman, B., and Meyer, H. Adolescent sexual behavior. *Medical Aspects of Human Sexuality*, 1985, 19, 28–31; 34–36.

Owen, E., and Kapila, H. Vasectomy reversal: Review of 475 microsurgical vasovasostomies. *Medical Journal of Australia*, 1984, 140, 398–400.

Owen, P. Prostaglandin synthetase inhibitors in the treatment of primary dysmenorrhea: Outcome trials reviewed. *American Journal of Obstetrics and Gynecology*, 1984, 148, 96–103.

Page, J. *The Other Awkward Age*. Berkeley, Calif.: Ten Speed Press, 1977.

Palson, C., and Palson, R. Swinging in wedlock. *Society*, 1972, 9, 43–48.

Pape, J. Paper presented at an international scientific conference on AIDS, Les Trois Ilets, Martinique, Jan. 1986.

Parrot, A., and Allen, S. Acquaintance rape: Seduction or crime? Paper presented at the Eastern Regional Annual Conference of the Society for the Scientific Study of Sex, Apr. 1984.

Pasquale, S. Rationale for a triphasic oral contraceptive. *Journal of Reproductive Medicine*, 1984, 29, 560–567.

Paul, J. The bisexual identity: An idea without social recognition. *Journal of Homosexuality*, 1984, 9, 45–63.

Paulsen, K., and Johnson, M. Sex role attitudes and mathematical ability in 4th-, 8th-, and 11th-grade students from a high socioeconomic area. *Developmental Psychology*, 1983, 19, 200–209.

Pauly, I. Female transsexualism: Part II. *Archives of Sexual Behavior*, 1974, 3, 509–526.

Paxter, J., O'Hare, D., Nelson, F., and Svigir, M. Two years' experience in New York City with the liberalized abortion law—progress and problems. *American Journal of Public Health*, 1973, 63, 524–535.

Penfield, J. Contraception and female sterilization. *New York State Journal of Medicine*, 1981, 81, 255–258.

Penrod, S., and Linz, D. Using psychological research on violent pornography to inform legal change. In N. Malamuth and E. Donnerstein (Eds.), *Pornography and Sexual Aggression*. Orlando, Fla.: Academic Press, 1984.

Pepitone-Rockwell, F. Counseling women to be less vulnerable to rape. *Medical Aspects of Human Sexology*, Jan. 1980, 145–146.

Peplau, L. What homosexuals want in relationships. *Psychology Today*, March 1981, 28–38.

———, Rubin, Z., and Hill, C. Sexual intimacy in dating relationships. *Journal of Social Issues*, 1977, 33, 86–109.

Perlmutter, J. A gynecological approach to menopause. In M. Notman and C. Nadelson (Eds.), *The Woman Patient*. New York: Plenum, 1978.

Perry, J., and Whipple, B. Pelvic muscle strength of female ejaculators: Evidence in support of a new theory of orgasm. *Journal of Sex Research*, 1981, 17, 22–39.

Peterson, J., Hartsock, N., and Lawson, G. Sexual dissatisfaction of female alcoholics. *Psychological Reports*, 1984, 55, 744–746.

———, Kretchmer, A., Nellis, B., Lever, J., and Hertz, R. The Playboy readers sex survey, Part 2. *Playboy*, March 1983, 90–92; 178–184.

Petrovich, M., and Templer, D. Heterosexual molestation of children who later become rapists. *Psychological Reports*, 1984, 54, 810.

Pfeiffer, E. Sex and aging. In L. Gross (Ed.), *Sexual Issues in Marriage*. New York: Spectrum, 1975.

Pfuhl, E. The unwed father: A "non-deviant" rule breaker. *Sociological Quarterly*, 1978, 19, 113–128.

Pheterson, G., Kiesler, S., and Goldberg, P. Evaluation of the performance of women as a function of their sex, achievement, and personal history. *Journal of Personality and Social Psychology*, 1971, 19, 114–118.

Philip, T., Guillebaud, J., and Budd, D. Complications of vasectomy: Review of 16,000 patients. *British Journal of Urology*, 1984, 56, 745–748.

Phoenix, C., Goy, R., Gerall, A., and Young, W. Organizing action of prenatally administered testosterone propionate on the tissues mediating mating behavior in the female guinea pig. *Endocrinology*, 1959, 65, 369–382.

Pietropinto, A., and Simenauer, J. *Husbands and Wives*. New York: Times Books, 1979.

Pinhas, V. Personal communication, June 1985.

Platt, R., Rice, P., and McCormack, W. Risk of acquiring gonorrhea and prevalence of abnormal adnexal findings among women recently exposed to gonorrhea. *The Journal of the American Medical Association*, 1983, 250, 3205–3209.

Polit-O'Hara, D., and Kahn, J. Communication and adolescent contraceptive practices in adolescent couples. *Adolescence*, 1985, 20, 33–43.

Pomeroy, S. *Goddesses, Whores, Wives, and Slaves: Women in Classical Antiquity*. New York: Schocken Books, 1975.

Pomeroy, W. Why we tolerate lesbians. *Sexology*, May 1965, 652–654.

Porreco, R., and Meier, P. Trial of labor in patients with multiple previous cesarean sections. *Journal of Reproductive Medicine*, 1983, 28, 770–772.

Portland Town Council, The. *A Legislative Guide to Gay Rights*. Portland, Ore., 1976.

Powdermaker, H. *Life in Lesu*. New York: Norton, 1933.

Powell, D., and Fuller, R. Marijuana and sex: Strange bedfellows. *Journal of Psychoactive Drugs*, 1983, 15, 269–280.

Press, A., McDaniel, A., Raine, G., and Carroll, G. A government in the bedroom. *Newsweek*, July 14, 1986, 36–38.

Preston, S. Estimating the proportion of American marriages that end in divorce. *Sociological Methods and Research*, 1975, 3, 435–460.

Price, V., Scanlon, B., Janus, M-D. Social characteristics of adolescent male prostitution. *Victimology*, 1984, 9, 211–221.

Prince, V. Sex without fear of AIDS, herpes, or pregnancy. Paper presented at the Western Region Annual Conference of the Society for the Scientific Study of Sex, Scottsdale, Ariz., January, 1986.

———, and Bentler, P. Survey of 504 cases of transvestism. *Pyschological Reports*, 1972, 31, 903–917.

Pritchard, J., MacDonald, D., and Gant, N. *Williams Obstetrics*, 17th ed. New York: Appleton-Century-Crofts, 1985.

Proctor, F., Wagner, N., and Butler, J. The differentiation of male and female orgasm: An experimental study. In N. Wagner (Ed.), *Perspectives on Human Sexuality*. New York: Behavioral Publications, 1974.

Przbyla, D., and Byrne, D. The mediating role of cognitive processes in self-regulated sexual arousal. *Journal of Research in Personality*, 1984, 18, 54–63.

Puolakka, J., and Tuimala, R. A comparison between oral ketoconazole and topical miconazole in the treatment of vaginal candidiasis. *Acta Obstetrica et Gynecologica Scandinavica*, 1983, 62, 575–577.

Purcell, S. Relation between religious orthodoxy and marital sexual functioning. Paper presented at a meeting of the American Psychological Association, Los Angeles, Aug. 25, 1985.

Purifoy, F., Martin, C., and Tobin, J. Age-related variation in female sexual arousal. Paper presented at the Twenty-Sixth Annual Meeting of the Society for the Scientific Study of Sex, Chicago, Nov. 18–20, 1983.

Puzo, M. *The Godfather*. Greenwich, Conn.: Fawcett, 1969.

Quinsey, V., Chaplin, T., and Upfold, D. Sexual arousal to nonsexual violence and sadomasochistic themes among rapists and non-sex-offenders. *Journal of Consulting and Clinical Psychology*, 1984, 52, 4, 651–657.

Quinsey, V., and Upfold, D. Rape completion and victim injury as a function of female resistance strategy. *Canadian Journal of Behavior Science*, 1985, 17, 40–50.

Raboch, J., Mellon, J., and Starka, L. Klinefelter's syndrome: Sexual development and activity. *Archives of Sexual Behavior*, 1979, 8, 333–340.

Rachman, S. Sexual fetishism: an experimental analogue. *Psychological Record*, 1966, 16, 293–296.

Rada, R. Alcoholism and forcible rape. *American Journal of Psychiatry*, 1975, 132, 444–446.

———. Alcoholism and the child molester. *Annals of the New York Academy of Sciences*, 1976, 273, 492–496.

———. Commonly asked questions about the rapist. *Medical Aspects of Human Sexuality*, 1977, 11, 47–56.

Radar, C. MMPI profile types of exposers, rapists, and assaulters in a court service population. *Journal of Consulting and Clinical Psychology*, 1977, 45, 61–69.

Rapaport, K., and Burkhart, B. Personality and attitudinal characteristics of sexually coercive college males. *Journal of Abnormal Psychology*, 1984, 93, 216–221.

Raphael, S., and Robinson, M. *Alternative Lifestyles*, 1980, 3, 207–229.

Rapp, F. Structure and function of the virus: Latency of herpes simplex virus. Paper presented at the Herpes Symposium, Oregon Health Sciences University, Portland, Oreg., Apr. 2, 1982.

Reamy, K., and White, S. Sexuality in pregnancy and the puerperium: A review. *Obstetrical and Gynecological Survey*, 1985, 40, 8–13.

Rebeta-Burditt, J. *The Cracker Factory*. New York: Bantam Books, 1978.

Redfield, R., Markham, P. Salahuddin, S., Wright, D., Sarngadharan, M., and Gallo, R. Heterosexually acquired HTLV-III/LAV disease (AIDS-related complex and AIDS): Epidemiologic evidence for female-to-male transmission. *The Journal of the Americal Medical Association*, 1985, 254, 2094–2096.

Reichman, R., Badger, G., Mertz, G., Corey, L., Richman, D., Connor, J., Redfield, D., Saupia, M., Oxman, M., Bryson, Y., Tyrrell, D., Portnoy, J., Creigh-Kirk, T., Keeney, R., Ashikaga, T., and Dolin, R. Treatment of recurrent genital herpes simplex infections with oral acyclovir: A controlled study. *Journal of the American Medical Association*, 1984, 251, 2103–2107.

Rein, M. Epidemiology of gonococcal infections. In R. Roberts (Ed.), *The Gonococcus*. New York: Wiley, 1977.

———. Condoms and STDs: Do the former prevent transmission of the latter? *Medical Aspects of Human Sexuality*, 1985, 19, 113; 116–117.

Reiss, A. The social integration of queers and peers. In H. Becker (Ed.), *The Other Side*. New York: Free Press, 1964.

Research Forecasts, Inc. *The Tampax Report: A Summary of Survey Results on a Study of Attitudes toward Menstruation*. New York: Tampax Incorporated, 1981.

Reuben, D. *Everything You Always Wanted to Know About Sex*. New York: Bantam Books, 1969.

Rhodes, R. Sex and sin in Sheboygan. *Playboy*, Aug. 1972, 186–190.

Rich, A. *Of Woman Born*. New York: Norton, 1976.

Ricks, D. Oregon doctor tells anti-herpes success. *The Oregonian*, Apr. 7, 1986.

Riedman, S. Change of life. *Sexology*, July 1961, 808–813.

Riley, A. Androgens and female sexuality. *British Journal of Sexual Medicine*, 1983, 10, 5–6.

Ritter, T. The people's home medical book. In R. Barnum (Ed.), *The People's Home Library*. Cleveland, Ohio: Barnum, 1919.

Ritz, S. How to deal with menstrual cramps. *Medical Self-Care*, Spring 1981, 17–22.

———. Growing through menopause. *Medical Self-Care*, Winter 1981, 15–18.

Robbins, M., and Jensen, G. Multiple orgasm in males. *Journal of Sex Research*, 1978, 14, 21–26.

Roberto, L. Issues in diagnosis and treatment of transsexualism. *Archives of Sexual Behavior*, 1983, 12, 445–473.

Robinson, D., and Rock, J. Intrascrotal hyperthermia induced by scrotal insulation: Effect on spermatogenesis. *Obstetrics and Gynecology*, 1967, 29, 217–223.

Robinson, P. What liberated males do. *Psychology Today*, July 1981, 81–84.

Roby, P. Politics and criminal law: Revision of the New York State penal law on prostitution. *Social Problems*, 1969, 17, 18–109.

Roel, J., and Gray, D. The crises of rape: A guide to counseling victims of rape. *Crises Intervention*, 1984, 13, 67–77.

Rogel, M. A critical evaluation of the possibility of higher primate reproductive and sexual pheromones. *Psychological Bulletin*, 1978, 85, 810–830.

Rogers, C. *Client-Centered Therapy: Its Current Practice, Implications, and Theory*. Boston: Houghton Mifflin, 1951.

Rooth, F., and Marks, I. Persistent exhibitionism: Short-term response to aversion, self-regulation, and relaxation treatment. *Archives of Sexual Behavior*, 1974, 3, 227–248.

Rosenkrantz, P., Vogel, S., Bee, H., Broverman, I., and Brovernman, D. Sex-role stereotypes and self concepts in college students. *Journal of Consulting and Clinical Psychology*, 1968, 32, 287–295.

Rosenman, M. *Loving Styles*. Englewood Cliffs, N.J.: Prentice-Hall, 1979.

Ross, M. *The Married Homosexual Man*. London: Routledge & Kegan Paul, 1983.

Rotheram, M., and Weiner, N. Androgyny, stress, and satisfaction. *Sex Roles*, 1983, 9, 151–158.

Roy, R., and Roy, D. Is monogamy outdated? In E. Morrison and V. Borosage (Eds.), *Human Sexuality: Contemporary Perspectives*. Palo Alto, Calif.: National Press Books, 1973.

Royston, J., Humphrey, S., Flynn, A., Marshall, J., and Zarzosa-Berez, A. An automatic electronic device (Rite Time) to detect the onset of the infertile period by basal body temperature measurements. *British Journal of Obstetrics and Gynaecology*, 1984, 91, 565–573.

Rubenstein, C. The modern art of courtly love. *Psychology Today*, July 1983, 39–49.

Rubin, A. Sexually open versus sexually exclusive marriage: A comparison of dyadic adjustment. *Alternative Lifestyles*, 1982, 5, 101–108.

Rubin, I. *Sexual Life After Sixty*. New York: Basic Books, 1965.

Rubin, J., Provenzano, F., and Luria, Z. The eye of the beholder: Parents' views on sex of newborns. *American Journal of Orthopsychiatry*, 1974, 44, 512–519.

Rubin, L. *Worlds of Pain: Life in the Working Class Family*. New York: Basic Books, 1976.

Rubin, R., Reinisch, J., and Haskett, R. Postnatal gonadal steroid effects on human behavior. *Science*, 1981, 1318–1324.

Rubin, Z. Measurement of romantic love. *Journal of Personality and Social Psychology*, 1970, 16, 265–273.

———. *Liking and Loving*. New York: Holt, Rinehart, and Winston, 1973.

Rubinow, D., and Roy-Byrne, P. Premenstrual syndromes: Overview from a methodologic perspective. *American Journal of Psychiatry*, 1984, 141, 163–172.

Ruble, D., and Brooks-Gunn, J. Menstrual myths. *Medical Aspects of Human Sexuality*, June 1979, 110–127.

Rush, F. *The Best Kept Secret: Sexual Abuse of Children*. Englewood Cliffs, N.J.: Prentice-Hall, 1980.

Russell, D. Pornography and violence: What does the new research say? In L. Lederer (Ed.), *Take Back the Night: Women on Pornography*. New York: Morrow, 1980.

———. *Rape in Marriage*. Riverside, N.J.: Macmillan, 1982.

Russell, M. Sterilization. In A. Ellis and A. Abarbanel (Eds.), *The Encyclopedia of Sexual Behavior*, Vol. 2. New York: Hawthorn, 1961.

Saario, T., Jacklin, C., and Tittle, C. Sex role stereotyping in public schools. *Harvard Educational Review*, 1973, 43, 386–416.

Sacks, H., Rose, D., and Chalmers, T. Should the risk of Acquired Immune Deficiency Syndrome deter hepatitis B vaccination? *The Journal of the American Medical Association*, 1984, 252, 3375–3377.

Safran, C. What men do to women on the job: A shocking look at sexual harassment. *Redbook*, November 1976, 148 ff.

———. Sexual harassment: The view from the top. *Redbook*, Mar. 1981, 47–51.

Saghir, M., and Robins, E. *Male and Female Homosexuality: A Comprehensive Investigation*. Baltimore, Md.: Williams and Wilkins, 1973.

Saldana, L., Schulman, H., and Reuss, L. Management of pregnancy after cesarean section. *American Journal of Obstetrics and Gynecology*, 1979, 135, 555–560.

Sales, E., Baum, M., and Shore, B. Victim readustment following assault. *Journal of Social Issues*, 1984, 40, 117–136.

Salovey, P., and Rodin, J. The heart of jealousy. *Psychology Today*, Sept. 1985, 22–29.

Salsberg, S. Is group marriage viable? *Journal of Sex Research*, 1973, 9, 325–333.

Sanders, B., Soares, M., and D'Aquila, J. The sex difference on one test of spatial visualization: A nontrivial difference. *Child Development*, 1982, 53, 1106–1110.

Sarlin, M., and Altshuler, D. Group psychotherapy with deaf adolescents in a school setting. *International Journal of Group Psychotherapy*, 1968, 18, 337–344.

Sarrel, P. Male rape. Paper presented at the Annual Meeting of the International Academy of Sex Research, Phoenix, Ariz., Nov. 1980.

Sarrel, P., and Masters, W. Sexual molestation of men by women. *Archives of Sexual Behavior*, 1982, 11, 117–131.

Satterfield, S., and Listiak, A. Juvenile prostitution: A sequel to incest. Paper presented at the 135th Meeting of the American Psychiatric Association, Toronto, May 15–21, 1982.

Saunders, J., and Edwards, J. Extramarital sexuality: A predictive model of permissive attitudes. *Journal of Marriage and the Family*, 1984, 46, 825–835.

Sawyer, C. Reproductive behavior. In J. Field (Ed.), *Handbook of Physiology. Section I: Neurophysiology*. Washington, D.C.: The American Physiological Society, 1960.

Saxena, B. Comparative evaluation of contraceptive efficacy of northiserone oenanthate (200mg) injectable contraceptive given every two or three months. *Contraception*, 1984, 30, 561–574.

Scanlon, J. Obstetric anesthesia as a neonatal risk factor in normal labor and delivery. *Clinics in Perinatology*, 1974, 1, 465–482.

Schecter, M., Jeffries, E., Constance, P., Douglas, B., Fay, S., Maynard, M., Nitz, R., Willoughby, B., Boyko, W., and MacLeod, A. Changes in sexual behavior and fear of AIDS. *The Lancet*, June 9, 1984, 1293.

Schellhammer, P., and Donnelly, J. A mode for treatment for incarceration of the penis. *Journal of Trauma*, 1973, 13, 171.

Schneebaum, T. Notes and observations on Mascho Amarataire and Huachipairi. In C. A. Tripp, *The Homosexual Matrix*. New York: McGraw-Hill, 1975.

Schon, M., and Sutherland, A. The role of hormones in human behavior. III. Changes in female sexuality after hypophysectomy. *Journal of Clinical Endocrinology and Metabolism*, 1960, 20, 833–841.

Schover, L., Friedman, J., Weiler, S., Heiman, J., and LoPiccolo, J. Multiaxial problem-oriented system for sexual dysfunctions. *Archives of General Psychiatry*, 1982, 39, 614–619.

Schreiner-Engel, P. Diabetes mellitus and female sexuality. *Sexuality and Disability*, 1984, 6, 83–92.

Schwartz, P. The changing nature of American relationships–heterosexual and homosexual. Paper presented at Regional Conference, American Association of Sex Educators, Counselors, and Therapists, Las Vegas, Nev., Oct. 1984.

————, and Blumstein, P. Bisexuality: Some sociological observations. Paper presented at the Chicago Conference on Bisexual Behavior, Oct. 6, 1973.

Scully, D., and Marolla, J. Convicted rapists' vocabulary of motives: Excuses and justifications. *Social Problems*, 1984, 31, 530–544.

Seaman, B., and Seaman, G. *Women and the Crisis in Sex Hormones*. New York: Bantam Books, 1978.

See, P. The more, the merrier? In J. R. Delora and J. S. Delora (Eds.), *Intimate Life Styles*, 2d rev. ed. Pacific Palisades, Calif.: Goodyear, 1975.

Seligmann, J. The date who rapes. *Newsweek*, Apr. 9, 1984, 91–92.

Semans, J. Premature ejaculation, a new approach. *Southern Medical Journal*, 1956, 49, 353–358.

Serbin, L. In *Nova*, The Pinks and the Blues. Boston: WGBH Transcripts, 1980.

Sevely, J., and Bennett, J. Concerning female ejaculation and the female prostate. *Journal of Sex Research*, 1978, 14, 1–20.

Sexuality Today. Negative vs. positive coercion key to adult sexual problems in molested girls. July 13, 1981, 4.

————. More men report rape, but it's still just the tip of the iceberg. April 5, 1982, 5.

Shainess, N., and Greenwald, H. Debate: Are fantasies during sexual relations a sign of difficulty? *Sexual Behavior*, 1971, 1, 38–54.

Shanegold, M. Sports and menstrual function. *The Physician and Sportsmedicine*. 1980a, 8, 66–70.

————. Pregnancy. In C. Haycock (Ed.), *Sports Medicine for the Athletic Female*. Oradell, N.J.: Medical Economics, 1980b.

————. Causes, evaluation, and management of athletic oligoamenorrhea. *Medical Clinics of North America*, 1985, 69, 83–95.

Shaul, S., Bogle, J., Hale-Harbaugh, J., and Norman, A. *Toward Intimacy: Family Planning and Sexuality Concerns of Physically Disabled Women.* New York: Human Sciences Press, 1978.

Sheehan, K., Casper, R., and Yen, S. Luteal phase defects induced by an agonist of luteinizing hormone-releasing factor: A model for fertility control. *Science,* 1982, 215, 170–172.

Sheehy, G. *Hustling.* New York: Delacorte, 1973.

Shen, W., Sata. L., and Hofstatter, L. Thioridazine and understanding sexual phases in both sexes. *Psychiatric Journal of the University of Ottawa,* 1984, 9, 187–190.

Sherfey, M. *The Nature and Evolution of Female Sexuality.* New York: Random House, 1972.

Sherris, J., Moore, S., and Fox, G. New developments in vaginal contraception. *Population Reports,* 1984, 12, 1.

Shettles, L. Predetermining children's sex. *Medical Aspects of Human Sexuality,* June 1982, 172.

Sholty, M., Ephross, P., Plaut, S., Fischman, S., Charnas, J., and Cody, C. Female orgasmic experience: A subjective study. *Archives of Sexual Behavior,* 1984, 13, 155–164.

Shostak, A. Abortion as fatherhood lost: Problems and reforms. *Family Coordinator,* 1979, 28, 569–574.

————, McLouth, G., and Seng, L. *Men and Abortions: Lessons, Losses and Love.* New York: Praeger, 1984.

Siegel, R. Cocaine and sexual dysfunction. *Journal of Psychoactive Drugs,* 1982, 14, 71–74.

Silber, S., and Cohen, R. Microsurgical reversal of tubal sterilization: Factors affecting pregnancy rate, with long-term follow-up. *Obstetrics and Gynecology,* 1984, 64, 679–682.

Simcock, B. Sons and daughters—a sex preselection study. *Medical Journal of Australia,* 1985, 142, 541–2.

Simenauer, J., and Carroll, D. *Singles: The New Americans.* New York: Simon and Schuster, 1982.

Singer, J., and Singer, I. Types of female orgasms. *The Journal of Sex Research,* 1972, 8, 255–267.

Singh, B., Cutler, J., and Utidijian, H. Studies on the development of a vaginal preparation providing both prophylaxis against venereal disease and other genital infections and contraception. *British Journal of Venereal Diseases,* 1972, 48, 57–64.

Sirkin, M., and Mosher, D. Guided imagery of female sexual assertiveness: Turn on or turn off? *Journal of Sex and Marital Therapy,* 1985, 11, 41–49.

Sivanesaratnam, V. Onset of azoospermia after vasectomy. *New Zealand Medical Journal,* May 8, 1985, 331–332.

Skene, A. Two important glands of the urethra. *American Journal of Obstetrics,* 1880, 265, 265–270.

Slater, P. Sexual adequacy in America. *Intellectual Digest,* Nov. 1973, 17–20.

Slone, D., Shapiro, S., Kaufman, D., Rosenberg, L., Miettinen, O., and Stolley, P. Risk of myocardial infarction in relation to current and discontinued use of oral contraceptives. *New England Journal of Medicine,* 1981, 305, 420–424.

Smith, D. The social content of pornography. *Journal of Communication,* Winter 1976, 16 24.

Smith, G., Taylor, G., and Smith, K. Comparative risks and costs of male and female sterilization. *American Journal of Public Health,* 1985, 75, 370–374.

Smith, J., and Smith, L. Co-marital sex and the sexual freedom movement. *Journal of Sex Research,* 1970, 6, 131–142.

Smith, K. The homophobic scale. In G. Weinberg, *Society and the Healthy Homosexual.* New York: Anchor, 1973.

Smith, M., and Paulson, D. The physiologic consequences of vas ligation. *Urological Survey,* 1980, 30, 31–34.

Smith, P., and Midlarsky, E. Empirically derived conceptions of femaleness and maleness: A current view. *Sex Roles,* 1985, 12, 313–328.

Smithyman, S. Characteristics of undetected rapists. In W. Parsonage (Ed.), *Perspectives on Victimology,* Beverly Hills, Calif.: Sage, 1979.

Sokolov, J., Harris, R., and Hecker, M. Isolation of substances from human vaginal secretions previously shown to be sex attractant pheromones in higher primates. *Archives of Sexual Behavior,* 1976, 5, 269–274.

Solomon, R. The love lost in cliches. *Psychology Today,* Oct. 1981, 83–94.

Sommer, B. The effect of menstruation on cognitive and perceptual motor behavior: A review. *Psychosomatic Medicine,* 1973, 35, 515–34.

Sontag, S. The double standard of aging. *Saturday Review,* Sept. 23, 1972, 29–38.

Sorenson, R. *Adolescent Sexuality in Contemporary America.* New York: World, 1973.

Spanier, G., and Furstenberg, F. Remarriage after divorce: A longitudinal analysis of well-being. *Journal of Marriage and the Family,* 1982, 44, 709–720.

Specter, M. Caution in sexual behavior is driving down the syphilis rate. *The Washington Post Weekly Edition,* Aug. 26, 1985, 32.

Spence, J., and Helmreich, R. *Masculinity and Femininity: The Psychological Dimensions, Correlates, and Antecedents.* Austin, Tex.: University of Texas Press, 1978.

————, ————, and Stapp, J. Ratings of self and peers on sex role attributes and their relation to self-esteem and conceptions of masculinity and femininity. *Journal of Personality and Social Psychology,* 1975, 32, 29–39.

Spengler, A. Manifest sadomasochism of males: Results of an empirical study. *Archives of Sexual Behavior*, 1977, 6, 441–456.

Speroff, L., Blass, R., and Kase, N. *Clinical Gynecologic Endocrinology and Infertility*. Baltimore, Md.: Williams and Wilkins, 1978.

Spezzano, C., and Waterman, J. The first day of life. *Psychology Today*, December 1977, 11, 110.

Spring-Mills, E., and Hafez, E. Male accessory sexual organs. In E. Hafez (Ed.), *Human Reproduction*. New York: Harper & Row, 1980.

Stadel, B., Rubin, G., Webster, L., Schlesselman, J., and Wingo, P. Oral contraceptives and breast cancer in young women. *The Lancet*, Nov. 2, 1985, 970–973.

Starcher, E., Kramer, M., Carlota-Orduna, B., and Lundberg, D. Establishing efficient interview periods for gonorrhea patients. *American Journal of Public Health*, 1983, 73, 1381; 1384.

Stark, E. The unspeakable family secret. *Psychology Today*, May 1984, 42–46.

Starr, B., and Weiner, M. *The Starr-Weiner Report on Sex and Sexuality in the Mature Years*. New York: Stein and Day, 1981.

Steege, J. Female factors which contribute to premature ejaculation. *Medical Aspects of Human Sexuality*, 1981, 15, 73–74.

Steen, E., and Price, J. *Human Sex and Sexuality*. New York: Wiley, 1977.

Steinberg, M., Juliano, M., and Wise, L. Psychological outcome of lumpectomy versus mastectomy in the treatment of breast cancer. *American Journal of Psychiatry*, 1985, 142, 34–39.

Steinem, G. Erotica and pornography: A clear and present difference. In L. Lederer (Ed.), *Take Back the Night: Women on Pornography*. New York: Morrow, 1980.

Stengel, R. Sex Busters. *Time*, July 21, 1986, 12–21.

Stephan, W., Berscheid, E, and Walster, E. Sexual arousal and heterosexual perception. *Journal of Personality and Social Psychology*, 1971, 20, 93–101.

Stevens, M. Lesbian mothers in transition. In G. Vida (Ed.), *Our Right to Love*. Englewood Cliffs, N.J.: Prentice-Hall, 1978.

Stevenson, J., and Umstead, G. Sexual dysfunction due to antihypertensive agents. *Drug Intelligence and Clinical Pharmacy*, 1984, 18, 113–121.

Stimson, A., Wase, J., and Stimson, J. Sexuality and self-esteem among the aged. *Research in Aging*, 1981, 3, 228–239.

Stock, W. The effect of pornography on women. Paper presented at a hearing of the Attorney General's Commission on Pornography, Houston, Tex., September 11–12, 1985.

Stock, W., and Geer, J. A study of fantasy-based sexual arousal in women. *Archives of Sexual Behavior*, 1982, 11, 33–47.

Stolkowski, J., and Choukroun, J. Preconception selection of sex in man. *Israel Journal of Medical Sciences*, 1981, 17, 1061–1067.

Stoller, R. *Sex and Gender*. New York: Science House, 1968.

———. The term "transvestism." *Archives of General Psychiatry*, 1971, 24, 230–237.

———. Etiological factors in female transsexualism: A first approximation. *Archives of Sexual Behavior*, 1972, 2, 47–64.

———. Sexual deviations. In F. Beach (Ed.), *Human Sexuality in Four Perspectives*. Baltimore, Md.: Johns Hopkins University Press, 1977.

———. Tranvestism in women. *Archives of Sexual Behavior*, 1982, 11, 99–115.

———, and Herdt, G. Theories of origins of male homosexuality. *Archives of General Psychiatry*, 1985, 42, 399–404.

Stone, M. *When God Was a Woman*. New York: Dial Press, 1976.

Storms, M. Theories of sexual orientation. *Journal of Personality and Social Psychology*, 1980, 38, 783–792.

Straus, S., Seidlin, M., and Takiff, H. Management of mucocutaneous herpes simplex. *Drugs*, 1984a, 27, 364–372.

———, Takiff, H., Seidlin, M., Bachrach, S., Lininger, L., Giovanna, J., Western, K., Smith, H., Lehrman, S., Creigh-Kirk, T., and Alling, D. Suppression of frequently recurring genital herpes: A placebo-controlled double-blind trial of oral acyclovir. *The New England Journal of Medicine*, 1984b, 310, 1545–1550.

Straw, T. Visual impairment. In D. Bullard and S. Knight (Eds.), *Sexuality and Physical Disability*. St. Louis, Mo.: Mosby, 1981.

Street, R. *Modern Sex Techniques*. New York: Archer House, 1959.

Stubblefield, P., Monson, R., Schoenbaum, S., Wolfson, C., Cookson, D., and Ryan, K. Fertility after induced abortion: A prospective follow-up study. *Obstetrics and Gynecology*, 1984, 63, 186–193.

Subak-Sharpe, G. Is your sex life going up in smoke? *Today's Health*, Aug. 1974, 37–41.

Sue, D. Erotic fantasies of college students during coitus. *The Journal of Sex Research*, 1979, 15, 299–305.

Suggs, R. *The Hidden Worlds of Polynesia*. New York: Harcourt, Brace, and World, 1962.

Sullivan, W. Boys and girls are now maturing earlier. *The New York Times*, Jan. 24, 1971.

Summit, R., and Kryso, J. Sexual abuse of children: A clinical spectrum. *American Journal of Orthopsychiatry*, 1978, 48, 237–251.

Sweet, R. Chlamydia, group B streptococcus, and herpes in pregnancy. *Birth*, 1985, 12, 17–24.

Tan, E., Johnson, R., Lambie, D., Vijayasenan, M., and Whiteside, E. Erectile impotence in chronic alcoholics. *Alcoholism: Clinical and Experimental Research*, 1984, 8, 297–301.

Tanner, M., Pierce, B., and Hale, D. Toxic shock syndrome. *Western Journal of Medicine*, 1981, 134, 477–484.

Tatum, H., and Connell-Tatum, E. Barrier contraception: A comprehensive overview. *Fertility and Sterility*, 1981, 36, 1–12.

Tauber, M. Sex differences in parent-child interaction styles in a free-play session. *Child Development*, 1979, 50, 981–988.

Tavris, C. Masculinity. *Psychology Today*, Jan. 1977, 34.
———, and Sadd, S. *The Redbook Report on Female Sexuality*. New York: Delacorte Press, 1977.

Taylor, J. In R. Haber and C. Eden (Eds), *Holy Living*, rev. ed. New York: Adler, 1971.

Taylor, M., and Lockwood, W. Toxic-shock syndrome. *Journal of the Mississippi State Medical Association*, 1981, 22, 194–198.

Taylor, R. *Sex in History*. New York: Harper & Row, 1970.

Tessler, A., and Krahn, H. Variocele and testicular temperature. *Fertility and Sterility*, 1966, 17, 201–203.

Thoman, E., Liderman, P., and Olsen, J. Neonate-mother interaction during breast feeding. *Developmental Psychology*, 1972, 6, 110–118.

Thompson, R. *The Brain*. New York: Freeman, 1985.

Thoresen, J. Lesbians and gay men: Complements and contrasts. Paper presented at the Society for the Scientific Study of Sex Conference, Philadelphia, Apr. 7, 1984.

Thornburg, H. Adolescent sources of information about sex. *Journal of School Health*, 1981, 51, 274–277.

Tolstedt, B., and Stokes, J. Relation of verbal, affective, and physical intimacy to marital satisfaction. *Journal of Counseling Psychology*, 1983, 30, 573–580.

Tordjman, G., Thierrée, R., and Michel, J. Advances in vascular pathology of male erectile dysfunction. *Archives of Sexual Behavior*, 1980, 9, 391–398.

Toth, A., Lesser, M., and Labriola, D. The development of infections of the genitourinary tract in wives of infertile males and the possible role of spermatozoa in the development of salpingitis. *Surgery, Gynecology, and Obstetrics*, 1984, 159, 565–569.

Tourney, G. Hormones and homosexuality. In J. Marmor (Ed.), *Homosexual Behavior*. New York: Basic Books, 1980.

Trause, M., Kennell, J., and Klaus, M. Parental attachment behavior. In J. Money and H. Musaph (Eds.), *Handbook of Sexology*. New York: Elsevier/North-Holland, 1977.

Tripp, C. *The Homosexual Matrix*. New York: McGraw-Hill, 1975.

Trussell, J., and Westoff, C. Contraceptive practice and trends in coital frequency. *Family Planning Perspectives*, 1980, 12, 246–249.

Tullman, G., Gilner, F., Kolodny, R., Dornbush, R., and Tullman, G. The pre- and post-therapy measurement of communication skills of couples undergoing sex therapy at the Masters and Johnson Institute. *Archives of Sexual Behavior*, 1981, 10, 95–99.

Tyrer, L. Who is a candidate for an IUD? *Urban Health*, 1983, Sept., 39–41.

Ubell, E. Sex in America today. *Parade*, 1984, October 28, 11–13.

Udry, J., Billy, J., Morris, N., Groff, T., and Raj, M. Serum androgenic hormones motivate sexual behavior in adolescent boys. *Fertility and Sterility*, 1985, 43, 90–94.

Unger, R. *Female and Male*. New York: Harper & Row, 1979.

United Nations Commission. Study on Traffic in Persons and Prostitution. ST/SOA/5D/8, 1959.

U.S. Attorney General's Commission on Pornography. *Final Report of the Attorney General's Commission on Pornography*. Washington, D.C.: U.S. Justice Department, 1986.

U.S. Bureau of the Census. *Statistical Abstract of the United States: 1978*, 99th ed. Washington, D.C.: U.S. Department of Commerce, 1978.

U.S. Bureau of the Census. *Statistical Abstract of the United States: 1985*, 105th ed. Washington, D.C.: U.S. Department of Commerce, 1985.

U.S. General Accounting Office. *Sexual Exploitation of Children—A Problem of Unknown Magnitude*. Gaithersburg, Md., 1982.

U.S. News and World Report. Sept. 2, 1985.

Valleroy, M., and Kraft, G. Sexual dysfunction in multiple sclerosis. *Archives of Physical Medicine and Rehabilitation*, 1984, 65, 125–128.

Vance, C. Is it really a novel law? *Psychology Today*, Apr. 1985, 40.

Van Dis, H., and Larsson, K. Induction of sexual arousal in the castrated male rat by intracranial stimulation. *Physiological Behavior*, 1971, 6, 85–86.

Van Wyk, P. Psychosocial development of heterosexual, bisexual, and homosexual behavior. *Archives of Sexual Behavior*, 1984, 13, 505–544.

Vaughn, E. and Fisher, A. Male sexual behavior induced by intracranial electrical stimulation. *Science*, 1962, 137, 758–760.

Veevers, J. Voluntarily childless wives: An exploratory study. *Sociology and Social Research*, 1973, 57, 356–366.

Veith, J., Buck, M., Getzlaf, S., Van Dalfsen, P., and Slade, S. Exposure to men influences the occurrence of ovulation in women. Paper presented at the Ninety-First Convention of the American Psychological Association, Anaheim, Calif., Aug. 27, 1983.

Velarde, A., and Warlick, M. Massage parlors: the sensuality business. *Society*, 1973, 11, 63–74.

Ventura, S. Trends in first births to older mothers, 1970–79. *NCHS Monthly Vital Statistics Report*, May 27, 1982.

Vessey, M., Peto, R., Johnson, B., and Wiggins, P. A long-term follow-up study on women using different methods of contraception: An interim report. *Journal of Biosocial Science*, 1976, 8, 373–427.

Vines, N. Psychological aspects of recurrent genital herpes. Paper presented at the Herpes Symposium, Oregon Health Sciences University, Portland, Oreg., Apr. 2, 1982.

Vinick, B. Remarriage in old age. *The Family Coordinator*, 1978, 27, 359–363.

Vogt, M., Craven, D., Crawford, D., Witt, D., Byington, R., Schooley, R., and Hirsch, M. Isolation of HTLV-III/LAV from cervical secretions of women at risk for AIDS. *The Lancet*, March 8, 1986, 525–527.

Vontver, L. Herpes: Managing pregnancies. *Sexually Transmitted Diseases Bulletin*, Aug. 1982, 1 and 5.

Wagner, G., Bro-Rasmussen, F., Willis, E., and Nielsen, M. New theory on the mechanism of erection involving hitherto undescribed vessels. *The Lancet*, Feb. 20, 1982, 416–418.

Wagner, N., and Sivarajan, E. Sexual activity and the cardiac patient. In R. Green (Ed.), *Human Sexuality: A Health Practitioner's Text*. Baltimore, Md.: Williams and Wilkins, 1979.

Walbroehl, G. Sexuality during pregnancy. *American Family Physician*, 1984, 29, 273–275.

———. Sexuality in cancer patients. *American Family Physician*, 1985, 31, 153–158.

Walfish, S., and Myerson, M. Sex role identity and attitudes toward sexuality. *Archives of Sexual Behavior*, 1980, 9, 199–203.

Walker, L. *The Battered Woman*. New York: Harper & Row, 1979.

Walker, P. Paper presented at the Western Regional Conference of The Society for the Scientific Study of Sex, San Francisco, Nov. 1982.

Wallerstein, E. *Circumcision*, New York: Springer, 1980.

Walnut Creek Contraceptive Drug Study. A prospective study of the side effects of oral contraceptives. NIH Publication No. 81-564, Jan. 1981, 111, 9.

Walster, E., and Walster, G. *A New Look at Love*. Reading, Mass.: Addison-Wesley, 1978.

Warren, M. Onset of puberty later in athletic girls. *Medical Aspects of Human Sexuality*, 1982, 4, 77–78.

Washington, A., Arno, P., and Brooks, M. The economic cost of pelvic inflammatory disease. *The Journal of the American Medical Association*, 255, 1986, 1735–1738.

———, Gove, S., Schachter, J., and Sweet, R. Oral contraceptives, *Chlamydia trachomatis* infection, and pelvic inflammatory disease. *The Journal of the American Medical Association*, 1985, 253, 2246–2250.

Watson, M. Sexually open marriage: Three perspectives. *Alternative Life Styles*, 1981, 4, 3–21.

Watson, R. *Gardnerella vaginalis*: Genitourinary pathogen in men. *Urology*, 1985, 25, 217–222.

Wax, J. Sex and the single grandparent. *New Times*, 1975, 5, 43–47.

Waxenberg, S., Drellich, M., and Sutherland, A. Changes in female sexuality after adrenalectomy. *Journal of Clinical Endocrinology*, 1959, 19, 193–202.

Wear, J., and Holmes, K. *How to Have Intercourse Without Getting Screwed*. Seattle, Wash.: Madrona, 1976.

Webb, J., Millan, D., and Stolz, C. Gynecological survey of American female athletes competing at the Montreal Olympic Games. *Journal of Sports Medicine and Physical Fitness*, 1979, 19, 405–412.

Weg, R. The physiological perspective. In R. Weg (Ed.), *Sexuality in the Later Years: Roles and Behavior*. New York: Academic Press, 1983.

Weidiger, P. *Menstruation and Menopause*. New York: Knopf, 1976.

Weinberg, G. *Society and the Healthy Homosexual*. New York: Anchor, 1973.

Weinberg, M., Williams, C., and Moser, C. The social constituents of sadomasochism. *Social Problems*, 1984, 31, 379–389.

Weis, D. Affective reactions of women to their initial experience of coitus. *Journal of Sex Research*, 1983, 19, 209–237.

———. The experience of pain during women's first sexual intercourse: Cultural mythology about female sexual initiation. *Archives of Sexual Behavior*, 1985, 14, 421–428.

Weller, R., and Halikas, J. Marijuana use and sexual pleasure. *The Journal of Sex Research*, 1982, 18, 1–17.

Wells, B. Nocturnal orgasms: Females' perceptions of a "normal" sexual experience. *Journal of Sex Education and Therapy*, 1983, 9, 32–38.

Wespes, E., and Schulman, C. Venous leakage: Surgical treatment of a curable cause of impotence. *Journal of Urology*, 1985, 133, 796–798.

Wesson, D. Cocaine use by masseuses. *Journal of Psychoactive Drugs*, 1982, 14, 75–76.

Westoff, C., and Jones, E. The secularization of U.S. Catholic birth control practices. *Family Planning Perspectives*, 1977, 9, 203–207.

Whitam, F. The prehomosexual male child in three societies: The United States, Guatemala, Brazil. *Archives of Sexual Behavior*, 1980, 9, 87–99.

———, and Diamond, M. A preliminary report on the sexual orientation of homosexual twins. Paper presented at the Western Region Annual Conference of the Society for the Scientific Study of Sex, Scottsdale, Arizona, January 1986.

White, D. Pursuit of the ultimate aphrodisiac. *Psychology Today*, September 1981, 9-11.

Whitley, M., and Berke, P. Sexual response in diabetic women. *Journal of Sex Education and Therapy*, 1983, 9, 51–56.

WHO Task Force on Sequelae of Abortion. Secondary fertility following abortion. *Studies in Family Planning*, 1984, 15, 291–295.

Wiesmeier, E., Lovett, M., and Forsythe, A. *Chlamydia trachomatis* isolation in a symptomatic university population. *Obstetrics and Gynecology*, 1984, 63, 81–84.

Wiest, W. Semantic differential profiles of orgasm and other experiences among men and women. *Sex Roles*, 1977, 3, 399–403.

Williams, L. The classic rape: When do victims report. *Social Problems*, 1984, 31, 459–467.

Williams, P., and Smith, M. Interview in *The First Question*. London: British Broadcasting System Science and Features Department film, 1979.

Willson, J., Carrington, E., and Ledger, W. *Obstetrics and Gynecology*. St. Louis, Mo.: Mosby, 1983.

Wilson, G. Alcohol and sexual function. *British Journal of Sexual Medicine*, 1984, 11, 56–58.

———, and Lawson, D. Effects of alcohol on sexual arousal in women. *Journal of Abnormal Psychology*, 1976, 85, 489–497.

———, and Niaura, R. Alcohol and the disinhibition of sexual responsiveness. *Journal of Studies of Alcohol*, 1984, 45, 219–224.

Wilson, M. Female homosexuals' need for dominance and endurance. *Psychological Reports*, 1984, 55, 79–82.

Wise, T., and Meyer, J. Transvestism: Previous findings and new areas for inquiry. *Journal of Sex and Marital Therapy*, 1980, 6, 116–128.

———, Rabins, P., and Gahnsley, J. The older patient with a sexual dysfunction. *Journal of Sex and Marital Therapy*, 1984, 10, 117–121.

Witkin, H., Mednick, S., Schulsinger, F., Bakkestrom, E., Christiansen, K., Goodenough, D., Hirschorn, K., Lundsteen, C., Owen, D., Philip, J., Rubin, D., and Stoking, M. Criminality in XYY and XXY men. *Science*, 1976, 193, 147–155.

Witkin, S., and Toth, A. Relationship between genital tract infections, sperm antibodies in seminal fluid, and infertility. *Fertility and Sterility*, 1983, 40, 805–808.

Wofsy, C., Hauer, L., Michaelis, B., Cohen, J., Padian, N., Evans, L., Levy, J. Isolation of AIDS-associated retrovirus from genital secretions of women with antibodies to the virus. *The Lancet*, March 8, 1986, 527–529.

Wolfe, L. *The Cosmo Report*. New York: Arbor House, 1981.

Wolfenden Report. See Great Britain Committee on Homosexual Offenses and Prostitution.

Wolner-Hanssen, P., and Mardh, P. In vitro tests of the adherence of *Chlamydia trachomatis* to human spermatozoa. *Fertility and Sterility*, 1984, 42, 102–107.

Women on Words and Images. *Dick and Jane as Victims*. Princeton, N.J., 1972.

———. *Channeling Children: Sex Stereotyping on Prime Time TV*. Princeton, N.J., 1975.

Wood, G., and Ruddock, E. *Vitalogy*. Chicago: Vitalogy Association, 1918.

Woods, N. *Human Sexuality in Health and Illness*. St. Louis, Mo.: Mosby, 1975.

Wooster, M. Reagan's smutstompers. *Reason*, April 1986, 26–33.

World Health Organization. Special program of research, development and research training in human reproduction. Seventh Annual Report, Geneva, Nov. 1978.

World Health Organization Scientific Group Review. *Steroid Contraception and the Risk of Neoplasm*. Technical Report Series No. 619, Geneva, 1978.

Wright, M., and McCary, J. Positive effects of sex education on emotional patterns of behavior. *Journal of Sex Research*, 1969, 5, 162–169.

Yates, E., Barbaree, H., and Marshall, W. Anger and deviant sexual arousal. *Behavior Therapy*, 1984, 15, 3, 287–294.

Young, W. Prostitution. In J. Douglas (Ed.), *Observations of Deviance*. New York: Random House, 1970.

Zabin, L., and Clark, S. Why they delay: A study of teenage family planning clinic patients. *Family Planning Perspectives*, 1981, 13, 205–217.

————, Hirsch, M. Smith, E., and Hardy, J. Adolescent sexual attitudes and behavior: Are they consistent? *Family Planning Perspectives*, 1984a, 16, 181–185.

————, Hardy, J., Streett, R., and King, T. A school-, hospital- and university-based adolescent pregnancy prevention program. *The Journal of Reproductive Medicine*, 1984b, 29, 421–426.

Zakin, D. Perforation of the bladder by the intrauterine device. *Obstetrical and Gynecological Survey*, 1984, 39, 59–66.

Zatuchni, G. *Current Problems in Obstetrics and Gynecology*, 1984, 7, 4–37.

Zelnick, M., and Kantner, J. Sexual and contraceptive experiences of young unmarried women in the United States, 1976 and 1971. *Family Planning Perspectives*, 1977, 9, 55–71.

————, and ————. First pregnancies to women aged 15–19: 1976 and 1971. *Family Planning Perspectives*, 1978, 10, 11–20.

————, and ————. Sexual activity, contraceptive use, and pregnancy among metropolitan-area teenagers: 1971–1979. *Family Planning Perspectives*, 1980, 12, 230–237.

————, and Kim, Y. Sex education and its association with teenage sexual activity, pregnancy and contraceptive use. *Family Planning Perspectives*, 1982, 14, 117–126.

Zilbergeld, B. Group treatment of sexual dysfunction in men without partners. *Journal of Sex and Marital Therapy*, 1975, 1, 204–214.

————. *Male Sexuality: A Guide to Sexual Fulfillment*. Boston: Little, Brown, 1978.

————, and Evans, M. The inadequacy of Masters and Johnson. *Psychology Today*, Aug. 1980, 29–43.

————, and Kilmann, P. The scope and effectiveness of sex therapy. *Psychotherapy*, 1984, 21, 319–326.

Zillmann, D., and Bryant, J. Pornography, sexual callousness, and the trivialization of rape. *Journal of Communication*, Autumn 1982, 10–21.

Zimmer, D. Interaction patterns and communication skills in sexually distressed, maritally distressed, and normal couples: Two experimental studies. *Journal of Sex and Marital Therapy*, 1983, 9, 251–265.

Zorgniotti, A. Practical diagnostic screening for impotence. *Urology*, 1984, 23, 98–102.

————, and Lefleur, R. Auto-injection of the corpus cavernosum with a vasoactive drug combination for vasculogenic impotence. *Journal of Urology*, 1985, 133, 39–41.

Zorn, J., McDonough, P., Nessman, C., Janssens, Y., and Cedard, L. Salivary progesterone as an index of the luteal function. *Fertility and Sterility*, 1984, 41, 248–253.

Zussman, L., Zussman, S., Sunley, R., and Bjornson, E. Sexual response after hysterectomy-oophorectomy: Recent studies and reconsideration of psychogenesis. *American Journal of Obstetrics and Gynecology*, 1981, 140, 725–729.

Credits

delka/Magnum Photos, Inc. **438**: © Paul Conklin. **442**: Polly Brown/Archive Pictures, Inc. **445**: Reproduced by permission of Planned Parenthood, Portland, Ore. **451**: © Bill Aron/Jeroboam, Inc. **456**: Ken Heyman. **471**: Alan Carey/The Image Works. **476**: © Elizabeth Hamlin/Stock, Boston, Inc, **494**: © Charles Harbutt, Archive Pictures, Inc. **500, left**: © James Motlow/Jeroboam, Inc. **500, right**: Patricia Hollander Gross/Stock, Boston, Inc. **510**: Anestis Diakopoulos/Stock, Boston, Inc. **512**: Chuck Fishman/Woodfin Camp & Associates. **513**: George Bellerose/Stock, Boston, Inc. **521**: © Judy S. Gelles/Stock, Boston, Inc. **527**: Frank Siteman/Jeroboam, Inc. **609**: Reed & Carnrick Pharmaceuticals. Courtesy The Centers for Disease Control. **640**: © Carl Miller. **650**: Ellis Herwig/Stock, Boston, Inc. **657**: © Bettye Lane. **676**: Mary Ellen Mark/Archive Pictures, Inc. **678**: Judy Lutticken. **689**: Photographie Giraudon. **690**: Sipa Press/Editorial Photocolor Archives. **700**: Charles Gatewood/Stock, Boston, Inc. **701**: Courtesy Amon Carter Museum, Fort Worth, Texas.

Excerpts

Pages 31, 426, 427: From *Sexual Response in the Human Female* by Alfred C. Kinsey, Wardell B. Pomeroy, and Clyde E. Martin. The Kinsey Institute for Sex Research, Bloomington, Ind., 1953. **108, 150, 157, 179**: From *Human Sexual Response* by William H. Masters and Virginia E. Johnson. Little, Brown and Company, 1966. **118–119**: Breast self-examination information from the American Cancer Society. **121**: Lines from "She Shall Be Called Woman" from *Collected Poems* (1930–1973) by May Sarton, reprinted by permission of W.W. Norton & Company, Inc. Copyright © 1974 by May Sarton. **128**: Castleman adaptation reprinted from *Medical Care* Magazine, Point Reyes, Calif. **170–171**: Reproduced by Special Permission of *Playboy* Magazine; copyright © 1978 by Playboy. **189, 325, 540, 563**: Reprinted with permission of Macmillan Publishing Co., Inc., from *The Hite Report* by Shere Hite. Copyright © 1976 by Shere Hite. **192**: From "Female Ejaculation: A Case Study" by F. Addiego, E. Belzer, J. Cornolli, W. Moger, J. Perry, and B. Whipple, *Journal of Sex Research*, 1981, 17, 13–21. Reprinted by permission of the Society for the Scientific Study of Sex, publisher of *The Journal of Sex Research*. **229–230**: From *The Cracker Box* by Joyce Rebeta-Burditt. Copyright © 1977 by Joyce Rebeta-Burditt. Macmillan Publishing Company, Inc. **298**: From "Sexuality and the Handicapped" by F. Bidgood, *SIECUS Report*, 1974, 2, 2. **312**: Smith excerpt from George Weinberg, *Society and the Healthy Homosexual*, St. Martin's Press, Inc., New York. Copyright © 1973 by

George Weinberg. **313, 315, 316, 319**: From *Sexual Preference: Its Development in Men and Women* by Allan Bell et al., Bloomington: Indiana University Press, 1981. **333**: Letter by Don Dufford. Used by permission. **349, 353, 369**: Tables adapted from Robert A. Hatcher et al., *Contraceptive Technology 1980–1981*, 10th rev. ed.; and *Contraceptive Technology 1986–1987*, 13th rev. ed. © 1980 and 1986 by Irvington Publishers, Inc., New York. Reprinted with permission from Irvington Publishers, Inc., New York. **405–406**: From *Of Woman Born: Motherhood as Experience and Institution* by Adrienne Rich. Copyright © 1976 by W.W. Norton & Company, Inc., New York. **407, 408**: From "The Pregnant Male" by D. Dailey, *Journal of Sex Education and Therapy*, 1978, 4, 43–44. Used with permission of *Journal of Sex Education and Therapy*. **418–419**: From "The First Day of Life" by C. Spezzano and J. Waterman, *Psychology Today*, December 1977, 11, 110. Reprinted from *Psychology Today* Magazine. Copyright © 1977 Ziff-Davis Publishing Company. **425**: From *Sexual Response in the Human Male* by Alfred C. Kinsey, Wardell B. Pomeroy, and Clyde E. Martin. The Kinsey Institute for Sex Research, Bloomington, Ind., 1948. **501**: From "The Double Standard of Aging" by Susan Sontag, *Saturday Review*, Sept. 23, 1972, 29–38. **501**: From "Sex and the Senior Citizen" by N. Lobsenz, *The New York Times Magazine*, Jan. 20, 1974, 87–91. Copyright © 1974 by The New York Times Company. Reprinted by permission. **510**: From "Remarriage in Old Age" by B. Vinick, *The Family Coordinator*, 1978, 27, 359–363. Copyright 1978 by the National Council on Family Relations. Reprinted by permission. **524**: From "Sexual Adequacy in America" by P. Slater, *Intellectual Digest*, November 1973, 17–20. **674**: From *Ms.* Magazine, September 1977, p. 89. Copyright © 1977 Ms. Foundation for Education and Comm., Inc. **677**: From "Sexual Harassment on the Job" by Karen Lindsey, *Ms.* Magazine, November 1977, pp. 47ff. Copyright © 1977 Ms. Foundation for Education and Comm., Inc.

Color Photographs

Plates 1, 2: Courtesy Federation of Feminist Women's Health Centers, West Hollywood, Calif. **Plate 3**: Copyright © David Scharf, 1982. Peter Arnold, Inc. **Plates 4, 5, 6**: Copyright © Lennart Nilsson. **Plate 7**: © Petit Format/Science Source. Photo Researchers, Inc. **Plate 8**: Courtesy STD Training Center, Harborview Medical Center, Seattle, Wash. **Plates 9–13**: Courtesy Centers for Disease Control, Atlanta, Georgia. **Plate 14**: Courtesy The Clinic, 1216 N.W. 21st, Portland, Ore. 97209.

Index

431, 520
nudity and, 455–457
privacy in, 458
psychosexual development in, 447–458
role models in, 451–455
sexual behavior in, 426–431
Child molestation, 336–337, 632, 669–672
prevention of, 674–676
rapists and, 664
Child rearing, androgynous, 463–464
Children, sexual exploitation of, 698
China. *See* People's Republic of China
Chlamydial infection, 589–592
gonorrhea and, 597
transmission, symptoms, and treatment of, 586
Chlamydia trachomatis, 583, 589–592, 600, 617
Chorionic villi sampling (CVS), 403
Christianity, homosexuality and, 309–310
Chromosomal sex, 52–53
Chromosomes, 52. *See also* X chromosomes; Y chromosomes
sex, 52–53; abnormalities of, 59–62
Cigarette smoking
cervical cancer and, 111–112
fertility and, 386
fetal development and, 402
oral contraceptives and, 353
sexual arousal and, 176
Cilia
fallopian tube, 113
sperm cell, 141
Circumcision
female, 102
penile, 144; sexual arousal and, 157; sexual functioning and, 155–157
Cleck, Margaret, 492
Climacteric, 502
Clitoral hood, circumcision of, 102
Clitoral orgasm, 188–189
Clitoridectomy, 102–103
Clitoris, 99–100
female orgasm and, 539–540
manual stimulation of, 287
mutilation of, 102–103
oral stimulation of, 288
sexual arousal and, 40, 100
Clotrimazole
moniliasis and, 588
trichomoniasis and, 589
Cocaine, sexual arousal and, 174
Codeine
neonatal addiction to, 402
sexual problems and, 530
Cohabitation, 471–475

law and, 686
Coital inorgasmia, 538
Coital pain, 546–548
Coital positions, 291–295
conception and, 388–389
premature ejaculation and, 566
Coitus. *See* Sexual intercourse
Colostrum, 405, 419
Colposcopy, 112
Combination pill, 350
side effects of, 352–353
Comfort, Alex, 197
Coming out, 328–333
Commitment, relationships and, 226
Communication. *See also* Sexual communication
premature ejaculation and, 567
relationships and, 230
sex therapy and, 556–557
Companionate love, 220–221
Comstock, Anthony, 343, 692
Conception
alternative methods of, 389–390
enhancing possibility of, 388–389
Condoms, 363–366
advantages/disadvantages of, 366
sexually transmitted diseases and, 621
use of in ancient times, 13
use of, 364–365
Congenital heart defects, alcohol use and, 402–403
Conjunctivitis, 590
Consensual adult statutes, 688
Contraception, 35
adolescent couples and, 442–444
cervical caps and, 358–360
condoms and, 363–366
as contemporary issue, 344
diaphragms and, 355–358
douching and, 373
history of, 13–14
intrauterine devices and, 366–369
menstrual cycle and, 369–372
methods of, 347–348
new methods of, 377–379
oral contraceptives and, 350–355
outercourse and, 349–350
in People's Republic of China, 10–11
postcoital, 373
shared responsibility in, 345–347
sterilization and, 374–377
in United States, 343
vaginal spermicides and, 360–363
withdrawal and, 373
Contraceptives. *See specific type*
Contraceptive sponge, 360
Coprophilia, 644
Corona, penile, 144

Corpora cavernosa, 143
Corpus luteum, 124
Corpus spongiosum, 143
Cowper's glands, 142
COYOTE, 704
Cremasteric muscle, 136
Cremasteric reflex, 137
Criticism, sexual communication and, 250–257
Crura
clitoral, 99
penile, 143
Cryosurgery, cervical cancer and, 112
Cryptococcal infection, 611
Cryptorchidism, 136–137
Culpotomy, 374
Cunnilingus, 288, 290
adolescents and, 437
vaginal spermicides and, 363
CVAs. *See* Cerebrovascular accidents
CVS. *See* Chorionic villi sampling
Cystitis, 585
diaphragms and, 358
honeymoon, 101
Cysts, breast, 118
Cytomegalovirus, 611

Daughters of Bilitis, 334
Davidson, Julian, 163
Deafness, sexuality and, 300–301
Decriminalization, prostitution and, 704
Degler, Carl, 17
Delgado, Jose, 166
Delivery. *See* Childbirth
Demographic bias, in sex research, 25
Depo-Provera. *See* Medroxyprogesterone acetate
Depression
inhibited sexual desire and, 532
oral contraceptives and, 355
sexual problems and, 526
DES. *See* Diethylstilbestrol
Desire, sexual response and, 177
Developmental disabilities, sexuality and, 301
DHT. *See* Dihydrotestosterone
Diabetes
erectile inhibition and, 537
oral contraceptives and, 354–355
sexual problems and, 529–530
urinary tract infections and, 101
Diaphragms, 355–358
advantages of, 357–358
disadvantages of, 358
introduction in United States, 13
urinary tract infections and, 101
use of, 355–357
Dick-Read, Grantly, 412

Diethylstilbestrol (DES), 402
Dihydrotestosterone (DHT)
    deficiency of, 65–67
    prenatal sexual differentiation and,
        55–57
Dilation and evacuation, 396
Dionysus, 152
Direct observation, in sex research, 27–
    28
Disabilities. *See* Developmental
    disabilities; Physical disabilities
Disclosure, homosexuality and, 330
Divorce, 490–494
    adjustment to, 492–494
Dodson, Betty, 95, 276
Double standard
    adolescent, 434–435
    adult sexual problems and, 522–523
    of aging, 499–501
Douching, 110
    contraception and, 373
    diaphragms and, 357
    sexually transmitted diseases and,
        620–621
Down's syndrome, 404
Doxycycline
    chlamydial infections and, 592
    gonorrhea and, 597
    lymphogranuloma venereum and,
        617
    nongonococcal urethritis and, 601
Drugs. *See also specific type*
    childbirth and, 416
    erectile inhibition and, 537
    inhibited sexual desire and, 532
    sexual arousal and, 174–176
    sexual problems and, 530–531
Drug therapy, homosexuality and, 311
Ductus deferens. *See* Vas deferens
Dysmenorrhea, 128–129
    intrauterine devices and, 368
    primary, 129
    secondary, 130
Dyspareunia, 546

Ectopic pregnancy, 113
    intrauterine devices and, 368
Educational level, sexual variety and,
    525
Effacement, cervical, 410
Efudex. *See* 5–Fluorouracil
Ehrhardt, Anke, 57, 63
Eighteenth Amendment, 18
Either/or questions, 244
Ejaculation, 148–151. *See also* Orgasm
    emission phase of, 149
    expulsion phase of, 149–150
    partial, 541
    premature, 542–543; sex therapy

and, 566–571
    pubococcygeus muscle and, 145
    retrograde, 150
    sex education and, 460–461
Ejaculatory ducts, 55, 140
Ejaculatory inhibition, 541–542
    faking orgasm and, 545
    infertility and, 387
    primary, 541
    secondary, 541
    sex therapy and, 574–575
Elderly, sexual behavior of, 43
Ellis, Albert, 212
Ellis, Havelock, 18, 177
Embryo transfer, 390
Empathy
    sexual communication and, 234
    sexual criticism and, 256
Encephalitis, 611
Endocrine system, 54
Endometrial cancer
    estrogen replacement therapy and,
        505
    oral contraceptives and, 351
Endometriosis
    dyspareunia and, 547
    oral contraceptives and, 351
    secondary dysmenorrhea and, 130
Endometritis, 590, 592
Endometrium, 112
Entrapment, homosexual men and,
    335, 688
Epididymis, 139–140
Epididymitis, 590–591, 595
Epilepsy, oral contraceptives and, 355
Episiotomy, 104, 416
Erectile inhibition, 535–537
    primary, 535
    secondary, 536
    sex therapy and, 571–574
Erection, 147–148, 180
Erikson, Erik, 222
Erogenous zones, 167
Erotica
    pornography and, 694, 696
    sexual arousal and, 168–169
    sexual communication and, 239
Erotic dreams, 268–275. *See also*
    Sexual fantasy
ERT. *See* Estrogen replacement therapy
Erythromycin
    chancroid and, 617
    chlamydial infections and, 592
    gonorrhea and, 597
    granuloma inguinale and, 617
    lymphogranuloma venereum and,
        617
    nongonococcal urethritis and, 601
    syphilis and, 599–600

Estradiol, 54
Estrogen replacement therapy (ERT)
    female sexual behavior and, 164
    menopause and, 504–505
Estrogens
    female sexual behavior and, 163–164
    follicle-stimulating hormone and,
        124
    homosexuality and, 317–318
    hypothalamus and, 58
    menstrual cycle and, 54, 114
    morning-after contraception and,
        373
    oral contraceptives and, 350
    sexual problems and, 530–531
Ethnography, 8
Evans, Michael, 36–37
Excitement, sexual response and, 177,
    180–181
Exercise
    amenorrhea and, 131
    menopause and, 505
    pregnancy and, 400–401
Exhibitionism, 630–633
    rapists and, 664
Experimental research, in sex research,
    28–29
Extramarital relationships, 482–490
    consensual, 484–490
    nonconsensual, 482–484
Eye contact, sexual communication
    and, 240–241

Facial expression, sexual
    communication and, 260
Fallopian tube infections, infertility
    and, 387
Fallopian tubes, 113
    intrauterine devices and, 368
Fallopius, 363
Falwell, Jerry, 312
Fantasy. *See* Sexual fantasy
FAS. *See* Fetal alcohol syndrome
Feedback, sexual communication and,
    241
Feeling statements, sexual
    communication and, 256–257
Fellatio, 288, 290
    adolescents and, 437
    AIDS and, 616
    anger rape and, 665
    homosexuality and, 328
Female genitals
    external, 97–104; sexual response
        cycle and, 182
    manual stimulation of, 287
    mutilation of, 102–103
    underlying structures of, 104–106
Female reproductive system, internal

structures of, 106–114
Female sexual differentiation
  brain and, 57–59
  sex hormones and, 54–57
Femininity, 49
  cultural basis of, 50–51
  sexual fantasy and, 271
Fertility
  hypothalamus and, 58
  nursing and, 372
Fertility awareness, 369
Fetal alcohol syndrome (FAS), 402–403
Fetal development, 399–400
  risks to, 400–403
  sexual differentiation during, 53–54
Fetishism, 638–639
Fibroadenomas, breast, 118
Fimbriae, fallopian tube, 113
5–Fluorouracil, genital warts and, 610
Follicles, 124
  graafian, 125
Follicle-stimulating hormone (FSH), 124
  menstrual cycle and, 125–126
  oral contraceptives and, 350
Foods, sexual arousal and, 171–176
Forceps delivery, 416
Foreplay, 5
Foreskin, penile, 144
Fornication, 685
Freedom of speech, pornography and, 692–693
Frenum, penile, 144
Freud, Sigmund, 18, 188–190, 275, 316
Friendships, nonsexual, 215–216
Fromm, Erich, 209, 220, 225, 229
Frotteurism, 644–645
FSH. See Follicle-stimulating hormone
Fundus, uterine, 112

Gall bladder disease, oral contraceptives and, 354
Gamma benzene hydrochloride, pubic lice and, 609
Garden of Eden, 16
Gardnerella vaginalis, 583–585
  transmission, symptoms, and treatment of, 586
Gay, 305, 330. See also Homosexuality
Gay rights, 334–337
Gebhard, Paul, 29
Gender, definition of, 49
Gender assumptions, 50
Gender dysphoria. See Transsexualism
Gender identity
  definition of, 50
  development of, 51–74

social learning of, 67–69
Gender nonconformity, 318–319
Gender roles, 50, 75–76
  adolescence and, 434–435
  androgynous child-rearing and, 463–464
  androgyny and, 86–89
  historical development of, 14–18
  homophobia and, 313
  homosexual relationships and, 321
  human potential and, 5
  rape and, 651
  sexual fantasy and, 273
  sexual interaction and, 168
  sexuality and, 81–86
  sexual problems and, 527
  socialization of, 77–81
Genes, 53
Genetic sex, 49
Genital folds, 55
Genital herpes. See Herpes
Genital infibulation, 102–103
Genitality, relationships and, 224–225
Genitals. See also Female genitals; Male genitals
  external, differentiation of, 55–57
Genital self-exam, 95–97, 280–281
Genital tubercle, 55
Genital tuberculosis, castration and, 162
Genital warts, 610
  cervical cancer and, 111–112
  transmission, symptoms, and treatment of, 587
Gentamicin, granuloma inguinale and, 617
George, Linda, 43
Gerontophilia, 643
Geschwind, Norman, 59
Gigolos, 702
Giving permission, sexual communication and, 246
Glans
  clitoral, 99–100
  penile, 143
Gonadal sex, 53–54
Gonadotropic releasing factors, 124
Gonadotropin-releasing hormone inhibitor, male contraception and, 378
Gonadotropins, 124
  puberty and, 431–432
Gonorrhea, 583–584, 592–597, 621
  transmission, symptoms, and treatment of, 586
Gossypol, male contraception and, 378
Graafian follicle, 125
Grafenberg, Ernest, 190
Grafenberg spot, 109, 190–192

Graham, Reverend Sylvester, 275
Granuloma inguinale, 617
Greenwald, Harold, 27
Groth, Nicholas, 664–665
Group marriage, 487–490
G spot. See Grafenberg spot
Gynecology, 96, 164

Hamilton, Eleanor, 278
Hammersmith, Sue Kiefer, 43, 313–314
HCG. See Human chorionic gonadotropin
Hearing, sexual arousal and, 170–171
Heart attack, sexual problems and, 530
Heath, Robert, 166
Heckler, Margaret, 670
Heider, Karl, 10
Heiman, Julie, 560
Hemophilus ducreyi, 617
Hepatitis. See Viral hepatitis
Hermaphroditism, 62, 86
Hermaphroditus, 62
Heroin
  neonatal addiction to, 402
  sexual arousal and, 176
Herpes, 583, 598, 601–607
  genital, 602
  oral, 602–603
  transmission, symptoms, and treatment of, 587
Herpes keratitis, 605
Herpes simplex (HSV), 601–602
Heterosexuality, 33–34, 37, 44
  AIDS and, 613–614
  anal stimulation and, 290
  oral-genital stimulation and, 289
  sex-equals-coitus model of, 524
Hite, Shere, 39–41, 189, 282, 325, 524, 540, 544
HIV. See Human immunodeficiency virus
Hobson, William, 664–665
Home birth, 415
Homophobia, 311–314
Homosexuality, 13, 18–19, 25–26, 33–37, 42–44, 70, 305–306
  adolescent, 440–441
  aging and, 509–510
  AIDS and, 611–616
  anal stimulation and, 290
  biological theories of, 317–320
  in childhood, 430
  coming out and, 328–333
  cross-cultural perspectives on, 310
  development of, 314–320
  gender-role stereotypes and, 82
  homophobia and, 311–314
  law and, 688

Homosexuality (*Continued*)
    lifestyles and, 320–333
    in nursing homes, 501
    oral-genital stimulation and, 289
    parenthood and, 324–325
    psychosocial theories of, 314–317
    relationships and, 321–324
    sexual behavior and, 327–328
    sexual expression and, 325–328
    sexual problems and, 528–529
    societal attitudes and, 308–311
Homosexual parents, 324–325
Honeymoon cystitis, 101
Hormonal sex, 54
Hormones. *See specific type*
Hormone therapy
    breast cancer and, 119
    homosexuality and, 311, 320
    hypogonadism and, 163
    male infertility and, 387
    prostatic cancer and, 508
    transsexualism and, 72
Hospital births, 413–414
Hot flashes, 503–504
HSV. *See* Herpes simplex
HTLV-III. *See* Human T-lymphotropic
    virus III
Human chorionic gonadotropin
    (HCG), pregnancy detection and,
    391
Human immunodeficiency virus (HIV),
    611
Human T-lymphotrophic virus III
    (HTLV-III), 611
Hunt, Morton, 38, 292, 306, 326,
    480, 636, 672
Hustlers, 702
H-Y antigen, sexual differentiation and,
    54
Hymen, 101–104
    imperforate, 102
Hypertension, oral contraceptives and,
    353, 355
Hypnosis, homosexuality and, 311
Hypogonadism, 163
Hypothalamic releasing factors, 124
Hypothalamus
    male refractory period and, 195
    menstrual cycle and, 123–124
    sexual differentiation and, 57–58
    sexual functioning and, 166
Hysterectomy, 114
    cervical cancer and, 112
    intrauterine devices and, 368

Immunotherapy, breast cancer and, 119
Imperforate hymen, 102
Impotence. *See* Erectile inhibition
Incest, 25–26, 526, 534, 632, 670,

672–674
    rapists and, 664
Inclusion, relationships and, 222, 227
Independence, in childhood and
    adolescence, 457–458
Induced abortion, 392
Infatuation, 219–220
Infertility, 35, 386–388
    female, 386–387
    male, 387–388; scrotal temperature
        and, 137
    sexuality and, 388
Inguinal canal, 136
Inhibited sexual desire (ISD), 531–533
    sex therapy and, 576
Inorgasmia, 538–540
    coital, 538
    primary, 538–539
    secondary, 538
    situational, 538
Intercourse. *See* Sexual intercourse
Interpersonal distance, sexual
    communication and, 260–261
Interstitial cells, 139
Interviews, in sex research, 22–26
Intimacy, 206. *See also* Relationships
    development of, 221–225
    in later years, 510
    self-love and, 222
Intrauterine death, alcohol use and,
    402
Intrauterine devices (IUDs), 366–369
    advantages of, 367–368
    disadvantages of, 368–369
    introduction of, 14
    morning-after insertion of, 373
    safety of, 347
    secondary dysmenorrhea and, 130
    use of, 366–367
Introitus, 101
Intromission, 291
In vitro fertilization, 389
Iron deficiency anemia, oral
    contraceptives and, 351
ISD. *See* Inhibited sexual desire
IUDs. *See* Intrauterine devices

Jacklin, Carol, 79
Jealousy, love and, 207–209
Johnson, Lyndon, 694
Johnson, Virginia, 18, 25, 28, 34–37,
    108, 150, 157, 168, 176–179,
    185, 189–190, 194, 196, 198,
    285–286, 316, 409, 419, 503–
    504, 522, 536, 542, 547, 553,
    555, 557, 562, 565, 567–568,
    577

Kama Sutra, 152, 689

Kantner, John, 42, 439–440
Kaplan, Helen Singer, 177, 520, 531,
    539, 554, 564
Kaposi's sarcoma, 611
    amyl nitrate and, 175
Kegel, Arnold, 105
Kegel exercises, 105–106, 145, 561,
    564
Kellogg, John Harvey, 275
Kept boys, 702
Ketoconazole
    moniliasis and, 588
Kinsey, Alfred, 18, 22, 25, 29–34, 38,
    40, 168, 196, 269, 275, 279, 280,
    292, 305–307, 318, 325, 425,
    430, 432, 437, 439–440, 525,
    669, 685
Klagsburn, Francine, 478
Klinefelter's syndrome, 61
Klismaphilia, 644
Kwell. *See* Gamma benzene
    hydrochloride

Labia majora, 99
Labia minora, 99
    oral stimulation of, 288
Labioscrotal swelling, 55
Labor, stages of, 410–411
Lactation, 419
Lamaze, Bernard, 412
Laminaria, suction curettage and, 395
Laparoscopy, 374
Latent syphilis, 599
Law
    prostitution and, 703–704
    sexual behavior and, 335–336, 685–
        688
L-dopa, sexual arousal and, 175
LeBoyer, Frederick, 412
Lesbianism, 15, 44, 305. *See also*
    Homosexuality
    biological theories of, 317–320
    psychosocial theories of, 314–317
    sexual behaviors in, 325–327
Leukorrhea, 584
Levine, Ellen, 697
Lewis, Denslow, 36
Leydig's cells, 139
LGV. *See* Lymphogranuloma venereum
LH. *See* Luteinizing hormone
Lifestyles, homosexual, 320–333
Limbic system, sexual behavior and,
    165–167
Listening, sexual communication and,
    240
Liver tumors
    estrogen replacement therapy and,
    505

Narcotics. *See also specific type*
  erectile inhibition and, 537
  inhibited sexual desire and, 532
Narratophilia, 643
Natural family planning, 369
Necrophilia, 644
Needle aspiration, 119
Negative feedback mechanism,
    menstrual cycle and, 125
Neisseria gonorrhoeae, 592, 597
Nelson, James B., 309
New Guinea, sexual behavior in, 10
New Testament, 13
NGU. *See* Nongonococcal urethritis
Nicotine, sexual arousal and, 176
Night-crawling, 9
Nipple, 116
Nixon, Richard, 694
Nocturnal emissions, 150
  sex education and, 460–461
Nocturnal penile tumescence (NPT)
    test, 531
Nongonococcal urethritis (NGU),
    590–591, 600–601, 621
  transmission, symptoms, and
    treatment of, 587
Nonresponse, in sex research, 23–24
Nudity, psychosexual development and,
    455–457
Nursing, 419–420
  fertility and, 372
Nursing homes, sexuality and aging in,
    501–502
Nutrition
  infertility and, 386
  menopause and, 505
  pregnancy and, 400
Nystatin, moniliasis and, 588

Obscene phone calls, 633–634
Ocular herpes, 605
O'Neill, George, 484
O'Neill, Nena, 484
Olds, James, 166
Old Testament, 15
Oophorectomy, 114
  female sexual behavior and, 164
Open-ended questions, 243–244
Open marriage, 484–486
Opiates, sexual arousal and, 176
Opium, neonatal addiction to, 402
Oral contraceptives, 350–355. *See also*
    Birth control pill
  advantages of, 351
  disadvantages of, 352–354
  for men, 377–378
  nursing and, 419
  sexual problems and, 531
Oral-genital stimulation, 287–290

Orchidectomy. *See* Castration
Orgasm. *See also* Ejaculation
  blended, 190
  clitoral, 100, 188–189
  erotic dreams and, 269
  faking of, 544–546
  female, inhibition of, 538–540;
    premature, 544
  Grafenberg spot and, 109, 190–192
  male, inhibition of, 541–542
  marital satisfaction and, 480
  multiple, 195–198
  older female and, 504
  sexual response and, 177, 187–192
  during sleep, 150
  uterine, 190
  vaginal, 188–189
  vulval, 190
Orgasmic platform, 185
Outercourse, contraception and, 349–
    350
Ovarian cancer, oral contraceptives and,
    351
Ovarian cysts, oral contraceptives and,
    351
Ovarian infections, infertility and, 387
Ovaries, 114
  development of, 54
  menstrual cycle and, 123, 125–126
  surgical removal of, 114
Ovotestes, 62
Ovral, 373
Ovulation, 114, 125–126
  nursing and, 419
Ovulation method, contraception and,
    370
Ovum, 52
  luteinizing hormone and, 124

PAINS (for the IUD), 369
Papaverine, erectile inhibition and, 574
Pap smear, 111–112
  classes of, 112
Papules, genital herpes, 602
Paraphilia, 629, 642–645
Paraphrasing
  sexual communication and, 242
  sexual criticism and, 256
Paraplegia, sexuality and, 299–300
Parenthood, optional, 383–386
Parents
  gender-role formation and, 77–78
  homosexual, 324–325
Parkinson's disease, 175
Partial ejaculation, 541
Partial mastectomy, 119
Passing, homosexuality and, 330
Passionate love, 219–220
Paul of Tarsus, 13, 15

Pearson, Allan, 492
Pederasty, 6
Pedophilia. *See* Child molestation
Peer-delinquent prostitutes, 702
Peer groups, gender-role formation
    and, 79
Pelvic exam, pregnancy detection and,
    391
Pelvic floor muscles, Kegel exercises
    and, 105–106
Pelvic inflammatory disease (PID),
    590–592
  gonorrhea and, 596
  intrauterine devices and, 367–368
  nongonococcal urethritis and, 600
  secondary dysmenorrhea and, 130
  vaginal spermicides and, 362
Penicillin
  nongonococcal urethritis and, 601
  syphilis and, 599–600
Penicillin G, gonorrhea and, 597
Penile cancer, uncircumcised males and,
    155
Penile implants, 573–574
Penile strain gauge, 30, 172
Penile tumescence, alcohol and, 29,
    172
Penis, 143–147
  erection of, 147–148
  fractures of, 146–147
  oral stimulation of, 288–289
  size of, sexual functioning and, 151–
    155
People's Republic of China, sexual
    behavior in, 10–12
Perineum, 104
Personal space. *See* Interpersonal
    distance
Petting, adolescent, 436–437
Peyronie's disease, 548
Pheromones, 169–170
Phimosis, 157
Phthirus pubis, 608
Physical appearance, 209–210
Physical disabilities
  body image and, 297–298
  sexuality and, 295–301
Pictophilia, 643
PID. *See* Pelvic inflammatory disease
Pill. *See* Birth control pill
Pimps, 703
Pituitary gland, menstrual cycle and,
    123–124
Placenta, 400–401
  attachment to uterine wall, 402
Placenta previa, 414
Plateau, sexual response and, 177,
    185–186
Playfulness, relationships and, 224